THE BALLPLAYERS

BASEBALL'S ULTIMATE BIOGRAPHICAL REFERENCE

VOLUME ONE
HANK AARON TO JIM LYTTLE

THE BALLPLAYERS

BASEBALL'S ULTIMATE BIOGRAPHICAL REFERENCE

VOLUME ONE
HANK AARON TO JIM LYTTLE

EDITED BY MIKE SHATZKIN

MANAGING EDITOR: STEPHEN HOLTJE

PICTURE EDITORS: MARK RUCKER & JOHN THORN

Created and Developed by
Mike Shatzkin & Jim Charlton

The Idea Logical PRESS

NEW YORK, NEW YORK
www.idealog.com

3 1969 01853 1565

Idea Logical Press Edition Copyright © 1999 by The Idea Logical Company

Copyright © 1990 by Mike Shatzkin & Jim Charlton

Editor: Mike Shatzkin
Managing Editor: Stephen Holtje

Picture Editors: Mark Rucker & John Thorn
Associate Editors: Bob Carroll Jane Charnin-Aker, Shepard C. Long
Copy Editor: Frederic Schwartz

Created and developed by Mike Shatzkin & Jim Charlton
Design & layout by Robert Bull Design

Inquiries should be addressed to: The Idea Logical Press
240 East 56th Street
New York, NY 10022
www.idealog.com/theballplayers
email: books@idealog.com

ISBN 0-9671037-0-3   THE BALLPLAYERS
VOLUME ONE: HANK AARON TO JIM LYTTLE
ISBN 0-9671037-1-1   THE BALLPLAYERS
VOLUME TWO: DUKE MAAS TO DUTCH ZWILLING
ISBN 0-9671037-2-X   THE BALLPLAYERS
TWO VOLUME SET

INTRODUCTION TO THE IDEA LOGICAL EDITION

Between 1986 and the end of the 1989 season, during a period of nearly four years, over a hundred people helped us create this massive compendium of baseball biography. We called the book *The Ballplayers,* even though the subjects of the biographies extend far beyond just ballplayers. Included in here are biographies of owners, managers, scouts, umpires, announcers, writers, teams, leagues, ballparks, and even a couple of fans! The idea behind this book was to tell the stories behind the stats, or the stories that stats just don't tell.

Over thirty-five thousand copies of *The Ballplayers* were printed and distributed in the William Morrow edition that was published in 1990 but, since about 1994, the book has been out of print. Search services have told us consistently that used copies cost at least double the book's original $39.95 retail price; not a spring goes by without our office receiving a call from a writer or sports announcer or just plain fan who is desperate for a copy. Do I have one to spare in my attic?

For the past several years, we have not even been able to meet those requests with books. But we have, since 1996, had *The Ballplayers* available as an online, searchable database housed in the Sportsline USA Web site (get to it through us: www.idealog.com/theballplayers). There, thousands of new fans have discovered the magic of narrative baseball history, organized by the names of the people and entities that made that history.

The scope of this project is repeatedly brought home to us by the attempt to update it sufficiently to publish a new edition. Doing so is an enormous task and, despite the best efforts of a staff dedicated to sports content on the Web, it will not be completed soon.

But now, new technology enables the creation of an Idea Logical Press presentation of the original Morrow book. This Idea Logical Press edition is delivered in two volumes instead of one, which we believe makes it easier and more comfortable to use. The complete original edition is presented here, at a price somewhat lower than you'd pay for the original, if you could find it.

Mike Shatzkin
Founder & CEO
The Idea Logical Press
June, 1999

ACKNOWLEDGMENTS

A project this big doesn't get done without a lot of help from a lot of people.

Stephen Holtje handled the enormous job of trafficking about 6,000 entries to and from contributors and editors and in and out of computer files, wrote many entries, and edited many others.

Shep Long contributed to every aspect of this book's creation during over two years on the project.

Jim Charlton helped nurture the idea for *The Ballplayers* into a real concept, assembled much of the SABR research team, and gave us the benefit of his special knowledge of the Chicago Cubs.

Lee Simmons was the original acquiring editor of this book and provided cogent early criticism to assure the book's consistency and authority.

Alan Williams added his special touch to sharpen our style.

Bob Carroll and Jane Charnin-Aker drafted a large portion of the book from the contributions of our researchers and provided a great number of entries themselves.

Many of our researchers made special contributions in particular areas of baseball history: Merritt Clifton on Japanese, Mexican, and minor leaguers; Fred Ivor-Campbell on the 19th century figures; A.D. Suehsdorf on the early 20th century; Frank Phelps on scouts and in drawing up lists of other non-player categories. Norman Macht, Jack Kavanagh, and Morris Eckhouse deserve special thanks for the sheer number of entries they researched. Stewart Wolpin and Chris Renino handled many of the most important subjects. Dick Clark not only double-checked statistics in Negro League articles against the latest research, he also coordinated the survey used to decide which players should be included and assembled the researchers for the bios.

Richard Topp, former chairman of SABR's Biographical Committee and currently SABR's president, gave us special expertise on birth and death dates and managerial records. Fred Schwarz meticulously checked every word and semi-colon, and John Metcalf gave us valuable criticism on our content.

Thelma Morris and Mike Sparrow of the Cleveland Public Library assisted in the use of their wonderful baseball collection, and Rick Minch and Sue Gharrity of the Indians' public relations office provided help far beyond their normal duties.

Special thanks to Mark Rucker and John Thorn for the pictures, to Bob Bull for an inviting and readable design, to Vance Weaver for his patient typesetting expertise, to Stephen Dydo and Cory Lynn for computer help, and to Andy Dutter for fostering, orchestrating, and coordinating more help from our publisher than any author has the right to expect.

My personal thanks go to my parents, Leonard and Eleanor Shatzkin, for a lifetime of indulging my interest in baseball and fostering my interest in books; to my wife, Martha Moran, the special person who makes many things possible; and to Mary Foster, who in 1955 introduced me to this wonderful game.

Mike Shatzkin
December 6, 1989

THE METHODOLOGY OF THE BALLPLAYERS

The nature of *The Ballplayers* required that we the select the subjects for entries. Clearly the concept of "complete," which is a useful guideline for *The Baseball Encyclopedia*, would be impossible even to define for a book including so many subjects other than ballplayers and managers–club and league histories, awards, publications, scouts, Japan Leaguers, Negro Leaguers, Mexican Leaguers, executives, umpires, journalists, and broadcasters.

We set an objective standard for inclusion of 20th-century ballplayers, progressively tougher as we went further back in time:

    1950-present: 500 at-bats or 100 innings pitched
        through the 1989 season
    1920-1950: 750 at-bats or 250 innings pitched
    1900-1920: 1,000 at-bats or 500 innings pitched

The objective standard required the inclusion of nearly 5,700 ballplayers and managers. We added ballplayers who did not play enough to meet the numerical criteria, but whom we thought people would want to look up. So Choo-Choo Coleman, Jim Thorpe, Herb Washington, and Eddie Gaedel, among others, got in the book.

It was also necessary to assign each entry an appropriate length. The "text value" of a particular subject is often based on facts not contained in statistics. So Mickey Rivers, Moe Berg, and Germany Schaefer got more space than their statistical records would have indicated.

We made subjective decisions as to which 19th-century ballplayers, Negro Leaguers, etc. to include. *The Ballplayers* includes entries for over 1,000 names and topics other than 20th-century ballplayers and managers.

There is a statistical summary for the ballplayers and managers which we call the top line. With the understanding that comprehensive individual statistics are published elsewhere, our objective for the top lines was to create a factual snapshot of the player or manager's career. A unique element of the top lines in *The Ballplayers* is the assembled All-Star selection information, which is not part of the player records in *The Baseball Encyclopedia* or *Total Baseball*, but which we felt was an important component of the quick summary we wanted to present.

We also present the player's major awards (MVP, Cy Young, Rookie of the Year, and Gold Glove), usually available only in year-by-year lists.

The statistics (games, batting average, home runs, and RBI for hitters; innings pitched, won-lost record, and earned-run average for pitchers), seasonal accomplishments (league leaderships, awards, 20-win seasons, and All-Star selections), post-season play information, and Hall of Fame induction dates in the top lines provide a quick locator of an entry's place in baseball history. Even the basic information for these rudimentary top lines came from a variety of sources and required some interpretation.

The 1988 edition of *The Baseball Encyclopedia* was our principal source for major league stats, but Neft & Cohen's *Sports Encyclopedia: Baseball* (St. Martins, 1988 edition) and *Total Baseball* were used to check facts. All statistics are up to date through the 1989 season.

We were fortunate to have the services of Richard Topp, the former chairman of SABR's Biographical Committee. He reviewed entries for birth and death dates, kept us current with new research in career statistics and managerial records, and let us know whenever he noticed a major omission from the body of an article.

Dick Clark made SABR's monumental, ongoing compilation of statistics from the Negro Leagues available to us, keeping us up to date with new research.

Top line information for stadiums was taken from the landmark SABR publication *Green Cathedrals,* by Philip Lowry.

In the course of creating *The Ballplayers*, we also used every book on baseball history we could get our hands on, team media guides going back over many years, and the personal recollections of trustworthy observers. We checked every fact we could and tried to label uncheckable speculation for what it is. The "editorial office" for *The Ballplayers* remains open to improve future editions with new information and leads on information that we get from any source, as well as to add the continuing developments about the people involved with our national pastime. Contributions of additional information from our readers are greatly appreciated and will be carefully reviewed for inclusion in subsequent editions. Unfortunately, the sheer paperwork demands prevent us from acknowledging each contribution. Please write to us at:

The Ballplayers
c/o William Morrow & Company
105 Madison Avenue
New York, NY 10016

AN EXPLANATION OF

1. Name most known by during career.
2. Given first and middle names, if significantly different from name known by during career.
3. Nickname(s).
4. Years of birth and death.
5. Positions played for significant amounts of time. These may not include all positions; included are the player's primary position for each year of his career, positions played for more than 50 games over the course of his career, and positions played for 5% of his career.
6. Years in the major leagues, but not including years in which the player was on the roster but did not play.

1 **5** **2** **6** **7**

3 **Stretch Rickenbach** - [Johann Sebastian]
4 (Spandex) - 1931 - . 1B-OF-LHP 1949, 53-65, 69 Yankees, **Browns/Orioles**, Angels, Braves 1745 g, .289, 357 hr, **10**
1157 rbi; 365 ip, 27-30, 3.68. 20 wins: 49 *1 LCS, 1 g, —.*
8/9 *3 WS, 16 g, .326, 3 hr, 7 rbi*
 Manager 1972-75 **Braves** 285-237, .549. First place: **12**
11 73 1 LCS, 3-4, .429
☞ Rookie of the Year - 49; MVP - 49, 57-58; Cy Young -
15 49; Led League - ba 56-58, 60, rbi 56, w 49, All-Star - 49, **14**
57-62; Gold Glove - 62; Hall of Fame - 1987
The rookie sensation of 1949 etc. etc. (QED)

16 **17** **18**

7. Teams played for in the majors, not including teams of which the player was the property but for whom he did not appear in a major league game. The current team name is used for all teams still in existence; well-known defunct teams of the 20th century are also identified by name.

 Teams are listed in the order in which the player appeared with them, but are listed only once even if the player returned to them later.
8. The boldfaced team is that for which the player played the most, determined by games (offensive players) or innings pitched (pitchers).
9. If a team name changed because of a franchise move, the continuity of the franchise is shown by a backslash.
10. Career batting average , home runs, runs batted in.
11. Career innings pitched (rounded off to the nearest full inning), wins-losses, earned-run average.
12. "—" stands for "no average" (no official at-bats).
13. In a player's career statistics, a lack of home runs or RBI is significant, so topline data would show "0 hr" or "0 rbi." However, many players have no home runs or RBI in either LCS or World Series play; in such cases, the statistic is simply omitted.
14. Managerial statistics are won-lost record and winning percentage.
15. Years of awards and achievements are shown by the last two numbers, since the century is

easily deduced from context. Awards are complete through 1988; 1989 awards available when we went to press are included. MVP awards include the Chalmers Award and league awards given prior to the inauguration of the BBWAA MVP Award.
16. "Led League" includes ties for the lead and follows *The Baseball Encyclopedia* by generally using the qualifying standards of the time.
17. All-Star selections include years in which a player was selected by the All-Star manager or elected by the fans but was unable to play in the game due to injury, military service, or retirement. Sources were *The Sporting News Dope Book* and *Official Baseball Register* and *USA Today*.
18. The initials of the primary researcher(s) of the article. A key to researchers' identities is at the back of the book, followed by short biographical sketches.
19. If a player was born with a different name than he used during his career, that name is given.
20. Despite our best efforts, some birth and death dates could not be tracked down. This is shown by "Unk." If a possible but not definitely established date exists, it is shown with a question mark.
21. Defunct teams are identified by the city name followed by the initials of the league.

THE TOP-LINE FORMAT

(13)   **(19)**

Crotchety Ghiezer - [Albert Colin, born **(20)**
Shtablinow Zbnivfstieck] (Old Steak 'n Brains, The **(22)**
(21) Russian Wrassler) - Unk.-1936. SS-2B-C 1875-96,
1903 Hartford (NA), Indianapolis (NL), Reds, Chicago-
Pittsburgh (UA), Louisville (AA), **Dodgers**, Braves,
(23) Yankees NA: 29 g, .253; ML: 2149 g, .301, 0 hr, 1006
rbi (inc.)
(24)   *Manager* 1914 *Pittsburgh (FL)* 22|44, .333.
Umpire NL 1899-1902, AL 1904-09, 29-35 *3 WS,
1 ASU*
The yclept Russian from Chicago . . . . (GS)

(25)

22. A few 19th-century teams switched cities midseason; they are shown
with a hyphen.
23. National Association statistics are shown separately, because fewer
categories are available.
24. Some statistical categories are not complete, especially RBI, which
were not kept track of by the American Association or by the National
League in some years. SABR is currently reconstructing these
statistical gaps.
25. Umpires' records include years umpiring (broken down by league) and
numbers of World Series, LCS, and All-Star Games worked (for many
years the umpires for these contests were chosen by their respective
leagues on merit).

ADDITIONAL NOTES

There is often insufficient information regarding Negro, Japan, and
Mexican leaguers; the toplines of players in these categories often contain
frustrating gaps. Japanese statistics are available–in Japanese. We will
have them in the next edition. SABR's Negro Leagues committee is
currently attempting to reconstruct complete career statistics, but their
efforts are proceeding year-by-year; thus, we have some yearly statistics
for most players, but career statistics for very few. Mexican statistics are
interrupted in 1984, when they were lost in a devastating earthquake.

Negro Leaguers who also played in the white major leagues have their
statistics listed separately. Their All-Star selections in both leagues are
listed on the same line, but are separated; the same applies to league leads
in major categories.

No headings in categories such as "Executive," "Scout," or
"Broadcaster" are given in the toplines of men who had major league
playing careers.

LIST OF ABBREVIATIONS
AA - American Association
AB - at-bats
AL - American League
ALCS - American League Championship
  Series
ASU - All-Star umpire
BA - batting average
BAA - Basketball Association of America
BBWAA - Base Ball Writers Association
  of America
BWS - Black World Series
C - catcher
DH - designated hitter
DL - disabled list
ERA - earned-run average
FL - Federal League
G - games
GM - general manager
HBP - hit by pitch(es)
HR - home run(s)
IL - International League
IP - innings pitched
JWS - Japan World Series
K - strikeouts
LCS - League Championship Series
LHP - lefthanded pitcher
ML - major league
MVP - most valuable player
NA - National Association
NBL - National Basketball League
NL - National League
NLCS - National League Championship
  Series
NNL - Negro National League
OF - outfield(er)
P - pitcher
PCL - Pacific Coast League
PL - Players' League
RBI - run(s) batted in
RHP - righthanded pitcher
SABR - Society for American Baseball
  Research
SS - shortstop
TSN - *The Sporting News*
UA - Union Association
WS - World Series
1B - first base(man)
2B - second base(man)
3B - third base(man)

THE BALLPLAYERS

BASEBALL'S ULTIMATE BIOGRAPHICAL REFERENCE

VOLUME ONE

HANK AARON TO JIM LYTTLE

Hank Aaron [Henry Louis] (Hammerin' Hank) — 1934–
. OF-1B 1954–1976 **Braves**, Brewers 3298 g, .305,
755 hr, 2297 rbi. *1 LCS, 3 g, .357, 3 hrs, 7 rbi. 2 WS, 14 g,
.364, 3 hr, 9 rbi*
☛ *Most Valuable Player—57. Led League—ba 56, 59.
Led League—hr 57, 63, 66–67. Led League—rbi 57, 60,
63, 66. All-Star—54–76. Gold Glove—58–60. Hall of
Fame—1982.*

Aaron was normally not an excitable sort. One
observer remarked that Aaron seemed to be looking
for a place to sit down when he approached the
batter's box. Robin Roberts, who gave up Aaron's
first home run, remarked that Aaron was the only
batter he knew that "could fall asleep between
pitches and still wake up in time to hit the next
one."

On a muggy April night in Atlanta in 1974, relief
pitcher Tom House carried a baseball in from the
left-field bullpen. When he handed the ball that had
eclipsed the most important record in baseball to the
unemotional record breaker, House reported that
there were tears in Aaron's eyes. Perhaps the emo-
tion was in response to his 715th home run,
breaking Babe Ruth's career record, but more likely
it was in thanks that the ordeal was finally over. It
was an ordeal similar to the one undergone by Roger
Maris 23 summers earlier, one difference being that
Aaron's pursuit of Ruth had racial implications to
many. Aaron received hate mail and death threats
and, when he failed to get number 714 at the end of
the 1973 season, he left an entire off-season for
speculation and building expectations. The tears
may have been the reaction to a giant weight being
lifted off his shoulders.

Aaron was able to become the all-time home run
champ by sustaining a relatively unspectacular but
remarkably consistent career. He was never hurt
badly enough to be out of the lineup for an extended
period of time. He was not a particularly aggressive
baserunner, so his legs suffered little wear and tear.
He controlled his weight throughout his career. His
remarkable physical condition allowed him to average 33 HR a year, hitting between 24 and 45 HR for
19 straight years. He drove in more than 100 runs
15 times, including a record 13 seasons in a row. He

was an All-Star in each of the 23 seasons he played.
Sometimes lost among the home run hullaballoo are
Aaron's two batting titles and four Gold Gloves for
his play in right field. He was consistent and
dangerous, and he quickly gained the respect he was
to enjoy through his entire career. Early in his
career, the Braves played the Dodgers with Jackie
Robinson at third. Aaron twice faked bunts, but
Robinson didn't budge. After the game, Aaron
asked him why he didn't move in. Robinson told
him, "We'll give you first base anytime you want
it."

Aaron had an understated style that could make
him look lazy. He wasn't. He didn't play high school
ball in Mobile, Alabama, which somehow hatched
the strange story that he batted crosshanded early in
his career. He played semi-pro ball when he was 15,
and was the shortstop for two seasons with the
Indianapolis Clowns in the Negro leagues. In May
1952, the Braves paid $7,500 for Aaron, who spent
the next season and a half tearing up three different
minor and winter leagues. He desegregated the
Braves in 1954 after Bobby Thomson broke a leg in
spring training to open a spot. Aaron joined a
powerful lineup featuring Eddie Mathews and Del
Crandall that needed a final link.

Aaron won his first batting title in 1956, his third
ML season. He came close to the Triple Crown the
following year with league bests of 44 homers and
and 132 RBI, but he finished third in the batting
race behind Stan Musial and Willie Mays. Aaron
blamed an ankle injury (he twisted it when he
stepped on a bottle thrown onto the field) for
slowing him up at bat. One of those 1957 homers is
reputedly Aaron's own favorite: the homer that
clinched the 1957 NL pennant. For his efforts that
season, he won his only MVP award. In the Braves'
World Series win over the Yankees, he batted .393
with three more homers and seven RBI.

In 1959, Aaron won his second batting title with
a .355 average and led the league in slugging with a
.636 average. In that year's All-Star Game, he
singled in the tying run in the eighth inning, then
scored the eventual winner on Mays's triple. In
1963, he again threatened to win the Triple Crown.
He led the league with 44 HR and 130 RBI, but

1

Hank Aaron

again finished third in the batting race with a .319 average, beaten by Tommy Davis (.326) and Roberto Clemente (.320). He won HR titles in 1966, when he also won his final RBI crown, and in 1967, the Braves' first two seasons in Atlanta. The Braves won a wild NL Western Division race in 1969, but lost in the LCS in three games to the Mets, despite an Aaron homer in each game, seven RBI, and a .357 average.

It was around this time that Aaron was acknowledged to be a serious threat to Ruth's lifetime record. Heretofore soft-spoken and reserved, Aaron became more vociferous on the treatment of blacks in baseball's upper echelon. In 1970, soon after collecting his 3,000th hit, he stated frankly: "I have to tell the truth, and when people ask me what progress Negroes have made in baseball, I tell them the Negro hasn't made any progress on the field. We haven't made any progress in the commissioner's office. Even with Monte Irvin in there, I still think it's tokenism. I think we have a lot of Negroes capable of handling front-office jobs. We don't have Negro secretaries in some of the big league offices, and I think it's time that the major leagues and

baseball in general just took hold of themselves and started hiring some of these capable people." His quest for racial equality did not interrupt his chase of Ruth. In 1971, he had a career-high .669 slugging average and slammed 47 HR to climb to third place on the all-time list with 639, behind Ruth and Willie Mays. With 34 more in 1972, he passed Mays to go into second place. At the age of 39 in 1973, he cracked 40, the most HR ever for a player his age, ending the season one homer off the record. When the 1974 season opened, the Braves preferred he sit out the first series in Cincinnati so he'd hit the record shots in Atlanta. Aaron and Commissioner Bowie Kuhn thought not. And Aaron didn't leave people in suspense long, hitting a 3–1 pitch off Jack Billingham in his second at-bat on Opening Day, the first homer to be struck at the new Riverfront Stadium. He sat out the next game before the scene shifted back to Atlanta. On April 8, a Monday night game on national TV, he leaned into a 1–0 fastball from Dodger lefty Al Downing. He hit the ball with his weight on his front foot, as was his custom, on a slow arc into the left-field bullpen, where reliever House made a nice catch. As he jogged around the bases, easily and emotionlessly with his head down, he was congratulated by the Dodger infielders. He was met at home plate by a small mob, including his mother.

Aaron finished the year with 20 homers. Soon after the season was over, the Braves sent him to Milwaukee, where he hit 22 HR in two seasons for the Brewers. He finished his career tops all-time in HR, RBI, total bases, and extra-base hits, second in at-bats and runs (tied with Ruth), and third in games played and hits (3,771). He currently works in the Braves' front office. /(SEW)

Tommie Aaron — 1939–1984. 1B-OF 1962–63, 65, 68–71 **Braves** 437 g, .229, 13 hr, 94 rbi. *1 LCS, 1 g, .000*

Half the answer to the trivia question, "What brother combination hit the most homers?" the younger Aaron played regularly only as a rookie, batting .231. He managed in the minors and coached for the Braves until dying of leukemia at age 45. /(BC)

Don Aase — 1954– . RHP 1977–82, 84– Red Sox, **Angels, Orioles, Mets** 1071 ip, 63–59, 3.76 ☛ *All-Star—86.*

Aase was an erratic starter his first four seasons with Boston and California, and was permanently switched to relief in August 1980. Undergoing elbow surgery, he didn't pitch in the majors from late 1982 until June 1984. He signed with the Orioles as a free agent in 1985, went 10–6 with 14 saves, and became a All-Star in 1986, earning a club-record 34 saves. An arm injury held him to only eight innings in 1987. /(BC)

Ed Abbaticchio — 1877–1957. 2B-SS 1897–98, 1903–05, 07–10 Phillies, **Braves**, Pirates 855 g, .254, 11 hr, 324 rbi. *1 WS, 1 g, .000*

Abbaticchio was the first prominent player of obvious Italian ancestry. He led the National League with 610 at-bats for Boston in 1905. When the 1908 season ended with a playoff between the Cubs and Giants, Abbaticchio's Pirates were a half-game out. They had lost the pennant when Abbaticchio's apparent grand slam against the Cubs was called foul. Later, a woman who was struck by the ball sued for damages and swore in court that the ball had been fair. /(JK)

Abbott & Costello — *Comedians*

The Baseball Hall of Fame has a gold-plated recording of Abbott & Costello performing their best-known routine, "Who's on First?" in which a befuddled Costello asks Abbott about the peculiarly-named players of a baseball team. Who is the first baseman, What plays second, I Don't Know is the third baseman, and the shortstop is named I Don't Give a Darn.

Straight man William "Bud" Abbott came from a circus family. In 1936 he teamed up with Lou Costello (nee Cristillo), a fellow burlesque performer who had been a Hollywood stunt man. Their early radio success on the "Kate Smith Show" led to a program of their own and (beginning in 1940) a film career of 38 Grade-B movies. By the time they had a TV series in the early 1950s, their act had gone stale and the two comedians had developed a strong mutual antipathy. /(TF)

Glenn Abbott — 1951– . RHP 1973–81, 83–84 A's, **Mariners**, Tigers 1285 ip, 62–83, 4.39. *1 LCS, 1 ip, 0.00*

On the final day of the 1975 season, the 6'6" Abbott combined with three other A's pitchers (Vida Blue, Paul Lindblad, and Rollie Fingers) to no-hit the Angels. Claimed by Seattle in the expansion draft in 1977, he played for the Mariners longer than any other player on their original Opening Day roster, twice winning 12 games. He missed the entire 1982 season due to illness. /(NLM)

Jim Abbott — 1967– . LHP 1989– **Angels** 181 ip, 12–12, 3.92

Abbott is the most successful pitcher ever to go directly from college to the majors. Angels manager Doug Rader raised eyebrows when he put Abbott, who was born without a right hand, into his rotation out of spring training. Many thought it was done for the publicity, but after struggling early, Abbott proved the doubters wrong. /(WOR)

Spencer Abbott — 1877–1951. *Minor League* Star.

A troublesome nature kept Abbott moving from club to club, mostly in the lower reaches of the Giants' system. His 34 years of managing (1903–06, 1910–11, 1913–14, 1919–34, 1936–43, 1946–47) set a since-broken minor league record; he spent that time with 24 teams, winning five pennants. He was a coach with the Senators in 1935. /(MC)

Ferdinand A. Abell — 1833–1913. *Executive.*

One of the founders of the Brooklyn club in 1883, Abell put up the money to build Washington Park, Brooklyn's home grounds until Ebbets Field was built. Brooklyn joined the National League in 1890; their players were paid so well none went over to the Players' League and the Superbas won the pennant. In 1898 Abell consolidated the team with Baltimore and won two pennants, but the Brooklyn club was heavily raided by the American League in 1901 and Abell refused to raise salaries to meet the competition. /(NLM)

Al Aber (Lefty) — 1927– . LHP 1950, 53–57 Indians, **Tigers**, A's 389 ip, 24–25, 4.18

The Cleveland native won 24 games for Spartanburg in 1949 and threw a five-hitter for the Indians in his only ML appearance before serving overseas in 1951–52. Despite the long layoff, the sinkerballer returned to become a competent Tiger reliever. /(JCA)

Ted Abernathy — 1933– . RHP 1955–57, 60, 63–72 Senators, Indians, Cubs, Braves, **Reds**, Cardinals, Royals 1148 ip, 63–69, 3.46

Ironman submariner Abernathy struggled with control and injuries before finally enjoying his first good year in the majors at age 29 with Cleveland in 1963 (7–2, with 12 saves). With the Cubs in 1965, he was named NL Fireman of the Year when he led the league with 31 saves. Two years later with the Reds he again was Fireman of the Year and again led in saves (28). He had 148 career saves. /(MC)

Al Abrams — 1904-1977. *Writer*

Abrams joined the Pittsburgh *Post-Gazette* in 1926 and was its sports editor from 1947 to 1974. He continued his column, "Sidelights on Sports," after he retired. /(NLM)

Cal Abrams — 1924- . OF 1949-56 Dodgers, Reds, Pirates, **Orioles**, White Sox 567 g, .269, 32 hr, 138 rbi

Abrams, who was pegged out at home by Richie Ashburn to preserve the Phillies' 1950 pennant, was a weak-armed singles hitter. After three bench-warming years with Brooklyn, his best season came with the 1953 Pirates (.286, 15 HR). /(BC)

Jim Acker — 1958- . RHP 1983- **Blue Jays**, Braves 694 ip, 26-40, 3.78. *2 LCS, 12 ip, 0-0, 0.73*

Originally a Braves farmhand, Acker slipped badly after his 7-2, 10-save season with Toronto in 1985, and was traded back to Atlanta in mid-1986. In 1987 Acker led the Braves with 14 saves. His brother Bill was an NFL lineman. /(BC)

Tom Acker (Shoulders) — 1930- . RHP 1956-59 **Reds** 380 ip, 19-13, 4.12

Acker was a hard-throwing reliever who was 10-5 with four saves for the Reds in 1957, but his ERA was 4.97 and stayed over 4.00 in his remaining two ML seasons. /(FK)

Cy Acosta [Cecilio] — 1946- . RHP 1972-75 **White Sox**, Phillies 187 ip, 13-9, 2.65

The Mexican-born reliever was the ace of the Chicago bullpen in 1973, winning 10 and saving 18. After shoulder, elbow, and eye injuries disabled him for much of 1974, he never won another game. /(JCA)

Jose Acosta — 1891- . RHP 1920-22 **Senators**, White Sox 213 ip, 10-10, 4.51

Jose Acosta was one of a host of Cubans (which included his younger brother Merito, an outfielder) signed by Washington during the 1920s. The 5'6" 134-lb hurler had back-to-back 5-4 seasons in 1920-21. /(NLM)

Jerry Adair — 1936-1987. 2B-SS 1958-70 **Orioles**, White Sox, Red Sox, Royals 1165 g, .254, 57 hr, 366 rbi

The often dour Adair brought a light bat, steady hands, and a tough attitude to the game. Hit in the mouth by a wild throw during the first game of a doubleheader in 1964, he took 11 stitches and returned to play the entire second game. He holds the ML record (with Bobby Grich and Joe Morgan)

for fewest errors in a season by a second baseman (five, in 1964). He also set ML records with 89 consecutive games and 458 chances without an error from July 22, 1964 to May 6, 1965 with the Orioles.

After hitting .300 for Hankyu in Japan in 1971, he returned to the States and was a coach for the A's and the Angels. /(BC)

Ace Adams — 1912- . RHP 1941-46 **Giants** 553 ip, 41-33, 3.47
☛ *All-Star—43.*

Ace (his given name) was the relief star of Mel Ott's wartime Giants. Beginning in 1942, he led the NL in games pitched three straight years and in games finished four straight. His 70 appearances and 67 in relief in 1943 set ML records. He topped the league in saves in 1944 and 1945 (13 and 15), but the next year he jumped to the then-outlaw Mexican League. /(JD)

Babe Adams [Charles Benjamin] — 1882-1968. RHP 1906-07, 09-16, 18-26 Cardinals, **Pirates** 2995 ip, 194-140, 2.76. 20 wins: 11, 13 *2 WS, 28 ip, 3-0, 1.29*

Except for a single game he lost for St. Louis in 1906, Adams pitched his entire major league career with Pittsburgh. After a brief stay with the Pirates in 1907, the quiet Hoosier rejoined the team as a 27-year-old rookie in 1909 and helped them win the pennant with a 12-3 mark. The Pirates went into the World Series against Ty Cobb and the Detroit Tigers with staff ace Howie Camnitz laid up with tonsillitis. Even though Adams ranked fifth on the club in wins, manager Fred Clarke chose him as the opening game pitcher on a tip that the righthander's style resembled that of Dolly Gray, an AL pitcher who'd handled the Tigers well during the season. Adams won Game One 4-1, Game Five 8-4, and, on two day's rest, clinched the series 8-0 to become the first pitcher to win three games in a seven-game series.

Over the next half-dozen years, Adams was the Pirates' ace, winning 22 games in 1911 and 21 in 1913. A sore arm threatened his career in 1916, and he returned to the minors. He was 34-16 in less than two minor league seasons before the Pirates brought him back. In both 1919 and 1920 he posted 17-win totals. He led the NL with eight shutouts in 1920. In 1925, when he was a 43-year-old reliever, he made another World Series appearance, pitching one scoreless inning against the Senators.

Adams was never a hard thrower and his sore arm cost him what speed he had, but he could put the

Babe Adams with the Pirates

ball exactly where he wanted to. In 1920, he walked only 18 men in 263 innings. He allowed a mere 430 bases on balls for his career. /(BC)

Bobby Adams — 1921- . 3B-2B 1946–59 **Reds,** White Sox, Orioles, Cubs 1281 g, .269, 37 hr, 303 rbi

Adams fashioned a 14-year career after spending 3 years in the military, but was a regular only in 1952–53. He was a handy infielder and a dependable pinch hitter who rapped six consecutive pinch hits in 1958. On April 19, 1952, Adams and Grady Hatton led off a game with back-to-back home runs against Pittsburgh's Mel Queen. Adams's brother Dick was with the A's briefly and his son Mike lasted parts of five seasons with three different teams. /(JK)

Buster Adams [Elvin] — 1915- . OF 1939, 43–47 Cardinals, **Phillies** 576 g, .266, 50 hr, 249 rbi

A wartime slugger, Adams's top year was 1945, when he hit .287 with 22 homers and 109 RBI splitting time between the Phillies and Cardinals. His nickname stemmed from his resemblance to the Buster Brown shoe company logo. /(MC)

Franklin P. Adams — 1881-1960. *Writer.*

Franklin P. Adams was a columnist for the New York *Globe*. On July 10, 1908, the composition room called to tell him that his column was eight lines short. Adams, on his way to a Giant-Cub matchup at the Polo Grounds, quickly scrawled out eight lines entitled "Baseball's Sad Lexicon": "These are the saddest of possible words, Tinker-to-Evers-to-Chance. Trio of bear cubs and fleeter than birds, Tinker-to-Evers-to-Chance. Ruthlessly pricking our gonfalon bubble, Making a Giant hit into a double, Words that are weighty with nothing but trouble. Tinker-to-Evers-to-Chance." Adams was later an ace panelist on the radio show "Information Please." /(WOR)

Glenn Adams (Addie) — 1947- . DH-OF 1975–82 Giants, **Twins**, Blue Jays 661 g, .280, 34 hr, 225 rbi

The DH in 326 ML games, Adams pinch-hit in more than half of his other appearances. With the help of his only ML grand slam, he drove in eight runs in one game, June 26, 1977, setting a Twins record. /(AB)

Sparky Adams [Earl John] — 1894-1989. 2B-3B-SS 1922–34 **Cubs**, Pirates, Cardinals, Reds 1424 g, .286, 9 hr, 394 rbi

The versatile Adams spent 1923 and 1924 as the Cubs' semi-regular shortstop, but came into his own when he was switched to second base for 1925 after second baseman George Grantham was traded to Pittsburgh for shortstop Rabbit Maranville. Adams led NL 2B in putouts, assists, total chances per game, and fielding average at his new position. Playing regularly, he led the league in at-bats for the first of three straight seasons and finished third in steals with 26, scoring 95 runs while batting .287. The leadoff batter improved to .309 in 1926, again scoring 95 runs, and finished second in steals (27) and third in hits. In 1927 he was moved around the infield more, playing 60 games at second base, 53 at third base, and 40 at shortstop. He scored a career-high 100 runs, finished fourth in the league in steals with 26, and hit .292. NL champion Pittsburgh sent Kiki Cuyler, who had fallen into disfavor with management, to the Cubs for Adams and Pete Scott in 1927. Adams once again replaced Grantham at second base as Grantham moved to first.

Adams's average fell off over the next two seasons, and in 1929 he was used in a utility role. After the season he was sold to the Cardinals. Used at third base, he helped St. Louis to two straight pennants, leading NL third basemen in fielding both seasons and in double plays in 1931. In the notorious rabbit-ball season of 1930, when the league batting average was .303, all eight Cardinal regulars (300-plus at-bats) hit .300, the only time in history that has happened. Adams contributed a career-high .314. In St. Louis's 1931 World Championship year, he led the league with 46 doubles and tied with teammate Pepper Martin for third in steals with 16. Another member of the Gas House Gang, Frankie Frisch, finished first with 28 and the Cardinals led the league in stolen bases.

In 1932 a knee injury kept Adams out for most of the year. In early May 1933 he went to the Reds along with Paul Derringer and Allyn Stout for Leo Durocher, Dutch Henry, and Jack Ogden in the deal that completed the cast of characters in the classic Gas House Gang. In Cincinnati Adams joined George Grantham again. But Adams's knee injury had deprived him of his speed, and although he was a regular for a year and a half, his average dropped off and his major league career ended. /(SFS)

Joe Adcock — 1927– . 1B-OF 1950–66 Reds, **Braves**, Indians, Angels 1959 g, .277, 336 hr, 1122 rbi. *2 WS, 9 g, .250, 2 rbi.*
*Manager 67 **Indians** 75–87, .463*
☛ *All-Star—60..*

Although he was played out of position, platooned, and frequently injured, Adcock retired as the twentieth most prolific home run hitter of all time and seventh among righthanded hitters. A natural first baseman, the 6′4″ 220-lb slugger platooned with Ted Kluszewski when he joined the Reds in 1950, then switched to left field to keep both bats in the lineup. Traded to the Braves in 1953, he returned to first base and appeared in a career-high 157 games. On July 31, 1954, he hit four home runs and a double in a game against the Dodgers at Ebbets Field. His 18 total bases still stand as the one-game record. A broken arm in 1955 and broken leg in '57 held him to half-seasons, but in his healthy 1956 he hit .291, with 38 homers and 103 RBI. He was often platooned in later years, but in 1961, when he played in 152 games, he had 35 home runs and a career-high 108 RBI. Traded to the Indians in 1963 and sent on to the Angels the next year, Adcock

played through the '66 season as a platoon player and pinch-hitter. In 1967 he became manager of the Indians, but when the team finished eighth he was fired. Ironically, the main criticism of his managing was that he insisted on platooning the team's top sluggers, Leon Wagner and Rocky Colavito. /(MC)

Bob Addie — 1911–1982. *Writer*
Addie covered the Senators for 37 years with the Washington *Times-Herald* and the Washington *Post*. His column, "Addie's Atoms," appeared in *The Sporting News*. In 1981 Addie received the J.G. Taylor Spink Award. He was married to Pauline Betz, four-time U.S. women's tennis champion. /(NLM)

L.H. Addington (Leroy) — 1894–1956. *Writer*
For many years a member of the editorial staff of *The Sporting News* and publicity director for the National Association, Addington wrote a column, "In the Bullpen," that appeared regularly in *TSN* in the 1920s and 30s. /(NLM)

Bob Addis — 1925– . OF 1950–53 Braves, **Cubs**, Pirates 534 g, .281, 2 hr, 47 rbi
Addis was speedy but lacked power. After hitting .295 with 13 doubles in 93 games for the 1952 Cubs, he was given just 15 at-bats in 1953, and left the majors. /(BC)

Grady Adkins — 1897–1966. RHP 1928–29 **White Sox** 363 ip, 12–27, 4.34
Adkins showed promise as a 31-year-old rookie, going 10–16 with the fifth-place 1928 White Sox. But the next year he couldn't get anyone out, finishing 2–11 with a 5.33 ERA. /(BC)

Tommie Agee — 1942– . OF 1962–73 Indians, White Sox, **Mets**, Astros, Cardinals 1129 g, .255, 130 hr, 433 rbi. *1 LCS, 3 g, .357, 2 hr, 4 rbi. 1 WS, 5 g, .167, 1 hr, 1 rbi*
☛ *Rookie of the Year—66. All-Star—66–67. Gold Glove—66, 70.*

The speedy outfielder originally signed with the Indians for a $60,000 bonus. He was later sent to the White Sox along with Tommy John in a three-team trade. In 1966, his first full season, he hit 22 homers and led AL outfielders in putouts to earn Rookie of the Year honors. Traded to the Mets two years later, Agee helped them win the 1969 pennant with his leadoff hitting, including a career-high 26 homers. In the WS, he starred in the Mets' Game Three victory with a home run and two outstanding catches. /(AB)

Harry Agganis (The Golden Greek) — 1930–1955. 1B 1954–55 **Red Sox** 157 g, .261, 11 hr, 67 rbi

A brilliant athlete and a New England favorite, Agganis was a baseball and football star at Lynn Classical H.S. and Boston University, making All-American as a quarterback. He signed for a reported $35,000 with the Red Sox and after only one minor league season jumped to the majors. His death of leukemia during the 1955 season set Boston hopes for the future back for several seasons. A good fielder who led AL first basemen in assists in 1954, he had 11 HR in 434 at-bats in his rookie season and was hitting .313 at the time of his death. /(EW)

Sam Agnew — 1887–1951. C 1913–19 **Browns**, Red Sox, Senators 560 g, .204, 2 hr, 98 rbi. *1 WS, 4 g, .000*

Agnew was a Browns regular for three seasons (1913 through 1915) and led American League catchers in errors in two of them because of a scattergun arm. In 1915 he committed 39 errors. /(WAB)

Juan Agosto — 1958– . LHP 1981– **White Sox**, Twins, Astros 392 ip, 24–18, 3.46. *1 LCS, 0.1 ip, 0–0, 0.00*

The Puerto Rican born Agosto was signed at age 16 by the Red Sox in 1974, but spent his first full ML season with the 1984 White Sox. Chicago fans unkindly labelled the reliever "Juan Disgusto: the Master of Disaster" when he failed too often with the game on the line. He matured with the Astros; in 1988, he went 10–2. /(RL)

Luis Aguayo — 1959– . SS-2B-3B 1980– **Phillies**, Yankees, Indians 568 g, .236, 37 hr, 109 rbi

A utility infielder and pinch-hit specialist for the Phillies, Aguayo made his ML debut in 1980, but did not have 100 plate appearances in a season until 1985. In 1987 he hit 12 HR in only 209 at-bats, and his final home run eliminated the Mets from the pennant race in the last week of the season. /(SG)

Rick Aguilera (Aggie) — 1961– . RHP 1985– **Mets**, Twins 549 ip, 40–32, 3.53. *2 LCS, 12 ip, 0–0. 0.75. 1 WS, 3 ip, 1–0, 12.00*

As the Mets' fifth starter, Aguilera went 10–7 each of his first two years. He pitched three innings of scoreless relief in the Mets' dramatic 16-inning LCS clincher over the Astros in 1986. He was hit hard in Game Two of the World Series in relief of loser Dwight Gooden. Aguilera also surrendered two tenth-inning runs in Game Six, but was the winning pitcher after the Mets' spectacular three-run comeback in the bottom of the inning.

His best season, an 11–3 mark in 1987, was interrupted by three months on the DL in the middle of the year. An elbow operation kept Aguilera out for most of 1988, and David Cone took his place in the rotation. Aguilera was used in relief in 1989 and, throwing harder than previously, he soon won the righthanded closer role from Roger McDowell. Dealt to the Twins in mid-season in the five-man package that brought Frank Viola to the Mets, Aguilera returned to a starting role.

Aguilera hit .278 in his first major league season and has been used as a pinch-hitter. He was a third baseman at Brigham Young University and played on the same team with Cory Snyder, Wally Joyner, and Scott Nielsen. /(SH)

Hank Aguirre — 1932– . LHP 1955–70 Indians, **Tigers**, Dodgers, Cubs 1375 ip, 75–72, 3.25 ☛ *Led League—era 62. All-Star—62.*

Equally adept at delivering screwballs and one-liners, Aguirre was switched from the bullpen to the starting rotation by the Tigers in 1962 and responded by leading the AL in ERA (2.21) while posting a 16–8 mark. A notoriously poor hitter, he hit below .040 in seven seasons and had a career BA of .085. /(AB)

Willie Aikens — 1954– . 1B-DH 1977, 79–85 Angels, **Royals**, Blue Jays 774 g, .271, 110 hr, 415 rbi. *1 LCS, 3 g, .364. 1 WS, 6 g, .400, 4 hr, 8 rbi*

In 1980 Aikens became the first player ever to have two multiple home run games in the same World Series when he blasted a pair in Game One for the Royals and repeated in Game Four. Named Willie Mays Aikens for the Hall of Famer, the 220-pound slugger topped 20 homers three times. Aikens's lack of fielding skills was legendary, and he should have been a DH, but Hal McRae already filled that role for the Royals. Aikens's involvement with drugs led to his suspension by the Royals and a 1984 trade to Toronto, where he DHed with little success. /(FJO)

Danny Ainge — 1959– . 2B-3B-OF 1979–81 **Blue Jays** 211 g, .220, 2 hr, 37 rbi

A basketball star at Brigham Young, the fiery Ainge was a 6'4" infielder-outfielder with the Blue Jays. After three years of failing to hit major league pitching, he quit baseball to join the NBA Boston Celtics. /(BC)

Eddie Ainsmith — 1892–1981. C 1910–24 **Senators**, Tigers, Cardinals, Dodgers, Giants 1068 g, .232, 22 hr, 317 rbi

A steady catcher for 15 seasons despite little offensive production, Ainsmith was a smooth handler of pitchers and an aggressive player. In a one-sided game on June 26, 1913, the Senators' catcher stole second, third, and home in the ninth inning, courtesy of the casual attitude taken by Athletics' pitcher Chief Bender. All of Ainsmith's excursions went unchallenged, but were scored as stolen bases. /(JK)

Jack Aker (Chief) — 1940- . RHP 1964-74 **A's**, Pilots, Yankees, Cubs, Braves, Mets 747 ip, 47-45, 3.28

A rugged, sidearming sinkerballer, Aker relieved in all 495 of his ML games, saving 123. The nickname "Chief" refers to his Potowatomie Indian ancestry, fierce presence, and effectiveness. He was AL Fireman of the Year with the 1966 A's, going 8-4 with a 1.99 ERA and 32 saves—a ML record until 1970. In August 1967, the Kansas City players, with Aker as their representative, became embroiled in a feud with owner Charley Finley. Having enraged Finley, Aker found himself pitching less and less. He was chosen by the Pilots in the 1968 expansion draft and was soon traded to New York. As a Yankee, he led the staff in saves in 1969 and recorded a 2.06 ERA in both 1969 and 1970, despite undergoing career-

Jack Aker

threatening spinal surgery over the intervening winter. He pitched with pain the rest of his career. When the Yankees acquired Sparky Lyle in 1972, Aker was dealt to the Cubs, and led their bullpen in saves and wins. He later became a successful minor league manager and Cleveland's pitching coach. /(JCA)

Vic Albury — 1947- . LHP 1973-76 **Twins** 372 ip, 18-17, 4.11

Vietnam veteran Albury was sometimes impressive with the Twins but erratic, a victim of wildness and a chronic sore arm. He sometimes played in the field in the minors, but his hitting ability was of no use in the DH-employing AL. /(MC)

Santo Alcala — 1952- . RHP 1976-77 **Reds**, Expos 68 g, 249 ip, 14-11, 4.76

The 6'5" Dominican had a flashy 11-4 mark in 1976 with the "Big Red Machine," but his 4.70 ERA revealed his reliance on the Cincinnati bats. Traded to Montreal, he fell to 3-7. /(BC)

Mike Aldrete — 1961- . OF-1B 1986- **Giants**, Expos 425 g, .277, 15 hr, 138 rbi. *1 LCS, 5 g, .100, 1 rbi*

A lefthanded reserve who can play anywhere in the outfield, Aldrete enjoyed his best season in 1987, hitting .325 with 9 HR and 51 RBI when Giants regulars Candy Maldonado and Jeffrey Leonard were injured much of the season. He was traded to the Expos for Tracy Jones before the 1989 season. /(SCL)

Vic Aldridge — 1893-1973. RHP 1917-18, 22-28 **Cubs**, Pirates, Giants 1601 ip, 97-80, 3.76. *2 WS, 26 ip, 2-1, 4.91*

Aldridge was a steady hurler for the Cubs, going 47-36 from 1922 through 1924, and the Pirates, for whom he won 15 games in each of their 1925 and 1927 pennant-winning seasons. He had complete game wins over Coveleski and the Senators in Games Two and Five of the 1925 World Series, winning 3-2 and 6-3. In the seventh and deciding game, he couldn't get out of the first inning, but though the score was 4-0 after one, the Pirates came back to win 9-7.

In February 1928, the disgruntled Aldridge was traded to the Giants for 34-year-old Burleigh Grimes, who had clashed with New York manager John McGraw. Aldridge held out, joined the Giants late, and was waived after a dismal showing. Grimes, meanwhile, led the NL with 25 wins. /(JK)

Dale Alexander (Moose) — 1903–1979. 1B 1929–33 **Tigers**, Red Sox 662 g, .331, 61 hr, 459 rbi
☛ *Led League—ba 32.*

In his first two years with the Tigers, the right-handed-hitting Alexander showed a powerful bat but an iron glove. Then in 1931, as his fielding began to improve, he lost his home run swing, hitting only 3 after two 20-plus seasons. When his BA dipped to .250 in June of the next year, the Tigers traded him to the Red Sox for aging outfielder Earl Webb. "Moose" suddenly went on a batting tear, hitting .372 for the rest of the season to end with an AL-high .367 BA. But his fielding was still a liability and his power was gone. When he hit a weak .281 as a part-timer in 1933, his ML career was over. /(EC)

Doyle Alexander — 1950– . RHP 1971– Dodgers, **Orioles**, Yankees, Rangers, Braves, Giants, Blue Jays, Tigers 3367 ip, 194–174, 3.76. *3 LCS, 23 ip, 0–4, 8.61. 1 WS, 6 ip, 0–1, 7.50*
☛ *All-Star—88.*

Dour Doyle Alexander moved around enough to become the fourth pitcher to record wins over all 26 teams. He became increasingly effective late in his career, by developing an assortment of pitches, speeds, and deliveries, and relying more on guile and control than overpowering stuff. In 1983 Alexander seemed like a journeyman pitcher at the end of his career when he put himself on the disabled list (and in Yankee owner Steinbrenner's doghouse) by injuring his hand punching a concrete wall in frustration. He was picked up by the Blue Jays and, though he started out by losing his first six games, he turned it around with a club record 8-game winning streak. He went on to win a club record 17 games the following season. In 1985 he won 17 games again, including the game that clinched the AL East pennant on the penultimate day of the season. He accused Toronto management of not wanting to win badly enough to pay him what he felt he was worth, and after badmouthing local fans, was traded to Atlanta, where his pitching was uninspiring. Traded to Detroit midway through the 1987 season, Alexander had a 1.53 ERA and a 9–0 record in an exciting pennant race for the Tigers, including two dramatic victories over the Blue Jays in the final days of the season. Often a slow starter, he had a surprisingly good first half in 1988, earning his first All-Star selection. However, he pitched less well for the remainder of the season as the weak Tigers were beset by injuries and fell out of first place. /(TF)

Gary Alexander — 1953– . C-DH 1975–81 Giants, A's, **Indians**, Pirates 432 g, .230, 55 hr, 202 rbi

Strikeouts and throwing errors short-circuited Alexander's ML career. Splitting the 1978 season between Oakland and Cleveland, he led all ML catchers with 27 homers but also led the ML with 166 strikeouts while batting only .225. The next year, his 18 errors led all ML catchers. /(ME)

Grover Cleveland Alexander
(Pete) — 1887–1950. RHP 1911–30 **Phillies**, Cubs, Cardinals 5189 ip, 373–208, 2.56. 20 wins: 11, 13–17, 20, 23, 27 *3 WS, 43 ip, 3–2, 3.35*
☛ *Led League—w 11, 14–17, 20. Led League—era 15–17, 19–20. Led League—k 12, 14–17, 20. Hall of Fame—1938.*

Pete had difficulty with everything in life except pitching. He was a solitary man and said little, and that in a small, whispery voice. His teammates respected him, and his longtime catcher, Reindeer Bill Killefer, was his friend.

Alexander's alcoholism was well known even before Ronald Reagan portrayed it in the movie "The Winning Team." But in spite of rumors of his pitching drunk or badly hung over, alcohol had no discernible effect on Alexander's performance until late in his career. He also suffered from epilepsy, which was sometimes mistaken for drunken behavior. The disease first appeared in 1918 during his service in France with the artillery, which partially deafened him. Despite his problems, Alexander was one of the most successful pitchers in ML history.

Many of his minor league experiences were inauspicious. Playing for Galesburg, IL, of the Central Association in 1909, he tried to break up a double play and took the shortstop's relay directly in the head. Unconscious for two days, he awoke with double vision. Galesburg sent him to Indianapolis (American Association), but, still disoriented, he broke three of the manager's ribs with his first pitch. Indianapolis sent him home and sold his contract to the Syracuse Chiefs of the International League over the winter. By spring, his vision had cleared and he won 29 for the Chiefs, including 15 shutouts.

The Phillies acquired Alexander for $750 in 1911. As a rookie, he led the NL in wins (28), complete games (31), innings pitched (367), and shutouts (7). Four of the shutouts were consecutive; one was a 1–0 win over Cy Young, then in his final season.

Alexander's greatest years were in Philadelphia (1911–17), despite a right-field wall in the Baker Bowl that was only 272 feet from home plate. He won 190 games (one-third of the team's total for the period), won 30 or more three straight years, 1915–17, and led the NL in every important pitching statistic at least once. His 16 shutouts in 1916 is still the ML record.

Traded with catcher Bill Killefer to the Cubs in 1917 for a battery of considerably lower caliber and $55,000, Pete won another 128 games for Chicago. But when Joe McCarthy took over as manager in 1926, he sent his drinking pitcher to the Cardinals for the $6,000 waiver price.

Alexander was ungainly, with a shambling walk; his uniform never seemed to fit properly, and his cap looked a size too small. Yet his pitching motion was economical, apparently effortless, and marvelously graceful. His windup was minimal, his stride short, his delivery three-quarters overhand. His right arm swung across his chest and the ball seemed to emerge from his shirtfront. He warmed up quickly. On the mound he was deliberate but without wasted time or motion.

He had a live fastball that moved in on right-handed hitters and a sharp-breaking curve. He had no changeup as such, but could change speeds on both the fastball and the curve to achieve the same effect. He kept the ball low and on the outside of the

Grover Cleveland Alexander

plate. His control was extraordinary (career: 1.65 walks per 9 innings), and batters who tried to wait him out usually fanned.

His most famous victim was Tony Lazzeri of the Yankees. In the seventh inning of the final game of the 1926 WS, with the Cardinals ahead 3–2, the Yankees had two out and the bases loaded. Alexander, who'd won two games, including a complete game the day before, relieved for St. Louis. On four knee-high pitches, he struck out Lazzeri, then pitched two more hitless innings to wrap up the World Championship.

After his 1926 heroics, Alexander got his best contract ever: $17,500. He responded with 21 wins in 1927, but he was 40 years old. The whiskey and age were taking their toll. After leaving the majors, he pitched in demeaning circumstances with touring teams until he was 51. He retired believing his 373 wins placed him one ahead of Christy Mathewson for the most career NL victories, but later statistical research added another win to Matty's total. /(ADS)

Hughie Alexander — 1917– . OF 1937 **Indians** 7 g, .091, 0 hr, 0 rbi

A fast, strong centerfielder, Alexander was an All-Star in both his minor league seasons, hitting .348 with 28 HR and 102 RBI for Fargo-Moorehead (Northern League) in 1936 and .344 with 29 HR in only 79 games for Springfield (Mid-Atlantic League) in 1937. He played in seven games with the Indians that year, but in December 1937 he mangled his left hand in an oil-drill accident and it was amputated.

Alexander became a scout for Cleveland in 1938 and signed Allie Reynolds and Dale Mitchell for the Indians. He joined the White Sox in 1952 and the Dodgers in 1956. Before he left the Dodgers for Philadelphia in 1970, he signed three-quarters of their 1970s infield: Steve Garvey, Ron Cey, and Bill Russell. He was made chief scout of the Phillies in 1979, and in 1987 followed Dallas Green to the Cubs as special player consultant. /(FVP)

Andy Allanson — 1961– . C 1986– **Indians** 395 g, .246, 12 hr, 112 rbi

A lithe, take-charge catcher, Allanson's handling of the 1986 Cleveland pitching staff was in part responsible for the Indians' resurgent, 84–78 mark. He was named the Topps All-Rookie catcher. Despite his size (6'5", 220-lb), he didn't homer until his 1,025th pro at-bat, in the Kingdome that June 23. The Indians, feeling they were perhaps a better-hitting, veteran catcher away from contention, signed Rick Dempsey for 1987, demoting Allanson. Cleveland

finished dead last (61–101). Allanson was again the starting catcher in 1988. /(JCA)

Bernie Allen — 1939– . 2B 1962–73 **Twins**, Senators, Yankees, Expos 1139 g, .239, 73 hr, 351 rbi

Allen, a T-quarterback from Purdue, had his best major league season his rookie year, with career highs in homers (12), RBI (64), and BA (.269). After that, his bat faded, and he was mostly a part-time defensive specialist. In five seasons with the Twins, he hit .318 as a visitor in Washington, but batted just .193 in 1967 after his trade to the Senators. /(BC)

Bob Allen — 1937– . LHP 1961–63, 66–67 **Indians** 274 ip, 7–12, 4.11

Allen posted a 2.98 ERA with five saves in his final season as an Indians reliever, but his 0–5 mark earned him a one-way ticket to the Pacific Coast League. /(MC)

Dick Allen — 1942– . 1B-3B-OF 1963–77 **Phillies**, Cardinals, Dodgers, White Sox, A's 1749 g, .292, 351 hr, 1119 rbi. *1 LCS, 3 g, .222*
☛ *Rookie of the Year—64. Most Valuable Player—72. Led League—hr 72, 74. Led League—rbi 72.*

Talented, controversial, charming, and abusive, Allen put in 15 major league seasons, hitting prodigious homers and paying prodigious fines. Called "Richie" at first, in mid-career he became, adamantly, "Dick." He was praised as a money player and condemned as a loafer.

He made 41 errors at third base (which he had not played in the minors) for the Phillies in 1964, but his 29 home runs, 91 RBI, 201 hits, and .318 BA earned him Rookie of the Year honors. A deep cut on his right hand, which he reported having suffered while pushing a stalled car, affected his throwing and the Phillies made him a first baseman/outfielder in 1967. He hit 40 home runs in 1966 and 177 through 1969, but off-the-field behavior brought him a 28-day suspension, a $500-a-day fine, and a trade to the Cardinals at the end of '69. The swap proved doubly controversial when Curt Flood refused to report to the Phillies and challenged the reserve clause in court, forcing St. Louis to substitute Willie Montanez. The Cardinals passed Allen on to the Dodgers after one year, and they traded him to the White Sox a year later. Each trade added to Allen's reputation as an unmanageable loner.

In 1972, with easygoing Chuck Tanner as his White Sox manager, he led the AL in homers (37),

Dick Allen

RBI (113), walks (99), and slugging percentage (.603) and was named MVP. In 1974, he was on his way to a similar year when he "retired" with a month left to play, giving no reason. Despite his vacation, he led the AL with 32 home runs.

The Sox traded him to Atlanta for cash and a player to be named later in December 1974, but before he could play for the Braves they sent him to the Phillies in May 1975 for Barry Bonnell, Jim Essian, and cash. When Essian was turned over to Chicago as Atlanta's player to be named later, he'd been swapped for Allen twice in less than half a year. After two sub-par years in Philadelphia and one in Oakland, Allen retired for good, still an enigma. His brothers Ron and Hank played in the majors./(BC)

Ethan Allen — 1904- . OF 1926-38 **Reds**, Giants, Cardinals, Phillies, Cubs, Browns 1281 g, .300, 47 hr, 501 rbi

Allen, who never played in the minors, was a trim, lefthanded-hitting outfielder, who hit consistently

well over a 13-year ML career. A bright, articulate man, he later served as the motion picture director of the NL, became a successful college baseball coach, and authored several books on baseball playing techniques. /(FS)

Frank Allen (Thin Man) — 1889-1933. LHP 1912-17 **Dodgers**, Pittsburgh (FL), Braves 970 ip, 50-66, 2.93

Allen suffered through three losing seasons with the Dodgers (in the best of them, 1913, he went 4-18—the worst record in the majors—despite a better-than-average 2.83 ERA). He was making $2,000 a year in 1914 when he jumped to the Federal League at the end of the season. It proved fortunate for the 6'1" 158-lb Allen, who finished second in the league with 23 wins and six shutouts in 1915. The highlight of his season came early, when, on April 24, he no-hit St. Louis, walking four and striking out two to defeat Bob Groom 2-0.

After the demise of the Federal League, he became a Brave and continued to pitch well (8-2, 2.07), but dropped off to 3-11, 3.94 in 1917./(NLM)

Hank Allen — 1940- . OF 1966-70, 1972-73 **Senators**, Brewers, White Sox 389 g, .241, 6 hr, 57 rbi

The older brother of Dick and Ron Allen shuttled between Triple-A and Washington from 1966 through 1970. Tabbed "indifferent" by several managers, he had good speed, a fair arm, and trouble hitting righthanders./(JCA)

Johnny Allen — 1905-1959. RHP 1932-44 Yankees, Indians, Browns, Dodgers, Giants 1950 ip, 142-75, 3.75. 20 wins: 36 *2 WS, 4 ip, 6.23*
☛ *All-Star—38.*

The tempestuous, hard-throwing Allen had shouting matches with team officials and umpires. He had a spectacular 17-4 rookie record with the Yankees in 1932, but a sore arm two years later and his habitual angry holdouts provoked his trade to the Indians in 1936. He was 20-10 that year, and won his first 15 decisions in 1937 before dropping a final 1-0 heartbreaker to Detroit. In 1938, he put together a string of 12 wins in a row before hurting his arm, and from then on was used as a spot starter and reliever. Pitching for Brooklyn in the 1941 WS, he held the Yankees scoreless in three relief appearances./(JD)

Lee Allen — 1915-1969. *Writer.*

For ten years the historian at the Baseball Hall of Fame, Allen was formerly a feature writer for the

Cincinnati *Enquirer*, served as public relations director for the Reds, and also conducted radio and TV programs in Cincinnati and Philadelphia. Known as "Baseball's Walking Encyclopedia," he brought 55 cartons of books and record files with him to Cooperstown. Allen often spent time in small towns ferreting out information about old players. Among his books: *The Official History of the Cincinnati Reds, The History of the World Series, The National League Story,* and *The American League Story.* He played a major role in the compilation of the original *Baseball Encyclopedia.* /(NLM)

Lloyd Allen — 1950- . RHP 1969-75 **Angels,** Rangers, White Sox 297 ip, 8-25, 4.70

Allen was an Angels' bullpen hopeful in the early 1970s, and had his best year in 1971 (15 saves, 2.49). Although he pitched a seven-inning no-hitter for San Jose (California League) in 1968, he had a 1-12 record in the majors as a starting pitcher. /(SFS)

Maury Allen — 1932- . *Writer.*

Allen, a writer for the New York *Post* and *Sports Illustrated,* wrote *Where Have You Gone, Joe DiMaggio?* in 1975. His other books include *Baseball's 100* and *Now Wait a Minute, Casey.* /(NLM)

Mel Allen [Melvin Allen Israel] — 1913- . *Broadcaster.* ☛ *Hall of Fame—1978.*

The voice of Mel Allen is as resonantly warm and friendly as it is deep and authoritative. First heard on the radio in 1935, when he did football games for the University of Alabama, Allen continued on the air through the 1980s narrating television's "This Week In Baseball."

He became famous as the "Voice of the Yankees" (1939-64), a job and a team he loved. His home-run call, "That ball is going, going, gone!" became a trademark, as did his frequent exclamation, "How about that!" In 1978 he and Red Barber were the first broadcasters voted into the Hall of Fame (in the so-called Writers' Wing). /(MG)

Neil Allen — 1948- . RHP 1979-88 **Mets,** Cardinals, Yankees, White Sox 985 ip, 58-69, 3.85

Allen's emergence as a bullpen stopper in 1980 was one of the Mets' few bright spots in the first part of the decade. The clubhouse cut-up had seasons of 22, 18, and 19 saves (1980-82). After a poor start in 1983, at which point Allen confessed an alcohol problem, the Mets traded him to the Cardinals, who were unloading Keith Hernandez for suspected drug use. Hernandez became a team leader on the Mets;

Allen bounced around and hit bottom in 1987, when he was 0-8 for the White Sox and the Yankees. It was his second stint with the Yankees; in 1988 he pitched an unusual shutout for them. Relieving in the first inning with none out and a runner on first base, he picked off the runner; a special scorer's decision gave him a shutout, but not a complete game. /(SH)

Newt Allen [Newton Henry] (Colt) — 1901-1988. 2B-SS-OF-MGR Negro Leagues 1920-48 Kansas City Tigers, All-Nations, Kansas City Monarchs, St. Louis Stars, Detroit Stars, Homestead Grays, Cincinnati Clowns 640 g, .293, 16 hr

For 23 years, Newt Allen was the foundation of the powerhouse Kansas City Monarch teams that won 10 league championships. He was just 5'7" and 169 lbs, but displayed amazing strength and endurance in his baseball travels. Considered the premier second baseman during the formative years of the Negro National League, he made fielding his position an art. Former teammate Chet Brewer said, "Newt was a real slick second baseman, he could catch the ball and throw it without looking. Newt used to catch the ball, throw it up under his left arm; it was just a strike to first base. He was something! Get that ball out of his glove quicker than anybody you ever saw."

Allen attended Lincoln High School in Kansas City, MO with future Monarch teammates Frank Duncan and Rube Currie. The three organized a local team called the Kansas City Tigers, named after the school mascot. After a brief amateur career, in 1921 Allen joined the semi-pro Omaha Federals, for whom he was playing second base when discovered by Monarch owner J.L. Wilkinson. He signed with the All-Nations, toured with them for most of 1922, and was promoted to the Monarchs in October.

The switch-hitting Allen was a line-drive hitter and a skilled bunter. Aggressive on the basepaths, he was not afraid to break up a double play. He twice led the Monarchs in hits, doubles, and stolen bases. He paired with shortstops Willie Wells, Jesse Williams, and Dobie Moore to form extraordinary DP combinations. As Monarch captain, he led his club to the Black World Series in 1924, 1925, and 1945. In the first BWS, against Hilldale in '24, he had seven doubles and batted .281. His best year was 1929, when he hit .330 and led the team with 24 doubles and 23 stolen bases. In 1930 he batted .356.

Allen spent parts of the 1931 and 1932 seasons with the St. Louis Stars, Detroit Stars, and Homestead Grays, as well as with the Monarchs. In 1937 the Monarchs joined the newly-formed Negro American League; with Allen as their manager, they won five pennants (1937, 1939–42). In 1942, at the age of 41, Allen made his final BWS appearance; he batted .267 in the Monarchs' four-game sweep of the Homestead Grays.

Playing in Cuba for two winters, he batted .313 for the Almendares club in 1924–25 and .269 for the Habana team in 1937–38. He toured Japan, the Philippines, and the Hawaiian Islands with other Negro Leaguers. In 24 recorded games against major league competition, he batted .301. /(LL)

Gary Allenson (Hardrock) — 1955– . C 1979–85 **Red Sox**, Blue Jays 416 g, .221, 19 hr, 131 rbi

Allenson was International League MVP with Pawtucket in 1978. He shared catching duties in Boston with Carlton Fisk, and later Rich Gedman. He might have lasted longer had he been better able to hit major league breaking pitches. /(JCA)

Gene Alley — 1940– . SS-2B 1963–73 **Pirates** 1195 g, .254, 55 hr, 342 rbi. *3 LCS, 8 g, .040. 1 WS, 2 g, .000*
☛ *All-Star—67–68. Gold Glove—66–67.*

In 1966, the slight, soft-spoken Virginian teamed with second baseman Bill Mazeroski for a ML-record 215 double plays. A mediocre hitter, Alley was a good bunter, and an excellent hit-and-run man. He won Gold Gloves in 1966 and '67. A 1967 shoulder injury reduced his effectiveness and along with knee problems caused him to consider early retirement several times. He persevered through 1973. /(JCA)

Bob Allison — 1934– . OF 1958–70 **Senators/Twins** 1541 g, .255, 256 hr, 796 rbi. *2 LCS, 5 g, .000, 1 rbi. 1 WS, 5 g, .125, 1 hr, 2 rbi*
☛ *Rookie of the Year—59. All-Star—59, 63–64.*

A college fullback and all-around athlete, Allison admitted, "Hitting is the hardest thing I have ever tried to learn in my life." Learn he did. The Missourian ranks third among Twins home run hitters. His 30 in 1959 helped him become AL Rookie of the Year, and five times he hit 29 or more. He and roommate Harmon Killebrew were the first ML players to combine for two grand slams in one inning (7/18/62). In 1963 he led the AL in runs scored (99) and he hit homers in three consecutive at-bats on May 17. Burly #4 was a hustling fielder—his backhand diving catch in Game Two of the 1965 World Series was a typical effort—and an aggressive, hard-sliding baserunner. Killebrew once said of him: "He wants to win at everything—cards,

ping pong, handball, or baseball. He wants to be first on the airplane and first on the bus." /(JCA)

All-Star Game — 1933–

Arch Ward, the sports editor of the Chicago *Tribune*, put together the first All-Star Game in 1933 as a part of Chicago's Exposition that year. The contest has retained its basic form ever since: teams of NL and AL stars, usually chosen by the fans and the year's All-Star managers, compete against each other in a mid-summer exhibition game.

For the first game, played in Comiskey Park, the managers were the senior pilots of their respective leagues: the recently retired John McGraw for the National League and Connie Mack, still going strong in his thirty-third straight year as manager of the Philadelphia Athletics. In subsequent years the pennant-winning managers of the previous season guided the teams, and in the years 1935–46 they selected the entire lineup. From 1947 to 1957 the vote for the starting lineup was returned to the fans, but Cincinnati fans stuffed the ballot box in 1957, producing a starting lineup with only one non-Reds player. The Cardinals' Stan Musial joined Reds Ed Bailey, Johnny Temple, Roy McMillan, Don Hoak, Wally Post, Frank Robinson, and Gus Bell. Commissioner Ford Frick kicked Post and Bell off the team to make room for Hank Aaron and Willie Mays, and took the vote away from the fans, giving it to the players, coaches, and managers. It was returned to the fans in 1970. Each year, various sportswriters and broadcasters decry the injustices of the latest vote, as reputations, rather than current performances, govern voter preferences. Ballot stuffing in Oakland and a weak crop of AL catchers made the A's Terry Steinbach a starter in 1987 (he was batting .218 at the time), but Steinbach became the hero of the game, winning the MVP award with a solo homer and two RBI. In 1989, Mike Schmidt was elected to start at third base for the NL despite having retired in May, and Jose Canseco was named to the AL starting lineup after missing the entire first half of the season with an injured wrist (neither one played).

There have been many memorable moments in the All-Star Games. The aging Babe Ruth won the first Game with a three-run homer, setting an early pattern of AL dominance by the younger league's abundance of superstar sluggers. The 1934 game featured Carl Hubbell striking out Ruth, Gehrig, Foxx, Simmons, and Cronin consecutively, the first three on twelve pitches with two runners on in the first inning. He then struck out Lefty Gomez, the

AL pitcher; Hubbell's six strikeouts in an All-Star Game have since been tied but not bettered. However, the AL won the game and took the 1935 contest too, before the NL finally won in 1936.

An unfortunate incident occurred in the 1937 game when Earl Averill's line drive hit Dizzy Dean on the toe. When told by the doctor that the toe was fractured, Dean said, "Fractured, hell! The damn thing's broke!" He hurt his arm by favoring his foot when he came back, shortening his Hall of Fame career.

The first shutout was recorded by the NL in a 4–0 victory in 1940, Paul Derringer getting the victory with support from Bucky Walters, Whit Wyatt, Larry French, and Hubbell. The AL was 12–4 in the first sixteen years of the mid-summer contest, including a thrilling 1941 victory on Ted Williams's three-run homer with two out in the bottom of the ninth inning and the AL down 5–4. The 1942 contest was followed a day later by a game won by the AL All-Stars 5–0 over Mickey Cochrane's Service All-Stars (mostly major leaguers in the military). In a losing cause in 1943, the NL's Johnny Vander Meer was the first pitcher to equal Hubbell's six strikeouts. The 1944 Game featured Phil Cavaretta setting an All-Star mark by reaching base five times (triple, single, three walks). In 1946 Ted Williams returned from military service to hit two HR (including the famous clout off Rip Sewell's blooper pitch) with four hits and five RBI as the AL won 12–0.

The 1949 game saw the first black All-Stars: Jackie Robinson, Don Newcombe, and Roy Campanella for the NL, and Larry Doby for the AL. In the 1950s the NL began to even the overall record, winning seven of the eleven contests (there were two All-Star Games each season starting in 1959). The most exciting All-Star Game of the decade was the 14-inning contest of 1950, tied on a Ralph Kiner HR in the ninth and won by a Red Schoendienst homer. Larry Jansen pitched one-hit ball for five innings and struck out six. Ted Williams broke his elbow while robbing Kiner with a catch against the wall in the first inning, but Williams stayed in the game and had an RBI single in the fifth inning. Williams had also saved the 1949 contest with a running catch of a Don Newcombe liner that was slicing away from him with the bases loaded in the second inning.

In the 1960s the NL went 11–1, with one tie. Some have attributed this to senior circuit teams' earlier willingness to sign black players who became superstars, such as Willie Mays, Ernie Banks, Willie Stargell, and Bob Gibson. Stan Musial, helped by the two-contest-a-year format that continued through 1962, set an All-Star record by playing in 24 games. Denny McLain pitched three perfect innings in the 1966 contest, but the NL won yet again on a game-winning 10th-inning single by Maury Wills that drove in Tim McCarver. In 1967 Tony Perez homered in the 15th inning off Catfish Hunter to give the NL a 2–1 victory in the longest All-Star Game ever. Pitching dominated the game to such an extent that there were 30 strikeouts, including 6 by Ferguson Jenkins. Rico Carty became the first player elected as a write-in candidate as his comeback season caught the ballot makers by surprise in 1970. The NL won that year on 12th-inning singles by Pete Rose, Billy Grabarkewitz, and Jim Hickman. Rose scored the winning run in a famous home-plate collision with catcher Ray Fosse that broke Fosse's collarbone. He was never the same afterwards. The win was the NL's eighth in a row, and they started a new streak of 11 straight in 1972. Lee Mazzilli was the surprise hero in 1979, tying the game with an eighth-inning HR in his first All-Star at-bat and then walking in the ninth with the bases loaded for the win. The only AL win in the 1970s came in 1971, when Reggie Jackson crushed a mammoth home run that caromed off a light standard atop the right-field roof at Tiger Stadium.

The AL finally reached parity in the mid-1980s starting with their 1983 victory, which featured the first-ever All-Star grand slam, by Fred Lynn. Dwight Gooden was the youngest All-Star ever in 1984 at the age of 19, and he and Fernando Valenzuela struck out six consecutive batters between them, breaking Hubbell's mark. Valenzuela equaled Hubbell's individual feat in 1986, striking out Don Mattingly, Cal Ripken, Jesse Barfield, Lou Whitaker, and pitcher Ted Higuera consecutively. The NL won another extra-inning game in 1987 on a two-out 13th-inning triple by Tim Raines; they have won all eight extra-inning affairs and lead the series, 37–22./(SH)

Mel Almada — 1913–1988. OF 1933–39 **Red Sox**, Senators, Browns, Dodgers 646 g, .284, 15 hr, 197 rbi

The Browns traded their longtime star, Sammy West, to Washington for this Mexican-born leadoff hitter in June 1938, and Almada batted .342 the rest of the way. His skills disappeared during the off-season, and a poor start in 1939 resulted in his sale to Brooklyn./(JK)

Bill Almon — 1952– . SS-3B-OF-2B-1B 1974–88
Padres, Expos, Mets, White Sox, A's, Pirates, Phillies
1236 g, .254, 36 hr, 296 rbi

Almon attended Brown University in his native
Providence, Rhode Island, was named *TSN* College
Player of the Year, and was the first player chosen in
the June 1974 draft, signing with the Padres for
$100,000. Tall and rangy, Almon became starting
shortstop for San Diego in 1977, but Ozzie Smith
came along in 1978 and Almon was relegated to
utility duty. Released by the Mets in 1980, in 1981
Almon was second in AL Comeback Player of the
Year voting, batting .301 for Chicago, the best
batting average for a starting AL shortstop in 11
years. He returned to a utility role with Oakland and
Pittsburgh. /(ME)

Roberto Alomar — 1968– . 2B 1988- **Padres** 301 g,
.282, 16 hr, 97 rbi

The younger son of Sandy Alomar, Sr., who is now a
Padre coach, Roberto became the regular Padres
second baseman in 1988, hitting .266 with 24 stolen
bases. /(JFC)

Sandy Alomar [Santos Conde] — 1943– . 2B-SS-3B
1964–78 Braves, Mets, White Sox, **Angels,** Yankees,
Rangers 1481 g, .245, 13 hr, 282 rbi. *1 LCS, 2 g, .000*
☛ *All-Star—70.*

Alomar played every position but pitcher and
catcher in the majors. A light hitter, he became a
regular with the 1968 White Sox after he learned to
switch hit. Though he led AL second basemen in
errors in 1968 and 1969, most observers considered
the errors a by-product of his exceptional range. He
was California's everyday second baseman for five
years, played 648 consecutive games from 1969 to
1973, and in 1971 led the league with 689 at-
bats—a since-broken AL record for a switch hitter.
Sold to the Yankees in 1974, he led the AL in
fielding at 2B in 1975. He stole 20 or more bases in
seven seasons, and 227 lifetime. He became a
manager in his native Puerto Rico, and a coach for
the Padres, the team that signed his sons Roberto,
an infielder, and Sandy, Jr., a catcher. /(MC)

Felipe Alou — 1935– . OF-1B 1958–74 Giants,
Braves, A's, Yankees, Expos, Brewers 2082 g, .286,
206 hr, 852 rbi. *1 LCS, 1 g, .000. 1 WS, 7 g, .269, 1 rbi*
☛ *All-Star—62, 66, 68.*

The oldest and the only power hitter of the Alous,
Felipe spoke out loudly and often for Latin American players, arguing that they were underpaid and
overly criticized for being "hot dogs." A tall, solemn
man, Felipe was among the first born-again Chris-
tians to come to the big leagues. His finest year was
1966 with the Braves when he hit 31 homers and
batted .327, his 218 hits and 122 runs leading the
league. Felipe seldom struck out. Later he became a
batting coach and minor league manager with the
Montreal Expos. San Francisco fans still recall he
scored the winning run in the Giants' come-from-
behind victory over the Dodgers in the final game of
the 1962 playoff. /(JD)

Jesus Alou (Jay) — 1942– . OF 1963–79 **Giants,**
Astros, A's, Mets 1380 g, .280, 32 hr, 377 rbi. *2 LCS, 5 g,*
.429, 1 rbi. 2 WS, 8 g, .150, 3 rbi

Jesus, the biggest but slowest of the three Alou
brothers, was usually called "Jay" by broadcasters,
who feared a report "Jesus strikes out!" might be
construed as blasphemy. When he joined Felipe and
Matty on the Giants late in 1963, they appeared as
the only ML all-brother outfield. The next season,
when Felipe was traded, Jesus replaced him as the
Giants' rightfielder. A competent contact hitter, he
lacked Felipe's home run power and Matty's speed.
He later played on Oakland's 1973-'74 World
Champions, mostly as a DH or pinch hitter. /(JD)

Matty Alou — 1938– . OF-1B 1960–74 Giants, **Pirates,**
Cardinals, A's, Yankees, Padres 1667 g, .307, 31 hr,
427 rbi. *2 LCS, 8 g, .333, 2 rbi. 2 WS, 13 g, .139, 1 rbi*
☛ *Led League—ba 66. All-Star—68–69.*

The 5'9" 160-lb Matty was the best hitter for
average and the fastest of the three Alou brothers as
well as the smallest. The feisty Dominican had his
finest year when he came from the Giants to the
Pirates in 1966, leading the league in batting at .342.
In 1969 he topped the NL in hits and doubles. The
only lefty of the Alous, he lined hits to all fields and
batted .300 seven times. As a late-season pick-up in
1972, he hit .381 in the LCS and helped Oakland to
their first World Championship. He and Felipe
played together in the 1962 Series against the
Yankees, and played together near the ends of their
careers on the 1973 Yankees. The three brothers
were together on the same team only briefly when
Jesus came up in 1963 to join the Giants, but did all
start one game together in the outfield. /(JD)

Whitey Alperman [Charles Augustus] — 1879–1942.
2B 1906–09 **Dodgers** 450 g, .237, 7 hr, 141 rbi

Alperman was the Dodgers' starting second baseman in 1906, '07, and '09. He hit a career-high .252

in 1906 and tied for the NL lead in triples in 1907 with 16. He also led NL second basemen with 6.2 chances per game in 1907 and 42 errors in 1909. /(JM)

Walt Alston (Smokey) — 1911–1984. 1B 1936 **Cardinals** 1 g, .000, 0 hr, 0 rbi.
   Manager 1954–76 **Dodgers** 2040–1613, .558. First place: 55–56, 59, 63, 65–66, 74 *1 LCS, 3–1, .750. 7 WS, 20–20, .500*

Alston carved out a Hall of Fame career as a manager of the Brooklyn and Los Angeles Dodgers. A product of the "Cradle of Coaches," Miami (Ohio) University, Alston tried almost every position during a 13-year minor league playing career (1935–47). Initially a third baseman, he moved to first base in 1936 and led the Mid-Atlantic League with 35 homers. Promoted to St. Louis, Alston struck out in his only major league at-bat. His first managerial assignment came while he was still a player, with Portsmouth (Mid-Atlantic League) in 1940. He led the circuit in homers (28), but the club finished sixth. The following two years, Alston led the Mid-Atlantic League in homers and RBI. He moved up, as player only, to Rochester (International League), but was released in 1944. Branch Rickey, who knew Alston from his days as the Cardinal's GM, hired him as player-manager at Trenton (Interstate League) on July 28, 1944, beginning Alston's 33-year run as a skipper in the Dodgers' organization. He spent two seasons at Trenton, one at Nashua, one at Pueblo, and two at St. Paul. After leading St. Paul to the Junior World Series in 1949, Alston was promoted to Brooklyn's top minor league club, Montreal. During four seasons in Canada, guiding many of Brooklyn's future stars, Alston's Royals never finished below second place. Finally, on November 24, 1953, Walter O'Malley named Alston to replace Charlie Dressen, who wanted a multi-year contract, a Dodger taboo. Alston served under 23 consecutive one-year contracts. Following charismatic helmsmen like Leo Durocher, Bert Shotton, and Dressen, Alston kept a low profile in the dugout. A quiet, dignified leader, Walt refused to panic following a disappointing second-place finish in 1954. He proved he was boss in 1955, quelling clubhouse turmoil just before the start of the season. With a lineup of stars, Alston led Brooklyn to its only World Series victory in 1955 and a pennant in 1956. Alston adapted to his talent: the power-laden Brooklyn clubs, the pitching-rich Los Angeles Dodgers of the 1960s, and the young team of the 1970s. Sandy Koufax, Don Drysdale,

Walter Alston

and Maury Wills led the group that earned four pennants in eight seasons from 1959 to 1966. Steve Garvey, Dave Lopes, and Ron Cey headed Alston's last great team. At age 62, Alston guided his 1974 Dodgers to a seventh and final World Series. He was honored as Manager of the Year six times by Associated Press and five times by United Press International. In eight All-Star Game assignments, he was the winning manager a record seven times. Alston was the first 1970s manager inducted into the Hall of Fame. /(ME)

Dave Altizer (Filipino) — 1876–1964. SS-OF-1B-2B-3B 1906–11 **Senators**, Indians, White Sox, Reds 514 g, .250, 3 hr, 116 rbi

After serving with the Army in China and the Philippines during the Boxer Rebellion and the Spanish-American War, Altizer played every position but pitcher and catcher. He was known for shouting "No, no, no" whenever he was tagged out. In 1908 he invented a postcard with a photo of William Jennings Bryan which, when held up to the light, also showed a photo of the White House. Altizer later umpired in the minors. /(NLM)

George Altman — 1933- . OF 1959-67 **Cubs**, Cardinals, Mets 991 g, .269, 101 hr, 403 rbi
☛ *All-Star—61-62.*

The lefthanded hitter improved his average each of his four years as a Cub regular, reaching a career-high .318 in 1962. In 1961 he had 27 home runs, led the NL in triples (12), and hit an All-Star Game pinch homer. Traded to the Cardinals in 1963, his home run production and BA plummeted. After another poor year with the Mets, he returned to the Cubs for three years as a pinch hitter.

Playing in Japan for Lotte and Hanshin, 1968–75, he hit .309 with 205 HR, and credited martial arts training for his improvement. /(JCA)

Joe Altobelli — 1932- . 1B-OF 1955, 57, 61 **Indians**, Twins 166 g, .210, 5 hr, 28 rbi.
Manager 1977–79, 83–85 **Giants**, Orioles 439–406, .520. First place: 83 *1 LCS, 3-1, .750. 1 WS, 4-1, .800*

Although only a weak-hitting utility man in three ML seasons, Altobelli was successful as a manager. He was Manager of the Year three times in 11 minor league seasons, and earned the same honor in 1978 when he brought the San Francisco Giants in third. In 1983, his first year as manager of the Orioles, he won the AL pennant and defeated the Phillies in the WS. /(FK)

Nick Altrock — 1876–1965. LHP 1898, 1902–09, 12–15, 18–19, 24, 29, 31, 33 Louisville (NL), Red Sox, **White Sox**, Senators 1515 ip, 82–75, 2.67. 20 wins: 05–06 *1 WS, 18 ip, 1-1, 1.00*

Altrock was a standout for the early White Sox, winning 20 games plus one in the WS for the 1906 "Hitless Wonders." A sore arm ended his active career, but in his many years as a ML coach he made token playing appearances through 1933. Florid-faced, with a shock of unruly hair that whitened with age, Altrock was famous for his clowning in the coaching box and before games, teaming first with Germany Schaefer and later with Al Schacht. /(JK)

George Alusik (Turk, Glider) — 1935- . OF 1958, 61–64 Tigers, **A's** 298 g, .256, 23 hr, 93 rbi

The 6'4" 175-lb Alusik had fair home run power in his lanky frame but no chance of breaking into the Tigers' Colavito-Bruton-Kaline outfield. Sold to the A's, he platooned with lefthanded hitter Manny Jimenez and became a useful pinch-hitter. /(FJO)

Luis Alvarado (Pimba) — 1949- . SS-2B-3B 1968–74, 76–77 Red Sox, **White Sox**, Indians, Cardinals, Tigers, Mets 463 g, .214, 5 hr, 84 rbi

Named International League MVP in 1969, Alvarado failed to hit in three trials with Boston. Traded to the White Sox on December 1, 1970 with Mike Andrews for Luis Aparicio, he was expected to replace Aparicio at shortstop. But the slick-fielding Puerto Rican with the quick release never hit above .232. /(RL)

Jose Alvarez — 1956- . RHP 1981-82, 88 **Braves** 162 ip, 8-9, 2.99

This relief pitcher finally stuck in the majors at the age of 32. He began his career in the Braves' system, was let go by them and by three other organizations, and was picked up again by the Braves in 1986. /(SFS)

Max Alvis — 1938- . 3B 1962–70 **Indians**, Brewers 1013 g, .247, 111 hr, 373 rbi
☛ *All-Star—65, 67.*

The consistent and popular Texan had lifetime highs of .274 and 22 homers as a rookie in 1963. A career-threatening bout with spinal meningitis disabled him for six weeks in 1964, but he made a remarkable comeback and was an All-Star in 1965. In both 1963 and 1967, he was voted the Indians' Man of the Year. /(JCA)

Brant Alyea [Garrabrant Ryerson] — 1940- . OF 1965, 68–72 Senators, **Twins**, A's, Cardinals 371 g, .247, 38 hr, 148 rbi. *1 LCS, 3 g, .000*

Slow afoot and a frequent strikeout victim, Alyea had one outstanding season. In 1970, in only 94 games, he hit .291, with 16 homers and 61 RBI, to help push the Twins to the AL West title. /(MC)

Joey Amalfitano — 1934- . 2B-3B 1954-55, 60-67 **Giants**, Astros, Cubs 643 g, .244, 9 hr, 123 rbi.
Manager 1979-81 **Cubs** 66-116, .363

Amalfitano signed with the Giants as an 18-year-old bonus baby in 1954, and under the rule of the time had to be kept on the ML roster, hindering both the Giants' pennant chances and his own development. After finally receiving some minor league training (1956–59), he returned to the Giants as a utility infielder, never hitting enough to hold a regular position. He coached for several ML teams, and in 1979–82 he was one of the Cubs' "rotating" managers. /(JD)

Ruben Amaro — 1936– . SS-1B 1958, 1960–69 Cardinals, **Phillies**, Yankees, Angels 940 g, .234, 8 hr, 156 rbi

☛ *Gold Glove—64.*

Although his weak bat and some hard luck limited him to reserve roles most of the time, the personable Mexican's glove, range, and versatility kept him in the majors for 11 years. When Yankee shortstop Tony Kubek was forced to retire after the 1965 season, New York traded infielder Phil Linz to the Phillies for Amaro. His three years in New York were plagued by injuries, which started with a collision with leftfielder Tom Tresh in his first week in a Yankee uniform./(AB)

Wayne Ambler — 1915– . SS-2B 1937–39 **Athletics** 271 g, .224, 0 hr, 73 rbi

Although he was offered a $5,000 bonus by a NL club just before his graduation from Duke University, Ambler signed with Connie Mack's Athletics, explaining: "Mr. Mack paid for my entire college education without ever asking for an accounting or my signature on a contract."/(NLM)

American Association — 1882–1892. League.

The American Association was formed by midwestern clubs who resented the National League's ban on beer and Sunday baseball. Dominated by the St. Louis Browns of brewing magnate Chris von der Ahe, the league thrived, quickly making peace with the NL. However, the Players' League revolt undid the AA, which (on the advice of the NL) expanded to 12 teams in 1890 to directly compete with the PL, a disastrous move that exacerbated the ills of that strife-torn year and led to the AA's being absorbed by the NL after the 1891 season./(SH)

American League — 1901–

The American League was the brainchild of Ban Johnson, the president of the Western League, which was the strongest minor league in the 1890s. It was upgraded by Johnson and former major leaguer Charles Comiskey, the owner of the St. Paul franchise. By 1900 it was renamed the American League, and in 1901 it went into open competition with the National League, the only other major league at the time. Comiskey moved the St. Paul club to Chicago, and the new league also competed with the NL head-on in Boston and Philadelphia; the other franchises were in Detroit, Milwaukee, Cleveland, Baltimore, and Washington.

Johnson stocked his new league with major league players by starting a bidding war for their services, ignoring the reserve clause in the NL contracts. The low salaries paid by NL clubs, enforced with a $2,400 salary maximum, made it easy to lure stars such as Cy Young, John McGraw, Willie Keeler, Napoleon Lajoie, Ed Delahanty, Jesse Burkett, and others. Connie Mack signed Lajoie for the Philadelphia Athletics by offering him a $6,000 contract, and Lajoie won the Triple Crown with 14 HR, 125 RBI, and a tremendous .422 average (still the AL record). When a Pennsylvania court ruled that Lajoie had to return to the Phillies, Johnson convinced Mack to transfer the highly desirable star to the Cleveland franchise to keep him in the AL. For a while, Lajoie did not accompany the team on trips to Philadelphia, a small consolation to Mack. This kind of owner solidarity helped the young league survive the war with the senior circuit, although it certainly helped that the AL outdrew the NL in all three cities in which they both competed in 1901. The Milwaukee franchise moved to St. Louis for 1902 and, now competing in four cities, the AL once again outdrew the NL in head-to-head competition; overall attendance for the eight-team league was 2,228,000 in a 136-game schedule compared to the NL's 1,684,000.

After the 1902 season, there was a peace settlement between the two leagues; the NL sought a merger, but Johnson knew he had the upper hand, and held out for full acceptance by the NL. The only concession the AL had to make was to promise not to place a franchise in Pittsburgh; they did move the Baltimore club to New York, they were allowed to keep all the players they had taken from the NL, and the AL reserve clauses were to be respected. The American League based its popularity on its contrast to the rowdyism of the National League, with Johnson especially noted for his strong support of the league's umpires. In the NL an arbiter's authority depended largely on his own presence (which is how Bill Klem became famous), but Johnson stood behind all of his umpires and tolerated very little abuse of them by players or managers. This was a major element in John McGraw's decision to move to the NL's New York franchise, and McGraw tried to block the AL's move of the Baltimore club to New York. The bad feelings between McGraw and Johnson led to another conflict the next year. The revival of the two-league concept allowed the resumption of postseason play in 1903 with the inaugural World Series, won by the Boston Pilgrims over the Pirates, but when McGraw's Giants won in 1904, he refused to play the Pilgrims. He did deign to meet Mack's Athletics in 1905, and the Series has continued uninterrupted ever since, as has the peace between the two leagues.

The profitable American League expanded its schedule to 154 games in 1904. It had good luck in attracting young talent that turned out to be of superstar caliber. Ty Cobb, Shoeless Joe Jackson, Ed Walsh, Addie Joss, Tris Speaker, Walter Johnson, and most of all Babe Ruth brought the AL more publicity, and helped the junior circuit win twice as many World Series as the NL through 1918.

In 1919 the Black Sox scandal rocked the game as key members of the seemingly invincible White Sox threw the WS to the Reds for payoffs from gamblers. The AL's antidote was the legendary Babe Ruth. He had set what many considered to be an unbreakable record in 1919 by hitting 29 HR for Boston (19 ahead of the runners-up). After being sold to the Yankees for the 1920 season, Ruth benefited from several changes regarding the ball: it was livelier, it was cleaner (the spitball was outlawed), and it wasn't kept in play until it was falling apart. Ruth hit an unprecedented 54 HR in 1920 with his then unorthodox (and later much-copied) uppercut swing, and he proved to be quite a gate attraction. League attendance was over five million, more than a million and a half above the previous high and a million better than the NL total. Ruth's 54 HR was 35 ahead of runner-up George Sisler, but Ken Williams adopted the new strategy and soon he, Bob Meusel, Al Simmons, Lou Gehrig, and Joe Hauser were breaking the 20-HR barrier as Ruth set a new standard with 60 HR in 1927. When the next generation came along in the 1930s with the new style as a normal part of their repertoire, stars like Jimmie Foxx, Earl Averill, Hank Greenberg, Indian Bob Johnson, Joe DiMaggio, Hal Trosky, and Rudy York hit 30 HR regularly, occasionally challenged Ruth's record, and enabled the AL to dominate in the early years of the All-Star Game.

Ban Johnson continued as the autocrat of the American League until 1927, but his control over all of baseball slipped after the Black Sox scandal led to the appointment of Judge Landis to the new office of Commissioner. The peace settlement back in 1903 had included the founding of the National Commission, a triumvirate composed of the AL and NL presidents and Cincinnati owner Garry Herrmann that decided disputes between clubs and between clubs and players. Johnson had been able to dominate this board, but met his match in Landis. It didn't help that the scandal also precipitated a break between Johnson and Comiskey. Johnson resigned when it became apparent to him that he was never going to remedy the situation. Ernest S. Barnard became AL president, but he died in 1931 and was succeeded by Will Harridge, who lasted a record 28 years.

Meanwhile, the Yankee dynasty that Ruth had started shared power with such mini-dynasties as the Senators (1924–25, '33), the Athletics (1929–31), and the Tigers (1934–35); New York won 14 AL pennants between 1921 and 1943. The Yankees also won the World Series ten times in that period; four additional AL victories added to American League domination of the postseason. In the tradition of Ruth, the AL was a hitters' league, and offense drew in the fans in numbers the NL couldn't match. In Boston, owner Tom Yawkey and general manager Eddie Collins paid dearly for West Coast stars Ted Williams and Bobby Doerr, and the Red Sox became respectable for the first time since Harry Frazee had sold off Ruth and others to pay the debts on his Broadway shows. But the two Hall of Famers brought Boston only one pennant (1946).

Yankee hegemony reached its peak after the war: from 1947 to 1964 they won fifteen AL pennants and ten World Series, including a record five straight under manager Casey Stengel (1949–53). This new Yankee dynasty was built around Mickey Mantle, Yogi Berra, and Whitey Ford and featured strength at every position and the solid pitching of the "Big Three": Allie Reynolds, Vic Raschi, and Ed Lopat. GM Ed Barrow and farm director George Weiss had put together the AL's best minor league system, and the dynasty seemed self-perpetuating. Al Lopez was elected to the Hall of Fame as a manager largely on the strength of being the only manager to take the flag away from New York in the 1950s, winning in 1954 and 1959. Managing Cleveland from 1951 to 1956 and Chicago starting in 1957, he finished second every other year in the decade.

The first AL franchise move in 50 years came when the St. Louis Browns moved to Baltimore for the 1954 season. Harridge's reign ended in 1959, and former All-Star Joe Cronin succeeded him as AL president. The 1960s brought more change, and (eventually) the end of the Yankee dynasty. The AL jumped the gun on expansion to get a California franchise (the Los Angeles Angels) and to let Calvin Griffith get out of Washington. Griffith's original Senators became the Minnesota Twins and a new franchise took their place in Washington. The ten-team structure required a 162-game schedule, which instantly led to controversy. Roger Maris, having adapted his swing to the short right-field porch at

Yankee Stadium, hit 61 HR in 1961 to break Ruth's season record. But Ruth had hit 60 in only 154 games. Commissioner Ford Frick, a former ghostwriter and drinking buddy of Ruth's, ruled that Maris had to match or set the record in the same 154 games; after that span of time, Maris had 59 HR. The infamous asterisk that Frick placed next to Maris's record was later overturned by the rules committee.

The biggest change in baseball was not the length of the schedule or the location of the franchises. In 1962 the Player Development Plan was adopted to deal with the troubled minor leagues, which had been losing money and teams for years. A plan to distribute the talent to stock the minors (and eventually, of course, the majors too) followed in 1965 with the introduction of the annual free-agent draft. The Yankee franchise had already developed the problems that would bring it crashing down to last place in 1966 after a sixth-place finish in 1965, but their inability to buy up all the young talent in the future doomed them to a lengthy stretch of mediocrity. The Yankee collapse ended the last vestiges of AL dominance. New York had lost the last two World Series, and the NL was winning the All-Star Game almost every year; AL teams had been slower than their NL counterparts to sign up minority talent, and the imbalance was great. AL attendance dropped off radically in 1965. As the Yankees lost their attraction, the NL drew five million more fans than the AL.

Baltimore became the new league dynasty thanks to their fine farm system and to the wise acquisition of Frank Robinson from the NL's Reds. Robinson won the Triple Crown in his first AL season (1966) and led the Orioles to their first-ever World Championship, something their precursors, the Browns, had never won. Baltimore became truly dominant after the second expansion in 1969, when the 12-team league was split into two divisions. They won three straight AL flags (1969–71), with division titles in 1973–74, and added another AL pennant in 1979.

The move to divisional play was an effort to get around the problem of too many losers each season. With two divisions in each league, more teams could contend, and do so later in the season. The newly minted Pilots lasted just one season in Seattle, moving to Milwaukee in 1970. The Kansas City Royals, better judges of young talent, became a Western Division dynasty later in the decade. Kansas City was available for an expansion franchise because Charlie Finley, the maverick owner of the Athletics (whom he rechristened the A's), had

moved his team to Oakland in 1968 in an effort to duplicate the attendance success of the Dodgers, Giants, and Angels on the West Coast. He failed at that, but he succeeded in building one of the most exciting teams in the league. Based on the superstar talents of Catfish Hunter, Vida Blue, Reggie Jackson, and Rollie Fingers, the team won five consecutive division titles (1971–75) and three straight World Championships (1972–74) and led the league each year in clubhouse vendettas and player-owner squabbles. Just to make sure they got attention, Finley literally changed the face of baseball by offering them rewards for growing mustaches, and also outfitted them in a variety of green, gold, and white uniforms.

Meanwhile, the league dealt with continuing attendance problems by approving a radical rule change, the designated hitter (DH). Allowing another player to bat for the pitcher perked up offense and attendance. This step was taken in the last year of Joe Cronin's administration. In 1974 Lee McPhail (the son of former owner Larry McPhail) took over the AL presidency.

What broke up the A's, and revived the fortunes of the Yankees, was the advent of free agency. Hunter showed the shape of things to come when he became a free agent after Finley reneged on part of his contract. George Steinbrenner, the New York owner, acquired Hunter's services with an unheard-of $3.5– million-dollar, five-year contract in 1975. Pitchers Andy Messersmith and Dave McNally challenged the reserve clause that year and won. Thereafter, players could, with varying restrictions, sell their services to the highest bidder after fulfilling certain requirements as to length of service. Finley's players hated him and seized the chance to escape. Finley saw trouble coming and traded or sold his best players when he could. Jackson and Ken Holtzman were traded to Baltimore for Don Baylor and Mike Torrez (although Finley was unable to hang onto Baylor and traded Torrez to the Yankees after less than two seasons). The sales of Joe Rudi and Rollie Fingers to the Red Sox and Vida Blue to the Yankees, for a million dollars each, were voided by Commissioner Bowie Kuhn "in the best interests of baseball."

The Yankees, besides signing many former A's—in addition to Hunter in 1975, they got Jackson and Ken Holtzman for 1977—assumed the characteristics of those Oakland teams: internecine feuding ameliorated by common opposition to the owner. They also had the success typical of the A's, winning three straight league titles (1976–78) and two World Series (1977–78). At the end of the

1980s, they were still the last team to repeat as World Champions.

Free agency is seen as a major factor in the new era of parity, with almost every team winning at least one division title, the exceptions in the AL being Cleveland and Texas. The Texas franchise has largely continued the losing tradition of its ancestors, the Senators. The team moved to Arlington, Texas after the 1971 season, bringing about a league realignment, with Milwaukee and Texas switching divisions. But the biggest change came in 1977, when the AL expanded again (this time without corresponding expansion by the NL). The addition of the Toronto Blue Jays and Seattle Mariners gave the AL 14 teams, and it adopted a much-criticized balanced schedule that resulted in each team playing more games outside its division than within it. At the time, the Western Division was considerably weaker than the East, and the Western clubs wanted more home dates against the East's more established and better-drawing teams.

Red Ames with the Giants

Interest in baseball boomed after the 1977 expansion, linked by many observers to the fact that almost every team had a turn at winning (the Mariners joined Texas and Seattle as the have-nots, but Toronto won its division in 1985). Dr. Bobby Brown, a former Yankee star and former part-owner of the Texas club, succeeded McPhail as AL president in 1984. /(SH)

Red Ames [Leon Kessling] — 1882–1936. RHP 1903–19 **Giants**, Reds, Cardinals, Phillies 3192 ip, 183–167, 2.63. 20 wins: 05 *3 WS, 11 ip, 0–1, 2.45*

In his major league debut, Ames threw a five-inning no-hitter against the Cardinals (9/14/03). He went on to pitch on four Giants pennant-winners; for the 1905 World Champions, Ames went 22–8, Christy Mathewson 31–8, and Joe McGinnity 21–15. Though Ames never again won more than 15, he remained a dependable New York starter through 1912. In the season opener on April 15, 1909, he no-hit Brooklyn into the 10th inning and went the route, losing 3–0 in the 13th.

Ames lost a league-high 23 games for Cincinnati in 1914 but, oddly, tied for the NL lead with six saves. With the Cardinals, his seven saves in 1916 and eight relief wins in 1917 were also NL highs. /(JK)

Sandy Amoros — 1930– . OF 1952, 1954–57, 1959–60 **Dodgers**, Tigers 517 g, .255, 43 hr, 180 rbi. *3 WS, 12 g, .161, 1 hr, 4 rbi*

The Cuban native, who spoke almost no English, was never more than a semi-regular in the Dodger outfield, but he's remembered for one great play, generally listed among the most outstanding in World Series history. In Game Seven of the 1955 WS, his sprinting catch of Yogi Berra's drive down the leftfield line was the key to Brooklyn's victory. According to winning pitcher Johnny Podres: "As great a catch as Amoros made, his relay to Pee Wee [Reese] (to double up Gil McDougald) was even better." When a reporter asked Amoros if he thought he would make the catch, he said, "I dunno. I just run like hell." /(TG)

Anaheim Stadium (The Big A) California Angels 1966– . LF-333, CF-404, RF-333

A modern, three-level stadium 36 miles from Los Angeles, Anaheim Stadium was designed for baseball, opening in 1966 with almost all of its 43,250 seats along the foul lines, and unenclosed in the outfield. It took its nickname, The Big A, from the massive left-field scoreboard, which was supported by a 230-foot-high Angels logo, a letter A with a halo. That scoreboard was forced into the parking lot in 1980 when double-decked outfield seating was added to accommodate the NFL's Rams, making Anaheim a fully enclosed ballpark and raising the baseball capacity to its present 64,593. The playing field remains natural grass. /(SCL)

Larry Andersen — 1953- . RHP 1975, 77, 79, 81–89 Indians, Mariners, Phillies, **Astros** 724 ip, 27–28, 3.33. *1 LCS, 5 ip, 0–0, 0.00. 1 WS, 4 ip, 0–0, 2.25*

A well-known clubhouse prankster and cutup, Andersen spent 10 years in the minors with brief stints in the ML every other year from 1975 to 1981, when he arrived to stay with Seattle. His 2.65 ERA as a middle reliever that year led the Mariners' staff. His offbeat questions, such as "why do we drive on the parkway and park in the driveway," gained him national attention with the Astros. /(SG)

Allan Anderson — 1964- . LHP 1986–88 **Twins** 496 ip, 37–25, 3.72
☛ *Led League—era 88.*

A second-round draft pick in 1982, Anderson finally lived up to his potential in 1988, going 16–9 and leading the AL with a 2.45 ERA despite pitching in the batter-friendly Metrodome. /(WOR)

Bob Anderson — 1935- . RHP 1957–63 **Cubs**, Tigers 841 ip, 36–46, 4.26

Anderson was the number-two man in the Cubs' rotation in 1959 (12–13, 4.13) and 1960 (9–11, 4.11). Moved to the bullpen by Chicago's "College of Coaches" in 1961, he was less effective. Traded to Detroit for Steve Boros after the 1962 season, he had his only winning record in 1963, his final year, going 3–1 in limited relief use. Traded to Kansas City in the Rocky Colavito deal that winter, he never made it back to the majors. /(JFC)

Brady Anderson — 1964- . OF 1988- Red Sox, **Orioles** 188 g, .210, 5 hr, 37 rbi

This Maryland native came to the Orioles in the deal that sent Mike Boddicker to Boston. The speedy centerfielder proved to be a high-percentage basestealer with the ability to draw walks. /(JFC)

Bud Anderson — 1956- . RHP 1982–83 **Indians** 149 ip, 4–10, 3.68

A minor league starter, Anderson was twice called up in mid-season as a reliever for the Indians. He had 7 saves in 1983 but only a 1–6 record. /(ME)

Craig Anderson — 1938- . RHP 1961–64 Cardinals, **Mets** 192 ip, 7–23, 5.10

The name Craig was unlucky with the early Mets. Anderson lost 16 straight with the original 1962 team and 19 in a row over three years. In NL history, the latter streak was rivaled only by teammate Roger Craig's 18 straight defeats in 1963. /(JCA)

Dave Anderson — 1960- . SS-3B-2B 1983- **Dodgers** 662 g, .232, 13 hr, 116 rbi. *1 LCS, 4 g, .000. 1 WS, 1 g, .000*

A bad back hindered Anderson's quest for the Dodgers' starting shortstop job after he was voted the Pacific Coast League's top prospect at Albuquerque. While he didn't continue the Pee Wee Reese, Maury Wills, and Bill Russell legacy as an everyday player, he became a valuable utility man. He contributed significantly in the Dodgers' 1988 World Championship season by filling in for injured regular Alfredo Griffin. /(TG)

Fred Anderson (Spitball) — 1885–1957. RHP 1909, 13–18 Red Sox, Buffalo (FL), **Giants** 986 ip, 53–58, 2.86

The 6'2" 180-lb Anderson spent his most productive years with Buffalo of the Federal League, going 13–16 in 1914 and 19–13 in 1915. He had an 8–8 mark for the NL champion 1917 Giants, with a 1.44 ERA. He had three saves in 1918 to tie for the NL lead. /(JM)

George Anderson — 1889–1962. OF 1914-15, 18 **Brooklyn FL**, Cardinals 269 g, .287, 5 hr, 69 rbi

A lefthanded-hitting leadoff man with reported 3.2-second speed to first, Anderson was a solid Federal League player unable to earn a job in the ML after the Feds folded. /(NLM)

Harry Anderson — 1931- . OF-1B 1957–61 **Phillies**, Reds 484 g, .264, 60 hr, 242 rbi

An outstanding spring training in 1957 won the lefthanded slugger promotion from Class A to the majors. In his sophomore year, he batted .301 with 23 HR and finished third in the NL with 97 RBI. But he led the league in strikeouts, and a chronic problem making contact hastened his ML exit. /(AL)

Jim Anderson — 1957- . SS-3B 1978–81, 83–84 Angels, **Mariners**, Rangers 419 g, .218, 13 hr, 86 rbi. *1 LCS, 4 g, .091*

A high school All-American at Granada Hills, CA in 1975, Anderson played six ML positions, including catcher, but failed to hit in any of them. /(NLM)

John Anderson (Honest John) — 1873–1949. OF-1B 1894–99, 1901–08 **Dodgers**, Washington (NL), Milwaukee (AL)/Browns, Yankees, Senators, White Sox 1627 g, .290, 48 hr, 976 rbi

Anderson was born in Norway. He broke in as an outfielder, and while the switch-hitter batted well, his fielding was terrible; he was moved back and forth between the OF and first base several times. For Brooklyn and Washington in 1898, he led the NL with 22 triples and a .494 slugging average. He hit .330 for the 1901 Milwaukee AL franchise in its only year of existence; the team became the St. Louis Browns in 1902. As a 1906 Senator, Anderson led the AL with 39 stolen bases./(AJA)

Mike Anderson — 1951– . OF 1971–79 **Phillies**, Cardinals, Orioles 721 g, .246, 28 hr, 134 rbi

Before injuries and illness spoiled his career, Anderson excelled as a defensive rightfielder and showed promise as a hitter./(AB)

Ollie Anderson — Unk.–1945. *Umpire* FL 1914

Anderson, who umpired for 40 years in 14 different minor leagues, including Texas, Pacific Coast, and American Association, worked 5,000 consecutive games before an auto accident hospitalized him in 1936. When players objected to his calls, his standard reply was, "I wish I were Santa Claus so I could give you everything you want."/(RTM)

Rick Anderson — 1956– . RHP 1986–88 **Mets**, Royals 97 ip, 4–4, 4.75

Anderson finally got the call at the age of 29 and contributed a 2–1, 2.72 record to the 1986 World Champion Mets. He was traded to the Royals in the deal that brought David Cone to New York.

Anderson pitched an 8–0 no-hitter against Shreveport on May 12, 1979 while with Jackson (Texas League)./(SFS)

Sparky Anderson [George Lee] (Captain Hook) — 1934– . 2B 1959 **Phillies** 152 g, .218, 0 hr, 34 rbi.

Manager 1970– Reds, **Tigers** 1758–1362, .563. First place: 70, 72–73, 75–76, 84, 87 *7 LCS, 18–9, .667. 5 WS, 16–12, .571*

Named Manager of the Year twice in the NL and once in the AL, Anderson is the first manager to win more than 600 in both the NL and the AL and the first to win World Championships in both leagues. His 18 LCS wins lead all managers. He won the NL pennant in his first season, and in nine years at Cincinnati, he won five division titles, four pennants, and two world championships, only once

finishing below second place. He became known as Captain Hook for his frequent early removal of his starting pitchers in an era when that strategy was still unusual. It was a policy dictated by necessity. The "Big Red Machine" was based on offense, and often Anderson lacked a quality rotation. Also, many of the Reds' best starters—Gary Nolan, Don Gullett, and Wayne Simpson—were injury-prone and could not be overworked. But the Reds developed some of the best relief corps in the majors, including Clay Carroll, Wayne Granger, Tom Hall, and Pedro Borbon.

Moving to Detroit in June 1979, Anderson won the World Championship in 1984 and a division title in 1987. He became known for his unbounded optimism and a tendency to overstate his case to reporters. He called Kirk Gibson "the next Mickey Mantle" and handed less-talented players such as Chris Pittaro and Torey Lovullo regular jobs, praising their talents to the maximum, only to see them play themselves back to the minors within months. White-haired since his playing days, the avuncular

Sparky Anderson

Anderson missed time due to nervous exhaustion in 1989, when the Tigers finished a distant last. That season was only his second losing record in his first 20 years of managing.

Starting out with six seasons in the minor league farm system of the Dodgers, Anderson was traded to the Phillies and became their regular second baseman in 1959, his only big league season. After returning to the minors, he became a manager in 1964 at Toronto. Following four more seasons as minor league manager, he returned to the NL in 1969 as a coach for San Diego. He accepted a coaching post with California for 1970 but then was hired to manage Cincinnati. /(AL)

Ivy Andrews (Poison) — 1907–1970. RHP 1931–38 Yankees, Red Sox, **Browns**, Indians 1041 ip, 50–59, 4.14. *1 WS, 6 ip, 3.18*

Periodic arm miseries led Andrews to develop an assortment of pitches to replace his lost fastball. His best year was 13–7 in 1935 with the seventh-place Browns. /(JL)

Mike Andrews — 1943– . 2B 1966–73 **Red Sox**, White Sox, A's 893 g, .258, 66 hr, 316 rbi. *1 LCS, 2 g, .000. 2 WS, 7 g, .250, 1 rbi*
☛ *All-Star—69.*

Erratic in the field, Andrews had some sting at bat. Oakland picked him up in mid-1973 as a backup second baseman for the pennant drive, but when he made two key WS errors, owner Charlie Finley maneuvered him onto the disabled list, enraging teammates, fans, press, and Commissioner Bowie Kuhn. Andrews was reinstated and received a standing ovation at Shea Stadium. Angry at Finley for provoking the embarrassing incident, A's manager Dick Williams resigned during the off-season. Mike's brother Rob later played in the NL. /(AB)

Nate Andrews — 1913– . RHP 1937, 39–41, 43–46 Cardinals, Indians, **Braves** 773 ip, 41–54, 3.46
☛ *All-Star—44.*

After four failed trials lasting less than 40 innings, Andrews escaped the minors during WWII to lead the NL with 20 losses in 1943 and was 16–15 in 1944. His career fizzled when the regulars returned from the war. /(JK)

Rob Andrews — 1952– . 2B 1975–79 Astros, **Giants** 493 g, .251, 3 hr, 91 rbi

The younger brother of Mike Andrews had no power, but his fielding consistency made him a useful backup second baseman. /(EW)

Joaquin Andujar — 1952– . RHP 1976–88 **Astros**, Cardinals, A's 2153 ip, 127–118, 3.58. 20 wins: 84–85 *3 LCS, 18 ip, 1–1, 5.00. 2 WS, 17 ip, 2–1, 3.12*
☛ *Led League—w 84. All-Star—77, 79, 84.*

Referring to himself as "one tough Dominican," the colorful Andujar reached his peak in the mid-1980s as a Cardinal workhorse who worked well on three days' rest. Coming from the Astros, who hadn't been able to handle his unique personality and had misused him in the bullpen, Andujar's 15–10, 2.47 record in 1982 helped St. Louis to a World Championship. He won the LCS clincher 6–2 as the Braves were swept in three games, and had a 1.35 ERA in the World Series, winning Games Three and Seven.

After dropping off to 6–16 in 1983, Andujar led the NL in wins, shutouts, and IP in 1984, going 20–14 with a 3.34 ERA and four shutouts in 261.1 IP. His 21–12 record in 1985 led the Cardinals as they captured the NL pennant, although he pitched poorly in the last two months after four great months and was 1–5 with a 5.76 ERA after August. He continued to struggle in the postseason, getting hit hard in two LCS starts and losing Game Two to the Dodgers. In the World Series, the Royals knocked him out in the fifth inning of Game Three as he lost 6–1, and he had a disastrous relief appearance in Game Seven. Called in in the fifth inning when the Cardinals were already losing by a wide margin, he gave up a hit and a walk and was then ejected, along with manager Whitey Herzog, for complaining vociferously about the umpiring.

Andujar was traded to Oakland that winter and his career wound down amidst injuries and accusations by him that his downfall was caused by a conspiracy against him (he never offered any specifics). One of his injuries with the A's came while taking batting practice despite being in the AL, where the DH rule prevented him from hitting. Although he batted just .127 lifetime, he considered himself quite a hitter, and switch-hit by an unusual system: if he didn't trust the control of the pitcher he was facing, he would go against the usual lefty-righty percentages and bat so that his pitching arm was the more protected back arm. /(SH)

Roger Angell — 1921– . *Writer*

A 1942 graduate of Harvard, Angell joined *The New Yorker* in 1962. His regular reports about baseball for that magazine have been collected into successful and respected books, including *The Summer Game* (1972), *Five Seasons* (1977), *Late Innings* (1982) and *Season Ticket* (1988). /(NLM)

Cap Anson [Adrian Constantine] (Pop)1851–1897. 1B-3B-C 1871–97 Rockford NA, Philadelphia NA, **Cubs** NA 245 g, .352; NL 2276 g, .334, 96 hr, 1715 rbi (inc.)
Manager 1879–98 **Cubs**, Giants 1297–957 .575
☛ *Led League—ba 79, 81, 88. Led League—rbi 81, 86, 88, 91 . Hall of Fame—1939.*

A premier batsman and leader, Anson is widely regarded as the foremost on-field baseball figure of the 19th century. He led the NL in hitting three times and was the first man to get 3,000 hits. As a manager, he took his Chicago team to five pennants. Counting five years in the National Association, he played 27 seasons at the highest level of baseball competition and was a regular each year. He was stern, iron-willed, and incorruptible, and his influence went far beyond the field as baseball became the national game.

After a year at Notre Dame, the 19-year-old Iowan turned pro in 1871 with the Rockford Forest

Cap Anson

Citys of the National Association, the forerunner of the NL. The following season, he joined the Philadelphia Athletics as a third baseman and first baseman. In five NA seasons, he hit over .350 four times. One of the first players signed by William Hulbert when he launched the NL in 1876, Anson helped the Chicago team (then called White Stockings) to the first NL pennant, hitting .356.

Although he'd played mostly as a third baseman and catcher in his early years, when he became playing manager in 1879, he put himself permanently at first base. The stocky six-footer was no artist in the field. He holds the all-time record for most errors committed by a first baseman, but he played at a time when gloves were not used and errors were common. Longevity also helped account for his error record.

He made up for his fielding shortcomings with his bat. In all but two of his 22 NL seasons, he topped .300. He led the league in 1879, 1881, and 1888, with his .399 in '81 his personal high. He led the league in RBI four times and five times drove in more than 100 even though teams played fewer than 100 games each season until 1884. Line-drive singles were his hallmark, although he twice led in doubles and totaled 532 two-base hits over his long career. He hit 96 home runs, but 21 came in 1884, when the White Stockings played at Lake Front Park, with a 180-foot left-field foul line. He had five homerless seasons.

Anson managed the White Stockings to three straight pennants from 1880 to 1882 and two more flags in 1885 and 1886. An innovator, he encouraged basestealing, devised hit-and-run plays, and was one of the first to rotate pitchers. The first manager to institutionalize preseason training, he laid down strict training rules for his players and sometimes enforced them with his fists. He had an explosive temper and could be a cruel bench jockey and umpire baiter. Many of the greatest stars of the 19th century played for him, but none outshone him.

Anson participated in baseball tours of England in 1874 and of the world in 1888–89. He improved the quality of play in his time and spread the game's popularity. He raised the caliber of players with his own integrity and principles. Yet, at the same time, he was a bigot who once pulled his team off the field rather than play against a team with a black player. He is often cited as a force in the banning of black players from ML baseball, an unwritten rule that persisted until 1947. That Anson was a racist is beyond question. The extent of his influence in keeping blacks out of the majors in the 19th century is debatable.

Anson became part-owner of the White Stockings in 1888, but he won no more pennants in the 1890s. The team was so linked with his image that when he finally left after the 1897 season, they were known for a while as the "Orphans." He managed the Giants for 22 games in 1898, then left baseball. When he later had financial problems, the NL attempted to establish a pension for him, but he rejected it. In 1939, he was named to baseball's Hall of Fame. /(AJA)

Johnny Antonelli — 1930- . LHP 1948–50, 1953–61 Braves, **Giants**, Indians 1992 ip, 126–110, 3.34. 20 wins: 54, 56 *1 WS, 11 ip, 1–0, 0.84*
☛ *Led League—era 54. All-Star—54, 56–59.*

One of the first "bonus babies," the tall, dark-eyed Antonelli signed with the Boston Braves for $65,000 in 1948 and pitched only in spots, mostly in relief, before leaving for military service in 1951–52. His 1954 trade to the Giants for Polo Grounds hero Bobby Thomson temporarily infuriated New Yorkers, but Antonelli silenced the critics with a 21–7 mark for Durocher's world champions. He led the NL in winning percentage (.750), ERA (2.30), and shutouts (6), and had a win and a save in the WS. He won 20 again in 1956 and 19 for the San Francisco transplants of 1959, leading the NL in shutouts again in both seasons. His 26 career shutouts constitute 21% of his ML wins. /(JD)

Luis Aparacio (Little Looie) — 1934- . SS 1956–73 **White Sox**, Red Sox 2599 g, .262, 83 hr, 791 rbi. *2 WS, 10 g, .286, 2 rbi*
☛ *Rookie of the Year—56. All-Star—58–64, 70–72. Gold Glove—58–62, 64, 66, 68, 70. Hall of Fame—1984.*

Playing side by side with Nellie Fox during the late 1950s and early 1960s, Aparicio helped form the nucleus of one of the slickest-fielding infield combinations in baseball. His 506 stolen bases ranked him seventh all-time when he retired, and he holds the lifetime shortstop records for games, double plays, and assists and the AL records for putouts and total chances. He dominated on a season-to-season basis too; in the first thirteen years of his career, he led AL shortstops eight consecutive years in fielding, seven times in assists, four times in putouts, twice each in total chances per game and double plays, and only once in errors.

Aparicio succeeded Chico Carrasquel, continuing the Venezuelan connection that gave the White Sox amazing depth at shortstop for years. Chicago was so confident in him as a rookie that they traded Carrasquel, a perennial fan favorite, to Cleveland for Larry Doby. Named Rookie of the Year in 1956, Aparicio led the league in stolen bases for the first of nine straight years. White Sox manager Marty Marion advised Aparicio to shorten his stance and stride into the pitch. Then he was told to play deeper to gain more range. His cannonlike arm took care of the rest. Bill Veeck arrived on the scene in 1959 and was amazed. "He's the best I've ever seen. He makes plays which I know can't possibly be made, yet he makes them almost every day."

Always a steady hitter, but never one of the great ones, Aparicio relied on his speed to make things happen in an era known for lead-footed sluggers. With Aparicio leading off followed by Fox in the lineup, Chicago had a deadly hit-and-run duo that helped catapult them to their first pennant in 40 years. Fittingly, it was Aparicio who fielded the ground ball off of Vic Power's bat that clinched it on September 22, 1959. In 1963, a new general man-

Luis Aparicio

ager decided a house-cleaning was in order, so Aparicio was sent to the Orioles. He established a since-broken AL shortstop record for fielding percentage that year (.983) and remained long enough to get into another World Series in 1966. He had lost some speed, but compensated by becoming a better hitter. Returning to Chicago in 1968, he enjoyed some of his finest years. He topped the .300 mark for the only time in his career in 1970, a year in which his team finished dead last in the standings with 106 losses. Aparicio played his 2,219th game on September 25, 1970 in front of a mere 2,000 fans to break Luke Appling's record of games played at shortstop. Rumors abounded that he was to be the Sox manager at the start of the 1971 season, but instead the club traded him to Boston for Mike Andrews. Aparicio finished his career in 1973, and in 1984 he took his place in the Hall of Fame. Now residing in Venezuela, his son's name is Nelson, after Luis's long-time sidekick Nellie Fox. /(RL)

Bob Apodaca — 1950- . RHP 1973-77 **Mets** 362 ip, 16-25, 2.86

The righthanded reliever was 3-4 with 13 saves and a 1.48 ERA for the Mets in 1975, despite suffering a broken nose during the season. He retired after spending all 1978 and '79 on the disabled list with an elbow injury. /(KT)

Luis Aponte — 1953- . RHP 1980-84 **Red Sox**, Indians 220 ip, 9-6, 3.27

This successful Venezuelan reliever retired for three years after four years in the Red Sox system. Playing in the Inter-American League in 1979, he developed an amazing fork ball and was resigned by the Red Sox. /(EW)

Pete Appleton [born Peter William Jablonski] — 1904-1974. RHP 1927-28, 1930-33, 36-42, 1945 Reds, Indians, Red Sox, Yankees, **Senators**, White Sox, Browns 1141 ip, 57-66, 4.30

An accomplished pianist and college bandleader at the University of Michigan, Pete opted for a baseball career at graduation. He played under his real name until 1933, then had it legally changed to Appleton. Used mainly in relief for most of his ML career, his best year was 1936, when he started 20 games for the Senators and finished 14-9. /(LRD)

Luke Appling (Old Aches and Pains) — 1909- . SS-3B 1930-43, 45-50 **White Sox** 2422 g, .310, 45 hr, 1116 rbi ☛ All-Star—36, 39-43, 46-47. Hall of Fame—1964.

Voted the greatest living White Sox player in a 1969 fan poll, Appling was almost a member of the Chicago Cubs. After two years at Oglethorpe University, Appling signed with the Atlanta Crackers (Southern Association). He was sold to the Cubs late in the 1930 season, but thanks to the intervention of Milt Stock (Eddie Stanky's father-in-law), Appling joined the White Sox in a cash transaction that also involved little-known outfielder Doug Taitt. There was nothing remarkable about Appling's first two seasons. His arm was powerful, but his throws were inaccurate, and sometimes wound up in the stands. Worse yet was his penchant for muffing the most routine ground ball.

The arrival of Jimmy Dykes as manager in 1934 had a positive effect on the young shortstop. Dykes cajoled, pleaded, and instilled confidence. When Appling finally realized that he wasn't going to drive the ball out of spacious Comiskey Park, he adjusted his stance and became one of the most productive hitters of the decade. With a keen batting eye, the leadoff hitter would foul off pitch after pitch before selecting just the right one, or drawing one of his many bases on balls. Legend has it that on one occasion, Appling fouled off seventeen straight pitches before hitting a triple, and his 1,302 lifetime walks (with a high of 122 in 1935) ranks 23rd all-time.

In his greatest year, 1936, Appling led the AL with a .388 average. It was the first batting title won by a White Sox player. He also had a club-record 27-game hitting streak and a seven-for-seven performance over three games. In 1943, at age 35, he won his second batting title. He hit .300 15 times.

Appling held down the shortstop position for nearly twenty years. In that time, he established ML shortstop records for games played and double plays and AL records for putouts and assists; all were later broken by Luis Aparicio. In spite of his everyday play, he acquired the epithet "Old Aches & Pains" through 20 years of complaining about his various physical ailments, the condition of the infield ("I swear, that park must have been built on a junkyard!" As it turned out, he was right), and salary disputes with General Manager Harry Grabiner. A $5,000 bonus promised him for winning the batting title in 1936 was later rescinded. In disgust he tore

Luke Appling

up his 1937 contract. Owner J. Lou Comiskey weathered the storm, and when Appling was ready to play, he was given a new contract. This time he signed on for another year, even though it was $2,500 less than what he wanted. Elected to the Hall of Fame in 1964, Appling worked as a batting instructor for the Atlanta Braves in the 1980s and rekindled memories with a home run off Warren Spahn in the first Cracker Jack Old-Timers' Game. /(RL)

Luis Aquino — 1965– . RHP 1986, 88– Blue Jays, **Royals** 182 ip, 8–9, 3.57

Aquino was converted to starting in 1989 and thrived in the new role. The Puerto Rican native pitched a 2–0 no-hitter against Columbus (International League) on June 20, 1988 while with Omaha (American Association). /(WOR)

Ramon Arano — 1939– . Mexican League.

The 5'8″ 160-lb Arano didn't impress big league scouts but nonetheless became the only pitcher ever to win over 300 games in a single minor league, setting Mexican career marks for games, innings, wins, losses, hits, runs, earned runs, and strikeouts. His totals are complete only through 1984, as 1985 records were lost in the Mexico City earthquake. Except for three games with Oklahoma City at the end of '62, Arano never pitched outside of Mexico. Breaking in with Aguascaliente, he spent 11 years with the Mexico City Reds and eight with Cordoba, where he twice won 19 games. Arano also pitched for Poza Rica, Veracruz, Saltillo, Reynosa, and Coatzcoalcos. /(MC)

Jimmy Archer — 1883–1958. C-1B 1904, 07, 09–18 Pirates, Tigers, **Cubs**, Dodgers, Reds 846 g., .250, 16 hr, 296 rbi, *2 WS, 4 g, .143*

Dublin-born Archer took over as the Cubs' catcher in 1909 when star Johnny Kling was a season-long holdout. Archer, perhaps the best-throwing catcher of his time, made Kling expendable in 1911. Archer's right arm had been terribly burned by hot tar in an industrial accident. In healing, the muscles shortened but were left with a unique strength, enabling him to throw from the squat. This became his trademark. He led NL catchers in assists in 1912. /(JK)

Jose Arcia (Flaco) — 1943– . SS-2B-OF 1968–70 Cubs, **Padres** 293 g, .215, 1 hr, 35 rbi

This native Cuban's nickname, Flaco, means "thin," an apt description for the 6'3″ 170-lb utility man. He hung on with the expansion Padres for two years, but didn't hit enough to last. /(WOR)

Frank Arellanes — 1882–1918. RHP 1908–10 **Red Sox** 410 ip, 24–22, 2.28

In 1909, as the replacement for Cy Young in the Red Sox pitching rotation, the swarthy Arellanes had his one decent year, (16–12, 2.18 ERA), giving up only 1.68 walks per nine innings. He relieved between starts and led the AL with 8 saves. /(EC)

Hank Arft (Bow-Wow) — 1922– . 1B 1948–52 **Browns** 300 g, .253, 13 hr, 118 rbi

A long-ball hitter, Arft hit a triple and a homer in his first game. He led the league in fielding in 1948 and 1950. He lives in St. Louis and runs a successful mortuary business. /(WB)

George Argyros — 1937– . Owner.

Argyros was described by then-NL president A. Bartlett Giamatti as "the James Watt of baseball" (after Reagan's Secretary of the Interior). The deforestation of the Mariners under Argyros has included the trades of such stars as Bill Caudill, Shane Rawley, Ivan Calderon, Danny Tartabull, Phil Bradley, and Mark Langston for a few overage catchers and minor leaguers unlikely to become major league stars. When Argyros bought the Mariners in 1981, he made himself the focus of an advertising campaign called "Playing Hardball" and promised to stamp the team with his own personality. When he sold the franchise in 1989, the Mariners had yet to have their first winning season. A friend of former Commissioner Peter Ueberroth, Argyros has led the major leagues in fiscal restraint, with the lowest salaries to go with the lowest winning percentage. Having the parsimony of a Calvin Griffith without the baseball acumen, Argyros has hired executives from his real estate and airline investments rather than baseball people. His managerial genius was best demonstrated in the 1986–87 off-season when the Mariners gave all their players salary cuts (including the few who played well), and then suggested they attend seminars on positive thinking. /(TF)

Buzz Arlett [Russell Loris] — 1899–1964. OF-1B 1931 **Phillies** 121 g, .313, 18 hr, 72 rbi

The handsome switch-hitter did not reach the majors until he was 32, despite an awesome minor league record. In his one ML year with the Phillies, he hit well but was a lackadaisical fielder. The 6'3" 225-lb Californian began as a pitcher with Oakland of the Pacific Coast League in 1918 and won 108 before becoming a full-time outfielder in 1923. When he retired after 1937, his minor league career marks included a .341 BA and 432 HR. He hit four home runs in a game on two occasions with Baltimore (International League) in 1932. In 1984, the Society for American Baseball Research voted him the outstanding player in minor league history. /(LRD)

Harold Arlin — Unk.–Unk. *Broadcaster.*

On August 5, 1921, Arlin called the first baseball game ever to be broadcast on radio, describing the Pirates' 8–5 victory over the Phillies from a Forbes Field box seat for Pittsburgh's station KDKA. That fall, Arlin worked the first-ever football broadcast as well, a college game between Pitt and West Virginia. /(SL)

Steve Arlin — 1945– . RHP 1969–74 **Padres**, Indians 790 ip, 34–67, 4.32

Arlin threw an Eastern League no-hitter as a Phillies farmhand on July 25, 1967. With the struggling young Padres, he led the NL with 19 losses in 1971 and 21 in 1972. On July 18, 1972, he had a no-hitter with two outs in the ninth when Philadelphia's Denny Doyle singled. That season, he also had a one-hit 1–0 victory, went 10 innings allowing one hit before being relieved in another game, and had two other two-hitters. Of his 34 career wins, 11 were shutouts. Arlin practiced dentistry while still an active player. Arlin's grandfather, Harold Arlin, was the first announcer to broadcast a baseball game. /(MC)

Arlington Stadium Texas Rangers 1972– . LF-330, CF-400, RF-300

Arlington Stadium opened in 1965 as Turnpike Stadium for the local Texas League club, before joining the ML when the expansion Senators moved in as the Rangers. It is a single-level bowl-shaped stadium with no roof at all over the grandstand. Because of its openness it appears larger than its 35,698 capacity, second smallest in the ML. The field is natural grass with little foul territory, and is sunk below ground, so fans enter the stadium in the upper levels of the grandstand. A large Texas-shaped scoreboard stands behind the left-center field seats, and eight tall light towers ring the stadium. Almost all the Rangers' home games (including Sundays) are played at night due to the oppressive summer afternoon heat. Arlington Stadium is adjacent to the Six Flags Over Texas amusement park and is halfway between Dallas and Fort Worth. /(SCL)

Tony Armas — 1953– . OF-DH 1976– Pirates, **A's**, Red Sox, Angels 1432 g, .252, 251 hr, 815 rbi
☛ *Led League—hr 81, 84. Led League—rbi 84. All-Star—81, 84.*

A popular power hitter, Tony Armas was one of baseball's top sluggers until injuries took their toll. Developed in the Pittsburgh organization, he went to Oakland in a blockbuster, nine-player deal on March 15, 1977. Various injuries held him back until 1980, when he hit .279 with 35 HR and 109 RBI. He was *TSN* AL Player of the Year in 1981, tying for the league lead in homers and games played, but leading the league in strikeouts. The free swinger was traded to Boston for the more consistent Carney Lansford in a five-player deal. Armas peaked in 1984 (.268, 43 HR, 123 RBI). He was named to *TSN* and *UPI* postseason AL all-star teams and was Boston's co-MVP. From 1980 to 1985, Armas hit more homers than any AL player. The Venezuelan's next two seasons were ruined by leg injuries. He was replaced by Dave Henderson in the Boston outfield and released after batting just once in the 1986 World Series. He became a valuable role player for the Angels. /(ME)

Bill Armour — 1869-1922. Manager 1902-06 **Indians**, Tigers 382-347, .524

Armour was credited with finding and buying Ty Cobb for $500 while he was Tigers manager. In 1907 he bought a one-third interest in the Toledo club of the American Association. He later scouted for the Cardinals and was business manager for the minor league Milwaukee Brewers and Kansas City Blues in 1914-15. /(NLM)

Jack Armstrong — 1965- . RHP 1988- **Reds** 108 ip, 6-10, 5.33

The Reds made Armstrong their first-round draft pick in June 1987. He pitched a 4-0 no-hitter against Indianapolis on August 7, 1988 while with Nashville (American Association). /(JFC)

Mike Armstrong — 1954- . RHP 1980-87 Padres, **Royals**, Yankees, Indians 338 ip, 19-17, 4.10

Armstrong was a reliable set-up man for Dan Quisenberry in the Royals' bullpen in 1982 and 1983. He relied on a sinking fastball, hard slider, and forkball, and a submarine motion that was difficult to follow. /(FJO)

Morrie Arnovich (Snooker) — 1910-1959. OF 1936-41, 46 **Phillies**, Reds, Giants 590 g, .287, 22 hr, 261 rbi. *1 WS, 1 g, .000*
☛ *All-Star—39.*

A stocky, line drive hitter with little home run power, Arnovich hit a career-high .324 in 1939. /(JD)

Jerry Arrigo — 1941- . LHP 1961-70 Twins, **Reds**, Mets, Cubs 620 ip, 35-40, 4.14

After four years working mostly in relief, Arrigo started 31 games for the 1968 Reds. He responded with his best season, 12-10 and a 3.33 ERA. /(MC)

Fernando Arroyo — 1952- . RHP 1975, 77-82 **Tigers**, Twins, A's 535 ip, 24-37, 4.44

Never a hard thrower, Arroyo finessed his way into the Detroit rotation after Mark Fidrych's injury in 1977, but lost 18 games. In the 1981 strike-

shortened season, he went 7-10 with his only sub-4 ERA (3.94). /(CC)

Luis Arroyo (Yo-Yo) — 1927- . LHP 1955-57, 59-63 Cardinals, Pirates, Reds, **Yankees** 531 ip, 40-32, 3.93. *2 WS, 5 ip, 1-0, 3.86*
☛ *All-Star—55, 61.*

On July 22, 1960, the pudgy Arroyo's acquisition by the Yankees was little noticed; he'd had mixed results in previous trials with three NL clubs, but he mystified AL batters with his screwball. In 1961, he was recognized as the league's top reliever, having taken a direct hand in 44 of the Yankees' 109 victories with 15 relief wins and 29 saves, both AL highs. His reliability contributed to Yankee ace Whitey Ford's first 20-win season. Arroyo then added a WS win, but a sore arm the following spring ended his dominance. /(GDW)

Richie Ashburn — 1927- . OF 1948-1962 **Phillies**, Cubs, Mets 2189 g, .308, 29 hr, 586 rbi. *1 WS, 4 g, .176, 1 rbi*
☛ *Led League—ba 55, 58. All-Star—48, 51, 53, 58, 62.*

The ultimate singles hitter, Ashburn hit leadoff for 15 years, batting over .300 nine times, winning two batting titles and finishing second three times. He is

Richie Ashburn

also the most recent player to hit .300 in his last season; he batted .306 for the expansion Mets and was their only All-Star. He became a Phillies broadcaster in 1963 and is a familiar short and smiling figure who wears an Irish hunting cap.

An All-Star in his first season, Ashburn knew how to get on base, leading the NL in walks four times. He was a model of consistency. He batted 6-for-10 and scored four runs in five All-Star games, and only once did he fail to score at least 84 runs in a season for the Phillies. A spray hitter with little power, 86 percent of his hits were singles. He reached his season high for homers (seven) with the Mets in his last year, playing in the Polo Grounds with its short distances down the lines.

Together with Robin Roberts, Jim Konstanty, Del Ennis, Curt Simmons, and Granny Hammer, he was a core player on the 1950 Philadelphia Whiz Kids, who won the NL pennant on the last day of the season over the Dodgers. On May 20, 1951, he singled eight times in a doubleheader. /(SEW)

Alan Ashby — 1951- . C 1973- Indians, Blue Jays, **Astros** 1370 g, .245, 90 hr, 513 rbi. *2 LCS, 8 g, .129, 1 hr, 3 rbi*

Ashby provided the Astros with 10 seasons of fine catching, quality game calling, and respectable hitting. Houston often tried to displace him with prospects like George Bjorkman, Luis Pujols, John Mizerock, and Mark Bailey, but Ashby beat off successive challenges to keep the regular job year after year. It finally took a bad back and Craig Biggio in 1989 to send Ashby packing; he was released after refusing a trade to Pittsburgh. From 1979 into 1985, he was battered by Joe Niekro's knuckleballs. "All the broken fingers and broken toes I can remember were caused by the knuckler," Ashby said. He was disabled five times with Houston. He tied a NL record for most no-hitters caught: Ken Forsch's (4/7/79); Nolan Ryan's (9/26/81); and Mike Scott's division title clincher (9/25/86). A switch-hitter who was much stronger lefthanded, he became the first Astro to homer from both sides of the plate in the same game on September 27, 1982. /(JCA)

Emmett Ashford (Ash) — 1914-1980. *Umpire* AL 1966-70 *1 WS, 1 ASU*

The first black umpire in the majors, Ashford was hired at age 51 to get five years to qualify for a pension. A loner off the field, Ash was a showboat on the diamond who dressed impeccably for the job wearing jewelry that included flashy cufflinks. In 1982 a Little League field in Los Angeles was named in Ashford's honor. /(RTM)

Tucker Ashford (Thomas) — 1954- . 3B 1976-78, 80-81, 83-84 **Padres**, Rangers, Yankees, Mets, Royals 222 g, .218, 6 hr, 55 rbi

The second player in the 1974 draft, Ashford's weak bat kept him from sticking as the Padres' regular third baseman in 1977. After 18 ML and minor league stops as a player, he became a manager in the Mets' farm system. /(FJO)

Bob Aspromonte — 1938- . 3B 1956, 1960-71 Dodgers, **Astros**, Braves, Mets 1324 g, .252, 60 hr, 457 rbi. *1 LCS, 3 g, .000*

One of many major leaguers produced by Brooklyn's Lafayette High School (including his brother Ken and Sandy Koufax), Aspromonte debuted at age 18 and struck out in his one at-bat with Brooklyn. At the time of his retirement, he was the last active ex-Brooklyn Dodger. He was a regular with the original Houston expansion team in 1962 and stayed through 1968. The celebrated bachelor set a NL record for third basemen with 57 consecutive errorless games in 1962 and added a since-broken NL record for fewest errors at 3B (11) in 1964. He was strictly pull hitter until 1967, when he batted a career-high .294 by hitting to all fields. Supplanted by Doug Rader the following season, he was the last original Colt .45 to leave the franchise. /(JCA)

Ken Aspromonte — 1931- . 2B-3B 1957-63 Red Sox, Senators, **Indians**, Angels, Braves, Cubs 475 g, .249, 19 hr, 124 rbi.
    Manager 1972-74 **Indians** 220-260, .458

The elder of the Brooklyn-born brothers, this flashy-fielding second baseman led the Pacific Coast League in hitting in 1957 (.337) but was inconsistent in the majors. During the 1959 season Ken collected three hits in a game on five different occasions for the Senators. He came closest to being an everyday player in 1960 after being traded to the Indians, for whom he played 117 games, finishing with a career-high .288 average. /(RTM)

Brian Asselstine — 1953- . OF 1976-81 **Braves** 284 g, .254, 12 hr, 68 rbi

A speedy outfielder who showed flashes of power, Asselstine spent much of his career shuttling between the Braves and their Richmond farm club. He had finally won a regular ML job in 1978 when he broke his ankle after 39 games and missed the rest of the season. /(JCA)

Paul Assenmacher — 1960- . LHP 1986- **Braves,** Cubs 279 ip, 19-15, 3.58. *1 LCS, 0.2 ip, 0-0, 13.50*

Assenmacher was signed by the Braves out of a 1983 tryout camp. As a rookie in 1986, he went 7–3 (2.50) with seven saves in 61 appearances, mostly as a lefthanded setup man for Gene Garber. He spent the first month of 1987 on the DL and in 1988, he was tied for the NL lead in appearances, with 54, when he was disabled with recurring shoulder problems. He was 8–7 with five saves in 1988, posting a 1.16 ERA away from Atlanta-Fulton County Stadium but a 4.87 ERA at home. In mid-1989 he was acquired by the Cubs for their successful stretch drive. /(JCA/SCL)

National Association — 1871-1875. League.

The National Association of Professional Base Ball Players, formed in March 1871, was the game's first professional league. Any professional or semi-pro club could enter the NA pennant race simply by paying a $10 fee, and each club was responsible for scheduling its own games with the other contenders. Eight to thirteen clubs began each of the association's five seasons, but each year one to six clubs failed to finish. Only three of the twenty-three clubs that competed in the NA played all five years: Mutual of New York, Athletic of Philadelphia (which won the first NA pennant), and Boston's Red Stockings (who won the other four). /(FIC)

Astrodome Houston Astros 1965- . LF-330, CF-400, RF-330

Called the Eighth Wonder of the World when it opened in 1965, Houston's cavernous Astrodome was the world's first domed stadium. It was erected adjacent to Colt Stadium, home of the Astros in their three seasons as the Colt .45s, and was intended to protect players and fans from the sweltering Texas heat more than to prevent rainouts. In its first season, the Astrodome had a natural grass playing field, and the 4,796 panes of glass in the roof were clear, allowing light through to help the grass grow. Unfortunately, during day games the intense glare made it difficult to see fly balls, and the indoor grass was dying anyway. The roof was painted for the 1966 season, and an artificial playing surface—AstroTurf—was developed. On April 8, 1966 the Astros and Dodgers played baseball's first game on artificial turf.

Inside, the Astrodome is indeed a marvel. Circu-

lar, with five seating levels and air conditioning to keep the temperature at 72 degrees for every game, it has a roof 208′ above the playing field at its highest point, the equivalent of an 18-story building. A huge American flag is suspended in dead center field, and baseball's largest scoreboard runs 474′ across the back wall. Still, the stadium proved to be not quite large enough when Mike Schmidt hit a speaker hanging from the roof in center on June 10, 1974 (the ball fell for a single). And on June 15, 1976, the Astrodome suffered its only rainout when torrential storms flooded the Houston streets and made it impossible to get to the stadium.

The Astrodome has always favored pitchers, and although the dimensions have been shortened from their original 360–420–360, the ball still does not carry well here, reducing the number of home runs. Only three home runs have ever been hit into the stadium's highest level, by Jimmy Wynn, Doug Rader, and Andre Dawson.

Today the Astrodome is hardly as unique as when it opened. The Twins and Mariners both play in larger domed stadiums, and the Astrodome's 45,000 capacity makes it the NL's second-smallest facility. /(SCL)

Joe Astroth — 1922- . C 1945-46, 49-56 **A's** 554 g, .254, 13 hr, 156 rbi

On September 23, 1950, Astroth had six RBIs in an inning, a feat accomplished by only nine others in modern baseball. A fine handler of pitchers, Astroth was Bobby Shantz's personal catcher in 1952, when Shantz won 24 games and the MVP award. /(RTM)

Keith Atherton (Country) — 1959- . RHP 1983-88 A's, **Twins** 527 ip, 33-38, 3.98. *1 LCS, 0.1 ip, 0-0, 0.00 1 WS, 1 ip, 0-0, 6.75*

It took a switch from starting to relief in his sixth year as an A's farmhand to get Atherton to Oakland. With the fastball his only good pitch, he was often touched for home runs. Traded to Minnesota in May 1986, he went 0–7 in August but saved 10 on the season, then was a set-up man for Jeff Reardon and the 1987 World Champions. /(JCA)

Atlanta Braves — 1966- . Team. 1773-2040, .465. *NL West Champions 69, 82*

The first major league team to move to the rich baseball territory of the Southeast, the Braves have struggled despite being located in a booming city and establishing a strong regional (later national) broadcasting network. Ten years after their arrival, attendance had sunk to 534,672 and only the club's purchase by Ted Turner kept the franchise in Georgia. Divisional championships in 1969 and 1982 and Henry Aaron's successful quest for Babe Ruth's career HR record have been the team's high points. In 1973 the Braves became the only team in history with three 40-HR sluggers, as Aaron, Darrell Evans, and Davey Johnson all topped that mark. /(PB)

Atlanta-Fulton County Stadium (The Launching Pad) Atlanta Braves 1966- . LF-330, CF-402, RF-330

One of baseball's earliest circular multi-decked stadiums, Atlanta-Fulton County Stadium was completed in 1965 and by the mid-70s had become known as The Launching Pad for the frequency with which home runs were hit there. Despite reasonable distances to all the fences, local atmospheric and weather conditions make the stadium a slugger's heaven, regularly the scene of more home runs than any other NL park. From 1967 until the early 1980s, Chief Noc-A-Homa, the Braves mascot, who resided in a teepee behind the outfield fence, would celebrate each Braves homer with victorious whooping and dancing, and on April 8, 1974, Hank Aaron hit his 715th career HR to pass Babe Ruth for the all-time ML lead. The stadium features a natural grass surface and distinctive vertical supports on the exterior and is located near three major interstate highways, providing easy access to fans from around the Southeast. It has a capacity of 52,003 and is also home to football's Atlanta Falcons. /(SCL)

Toby Atwell [Maurice Franklin] — 1924- . C 1952-56 Cubs, **Pirates**, Braves 378 g, .260, 9 hr, 110 rbi
☛ *All-Star—52.*

This Army Air Corps veteran almost saw his career come to an end when he hurt his knee sliding while playing for Montreal in 1949. Atwell's 1952 rookie season was his most productive offensively; he hit .290 for the Cubs. /(RTM)

Bill Atwood (Dad Gum) — 1911- . C 1936-40 **Phillies** 342 g, .229, 7 hr, 112 rbi

Nicknamed "Dad Gum" because it was his strongest expletive, the mild-mannered Atwood hit .302 as a rookie for the Phillies, but was never more than a part-time player. /(JK)

Rick Auerbach — 1950- . SS-2B-3B 1971-81 **Brewers**, Dodgers, Reds, Mariners 624 g, .220, 9 hr, 86 rbi

Handed the Brewers shortstop job at age 21, Auerbach kept it for part of 1971 and all of 1972. His weak bat cost him the starting job, but he lasted

seven seasons as a utility man and pinch hitter elsewhere. /(MC)

Don August — 1963- . RHP 1988- **Brewers** 291 ip, 25-19, 4.18

A member of the 1984 Olympic baseball team, August was the Astros' first-round pick in the June '84 draft. Acquired by Milwaukee in the Danny Darwin deal in 1986, he moved into the Brewer rotation in 1988 and had his best season, going 13-7 with a 3.09 ERA. /(SFS)

Jerry Augustine — 1952- . LHP 1975-84 **Brewers** 944 ip, 55-59, 4.23

Named to the 1976 AL All-Rookie Team (9-12, 3.30) as a starter, most of Augustine's career was spent in the bullpen. He retired in the Brewer's top ten in eight major pitching categories. /(JCA)

Eldon Auker (Big Six) — 1910- . RHP 1933-42 **Tigers**, Red Sox, Browns 1963 ip, 130-101, 4.42. *2 WS, 17 ip, 1-1, 4.67*

A submarine pitcher, Auker lost Game Seven of the 1934 World Series to Dizzy Dean after winning Game Four 10-4. In 1935 his 18-7 (.720) mark led the league in winning percentage. He pitched the first night game in St. Louis on May 24, 1940, losing to Bob Feller and Cleveland 3-2. He was a good-hitting pitcher, compiling a .308 mark in 1936. His lifetime average was a capable .187 with six homers. He developed his underhanded style of pitching because of a shoulder injury he had suffered while playing football for Kansas State University, where he starred in basketball as well as baseball. /(WB)

Doug Ault — 1950- . 1B-DH 1976-78, 80 Rangers, **Blue Jays** 256 g, .236, 17 hr, 86 rbi

Chosen by the Blue Jays in the November 1976 expansion draft, Ault helped them win their first-ever game and tied an Opening Day record with two homers. He had career highs of 11 HR and 64 RBI in 1977, his only season as a regular. /(WOR)

Jimmy Austin (Pepper) — 1879-1965. 3B-SS-C 1909-23, 25-26, 29 Yankees, **Browns** 1580 g, .246, 13 hr, 390 rbi.
Manager 1913, 18, 23 **Browns** 31-43, .419

Born in Wales, Austin was one of the best third basemen of his day. In his twelve seasons as a regular, he led the AL five times in total chances per game, four times in double plays, twice each in putouts and assists, and once in fielding average. An inconsistent hitter, he compensated by drawing walks and stealing bases, pilfering 244 lifetime with a high of 37. The switch-hitting chatterbox is most famous for a photo of him at third base, attempting to avoid the flying spikes of Ty Cobb. He signed with Pittsburgh of the Federal League but never reported, as the Browns matched the contract.

Austin was the first of Branch Rickey's "Sunday Managers" with the Browns (Rickey would not enter a ballpark on a Sunday due to an early promise to his mother). Austin had three short stints as the Browns' interim manager. The last four years of his playing career each consisted of just one game, including his sole appearance behind the plate. He coached with the Browns until 1932, when he joined the White Sox for seven years./(WB)

Rick Austin — 1946- . LHP 1970-71, 75-76 **Indians, Brewers** 136 ip, 4-8, 4.62

Up and down for two years with the Indians, Austin earned a second chance with the Brewers with a strong season (2.33 ERA) in 1974 with the Hankyu Braves of the Japan Pacific League./(MC)

Sam Austin — Unk.-Unk. *Writer.*

One of the earliest and best New York baseball writers, Austin covered the game for the New York *Herald* for more than 30 years beginning in the 1880s./(NLM)

Earl Averill [Howard Earl] — 1902-1983. OF 1929-41 **Indians, Tigers, Red Sox** 1669 g, .318, 238 hr, 1165 rbi. *1 WS, 3 g, .000*
☛ *All-Star—33-38. Hall of Fame—1975.*

The Veterans Committee named outfielder Averill to the Hall of Fame 34 years after his final season. He is still the Indians' all-time home run leader with 226 (thanks in part to the short fence in old League Park) and holds Cleveland career records in six offensive categories. His number 3 is one of only three retired by the Indians.

"The Earl of Snohomish" (his hometown) grew up in the state of Washington and played semi-pro ball before signing with San Francisco of the Pacific Coast League in 1926. After three .300 seasons in the PCL, including .354 with 36 home runs and 173 RBI in 1928, the 5'9" 172-lb lefthanded hitter was purchased for a reported $50,000 by Cleveland. On Opening Day, 1929, he became the first AL player to homer in his initial big league at-bat. His 18 HRs (then a team record) and .331 BA in his rookie season helped establish him as one of the Indian's most popular players. A graceful but unspectacular

Earl Averill, Sr. with the Indians

centerfielder, he led all AL outfielders that year with 388 putouts, but his arm, injured in high school, was not strong.

In 1930, Averill hit .339, and on September 17 walloped three home runs in the first game of a doubleheader and another in the second game to become the first ML player to hit four homers in a twin bill. His 11 RBI that day set an AL record. A dead pull hitter, he slammed 32 homers in both 1931 and '32. He became one of the most feared hitters in the league; on August 29, 1932, Red Sox pitchers walked him five consecutive times. He had an off-year (.288) in 1935, largely because he burned his hand testing Fourth of July fireworks, but he bounced back in 1936 to lead the AL with 232 hits, and hit .378, second only to Luke Appling's .388.

His line drive in the 1937 All-Star Game broke Dizzy Dean's toe, an injury that indirectly ended Dean's career. That same year, just before a June game, Averill suffered temporary paralysis in his legs. X-rays revealed a congenital spinal malformation which forced him to change his batting style. His BA and home run output slipped.

He was showered with gifts, including a new Cadillac, on "Earl Averill Day" in Cleveland in 1938. Cleveland fans were outraged the following June when he was traded to Detroit for marginal pitcher Harry Eisenstat and cash. Averill hit .280 in a part-time role for the 1940 pennant-winning Tigers. His son, Earl Douglas, played seven years in the majors. /(JCA)

Earl Averill [Earl Douglas] — 1931– . C-OF-3B 1956, 58–63 Indians, Cubs, White Sox, **Angels**, Phillies 449 g, .242, 44 hr, 159 rbi

Averill came up as a catcher with the Indians, the team with which his father, Howard Earl Averill, fashioned a Hall of Fame career. In 1961, his only solid season, the righthanded hitter batted .266 with 21 home runs for the Angels in their first year. /(JM)

Bobby Avila (Beto) — 1924– . 2B 1949–59 **Indians**, Orioles, Red Sox, Braves 1300 g, .281, 80 hr, 465 rbi. *1 WS, 4 g, .133*
☛ *Led League—ba 54. All-Star—52, 54–55.*

The Indians signed Avila for only $17,500 out of the Mexican League, where he was already a star. The first Mexican to have real ML success, he was the Indian second baseman for eight years and became a national hero in his own country. In a 1951 game at Boston, he hit three homers, a single, and a double. In 1952 he led the AL in triples (11). He won the AL batting title in the Indians' 1954 pennant-winning year when he hit .341 despite playing half the season with a broken thumb.

An adept bunter and daring baserunner, his soccer training paid off several times when he intentionally kicked the ball out of defenders' mitts while sliding. Cleveland manager Al Lopez said Avila had "a fine swing, a sharp eye, a good spirit of competition . . . and a world of confidence in himself."

Dealt three times between December 1958 and July 1959, the dapper, well-educated Avila returned to Mexico in 1960, becoming a politician and, later, president of the Mexican League. /(JCA)

Benny Ayala [Benigno] — 1951– . OF-DH 1974, 76–77, 79–85 Mets, Cardinals, **Orioles**, Indians 425 g, .251, 38 hr, 145 rbi. *1 LCS, 1 g, --, 1 rbi. 2 WS, 5 g, .429, 1 hr, 3 rbi*

Puerto Rico-born Ayala homered in his first ML at-bat (8/27/74) but didn't stick on a ML roster until the Orioles acquired him in 1979. One of the Orioles' role players, he hit 33 homers and had 120 RBI in only 692 Oriole at-bats. /(MC)

Doc Ayers [Yancy Wyatt] — 1890–1968. RHP 1913–21 **Senators**, Tigers 1429 ip, 66–79, 2.84

Ayers earned his nickname by studying medicine. As a ballplayer, he spread germs through the AL as a spitball pitcher. His best year was 14–9 with the 1915 Senators. He was one of the pitchers given special dispensation to continue throwing the spitter after it was banned following the 1919 season. /(JK)

Joe Azcue [Jose Joaquin] (The Immortal Azcue) — 1939– . C 1960, 62–70, 72 Reds, A's, **Indians**, Red Sox, Angels, Brewers 909 g, .252, 50 hr, 304 rbi
☛ *All-Star—68.*

"The Immortal Azcue" was traded to Cleveland in 1963, just hours before their starting catcher broke his hand. The Cuban was less fortunate when he hit into the ML's first unassisted triple play in 41 years (July 29, 1968), turned by Washington's Ron Hansen. He caught no-hitters by Sonny Siebert of the Indians (6/10/66) and Clyde Wright of the Angels (7/3/70) and hit .280 in 1968, his All-Star year. He was a season-long holdout in 1971. /(JCA)

Charlie Babb — 1873–1954. SS 1903–05 Giants, **Dodgers** 347 g, .243, 0 hr, 116 rbi

After his rookie year with the Giants, Babb was traded to Brooklyn along with pitcher John Cronin for veteran shortstop Bill Dahlen. Babb hit .265 in 1904 for the Dodgers but was only fair in the field./(BC)

Johnny Babich — 1913– . RHP 1934–36, 40–41 Dodgers, Braves, **A's** 592 ip, 30–45, 4.93

After pitching without much success in the NL during the mid-1930s, Babich went 14–13 with the Athletics in 1940. Five of his wins helped deny a fifth straight pennant to the Yankees, who finished two games behind the league-leading Tigers./(JK)

Wally Backman — 1959– . 2B 1980– **Mets**, Twins 852 g, .277, 15 hr, 191 rbi. *2 LCS, 13 g, .256, 4 rbi. 1 WS, 6 g, .333, 1 rbi*

Backman was a Mets platoon regular whose speed and high on-base percentage made him a valuable number-two hitter. The switch-hitter teamed with leadoff hitter Len Dykstra (both used against right-handers) to become known as the "Partners in Grime" for their hustling, dirty-uniform style of play for the 1986 World Champions. Backman hit .320 that season and led the Mets with five runs in the LCS against the Astros. In Game Three he led off the ninth inning with a bunt single and scored on Dykstra's HR as the Mets won 6–5, and in Game Five he led off the 12th with an infield hit, advanced to second on a wild pickoff throw, and scored the winning run on Gary Carter's single. In the climactic Game Six, his 14th-inning single drove in a go-ahead run in the seesaw finale, and he scored the Mets' third and final run in the game-winning 16th-inning rally.

Backman was the Mets' first-round pick in the June 1977 draft, but although he hit .323, .278, and .272 in his first three trials with the Mets (1980–82), his mediocre fielding kept him from winning the second-base job. He impressed Tidewater (International League) manager Davey Johnson in 1983, and when Johnson became the Mets' manager in 1984 he brought Backman with him and was

rewarded with 68 runs and 32 stolen bases. In Backman's only year as a regular, 1985, he led NL second basemen in fielding.

The Mets traded Backman to Minnesota after Gregg Jefferies hit .321 in the final months of 1988, and in 1989 he played every day for the Twins when not injured./(SH)

Mike Bacsik — 1952– . RHP 1975–77, 79–80 **Rangers**, Twins 173 ip, 8–6, 4.43

Ranger pitching coach Sid Hudson called Bacsik "one of those kids who didn't quite have enough to make it." Bacsik was 4–2 in relief for the Twins in 1979./(KT)

Fred Baczewski (Lefty) — 1926–1976. LHP 1953–55 Cubs, **Reds** 279 ip, 17–10, 4.45

The highlights of Baczewski's brief career were an 11–4 record for the sixth-place 1953 Reds and an 11-hit shutout of Pittsburgh in 1954./(FK)

Red Badgro [Morris Hiram] (Bad Girl) — 1902– . OF 1929–30 **Browns** 143 g, .257, 2 hr, 45 rbi

Like Jim Thorpe, Ernie Nevers, and George Halas, Badgro made more of a name for himself as a football player than a baseball player. An end who had starred at the University of Southern California, he played with all three New York football teams, the Yankees, Giants, and Dodgers, from 1927 to 1936. In 1981 he was the oldest man ever elected to the Professional Football Hall of Fame.

In baseball, he hit a powerless .284 in 1929 and dropped to .239 in 1930./(WB)

Bugs Baer (Arthur) — 1876–1969. *Writer.*

Baer was a columnist and cartoonist for King Features Syndicate. His column, "One Word Led to Another," ended with the closing of the New York *World-Journal-Tribune.* His quips were widely admired. Among the more famous: "Bodie was out trying to steal second. His head was full of larceny, but his feet were honest," and "DiMaggio, who popped out in his first four at-bats, could have done all his hitting in a chimney."/(NLM)

Jim Bagby, Sr. (Sarge) — 1887–1954. RHP 1912, 16–23 Reds, **Indians**, Pirates 1828 ip, 127–87, 3.10. 20 wins: 17, 20 *1 WS, 15 ip, 1–1, 1.80*
☛ *Led League—w 20.*

The slender, strong-armed Bagby won 23 games in 1917 and 17 in each of the next two seasons. In 1920, when Cleveland won its first pennant, he led the AL in wins (31), winning percentage (.721), innings (339–2/3), hits allowed (338), and relief wins (6). In the WS against Brooklyn he lost Game Two but came back to win the Game Five. Bagby went the distance, giving up 13 hits but only one run, and became the first pitcher to hit a WS home run. Two other WS firsts by teammates helped him: Elmer Smith's grand slam homer and Bill Wambsganss's unassisted triple play. Bagby's son Jim, Jr., also became a major league pitcher./(ME)

Jim Bagby, Jr. — 1916–1988. RHP 1938–47 Red Sox, **Indians**, Pirates 1668 ip, 97–96, 3.96. *1 WS, 3 ip, 0–0, 3.00*
☛ *All-Star—42–43.*

The son of Jim Bagby, Sr., this 6'2" 170-lb right-hander reached his career high of 17 wins in each of his All-Star years (1942–43). He led the AL in starts both years, but he missed much of 1944 in the Merchant Marine and thereafter never won more than eight games./(SFS)

Stan Bahnsen — 1944– . RHP 1966, 68–82 Yankees, White Sox, A's, **Expos**, Angels, Phillies 2528 ip, 146–149, 3.61. 20 wins: 72
☛ *Rookie of the Year—68.*

Bahnsen was 1968 AL Rookie of the Year, going 17–12 (2.05) for the Yankees. He had thrown a seven-inning no-hitter with Toledo in 1966 and a seven-inning perfect game with Syracuse in 1967. In his 1966 major league debut, he struck out the side at Boston.

Bahnsen faltered in 1969 and then had two 14-win seasons. Desperate for third-base help, the Yankees dealt him to the White Sox straight up for Rich McKinney in December 1971. Bahnsen went 21–16 in 1972 but set a since-broken ML record by being removed in 36 of his 41 starts. On August 21, 1973, against Cleveland, he had a no-hitter with two outs in the ninth when Walt Williams bounced a single over a drawn-in Bill Melton at third. Bahnsen won 18 in 1973 but lost a league-high 21. On May 15, 1974, Bahnsen defeated Minnesota 1–0, retiring the first 23 batters before allowing a Bobby Darwin single.

In a second career as a reliever, Bahnsen appeared in 55 and 57 games for the 1979 and 1980 Expos, and 25 games for the 1981 Eastern Division Champions./(RL)

Ed Bahr — 1919– . RHP 1946–47 **Pirates** 219 ip, 11–11, 3.37

The Canadian was a rookie success in 1946 (8–6, 2.63), leading the Pirate staff in ERA. The next year his control problems made him a victim of the "sophomore jinx."/(ME)

Scott Bailes — 1961– . LHP 1986– **Indians** 492 ip, 31–41, 4.70

When the Indians were owed a player from Pittsburgh in mid-1985, they chose Bailes, a Double-A reliever with sharp breaking stuff. He jumped to the majors the next spring and went 10–10 with seven saves, setting a Cleveland rookie record for most relief wins (eight). Though unable to throw too often, making him better suited to starting, he continued to be shuttled between the rotation and the bullpen./(JCA)

Bill Bailey — 1889–1926. LHP 1907–12, 14–15, 18, 21–22 **Browns**, Baltimore (FL), Chicago (FL), Tigers, Cardinals 1084 ip, 36–76, 3.57

After an impressive 4–1 debut in 1907 with the Browns, Bailey's career consisted entirely of losing records, including a 3–18 mark in 1910 and an 8–20 record in 1915 in his second year in the Federal League./(WB)

Bob Bailey — 1942– . 3B-OF 1962–78 Pirates, Dodgers, **Expos**, Reds, Red Sox 1931 g, .257, 189 hr, 773 rbi

Bailey signed with the Pirates for what was believed to be a record bonus of $175,000 in 1961. He was *TSN* Minor League Player of the Year in 1962 and the regular Pirate third baseman for the next four years. The Dodgers traded Maury Wills for Bailey and Gene Michael in December 1966, but Bailey hit only .227 for two consecutive years, and Los Angeles sold him to the expansion Expos.

Bailey hit well for the Expos. Manager Gene Mauch often said: "Bailey means wood. Bailey doesn't mean leather." An opponent added: "They called him Beetle, after the comic strip character. He fielded like a comic strip character." As the starting third baseman in 1972–73, he made 39 errors. Mauch also tried him at 1B and OF.

The Montreal fans developed a love-hate relationship with the slow-footed streak hitter who grounded into 216 lifetime double plays. In 1970 Bailey hit .287 with 28 homers, including one of the longest shots in Astrodome history on August 16. When he was traded in December 1975, he was the leader in nine of ten Expo career batting categories./(JCA)

Ed Bailey — 1931- . C 1953–66 **Reds**, Giants, Braves, Cubs, Angels 1212 g, .256, 155 hr, 540 rbi. *1 WS, 6 g, .071, 1 hr, 2 rbi*
☛ *All-Star—56–57, 60–61, 63.*

Sharing catching duties with Smokey Burgess on the 1956 Reds, the 6′2″ 205-lb Bailey hit 28 home runs as the team tied a National League record by hitting 221. Bailey hit 20 homers in 1957 and 21 in 1963, and was in double figures five other years, but he never drove in more than 75 runs. Platooned throughout his career, he had eight pinch-hit homers, two of which were grand slams. His career featured two very productive games (he hit three home runs in one 1956 game and drove in eight runs in a 1965 contest) and he made two unassisted double plays. When pitcher Jim Bailey was promoted to the 1959 Reds, Ed briefly became part of one of baseball's few "brother batteries." /(FK)

Howard Bailey — 1958- . LHP 1981–83 **Tigers** 119 ip, 6–9, 5.22

The Michigan native went from non-roster player to the Tiger starting rotation in April 1981, only to be sent down five starts later. He recorded four of his five 1983 wins in long relief. /(CC)

Mark Bailey — 1961- . C 1984- **Astros** 322 g, .223, 23 hr, 97 rbi

Signed as a third baseman, the 6′5″ Bailey had been catching less than a year when he vaulted from Double-A to Houston in April 1984 to replace an injured Alan Ashby. He homered in three consecutive games from July 15 to 17, and homered from both sides of the plate September 16. His short apprenticeship as a catcher showed as time went on; he couldn't handle Joe Niekro's knuckleball, and had problems with his catching mechanics and throwing. His shoulder began troubling him in 1986. Although he was extremely patient at the plate (he had more walks than hits in 1986), he still struck out frequently. He began the 1988 season with Houston, but his declining batting average and increasing weight prompted a demotion to Tucson (Pacific Coast League), and in July he was traded to the Expos' organization for infielder Casey Candaele. /(JCA)

Bob Bailor — 1951- . OF-SS-2B-3B 1975–85 Orioles, **Blue Jays**, Mets, Dodgers 955 g, .264, 9 hr, 222 rbi. *1 LCS, 2 g, .000*

The Blue Jays made Bailor, a shortstop in the Orioles' organization, their first pick in the 1976 expansion draft. As a rookie, he hit .310, a record for a player on a first-year expansion franchise. Bailor was hustling, versatile, and injury-prone. After four years as a Toronto regular, he spent 1981–83 as a much-used Mets utility man. He was traded to the Dodgers with Carlos Diaz for Sid Fernandez and Ross Jones, a trade that helped the Mets more than Bailor ever did. /(TF)

Harold Baines (Hal) — 1959- . OF-DH 1980- **White Sox**, Rangers 1428 g, .288, 189 hr, 835 rbi. *1 LCS, 4 g, .125*
☛ *All-Star—85–87, 89.*

Baines was a 12-year-old little leaguer in Easton, MD when he caught the eye of White Sox owner Bill Veeck. When Chicago made him the first pick in the June 1977 draft, Paul Richards said Baines "was on his way to the Hall of Fame. He just stopped by Comiskey Park for 20 years or so." There was much pressure on the soft-spoken 20-year-old when he became a regular in 1980. It wasn't until 1982 that he began to produce, hitting 25 home runs with 105 RBI. With a batting style reminiscent of Mel Ott, the lefthanded hitter led the AL in 1983 with a then-ML record 22 game-winning RBI.

Baines's HR off Milwaukee's Chuck Porter on May 9, 1984 ended the major leagues' longest game ever by time (8:06) and the AL's longest game by innings (25). The bat went to the Hall of Fame. In 1986 Baines suffered a serious knee injury that required two operations, and forced him to DH. His 155th career HR in 1987 set the all-time White Sox record, and he became the first White Sox batter to hit 20 HR in six consecutive seasons. In mid-1989 he was traded to the contending Rangers to give him a chance at another pennant. /(RL)

Doug Bair — 1949- . RHP 1976–86, 89 Pirates, A's, Reds, Cardinals, Tigers 884 ip, 55–43, 3.60. *2 LCS, 2 ip, 0–1, 4.50. 2 WS, 3 ip, 0–1, 6.75*

The epitome of the longtime reliever with one supreme season, Bair had his in 1978 with the Reds. Theretofore an erratic hard thrower, he was suddenly brilliant, winning 7, saving 28, and posting a 1.98 ERA in 70 appearances. His ERA ballooned to 4.31 the next year, although he won 11 and saved 16. Although he would pitch well later in his career, he never again approached the numbers of his one great season. /(MC)

Doug Baird — 1891–1967. 3B-OF-2B 1915–20
Pirates, Cardinals, Phillies, Dodgers, Giants 617 g, .234,
6 hr, 191 rbi

Pittsburgh's Doug Baird and Max Carey were the
NL's best base-stealing tandem in 1915 and 1916.
But Baird batted just .218 over those two seasons
and fanned a league-high 88 times in '15. In 1921 he
broke an American Association record by stealing
72 bases for Indianapolis. /(ME)

Baker Bowl Philadelphia Phillies 1895–1938. LF-341,
CF-408, RF-281

Named for Phillies owner William F. Baker, the
Baker Bowl was a marvel when it opened with
18,000 seats on April 30, 1887, but was the most
outdated park in ML baseball when it was finally
abandoned. A simple wooden grandstand with a 40-
foot-high right-field wall (later increased to 60 feet),
it was badly damaged in an 1894 fire. During an
August 8, 1903 doubleheader the third base stands
collapsed, killing twelve people. The Phillies clung to
their decaying park until 1938, when they joined the
Athletics at Shibe Park, and in 1950 the Baker Bowl
was torn down. No ball ever cleared the 35′ wall of
the centerfield clubhouse. /(SCL)

Del Baker — 1892–1973. C 1914–16 **Tigers** 172 g,
.209, 0 hr, 22 rbi.
　Manager 1933, 38–42 **Tigers** 358–317, .530. *1 WS,
3–4, .429*

A catcher during his 22-year playing career, which
included only three ML seasons with the Tigers,
Baker became a minor league manager in 1927. A
Tiger coach, he replaced Mickey Cochrane as Detroit manager in 1938. An expert sign stealer, he
took the Tigers to the 1940 pennant but lost the WS
to the Reds in seven games. At the time of his death
he was a coach at Trinity College in San
Antonio. /(NLM)

Dusty Baker [Johnnie B., Jr.] — 1949– . OF-1B
1968–86 Braves, **Dodgers**, Giants, A's 2039 g, .278,
242 hr, 1013 rbi. *4 LCS, 17 g, .371, 3 hr, 13 rbi. 3 WS,
18 g, .232, 2 hr, 7 rbi*
☛ *All-Star—81–82. Gold Glove—81.*

Hank Aaron said, "Dusty Baker has more potential
than any outfielder I've seen in all my seasons with
the Braves." Although only a 27th-round draft
choice, Baker seemed ready to realize that potential
when he batted .321 (third in the NL) in 1972, his
first full season in the ML. But after three straight
subpar seasons, he was traded to the Dodgers in
November 1975. Another poor season followed, but
in 1977 he rebounded (.291, 30 HR, 89 RBI). He set

Dusty Baker

a club record against San Diego with five RBI in one
inning, hit .357 with a four-game-record eight RBI
in the LCS, and batted .292 in the World Series. His
two-run homer off Steve Carlton provided the game-
winning RBI in the LCS. In three more LCS, he
never hit less than .316. In 1981, the muscular
leftfielder again finished third in batting (.320), won
a Gold Glove, and made an outstanding catch in the
All-Star Game at Cleveland. A prolonged contract
dispute sent him to the Giants on April 1, 1984; that
year, he hit .292 without the benefit of spring
training. /(ME)

Floyd Baker — 1916– . 3B-2B-SS 1943–55 Browns,
White Sox, Senators, Red Sox, Phillies 874 g, .251, 1 hr,
196 rbi

Baker turned down a football scholarship to sign
with the Browns. After an unimpressive beginning
epitomized by his two strikeouts as a pinch hitter in
the 1944 World Series, Baker developed into one of
the best fielders in the AL. His .317 mark for the
1950 White Sox marked the high point of the
taciturn Virginian's career. /(WB)

Frank Baker (Home Run) — 1886–1963. 3B 1908–14,
16–19, 21–22 **A's**, Yankees 1575 g, .307, 96 hr, 1013 rbi.
6 WS, 25 g, .363, 3 hr, 18 rbi
☛ *Led League—hr 11, 13–14. Led League—rbi 12–13..
Hall of Fame—1955.*

A Maryland farm boy, Baker was a powerful slugger
in the dead ball era, leading or tying for the league
lead in homers four consecutive seasons (1911–14),
although 12 was his top total. Baker earned his
memorable nickname in the 1911 World Series,

when he hit game-winning home runs on successive days against the Giants' future Hall of Fame pitchers Rube Marquard and Christy Mathewson.

The lefthanded hitter was the third baseman in Connie Mack's fabled Philadelphia A's "$100,000 Infield," together in the years 1911–14. Teamed with him were Stuffy McInnis, Eddie Collins, and Jack Barry. Connie Mack broke his team up rather than pay the higher salaries brought on by Federal League competition, and after Baker sat out 1915 in protest, Mack sold him to the Yankees in 1916 for $35,000.

In 1920, Baker was again out of the game, due to the illness and subsequent death of his first wife. He returned to the Yankees as a part-time player and helped the team win its first two World Championships in 1921 and '22. His final at-bat was in the 1922 WS.

Baker managed in the Eastern Shore League in 1924–25 and discovered Jimmie Foxx, delivering him to Connie Mack after the 1924 season. He lived a quiet life on his farm near Trappe, MD, where he was born, making appearances at Old Timers' Games in New York and Philadelphia until his death in 1963. /(JK)

Gene Baker — 1925– . 2B-3B 1953–58, 1960–61 **Cubs**, Pirates 630 g, .265, 39 hr, 227 rbi. *1 WS, 3 g, .000* ☛ *All-Star—55.*

An all-star shortstop in the Pacific Coast League, Baker switched to second base as a rookie with the Cubs in 1954 and, along with shortstop Ernie Banks, was named to the all-rookie team by *TSN*. Although he led NL second basemen in errors for three straight years, he had excellent range and his bat showed occasional home run power. In 1957, Baker was traded to the Pirates along with Dee Fondy for Dale Long and Lee Walls. Early the next season, he injured his knee. He missed all of 1959 and played only a few games in 1960–61 before turning to coaching and scouting for the Pirates. /(MN)

Steve Baker — 1956– . RHP 1978–79, 82–83 **Tigers**, A's, Cardinals 237 ip, 7–16, 5.13

With an explosive but uncontrolled fastball, Baker was 3–11 in parts of two seasons as a starter with the Tigers. He later returned to the ML as a reliever. /(MC)

Steve Balboni (Bones, Bye-Bye) — 1957– . 1B-DH 1981–Yankees, **Royals**, Mariners 842 g, .232, 164 hr, 461 rbi. *2 LCS, 10 g, .111, 1 rbi. 1 WS, 7 g, .320, 3 rbi*

A free-swinging power hitter, Balboni hit 152 HR in the minors from 1979 to 1983, leading his

Frank Baker

league four straight years (1979–82). After three trials with the Yankees he was acquired by the Royals to replace Willie Aikens and averaged nearly 30 HR annually in four seasons, reaching a high of 36 in Kansas City's 1985 World Championship year. However, the streaky low-average hitter (he never batted above .240) set a team record with 166 strikeouts that year, leading the AL. At other times he struck out in nine consecutive plate appearances and in 13 straight games. He led league first basemen in errors in 1986 and tied for the lead in 1984, and became a DH after back trouble reduced his mobility. Released by the Royals in May 1988, he signed with the Mariners that June and resurrected his career with 21 HR and 61 RBI in 350 at-bats with Seattle. When he was awarded a big contract in arbitration that winter, he was traded to the Yankees just before the start of the 1989 season and hit 17 HR with 59 RBI in 300 at-bats, mostly as their DH. /(FO)

Jack Baldschun — 1936– . RHP 1961–67, 69–70 **Phillies**, Reds, Padres 704 ip, 48–41, 3.70

The red-haired screwballer was the workhorse of the Phillies bullpen from 1961 through 1965, saving 59 games, appearing in 65 or more games each year, and leading the NL with 12 relief wins in 1962. He won both ends of an April 14, 1962 doubleheader. /(JCA)

Dave Baldwin — 1938– . RHP 1966–70, 73 **Senators**, Brewers, White Sox 224 ip, 6–11, 3.09

A zoologist and anthropologist who later earned a Ph.D., this relief pitcher's wicked sidearm delivery was particularly effective against righthanded hitters.

His best year was as a rookie in 1967 when he saved 12 for the Senators and had a 1.70 ERA. /(JCA)

Lady Baldwin [Charles Busted] — 1859–1937. LHP 1884–90 Milwaukee (U),**Detroit (NL)**, Brooklyn, Buffalo (PL) 1017 ip, 73–41, 2.85. 20 wins: 86

In 1886, his one outstanding ML season, the Detroit ace led the NL with seven shutouts, tied for the league lead with 42 wins, and ranked second in strikeouts (323). Teammates gave him his odd nickname because he didn't smoke, curse, or join them in drinking bouts. /(FIC)

Mark Baldwin (Fido) — 1865–1929. RHP 1887–93 Cubs, Columbus (AA), Chicago (P), **Pirates**, Giants 2811 ip, 154–165, 3.36. 20 wins: 89–92

Baldwin's 34 losses led the American Association in 1889, but he also won 27 that year for sixth-place Columbus, and struck out 368 (a season high since topped only by Nolan Ryan and Sandy Koufax). The next year with Chicago his 32 wins tied for the Players' League lead. /(FIC)

Rick Baldwin — 1953– . RHP 1975–77 **Mets** 183 ip, 4–7, 3.59

The bible-toting sinkerballer led the Mets staff with 54 relief appearances as a rookie in 1975, when he had a respectable 3.34 ERA. After spending most of 1976 at Tidewater (International League), he earned only one win and one save in 40 appearances with the Mets in 1977. /(JCA)

Neal Ball — 1881–1957. SS-2B 1907–13 Yankees, **Indians**, Red Sox 496 g, .251, 4 hr, 151 rbi. *1 WS, 1 g, .000*

After leading AL shortstops with 80 errors in 1908, on July 19, 1909, the Cleveland infielder executed the major leagues' first unassisted triple play, catching a liner, doubling one Red Sox runner off second, and tagging another from first. He also hit an inside-the-park homer that inning. /(ADS)

Phil deCateesby Ball — 1864–1933. *Executive*
Ball became wealthy building refrigeration plants and, with Harry Sinclair, financed the St. Louis club in the Federal League. As part of the settlement with that league, the AL allowed him to buy the Browns in 1916 for $750,000. He remained owner until 1932. Ball became a strong supporter of Ban Johnson, opposed the hiring of Judge Landis, and for six years never voted in support of Landis. An early aviation enthusiast, he was director of several airplane companies and bought the factory where Lindbergh's plane was built. /(NLM)

Lee Ballanfant — 1895–Unk. *Umpire* NL 1936–57
4 WS
☛ *All-Star—4.*

A respected NL umpire for 22 years, Ballanfant had his most embarrassing moment in the heat of the 1940 pennant race. In the first inning of an important game between the Dodgers and Cardinals, he got in the way of a ball thrown to first base, preventing the Dodgers from completing an apparent double play. The ball remained in play, over the protests of the irate Dodgers. /(RTM)

Jeff Ballard — 1963– . LHP 1987– **Orioles** 438 ip, 28–28, 4.27

On the surprising 1989 Orioles, this finesse pitcher was 9–2 by the All-Star break. He finished 18–8, 3.43. /(WOR)

Jay Baller — 1960– . RHP 1982, 85–87 Phillies, **Cubs** 143 ip, 4–8, 4.85

Baller led the Eastern League with a 2.68 ERA at Reading in 1982 while striking out 155 batters in 151.1 innings, and was one of five players traded from the Phillies to the Indians for Von Hayes that December. The 6'6" reliever never pitched for the Indians, but resurfaced in the Cubs bullpen in 1985. In 1986 Baller recorded five of his six career saves. /(SCL)

Ed Ballinger — 1869–1966. *Writer*
Ballinger traveled a half-million miles covering the Pirates from the time he joined the Pittsburgh *Post* in 1903 until he retired 43 years later as sports editor of the *Post-Gazette.* /(NLM)

Win Ballou [Noble Winfield] (Old Pard) — 1897–1963. RHP 1925–27, 29 Senators, **Browns**, Dodgers 330 ip, 19–20, 5.11. *1 WS, 2 ip, 0–0, 0.00*

Ballou took credit for Washington's 1925 pennant when, in a crucial, late-season game with the Athletics, a ball hit up the middle caromed off his shin, resulting in a double play. His only solid ML season was 1926 with the Browns (11–10), but he pitched in the Pacific Coast League well into his forties. /(WAB)

Baltimore Orioles — 1954– . Team. 3059–2632, .538. *AL East Champions 69–71, 73–74, 79, 83 AL Champions 66, 69–71, 79, 83 World Champions 66, 70, 83*

In 1954 Bill Veeck sold the St. Louis Browns to a Baltimore-based group of investors, who moved the perpetual losers to their hometown. With Paul Richards at the helm both on the field and in the front office, the Orioles developed a highly productive farm system and by 1960 were contending for the pennant. The Orioles were built on the arms of the "Baby Birds," a group of young pitchers who included Wally Bunker and Milt Pappas, as well as the brilliant fielding of Brooks Robinson. The addition of Frank Robinson in 1966 brought Baltimore its first WS victory, a four-game sweep of the Dodgers. The Orioles soon became a mini-dynasty, reaching the WS three straight years (1969–71) with a lineup that included Boog Powell, Mark Belanger, and Paul Blair, and pitchers Mike Cuellar, Dave McNally, and Jim Palmer. Known for strong organizational unity and "The Oriole Way," which emphasized fundamentals and careful, measured development in the minor leagues, Baltimore has also produced a slew of pitching coaches (George Bamberger, Ray Miller, Wes Stock), managers (Earl Weaver, Frank Robinson), and front-office talent (Harry Dalton, Frank Cashen). A short period of decline in the 1980s was stemmed by Roland Hemond with a typical infusion of young pitching talent. /(SH)

Baltimore Orioles — 1882–1899. Team 1882–91 AA, 1892–99 NL 644–447, .590. *NL Champions 1894–96*

After an undistinguished run in the American Association that was actually interrupted in 1890, when the team chose to be a minor league club, the original Baltimore Orioles were absorbed by the National League after the AA fell apart following the 1891 season. Part-owner and manager Ned Hanlon built a dynasty around the Hall of Fame talents of John McGraw, Hughie Jennings, Willie Keeler, Joe Kelley, and Wilbert Robinson, and the team pioneered a cutthroat style of play that was simultaneously heady and dirty. The owners bought the Brooklyn club later in the decade and transferred most of the Orioles' best players to their new team, and when the NL dropped four teams after the 1899 season, the fabled Orioles were no more. /(SH)

George Bamberger (Bambi) — 1925– . *Manager* 1978–80, 82–83, 85–86 **Brewers**, Mets 458–478, .489

The genial Bamberger recorded 213 victories in 18 years as a minor league pitcher but won more recognition as a ML pitching coach and manager. He was the Orioles pitching coach for a decade beginning in 1967. During that time, Baltimore had such standouts as Jim Palmer, Dave McNally, Mike Cueller, and Pat Dobson, all of whom won 20 games in 1971.

Offered the Milwaukee helm in 1978, Bamberger led the Brewers to a third-place finish and was named *TSN* and *UPI* Manager of the Year. In the spring of 1980, he underwent coronary bypass surgery but returned to manage from June 6 until his retirement in September. He was given a lifetime job in Milwaukee's front office but was lured away by the Mets. He managed New York from 1982 until he resigned voluntarily in June 1983, citing health reasons. In 1985 and '86 he managed the Brewers to sixth-place finishes. /(JCA)

Dave Bancroft (Beauty) — 1891–1972. SS 1915–30 **Phillies**, Giants, Braves, Dodgers 1913 g, .279, 32 hr, 591 rbi. *4 WS, 24 g, .172, 7 rbi.*
    Manager 1924–27 **Braves** 249–363, .407
☛ *Hall of Fame—1971.*

Bancroft was the classic shortstop. He had quick hands for a ground ball or a deft tag, quickness afoot for covering a middle infielder's territory, and quick-wittedness for lightning response to defensive opportunity. At bat, he was a dexterous switch-hitter,

Dave Bancroft with the Giants

ideal for the leadoff or second spot. In his time, he was considered by most to be better than Maranville, which meant he was the best.

The formidable Mickey Doolan had been the Phillies' shortstop for nine years before jumping to Baltimore of the Federal League in 1914, and the team floundered until Bancroft arrived from Portland (Pacific Coast League). A beauty from the start, he was a key player in the 1915 pennant drive and two subsequent second-place finishes. Thereafter, the team descended to the cellar, where owner William Baker's policy of selling stars for cash would keep it for a generation. For Bancroft, the Giants gave Baker plenty of money, 35-year-old Art Fletcher, and the first, and lesser, of two Giant pitchers named Hubbell.

Bancroft's three-plus years with the Giants were his best. He was McGraw's field leader and designated cutoff man. In 1921–22, he led the league in putouts, assists, and double plays. He became a .300 batter, had a six-for-six day in 1920, and hit for the cycle in 1921.

In late 1923, he was dealt to the Braves with Casey Stengel and Bill Cunningham for Billy Southworth and Joe Oeschger. McGraw, all heart, said he was giving up the league's best shortstop as a favor to Christy Mathewson (then fronting the listless Braves as their president) and to Bancroft, who would become their playing manager. The truth was that Bancroft was an aging 32, and New York had 20-year-old hotshot Travis Jackson with no place to put him.

A step slower in the field, Bancroft still was a class act, but he couldn't pry the Braves out of the second division. His fine career ended with two years at Brooklyn and a few games with the Giants as he made the inevitable transition to coaching. He ran a downhill course through the minors. Briefly, the old roughneck even managed a women's softball team.

Lifetime, Bancroft remains sixth in total chances for shortstops with 11,844, first in average putouts per game (2.5) and tied for second in average chances per game (6.3). /(ADS)

Frank C. Bancroft — 1846–1921. *Manager* 1880–85, 87, 89, 1902 Worcester (NL), Detroit (NL), Cleveland (NL), **Providence (NL)**, Philadelphia (AA), Indianapolis (NL), Reds 372–328, .531. First place: 84

Bancroft introduced baseball to Cuba in 1879 when he took a touring team to the Caribbean. He managed six ML clubs through the 1880s, including the 1884 Providence Grays, who won the first World Series. He spent 30 years as business manager for the Cincinnati Reds. /(JK)

Chris Bando (C.B.) — 1956– . C 1981–88 **Indians**, Tigers 497 g, .227, 27 hr, 141 rbi

Never the hitter brother Sal was, switch-hitting Cleveland native Chris Bando kept his job as the Indians' second-string catcher with his defense and uncomplaining attitude. He proved exceptional at handling the knuckleballs of Tom Candiotti and Phil Niekro. /(ME)

Sal Bando — 1944– . 3B 1968–1981 **A's**, Brewers 2019 g, .254, 242 hr, 1039 rbi. *5 LCS, 20 g, .270, 5 hrs, 8 rbi. 3 WS, 19 g, .206, 1 hr, 4 rbi*
☛ *All-Star—69, 72–74.*

Bando was a power-hitting third baseman and co-captain of the raucous Oakland A's dynasty that won five straight AL Western Division titles (1971–75) and three straight World Series (1972–74). He was the glue of the infield, although, characteristically for that team, he didn't always show respect for management. In June 1974, after a disappointing loss, he observed that A's manager Alvin Dark "couldn't manage a meat market." And although he was chosen for four All-Star teams, he never started, having the misfortune to play during Brooks Robinson's final years.

Bando managed to stick with colorful A's owner Charlie Finley for 11 seasons, including the last two years the franchise was in Kansas City. In both 1969 and 1971, Bando hit two grand slams. In the seventh game of the 1972 World Series, he knocked in a run with a double, then scored the eventual winning run on Gene Tenace's double in the sixth inning of a 3–2 A's victory.

Bando's best year came in 1973, when he led the league in doubles with 32 and hit a career-high .287 with 29 HR and 98 RBI. In the 1973 playoffs against Baltimore, he nearly hit three homers in the second game, a 6–3 Oakland win. In the third inning Al Bumbry made a spectacular leaping catch of Bando's first long drive. Following Game Two of the 1973 Series, he prompted the black armbands the players wore to show their feelings over the Mike Andrews incident, when Finley roasted the unfortunate second baseman's two-error performance. In the 1974 playoffs against Baltimore, Bando hit two homers. His solo homer off Jim Palmer in Game Three provided the game's only run, and in the fourth and final game Bando scored the eventual winning run on Reggie Jackson's seventh-inning double, the only hit for Oakland that afternoon.

Sal Bando

Bando escaped Finley in 1977 when he signed with the Brewers as a free agent, and stayed around long enough to see his younger brother, Chris, reach the majors in 1981 with Cleveland. /(SEW)

Eddie Bane — 1952- . LHP 1973, 75-76 **Twins** 168 ip, 7-13, 4.66

The curveballer was 40-4 in three years at Arizona State, and the Twins signed him for the largest bonus they had ever paid a pitcher. He debuted before 45,890 expectant Minnesota fans (7/4/73), but in three seasons he never lived up to their hopes. /(JCA)

Ed Bang — 1880-1968. *Writer*

After working for several newspapers in Ohio, Bang succeeded Grantland Rice as sports editor of the Cleveland *News* in 1907 and remained there for 53 years until the newspaper closed. In 1942, he estimated he'd written more than 50 million words for the *News*. Known for his distinctive foghorn voice and for answering every letter or call, whether from an important sports figure or only a fan, Bang was among those who once carried card No. 1 of the BBWAA and was a regular contributor to *The Sporting News*. /(NLM)

Dan Bankhead — 1920-1976. RHP 1947, 50-51 **Dodgers** 153 ip, 9-5, 6.52

Bankhead was the major leagues' first black pitcher, but enjoyed little success at that level. He pitched a no-hitter for Nashua in 1948, and, in his first big league at-bat, homered off Pittsburgh's Fritz Ostermueller. /(EGM)

Sam Bankhead — 1910-1976. SS-OF-2B-RHP-MGR Negro Leagues 1930-50 Birmingham Black Barons, Nashville Elite Giants, Louisville, Pittsburgh Crawfords, **Homestead Grays** statistics not available
☛ *All-Star—33-34, 36, 38, 42-44.*

The oldest of five brothers who played in the Negro Leagues, Sam Bankhead appeared in seven East-West all-star games between 1933 and 1946, during which time he played three different positions for three different teams and batted .346. He was an integral part of the Pittsburgh Crawfords and Homestead Grays of the 1930s and 1940s. He was known for his strong arm, consistent hitting, and versatility in the field. He interrupted his Negro National League career for several years to play in the Cuban winter league. In 21 documented games against white major leaguers, he batted .342. /(BP)

Scott Bankhead — 1963- . RHP 1986- Royals, **Mariners** 616 ip, 38-32, 4.03

Bankhead pitched for the 1984 U.S. Olympic team and appeared in only 31 games in the minors before being called up by the Royals. He was traded to Seattle in the deal for Danny Tartabull. In his first month with the Mariners, Bankhead went 4-1 with a 2.94 ERA, but he developed tendinitis and ended the season with a less impressive 9-8 record and 5.42 ERA. His usually sharp control and strikeout ability were established by 1988, but it wasn't until 1989, when he went on a hot streak after the All-Star break, that he proved himself a winning pitcher. He finished that year 14-6 with a 3.34 ERA. /(TF)

Ernie Banks (Mr. Cub) — 1931– . 1B-SS 1954–1971
Cubs 2528 g, .274, 512 hr, 1636 rbi
☛ *Most Valuable Player—58–59. Led League—hr 58, 60.*
Led League—rbi 58–59. All-Star—55–62, 65, 67, 69.
Gold Glove—60. Hall of Fame—1977.

He will always be "Mr. Cub," the most popular
player the Cubs ever had. His sunny personality is
legend, as is his refrain on a sunny day: "Let's play
two!" The first black player on the Cubs, Banks
came up as a shortstop, where he won consecutive
MVP awards, but actually played more games at
first base. He is also one of a handful of Hall of
Famers never to get into postseason play.

Growing up in Dallas, Banks had to be bribed
with nickels and dimes by his father to play catch.
Banks, more interested in softball than baseball, was
a high school star in both football and basketball,
and once ran a 52-second quarter mile. At the age of
17, he signed on to play baseball with a Negro
barnstorming team for $15 a game. Cool Papa Bell
later signed him for the Kansas City Monarchs. He

Ernie Banks

returned to them after two years in the army, and
the Cubs discovered him there at the end of the
1953 season. The 22-year-old went right to the Cubs
and hit his first homer on September 20, 1953, off
Gerry Staley in St. Louis. He quickly replaced Roy
Smalley, Sr., as the regular Cub shortstop in 1954.
Starting with his first game in 1953, he played 424
consecutive games until fracturing his hand midway
through the 1956 season.

Like his contemporary, Hank Aaron, Banks
didn't look like a power hitter. He was slim, with
powerful thighs, and he held his bat high, wiggling it
nervously while waiting for the pitch. Like Aaron he
got his power from amazingly quick and strong
wrists. A teammate of his once remarked that Banks
had "wrists right up to his armpits." An opposing
player noted that he often "hits the ball right out of
the catcher's mitt." In 1955, he switched to a lighter
bat, starting a trend. He then went out and smacked
44 HR, the most ever for a shortstop, including
three in one day at Wrigley against Pittsburgh and
an NL-record five grand slams. His best years were
his consecutive MVP years in 1958 and 1959. He
hit .313 and .304 respectively—his only full years
over .300 --and led the league in RBI both years,
with 129 and a career-high 143. He also hit a
league-leading and career-high 47 HR in 1958 and
added another 45 in 1959.

From 1955 to 1960, Banks hit more homers than
anyone in the majors, including Mantle, Mays, and
Aaron. At the end of the 1959 season, he was so
popular that the Cubs wanted to give him his own
day. The modest Banks gratefully declined, saying
that he hadn't been around long enough to be so
honored. By 1964, Banks had relented, and the
honorary day was held.

At first, Banks's fielding was erratic. He posted
error totals of 34, 22, and 25 early in his career,
culminating in a league-leading 32 in 1958. He
worked dilligently to cut his errors down to 12 in
1959, then a record for shortstops, and led NL
shortstops in fielding in both 1960 (he won a Gold
Glove) and 1961. Meanwhile, he kept hitting. In the
first 1960 All-Star game he had a two-run homer in
a 5–3 NL victory, and he ended the season leading
the league in HR for the second time, with 41.

Even though Banks had led the league in fielding
the previous two seasons, injuries to his legs had cut
down his range, so he accepted a move to first base
in 1962. When Leo Durocher took over the team in
1966, he kept bringing up young phenoms to replace
Banks, but none did. Banks won the fielding title at
his new position in 1969, and led NL first basemen

in assists five times. By 1970, his legs had begun to weaken from nagging injuries and arthritis. On May 12, 1970, he hit his 500th homer, the most avidly anticipated event in Wrigley Field history, with the possible exception of the first night game. After Banks's retirement in 1971, the Cubs hoisted a pinstriped pennant with his number 14 atop the left field foul pole at Wrigley Field. He was the first Cubs player to have his number retired. /(SEW)

Alan Bannister — 1951- . OF-2B-SS-DH 1974–85 Phillies, **White Sox**, Indians, Astros, Rangers 972 g, .270, 19 hr, 288 rbi

Highly touted in college, Bannister was the Phillies' first-round pick in the 1973 draft. Although versatile (he played every position but pitcher and catcher) he never lived up to his college raves and was rarely a regular. Only once, as the 1977 White Sox' shortstop, did he play in over 100 games at a position, and then he led all AL shortstops in errors (40). /(JCA)

Floyd Bannister — 1955- . LHP 1977- Astros, Mariners, **White Sox**, Royals 2,326 ip, 133–142, 4.03. *1 LCS, 6 ip, 0–1, 4.50*
☛ *Led League—k 82. All-Star—82.*

A standout at Arizona State, Bannister was named *TSN* College Player of the Year in 1976 and was the nation's first draft pick that June. He reached the Astros in 1977, but was ill and had blister problems in 1978 and was traded to the Mariners for Craig Reynolds. With his 90 mph fastball, sharp slider, and excellent curveball, Bannister notched many strikeouts but few wins. He fanned an AL-high 209 batters in 1982, but averaged just 10 wins a season in Seattle. Playing out his option, he signed with the White Sox for 1983. After losing nine of his first 12 decisions, he became the catalyst of Chicago's '83 pennant drive, going 13–1 (2.23) after the All-Star break. But, lacking the killer instinct and refusing to pitch inside, he was frequently victimized by the long ball, and was perceived as not living up to his potential. After he increased his value by going 16–11 in 1987, the White Sox traded him to the Royals for four young players, including pitching prospects Melido Perez and John Davis. /(RL)

Jack Banta — 1925- . RHP 1947–50 **Dodgers** 205 ip, 14–12, 3.78. *1 WS, 3 g, 3.18*

Banta, a sidearming reliever, had a 10–6 record for the 1949 Dodgers, winning the pennant-clinching game on the last day of the season. A 1950 arm injury ended his promising career. /(EGM)

Walter Barbare (Dinty) — 1891–1965. 3B-SS-2B 1914–22 Indians, Red Sox, Pirates, **Braves** 500 g, .260, 1 hr, 156 rbi

A light-hitting, long-armed infielder, Barbare went in a 1921 trade from Pittsburgh to the Braves for star shortstop Rabbit Maranville. He responded with his only solid season, batting .302. Barbare also managed and umpired in the minors. /(JK)

Red Barber [Walter] — 1908- . *Broadcaster 1934–66*

Barber was New York City's first baseball radio broadcaster, and the first baseball telecaster anywhere. He chronicled the rise of the Dodgers with phrases like "tearin' up the pea patch" and "the bases are FOB"—full of Brooklyns. The Mississippi-born Barber said, "(I) didn't broadcast with a Brooklyn accent, but I did broadcast with a Brooklyn heart." When fired by the Yankees, he ended his farewell interview by blowing a kiss to Brooklyn. /(TG)

Red Barber

Steve Barber — 1939– . LHP 1960–74 **Orioles**, Yankees, Pilots, Cubs, Braves, Angels, Giants 2000 ip, 121–106, 3.36. 20 wins: 63
☛ *All-Star—63, 66.*

One of the Orioles' "Baby Birds" (a group of promising young pitchers), Barber came up as a flame-thrower with a reputation for wildness. He led the AL in walks his rookie year, but by 1963 had settled down to become Baltimore's first modern-day ML 20-game winner. Tendinitis in his elbow sidelined him for the second part of 1966, and Barber missed pitching in the All-Star Game and World Series. He went 8–1/3 innings in his first start of 1967 before giving up a hit to Jim Fregosi, and threw a combined no-hitter with Stu Miller against Detroit two weeks later (Baltimore lost that game 2–1). He was traded to the Yankees in mid-'67. Problems with his elbow and his pitching mechanics limited his success with five more teams. /(JCA)

Turner Barber — 1893–1968. OF-1B 1915–23 Senators, **Cubs**, Dodgers 491 g, .289, 2 hr, 185 rbi. *1 WS, 3 g, .000*

Barber was a substitute except for 1921, when he and Cubs teammates George Maisel and Max Flack formed one of the least-renowned .300-hitting outfields. It was also Maisel's only season as a regular; Flack hit .300 three times. /(JK)

Curt Barclay — 1931– . RHP 1957–59 **Giants** 199 ip, 10–9, 3.48

After turning down a basketball contract with the Boston Celtics, the 6'3″ Barclay joined the sixth-place Giants in their final year in New York. He posted a 9–9 rookie record, but the next season a shoulder injury ended his career. /(JK)

George Barclay (Deerfoot) — 1876–1909. OF 1902–05 **Browns**, Braves 401 g, .248, 4 hr, 140 rbi

Barclay never equalled his rookie season, when he hit .300 and stole 30 bases. /(WB)

Ray Bare — 1949– . RHP 1972, 74–77 Cardinals, **Tigers** 339 ip, 16–26, 4.80

Bare is remembered by Tiger fans for snapping a club-record 19-game losing streak in 1975 with a two-hit, 8–0 performance at California. /(CC)

Jesse Barfield — 1959– . OF 1981– **Blue Jays**, Yankees 1161 g, .263, 197 hr, 583 rbi. *1 LCS, .280, 1 hr, 4 rbi*
☛ *Led League—hr 86. All-Star—86. Gold Glove—86–87.*

Barfield has the best outfield arm of the 1980s. He led AL outfielders each year from 1985 to 1987 despite few runners being so foolhardy as to challenge him, and won Gold Gloves in 1986 and '87. He also has shown prodigious home run power, leading the ML with 40 HR in 1986, and was the Blue Jays' career HR leader as of the beginning of the 1988 season. Barfield was the first Blue Jay to hit a pinch grand slam, and the first to hit 20 homers and steal 20 bases in the same season. With George Bell and Lloyd Moseby, Barfield starred in what was considered by some the best outfield of the 1980s, but in early 1989 he was traded to the Yankees for pitching prospect Al Leiter. /(TF)

Clyde Barfoot — 1891–1971. RHP 1922–23, 26 **Cardinals**, Tigers 250 ip, 8–10, 4.10

Barfoot was in his early thirties before he got a chance as the second reliever in the Cardinals' bullpen. A longtime star in the Texas League, Pacific Coast League, and Southern Association, he won 314 minor league games in a career that spanned 25 years. /(FJO)

Cy Barger [Eros] — 1885–1964. RHP 1906–07, 10–12, 14–25 Yankees, **Dodgers**, Pittsburgh FL 975 ip, 47–62, 3.56

Barger's father wanted to give him an impressive-sounding Greek name, and chose Eros (the god of love) without knowing its source. Cy was sometimes impressive, as when he went 15–15 for the 1910 Dodgers, but he dropped to 1–9 two years later. He was 20–23 in two years with Pittsburgh of the Federal League. /(NLM)

Len Barker — 1955– . RHP 1976–85, 87 Rangers, **Indians**, Braves, Brewers 1322 ip, 74–76, 4.35
☛ *Led League—k 80–81.*

Flame-throwing Barker three-hit the White Sox in his first ML start with the Rangers, but his wildness caused his trade to Cleveland in 1979. There he learned to control his 96-mph fastball and posted a 19–12 mark in 1980 while leading the AL in strikeouts. He pitched a 3–0 perfect game against Toronto (5/15/81) and started that year's All-Star Game. He led in strikeouts again in 1981 and was 15–11 in 1982. The Braves gave up Brett Butler, Brook Jacoby and Rick Behenna to get him in late 1983, but he never managed a winning record for Atlanta. /(MC)

Al Barlick — 1915– . *Umpire* NL 1940–43, 46–55, 58–70 *7 WS, 7 ASU*

Al Barlick

A WWII Coast Guard veteran with a salty tongue, Barlick was firm and tough and demanded respect. He umpired a record seven All-Star Games, spanning four decades. He was the plate umpire in the 1970 game when Pete Rose flattened catcher Ray Fosse. A no-nonsense type, he stopped a game at Shea Stadium to have the coaching box rechalked and forfeited a game in Philadelphia when unruly fans hit him with a tomato and fellow ump Lee Ballanfant with a bottle. In 1949 his call of a trap by the Cubs' Andy Pafko produced one of the shortest home runs in history. While Pafko argued the call, batter Rocky Nelson circled the bases for a 220-foot homer. /(RTM)

Mike Barlow — 1948- . LHP 1975-81 Cardinals, Astros, **Angels**, Blue Jays 247 ip, 10-6, 4.63. *1 WS, 1 ip, 0.00*

The 6′6″ reliever grew up near (but was no candidate for) Cooperstown, NY. He had a terrific September 1977 with the Angels, winning four games, more than he ever won again in a full ML season. /(JCA)

Ernest S. Barnard — Unk.-1931. *Executive.*

Barnard was sports editor of a Columbus, Ohio, newspaper when he joined the Indians as road secretary in 1904. He became president of the club in 1922 and in 1928 succeeded Ban Johnson as president of the AL, a position he held until his death. /(NLM)

Jesse Barnes — 1892-1961. RHP 1915-27 **Braves, Giants,** Dodgers 2569 ip, 153-149, 3.22. 20 wins: 19-20 *2 WS, 26 ip, 2-0, 1.71*
☛ *Led League—w 19.*

Barnes was a hard thrower who came to the ML with the Braves the year after their 1914 "miracle" pennant. By the time he became a regular starter, the team had strong pitching but little else. Barnes led the NL in losses (21) in 1917. After being traded to the Giants with Larry Doyle for aging Buck Herzog in January 1918, Barnes spent most of the season in the infantry but was 6-1 in nine starts for New York. The next year he was John McGraw's ace, leading the NL in wins with a 25-9 record and a 2.40 ERA. He was one of three Giants with 20 wins the following year with a 20-15 mark. In 1921 he contributed 15 wins to the Giants' pennant and won twice in the WS. Although his win total fell to 13 in 1922, one of the victories was a no-hitter against the Phillies (5/7/22). That fall he was on the mound for the Giants in the 10th inning of Game Two of the WS with the score tied at 3-3 when umpire George Hildebrand called the game because of darkness. Most observers insisted there was still plenty of light, and Commissioner Landis was so incensed he gave the gate receipts to charity. Barnes's younger brother Virgil pitched for the Giants during these years but did not become a regular starter until after Jesse was traded back to the Braves in 1923. They pitched against each other ten times, five as starters, with Jesse winning five and losing three. With the Braves, Jesse again led the NL in losses (20) in 1924. A lifetime .214 hitter, he is the only NL pitcher to walk twice in one inning (10/2/17). /(NLM)

Red Barnes [Emile Deering] — 1903-1959. OF 1927-30 **Senators,** White Sox 286 g, .268, 8 hr, 97 rbi

As a rookie centerfielder in 1928 Barnes formed part of the Senators' all-.300 outfield. Flanked by Hall of Famers Sam Rice (.328) and Goose Goslin (.379), Barnes hit .302 with 15 triples. /(JK)

Ross Barnes [Roscoe Charles] — 1850-1915. 2B-SS 1871-77, 79, 81 **Red Sox (NA),** Cubs, Reds, Braves *NA*: 266 g, .379; *NL*: 234 g, .319, 2 hr, 111 rbi
☛ *Led League—ba 73, 75-76.*

The clever second baseman was the NL's first batting leader (.429) with Chicago in 1876. Having already won two National Association titles (1873, '75), he was also the first player to lead two different leagues in batting. He specialized in "fair-foul" hits— squibbed bunts that landed fair, rolled foul, but remained in play under the rules of the time. When the rules were changed before the 1877 season his BA plummeted. /(ADS)

Virgil Barnes (Zeke) — 1897–1958. RHP 1919–20, 22–28 **Giants**, Braves 1094, 61–59, 3.66. *2 WS, 17 ip, 0–1, 4.15*

Barnes joined the Giants after his older brother Jesse had become their star pitcher. Virgil did not establish himself until after Jesse was traded away. From 1924 to 1927 he won 53 games for New York. An injury to the deltoid and bursa tendons in his shoulder forced Barnes's retirement. /(NLM)

Walter S. Barnes — 1860–Unk. *Writer.*

A graduate of Harvard, Barnes began writing baseball for the Boston *Post* in 1880, then was sports editor of the *Journal, Herald,* and *Globe.* In 1939, he was the oldest member of the BBWA, holding card 1. /(NLM)

Barney Barnett (Larry) — 1945– *Umpire* AL 1968–87 *5 LCS 3 WS, 3 ASU*

Barnett was the plate ump in the third game of the 1975 WS when a controversial 10th-inning call took place. Reds batter Ed Armbrister bunted and seemed to interfere as Boston catcher Carlton Fisk went after the ball. Fisk's throw sailed into centerfield. Over Red Sox objections Barnett ruled no interference. The Reds later scored the winning run. /(RTM)

Rex Barney — 1924– . RHP 1943, 1946–50 **Dodgers** 598 ip, 35–31, 4.34. *2 WS, 9 ip, 0–2, 6.75*

Barney's fastball was unhittable but all too often unreachable. In six Dodger seasons of unfulfilled promise, only in 1948 did he strike out more batters than he walked (138 to 122). That season he went 15–13 with a 3.10 ERA and pitched a no-hitter against the Giants. After that he grew progressively wilder, to the frustration of Dodger boss Branch Rickey, who even tried a hypnotist on him. Barney later became a successful baseball broadcaster. /(JD)

Clyde Barnhart (Pooch) — 1895–1980. OF-3B 1920–28 **Pirates** 814 g, .295, 27 hr, 436 rbi. *2 WS, 11 g, .273, 9 rbi*

Barnhart was the Pirates' third baseman until Pie Traynor arrived, when he was moved to the outfield. Tough to strike out, he fanned only 149 times in 2673 at bats. He drove in a career-high 114 runs and hit .325 as the Pirates leftfielder in 1925. Lloyd Waner replaced Barnhart in 1927 but Waner moved to center when Kiki Cuyler fell into manager Donie Bush's doghouse and was benched. The slow-footed Barnhart went back to left and hit .319. In the four-game '27 WS, he drove in four of Pittsburgh's ten runs. His son, Vic, was a Pittsburgh shortstop in the 1940s. /(ME)

David Barnhill (Impo) — 1914–1983. RHP Negro Leagues 1937–49 Miami Clowns, Ethiopian Clowns, **New York Cubans**
☛ *All-Star—41–43.*

A small, fireballing strikeout artist, Barnhill was the ace of the New York Cubans' staff during the early 1940s, compiling an 18–3 record in 1941. He pitched in the 1941–43 East-West all-star games, defeating Satchel Paige in the 1942 contest. That year, the Pirates considered Barnhill for the role of breaking baseball's color line, but the opportunity did not materialize. In 1947, he shut out the Cleveland Buckeyes in the Negro World Series to help the Cubans to the championship. He was signed by the New York Giants in 1949, and in 1950 he compiled an 11–3 record for the AAA champion Minneapolis Millers (American Association). Since he was already 35, his age kept him from getting a shot at the majors. He continued to play in the Pacific Coast League and Florida International League until 1953. /(JR)

Bill Barnie (Bald Billy) — 1853–1900. C-OF 1883, 86 **Baltimore (AA)** 19 g, .180, 0 hr, inc rbi.
Manager **1883–94, 97–98** Baltimore AA, Brooklyn-Baltimore (AA), Philadelphia (AA), Washington (NL), Louisville (NL), Dodgers 646–829, .438

Barnie was working in a brokerage office when he broke into baseball in 1871 as a catcher/outfielder. While managing Baltimore's American Association team in the 1880's, he occasionally caught for his team, but his .180 BA hardly indicated "leading by example." His third-place finish in 1887 was his best season, but "Bald Billy" managed for 14 ML seasons. In 1900, while managing Hartford of the Eastern League, he died in midseason from asthmatic bronchitis. /(NLM)

Salome Barojas — 1957– . RHP 1982–85 **White Sox**, Mariners 381 ip, 18–21, 3.85. *1 LCS, 2 ip, 0–0, 18.00*

On a scouting trip to Mexico during the 1981 players' strike, White Sox manager Tony LaRussa signed Barojas out of the Mexican League. In 1982, the rookie reliever, who spoke no English, won 6 and saved 21 for the Sox. /(NLM)

George Barr — 1897–1974. *Umpire* NL 1931–49 *4 WS, 1 ASU*

Barr was the only modern umpire to be assigned consecutive WS (1948–49). As the plate umpire during a rainy 1949 game in Boston, Barr ejected the Braves' Connie Ryan after Ryan protested the decision not to call the game by kneeling in the on-deck circle wearing a raincoat. /(RTM)

Jim Barr — 1948– . RHP 1971–80, 82–83 **Giants**, Angels 2064 ip, 101–112, 3.56. *1 LCS, 1 ip, 0–0, 9.00*

Barr signed with the Giants after starring for a University of Southern California team that included Bill Lee, Brent Strom, and Dave Kingman. Called up for long relief in August 1971, he helped the Giants to a Western Division title. The next August, he earned a starting slot after retiring 41 consecutive batters in relief. He won at least 11 games each season from 1973 through 1977, with a peak year of 15–12 in 1976. In 1974 he allowed only 1.76 walks per nine innings. He signed as a free agent with the Angels in 1979, but after arm trouble, returned to the Giants in 1982. /(MC)

Bill Barrett (Whispering Bill) — 1900–1951. OF-SS 1921, 23–30 A's, **White Sox**, Red Sox, Senators 716 g, .288, 23 hr, 328 rbi

The gentlemanly, soft-spoken Barrett was primarily a singles hitter and batted .307 in 1926, his best full season. He was the league's worst fielding shortstop (.904) with the White Sox in 1924, after which he usually played right field. /(EC)

Charles Barrett — 1871–1939. *Scout.*

Barrett was a mediocre minor league outfielder. He joined the St. Louis Browns as a scout in 1909 and worked one season for the Tigers before joining Branch Rickey's Cardinals from 1918 until his death. He helped Rickey develop the Cardinals' phenomenal minor league system, securing such players as Pepper Martin, Chick Hafey, and Jim Bottomley. /(FVP)

Dick Barrett (Kewpie) — 1906–1966. RHP 1933–34, 43–45 A's, Braves, Cubs, **Phillies** 739 ip, 34–58, 4.30

This roly-poly wartime big leaguer was a Pacific Coast League standout, with seven 20-win seasons, 234 wins, and the league's most career strikeouts. After an 0–4 start with the Cubs in 1943, he was sold to the Phillies and responded with a 14-inning, 1–0 blanking of Cincinnati. His 20 losses led the NL in 1945. /(JK)

Frank Barrett (Red) — 1913– . RHP 1939, 44–46, 50 Cardinals, **Red Sox**, Braves, Pirates 218 ip, 15–17, 3.51

Barrett was one of many career minor leaguers who played in the majors during WWII. As a 30-year-old rookie reliever, he won eight and saved eight for the 1944 Red Sox. /(ME)

Jimmy Barrett — 1875–1921. OF 1899–1908 Reds, **Tigers**, Red Sox 865 g, .291, 16 hr, 255 rbi

A solidly built lefthanded hitter, Barrett had an exceptional arm and led outfielders in assists in three of the first four AL seasons. He twice led the league in drawing walks. A knee injury ended his career prematurely. /(JK)

Johnny Barrett — 1915–1974. OF 1942–46 **Pirates**, Braves 588 g, .251, 23 hr, 220 rbi

The fleet lefthanded hitter led the NL in stolen bases (28) and triples (19) with the Pirates in 1944. Two years later, a knee injury diminished his speed and ended his ML career. /(ME)

Marty Barrett — 1958– . 2B 1982– **Red Sox** 867 g, .281, 17 hr, 298 rbi. *2 LCS, 11 g, .267, 5 rbi. 1 WS, 7 g, .433, 4 rbi*

Steady but unspectacular both in the field and at the plate, Barrett starred in the 1986 postseason, winning ALCS MVP honors and setting a ML record with 24 hits in 14 postseason games. He hit a career-high .303 in his first full ML season (1984) and has remained an excellent number-two hitter. He rarely strikes out and is a skillful bunter, leading the AL in sacrifice hits three straight years from 1986 to 1988. Renowned for his savvy at second base, Barrett constantly confounds baserunners with decoys, bluffs, and an occasional hidden-ball trick. His younger brother Tom played 36 games for the Phillies in 1988. /(SCL)

Red Barrett [Charles Henry] — 1915– . RHP 1937–40, 43–49 Reds, **Braves**, Cardinals 1263 ip, 69–69, 3.53. 20 wins: 45 *1 WS, 4 ip, 0.00*
☛ *Led League—w 45.*

With the Braves and Cardinals in 1945, Barrett led the NL in wins (23), complete games (24), innings pitched (284.2), and most hits allowed (287). On August 10, 1944, he threw just 58 pitches in defeating the Reds, 2–0. In 1947, Pirate slugger Ralph Kiner had hit seven homers in three games and faced Barrett the next day. "Barrett predicted that I wouldn't hit one off him," recalled Kiner. "I did, which made it eight homers in four games."/(RTM)

Francisco Barrios [born Francisco Javier Jimenez Jimenez] — 1953–1982. RHP 1974, 76–81 White Sox 717 ip, 38–38, 4.15

Big-city life was too much for Barrios, an excitable, gregarious Mexican. Possessing a 90-mph fastball, Barrios joined Chicago in 1976 and combined with Blue Moon Odom to no-hit Oakland on July 28. They walked 11, but prevailed 2–1. Barrios had a flush of success in 1977 with a 14–7 mark. But, bad tempered, he engaged umpires in verbal tirades, and once slugged it out with teammate Steve Trout in a Cleveland hotel. In 1981 he was arrested on a narcotics charge, and a year later he died of a drug overdose./(RL)

Ed Barrow (Cousin Ed) — 1868–1953. *Executive Manager* 1903–04, 18–20 Tigers, **Red Sox** 310–320, .492. *1 WS, 4–2, .667*
☞ *Hall of Fame—1953..*

Ed Barrow was the man most responsible for the success of the New York Yankees between 1921 and 1945. With Barrow as general manager, the Yankees won 14 pennants and ten World Series, sweeping five of them. He achieved his foremost success by organizing and developing their farm system. After he became club president in 1939, he and George Weiss developed the Yankees into the most consistent pennant-winning organization in major league history.

Barrow worked for two newspapers in Des Moines, IA, before moving east in 1890. He formed a partnership with baseball concessioner Harry Stevens, and they got the scoreboard and pop concessions at the Pirates' Exposition Park. In 1894 Barrow became manager and GM at Wheeling, WV (International League). In 1895 he acquired the Paterson, NJ franchise in the Atlantic League, signed Honus Wagner, and served as president of the circuit from 1897 to 1899. He then purchased a part interest of the Toronto (International League) club, became its manager, and won a pennant in 1902. The Detroit Tigers then made him their manager,

Ed Barrow

but he resigned during 1904 following a dispute with the GM. When two unsuccessful years of managing in the minors followed, Barrow left baseball.

Barrow returned in 1910 as president of the Eastern League. He was named manager of the Boston Red Sox in 1918 and immediately led them to the World Championship. That season, he acknowledged Babe Ruth's prowess as a hitter by increasingly working the ace pitcher into the lineup as an outfielder. The Red Sox sold Ruth to the Yankees in 1920, and at the close of the season, Barrow became the Yankee GM. In 1921–23, the Yankees won their first three pennants.

The forceful, straightforward Barrow possessed an explosive temper and once challenged Babe Ruth to a fight. He exercised strict discipline as manager and executive. In 1937 and 1941, he was named *TSN* Major League Executive of the Year. When the Yankees were sold to Larry McPhail, Dan Topping, and Del Webb in 1945, Barrow became chairman of the board, but he retired two years later. He was elected to the Hall of Fame by the Committee on Baseball Veterans in 1953, the year he died./(JLE)

Jack Barry — 1887–1961. SS-2B 1908–17, 19 **A's,** Red Sox 1222 g, .243, 10 hr, 429 rbi. *5 WS, 25 g, .241, 8 rbi.*
Manager 1917 **Red Sox** 90–62, .592

Barry spent most of his career with pennant-winning teams and was the shortstop in the Athletics' famous "$100,000 Infield." A key component of Connie Mack's first dynasty, Barry was signed off the campus of Holy Cross and helped the Athletics to World Championships in 1910–11 and '13. Observers considered Barry vital to the A's chances. Ty Cobb's spiking of Barry in the heat of the 1909 pennant race, depriving Philadelphia of his services, is often cited as the reason Detroit won the flag, even though Barry hit only .215 that season.

Not a great fielder, he was at least reliable, and he led AL shortstops in double plays in 1912. He was rated very highly by contemporaries, although he led in errors in 1910. That year he improved his batting to .259 with 60 RBI, 64 runs, and 52 walks in 487 at-bats. In the World Series, he had three runs scored and three RBI in the Athletics' 12–5 victory in Game Three. In 1911 he stole a career-high 30 bases and hit .368 in the World Series. The number-seven hitter's best year came in 1913, when he had career highs in batting (.275) and RBI (85). In 1914 he hit .071 in the World Series as Philadelphia was upset by the Miracle Braves. The disappointed and financially pressed Mack sold stars Barry and Eddie Collins to raise money to prevent further losses to defections to the Federal League.

New Red Sox owner Joe Lannin paid $8,000 for Barry in mid-1915. Used exclusively at second base, he hit .262 for Boston and proved to be the last piece in the pennant puzzle. Boston won consecutive World Championships in 1915 and 1916. Barry played only 94 games, hit just .203, and did not play in the World Series. His winning ways netted him $17,930 in WS shares over the course of his career.

Boston manager Bill Carrigan quit after the season to go into business, and Barry was named to replace him. He won 90 games, just one less than the 1916 team, but finished second to Chicago. As a player, he led AL second basemen in fielding but hit just .214. After spending all of 1918 in the military, he returned to a team, now managed by Ed Barrow, that was being sold off to bankroll new owner Harry Frazee's Broadway shows. When Barry hit .241 with only two RBI in 31 games, he was traded back to the Athletics in June. He chose to retire instead of reporting. /(SFS)

Shad Barry [John C.] — 1876–1936. OF-1B 1899–1908 Washington (NL), Braves, **Phillies,** Cubs, Reds, Cardinals, Giants 1099 g, .267, 10 hr, 390 rbi

Barry played every position except pitcher and catcher for seven teams in 10 years. He hit a career-high .304 as the Reds' first baseman in 1905, and during WWI was in charge of all baseball programs for the American Expeditionary Force. /(JK)

Dick Bartell (Rowdy Richard) — 1907– . SS 1927–43, 46 Pirates, Phillies, **Giants,** Cubs, Tigers 2016 g, .284, 79 hr, 710 rbi. *3 WS, 18 g, .294, 1 hr, 7 rbi*
☛ *All-Star—33, 37.*

"Rowdy Richard" battled rivals and umpires with his fists and mouth for 18 major league seasons. Although the 160-lb scrapper was best known for his aggressiveness, he was a good shortstop with occasional sting in his bat, six times batting over .300.

Dick Bartell

Nevertheless, his volatile personality wore out its welcome after a few seasons. He broke in with the Pirates (who kept him instead of young Joe Cronin), becoming the regular shortstop in 1928. In 1931, he was traded to the Phillies, and after four seasons there was traded again to the Giants. He helped New York win pennants in 1936 and '37. After a year with the Cubs, he was traded to Detroit just in time for their 1940 pennant. *Rowdy Richard*, his autobiography (with Norman Macht), was published in 1987. /(JD)

Tony Bartirome — 1932– . 1B 1952 **Pirates** 124 g, .220, 0 hr, 16 rbi

In his only ML season, the slick-fielding Pittsburgh native set a Pirate record by not hitting into a double play in 355 at-bats. His ML career was cut short by military service, but he played in the minors until 1963. After 19 years as the Pirate trainer, he moved with manager Chuck Tanner to the Braves as a coach in 1986. /(ME)

Bob Barton — 1941– . C 1965–74 Giants, **Padres**, Reds 393 g, .226, 9 hr, 66 rbi

Barton's most active year came in 1971 with the three-year-old Padres, when the strong thrower caught 119 games and set career highs in most offensive categories, but led NL catchers with 15 errors. It was his only season as anything but a reserve catcher. /(SFS)

Base Ball Writers Association of America — 1908–

Jack Rider of the Cincinnati *Enquirer* was traveling with the Reds in 1906 when he began discussing with other writers the need to improve working conditions. Sid Mercer of the New York *Globe* agreed. An earlier attempt to organize writers had failed; very few were on the road with teams. They enlisted Ernest Lanigan of the New York *Press* to do the missionary work because the *Press* had the most extensive baseball coverage.

According to a mistaken legend, the idea began when Hugh Fullerton of the Chicago *Examiner* found actor Louis Mann in his pressbox seat at the 1908 WS. Fullerton did indeed confront Mann, who often sat in the pressbox at the Polo Grounds, but that was a fairly common nuisance at the time.

The organization was formally constituted in Detroit on October 14, 1908, but a formative meeting of a few writers from New York, Brooklyn, Chicago, and Cincinnati had occurred in the NL offices in New York on August 11. NL president Harry Pulliam supported the idea.

In 1910, the New York teams gave the group a boost. At a city series they admitted only BBWAA members to the press box. As a result, the organization collected a high number of $2 annual dues. Among the goals of the BBWAA were better facilities, promoting uniform scoring, and acting with the leagues in making rules suggestions. Chapters were formed in most ML cities; their annual winter dinners have become big events. /(NLM)

Monty Basgall [Romanus] — 1922– . 2B 1948–49, 51 **Pirates** 200 g, .215, 4 hr, 41 rbi

Long a Los Angeles Dodger coach, Basgall originally signed with Brooklyn at age 19 in 1942, but he spent most of his playing career in the Pirates' organization. In 1949, he played in 107 games and hit .218 as Pittsburgh's sub for injured Danny Murtaugh. /(MC)

Eddie Basinski (Fiddler) — 1922– . SS-2B 1944–45, 47 **Dodgers**, Pirates 203 g, .244, 4 hr, 59 rbi

Basinski went straight from the University of Buffalo to the Dodgers, where he was the regular Brooklyn shortstop in 1945 while Pee Wee Reese was in the service. /(ME)

Kevin Bass — 1959– . OF 1982– Brewers, **Astros** 947 g, .275, 78 hr, 396 rbi. *1 LCS, 6 g, .292* ☛ *All-Star—86.*

One of three players the Brewers sent to Houston when they acquired veteran pitcher Don Sutton for their 1982 pennant drive, Bass was hitting .315 at Vancouver (Pacific Coast League) at the time of the trade, and has been with the Astros ever since. The switch-hitting Bass led the Astros in pinch hits in 1983 and 1984 before winning the starting centerfield job in 1985, then moved to right field when the club acquired Billy Hatcher. He has both power and speed, and was an NL All-Star in 1986 when he hit .311 with 20 HR and 22 stolen bases, helping the Astros to the NL West title. In the 1986 NLCS, Bass had three two-hit games. /(SCL)

Norm Bass — 1939– . RHP 1961–63 **A's** 253 ip, 13–17, 5.32

As a rookie, Bass hit his only ML home run, tossed two shutouts, and led the A's in wins with 11, but his ERA was an inflated 4.69. Lacking a reliable out pitch and consistent control, he faded from an improving Kansas City staff. /(FJO)

Johnny Bassler — 1895–1979. C 1913–14, 21–27 Indians, **Tigers** 811 g, .304, 1 hr, 318 rbi

Bassler was an excellent catcher and a steady .300 hitter with little power for the Tigers, finishing sixth, seventh, and fifth in AL MVP voting, 1922–24. He enjoyed the California lifestyle so much he cut short his ML career and spent many years playing and managing in the Pacific Coast League. /(JK)

Emil Batch (Heinie) — 1880–1926. 3B-OF 1904–07 **Dodgers** 348 g, .251, 7 hr, 98 rbi

Fans called this East New York boy "Ace" when he broke in at third base for Brooklyn late in 1904, but his NL-leading 57 errors the next year got him moved to the outfield for the rest of his career. /(TG)

John Bateman — 1942– . C 1963–72 **Astros**, Expos, Phillies 1017 g, .230, 81 hr, 375 rbi

Bateman battled weight problems throughout his career, paying over $2,000 in overweight fines. His best year was 1966, when he batted .279 and hit 17 homers for Houston. On September 29, 1970, he hit the final home run at Philadelphia's Connie Mack Stadium. During the late 1970s he traveled with Eddie Feigner's *King and His Court* four-man softball team. /(RTM)

Johnny Bates — 1882–1949. OF 1906–14 **Braves**, Phillies, Reds, Cubs, Baltimore FL 1163 g, .277, 25 hr, 417 rbi

Journeyman outfielder Bates hit .305 for the 1910 Phillies in his best year. He later became an off-season pool hall owner and breeder of show dogs. /(NLM)

Earl Battey — 1935– . C 1955–67 White Sox, **Senators/Twins** 1141 g, .270, 104 hr, 449 rbi. *1 WS, 7 g, .120, 2 rbi*
☛ *All-Star—62–63, 65–66. Gold Glove—60–62.*

From 1961 through 1966 the durable Battey played in 805 of the Twins' first 970 games despite injuries. Besides a perennial bad knee, several dislocated fingers, and a goiter problem (at times he ballooned to 60 pounds over his listed weight), he twice had cheekbones broken by pitched balls and wore a special helmet after 1962. In Game Three of the 1965 WS, he ran into a neck-high crossbar in Dodger Stadium while chasing a foul pop. He played the remainder of the series even though he could barely speak or turn his head.

   A three-time Gold Glove winner, Battey topped all ML catchers in 1962 with a .280 BA, threw out

24 runners, and picked off 13. He had career highs of 26 homers and 84 RBI in 1963. He was the top vote-getter on the 1965 AL All-Star squad. /(JCA)

Matt Batts — 1921– . C 1947–56 Red Sox, Browns, **Tigers**, White Sox, Reds 546 g, .269, 26 hr, 219 rbi

A backup catcher, the husky Texan played ten years in the ML but only in 1953 with the Tigers did he appear in more than 100 games, hitting .278 with 42 RBI. /(CC)

Hank Bauer — 1922– . OF 1948–61 **Yankees**, A's 1544 g, .277, 164 hr, 703 rbi. *9 WS, 53 g, .245, 7 hr, 24 rbi.*
   Manager 1961–62, 64–69 A's, **Orioles** 594–534, .527. First place: 66 *1 WS, 4–0, 1.000*
☛ *All-Star—52–54.*

One of Casey Stengel's favorites, Bauer didn't give away runs or make mental mistakes, and he had a fierce determination to win. He collected nine WS checks while with the Yankees and would snarl "Don't mess with my money!" to teammates who didn't hustle. The ex-Marine exuded authority; his face was likened to a clenched fist. Stengel platooned Bauer for much of his Yankee career, but he still emerged as a solid hitter with both power and speed. He started three straight All-Star games (1952–54) and hit 26 HR in 1956 and 18 first-inning leadoff HR in his career. He hit a three-run triple in the finale of the 1951 WS, and secured the 4–3 win over the Giants with a sliding catch in right field as the would-be tying run was streaking home. From 1956 to 1958 he set a WS record with a 17-game hitting streak. Bauer was eventually traded to the A's in the deal that brought Roger Maris to New York. He managed the Orioles to the 1966 World Championship. /(MG)

Russ Bauers — 1914– . RHP 1936–41, 46, 50 **Pirates**, Cubs, Browns 599 ip, 31–30, 3.53

Bauers led Pittsburgh starters in winning percentage (.684, 13–6) and ERA (2.88) as a rookie in 1937. He lost a one-hitter to Boston in 1938. He saw little major league action after a sore arm in 1939. /(ME)

Joe Bauman — 1922– . 1B *Minor League*.

Bauman was a minor league slugger who batted .337 and collected 337 home runs and 1057 RBI in 1019 games. First signed by the Braves, he lost four years to WWII, and held out from 1949–51. He won four HR titles in the nine years he played, but only once played above Class A. After hitting 103 HR for

Artesia in 1952–53, he won the Longhorn League (Class C) triple crown by batting .400 with 72 HR and 224 RBI for the Roswell Rockets in 1954. The 72 HR and .916 slugging average he achieved that season are all-time pro records. /(MC)

Frank Baumann (The Beau) — 1933– . LHP 1955–65 Red Sox, **White Sox**, Cubs 797 ip, 45–38, 4.11
☛ *Led League—era 60.*

Touted early as "a Herb Score with control," the burly lefthander received a $90,000 signing bonus from the Red Sox in 1952 and Sox owner Tom Yawkey nicknamed him "The Beau." His only good year was 1960, when he went 13–6 for the White Sox with an AL-best 2.67 ERA. /(JCA)

George Baumgardner — 1891–1970. RHP 1912–16 **Browns** 686 ip, 36–48, 3.22

Naive to a fault, Baumgardner never got paid what he was worth. The Browns paid the "rube" West Virginian in dollar bills to make his salary seem more substantial. His best record came when he was 14–13 in 1914 and led the AL in relief wins (6) and losses (5). /(WB)

Ross Baumgarten — 1955– . LHP 1978–82 **White Sox**, Pirates 496 ip, 22–36, 3.99

Baumgarten threw a shutout in his second ML start and authored two one-hitters (both against California, on 5/25/79 and 7/2/80). A series of ailments weakened his shoulder. His arm gone, he lost his last ten decisions. /(JCA)

Stan Baumgartner — 1894–1955. LHP 1914–16, 21–22, 24–26 Phillies, **A's** 506 ip, 27–21, 3.70

Baumgartner played on the University of Chicago's 1913–14 Big Ten football, baseball, and basketball champions; he later coached those three sports at the University of Delaware. In his only major league season of note, he went 13–6 for the 1924 Athletics. For 20 years he was a sportswriter for the Philadelphia *Inquirer*. /(NLM)

Frankie Baumholtz — 1918– . OF 1947–49, 51–57 Reds, **Cubs**, Phillies 1019 g, .290, 25 hr, 272 rbi

Baumholtz's career had a promising start when he finished fifth in the inaugural 1947 Rookie of the Year voting. He hit .283 with 32 doubles and a career-high 96 runs scored as the Reds' everyday right fielder and had 18 assists. His average rose to .296 in 1948, but his production fell off in all other categories. He was traded to the Cubs with Hank Sauer for Harry Walker and Peanuts Lowery in

1949 while batting .235. Baumholtz hit just .226 for Chicago and was out of the league the next year.

He made it back as the Cubs' centerfielder in 1951, and although he never equaled the production of his rookie season, he hit for a good average. His highest-average year, 1952, was interrupted by a broken hand; he finished at .325 while mostly playing right field. Back in centerfield in 1953, he had the arduous responsibility of covering most of the outfield between sluggardly sluggers Sauer and Ralph Kiner. Years later, Kiner would remember that all the centerfielder ever heard was, "You take it!"

In 1954 Baumholtz played part-time and began pinch hitting, although with little success (2-for-17). He grew into the role in 1954, leading the league in pinch hits (15-for-37). Sold to the Phillies after the season, he again led in pinch hits (14-for-52) in 1956, and played only 15 games in the outfield. He was out of the majors after only two at-bats in 1957.

Before breaking into the majors, Baumholtz played professional basketball for two seasons in the NBL and the BAA. /(JFC)

Ed Bauta — 1935– . RHP 1960–64 **Cardinals**, Mets 149 ip, 6–6, 4.35

The Pacific Coast League's top reliever in 1961 with Portland, this righthanded Cuban was the losing pitcher in the first game ever played at Shea Stadium, April 17, 1964, as the Mets bowed to Pittsburgh, 4–3. /(RTM)

Jose Bautista — 1964– . RHP 1988- **Orioles** 250 ip, 9–19, 4.61

After seven years in the Mets system, this Dominican was drafted by the Orioles and immediately moved into their rotation in 1988, posting a 6–15, 4.30 record. /(JFC)

Harry Bay (Deerfoot) — 1878–1952. OF 1901–08 Reds, **Indians** 673 g, .277, 5 hr, 141 rbi

Bay was the American League stolen base champion in 1903 with 45. He had 169 career stolen bases and remains among Cleveland's all-time leaders. He set a since-tied major league record with 12 outfield putouts in a July 19, 1904 game against Boston (12 innings). /(ME)

Don Baylor (Groove) — 1949– . DH-OF-1B 1970–88 Orioles, A's, **Angels**, Yankees, Red Sox, Twins 2292 g, .260, 338 hr, 1276 rbi. *7 LCS, 28 g, .271, 3 hr, 17 rbi. 3 WS, 10 g, .280, 1 hr, 4 rbi*
☛ *Most Valuable Player—79. Led League—rbi 79. All-Star—79.*

Don Baylor, batting

A durable power hitter, Don Baylor will probably be most noted as the major league record holder for being hit by a pitch. He was hit a major league-high 28 times in 1987, setting the career record (244) when plunked by Rick Rhoden on June 28. He was fast in the first half of his career, and retired with 285 stolen bases to go with his 338 HR.

Baylor was *TSN* Minor League Player of the Year in 1970. Part of the 1976 Reggie Jackson trade, Baylor stole a career-high 52 bases in his first season with Oakland, then signed with California as a free agent. He peaked in his 1979 MVP season, hitting .296 with 36 HR and leading the league with 139 RBI and 120 runs scored. After three successful but unhappy seasons in New York, he went to the Red Sox. He was voted the AL's top DH in 1985 and 1986, reaching the 2,000-hit plateau the latter year. Baylor received the Roberto Clemente Award for humanitarian service in 1985.

Known for his leadership, he played on seven first-place teams, and played in the World Series with three different teams in his last three seasons. /(ME)

Bill Bayne (Beverly) — 1899–1981. LHP 1919–24, 28–30 **Browns**, Indians, Red Sox 661 ip, 31–32, 4.82

Bayne had such a wicked curveball that it once led Ty Cobb to pinch-hit a righthanded hitter for himself. Bayne's best season was with the Browns in 1921, when he was 11–5, but he slumped to 4–5 during St. Louis's pennant run in 1922. He was a lifetime .290 hitter. /(WB)

Belve Bean [Beveric Benton] (Bill) — 1905–1988. RHP 1930–31, 33–35 **Indians**, Senators 235 ip, 11–7, 5.32

Used in relief and given a few starts by Cleveland, Bean was never able to establish himself. He won 17 of his last 20 decisions at Toledo (American Association) in 1932 to earn another shot. /(ME)

Dave Beard — 1959– . RHP 1980–85 **A's**, Mariners, Cubs 270 ip, 19–18, 4.69. *1 LCS, 0.2 ip, 0–0, 40.50*

Beard had only 21 innings of ML experience when he saved the deciding game of the 1981 AL Western Division playoff against the Royals. In the LCS, he retired two batters and surrendered a three-run home run to the Yankees' Lou Piniella. Beard led Oakland in saves in 1982 and 1983 with 11 and 10, then was traded to Seattle with catcher Bob Kearney for ace reliever Bill Caudill. He had a 5.80 ERA in 43 appearances for the Mariners in 1984, while Caudill saved 36 games for Oakland. /(SCL)

Mike Beard — 1950– . LHP 1974–77 Braves 118 ip, 4–2, 3.74

Beard's unhappiness at being farmed out to Richmond (International League) in 1976 sealed his fate with Atlanta manager Dave Bristol. "People who play baseball for a living never do grow up," groused Beard, a guitar-playing reliever. /(PB)

Gene Bearden (The Arkansas Traveler) — 1920– . LHP 1947–53 **Indians**, Senators, Tigers, Browns, White Sox 788 ip, 45–38, 3.96. 20 wins: 48 *1 WS, 11 ip, 1–0, 0.00*
☛ *Led League—era 48.*

The knuckleballer was a rookie sensation in 1948 when he went 20–7 and led the AL with a 2.43 ERA. His 20th win was the Indians' pennant-deciding playoff versus Boston. In the WS, he had a win and a save without giving up a run. He never again approached his rookie record. He winked at training rules, suffered a lingering thigh injury in 1949, and batters learned to lay off his nasty knuckler. /(JCA)

Gary Beare — 1952– . RHP 1976–77 **Brewers** 100 ip, 5–6, 5.13

A hard-luck hurler cut down by a sore arm in 1978, Beare got a 17-run explosion from the Brewers to beat the Indians in 1976. /(MC)

Larry Bearnarth — 1941– . RHP 1963–66, 71 **Mets**, Brewers 323 ip, 13–21, 4.13

Sinker-baller Bearnarth led the 1963 Mets with 58 appearances. Casey Stengel referred to the 6'2" 205-lb intellectual as "Big Ben." In the 1980s he was the Expo pitching coach. /(KT)

Jim Beattie — 1954– . RHP 1978–86 Yankees, **Mariners** 1149 ip, 52–87, 4.17. *1 LCS, 5 ip, 1–0, 1.69. 1 WS, 9 ip, 1–0, 2.00*

Beattie was a college basketball star at Dartmouth. He pitched brilliantly for the Yankees in the 1978 LCS and World Series, but the next season was on owner George Steinbrenner's shuttle to Triple-A, before being traded to Seattle as part of the deal for Ruppert Jones. In seven seasons with the Mariners, Beattie was a workhorse starter, setting club records (subsequently broken) for walks, runs, and earned runs allowed in a season. In 1982, Beattie set a club record for a starter by pitching 19 consecutive scoreless innings. On September 27, 1983, Beattie threw the first one-hitter in Mariners history, the only baserunner being the Royals' U.L. Washington, who singled in the third inning. He also surrendered Carl Yastrezemski's 3,000th hit. /(TF)

Jim Beauchamp — 1939– . 1B-OF 1963–65, 67–73 **Cardinals**, Astros, Braves, Reds, Mets 393 g, .231, 14 hr, 90 rbi. *1 WS, 4 g, .000*

In the minors, Beauchamp proved a good defensive outfielder and basestealer while hitting 186 home runs. The majority of his big league appearances came as a pinch hitter, and he collected 46 hits that way. His son, James, Jr., signed with Toronto in 1982. /(FJO)

Ginger Beaumont [Clarence] — 1876–1956. OF 1899–1910 **Pirates**, Braves, Cubs 1444 g, .311, 38 hr, 617 rbi. *2 WS, 11 g, .250*
☛ *Led League—ba 02.*

The first player ever to bat in a World Series was an outstanding leadoff hitter. Beaumont's chunky build (5'8", 190 lb) belied blazing speed that helped him beat out many infield hits. On July 22, 1899, at the Pirates' Exposition Park, he got six infield hits in six at-bats and scored six runs. Nicknamed for a shock of red hair, Beaumont batted .352 as a rookie and led the NL with .357 in 1902, and scored 100 or more runs each season from 1900 to 1903, with a league-high 137 in '03. /(ME)

Johnny Beazley (Beaz, Two-game Johnny) — 1918– . RHP 1941–42, 46–49 **Cardinals**, Braves 374 ip, 31–12, 3.01. *2 WS, 19 ip, 2–0, 2.37*

Beazley had a marvelous season in 1942, going 21–6 with a 2.13 ERA and finishing second in the NL in wins, winning percentage, and ERA. He capped it off with two wins in the Cardinals' World Series upset of the Yankees. While serving in the Air Force during WWII, the quiet Tennessean failed to warm up properly for an exhibition against his old teammates and severely hurt his arm. He tried in vain to regain his form after coming out of the service. /(WB)

Boom-Boom Beck [Walter William] — 1904–1987. RHP 1924, 27–28, 33–34, 39–45 Browns, Dodgers, **Phillies**, Tigers, Reds, Pirates 1034 ip, 38–69, 4.30

Boom-Boom Beck supposedly earned his nickname while pitching for Casey Stengel's Dodgers in 1934. Becoming upset when Stengel came out to remove him when the Dodgers still had a lead, Beck angrily threw the ball into right field at the old Baker Bowl in Philadelphia. The ball hit the tin-plated wall and caromed to center. The "boom-boom" of the rebound roused centerfielder Hack Wilson, who was relaxing during the pitching change and thought the game had resumed. Wilson pursued the ball and fired a strike back to the infield.

As an after-dinner speaker, the loquacious Beck later left audiences shaking their heads as he lamented that America was in danger of giving baseball back to the Indians. Pitching for atrocious teams but performing none too well himself, he had only two winning records in 12 major league seasons, a 1–0 mark in six games in 1927 and an 8–5 record split between the Reds and the Pirates in the war-weakened 1945 season, his last. He won his last game while coaching at Toledo (American Association) in 1951, pitching a 10–2 win over Minneapolis at the age of 46 to bring his total professional mark to an even 236–236. /(WB)

Clyde Beck (Jersey) — 1902– . 3B-2B-SS 1926–31 **Cubs**, Reds 468 g, .232, 12 hr, 162 rbi

When the Cubs hit four homers in the seventh inning on May 12, 1930, they were only the second team in history to accomplish the feat; utility man Beck hit the record-tying HR. He hit a career-high six HR in that rabbit-ball season but batted only .213, 90 points below the league average. /(WOR)

Fred Beck — 1886–1962. 1B-OF 1909–11, 14–15 Braves, Reds, Phillies, **Chicago (FL)** 635 g, .252, 34 hr, 251 rbi
☛ *Led League—hr 10.*

In 1910, Beck hit ten homers to tie for the NL lead. After dropping back to the minors, he returned as

the Chicago Whales' (Federal League) regular first baseman for 1914–15. His long minor-league career ended in 1928. /(JK)

Beals Becker — 1886–1943. OF 1908–15 Pirates, Braves, Giants, Reds, **Phillies** 876 g, .276, 45 hr, 292 rbi. *3 WS, 7 g, .263*

Becker was a fair fielder and a lefthanded batter who had trouble with southpaw pitching. His top year was 1914, when he hit .325 with 9 homers and 66 RBI for the Phillies. He played better on the road than at home, reportedly because he had "rabbit ears" and reacted to hometown heckling. /(NLM)

Glenn Beckert (Bruno) — 1940– . 2B-3B 1965–75 **Cubs**, Padres 1320 g, .283, 22 hr, 360 rbi
☛ *All-Star—69–72. Gold Glove—68.*

The Cubs' regular second baseman for nine years, Beckert was a reliable contact hitter who hit second in the batting order for most of his career. He was the most difficult batter to strike out in the NL five times (in 1968 he whiffed only 20 times in 643 at-bats), and he walked only slightly more often, but nonetheless led the NL in runs scored with 98 in '68. Although never considered a power hitter, he had 20 or more doubles in six seasons.

Beckert was a minor league shortstop, but switched to second base after Ken Hubbs died. He won the Cubs' second-base job in 1965 and adjusted quickly to his new position, leading the NL in assists while finishing second in double plays and total chances per game. For his entire Cub career, he played alongside shortstop Don Kessinger (who often led off in front of Beckert), giving the Cubs an outstanding defensive keystone combo. Throughout Beckert's career, he was overshadowed by two of the greatest second basemen in baseball history. When he first came up, Bill Mazeroski was regularly leading the league in most defensive categories; after Maz faded, Joe Morgan grabbed the second-base spotlight. Beckert was second in the NL in assists from 1966 to 1969, and in 1971 he won a Gold Glove. He received his nickname, Bruno (after the wrestler Bruno Sammartino), from teammate Paul Popovich in the minor leagues, because Beckert frequently knocked down other infielders in pursuit of pop-ups.

Although he hit only .239 as a rookie, Beckert quickly improved and went on to hit .280 or better the next six seasons, peaking at .342 in 1971. On June 3, 1971, he drove in Ken Holtzman with the only run of the game in Holtzman's no-hitter against the Reds.

After his skills were eroded by knee and heel injuries over the next two seasons, Beckert was traded to the Padres for outfielder Jerry Morales. In San Diego, Beckert was a part-time infielder and pinch hitter limited again by ankle and finger injuries. /(SH)

Jake Beckley (Eagle Eye) — 1867–1918. 1B 1888–1907 **Pirates**, Pittsburgh (PL), Giants, Reds, Cardinals 2386 g, .308, 88 hr, 1575 rbi
☛ *Hall of Fame—1971.*

The lefthanded Beckley is first all-time in games played at first base. The powerful 5'10" 200-lb slugger hit .300 or better 13 times, including six straight years, 1899–1904. He had 2930 hits lifetime, and his 244 triples rank fourth on the career list. He scored 100 runs five times in the 1890s, and stole 315 bases in his career. On September 26, 1897 he hit three homers against the Cardinals while playing for the Reds. When on a hitting spree, his blood-curdling cry of "Chickazoola" rattled pitchers.

Jake Beckley

Beckley also won fame with his glove. His 25,000 chances and 23,696 putouts rank first all-time among first basemen. However, he had a notorious scatter-gun arm, and runners always took the extra base on him. He also had a unique hidden-ball trick: He hid the ball under one corner of the base. /(WB)

Bill Beckmann — 1907– . RHP 1939–42 A's, Cardinals 440 ip, 21–25, 4.79

Beckman first made the majors at age 32 in 1939 and enjoyed his best season the next year, going 8–4 with the A's. He was sent down to Rochester early in 1942, but earned a September call-up by the Cardinals. The Cards won the pennant by two games, one of which was Beckmann's clutch win in his last ML appearance. /(MC)

Joe Beckwith — 1955– . RHP 1979–80, 82–86 **Dodgers**, Royals 422 ip, 18–19, 3.54. *1 LCS, 2 ip, 0–0, 0.00. 1 WS, 2 ip, 0–0, 0.00*

A freak spring-training eye injury caused Beckwith to sit out 1981. The situation was remedied by an equally unusual operation, which reduced the vision of his good eye to that of his bad eye. Beckwith was almost exclusively a reliever, and in 1984 he won a career-high eight games from the Royals' bullpen. /(TG)

John Beckwith (The Black Bomber) — 1902–1956. SS-3B-C-0F-MGR Negro Leagues 1919–38 Chicago Giants, Chicago American Giants, Baltimore Black Sox, Homestead Grays, Harrisburg Giants, New York Lincoln Giants, Bacharach Giants, New York Black Yankees, Newark Dodgers, Brooklyn Royal Giants 452 g, .348, 71 hr (inc.)
☛ *Led League—hr 30–31(NAL).*

Beckwith was a 230-lb righthanded slugger who smashed some of the longest and most memorable home runs in Negro League baseball during the 1920s and early 1930s. A pull hitter who swung a huge 38" bat, he hit against a severe fielder shift that did little to curtail his effectiveness. In 1921, as a 19-year-old rookie with the Chicago Giants, he became the first player, white or black, to hit a ball over the laundry roof behind Cincinnati's Crosley Field. His longest blast, according to Hosely Lee, who pitched against Beckwith in the Eastern Colored League, came at Washington's Griffith Stadium, which had the longest leftfield fence in the majors at the time. Beckwith's home run hit an advertising sign, approximately 460' from home plate and 40' above the ground, behind the leftfield bleachers. Negro

League great Ted Radcliffe said of Beckwith, "Nobody hit the ball any farther than him—Josh Gibson or nobody else."

Beckwith played several positions, yet, despite his great size, appeared most frequently at shortstop. The core of his career spanned 1921–31, for which time only partial statistics are available. Only twice during those years did he hit less than .322, but though he topped the .360 mark six times, he never won a batting title. He finished second three times— twice to Hall of Famer Oscar Charleston, and once to Chino Smith. In 1925, he hit .419 to Charleston's .430. He won two HR crowns, with nine in 1930 and seven in 1931, but lost two others to Charleston by one HR. He batted .398 as a rookie in 1921, and in 1924 batted .417 for the Baltimore Black Sox of the Eastern Colored League, hitting 40 HR against league and non-league competition. In 1927, he hit 12 HR in league competition, but reportedly hit an astounding 72 for the whole year. In 1930, with the N.Y. Lincoln Giants, he is said to have batted .546, including a documented .494 (40-for-81) in 20 league games.

Beckwith was temperamental, and had the reputation of being somewhat lazy and mean. He once punched out teammate Bill Holland, a pitcher, who had thrown his glove when Beckwith's fielding error cost him a game. Because of his fiery disposition, he was traded often. In his last appearance documented by a newspaper boxscore (1934), he went 1-for-3 against Hall of Famer Dizzy Dean. He played a handful of games from 1932 to 1934, and supposedly finished his career in 1938 with the Brooklyn Royal Giants, though no records of his last four years exist. /(JM)

Julio Becquer — 1931– . 1B 1955, 1957–61, 1963 **Senators**, Angels, Twins 488 g, .244, 12 hr, 114 rbi

Becquer had 63 career pinch hits and was the AL's top pinch hitter in 1957 and '59. He stole three bases for the 1957 Senators, a team which stole only 13. /(FK)

Hugh Bedient — 1889–1965. RHP 1912–15 **Red Sox**, Buffalo (FL) 937 ip, 58–53, 3.08. 20 wins: 12 *1 WS, 18 ip, 1–0, 0.50*

Bedient won 20 games as a Red Sox rookie in 1912 and another in the WS when he outpitched Christy Mathewson 2–1 in the fifth game. He also pitched the first seven innings of the final game, won by the Red Sox in the tenth. /(JK)

Steve Bedrosian (Bedrock) — 1957– . RHP 1981- **Braves**, Phillies, Giants 910 ip, 56–61, 3.23. *2 LCS, 4 ip, 0–0, 6.23. 1 WS, 3 ip, 0–0, 0.00*
☛ *Cy Young Award—87. All-Star—87.*

One of the NL's star relievers of the 1980s, Bedrosian was *TSN* NL Rookie Pitcher of the Year in 1982 and in 1987 won the NL Cy Young Award. He made only one relief appearance in four minor league seasons, and already had a hard slider and a good change of pace to go with his 96-mph fastball when he reached the ML. Encouraging him to throw as hard as possible, the Braves started him out in middle relief, and he led NL relievers with 123 strikeouts as a rookie, finishing with a 2.42 ERA and 11 saves. Bedrosian had continued success out of the bullpen in 1983–84, but in 1985 the Braves made him a starter. He didn't complete any of his 37 starts that year, and was 7–15. Before the 1986 season Bedrosian was traded to Philadelphia, where the Phillies made him their ace in the bullpen. He saved 29 games in 1986, and a ML-high 40 in 1987 to edge Rick Sutcliffe for the Cy Young Award. In 1988, he missed the first month of the season with walking pneumonia, but managed to save 28 of the Phillies' paltry 65 victories. In 1989 the Giants acquired Bedrosian for their successful pennant bid in exchange for three young prospects. /(SG)

Fred Beebe — 1880–1957. RHP 1906–11, 16 Cubs, Cardinals, Reds, Phillies, Indians 1294 ip, 63–84, 2.86
☛ *Led League—k 06.*

This workhorse led the NL in starts in 1909 while going 15–21 for the Cardinals. His rookie season was his best; he led the NL in strikeouts and was 16–10 overall, going 7–1 for the World Champion Cubs before being traded to St. Louis. /(WB)

Fred Beene — 1942– . RHP 1968–70, 72–75 Orioles, **Yankees**, Indians 288 ip, 12–7, 3.62

An excellent fielder and a fierce competitor, the 5'9" 155-lb Beene spent eight years in the Baltimore farm system. He was 6–0 with a 1.68 ERA with the 1973 Yankees. /(JCA)

Joe Beggs — 1910–1983. RHP 1938, 40–44, 46–48 Yankees, **Reds**, Giants 694 ip, 48–35, 2.96. *1 WS, 1 ip, 9.00*

Beggs failed as a starter with the Yankees in 1938 after a 21-4 record at Newark. Using his breaking ball and sinker, his strong relief pitching (12 wins, 7 saves) helped the 1940 Reds to the World Championship. /(JK)

Hank Behrman — 1921– . RHP 1946–49 **Dodgers**, Pirates, Giants 430 ip, 24–17, 4.40. *1 WS, 6 ip, 7.11*

The native Brooklynite went 11–5 his rookie season. Manager Burt Shotton said poor work habits kept Behrman from reaching his potential. /(EGM)

Ollie Bejma [Aloysius Frank] (The Polish Falcon) — 1907– . 2B-SS 1934–36, 39 **Browns**, White Sox 316 g, .245, 14 hr, 117 rbi

The colorful 5'10" 115-lb infielder hit a home run in his first start that provided the winning margin over the Red Sox. In 1937, he was co-MVP of the American Association, just ahead of Ted Williams. /(WB)

Mark Belanger (Blade) — 1944– . SS 1965–82 **Orioles**, Dodgers 2016 g, .228, 20 hr, 389 rbi. *6 LCS, 21 g, .200, 1 hr, 5 rbi. 4 WS, 22 g, .164, 2 rbi*
☛ *All-Star—76. Gold Glove—69, 71, 73–78.*

When the Orioles traded shortstop Luis Aparicio after the 1967 season, they replaced him with his roommate, Belanger. The slender "Blade" didn't relinquish the position until 1982. An eight-time Gold Glove winner, he played in 43 postseason games during a decade of strong Baltimore teams and holds several ALCS defensive records for short-stops. Seldom spectacular, Belanger rarely fielded a ball one-handed or sidearmed a throw, but he moved around short with sure-handed ease and grace. Although an unimpressive hitter, he had the distinction of swatting a home run in the first ALCS game played, versus Minnesota (10/4/69). That year was his best offensively, as he hit .287 with 50 RBI.

Granted free agency after 1981, Belanger signed with the Dodgers for his final season. A longtime player representative with Baltimore, he became a special assistant with the Major League Baseball Players' Association after retiring as a player. /(JCA)

Wayne Belardi (Footsie) — 1930– . 1B 1950–51, 53–56 Dodgers, **Tigers** 263 g, .242, 28 hr, 74 rbi. *1 WS, 2 g, .000*

Belardi hit 11 homers in just 163 at-bats for the 1953 NL Champion Dodgers. After his trade to Detroit, "Footsie" had his most active season in 1954, hitting 11 HR in 99 games. /(CC)

Tim Belcher — 1961– . RHP 1987– **Dodgers** 444 ip, 31–20, 2.82. *1 LCS, 15 ip, 2–0, 4.11. 9 WS ip, 1–0, 6.23*

Belcher began 1988 in the Dodger bullpen and earned a starting spot. His 12–6, 2.91 record helped the Dodgers to their storybook pennant, and he was

named NL Rookie Pitcher of the Year by *TSN*. He was 3–0 in postseason play, but actually pitched rather poorly. In 1989 he led the NL with eight shutouts while going 15–12, 2.82, but when not pitching a shutout his ERA was 4.10.

Belcher was the center of controversy before he ever pitched in pro ball. Drafted by the Yankees in the January 1984 supplemental phase, he was taken by Oakland from the compensation pool after Baltimore signed Type A free agent Tom Under-wood. The Yankees had not had a chance to protect him. The incident pointed up the inadequacy of the compensation system, which was abandoned soon thereafter. The Dodgers acquired Belcher in return for Rick Honeycutt. /(SFS)

Bo Belinsky [Robert] — 1936– . LHP 1962–67, 69–70 **Angels**, Phillies, Astros, Pirates, Reds 666 ip, 28–51, 4.10

One of the most colorful players of the 1960s, the pool-hustling playboy was picked up from the Ori-oles organization by the Angels in the 1961 expan-sion draft. Undefeated in his first three ML starts, he pitched the first big-league no-hitter on the West Coast against the Orioles on May 5, 1962. Acting appearances in several TV shows, dates with Hollywood starlets Ann-Margaret, Connie Stevens, and Tina Louise, and a much-publicized romance with actress Mamie Van Doren helped keep Belin-sky in the spotlight even after his pitching deteriorated. /(RTM)

Beau Bell [Roy Chester] — 1907–1977. OF-1B 1935–41 **Browns**, Tigers, Indians 767 g, .297, 46 hr, 437 rbi
☛ *All-Star—37.*

For two seasons, 1936 and '37, Bell was one of the best righthanded hitters in the game. In 1936 he hit .344 with 123 RBI and 100 runs scored for the Browns, and he led the AL in hits (218) and doubles (51) in 1937 while hitting .340 with 117 RBI. Bell was a graduate of Texas A&M College, where he studied to be a teacher. When he batted .250 for the Browns in 1935, they farmed him out, calling him the "$17,500 Lemon." Following the advice of manager Rogers Hornsby, whose style Bell adopted, he raised his average nearly 100 points the next season. Alcohol problems hastened his decline, and he was out of the majors by 1942. He coached at the University of Texas for many years. /(WB)

Buddy Bell [David Gus] — 1951– . 3B-OF-SS 1972–89 **Indians**, Rangers, Reds, Astros 2405 g, .279, 201 hr, 1106 rbi

 *All-Star—73, 80–82, 84. Gold Glove—79–84.*

Buddy and his father Gus hold the all-time father-son record for hits (4,337) and combined for 407 HR, tied for the second-best father-son total. A surehanded third baseman with enough range to play shortstop when needed, Buddy won six straight Gold Gloves and led AL third basemen five times in total chances per game, three times each in putouts and assists, and twice each in double plays and fielding.

Breaking in with the Indians in 1972 when Graig Nettles had third base locked up, Bell played out-field most of the season and was named to the *Baseball Digest* Rookie All-Star Team. Nettles was traded in the off-season, and in 1973 Bell showed himself to be among the league's best third base-

Buddy Bell with the Indians

man, leading in putouts and double plays. The Indians traded Bell to Texas in December 1978 for Toby Harrah. Bell responded with his best year to that point, hitting .299 with 18 HR, 101 RBI, and a league-leading 16 game-winning RBI, and won his first Gold Glove. The line-drive hitter eventually became the all-time Texas leader in doubles, RBI, extra-base hits, and total bases. A clutch hitter and smart baserunner, he also had a good batting eye.

A lackluster start in 1985, and the presence of prospect Steve Buechele, prompted Bell's trade to the Reds on July 19. The Cincinnati native filled a long-standing void at third. By joining the Reds, Bell gave the club five active members of the 2,000-hit club (with Pete Rose, Tony Perez, Dave Concepcion, and Cesar Cedeno). After weathering a lengthy adjustment to NL pitching and rumors that he was finished, Bell starred for the Reds in 1986 and '87, leading NL third basemen in fielding in '87. When he started 1988 on the disabled list, he lost his job to star rookie Chris Sabo, and was traded to the Astros in June. He returned to the Rangers as a free agent after the season and was projected as their DH, but injuries and what was becoming an annual first-half slump prompted him to retire. /(ME)

Cool Papa Bell [James] — 1903– . OF Negro Leagues 1922–50 St. Louis Stars, Pittsburgh Crawfords, Homestead Grays, Kansas City Monarchs Statistics incomplete

Hall of Fame—1972.

Bell was offered a chance to play for the Browns in 1951, but he turned it down; he was nearly 48 years old. He earned his nickname for his demeanor under pressure while pitching for the St. Louis Stars as a 19-year-old in 1922. A sterling fielder and an outstanding batter, what made Bell stand out more than anything else was his uncanny speed. Two exaggerated stories demonstrate the effect it had on his contemporaries. Satchel Paige often regaled audiences with the story that when he and Bell roomed together, Bell was so fast that he could turn out the light and be in bed before the room got dark. In truth, he did it one night, but only because there was a short in the wires. Another story has him hitting a ball up the middle and being struck by it as he slid into second base.

A verified story is that during an inter-racial all-star exhibition game on the West Coast, Paige laid down a bunt with Bell on first base. As catcher Roy Partee of the Indians set to throw to first, Bell brushed by him to score. By his own count, Bell once stole 175 bases in a 200-game season. The

Cool Papa Bell

scanty statistics of the Negro Leagues credit him with several years over .400.

There is little doubt that Bell could have starred in the major leagues had there been no color ban during his prime. An unselfish man off the field and on, in 1946 (Jackie Robinson's first year in white organized baseball), Bell deliberately forfeited the batting title to Monte Irvin to enhance Irvin's chance to follow Robinson to the majors. While

coaching and playing with the Monarchs, Bell demonstrated to the young Robinson that he would never make it with his weak arm at shortstop. Bell, in his forties, beat out everything hit to Robinson's right. /(WB)

Eric Bell — 1963– . LHP 1985–87 **Orioles** 194 ip, 11–15, 5.38

Bell was one of only two pitchers to last the entire 1987 season on the Orioles' roster (Mike Boddicker was the other), and he tied Boddicker for the club lead in wins with 10. Elbow surgery sidelined him for the entire 1988 season and left his career in jeopardy. /(ME)

Gary Bell (Ding Dong) — 1936– . RHP 1958–69 **Indians**, Red Sox, Pilots, White Sox 2015 ip, 121–117, 3.68. *1 WS, 5 ip, 0–1, 5.06*
☛ *All-Star—60, 66, 68.*

Bell used a blazing fastball to win 28 games in his first two ML seasons. He later learned to control his curve and developed a slider. In nine years at Cleveland he went through seven managers, who shifted him back and forth between starting and relieving. In 1962 he led the AL with nine relief victories, but he hated relieving, calling it a "rotten, thankless job." Starters received more money and prestige, and the wisecracking Bell preferred four days off to joke around on the bench. After saving 17 in 1965, he returned to starting and won 14 in 1966. Traded to the Red Sox early in 1967, he won 12 during their pennant drive. He had a loss and a save in the WS.

"Ding Dong" was drafted by the expansion Pilots in 1969 and won Seattle's home opener. As author Jim Bouton's roommate, he was prominently mentioned in *Ball Four.* /(JCA)

George Bell — 1959– . OF 1981, 83– **Blue Jays** 1039 g, .289, 181 hr, 654 rbi. *2 LCS, 12 g, .271, 1 hr, 3 rbi*
☛ *Most Valuable Player—87. Led League—rbi 87. All-Star—87.*

From 1984, when he became a regular in the Blue Jay lineup, through 1988, Bell averaged 31 home runs and 104 RBI per season to establish himself as one of the American League's dominant power hitters. Drafted by Toronto from the Phillies' organization at the end of 1980, he spent the next four seasons either on the Toronto bench or with the Blue Jays' Triple-A team at Syracuse. A torrid spring training served as a springboard for his 1984 season of 26 homers, 87 RBI, and a new team record of 69 extra-base hits, and established him as a regular, with Lloyd Moseby and Jesse Barfield, in perhaps baseball's finest outfield of the 1980s. His HR, RBI, and extra-base-hit totals climbed in each of his next three seasons. In August 1985 he clubbed homers in a Blue Jay-record four consecutive games. Two of the homers cleared the roof at Comiskey Park, and another landed in the centerfield bleachers. His high point as a slugger came in 1987 as he set team records with 47 home runs, 134 RBI (which led the AL), 16 game-winning RBI, 83 extra-base hits, 369 total bases, and a .605 slugging average.

Bell's selection as the 1987 American League MVP generated quite a bit of controversy in light of his poor performance in two crucial series at the end of the 1987 campaign against the Tigers, who defeated Toronto on the final day of the season to win the division. No stranger to discord, the hot-tempered native of San Pedro de Macorís in the Dominican Republic had incurred the hatred of Boston fans by directing a karate kick at Red Sox pitcher Bruce Kison, who seemed to be throwing at Blue Jay batters. His general surliness, lackadaisical defensive play, and team-record outfield errors incurred the wrath of Toronto management and fans, and prompted manager Jimy Williams's 1988 spring-training announcement that Bell would be moved to DH in order to improve team defense and save his knees. Bell bristled, then hit three home runs on Opening Day (the first player ever to do so). Nevertheless, a bitter, season-long feud with Williams ensued and played a decisive role in the downfall of the 1988 team. /(TF)

George Bell (Farmer) — 1874–1941. RHP 1907–11 **Dodgers** 1086 ip, 43–79, 2.85

Bell made his ML debut as a 32-year-old rookie, but was given little support by his team. In 1910 he led the NL in losses with 27 while winning only 10, yet posted an excellent 2.64 ERA. Nearly 40% of his wins came on 17 shutouts. /(TG)

Gus Bell [David Russell] — 1928– . OF 1950–64 Pirates, **Reds**, Mets, Braves 1741 g, .281, 206 hr, 942 rbi. *1 WS, 3 g, .000*
☛ *All-Star—53–54, 56–57.*

David Bell's parents so admired catcher Gus Mancuso they nicknamed their son Gus, but instead of a catcher, he became a power-hitting outfielder. Bell was hitting .400 at Indianapolis when he was called up to the Pirates in 1950, joining Ralph Kiner in the

Bucs' outfield. After two strong seasons, he spent part of 1952 back in the minors because of a dispute with the Pirate front office; he had wanted his family to travel with him, including his son Buddy, later an outstanding ML third baseman.

Traded to Cincinnati, Bell hit a career-high 30 homers in 1953. He had his best years with the Reds (1953–61), four times topping 100 RBI.

In the 1957 All-Star voting, Cincinnati fans sent in so many ballots they succeeded in having seven Reds named to the starting lineup. Commissioner Ford Frick removed Bell and Wally Post as starters, but Manager Walter Alston named Bell to the squad and he doubled in two runs in the seventh.

Selected by the Mets in the expansion draft, he collected the first Met hit, a single on April 11, 1962. /(RTM)

Hi Bell [Herman S] — 1897–1949. RHP 1924, 26–27, 29–30, 32–34 **Cardinals**, Giants 663 ip, 32–34, 3.69. *3 WS, 4 ip, 0–0, 4.50*

Bell was the last pitcher to start and win both games of a doubleheader. He did it for the Cardinals in 1924 and duplicated the feat for Rochester (International League) in 1928. He spent much of his career in relief and led the NL with eight saves in 1930, long before it was a statistic. /(WB)

Jay Bell — 1965– . SS-2B 1986– **Indians**, Pirates 194 g, .238, 7 hr, 65 rbi

Bell homered in his first big-league at-bat (9/29/86). He came to the majors as an error-prone shortstop coveted for his heavy hitting (17 HR in 362 at-bats for Buffalo, American Association, 1987) but proved to be an excellent fielder who just couldn't hit enough to keep his job.

Bell was the Twins' first-round pick in the June 1984 draft. He came to Cleveland as part of the package that sent Bert Blyleven to Minnesota. /(WOR)

Jerry Bell — 1947– . RHP 1971–74 **Brewers** 284 ip, 17–11, 3.27

Sinker-slider specialist Bell was 5–1 with a 1.65 ERA in 1972 and 9–9 in 1973, but a chronic back ailment shortened his career. /(JCA)

Kevin Bell — 1955– . 3B 1976–80, 82 **White Sox**, A's 297 g, .222, 13 hr, 64 rbi

Highly touted by White Sox manager Paul Richards, Kevin Bell proved a weak hitter and an average fielder. He hit an inside-the-park grand slam in

Royals Stadium on June 22, 1976 as the leftfielder was knocked unconscious in a collision with the wall. In June 1977 a knee injury ended his season, and he never won a regular job./(RL)

Les Bell — 1901- . 3B 1923-31 **Cardinals**, Braves, Cubs 896 g, .290, 66 hr, 509 rbi. *1 WS, 7 g, .259, 1 hr, 6 rbi*

An early product of the Cardinals farm system, Bell led the American Association in BA in 1924 as a shortstop. Switched to third base, he helped the Cardinals win their first pennant in 1926 (.325, 17 HR, 100 RBI). With the Braves in 1928, he hit three homers and a triple in a single game./(JK)

Rafael Belliard — 1961- . SS-2B 1982- **Pirates** 437 g, .219, 1 hr, 66 rbi

A fine-fielding shortstop, Belliard became Pittsburgh's starter midway through the 1986 season and hit a career-high .233. Returning to the Pirates in 1987 after being sent down midway through the season, he suffered a fractured left fibula, a recurrence of an injury he suffered twice in 1984. When Jose Lind slumped in 1989, Belliard won the second base job in the second half of the season./(ME)

Harry Bemis — 1874-1947. C 1902-10 **Indians** 703 g, .255, 5 hr, 234 rbi

The 5'6" Bemis never hit higher than the .312 mark of his rookie 1902 season. In eight subsequent years with Cleveland, he shared catching duties as the lefthanded hitter./(ME)

Johnny Bench — 1947- . C 1967-83 **Reds** 2158 g, .267, 389 hr, 1376 rbi. *6 LCS, 22 g, .253, 5 hr, 6 rbi. 4 WS, 23 g, .279, 5 hr, 14 rbi*
☛ *Rookie of the Year—68. Most Valuable Player—70, 72. Led League—hr 70, 72. Led League—rbi 70, 72, 74. All-Star—68-77, 80, 83. Gold Glove—68-77. Hall of Fame—1989.*

Considered by some the greatest catcher of all time, Bench got a "can't miss" tag when Peninsula of the Carolina League retired his uniform after he hammered 22 homers in 98 games as an 18-year-old in 1966. He spent the first four months of the 1967 season at Buffalo, then took over the Cincinnati catching job in August 1967. In spring training of 1968, Ted Williams autographed a baseball "To Johnny Bench, a Hall of Famer for sure." Bench met expectations quickly by catching a rookie-record 154 games that season, setting a record for catchers with 40 doubles, and becoming the first

catcher to win National League Rookie of the Year honors. He went on to become the National League's dominant catcher for nearly a decade and a half.

Bench batted either fourth or fifth for the Big Red Machine team that dominated the National League in the 1970s and won six division titles, four pennants, and two World Series. From 1970 to 1977, Cincinnati players won six of eight MVP awards; Bench won two of them. The first came in 1970 following his league-leading 45 home runs and 148 RBI, all-time records for catchers. After holding out and slumping somewhat in 1971, Bench rebounded in 1972 to win his second MVP award. That year, he had the hottest streak of his career, hitting seven homers in five straight games from May 30 through June 3, and he finished with 40 homers and 125 RBI, leading the league in both categories for the second time. He homered three times on July 26, 1970, en route to setting a record of 36 homers by July 31, and twice more had three-homer games, on May 9, 1973 and May 29, 1980. He won his third RBI crown in 1974, driving in 129 runs and leading the NL with 314 total bases.

Of partial Native American descent, Bench was named to the All-Star team in 13 consecutive seasons, and he faced fellow Native American catcher Bill Freehan in five of them. He batted .370 in All-Star competition, hitting homers in the 1969, 1971, and 1973 games and narrowly missing a second homer in 1969. His selection as an All-Star was based as much on his defensive abilities as his offensive skills. He won ten straight Gold Glove Awards and set a NL record by catching at least 100 games in each of his first 13 seasons. He established career records for putouts and chances. Blessed with exceptionally large hands, he was one of the first catchers after the Cubs' Randy Hundley to use a hinged mitt and a one-handed catching style. His throwing arm was unrivaled by catchers of his era.

Bench suffered his worst year as a regular in 1976 when he hit .234 with 16 homers, and some thought he was finished at the age of 29. But competing head-to-head in the World Series against Thurman Munson, the American League's best catcher, brought him alive. He outhit Munson .533 to .529 and won the Series MVP award. Bench recorded his last super season in 1977, hitting .275 with 31 home runs and 109 RBI.

Worn out by catching, Bench repeatedly requested a shift to another position, but the Reds lacked a suitable replacement, and were reluctant to

Johnny Bench, catching

accommodate him. They finally moved him to first base in 1981. On May 28, Bench fractured his ankle, with his batting average at .343. He missed two months and finished the season at .309, his only year over .293. Bench played primarily third base the next two seasons, but went back behind the plate for his last game at the end of 1983. He was elected to the Hall of Fame in his first year of eligibility and was inducted in 1989./(MC/CR)

Chief Bender [Charles Albert] — 1883–1954. RHP 1903–17, 25 A's, Baltimore (FL), Phillies, White Sox 3017 ip, 210–127, 2.46. 20 wins: 10, 13 *5 WS, 85 ip, 6–4, 2.44*
☛ *Hall of Fame—53.*

Bender, for many years the only American Indian elected to the Hall of Fame, boldly created his own opportunities in a world still basically hostile toward his race. His father was a German settler in Minnesota, his mother a Chippewa. He grew up on a reservation, and was sent to a church-run school in Philadelphia when he was eight. After being returned to his mother, he bolted the reservation at 13 to attend the Carlisle Indian School in Pennsylvania.

He accepted his Indian identity, stoically doffing his cap to cheers for "The Chief," but signed

Chief Bender

autographs "Charley Bender." Being an Indian gave him separate glamour among the sons of white immigrants with whom he played, and small boys whooped their admiration. But it was his pitching skills that made him stand out.

Bender's career with the Athletics included two seasons as league leader in winning percentage (1910: 23–5; 1914: 17–3). He pitched a no-hitter against Cleveland in 1910. In the 1905 World Series, in which every game was a shutout, Bender blanked the Giants 3–0 in Game Two, the only game Connie Mack's club won. Christy Mathewson dominated the Series with three shutouts, and Joe McGinnity added his. Bender's 6–4 career WS record included nine complete games, three coming in 1911 when he twice came up against Mathewson, and defeated him once. Bender jumped to the outlaw Federal League for its final, 1915 season, and experienced his most dismal record (4–16).

An all-around player, Bender appeared in several games in the infield and outfield and pinch hit 29 times. He was an expert sign stealer, practicing his art from the coaching box between starts. He steered clear of temptations which wrecked others' careers, such as that of the briefly phenomenal Louis Sockalexis, whose disastrous misadventures were used to deny opportunity to other Native Americans. After his playing career effectively ended with the Phillies in 1917, Bender managed in the minors and coached in the majors. He maintained a solid family life in Philadelphia, based on values adopted while living on a Quaker farm during his school boy summers. /(JK)

Bruce Benedict — 1955– . C 1978- **Braves** 982 g, .242, 18 hr, 260 rbi. *1 LCS, 3 g, .250*
☛ *All-Star—81, 83.*

Benedict was Atlanta's starting catcher from 1980 to 1983, and made the NL All-Star team twice, but a weak bat relegated him to backup status thereafter. In 1982 he led NL catchers in fielding percentage and hit .389 down the stretch as Atlanta won the AL West. His .242 average in 1988 was his best since 1983, when he hit a career-high .298, and in 1989 starting catcher Jody Davis's poor hitting gave Benedict increased playing time. /(ME)

Ray Benge (Silent Cal) — 1902– . RHP 1925–26, 28–36, 38 Indians, **Phillies**, Dodgers, Braves, Reds 1875 ip, 101–130, 4.52

Although he spent only one of his nine full major league seasons with a first-division team, Benge won ten or more games six times. He was not a strikeout pitcher, but on June 16, 1929, he tied what was then a Phillies record with 13 strikeouts in a 7–2 victory at Chicago. /(AL)

Benny Bengough — 1898-1968. C 1923-32 Yankees, Browns 411 g, .255, 0 hr, 108 rbi. *2 WS, 6 g, .176, 1 rbi*

Born in Liverpool, England, Bengough came close to being a Catholic priest. A bullpen catcher in Buffalo, his mother insisted that the manager use him in a game. In his first start, he threw out four Browns baserunners in an exhibition game.

Bengough became a regular on the same day Lou Gehrig replaced Wally Pipp in the lineup in 1925; it was Bengough's only season of more than 58 games. A talkative catcher behind the plate, he would get laughs and distract hitters by running his fingers through his "imaginary" hair. He later coached the Browns, Senators, Braves, and Phillies. /(WB)

Juan Beniquez — 1950- . OF 1971-72, 74-88 Red Sox, Rangers, Yankees, Mariners, **Angels**, Orioles, Royals, Blue Jays 1500 g, .274, 79 hr, 476 rbi. *2 LCS, 5 g, .250, 1 rbi. 1 WS, 3 g, .125, 1 rbi*
☛ *Gold Glove—77.*

Versatile and dependable off the bench, Beniquez fared best late in his career, batting .300 four straight years (1983–86) when he was used primarily against lefthanded pitchers. He was a shortstop in the minors, and set a modern ML record with six errors there in two consecutive games for Boston in 1972. The Red Sox converted him to an outfielder, and he won a Gold Glove with Texas in 1977. Beniquez played for eight different AL clubs, an all-time record. /(ME)

Stan Benjamin — 1914- . OF 1939-42, 45 **Phillies**, Indians 242 g, .229, 5 hr, 41 rbi

Benjamin joined the Phillies in September of 1939 after batting .323 with Chattanooga (Southern Association). His only season as a major-league regular was 1941, when he hit just .235. /(AL)

Bennett Park — Detroit Tigers 1901-11

Named for Tiger catcher Charlie Bennett, the field was originally laid over cobblestones. It was rebuilt as Navin Field (now Tiger Stadium) in 1912, with the playing field turned 90 degrees. /(SCL)

Charlie Bennett — 1854-1927. C 1878, 80-93 Milwaukee (NL), Worcester (NL), **Detroit (NL)**, Braves 1062 g, .256, 56 hr, 420 rbi

Bennett's 15-year career as a part-time catcher was ended when he lost both legs in a train accident. He had been a fan favorite in Detroit, where he played from 1881 to 1888, and when the Tigers became an entry in the new American League in 1901, their new ballpark was named Bennett Park in his honor. It remained Bennett Park until 1912, when it became the site of the present Tiger Stadium. /(JK)

Dennis Bennett — 1939- . LHP 1962-68 **Phillies**, Red Sox, Giants, Angels 863 ip, 43-47, 3.69

An auto accident in Puerto Rico while playing winter ball after the 1962 season set the rangy Bennett back, and a sore left shoulder, incurred during his second straight 1–0 shutout in mid-September 1964, may have cost the Phillies the pennant. When Bennett went down, manager Gene Mauch went essentially to a two-man rotation, wearing out Jim Bunning and Chris Short in the stretch run. In subsequent seasons he never recovered his earlier form. /(AL)

Herschel Bennett — 1896-1964. OF 1923-27 Browns 317 g, .276, 7 hr, 104 rbi

A capable substitute outfielder, Bennett was hitting .330 in 1924 when a broken arm cost him the rest of the season. A later injury caused by crashing into a wall in Philadelphia hastened the end of his career. The son of a farmer, Bennett later served as the Springfield, Missouri, Commissioner of Revenue. /(WB)

Gene Benson — 1913- . OF Negro Leagues 1934-48 Bacharach Giants, Pittsburgh Crawfords, Newark Eagles, **Philadelphia Stars** statistics not available
☛ *All-Star—40, 46.*

Benson, an all-around performer in the Negro National League, was a 5'8" 185-lb outfielder who displayed great range in center while popularizing the basket catch. He was a starter on the 1940 and 1946 Eastern all-star squads. While he spent most of his career with the Philadelphia Stars, he was one of the players added to the Washington Elite Giants roster for the 1936 Black Title series with the Pittsburgh Crawfords, which was aborted when each club attempted to replace three defecting regulars. He also played winter ball in Venezuela (1945) and Cuba (1947–48). Available data places his lifetime batting average at more than .300, with a peak mark of .370, fifth-best in the NNL in 1945, when he shared the league lead with 57 hits. /(MFK)

Jack Bentley — 1895–1969. LHP-1B 1913–16, 23–27 Senators, **Giants**, Phillies 287 g, .291, 7 hr, 71 rbi; 714 ip, 46–33, 4.01. *2 WS, 10 g, .417, 1 hr, 2 rbi; 24 ip, 1–3, 4.94*

In Game Five of the 1924 World Series, Bentley pitched the Giants to a 6–2 win over the Senators and hit a two-run homer off Walter Johnson. However, he lost Game Two 4–3 and dropped the finale in relief when Earl McNeely's double-play grounder hit a pebble and bounced over third baseman Fred Lindstrom's head in the 12th inning after two other fielding blunders.

Bentley was an excellent hitter; while going 13–8 in 1923, his first year with the Giants, he hit .427 in 89 at-bats, including a league-leading 10 pinch hits in 20 pinch at-bats. He had been acquired after going 41–5 in three years with the Baltimore Orioles of the International League. Also playing in the outfield and at first base, he had hit .349 for Baltimore in 1922 and was considered "the next Babe Ruth." After going 16–5 in 1924, weight problems took their toll in 1925, as he went 11–9 with a 5.04 ERA, and he was traded to the Phillies. Playing first base in Philadelphia, he hit .258 in 75 games, pitching only eight times, and returned to the Giants near the end of the season. /(SH)

Joe Benz (Blitzen, Butcher Boy) — 1886–1957. RHP 1911–19 **White Sox** 1358 ip, 76–75, 2.42

Benz had a good spitter and knuckleball. In 1914, though he led the AL with 19 losses, he had one incredible stretch. On May 31, despite three White Sox errors, he no-hit Cleveland 6–1. Then, on June 6, he two-hit the Highlanders in a nine-inning 1–1 tie halted by rain. Six days later, he squared off against Walter Johnson, whom Benz had boasted he could beat. He held the Senators hitless for eight innings while the White Sox scored twice off the Big Train. In the ninth, Eddie Ainsmith hit a bounder toward Buck Weaver at short, but third baseman Scotty Alcock stuck his glove out and deflected the ball into left field, spoiling Benz's no-hitter. Nonetheless, he notched one of two wins he would get in ten lifetime decisions against Johnson. /(RL)

Todd Benzinger — 1963– . OF-1B 1987– **Red Sox**, Reds 354 g, .254, 38 hr, 189 rbi. *1 LCS, 4 g, .091*

A baby-faced switch-hitter with moderate power, Benzinger overcame an injury-riddled minor league career to make the Red Sox as an outfielder. He switched to to first base when Dwight Evans was returned to right field. The Red Sox traded him to Cincinatti with Jeff Sellers for Nick Esasky and Rob

Murphy, and he became the Reds' starting first baseman in 1989. He had seven RBI in one game against Detroit on September 15, 1987. /(SCL)

Johnny Berardino — 1917– . 2B-SS-3B 1939–42, 46–52 **Browns**, Indians, Pirates 912 g, .249, 36 hr, 387 rbi

After three years as a regular at the beginning of his career, including a 16-HR season in 1940, Berardino became a utility man who was called a "one-man infield" for his versatility. He hit a grand slam off Yankee relief ace Johnny Murphy in 1940. After playing for the Browns, Indians, and Pirates by the end of 1950, Berardino appeared with all three teams, in the same order, over the last two years of his career.

Following his release by Pittsburgh in 1952, Berardino had to hock his 1948 Indians World Series ring. He had appeared in a few of the "Our Gang" comedies as a child actor, and Bill Veeck once insured the infielder's face as a publicity stunt. Berardino dropped the second "r" from his name and returned to acting, spending over 25 years as Dr. Steve Hardy on the popular soap opera "General Hospital." /(WB)

Lou Berberet — 1929– . C 1954–60 Yankees, Senators, Red Sox, **Tigers** 448 g, .230, 31 hr, 153 rbi

One of only four regular catchers to field 1.000 for a full season, the stocky Berberet was perfect in 77 games for Washington in 1957 and made only one error in 59 games the year before. /(RM)

Juan Berenguer (Pancho Villa) — 1954– . RHP 1978– Mets, Royals, Blue Jays, Tigers, Giants, **Twins** 963 ip, 55–49, 3.93. *1 LCS, 6 ip, 0–0, 1.50. 1 WS, 4 ip, 0–1, 10.38*

A perennial prospect with the Mets, Berenguer had winning seasons as a part-time starter for Detroit in 1983–84 but found a true home in Minnesota in 1987. As set-up man for closer Jeff Reardon, he went 8–1 (3.94) for the '87 World Champions and 8–4 (3.96) in 1988. Extremely wild as a youngster, he learned to harness his 90-plus-mph fastball, which he liked to throw inside, and added a forkball. His effectiveness was aided by his intimidating appearance and disposition. A mean-looking, husky Panamanian with long hair and a mustache, he was called "Pancho Villa" by his teammates. "If I pulled up in front of a restaurant," said Giants catcher Bob Brenly, "and he came out to park my car, I'd eat somewhere else." /(JCA)

Bruce Berenyi — 1954- . RHP 1980-86 **Reds**, Mets 782 ip, 44-55, 4.03

A promising flamethrower whose career was cut short by injury, Berenyi came up to the Reds at the end of 1980 after leading the American Association in both strikeouts and walks. In strike-shortened 1981, he led the NL with 77 walks. Lack of control combined with the Reds' weak offense in 1982 (last in the NL in runs scored) resulted in a league-leading 18 losses despite a 3.36 ERA.

The Mets, contending for the pennant in 1984, traded Jay Tibbs, Eddie Williams, and pitcher Matt Bullinger to acquire Berenyi that June. He was 9-6 the rest of the way with a 3.76 ERA, and got off to an even better start in 1985. However, on April 24 he tore his rotator cuff while trying to pitch after his arm had tightened up during a rain delay.

Berenyi revealed later that his shoulder had hurt most of his career, but he'd gotten used to it; the trouble had first cropped up in 1978. Out for the rest of the year, he was unable to come back in 1986, contributing only two wins in the Mets' World Championship season. His uncle was former Browns' ace Ned Garver. /(SH)

Moe Berg [Morris] — 1902-1972. C-SS 1923, 26-39 Dodgers, **White Sox**, Indians, Senators, Red Sox 662 g, .243, 6 hr, 206 rbi

Among the most scholarly professional athletes ever, Berg was an alumnus of three universities, lawyer, mathematician, linguist, and poor hitter, eliciting the comment: "He can speak 12 languages but can't hit in any of them." His ability to handle young pitchers and his reputation as a bullpen mystic kept him in the majors, where his roommates wondered at his sacrosanct clutter of books and newspapers stacked in dozens of piles. He professed the belief that his newspapers were "alive" and could "die" from being looked at by someone else. On occasion he braved snowstorms to purchase replacements for "deceased" newspapers.

Casey Stengel called him "the strangest man ever to play baseball" even before it was known he had served America as a spy. Some may have wondered why a third-string catcher like Berg went to Japan in the early 1930s with the likes of Ruth and Gehrig on an all-star traveling team. In fact, Berg was assigned to take espionage photos. During WWII, he became one of America's most important atomic spies, gathering vital information on top German scientists and even performing some missions that might have required assassination. He declined the Medal of Merit for his wartime service and never wrote his memoirs after being angered by an assigned co-author who confused him with "Moe" of the Three Stooges.

Berg fit the classic spy image: dark, heavy-featured, mysterious, sybaritic, courageous, and impeccably mannered. Women were attracted to the cultured, lifelong bachelor. When he was criticized for "wasting" his intellectual talent on the sport he loved, Berg replied: "I'd rather be a ballplayer than a justice on the U.S. Supreme Court." /(DB)

Bill Bergen — 1873-1943. C 1901-11 Reds, **Dodgers** 947 g, .170, 2 hr, 193 rbi

The worst hitter ever to play regularly in the ML, his .170 career BA is 42 points below any other batter with 2500 or more at-bats. His .139 in 1909 is the lowest mark ever for a batting title qualifier. In the lineup for his arm, his 202 assists the same year are the ninth best by a catcher; that July 24, he set a 20th-century record by throwing out seven would-be basestealers. His brother Marty was also a ML catcher. /(TG)

Boze Berger [Louis William] — 1910- . 2B-SS-3B 1932, 35-39 Indians, **White Sox**, Red Sox 343 g, .236, 13 hr, 97 rbi

Berger was the MVP with New Orleans in 1934. He was Cleveland's starting second baseman in 1935, but was relegated to utility duty thereafter due to marginal hitting. When WWII started, Berger made a career of the military, staying in until 1962. /(LRD)

Heinie Berger [Charles] — 1882-1954. RHP 1907-10 **Indians** 609 ip, 32-29, 2.56

A spitball master, Berger made the majors after two 20-win seasons in the American Association. He twice won 13 for Cleveland, and established the club record for righthanders with 162 strikeouts in 1909. /(ME)

Wally Berger — 1905-1988. OF 1930-40 **Braves**, Giants, Reds, Phillies 1350 g, .300, 242 hr, 898 rbi. *2 WS, 7 g, .000, 1 rbi*
☛ *Led League—hr 35. Led League—rbi 35. All-Star—33-36.*

Had there been an award for Rookie of the Year in 1930, Wally Berger would have won it. He hit .310 that year for the Braves and established National League rookie records with 38 homers and 119 RBI. The powerfully built centerfielder was the heart of the Boston offense for seven seasons. Berger had torn up the Pacific Coast League with Los Angeles in 1929, establishing a club record with 40 HR, but he was the property of the Cubs, who in 1930 had the only all-100 RBI outfield ever, with Riggs Stephenson, Hack Wilson, and Kiki Cuyler. Berger was traded to Boston, where he batted over .300 in each of his first four seasons. In 1933 he led the Braves into the first division for the first time in 12 years. He hit .313, and though he missed nearly three weeks with illness, had 27 HR, exactly half his team's total, and second in the league to Chuck Klein. He was the NL's starting centerfielder in the 1933 and 1934 All-Star games. Berger's power statistics were not helped by his home ballpark. Still, he hit 105 home runs in Braves Field, more than any player in history. He had success with curveball pitchers, but his nemesis was Carl Hubbell, whose screwball would upset Berger's timing for several games. After his league-leading performances of 1935 (34 HR, 130 RBI), Berger suffered a shoulder

Wally Berger

injury in 1936. It worsened in 1937, when he was traded to the Giants, and he saw limited duty before being sent to the Reds, for whom he batted .307, in May 1938. Relegated to part-time play again in 1939, he was released to the Phillies in May 1940. Despite hitting .302 in 22 games, he was let go a month later. /(DBev)

Dave Bergman — 1953– . 1B-OF 1975, 77– Yankees, Astros, Giants, **Tigers** 1076 g, .260, 44 hr, 224 rbi. *3 LCS, 10 g, .375, 4 rbi. 1 WS, 5 g, .000*

Bergman was a batting champ and league MVP in each of his first two minor league seasons, but with little power has never been an everyday starter in the ML. He hit a career-high .294 for the Tigers in 1988, and his lefthanded bat and steady glove are assets on the bench. On March 24, 1984, he was traded twice; from the Giants to the Phillies, and then from the Phillies to the Tigers. /(SCL)

Jack Berly — 1903–1977. RHP 1924, 31–33 Cardinals, Giants, **Phillies** 215 ip, 10–13, 5.02

Berly suffered from poor control and was generally better as a reliever. He saw his most action in 1931 with the Giants, going 7–8 with a 3.88 ERA, both career bests, but even then he had a 2.88 ERA in 16 relief outings compared with 4.32 in his 11 starts. His career was ended in 1933 by a broken leg. /(WOR)

Chris Berman — 1955– . *Broadcaster.*

Well known as a co-host of ESPN's "SportsCenter," a nightly wrap-up of the day's sporting events, Berman has a memorable rapid-fire home run call ("Back, back, back, back, back, back . . .") and bestows humorous nicknames on players, like Bert "Be in" Blyleven and Dave "Parallel" Parker. /(SCL)

Dwight Bernard — 1952– . RHP 1978–79, 81–82 **Mets**, Brewers 176 ip, 4–8, 4.14. *1 LCS, 1 ip, 0.00. 1 WS, 1 ip, 0.00*

Bernard spent parts of two seasons in the Met bullpen with little success. A trade for Mark Bomback sent him to Milwaukee, where he won three and saved six for the 1982 pennant winners. /(GEB)

Tony Bernazard — 1956– . 2B 1979–87 Expos, White Sox, Mariners, **Indians**, A's 1065 g, .262, 75 hr, 391 rbi

Bernazard had an 0-for-44 streak at the plate with the 1984 Indians, finishing at .221. He peaked in 1986, when he batted .301 and set a club record for homers by a switch hitter (17). That July 1, he became the first Indian to homer from both sides of the plate in one game. Eventually, his bat could not compensate for his inadequacy as a fielder, and he was traded to Oakland in July of 1987. The next year he was playing in Japan. He was taught to play by Vic Power in his native Puerto Rico. /(ME)

Bill Bernhard (Strawberry Bill) — 1871–1949. RHP 1899–1907 Phillies, A's, **Indians** 1792 ip, 116–82, 3.04. 20 wins: 04

Bill Bernhard was the first Cleveland pitcher to lead the American League in winning percentage, with a .783 mark (18–5) in 1902. Like Nap Lajoie, Bernhard was barred from playing in Philadelphia after jumping from the Phillies to the Athletics in 1901. He joined Cleveland after one game in 1902. In 1904, after being slowed by a broken finger in 1903, he again led his staff in winning percentage, going 23–13. Bernhard later had a long managerial career in the Southern Association. /(ME)

Juan Bernhardt — 1953– . DH-3B-1B 1976–79 Yankees, **Mariners** 154 g, .238, 9 hr, 43 rbi

Bernhardt hit the first home run by a Mariner in the Kingdome, April 10, 1977. The Dominican played for his country's team in the 1971 Pan Am games. /(NLM)

Dale Berra — 1956– . SS-3B 1977–87 **Pirates**, Yankees, Astros 853 g, .236, 49 hr, 278 rbi

Yogi Berra's son was a highly-touted prospect from the time of his first-round selection by Pittsburgh in the 1975 draft. At first a utility infielder, Dale finally became a regular at shortstop in 1982. A productive bat (.263, 10 HR, 61 RBI) could not compensate for poor defense. Traded to the Yankees after drug problems, he played just 16 games with his father as manager before Yogi was fired. Dale was a spare part the rest of his career. He established a major league record in 1983 by reaching base seven times on catcher's interference. Dale and Yogi held the record for father-son home runs (407) until Bobby and Barry Bonds broke it in 1989. /(ME)

Yogi Berra [Lawrence Peter] — 1925– . C-OF 1946–63, 65 **Yankees**, Mets 2120 g, .285, 358 hr, 1430 rbi. *14 WS, 75 g, .274, 12 hr, 39 rbi.*
    Manager 1964, 72–75, 84–85 Yankees, **Mets** 484–444, .522. First place: 64, 73 *2 WS, 6–8, .429* ☛ *Most Valuable Player—51, 54–55 . All-Star—48–62. Hall of Fame—1972.*

Yogi Berra is known to millions who don't even follow baseball. His persona transcends the game. Berra is funny and, at a squat 5′8″, was a seemingly improbable star. But a star he was—a Hall of Famer. "To me," Casey Stengel said, "he is a great man. I am lucky to have him and so are my pitchers . . .He springs on a bunt like it was another dollar."

    Through hard work and the help of Bill Dickey, Berra became a great catcher. He led the American

Yogi Berra

League in games caught and chances accepted eight times, and led the league in double plays six times. He is one of only four catchers to ever field 1.000 in a season (1958), and between July 28, 1957, and May 10, 1959, Berra set major league records by catching in 148 consecutive games and accepting 950 chances without making an error.

Yogi was a master at calling pitches and handling a pitching staff. He caught two no-hitters by Allie Reynolds in 1951 and Don Larsen's perfect game in the 1956 World Series. He treated every Yankee pitcher differently; some he goaded and some he babied, depending on their temperament. An excellent, cat-like athlete, he was also a good defensive left fielder late in his career.

As a slugger, he was feared throughout the league. Berra set American League records for home runs hit while playing catcher with his 30 home runs in both 1952 and 1956 and his 306 lifetime (these were later broken by Carlton Fisk). He also had five 100-RBI seasons. Between 1949 and 1955, when he was the heart of the Yankees' batting order, he led the club in RBI each season and won three MVP awards.

Berra was one of the greatest clutch hitters of all time—"the toughest man in the league in the last three innings," according to Paul Richards, a rival manager. Along with Roberto Clemente, Berra was probably the best bad-ball hitter in the game's history. He was skilled at golfing low pitches for deep home runs and chopping high pitches for line drives. Yet for all his aggressiveness at the plate, he was hard to strike out. In 1950, he fanned only 12 times in 597 at-bats.

As Lawrence Peter Berra had a way with the bat, so does he have a way with words. One of Berra's first notable quotes came in 1947, when the people of his hometown St. Louis threw Berra a "night" before a Yankees-Browns game. Grateful, Berra told the crowd: "I want to thank everyone for making this night necessary." He once said of a restaurant: "Nobody goes there anymore, it's too crowded." And as a veteran, he noted, "I've been with the Yankees 17 years, watching games and learning. You can see a lot by observing." "A nickel ain't worth a dime anymore," was his pithy comment on inflation. When asked as a child how he liked school he replied: "Closed." His colorful expressions that got to the heart of things became known as "Yogi-isms."

After playing briefly in the Yankee farm system, Berra enlisted in the navy in 1944. After his discharge in 1946 he reported to the Yankees'

Newark club in the International League. He had a great year (.314, 15 HRs, 59 RBI in only 277 at-bats) and was called across the Hudson.

Berra came up as an outfielder before being converted to catcher, and he shared New York's catching duties with Aaron Robinson at first, and later with Gus Niarhos, before becoming the Yankees' regular catcher from 1949 to 1959. Except for a few games with the Mets in 1965, Berra played his entire career as a Yankee, serving as an outfielder and pinch hitter as well as catcher in 1960–63.

When his career was over, Berra had played on a record ten World Series champions. He also played in an unmatched 14 World Series and holds WS records for games (75), at-bats (259), hits (71), and doubles (10).

Berra was named the Yankees' manager for the 1964 season, the final season of the mighty New York dynasty. The Yankees won the pennant but were defeated by St. Louis in a seven-game World Series. The day after the Series ended, the Yankees fired Berra and hired St. Louis Manager Johnny Keane. New York finished sixth in 1965.

Berra, meanwhile, rejoined Stengel with the Mets. He took over as the Mets' manager when Gil Hodges died suddenly in 1972 and led them to the NL pennant in 1973, thus joining Joe McCarthy as the second manager to win pennants in both leagues.

In 1976 Berra returned to the Yankees as a coach, and he managed the club again in 1984 and the beginning of 1985. He later coached for Houston. Wherever he goes, Berra remains one of baseball's most popular figures./(MG)

Ray Berres — 1908– . C 1934, 36–45 Dodgers, Pirates, **Braves**, Giants 561 g, .216, 3 hr, 78 rbi

Despite his weak bat, Berres's defense kept him in the majors for eleven seasons, usually in a backup role. He was a White Sox coach for more than 20 years./(ME)

Charlie Berry [Charles Francis] — 1902–1972. C 1925, 28–36, 38 A's, **Red Sox**, White Sox 657 g, .267, 23 hr, 256 rbi.
Umpire AL 1942–62 5 WS, 5 ASU

Chosen at end on Walter Camp's last All-America team, Lafayette star Berry played both baseball and football on a ML level. In 1925–26 he starred for Pottsville of the NFL, leading the league in scoring in '25 with 74 points. His ML baseball career was longer but less distinguished, mostly as a reserve. He became an AL umpire in 1942 and remained for 21 years. At the same time he was a head linesman for the NFL, officiating in 12 championship games. In 1958, he umpired in the WS and later that year served as head linesman for the famous "Sudden Death" championship game between the Colts and Giants. His father, Charles Joseph Berry, played for three ML teams in 1884. /(RTM)

Joe Berry (Jittery Joe) — 1904–1958. RHP 1942, 44–46 Cubs, **A's**, Indians 294 ip, 21–22, 2.45

Jittery Joe was a fidgety righthander with a herky-jerky delivery who spent 18 years in the minors before leading the AL in relief wins (10) and saves (12) as a 39-year-old A's rookie in 1944. The 145-lb Berry was once blown off the mound by a gust of wind. /(JCA)

Ken Berry — 1941– . OF 1962–75 **White Sox**, Angels, Brewers, Indians 1383 g, .255, 58 hr, 343 rbi
☛ *All-Star—67. Gold Glove—70, 72.*

An extraordinary outfielder, Berry won two Gold Gloves. Leaping catches above the Comiskey Park fence became his trademark. An All-Star with the White Sox in 1967 when he had a 20-game hitting streak, Berry batted over .280 only twice, in 1972 and '73 with the Angels. From September 16, 1971 through July 27, 1973, he accepted a record 510 consecutive outfield chances without an error. /(JCA)

Neil Berry [Cornelius John] — 1922– . SS-2B 1948–54 **Tigers**, Browns, White Sox, Orioles 441 g, .244, 74 rbi

Sometimes called Connie, Berry was a reliable utility infielder with a weak bat. He played in more than 100 games only in 1949. /(RTM)

Damon Berryhill — 1963– . C 1987– **Cubs** 198 g, .255, 12 hr, 80 rbi

Berryhill relegated Jody Davis to the bench with a seven-HR, 38-RBI, .259 performance after being called up in 1988. He hit .257 with five HR and 41 RBI in 1989, but missed almost half the season with injuries. /(JFC)

Frank Bertaina — 1944– . LHP 1964–70 Orioles, Senators, Cardinals 413 ip, 19–29, 3.84

In his first ML game (9/12/64), Bertaina matched one-hitters with A's pitcher Bob Meyer. Known for his daffy behavior, he was dubbed "Toys in the Attic" by Moe Drabowsky. /(RTM)

Dick Bertell — 1935– . C 1960–65, 67 **Cubs**, Giants 444 g, .250, 10 hr, 112 rbi

Bertell hit .273 and .302 as a part-timer in 1961 and 1962. Catching a career-high 110 games for the Cubs in 1964, Bertell tied for the NL lead in errors (11). Traded to the Giants in May 1965, Bertell hit just .188 in 22 games for San Francisco. A knee injury kept him out for all of 1966, and a return to Chicago in 1967 was unsuccessful. /(SFS)

Reno Bertoia — 1935– . 3B-2B 1953–62 **Tigers**, Senators/Twins, A's 612 g, .244, 27 hr, 171 rbi

A Tiger bonus baby, the handsome, Italian-born infielder had speed and good hands but a light bat. In 1960, the only season in which he played in more than 100 games, he hit .265 as the Senators third baseman. /(GEB)

Bob Bescher — 1884–1942. OF 1908–18 **Reds**, Giants, Cardinals, Indians 1228 g, .258, 28 hr, 345 rbi

The 200-pound Bescher was a college football star at Wittenberg (Ohio). The winner of four consecutive stolen base titles (1909–12), he held the NL single-season record (81 in 1911) until Maury Wills broke it in 1962. A classic leadoff batter, he led the NL in runs (120) in 1912 and walks (94) in 1913. /(CG)

Herman Besse (Long Herm) — 1911–1972. LHP 1940–43, 46 **A's** 242 ip, 5–15, 6.97

Besse pitched one full season and parts of four others for Connie Mack's woebegone A's of the early 1940s. In 1942, his one year of steady work, he was 2–9 with a 6.50 ERA. /(MC)

Don Bessent (The Weasel) — 1931– . RHP 1955–58 **Dodgers** 211 ip, 14–7, 3.33. *2 WS, 13 ip, 1.35, 1–0*

A relief specialist, Bessent had an 8–1 record for the World Champion 1955 Dodgers and a staff-best 2.70 ERA. He was the winning pitcher in Game Two of the 1956 World Series. /(FK)

Takehiko Bessho — Unk.–Unk. P 1942–60 **Yomiuri Giants**

In 1949, his eighth season pitching, Bessho came to the fore by winning 42 games, a Japanese record equaled only by Iron Man Inao. He continued as Yomiuri's ace throughout the 1950s. With the Yakult Atoms in 1970, he became the first Japanese manager forced to resign in mid-season; previously, managers had only been sent away for periods of rest and meditation. /(MC)

Karl Best — 1959– . RHP 1983–86, 88 **Mariners**, Twins 92 ip, 5–6, 4.04

Best could never stick in the majors despite annual call-ups by the pitching-poor Mariners. The reliever's best stint by far came at the end of 1985, when he was 2–1 with a 1.95 ERA in 32 innings. /(SFS)

Larry Bettencourt — 1905–1978. OF-3B 1928, 31–32 **Browns** 168 g, .258, 8 hr, 53 rbi

A member of the College Football Hall of Fame, Bettencourt was a consensus All-America center at St. Mary's College in 1927 when he scored 12 touchdowns on intercepted passes, blocked punts, and recovered fumbles. He signed a baseball contract with the St. Louis Browns for $6,000, then the largest bonus ever paid a rookie just out of school, but failed to stick in three ML trials. In 1933 he played pro football for the Green Bay Packers. /(NLM)

Kaoru Betto — 1920– . 1B-OF 1948–57 **Yokohama Taiyo Whales**

☛ *Most Valuable Player—50. Led League—hr 50.*

One of Japan's first home run threats, Betto served in WWII and struggled at other jobs before turning to pro baseball at age 28. In 1950, he challenged Tomio Fujimara's Japanese HR record of 45, falling two short. Among the most flamboyant early Japanese stars, he married a beauty queen, and boasted that he never faced a pitcher he couldn't hit. As interim manager of the Taiyo Whales in 1967, he won ten games in a row before persuading the man he replaced to return. He did later become Taiyo's manager. /(MC)

Huck Betts [Walter Martin] — 1897–1987. RHP 1920–25, 32–35 **Phillies**, Braves 1366 ip, 61–68, 3.93

Betts was a curveballing righthander who was hampered by weak clubs and the lack of a fastball. The 5′11″ 170-lb Huck (derived from his love for huckleberries) pitched mostly in relief for the Phillies, but had three solid seasons as a starter for the Braves. He won a career-high 17 games in 1934. /(FS)

Bruno Betzel — 1894–1965. 2B-3B-OF 1914–18 **Cardinals** 448 g, .231, 2 hr, 94 rbi

A light-hitting ML infielder, Betzel managed for 26 years in the minors (1928–56). He won seven pennants with seven different teams, the last with Toronto of the International League in his final managerial season. /(JK)

Kurt Bevacqua (Dirty) — 1947– . 3B-2B-1B-OF 1971–85 Indians, Royals, Brewers, Rangers, **Padres**, Pirates 970 g, .236, 27 hr, 275 rbi. *1 LCS, 2 g, .000. 1 WS, 5 g, .412, 2 hr, 4 rbi*

Bevacqua put in 15 ML years although he never played more than 64 games at any one position in a season. Nicknamed "Dirty" for his aggressive, diving, hard-sliding style, he pinch-hit more than 300 times. In 1980, he led the NL in both pinch hits and pinch at-bats. His career batting average as a pinch hitter was 30 points higher than his BA as a starter.

In the 1984 WS, manager Dick Williams surprised many by selecting Bevacqua as the DH for the Padres. He was a goat in Game One when he tripped and was thrown out trying to stretch a double in a 3–2 loss. But he blasted a game-winning homer in Game Two and kept the Padres' hopes alive for several innings with another homer in the fifth and final game. He won Topps' bubblegum-blowing contest in 1972 and was pictured on a special card in the following season's Topps set, with Joe Garagiola measuring the winning bubble. /(MC)

Bill Bevens — 1916– . RHP 1944–47 **Yankees** 642 ip, 40–36, 3.08. *1 WS, 11 ip, 0–1, 2.38*

Bevens pitched and lost one of the most famous games in baseball history, Game Four of the 1947 WS. Only 7–13 for the Yankees during the regular season, he survived a record 10 walks while holding the Dodgers hitless, and led 2–1 with two outs in the bottom of the ninth inning. Veteran Cookie Lavagetto's pinch-hit double off the right-field wall (his last major league hit) not only ended Bevens's bid for the first WS no-hitter, but also drove in the tying and winning runs for the Dodgers. /(GEB)

Buddy Biancalana [Roland America] — 1960– . SS-2B 1982–87 **Royals**, Astros 311 g, .205, 6 hr, 30 rbi. *2 LCS, 9 g, .211, 1 rbi. 1 WS, 7 g, .278, 1 rbi*

Biancalana made the majors with a strong arm and good glove. He battled Onix Concepcion for the Royals' shortstop job, but neither hit well enough. Lack of discipline at the plate handicapped Biancalana's hitting, but he started all 14 postseason games for the 1985 Royals and handled 55 chances flawlessly while making several dazzling plays. /(FJO)

Jim Bibby — 1944– . RHP 1972–81, 83–84 Cardinals, Rangers, Indians, **Pirates** 1723 ip, 111–101, 3.76. *1 LCS, 7 ip, 1.29. 1 WS, 10 ip, 2.61*

☛ *All-Star—80.*

Wildness, inconsistency, and injuries plagued the unusually muscular 6'5" 235-lb Bibby. Drafted first by the Mets and then by Uncle Sam, he spent two years in Viet Nam, one on the disabled list (after a spinal fusion operation), and five in the minors before reaching the majors in 1972. With Texas in 1973, he no-hit Oakland on July 30, and also pitched a one-hitter and a two-hitter. He went 12–4 with a 2.80 ERA for Pittsburgh in 1979 and pitched well in the LCS and WS. His .760 winning percentage (19–6) in 1980 was the NL's best. On May 19, 1981 the overpowering Bibby allowed a leadoff single to Atlanta's Terry Harper and then retired 27 Braves in a row. Shortly after that he suffered a rotator cuff injury that eventually ended his career. His brother, Henry, played in the NBA. /(JCA)

Vern Bickford — 1920–1960. RHP 1948–54 **Braves,** Orioles 1076 ip, 66–57, 3.71. *1 WS, 3 ip, 0–1, 2.70*
☛ *All-Star—49.*

The famous cliche about the 1948 Boston Braves NL championship team, "Spahn, Sain and two days of rain," did not do justice to Bickford's strong 11–5 record. His top season was 1950, when he went 19–14 and led the league in games started (39), complete games (27), and innings pitched (311 2/3). On August 11 of that year he no-hit the Dodgers, 7–0. In 1951, he broke a finger on his pitching hand and never regained his effectiveness. /(GEB)

Les Biederman — Unk.–1981. *Writer*

Biederman retired in 1969 after 39 years with the Pittsburgh *Press* and 20 years as a correspondent for *The Sporting News*. He ranked Harvey Haddix's 12-inning perfect game his greatest thrill in sports. A graduate of Ohio State, he was president of the BBWAA in 1959 and was credited with raising a half-million dollars for Children's Hospital in Pittsburgh. /(NLM)

Mike Bielecki (Bie) — 1959– . RHP 1984– **Pirates,** Cubs 505 ip, 30–26, 3.85. *1 LCS, 12 ip, 0–1, 3.72*

Baseball America's 1984 Minor League Player of the Year, Bielecki led NL rookies in starts and innings in 1986 but went winless in the second half (0–6) and spent most of 1987 in the minors. His 18–7, 3.14 record for the 1989 Cubs was a major factor in their surprising division title. He lost a heartbreaker in the LCS, dropping the final game after taking a 1–1 tie into the ninth inning. He had a no-decision in Game Two. /(ME)

Lou Bierbauer — 1865–1926. 2B 1886–98 Philadelphia (AA), Brooklyn (PL), **Pirates,** Cardinals 1383 g, .267, 33 hr, 706 rbi

Bierbauer jumped Philadelphia's American Association club to join the Players' League in 1890. When the PL folded, players were supposed to rejoin their previous clubs. Pittsburgh became known as the Pirates when they swiped Bierbauer from Philadelphia through a clerical error in 1891. Bierbauer tied a then-ML record with 12 putouts at 2B in an 1888 game. In 10 years as a regular, he led his league's second basemen in assists five times. /(ME)

Carson Bigbee (Skeeter) — 1895–1964. OF 1916–26 **Pirates** 1147 g, .287, 17 hr, 324 rbi. *1 WS, 4 g, .333, 1 rbi*

A reliable contact hitter, Bigbee peaked in 1922, when he scored 113 runs and hit .350 with 215 hits. Illness and poor vision handicapped the University of Oregon alumnus for the rest of his career. His brother Lyle played briefly in the ML. /(JK)

Craig Biggio — 1965– . C 1988– **Astros** 184 g, .247, 16 hr, 65 rbi

The Astros' first-round draft pick in June 1987, when Alan Ashby was hurt in 1988 Biggio was rushed and hit only .211. But in 1989 he hit .257 with 13 HR, 60 RBI, and 64 runs in 134 games. Unusually fast for a catcher, he often hit leadoff and stole 21 bases in 24 attempts, the second-best percentage in the NL. /(WOR)

Helene Hathaway Robinson Bigsby — 1878–1950. *Executive.*

The first woman club owner in the major leagues, she was president of the St. Louis Cardinals in 1916 while the wife of Schuyler P. Britton. /(NLM)

Larry Biittner — 1946– . OF-1B 1970–83 Senators/ Rangers, Expos, **Cubs,** Reds 1217 g, .273, 29 hr, 354 rbi

Biittner finished the 1980s tied for 12th on the all-time list for pinch hits with 95 (in 370 pinch at-bats). He was an inconsistent batter who sometimes had respectable averages, with a high of .315 in 1975 for Montreal. He showed power only in 1977, his first full season in Wrigley Field, when he hit .298 with career highs of 12 HR, 28 doubles, 62 RBI, and 74 runs. /(JFC)

Dann Bilardello — 1959– . C 1983–86, 89 **Reds,** Expos, Pirates 331 g, .212, 18 hr, 82 rbi

Bilardello struggled with injuries as a Dodger farm-hand before the Reds claimed him and made them their catcher for 1983. A dead-pull hitter, he batted .238 as a rookie and went downhill from there. His catching mechanics were excellent, but his game-calling was found lacking. He welcomed his trade to Montreal in 1986, but didn't last the season. He spent all of 1987–88 in the minors before resurfacing briefly with the Pirates in 1989 when Mike LaValliere missed half the season with a knee injury. /(JCA)

Steve Bilko — 1928–1978. 1B 1949–54, 58, 60–62 **Cardinals,** Cubs, Reds, Dodgers, Tigers, Angels 600 g, .249, 76 hr, 276 rbi

Bilko was a slugger who posted phenomenal numbers in the minor leagues but never met expectations in the majors. He got his first call-up with the Cardinals in 1949 after hitting 34 HR in 139 games at Rochester (International League), but didn't stick for a full season until 1953 (he had a broken arm in 1952). He played every game for St. Louis that year, but his 125 strikeouts, just 9 fewer than the ML record at the time, cut into his productivity. On May 28, 1953, he struck out five times in a ten-inning game. He hit .251, and his 21 HR, 84 RBI, 72 runs, and 70 walks were all career highs. He never played regularly again. Bilko was sold to the Cubs for $12,500 in April 1954 and was let go after the season.

In the next three years, Bilko built a legend. Playing for Los Angeles in the Pacific Coast League (which had an extended schedule due to the good weather—in 1955 he played 168 games), he led the league in HR each year, with totals of 37, 55, and 56. He won the Triple Crown in 1956 with a .360 batting average and 164 RBI while also leading the league with 163 runs scored, and he hit .300 all three seasons. This earned the 6'1" slugger, charitably listed at just 240 pounds, another major league trial in 1958, with the Reds. He hit .264 with four HR in 31 games and was traded to the Dodgers with Johnny Klippstein for Don Newcombe in June. He hit just .208 with seven HR for Los Angeles. After spending 1959 at Spokane (Pacific Coast League), where he hit 26 HR and led with 92 RBI, he was picked up by Detroit for 1960 and recorded nine HR and a .208 average. In 1961 the expansion Angels were desperate enough to try Bilko, and he had his best season, hitting .279 with 20 HR (but 81 strikeouts) in 294 at-bats. He hit .287 in 1962, but a leg injury cut into his season. After one last tour with Rochester (International League) in 1963, he retired. He hit 313 HR and batted .312 in his minor league career. /(WOR)

Jack Billingham — 1943– . RHP 1968–80 Dodgers, Astros, **Reds,** Tigers, Red Sox 2231 ip, 145–113, 3.83. *2 LCS, 17 ip, 0–1, 4.32. 3 WS, 25 ip, 2–0, 0.36* ☛ *All-Star—73.*

Billingham, a distant relative of Christy Mathewson, was groomed as a reliever in the Dodger organization. He became a starter with Houston, and by 1972 was a mainstay in the rotation of Cincinnati's "Big Red Machine." The gentle, 6'4" righthander won at least 10 games for 10 consecutive seasons (1970–79), with 19 victories in both 1973 and '74. He didn't miss a turn in '73 **as** he led the NL with 40 starts, 293 IP, and seven shutouts. In three World Series, Billingham allowed just one earned run in 25 1/3 innings; in Game Three of the 1972 WS, he threw eight shutout innings to defeat Oakland, 1–0.

In his first 1974 start, he gave up Hank Aaron's record-tying 714th home run. In 1978, after winning 87 games in six years with Cincinnati, Billingham was traded to Detroit. Two years later he finished with Boston. /(JCA)

Dick Billings — 1942– . C-OF 1968–75 **Senators/ Rangers,** Cardinals 400 g, .227, 16 hr, 142 rbi

Billings, who earned a B.S. degree at Michigan State, hit .305 in the minors but never hit higher than .254 in the major leagues. /(GEB)

George Binks (Bingo) [born George Binkowski] — 1914– . OF-1B 1944–48 **Senators,** A's, Browns 351 g, .253, 8 hr, 130 rbi

The speedy Binks got his ML opportunity at age 30 because of the World War II player shortage. He hit .278 with 81 RBI as centerfielder for the 1945 Senators, a team that missed the AL pennant by one game. His play earned him three more postwar seasons in the ML. /(MC)

Doug Bird — 1950– . RHP 1973–83 **Royals,** Phillies, Yankees, Cubs, Red Sox 1212 ip, 73–60, 3.99. *3 LCS, 8 ip, 1–1, 2.35*

Bird had a lively fastball, a nasty slider, and a palm ball. A reliever in five of his six years with Kansas City, he saved 20 as a rookie and went 11–4 with 14 saves in 1977. When he left KC after the 1978 season, he held the club's career marks in games pitched and saves. Over a three-year span with the Phillies, Columbus (International League), and the Yankees, Bird had an 18-game winning streak. The day after he finally lost (6/11/81), the Yankees traded him to the Cubs. /(JCA)

Mike Birkbeck — 1961- . RHP 1986- **Brewers** 236 ip, 12-17, 5.12

Birkbeck was 10-8 with a 4.72 ERA in 1988, but in 1989 he started the year 0-4 and went on the DL with a weakened rotator cuff. /(JFC)

Ralph Birkofer (Lefty) — 1908-1971. LHP 1933-37 **Pirates**, Dodgers 544 ip, 31-28, 4.19

The chunky Birkofer's excellent fastball and sharp-breaking curve stamped him an excellent prospect, but arm trouble forced his retirement after only five ML seasons. /(FS)

Joe Birmingham (Dode) — 1884-1946. OF 1906-14 **Indians** 772 g, .254, 6 hr, 265 rbi.
  Manager 1912-15 **Indians** 170-191, .471

A so-so hitter but an outstanding defensive centerfielder, Birmingham led AL outfielders with 33 assists in 1907. On October 2, 1908, he scored the only run in Addie Joss's perfect game against Ed Walsh. As the manager of the 1913 Cleveland team, then called the "Naps" in honor of second baseman Nap Lajoie, he caused a local furor by benching the star. /(CG)

Babe Birrer [Werner Joseph] — 1928- . RHP 1955-56, 58 **Tigers**, Orioles, Dodgers 120 ip, 4-3, 4.36

"Babe" earned his nickname on a July day in 1955 when, while working four innings in relief for Detroit, he smacked two three-run homers. He never hit another home run. /(CC)

Tim Birtsas — 1960- . LHP 1985-86, 88- **A's**, Reds 277 ip, 13-11, 4.12

After a 10-6 season as a rookie for Oakland in 1985, Birtsas spent most of 1986 disabled or in the minors. Originally drafted by the Yankees, he was part of the trade package that pried Rickey Henderson from the A's in 1984, and was sent to Cincinnati with Jose Rijo for Dave Parker in December 1987. /(ME)

Charlie Bishop — 1924- . RHP 1952-55 **A's** 294 ip, 10-22, 5.33

The swarthy fireballer threw a no-hitter in the Piedmont League in 1948. He pitched a shutout for the Athletics in his first big league start, but went 3-14 in 1953, his only full ML year. /(JCA)

Max Bishop (Tilly, Camera Eye) — 1899-1962. 2B 1924-35 **A's**, Red Sox 1338 g, .271, 41 hr, 379 rbi. *3 WS, 18 g, .182, 1 rbi*

Max Bishop

The leadoff man for Connie Mack's AL champions (1929-31), Bishop specialized in drawing walks in front of A's sluggers Al Simmons, Mickey Cochrane, and Jimmie Foxx. Seven times he topped 100 bases on balls, leading the AL with 128 in 1929. In one doubleheader, he walked eight times. He led AL second basemen in fielding four times. The quiet, gentlemanly Bishop later served 24 years as baseball coach at the U.S. Naval Academy, compiling a 306-143 record. /(JK)

Del Bissonette [Adelphia Louis] — 1899-1972. 1B 1928-31, 33 **Dodgers** 604 g, .305, 65 hr, 391 rbi.
  Manager 1945 **Braves** 25-36, .410

In his injury-shortened career, Bissonette set a Dodger rookie home run record with 25 in 1928 but led NL first basemen in errors in two of his three full seasons. A Brooklyn limerick of the time went: The Dodgers have Del Bissonette. No meal has he ever missed yet. The question that rises Is one that surprises: Who paid for all Del Bissonette? /(TG)

Hi Bithorn — 1916-1952. RHP 1942-43, 46-47 **Cubs,** White Sox 509 ip, 34-31, 3.16

Only 9-14 as a Cub rookie in 1942, the burly righthander blossomed to 18-12 the next year, fourth in the NL in wins. He led the league in shutouts (7) and posted a 2.60 ERA. He spent the next two seasons in military service, ballooning to 225. In 1946 he pitched mostly in relief with sporadic success. Sold to the Pirates, who released him in spring training, he pitched two innings for the White Sox in 1947 before a sore arm ended his ML career. He was shot to death on New Year's Day 1952 while attempting a comeback in the Mexican winter league. /(MC)

Jeff Bittiger — 1962- . RHP 1986- Phillies, Twins, **White Sox** 94 ip, 4-6, 4.77

Originally signed by the Mets in 1980, Bittiger couldn't balance strikeouts and control well enough to win in the majors. He was Texas League Pitcher of the Year in 1982. /(SFS)

Black Sox Scandal

The heavily favored Chicago White Sox were upset in the 1919 World Series by the Cincinnati Reds, five games to three. At the apex of the pennant race the following year, eight players were indicted for throwing the Series in return for payoffs from gamblers. Although they were all cleared by a conciliatory grand jury, newly appointed Commissioner Kenesaw Mountain Landis banned for life the eight so-called Black Sox—left fielder Shoeless Joe Jackson, first baseman and ringleader Chick Gandil, shortstop Swede Risberg, third baseman Buck Weaver, centerfielder Happy Flesch, pitchers Eddie Cicotte and Lefty Williams, and utility infielder Fred McMullin—from organized baseball. Only a handful of them actually received any payment, and Jackson hit .375 in the Series to lead both teams. Landis's office had been created because of the scandal, and he was chosen to fill it because he had shown a friendly attitude toward the baseball establishment when he was a judge. He justified banning all eight players on the grounds that not reporting the plot was as bad as actually taking part in the fix. The plan was apparently hatched by local Chicago gamblers, but New York gangster Arnold Rothstein was rumored to be its major backer. The players were easily tempted. They were not paid well by tight-fisted owner Charles Comiskey. Legend has it that upon Jackson's leaving the courthouse, a little boy cried, "Say it ain't so, Joe!" There have been

movements to have Jackson, who owns the third-highest batting average in baseball history, posthumously reinstated for election to the Hall of Fame. This revisionist sympathy has risen considerably with the release of two films connected to the scandal: "Eight Men Out" in 1988, based on the definitive Eliot Asinof book, and "Field of Dreams" in 1989, based on the W.P. Kinsella novel "Shoeless Joe." An off-Broadway play, "Out!" was also produced in New York in 1986. /(SEW)

Bud Black [Harry Ralston] — 1957- . LHP 1981- Mariners, **Royals,** Indians 1260 ip, 70-71, 3.72. *2 LCS, 16 ip, 0-1, 3.45. 1 WS, 5 ip, 0-1, 5.06*

Black's effectiveness hinged on constantly mixing his fastball, curve, slider, and change-up to keep hitters guessing. Used initially as a middle reliever, he led Royals' starters in IP, wins, ERA, and strikeouts in 1984.

His fortunes fell in 1985, when he seemed to lose something off his set-up pitch, the fastball. The only Royal starter with a losing record in Kansas City's World Championship season, Black was put back in the bullpen in 1986 and was traded to the Indians in mid-1988. /(FO)

Don Black — 1916-1959. RHP 1943-48 **A's,** Indians 797 ip, 34-55, 4.35

After three years of trying to control Black's drinking problem, the A's suspended him in 1945, then sold him to Cleveland. Against the A's on July 10, 1947, he pitched the first no-hitter in Municipal Stadium before the largest crowd (47,871) ever to see a no-hitter up until then. The crowd was drawn by the expectation of the first appearance of Cleveland's Larry Doby, the AL's first black player, but Doby didn't play in the game. On September 13, 1948, Black collapsed at home plate after suffering a brain hemorrhage. While still in critical condition, he was given a night by Indians fans, who raised $40,000 for him. He recovered but never pitched again. /(NLM)

Joe Black — 1924- . RHP 1952-57 **Dodgers,** Reds, Senators 414 ip, 30-12, 3.91. *2 WS, 22 ip, 1-2, 2.82*

Joe Black, who began in the Negro Leagues, won Rookie of the Year honors as a 28-year-old reliever for the 1952 Dodgers. He won 14 in relief and added 15 saves, using a blazing fastball and tight curve. At season's end, Dodger manager Chuck Dressen started him twice (a win and a loss) to prepare him for starting the first game of the WS. He won 4-2, but then lost two close games (also starts) 2-0 and

4–2. His victory was the only one by a black pitcher in the WS until Mudcat Grant won in 1965.

In spring training the next year, Dressen insisted that Black learn several new pitches. He lost control of the two that had brought him success and was never effective again./(GEB)

Ron Blackburn — 1935– . RHP 1958–59 **Pirates** 108 ip, 3–2, 3.50

An unheralded prospect at the Pirates' 1958 training camp, this righthanded reliever impressed the brass with his sinker and made the club. In 1959, he batted only five times, but his one hit was a homer against the Cubs./(RTM)

Lena Blackburne [Russell Aubrey] (Slats) — 1886–1968. SS-3B-2B-RHP 1910, 12, 14–15, 18–19, 27, 29 **White Sox**, Reds, Braves, Phillies 548 g, .214, 4 hr, 139 rbi

Blackburne made an unusual contribution to baseball when he discovered and marketed the special mud from the Delaware River used by umpires to rub the gloss off new baseballs. His feminine nickname came from a leather-lunged minor league fan who compared him to another player, Cora Donovan, but Blackburne claimed it was because he had a "lean" physique. More successful as a minor league manager and coach, his term as White Sox skipper (1928–29) was most notable for his savage fistfight with one of his own players, Art (The Great) Shires. Blackburne's one outing as a pitcher came in his only appearance of 1929./(JK)

Ewell Blackwell (The Whip) — 1922– . RHP 1942, 46–53, 55 **Reds**, Yankees, A's 1321 ip, 82–78, 3.30. 20 wins: 47 *1 WS, 5 ip, 7.20*
☛ *Led League—w 47. All-Star—46–51.*

A 6'6" stringbean with a wicked sidearm delivery, Blackwell was virtually unhittable for righthanded batters as the ball seemed to explode at them from third base. As a Reds rookie in 1946 he had only a 9–13 record but a NL-leading six shutouts. In 1947 he was dubbed The Whip, as he led the NL in wins (22–8), complete games (23), and strikeouts (193) for the fifth-place Reds. His 16 consecutive wins set a NL mark for righthanders. He came very close to tying teammate Johnny Vander Meer's feat of back-to-back no-hitters. On the night of June 18, he no-hit the Braves; in his next outing he held the Dodgers hitless into the ninth before Eddie Stanky's one-out single.

Arm miseries the next couple of years took the snap out of "The Whip." In 1950 and '51, he came back partway with 17 and 16 wins, but his arm problems returned. He was 3–12 in 1952 when the Reds traded him to the Yankees on August 28. "I wish it could have been earlier in my career," he said later. "There was no great difference between the two leagues, but I'd have to say it was easier pitching in Yankee Stadium." He won a game down the stretch for New York and started the fifth game of the WS (no decision). The next season, he had two wins before his arm problems ended his career./(RTM)

Tim Blackwell — 1952– . C 1974–83 Red Sox, Phillies, Expos, **Cubs** 426 g, .228, 6 hr, 80 rbi

The strong-armed receiver was usually a backup to better-known catchers. His only starting job came in 1980 with the Cubs when Barry Foote injured his back. Blackwell responded by hitting a career-high .272./(JCA)

Ray Blades — 1896–1979. OF 1922–32 **Cardinals** 767 g, .301, 50 hr, 340 rbi. *3 WS, 8 g, .083. Manager 1939–40* **Cardinals** 107–85, .557

Blades was an intelligent, aggressive reserve player for most of his 10 ML seasons, and he hit .300 in each of his three seasons as a starting outfielder for the Cardinals (1924–26). After managing in the Cardinals farm system in the mid-1930s, Blades managed the parent club to 92 wins and second place 1939, but was replaced when the Cardinals sputtered early in 1940./(FS)

George Blaeholder — 1904–1947. RHP 1925, 27–36 **Browns**, A's, Indians 1914 ip, 104–125, 4.54

The hard-working Blaeholder was one of the original exponents of the slider, perfecting the "nickle curve" while pitching for the hapless St. Louis Browns. Although he never had a winning season for the Browns, he had ten wins or more for seven consecutive years. His four shutouts led the AL in 1929./(JK)

Dennis Blair — 1954– . RHP 1974–76, 80 **Expos**, Padres 339 ip, 19–25 3.69

Called up to the Expos in 1974, the 6'5" Blair beat the Phillies in his debut (on May 26), ten days before his 20th birthday. That season proved to be his best (11–7, 3.27)./(RM)

Footsie Blair [Clarence Vick] — 1900–1982. 2B-1B-3B 1929–31 **Cubs** 246 g, .273, 9 hr, 96 rbi. *1 WS, 1 g, .000*

In Blair's only season as a regular, he hit .273 with six HR and 97 runs scored in 1930. But in that rabbit-ball season, he was 30 points below the league average. /(SFS)

Paul Blair (Motormouth) — 1944– . OF 1964–80 **Orioles**, Yankees, Reds 1947 g, .250, 134 hr, 620 rbi. *7 LCS, 25 g, .238, 2 hr, 10 rbi. 6 WS, 28 g, .288, 1 hr, 5 rbi* ☛ *Gold Glove—67, 69–75.*

An intuitive centerfielder whose speed going back allowed him to play unusually shallow, the loquacious Blair won eight Gold Gloves. An Oriole from 1964 through 1976, he finished among Baltimore's all-time top five in a dozen offensive categories. His average was augmented by his bunting skills, and he had 171 career stolen bases. He had his best year in 1969 (.285, 26 HR, 76 RBI). In 1970, he suffered serious eye and facial injuries from a Ken Tatum beaning. Lingering fear at the plate caused him to seek help from a hypnotherapist. In 1971 he tried switch-hitting, but stopped after going 11–57.

Blair appeared in 53 postseason games with Baltimore and the Yankees. His 430-foot home run in Game Three of the 1966 WS gave the Orioles a 1–0 victory over the Dodgers, and he tied the record for most hits in a five-game WS, going 9–19 (.474) in 1970. He made several sensational catches in the '66 and '70 WS and '70 LCS. /(JCA)

Walter Blair (Heavy) — 1883–1948. C 1907–11, 14–15 Yankees, **Buffalo (FL)** 442 g, .217, 3 hr, 106 rbi

A product of Bucknell University (as was Christy Mathewson before him), Blair hit .196 over five seasons as a Yankee reserve catcher. He was a regular for two seasons with Buffalo of the Federal League, hitting slightly better and filling in as a manager for two games. /(MG)

Sheriff Blake [John Frederick] — 1899–1982. RHP 1920, 24–31, 37 Pirates, **Cubs**, Phillies, Browns, Cardinals 1620 ip, 87–102, 4.13. *1 WS, 1 ip, 0–1, 13.50*

Blake was the second of three Cubs relievers (and the losing pitcher) during the famous seventh inning of Game Four of the 1929 WS, when the A's rallied for ten runs to overcome an 8–0 deficit. For most of his career he was a solid starter for the Cubs, with all but 6 of his 87 career wins coming in a Chicago uniform, including a 17–11 season in 1928. /(ME)

Johnny Blanchard — 1933– . C 1955, 59–65 **Yankees**, A's, Braves 516 g, .239, 67 hr, 200 rbi. *5 WS, 15 g, .345, 2 hr, 5 rbi*

Blanchard savored his position as the Yankees' third-string catcher for most of his career. A defensive liability, he nearly quit in 1960 when Casey

Stengel considered activating 40-year-old bullpen coach Jim Hegan to back up Yogi Berra while Elston Howard was injured. Stengel reconsidered, and Blanchard responded in 1961 with adequate defense and a career-best .305, 21 HR season. Blanchard holds the record with ten World Series pinch-hitting appearances. /(GDW)

Fred Blanding — 1888–1950. RHP 1910–14 **Indians** 814 ip, 45–46, 3.13

A former University of Michigan pitcher, Blanding made his ML debut against Washington (9/15/10) by defeating Walter Johnson, 3–0, on a six-hitter. Blanding had his best year in 1912, going 18–14 for the Indians. /(NLM)

Ted Blankenship — 1901–1945. RHP 1922–30 **White Sox** 1321 ip, 77–79, 4.32

Ted, brother of pitcher Homer (Si) Blankenship, was a stalwart Texan with the mediocre White Sox of the 1920s. In 1925, his best year, he was 17–8, and battled Grover Cleveland Alexander to a 19-inning, 2–2 tie in the Chicago City Series. He broke a finger in 1926 (13–10, 3.61) and was never the same after that. /(ADS)

Larvell Blanks (Sugar Bear) — 1950– . SS-2B 1972–80 Braves, **Indians**, Rangers 629 g, .253, 20 hr, 172 rbi

Called Sugar Bear after a cartoon character on a cereal box, Blanks was Atlanta's starting shortstop in 1975. He was traded twice in the same day (December 12, 1975): from the Braves to the White Sox to the Indians, with whom he was a utility man. /(JCA)

Cy Blanton [Darrell] — 1908–1945. RHP 1934–42 **Pirates**, Phillies 1218 ip, 68–71, 3.55 ☛ *Led League—era 35. All-Star—37, 41.*

Blanton broke into the majors as the top rookie pitcher of 1935. He was 18–13 with the Pirates, led the NL in ERA (2.58), and tied for the league lead in shutouts (4). Although he was named twice to the NL All-Star team in later years, he never pitched as well as in that first year. He died in 1945 in an Oklahoma state hospital for the mentally ill. /(ME)

Don Blasingame (The Blazer, The Corinth Comet) — 1932– . 2B 1955–66 **Cardinals**, Giants, Reds, Senators, A's 1444 g, .258, 21 hr, 308 rbi. *1 WS, 3 g, .143* ☛ *All-Star—58.*

A hustling everyday second baseman with four ML teams, Mississippi's "Corinth Comet" was a spray hitter and skillful bunter. As a rookie with St. Louis in 1956, he had 587 at-bats without once homering. He had eight HR the next year, but after that never hit more than two. Four times he spoiled no-hitters, twice in August 1963. "The Blazer" was particularly fast getting down the line, hitting into fewer double plays (one in every 123 at-bats) than anyone in history except Don Buford.

In 1960, he married the daughter of catcher Walker Cooper, a 1956–57 teammate. Blasingame later played, coached, and managed in Japan. /(JCA)

Wade Blasingame — 1943– . LHP 1963–72 **Braves**, Astros, Yankees 863 ip, 46–51, 4.52

The Braves gave Blasingame $100,000 to sign, and manager Bobby Bragan said the southpaw had the NL's best curveball when he went 9–5 in 1964. He was 16–10 at age 21 in 1965, but after a fractured finger and sore arm in 1966, he never had another winning season. /(JCA)

Steve Blass — 1944– . RHP 1964, 66–74 **Pirates** 1598 ip, 103–76, 3.63. *2 LCS, 23 ip, 1–1, 4.76. 1 WS, 18 ip, 2–0, 1.00*
☛ *All-Star—72.*

Blass presents one of baseball's great unsolved mysteries. Why did one of the NL's most consistent winners from 1968 through 1972 suddenly collapse? The slender, intelligent pattern pitcher with the jerky, unorthodox motion went 18–6 with a 2.12 ERA in 1968. His three-hit and four-hit victories in Games Three and Seven of the 1971 WS earned him the series MVP award. His 1972 season was his best: 19–8, 2.49 ERA.

Suddenly, in 1973, he couldn't cut his fastball loose and he was so wild he often threw behind batters. Yet there was no pain or stiffness in his arm. The once ebullient winner became emotionless on the mound. Teammates said he "looked relieved" when taken from a game. He struggled, going 3–9 with a 9.81 ERA. He pitched one game for the Pirates in 1974, walked seven and gave up five earned runs in five innings, and was sent to Charleston.

Everyone had a theory: "too nice a guy, afraid he'd hit a batter"; "his jittery motion finally let him down"; "he was afraid he couldn't duplicate his '72 record." Some said he was devastated by the tragic death of Roberto Clemente, whose eulogy he gave in Puerto Rico. He tried psychotherapy, transcendental meditation, optometherapy, and various mechanical experiments. Nothing helped. Blass later became a Pirate broadcaster. /(JCA)

Buddy Blattner [Robert Garnett] — 1920– . 2B-3B-SS 1942, 46–49 Cardinals, **Giants**, Phillies 272 g, .247, 16 hr, 84 rbi

A table tennis champion in his youth and a smooth-fielding, weak-hitting infielder over five ML seasons, Blattner became a baseball broadcaster after his playing career ended, working for the Cardinals, Angels, and Royals. As a player, his best season was 1946, when he hit .255 with 11 HR as the Giants' regular second baseman. /(FS)

Jeff Blauser — 1965– . 2B-SS-3B **Braves** 211 g, .260, 16 hr, 68 rbi

Blauser was a good-fielding shortstop in the minors, but was forced out of position by Andres Thomas. Hitting .270 in 1989, Blauser won back the short-stop job. /(WOR)

Marv Blaylock — 1929– . 1B 1950, 55–57 Giants, **Phillies** 287 g, .235, 15 hr, 78 rbi

Blaylock occasionally showed some power, particularly in 1956 when he batted .254 with 10 home runs, but he lost his first base spot to Ed Bouchee the next season. /(GEB)

Curt Blefary (Clank) — 1943– . OF-1B-C 1965–72 **Orioles**, Astros, Yankees, A's, Padres 974 g, .237, 112 hr, 382 rbi. *1 LCS, 1 g, .000. 1 WS, 4 g, .077*
☛ *Rookie of the Year—65.*

The Brooklyn-born Blefary originally signed with the Yankees, but was sold to Baltimore while still in the minors. He was named Rookie of the Year with the Orioles in 1965 when he hit .260 with 22 HR and 70 RBI. Nicknamed "Clank" by his teammates for his iron glove, Blefary was tried at first base and then catcher in an effort to keep his bat in the lineup. He caught Tom Phoebus's April 27, 1968 no-hitter. He blamed the constant defensive shuffling for his offensive decline. He was traded to Houston in 1969 as part of the deal that brought Mike Cuellar to Baltimore. /(JCA)

Cy Block — 1919– . 3B 1942, 45–46 **Cubs** 17 g, .302, 0 hr, 5 rbi. *1 WS, 1 g, --*

When spirited, determined Cy Block came up for nine games with the 1942 Cubs, he and Stan Musial were considered among the year's most promising rookies. Block then spent three seasons with the Coast Guard and appeared in only eight more ML games, but pinch-ran in the 1945 World Series. Trying the insurance business, he milked his brief ML career by renting a huge billboard on Broadway in New York City featuring himself in a Cub uniform and the slogan: "Life insurance is the home run investment, with it you can't strike out." Block became a millionaire businessman./(DB)

Ron Blomberg — 1948- . DH-1B-OF 1969, 71–76, 78 **Yankees**, White Sox 461 g, .293, 52 hr, 224 rbi

The strapping, ebullient Southerner was the nation's and the Yankees' first draft pick in 1967. A powerful lefthanded hitter and terrible fielder, on Opening Day, 1973 he became baseball's first designated hitter; the irrepressible Blomberg commented: "I've been a DH all my life: Designated Hebrew." Accused of being a Designated Hypochondriac, the perennial prospect spent months and years sidelined with a variety of muscle injuries. Even when he was healthy, he was seldom permitted to face lefthanded pitching. In 1973 he hit a career-high .329 while playing in 100 games—for him, a full season./(JCA)

Clifford Bloodgood — 1894–1957. *Writer*

Beginning in 1919 and for more than 30 years, readers of *Baseball Magazine* saw many articles by Bloodgood, who was the magazine's art and associate editor./(NLM)

Jimmy Bloodworth — 1917- . 2B 1937, 39–43, 46–47, 49–51 **Senators**, Tigers, Pirates, Reds, Phillies 1002 g, .248, 62 hr, 453 rbi. *1 WS, 1 g, --*

Bloodworth was an adequate second baseman over eleven ML seasons but a subpar hitter. In 1943 with Detroit he set a since-broken AL record by grounding into 29 double plays. During one spring training game, he was credited with an "unpatriotic" base hit when he tapped the ball back to pitcher Elmer Riddle. Suddenly, the National Anthem blared forth from a loudspeaker, and, while Riddle stood at attention, Bloodworth scurried safely to first./(GEB)

Lu Blue — 1897–1958. 1B 1921–33 **Tigers**, Browns, White Sox, Dodgers 1615 g, .287, 44 hr, 692 rbi

Blue broke in with the Tigers in 1921, hitting .308. Although he and manager Ty Cobb were less than friendly, he held the Detroit first base job for seven years. Small for a first baseman at 5'10", Blue fielded his position well. He was a switch-hitter, adept at drawing bases on balls. He finished second in the AL in drawing walks four times, and ended with a career on-base percentage near .400. His career totals included 1092 walks, 1151 runs scored, 109 triples, and 150 stolen bases. In six of his twelve years as a regular, he scored at least 100 runs. A

veteran of World War I, the Washington, D.C. native is probably the best-known former major leaguer to be buried in Arlington National Cemetery./(LRD)

Vida Blue — 1949- . LHP 1969–83, 85–86 **A's**, Giants, Royals 3344 ip, 209–161, 3.26. 20 wins: 71, 73, 75 *5 LCS, 31 ip, 1–2, 4.60. 3 WS, 33 ip, 0–3, 4.05* ☛ *Most Valuable Player—71. Led League—era 71. Cy Young Award—71. All-Star—71, 75, 78, 81.*

Blue signed with the Athletics at age 19 instead of accepting one of numerous scholarship offers to become a major-college quarterback. He had his first wrangle with A's owner Charles O. Finley right away, when Finley wanted Blue to change his first name to "True."

Vida Blue

He was called up to the A's late in 1970. On September 21, 1970, he no-hit the Twins, who narrowly edged the Athletics for the division title. As a sophomore, Blue won 17 games by the All-Star break, then was the winning pitcher in the only All-Star game won by the American League between 1962 and 1983, when the NL was 19–1. Blue finished 1971 at 24–8, with 301 strikeouts in 312 innings. Though bombed in the ALCS by Baltimore, he was named both MVP and Cy Young Award winner.

Blue's prolonged holdout in 1972 was only resolved through the intervention of baseball commissioner Bowie Kuhn. Blue slumped to 6–10. Rumors flew that he'd hurt his arm by pitching without spring training and reporting overweight. Blue denied serious arm pain, but his strikeout record was never as spectacular the rest of his career as it was in 1971. Much later, he acknowledged that his drug problems had begun in 1972. As the Athletics won their first of their three straight World Championships, Blue contributed four shutout innings in relief of Blue Moon Odom to save the fifth and final playoff game.

He rebounded with 20–9 in 1973, when the Athletics had three 20-game winners, and was 17–15 in 1974, 22–11 in 1975, and 18–13 in 1976, as the Athletics chased the Royals to the wire in the last year the nucleus of their dynasty remained together. Already Finley had attempted to sell Blue to the Yankees in mid-season, for $1.5 million. Kuhn vetoed that deal. While most of the other Oakland stars departed through free agency, Finley tried to send Blue to the Reds for $1.75 million plus Dave Revering. Kuhn vetoed that, too. After suffering through a 14–19 season in 1977, Blue was finally traded to the Giants for eight players and $390,000. He gave the Giants an 18–10 season, becoming the first pitcher ever to start an All-Star game for each league, and earning NL Pitcher of the Year honors from *TSN*. Erratic pitching over the next few years continued after he was traded to the Royals after 1981. Drug rumors concerning Blue were confirmed in 1983. Blue was one of five members of the Kansas City Royals who eventually served prison time plus a suspension from baseball (a year in Blue's case) for cocaine use.

Given another chance by the Giants in the Bay Area where he remained popular, Blue was 18–18 in 1985–1986. The Athletics signed Blue for 1987, promoting a reunion with slugger Reggie Jackson, who also rejoined the club after 11 years away.

However, Blue flunked a urine test to detect cocaine use, and retired rather than face further scandal. /(MC)

Ossie Bluege — 1900– . 3B-SS-2B 1922–39 **Senators** 1867 g, .272, 43 hr, 848 rbi. *3 WS, 17 g, .200, 5 rbi.*
   Manager 1943–47 **Senators** 375–394, .488

"If it's a ground ball, I can field it," said the rookie shortstop in 1922 when asked if he could adjust to playing third. He spoke truly. Bluege (pronounced Blu-ghy) held down third base at Washington for much of the following 17 years. His numbers were modest, but he was consistent and mild. He neither smoke nor drank, and was an accountant in the off-season, with Washington's best hotels among his clients. Clark Griffith, the Senators' frugal owner, feared that poring over figures would ruin Bluege's batting eye, and ordered him to quit. As he never earned over $10,000, Bluege couldn't afford to.

Bluege was Griffith's organization man. After playing, he was a Senator coach (1940–42), manager (1943–47, including two well-handled second-place finishes), and farm director (1948–56). From 1957–71, for the Senators and Twins, he was club comptroller. Ossie's younger brother, Otto, or "Squeaky," had one season plus one game as a Cincinnati shortstop. /(ADS)

Jim Bluejacket — 1887–1947. RHP 1914–16 **Brooklyn (FL)**, Reds 237 ip, 13–17, 3.46

Sportswriters disparaged the American Indian as an oddball redskin righthander, but despite eccentricities, he was no fool. After a marginal life in baseball, Bluejacket (born James Smith) had a successful career in the oil industry. /(ADS)

Bert Blyleven — 1951– . RHP 1970– **Twins**, Rangers, Pirates, Indians 4703 ip, 271–231, 3.22. 20 wins: 73 *3 LCS, 24 ip, 3–0, 2.59. 12 WS, 23 ip, 2–1, 2.35* ☛ *Led League—k 85. All-Star—73, 85.*

Possessing the premier curveball of his era, Bert Blyleven carved out a great career despite frequent accusations of underachievement. Born in the Netherlands, Blyleven was *TSN* AL Rookie Pitcher of the Year in 1970. His early career coincided with the collapse of the aging Minnesota club. Despite six straight years of better than 200 strikeouts and five of 15 or more wins with poor teams, more was expected of him. He was traded to the Rangers with Danny Thompson for Bill Singer, Roy Smalley, Mike Cubbage, Jim Gideon, and $250,000 on June 1, 1976. Blyleven pitched a no-hitter against California on September 22, 1977. He and John Milner

Bert Blyleven

were traded to the Pirates for Al Oliver and Nelson Norman in another blockbuster deal on December 8, 1977.

Blyleven helped Pittsburgh to its 1979 World Series win, but he became increasingly unhappy with manager Chuck Tanner's strategy of going to the bullpen in close games. Openly admitting his pursuit of statistical goals, Blyleven announced his intention to retire, unless he was traded, on April 30, 1980. After being placed on the disqualified list, Blyleven agreed to rejoin the Pirates May 13. The slender righthander was virtually given to Cleveland in a six-player deal on December 9, 1980.

A severe elbow injury sidelined Blyleven for most of 1982. He struggled in 1983 but rebounded with one of his best seasons (19–7, 2.87) in 1984. Unhappy playing for a non-contender, he forced a trade back to Minnesota in 1985. His ERA skyrocketed in the Metrodome, but Blyleven continued to accumulate wins and strikeouts. He also surrendered a ML-record 50 homers in 1986 and a league-high

46 in 1987. The homers were partially due to his outstanding control. He maintained a strikeout-to-walk ratio of nearly 3:1 while passing the 3000-strikeout mark in 1986. His eighth AL season with 200 or more strikeouts (1986) established a league record. Blyleven had 196 strikeouts in 1987, his ninth season of 15 or more wins (15–12) and turned in outstanding performances in postseason play, winning twice in the LCS and once in the World Series. After a mediocre 1988 season for the Twins, he moved on to the Angels and went 17–5 with a 2.73 ERA (fourth in the AL) in 1989. Leading the AL with five shutouts in '89, he finished the 1980s as the active career leader in that category and trailed only all-time leader Nolan Ryan among active players in strikeouts. /(ME)

Mike Blyzka — 1928– . RHP 1953–54 **Browns/ Orioles** 181 ip, 3–11, 5.58

The chunky reliever was included in the 18-player deal that sent Bob Turley and Don Larsen to the Yankees. /(GEB)

John Boccabella — 1941– . C-1B-OF 1963–74 Cubs, **Expos**, Giants 551 g, .219, 26 hr, 148 rbi

An original Expo after six part-time years with the Cubs, the versatile Boccabella hit two homers in one inning for Montreal (7/6/73). Expo Manager Gene Mauch called him "one of the most underrated players in the league." /(JCA)

Bruce Bochte — 1950– . 1B-OF 1974–82, 84–86 Angels, **Mariners**, A's 1538 g, .282, 100 hr, 658 rbi
☛ *All-Star—79.*

Bochte was an AL All-Star in 1979 when he hit .316 for the Mariners and his .300 the next season earned him the club MVP award. After hitting .297 in '82, he abruptly retired, explaining, "I was the Mariners' player rep for three years and became aware of a cold, impersonal attitude on the part of management, and wanted no part of that." Lured back to baseball by the A's in '84, he put in three more solid seasons. /(NLM)

Bruce Bochy — 1955– . C 1978–80, 82–87 Astros, Mets, **Padres** 358 g, .239, 26 hr, 93 rbi. *1 LCS, 1 g, .000. 1 WS, 1 g, 1.000*

Bochy was a backup catcher and pinch hitter with some power who never started more than 29 games behind the plate in one season. His bigger-than-normal hat size caused him trouble in 1982 when he was called up to the Mets. When he arrived in New

York, he could not find a helmet to fit him, and had to wait until his was rushed up from Tidewater (International League) before he could play. He became a minor league manager for the Padres when his playing days ended. /(JCA)

Hal Bock — 1939– . *Writer*

Bock has been covering baseball in New York for the Associated Press since 1963. His twice-weekly column, "Bock's Score," is published by 1700 newspapers. /NLM)

Eddie Bockman — 1920– . 3B 1946–49 Yankees, Indians, **Pirates** 249 g, .230, 11 hr, 56 rbi

After four years of military service during WWII, Bockman saw brief ML action as a reserve third baseman, and he has been a scout for the Phillies since 1960. His notable signees and discoveries include Bob Boone, Larry Bowa, Mark Davis, and Joe Charboneau. /(FVP)

Randy Bockus — 1960– . LHP 1986– **Giants** 56 ip, 2–1, 4.15

The injury-prone Giants staff afforded this reliever several opportunities in the majors. /(JFC)

Mike Boddicker — 1957– . RHP 1980– **Orioles**, Red Sox 1574 ip, 101–87, 3.70. 20 wins: 84 *2 LCS, 12 ip, 1–1, 4.63. 1 WS, 9 ip, 1–0, 0.00*
☛ *Led League—w 84. Led League—era 84. All-Star—84.*

Boddicker was outstanding in his first two ML seasons, baffling AL hitters with a collection of slow breaking balls. He was *TSN* AL Rookie Pitcher of the Year in 1983 and tied an LCS record with 14 strikeouts in a shutout win in the '83 ALCS. As a sophomore, he led the AL in both wins (20) and ERA (2.79). After three more seasons as Baltimore's most consistent starter, he was traded to the Red Sox in July 1988. He helped the Red Sox win the AL East by going 7–3 with a 2.63 ERA; he had been 6–12 with a 3.86 for the Orioles. He was 15–11, 4.00 in 1989 and gave up 217 hits in 211.2 innings, but won by holding opposing batters to a league-leading .212 batting average with runners in scoring position. /(ME)

Ping Bodie [Frank Stephan; born Francesco Stephano Pezzullo] — 1887–1961. OF 1911–14, 17–21 **White Sox**, A's, Yankees 1049 g, .275, 43 hr, 516 rbi

The burly, colorful, but modestly talented slugger took "Bodie" from the California town in which he once lived, while "Ping" approximated the sound of the ball off his bat. A fair hitter with a good arm (AL leader in outfield assists with 32 in 1917), Bodie was naturally funny and garrulous. Supposedly Ring Lardner blended elements of Bodie into the brash ballplayer of his "You Know Me, Al" stories. Asked about rooming with the gallivanting Babe Ruth, Ping cracked: "I don't room with Ruth; I room with his suitcase!" When the slowfooted Bodie was out by yards in an attempted steal, columnist Bugs Baer wrote: "There was larceny in his heart, but his feet were honest." /(ADS)

Tony Boeckel (Elmer) — 1892–1924. 3B 1917, 19–23 Pirates, **Braves** 777 g, .282, 27 hr, 337 rbi

Before he died in an automobile crash at age 30, Boeckel was an aggressive if error-prone third baseman with occasional power. In his final season he hit .298. /(JK)

George Boehler — 1892–1958. RHP 1912–16, 20–21, 23, 26 **Tigers**, Browns, Pirates, Dodgers 201 ip, 6–12, 4.74

Although he didn't stick in the ML in nine tries, Boehler won 210 games in the minors during his 18-year career. Six times he won over 20, including a 38–13 mark with Tulsa of the Western League in 1922. /(NLM)

Joe Boehling — 1891–1941. LHP 1912–17, 20 **Senators**, Indians 925 ip, 55–50, 2.97

Although he never improved on his 17–7 rookie record in 1913, the slender Boehling turned in several solid seasons for Washington. He dropped out of baseball for several years, then returned for a lengthy minor league career. /(JK)

Joe Boever — 1960– . RHP 1985– Cardinals, **Braves** 159 ip, 5–14, 3.79

In 1989 Boever (pronounced BAY-vur) was the Braves' bullpen ace until a weight problem in the second half of the season. He saved 21 games but was 4–11, 3.94. /(SFS)

Dusty Boggess Lynton — 1904–1968. *Umpire* NL 1944–48, 50–62 *4 WS, 5 ASU*

Boggess spent 21 years in the minors, 16 as an infielder and catcher. His nickname stemmed both from his dusty red hair and his habit of scooping up dirt while he batted. A NL umpire for 18 years, he kept a souvenir ball autographed by every umpire he'd worked with. It was buried with him, as specified in his will. /(RTM)

Tommy Boggs — 1955– . RHP 1976–83 Rangers, **Braves** 577 ip, 20–44, 4.14

The second pick in the nation in June 1974, Boggs debuted with Texas at age 20. His record was 3–20 in parts of four seasons before he had his only winning year, 12–9 with Atlanta in 1980. /(JCA)

Wade Boggs — 1958– . 3B 1982– **Red Sox** 1183 g, .352, 64 hr, 523 rbi. *2 LCS, 11 g, .279, 5 rbi. 1 WS, 7 g, .290, 3 rbi*

☛ *Led League—ba 83, 85–88. All-Star—85–89.*

With an easy lefthanded stroke that sprays line drives to all fields, an outstanding eye for the strike zone, and a litany of routines that borders on the fanatical, Wade Boggs, the AL's perennial batting champion, has become a baseball anomaly, a player whose statistics are so staggering as to defy contemporary comparison. In the post-WWII era of declining batting averages, Boggs's .356 career mark through 1988 is the fourth-highest in ML history, behind Ty Cobb, Rogers Hornsby, and Joe Jackson. He has hit .349 or higher in six of his seven seasons (Rod Carew did so five times in 19 seasons), and in 1988 he became the only player in ML history with 200 or more hits in six consecutive seasons. As remarkable as his hitting ability is his patience at the plate. He routinely draws 100 walks in a season, leading the AL in both 1986 and '88, while his on-base percentage for his first seven seasons is a phenomenal .448. In 1985, Boggs reached base 340 times. Only Babe Ruth, Ted Williams, and Lou Gehrig have done better.

Still, Boggs is not without his detractors. He has a reputation as an egotistical statistics-minded player with little regard for his team's fortunes (although he did cry in the dugout after the Red Sox lost Game Seven of the 1986 WS to the Mets). He is criticized both for his lack of speed (12 career stolen bases) and an alleged lack of run-producing ability. Usually batting leadoff, Boggs finished the 1980s with 100 or more runs scored in seven consecutive seasons, and has rapped 40 or more doubles five times. In 1987, batting third most of the year, Boggs hit 24 HR and his .588 slugging percentage was third in the AL, but he has hit no more than eight HR in any other season.

Boggs's ML success did not come quickly. He toiled for six seasons in the Red Sox' minor league chain, always among his league's batting leaders, but stigmatized as an inadequate fielder. He reached the ML in 1982, and improved enough at third base to finish second in the AL Gold Glove voting in 1987. Boggs got his opportunity to play regularly when Carney Lansford injured his ankle in June 1982. He hit .349 the rest of the season to set an AL rookie record and finish third in the Rookie of the Year voting behind Cal Ripken and Kent Hrbek. The following season, Boggs won his first batting title with a .361 average and topped 200 hits and 100 runs for the first of six consecutive seasons. He

Wade Boggs

"slumped" to a career-low .325 in 1984, and has not hit below .357 since, winning the AL batting title every year.

To Boggs, perhaps the game's most superstitious player today, his cherished and obsessive rituals both before and during games are the keys to his consistency. His diet consists almost exclusively of chicken, and he runs pregame windsprints precisely at 7:17 each evening. He draws a Hebrew letter in the batter's box before each at bat, and his route to and from the playing field is so precise that by late summer his footprints are clearly visible in the grass in front of the Fenway Park dugout.

In 1988, the details of Boggs's long-term extramarital affair with Margo Adams became public, and Adams's lawsuit created dissension among the Red Sox, many of whom were asked to give depositions. Despite rumors he would be traded because of the scandal, Boggs remained in Boston through 1989./(SCL)

Sammy Bohne [born Sammy Cohen] — 1896–1977. 2B-SS-3B 1916, 21–26 Cardinals, **Reds**, Dodgers 663 g, .261, 16 hr, 228 rbi

One of four Cincinnati infielders in the early 1920s who were graduates of the San Francisco sandlots, Bohne broke up Dodger Dazzy Vance's bid for a no-hitter with two outs in the ninth (6/17/23). That year a Chicago newspaper story implied that Bohne and Pat Duncan were associated with gamblers. The players were cleared by a federal judge, and later Bohne was awarded damages in a libel suit. /(NLM)

Bruce Boisclair — 1952– . OF 1974, 76–79 **Mets** 410 g, .263, 10 hr, 77 rbi

The lefty Met outfielder hit .287 in his rookie 1976 season, when he was the NL's best pinch hitter (12 for 21, .571). He was used mainly as a pinch hitter through 1979, when a broken wrist and a .184 BA ended his ML career. /(JCA)

Bernie Boland — 1892–1973. RHP 1915–21 **Tigers**, Browns 1063 ip, 68–53, 3.24

A regular starter for the Tigers for five years before suffering a broken arm, Boland had a top season of 16–11 in 1917. He used a sharply breaking curve ball to strike out Babe Ruth three times in one game. As a rookie in 1915 he came within one out of pitching a no-hitter against the Yankees. /(NLM)

Joe Boley [John Peter] — 1896–1962. SS 1927–32 **A's**, Indians 538 g, .269, 7 hr, 227 rbi. *3 WS, 12 g, .154, 2 rbi*

An exceptional fielder, steady hitter, and member of the Baltimore team that won seven consecutive International League championships (1919–25), Boley's reputed $100,000 price tag kept major-league bidders at bay for years. Connie Mack wrested him away for $60,000 in 1927, and the 28-year-old rookie batted .311 for the A's. Boley joined Jimmie Foxx, Max Bishop, and Jimmy Dykes in Mack's "Million Dollar Infield," which sparked the A's to three pennants and two world championships (1929–31). /(JL)

Jim Bolger (Dutch) — 1932– . OF 1950–51, 54–55, 57–59 **Reds**, **Cubs**, Indians, Phillies 312 g, .229, 6 hr, 48 rbi

Bolger couldn't stick with his hometown Reds, but he found a niche with the Cubs in 1957. He led the NL in pinch hits (17) and pinch at-bats (48), but that .354 pinch BA was followed by pinch averages of .196 and .125, ending his career. /(SFS)

Bobby Bolin — 1939– . RHP 1961–73 **Giants**, Brewers, Red Sox 1576 ip, 88–75, 3.40. *1 WS, 3 ip, 6.75*

The sidearming Bolin pitched two no-hitters in the minors and had a top ML mark of 14–6 in 1965. The next year he tied a then-ML record by striking out the first five Dodger batters he faced. He was the winning pitcher in the Milwaukee Brewers' first victory. /(GEB)

Frank Bolling — 1931– . 2B 1954, 56–66 **Tigers**, Braves 1540 g, .254, 106 hr, 556 rbi
☛ *Gold Glove—58.*

The younger brother of Milt Bolling, Frank twice hit 15 homers in a season. During his dozen ML years he never played an inning at any position other than second base. With the Tigers, he led AL second basemen in fielding in 1958. Traded to the Braves for centerfielder Billy Bruton after the 1960 season, he led NL second basemen in fielding in 1961, '62, and '64, finishing with a career mark of .982. /(GEB)

Milt Bolling — 1930– . SS-2B 1952–58 **Red Sox**, Senators, Tigers 400 g, .241, 19 hr, 94 rbi

The former Spring Hill college basketball star showed promise as a young shortstop, but injuries to his legs and elbows cost him first-string status. While with Detroit, he played a few games alongside brother Frank. Their uncle, John Bolling, played first base for the Phillies and Dodgers. /(EW)

Cliff Bolton — 1907–1979. C 1931, 33–37, 41 **Senators**, Tigers 335 g, .291, 6 hr, 143 rbi. *1 WS, 2 g, .000*

This North Carolina farm boy hit .304 for the Senators in 1935, the only year he played in more than 100 games. His small size and lack of power kept him in a backup role most of his career. /(GEB)

Tom Bolton — 1962– . LHP 1987– **Red Sox** 110 ip, 2–7, 5.10

Bolton's hittability confined him to middle relief in his short major league stints. /(WOR)

Mark Bomback — 1953– . RHP 1978, 80–82 Brewers, **Mets**, Blue Jays 314 ip, 16–18, 4.47

In his ninth minor league season, Bomback was named *TSN* 1979 Minor League Player of the Year with a 22–7 mark in the Pacific Coast League. He was 10–8 as a Met rookie the next year. /(GEB)

Tommy Bond — 1856–1941. RHP-OF 1874–82, 84 Brooklyn/Hartford (NA), Hartford (NL), **Boston (NL)**, Worcester (NL), Boston (UL), Indianapolis (AA) *NA:* 41–48; 126 g, .242; *ML:* 2780 ip, 193–115, 2.25; 361 g, .236, 0 hr, 121 rbi. 20 wins: 1874, 76–80
    Manager 1882 **Worcester (NL)** 5–22, .185
☛ *Led League—w 1877–78. Led League—k 1877–78. Led League—era 1877, 79.*

Bond became the first "triple crown" pitcher when he led the National League with 40 wins, 170 strikeouts, and a 2.11 ERA for Boston in 1877. In 1878 he repeated as leader in wins, strikeouts, shutouts, and winning percentage, while working more games and innings than any other NL pitcher. He won a career-high 43 games in 1879, again was the NL's ERA champion, and threw 12 shutouts while the entire league had only 42. In his first four NL seasons, he compiled a 154–68 record.

Bond was one of the first curveball pitchers. Born in Ireland, at age 18 he joined the 1874 National Association Brooklyn Atlantics. He remained with that team when it moved to Hartford in 1875 and became a pioneer entry in the NL in 1876. He was virtually his team's only pitcher for most of his career, particularly while with Boston. In 1880 Boston was shut out in eight of Bond's games, and Bond began phasing out his pitching career. He coached at Harvard and was a New England League umpire in 1882–83. He lived to be the last survivor of the National League's first season./(JK)

Walt Bond — 1937–1967. OF-1B 1960–62, 64–65, 67 Indians, **Astros**, Twins 365 g, .256, 41 hr, 179 rbi

This gigantic 6'7" 235-lb Kansas City Monarch and minor-league slugger battled leukemia as a player. During a four-year remission, he put together one productive major-league season, for the 1964 Colt .45's (20 HR, 85 RBI). Bond began 1967 with the Twins, but died in September./(JK)

Barry Bonds — 1964– . OF 1986– **Pirates** 566 g, .256, 84 hr, 223 rbi

Bobby Bonds's son came to the majors with talents similar to those of his father. Barry became the second 20-HR, 20-steal Pirate ever in 1987. He led 1986 NL rookies with 16 HR, 36 steals, 48 RBI, and 65 walks. Batting both third and leadoff, he started several games with home runs. Injuries slowed him from mid-1988 on, but he retained his 20-HR power. In 1989 he and Bobby took over the father-son HR title from the Berras./(ME)

Bobby Bonds — 1946– . OF-DH 1968–81 **Giants**, Yankees, Angels, White Sox, Rangers, Indians, Cardinals, Cubs 1,849 g, .268, 332 hr, 1,024 rbi. *1 LCS, 3 g, .250* ☛ *All-Star—71, 73, 75. Gold Glove—71, 73–74.*

The enigmatic Bonds, the quintessential 30–30 player, never quite lived up to his predicted potential and could never find a permanent home. After spending seven productive seasons with the Giants, most under the shadow of Willie Mays, he spent the final seven years of his career playing for seven different teams. He hit 30 homers for five different teams, a major league record. Bonds debuted auspiciously on June 25, 1968, hitting a grand slam in the seventh inning against the Dodgers in Candlestick, the only player in the 20th century to collect a grand slam as his first hit. In his first full season in 1969, he reached the 30–30 club with 45 stolen bases and 32 homers and led the league in runs, but also led the league in strikeouts, setting a major league record with 185. He repeated that feat the following year, setting a new strikeout record of 189. After Mays was dealt to the Mets, Bonds's career took off. He

Bobby Bonds

had his best year in 1973, narrowly missing the first 40-homer, 40-stolen base season with 39 dingers and 43 steals, but again leading the league in strikeouts. Bonds insists that he had five homers rained out, including two in a game against Atlanta. Against Pittsburgh, he led off consecutive games with homers on June 5 and 6, and set a then-ML record of 11 leadoff homers. He ended the 1973 season in a slump that carried into 1974, when he was benched and fined by Charlie Fox. He regained his batting eye, but was traded after the season to the Yankees for Bobby Murcer, starting his nomadic period. The Yankees made him their number three hitter, and Bonds responded with another 30–30 effort with 85 RBIs, and became the last NL outfielder to have an unassisted double play in a game against the Mets on May 31. But after the season, the Yankees traded him to California, where he played just 99 games because of an injured hand. He rebounded in 1977 for the Angels with his third 30–30 year, with 37 homers and 41 stolen bases and driving in a career high 115 runs. In a nine-game span from August 2 to 11, he smacked eight homers. Despite his fine season, he was traded in the off season to the White Sox, but played only 26 games before being shipped to the Rangers. His combined totals for the season gave him his second straight and fifth 30–30 season, yet he was again traded in the off season to the Indians. He had his last effective season, hitting 25 homers in spacious Municipal Stadium, and wanted his contract renegotiated. The Indians responded by trading him to the Cardinals, but he didn't hit well and was platooned. He was then sold to the Cubs, but appeared in just 45 games. Bonds was named batting coach of the Indians in 1984. In his career, he set a major league record of 35 leadoff homers, a mark eclipsed by Rickey Henderson in 1988. He and his son Barry are also the all-time leading father-son homer duo, passing the Bells and the Berras in 1989. /(SEW)

Bill Bonham — 1948– . RHP 1971-80 **Cubs**, Reds 1488 ip, 75–83, 4.00

Reliever Bonham was converted to starting midway through 1973, and the following season his 22 losses tied for the league lead despite his 7.07 strikeouts-per-nine-innings, third best in the NL. Plagued by wildness and playing for bad Cubs teams, he improved his record only marginally. On July 31, 1974, he struck out four batters in one inning; that season, his eight balks tied what was then the ML record. On August 5, 1975, he set a ML record when he allowed seven consecutive hits to start the

game. A trade to the Reds for the 1978 season (for Woodie Fryman and Bill Caudill) turned his career around, and he finally had a winning season as a starter (11–5, 3.54). He contributed a 9–7 record to the 1979 Reds' division championship. /(JFC)

Ernie Bonham (Tiny) — 1913-49. RHP 1940-49 **Yankees**, Pirates 1551 ip, 103–72, 3.06. 20 wins: 42
1 WS, 28 ip, 1–2, 3.21
☛ *Led League—era 40. All-Star—42-43.*

Bonham was an important contributor to the 1941–43 Yankee pennants. The 6′2″ 215-lb hulk ("Tiny") was the first successful pitcher to use the forkball, and had excellent control. He led the AL with a 1.90 ERA as a rookie in 1940. In 1942 his .808 winning percentage (21–5), six shutouts, and 22 complete games were the league's best. Chronic back problems reduced his effectiveness his final five seasons, but he remained a tough competitor, winning his last six games. He died suddenly from appendicitis complications just two weeks after pitching his last game. /(GDW)

Bobby Bonilla — 1963– . 3B-OF 1986– White Sox, **Pirates** 601 g, .278, 66 hr, 306 rbi
☛ *All-Star—88-89.*

Pittsburgh's lost and found star was originally signed by the Pirates in 1981, but he was left unprotected and lost to the White Sox in 1985. Originally recommended to the Pirates by Syd Thrift, he was reacquired after Thrift became their GM in 1986. The powerful switch-hitter hit the seventh upper-deck HR in Three Rivers Stadium history on July 12, 1987 and hit a career-high .300 that year. In 1988 a hot first half had him leading the NL in HR and RBI and challenging for the Triple Crown, but he cooled off and finished with 24 HR and 100 RBI. Finally given a permanent position at third base in 1988, he was error-prone but showed fair range using an unusual sideways-facing stance in the field. /(ME)

Juan Bonilla — 1956– . 2B 1981-83, 85-87 **Padres**, Yankees, Orioles 429 g, .256, 7 hr, 101 rbi

Although he led NL second basemen with 13 errors in strike-shortened 1981, Bonilla made a good beginning with the Padres, hitting .290 in 99 games and showing good range afield. A broken wrist and rehabilitation from drug abuse shelved him for most of the 1982 season. In 1983 his BA skidded to .237. When he held out the following year, he was released. In subsequent tries with the Yankees and Orioles, he was unable to win a regular job. /(MC)

Barry Bonnell — 1953- . OF-3B 1977–86 Braves, **Blue Jays**, Mariners 976 g, .272, 56 hr, 355 rbi

Bonnell was a platoon outfielder with a good arm who would sometimes be among the league batting leaders during the season, but seldom at the end. An exception was 1983, when he hit .318 (10 HR and 54 RBI) for the Blue Jays. That December he was traded to Seattle for pitcher Bryan Clark. /(TF)

Zeke Bonura [Henry John] (Banana Nose) — 1908–1987. 1B 1934–40 **White Sox**, Senators, Giants, Cubs 917 g, .307, 119 hr, 704 rbi

A fans' delight and manager's nightmare, Bonura led AL first basemen in fielding in 1936 by refusing to become involved. As easy grounders bounded by untouched, Zeke waved his "Mussolini salute" with his glove. Known affectionately as "Banana Nose," the colorful and outspoken Bonura was the White Sox' first bona fide home run hitter, with 27 in his rookie year. He continued slugging, but his nonchalant fielding, aggravating annual hold-outs, and rumored interest in owner J. Lou Comiskey's daughter got him traded to Washington in 1938 in exchange for Joe Kuhel, the AL's top fielding first baseman. /(RL)

Greg Booker — 1960- . RHP 1983- **Padres** 253 ip, 5–7, 3.80. *1 LCS, 2 ip, 0–0, 0.00. 1 WS, 1 ip, 0–0, 9.00*

A 6'6" reliever, Booker shuttled between San Diego and Las Vegas (Pacific Coast League) from 1983 to 1986 before finally spending full seasons with the Padres in 1987 and 1988. Originally drafted as a first baseman, he switched to pitching full-time in his second pro season (1982) and led the California League in losses, walks, and wild pitches. He still reached the ML at the tail end of the 1983 season, and in 1984 he pitched one inning in Game Three of the WS, walking four batters. Booker's father-in-law is Padres manager Jack McKeon. /(SCL)

Bob Boone — 1947- . C 1972–89 **Phillies**, Angels 2224 g, .254, 105 hr, 817 rbi. *6 LCS, 27 g, .310, 2 hr, 9 rbi. 1 WS, 6 g, .412, 4 rbi*
☛ *All-Star—76, 78–79, 83. Gold Glove—78–79, 82, 86–89.*

The most durable catcher in ML history, Boone had caught a ML-record 2066 games entering the 1990 season. The son of Tigers All-Star third baseman Ray Boone, Bob attended Stanford University before reaching the ML in late 1972, and although he had several good seasons at the plate, his value lay in his defensive skills and his handling of

Bob Boone

pitchers. In 1977, his eight errors and three passed balls were the lowest totals among NL catchers. He started for Philadelphia's three straight division champions (1976–78) as well as the World Championship club of 1980. After Boone's off-year in 1981 (.211, 4 HR, 24 RBI), the Phillies decided that Keith Moreland was ready to take over behind the plate, and Boone was traded to the Angels. He quickly proved the Phillies wrong. While Moreland struggled, Boone threw out 21 of the first 34 AL runners attempting to steal against him and steadied the Angels' pitching staff en route to the AL West title. He remained the Angels' starting catcher for seven years, but was let go after hitting a career-high .295 in 1988 at the age of 40. He signed with the Royals as a free agent and led them in 1989 with a .350 batting average with runners in scoring position. /(SG)

Ike Boone — 1897–1958. OF 1922–25, 27, 30–32 Giants, **Red Sox**, White Sox, Dodgers 356 g, .319, 26 hr, 192 rbi

A product of the University of Alabama, Boone hit well in several trials in the majors, but his lack of speed handicapped him in the field and on the bases. He had a career BA of .370 in the minor leagues, and in 1929 (over the course of 198 games in the Pacific Coast League), he set an organized baseball record with 553 total bases while batting .407 with 55 homers and 218 RBI. /(LRD)

Luke Boone (Danny) — 1890–1982. 2B-SS-3B 1913–16, 18 **Yankees**, Pirates 314 g, .209, 6 hr, 76 rbi

The regular second baseman for the Yankees in 1914–15, Boone's fielding couldn't make up for his poor hitting. The Pittsburgh native played in the American Association until 1936. /(ME)

Ray Boone (Ike) — 1923– . 3B-SS-1B 1948–60 Indians, **Tigers**, White Sox, A's, Braves, Red Sox 1373 g, .275, 151 hr, 737 rbi. *1 WS, 1 g, .000*
☛ *Led League—rbi 55. All-Star—54, 56.*

Boone was hitting .355 in the Texas League in late 1948 when Cleveland shortstop-manager Lou Boudreau was hurt. Boone, who had been converted from catcher to shortstop that year, was called up in time to earn a World Series share. Before long he forced Boudreau to switch to third base.

Boone had a powerful throwing arm, but bad knees and ankles limited his range. He led AL shortstops in errors in 1951. Traded to Detroit in an eight-player deal in 1953, he was switched to less-demanding third base, and his hitting improved. He more than doubled his HR and RBI output, hitting 26 HR, including four grand slams. A righthanded line-drive hitter who could handle the curveball, in 1955 he led the AL in RBI with 116.

Ray's son Bob Boone starred as a ML catcher. /(JCA)

John Boozer — 1939– . RHP 1962–64, 66–69 **Phillies** 394 ip, 14–16, 4.09

Boozer bounced between the minors and the Phillies five times on option, never able to keep a starting slot. Despite occasional streaks of wildness, he saved 11 games in relief for Philadelphia during his last two ML years. /(JK)

Pedro Borbon — 1946– . RHP 1969–80 Angels, **Reds**, Giants, Cardinals 1026 ip, 69–39, 3.52. *4 LCS, 14 ip, 1–0, 0.63. 3 WS, 11 ip, 0–1, 3.86*

An unabashed cockfighting enthusiast, macho Borbon reportedly could warm up faster and throw a ball farther than anyone else in the NL during the mid-1970s when he was a top reliever for Cincinnati's "Big Red Machine." He liked to show off by throwing strikes to home plate from the center field warning track during batting practice. His best seasons were 1973 (11–4 with 14 saves) and 1977 (10–5 with 18 saves). /(MC)

Frenchy Bordagaray [Stanley George] — 1910– . OF-3B 1934–39, 41–45 White Sox, **Dodgers**, Cardinals, Reds, Yankees 930 g, .283, 14 hr, 270 rbi. *2 WS, 3 g, --*

Frenchy fit Casey Stengel's Brooklyn Dodgers like fingers in a glove. Gifted but erratic, he mixed brilliant plays with bonehead ones. He ran when he wanted, failed to slide when he should have, and ignored signs. In 1935, he showed up at spring training with a mustache, a no-no in those days. They made him shave it off, which he blamed for a subsequent slump. With the Cardinals in '38, he led the league with 20 pinch hits in 43 at-bats. /(NLM)

Pat Borders — 1963– . C 1988– **Blue Jays** 150 g, .263, 8 hr, 50 rbi. *1 LCS, 1.000, 1 rbi*

Borders won platoon time with his bat, but poor throwing mechanics made this converted third baseman easy to steal on. /(JFC)

Rich Bordi — 1959– . RHP 1980– A's, Mariners, Cubs, **Yankees**, Orioles 371 ip, 20–20, 4.34

The 6'7" Bordi was the last player signed by A's owner Charley Finley. He made his ML debut with the A's in 1980 after pitching only 11 games in the minors. Traded or released six times thereafter, Bordi didn't spend a full season in the ML until 1984 with the Cubs, then appeared in 51 games for the Yankees in 1985 and 52 games for the Orioles in 1986. He was released by the Yankees after the 1987 season and made two starts for the World Champion A's in 1988, lasting less than eight innings total. /(SCL)

Glenn Borgmann — 1950– . C 1972–80 **Twins**, White Sox 474 g, .229, 16 hr, 151 rbi

Light-hitting but rifle-armed Borgmann set a Minnesota record when he led all ML catchers with a .997 fielding average in 1974, his first of two years as the Twins' regular catcher. Injuries, the emergence of Butch Wynegar, and Borgmann's poor hitting relegated him to reserve duty thereafter. /(MC)

Bob Borkowski (Bush) — 1926– . OF 1950–55 Cubs, **Reds**, Dodgers 470 g, .251, 16 hr, 112 rbi

Originally signed as a pitcher, "Bush" went 18–9 for Elizabethton, but his .384 BA convinced the Cubs to switch him to the outfield. Although he never earned a regular spot in the majors, he was a useful sub and righthanded pinch hitter, with a knack for hitting Giants and Phillies pitching. /(RM)

Steve Boros — 1936– . 3B-1B-2B 1957–58, 61–65 **Tigers**, Cubs, Reds 422 g, .245, 26 hr, 149 rbi.
　Manager 1983–84, 86 **A's**, Padres 168–200, .457

Boros signed with Detroit for $25,000 while a student at the University of Michigan, where he received a B.A. in literature. He was voted American Association MVP with Denver in 1960 and had an excellent rookie season with the Tigers in 1961 until sidelined by a broken collarbone. After that the intellectual infielder was better known for his B.A. than his BA. Later a ML manager, in his only two full seasons (1983 A's and 1986 Padres) his teams finished with identical 74–88 records. He was considered a masterful teacher of baserunning. /(RM)

Hank Borowy — 1916– . RHP 1942–51 **Yankees**, Cubs, Phillies, Pirates, Tigers 1716 ip, 108–82, 3.50. 20 wins: 45 *3 WS, 29 ip, 3–2, 4.97*
☛ *Led League—era 45. All-Star—44.*

Borowy pitched reliably for the Yankees during WWII, going 15–4 as a 1942 rookie and following with 14–9 and 17–12 years. After a 10–5 start in 1945, he was suddenly sold to the Cubs on July 27 for $97,000. He went 11–2 for the remainder of the season, leading the NL in winning percentage (.846) and ERA (2.14), as the Cubs won the pennant. In the WS, he shut out the Tigers in the first game, lost the fifth game, and then came back to win the sixth with four scoreless relief innings. He started the final game on one day's rest but gave up hits to the first three batters before leaving. *TSN* named him to the all-star ML team for 1945. During the remainder of his career, he was plagued by finger blisters and a sore shoulder. /(ME)

Rick Bosetti — 1953– . OF 1976–82 Phillies, Cardinals, **Blue Jays**, A's 445 g, .250, 17 hr, 133 rbi. *1 LCS, 2 g, .250*

Bosetti was a flashy fielder who, with Toronto in 1979, led AL outfielders in putouts, assists, and errors. *The Rick Bosetti Baseball Book* was the Blue

Jays' first publication of tips from a big leaguer, though it was scarcely believable looking at the off-balance swings on Bosetti's bubblegum cards. Recognizing his own modest talents as a player, Bosetti had other goals—notably to urinate in the outfield of every major league park, a goal he was able to achieve. /(TF)

Chris Bosio — 1963– . RHP 1986- **Brewers** 621 ip, 33–37, 3.93

A hard thrower who can start or relieve, Bosio joined the Brewers' rotation midway through 1987 and tossed a two-hit shutout against Minnesota August 28. In 1988 he was 6–12 as a starter (despite a 3.36 ERA) and also saved six games. Bosio became the anchor of Milwaukee's staff in 1989 with a 15–10, 2.95 record. /(SCL)

Thad Bosley — 1956– . OF 1977- Angels, White Sox, Brewers, Mariners, **Cubs**, Royals 754 g, .274, 19 hr, 155 rbi. *1 LCS, 2 g, .000*

The often-injured Bosley usually hit well when given the chance, but never got more than 180 at-bats in any one season. He led the ML in pinch hits in both 1985 and 1987 and hit six pinch home runs for the Cubs in '85. He was on the DL seven different times in his career. Bosley led the California League with 90 stolen bases for Salinas in 1976. /(ME)

Dick Bosman — 1944– . RHP 1966–76 **Senators/ Rangers**, Indians, A's 1591 ip, 82–85, 3.67. *1 LCS, 0.1 ip, 0.00*

A highly competitive control pitcher who told teammates, "If you don't hustle when I'm pitching, I'll kick your ass," Bosman was 14–9 with an AL-best 2.19 ERA for the 1969 Senators. He won a career-high 16 in 1970, and no-hit the A's while with Cleveland (7/19/74), losing a perfect game on his own error. Bosman won 11 to help Oakland to a division title in 1975, but the A's cut him in 1977. /(KT)

Lyman Bostock — 1950–1978. OF 1975–78 **Twins**, Angels 526 g, .311, 23 hr, 250 rbi

Bostock, the son of Negro League player Lyman Bostock, Sr., appeared headed for stardom before he was fatally wounded in 1978. In 1976, he hit .323 and received the Calvin R. Griffith Award for the most improved Twin. In 1977, he finished second to teammate Rod Carew in the AL batting race (.336 to Carew's .388). The well-liked Alabaman was shot in Gary, Indiana, in the back seat of a car driven by his uncle. Police later arrested the estranged husband of one of two women in the car. /(RM)

Boston Braves — 1871–1952. Team. 5118–5598, .478. *National Association Champions 72–75 NL Champions 1877–78, 83, 91–93, 97–98, 1914, 48, 57–58 World Champions 14, 57*

The franchise that is now the Atlanta Braves, after a 13-year stopover in Milwaukee, is the longest continuously active club in baseball history. A charter member of the National Association, the first professional league, the team called itself the Boston Red Stockings because manager Harry Wright and three other members of the Cincinnati Red Stockings, baseball's first pro team, were on the original club in 1871. They finished first four straight years (1872–75) and continued in the National League when that organization supplanted the NA in 1876.

Boston won eight NL pennants before the end of the 19th century, becoming known as the

Beaneaters in the process. The 20th century wasn't as kind to the team, which finally assumed the familiar Braves name. Boston did make history in 1914 when the "Miracle Braves" took less than two months to go from last to first in the second half of the season and proceeded to stun the Athletics in the World Series, becoming in the process the first team to successfully utilize platooning. Financial difficulties took their toll over the next thirty years, as the Braves finished over .500 only five times from 1917 through 1945, but contractor Lou Perini bought the franchise for 1946. With a turnover of personnel on the field and in the front office, the team won the NL pennant in 1948, but declining attendance resulted in the move to Milwaukee only five years later. Babe Ruth hit his final home runs in a Boston Braves uniform in 1935, and Casey Stengel managed the club during the lean years of the late 1930s and early 1940s. /(SH)

The 1914 Boston Braves

Boston Red Sox [aka Puritans] (BoSox) — 1901- .
6996-6720, .510. *AL East Champions 75, 86, 88 AL
Champions 03-04, 12, 15-16, 18, 46, 75, 86 World
Champions 03, 12, 15-16, 18*

Red Sox fans like to moan about how their team
always lets them down, but in fact it is one of the
more successful franchises in the American League.
It's just that they haven't won a World Championship since 1918 . . .

Originally called the Puritans, the franchise was
quite successful in the first two decades of the
American League. Their first pennant came in 1903,
when Cy Young led the AL in wins and Buck
Freeman led in HR and RBI, and they won the first
World Series. They repeated in 1904, but Giants
manager John McGraw refused to let his team play
the WS. The Puritans were rebuilt over the rest of
the decade, and when they won the AL flag in 1912,
they featured Tris Speaker, who led AL outfielders
with 35 assists and tied for the lead in HR, and

Smoky Joe Wood, who had a spectacular 34–5
record that included a string of 16 straight victories.
Boston won the Series from the Giants in Game
Seven on errors by Snodgrass and Merkle. The Red
Sox then won back-to-back World Championships
in 1915 and 1916, with Babe Ruth winning the
ERA title in 1916. That year, he won a 14-inning
2–1 contest in Game Two. The Red Sox' fifth World
Championship in as many chances came in 1918,
and Ruth set a scoreless streak record of 29.2
innings dating back to 1916.

But owners Hugh Ward (largely an absentee
owner) and Harry Frazee (unfortunately quite present) suffered losses on the New York stage and
made up the difference by selling off the Red Sox'
most talented players. Babe Ruth had been moved
to the outfield in 1919 and proceeded to set a ML
record with 29 HR. That winter he was sold to the
Yankees in a complicated deal that included
$100,000 cash and a $300,000 mortgage on Fenway

The 1908 Boston Red Sox

Park. He was only the first to go, and the Red Sox soon took up residence in the lower levels of the standings, finishing last nine times before Tom Yawkey bought the franchise in 1933 and brought in a new era.

Yawkey bought up established stars such as Lefty Grove, Joe Cronin, and Jimmie Foxx, who gave him an MVP season in 1938. Later in the decade GM Eddie Collins found Ted Williams and Bobby Doerr in the Pacific Coast League. These efforts produced an AL pennant in 1946 (when Ted Williams won the first of his two MVP awards) and a storied loss to the Cardinals in the World Series that began the legend of the Red Sox being fated to lose the big games. In the bottom of the eighth inning of Game Seven, Enos Slaughter scored the winning run from first on a single, while Red Sox shortstop Johnny Pesky supposedly held the ball. Actually, Pesky had his back to the play, which was fumbled by Leon Culberson; Pesky hesitated only slightly before relaying the ball to the plate, but it was too late.

The Red Sox contended for the next few seasons, losing a one-game playoff to the Indians in 1948, but by the mid-1950s slumped to mediocrity, and sometimes less than that. A continual cry for more pitching was unassuaged, and Boston fans had little to do but watch Williams, perhaps the greatest hitter of all time, until his retirement in 1960 took even that solace from them. But the rise of a younger set of stars in the 1960s, especially Carl Yastrzemski, brought the "Impossible Dream" pennant of 1967 after two straight ninth-place finishes. Yaz won the MVP award on the strength of a Triple Crown performance, the last in the majors. Once again it was the Cardinals who denied Yawkey's dreamed-of World Championship, as the Red Sox lost again in seven games.

The Red Sox once again entered a period of mediocrity, although they didn't suffer any losing seasons and contended occasionally. Once again it was the arrival of young blood that brought a pennant. Fred Lynn and Jim Rice had great rookie seasons in 1975, with Lynn capturing both MVP and Rookie of the Year honors, the only man ever to win the MVP in his first season. Rice succeeded Yastrzemski and Williams in the line of great Boston left fielders, and like them became the focus of the fans' love for and dissatisfaction with their team. Once again the Red Sox took the Series to seven games, getting there with a thrilling victory in Game Six (THE Game Six, in Boston; years later it was still referred to as such, with no confusion ever resulting from intervening sixth games of other

Series). Bernie Carbo's game-tying pinch-homer in the 8th inning and Carlton Fisk's dramatic, body-English-directed shot in the 12th inning were the main ingredients. But of course the Reds won Game Seven, and the fatalism of Boston rooters became legend. Tom Yawkey, who had often been accused of pampering and overpaying his favorite stars, died the following year without ever having achieved the World Championship he desired so ardently.

Another lost playoff game in 1978 varied the motif, harking back to the loss to the Indians 30 years earlier. Lost in the disapointment was a great Red Sox comeback at the end of the season after they had been overtaken by the Yankees. After that the triumvirate ownership of Mrs. Tom Yawkey, Haywood Sullivan, and Buddy LeRoux began feuding, and the team entered another fallow period. The arrival of Wade Boggs in 1982 and Roger Clemens in 1984 brought a pennant in 1986, with a dramatic Game Five HR by instant hero Dave Henderson turning the team around. But, one strike away from a World Championship in Game Six against the Mets, reliever Bob Stanley threw a wild pitch, and then Mookie Wilson hit a roller through Bill Buckner's legs at first base. Manager John MacNamara was criticized for not replacing Buckner with a defensive substitute for sentimental reasons. The speedy Wilson would have been safe anyway, but the error allowed the winning run to score, and the Red Sox once again lost in Game Seven. The inertial MacNamara was replaced in mid-1988 by Joe Morgan, nine and a half games back in fourth place at the All-Star break. Morgan led them on a hot streak that carried them to the division title. They won 19 of his first 20 games, and won an AL-record 24 straight games at home (the first five under MacNamara). They were swept by the overwhelming A's in the LCS./(SH)

Daryl Boston — 1963– . OF 1984– **White Sox** 495, .239, 38 hr, 123 rbi

The lefthanded-hitting, 6'3" 185-lb Boston was the White Sox' first pick in the 1981 June draft. In 1984 he batted .312 in the American Association and led the league with 19 triples. In his debut with Chicago that May 13, he collected three hits before striking out. Over the next four seasons he shuttled between the majors and Triple-A, his occasional power not compensating for what was perceived as a lack of hustle in the outfield and aggressiveness at the plate. The White Sox' new batting coach in 1989, Walt Hriniak, helped him raise his average 30 points, but Boston lost his power in the process./(RL)

Dave Boswell — 1945– . RHP 1964–71 **Twins**, Tigers, Orioles 1066 ip, 68–56, 3.52. *1 LCS, 11 ip, 0–1, 3.52. 1 WS, 3 ip, 3.38*

Pitching for the Twins in 1967, Boswell racked up 204 strikeouts as he, Jim Kaat, and Dean Chance became the first three pitchers on the same team to strike out 200 each in one season. In 1969 he went 20–12 and was involved in an off-the-field scuffle with teammate Bob Allison which resulted in Boswell getting punched by manager Billy Martin. In the 1969 LCS, he lost to the Orioles 1–0 in ten innings./(RTM)

Ken Boswell — 1946– . 2B 1967–77 **Mets**, Astros 930 g, .248, 31 hr, 244 rbi. *2 LCS, 4 g, .308, 2 hr 5 rbi. 2 WS, 4 g, .667*

Known for his "bad hands" when he broke in with the Mets, Boswell made three errors on Opening Day, 1969. But in 1970, he set the major-league fielding mark for second basemen (.996) and played a then-record 85 consecutive errorless games. Always a platoon player, he tied a record with three pinch hits in the 1973 World Series. His career-high .279 BA came in the Mets' 1969 championship season./(KT)

Tom Boswell — 1947– . *Writer.*

A writer and columnist for the Washington *Post* since 1969, Boswell has published two collections of baseball essays: *How Life Imitates the World Series* (1982); and *Why Time Begins on Opening Day* (1984)./(NLM)

Jim Bottomley (Sunny Jim) — 1900–1959. 1B 1922–37 **Cardinals**, Reds, Browns 1991 g, .310, 219 hr, 1422 rbi. *4 WS, 24 g, .200, 1 hr, 10 rbi.*
    Manager 1937 **Browns** 21–58, .266
☛ *Most Valuable Player—28 . Led League—hr 28. Led League—rbi 26, 28. Hall of Fame—1974.*

"Sunny Jim" was the first MVP to emerge from a team's own farm system. A product of Branch Rickey's Cardinal chain, he arrived at the parent club in 1922. Within a year, he replaced Jack Fournier at first base, as expected, and held the job until traded to Cincinnati after the 1932 season to make room for another farm boy, Ripper Collins.

A lefty cleanup man with a career slugging average of .500, Bottomley had a pleasant nature and smiling face, and the habit of wearing his cap tilted over his left eye. He batted his career-high .371 in his first full season (1923). On September 16, 1924, against the Dodgers, he drove in a record 12

Jim Bottomley

runs with two homers, a double, and three singles. The MVP in 1928, he batted .325, led the league in triples (20) and RBI (136), and tied Hack Wilson for the home run lead (31). He contributed mightily to the Cardinals' triumph in the 1926 WS, but did poorly in three others. In 1931, though limited by injury to 108 games, Bottomley finished third in the closest batting race in NL history (Chick Hafey—.3489; Bill Terry—.3486; Bottomley—.3482).

At 32 and no longer the .300 hitter he had been, the Cardinals sent Sunny Jim to Cincinnati for pitcher Ownie Carroll and outfielder Estel Crabtree—a trade of washed-up players. The Reds dealt him in 1936 to the Browns, where he was doing mostly pinch hitting when, in 1937, he was named to succeed his old friend, Rogers Hornsby, as manager. The hopeless Browns were last when he took over, and last when the season ended, eighty games later. He was bounced in favor of another old Card, Gabby Street.

Bottomley managed a bit in the minors, but no longer needed baseball. With savings from his salary ($15,000 tops) and World Series winnings (another

$22,000), he bought a Missouri cattle farm. Shortly before his death, he returned as a scout for the Cubs and manager in the Appalachian League. On the basis of strong career marks in doubles, hits, RBI, putouts, chances, and DP, he was posthumously elected to the Hall of Fame. /(ADS)

Ed Bouchee — 1933- . 1B 1956-62 **Phillies**, Cubs, Mets 670 g, .265, 61 hr, 290 rbi

Bouchee peaked in his rookie 1957 season, batting .293 with 17 HR and 76 RBI. The husky lefthanded hitter was a Brave-killer, hitting 11 of his first 41 homers against Milwaukee. In 1958, illness kept him out until July. /(AL)

Lou Boudreau — 1917- . SS 1938-52 **Indians**, Red Sox 1646 g, .295, 68 hr, 789 rbi. *1 WS, 6 g, .273, 3 rbi.*
   Manager 1942-50, 52-57, 60 **Indians**, Red Sox, A's, Cubs 1162-1224
☛ *Most Valuable Player—48. Led League—ba 44. All-Star—40-44, 47-48. Hall of Fame—1970 .*

A slick-fielding shortstop, steady hitter, and pennant-winning manager, Boudreau's career peaked in his fairy-tale 1948 season, but he was voted into the Hall of Fame for a career of distinguished play. He was captain of the basketball and baseball teams at the University of Illinois when he signed an agreement to join the Indians following graduation. Big Ten officials ruled him ineligible for amateur participation for the remainder of his college career. Free to work with the pros, he appeared in one ML game in 1938 as a pinch-hitter. He also played pro basketball with Hammond (IN) of the National Basketball League.

In 1939 he started with the Buffalo Bisons of the International League under manager Steve O'Neill. Originally a third baseman/catcher, Boudreau was moved to shortstop and teamed with second baseman Ray Mack. The young keystone combo gained attention for solid batting and adept fielding, particularly in turning double plays. Both were called up to Cleveland in the second half of the season.

In 1940, Boudreau's first full season, he was named to the AL All-Star team and hit .295 with 101 RBI. Boudreau played no part in the "Cleveland Crybabies" incident and the subsequent firing of manager Ossie Vitt. Cleveland struggled through a lackluster 1941 season, and in 1942 Boudreau was named player-manager. At 24, he was the youngest ever to manage a ML team from the outset of the season.

The innovative Boudreau oversaw the transformation of Bob Lemon from an infielder to a pitcher

Lou Boudreau

and created the "Williams Shift" and other tactics, but was unable to lift the Indians out of the middle of the pack. His shortstop play continued to win plaudits. He compensated for limited range by intelligent positioning and sure hands, and he led AL shortstops in fielding eight times. He won the 1944 AL batting title (.327) and led the league in doubles in 1941, 1944, and 1947.

When Bill Veeck purchased the Indians in 1946, he planned to replace Boudreau as manager. When word leaked out, a public clamor arose and Boudreau was retained. In 1948 Boudreau produced one of the greatest individual seasons ever. His team won the AL pennant and WS. He batted .355, hit 18 homers, batted in 106 runs, and scored 116. He was easily AL MVP. His play was inspirational. On August 8, he was sidelined with an ankle injury for a doubleheader with the Yankees before 73,484 Indian fans at Municipal Stadium. With the Tribe trailing 6–4, he limped to the plate and delivered a game-tying single. Cleveland swept the twin bill. The Indians and Red Sox ended the season tied for first. In the one-game playoff, Boudreau keyed the victory by going four-for-four with two homers.

Boudreau had little success in later seasons as a bench manager. He became a popular baseball broadcaster in Chicago. The greatest shortstop in Cleveland history, he saw his number 5 retired and the street bordering Municipal Stadium renamed Boudreau Boulevard. /(ME)

Jim Bouton (Bulldog) — 1939– . RHP 1962–70, 78 **Yankees**, Pilots, Astros, Braves 1239 ip, 62–63, 3.57. *2 WS, 24 ip, 2–1, 1.48*
☛ *All-Star—63.*

Bouton was a good pitcher before arm trouble deprived him of his fastball, but the personable nonconformist is best remembered for his book. *Ball Four*, a combination of his diary of the 1969 season (split between the expansion Pilots and the Astros) and his recollections of his Yankee career, broke baseball taboos by revealing the personal lives of his teammates past and present. Sometimes less-than-admirable but usually amusing details were included. Until then, the whole of baseball journalism had protected the public from such supposedly shocking knowledge as the drinking habits of Mickey Mantle and his Yankee buddies, the use of "pep pills," and the womanizing of most ballplayers on road trips. Commissioner Bowie Kuhn called it "detrimental to baseball."

Bouton first gained notice as an integral member of the Yankee staff in the final three seasons (1962–64) of the four-decade New York dynasty. His style was energetic, with his cap often flying off as he hurled both the ball and his body toward the plate. He was 7–7 as a rookie, then had an All-Star season in 1963. He was 21–7 with a 2.53 ERA and placed among the league leaders in most categories: second in winning percentage, shutouts (6), and fewest hits per nine innings (6.89), tied for second in wins, and fourth in ERA. He took a tough loss in Game Three of the World Series, opposing the Dodgers' Don Drysdale. Bouton surrendered the lone run of the game on a first-inning walk, a wild pitch, and a single; he tied a WS record with two wild pitches in the game.

Bouton was solid again in 1964, going 18–13 with a 3.02 ERA and leading the AL in starts. He had a fine World Series, winning Game Three 2–1 on a complete-game six-hitter (St. Louis's run was unearned) and also capturing Game Six, which was a 1–1 tie through six innings, by the score of 8–3.

But the Yankee dynasty and Bouton's career both came crashing down in 1965. He blew out his arm and the New York offense failed. He doggedly pitched through pain for two seasons, going 4–15, 4.82 in '65 and 3–8, 2.69 in 1966, the year the Yankees fell to last place.

Bouton spent most of the rest of his career in the bullpen, and began to throw a knuckleball in 1968. He retired after the 1970 season and spent some time as a TV sports reporter in New York. A successful minor league comeback in 1975 didn't lead to any offers, but he tried again in 1977; it was at this point that he said, "This winter I'm working out every day, throwing at a wall. I'm 11–0 against the wall." He was still unpopular among his ML peers, but he made it back with the Braves (owned by anti-establishment Ted Turner) in 1978 and went 1–3 in five starts. After finally calling it a career, he wrote about his comeback in an update of his first book called *Ball Five*. Since his retirement, he has gone into various baseball-related businesses and was one of the inventors of "Big League Chew," bubblegum shredded to resemble tobacco. /(SH)

Larry Bowa — 1945– . SS 1970–85 **Phillies**, Cubs, Mets 2247 g, .260, 99 hr, 525 rbi. *5 LCS, 21 g, .234, 3 rbi. 1 WS, 6 g, .375, 2 rbi.*
Manager 1987–88 **Padres** 81–127, .389
☛ *All-Star—74–76, 78–79. Gold Glove—72, 78.*

Fast feet, a strong arm, soft hands, a quick temper, and unlimited determination characterized Bowa's years as an outstanding ML shortstop. Often at odds with teammates, managers, and members of the media, Bowa never let distractions influence his play in the field. When he finished his playing career in 1985, he held the NL record for games played at shortstop (2,222), years leading NL shortstops in fielding (6), and for fewest errors in a season of 150 or more games (9). He also holds the ML record for highest fielding percentage for a career (.980) and for a season of over 100 games (.991).

A powerless switch-hitter early in his career, he developed into a tough out, hitting .280 or better four times, with a high of .305 in 1975, and seldom struck out. He was always a good basestealer, finishing with 318 for his career. With Bowa at

Larry Bowa

short, the Phillies won division titles from 1976 to 1978 and the world championship in 1980.

Bowa was named manager of the Padres before the 1987 season, but his aggressive and often angry style was ineffective, and he was fired after leading San Diego to a 16–30 start in 1988. /(AL)

Sam Bowens — 1939– . OF 1963–69 **Orioles**, Senators 479 g, .223, 45 hr, 143 rbi

Bowens hit 22 of his 45 homers in 1964, his first full season, tying an Oriole rookie HR record since surpassed by Cal Ripken, Jr. He was noted for his slow and easy lifestyle; when the Senators sent him to Buffalo in 1969, Sam took 13 days to report. /(RTM)

Frank Bowerman (Mike) — 1868–1948. C-1B 1895–1909 Baltimore (NL), Pirates, **Giants**, Braves 1045 g, .251, 13 hr, 392 rbi.
  Manager 1909 **Braves** 23–55, .295

Although overshadowed by Wilbert Robinson and Boileryard Clarke at Baltimore, and by Roger Bresnahan in New York, dour Frank was a capable backstop and the first to catch young Christy Math-

ewson. He also played 132 games at first, and a few at every other position, including one inning of pitching. Sent to Boston in the 1907 trade for Fred Tenney, he spent half a season managing the Doves. /(ADS)

Bob Bowman [Robert Leroy] — 1931– . OF 1955–59 **Phillies** 256 g, .249, 17 hr, 54 rbi

Husky and handsome, Bowman looked like a star, but his only real asset was a strong throwing arm. His hitting never measured up, and before leaving the Phillies he briefly tried pitching. /(AL)

Bob Bowman [Robert James] — 1910–1972. RHP 1939–42 **Cardinals**, Giants, Cubs 365 ip, 26–17, 3.82

As a Cardinal rookie in 1939, Bowman had a 13–5 record (including 7 relief wins) and tied for the NL lead in saves (9). Never effective after that, he is remembered for his near-fatal beaning of former teammate Joe Medwick after the two had argued in a hotel elevator before a game. /(JK)

Joe Bowman — 1910– . LHP 1932, 34–41, 44–45 A's, Giants, Phillies, **Pirates**, Red Sox, Reds 1466 ip, 77–96, 4.40

The 6'1" 190-lb Bowman was one of two 20-game losers with the last-place 1936 Phillies, and 33–38 in five years with stronger Pirate teams. After a sore arm and a sojourn in the minors, he bounced back with a 12–8 season for the wartime Red Sox. Often used as a pinch hitter, he twice batted over .300. /(ME)

Roger Bowman — 1927– . LHP 1949, 51–53, 55 Giants, **Pirates** 118 ip, 2–11, 5.81

A bright prospect in the Giants' system, a 1952 arm injury ruined the hard-throwing lefty's chances. He had a distinctive follow-through which left him vulnerable to ground balls up the middle. In 1954 he pitched a seven-inning perfect game for Hollywood (Pacific Coast League) on the last day of the season to clinch a tie for the pennant. /(DB)

Ted Bowsfield — 1936– . LHP 1958–64 Red Sox, Indians, **Angels**, A's 662 ip, 37–39, 4.35

In 1958, this Canadian had four wins, three against the Yankees. Casey Stengel called him, "that fella that throws them ground balls." Bowsfield won 11 games for the expansion Angels. /(RTM)

Bob Boyd (The Rope) — 1926– . 1B 1951, 53–54, 56–61 White Sox, **Orioles**, A's, Braves 693 g, .293, 19 hr, 175 rbi

Nicknamed "Rope" for his line-drive hitting, Boyd was the first Oriole regular to bat over .300 with .318 in 1957 and .309 the next year. Despite his high BA, he lacked the home run punch expected from a first baseman and was primarily a pinch hitter in his last seasons. /(RTM)

Oil Can Boyd [Dennis Ray] — 1959- . RHP 1982- **Red Sox** 1017 ip, 60–56, 4.16. *1 LCS, 14 ip, 1–1, 4.61. 1 WS, 7 ip, 0–1, 7.71*

One of 14 children of Negro Leaguer Willie James Boyd, the flamboyant, moody, and high-strung Oil Can is one of baseball's underachievers, plagued by a hot temper and persistent shoulder problems. Boyd emerged as one of the AL's top starters in 1985, pitching 272.1 innings despite an emaciated-looking 6'2" 160-lb frame, fanning 12 batters in a game twice, and winning 15 games. At the same time, he became disliked around the league for his cocky demeanor and animated fist-pumping and finger-wagging on the mound. In 1986 Boyd had 11 wins by mid-July, but flew into a rage when he was left off the All-Star squad and was suspended by the Red Sox before checking into a hospital with emotional problems. He returned in August to add five more wins during Boston's pennant run, but a recurring blood clot in his right shoulder forced him onto the DL five times from 1987 to 1989 and has threatened to end his career. His nickname comes from his Mississippi hometown, where beer is called oil. /(SCL)

Clete Boyer — 1937- . 3B-SS 1955–57, 59–71 A's, **Yankees**, Braves 1725 g, .242, 162 hr, 654 rbi. *1 LCS, 3 g, .111, 3 rbi. 5 WS, 27 g, .233, 2 hr, 11 rbi*
☛ *Gold Glove—69.*

One of three Boyer brothers to reach the majors, Clete ranked as a top AL defensive third baseman during his eight years with the Yankees, overshadowed only by Baltimore's Brooks Robinson. In the 1962 World Series, he batted .318 against the Giants, including a home run in the opening game. When he homered in the seventh game of the 1964 WS two innings after his brother Ken had homered for the Cardinals, it marked the only time that brothers had connected for home runs in the same WS game. He holds the WS record for most career assists by a third baseman (66).

Traded to the Braves after the 1966 season, he enjoyed his best offensive year in 1967 with 26 homers and 96 RBI. He led NL third basemen in fielding in 1967 and 1969.

On August 31, 1969, as he approached the plate locked in a 1-for-17 batting slump, he fell "victim" to Morganna, a buxom blonde who'd earned notoriety by dashing on the field and kissing ballplayers. After the kiss, Clete got an RBI-single, two more hits in the game, and racked up eight hits in his next 15 at-bats.

After his release by the Braves in 1971, he played for Hawaii in the Pacific Coast League, where he became the first American professional to be traded to a Japanese league when he was dealt to the Tayio Whales for John Werhas.

Boyer coached for the A's and Yankees in the 1980s, often under his old teammate Billy Martin. /(RTM)

Cloyd Boyer (Junior) — 1927- . RHP 1949–52, 55 **Cardinals**, A's 396 ip, 20–23, 4.73

The older brother of Ken and Clete, Cloyd had less success as a pitcher than his siblings did at third base. He achieved consistency, however, by compiling winning percentages of exactly .500 in three different seasons. /(FK)

Ken Boyer — 1931–1982. 3B 1955–69 **Cardinals**, Giants, White Sox, Dodgers 2034 g, .287, 282 hr, 1141 rbi. *1 WS, 7 g, .222, 2 hr, 6 rbi.*
*Manager 1978–80 **Cardinals** 166–191, .465*
☛ *Most Valuable Player—64. Led League—rbi 64. Gold Glove—58–61, 63.*

This quiet but dominant All-Star third baseman was a splendid fielder and consistently productive and clutch hitter. Signed as a pitcher by the Cardinals for $6,000, his poor pitching and strong hitting prompted his move to third base. He played brilliantly there for most of his 11 years in St. Louis. He won five Gold Gloves and led third basemen in double plays a record-tying five times. In eight different seasons, he hit over 20 homers, and combined with brother Clete for 444 HR. (Only the Aarons and DiMaggios hit more homers than the Boyers.) Ken's 255 as a Cardinal put him second only to Stan Musial.

After solid rookie and sophomore years, to Boyer's dismay he was sent to centerfield for most of the 1957 season, and GM Frank Lane criticized the soft-spoken Cardinal as an "unaggressive player." The arrival of Curt Flood in 1958 allowed Boyer to return to third base. It was during Solly Hemus's tenure as Cardinal manager that Boyer was named team captain. Hemus said, "Boyer is the guy everybody walks up to in the clubhouse and talks to." He led by example and through subtle prodding.

In 1959, Boyer went on a 29-game hitting streak,

Ken Boyer, running

the longest in the majors since Stan Musial's 30-game string in 1950. In 1960 and '61, he led the Cardinals in batting, HR, and RBI, hitting a career-high 32 homers in 1960. He twice hit for the cycle, once in 1961, and again in 1964. His 1964 MVP season (.295, 24 HR, 119 RBI) was climaxed by his clutch performance in the World Series against the Yankees. In Game Four, he stroked a grand slam off Al Downing to give the Cardinals a 4–3 win, and his seventh-inning shot in Game Seven off Steve Hamilton catapulted the Cardinals to a 7–5 win and the world championship.

Boyer slumped in 1965 and was traded to the Mets for third baseman Charlie Smith and pitcher Al Jackson. His glittering career ended four years later with the Dodgers. He was a Cardinal coach in 1971–72, and took over as manager early in 1978. In 1979, he led the Redbirds to a third-place finish, but after winning only 18 of 51 in 1980, he was replaced by Whitey Herzog. Boyer died of lung cancer in 1982, and his uniform number 14 was retired by the Cardinals in 1984. /(RTM)

Buzz Boyle [Ralph] — 1908–1978. OF 1929–30, 33–35 Braves, **Dodgers** 366 g, .290, 12 hr, 125 rbi

The speedy rightfielder led NL outfielders in assists (20) in 1934 when he hit .305 for the Dodgers. His older brother Jim caught one game for the Giants in 1926. /(TG)

Gene Brabender — 1941– . RHP 1966–70 **Orioles,** Pilots/Brewers 621 ip, 35–43, 4.25

This mighty 6′5″ 225-lb hurler would playfully bend the spikes used to fasten the tarpaulin. His busiest year was 1969, when he went 13–14 for the Pilots. Used in relief by the World Champion 1966 Orioles, the bespectacled Brabender was 4–3. /(RTM)

William G. Brabham — 1875–1947. *Executive.*

A lawyer from the University of North Carolina, Brabham was president of four different minor leagues at one time. In 1932, when the minors formed their own National Association, he was elected president and given powers over the minor leagues similar to those Judge Landis held for the majors. /(NLM)

Gib Brack (Gibby) — 1908–1960. OF 1937–39 Dodgers, **Phillies** 315 g, .279, 16 hr, 113 rbi

As a rookie outfielder with the Brooklyn Dodgers in 1937, Brack was among the top five NL hitters through May, but he slid back to mediocrity for the rest of his brief career. /(AL)

Buddy Bradford [Charles William] — 1944– . OF 1966–76 **White Sox,** Indians, Reds, Cardinals 697 g, .226, 52 hr, 175 rbi

Bradford provided speed, power, and defense, mostly as a fourth outfielder. On April 25, 1969, he became only the fourth White Sox player to hit a home run over the Comiskey Park roof, pounding one off the Twins' Tom Hall. Bradford hit a career-high 11 HR that season, during the first of his three stints with the White Sox. /(RL)

Larry Bradford — 1951– . LHP 1977, 79–81 **Braves** 104 ip, 6–4, 2.51

Returning from arm trouble, Bradford had an 0.95 ERA in 21 relief appearances in 1979. On his way to a 2.45 ERA in 56 appearances (with 4 saves) in 1980, he held opponents to 1.08 in his home park at

Atlanta, one of the best hitters' parks in the NL. /(MC)

Bill Bradley — 1878–1954. 3B 1899–1910, 14–15 Cubs, **Indians,** Brooklyn (FL), Kansas City (FL) 1461 g, .271, 33 hr, 552 rbi.
   Manager 1914 **Brooklyn (FL)** 77–77, .500

Until he was injured in 1906, Bill Bradley was the greatest third baseman in the short history of the American League. In his first season as a regular, with the Cubs in 1900, the 22-year-old hit .282, but he showed a bit of what was to come by leading NL third basemen in total chances per game. When the AL declared itself a major league in 1901, Bradley jumped to his hometown Cleveland Blues (later the Indians). In the first seven years of the league, he led

Bill Bradley with Brooklyn of the Federal League

its third basemen in at least one fielding category every year except his injury-shortened season of 1906, and his .955 fielding average in 1904 set an AL record that stood for ten years. All told, he led AL third basemen four times in fielding, three times in double plays, twice in putouts, and once each in assists and errors. His AL career 3B marks in games, putouts, assists, double plays, total chances, and errors all stood until Frank "Home Run" Baker broke them.

But what also helped place Bradley above such contemporaries as Hall of Famer Jimmy Collins was his potent bat. In the first four years of the league, Bradley was consistently among the league's offensive leaders. His 29-game hitting streak in 1902 set an AL record that Ty Cobb broke in 1911. Bradley's streak helped him to his best season offensively, as he reached career highs in BA (.340, sixth in the AL), runs (104, fourth), doubles (39, tied for third), and HR (11, tied for second). On July 28, 1903 he hit three triples in a game, tying a still-standing AL record, and he hit for the cycle that September 24.

His hitting declined starting in 1905, and after 1907 his fielding slipped a bit; he hit .186 in 1909 and .196 in 1910, which cut down on his playing time. Managing the Brooklyn franchise in the Federal League in 1914, he hit .500 using himself as pinch hitter (3-for-6). The following season, 37 years old, he played 66 games for the FL's Kansas City team despite hitting .187. /(WOR)

George Bradley (Grin) — 1852–1931. RHP-3B-OF-SS 1875–1877, 79–84, 86, 88 St. Louis (NA) Cardinals, Cubs, Troy (NL), Providence (NL), **Cleveland (NL)**, Philadelphia (AA), Cincinnati (UA), Baltimore (AA) *NA*: 61 g, .268; 33–26; *ML*: 507 g, .228, 3 hr, 110 rbi; 2404 ip, 138–127, 2.50. 20 wins: 76, 84
☛ *Led League—era 76.*

On July 15, 1876, during the NL's first season, Bradley pitched the league's first no-hitter, defeating Hartford 2–0. That year, the perpetually grinning righthander pitched every one of St. Louis's 64 games and led them to a second-place finish with 45 wins. His 16 shutouts set a ML record tied only by Grover Alexander 40 years later. Brought to Chicago the next season to take over the pitching for Al Spalding, he was far less effective, and for the rest of his career played at third base as often as he pitched. /(FIC)

Phil Bradley — 1959– . OF 1983– **Mariners**, Phillies, Orioles 905 g, .290, 74 hr, 345 rbi

After an unsuccessful 1988 season with the Phillies distinguished only by his league-leading 16 HBP,

Bradley returned to the AL and became a key part of the resurgent 1989 Orioles. The former University of Missouri quarterback began his career with the Mariners. He hit 26 homers for them in 1985 but never hit more than 14 in any subsequent season, and he settled into his role as a hustling leadoff hitter with good extra-base-hit power and base-stealing ability. Despite hitting poorly at the start of most seasons and striking out frequently, Bradley batted at least .297 in each of his four full seasons with Seattle and is the only player to have a .300 batting average for his career as a Mariner. His complaints about the Mariners, their ballpark, and their fans led to his trade to Philadelphia. At the time of his departure, he held the Mariner season records for batting average, hits, total bases, and on-base percentage, and was tied for season team records for hits, consecutive hits, triples, and runs in a game. He was also the Mariners' career leader in triples and was second in career stolen bases. /(TF)

Scott Bradley — 1960– . C-3B-1B 1984– Yankees, White Sox, **Mariners** 413 g, .271, 17 hr, 144 rbi

Bradley had a finger broken in a home-plate collision in his first major league start as a catcher for the Yankees. He was traded to the White Sox and, after appearing in only nine games for Chicago, to the Mariners for Ivan Calderon. In his first season with Seattle, the hustling Bradley was the Mariners' top pinch hitter and the most difficult batter in the American League to strike out. Displaced by Dave Valle as the regular catcher, Bradley finished the 1980s as a backup catcher and designated hitter. /(TF)

Tom Bradley — 1947– . RHP 1969–75 Angels, **White Sox**, Giants 1017 ip, 55–61, 3.72

Behind Bradley's horn-rimmed glasses lurked an intellectual with a degree in Latin from the University of Maryland. The hard thrower fanned over 200 batters and won 15 games in each of his two seasons with the White Sox (1971 and 1972). /(RL)

Bobby Bragan — 1917– . SS-C 1940–44, 47–48 **Phillies**, Dodgers 597 g, .240, 15 hr, 172 rbi. *1 WS, 1 g, 1.000, 1 rbi.*
 Manager 1956–58, 63–66 Pirates, Indians, **Braves** 443–478, .481

Bragan served in almost every capacity in his lengthy baseball career. He was the Phillies' regular shortstop his first three years in the major leagues, then became a catcher. A minor-league manager for seven years, he attracted attention as a major-league skipper for wrangling with umpires. He made every sports section when, one day, he walked on the field sipping a soft drink through a straw, discussing the play in question with the umpires and offering each a taste of his drink. A scout and major-league coach, Bragan was also, for many years, president of the Texas League. /(AL)

Glenn Braggs — 1962– . OF 1986- **Brewers** 406 g, .256, 42 hr, 203 rbi

A swift, muscular outfielder, Braggs capped a stellar minor league career by hitting .360 in the Pacific Coast League in 1986 to win *Baseball America*'s Triple-A Player of the Year honors. He won Milwaukee's right field job in 1987 and was leading the Brewers with 42 RBI in July 1988 when a shoulder nerve problem ended his season. In 1989 he maintained the same level of play while adding high-percentage basestealing to his repetoire. /(JCA)

Dave Brain — 1879–1959. 3B-SS 1901, 03–08 White Sox, **Cardinals**, Pirates, Braves, Reds, Giants. 679 g, .252, 27 hr, 303 rbi

An unreliable fielder with good speed on the basepaths, the English-born Brain had power at the plate but no consistency. He cracked 15 triples for the Cardinals in 1903 and led the NL with 10 home runs in 1907 for the Braves. /(FJO)

Asa Brainard (Count) — 1841–1888. RHP-2B Washington (NA), Middletown (NA), **Lord Baltimores (NA)** 108 g, .239; 84 g, 24–56

In 1869 Brainard was brought to Cincinnati by Manager Harry Wright to pitch for the Cincinnati Red Stockings, baseball's first all-professional team. Paid $1,100 for his efforts, he was reportedly a "scientific" pitcher who succeeded by changing speeds with good control. The Red Stockings toured the country, taking on all challenges in 1869 and not losing a game until the following year. After the formation of the National Association in 1871, Brainard pitched for the Washington Olympians and then the Lord Baltimores but was unable to recapture the success of his Red Stocking days. In 1874, his final season, he was 5–24. When he died in 1888, he was the first of the old Red Stockings to pass on. /(BC)

Erv Brame — 1901–1949. RHP 1928–32 **Pirates** 791 ip, 52–37, 4.76

Brame was Pittsburgh's workhorse in 1929 and 1930, leading the club in complete games both years and tying for the NL high (22) in '30. Often used as a pinch-hitter, he hit .306 with eight homers during his career. /(ME)

Ralph Branca — 1926– . RHP 1944–54, 56 **Dodgers**, Tigers, Yankees 1484 ip, 88–68, 3.79. *2 WS, 17 ip, 1–2, 6.35*
☛ *All-Star—47–49.*

The fact that he threw the pitch Bobby Thomson hit for "the shot heard round the world" to win the 1951 playoff has obscured much of the rest of Branca's career. The one-time N.Y.U. basketball player was the starter and loser of the first two NL playoff games in 1946 and 1951. In 1947, he won 21 games for the Dodgers at age 21. In the WS that year, he won the Sixth Game, saved by Al Gionfriddo's famous catch of DiMaggio's drive. Before the '51 playoffs, Branca had worn number 13 and good-naturedly posed with black cats. Afterward, he changed his number, but not his luck. An off-season pelvis injury all but ended his career and he won only twelve more games over the next five years. He later became a broadcaster for the Mets. /(TG)

Ron Brand — 1940– . C-SS 1963, 65–71 Pirates, **Astros**, Expos 568 g, .239, 3 hr, 106 rbi

This 5'8" 175-lb catcher had a shotgun arm, and also played outfield, shortstop, third base, and second base. Brand collected Houston's first hit in the Astrodome, a triple off the Yankees' Mel Stottlemyre in an exhibition game. /(RTM)

Darrell Brandon (Bucky) — 1940– . RHP 1966–69, 71–73 Red Sox, Pilots, Twins, **Phillies** 590 ip, 28–37, 4.04

Brandon started 19 games for the AL champion 1967 Red Sox, but an arm injury shelved him for the World Series. He came back from the minors in 1971 for three moderately successful years in the Phillies' bullpen. /(PB)

Edgar G. Brands — 1888–1970. *Writer.*

A graduate of the U. of Illinois, Brands worked for newspapers in Illinois and Montana before becoming managing editor of Collyer Publishing Co., specialists in sports publications. In 1930, he joined *The Sporting News*, writing features, editorials, and a regular column, "Between Innings," and serving as editor until he retired in 1954. /(NLM)

Dr. William E. Brandt — Unk.–1963. *Writer.*

A practicing osteopathic physician, Dr. Brandt succeeded Ford Frick as manager of the NL Service Bureau and held the job for ten years until he resigned to do a daily radio show, "The Inside of

Sports." A graduate of Muhlenberg College, he began with the Philadelphia *Record* in 1912, and worked for the *Bulletin* and *Ledger* in that city and the *New York Times* before going to work for the NL. He wrote for several magazines and the *Encyclopaedia Britannica*. A 1921 graduate of Philadelphia College of Osteopathy, he was president of the school from 1953 to 1958. /(NLM)

Ed Brandt — 1905-1944. LHP 1928-38 **Braves**, Dodgers, Pirates 2268 ip, 121-146, 3.86

The forkballer led the NL in losses (21) as a rookie and was 21-45 in his first three seasons with the weak Braves. But he started 1931 with eight straight wins on his way to an 18-10 mark, and followed with several more strong seasons. He often pinch hit, and he led all pitchers in hitting with a .309 BA in 1933. /(ME)

Jackie Brandt — 1934- . OF 1956, 58-67 Cardinals, Giants, **Orioles**, Phillies, Astros 1221 g, .262, 112 hr, 485 rbi
☛ *All-Star—61.*

Some historians link the derivation of the baseball term "flake" to this nail-biting outfielder, since a teammate once commented that "things seem to flake off his mind and disappear." Brandt split his outstanding rookie season with the Cards and Giants, hitting a career-high .298 while leading the NL in fielding (.990). 1958 was spent in the military. He won a Gold Glove for his play in left field with San Francisco in 1959. /(RTM)

Kitty Bransfield [William Edward] — 1875-1947. 1B 1898, 1901-11 Braves, Pirates, **Phillies**, Cubs 1330 g, .270, 14 hr, 637 rbi. *1 WS, 8 g, .200, 1 rbi*

The slick-fielding Bransfield joined the Pirates in 1901 and was the regular first baseman on three straight pennant winners. Although he twice edged his BA over .300 (1902 and '08), his first season was the best overall performance of his career (.295, 92 runs, 91 RBI, 17 triples). He led NL first basemen in fielding in 1909 while with the Phillies. /(ME)

Mickey Brantley — 1961- . OF 1986- **Mariners** 302 g, .259, 32 hr, 125 rbi

Brantley hit .302 in 1987 while leading the Mariners with a club rookie-record 12-game hitting streak and tying team records with five hits and three home runs in one game against Cleveland September 14. Over the first half of the 1988 season, Brantley was among club leaders in hits and homers while playing centerfield for the Mariners. Brantley was world

heavyweight boxing champion Mike Tyson's "Big Brother" when Tyson was a youth in Catskill, New York. /(TF)

Steve Braun — 1948- . OF-3B-DH 1971-84 **Twins**, Mariners, Royals, Blue Jays, Cardinals 1361 g, .272, 51 hr, 382 rbi

After jumping to the Twins from Class A, Braun spent six seasons in Minnesota playing every infield and outfield position while batting .284. In August of 1978, he tied a Royal record by reaching base eleven consecutive times. Braun developed into a top pinch hitter with the Royals and Cardinals, retiring with 113 pinch hits, sixth on the all-time list. In 1986, Braun became a coach in the Cardinal farm system. /(FJO)

Braves Field Boston Braves 1915-52. LF-337, CF-370, RF-319

Braves Field was baseball's largest park at the time it opened, August 18, 1915, when over 40,000 fans jammed the single-decked grandstand to see the Braves defeat St. Louis 3-1 on a spacious field that was 402' down the left-field line and 520' to center. Those distances were shortened over the years, but the left-field fence remained 25' high, and a 10' wall in right guarded the "Jury Box," a small bleacher section with extremely boisterous fans. Home to the Braves until their move to Milwaukee, the park also hosted the Red Sox' home WS games in 1915 and 1916 and their Sunday games from 1929 to 1932, and was the scene of ML baseball's longest game, a 26-inning tie between the Dodgers and Braves on May 1, 1920. It is now the site of Boston University's Nickerson Field, and the seats along the right field foul line and the Gaffney Street entrance still stand. /(SCL)

Garland Braxton — 1900-1966. LHP 1921-22, 25-31, 33 Braves, Yankees, **Senators**, White Sox, Browns 938 ip, 50-53, 4.13
☛ *Led League—era 28.*

The lefthanded screwballer led the AL in relief appearances (56) and tied for the lead in saves (13) with the Senators in 1927. The next year, as a regular starter, he topped the league in ERA (2.51). A scratch golfer, he won senior titles in retirement. /(JK)

Al Brazle (Cotton, Ol' Boots and Saddles) —
1913–1973. LHP 1943, 46–54 **Cardinals**
1377 ip, 97–64, 3.31. *2 WS, 14 ip, 0–2, 4.50*

The side-arming Brazle spent eight years in the
minors before landing a job with the Cardinals in
1943 at age 28. In Game Three of the '43 World
Series, the sinkerballing rookie held a 2–1 lead over
the Yankees until the eighth, when New York
exploded for five runs. Exclusively a reliever his last
few years, Brazle led the NL in saves in 1952 and
'53./(RTM)

Sam Breadon — 1876–1949. *Executive.*

Breadon's first business venture was vending popcorn at the 1904 St. Louis World's Fair. He owned
an automobile agency until the 1930s. As a favor to
a friend, he invested $200 in the Cardinals, and 27
years later he controlled the team. Under Breadon,
the Cards won nine pennants and six WS. He
succeeded Branch Rickey as Cardinals president in
1920, but Rickey stayed on as GM. They began the
first farm system. At its peak, they owned 16 teams
outright and had 12 working agreements./(NLM)

Sid Bream — 1960– . 1B 1983– Dodgers, **Pirates**
562 g, .262, 45 hr, 240 rbi

The lanky, lefthanded first baseman came to Pittsburgh in the 1985 Bill Madlock deal. A career .329
hitter in the minors, Bream set a NL record with
166 assists at first base in 1986, his first full season,
and finished third in the league in doubles./(ME)

Harry Brecheen (The Cat) — 1914– . LHP 1940,
43–53 **Cardinals**, Browns 1908 ip, 132–92, 2.92. 20 wins:
48 *3 WS, 33 ip, 4–1, 0.83*
☛ *Led League—era 48. Led League—k 48. All-
Star—47–48.*

Brecheen became the first lefthander to record three
wins in a World Series, doing so against the Red Sox
in 1946. The screwballer blanked Boston 3–0 in
Game Two on a four-hitter. In addition, he singled
in the Cardinals' first run, and his sacrifice bunt set
up his team's two other runs. In Game Six, "The
Cat," named for his expert fielding and cat-like
movements, once again beat Mickey Harris. With
one day's rest, he pitched two innings of relief in
Game Seven to pick up his third win. He had a 0.45
ERA in the Series, and his lifetime WS ERA of 0.83
is the best ever.
  Brecheen's finest season came in 1948 when he
led the NL in winning percentage (.741, 20–7), ERA
(2.24), strikeouts (149), and shutouts (7). He was

Harry Brecheen

one of 61 players to play for both the Cardinals and
Browns./(RTM)

Hal Breeden — 1944– . 1B 1971–75 Cubs, **Expos**
273 g, .243, 21 hr, 76 rbi

The younger brother of former ML catcher Danny
Breeden, Hal had good power numbers in the
minors and the Cubs traded Hoyt Wilhelm to get
him from Atlanta. He was only used as a platoon
player and pinch hitter in the ML. With the Expos
in 1973, his most active season, he batted 258 times
and had 15 homers. On July 13 that year he became
only the second player to hit pinch homers in both
games of a doubleheader. From 1976 to 1978 he
played for the Nippon Ham Fighters of Japan's
Pacific League./(MC)

Marv Breeding — 1934– . 2B 1960–63 **Orioles**,
Senators, Dodgers 415 g, .250, 7 hr, 92 rbi

Breeding enjoyed a fine rookie season with Baltimore, batting a career-high .267. Though he led the
Pacific Coast League in stolen bases (27) in 1959

with Vancouver, he had only 19 in his ML career. /(RTM)

Fred Breining — 1955– . RHP 1980–84 **Giants**, Expos 437 ip, 27–20, 3.33

A throw-in to the Giants in the deal that sent Bill Madlock to the Pirates, Breining earned a spot in the San Francisco bullpen with a 2.54 ERA in 1981. He became a starter late the next season and finished 11–6. After an 11–12 year in '83, he was traded to the Expos for Al Oliver but reported with a career-ending rotator cuff injury. The Giants sent Andy McGaffigan to Montreal as a replacement. /(MC)

Ted Breitenstein — 1869–1935. LHP-OF 1891–1901 St. Louis (AA), **Cardinals**, Reds 2964 ip, 166–170, 4.04; 447 g, .216, 4 hr, 126 rbi. 20 wins: 94, 97–98
☛ *Led League—era 93.*

The handsome native St. Louisan dazzled hometown fans by tossing a no-hitter again Louisville in his first major league start (October 4, 1891). Seven years later, he no-hit Pittsburgh. The 5'9" lefty paired with St. Louis-born catcher Heinie Peitz, forming what fans called "the Pretzel Battery." Breitenstein twice led the NL in starts and complete games, but was a 20-game loser five straight seasons (1892–96) with weak Browns teams. He also played 65 games in the outfield. /(FJO)

Nick Bremigan — 1945– . *Umpire* AL 1974–87 *4 LCS 1 WS, 2 ASU*

Considered one of the top rule interpreters, Bremigan has been a syndicated columnist and given clinics to American armed forces in Spain, England, and Germany. He was one of the umpires involved in the famous George Brett pine tar incident. /(RTM)

Bob Brenly — 1954– . C 1981– **Giants**, Blue Jays 871 g, .247, 91 hr, 333 rbi. *1 LCS, 6 g, .235, 1 hr, 2 rbi*
☛ *All-Star—84.*

Brenly was the Giants' starting catcher from 1984 to 1987, averaging 18 home runs per season and providing steady defense. The burly righthanded hitter was signed as a third baseman out of Ohio University (where he tied Mike Schmidt's single-season HR record), then switched to catcher in 1979, his fourth pro season. He continued to fill in at third or first base when necessary in the ML, and played 45 games at third in 1986.

Brenly won the Giants' starting catching job in 1984, hitting .291 with 20 HR and 80 RBI. He

would never hit better than .267 again but he remained a consistent power threat. In Game Four of the 1987 NLCS he homered off the Cardinals' Danny Cox.

On September 14, 1986 against the Braves, in the fourth inning, Brenly tied a ML record with four errors at third base, booting three grounders and throwing wildly once to allow four unearned runs. In the fifth inning he hit a solo home run, and in the seventh he added a two-run single to tie the score, 6–6. In the bottom of the ninth with two out and the count full, he homered to win the game.

Brenly was released by the Giants after hitting only .189 in 1988. The Blue Jays signed him but released him in mid-1989. Popular in San Francisco, he was signed for their stretch drive. /(SCL)

Ad Brennan [Addison Foster] — 1881–1962. LHP 1910–15, 18 **Phillies**, Chicago (FL), Senators, Indians 677 ip, 38–35, 3.11

Although the Kansan had two double-digit winning seasons with the Phillies before he jumped to the Federal League in 1914, he is most often remembered for decking Giant Manager John McGraw in a fistfight beneath the stands. /(JK)

Don Brennan — 1903–1953. RHP 1933–37 Yankees, **Reds**, Giants 397 ip, 21–12, 4.19. *1 WS, 3 ip, 0–0, 0.00*

Burly Don Brennan showed early promise with his fastball as a starter for the Yankees, but control problems prompted his release, and he spent the remainder of his career working primarily from the bullpen. /(FS)

Tom Brennan (The Gray Flamingo) — 1952– . RHP 1981–85 **Indians**, White Sox, Dodgers 219 ip, 9–10, 4.40

Brennan was the Indians' first pick in the June 1974 draft. He finally reached Cleveland in 1981 and lasted one-plus season as a long reliever given an occasional start. "The Gray Flamingo" had an unorthodox delivery, pausing while standing on one leg. /(JCA)

Roger Bresnahan (The Duke of Tralee) — 1879–1944. C-OF-RHP 1897, 1900–15 Senators, Cubs, Orioles, **Giants**, Cardinals 1430 g, .279, 26 hr, 530 rbi; 50 ip, 4–1, 3.93. *1 WS, 5 g, .313, 1 rbi.*
Manager 1909–12, 15 **Cardinals**, Cubs 348–432, .432
☛ *Hall of Fame—1945.*

Bresnahan was one of several players who became a close friend of John McGraw. With Christy Mathewson, another friend, it was an attraction of opposites. Roger could have been McGraw's twin:

Roger Bresnahan with the Giants

compact, pugnacious, fiercely concentrated on the game, and skilled in all the ways it takes to play it. Temperamental like his manager, he was an unabashed Irish brawler, tough on teammates who did less than their best, tough on opponents, toughest on umpires, whom he baited and bedeviled. He was frequently ejected, fined and suspended, gave headaches to League officials, and engaged in noisy confrontations with at least three club owners. He could play any position on the field.

Washington had him first as an 18-year-old pitcher who shut out the Browns, 3–0, on six hits in his major-league debut. His repertoire was dazzling. The papers credited him with "a speedy shoot, outcurve, inshoot, drop ball." Roger won three more games that season, but the Senators let him go the next spring when he insisted on more money than they would pay. The Cubs brought him up after two years in the high minors, played him for two innings, and lost him to McGraw's Orioles in 1901. Rapped hard in two outings, he was tried at second, third, the outfield, and when Wilbert Robinson was hurt, behind the plate. He played well wherever they put him, but catching was his forte.

When McGraw departed the American League for the Giants at mid-year, Bresnahan made the leap with him. The Giants had Jack Warner and Frank Bowerman as their catchers, so Roger became the centerfielder. The season was a romp. Despite his hefty build, he was fast and agile enough not only to cover the outfield expanse, but to bat leadoff. He played 116 games, got 142 hits and batted a handsome .350, his career high and a mere .005 behind Honus Wagner.

By 1905 Bresnahan was the Giants' first-string catcher. Some say Mathewson urged McGraw to make the move, although Mac had known Roger's capabilities for years and could have figured it for himself, particularly now that he had acquired Turkey Mike Donlin for the outfield. Roger had another good year, hitting .302 and catching 87 games. He caught all five Series games against the Athletics, which meant Matty's three shutouts, Joe McGinnity's one, and Joe's shutout loss to Chief Bender. He also hit a sparkling .313.

Perhaps his most notable contributions to the game were in protective equipment. In 1905, after being hospitalized for a head injury from a beaning, he experimented with a batting helmet manufactured by the A.J. Reach Company. It was like the leather football helmet of the period sliced vertically: one half for covering the left side of a righthanded batter's head, the other for the lefty hitter. Although beanballs were frequent, the idea did not find favor. Two years later he devised catcher's shin guards. The first ones, evidently modeled after a cricketer's leg pads, were large and bulky, with a knee flap that came up to the thigh. They were greeted with ridicule and protest, but soon caught on. By 1909 they had more utilitarian shape and size, and were in general use. About 1908 he improved the flimsy wire catcher's mask with leather-bound rolls of padding to absorb the shock of foul-tips.

In winter that year, McGraw traded his friend to St. Louis. Roger had caught 139 games during the season, but he was 29 and slowing down. McGraw could afford to let him go. He had the young Chief Meyers on deck and the Cardinals eager to make a deal. Long a lackluster club and a cellar-dweller for two years, its owners thought a manager like the fiery Duke of Tralee might energize the players. To get him they gave up three of their few talents: Red Murray, a first-rate outfielder, Bugs Raymond, an eccentric but effective pitcher, and an experienced backup catcher, Admiral Schlei, acquired from Cincinnati.

Manager Bresnahan acquired some good players

and got them above .500 and in fifth place by 1911. The Cardinals' owner, Mrs. Schuyler Britton, who had recently inherited the club on the death of her uncle, Stanley Robison, was pleased with the improvement and rewarded Roger with a five-year contract at $10,000 per year, plus a percentage of the profits, if any. During the disappointing sixth-place season of 1912, however, Mrs. Britton, like owners before and since, second-guessed her manager publicly. Roger blistered her ears with some choice dugout repartee and was fired forthwith. Roger demanded to be paid as manager and player for the remaining four years of his contract. The Cardinals, unable to clear waivers for a trade, finally sold him to the Cubs. He backstopped Jimmy Archer in 1913, managed Chicago to a fourth-place finish in 1915, all the while continuing his contract fight with the Cardinals. He finally won a $20,000 settlement. His playing career ended in 1916. He was owner-manager of his hometown Toledo Mud Hens through 1923, then coached the Giants (1925–28) and Tigers (1930–31). /(ADS)

Rube Bressler [Raymond Bloom] — 1894–1966. OF-1B-P 1914–32 Phillies, **Reds**, Dodgers, Cardinals 1305 g, .301, 32 hr, 586 rbi; 540 ip, 26–32, 3.40

Nicknamed Rube in the tradition of more successful lefthanded pitchers (Waddell, Marquard), Bressler became a righthanded-hitting outfielder/first baseman in mid-career. He gripped the bat with his hands apart (as did Ty Cobb), and slap-hit his way to a .301 lifetime BA. Although he played for two pennant winners (1914 A's and '19 Reds), he never appeared in a WS game. /(JK)

Ed Bressoud — 1932– . SS-2B-3B 1956–67 Giants, **Red Sox**, Mets, Cardinals 1186 g, .252, 94 hr, 365 rbi. *1 WS, 2 g, --*
☛ *All-Star—64.*

Bressoud was a dependable shortstop whose arrival in 1956 allowed the Giants to send Alvin Dark to the Cardinals in a deal for Red Schoendienst. He spent just two of his six Giant seasons as their regular SS, but was successful in three years with the Red Sox because he adapted his swing to Fenway's leftfield wall; he hit 20 HR in 1963. Made expendable by Rico Petrocelli's emergence in 1965, Bressoud concluded his career against the Red Sox as a Cardinal utility man in the 1967 World Series. /(PB)

George Brett — 1953– . 3B-1B 1973- **Royals** 2137 g, .310, 267 hr, 1311 rbi. *6 LCS, 27 g, .340, 9 hr, 19 rbi. 2 WS, 13 g, .373, 1 hr, 4 rbi*
☛ *Most Valuable Player—80. Led League—ba 76, 80. All-Star—76–88. Gold Glove—85.*

If a player ever had claim to the title "The Franchise," it would be George Brett in Kansas City. He came from a baseball family. Older brother Ken pitched 13 years in the majors while two other brothers played minor league ball. Yet his beginnings in professional baseball were modest. He batted .281 over three-plus seasons in the minors. He led the California League in errors at third base in his second pro season. He hit only .125 in his first major league call-up and hit but two home runs with 47 RBI in his first full season with Kansas City.

Royals' batting coach Charlie Lau worked with Brett on hitting to all fields on every type of pitch. Brett learned to adapt to what pitchers offered instead of waiting for fastballs. Hal McRae, acquired by the Royals the year Brett came up, taught him

George Brett

resolute baserunning. In his second full season Brett led the AL in hits and triples while batting .308.

Season after season Brett put up star-studded batting statistics. From 1975 to 1988 he batted above .300 ten times, drove in over 100 runs four times, and topped 100 runs scored four times. In 1979 Brett tallied 85 extra-base hits and became the sixth player in history with 20 or more doubles, triples, and home runs in the same season.

Brett flirted with a .400 batting mark in 1980 and finished at .390, the highest major league average since Ted Williams's .406 in 1941. His incredible season included a 37-game hitting streak and Player of the Year Awards from *TSN*, *Baseball Digest*, UPI, and the Associated Press. One wonders what might have been had Brett been healthy. He suffered through a bruised heel, tendinitis, and torn ligaments that summer. However, the highlight of his season was capturing the AL pennant. "I know I captured a lot of the media's attention this past season," Brett explained, "but the Royals have a team built on teamwork, not on individuals."

George put together numbers in 1985 that rivaled 1979 and 1980. He surpassed the century mark in RBI, runs, and walks while hitting .335 with a career-high 30 HR.

Brett proved more than a one-dimensional player by continually improving his defense and baserunning. The most productive player in Royals' history, he was rewarded with a lifetime contract. He was a terror in postseason play as well. His nine career home runs and .728 slugging average are LCS records, as is his single-series slugging average of 1.056 (1978).

Brett had to overcome numerous injuries during his career that kept him on the disabled list more than 32 weeks from 1978 to 1989. He moved to 1B in 1987, opening up third base for rookie phenom Kevin Seitzer. The transition proved a success as George was named first baseman on *TSN*'s 1988 AL All-Star and Silver Slugger Teams. At 35 he showed no signs of slowing down, with 42 doubles, 24 home runs, and a .306 average.

Brett holds Royals' team records for career games, hits, runs, doubles, triples, home runs, runs batted in, and batting and slugging average. George and his three brothers own and operate the Spokane, WA franchise in the Northwest League. /(FO)

Ken Brett — 1948- . LHP 1967, 69–81 Red Sox, Brewers, Phillies, **Pirates**, Yankees, White Sox, Angels, Twins, Dodgers, Royals 1526 ip, 83–85, 3.93. *2 LCS, 5 ip, 3.86 1 WS, 1 ip, 0.00*
☛ *All-Star—74.*

Although later overshadowed by younger brother George, in 1967 Ken became the youngest pitcher (19 years, one month) to pitch in a WS game. He went on to tie the modern record for playing with the most teams (10). A three-time 13-game winner, the clever lefty was the winning pitcher while representing the Pirates in the 1974 All-Star Game at Pittsburgh. A good hitter (.262), he set a record for pitchers in 1973 by homering in four straight starts with the Phillies. /(ME)

Marv Breuer (Baby Face) — 1914- . RHP 1939–43 **Yankees** 484 ip, 25–26, 4.03. *2 WS, 3 ip, 0.00*

Breuer earned his engineering degree from the Missouri School of Mines, a college without a baseball team. The youthful, soft-spoken right-hander failed to live up to Yankee expectations after starring for Newark in the minors. /(JK)

Chet Brewer — 1907- . RHP Negro Leagues 1925–48 Kansas City Monarchs, Washington Pilots, Chicago American Giants, Philadelphia Stars, New York Cubans, Cleveland Buckeyes, Tennessee Rats 81–39 (inc.)
☛ *All-Star—34, 37, 48.*

Brewer was one of a stable of Kansas City Monarch pitchers that included the legendary Satchel Paige and Bullet Joe Rogan. He defeated some of the best hurlers of his day, both black and white—Willie Foster, Slim Jones, Smokey Joe Williams, Bob Feller, and Paige. He had a lively fastball and a devastating overhand "drop ball," which was especially tough on lefthanded hitters. He also threw a legal emery ball.

In 1926, his first full season with the Monarchs, Brewer went 12–1 with eight complete games. His .842 winning percentage (16–3) led the league in 1929; that season, he pitched 31 consecutive scoreless innings against league competition. One of his greatest performances came under the lights in 1930 against the Homestead Grays' Smokey Joe Williams. Brewer struck out 19, including 10 in a row, only to lose 1–0 in 12 innings on a fluke hit by Chaney White. Brewer won 30 games that year. He won 16 straight games in 1934 and finished the season with 33 victories against league and non-league opponents. Pitching in Mexico in 1939, he threw two no-hitters.

Brewer was a Pittsburgh Pirates scout from 1957 to 1974 and later worked for the Major League Scouting Bureau. /(LL)

Jack Brewer (Buddy) — 1919- . RHP 1944-46 **Giants** 217 ip, 9-10, 4.36

Brewer joined the Giants after his discharge from the Navy in 1944 and was an effective starter in 1945 (8-6, 3.83), but lost his job when the remaining ML players returned from WWII in 1946. /(FS)

Jim Brewer — 1937-1987 . LHP 1960-76 Cubs, **Dodgers**, Angels 1039 ip, 69-65, 3.07. *3 WS, 3 ip, 2.70* ☛ *All-Star—73.*

With a tip from Warren Spahn, Brewer developed a screwball in 1964, and became one of the most successful relievers in the NL. He averaged better than 19 saves a season for the Dodgers in the years 1968-73, with a career-high 24 in 1970. In 1972 his ERA was 1.26, and he averaged an outstanding 4.69 hits per nine innings. Dodger manager Walter Alston said, "We've had a lot of great relief pitchers, but I've never seen one better than Brewer."

In 1960 as a Cub rookie, the even-tempered lefty was the victim in a much-publicized mound altercation. Cincinnati's Billy Martin accused Brewer of throwing at him, charged the mound, and punched Brewer, breaking his jaw.

Brewer died at the age of 50 in an auto accident. /(JCA)

Tom Brewer — 1931- . RHP 1954-61 **Red Sox** 1509 ip, 91-82, 4.00 ☛ *All-Star—56.*

The Red Sox' most effective righthanded starter during the 1950s, Brewer pitched for teams that finished in the middle of the pack. His best year was 1956, when he finished 19-9 and pitched two innings of the All-Star Game. Throughout his career, he was especially tough on the Indians and A's. /(PB)

Fred Brickell — 1906-1961. OF 1926-33 **Pirates**, Phillies 501 g, .281, 6 hr, 131 rbi. *1 WS, 2 g, .000*

The Kansan reached the majors at age 19 and hit .312 during four-plus years as a Pirates sub. His BA dipped when the Phillies gave the him a chance to play regularly. His son Fritzie played briefly in the majors. /(ME)

Jack Brickhouse — Unk.- . *Broadcaster.*

Brickhouse began his radio career at the age of 18 in Peoria, Illinois. In 1940 he became the first radio broadcaster for both Cubs and White Sox games. He became the WGN telecaster when the station began its baseball coverage in 1948. He also broadcast Chicago Bears football for 21 years. In 1983, Brickhouse was given the Ford Frick Award and a place on the Hall of Fame Broadcasters' Honor Roll. /(NLM)

Jim Brideweser — 1927- . SS-2B 1951-57 Yankees, **Orioles**, White Sox, Tigers 329 g, .252, 1 hr, 50 rbi

Signed off the USC campus by the Yankees, Brideweser was mostly a backup shortstop. His busiest year came in 1957, when he batted .268 for the Orioles. /(RTM)

Marshall Bridges (Sheriff) — 1931- . LHP 1959-65 Cardinals, Reds, **Yankees**, Senators 345 ip, 23-15, 3.75. *1 WS, 4 ip, 0-0, 4.91*

A hard-throwing southpaw reliever, Bridges surprised everyone with his stellar Yankee performance in 1962 (8-4, 18 saves). "The Sheriff" lost his winning momentum after he was shot during a barroom incident the following winter. /(GDW)

Rocky Bridges [Everett Lamar] — 1927- . SS-2B-3B 1951-61 Dodgers, **Reds**, Senators, Tigers, Indians, Cardinals, Angels 919 g, .247, 16 hr, 187 rbi ☛ *All-Star—58.*

The wisecracking Bridges fashioned a second career as an eminently quotable minor league manager. Always chewing a huge wad of tobacco, he was responsible for such wry gems as "Tommy Lasorda's curve had as much hang time as a Ray Guy punt" and "There are three things the average man thinks he can do better than anybody else: build a fire, run a hotel, and manage a baseball team."

Before starting his minor league managing career, Bridges was a versatile utility man. In two rare seasons in which he held down just one position, he led NL second basemen (1953) and AL shortstops (1957) in total chances per game, but he never hit enough to be an everyday player. /(JFC)

Tommy Bridges — 1906–1968. RHP 1930–43, 45–46 **Tigers** 2826 ip, 194–138, 3.57. 20 wins: 34–36
4 WS, 46 ip, 4–1, 3.52
☛ *Led League—w 36. Led League—k 35–36..*

Bridges's victory totals fell tantalizingly short of satisfying the demanding writers who elect players to baseball's Hall of Fame. He had won 192 when, in 1943, at 37, he was called to military service. He missed the soft pickings of wartime baseball in 1944 and rejoined the Tigers in 1945 to record a lone win. The next year, when baseball resumed with its

Tommy Bridges

younger stars, there was no room for the veteran who had helped the Tigers win four pennants. There were victories remaining in him, but they were gained in the Pacific Coast League where, at age 40, Bridges led the league with a 1.64 ERA.

The son of a country doctor, Bridges graduated from the University of Tennessee and was expected to follow in his father's footsteps. He chose baseball instead, and the only doctoring he did was intended to induce sharp, breaking curves. Bridges's frail appearance was deceptive. Though he had a blazing fastball, his curve was the wonder of the AL for over a decade. He once fanned 20 in a minor league game, and led the AL in strikeouts in 1935 and 1936.

In 1932 Bridges lost a bid for a perfect game in dramatic fashion that either proved the integrity of the game, or was just poor sportsmanship. Walter Johnson was the Washington manager, and his Senators trailed Detroit, 13–0, with two out in the ninth. Young Bridges was doing something Johnson had never done: pitch a perfect game. The Washington pitcher, Bobby Burke, was due up. Instead, Johnson sent gifted pinch hitter Dave Harris to bat. Harris led the AL that season with 14 pinch hits. A notoriously good curveball hitter, Harris out-dueled Bridges, stroking a clean single to left to break up the perfect game. The next batter was a routine out, and Washington still lost by 13 runs.

Bridges won over 20 games for three straight seasons (1934–36) and led the AL with 23 victories in '36. Among his memorable feats was his clutch performance in Game Six of the 1935 World Series. With the score tied 3–3, Stan Hack opened the top of the ninth with a triple. He remained there as Bridges retired the next three batters. The Tigers scored in the bottom of the inning, winning the Series, and Bridges had his second victory.

During the 1930s, Bridges was named to the AL All-Star staff six times, and gained a victory in 1939. With 194 regular season victories, four in the WS, and one in an All-Star game, Bridges had 199 career wins. /(JK)

Al Bridwell — 1884–1969. SS-2B-3B 1905–15 Reds, Braves, **Giants**, Cubs, St. Louis (FL) 1251 g, .255, 2 hr, 348 rbi

Bridwell was a useful lefthand-hitting infielder who led NL regular shortstops in fielding in 1907 but is chiefly remembered today for hitting the single that began the infamous "Merkle Boner" rally in 1908. /(JK)

Bunny Brief [Anthony Vincent, born Antonio Bordetzki] — 1892–1963. 1B-OF 1912–13, 15, 17 **Browns**, White Sox, Pirates 183 g, .223, 5 hr, 59 rbi

Brief had 42 homers and 191 RBI for Kansas City (American Association) in 1921. He led his league in home runs eight times and twice led all minor leagues. He chose an apt alias, as his major-league career was just that. /(LRD)

Buttons Briggs [Herbert] — 1875–1911. RHP 1896–98, 1904–05 **Cubs** 855 ip, 44–47, 3.41

Briggs won 19 games for the 1904 Cubs but slumped to 8–8 the next year. By 1906 he was pitching semi-pro ball for Elyria of the Ohio Trolley League. His first pitch of that season was smashed for a homer by Wooster catcher Charles Follis, the first black pro football player. /(BC)

Dan Briggs — 1952– . 1B-OF 1975–79, 81–82 **Angels**, Indians, Padres, Expos, Cubs 325 g, .195, 12 hr, 53 rbi

Originally signed by the Angels as a pitcher, the mustachioed lefty hit well over .300 in several Triple-A seasons as a first baseman-outfielder, but never hit better than .226 in trials with five ML clubs. /(JCA)

John Briggs — 1944– . OF-1B 1964–75 **Phillies**, Brewers, Twins 1366 g, .253, 139 hr, 507 rbi

Perennial prospect John Briggs was a fast, well-built, lefthanded-hitting outfielder. Because of the rules regarding bonus players when he signed, Briggs spent only one season in the low minors, and then was retained by the Phillies in 1964. He only once hit over .270, and didn't play regularly until his trade to Milwaukee, where he hit a career-high 21 homers in 1971 and 1972. /(AL)

Johnny Briggs — 1934– . RHP 1956–60 **Cubs**, Indians, A's 165 ip, 9–11, 5.00

A promising youngster who never lived up to it, Briggs started 17 games for the 1958 Cubs with a 5–5 mark. He was 4–4 as a reliever with the Indians and A's in 1960, but his ERA was 6.42. /(FK)

Walter O. Briggs, Sr. — 1877–1952. Owner.

As a young man, Briggs was a vociferous Tiger fan; in 1902 he was nearly ejected from the ballpark by umpire Tom Connolly for loudly and vehemently castigating the ump. He made a fortune in the auto-body industry, and in 1920 he bought 25 percent of the Tigers. Later, he bought another 25 percent, and, when Frank Navin died in 1935, Briggs bought

Briggs Stadium, named for Walter Briggs and later renamed Tiger Stadium

the remainder of the club. He took no money out of the club, reinvesting profits (and adding his own money) to improve the team and the ballpark. In 1941 he was *TSN* Executive of the Year. On two occasions he bought each of his players a new suit and hat after outstanding victories, causing a league rule to be passed prohibiting such rewards for single-game efforts. /(NLM)

Harry Bright — 1929- . 1B-3B-C 1958–65 Pirates, **Senators**, Reds, Yankees, Cubs 336 g, .255, 32 hr, 126 rbi. *1 WS, 2 g, .000*

It took expansion to give versatile, tenacious Harry Bright his only season as a regular, as he hit 17 homers for the lackluster 1962 Senators. Pinch hitting for the Yankees in Game One of the 1963 WS, he became Sandy Koufax's 15th strikeout victim, then a WS record. /(JK)

Nellie Briles [Nelson] — 1943- . RHP 1965–78 **Cardinals**, Pirates, Royals, Rangers, Orioles 2112 ip, 129–112, 3.43. *1 LCS, 6 ip, 3.00. 3 WS, 31 ip, 2–1, 2.59*

A gritty control artist, Briles moved into the St. Louis starting rotation when Bob Gibson suffered a broken leg in 1967. He won nine straight games and led the NL in winning percentage (.737, 14–4) and the Cardinals in ERA (2.43). He was 19–11 in 1968, but slumped the next two years. Traded to the Pirates in 1971, he helped Pittsburgh to the pennant and pitched a two-hit shutout against Baltimore in Game Five of the WS. After winning 14 games in each of the next two seasons, he was traded to the AL, where he finished his career. Briles, who sang the National Anthem before Game Four of the 1973 WS, later became a TV baseball announcer. /(ME)

Jim Brillheart — 1903–1972. LHP 1922–23, 27, 31 **Senators**, Cubs, Red Sox 286 ip, 8–9, 4.19

Brillheart spent only parts of four seasons in the ML, but his career lasted from 1921 (with Greenville, SC of the Sally League) through 1946 (with San Diego of the Pacific Coast League). He is one of the few pitchers to work in over 1,000 games—928 in the minors and 86 in the majors. /(NLM)

Ed Brinkman — 1941- . SS 1961–75 **Senators**, Tigers, Cardinals, Rangers, Yankees 1845 g, .224, 60 hr, 461 rbi. *1 LCS, 2 g, .250*
☛ *All-Star—73. Gold Glove—72.*

The wiry, durable Brinkman was a poor hitter until manager Ted Williams changed his batting style in 1969; his BA jumped nearly 80 points to .266. In 1972 with Detroit, he won a Gold Glove while

setting four single-season records for shortstops: consecutive errorless games (72), consecutive errorless chances (331), fewest errors (7), and best fielding percentage (.990). The older brother of ML catcher Chuck Brinkman, Ed was a teammate of Pete Rose at Cincinnati's Western Hills High. He joined the White Sox as a coach in 1983. /(JCA)

Joe Brinkman — 1944- . *Umpire* AL 1973–87 *3 LCS 2 WS, 2 ASU*

Brinkman, who for several years operated the Joe Brinkman Umpires' School in Cocoa, FL, was an All-Army baseball and football standout who hoped for a pro football career. He was chief of the umpiring crew that ruled George Brett out after he hit a home run with a bat deemed to have pine tar beyond the 18-inch limit. AL president Lee McPhail overturned the call. /(RTM)

Lou Brissie [Leland Victor] — 1924- . LHP 1947–53 **A's**, Indians 898 ip, 44–48, 4.07

Lou was the only survivor of his WWII infantry unit, which was wiped out in battle. However, an exploding shell shattered his left leg, causing him to wear a brace during his pitching career. The courageous 6′4″ southpaw went 16–11 in 1949 for the Athletics and helped himself by batting .267. Brissie later became the National Director of the American Legion baseball program. /(RM)

Dave Bristol — 1933- . *Manager* 1966–72, 76–77, 79–80 **Reds**, Brewers, Braves, Giants 658–764, .463

Bristol led the Reds to third place in 1969, but was replaced after the season by Sparky Anderson, who won the pennant in 1970. Bristol never again had a winning record, saddled as he was from then on with some of the worst teams in the majors. /(SH)

Jim Britt — 1911–1981. *Broadcaster.*

The voice of the Braves and Red Sox for ten years in the 1940s and '50s, Britt concentrated on the Braves when the Red Sox began airing road games. When the two Boston clubs decided to employ separate announcers, Britt was given his choice. He chose the Braves, and Curt Gowdy got the Red Sox job. When his team moved to Milwaukee in 1954, Britt went to Cleveland for four years, returning to Boston in 1958 to work TV news. He broadcast seven All-Star games and five WS, as well as doing football telecasts during the 1950s. /(NLM)

Jim Britton — 1944- . RHP 1967-69, 71 **Braves**, Expos 238 ip, 13-16, 4.01. *1 LCS, 0.1 ip, 0-0, 0.00*

The 6'5" 215-lb Britton declined a football scholarship to Penn State and signed with the Orioles. Drafted by the Braves, he pitched a Texas League no-hitter against Little Rock on Opening Day, 1967. Atlanta used him as a spot starter in 1968-69, but he sat out 1970 with arm trouble. /(MC)

Johnny Broaca — 1909- . RHP 1934-37, 39 **Yankees**, Indians 674 ip, 44-29, 4.08

The bespectacled Yale graduate puzzled more than batters. He confused everyone by bolting the Yankees twice, taking up professional boxing when he could have been pitching in the World Series, and, eventually, rejecting a baseball career altogether. /(JK)

Pete Broberg — 1950- . RHP 1971-78 **Senators/Rangers**, Brewers, Cubs, A's 963 ip, 41-71, 4.56

Broberg possessed great natural skills: "I thought we had another Bob Feller," said Ranger pitching coach Sid Hudson, "but he's a hardhead." In his best year, Broberg was 14-16 for the 1975 Brewers. /(KT)

Greg Brock — 1957- . 1B 1983- **Dodgers**, Brewers 859 g, .247, 102 hr, 406 rbi. *2 LCS, 8 g, .048, 1 hr, 2 rbi*

The man who replaced Steve Garvey at first base for the Dodgers had impossible press notices to live up to. Called "the best power hitting prospect the Dodgers have had since Duke Snider" after breaking home run records at Albuquerque and San Antonio, Brock most resembled Snider in his inability to hit lefthanded pitching. After being traded to the Brewers, Brock cut down his stroke and raised his average at the expense of some power. /(TG)

Lou Brock — 1939- . OF 1961-79 Cubs, **Cardinals** 2616 g, .293, 149 hr, 900 rbi. *3 WS, 21 g, .391, 4 hr, 13 rbi* ☛ *All-Star—67, 71, 74-75. Hall of Fame—1985.*

Signed out of Southern University for a $30,000 bonus in 1961, Brock moved up to the Cubs within one season. He hit only .263 and .258 in two full seasons with Chicago while showing flashes of both speed and power, including a 450-foot home run into the centerfield bleachers at the Polo Grounds, one of only four homers ever to land there. He came into his own after moving to St. Louis in a six-man trade on June 15, 1964. The deal was essentially Brock for pitcher Ernie Broglio, and is regarded as one of the worst the Cubs ever made. Brock averaged .348 in the 1964 stretch drive and finished

Lou Brock

the season at .315, with 111 runs scored, 200 hits, 30 doubles, 11 triples, and 43 stolen bases. In fourth place when Brock joined them, the Cardinals overtook the Phillies, Giants, and Reds to claim the pennant in the last week of the season. Brock then batted .300 with a homer as the Cardinals beat the Yankees in the World Series.

He scored 107 runs and stole 63 bases in 1965, then won his first of four straight and eight total stolen-base championships with 74 in 1966. Brock's greatest season was probably 1967, when he led the Cardinals to another World Championship with a league-leading 113 runs scored, 52 steals, and career highs of 21 homers, 76 RBI, and a .472 slugging average. Brock batted .414 with seven steals against Boston in the WS, breaking or tying four Series records. Although he slumped to .279 in 1968, Brock helped St. Louis win the pennant again by leading the NL in doubles (46) and triples (14) as well as steals (62). The Cardinals lost the World

Series to the Tigers in seven games, but Brock was sensational. He hit .464 to lead both clubs, with two homers and seven steals. At that time he had the highest average (.391) of any player in two or more World Series, along with a Series-record 14 steals. His .655 slugging average ranked fifth and his seven doubles ranked eighth.

Brock hit between .297 and .313 in each season from 1969 through 1976 and led the NL with 126 runs in 1971. Former teammate Bobby Tolan edged Brock, 57 to 51, for the 1970 stolen-base championship, but Brock then won four more titles in a row with 64, 63, 70 and 118.

Brock's 118 steals in 1974 shattered Maury Wills's major league record of 104, set in 1962, and remains the National League record through the 1980s (Rickey Henderson broke the ML record with 130 in 1982). At 35, Brock was by far the oldest man to steal 100 bases. "I figured it was now or never," he said.

He dropped off to "only" 56 steals in each of the next two seasons. Dipping to .221 and 17 steals in 1978, Brock lost his regular job and was urged to retire. Instead he rebounded to .304 with 21 steals, retiring first all-time in stolen bases with 938. He was elected to the Hall of Fame in 1985, his first year of eligibility.

Despite Brock's high averages and electrifying feats on the bases, his stature is disputed by baseball experts. He struck out over 100 times in nine seasons, over 90 times in 12 seasons, and fanned more often than he scored in 11 seasons. He also struck out 1,730 times career, the most all-time at his retirement, while walking only 761 times, a poor ratio for any player and horrendous for a leadoff man. Brock also led the NL in errors seven times, including five years consecutively, never committing fewer than 10 from 1964 through 1973. He was shifted from centerfield to right before settling in left in 1966, primarily because of his defensive shortcomings. /(MC)

Steve Brodie [Walter Scott] — 1868-1935. OF 1890-99, 1901-02 Boston (NL), Cardinals, Baltimore (NL), Pirates, Baltimore (AL), Giants 1438 g, .303, 25 hr, 900 rbi

Brodie was a solid, lefthanded-hitting outfielder who from 1893 to 1897 played 574 consecutive games. He batted .329 over those seasons. He was an important cog in the Baltimore Oriole machine that won National League pennants in 1894–96. Playing centerfield, he led NL outfielders in fielding with Pittsburgh in 1897 and with the Orioles in 1899. In

1900 he left the disbanded Baltimore franchise for the Chicago White Sox of the minor American League. In 1901 he was back in the majors with John McGraw's AL Baltimore Orioles. /(AJA)

Dick Brodowski — 1932- . RHP 1952, 55-59 **Red Sox**, Senators, Indians 215 ip, 9-11, 4.76

The baby-faced Brodowski reached Boston after less than two years of pro ball, then spent two years in the military, and was ineffective after his return. /(DB)

Bob Broeg — 1918- . *Writer.*

Broeg joined the *St. Louis Post-Dispatch* in 1945 and became sports editor in 1958. He is a member of the Board of Directors of the National Baseball Hall of Fame and the only person eligible to vote in the elections for the baseball, pro football, and college football Halls of Fame. He has authored nine books, including the popular *Redbirds: A Century of Cardinal Baseball.* In honor of his many contributions to baseball, the St. Louis chapter of SABR is named for him. /(FJO)

Ernie Broglio — 1935- . RHP 1959-66 **Cardinals**, Cubs 1337 ip, 77-74, 3.74

Broglio won 21 games, 7 in relief, for the 1960 Cardinals. Following an 18–8 record in 1963, he was dealt in June of 1964 for an unproven Cub outfielder, Lou Brock. Broglio won only seven more games in the majors. /(FJO)

Jack Brohamer — 1950- . 2B-3B 1972-80 **Indians**, White Sox, Red Sox 805 g, .245, 30 hr, 227 rbi

Small, gutsy, and bow-legged, Brohamer became Cleveland's second baseman in 1972 and was named to the *TSN* All-Rookie Team. He hit a career-high .270 in 1974. With the White Sox on September 24, 1977, he hit for the cycle. Brohamer, who started two ML triple plays, was a utility man for the second half of his career. /(JCA)

Tom Brookens — 1953- . 3B-2B-SS **Tigers**, Yankees 1272 g, .245, 70 hr, 411 rbi. *2 LCS, 7 g, .000. 1 WS, 3 g, .000*

Brookens first became Detroit's third baseman in 1980, and, as the decade progressed, alternately fended off challengers for his job and served in a utility role. A mediocre fielder, he led the AL in errors at 3B in 1980 and 1985, and tied an AL 3B record on September 6, 1980 with four errors in an inning. Though short on power and struggling to hit over .240, his clutch, heads-up play and team-first attitude kept him on Detroit clubs that saw post-season action in 1984 and 1987. Tom's twin brother, Tim, played in the Tigers organization, and their cousin, Ed "Ike" Brookens, pitched briefly with Detroit in 1975. /(JCA)

Brooklyn Dodgers [aka Bridegrooms, Trolley Dodgers, Superbas, Robins] (Daffiness Boys, Flock, Bums) — 1884–1957. Team AA 1884–89; NL 1890–1957 NL: 5214–4927, .514. *American Association Champions 1890 NL Champions 1899, 1900, 16, 20, 41, 47, 49, 52–53, 55–56 World Champions 55*

The only major league team whose named location was a borough (rather than a city or state), the Brooklyn Dodgers entered American mythology as a metaphor for lost innocence and community. They became a symbol of the decline of the eastern city. Many in Brooklyn agreed with columnists Pete Hamill and Jack Newfield when they named the three most evil men of the 20th century as "Hitler, Stalin, and Walter O'Malley." O'Malley moved the "Boys of Summer" to Los Angeles only ten years after their proudest moment, the breaking of the color barrier with Jackie Robinson, and two years

after their greatest triumph, beating the hated Yankees in the World Series after five losses.

The Dodgers are best remembered for their free-wheeling days as manager Wilbert Robinson's Daffiness Boys, for their legendary Ebbets Field fans, and for the cry of "Wait until next year." Brooklyn lost the only two league playoffs played during their tenure, in 1946 and 1951, and were the only major league team to finish in the cellar only once. They played the longest major league game ever, a 26-inning tie with the Braves in 1920. /(TG)

Hubie Brooks [Hubert] — 1956– . 3B-SS-OF 1980-Mets, **Expos** 1198 g, .276, 103 hr, 609 rbi
☛ *All-Star—86–87.*

Originally a third baseman, and the third player chosen in the June 1978 draft, Hubie Brooks was an early key to the rebuilt fortunes of the Mets. Though he gave the club its first real stability at third base, Brooks was shifted to shortstop in 1984 to make room for Ray Knight and was then traded with Floyd Youmans, Mike Fitzgerald and Herm Winningham to the Expos for Gary Carter after the season. An outstanding clutch hitter, in 1985 Brooks

The 1955 Brooklyn Dodgers

became the first NL shortstop since Ernie Banks (1960) to drive in 100 runs. Off to his greatest season in 1986, when he hit .340, Hubie was sidelined by a series of injuries, the most severe being torn ligaments and bone chips in his left thumb. His 1987 season was shortened by a broken wrist, suffered when he was hit by a Danny Darwin pitch. Brooks earned Silver Slugger Awards in 1985 and 1986.

Never a good fielder even at third base (he led NL third basemen in errors in 1981), Brooks's extreme lack of range at shortstop led the Expos to move him to right field in 1988. The move may have helped his durablity, but even in the outfield his defense proved barely adequate. /(ME)

Jim Brosnan (Professor) — 1929– . RHP 1954, 56–63 Cubs, Cardinals, **Reds**, White Sox 831 ip, 55–47, 3.54. *1 WS, 6 ip, 7.50*

Had pitching been his only talent, the 6'4" 200-lb Brosnan would be recalled as a consistent reliever whose ERA for eight consecutive years never topped 3.79. Used exclusively in relief for the pennant-winning 1961 Reds, he compiled a 10–4 record and a 3.04 ERA in 53 appearances. But the spectacled and scholarly "Professor" became best known as the author of the autobiographical baseball book classics *The Long Season* and *Pennant Race*. /(FK)

Brotherhood of Ballplayers

In 1885 the owners put a $2,000 salary limit into the National Agreement. In response, John Montgomery Ward, star shortstop of the New York National League team, secretly formed the Brotherhood of Ballplayers. Its existence was announced in August 1886; in fall 1887 the Brotherhood demanded recognition by the owners, with members not signing contracts until it was granted. The Brotherhood Committee of Ward, Ned Hanlon, and Dan Brouthers held meetings with the NL, leading to a new form of contract that defined all relations between the league and its players, with no additional restrictions contained in outside documents. Section 18 of the new contract contained a clause allowing the club to reserve the player for the next season, provided that the full salary be written in the contract; a salary reduction constituted a release. Because of the $2,000 limit (broken by all teams in under-the-table deals with star players), the clause was not consistent with the status quo. The League Committee solved the problem by promising to strike the limit from the National Agreement. Players went ahead and signed contracts for the next season, but the limit wasn't stricken, "owing to the alleged refusal of the other party to the agreement, the American Association [the other major league at the time], to consent," according to the Reach Guide. At this point, the American Association was in no position to buck the National League, so it was probably acting under NL orders. As a result, clubs were able to reserve players at reduced salaries the following fall.

At the same time, three NL clubs (Indianapolis, Pittsburgh, and Washington) stated that they needed a larger share of the gate receipts in big cities. The other owners voted down a change in the division of the gate, so John T. Brush of Indianapolis proposed a reduction of players' salaries on these clubs (despite the fact that these teams already paid lower salaries than other clubs). This was done by setting player ratings from "A" to "E" with prescribed salaries for each rating. This action was taken while Ward was overseas on tour with Al Spalding; Ward returned in April and insisted on the repeal of this rule, which would eventually reduce salaries throughout the league. Spalding, the chairman of the league committee appointed to deal with this controversy, stonewalled.

The Brotherhood, in a July 4, 1889 meeting in New York City, secretly organized the Players' League for the following season. Word leaked out in September, but all was denied until November. Chicago star Cap Anson was the only player who remained with the NL at first. The NL repealed the classification system, invoked the reserve clause, and moved Cincinnati and Brooklyn from the AA to the NL. In response to these moves and to generous contract offers, some players abandoned the new league. But a lawsuit against Ward failed when, in January 1890, it was ruled that the "contract was lacking in mutuality, unconscionable and inequitable." The National League transferred Indianapolis's players to New York, which had lost all but three of its members to the Players' League, and then bought out Indianapolis and Washington for $65,000. The NL played an eight-team schedule, with the former AA teams, Brooklyn and Cincinnati, carrying the NL at first. Pittsburgh played most of its games on the road. Although a good pennant race saved attendance after a bad slump in June, the NL as a whole lost $300,000 for the season, a tremendous sum at the time. On October 4, Cincinnati was lost to the Players' League, sold for $40,000. But the financial backers of the Players' League had also taken a licking and, unaware of the extent of the NL's losses, they caved in to the NL that winter. /(SH)

Mark Brouhard — 1956- . OF-DH 1980–85 **Brewers** 304 g, .258, 25 hr, 104 rbi. *1 LCS, 1 g, .750, 1 hr, 3 rbi*

Slow-footed slugger Brouhard was a reserve out-fielder and DH for the Brewers. In the fourth game of the 1982 LCS, he played for injured Ben Oglivie after 28 days of inactivity. He had three hits, including a homer and three RBI, and tied an AL record with four runs scored. In 1986 he played for the Yakult Swallows of Japan's Central League (.258, 21 HR, 64 RBI) but was dropped from their roster in 1987 to make room for Bob Horner. /(MC)

Heywood C. Broun — 1888–1939. *Writer.*

Broun was a copy reader, sports writer and editor, drama critic, war correspondent, and columnist in his 31-year career. He could reputedly bat out a column in 30 minutes. He was a big eater (6'3", 250-lb) and a messy dresser who sported an old broad-brimmed hat. Broun attended Harvard but did not graduate before he began his journalism career in 1910 with the New York *Morning Tele-graph*, a racing and theatrical paper. He moved to the *Tribune* in 1912, where he became drama critic in 1916. He began his column, "It Seems to Me," at the *World* in 1921. One of his most quoted lines appeared in 1915, when John McGraw frequently started pitcher Rube Schauer and relieved him with Ferdie Schupp: "It never Schauers but it Schupps."

Broun was the founder of the American Newspaper Guild in 1933. He moved to the *New York Post* in 1939, but died of pneumonia after writing only one column. His only baseball book, *The Sun Field*, was published in 1923. He received the J.G. Taylor Spink Award from the Hall of Fame in 1970. /(NLM)

Dan Brouthers [Dennis Joseph] (Big Dan) — 1858–1932. 1B 1879–96, 1904 Troy (NL), **Buffalo (NL)**, Detroit (NL), Braves, Boston (PL), Boston (AA), Dodgers, Baltimore (NL), Louisville (NL), Phillies, Giants 1673 g, .343, 106 hr, 1056 rbi
☛ *Led League—ba 82–83, 89, 91–92. Led League—hr 81, 86. Led League—rbi 92. Hall of Fame—1945.*

Dan Brouthers was one of baseball's 19th-century superstars, a five-time batting champion who also led the NL in slugging percentage each of his first six full seasons. Particularly large for his era at 6'2" and 205 lbs., mustachioed Big Dan sported a lusty lefthanded swing that produced a career .343 batting average, ninth-best of all time.

After parts of 1879–80 with Troy, which in-cluded two unsuccessful starts as a pitcher,

Brouthers became a regular in Buffalo in 1881 and led the NL in home runs and slugging percentage. He won his first batting title in 1882 with a .368 mark, and repeated the next season by batting .374. His average would not dip below .300 until his token appearence with the Giants in 1904, eight years after his initial retirement.

Brouthers joined Detroit in 1886 and hit .370 while leading the league in home runs (11), doubles (40), and, for the sixth consecutive season, slugging percentage. Although his average dropped to .338 and .307 the next two years, he led the league in doubles and runs each time, then moved on to Boston, where he regained the batting title with .373 in 1889. He jumped to the one-year Players League

Dan Brouthers

in 1890, helping Boston to the league championship, then joined Boston's American Association club in 1891, where he edged teammate Hugh Duffy for his fourth batting title. Back in the NL with Brooklyn in 1892, he led the league in hitting once again (.335) and also led in hits and RBI.

A capable barehanded fielder at first base, Brouthers made his best contributions at the plate. He went 6-for-6 on July 19, 1883, and on September 10, 1886, he blasted three home runs, a double, and a single for 15 total bases. When his ML career was done, he played in the Eastern League, winning a final batting title with a .415 average. He remained in baseball when former teammate and Giant manager John McGraw placed him in charge of the Polo Grounds press gate for many years. In 1945, when a dearth of turn-of-the-century stars was addressed by the Hall of Fame Veterans Committee, Big Dan Brouthers was among the eight inducted. /(JK)

Bob Brower — 1960- . OF 1986- **Rangers**, Yankees 256 g, .242, 17 hr, 60 rbi

Brower showed great promise in 1987, when he hit .261 with 14 HR as a part-time outfielder with Texas, but he dropped off to .224 with 1 HR in 1988 after starting the season on the DL. He replaced the injured Dave Winfield in the Yankee outfield in 1989, but erratic fielding and the acquisition of Jesse Barfield relegated Brower to Columbus. /(JFC)

Frank Brower — 1893-1960. OF-1B 1920-24 **Senators**, Indians 450 g, .286, 30 hr, 205 rbi

Signed as a pitcher by the Cardinals, Brower became an everyday player in the minors. He was called "The Babe Ruth of the Bushes" in 1920 when he hit .394 with 23 homers for Reading of the International League. The Senators purchased his contract but he produced no Ruthian ML stats. In 1923, his top year, he hit 16 homers for Cleveland. /(NLM)

Boardwalk Brown [Carroll] — 1889-1977. RHP 1911-15 **A's**, Yankees 731 ip, 38-40, 3.47

Brown got his nickname because he was discovered playing on the sandlots of Atlantic City by a scout for Connie Mack. He was 13-11 for the A's in 1912 and followed with 17-11 for the pennant winners of 1913, but was not used in the A's WS victory as Connie Mack used only three pitchers. After a 1-6 start in 1914, he was sold to New York. /(NLM)

Bob Brown — 1911- . RHP 1930-36 **Braves** 364 ip, 16-21, 4.48

Brown was a promising 14-7 (3.30) as a 21-year-old rookie in 1932, but only won two more games in four more seasons. /(JK)

Bobby Brown (Doc) — 1924- . 3B-SS-2B-OF 1946-52, 54 **Yankees** 548 g, .279, 22 hr, 237 rbi. *4 WS, 17 g, .439, 9 rbi*

After signing with the Yankees for a substantial bonus, Brown hit .300 in 1947 in 69 games and led the AL in pinch hits (9). The next year he again hit .300 in a career-high 113 games. Because he was a weak fielder, he was platooned at third base and occasionally used at other positions when his potent lefthanded bat was needed. After serving in the military for most of 1952 and all of '53, he retired from baseball in mid-1954 to practice medicine. He was a hitting star in four WS. His pinch-double tied the seventh game of the 1947 WS, he tripled with the bases loaded in the 1949 WS, and his double led to the only run in Game One of the 1950 WS. In 1984, Brown left a successful career as a surgeon and re-entered baseball as the successor to Lee MacPhail as president of the American League. /(FK)

Bobby Brown [Rogers Lee] — 1954- . OF 1979-85 Blue Jays, Yankees, Mariners, **Padres** 502 g, .245, 26 hr, 130 rbi. *3 LCS, 9 g, .067. 2 WS, 9 g, .063, 2 rbi*

The speedy Brown played in seven organizations, and in 1979 shared International League MVP honors (with Dave Stapleton), batting .349 for Columbus. While playing for Seattle on September 13, 1982, he broke up a Vida Blue no-hitter. /(NLM)

Buster Brown [Charles] — 1881-1914. RHP 1905-13 Cardinals, Phillies, **Braves** 1452 ip, 51-105, 3.20

Often disgruntled, saddled with poor teams, and plagued by wildness, Brown never had a winning ML season despite posting some good ERAs. In 1909, the former Ames College star kept his ERA for the Braves to 2.67 but went 9-23. /(NLM)

Chris Brown (Tin Man) — 1961- . 3B 1984- **Giants**, Padres, Tigers 449 g, .269, 38 hr, 184 rbi
☛ *All-Star—86.*

"Chris has the talent to be an MVP," said former teammate Mike Krukow in 1989, but the enigmatic Brown showed little desire to play like one, or often to play at all. Instead, he would infuriate both managers and teammates with a careless attitude and a litany of nagging, minor injuries that were usually described as imaginary. From 1984 to 1988, Brown missed over 250 games with ailments as ludicrous as a "bruised tooth," but was placed on the DL only once, when a Danny Cox pitch broke his jaw.

Brown made the *Topps* and *Baseball Digest* all-rookie teams in 1985 after hitting .271 with 16 HR, and in 1986 he was hitting .348 on June 25 and made the NL All-Star team. Brown had led the Giants in hitting in both 1985 and '86, but by July 4, 1987 the club was fed up with its moody third baseman and traded him to San Diego in a seven-player swap that brought Kevin Mitchell to San Francisco. Brown hit only .237 with 12 HR in 1987, and .235 in 80 games (though he was never on the DL) in 1988 before being traded to the Tigers in the off-season. Detroit manager Sparky Anderson believed he could motivate Brown, but Brown quickly came up with shoulder and back "problems" and was released in June. He then signed a minor league contract with the Pirates. Brown was called "Tin Man" by both teammates and opponents, a disparaging reference to the "Wizard of Oz" character who had no heart. /(SCL)

Clint Brown — 1903–1955. RHP 1928–42 **Indians**, White Sox 1486 ip, 89–92, 4.26

One of the first relief aces, the righthanded junk-baller threw underhand, sidearm, and three-quarters. His 61 appearances in 1939 set the (since broken) ML record for relievers. A fair starter for the Indians from 1930 through 1933, with a 15–12 mark in 1932 his best, he was switched to relief in 1934 and then sold to the White Sox two years later. He led the AL in saves (18) in 1937 and relief wins (11) in 1939. /(JK)

Darrell Brown — 1955– . OF-DH 1981–84 Tigers, A's, **Twins** 210 g, .274, 1 hr, 44 rbi

A singles hitter, Brown was a three-time first draft choice before signing with Detroit. He usually played centerfield and batted leadoff during his two years in Minnesota. /(CC)

Dave Brown — 1896– . LHP Negro Leagues 1918–25 Chicago American Giants, New York Lincoln Giants statistics not available

To aquire Dave Brown for the Chicago American Giants, Rube Foster put up a $20,000 bond to get Brown a parole from a highway robbery conviction. While leading the 1920–22 team to three straight championships, Brown was generally considered the best lefthander in the Negro Leagues. In 1921 he

was 11–3 with five shutouts and a league-leading 2.47 runs per game (ERA unknown). For the four years for which league records are available, he was 41–18. He also played in the winter Cuban League, compiling a 17–12 record over four years. His career came to a sudden halt in 1925 when, sought in connection with a New York homicide, he disappeared. /(BP)

Dick Brown — 1935–1970. C 1957–65 Indians, White Sox, **Tigers**, Orioles 641 g, .244, 62 hr, 223 rbi

A dependable catcher with occasional home run power, Brown's career ended in 1965 after surgery for a brain tumor. He scouted for the Orioles until his death five years later. His brother, Larry, played 12 years as a ML infielder. /(JK)

Eddie Brown (Glass Arm Eddie) — 1891–1956. OF 1920–21, 24–28 Giants, Dodgers, **Braves** 790 g, .303, 16 hr, 407 rbi

The 6'3" 190-lb righthanded speedster lacked power and had a notoriously weak arm, but became a ML regular at age 31 and had four straight .300-plus seasons, with a career-high 99 RBI in 1925 and a NL-leading 201 hits in 1926. /(JK)

Fred Brown — 1879–1955. OF 1901–02 **Braves** 9 g, .200, 0 hr, 2 rbi

His ML career consisted of only nine games, but Brown was far more successful in the political arena. In 1923 he became the first Democratic governor of New Hampshire in 65 years. He served as U.S. Senator from 1933 to 1939. In 1939 he was appointed Comptroller General of the United States. /(BC)

Gates Brown [William James] — 1939– . OF-DH 1963–75 **Tigers** 1051 g, .257, 84 hr, 322 rbi. *1 LCS, 3 g, .000. 1 WS, 1 g, .000*

Brown never knew why his mother called him "Gates," but he preferred it to Billy, and the nickname stuck. In his first ML at bat (6/19/63), he hit a pinch homer, a fitting beginning for one of baseball's most successful pinch hitters. The squat, popular Brown had limited defensive skills and couldn't break into the regular Tiger outfield, but he collected 107 career pinch hits and 16 pinch homers. In both 1968 and 1974 he led the AL in total pinch hits. /(JCA)

Hal Brown (Skinny) — 1924- . RHP 1951–64 White Sox, Red Sox, **Orioles**, Yankees, Astros 1680 ip, 85–92, 3.81

A knuckleball pitcher with outstanding control, Brown was both a starter and a reliever. With Houston in 1963, he walked just eight in 141 innings. Chunky as a youngster, his parents facetiously nicknamed him "Skinny." He was 12–5 with Baltimore in 1960, his best season, and pitched 36 consecutive shutout innings the next year to set the Oriole record. Although his ERAs with Houston in 1963–64 were as good as they had been with Baltimore, his record with the anemic Colt .45's (later the Astros) was 8–26./(JCA)

Ike Brown — 1942- . 2B-1B-OF 1969–74 **Tigers** 280 g, .256, 20 hr, 65 rbi. *1 LCS, 1 g, .500, 2 rbi*

Brown's first hit was a homer at Yankee Stadium. The stocky jack-of-all-trades was often called on to pinch-hit, batting .320 in that role in 1970–71. He hit eight homers in just 110 at-bats in '71./(CC)

Jackie Brown — 1943- . RHP 1970–71, 73–77 **Senators/Rangers**, Indians, Expos 893 ip, 47–53, 4.18

Curveball specialist Jackie Brown and his older brother Paul both signed with the Phillies after starring together in high school. Paul jumped to the majors as a phenom at 20 but was finished at 27, having gone 0–8 in four seasons. Jackie was 27 when he got his first shot at the majors in 1970. His best year was 1974, when he went 13–12 with a 3.57 ERA for the Rangers./(MC)

Jimmy Brown — 1910–1977. 2B-3B-SS 1937–43, 46 **Cardinals**, Pirates 890 g, .279, 9 hr, 319 rbi. *1 WS, 5 g, .300, 1 rbi*
☛ *All-Star—42.*

A product of the Cardinal farm system, the switch-hitting Brown was a leadoff hitter who seldom walked; he twice led the NL in at-bats (1939 and '42). He led Cardinal hitters with a BA of .300 in their 1942 WS win over the Yankees./(JK)

Jumbo Brown [Walter George] — 1907–1966. RHP 1925, 1927–28, 1932–33, 1935–41 Cubs, Indians, Yankees, Reds, **Giants** 598 ip, 33–31, 4.06

The 6′4″ 295-lb giant fielded his position with surprising agility, but his fastball was ineffective after four innings. An undistinguished reliever throughout most of his career, he was most effective with the Giants in his final four seasons. He tied for the NL lead in saves in 1940 (7) and led in 1941 (8)./(JK)

Kevin Brown — 1965- . RHP 1986, 88- **Rangers** 219 ip, 14–10, 4.02

Brown was the fourth player taken in the June 1986 draft and was in the majors by the end of the year. He moved into the Rangers' rotation in 1989 and went 12–9 with a 3.35 ERA as their number-two starter./(SFS)

Larry Brown (Iron Man) — 1902–1972. C-MGR Negro Leagues 1919–49 Birmingham Black Barons, Pittsburgh Keystones, Indianapolis ABC's, **Memphis Red Sox**, Detroit Stars, Chicago American Giants, New York Lincoln Giants, New York Black Yankees, Cole's American Giants, Philadelphia Stars statistics not available
☛ *All-Star—33–34, 38–41.*

Recognized as one of the best defensive catchers in Negro League history, husky Larry Brown was known for his rifle arm and unusual habit of leaving his mask on when catching pop-ups. Referred to as "Iron Man," he prided himself on catching nearly every day, sometimes three games a day; in 1930, he caught 234 games. Though mediocre offensively, he excelled in his six all-star appearances, hitting .308. His best single season on record was 1928, when he batted .294 and led the Memphis Red Sox in games, at-bats, hits, and doubles. After starring for the Chicago American Giants in the early 1930s, he finished his career as player-manager for Memphis throughout the 1940s./(PG)

Larry Brown — 1940- . SS-2B-3B 1963–74 **Indians**, A's, Orioles, Rangers 1129 g, .233, 47 hr, 254 rbi. *1 LCS, 1 g, --*

An outstanding fielder, Brown was Cleveland's regular second baseman in 1964 and regular shortstop from 1965 to 1969. A confirmed .230 hitter, he showed some power with 12 homers in 1964, but his slugging declined after he suffered fractures of the skull, nose and cheekbone in a 1966 collision with another player. His brother Dick was an AL catcher for nine seasons./(MC)

Lloyd Brown (Gimpy) — 1904–1974. LHP 1925, 28–37, 40 Dodgers, **Senators**, Browns, Red Sox, Indians, Phillies 1693 ip, 91–105, 4.20

This Texan won 46 games over three years with Washington, 1930–32, after which he went 33–53. He is chiefly remembered as the pitcher who gave up the most home runs to Lou Gehrig (15), including two grand slams. Brown pitched for 30 years in pro ball, 1923–53, and scouted for the Phillies and Senators./(LRD)

Mace Brown — 1909- . RHP 1935-43, 46 **Pirates**, Dodgers, Red Sox 1075 ip, 76-57, 3.47. *1 WS, 1 ip, 0-0, 27.00*

One of the first relief specialists, Brown set a record in 1937 by making 50 appearances without recording a complete game. He led Pittsburgh in wins (15, all in relief) in 1938, in a major league high 51 appearances, but surrendered the "Homer in the Gloamin'" to Gabby Hartnett that propelled Chicago past Pittsburgh and on to the NL pennant. Brown again led the AL with 49 games in 1943. He is credited with 48 career saves. /(ME)

Mike Brown — 1959- . RHP 1982-87 **Red Sox**, Mariners 254 ip, 12-20, 5.75

After jumping directly from Class AA to the pitching-poor Red Sox in 1983, Brown warned, "I'm a rookie, not a savior." His six wins that season were a career high. /(SCL)

Mike Brown — 1959- . OF 1983-86 **Angels**, Pirates 297 g, .267, 23 hr, 110 rbi

The Angels' top minor leaguer in 1983, Brown hit .322 after a mid-1985 trade to the Pirates. He struggled as a platoon player in 1986, was farmed out, hit .379 in the Pacific Coast League, but was released prior to the 1987 season. /(ME)

Ollie Brown (Downtown) — 1944- . OF 1965-77 Giants, **Padres**, A's, Brewers, Astros, Phillies 1218 g, .265, 102 hr, 454 rbi. *2 LCS, 3 g, .000*

Brown earned the nickname "Downtown" by hitting 40 homers for Fresno in 1964, but he was disappointing in San Francisco. San Diego's first choice in the 1968 expansion draft, he hit 20 homers for the Padres in 1969 and had career highs of 23 homers and 89 RBI in 1970. Originally signed as a pitcher, his strong arm was an asset in the outfield. His older brother Oscar was a Braves outfielder, and another brother, Willie, played in the NFL. /(JCA)

Raymond Brown — 1908-before 1972. RHP-OF-MGR Negro Leagues 1930-53 Dayton Marcos, Indianapolis ABC's, Homestead Grays

Ray Brown played for Cum Posey's Homestead Grays from 1932-45 and married Posey's daughter before moving on to Mexico (1946-49) and the Canadian Provincial League (1950-53). He started the 1935 East-West all-star game, threw a no-hitter for Santa Clara (Cuban Winter League) in 1936, and pitched them to the 1938 Cuban crown. He was 9-3 for the 1944 Black World Champion Homestead

Grays, and threw a one-hit shutout in the World Series. In 1945, he had a seven-inning perfect game for the Grays. He helped Sherbrooke to the 1951 Provincial title with an 11-10 record and a 3.31 ERA. A good batter who switch-hit at times, he often played the outfield and pinch hit. He was one of five players mentioned as being of major league caliber in a 1938 wire sent to the Pittsburgh Pirates by *The Pittsburgh Courier*. The other four were Hall of Famers Josh Gibson, Buck Leonard, Cool Papa Bell, and Satchel Paige. /(MFK)

Three-Finger Brown [Mordecai Peter Centennial](Miner) — 1876-1948 . RHP 1903-16 Cardinals, **Cubs**, Reds, St. Louis (FL),Brooklyn (FL), Chicago (FL) 3172 ip, 239-129, 2.06. 20 wins: 06-11 *4 WS, 58 ip, 5-4, 2.81.*
   Manager 1914 **St. Louis (FL)** 50-63, .442
☛ *Led League—era 06. Led League—w 09. Hall of Fame—1949.*

Some players overcome handicaps. Brown turned his to an advantage. As a seven-year-old boy he caught his right hand in a corn grinder on his uncle's

Three-Finger Brown

farm. It was necessary to amputate almost all the forefinger, and, although saved, the middle finger was mangled and left crooked. His little finger was also stubbed. Later, newspapers called him "Three-Finger," although to his teammates he was "Miner" because he'd worked several years in a coal mine before beginning in baseball at age 24. He started as an infielder, but when he learned to add spin to the ball by releasing it off his stub, he became a pitcher.

Brown was the pitching mainstay of the great "Tinker-to-Evers-to-Chance" Cub teams that won four pennants and two world championships, 1906–10. He won 20 or more games for six consecutive years, starting in 1906, and four of his five WS wins were shutouts.

The peak years of Brown's career coincided with those of Christy Mathewson, and they were often matched when the Giants and Cubs met. One game he lost to Mathewson was Matty's no-hitter in 1905. After that, Brown rolled off nine consecutive victories over Mathewson, the ninth coming in the playoff that decided the famous 1908 pennant race after the "Merkle Boner." In 1916, they faced each other for the final time, each with 12 wins. Mathewson beat Brown, in what turned out to be the last game for each.

Brown was a strong, durable pitcher, admired for his fitness. In 1914, *American Monthly*, a national magazine, published photos of his exercise program, a rugged series of body-building routines. Always in the starting rotation, he was still able to relieve frequently. He led the NL four times in saves and had 48 lifetime, in addition to his 239 career wins. /(JK)

Tom Brown — 1860–1927. OF 1882–98 Baltimore (AA), Columbus (AA), Pittsburgh (AA), Pirates, Indianapolis (NL), Braves, Boston (P), Boston (AA), **Louisville (NL)**, Cardinals, Washington (NL) 1786 g, .265, 64 hr, 528 rbi

When Brown reached England as one of the players on the 1888–89 World Tour, it was a homecoming for the Liverpool-born outfielder. A fleet ball hawk and basestealer, he usually batted leadoff although he led his league in striking out five times. In 1891 with Boston, he topped the American Association with 106 stolen bases and 177 runs scored. /(JK)

Tommy Brown [Thomas Michael] (Buckshot) — 1927– . SS-OF-3B 1944–45, 47–53 **Dodgers**, Phillies, Cubs 494 g, .241, 31 hr, 159 rbi. *1 WS, 2 g, .000*

Brown was just 16 when he broke in at shortstop with the wartime Dodgers in 1944, the youngest player ever to see regular action. On August 20,

1945, at age 17, he became the youngest player to homer in the majors. His weak hitting made him a utility infielder after the war. However, he hit three consecutive homers in a September 18, 1950 game. /(LRD)

Warren Brown — 1894–Unk. *Writer.*

A tall first baseman at the University of San Francisco, Brown once hit two bases-loaded triples in one inning. He signed with Sacramento of the PCL in 1914 but never went any higher. He became sports editor of the San Francisco *Call-Post*, then the New York *Evening Mail*. In 1923, he took over as sports editor of the Chicago *Herald Examiner*. He covered every World Series from 1920 to 1964. He was chairman of the Veterans Committee of the Hall of Fame. His books included *The Chicago Cubs, The Chicago White Sox*, and *Knute Rockne*. In 1973 he received the J.G. Taylor Spink Award from the Hall of Fame. /(NLM)

Willard Brown (Home Run, El Hombre) — 1913– . OF-SS Negro Leagues 1934–52 Monroe Monarchs, **Kansas City Monarchs** statistics not available; *ML:* OF 1947 Browns 21g, .179, 1 hr, 6 rbi
☛ *All-Star—37, 39–42, 46, 50.*

Brown was a longtime star with the Negro National League's Kansas City Monarchs. He was nicknamed "Home Run" by Hall of Famer Josh Gibson for out-slugging Gibson in their head-to-head confrontations. He began as a shortstop for the Monroe, LA Monarchs, and was later discovered by Kansas City Monarchs owner J.L. Wilkinson. Wilkinson offered Brown a $250 bonus, a $125-a-month salary, and $1 a day as meal money. Brown accepted the increase over his $10-a-week stipend in Monroe.

Brown matured into a complete and dangerous hitter. With Brown batting cleanup, the 1942 Monarchs routinely beat the Dizzy Dean All-Stars in exhibition games played in Chicago and Buffalo. Brown played in the 1942 and 1946 Negro World Series, and hit a combined .304 with three HR and 14 RBI.

Brown became a hero in Puerto Rico by winning three home run and three batting titles from 1946 through 1950, earning the nickname "El Hombre"—The Man. In 1947–48, he won the Triple Crown, hitting .432 with 27 HR and 86 RBI in 60 games.

While leading the NNL with a .372 average in the fall of 1947, the 34-year-old Brown signed with the St. Louis Browns. He became the first black player to hit a home run in the American League. But he felt the St. Louis club was not as talented as the Monarchs: "The Browns couldn't beat the Monarchs no kind of way, only if we was all asleep. That's the truth. They didn't have nothing. I said, 'Major league team? They got to be kidding'" After playing only 21 games, and frustrated with a .179 average, he quit the Browns because of racial pressures and the team's lack of a winning attitude, and rejoined the Monarchs. /(LL)

Byron Browne — 1942- . OF 1965–72 Cubs, Astros, Cardinals, **Phillies** 349 g, .236, 30 hr, 102 rbi

A fleet, strong-armed outfielder with modest power, Browne struck out in more than a fourth of his at-bats, including a NL-high 143 in 1966 and a record-tying eight in two consecutive games that June. One of his 14 siblings was the ABA's Dennis Browne. /(JCA)

George Browne — 1876–1920. OF 1901–12 Phillies, **Giants**, Braves, Cubs, Senators, White Sox, Dodgers 1102 g, .273, 18 hr, 303 rbi. *1 WS, 5 g, .182, 1 rbi*

Browne's speedy, aggressive play in right field and at the top of McGraw's batting order helped the Giants win pennants in 1904–05. The lefthanded hitter led the NL in runs scored in '04. /(JK)

Jerry Browne (Guv'nor) — 1966- . 2B 1986- **Rangers**, Indians 370 g, .280, 7 hr, 103 rbi

A slightly built, slap-hitting Virgin Islander, Browne was the Rangers' 1987 Rookie of the Year, winning their second-base job and batting .271 with 27 stolen bases. He was hitting .197 in June 1988 when he was returned to the minors. Traded to the Indians in the Julio Franco deal, he had his best season in 1989, hitting .299 with 83 runs scored. /(JCA)

Pete Browning (The Gladiator) — 1861–1905. OF 1882–94 **Louisville (AA)**, Cleveland (PL), Pirates, Reds, Louisville (NL), Cardinals, Dodgers 1185 g, .343, 47 hr, 352 rbi
☛ *Led League—ba 82, 85, 90.*

The famous Louisville Slugger line of baseball bats made by the Hillerich & Bradsby Company is named after the Louisville-born, bred, and employed Browning, who ordered the first customized bat in 1884. Browning himself was called "The Gladiator" for his desperate fights with fly balls. The epitome of the clumsy slugger (lifetime fielding average, .874), he was nearly deaf from mastoiditus, illiterate, and alcoholic. But he also compiled the

third-highest career BA for a righthanded batter and won three batting titles. /(JK)

Tom Browning — 1960- . LHP 1984- **Reds** 1211 ip, 78–52, 3.73. 20 wins: 85

Browning broke into the ML with 20 wins for the Reds in 1985, becoming the first rookie to win 20 since the Yankees' Bob Grim in 1954, and on September 16, 1988 he pitched a perfect game against the Dodgers en route to an 18–5, 3.41 record. In between, he suffered through two weak seasons and one trip to the minors. His 11 straight wins in 1985 was the best streak by a Reds pitcher in 30 years. /(ME)

Bill Brubaker — 1910–1978. 3B-2B 1932–40, 43 **Pirates**, Braves 479 g, .264, 22 hr, 225 rbi

Brubaker replaced Pie Traynor at third base for Pittsburgh in 1936. He had 102 RBI despite a league-leading 96 strikeouts. He slumped the next year and became the Pirates' utility man. /(ME)

Bob Bruce — 1933- . RHP 1959–67 Tigers, **Astros**, Braves 1122 ip, 49–71, 3.85

The Detroit native spent a little over a year with the Tigers. Traded to Houston's expansion team, he was the leading winner in two of their first three years, with a career best of 15–9 in 1964. /(JCA)

Mike Brumley — 1938- . C 1964–66 **Senators** 224 g, .229, 5 hr, 50 rbi

The lefthanded-hitting Brumley was an all-star three consecutive years in the minors, but hit only .244 as the Senators' regular catcher in 1964. His son, Mike, Jr., reached the majors with the Cubs in 1987. /(JCA)

Tom Brunansky (Bruno) — 1960- . OF 1981- Angels, **Twins**, Cardinals 1228 g, .247, 208 hr, 639 rbi. *1 LCS, 5 g, .412, 2 hr, 9 rbi. 1 WS, 7 g, .200, 2 rbi*
☛ *All-Star—85.*

Chosen by California in the first round of the June 1978 draft, Brunansky exhibited consistent, if unspectacular, power throughout his career. He played just 11 games for the Angels in 1981 before being traded with pitcher Mike Walters for Doug Corbett and Rob Wilfong in May 1982. He was the rightfielder on the 1982 Major League All-Rookie team and set a club record with 15 game-winning RBI the following year. One of seven players with 20 or more homers each season from 1982 to 1987 and one of six to play 150 or more games each of those six years, Brunansky's power was hurt in the Metrodome, which favors left-handed pull hitters. He led all players in the 1987 ALCS in batting average, total bases, doubles, and RBI, and tied for the lead in runs, hits, and homers. He was Minnesota's active home run leader, fourth overall, when traded to St. Louis for Tommy Herr in 1988. /(ME)

George Brunet (Lefty) — 1935- . LHP 1956-57, 59-71 A's, Braves, Astros, Orioles, **Angels**, Pilots, Senators, Pirates, Cardinals 1432 ip, 69-93, 3.62

Brunet made over 30 minor and major league moves before sticking with the Angels for four-plus years starting in 1965. A hard-luck pitcher, he led the AL in losses in 1967 (19) and '68 (17) despite good ERAs of 3.31 and 2.85. In 15 of his losses in 1967, his teammates scored two runs or less. Brunet was still pitching in the Mexican League past age fifty. He holds the minor league strikeout record with more than 3100. /(JCA)

Tom Bruno — 1953- . RHP 1976-79 Royals, Blue Jays, **Cardinals** 123 ip, 7-7, 4.24

As a Royals farmhand, 6'5" Tom Bruno threw seven-inning no-hitters in the Midwest League in 1972 and in the Southern League in 1974. An original Blue Jay, he was traded to St. Louis in 1978 and recorded a 1.98 ERA in 18 appearances, but was hit hard in 1979 and demoted. /(MC)

John T. Brush — 1845-1912. *Executive.*

One of the organizers of the original NL franchise in Indianapolis, where he owned a large clothing store, Brush became president of the club in 1887 and decided to become a leader in the game. The next year he pushed through the salary-limit rule, which helped spark the Players' League revolt in 1890. When his club dropped from the NL in 1889, Brush invested in the Giants, and in 1891 he was awarded the Cincinnati franchise in the reorganized, 12-team NL. He continued to own Indianapolis in the Western League. Ban Johnson, president of the league, accused him of using Cincinnati to draft players to send to Indianapolis. In 1902 he sold the Reds and bought control of the Giants. He tried to push through the idea of a trust holding all NL teams. The idea didn't get anywhere, and Brush made many enemies in the game. A diehard opponent of Ban Johnson, he fought the AL's attempts to put a team in New York and opposed the peace treaty between the AL and NL. Brush and his manager John McGraw refused to let the Giants play a WS in 1904. He won his fourth pennant with the Giants in 1912, then left for California to

recuperate from ill health after losing the WS to the Red Sox in seven games. He died on the train as it was passing through Missouri. /(NLM)

Warren Brusstar — 1952- . RHP 1977-84 **Phillies**, White Sox, Cubs 410 ip, 24-13, 3.05. *4 LCS, 13 ip, 1-0, 1.42. 1 WS, 2 ip, 0-0, 0.00*

A sinker-slider pitcher, Brusstar was a middle reliever who never started a game. Plagued by shoulder problems, he always pitched well in postseason play, and beat the Astros in Game Four of the 1980 LCS. /(AL)

Bill Bruton — 1929- . OF 1953-64 **Braves**, Tigers 1610 g, .273, 94 hr, 545 rbi. *1 WS, 7 g, .412, 1 hr, 2 rbi*

Bruton was a fleet centerfielder who led the NL in stolen bases in each of his first three seasons. His first ML homer (and his only one in 151 games in 1953) was the first home run hit at Milwaukee's County Stadium and gave the Braves a 3-2 victory over the Cardinals in ten innings.

Later his power output improved. Twelve times he led off games with home runs. In 1961, after being traded to the Tigers, he hit 17 homers. A knee injury cost him half of the 1957 season and a chance to appear in that year's WS. He came back strong the next season and hit .412 in the Series. His best season was probably 1960, his last with the Braves; he hit .286 and led the NL in runs scored (112) and triples (13). /(FK)

Billy Bryan — 1938- . C 1961-68 **A's**, Yankees, Senators 374 g, .216, 41 hr, 125 rbi

The 6'4" Georgian was a backup most of his career. He caught 95 games for Kansas City in 1965 and achieved career highs of 14 homers, 51 RBI, and a .252 BA. /(JCA)

Clay Bryant — 1911- . RHP 1935-40 **Cubs** 543 ip, 32-20, 3.73. *5 WS ip, 0-1, 6.75*
☛ *Led League—k 38.*

Bryant spent 45 years in baseball as a pitcher, coach, and minor league manager. A .266 lifetime hitter, he won his own game on August 28, 1937 with a 10th inning grand slam. He went 19-11 for the 1938 pennant-winning Cubs, leading the NL in strikeouts (and walks). In his World Series start in Game Three, he pitched almost five hitless innings before Joe Gordon started a Yankee stampede with a home run. Bryant's career was ruined by arm trouble the next year. /(DB)

Ron Bryant — 1947- . LHP 1967, 1969–75 Giants, Cardinals 917 ip, 57–56, 4.02. *1 LCS, 2 ip, 0–0, 4.50.* 20 wins: 73
☛ *Led League—w 73.*

Bryant adopted a huge stuffed bear (that he called "Bear Bryant") as his lucky charm in 1972. It seemed to turn his fortunes around. From 7–10 in '71, his record improved to 14–7. In 1973 he led the NL in victories, compiling a 24–12 mark for the Giants. Unfortunately, a diving-board accident stemming from an alcohol problem caused him a serious back injury in the spring of 1974. He slumped to 3–15, was traded to the Cardinals, and was cut after 10 games. /(MC)

Steve Brye — 1949- . OF 1970–78 Twins, Brewers, Pirates 697 g, .258, 30 hr, 193 rbi

Brye was called up to the Twins after leading the Southern Association in batting in 1970, but he was seldom more than a platoon player in his nine ML years. In 1974, his most active season, he hit .283 in 135 games, but he had only two homers and 41 RBI. /(MC)

Jerry Buchek — 1942- . 2B-SS-3B 1961, 63–68 Cardinals, Mets 421 g, .220, 22 hr, 108 rbi. *1 WS, 4 g, 1.000*

Cardinals utility man Buchek pinch ran three times in the 1964 World Series, scoring a run in Game One as St. Louis's three-run ninth inning put the game out of the Yankees' reach. He also singled in his only WS at-bat. When Julian Javier was out with a broken finger in 1965, he filled in and hit a career-high .247. Traded to the Mets for 1967, Buchek saw his most action, playing in 124 games and hitting 14 HR, but he struck out 101 times in 411 at-bats. In 1968 he was moved from second base to third base, hitting only .182 in limited duty. /(WOR)

Jim Bucher — 1911- . 3B-2B-OF 1934–38, 44–45 Dodgers, Cardinals, Red Sox 554 g, .265, 17 hr, 193 rbi

The defensively versatile lefthanded hitter had his best season with the 1935 Dodgers, batting .302. In 1937, Brooklyn traded Bucher, Johnny Cooney, Joe Stripp and Roy Henshaw to the Cardinals for Leo Durocher. /(EGM)

Jack Buck — 1925- . *Broadcaster.*

Buck has been play-by-play announcer for the Cardinals since 1954. Virtually an institution in St. Louis, Jack is highly respected by his peers and has called NFL games for CBS and NBC since 1974. He received the Spink award in 1987. /(FO)

Al Buckenberger — 1861-1917. Manager 1889–90, 92–95, 02–04 Columbus (AA), Pirates, Cardinals, **Braves** 493–540, .477

Buckenberger was not a hard driver; he was a kind and tolerant leader who insisted that his players be sober gentlemen at a time when such conduct was not the rule. A light-hitting minor league infielder, he began managing in 1884 at Terre Haute in the Northwest League. His highest ML finish was second with Pittsburgh in 1893. After a seventh-place finish in 1894, he was replaced by Connie Mack. /(RLM)

Garland Buckeye (Gob) — 1897-1975. LHP 1918, 25–28 Senators, **Indians**, Giants 565 ip, 30–39, 3.90

A guard for the football Cardinals from 1921–24, the 260-lb southpaw cast the biggest shadow in baseball with Cleveland in 1925, and backed it up with a 13–8 record. In 1927 he was one of two pro footballers to surrender a homer to Babe Ruth (the other was Ernie Nevers). /(LRD)

Bill Buckner (Billy Bucks) — 1949- . 1B-OF-DH 1969–Dodgers, **Cubs**, Red Sox, Angels, Royals 2495 g, .289, 173 hr, 1205 rbi. *2 LCS, 11 g, .196, 3 rbi. 2 WS, 12 g, .212, 1 hr, 2 rbi*
☛ *Led League—ba 80. All-Star—81.*

Bill Buckner will forever be remembered for the Mookie Wilson ground ball that went through his legs in the sixth game of the 1986 World Series and cost Boston the championship, but he should be

Bill Buckner

remembered as an outstanding hitter and fielder who overcame serious injuries. A consistent outfielder with the Dodgers (1969–76), he went with Ivan DeJesus to the Cubs for Rick Monday. Shifting to first base, Buckner hit .300 with Chicago (1977–84), won the 1980 batting title and twice led the league in doubles (1981 and '83). Playing on gimpy ankles, Buckner had outstanding seasons at Boston in 1985 and 1986 after coming over for Dennis Eckersley. He tied a major league record by playing 162 games at first base in 1985 and broke the ML record he set in 1983 for assists at the position with 184. Entering the 1990 season, he led all active players with 2,707 career hits. /(ME)

Don Buddin — 1934– . SS 1956, 58-62 **Red Sox**, Astros, Tigers 711 g, .241, 41 hr, 225 rbi

Buddin, the regular Red Sox shortstop in 1956 and 1958–61, was often the target of Fenway Park fans because of his erratic fielding. He led AL shortstops in errors in '58 and '59. Only a fair hitter, he had 12 homers in '59 and a career-high BA of .263 in 1961, the season before the Sox traded him to Houston for Eddie Bressoud. /(RMu)

Steve Buechele (Boo) — 1961– . 3B-2B 1985-**Rangers** 668 g, .239, 69 hr, 242 rbi

Buechele became the Rangers' third baseman when Buddy Bell was traded to Cincinnati in mid-1985. A competent fielder and a righthanded hitter with some power, his failure to hit righthanded pitchers made him one of the players most pinch-hit-for in 1987. He roomed with quarterback John Elway at Stanford. /(JCA)

Fritz Buelow [Frederick William] — 1876–1933. C 1899–1907 Cardinals, **Tigers**, Indians, Browns 430 g, .192, 6 hr, 112 rbi

A dreadful hitter, Berlin-born Buelow was competent enough in the field to share catching duties on three AL teams. /(JK)

Charlie Buffinton — 1861–1907. RHP 1882-92 **Braves**, Phillies, Philadelphia (PL), Boston (AA), Baltimore (NL) 3404 ip, 231-151, 2.96. 20 wins: 83-85, 87-89, 91.
  Manager 1890 **Philadelphia (PL)** 21-25, .457

"Big Buff" was an ace in the days of minimal pitching staffs. A righthander noted for his "downer" (a sinking, overhand curve), Buffinton was key in Boston's 1883 pennant, combining with Grasshopper Jim Whitney for 61 of the team's 63 wins. Two years later, they were responsible for 59 of its 66 losses. Buff's best year came in between: 47

Charlie Buffinton with the Phillies

victories, 2.15 ERA, and 63 complete games. He struck out 17 Clevelanders in one game, eight of them in a row. For part of 1890, he managed Philadelphia's Players' League team. He led the American Association with a .757 winning percentage (28–9) in 1891, but retired with Baltimore in 1892 rather than take a NL-ordered mid-season salary cut. /(ADS)

Don Buford — 1937– . OF-2B-3B 1963–72 White Sox, **Orioles** 1286 g, .264, 93 hr, 418 rbi. *3 LCS, 7 g, .357, 1 hr, 4 rbi. 3 WS, 15 g, .207, 4 hr, 7 rbi*
☛ *All-Star—71.*

The compact, switch-hitting outfielder-handyman was a key member of the 1969–71 AL champion Orioles. After four years as a regular infielder with the White Sox, he went to Baltimore in the 1968 deal for Luis Aparicio. The 5'7" team player was a top leadoff man, drawing walks, stealing bases, and scoring runs (99 in three consecutive years, leading the AL in '71). He was also the most difficult man in modern baseball history to double up, grounding into only 33 double plays in 4553 at-bats. Buford led off the 1969 WS with a homer off Tom Seaver. After a disappointing 1972 season, he left the Orioles to play in Japan. Known there as "the greatest leadoff man in the world" for his heroics on the Orioles' 1971 tour of Japan, he hit .270 with 65 HR in 1973–76. /(JCA)

Bob Buhl — 1928– . RHP 1953–67 **Braves**, Cubs, Phillies 2587 ip, 166–132, 3.55. *1 WS, 3 ip, 0–1, 10.80* ☛ *All-Star—60.*

Although he won in double figures six times with the Braves, this fast worker pitched in the shadows of Warren Spahn and Lew Burdette in the 1950s. A paratrooper in Korea in 1952, Buhl broke in with the Braves in 1953 and went 13–8 (2.97).

In 1956 a fractured finger on his pitching hand in August kept him from winning 20; he finished 18–8. His herky-jerky motion caused arm problems, and though he missed a month in 1957, he went 18–7 (2.74 ERA) to help Milwaukee win the pennant.

Buhl was a famed Dodger-killer, beating them eight times in 1956 alone. After his April 1962 trade to the Cubs, his first Chicago victory came two days later against Los Angeles. He had a large repertoire of pitches and fielded well, but he was a notoriously poor hitter. In 1962 he went 0-for-70, the worst ML "0-fer" by a pitcher in a season. He hit .089 lifetime, striking out in 45% of his at-bats. /(JCA)

Jay Buhner — 1964– . OF 1987– Yankees, **Mariners** 150 g, .240, 22 hr, 72 rbi

Buhner's blond good looks, power, and daring outfield play evoked comparisons to Mickey Mantle in New York, but he had a big hole in his swing. He was the main player in the mid-1988 deal that brought Ken Phelps to the Yankees. Buhner played regularly for the Mariners the rest of the season, but ended with a .215 batting average for the year, although he did have 13 HR in 261 at-bats. The arrival of Jeff Leonard, Ken Griffey, Jr., and Darnell Coles reduced his playing time in 1989, but he greatly improved his average without losing any of his power. /(WOR)

DeWayne Buice — 1957– . RHP 1987– **Angels**, Blue Jays 172 ip, 9–11, 4.23

Buice had pitched ten years in the minors, including two in Mexico, before going 6–7 with a club-high 17

saves as a 29-year-old Angels rookie in 1987. He averaged almost a strikeout an inning. He was leading the staff in games but had a 5.11 ERA in June 1988 when he was disabled with a leg injury. /(JCA)

Bozeman Bulger — Unk.–Unk. *Writer.*

The clown prince of baseball writers during the early years of the century, Bulger was a witty, literate reporter whose work was mostly filed with the New York *Evening World.* He took a cavalier attitude toward his responsibilities as a statistics-keeping official scorer. He once balanced his boxscore by arbitrarily assigning an unaccounted-for hit to Larry Doyle of the Giants on the grounds that, "if anyone got it, he did it." Fortunately, Doyle's league-leading .320 average was five points better than anyone else's in 1915.

Bulger was commissioned a Lt. Col. during WWI and was Gen. Pershing's Press Officer in the AEF. /(JK)

Morgan G. Bulkeley — 1837–1922. *Executive.*

Bulkeley was elected to the Hall of Fame because he was the first president of the National League. Actually, it was William Hulbert who had the foresight and determination to create a strong league to replace the National Association, but Hulbert was from Chicago and the politics of the situation called for an Easterner to provide titular leadership for the new league. Insisting he could only serve for a year, Bulkeley accepted the position. He had been the principal backer of the Hartford team in the National Association, and continued to own the city's team during the National League's first season in 1876. He had no connection with baseball after 1876, a casual fan more interested in sulky races than pennant races (he was a member of the National Trotting Association for 30 years). Hulbert slipped into the president's chair the next year and directed the new league to its success. In 1937, when a Cooperstown committee decided whom to install for the 1939 opening ceremonies, an obvious choice was Ban Johnson, founder and president of the American League. It was necessary to equally represent the National League; thus Morgan Bulkeley, seemingly the logical counterpart of Johnson, was inducted.

Bulkeley's father had founded the Aetna Insurance Company, and when he died, Morgan gave up a prosperous merchandising business in New York to run Aetna. After his brief fling with baseball, he entered politics and served as alderman in Hartford

Morgan Bulkeley

Al Bumbry — 1947- . OF 1972-84 **Orioles** 1428 g, .283, 53 hr, 392 rbi. *4 LCS, 11 g, .156, 1 rbi. 2 WS, 11 g, .125, 2 rbi*
☛ *Rookie of the Year—73.*

The speedy Bumbry stole 254 bases during his career and set the Orioles' record with 252 lifetime. With 1403 Oriole hits, he left among the Birds' top five all-time. In 1973, he was the AL Rookie of the Year as he batted .337, and in 1980 became the first Oriole to get 200 hits in a season. The good defensive outfielder won a Bronze Star in Vietnam. /(EW)

Wally Bunker — 1945- . RHP 1963-71 **Orioles**, Royals 1085 ip, 60-52, 3.51. *1 WS, 9 ip, 1-0, 0.00*

In 1964, poised 19-year-old Wally Bunker burst into the ML with a one-hit shutout, victories in his first six starts, and a 19-5 rookie year with Baltimore. He developed a sore arm the next year and was only a part-time pitcher after that. He threw a six-hit shutout in the 1966 WS and won 12 games for the expansion Kansas City Royals in 1969 before arm miseries ended his career. /(JK)

Jim Bunning — 1931- . RHP 1955-71 **Tigers**, Phillies, Pirates, Dodgers 3760 ip, 224-184, 3.27. 20 wins: 57
☛ *Led League—w 57. Led League—k 59-60, 67.*

His career evenly split between the major leagues, Bunning was the first pitcher since Cy Young to win over 100 or to strike out over 1,000 in each league. He retired second only to Walter Johnson with 2,885 strikeouts. He pitched a no-hitter for Detroit in 1958 and a perfect game for the Phillies against the Mets in 1964.

The 6'3" righthander's unusual pitching style, a sweeping sidearm delivery that finished with his glove hand touching the ground well in front of the mound, made him especially difficult for right-handed batters.

Bunning was 20-8 for the Tigers in 1957 but never again won 20. He had 19 victories for Detroit in 1962; then, after being traded to the Phillies in 1964, he won 19 in each of his first three years in Philadelphia. In 1967, when he won 17, he set a ML record with five 1-0 losses.

After retiring as a player, Bunning managed in the minors for five years, then entered Kentucky politics. He was elected to the state legislature and ran unsuccessfully for governor. In 1986, he was elected to the U.S. House of Representatives as a Republican from a heavily Democratic district. /(AL)

before becoming a four-term mayor of the city starting in 1880. He next became governor of Connecticut, holding that office through a series of stormy administrations. A Republican, he was locked out of his office in the State Capitol by a Democratic legislature and became known as "The Crowbar Governor" when he pried the door open.

Bulkeley was elected to the United States Senate in 1904 and served one term, notable for his conflicts with President Theodore Roosevelt. He continued to direct the Aetna Insurance company, which became the nation's largest under his leadership, until his death at 84. /(JK)

Jim Bunning

Bill Burbach — 1947- . RHP 1969-71 **Yankees**
161 ip, 6-11, 4.48

Despite some erratic rookie pitching, this 6'4"fireballer was counted on in 1969 as a cornerstone of the Yankees' rebuilding plans. Ill with mononucleosis the next spring, he never regained his freshman form./(GDW)

Al Burch — 1883-1926. OF 1906-11 Cardinals, **Dodgers** 611 g, .254, 4 hr, 103 rbi

A stocky utility outfielder with a sub-.300 career slugging average, Burch had his only good season with Brooklyn in 1909, stealing 38 bases and batting .271./(JK)

Bob Burda — 1938- . 1B-OF 1962, 1965-66, 1969-72 Cardinals, **Giants**, Brewers, Red Sox 388 g, .224, 13 hr, 78 rbi

Burda's ten-year career was spent shuttling between the majors and minors. The lefthanded hitter led the NL with 14 pinch hits in 1971./(EW)

Lew Burdette — 1926- . RHP 1950-67 Yankees, **Braves**, Cardinals, Cubs, Phillies, Angels 3068 ip, 203-144, 3.66. 20 wins: 58-59 *2 WS, 49 ip, 4-2, 2.92* ☞ *Led League—w 59. Led League—era 56. Led League—k 59-61. All-Star—57, 59.*

On October 10, 1957, Burdette shut out the Yankees for the second time in four days. He was the first pitcher in 37 years to win three complete games in a single WS and the first since Christy Mathewson (1905) to throw two shutouts in a single Series. The win gave Milwaukee the world championship and earned Burdette Series MVP honors.

Lew Burdette

Hall of Fame lefty Warren Spahn and righthander Burdette gave the Braves a formidable one-two punch, with 443 victories between them in 13 seasons. A slider and sinkerball pitcher, Burdette was widely accused of throwing a spitball as well. His constant fidgeting on the mound fed that suspicion; it didn't indicate nervousness. Teammate Gene Conley said, "Lew had ice water in his veins. Nothing bothered him, on or off the mound. He was a chatterbox out there . . . He would talk to himself, to the batter, the umpire, and sometimes even to the ball."

Besides winning 20 games in 1958 and 21 in '59, Burdette won 19 twice and 18 once. His 2.70 ERA topped the NL in 1956. In two All-Star Games, he allowed only one run in seven innings. He no-hit the Phillies on August 18, 1960.

On May 26, 1959, he was the winning pitcher when Pittsburgh's Harvey Haddix hurled 12 perfect innings against the Braves, only to lose in the 13th. That winter, the puckish Burdette asked for a $10,000 raise, explaining: "I'm the greatest pitcher that ever lived. The greatest game that was ever pitched in baseball wasn't good enough to beat me, so I've got to be the greatest!"/(TJ)

Smoky Burgess [Forrest Harrill] — 1927- . C 1949, 51–67 Cubs, Phillies, Reds, **Pirates**, White Sox 1718 g, .295, 126 hr, 673 rbi. *1 WS, 5 g, .333*
☛ *All-Star—54, 55, 59–61, 64.*

Old Smoky, who inherited his name from his father, was a National League All-Star with three different teams. Built short and squat, he was a fine catcher and became of one of the best pinch hitters of his era. He retired with a record 507 pinch at-bats. Only Manny Mota has surpassed Burgess's 145 pinch hits.

Burgess batted .368 in 108 games for the Phillies in 1954. Always a strong, lefthanded hitter, he drove in nine runs for the Reds against Pittsburgh on July 29, 1955. Three of his four hits were home runs—one a grand slam off future batterymate Vern Law. He finished 1955 with a career-high 21 HR. He reported that his most satisfying pinch hit was his home run off Chicago's Sam Jones with two games left in the 1956 season. The Reds needed just one HR to equal the NL record of 221 set by the Giants. Manager Chuck Dressen ordered Burgess to hit for Roy McMillan, barking, "Make it a home run—or nothin'!" The ball landed on Sheffield Avenue. On May 26 of that season, he had caught a three-pitcher no-hitter when Johnny Klippstein, Hersh Freeman, and Joe Black combined to skunk the Braves. Exactly three years later, he was Harvey

Haddix's batterymate when the Pirate hurler pitched his famous 12-inning perfect game against the Braves.

After almost six seasons in Pittsburgh, Burgess was sold to the contending White Sox late in 1964. In his first AL appearance he hit a pinch homer off Detroit's Dave Wickersham to tie a crucial stretch-drive game. Much heavier than in his NL prime, Burgess almost seemed to roll out of the dugout for his frequent pinch-hitting appearances. From 1965 through 1967, he appeared in 237 games, catching only seven. He led the AL in pinch at-bats all three seasons, and in pinch hits the first two. He retired as a .286 lifetime pinch hitter. During the 1980s he coached in Atlanta's farm system./(RL)

Tom Burgmeier (Bugs) — 1943- . LHP 1968–84 Angels, Royals, Twins, **Red Sox**, A's 1258 ip, 79–55, 3.23 ☛ *All-Star—80.*

A consistent and durable reliever until shoulder tendinitis ended his career at age 40, the savvy, fine-fielding Burgmeier had 102 lifetime saves. Signed by Houston, he debuted with California, and went to the Royals in the 1968 expansion draft. In 1971, he was 9–7 with 17 saves and a 1.74 ERA. He had a career-high 24 saves for Boston in 1980./(EW)

Si Burick — 1909–1986. *Writer.*

Sports editor of the Dayton *Daily News* for 54 years, Burick won the J.G. Taylor Spink Award in 1982, the first writer from a city with no ML team to be so honored. He covered his first opening game in Cincinnati in 1929 and never missed one until his death. Burick wrote *Alston of the Dodgers*; *The Main Spark*, a biography of Sparky Anderson; and *Byline: Si Burick*, an anthology of his columns./(NLM)

Bobby Burke (Lefty) — 1907–1971. LHP 1927–35, 37 Senators, Phillies 919 ip, 38–46, 4.29

A starter and reliever, Burke's best day came on August 6, 1931. After pitching a no-hitter to blank the Red Sox, he claimed to have thrown only six curves./(EW)

Glenn Burke — 1952- . OF 1976–79 Dodgers, A's 225 g, .237, 2 hr, 38 rbi. *1 LCS, 4 g, .000. 1 WS, 3 g, .200*

This speedster, who led three minor leagues in steals, is sometimes given credit for inventing the "high five." After his ML days, he participated in the Bay Area Gay Games./(TG)

Jimmy Burke (Sunset Jimmy) — 1874–1942. 3B 1898, 1901–05 Cleveland (NL), Milwaukee (AL), White Sox, Pirates, **Cardinals** 548 g, .244, 1 hr, 187 rbi.
Manager 1905, 18–20 Cardinals, **Browns** 189–213, .470

Burke was a St. Louis native who not only played in his hometown as a scrappy, light-hitting infielder (1903–05), but also managed both the Cardinals ('05) and Browns (1918–20). His ML teams never had a winning season, but he managed successfully in the minors and later coached for Joe McCarthy's 1929 Cubs pennant-winners and 1932 Yankee champions. A 1933 stroke left him an invalid. /(JK)

Tim Burke — 1959– . RHP 1985– **Expos** 479 ip, 37–19, 2.48
☛ *All-Star—89.*

Burke was a starter in the Pirates' and Yankees' organizations, but was brought to the majors as a reliever by Montreal's Buck Rodgers, who had managed Burke in Triple-A. A sinker-slider special-ist with a back-to-the-batter delivery, Burke set an NL rookie record with a league-leading 78 appear-ances in 1985; as set-up man for Fireman of the Year Jeff Reardon, he won his first eight ML decisions, and finished 9–4 with eight saves. He became the leader of Montreal's fine bullpen-by-committee when Reardon was traded in 1987, going 7–0 with 18 saves and a 1.19 ERA, and walking fewer batters per inning than any other NL reliever (19 in 91 innings). He saved 28, went 9–3, and made the All-Star team in 1989. /(JCA)

Jesse Burkett (The Crab) — 1868–1953. OF 1890–1905 Giants, **Cleveland (NL)**, Cardinals, Browns, Red Sox 2072 g, .341, 75 hr, 952 rbi
☛ *Led League—ba 95–96, 01. Hall of Fame—1946.*

Burkett batted over .400 three times, a feat dupli-cated only by Ty Cobb and Rogers Hornsby. A lefthanded line-drive hitter and clever bunter, his ability to foul pitches off was one of the reasons for the introduction of the rule making foul balls strikes. He said he owed his success to "that old con-feedence," but his speed helped him leg out many hits. He scored more than 100 runs in nine different seasons, twice topping the NL.

The 5'8" 155-lb Burkett starred in the outfield for the Cleveland Spiders during the 1890s and was one of the players switched to St. Louis in 1899 when the Cleveland franchise was stripped.

Called "The Crab" because of his caustic barbs and constant complaining, he insulted rivals, fans,

Jesse Burkett with the Cleveland Spiders

and teammates with equal venom. He was particu-larly sensitive to suggestions that he and Jack Glasscock, whom he resembled, were father and son, and would fight anyone who said so.

After leaving the ML, Burkett owned and man-aged the Worcester club of the New England League, 1906–13, making regular appearances in the outfield until he was 45. He later managed other minor league clubs and coached several college teams. In 1921, he coached for John McGraw's New York Giants, still as salty and bitter-tongued as ever. When the Giants won the WS, McGraw had to dig into his own pocket for a bonus for "The Crab"; the players refused to vote him a share. /(JK)

Ken Burkhart — 1916– . RHP 1945–49 **Cardinals**, Reds 519 ip, 28–20, 3.84.
Umpire NL 1957–73 *3 WS*
☛ *All-Star—4.*

Burkhart led the NL in winning percentage with a 19–8 (.704) mark as a Cardinals rookie in 1945. When the veteran players returned from WWII, he faded. Following an arm injury, he had to use an unusual shot-put delivery.

An excellent umpire, he umpired in back-to-back no-hitters in September 1968, Gaylord Perry on the 17th and Ray Washburn the next day. Burkhart was involved in a controversial play in the opening game of the 1970 WS when he became entangled with Orioles catcher Elrod Hendricks in a play at the plate. Burkhart called the Reds' Bernie Carbo out although replays showed Hendricks had tagged Carbo with his mitt while holding the ball in his other hand. /(RTM)

Ellis Burks — 1964- . OF 1987- **Red Sox** 374 g, .289, 50 hr, 212 rbi. *1 LCS, 4 g, .235, 1 rbi*

Tabbed a future MVP by Twins manager Tom Kelly, the speedy Burks earned the Red Sox' starting centerfield job at the age of 22, and as a rookie in 1987 became only the third player in club history to hit 20 HR and steal 20 bases in one season. He earned spots on both the *Baseball Digest* and *Topps* all-rookie teams, and in 1988 hit .294 with 92 RBI and 25 stolen bases. Defensively, Burks is one of the best centerfielders in the ML, with great range and a sure glove offsetting a somewhat erratic arm. His rise to stardom was interrupted by shoulder surgery in 1989. /(SCL)

Rick Burleson (Rooster) — 1951- . SS-2B 1974-84, 86-87 **Red Sox**, Angels, Orioles 1346 g, .273, 50 hr, 449 rbi. *2 LCS, 7 g, .350, 1 rbi. 1 WS, 7 g, .292, 2 rbi*
☛ *All-Star—77-79, 81. Gold Glove—79.*

Burleson sparked the Red Sox with his aggressive play at shortstop and as a lead-off hitter. He overcame a three-error debut in 1974 to become one of Boston's favorite players, relying on a tremendous arm to make up for anything he lacked in range. A Gold Glove winner in 1979, he set the ML record for double plays by a shortstop in 1980 with 147. Traded to the Angels in December of 1980, he injured the rotator cuff of his throwing arm in 1982, then retore it in '84. After a year off, he was voted AL Comeback Player of the Year in 1986, when he hit .284 in 93 games for the Angels. /(PB)

Johnny Burnett — 1904-1959. SS-3B-2B 1927-35 Indians, Browns 558 g, .284, 9 hr, 213 rbi

The Floridian had his first real shot with the Indians in 1930, and was hitting .312 on July 19 when he fractured a wrist, ending his season. He bounced back to bat .300 in 1931, and in an 18-inning game

on July 10, 1932, set a single-game ML record with nine hits. The day before, he had had two hits, giving him 11, an AL record for most hits in two consecutive games. /(EW)

Wally Burnette — 1929- . RHP 1956-58 **A's** 262 ip, 14-21, 3.56

Burnette was 6–8 as a starter for the last-place 1956 A's but had a 2.89 ERA. Used mostly in relief the next year, his ERA ballooned to 4.30. /(FK)

Bill Burns (Sleepy Bill) — 1880-1953. LHP 1908-12 Senators, White Sox, **Reds**, Phillies, Tigers 725 ip, 30-52, 2.69

Burns was shuffled to five teams in his five ML seasons, and not only because he never had a winning year. He was a crap-shooting, card-playing gambler with good stuff but no ambition, known to read newspapers or doze on the bench during games. In 1919, while in Cincinnati selling oil stock, he reportedly learned of the Black Sox' World Series plans. He won $4,000 on the first two games, then lost it all when honest Dickie Kerr won the third game. /(NLM)

Britt Burns — 1959- . LHP 1978-85 **White Sox** 1095 ip, 70-60, 3.66. *1 LCS, 9 ip, 0-1, 0.96*
☛ *All-Star—81.*

Burns was actually discovered by *Chicago Tribune* book critic Bob Cromie. While in Birmingham in 1978, he read about a local whiz kid who had fanned 18 batters in one game. Cromie sent the clipping to his friend Bill Veeck, the White Sox owner. Later that season Burns made his Chicago debut at age 19. In 1980 the 6'5" Burns was named *TSN* Rookie Pitcher of the Year on the strength of a 15-13 (2.84 ERA) season. He pitched 30 consecutive scoreless innings in 1981, a year marred by his father's death two months after being hit by a car. Over the next three seasons, injuries set in, and Burns's ERA ballooned. But he pitched his heart out in the last game of the 1983 LCS, holding the powerful Orioles in check for nine innings. The White Sox could not score either, and Tito Landrum's tenth-inning home run beat Burns. After rebounding in 1985 to go 18-11, he was traded to the Yankees, for whom he never pitched: A chronic, degenerative hip condition ended his career. /(RL)

Ed Burns — 1891–1955. *Writer.*

Burns, who broke in with the Chicago *Herald* in 1914, joined the Chicago *Tribune* in 1925 and was also a longtime correspondent for *The Sporting News.* A large, round man, Burns wrote with an acerbic wit and could wield a sharp needle. More often, he was whimsical, as when he blamed the Cubs' loss of the 1930 pennant on a pair of peacocks manager Rogers Hornsby had purchased from owner William Wrigley. Peacocks were bad luck, he said. "Back in Indiana, we tolerated 'em only on millinery. And then only on certain folks." He was president of the BBWAA in 1947. /(NLM)

George Burns [George Joseph] — 1889–1966. OF 1911–25 **Giants**, Reds, Phillies 1853 g, .287, 41 hr, 611 rbi. *3 WS, 19 g, .257, 5 rbi*

Silent and self-effacing—the antithesis of hot-tempered mentor John McGraw—Burns was a country boy and pool shark from Utica, N.Y. An outstanding leadoff batter who led the NL five times in runs scored and walks, Burns twice topped the league in stolen bases, with a high of 62 in 1914. He had a special knack for playing the Polo Grounds' notorious sun field in left, abetted by a long-billed cap and

George J. Burns with the Giants

primitive sunglasses. He was beloved by the rooters in the left field bleachers, or "Burnsville." "Silent George" spent eleven seasons with the Giants, and was sent to Cincinnati after the 1921 World Series in a trade for third baseman Heinie Groh. On his first visit to the Polo Grounds with the Reds, Burns was honored with a day and given a diamond-studded watch. /(JK)

George Burns (Tioga George) — 1893–1978. 1B 1914–29 Tigers, A's, **Indians**, Red Sox, Yankees 1866 g, .307, 72 hr, 948 rbi. *2 WS, 6 g, .250, 3 rbi*
☛ *Most Valuable Player—26.*

Burns was in his thirteenth major league season in 1926 when he was named MVP, shining among the AL's greatest luminaries. Babe Ruth hit more home runs (47 to Burns's four), but Burns was second to Ruth in RBI, with 114. He tied Hall of Famer Sam Rice for most hits, 216, broke Tris Speaker's doubles record with 64, and batted .358.

Burns drove in the winning run for Cleveland in Game Seven of the 1920 WS, but the Indians traded him to Boston in 1921. Burns reciprocated by turning an unassisted double play against Cleveland in 1923. Somewhat error-prone, he led the AL in that category four of the 12 seasons in which he played over 100 games at first base. Slumping at bat after 1927, he hung on for two final lackluster seasons. He found rejuvenation, though, in the Pacific Coast League, where he played and managed for five more years, hitting .335. /(JK)

Jack Burns (Slug) — 1907–1975. 1B 1930–36 **Browns**, Tigers 890 g, .280, 44 hr, 417 rbi

A graceful, lefthanded-batting first baseman who rose rapidly on the strength of three high-average minor league seasons, Burns hit a career-high .305 for the Browns in 1932. He twice led AL first basemen in assists, three times in double plays. The Bostonian became a Red Sox coach and scout, covering New England until 1973. /(JK)

Oyster Burns [Thomas P.] — 1864–1928. OF-SS 1884–1885, 87–95 Wilmington (U), Baltimore (AA), Brooklyn (AA), **Dodgers**, Giants 1188 g, .301, 66 hr, 674 rbi
☛ *Led League—rbi 90.*

"Erster Boins" was a popular Brooklyn outfielder and utility man who led the NL with 123 RBI and finished second in HR (13) with the 1890 pennant winners. Burns reportedly earned his nickname selling shellfish in the off-season. /(JK)

George Burns with the Indians, batting

Todd Burns — 1963– . RHP 1988– **A's** 199 ip, 14–7, 2.71. *2 WS, 2 ip, 0–0, 0.00*

Burns proved to be a valuable man on the A's pennant-winning 1988 staff, relieving, filling in for injured rotation members when needed, and compiling an 8–2, 3.16 record. In 1989 he was effective replacing the injured Dennis Eckersley in the role of bullpen stopper. /(JFC)

Pete Burnside — 1930– . LHP 1955, 1957–63 Giants, Tigers, **Senators**, Orioles 567 ip, 19–36, 4.81

This well-traveled Dartmouth man won a career-high seven games for the 1960 Tigers as both a starter and reliever. /(CC)

Ray Burris — 1950– . RHP 1973–87 **Cubs**, Yankees, Mets, Expos, A's, Brewers, Cardinals 2189 ip, 108–134, 4.17. *1 LCS, 17 ip, 1–0, 0.53*

After two years in the Cubs' bullpen, Burris became Chicago's ace starter in 1975, going 15–10 for a mediocre team and following with a 15–13, 3.11 record in 1976. He dropped to 14–16 in 1977 and 7–13 in 1978. He was traded to the Yankees for Dick Tidrow in May 1979 and was sold to the Mets that August; he spent time on the DL in both 1979 and 1980. He recovered to help the Expos to their only division title with a 9–7, 3.04 record during the strike-shortened 1981 season and pitched well in the LCS. He pitched a five-hit shutout to beat the Dodgers in Game Two and left Game Five tied 1–1, only to see Steve Rogers give up a ninth-inning HR to lose the game and the series. He had only one more winning season after that, going 13–10 for Oakland in 1984./(WOR)

Jeff Burroughs — 1951– . OF-DH 1970–84 **Senators/Rangers**, Braves, Mariners, A's 1603 g, .261, 234 hr, 854 rbi
☛ *Most Valuable Player—74. Led League—rbi 74.*

Burroughs was a top young power hitter, but by his late twenties had declined to the journeyman stage. The nation's first draft pick in 1969, he joined the Senators at 19. There, he often clashed with manager Ted Williams, though Burroughs later credited Williams for teaching him to concentrate. Burroughs hit 30 homers in 1973, his first season as the Rangers' regular right fielder. That set the stage for his MVP year in 1974, when he batted .301 with 25 homers and a league-leading 118 RBI. But the south wind at Arlington Stadium gave him fits (he fanned a league-high 155 times in 1976), and he profited from a trade to Atlanta, where he hit 41 homers with 114 RBI in 1977. Defensively, Burroughs was capable but slow. When he announced his goal was to win a Gold Glove, teammate Joe Lovitto said, "You won't make any errors. You don't get to a ball until it stops rolling."/(KT)

Dick Burrus [Maurice] — 1898–1972. 1B 1919–20, 25–28 A's, **Braves** 560 g, .291, 11 hr, 211 rbi

A three-sport star at North Carolina State, Burrus failed to stick in a trial with the A's. After four years in the minors, he returned to the ML to hit .340 for the 1925 Braves. However, he had little home run power, and when his batting average dropped to .270 he went on the bench./(NLM)

Ellis Burton — 1936– . OF 1958, 60, 63–65 Cardinals, Indians, **Cubs** 215 g, .216, 17 hr, 59 rbi

Burton's only memorable season was 1963, when he tagged 13 home runs and drove in 42 runs while playing 26 games for the Indians and 93 for the Cubs. A switch-hitter, he twice homered from both sides of the plate in a game./(FK)

Moe Burtschy [Edward] — 1922– . RHP 1950–51, 54–56 A's 185 ip, 10–6, 4.71

In 1954, his only full season in the majors, Burtschy was 5–4 with four saves in 46 appearances. The next year he had more luck than stuff before returning to the minors: despite a 10.42 ERA in 11 innings, his record was 2–0./(MC)

Jim Busby — 1927– . OF 1950–62 White Sox, **Senators**, Indians, Orioles, Red Sox, Astros 1352 g, .262, 48 hr, 438 rbi
☛ *All-Star—51.*

Busby led AL outfielders twice in putouts and once in fielding percentage. He was among the top five stolen base leaders three times, and batted a career-high .312 for Washington in 1953. A cousin of pitcher Steve Busby, Jim coached for fellow Texan Paul Richards at Baltimore, Houston, Atlanta, and Chicago./(TJ)

Steve Busby — 1949– . RHP 1972–76, 1978–80 **Royals** 1060 ip, 70–54, 3.72. 20 wins: 74
☛ *All-Star—74–75.*

Busby was the first pitcher to hurl no-hitters in each of his first two full major-league seasons (1973–74). The *TSN* AL Rookie Pitcher of the Year in 1973, he won 16 and no-hit Detroit on April 27. His second no-hitter came on June 19, 1974, as he retired the last 24 Milwaukee batters. During his next start, he retired the first nine, for an AL-record 33 straight. Over a 17-inning stretch he faced 54 batters, allowing no hits and three walks. A two-time All-Star, Busby set a Royal record with 22 wins in 1974. After three stellar seasons, knee and rotator cuff injuries ended his career./(FJO)

Gussie Busch [August Anheuser, Jr.] — 1899–1989. *Executive.*

In 1953 Busch convinced the board of directors of the St. Louis-based brewery Anheuser-Busch to purchase the hometown Cardinals and renovate Sportsman's Park. Busch became president and chief executive officer of the team and rose to become one of the National League's most powerful owners. In the 1970s, when developers ran out of funds while building the new downtown stadium, he raised the final $3 million and the park was named Busch Stadium.

Referred to at his death as "the last of the old-time beer barons," Busch began working for his father, August Anheuser Busch, Sr., at the brewery started by his grandfather, Adolphus A. Busch, and Eberhard Anheuser. Control of the company passed to Gussie and his brother, Adolphus III, in 1934, and solely to Gussie on his brother's death in 1946. Busch built the ailing company into the largest brewery in the world by the time he retired from an active role in 1975. The brewery's ownership of the Cardinals led the team organist to use the Budweiser theme, and before each home game a team of Clydesdales, the symbol of Budweiser Beer, paraded around the playing field./(SFS)

Busch Stadium

Busch Stadium St. Louis Cardinals 1966– . LF-330, CF-404, RF-330

A circular multi-purpose facility, Busch Stadium opened in 1966 with a natural grass field, but was converted to artificial turf in 1970. The infield dirt remained, however, until 1974, when it too was eliminated except for the areas around the bases. As with most modern parks, its outfield fences are symmetrical, but Busch's playing surface is extremely hard and fast, making it a haven for line-drive-hitting speedsters and dictating the makeup of recent Cardinals clubs. Named for the brewery family that owns the Cardinals, Busch has a small roof that is ringed with replicas of the famous St. Louis arch, which is only blocks away. The stadium has a capacity of 53,138 and was also home to the football Cardinals until their move to Phoenix in 1988./(SCL)

Donie Bush [Owen Joseph] — 1887–1972. SS 1908–23 Tigers, Senators 1946 g, .250, 9 hr, 436 rbi. *1 WS, 7 g, .261, 2 rbi.*
   Manager 1923, 27–31, 33 Senators, **Pirates**, White Sox, Reds 497–539, .480. First place: 27 *1 WS, 0–4, .000*

The 5′6″ 140-lb Tiger shortstop was a clever leadoff man who led the league in bases on balls five times. Despite a long, respectable playing career, Bush is best remembered as a manager. He led the Pirates to the World Series in 1927, where they were swept by the powerhouse Yankees. His vindictiveness may have been a factor; angry with future Hall of Famer Kiki Cuyler over a minor transgression, Bush benched him during the WS. After managing for seven major league seasons, Bush skippered in Triple-A, and became owner of the Indianapolis club. He later scouted for the Red Sox and worked for the White Sox to complete 65 years in organized baseball./(JK)

Guy Bush (The Mississippi Mudcat) — 1901- . RHP 1923–38, 1945 **Cubs**, Pirates, Braves, Cardinals, Reds 2721 ip, 176–136, 3.86. 20 wins: 33 *2 WS, 17 ip, 1–1, 5.40*

One of the winningest Cubs pitchers (152–101), Bush did double duty throughout his career, starting 308 games and relieving in 234. He led the NL in either relief wins or saves in four different seasons (1925, 1926, 1929, 1935), yet started at least 15 times in each of those years. On May 4, 1927, he worked 18 innings as the Cubs outlasted the Braves 7–2.

Bush won 18 and saved eight for the 1929 Cub pennant winners, contributed 19 wins to the 1932 NL champs, and had his only 20-win season the next year.

He was traded to Pittsburgh in 1935. On May 25, Bush relieved against the Braves in a game at Forbes Field and gave up the last two home runs of Babe Ruth's career. /(ME)

Joe Bush (Bullet Joe) — 1892–1974. RHP 1912–28 **A's**, Red Sox, Yankees, Browns, Senators, Pirates, Giants 3092 ip, 194–183, 3.51. 20 wins: 22 *5 WS, 61 ip, 2–5, 2.67*

Because of veteran Jack Coombs's season-long illness, Connie Mack was forced to rush young pitchers into the breech in 1913. Twenty-year-old Joe

Donie Bush (l.) and Red Faber

Joe Bush

Bush came through with a 14–6 mark to help the A's to the pennant, then added a five-hit win in the WS. Although plagued by wildness, the durable youngster continued to pitch well in the next few years, but Mack sold off most of his hitting stars and Bush's record slumped. In 1916 he pitched a no-hitter but led the AL in losses (24). Traded to the Red Sox in 1918, he helped them to a wartime pennant. In 1921, when he found his curve would no longer break, he developed a fork ball, then an almost unknown pitch. Traded to the Yankees for 1922, he had his best record, 26–7, for an AL-high .788 winning percentage.

Bush was a good hitter (.253 BA) and was often used as a pinch hitter. He played a season as an outfielder in the Pacific Coast League after leaving the majors. /(JK)

Randy Bush — 1958– . OF-DH 1982– **Twins** 918 g, .252, 82 hr, 343 rbi. *1 LCS, 4 g, .250, 2 rbi. 1 WS, 4 g, .167, 2 rbi*

A lefthanded slugger who usually plays right field or is the Twins DH, Bush has reached double figures in home runs in five of his six full ML seasons despite never recording 400 at bats. As a rookie in 1982, he broke up Jim Clancy's perfect game with a ninth-inning single on September 28, and in 1986 he tied an AL record with two consecutive pinch-hit home runs. /(SCL)

Tom Buskey — 1947– . RHP 1973–80 Yankees Indians, Blue Jays 479 ip, 21–27, 3.66

As a rookie in 1974, Buskey was traded from the Yankees to the Indians and set a since-broken Cleveland record with 17 saves. After four seasons with Cleveland, he went to the minors, but re-emerged with the early Blue Jays, notching 7 of its staff's 11 saves during the dreadful 1979 season. Two of Buskey's three wins in 1980 came in a doubleheader against Cleveland. /(TF)

John Butcher — 1957– . RHP 1980–86 Rangers, Twins, Indians 833 ip, 36–49, 4.42

Sinker specialist Butcher was drafted four times before signing as a first-rounder with Texas. Although he one-hit the Royals (8/16/83), he did not establish himself as a regular starter until he was traded to the Twins in 1983 as part of the Gary Ward deal. He was 13–11 and 11–14 in two years in Minnesota before suffering a career-ending arm injury. /(MC)

Max Butcher — 1910–1957. RHP 1936–45 Dodgers, Phillies, **Pirates** 1786 ip, 95–106, 3.73

In mid-season 1939, the 6'2" 220-lb Butcher stood 2–13 with the Phillies when Pittsburgh acquired him in a trade for longtime Pirate first baseman Gus Suhr. Although the deal was unpopular in Pittsburgh at the time, by 1941 Suhr was out of the majors and Butcher was the staff ace at 17–12. A sore arm in 1942 reduced his effectiveness, but he posted three more winning seasons for the Pirates during the war years. /(MC)

Sal Butera — 1952– . C 1980– **Twins**, Tigers, Expos, Reds, Blue Jays 359 g, .227, 8 hr, 76 rbi. *1 LCS, 1 g, .667. 1 WS, 1 g, --*

The weak-hitting Butera played eight years in the Twins system before serving as Minnesota's backup catcher for 1980 through 1982. His experience as a batting practice pitcher paid off in the NL; he pitched a scoreless inning for the Expos in 1985, and one for the Reds in 1986. Released by Cincinnati, he re-signed with Minnesota to play for the 1987 World Champions. /(JCA)

Art Butler — 1887–1984. SS-2B 1911–16 Braves, Pirates, **Cardinals** 454 g, .241, 3 hr, 101 rbi

A utility infielder, in 1916 Butler led the NL with 54 pinch-hit appearances and 13 pinch hits. He roomed with Honus Wagner as a young Pirate, and was the oldest living ex-big leaguer before his death at 94. /(JK)

Bill Butler — 1947– . LHP 1969–72, 74–75, 77 **Royals**, Indians, Twins 592 ip, 23–35, 4.21

A Royals expansion draft pick from the Tigers, Butler was a Topps All-Star Rookie in 1969. Although his record was a modest 9–10, he struck out 156 in only 193 innings. He tumbled to 4–12 the next year as a sore elbow cost him his fastball. /(MC)

Brett Butler — 1957– . OF 1981– Braves, **Indians**, Giants 1200 g, .281, 36 hr, 318 rbi. *1 LCS, .211. 1 WS, 4 g, .286, 1 rbi*

The pint-sized, 160-lb Butler developed into one of baseball's surest and most wide-ranging centerfielders. He led the NL in triples in 1983, then was sent by the Braves to the Indians as part of a misguided trade for Len Barker. From 1984 through 1987, Butler was Cleveland's lefthanded leadoff hitter, drag-bunting and averaging 41 stolen bases. In 1985 he led AL outfielders with a .998 fielding percentage. His 14 triples in 1986 led the AL. After he jumped to his hometown Giants as a free agent for 1988, Cleveland's Andy Allanson called him a selfish player. /(ME)

Johnny Butler (Trolley Line) — 1894–1967. SS-3B 1926–29 **Dodgers**, Cubs, Cardinals 375 g, .252, 3 hr, 146 rbi

After 31-year-old shortstop Johnny Butler hit .339 and fielded sensationally in the American Association in 1925, the Dodgers sent seven players to Minneapolis for him, but he never topped .270 in the majors. /(JK)

Pee Wee Butts [Thomas] (Cool Breeze) — 1919–1973. SS Negro Leagues 1938–50 Atlanta Black Crackers, Indianapolis ABC's, **Baltimore Elite Giants** 203 g, .310, 3 hr (inc.)
☛ *Led League—ba 40.*

The 5'9" 145-lb Pee Wee Butts was one of the best shortstops in Negro League baseball of the 1940s. Lauded for his sure hands, exceptional range, and strong throwing arm, he combined with Baltimore Elite Giants teammate Junior Gilliam to form one of the great double play combinations in Negro League history, and Butts is credited with making the young Gilliam into a good infielder. Butts lacked power as a hitter but sprayed the ball to all fields, ringing up consistently high averages. He batted .308, .309, .287, and .321 in 1944–1947 (the only years of his career for which confirmed statistics exist) and was the Negro National League batting champion in 1940 with an unconfirmed .391 average. He appeared in six Negro League all-star games, starting five of them. /(JM)

John Buzhardt — 1936– . RHP 1958–68 Cubs, Phillies, **White Sox**, Orioles, Astros 1491 ip, 71–96, 3.66

The quiet South Carolinian broke in impressively, compiling a 3–0 record (1.85) in six games with the 1958 Cubs. The righthander hurled a one-hitter against the Phillies in 1959; after the season ended, the Phillies traded Richie Ashburn for Buzhardt, Alvin Dark, and Jim Woods. Buzhardt went 11–34 in two years with Philadelphia, but enjoyed a career-best 13–8 season with the 1965 Chisox. /(TJ)

Bud Byerly [Eldred] — 1920– . RHP 1943–45, 50–52, 56–60 Cardinals, Reds, **Senators**, Red Sox, Giants 491 ip, 22–22, 3.70. *1 WS, 1 ip, 0–0, 0.00*

Although he only once won as many as six games and never pitched more than 95 innings in a season, Byerly put in parts of 11 seasons in the majors. His top year came at age 36 when he was 6–6 with six saves for the 1957 Senators. /(FK)

Bill Byrd — 1907– . RHP Negro Leagues 1932–49 Columbus Turfs, Columbus Blue Birds, Cleveland Red Sox, Columbus Elite Giants, Washington Elite Giants, Nashville Elite Giants, **Baltimore Elite Giants** statistics not available
☛ *All-Star—36, 39, 41, 44–46.*

The 6'1" 210-lb Byrd was one of the last pitchers to legally throw the spitball, though he didn't depend on it entirely. He had excellent control and a repertoire of pitches that included the slider, fastball, curve, sinker, and two variations of the knuckler. A switch-hitter, he pinch-hit in one of his six East-West all-star game appearances, and batted .364 for the season with the 1934 Cleveland Red Sox. Although only partial statistics are available, it is known that he completed 56 of 85 league games he pitched between 1933–37 and 1944–47. His best year documented was 1945, when he was 10–6 with 79 strikeouts and 11 complete games. He played winter ball with Caguas in Puerto Rico in 1940–41, leading the league in wins (15)./(BP)

Harry Byrd — 1925- . RHP 1950, 52–57 **A's,** Yankees, Orioles, White Sox, Tigers 828 ip, 46–54, 4.35 ☛ *Rookie of the Year—52.*

Byrd, who wasn't afraid to throw a brushback pitch, earned AL rookie honors with 15 victories in 1952, when he and A's southpaw Bobby Shantz formed the league's winningest righty-lefty tandem (39). He lost a league-high 20 his sophomore year, and never again won more than 11./(TJ)

Sammy Byrd (Babe Ruth's Legs) — 1906–1981. OF 1929–36 **Yankees,** Reds 744 g, .274, 38 hr, 220 rbi. *1 WS, 1 g, --*

Byrd earned his nickname during six years as a Yankee sub by often replacing the aging Babe Ruth in late innings. Byrd later became a professional golfer and won 23 tournaments./(JK)

Bobby Byrne — 1884–1964. 3B-2B 1907–17 Cardinals, **Pirates,** Phillies, White Sox 1282 g, .254, 10 hr, 329 rbi. *2 WS, 8 g, .240*

Pittsburgh's August 1909 acquisition of the 5'7¹/₂" 145-lb infielder contributed key elements to the Pirates' pennant drive, including allowing Tommy Leach to stay in centerfield. Byrne had his best season in 1910, leading the NL in doubles (43) and tying teammate Honus Wagner in hits (178)./(JK)

Tommy Byrne — 1919- . LHP 1943, 46–57 **Yankees,** Browns, White Sox, Senators 1362 ip, 85–69, 4.11; .238, 14 hr, 98 rbi. *4 WS, 21 ip, 1–1, 2.53; .300, 2 rbi*

The slow-working southpaw and $10,000 Yankee bonus baby sometimes enjoyed informing batters what pitch was coming. Good thing, since he led the league in hit batsmen five times. He paced the AL in walks in 1949, '50, and '51, but triumphed despite his wildness, thrice winning 15 or more and leading the league with a .762 winning percentage (16–5) in 1955. A fine hitter who manager Joe McCarthy tried to talk into converting to first base, Byrne amassed 14 homers and pinch hit 80 times./(TJ)

Milt Byrnes (Skippy) — 1916–1979. OF 1943–45 **Browns** 390 g, .274, 16 hr, 154 rbi. *1 WS, 3 g, .000*

Kept out of the service by bronchial asthma, Byrnes was a three-year wartime regular with the Browns, hitting a career-high .295 as centerfielder for the 1944 team that won the only pennant in Browns history./(NLM)

Bill Byron — Unk.-Unk. *Umpire NL 1913-19 1 WS*

Byron was known as "The Singing Umpire" because he would sing some of his calls. His most famous rendition, to a rookie: "You'll have to learn before you're older, you can't get a hit with the bat on your shoulder."/(RTM)

Marty Bystrom — 1958- . RHP 1980–84 **Phillies,** Yankees 394 ip, 26–24, 4.11. *1 LCS, 5 ip, 0–0, 1.69. 2 WS, 6 ip, 0–0, 4.50*

The 6'5" righthander joined the Phillies in September of 1980 and seemed headed for stardom. He shut out the Mets in his first start, won his four others, and compiled a 1.50 ERA. He then started Game Five of the LCS and WS, and though Bystrom did not record a decision, Philadelphia won both games. Beleaguered by elbow and shoulder problems, Bystrom was traded to the Yankees in 1984./(AL)

Putsy Caballero [Ralph Joseph] — 1927– . 2B-3B 1944–45, 47–52 **Phillies** 322 g, .228, 1 hr, 40 rbi. *1 WS, 3 g, .000*

A New Orleans schoolboy star, Caballero joined the Phillies at age 16 in wartime 1944, but only in 1948 and 1951 did he have over 150 at-bats. A utility infielder, he was often employed as a pinch-runner. /(AL)

Ramiro Caballero *Mexican Leagues*

Spending much of his career outside organized baseball, Caballero set a Mexican all-time record in 1962 with 59 home runs, adding 170 RBI and a .414 average for Guanajuato of the Mexican Central League. He won the Triple Crown in the same league for Leon two years later, hitting .380 with 35 HR and 145 RBI. After hitting .355 with 34 HR and 113 RBI in 1965, Caballero retired. /(MC)

Enos Cabell — 1949– . 3B-1B-OF 1972–86 Orioles, **Astros**, Giants, Tigers, Dodgers 1688 g, .277, 60 hr, 596 rbi. *3 LCS, 13 g, .184*

The angular Cabell found his path to the big leagues blocked by Baltimore regulars Brooks Robinson and Boog Powell. A deal to Houston gave him his opportunity at third base, a change he took advantage of to become a solid everyday performer. Combining line drive hitting with speed, Cabell stole over 30 bases every year between 1976 and '79, having his best year overall in 1977, when he hit .282 with career highs of 16 HR, 101 runs, and 42 stolen bases. This bad-ball hitter improved with age, hitting over .300 in 1983 with Detroit and again the following season in his second tour of duty with the Astros, this time as a first baseman. /(CC)

Greg Cadaret — 1962– . LHP 1987– **A's**, Yankees 231 ip, 16–9, 3.77. *1 LCS, 0.1 ip, 0–0, 27.00. 1 WS, 2 ip, 0–0, 0.00*

Cadaret was an effective set-up man for the pennant-winning 1988 A's. He was traded with Eric Plunk and Luis Polonia to the Yankees for Rickey Henderson in mid-1989 and was moved to the starting rotation. /(SFS)

Leon Cadore — 1890–1958. RHP 1915–24 **Dodgers**, White Sox, Giants 1257 ip, 68–72, 3.14. *1 WS, 2 ip, 0–1, 9.00*

On May 1, 1920, at Braves Field, Brooklyn's Cadore faced Joe Oeschger in the longest major league game ever played. Curveballer Cadore allowed 15 hits, walked five, and struck out seven. Brooklyn scored one run in the fourth; Boston answered with a run in the fifth. After 26 innings, with both starters still pitching despite the cold, damp weather, darkness fell, and the game was called, tied 1–1. Cadore went on to win a lifetime high of 15 that season. /(ADS)

Ray Cahill — Unk.–1952. *Scout.*

Cahill was a minor league catcher whose playing days ended during WWI when he was gassed while serving in France, and he suffered from chronic asthma thereafter. He scouted for the Browns from 1924 to 1941 and discovered Browns regulars Harlond Clift, Bob Muncrief, and Jack Kramer. /(FVP)

Les Cain — 1948– . LHP 1968, 1970–72 **Tigers** 374 ip, 23–19, 3.97

An impressive rookie in 1970, the hard-throwing Cain recorded 12 victories and 156 strikeouts, but was hindered thereafter by injuries and control problems. /(CC)

Sugar Cain [Merritt] — 1907–1975. RHP 1932–38 **A's**, Browns, White Sox 987 ip, 53–60, 4.83

Cain was a disappointment, having been hailed as the pitcher on whose broad shoulders Connie Mack would rebuild the A's staff after selling off Lefty Grove, Rube Walberg, and George Earnshaw in the early 1930s. A fastball that he couldn't control earned Cain the AL lead in walks in 1935, a year he spent with the A's and Browns. /(JK)

Ivan Calderon [born Ivan Calderon Perez] — 1962– . OF 1984– Mariners, **White Sox** 502 g, .273, 67 hr, 249 rbi

The injury-prone Calderon, a native Puerto Rican, was gunning for 1985 AL Rookie of the Year honors when he hurt his hand in August. Rated below-average defensively, he was sent by Seattle to the White Sox for catcher Scott Bradley the next June. In 1987 he hit 28 homers—many of them tape-measure shots—and led Chicago in 10 offensive categories. But his 1988 season, already marred by a ribcage pull, was ended in July by the need to have his chronically ailing shoulder repaired./(RL)

Earl Caldwell (Teach) — 1905–1981. RHP 1928, 35–37, 45–48 Phillies, Browns, **White Sox**, Red Sox 587 ip, 33–43, 4.69

Caldwell shut out the Braves in his major league debut with the 1928 Phillies but did not win another ML game until called up by the Browns seven years later. His 7–16 (6.00) mark in 1936 resulted in banishment to the minors in 1937, where he pitched until his contract was purchased by the wartime 1945 White Sox. He threw fairly well as a 40-year-old that season, but, assigned to the bullpen in 1946, he became a sensation, winning an AL-high 13 in relief with eight saves./(RL)

Mike Caldwell (Iron Mike, Mr. Warmth) — 1949– . LHP 1971–84 Padres, Giants, Reds, **Brewers** 2408 ip, 137–130, 3.81. 20 wins: 78 *1 LCS, 1 g, 3 ip, 0–1, 15.00 1 WS, 18 ip, 2–0, 2.04*

Caldwell leaped from Class A to the Padres in 1971, his first pro year. Swapped to the Giants for Willie McCovey and Bernie Williams, he blossomed with a 14–5 mark in 1974. He then underwent elbow surgery and had trouble regaining his form. The property of the Cardinals and Reds in 1977, he finally landed in Milwaukee. In 1978 he was AL Comeback Player of the Year, going 22–9 (2.36) with a league-high 23 complete games and shutting out the World Champion Yankees three times. In 1979 his .727 winning percentage (16–6) was the AL best; his eight consecutive victories set a Brewers record. After helping Milwaukee to the 1982 pennant with a 17–13 mark, he was pounded by the Angels in his LCS start, but shut out the Cardinals in the World Series opener and also won Game Five.

Caldwell used a three-quarters delivery, but threw sidearm to some lefties. His sinker was most effective, though he was accused of throwing a spitter. By 1984 his arm wore out, and he lost his fastball. Iron Mike retired as the Brewers' leader in complete games./(MC)

Ray Caldwell (Slim) — 1888–1967. RHP 1910–21 **Yankees**, Red Sox, Indians 2242 ip, 133–120, 3.21. 20 wins: 20 *1 WS, .1 ip, 0–1, 27.00*

The 6'2″ spitballer was once struck by lightning while pitching for the Yankees. He recovered, finished the game, and beat the Athletics 2–1. Caldwell won 19 for New York in 1915, and had his only 20-victory season with Cleveland in 1920. One of the veteran spitballers allowed to continue using the pitch after it was banned, he helped pitch the Indians to a pennant, but lost his only WS start. A lifetime .248 batter, Caldwell played 46 games in the outfield, and in 1915 led the AL with 33 pinch-hitting at-bats./(JK)

Jeff Calhoun — 1958– . LHP 1984–88 **Astros**, Phillies 151 ip, 6–7, 2.51. *1 LCS, 1 ip, 0–0, 9.00*

A lefthanded, sinker-slider thrower, Calhoun proved an effective middle reliever, particularly against lefthanded hitters. He did not allow a run in his first six ML games for Houston in 1984, and in 1985 threw 20 consecutive scoreless innings./(JCA)

California Angels — 1961– . Team. 2252–2381, .486. *AL West Champions 79, 82, 86*

Formed in the 1961 AL expansion, the Los Angeles Angels finished above .500 in their second season, faster than any other expansion team in the 20th century. After playing their first season in Wrigley Field, an old Pacific Coast League stadium, the club moved in with the Dodgers for four years, always calling their new home field Chavez Ravine rather than Dodger Stadium. The club changed its name to the California Angels in 1965 and moved to its own park in Anaheim in 1966. Bankrolled by Gene Autry, a cowboy-movie star, they spent freely when the free-agent era arrived in the mid-seventies, but have never gotten farther than the division championship. All three of their AL West titles have been followed by losing seasons./(SFS)

Marty Callaghan — 1900–1975. OF 1922–23, 28, 30 Cubs, **Reds** 295 g, .267, 74 rbi

A reserve outfielder with little extra-base power, Callaghan tied a ML record with three at-bats in one inning (8/25/22) as the Cubs outslugged the Phillies 26–23. He had two singles and struck out./(NLM)

Nixey Callahan — 1874–1934. OF-RHP-3B-2B-SS 1894, 1897–1905, 11–13 Phillies, Cubs, **White Sox** 923 g, .273, 11 hr, 394 rbi; 1063 ip, 99–73, 3.39. 20 wins: 1898–99
    Manager 1903–04, 12–14, 16–17 **White Sox**, Pirates 393–458, .462

Player-manager Callahan alternated among the mound, outfield, and infield. A two-time 20-game

The 1986 California Angels

winner with the Cubs, he could hit, field, and run, and was a crowd-pleaser. He continued as an outfielder after turning over the White Sox leadership to Fielder Jones in 1904, but he quit pitching. /(JK)

Johnny Callison — 1939– . OF 1958–73 White Sox, **Phillies,** Cubs, Yankees 1886 g, .264, 226 hr, 840 rbi ☛ *All-Star—62, 64–65.*

"He can run, throw, field, and hit with power," Gene Mauch said of Oklahoma-born Johnny Callison. "There's nothing he can't do well on a ball field." Playing for Mauch with Philadelphia, the lefthanded hitter batted as high as .300, hit as many as 32 HR, twice knocked in over 100 runs, and twice scored over 100. He led the NL with 40 doubles in 1966, and twice hit three homers in a game. In the 1964 All-Star Game, he hit a dramatic homer with two on and two out in the ninth off Dick Radatz to give the NL a 7–4 victory. That year, Callison finished second to Cardinal Ken Boyer in NL MVP balloting. /(TJ)

Paul Calvert — 1917– . RHP 1942–45, 49–51 **Indians,** Senators, Tigers 302 ip, 9–22, 5.31

A bespectacled French Canadian, the University of Montreal graduate was limited by a chronic sore arm. Usually a reliever, Calvert started 23 times for the 1949 Senators and led the league with 17 losses, including 14 in a row, the fourth longest streak in AL history. /(JK)

Ernie Camacho — 1955– . RHP 1980– A's, Pirates, **Indians,** Astros 248 ip, 10–20, 4.14

Camacho, a favorite of manager Pat Corrales, set an Indians record with 23 saves in 1984, though few came easy. Relying on a 90-mph fastball and little else, his career was derailed by a fragile arm and a psyche to match. He missed most of 1985 due to elbow surgery, but recovered in 1986 to save 20 games. His start in 1987 was so dreadful that he was booed even while warming up in the bullpen. He once said that he suffered headaches on the mound because he never blinked while pitching. /(ME)

Moises Camacho — 1933– . 2B 1951–75 Mexican Leagues

Considered the Rogers Hornsby of the Mexican League, Camacho batted more than .340 three straight seasons and twice topped 100 RBI for Mexicali in 1953–55, as remnants of the bankrupt Mexican circuit merged into the Class-C Arizona-Texas League. Returning to the Mexican League in 1957, he hit at least 20 homers three times, and .300 six times. Appointed Poza Rica's manager in 1971, he retired as a player, but couldn't resist re-activating himself to pinch hit until, at age 42, his lifetime average finally dipped below .300. /(MC)

Ronaldo Camacho — 1935– . 1B-2B 1953–75 Minor and Mexican Leagues

Camacho struggled in the Cardinals chain as a middle infielder for several seasons before returning to his native Mexico in 1956 and becoming a first baseman. Over the next 20 years, he hit 317 homers, playing for nine Mexican League teams. He was the league's home run champion in 1962–63, and the RBI leader in 1963 and 1969. /(MC)

Joseph Cambria (Papa Joe) — Unk.–1962. *Scout.*

Cambria was brought to the US from his native Italy when he was three months old, and was a minor league outfielder until he broke his leg in 1916. He owned several minor league clubs from 1929 to 1939, and became a scout for the Washington Senators, staying with the club when it moved to Minnesota as the Twins. Cambria signed Mickey Vernon, Early Wynn, and Ed Yost for the Senators, but was best known for his scouting in Cuba, signing over 400 Cuban players to pro contracts in his career. /(FVP)

Dolf Camilli — 1907– . 1B 1933–43, 45 Cubs, Phillies, **Dodgers**, Red Sox 1490 g, .277, 239 hr, 950 rbi. *1 WS, 5 g, .167, 1 rbi*
☛ *Most Valuable Player—41. Led League—hr 41. Led League—rbi 41. All-Star—39, 41.*

Camilli combined graceful fielding with long ball power. When Larry McPhail assumed command of the decrepit Dodgers in 1938, Camilli was the first player he sought. A steady, low-key leader, Camilli became the Dodger captain, a counterbalance to excitable manager Leo Durocher. A former boxer whose brother had died in the ring fighting World Heavyweight Champion Max Baer, Camilli quelled clubhouse clashes with a quiet word and meaningful look. He also discouraged team veterans from hazing Dodger rookies Pee Wee Reese and Pete Reiser.

Camilli hit at least 23 HR eight straight seasons. He was named MVP in 1941 after leading Brooklyn to the pennant with league highs of 34 HR and 120 RBI. When Brooklyn traded him to the rival Giants in 1943, Camilli refused to report. His son Doug caught for the Dodgers and Senators in the 1960s. /(JK)

Doug Camilli — 1936– . C 1960–67, 69 **Dodgers**, Senators 313 g, .199, 18 hr, 80 rbi

Camilli's father, Dolf, starred as a homer-hitting first baseman in the NL, but Doug couldn't match his father's bat. The high point of his nine ML seasons as a reserve was catching Koufax's 1964 no-hitter. /(TG)

Ken Caminiti — 1963– . 3B 1987– **Astros** 254 g, .246, 14 hr, 102 rbi

Caminiti is an excellent fielder, but after a hot start in his first call-up, his hitting dropped off. He finally won the third base job in 1989, hitting .255 with 10 HR and 72 RBI. /(WOR)

Howie Camnitz (Red, The Kentucky Rosebud) — 1881–1960. RHP 1904, 06–15 **Pirates**, Phillies, Pittsburgh (FL) 2085 ip, 133–106, 2.75. 20 wins: 09, 11–12 *1 WS, 4 ip, 0–1, 12.27*

"The Kentucky Rosebud" blossomed in 1909, tying Christy Mathewson for both the NL lead in winning percentage (.806), and second-most NL wins (25). Camnitz became Pittsburgh's sixth 100-game winner in 1912, en route to his third 20-win season in four years. Traded to the Phillies on August 20, 1913, after a 6–17 start, he pitched in just nine games for them, then jumped to Pittsburgh in the Federal League. His brother, Harry, pitched briefly for the 1909 Pirates and 1911 Cardinals. /(ME)

Rick Camp — 1953– . RHP 1976–78, 80–85 **Braves** 942 ip, 56–49, 3.37. *1 LCS, 1 ip, 0–1, 36.00*

Arm trouble kept Camp out of the majors in 1979, but the sinkerballer returned in 1980 to save 22 games and set a Braves record with 77 appearances. He recorded a 1.78 ERA with 17 saves in 1981, and tied for the NL lead with nine relief wins. After that he was used in every pitching role, with mixed results. A notoriously poor hitter (.074), he surprised everybody with his only ML home run in the 18th inning of a July 4–5, 1985 marathon with the Mets; his post-3:00 AM blast with two out on an 0–2 pitch from Tom Gorman tied the game at 11–11, but he lost it 16–13 in 19 innings. /(JCA)

Roy Campanella (Campy) — 1921– . C Negro Leagues 1937–42, 1944–45 Baltimore Elite Giants statistics not available *ML: C 1948–57* **Dodgers** *1215 g, .276, 242 hr, 856 rbi. 5 WS, 32 g, .237, 4 hr, 12 rbi*
☛ *All-Star—41, 44–45*
☛ *Most Valuable Player—51, 53, 55. Led League—rbi 53. All-Star—49–56. Hall of Fame—1969.*

Campanella, one of the five black players signed by Brooklyn Dodgers owner Branch Rickey before the 1946 season, was the first catcher to break organized baseball's color line. Just 5'9" but solidly built, he had already proven himself as a catcher during nine years in the Negro National League, the winter leagues, and Mexico. In 12 additional seasons, 10 in the majors, he was one of the era's outstanding players, and his leadership and indefatigable enthusiasm made him one of the most popular players in the game.

Born in Philadelphia of a black mother and an Italian father, Campanella began his baseball career in 1937 with a hometown semi-pro team, the Bacharach Giants. So impressive was his play that the Baltimore Elite Giants of the Negro National League offered him a uniform that year, though he was only 15 years old. Still in school, he played only on weekends and caught only to spell veteran Biz Mackey. The next year, however, he left school and joined the team full-time. He won the first-string job in 1939 and led the Giants to playoff triumphs over the Newark Eagles and the Homestead Grays. In four games he collected five hits, including one HR, and drove in seven runs.

Campanella soon challenged the aging Josh Gibson as the dominant Negro League catcher. He was voted the MVP in the 1941 East-West all-star game, but after a dispute with Baltimore owner Tom Wilson, he jumped to the Mexican League for part of 1942 and all of 1943. Rejoining the Giants, he led the league in doubles in 1944 and in RBI in 1945.

In October 1945, Campanella caught for a black all-star team in a five-game exhibition series against a squad of white major leaguers managed by Charlie Dressen. Dressen had orders to arrange an appointment for Campanella with the Brooklyn Dodgers, who later signed the catcher for their Nashua, NH, Class-B farm team (Eastern League), a club run by Buzzie Bavasi and managed by Walter Alston. Campanella, who roomed with pitcher Don Newcombe, hit .290, led the league in putouts, assists, and errors, and won the MVP award. In 1947 he advanced to Montreal, the Dodgers' International League team, and again was named the MVP, despite a season-ending slump that cut his average to

Roy Campanella

.273. Paul Richards, then the Buffalo manager, called him "the best catcher in the business—major or minor leagues."

Campanella made the Dodgers in 1948, but his promotion to Brooklyn was delayed by Rickey's plan to have him integrate the American Association. The owner forced manager Leo Durocher to play the catcher in the outfield, where he was not successful, and then sent him to St. Paul (AA) in May. In 35 games, he had 40 hits (half for extra bases) and 39 RBI and batted .325 before being recalled.

Campanella returned to the Dodgers to stay. For the next nine years, he caught for outstanding Brooklyn teams whose members have been lionized as "The Boys of Summer." They won National League pennants in 1949, 1952, 1953, 1955, and 1956, narrowly missed two others, and climaxed

Brooklyn's baseball history with its only World Series triumph in 1955. Campanella's contributions to the Dodgers were remarkable. He won the MVP award three times in five years. In 1953, his best season, he batted .312, and scored 103 runs. Also, his 142 RBI (which led the league) and 41 HR set ML records for catchers (plus one HR as a pinch-hitter). He fielded with grace that belied his physique and handled with distinction a predominantly white pitching staff.

Like those of many catchers, Campanella's career was punctuated by injuries. In spring training of 1954, he chipped a bone in the heel of his left hand and damaged a nerve. It affected his hitting and limited him to 111 games. Surgery helped in 1955, but the problem returned the next year. Then, in January 1958, Campanella was permanently disabled in an automobile accident. Returning home from his liquor store, which he ran in the off-season, he lost control of his car on an icy street. The car slammed into a telephone pole and flipped over, pinning him behind the steering wheel. The crash fractured his fifth cervical vertebra and damaged his spinal cord. He survived and endured years of therapy, living far beyond the normal span for quadriplegics, but his career was over. He committed himself to decades of work in community relations for the Dodgers. /(SG)

Bert Campaneris (Campy) — 1942– . SS-3B-OF-2B 1964–81, 83 A's, Rangers, Angels, Yankees 2328 g, .259, 79 hr, 646 rbi. *6 LCS, 18 g, .221, 2 hr, 6 rbi. 3 WS, 19 g, .263, 1 hr, 5 rbi*
☛ *All-Star—68, 72–75, 77.*

Surrounded by superstars, Bert Campaneris was a key contributor to the great Oakland teams with his competitive spirit and superb play. His memorable debut with the Kansas City A's (July 23, 1964) included two home runs, one off the first major league pitch ever thrown to him. Bert became only the third player in big league history to hit two homers in his first game. He made headlines in one of club owner Charlie Finley's publicity stunts in 1965. On September 9, Campaneris played every position in a nine inning game. He also led the A's in hitting (.270), edged his cousin, Jose Cardenal, for the league lead in steals (51), and led the league in triples (12). Campy became one of baseball's all-time top base thiefs, stealing 649 bases to rank seventh all-time on his retirement and leading the American League six times, including his first four full seasons (1965–68).

When the A's moved to Oakland in 1968, Bert

Bert Campaneris

led the league in hits (177) and at-bats. Though he struck out more than some leadoff hitters and didn't walk much, he was a catalyst in the Oakland attack. Hitting from an extreme crouch, the Cuban right-hander would get on base and disrupt pitchers. He improved consistently on defense, leading AL short-stops with 795 chances in 1972. An adept bunter, he led the AL in sacrifice bunts in 1972 (20) and 1978 (40). Despite these credentials, Bert is most associated with an unfortunate incident in the 1972 American League Championship Series. In Game Two, he already had three hits, two steals and two runs scored as he faced Detroit hurler Lerrin LaGrow. When LaGrow's pitch hit Campaneris in the ankle, Bert flung his bat at the hurler. A near-riot ensued as Detroit manager Billy Martin charged Campaneris. The batter and pitcher were both ejected. Bert was suspended for the remainder of the playoffs, reinstated for the World Series (in which he was hit by pitches three times), and suspended for the first seven games of 1973. He was the shortstop on *TSN*'s post-season AL All-Star Team in 1973 and 1974. In 1976, his 52 steals helped the A's set an AL club record with 341 steals. Like most of the A's, Campaneris played out his option, moving to the Rangers. After a full season with Texas (1977), age and injuries limited Bert to part-time, utility duty. He spent 1982 in the Mexican League. In 1983, at the age of 41, Campaneris returned to the big leagues as a utility infielder with the Yankees, playing for Billy Martin. He responded with a career-high .322 batting average in 59 games and solid defense at second and third base. /(ME)

Al Campanis — 1916- . 2B 1943 **Dodgers** 7 g, .100, 0 hr, 0 rbi

Campanis worked for the Dodgers for 46 years, rising to vice-president in charge of player personnel. His career came to an unceremonious end early in 1987 when he made insensitive racial remarks in a network television interview.

He played seven games with the Dodgers in 1943 before leaving for WWII with the Navy, and when he returned he became a manager in the Dodgers' minor league system. Campanis became a scout in 1950 and director of scouting from 1957 to 1968, before finally settling in as a club vice-president in 1969. His son Jim was a ML catcher for parts of six seasons.

In the infamous 1987 interview, he provoked national ridicule by suggesting that black ballplayers lacked the "necessities" to become ML managers. /(FVP)

Bill Campbell — 1948- . RHP 1973-87 **Twins,** Red Sox, Cubs, Phillies, Cardinals, Tigers, Expos 1229 ip, 83-68, 3.55. *1 LCS, 2 ip, 0-0, .000. 1 WS, 4 ip, 0-0, 2.25*
☛ *All-Star—77.*

Like many relievers, Bill Campbell's career was marked by injury and a couple of brilliant seasons. Signed by the Twins in 1970, he was their bullpen ace in 1974 (19 saves) and 1976 (20 saves). He led the entire Minnesota staff with 17 wins in 1976, an AL relief record, also leading the league with a .773 winning percentage and 78 appearances. Signed by the Red Sox as a free agent, he again led his staff in wins (13), and he paced the AL with 31 saves to

become *TSN*'s Fireman of the Year for the second straight season. A severe elbow injury in 1978, probably caused by overwork, finished his career as a stopper. Still valuable, he found work with six teams from 1981 to 1987 and led the NL with 83 appearances for the 1983 Cubs. /(ME)

Billy Campbell — 1873-1957. LHP 1905, 07-09 Cardinals, **Reds** 408 ip, 23-25, 2.80

After going 3-0 in three starts for the Reds in 1907, Campbell followed with losing records the next two seasons. His ERAs (2.60, 2.67) were worse than average for those dead-ball years. /(SFS)

Bruce Campbell — 1909- . OF 1930-42 White Sox, Browns, **Indians,** Tigers, Senators 1360 g, .290, 106 hr, 766 rbi

Campbell beat the odds when he recovered from a 1935 bout with spinal meningitis. After leading the AL with 104 strikeouts as a rookie (1932), the lefthanded batter led the Browns with 106 RBI the following year. On November 20, 1934, Campbell came to Cleveland for Johnny Burnett, Bob Weiland, and cash. He quickly proved popular with the Tribe and was batting .325 in early August when he complained of a headache in Detroit. Soon he was in critical condition with cerebral spinal fever. Given a fifty-fifty chance to recover, Campbell was miraculously back in uniform in 1936. He collapsed again in May, but still batted a remarkable .372 in 76 games and was honored on Bruce Campbell Day at Cleveland's League Park. He had three hits that day and went 6-for-6 on July 2, 1936. Philadelphia writers honored Campbell as most courageous athlete of the year in 1936. /(ME)

Dave Campbell — 1942- . 2B-3B 1967-74 Tigers, **Padres,** Cardinals, Astros 428 g, .213, 20 hr, 89 rbi

Campbell's first ML hit was a home run for the World Champion 1968 Tigers. After three short trials, Detroit sent the 6'1" Michigan native to San Diego. In 1970, his only season as a regular, Campbell led NL second basemen in putouts, assists, and errors while hitting .219 with 12 HR for the Padres. /(TJ)

Dave Campbell (Chopper) — 1951- . RHP 1977-78 **Braves** 158 ip, 4-10, 3.82

Despite a 0-6 record, Campbell compiled 13 saves in 65 appearances as a rookie with the last-place 1977 Braves. Overworked and unappreciated, he developed arm trouble during 1978 and left the majors. /(PB)

Mike Campbell — 1964– . RHP 1987- **Mariners**
185 ip, 8–16, 5.74

Seattle native Campbell was the Mariners' first-round draft pick in June 1985, but was hampered by wildness. /(JFC)

Vin Campbell — 1888–1969. OF 1908, 10–12, 14–15
Cubs, Pirates, **Braves**, Indianapolis (FL), Newark (FL)
546 g, .310, 15 hr, 167 rbi

The Braves traded a worn Mike Donlin to get Campbell's bat into their lineup in 1912; Campbell led NL hitters in at-bats, and outfielders in errors. In 1914 he signed a three-year Federal League contract and had two .300-plus campaigns. When the Feds folded in 1916, he sued and won payment for the final year, but couldn't find work elsewhere. /(NLM/ ADS)

Casey Candaele — 1961– . 2B-OF-SS 1986- **Expos**,
Astros 225 g, .244, 1 hr, 34 rbi

In 1987 the spunky, 5'9" Candaele played six positions and finished fourth in NL Rookie of the Year balloting. His teammates had a pool to guess the date of his first home run; it came on July 19, and was the shortest ever to clear the fence at Olympic Stadium. A special yellow seat was set in the first row of bleachers to mark the shot. The switch-hitter was demoted and traded to Houston in mid-1988. Casey's mother, Helen Callahan St. Aubin, played in the professional All American Girls Baseball League of 1942–1954 and had 354 steals in 388 games. /(JCA)

John Candelaria (The Candy Man) — 1953– . LHP
1975–**Pirates**, Angels, Mets, Yankees, Expos 2368 ip,
167–107, 3.27. *3 LCS, 25 ip, 1–1, 2.13. 1 WS, 9 ip, 1–1,
5.00*
☛ *Led League—era 77. All-Star—77.*

Considered one of baseball's best "money" pitchers, Candelaria's toughest opponent was injury. From 1975 to 1988, he had only one losing season. His 1976 no-hitter was the first ever pitched by a Pirate in Pittsburgh. A gutsy competitor, Candelaria's biggest asset was great control of all his pitches from a tough three-quarter delivery. The 6'7" 205-lb lefty helped Pittsburgh win the NL East as a rookie in 1975 and set a NLCS record with 14 strikeouts in Game Three. In 1977 he became the first NL pitcher since Sandy Koufax (in 1965) to win 20 games and lead in ERA (2.34) and winning percentage (.800, 20–5). He was Pittsburgh's first 20-game winner since 1960 and their first lefthander to win 20 since 1924. He led the 1979 World Champions with 14 wins and pitched shutout ball in the crucial sixth game of the World Series.

Candelaria overcame a severe arm injury in 1981. Plagued by chronic back problems, the already disgruntled Candelaria was moved to the bullpen in 1985 and traded to California in August as the Pirates dumped their high-salaried players after finishing last in 1984 despite leading the league in ERA. Candelaria was the AL Comeback Player of the Year in 1986 as the Angels won their division. He gave up only one earned run in his two LCS starts, winning one but losing Game Seven on errors. Near the end of another injury-plagued season in 1987, the Brooklyn, NY native was sent to the Mets, who had lost Ron Darling to injury, but Candelaria's 2–0 record wasn't enough to help them win their pennant race. Not wanting to return to the bullpen, he went to the Yankees after the season and was their best pitcher in 1988 (13–7, 3.38) but spent the last part of the year on the DL again, this time with knee ailments. More injuries cut into his 1989 campaign. /(ME)

Milo Candini — 1917– . RHP 1943–44, 46–51
Senators, Phillies 538 ip, 26–21, 3.92

After a 7–0 start with the Senators, Candini finished at 11–7 in 1943. Hard-throwing and occasionally wild, he spent all of 1945 in the army, and never again won more than three games in a season. /(EW)

Tom Candiotti (Candy) — 1957– . RHP 1983–84, 86-
Brewers, **Indians** 970 ip, 56–64, 3.69

Candiotti was released by Milwaukee in 1985 after six years in the minors and two major league trials. He was in winter ball, working on a knuckler, when signed by the Indians. The surprise of their 1986 staff, he led with 16 wins and a 3.57 ERA, and topped the AL with 17 complete games. As the Indians fell in 1987, so did Candiotti, going 7–18 despite throwing two one-hitters; he lost one of them. /(JCA)

Candlestick Park (The Stick) San Francisco Giants
1960– . LF-335, CF-400, RF-335

Located on Candlestick Point, which juts into San Francisco Bay, Candlestick Park opened in 1960 as baseball's first truly "modern" stadium, only to quickly fall under criticism for its poor location. At first it was essentially round, but open in the outfield, and icy winds whipped in from the bay through the stadium's open end, often dropping the already cool temperatures an additional 15 to 20 degrees during the course of a night game. The most infamous incident occurred during the 1961 All-Star Game, when Giants pitcher Stu Miller was literally blown off the pitching rubber by a strong gust, forcing a costly balk. Originally natural grass, the stadium was converted to artificial turf and the open end enclosed for the NFL's 49ers in 1972, but it was converted back to grass in 1979. The additional seats made Candlestick the NL's largest park at the time and reduced the wind problem somewhat, but it remains the only uncovered stadium with a heating system. The field itself has substantial foul territory and a wire outfield fence well inside the permanent seats, and on home runs and deep fly balls dozens of fans leap from their seats to the field in hopes of catching a souvenir. /(SCL)

Eli Canel (Buck) — 1906–1980. *Broadcaster.*

Born in Buenos Aires of Scottish-Spanish descent, Canel worked as a reporter for the Associated Press in Latin America for seven years before moving to New York, where he broadcast Yankees home games in Spanish until 1972. Beginning in 1937, he broadcast 42 WS. His trademark line, translated, was "Don't go away, this game is really getting interesting." In 1985, the Hall of Fame voted him the Ford C. Frick Award for broadcasters. /(NLM)

John Cangelosi — 1963– . OF 1985– **White Sox**, Pirates 433 g, .242, 6 hr, 67 rbi

The 5'8" Cangelosi was the surprise of the White Sox' 1986 spring camp when he displaced Rudy Law and Daryl Boston to win the centerfield job. The spunky switch-hitter drew walks and stole 50 bases, an AL rookie record. But a 0-for-31 drought dropped his average below .230, and he was benched. Dealt to Pittsburgh in 1987, he batted .275, mostly pinch hitting, and on September 15 he became the first Pirate in 21 years to steal home. /(RL)

Chris Cannizzaro — 1938– . C 1960–65, 68–74 Cardinals, Mets, Pirates, **Padres**, Cubs, Dodgers 740 g, .235, 18 hr, 169 rbi
☛ *All-Star—69.*

Mispronouncing Cannizzaro's name, Casey Stengel said, "Canzoneri is the only defensive catcher who can't catch." In 1964, Cannizzaro batted .311, by far a career-high, in 60 games. Only with the 1969–70 expansion Padres was he a regular. /(TJ)

Jimmy Cannon — 1910–1973. *Writer.*

"Nobody asked me, but . . ." was Cannon's familiar lead. A protege of Damon Runyon and Mark Hellinger, Cannon's prose was admired by Ernest Hemingway. Cannon started as a copy boy for the New York *Daily News* in 1926 and joined the New York *American* as a sportswriter in 1936. In WWII he accompanied Gen. Patton's Third Army as a war correspondent. Cannon joined the New York *Post* in 1946 and, except for war correspondence duty in Korea, remained with the paper until hired away by the New York *Journal-American* in 1959; his $1,000 a week salary was believed to be the most in the country paid to a sports columnist. An early observer of the impact of black athletes on both sports and society, he made the immortal comment that boxer Joe Louis was a credit to his race—the human race. /(JK)

Jose Canseco — 1964– . OF 1985– **A's** 568 g, .270, 128 hr, 424 rbi. *2 LCS, 9 g, .303, 4 hr, 7 rbi. 2 WS, 9 g, .181, 2 hr, 8 rbi*
☛ *Rookie of the Year—86. Most Valuable Player—88. Led League—hr 88. Led League—rbi 88. All-Star—86, 88.*

Born in Havana, Cuba, Canseco became a baseball giant in both size and ability. The first-ever member of the "40–40" club with his 40 stolen bases and league-leading 42 HR in 1988, he also led with 124 RBI and won the MVP award in a landslide.

Canseco struck out in his first big-league at-bat and in 12 of his first 24 at-bats in 1985. Despite a club-record 175 strikeouts in 1986, his 33 HR earned him the Rookie of the Year award in a close decision over Wally Joyner. With great bat speed and power to all fields, he became the first Oakland player with back-to-back 100-RBI seasons and joined Dave Kingman as the A's only players with three straight 30-HR seasons. Two years of intense weight training improved his power, but he also improved greatly on defense and showed a strong arm, earning a move from left field to right field.

Canseco's three homers in the LCS matched George Brett's AL record, and his HR in Game Four went to dead center and dented a TV camera over 400' from the plate. In Game One of the WS, he hit his first major league grand slam in the second inning, the 16th slam in WS history, and just the second ever by a player in his first game (Dan Gladden had done it in 1987). But he went hitless for the rest of the Series as the Dodgers stunned the favored A's.

Canseco missed the first half of 1989 with a broken bone in his hand but stayed in the news with a string of speeding tickets that started before the season. His indentical twin brother, Ozzie, played in the Yankees' and A's systems. /(ME)

Ben Cantwell — 1902–1962. RHP 1927–37 Giants, **Braves**, Dodgers 1534 ip, 76–108, 3.91. 20 wins: 33

After Cantwell led NL relievers with 12 wins and 8 losses in 1932, Braves manager Bill McKechnie returned him to the rotation in 1933. Cantwell responded with a league-leading .667 winning percentage (20–10). But 1932–33 were by far his best years; in 1935, Cantwell suffered 25 losses, including 13 in a row. /(JK)

Doug Capilla — 1952– . LHP 1976–81 Cardinals, Reds, **Cubs** 293 ip, 12–18, 4.34

Not many pitchers have enjoyed the start that Capilla had breaking into professional ball. He struck out the first 21 batters he faced as a professional hurler while at Great Falls (Pioneer League). The Hawaiian was originally signed by San Francisco as an outfielder. The Cardinals drafted him from the Giants in 1973. At times he showed signs of being a standout, but he had control problems during his career. /(EW)

Buzz Capra [Lee William] — 1947– . RHP 1971–77 Mets, **Braves** 543 ip, 31–37, 3.88
☛ *Led League—era 74. All-Star—74.*

After being sold by the pitching-rich Mets, Capra earned a starter's role and turned in a stellar 1974 season in which he set an Atlanta Braves consecutive victory mark (9), won the league ERA crown (2.28), and averaged the fewest hits per nine innings of all NL pitchers. The following year he suffered the shoulder injury which drove him to early retirement. /(CR)

Pat Caraway — 1906–1974. LHP 1930–32 **White Sox** 478 ip, 22–40, 5.35

Caraway had a fair curveball and a bizarre, accordion-like windup, nearly doubling over his 6'4" frame before delivering. He went 10–10 as a rookie in 1930, but in 1931 came completely unglued. On July 23 in Boston, he pleaded in vain to be taken out after giving up 11 runs in 4–2/3 innings. Between innings, manager Donie Bush berated his pitcher unmercifully. Three days later in New York, Caraway was shelled 22–5, the worst loss in White Sox history. His 24 losses led the AL that year. Surpris-

ingly, he made the club the next spring, but was sent down in July. /(RL)

Harry Caray — 1920– . *Broadcaster.*

He has broadcast from the centerfield bleachers with a cooler full of beer. He sweeps foul balls from the backstop with a long fishing net. And he leads the most raucous choruses of "Take Me Out to the Ballgame," ever heard at the ballgame. Harry Caray is broadcasting's premier showman, as much an attraction at the ballpark as the teams for which he works.

He made his ML debut with the Cardinals in 1945, and by the mid-50s was heard across the Midwest on flagship station KMOX and baseball's largest radio network. Caray was fired in 1969 amid rumors of personal difficulties with the Busch family, then spent one season in Oakland before returning to the Midwest as the voice of the White Sox. From 1971 to 1981 his antics helped resurrect that nearly comatose franchise, but in 1982 he jumped to the Cubs. His fame reached new peaks with a national TV audience through superstation WGN and the natural affinity Wrigley Field has for his grandstanding antics.

At each stop, Caray has been an unapologetic homer, loudly cheering the locals while freely using "we" and "they" to describe the participants. But even his beloved hometown players are not exempt from the often caustic criticism he calls objectivity. As he put it, "If they're horseshit, there's nothing I can do about it." Caray fought off a stroke to continue in the Cubs' booth as the 1980s drew to a close, still barking his home run call, "It might be . . .It could be . . . It is!", and capping each victory with the simple and joyous exultation "Cubs win!" /(SCL)

Skip Caray — 1939– . *Broadcaster.*

The versatile son of Harry Caray became a Braves broadcaster in 1976 and has announced football, basketball, and hockey as well. Skip made his ML broadcasting debut on May 30, 1965, calling a Braves-Astros game for Atlanta TV station WSB as an emergency substitute for Mel Allen, who was attending his mother's funeral. /(SCL)

Bernie Carbo — 1947– . OF-DH 1969–80 Reds, Cardinals, **Red Sox**, Brewers, Indians, Pirates 1010 g, .264, 96 hr, 358 rbi. *1 LCS, 2 g, .000. 2 WS, 8 g, .200, 2 hr, 4 rbi*

The journeyman outfielder starred in the 1975 World Series, tying the Series record with two pinch homers; the second tied the score in the eighth inning of Game Six, setting the stage for Carlton Fisk's dramatic overtime home run. Carbo had been the Reds' number-one draft pick in the inaugural 1965 draft, ahead of Johnny Bench. He was *TSN* Rookie of the Year in 1970, batting .310 with 21 HR. But the lefthanded hitter slumped to .219 his sophomore year, and arrived in Boston in 1974. With the Red Sox, Carbo was given a giant stuffed animal for good luck. He tabbed it "Mighty Joe Young," and the beast became as well known in Boston as Bernie. His 1978 sale to Cleveland caused Boston pal Bill Lee to walk out (after the season, Lee was sent to the Expos); Lee claimed Carbo was "the best tenth man in baseball."/(EW)

Jose Cardenal — 1943- . OF-1B 1963-80 Giants, Angels, Indians, Cardinals, Brewers, **Cubs**, Phillies, Mets, Royals 2017 g, .275, 138 hr, 775 rbi. *1 LCS, 2 g, .167. 1 WS, 4 g, .200*

Colorful Cardenal played for nine teams in 18 ML seasons. The Cuban immigrant couldn't crack San Francisco's outfield and was traded to California following the 1964 season. He finished second in the AL in steals (37), showed good range and a strong arm in center field, but also developed a reputation as a moody player. After two subpar seasons, Cardenal was shipped to Cleveland. He led the Indians in steals twice and tied a ML record for outfielders by making two unassisted double plays in 1968. Traded to the Cardinals in 1970, he hit .293 with 74 RBI. In a 1971 season split between St. Louis and Milwaukee, he drove in a career-high 80 RBI. Finally reaching the Cubs in 1972, he stayed for six seasons. As the Cubs' right fielder in 1973, he led the team in hitting (.303), doubles (33), and steals (19). He was named Chicago Player of the Year by the Chicago baseball writers. In 1978-80, he played for the Phillies, Mets, and Royals, ending his ML career batting .340 down the stretch for Kansas City and starting two games in right field during the 1980 World Series. He is a cousin of longtime ML shortstop Bert Campaneris./(ME)

Leo Cardenas (Chico, Mr. Automatic) — 1938- . SS 1960-75 **Reds**, Twins, Angels, Indians, Rangers 1941 g, .257, 118 hr, 689 rbi. *2 LCS, 6 g, .167, 1 rbi. 1 WS, 3 g, .333*
☛ *All-Star—64-66, 68, 71. Gold Glove—65.*

Cardenas was one of baseball's best shortstops during the 1960s. The son of Rafael Cardenas, himself an outstanding pro shortstop in Cuba, Leo became known as "Mr. Automatic" for his fancy fielding. As a Cincinnati regular (1962-68), he won

a Gold Glove in 1965 and topped NL shortstops twice each in fielding and putouts and once in double plays. He hit 20 homers in 1966, a Reds record for shortstops. Traded to Minnesota for pitcher Jim Merritt in November 1968, Cardenas helped the Twins win a divisional championship in 1969, batting .280 and leading AL shortstops in assists, double plays, and putouts. His 570 putouts that year tied a 63-year-old league record. He led the AL in fielding again in 1971./(TJ)

Don Cardwell — 1935- . RHP 1957-70 Phillies, **Cubs**, Pirates, Mets, Braves 2123 g, 102-138, 3.92. *1 WS, 1 ip, 0-0, 0.00*

After three mediocre seasons in Philadelphia, Cardwell was traded to the Cubs in mid-1960 and pitched a no-hitter against St. Louis in his first start for his new team, the only pitcher ever to do so. The durable pitcher led the NL with 38 starts for the 1961 Cubs and won a career-high 15 games. He sandwiched two fine seasons in Pittsburgh around severe arm trouble in 1964. His 13-10 mark in 1965 was dragged down by six one-run losses. Cardwell was a valuable swingman for the Mets (1967-70) and helped them to their 1969 World Championship with his experience. After going 3-9 by late July, he won five straight, including a 1-0 game against the Pirates in which he drove in the only run./(ME)

Rod Carew — 1945- . 1B-2B 1967-85 **Twins**, Angels 2469 g, .328, 92 hr, 1015 rbi. *4 LCS, 14 g, .220, 1 rbi*
☛ *Rookie of the Year—67. Most Valuable Player—77. Led League—ba 69, 72-75, 77-78. All-Star—67-81, 83-84.*

"Carew had great hand action, probably as good as anyone who ever swung a bat. He always used the entire field. Because he could bunt so well, he brought the third baseman in close. He made the defense come to him instead of the other way around. He had a great sense of the strike zone, never chasing a bad ball, and had no fear at the plate," said Bill Rigney, one of Carew's managers.

Born on a train in the Panama Canal Zone, Carew moved with his mother to New York at age 17. After signing with the Twins a day out of high school in 1964, he played three minor league seasons before jumping from Class C to the majors in 1967. He got his first ML hit on Opening Day off Baltimore's Dave McNally; 18 years later, on August 4, 1985, with California, Carew singled off Minnesota's Frank Viola to become the 16th player to attain 3,000 hits.

Carew batted .292 in 1967 and was named AL Rookie of the Year. He hit .273 in 1968, but

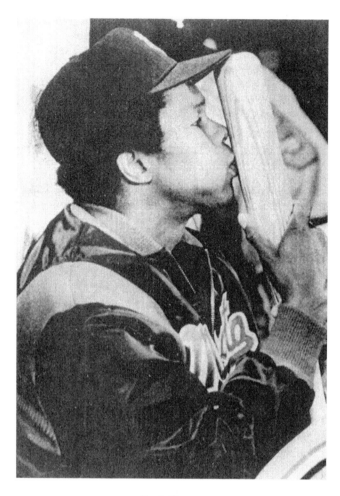

Rod Carew

followed with 15 consecutive seasons over .300. Only Ty Cobb, Stan Musial, and Honus Wagner have exceeded that achievement. Carew won seven AL batting championships, and won them by consistently larger margins than anyone except Rogers Hornsby. In his MVP 1977 season, Carew's .388 was 50 points higher than the next-best average in ML baseball, Dave Parker's NL-leading .338. This was the largest margin in ML history.

In 1970 Carew was off to his best start when he injured his knee, and he played just 51 games. In 1972 he became the first player to win a batting crown without hitting a home run. After capturing three more straight championships (1973–75) Carew batted .331 in 1976, but lost the title on the last day, to George Brett (.333) and Hal McRae (.332). He came back in 1977 to lead with his .388, and in 1978 led for the final time with .333.

Hitting was Carew's trademark, but he was also one of the game's best baserunners. Said Twins manager Frank Quilici, "There's nobody alive, nobody, who could turn a single into a double, a double into a triple the way Rod could. He may have been the most complete player of his time." Twins owner Calvin Griffith put Carew in the same class with Hall of Fame second basemen Hornsby and Charlie Gehringer.

Carew was moved from second to first base in 1975 to lengthen his career. After a dozen years with Minnesota, Carew forced a trade by announcing he would play out his option if the Twins did not deal him. (This was prompted in part by racist public statements by Griffith regarding black fans.) The club would receive nothing in return if he became a free agent. On February 3, 1979, he was traded to the Angels for Ken Landreaux, Dave Engle, Brad Havens, and Paul Hartzell. Carew, despite sitting out more than six weeks with a thumb injury that season, was instrumental in the Angels' drive to their first division title.

When Carew first came up, he was a loner—temperamental, often sullen—and didn't get along with his managers. He said in his autobiography, "I was always moody with managers . . .threatening to jump the club." Carew met with some racism in baseball, and following the announcement of his engagement to a Jewish woman, Marilynn Levy, he received death threats. As Carew matured, he became a family man, and a friendly, outgoing team leader.

Carew was on the losing club in four LCS, two with Minnesota and two with California. He would have played in 18 consecutive All-Star games, but was replaced due to injury in 1970 and 1979, and for the same reason was not chosen in 1982. In 1977 Carew received over four million All-Star votes, more than any other player ever. He established an All-Star record with two triples in the 1978 classic.

Always a base-stealing threat, Carew tied a ML record with seven steals of home in 1969, and amassed 348 career stolen bases. On May 18, 1969, he stole three bases in one inning. He led the league three times in base hits and once in runs scored, and led once and tied once in triples. He recorded 200 hits four times, and his 239 hits in 1977 was the highest total in the majors in 47 years. His 128 runs scored in '77 was the highest since 1961. Carew hit for the cycle in 1970, connected for five hits in a single game five times, and is 12th on the all-time hit list. His .339 average in 1983 set an Angels record, and he holds Twins season records for runs, hits, singles, triples, stolen bases, and batting average. /(JLE)

Andy Carey — 1931– . 2B 1952–62 **Yankees**, A's, White Sox, Dodgers 938 g, .260, 64 hr, 350 rbi. *4 WS, 16 g, .175, 2 rbi*

Carey was a $60,000 Yankee bonus baby out of St. Mary's College (CA). He was a notorious eater; because of him, the Yankees stopped allowing players to sign for meals. Carey became New York's regular third baseman in 1954, hitting .302. In July 1955 he helped turn four double plays in a game, tying a ML record for third basemen. The emergence of Clete Boyer made Carey expendable, and he was traded to Kansas City for Bob Cerv in 1960./(EW)

Max Carey [Maximilian Carnarius] (Scoops) — 1890–1976. OF 1910–29 **Pirates**, Dodgers 2476 g, .285, 69 hr, 800 rbi. *1 WS, 7 g, .458, 2 rbi.*
　　Manager 1932–33 **Dodgers** 146–161, .476
☛ *Hall of Fame—1961.*

Carey was the best-fielding centerfielder of his era. For 9 of his 17 seasons with Pittsburgh, he topped the league in putouts and total chances, and his career totals are exceeded only by Mays and Speaker for putouts, and by Speaker, Mays, and Cobb for total chances. Four years he led in outfield assists, and his lifetime total of 339 is the modern NL record. Most impressive were the range and speed which took him to the most fielding chances per game seven times, and the best NL career total for double plays (86), again topped only by Speaker and Cobb.

He also used his speed on the bases, leading the NL in steals ten times, six times topping 50. In 1922, he stole 51 bases in 53 attempts. His 738 SB put him among the all-time leaders. A switch-hitting leadoff man, Carey scored 42% of the time he reached base by a hit or walk. Playing in cavernous Forbes Field, he had a total of 159 triples. His average rose after the shift to the lively ball, from .273 between 1910 and 1919 to .304 between 1920 and 1926.

Carey had turned to baseball when he no longer had the money to continue as a Lutheran divinity student. He joined the Pirates in 1910, played alongside player-manager Fred Clarke for a season, and took over left field when Clarke quit. In 1916, he moved back to centerfield.

Carey played vigorously and with flair. He was team captain in 1926 when Clarke returned to the Pirate bench to advise Manager Bill McKechnie. Carey, in a slump, heard that hard-nosed old Fred had urged McKechnie to bench him, saying that the batboy couldn't do worse at the plate. Ruffied,

Max Carey with the Pirates

Carey called a team meeting to protest Clarke's harsh judgment. The challenge backfired. There was more support for Clarke's position than Carey expected. In retaliation the front office released two Carey supporters outright and sold Carey himself to Brooklyn for $4,000.

He played through 1929, scouted for the Pirates in 1930, and managed the Dodgers to third- and sixth-place finishes in 1932 and 1933. He scouted and managed in the minors off and on through 1956, and was inducted into the Hall of Fame in 1961./(ADS)

Tom Carey (Scoops) — 1908–1970. 2B-SS 1935–37, 39–42, 46 **Browns**, Red Sox 465 g, .275, 2 hr, 169 rbi

Carey had never played second base until his debut with Rogers Hornsby's Browns in 1935; he made a league-high 25 errors while still learning the position in 1936. He became a utility infielder and, after WWII service, a Red Sox coach. /(JK)

Tex Carleton [James Otto] — 1906–1977. RHP 1932–38, 40 Cardinals, **Cubs**, Dodgers 1607 ip, 100–76, 3.91. *3 WS, 11 ip, 0–1, 5.06*

In the minors, Carleton once had 13 consecutive wins and threw a no-hitter. In the majors, he was at least a .500 pitcher in all but his first season, and he won at least ten games in all but his last. On May 30, 1940, he threw a no-hitter for Brooklyn, beating the Reds, 3–0. /(EW)

Cisco Carlos [Francisco] — 1940– . RHP 1967–70 **White Sox**, Senators 237 ip, 11–18, 3.72

Called up to the White Sox in the midst of a four-team 1967 pennant race, Carlos went 2–0 in seven starts with an 0.86 ERA. He dipped to 4–14 the following year because he could not keep the ball down, and he was sold to the Senators in 1969. /(RL)

Hal Carlson — 1892–1930. RHP 1917–30 **Pirates**, Phillies, Cubs 2002 ip, 114–120, 3.97. *1 WS, 4 ip, 6.75*

Carlson was in his fourteenth ML season when he died of a stomach hemorrhage in May 1930. He won a career-high 17 in 1926, and was 64–48 from 1925 until his death. He spent his first seven seasons with the Pirates. A respectable batter, Carlson delivered a pinch homer for the Phillies on May 30, 1925. /(ME)

Steve Carlton (Lefty) — 1944– . LHP 1965–88 Cardinals, **Phillies**, Giants, White Sox, Indians, Twins 5217 ip, 329–244, 3.22. 20 wins: 71, 72, 76, 77, 80, 82 *5 LCS, 53.2 ip, 4–2, 3.52. 4 WS, 31.2 ip, 2–2, 2.56* ☛ *Led League—w 72, 77, 80, 82. Led League—era 72. Led League—k 72, 74, 80, 82–83.. Cy Young Award—72, 77, 80, 82. All-Star—68, 69, 71, 72, 74, 77, 79–82.*

The second-winningest lefthander of all time behind Warren Spahn, Carlton is also second on the all-time strikeout list behind Nolan Ryan. He is the only pitcher ever to win four Cy Young Awards, and had six 20-win seasons.

When he had his first tryouts in 1963, scouts questioned whether he could throw hard enough to make the ML, but Carlton, a dedicated worker at

Steve Carlton

conditioning throughout his career, built himself up with weights and his fastball became his strikeout pitch. He also had a decent curveball with a sharp downward drop, and a sneaky pickoff move that tested the limits of the balk rule. In 1969, he began to develop his slider, a pitch that broke down and in to righthanded batters, and it became a devastating complement to his fastball in mid-career. Carlton was also dangerous at the plate, with a .201 career average and 13 HR.

Carlton had a respectable 1967 season (14–9, 2.98) to help the Cardinals win the WS, but began to earn national recognition in 1969. He started and won the All-Star Game and set a since-broken ML record with 19 strikeouts against the Mets on September 15. Ironically, he lost the game 4–3 on a pair of home runs by Ron Swoboda.

In 1970, a contract dispute kept him out of spring training, and he had trouble controlling his breaking pitches all season and lost 19 games. He went back to his fastball more the following year and won 20 games for the first time.

Carlton asked for a $10,000 raise to $65,000 in that off-season and the Cardinals' management balked. Instead, they traded him to the Phillies for Rick Wise, a deal that will always be one of the most notorious in Cardinals history. Carlton was phenomenal in 1972, pitching as well for an entire season as any pitcher ever. He went 27–10 for a Phillies club that won only 57 games. He led the league in wins, ERA (1.97), strikeouts (310, only the second lefthander ever to reach 300), and complete games, and enjoyed a 15-game winning streak. Of course, he won his first Cy Young Award.

He was less impressive in the three seasons that followed, partly due to occasional soreness in his left elbow. Two changes helped him regain his form in 1976. He adjusted his stance on the rubber, which improved his control, and he began pitching to his old friend and former Cardinal batterymate, Tim McCarver, though Bob Boone was the Phillies regular catcher. Carlton's slider was crackling, and his combination of power and finesse gave him 20 victories in 1976. The Phillies won their first NL East title. In 1977, he led the NL in wins (23–10) for the second time and the Phillies won another division title.

By this time, Carlton was working out with Phillies conditioning coach Gus Hoefling up to two hours a day. Always an intense competitor and a private, seemingly unemotional personality, Carlton took umbrage at some items in the Philadelphia newspapers, and in 1978 he stopped talking to the press altogether. He led the league in strikeouts and wins in 1980, and posted a 2.34 ERA, his best since 1972. In the postseason that year, he was nearly flawless, winning once in the LCS and beating the Royals twice in the WS. In 1982 he topped the NL in wins, strikeouts, and shutouts to earn his fourth Cy Young Award.

Carlton began to show signs of wear in 1983, despite leading the league in strikeouts for the fifth time. He began to have trouble completing and winning his starts, and he lost his role as the Phillies' ace to John Denny. In 1984, at the age of 39, Carlton was 13–7 for a .500 ballclub. But his ERA was up and his strikeout total well down, and he only completed one game. The following year he was only 1–8 after 16 starts before going on the DL. The Phillies asked him to retire in 1986, but Carlton refused and was released. He then broke eight years of silence in the media to voice his reasons and

thank the Philadelphia fans for their support. He finished his career in brief, desperate flings with the Giants, White Sox, Indians, and Twins, but his ERA stayed above 5.00./(SG)

Don Carman — 1959– . LHP 1983–89 **Phillies** 797 ip, 47–50, 4.04

Carman debuted as a reliever, earning a save in his first ML appearance, but was converted to a starter prior to the 1986 All-Star Break, and finished the season 10–5, 3.22. He broke his pitching thumb in a January 1987 auto accident and surrendered a club-record 34 HR the following season while winning a career-high 13 games./(SG)

John P. Carmichael — 1902–1986. *Writer.*

Fresh out of the University of Wisconsin, Carmichael joined the Chicago *Herald Examiner* in 1924 after a brief stint with the Milwaukee *Leader*. Five years later, he started a 43-year stand as columnist ("The Barber Shop") and later sports editor for the Chicago *Daily News*. Known for poking fun rather than malice, near the end of his career he said, "I take pride in the fact that never in my 40 years did I use my column to attack anyone." For many years he and his boss, Lloyd Lewis, jousted in print, Carmichael covering the Cubs and Lewis the White Sox. Carmichael was given the J.G. Taylor Spink Award in 1974./(NLM)

Pat Carney (Doc) — 1876–1953. OF-LHP 1901–04 **Braves** 338 g, .247, 3 hr, 131 rbi; 109 ip, 4–9, 4.69

As the Braves' regular right fielder in 1902, Carney hit .270 with 75 runs, 65 rbi, and 27 stolen bases. His average declined to .240 and then .204, ending his major league career. He sometimes pitched, but was always easy to hit and lacked control. He coached four years at his alma mater, Holy Cross, and later became a physician./(NLM)

Bill Carpenter — Unk.–1952. *Umpire* **NL**, AL 1897, 04, 06–07

Carpenter umpired in the NL as a 23-year-old in 1897, but the bulk of his career, 21 years, was spent in the International League. In 1933 he became chief of staff of the league office, with duties that included umpire supervision and schedule-making. He became so proficient at the latter that other leagues used his services./(RTM)

Bob Carpenter — 1917- . RHP 1940-42, 46-47 **Giants**, Cubs 399 ip, 25-20, 3.60

As a teenager, Carpenter persuaded his father, whose ill health required him to leave Chicago, to move to Pensacola. There, he knew, Bill Terry ran a baseball school. For $25, Carpenter was taught the curveball and was placed with a minor league team. He worked his way to Terry's Giants, had 11-win seasons in 1941 and 1942, and then spent three years in the military. When he returned, an injury limited his ability to play, and he retired./(JK)

Cris Carpenter — 1965- . RHP 1988- **Cardinals** 116 ip, 6-7, 3.81

Carpenter signed for a $160,000 bonus after the Cardinals made him their first-round pick in the June 1987 draft. He showed good control but was too hittable./(SFS)

Charlie Carr — 1876-1932. 1B 1898, 1901, 03-06, 14 Washington (NL), A's, **Tigers**, Indians, Reds, Indianapolis (FL) 507 g, .252, 6 hr, 240 rbi

A journeyman first baseman, Carr made contacts in his travels that were useful later for his successful sporting goods manufacturing business, Bradley & Carr, which supplied baseballs to several minor leagues./(JK)

George Carr (Tank) — 1895-Unk. 1B-3B-OF-C Negro Leagues 1912-1934 Los Angeles White Sox, Kansas City Monarchs, Hilldale, Bacharach Giants, Philadelphia Stars 227 g, .318, 21 hr (inc.)

Carr was a hard-hitting Negro Leaguer whose surviving statistics show that he batted .339 in 1921, .300 in 1924, and .370 in 1925. He compiled a confirmed batting average of .318 over five documented seasons, and led the league with 23 stolen bases in 1925. He usually played winter ball in California. In one season in Cuba (1926-27), he batted a league-leading .416. He appeared in two Black World Series for Hilldale, hitting .316 in 1924 and .320 in 1925./(JM)

Alex Carrasquel — 1921-1969. RHP 1939-45, 49 **Senators**, White Sox 861 ip, 50-39, 3.73

One of many fine Latin-American players imported by Washington owner Clark Griffith, Carrasquel had a fine fastball, which complemented well the famed Senator knuckle-ball staffs of the early 1940s. The tall Venezuelan became more of an asset to the Senators as his pitching savvy increased and he

moved more into relief roles. All of his decisions came as a Senator and his brief fling with Chicago consisted of three appearances./(EW)

Chico Carrasquel [Alfonso] — 1928- . SS-3B-2B 1950-59 **White Sox**, Indians, A's, Orioles 1325 g, .258, 55 hr, 474 rbi
☛ *All-Star—51, 53-55.*

Venezuelan Chico Carrasquel was signed in 1949 by the Dodgers, who then sold him to the White Sox. Carrasquel's inability to speak English may have caused Branch Rickey to move him. White Sox GM Frank Lane solved the communication problem by trading journeyman pitcher Alex Carrasquel—Chico's uncle—for reliever Luis Aloma, who served as the interpreter between Chico and man-

Chico Carrasquel

ager Paul Richards. Replacing Luke Appling, Carrasquel soon established himself as a top shortstop and batted .282 with a 24-game hitting streak as a rookie in 1950. He broke an AL record by accepting 297 chances (in 53 games) without an error in 1951, and beat out reigning MVP Phil Rizzuto as the AL's starting All-Star SS. But Carrasquel had trouble controlling his weight, and in 1952 he was benched for lethargic play. In October 1955 Chicago traded him with Jim Busby to Cleveland for Larry Doby. They had another Venezuelan SS waiting in the minors—Luis Aparicio. Carrasquel became a legend in his native Caracas, serving as play-by-play man on their Game of the Week. /(RL)

Cam Carreon [Camilo] — 1937–1987. C 1959–66
White Sox, Indians, Orioles 354 g, .264, 11 hr, 114 rbi

Platooning with J.C. Martin on the White Sox in 1963, Carreon tied Yogi Berra for the best fielding average among AL catchers. He had speed and good defensive skills, but he was unable to take control of a ballgame. As a result, the slow-footed Martin won the job in 1964. A year later, Carreon was traded to Cleveland in a deal that brought Tommy John to Chicago. His son, Mark, was signed by the Mets in 1981 and made his major league debut with them on September 8, 1987, six days after his father's death. /(RL)

Bill Carrick (Doughnut Bill) — 1873–1932. RHP
1898–1902 **Giants**, Senators 1325 ip, 63–89, 4.14

It is often said that a pitcher who loses 20 games in a season must be very good to be allowed to pitch so often. So Bill Carrick must have been a wonder. He lost 26 for the Giants in 1899, 22 in 1900, and 23 for Washington in 1901. /(JK)

Bill Carrigan (Rough) — 1883–1969. C 1906, 08–16
Red Sox 706 g, .257, 6 hr, 235 rbi. *3 WS, 4 g, .167, 1 rbi.*
    Manager 1913–16, 27–29 **Red Sox** 489–500, .494.
First place: 15–16 *2 WS, 8–2, .800*

Carrigan was a dependable platoon catcher who took over a dissension-torn defending World Champion Red Sox team in 1913 as playing manager. He could not set things right until 1914, when he brought the team home second. In 1915 and 1916, with Babe Ruth added to his pitching rotation, Carrigan led Boston to two World Championships.

Carrigan quit at the peak of his success to become a banker in his native Maine. He made a surprise return as Red Sox manager in 1927, but the results were disastrous. The team finished last three straight seasons. While there was an absence of talent, it was

Bill Carrigan

also evident that the conservative Carrigan was out of his element in the free-swinging, lively-ball era. /(JK)

Don Carrithers — 1949– . RHP 1970–77 Giants,
Expos, Twins 565 ip, 28–32, 4.46. *1 LCS, 0 ip, infinite*

A likable power pitcher, Carrithers never found consistency on the ML level. He went 9–1 in Phoenix in 1970 but in two-plus seasons with the Giants was 12–14 as a starter and reliever. Traded to Montreal, he split time between the Expos and Triple-A in 1974 and 1975. He appeared in only seven games for the Twins in 1977 after he was injured in a car accident. /(JCA)

Clay Carroll (Hawk) — 1941– . RHP 1964–78 Braves, **Reds**, White Sox, Cardinals, Pirates 1353 ip, 96–73, 2.94. *4 LCS, 12 ip, 2–1, 1.50. 3 WS, 20 ip, 2–1, 1.33* ☛ *All-Star—71–72.*

Carroll was the mainstay of the "Big Red Machine" bullpen. The chunky stopper recorded 88 relief wins and 143 saves, including 37 in 1972, then a single-season record. His performance won him the Fireman of the Year award.

Carroll came up through the Braves farm system and led the NL with 73 appearances in 1966. The good-natured country boy went to Cincinnati in a mid-1968 deal and never had a losing season. He threw mostly fastballs, and also had a variety of effective breaking pitches. Johnny Bench explained, "Clay tells you he can do the job and then he goes out and does it." Carroll appeared in more than 50 games in each of his eight seasons in Cincinnati, and led the NL with nine relief wins in 1970.

The Reds lost the 1970 WS to Baltimore in five games, but Carroll had Cincinnati's only win and appeared in four games without allowing a run. He maintained his WS effectiveness in 1975, winning the seventh game over Boston. /(JCA)

Cliff Carroll — 1859–1923. OF 1882–88, 90–93 **Providence (NL)**, Washington (NL), Pirates, Cubs, Cardinals, Braves 991 g, .251, 31 hr, 346 rbi

A first baseman and catcher in the minors, Carroll played all his ML games in the outfield, three times leading NL left fielders in putouts. The Iowan quit baseball in 1889 to be a farmer, but missed the game and returned with Chicago in 1890 to enjoy his finest season, with career highs in three offensive and three defensive categories. His 134 runs scored ranked second in the NL. /(FIC)

Ownie Carroll — 1902–1975. RHP 1925, 1927–34 **Tigers**, Yankees, Reds, Dodgers 1331 ip, 65–89, 4.43

A handsome, smiling pitcher, Carroll had a sensational college career at Holy Cross, going 50–2 in three seasons. Doomed to pitch for non-contenders, Carroll never reached ML stardom. He led the 1928 Tigers with a career-high 16 wins, but, in 1932, led the NL with 19 losses for the last-place Reds. /(JK)

Tom Carroll — 1952– . RHP 1974–75 **Reds** 125 ip, 8–4, 4.18

Carroll went 3–0 in spot starts for the 1975 World Champion Reds, finishing 4–1 overall. /(WOR)

Kid Carsey [Wilfred] — 1870–1960. RHP 1891–99, 1901 Washington (AA), **Phillies**, St. Louis (NL), Cleveland (NL), Washington (NL), Brooklyn (NL) 2222 ip, 116–138, 4.95. 20 wins: 1893, 95
   Umpire 1894, 96, 1901 NL

As a 20-year-old rookie in 1891, Kid Carsey started 53 games for Washington, winning 14, but losing 37 to lead the American Association. He had four successive winning years with the Phillies, culminating with a career-best 24–16 in 1895. /(AJA)

Gary Carter (The Kid) — 1954– . C 1974- **Expos**, Mets 2008 g, .265, 304 hr, 1,143 rbi. *3 LCS, 18 g, .243, 6 rbi. 1 WS, 7 g, .276, 2 hr, 9 rbi* ☛ *All-Star—75, 79–88. Gold Glove—80–82.*

The premier and most popular catcher of the late 1970s and early 1980s after Johnny Bench retired, Carter was known for his ebullience, durability, clutch hitting (10 career grand slams), and handling of pitchers and balls in the dirt. He was also accused by many of his teammates of being a camera hog and a publicity hound. The gung-ho Carter was an All-American quarterback in high school in California, captain of his baseball, football and basketball teams, and a member of the National Honor Society. He signed a letter of intent to play football at UCLA, but chose baseball after being picked by Montreal in the third round of the 1972 free agent draft. Montreal gradually converted Carter from an outfielder to a catcher with help from Norm Sherry. In 1975 Carter was named *TSN* Rookie of the Year, losing the baseball writers' award to John Montefusco. He missed the first 60 games of the 1976 season after running into a wall in spring training chasing a long line drive. He became a full-time catcher in 1977 and, on April 20, hit homers in three consecutive at-bats. Known equally for his defensive skills, Carter set a record for fewest passed balls in 150 or more games, with just one. Between 1977 and 1982, he led the NL in most chances six times, in putouts five times, assists four times, and double plays three times. The Expos of those years were filled with talent, and were always expected to win the pennant but never did. In 1979 Carter tore ligaments in his thumb in the final week of the season as the Pirates overtook the Expos. He hit .360 in 1980 and drove in 22 runs in September, but Mike Schmidt's homer in the 11th inning on the last day of the season gave the Phillies the NL flag. Carter won 1981 All-Star Game MVP honors on the strength of two homers. He had a career-high 106 RBI in 1984 to lead the league, and again won

Gary Carter

MVP honors in the 1984 All-Star Game with another homer. In that game, he caught Dwight Gooden for the first time. He caught Gooden on a regular basis the following year after being swapped for four players to the Mets. On Opening Day 1985, he hit a grand slam to win the game. On September 3, 1985, he had three consecutive homers in a game, and he finished the season with 18 game-winning RBI. After two seasons of 100-plus RBI, in 1986 his 105 RBI (tying the team record) led the Mets to the World Series. Carter contributed a single in the two-out, 10th inning rally in the sixth game of the 1986 World Series against the Red Sox, won by the Mets. His production started to fall off after the championship. He began the 1988 season by hitting eight homers in April to give him 299 homers, then went more than 230 at-bats before hitting number 300 in August in Chicago. In 1989 he hit below .200 before going down with a knee injury in May. After returning to action, he was relegated to backup duty and then released after the season. /(SEW)

Joe Carter — 1960- . OF-1B 1983- Cubs, **Indians**
862 g, .268, 151 hr, 531 rbi
☛ *Led League—rbi 86.*

Wichita State's Joe Carter was *TSN*'s 1981 College Player of the Year; the Cubs, choosing second, made him their number-one draft pick that June. He played briefly in Chicago before going to Cleveland in a major seven-player deal for Rick Sutcliffe in June 1984. A disappointment at first, he struggled with injuries until 1986, when he burst forth with a .302 average, 29 homers, and a ML-leading 121 RBI. Blessed with one of the best physiques in baseball, he missed the 30–30 club by one HR and one stolen base in having the best offensive year by an Indian in decades. He did reach 30–30 in 1987, overcoming a salary dispute in spring training and constant shifting between the outfield and first base. Carter defeated incumbent Brett Butler to become the Indians' player representative, and took over centerfield when Butler signed with the Giants for 1988. /(ME)

Paul Carter (Nick) — 1894-1984. LHP 1914-20
Indians, **Cubs** 480 ip, 21-25, 3.32

Carter spent most of his seven ML seasons in the bullpen, where his antics and capers entertained the fans. He insisted his nickname (Nick) came from his "cutting up" on the field. He was 4–1 for the pennant-winning Cubs in 1918 until he was sidelined by illness and forced to miss the World Series. /(BC)

Alexander Cartwright — 1820-1892. *Executive.*
☛ *Hall of Fame—1938.*

One spring day in 1845, New York bank teller Alexander Cartwright suggested to his ballplaying companions that they organize formally into a club. From that humble start grew America's national game. Versions of baseball had been played long before; varieties of the children's game known in England as "rounders" and in America as "base ball" or "town ball" were popular throughout the northeastern states. But when the Knickerbocker Base Ball Club organized that September, Cartwright and his friends transformed the children's game into an adult sport, chiefly by three innovations still in effect today.

First, they increased the distance between bases to an adult-length 90 feet. This was 50% to more than 100% longer than in earlier versions. Second, they brought the game an adult sense of order by dividing the field into fair and foul territory, narrowing the

Alexander Cartwright

hitter's range to the space between the foul lines, and reducing the number of defensive players needed. The number of players wasn't specified in the first rules, but by 1846 the club was playing with nine to a side, and that was later made official. And third, Knickerbocker rules forbade the practice, permitted in earlier versions, of putting out baserunners by throwing the ball at them. This change not only brought dignity to baseball but also made it safe to use a harder ball, which led to faster, sharper play.

This "manly" version of baseball quickly took hold throughout metropolitan New York, and by 1860 was established as far afield as New Orleans and San Francisco. Cartwright himself helped spread the game. In 1849 he left New York to seek gold in California, traveling overland with his baseball and Knickerbocker rules, teaching the game along the way. In California he was taken ill with dysentery and abandoned thoughts of gold for the healthful climate of Hawaii. There he introduced baseball in 1852, even before it had taken hold in Philadelphia.

Cartwright became one of Honolulu's leading merchants and bankers, founded its library and fire department (he was fire chief for ten years), and managed the finances of Hawaii's royal family. Although he died one of Hawaii's most respected citizens, his contribution to baseball was all but forgotten until 1938, when a review of his journals prompted his election to the Hall of Fame. /(FIC)

Rico Carty — 1941- . OF-DH 1963–67, 1969–70, 1972–79 **Braves**, Rangers, Cubs, A's, Indians, Blue Jays 1651 g, .299, 204 hr, 890 rbi. *1 LCS, 3 g, .300*
☛ *Led League—ba 70. All-Star—70.*

High on any list of the great natural hitters, the powerful Dominican called himself "the Big Boy." In 1960, as a naive youngster, he signed ten pro contracts. When the mess was straightened out, he became the property of the Milwaukee Braves, who converted the slow-footed catcher into a poor outfielder. As a rookie in 1964 he hit .330, losing both the batting crown race (to Roberto Clemente) and the Rookie of the Year award (to Richie Allen). Tuberculosis sidelined him for the entire 1968 season; he spent five months in a sanitarium. Incredibly, he returned to hit .342 in 1969, despite seven shoulder dislocations. His .366 in 1970 (highest ML average since Ted Williams hit .388 in 1957) led the NL, and he started on the All-Star team as a write-in candidate. He broke his knee in a winter ball collision, costing him the 1971 season, and nearly his career. He was with three teams in 1973 and was playing in Mexico when the Indians signed him as a DH for 1974. His 31 home runs in 1978, with Toronto and Oakland, were a career high. /(JCA)

Bob Caruthers (Parisian Bob) — 1864–1911. OF-RHP 1884–93 **St. Louis (AA)**, Brooklyn (AA)/Dodgers, Cardinals, Cubs, Reds 705 g, .282, 29 hr, 213 rbi (inc.); 2829 ip, 218–97, 2.83. 20 wins: 85–90
☛ *Led League—w 85, 89. Led League—era 85.*

Caruthers is among the all-time leaders in winning percentage at .692. He won 40 games twice, posting league-leading marks of 40–13 (1885) and 40–11 (1889) while pacing his teams to pennants. He pitched a four-hitter in his September 1884 major league debut with the St. Louis Browns of the American Association. Considered a heady pitcher who figured out batters' weaknesses, he helped the team to three straight pennants. He earned his nickname when he traveled to France after the 1885 season and engaged in a trans-Atlantic salary battle, settling for the then-huge sum of $3,200.

Caruthers also became a good hitter, and in 1887 he had an amazing season. Playing 54 games in the outfield and 7 at first base in addition to his 39 pitching appearances, he overcame malaria to hit .357 (fifth in the AA) and slug .547 (second) with eight HR (tied for fourth) and 59 stolen bases. He also went 29–9 as a pitcher and won four of St. Louis's five postseason victories in a traveling 15-game series. Despite all this, eccentric owner Chris von der Ahe sold him to the Brooklyn Bridegrooms of the AA after the season for $8,250. Von der Ahe blamed carousing and card playing for his team's defeat in the series, and Caruthers, an expert billiards and poker player, was just one of several scapegoats sold off.

Signing for a $5,000 salary that made him the highest-paid player in the AA, Caruthers earned it by helping the theretofore pathetic Bridegrooms to second place. In 1889, playing only five games elsewhere than the pitching box, his 40–11 season gave Brooklyn its first pennant.

Caruthers was the fourth pitcher in ML history to homer twice in one game, on August 16, 1886; in the same game, he got a triple and a double, to become the third pitcher with four extra-base hits in a game. He lost 11–9 when he was tagged out in the ninth inning trying to stretch his triple into a third HR. In 1893, when the pitching distance was moved back to 60′6″ from the former 50′, he had a sore arm and only played outfield. It was his last major league season, although he played until 1898 in the minors. /(SFS)

Chuck Cary — 1960– . LHP 1985– **Tigers**, Braves, Yankees 180 ip, 6–8, 3.51

Cary was a fair reliever until a 1988 injury cost him most of the season. He came back in 1989 with the pitching-poor Yankees after being released by the Braves. /(WOR)

Jerry Casale — 1933– . RHP 1958–62 **Red Sox**, Angels, Tigers 370 ip, 17–24, 5.08

The Brooklynite was 13–8 as a Boston rookie in 1959 but never won more than two in any other season. A decent hitter, Casale teamed with Don Buddin and Pumpsie Green to hit three consecutive homers on September 7, 1959. /(JCA)

Paul Casanova — 1941– . C 1965–74 **Senators**, Braves 859 g, .225, 50 hr, 252 rbi
☛ *All-Star—67.*

The rangy, cat-like Cuban refugee was named *TSN* AL all-star catcher as a Senators rookie in 1966. An

enthusiastic, fun-loving spendthrift, he had a rifle arm and led AL catchers in double plays three times, but his hitting tailed off after his first two seasons. He caught all 22 innings and drove in the winning run against the White Sox in the longest night game in AL history (6/12/67). /(JCA)

Joe Cascarella (Crooning Joe) — 1907– . RHP 1934–38 **A's**, Red Sox, Senators, Reds 541 ip, 27–48, 4.84

In his rookie year with his hometown Philadelphia A's, he led the AL with seven relief wins, and was chosen for the all-star team which toured the Orient after the season. His fine tenor voice and a winning personality made him a popular figure on radio shows and in nightclubs. "Crooning Joe" later became operational vice president of Laurel Race Track. /(JK)

Charlie Case — 1879–1964. RHP 1901, 04–06 Reds, **Pirates** 396 ip, 24–18, 2.93

The Ohio native was the youngest member of Pittsburgh's pitching rotation in 1904–05. Case's .667 winning percentage (10–5) was second on the club in 1904. /(ME)

George Case — 1915– . OF 1937–47 **Senators**, Indians 1226 g, .282, 21 hr, 377 rbi
☛ *All-Star—39, 43–44.*

George Case is remembered as one of the greatest basestealers of all time, although his career was abbreviated by injuries. The Washington outfielder set a record by leading the ML in stolen bases five straight seasons (1939–43), and led again in 1945. Case's 61 stolen bases in 1943 was the highest ML single-season total in the period 1921–61. A three-time .300 hitter, Case scored an AL-leading 102 runs in 1943; that year, he was the AL's starting right fielder in the first night All-Star Game. In Bill Veeck's first ML promotion, Case raced Jesse Owens and lost. Case worked as a coach in the Mariner farm system. /(TJ)

Doc Casey [James Peter] — 1870–1936. 3B 1898–1907 Washington (NL), Dodgers, Tigers, **Cubs** 1114 g, .258, 9 hr, 354 rbi

Nap Lajoie credited Doc Casey for bringing him into pro ball. Lajoie, a Providence hack driver, was dubious about playing professionally until he saw the 5′6″ Casey catching for Pawtucket (New England League). Casey switched to third base, averaging 135 ML games a season from 1901 through 1907. He became a dentist and ran a Detroit drug store. /(JK)

Hugh Casey — 1913–1951. RHP 1935, 39–42, 46–49 Cubs, **Dodgers**, Pirates, Yankees 940 ip, 75–42, 3.45. *2 WS, 16 ip, 2–2, 1.72*

Hugh Casey was on the mound in the ninth inning of Game Four of the 1941 Yankee-Dodger World Series. Brooklyn led, 4–3, with two out, nobody on, and Tommy Henrich at bat. Henrich swung and missed Casey's 3–2 pitch, but the third strike eluded catcher Mickey Owen, and Henrich reached base, beginning a game-winning rally. Owen became a famous goat, and baseball historians since have differed as to whether the elusive pitch was a spitball.

Casey, who relieved in 287 of his 343 games, led the NL in saves twice and relief wins three times. A loner, a tough competitor, and a heavy drinker, Casey became friends with Ernest Hemingway. At Hemingway's house during spring training in Cuba, the drunken pair once put on boxing gloves. Teammate Kirby Higbe later recalled, "Ernest would belt Case one, and down he would go. Case would belt old Ernest, and down he would go . . .The furniture [really took] a beating." At age 37, allegedly despondent over the breakup of his marriage, Casey committed suicide./(TJ)

Dave Cash — 1948– . 2B 1969–80 Pirates, **Phillies**, Expos, Padres 1422 g, .283, 21 hr, 426 rbi. *4 LCS, 14 g, .288, 5 rbi. 1 WS, 7 g, .133, 1 rbi*
☛ *All-Star—74–76.*

The articulate Cash was an underrated second baseman who hit .300 four times and set a number of records, some significant and some trivial. His lifetime .984 fielding average is the NL record for second basemen.

Cash's career started slowly. In 1970 he hit .314 and showed fine range when filling in for aging All-Star Bill Mazeroski. However, Cash's 1970–72 seasons were interrupted each July for two weeks of military duty. Mazeroski didn't retire until after 1972, and Rennie Stennett appeared on the scene in 1971. Cash never became an everyday player with Pittsburgh, although he averaged almost 450 at-bats a year from 1971 to 1973 by occasionally playing third base. His best moments with the Pirates were in the 1971 LCS, when he hit .421, set a LCS record with eight hits in a four-game series (his 19 at-bats tied the record), and scored five runs, including the series clincher in Game Four.

Finally, in October 1973 (with Willie Randolph coming up through the farm system to compete with Stennett and Cash), the Pirates traded Cash to the Phillies for veteran pitcher Ken Brett. Cash played in all the Phillies' games in 1974 and 1975 and missed only two games in 1976. He set a since-broken ML record of 699 at-bats in 1975, and set a still-standing ML record for most at-bats with no sacrifice hits. He also tied the ML record with three consecutive seasons leading the majors in at-bats, and set the NL record for consecutive games at second base (443).

Cash not only played every day, he played well, making the All-Star team each year. He hit .300 in 1974, scored 89 runs, stole 20 bases, and drove in a career-high 58; in 1975 he upped his BA to .305 while leading the league with 213 hits, finishing second in the NL with 40 doubles and a career-high 111 runs (only one behind Pete Rose). Although his numbers fell off a bit in 1976 (.284, 92 runs), his 12 triples led the league, and he struck out only 13 times in 666 at-bats. To close out the year, he hit .308 in the LCS while the Phillies were being swept by the Reds. His weakness as a leadoff hitter was his failure to walk more often, but he was nonetheless one of the premier second basemen in the game. He led NL second basemen in assists and double plays in 1974, in putouts and double plays in 1975, and in fielding average and double plays in 1976.

After the 1976 season, Cash declared free agency and signed with the Expos. He maintained his level of play in 1977, finishing second in assists and batting .289 with 42 doubles (second in the NL), 91 runs, and a career-high 21 steals. But although his defense remained strong in 1978, as he again led the NL in putouts and fielding, his hitting declined (.252, 66 runs). Manager Dick Williams replaced Cash with Rodney Scott in 1979 despite the protests of some players and the front office. Scott hit .238 to Cash's part-time .321 that year, and although Scott stole 39 bases and led the NL in total chances per game, he was weak on the double play and scored only 69 runs in 151 games. Williams's dismissal during the 1981 season was ascribed by some to bad feelings dating back to this controversy. Meanwhile, Cash adjusted by becoming a valuable pinch hitter (10-for-30). That November, Cash was traded to the Padres for Bill Almon and Dan Briggs. He finished his career with a disappointing .227 average for the last-place Padres. After retirement he became the Phillies' minor league fielding coach./(SH)

Norm Cash — 1934-1986. 1B-OF 1958-74 White Sox, **Tigers** 2089 g, .271, 377 hr, 1103 rbi. *1 LCS, 5 g, .267, 1 hr, 2 rbi. 2 WS, 11 g, .333, 1 hr, 5 rbi*
☛ *Led League—ba 61. All-Star—61, 66, 71-72.*

Norm Cash had the greatest season of his career in 1961, but it was completely overshadowed by Roger Maris's 61 HR. Cash led the AL with 193 hits and a .361 batting average, 37 points ahead of the runner-up, teammate Al Kaline (they were only the eighth pair of AL teammates to finish one-two in a batting race). Only 12 players have topped his .488 on-base percentage that year, and none since. He had 132 RBI (fourth in the AL), 41 HR (sixth), eight triples (fourth), 119 runs (fourth), 11 stolen bases, 124 walks (second), a .662 slugging percentage (second, ahead of Maris), and 354 total bases (second). He finished fourth in the MVP voting, behind Maris, Mickey Mantle, and Jim Gentile.

Ironically, the season that was overlooked at the time was the apex of his career. All the performances cited were career highs. He dropped to .243 in 1962 and the 118-point drop is a record for a batting champ. Even on his own team, he was overshadowed by his roommate, Al Kaline. But although he never hit above .283 for the rest of his career, he was consistently one of the best first basemen in the majors. He hit 30 or more homers five times and 20 or more eleven times, including nine straight years (1961–69), and twice led the league in HR percentage (1965, 1971). He won *TSN* Comeback Player of the Year honors in 1965, finishing second in the AL in HR (30) and third in slugging (.512), then won the award again in 1971 when he hit 32 HR and slugged .531.

Cash never went on the DL, although some years he missed 20–40 games with minor injuries. His batting averages were actually well above average in the pitching-dominated late 1960s, and he walked frequently. Cash was a good fielder and at various times led the AL in putouts (1961), fielding average (1964, 1967), and assists (tied 1965, led 1966–67).

Cash was drafted in the 13th round by the NFL's Chicago Bears but he opted for baseball, beginning his career as an outfielder in the White Sox system. After missing 1957 for military service he made it to the majors briefly in 1958. He converted to first base and spent all of 1959 in the majors, although he played just 58 games in Chicago's AL championship season. In the off-season he was sent to Cleveland in the deal that brought Minnie Minoso back to Chicago, and then was picked up by Detroit in the most lopsided deal in their history: he was traded straight up for third baseman Steve Demeter, who had just five more at-bats in his ML career.

The genial, self-deprecating slugger tied two offbeat records. On June 27, 1963, he had no fielding chances at first base. And in the third inning of Game Six of the 1968 World Series, he had two hits as the Tigers scored 10 runs. He batted .385 for the Series, with five RBI and five runs, and hit a homer in Game Two. He also started the Series-winning rally in Game Seven with a two-out, seventh-inning single, and scored the first run of the game on Jim Northrup's triple. In the 1972 LCS,

Norm Cash after becoming Bob Gibson's record 16th strikeout victim in Game One of the 1968 World Series

Cash was part of the Tigers' "Over the Hill Gang". He homered in Game One in a losing cause and drove in the tying run of Game Four with a 10th-inning walk as the Tigers came from behind to force a fifth game.

Cash's 375 HR as a first baseman rank third in the AL, and his 377 HR overall were 30th all-time at the end of the 1980s. He and Kaline combined to hit 647 HR as teammates, the fourth-best AL total and eighth-best overall. His total of 317 hits and walks in 1961 is the 23rd-best in ML history; only seven people have bettered it, and only Wade Boggs has done it since Cash. He is seventh in lifetime assists among first basemen (1317) despite not being in the top ten in games at first base. Cash drowned in 1986 when he slipped on a boat, fell, and struck his head./(SH)

Joe Cashman — Unk.–Unk. *Writer.*

Cashman retired in 1970 after 53 years with the Boston *Record-American.* He was president of the BBWAA in 1953 and chairman of its Boston chapter for 22 years./(NLM)

Joe Cassidy — 1883–1906. SS-OF-3B 1904–05 **Senators** 303 g, .228, 2 hr, 76 rbi

A flashy fielder with cat-like agility, Cassidy was one of the first to play in the majors with no minor league experience. His 19 triples for the 1904 Senators tied him for the league lead and set a still-standing rookie record. He led AL shortstops with 520 assists and 66 errors in 1905, and was considered a top young shortstop when he died of malaria in the spring of 1906./(NLM)

George Caster — 1907–1955. RHP 1934–35, 37–46 **A's**, Browns, Tigers 1376 ip, 76–100, 4.54. *1 WS, 2/3 ip, 0–0, 0.00*

As a knuckleball starter for Connie Mack's hapless A's, Caster lost 19 games in 1937 and led the AL in losses in 1938 (20) and 1940 (19). Waived to the Browns after the 1940 season, he became an effective reliever, leading the AL in saves (12) in 1944 when the Browns won their only pennant./(NLM)

Pete Castiglione — 1921– . 3B-SS 1947–54 **Pirates**, Cardinals 545 g, .255, 24 hr, 150 rbi

In 1949, his first of two seasons as the Pirates' regular third baseman, he batted a career-high .268. The capable pinch hitter averaged .296 (16-for-54) lifetime in that role./(TJ)

Bob Castillo (Bobo) — 1955– . RHP 1977–85 **Dodgers**, Twins 688 ip, 38–40, 3.95. *2 LCS, 6 ip, 0–0, 2.84. 1 WS, 1 ip, 0–0, 9.00*

The Dodgers hoped Castillo, a three-time all-city player at Los Angeles's Lincoln High, would be their first star of Mexican origin. He wasn't. But he taught the screwball to Fernando Valenzuela, who was. In 1983, starting for Minnesota, he was 13–11 and voted Twins' Pitcher of the Year./(TG)

Carmen Castillo — 1958– . OF-DH 1982- **Indians**, Twins 558 g, .256, 55 hr, 185 rbi

Castillo, a fastball hitter, showed good power (11 HR in 184 at-bats in 1985), but could not win a regular job./(SFS)

Juan Castillo — 1962– . 2B-SS-3B 1986- **Brewers** 199 g, .215, 3 hr, 38 rbi

Another of the many middle infielders from San Pedro de Macoris in the Dominican Republic, Castillo is a fine fielder but has yet to hit consistently in the majors./(JFC)

Manny Castillo — 1957– . 3B 1980, 82–83 Royals, **Mariners** 236 g, .242, 3 hr, 73 rbi

The versatile Dominican was playing in the Mets organization at 16. In his ninth minor league season he hit .335 to earn a ML chance. As the Mariner third baseman in 1982, he set four team rookie records, hitting 29 doubles and striking out only 35 times in 506 at-bats./(JCA)

Marty Castillo — 1957– . 3B-C 1981–85 **Tigers** 201 g, .190, 8 hr, 32 rbi. *1 LCS, 3 g, .250, 2 rbi. 1 WS, 3 g, .333, 1 hr, 2 rbi*

A utility man for three complete seasons with the Tigers, Castillo hit his first ML homer to beat the Brewers in the ninth inning (6/28/83). His career highlight was a game-winning two-run homer in Game Three of the 1984 World Series./(MC)

John Castino — 1954– . 3B-2B-SS 1979–84 **Twins** 666 g, .278, 41 hr, 249 rbi
☛ *Rookie of the Year—79.*

Castino shared Rookie of the Year honors with Alfredo Griffin in 1979 when he hit .285 as the Twins' third baseman. He had career highs (.302, 13 HR, 64 RBI) the next year and led the AL in triples in 1981. Switched to second base in 1982 after the arrival of Gary Gaetti, Castino was hobbled by chronic back pain. A fused disc ended his career early in 1984./(MC)

Foster Castleman — 1931– . 3B-SS 1954–58
Giants, Orioles 268 g, .205, 20 hr, 65 rbi

Slick-fielding Castleman was the Giants' third baseman in 1956 and cracked 14 home runs, but his
.226 batting average put him back on the bench the
next year. Waived to the Orioles, he was handed the
shortstop job in 1958, but his weak bat (.170) kept
him from keeping it; Willie Miranda took it away by
hitting .200. /(MC)

Slick Castleman [Clydell] — 1913– . RHP 1934–39
Giants 587 ip, 36–26, 4.25. *1 WS, 4 ip, 2.08*

Neat and well-groomed, "Slick" went 4–7 and 11–6
for the 1936–37 pennant-winning Giants. A 1937
arm injury shortened his career. /(JK)

Bill Castro [Williams Radhames] (Checo,
Bills) — 1953– . RHP 1974–83 Brewers, Yankees, Royals
545 ip, 31–26, 3.33

The Dominican was an effective member of Milwaukee's bullpen for six years, beginning in 1975
when he led the Brewers staff with a 2.52 ERA. He
specialized in getting the double-play ball and seldom allowed a home run. He left Milwaukee as a
free agent in 1981 with a career 2.96 ERA. /(JCA)

Fidel Castro — 1926–

Castro was a star pitcher at Belen College and the
University of Havana in Cuba and attracted the
attention of several ML scouts with his wicked
curveball. He turned down a $5,000 bonus from the
Giants to pursue his law degree, and after graduating
became a leader of Cuba's revolutionary movement.
Although he never actually pitched in winter ball as
is often claimed, he did once pitch to Don Hoak
briefly during a game before being ejected from the
ballpark. /(SCL)

Danny Cater — 1940– . 1B-OF-3B 1964–75 Phillies,
White Sox, A's, Yankees, Red Sox, Cardinals 1289 g,
.276, 66 hr, 519 rbi

The strong, silent Texan signed as a shortstop with
the Phillies, but played first, third, and the outfield
in his 12-year ML career. He had an unusual batting
stance, with his feet close together, and a smooth,
lazy-looking swing. Some thought him lackadaisical;
he felt his low-key style was responsible for his being
traded five times. One of baseball's great worriers,
teammates said Cater could quote all his stats after
each at-bat.

As Oakland's regular first baseman in 1968, he
hit .290 to finish second to Carl Yastrzemski's .301

in an anemic AL batting race. Traded to the
Yankees, he hit .301 in 1970 but had only 10
homers in two seasons, and he was shipped to
Boston in 1972 for reliever Sparky Lyle. Lyle
became a three-time All-Star; Cater hit an abysmal
.237 that year. He rebounded in 1973 to hit .313 in
63 games. /(JCA)

Buster Caton [James Howard] — 1896–1948. SS
1917–20 Pirates 231 g, .226, 0 hr, 53 rbi

The 5'6" 165-lb Caton was one of several shortstops
to bridge the gap between Honus Wagner and
Rabbit Maranville in Pittsburgh. A WWI veteran,
Caton was later a Dodger scout. /(ME)

Bill Caudill — 1956– . RHP 1979–87 Cubs, Mariners,
A's, Blue Jays 667 ip, 35–52, 3.68
☛ *All-Star—84.*

Caudill was a fireballing reliever who saved 106
games while demonstrating pitching proficiency and
a wonderful sense of fun. He was nicknamed "The
Inspector" by his Mariners teammates when he
"investigated" their bats, sleuthing for hits that were
mysteriously missing. Caudill would come in from
the bullpen to the Pink Panther theme. During a
one-sided game against the Blue Jays, Caudill
emerged from the dugout between innings with one-
half of his beard shaved off. After setting franchise
records for saves, Caudill was traded to a stronger
Oakland team, where he had a 36-save season in
1984. Toronto traded Alfredo Griffin and Dave
Collins for Caudill and signed him to a hefty long-
term contract with the expectation that he would be
Toronto's first genuine bullpen ace. But because
Caudill's arrival in Toronto conicided with the
sudden emergence of Tom Henke, he didn't get
much opportunity to establish himself as a closer.
He had shoulder problems that ended his career
after a couple of seasons with the Blue Jays. His
attempts to catch on with the A's and Indians were
unsuccessful. /(TF)

Red Causey [Cecil Algernon] — 1893–1960. RHP
1918–22 Giants, Braves, Phillies 650 ip, 39–35, 3.59

The 6'1" 160-lb Causey had two stints with the
Giants. Sent to Boston in a 1919 trade for Art Nehf,
he was back for the Giants' championships in 1921
and 1922. /(JK)

Wayne Causey — 1936– . SS-2B-3B 1955–57,
61–68 Orioles, **A's**, White Sox, Angels, Braves 1105 g,
.252, 35 hr, 285 rbi

Causey was a hard-playing, steady infielder who
kept losing jobs to hotshot rookies. He was supposed
to have been one himself. Signed for a $50,000
bonus in 1955, contemporary rules regarding "bonus babies" required his presence on the Baltimore
roster until June 1957. After three years in the
minors, he was traded to Kansas City in 1961 but
lost his shot at shortstop to rookie Dick Howser. In
mid-season he won the third base position, but
injured his shoulder early in 1962. When he was
ready to play again, Ed Charles had taken over at
third base.

Causey's best years came in 1963–64, when he
was finally the A's starting shortstop and led the
team in hitting with .280 and .281 marks. But in
spring 1965, by then the team captain, he dislocated
his shoulder, opening the position for young Bert
Campaneris. Causey was shipped to Chicago in May
1966, where he mostly played second base. /(JCA)

Phil Cavarretta — 1916– . 1B-OF 1934–55 **Cubs**,
White Sox 2030 g, .293, 95 hr, 920 rbi. *3 WS, 17 g, .317,
1 hr, 5 rbi.*
    Manager 1951–53 **Cubs** 169–213, .442
☛ *Most Valuable Player—45 . All-Star—44, 46, 47.*

Cavarretta played 20 consecutive seasons with the
Cubs. A lefthanded schoolboy pitcher for Lane Tech
in Chicago, he signed a contract with Peoria (Central
League) before he finished high school. He hit for
the cycle as a right fielder in his first pro game in
1934. Brought up by the Cubs that September, he
struck out as a pinch hitter in his debut, but
homered in his first start for the only run of the
game. He became the everyday first baseman for the
1935 NL champions as an 18-year-old.

In a May 1939 game against the Giants, Cavarretta broke an ankle sliding; 13 months later he
repeated the same injury, also against New York.
Exempt from military service because of an ear
problem, he peaked during WWII. His 197 hits in
1944 tied with Stan Musial for the NL lead. In that
year's All-Star Game, he reached base a record five
times. He was the 1945 NL batting champion
(.355), helping the Cubs to the pennant and winning
MVP honors. He led all hitters in the 1945 WS with
a .423 average (11 for 26).

Cavarretta was the Cubs' player-manager in
1951–53, and led the NL with 12 pinch hits in '51.
Fired in spring training of 1954 because owner Phil

Wrigley bridled at Cavarretta's prediction of a
second-division finish, he finished his playing career
with the White Sox. He managed extensively in the
minors, coached and scouted for the Tigers, and
became an excellent batting instructor for the Mets'
organization. /(NLM)

Ike Caveney (James) 1894–1949. SS 1922–25 **Reds**
466 g, .260, 13 hr, 196 rbi

Caveney was a Reds shortstop for four seasons in the
1920s. Later, as manager of the San Francisco Seals
of the Pacific Coast League, he switched a young
shortstop named Joe DiMaggio to the
outfield. /(NLM)

O.P. Caylor — Unk.–Unk. *Writer.*

In 1880 Caylor organized the Cincinnati Reds and
played a series against Spink's St. Louis Browns, a
series that begat the American Association. A se-
date, dignified man, not close to the players, he was
baseball editor of the Cincinnati *Enquirer* for 20
years. Even though he was part owner and manager
of the New York Mets, he was barred from the 1887
American Association meeting because he was also
a writer. /(NLM)

Art Ceccarelli (Chic) — 1930– . LHP 1955–57,
59–60 **A's**, Orioles, Cubs 307 ip, 9–18, 5.05

Ceccarelli's best season was 1959, when he went
5–5 and threw two shutouts for the Cubs. /(TJ)

Cesar Cedeno — 1951– . OF-1B 1970–86 **Astros**,
Reds, Cardinals, Dodgers 2006 g, .285, 199 hr, 976 rbi.
2 LCS, 8 g, .174, 1 rbi. 1 WS, 5 g, .133, 1 rbi
☛ *All-Star—72–74, 76. Gold Glove—72–76.*

Cedeno's fine career pales only against the fact that
he was billed by Astros manager Leo Durocher as
"the next Willie Mays" (while the Cubs' manager,
Durocher had similarly touted Adolfo Phillips). The
comparisons to Mays were inevitable. Cedeno led
the NL in doubles twice, stole over 50 bases six
times, batted .320 twice, hit for the cycle twice, and
won five Gold Glove awards. But for all he accomplished, he never came up to the "another Mays"
prediction. He made something of a comeback in
1980 (.309, 10 HR, 73 RBI), helping Houston win
its first division title and earning his fourth selection
to *TSN*'s NL All-Star Team. Traded to the Reds
after the 1981 season, he improved his play after he
took a stress-relief course during the winter of
1983–84. On August 29, 1985, he was traded to the
Cardinals, who were seeking a replacement for
injured Jack Clark. He helped push St. Louis to the

Cesar Cedeno

home runs, 105 RBI, and .317. In 1961 he moved to first base, trading positions with Willie McCovey, and led the NL in home runs with 46 and RBI with 146, becoming more popular in San Francisco than teammate Willie Mays. Cepeda wrecked his knee in 1965, and was accused of malingering. Ultimately, he was traded to the Cardinals for Ray Sadecki. The 6'2″ 210-lb slugger led St. Louis to a pennant in 1967, topping the NL with 111 RBI and batting .325. Cepeda was nicknamed "The Baby Bull" after his father, "The Bull," an outstanding slugger sometimes called "The Babe Ruth of Puerto Rico." After his retirement as a player Cepeda served time in prison for marijuana smuggling. He admitted his guilt and served his time, but it is likely that the incident is a factor in his failure to gain election to the Hall of Fame. /(TJ)

Orlando Cepeda

pennant with a remarkable stretch drive: .434, 6 HR, 19 RBI in 28 games. However, after playing poorly in the postseason, he was released. /(ME)

Orlando Cepeda (The Baby Bull) — 1937– . 1B-OF **Giants**, Cardinals, Braves, A's, Red Sox, Royals 1958–74 2124 g, .297, 379 hr, 1365 rbi. *1 LCS, 3 g, .455, 1 hr, 3 rbi. 3 WS, 19 g, .171, 2 hr, 9 rbi*
☛ *Rookie of the Year—58. Most Valuable Player—67. Led League—hr 61, rbi 61, 67. All-Star—1959–64, 67.*

In his first ML game, the Giants' first regular-season game in San Francisco, Cepeda homered to help beat Don Drysdale and the Dodgers. It was a fitting beginning to a spectacular career that included nine .300 seasons and eight seasons with 25 or more homers. Bill Rigney, his manager for his first two ML seasons, called him "the best young righthanded power hitter I'd seen." He won Rookie of the Year honors in 1958 when he belted 25 homers, led the NL with 38 doubles, knocked in 96 runs, and batted .312. As a sophomore, he upped his figures to 27

Rick Cerone — 1954– . C 1975– Indians, Blue Jays, **Yankees**, Braves, Brewers, Red Sox 1257 g, .241, 54 hr, 402 rbi. *2 LCS, 6 g, .227, 1 hr, 2 rbi. 1 WS, 6 g, .190, 1 hr, 3 rbi*

Always a crowd favorite in New York, Cerone, a New Jersey native, was able to play near home when the Yankees acquired him from the Blue Jays after 1979. Cerone's finest season was 1980, when he finished seventh in AL MVP voting and had career highs in batting average (.277), home runs (14), and RBI (85).

Cerone earned the respect of his teammates by talking back to Yankees owner George Steinbrenner after the boss chewed out his team before the decisive Game 5 of the 1981 Divisional Playoffs. Cerone homered in that game, a 7–3 Yankees win.

Injuries hampered Cerone in 1982–84, and he was traded to Atlanta, where he played a year before being traded to Milwaukee. The Yankees signed him as a free agent before 1987, and he played in over 100 games for the first time since 1981. Twice he pitched, allowing no hits and only one walk in two innings, including a strikeout of Texas pitcher Bobby Witt, who was pinch hitting in a blowout. Let go by the Yankees in 1987, Cerone was picked up by the Red Sox and had renewed success sharing catching duties with Rich Gedman./(EG)

John Cerutti — 1960– . LHP 1985– **Blue Jays** 632 ip, 37–28, 3.67

Cerutti was shuttled back and forth between the Blue Jay bullpen and starting rotation in his first several seasons. While he never showed overpowering stuff, he was effective when he overcame a tendency to allow home runs. On July 2, 1986, Cerutti threw a club-record four wild pitches against Boston./(TF)

Bob Cerv — 1926– . OF 1951–62 Yankees, **A's**, Angels, Astros 829 g, .276, 105 hr, 374 rbi. *3 WS, 10 g, .258, 1 hr, 1 rbi*
☛ *All-Star—58.*

Cerv was sitting in the Yankee dugout one day in mid-1956 when manager Casey Stengel walked over and told him Enos Slaughter had been acquired from the A's. Casey said, "Nobody knows this, but one of us has been traded to Kansas City." Cerv looked around; he was the only player there. He had spent most of his first five years on the Yankee bench, but briefly became a star after going to the A's. In 1958 Cerv blasted 38 homers and was chosen over Ted Williams as the AL All-Star left fielder in the year of the Boston star's last batting

championship. He played a month of that season with his broken jaw wired shut. The Yanks reacquired Cerv in 1960 and, after the Angels claimed him in the expansion draft, traded for him again in 1961./(JCA)

Ron Cey (Penguin) — 1948– . 3B 1971–87 **Dodgers**, Cubs, A's 2073 g, .261, 316 hr, 1139 rbi. *5 LCS, 22 g, .268, 4 hr, 14 rbi. 4 WS, 23 g, .253, 3 hr, 13 rbi*
☛ *All-Star—74–79.*

Cey filled a traditional trouble spot when he became the Dodgers' regular third baseman in 1973. He held the position for ten seasons and became the leading home run hitter in Dodger history. Six times an All-Star in the 1970s, Cey got his nickname from his stocky build, short legs, and choppy running style. In 1981 his string of eleven seasons with 20 or more homers was interrupted by the players' strike and a late-season broken arm. He returned in time to play in the WS, where he was beaned by a Goose Gossage

Ron Cey

fastball. Nevertheless, he was co-MVP in the Series. In 1983 he was traded to the Cubs. His 25 homers and 97 RBI helped them win the 1984 Eastern Division title. /(ME)

Elio Chacon — 1936– . SS-2B 1960–62 Reds, **Mets** 228 g, .232, 4 hr, 39 rbi. *1 WS, 4 g, .250*

The 5'9" Venezuelan batted .265 as a reserve second baseman with the NL Champion Reds of 1961. In Game Two of that World Series, Chacon hit a key bloop single off the Yankees' Ralph Terry, and scored the winning run in the Reds' only victory. In 1962 Chacon was the shortstop for the original Mets. /(TJ)

Chet Chadbourne (Pop) — 1884–1943. OF 1906–07, 14–15, 18 Red Sox, **Kansas City (FL)**, Braves 347 g, .255, 2 hr, 82 rbi

An institution in the Pacific Coast League, "Pop" collected 3,216 minor league hits over 21 years. A far-ranging outfielder, his only full ML seasons came in the Federal League, where he led in assists one year and fielding percentage the other. /(JK)

Henry Chadwick — 1824–1908. *Writer.*
☛ *Hall of Fame—1938.*

As an English schoolboy, Chadwick played rounders, a forerunner of baseball. In his early twenties (a decade after emigrating with his parents to Brooklyn), he played baseball, but remained indifferent to the new game for several years. Then, in 1856, while witnessing a well-played match between two of New York's better clubs, he became a fan, and decided to do everything he could to make baseball "a national sport for Americans" as cricket was for the English. He set out to persuade *The New York Times* (for which he reported cricket matches) and other major metropolitan dailies to cover baseball, offering to report the games himself.

By the time the last New York paper began reporting baseball in 1862, Chadwick had taken on his next task: promoting changes—through his writing and his membership on an early baseball rules committee—that would move the game toward more balanced offense and defense, and would make it a more "manly," "scientific" game, demanding mental as well as physical ability. He expanded the box score and developed a scoring system that enabled reporters to record every play, allowing them to describe games in greater detail. A modified version of his system is standard today.

In 1860 Chadwick prepared baseball's first guide; he edited one or more annually until his death,

Henry Chadwick

including the famous and respected Spaulding Guide from 1881–1908. Through his rules committee work, his books and pamphlets, and his contributions to more than 20 periodicals, he did more than any other writer to shape the game and spread its popularity, and earned himself the appellation "father of baseball." His decades of vociferous opposition to gambling were largely responsible for keeping the game freer from corruption than other major sports.

Besides baseball, Chadwick wrote about many other sports and games, from yachting to billiards to chess. He was also a pianist, songwriter, drama critic, and, briefly, during the Civil War, a news correspondent in Virginia. He was enshrined in baseball's Hall of Fame in 1938, the only writer elected to the Hall itself (as opposed to the Writers Wing). /(FIC)

Leon Chagnon (Shag) — 1902–1953. RHP 1929–30, 32–35 **Pirates**, Giants 393 ip, 19–16, 4.51

After two early flops, Shag stuck with the Bucs in 1932 (at age 29) and turned in three good years from the Pittsburgh bullpen. In 1931 he was a 20-game winner for Fort Worth (Texas League). /(ME)

Bob Chakales (Chick, The Golden Greek) — 1927- .
RHP 1951–57 Indians, Orioles, White Sox, **Senators**, Red
Sox 420 ip, 15–25, 4.54

Chakales jumped from A-ball to the majors and
won two of his three 1951 victories with his bat. In
parts of seven seasons, primarily in relief, he struggled with his control, but hit a solid .271./(JCA)

Dave Chalk — 1950- . 3B-SS 1973–81 **Angels**,
Rangers, A's, Royals 903 g, .252, 15 hr, 243 rbi. *1 WS,
1 g, --*
☛ *All-Star—74–75.*

The Angels' (and baseball's) number-one pick in the
1972 free agent draft, Chalk led AL shortstops with
29 errors as a rookie in 1974 but with Jim Sundberg
was one of two rookies to make the All-Star team.
He became an outstanding fielder at both short and
third base. A notoriously slow starter at bat, he often
didn't hit for average until August and never showed
much home run power. His top season was 1977,
when he hit .277 with 69 RBI. A 1979 knee injury
finished him as a regular./(MC)

George Chalmers (Dut) — 1888–1960. RHP
1910–16 **Phillies** 646 ip, 29–41, 3.41. *1 WS, 8 ip, 0–1,
2.25*

The Scottish-born spitballer went 25–6 for Scranton
(New York State League) in 1910, and was purchased by the Phillies. He was 13–10, his ML best,
in 1911. He pitched well in Game Four of the 1915
World Series, but lost to the Red Sox 2–1./(AL)

Cliff Chambers (Lefty) — 1922- . LHP 1948–53
Cubs, **Pirates**, Cardinals 897 ip, 48–53, 4.29

After a disappointing 2–9 debut in 1948 with the
last-place Cubs, Chambers was dealt to Pittsburgh,
where he led Pirate pitchers with 13 victories in
1949 and 12 in 1950. The 6'3" Oregonian won a
career-high 14 games in 1951; he started that season
with Pittsburgh, but went to the Cardinals in the
seven-player June trade that moved Joe Garagiola to
the Pirates./(TJ)

Chris Chambliss — 1948- . 1B 1971–86, 88 Indians,
Yankees, Braves 2173 g, .279, 185 hr, 972 rbi. *4 LCS,
17 g, .286, 2 hr, 10 rbi. 3 WS, 13 g, .275, 1 hr, 5 rbi*
☛ *Rookie of the Year—71. All-Star—76. Gold Glove—78.*

On October 14, 1976, Chambliss hit one of base-
ball's most dramatic home runs. His ninth-inning,
Game Five shot off Mark Littell decided the
Yankees-Royals LCS. It snapped a 6–6 tie, ended
New York's 12-year pennant drought, and made
Yankee Stadium go wild. In that Series, Chambliss

batted .524 and tied or broke five LCS records for
hits and RBI.

Chambliss was twice drafted by the Reds, in 1967
and in 1969, but continued school and attended
UCLA for a year. Signing with the Indians when he
was drafted a third time in 1970, he led the
American Association in hitting with a .342 mark at
Wichita in 1970. He was the first player to lead the
AA in batting in his first pro season, and is believed
to be the first "rookie" to have won a Triple-A
batting title. In only his second pro season, Chambliss was the 1971 AL Rookie of the Year, Cleveland's second ever (Herb Score was the first). It was
the first time a player won consecutive Rookie of the
Year honors on the minor and major league levels.
Called up that May, he batted .275 and played solid
defense at first base. He led Indian regulars in
batting the next two seasons.

Chris Chambliss

On April 27, 1974, Chambliss was sent to the Yankees in a seven-player deal. After struggling that year, he became a key part of the potent New York offense. In 1975 he batted .304, but he was most productive for New York's 1976–78 pennants. His consistent performance matched his temperament; he averaged 92 RBI over those years, and in 1978 won a Gold Glove as he led AL first basemen in fielding (.997). He was the quiet, steady exception on a loud and turbulent club.

Chambliss was traded to Toronto and on to Atlanta after the 1979 season. He prospered in the NL, hitting a career-high 20 HR in both 1982, when he helped the Braves to a division title, and 1983. After averaging 141 games in his first 14 seasons, he was switched primarily to bench duty in 1985, and in 1986 led the NL with 20 pinch hits. He was named the Yankee hitting coach for 1988 and was activated very briefly, striking out in his only at-bat. His cousin Jo-Jo White performed in the NBA. /(MG)

Billy Champion — 1947– . RHP 1969–76 **Phillies, Brewers** 805 ip, 34–50, 4.68

Champion was 15–5 with an International League-leading 2.03 ERA in 1968, and was 7–1, 1.66, before the Phillies called him up in 1969. Only 12–31 in four NL seasons, the 6'4" redhead was considering quitting when he was traded to the Brewers. Originally a fastball-slider thrower, Champion added four more pitches and went 11–4 in 1974. An elbow injury sidelined him in August 1975 and forced him to retirement in 1976. /(JCA)

Mike Champion — 1955– . 2B 1976–78 **Padres** 193 g, .229, 2 hr, 49 rbi

Champion was the top-fielding Pacific Coast League second baseman in 1976 but hit only a weak .229 in his one year as the Padres' regular second baseman. /(MC)

Bob Chance — 1940– . 1B-OF 1963–67, 69 **Indians, Senators, Angels** 277 g, .261, 24 hr, 112 rbi

Chance won the Triple Crown with Charleston (Eastern League) in 1963 and followed with a strong 1964 rookie season with Cleveland (.279, 14 HR, 75 RBI), batting .340 versus Washington. The Senators traded for him and Manager Gil Hodges said he was "the kind of hitter who could wind up leading the league." But the unrelenting bench jockey had a tendency to gain weight and proved a disappointment. He split the 1965–67 seasons between Washington and Hawaii. /(JCA)

Dean Chance — 1941– . RHP 1961–71 **Angels, Twins, Indians, Mets, Tigers** 2148 ip, 128–115, 2.92. 20 wins: 64, 67 *1 LCS, 2 ip, 0–0, 13.50*
☛ *Led League—w 64. Led League—era 64, 67. Cy Young Award—64. All-Star—64, 67.*

Throwing hard from an unorthodox twisting windup, at the age of 23 in 1964 Chance won the Cy Young Award (when there was only one award including both leagues) in a landslide. Expectations were high, but he never evolved into a consistently dominant pitcher. With a touch of wildness and the disconcerting trait of never looking at home plate once he received the sign from his catcher, Chance would turn his broad back fully toward the hitter in mid-windup before spinning and unleashing a lively fastball, good sinker, or sidearm curve.

Chance was drafted by the Angels from the Orioles' organization in the 1960 expansion draft and as a rookie in 1962 was 14–10 with a 2.96 ERA starting in spots. He joined the rotation in 1963 and was 13–18 with meager support from his teammates. In 1964 he blossomed into the AL's most overpowering hurler. Pitching his home games in spacious Dodger Stadium (called Chavez Ravine by the Angels), Chance was 20–9 with a 1.64 ERA in '64 and tossed 11 shutouts, including 6 that he won 1–0. That June 6 he pitched 14 shutout innings against the Yankees, only to see the Angels lose 2–0 after he left the game. On September 10 he pitched a one-hitter against the Twins, allowing only an infield single to Zoilo Versalles in the eighth inning.

Chance slipped to 15–10 in 1965 and 12–17 in 1966 and began to berate his teammates for their poor play behind him. He was traded to Minnesota before the 1967 season and enjoyed a resurgence with the Twins, going 20–14 with a 2.73 ERA to win AL Comeback Player of the Year honors. He pitched a no-hitter against the Indians on August 25. On the final day of the season he faced the Red Sox with a chance to clinch the pennant. Chance lost, and Boston went to the World Series instead. Chance was 16–16 in 1968 and 5–4 in only 15 starts in 1969, then was traded to the Indians along with Graig Nettles in a six-player deal that brought Luis Tiant to the Twins. The Indians sold Chance to the Mets in mid-1970 and he spent his final season pitching mostly in relief with the Tigers in 1971.

Chance was a notoriously poor hitter, batting .066 in 662 career at-bats while striking out 353 times. /(SCL)

Frank Chance (Husk, The Peerless Leader) —
1877–1924. 1B-C-OF 1898–1914 **Cubs,**
Yankees 1286 g, .297, 20 hr, 596 rbi. *4 WS, 20 g, .310, 6 rbi.*
  Manager 1905–14, 23 **Cubs,** Yankees, Red Sox
946–648, .593. First place: 06–08, 10 *4 WS, 11–9, .550*
☛ *Hall of Fame—1946.*

Chance was the first baseman in the double-play trio
of "Tinker to Evers to Chance," immortalized by
Franklin Adams in the poem "Baseball's Sad Lexicon." He was dubbed "The Peerless Leader" as he
led the Cubs to pennants in 1906–08 and 1910 as
their player-manager. Some called him "Husk"
because he was husky, strong, and aggressive. He
made his opinions known and never backed down
from an argument. He ran his clubs with a clenched
fist, coming down hard on any player who gave less
than 100%. Eventually, he had trouble hearing
criticism, or anything at all. Since he crowded the

Frank Chance

plate, he too often was beaned, and his hearing was
eventually affected. As a result, he developed a
peculiar whine which grated on his teammates and
opponents.
  Chance reached the majors as a catcher and part-
time outfielder with Chicago, but when Johnny
Kling came along, he shifted to first base. He led the
NL with 67 stolen bases in 1903, and with 57 in
1906, when his 103 runs scored were also the league
high. In only six seasons (1903–08) did he play in
more than 100 games, but he batted better than
.300 in the first four of them.
  Chance's great success came as a young manager.
He was 27 when he took over the Chicago club from
Frank Selee in mid-1905; in seven full seasons, he
won at least 100 games four times, and never
finished lower than third. His .664 winning percentage (768–389) stands as the best in Cubs history. In
1906 the Cubs won 116 games—a major league
record—while losing just 36. They lost to the White
Sox in the '06 World Series, but defeated the Tigers
in the next two. Chance led all participants in the
'08 WS with a .421 batting average.
  Chance moved to the Yankees in 1913, but ill
health forced him to retire with New York in
seventh place in 1914. He returned to his native
California, and owned and managed the Los Angeles (Pacific Coast League) team in 1916–17. He
returned East in 1923 to try to rebuild the Red Sox,
decimated by the sale of stars (including Babe Ruth)
to the Yankees, but finished in the cellar. He was to
manage the White Sox in 1924, but his health
worsened, and he died that September. In 1946
Chance, Joe Tinker, and Johnny Evers were inducted into the Hall of Fame./(JK)

Happy Chandler [Albert B.] — 1907– . Commissioner.
☛ *Hall of Fame—1982.*

Chandler was the second Commissioner, succeeding
the legendary Judge Landis. He was elected in 1945,
after having served as Governor of Kentucky for
four years and U.S. Senator for six. He was perceived as a players' Commissioner, and he cautioned
owners to be less stubborn to avoid later confrontations. His advice was ignored.
  Despite the negative feelings of most club owners,
he supported the entry of Jackie Robinson into the
major leagues. When some players jumped to the
Mexican League in 1946, he suspended them for
five years (but gave them blanket amnesty in 1949).
He suspended Dodgers manager Leo Durocher for
one year for a series of actions detrimental to
baseball's image, including consorting with gam-

blers. He was the first to put six umpires on the field for the World Series.

Having made some decisions that riled several owners, he was fired after one term, receiving only nine of the twelve votes necessary to continue. When he left, his reputation for being good-humored, iron-willed, and honest remained intact. He had put the players' pension fund on a sound footing, averted threats to the reserve clause, and helped open the ML door for black players. In 1982 he was named to the Hall of Fame. /(NLM)

Spud Chandler [Spurgeon Ferdinand] — 1907- . RHP 1937-47 **Yankees** 1485 ip, 109-43, 2.84. 20 wins: 43, 46 *4 WS, 33 ip, 2-2, 1.62*
☛ *Most Valuable Player—43. Led League—w 43. Led League—era 43, 47. All-Star—42-43, 46-47.*

When Chandler retired after the 1947 season, he possessed the highest winning percentage (.717) of any pitcher with 100 or more major league victories. In addition to his 109 regular-season triumphs, Chandler won the 1942 All-Star Game and recorded two victories, including the clincher, for the Yankees in the 1943 World Series. Chandler led AL pitchers in wins (20), winning percentage (.883), ERA (1.64), complete games (20), and shutouts (five) in 1943, capturing the MVP award. After time out for military service, he went 20-8 in 1946 and led the league in ERA (2.46) for a second time in 1947. Chandler, who played baseball and football for the University of Georgia, threw 26 shutouts during his ML career. /(TJ)

Darrel Chaney — 1948- . SS-2B-3B 1969-79 **Reds**, Braves 915 g, .217, 14 hr, 190 rbi. *2 LCS, 10 g, .120, 1 rbi. 3 WS, 9 g, .000*

Chaney led the Southern League in homers with 23 in 1968, but never hit more than 3 in a ML season. He spent seven years with the Reds, mostly as backup to shortstop Dave Concepcion. "There's a whole bunch of clubs in the majors on which he could play regularly," said manager Sparky Anderson. After Chaney was traded to the Braves in 1976, he became their starting shortstop and had his best year offensively (.252, 50 RBI), but his 37 errors led NL shortstops. /(JCA)

Tiny Chaplin [James Bailey] — 1905-1939. RHP 1928, 30-31, 36 Giants, **Braves** 371 ip, 14-24, 4.25

"Tiny" Chaplin was a hard-throwing 6'1" 195-lb righthander. He was an ineffective reliever with the Giants for three seasons, and returned to the minors

for five more years before resurfacing as a starter for the Braves in 1936. /(FS)

Ben Chapman (Chappy) — 1908- . OF-3B-2B-RHP 1930-41, 44-46 **Yankees**, Senators, Red Sox, Indians, White Sox, Dodgers, Phillies 1716 g, .302, 90 hr, 977 rbi; 141 ip, 8-6, 4.39. *1 WS, 4 g, .294, 6 rbi.*
*Manager 1945-48 **Phillies** 197-277, .416*
☛ *All-Star—33-36.*

On a team best remembered for power, Chapman delighted Yankee fans with daring baserunning and fervent play from 1930 to 1936. An infielder in 1930, Chapman was moved to left field by new manager Joe McCarthy in 1931 to take advantage of his speed and throwing arm. Chapman led AL outfielders in assists in 1933 and 1935. He reached double figures in doubles, triples, HR, and steals in each of his first three seasons, and led the AL in stolen bases three straight years, 1931-33. He was the first batter for the AL in the inaugural 1933 All-Star Game.

Ben Chapman

Chapman moved to center in 1934, but he and his temper were displaced by Joe DiMaggio in 1936. Traded to Washington in mid-1936, Boston in mid-1937, and (despite batting .340) Cleveland after 1938, Chapman was a regular through 1940. In 1942, as pitcher-manager for Richmond (Piedmont League), he punched umpire I.H. Case and was suspended from playing for a year. He returned as a pitcher with Brooklyn in 1944, and went 5–3 (3.40). Two weeks after his trade to the Phillies in 1945, Chapman was named their manager. His spirited leadership brought initial improvement, but soon his temper and poorly timed comments, especially his widely publicized vicious baiting of Jackie Robinson in 1947, exasperated owner Bob Carpenter. Chapman was fired in 1948. /(ME)

Charles Chapman — 1880–1941. *Scout.*

A catcher at Princeton and a graduate of Harvard Law School, Chapman scouted part-time for the Cardinals from 1921 to 1931 and full-time for the Reds from 1931 to 1941, discovering or recommending Chick Hafey, Dom DiMaggio, and Eddie Joost. He eventually became a history professor at the University of California, and authored *Play Ball! Advice for Young Ballplayers* with ex-ML catcher Hank Severeid. /(FVP)

Jack Chapman (Death to Flying Things) — 1843–1916. OF 1874–76 **Brooklyn (NA)**, St. Louis (NA), Louisville (NL) *NA*: 96 g, .253; NL: 17 g, .239, 0 hr, 5 rbi.
      Manager 1877–78, 82–85, 89–92 Louisville (NL), Milwaukee (NL), Worcester (NL), Detroit (NL), Buffalo (NL), **Louisville (NL)** 306–428, .417

Chapman was one of the foremost players of the 1860s. Although his services were much in demand, he played most seasons with the Brooklyn Atlantics, the team that broke the Cincinnati Red Stockings' two-year winning streak in an extra-inning game in 1871. For defeating Cincinnati, each Brooklyn player received $364 from the Atlantics' share of the gate receipts. In an age that admired fielding prowess more than hitting ability, Chapman became famous for his many long running catches, and was the first to receive the colorful nickname "Death to Flying Things." He later played two seasons in the National Association and one in the National League. A weight problem brought about his retirement as a player, but he became a highly respected manager for many years. His Louisville team won the 1890 American Association pennant. /(BC)

Ray Chapman — 1891–1920. SS 1912–20 **Indians**
1050 g, .278, 18 hr, 364 rbi

Ray Chapman is the only modern major leaguer to have died as a direct result of being hit by a pitch. At the Polo Grounds on August 16, 1920, Chapman, crowding the plate as usual, was struck in the temple by a pitch from Yankee submariner Carl Mays that barely missed the strike zone. Chapman was taken to a hospital, never regained consciousness, and died twelve hours later. Rookie Joe Sewell replaced Chapman at short, beginning a Hall of Fame career. Cleveland players wore black arm bands, and manager Tris Speaker rallied his dejected men to win the first World Championship in club history.

The popular Chapman led the Indians in stolen bases four times, setting a team record with 52 in 1917 that stood until 1980. He led the AL in runs scored and walks in 1918. He was hitting .303 with

Ray Chapman

97 runs scored when he died. It is baseball analyst Bill James's opinion that Chapman was "probably destined for the Hall of Fame had he lived."/(ME)

Sam Chapman — 1916– . OF 1938–41, 45–51 **A's**, Indians 1368 g, .266, 180 hr, 773 rbi
☛ *All-Star—46.*

Chapman went right to the majors from the University of California, where he had been an All-American football player. He had it all: speed, power, and a strong arm. He hit 20 or more homers five seasons, but struck out often, leading the AL with 96 in 1940. Chapman became a popular team leader, and batted .322 with 25 HR in 1941. By 1942, he was a Navy flier. After he returned at the end of 1945, he never again hit .300, but he had not lost his power, and in 1949 drove in 108 runs. He led AL outfielders in putouts four times, assists once, and errors twice./(NLM)

Joe Charboneau — 1955– . OF-DH 1980–82 Indians 201 g, .266, 29 hr, 114 rbi
☛ *Rookie of the Year—80.*

They were writing songs in Cleveland about "Super Joe" when he was the 1980 AL Rookie of the Year (.289, 23 HR, 87 RBI). Then came one of the greatest downfalls in player history. He was sent down halfway through 1981 after hitting only .208. He underwent two back operations but never fully recuperated, and was released by the Indians' AA Buffalo affiliate in May 1983 after giving fans an obscene salute. A "flake" who would dye his hair exotic colors (or shave it off entirely), Charboneau impressed his teammates by opening beer bottles with an eye socket muscle./(JCA)

Ed Charles (The Glider, Pops) — 1935– . 3B 1962–69 **A's**, Mets 1005 g, .263, 86 hr, 421 rbi. *1 WS, 4 g, .133*

Nicknamed "The Glider" for his graceful baserunning and third base play, Charles spent eight tough seasons with the Braves organization in the still-segregated South, and wrote published poetry concerning the universe, racism, and baseball. With Eddie Mathews at third, Milwaukee had no place for Charles and finally traded him to Kansas City. His 1962 rookie marks included career highs of .288 and 17 HR. He remained a steady contributor for five seasons, but his home run production was cut in half when owner Charlie Finley moved the fences back in 1965. Traded to the Mets in early 1967, he was their oldest regular and was waived in November. He re-made the club in the spring of 1968 and batted .276 with 15 homers. In the Mets' 1969

World Championship season, he shared third base duties with Wayne Garrett and Bobby Pfeil./(JCA)

Oscar Charleston (The Hoosier Comet) — 1896–1954. OF-1B-MGR Negro Leagues 1915–54 Indianapolis ABC's, New York Lincoln Stars, Chicago American Giants, St. Louis Giants, Harrisburg Giants, Hilldale, Homestead Grays, **Pittsburgh Crawfords**, Toledo Crawfords, Indianapolis Crawfords, Philadelphia Stars, Brooklyn Brown Dodgers, Indianapolis Clowns statistics not available
☛ *Led League—ba 21(NNL). Led League—hr 21(NNL). All-Star—33–35. Hall of Fame—1976.*

Considered by many the greatest Negro League player of all, multi-talented Oscar Charleston was often compared with three great white contemporaries: his hitting and speedy, aggressive baserunning (and hard-sliding style) brought favorable comparison to Ty Cobb; his physique (he was barrel-chested, with spindly legs), power, and popularity, particu-

Oscar Charleston

larly with youngsters, were reminiscent of Babe Ruth; and his defensive style and skills, playing a shallow, far-ranging centerfield with a strong, accurate arm and excellent fly ball judgment, brought visions of Tris Speaker. The New York Giants' John McGraw, familiar with the untapped black talent available, considered the 6′ 190-lb Charleston the best, and coveted him.

A native of Indianapolis, Charleston grew up serving as batboy for the local ABC's. At age 15, he joined the army and was stationed in the Philippines. The military gave the underage runaway the opportunity to display his abilities in track and baseball; he ran the 220-yard dash in 23 seconds, and played in the otherwise all-white Manila League. Entering big-time black baseball with the ABC's, he was a vital cog in their 1916 Black World Series triumph over the Chicago American Giants, batting .360 in seven of the 10 games played. After stints with the American Giants and New York Lincoln Stars, he rejoined Indianapolis when the Negro National League was organized in 1920.

Through 1923, the lefthanded-hitting and throwing Charleston posted a .370 batting average with the NNL ABC's and St. Louis Giants, and in 1921 led the league in hitting (.446), triples (10), HR (14), total bases (137), slugging (.774), and stolen bases (28), finishing second with 79 hits in 50 games. From 1922 to 1925, he was player-manager for the Eastern Colored League Harrisburg Giants, and, after a second-division finish in 1924, he led them to three consecutive second-place finishes. In 1925, he batted .424. From 1928 to 1931, he hit .347 in two-year stints with the Hilldale club and the Homestead Grays. The Grays won a 10-game Eastern Championship Series from the New York Lincoln Giants in 1930.

In 1932 Gus Greenlee persuaded Charleston to manage his Pittsburgh Crawfords. Josh Gibson, Judy Johnson, and Satchel Paige joined him to give the club four future Hall of Famers. Operating independently, they went 99–36 as their 36-year-old manager batted .363, second on the club to Gibson. Often considered black baseball's greatest team, the Crawfords became the dominant member of the tough National Negro Association, which operated from 1933 to 1936. Pittsburgh claimed the 1933 pennant, as did the Chicago American Giants, without resolution. In 1935 the Crawfords won the first NNL's only undisputed title. In 1936 they posted the best overall record, winning the second half of the split season. A title series with the first-half champion Washington Elite Giants was never completed, though the Giants won the only game played, 2–0.

Charleston remained with the Crawfords through 1940, following them in moves to Toledo and Indianapolis. He became manager of the NNL Philadelphia Stars in 1941 and the Brooklyn Brown Dodgers when Branch Rickey formed the United States League in 1945. He was thus put in a position to scout and evaluate players for organized baseball's integration. He managed through 1954, leading the Indianapolis Clowns to the '54 Negro American League title, but died after the season.

Statistics so far compiled show that Charleston batted .353 lifetime. He twice led the Cuban Winter League in SB, and had 31 during the 1923–24 campaign, setting a record that stood for more than 20 years. In 53 exhibition games against white major leaguers, he hit .318 with 11 HR.

Charleston had a famous temper, and enjoyed brawling, resulting in legendary encounters with umpires, opponents, agents raiding his teams, a Ku Klux Klansman, and, on one occasion, several Cuban soldiers. As his legs gave out, he moved from centerfield to first base, yet as long as he played, he never lost his home run power, nor his meanness on the basepaths. He was sympathetic toward young players, and was protective of rookie teammates. A demanding manager who expected his players to perform as well as he did, his strength as a pilot lay in his understanding of the intricacies of the game. He was elected to the Hall of Fame by the Committee on Negro Baseball Leagues in 1976. /(MFK)

Norm Charlton — 1963– . LHP 1988– **Reds** 157 ip, 12–8, 3.33

The skinny, hard-throwing Charlton was the Expos' first-round draft pick in June 1984. He joined the Reds' excellent middle-relief staff in 1988 and became effective with more work in 1989. /(SFS)

Mike Chartak (Shotgun) — 1916–1967. OF-1B 1940, 1942–44 Yankees, Senators, **Browns** 256 g, .243, 21 hr, 98 rbi. *1 WS, 2 g, .000*

The broad-shouldered ex-coal miner languished in the talent-rich Yankee organization, but became a spare outfielder and pinch hitter with the Browns, playing 35 games in 1944 for their only pennant winner. Chartak retired a year later after contracting tuberculosis. /(JL)

Hal Chase (Prince Hal) — 1883-1947. 1B 1905-19 **Yankees**, White Sox, Buffalo (FL), Reds, Giants 1917 g, .291, 57 hr, 941 rbi.
 Manager 1910-11 **Yankees** 85-78, .521
☛ *Led League—ba 16. Led League—hr 15 .*

Among the most unsavory characters in the history of the game, Chase was an oddly charismatic star. He was considered by contemporary observers to be the best-fielding first baseman ever, but he repeatedly threw games for the quick money he could make betting against his own team, and he was eventually banned for life.

He led his league's first basemen in errors seven times, but only in 1911, as a playing manager, did he lead in any positive fielding categories (putouts and assists, but also errors once again). He holds the AL career first baseman's mark for errors (285). On September 21, 1906, he tied the ML record for putouts by a first baseman in a nine-inning game with 22; two other times he had 21.

The venal gate attraction jumped the Highlanders (later the Yankees) after the 1907 season, demanding a $4,000 salary. Management gave in to him, but he jumped anyway, playing for San Jose (California League) under an assumed name. He was suspended, then reinstated; when he returned to

Hal Chase

New York, his teammates presented the redhead with a silver loving cup. In 1910 manager George Stallings accused Chase of throwing games. Chase beat the charge and then used his popularity to take over the managerial post himself at the end of the season. In his first full year at the helm, the team dropped from second place (88-63) to sixth (76-76). Traded to the White Sox in June 1913 after his lackadaisical play became blatant, he jumped to the Federal League a year later. Playing in a small park, he hit an atypical 17 HR (his previous high was four) to lead the league in 1915. This made him much sought-after when the FL folded, and he was signed by the Reds. He led the NL in batting in 1916 with a career-high .339. He hit .300 four times, but usually with very few walks. He did steal as many as 40 bases (1910), and he finished his career with 363 steals. However, Chase never scored more than 85 runs or drove in more than 89, both highs coming in 1915.

In 1918, playing under the scrupulously honest Christy Mathewson, Chase was suspended for throwing games. He was initially cleared by an establishment eager to disbelieve Chase's accusers, but the charge was later proven. John McGraw of the Giants, always sure of his ability to reform the wayward, tried Chase in 1919, but by the end of the season wouldn't play him. Chase was implicated in the Black Sox scandal when the World Series was thrown at the end of the season, and thereafter he was persona non grata. /(JFC)

Ken Chase (Lefty) — 1913- . LHP 1936-43 **Senators**, Red Sox, Giants 1165 ip, 53-84, 4.27

Chase was a hard thrower who struggled with poor teams and poor control. He allowed 143 walks in 1940 to lead the AL. Chase retired after 1943 to run his family dairy farm near Cooperstown. /(JK)

Buster Chatham (Charles) — 1901-1975. 3B-SS 1930-31 **Braves** 129 g, .263, 6 hr, 59 rbi

The 5'5" 150-lb infielder played in more than 2,600 games, mostly in the minors, including a seven-season stretch with Atlanta (Sally League) in which he never missed a game. With Pueblo of the Western League, he once made nine straight hits in a doubleheader and hit two homers in his first two at-bats the next day for 25 total bases on 11 hits. Altogether he spent 53 years in baseball as player, coach, scout, and manager. /(NLM)

Charlie Chech — 1879–1938. RHP 1905–06, 08–09 **Reds**, Indians, Red Sox 606 ip, 33–31, 2.52

Using a puzzling curve and good control, Chech won a career-high 14 games as a rookie with the 1905 Reds. After Chech's best season, 1908 (11–7, 1.74), the Indians traded him with Jack Ryan and $12,500 for 41-year-old Cy Young. Chech's 2.95 ERA in 1909 was the sixth-worst in the AL among pitchers with 100 or more innings./(NLM)

Virgil Cheeves (Chief) — 1901–1979. RHP 1920–24, 27 **Cubs**, Indians, Giants 458 ip, 26–27, 4.73

Cheeves earned the name "Giant Killer" by beating the World Champion New Yorkers the first six times he faced them in 1921–22. He was much less effective against the rest of the NL, and a 12–11 mark in 1922 was his only winning season./(NLM)

Larry Cheney — 1886–1969. RHP 1911–19 **Cubs**, Dodgers, Braves, Phillies 1881 ip, 116–100, 2.70. 20 wins: 12–14
☛ *Led League—w 12.*

Brought up by the Cubs at the end of the 1911 season, Cheney beat the Dodgers in an extra-inning game, but was literally knocked out of the box. Zack Wheat hit a line drive at Cheney's head which the pitcher deflected with his hand, driving his thumb into his nose, breaking both. The next year he couldn't grip the ball tightly and changed his delivery. He would dig his fingernails into the ball, creating a knuckler. With it, he went 26–10 as a rookie that season, tying for the league lead in wins and leading with 28 complete games.

The spitball, which he picked up from its master, Ed Walsh, became Cheney's most effective pitch. In 1913 the workhorse went 17–14 as a starter and 4–0 as a reliever, with NL highs of 11 saves and 54 appearances. That September 14 he shut out the Giants on 14 hits—the most ever given up by a ML pitcher in a nine-inning shutout. His 50 games, 40 starts, and 140 walks topped the league in 1914, his last 20-win season./(JK)

Tom Cheney — 1934– . RHP 1957, 59–64, 66 Cardinals, Pirates, **Senators** 466 ip, 19–29, 3.77. *1 WS, 4 ip, 4.50*

Often spectacular when he was healthy, Cheney had eight shutouts among his 19 career wins. On September 12, 1962, he set a ML record with Washington by striking out 21 Orioles in a 16-inning 2–1 victory. A severe elbow injury suffered in July 1963 cut short his ML career./(JCA)

Jack Chesbro (Happy Jack) — 1874–1931. RHP 1899–1909 Pirates, **Yankees**, Red Sox 2897 ip, 198–132, 2.68. 20 wins: 01–04, 06
☛ *Led League—w 02, 04.*

When Chesbro's spitball sailed over the catcher's head and the winning run scored from third on the last day of the 1904 season, the Highlanders (later the Yankees) lost the pennant. At the time, it overshadowed Chesbro's outstanding season of 41 wins, in which he completed his first 30 starts. He pitched 454 innings in 55 games.

Chesbro's career began slowly, with a minor league career plagued by the misfortune of being with shaky franchises that folded in mid-season. Finally he joined the Atlantic League, organized by Ed Barrow, and worked his way to the majors. He joined Pittsburgh mid-season of 1899.

Chesbro's fame as a pitcher began when he pitched the Pirates to their first pennants in 1901 and 1902. In 1902 he picked up the spitball, at a

Jack Chesbro with the New York Highlanders

time when its peculiar properties were first being discovered by a number of pitchers. He strung together enough starring seasons to offset his relatively short career. He had only 12 seasons in the major leagues, 9 as a regular starter. Still, with his extraordinary 1904 season, he gained election to the Hall of Fame in 1948.

After Chesbro's pitching skills had dried up and he left the major leagues, he began a prosperous career as a merchant in New England, running a saw mill and lumber yard in North Adams, MA. He continued to pitch, appearing with semi-pro teams, traveling to take on mill town teams who found the pitching of the former major league superstar easy to hit.

He was baseball coach at Amherst College in 1911, and in 1924 Clark Griffith, his manager in 1904, brought him back to the major leagues for a brief role as a coach for the Washington Senators. Although the team was to win the pennant, fans were slow to respond and Chesbro was dropped for payroll reasons. /(JK)

Bob Chesnes — 1921–1979. RHP 1948–50 **Pirates** 379 ip, 24–22, 4.66

The Pirates paid over $100,000 for a one-year phenom. Although he was 14–6 in his rookie 1948 season, he was considered an eccentric and a discipline problem. He slipped to 7–13 as a sophomore and was out of the majors by 1950. /(JCA)

Hilda Chester (Queen of the Bleachers, Howling Hilda) — Unk.–Unk

Chester may be the most famous sports fan ever. Beginning in the 1920s, she attended most Dodger games to support her favorites, razz the opposition, and lead the fans in snake dances through the Ebbets Field aisles. The stentorian bleacherite acquired her trademark brass cowbell from the Dodger players in the late 1930s. It replaced the frying pan which she banged with an iron ladle after her doctor forbade her to yell following a heart attack.

The plump, gray-haired Chester once influenced a game. She gave centerfielder Pete Reiser a note for manager Leo Durocher (a favorite of hers after he visited her in the hospital after her second heart attack), and Durocher mistakenly thought the message was from team president Larry McPhail. It said "Get Casey hot. Wyatt's losing it." In the eighth inning, soon after Durocher got the note, pitcher Whit Wyatt gave up a hit. Despite having pitched a

good game up to that point, Wyatt was relieved by Hugh Casey, who just barely saved the game. /(SH)

Shigeru Chiba (Buffalo) — Unk.–Unk. 2B 1938–56 **Yomiuri Giants**, Kintetsu Pearls

Considered the greatest second baseman in Japanese baseball before the arrival of American John Sipin, Chiba was a mainstay of the Yomiuri Giants. He managed the Kintetsu Pearls, who were renamed the Buffaloes in his honor. /(MC)

Chicago Cubs [aka White Stockings, Colts, Orphans] — 1874– . Team. 8620–7977, .519. *NL East Champions 84, 89 NL Champions 1876, 80–82, 85–86, 06–08, 10, 18, 29, 32, 35, 38, 45 World Champions 07–08*

The Cubs have played continuously in one city longer than any other franchise. Originally an amateur club, the team, then called the White Stockings, played in the National Association's inaugural season in 1871, but dropped out for two years after that. After rejoining in 1874, the franchise has continued to the present day. The National League was formed in 1876 by White Stockings president William Hulbert after four stars of the dynastic Boston club were lured to Chicago; Hulbert feared reprisals by the Red Stockings and the NA. The team won the pennant that year on the strength of the four Boston stars, especially the pitching of Al Spalding. Superstar Adrian Anson earned his nickname "Cap" when he was named manager in 1879. Often less than admirable (he was a major force in the creation of the color line), he was nonetheless one of the best players in the NL, winning three batting titles and leading in RBI four times. He spent 22 years playing in the NL, all for Chicago, and led the team to pennants in 1880–82 and 1885–86.

After the elimination of competing leagues and the adoption of a 12-team structure in 1892, the team, now called the Colts for their young players, was frequently below .500. Anson was fired in 1898, his only non-playing year as a manager. The team was rebuilt by Frank Selee and came to fruition under playing manager Frank Chance, "The Peerless Leader." He led the club, finally called the Cubs, to a ML-record 116 victories in 1906 (against 36 losses) as they won the first of three straight NL pennants. Featured was the immortal double-play combination of Joe Tinker, Johnny Evers, and leader Chance, with a pitching staff starring Three-Finger Brown. They beat the Tigers in the World Series in 1907 and 1908 and won another pennant in 1910. Contending for much of the following decade, the Cubs won again in 1918, mostly on the strength of a rotation of Hippo Vaughn, Lefty Tyler, Claude Hendrix, and Phil Douglas. The team had been invigorated by the absorption of much of the Chicago Whales' roster after the Federal League folded and by the purchase of the Cubs by Whales owner Charles Weeghman, who moved them into the Whales' ballpark. Chewing-gum mogul William Wrigley, Jr., already a shareholder, bought controlling ownership of the club in 1921 and renamed the park Wrigley Field.

The Cubs were again strong in the late 1920s, and won a pennant in 1929 under manager Joe McCarthy. A Hall of Famer himself, McCarthy had three other Hall of Famers on his roster: Rogers Hornsby, Hack Wilson, and Kiki Cuyler. Wilson set the NL RBI and HR records of 190 and 56 in 1930, but declined due to poor conditioning and was out of the majors four years later. Hornsby managed the club from the end of 1930 into the middle of 1932, but it took the relaxed leadership of "Jolly Cholly" Grimm, the team's first baseman, to bring another pennant in 1932. Wilson was gone and Hornsby semi-retired, but two other Hall of Famers took up the slack, Gabby Hartnett and Billy Herman. They were swept in an acrimonious World Series that featured Babe Ruth's "called shot" off Cub pitcher Charlie Root. That year, William Wrigley died and Philip Wrigley inherited the team. Another mid-season managerial change sparked the team to another pennant in 1935, as Hartnett took over the reins and the team won a NL-record 21 straight games (no ties). Hartnett won the NL MVP award, and Phil Cavaretta became a regular at the tender age of 18 and went on to become a Chicago institution, playing 20 seasons with the Cubs. Another pennant came in 1938, when Hartnett delivered his famous "Homer in the Gloamin'" off the Pirates' Mace Brown in a crucial late-season game. However, an ominous pattern developed as the club lost another World Series; they had not had a World Championship since 1908, despite their many pennants.

They would have far fewer chances from then on. A freak pennant in war-weakened 1945 led to another WS loss to Detroit, in a Series that led one reporter to express doubts that either team could win. The Cubs started building the losing reputation that is their latter-day heritage. From 1940 to 1966, the franchise had only three winning seasons (1945, 1946, and 1963) and finished last six times; they were lucky that first the Pirates and then the expansion Mets monopolized the cellar. Even Ernie Banks's consecutive MVP seasons in 1958 and 1959 could only lift them to sixth place. Banks took over from Cavaretta and Stan Hack as the fans' favorite and became known as Mr. Cub. His 47 HR in 1958

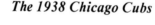

The 1938 Chicago Cubs

set the ML record for home runs by a shortstop and came among four straight seasons of 40 or more HR.

The Cubs' desperation led them to the infamous College of Coaches, a system of revolving managers. Used in 1961 and 1962, it "helped" them finish next-to-last both seasons. They went 82–80 in 1963, but blundered in June 1964 when they traded Lou Brock to the Cardinals in a six-player deal in which the best player they got was pitcher Ernie Broglio.

Leo Durocher took over in 1966, promising that "this is not a ninth-place club." He proved himself correct by finishing tenth, but the team contained the nucleus of a contender in regulars Banks, Billy Williams, Ron Santo, Don Kessinger, Randy Hundley, and Glenn Beckert. When Fergie Jenkins developed into a great pitcher in 1967, the Cubs moved up to third place for two years and looked like they'd win it all in 1969. Rooted on by the fanatical Bleacher Bums, they led the league for much of the season, but Durocher overworked his regulars and they wilted in the stretch, perhaps drained by being the only team that played all their home games in the day (when the temperature took more out of them than night games would). They finished second to the Miracle Mets that year, and second to the Pirates in 1970 and 1972; Durocher was replaced by Whitey Lockman in mid-1972. A fifth-place finish in 1973 signaled another era of losing ball. From 1973 through 1983 they had no winning seasons and finished last four times. Philip Wrigley died in 1977 and the Wrigley family sold the franchise to the Chicago *Tribune* in 1981.

GM Dallas Green, who came over from the Phillies, raided his old team for talent and came away with Ryne Sandberg as a throw-in in the swap of Larry Bowa for Ivan DeJesus. Just before the 1984 season, Green acquired outfielders Bob Dernier and Gary Matthews, and they combined with 90-RBI men Ron Cey, Jody Davis, and Leon Durham to put the club in contention. A mid-season trade brought pitcher Rick Sutcliffe, who went 16–1 for the Cubs and led them to a division title as the Cubs beat out the equally surprising Mets. But the Padres upset the Cubs in the LCS after Chicago had won the first two games, and Jim Frey's managing was criticized by many observers. The Cubs returned to their losing ways in 1985 and dropped to last place again in 1987. The 1988 season was brightened only by the installation of lights at Wrigley Field, which offended baseball purists but may have saved Wrigley as the venue for future Cubs games. The talent developed under

Green's administration (Mark Grace, Damon Berryhill, Jerome Walton, Greg Maddux, Dwight Smith) combined with Frey's acquisition of Mitch Williams and Mike Bielecki and the unorthodox managerial style of Don Zimmer to bring an unexpected division title in 1989. /(SFS)

Chicago White Sox — 1901- . Team. 6867–6810, .502. *AL West Champions 83 AL Champions 01, 06, 17, 19, 59 World Champions 06, 17*

White Sox fans have seen winners who couldn't hit and hitters who couldn't win, their team with short pants and opponents with long hits, scoreboards that exploded and phenoms who were duds, bright victories and baseball's blackest scandal, forty years mostly wandering in the wilderness of the AL second division, and some of the most glorious moments in American baseball history. They've often been frustrated but seldom bored.

The White Sox story began in St. Paul, Minnesota, where Charles Comiskey, a former first baseman and the son of a prominent Chicago politician, managed the Saints, one of the teams in Ban Johnson's successful but minor Western League. In 1900 Johnson and Comiskey, working in tandem, switched the Saints to Chicago's South Side as the first move in upgrading their circuit, which they renamed the American League.

Comiskey's nameless Chicago team won the 1900 AL pennant with a cast of former major leaguers and sandlot players. In 1901 Johnson broke away from the National Agreement and declared the AL a major league in open warfare with the established NL. The White Sox were quick to capitalize, signing such blue-chip players as Clark Griffith, Billy Sullivan, Sam Mertes, and Jimmy Callahan. They coasted to the 1901 title, their first ML pennant, and firmly established themselves in their tiny ballpark on 39th and Princeton Avenues. Comiskey added insult to injury by borrowing the former name of his crosstown rivals: "White Stockings" (shortened to "Sox" in 1902, reportedly to better fit headlines).

The 1906 "Hitless Wonders," short on hitting but very long on pitching and defense, earned the Sox' second AL pennant, then stunned the supposedly unbeatable Cubs of Tinker, Evers, and Chance by downing them in the first (and last) all-Chicago World Series. The next few years were highlighted by the pitching of "Big Ed" Walsh (40 wins in 1908) and the opening of Comiskey Park in 1910.

For all his demonstrated baseball smarts, Comiskey parted with dollars as readily as he parted with

The 1917 Chicago White Sox

blood, but the challenge of a Chicago Federal League franchise together with the presence of the Cubs forced him to revamp his ballclub in 1915. He acquired established stars Joe Jackson, Eddie Cicotte, and Eddie Collins to blend with rising youngsters like Buck Weaver, Red Faber, Lefty Williams, and Ray Schalk. By 1917, he had the best team in baseball, and one of the lowest-paid. His Sox won the world championship in 1917, slumped a year, then roared back stronger than ever in 1919. Surprisingly, they were upset by the Reds in the World Series that year, but they were well on their way to another pennant when the truth about their WS loss exploded. Eight players had conspired with gamblers to throw the Series. The eight "Black Sox"—Jackson, Cicotte, Williams, Hap Felsch, Swede Risberg, Chick Gandil, Fred McMullin, and Buck Weaver—were acquitted in court on technicalities, but new baseball Commissioner Kenesaw Mountain Landis banished them from organized baseball for life. Comiskey died in 1931, romantics insisted from a broken heart.

Stripped of their fallen stars, the Sox struggled for years despite occasional highlights from pitcher Ted Lyons, shortstop Luke Appling, and a few others. In 1936–37, under J. Louis Comiskey (Charles's son),

the team made serious pennant runs. But J. Louis's death in 1939, some catastrophic injuries (ace pitcher Monty Stratton lost his leg in a hunting accident), and WWII all combined to plunge the Sox to the bottom of the AL.

During the 1950s, a grab-bag aggregation built by frantic trader Frank Lane suddenly jelled into the "Go-Go Sox," an exciting contender fueled by Minnie Minoso, Nellie Fox, pitching, and aggressive baserunning. In 1959, shortly after Bill Veeck purchased controlling interest from the Comiskey family, the team won its first pennant in 40 years. Veeck's imaginative promotions, exploding scoreboard, and innovations (including players in short pants) helped take fans' minds off the Sox' slump in the 1960s.

The pennant drought continues, although there have been many outstanding players in White Sox stripes: Richie Zisk, Dick Allen, Wilbur Wood, Carlton Fisk, and Harold Baines, to name only a few. The team got as far as the AL West title in 1983. Owners have come and gone: Veeck to John Allyn, back to Veeck, and on to Jerry Reinsdorf and Eddie Einhorn. Attendance has sometimes dwindled, but hope springs from the promise of a new stadium in the 1990s. /(RL)

Floyd Chiffer — 1956– . RHP 1982–84 **Padres** 130 ip, 5–5, 4.02

Chiffer had a fine rookie 1982 season as a reliever with the Padres, compiling a 2.95 ERA in 51 games. He spent most of the next two seasons in Triple-A, had recurring arm trouble, and was traded to Minnesota. /(MC)

Rocky Childress [Rodney Osborne] — 1962– . RHP 1985–88 Phillies, **Astros** 108 ip, 2–3, 4.76

This finesse pitcher never stuck in the majors. His best and longest stint came in relief in 1987, when he was 1–2 with a 2.98 ERA for the Astros. /(WOR)

Cupid Childs [Clarence Algernon] — 1867–1912. 2B 1888, 90–1901 Phillies, Syracuse (AA), **Cleveland (NL)**, Cardinals, Cubs 1467 g, .306, 20 hr, 654 rbi

Childs hit .345 with a league-high 33 doubles in the 1890 American Association, setting a since-tied major league record with 18 chances accepted at second base in a nine-inning game that June 1. He joined the Cleveland Spiders (NL) in 1891 and became a vital cog in their offense, topping .300 in five of eight seasons and leading the league in runs scored in 1892 (136). His sharp batting eye made him an ideal lefthanded leadoff hitter; he walked 120 times while striking out only 12 in 1893. In 1894 he batted a career-high .353. /(AJA)

Rich Chiles — 1949– . OF-DH 1971–73, 76–78 Astros, Mets, **Twins** 284 g, .254, 6 hr, 76 rbi

Chiles set a team pinch-hitting record (11 hits) with Houston in 1971, and went to the Mets in a 1972 trade for Tommy Agee. His most productive season was 1977 with Minnesota (36 RBI), mostly as a DH/pinch hitter. /(JCA)

Lou Chiozza — 1910–1971. 2B-3B-OF 1934–39 **Phillies**, Giants 616 g, .277, 14 hr, 197 rbi. *1 WS, 2 g, .286*

Chiozza became the first man to bat in a major league night game when he led off for the Phillies in Cincinnati on May 24, 1935. Lean, swift, and swarthy, he had steel-gray hair even as a rookie. His brothers Dino and Joe also played pro ball; Dino appeared in two games for the 1935 Phillies. /(JCA)

Bob Chipman (Mr. Chips) — 1918–1973. LHP 1941–52 Dodgers, **Cubs**, Braves 880 ip, 51–46, 3.72. *1 WS, 0.1 ip, 0–0, 0.00*

Chipman alternated between long relief and spot starts over his ML career. Never a hard thrower, he failed to impress Dodger manager Leo Durocher

although he did not allow an earned run in four appearances spread over three years (1941–43). Traded to the Cubs for Eddie Stanky in 1944, he went 12–10 that season, his career best. /(MC)

Harry Chiti — 1932– . C 1950–52, 55–56, 58–62 **Cubs**, A's, Tigers, Mets 502 g, .238, 41 hr, 179 rbi

The husky catcher broke in with the Cubs at age 17 and made infrequent appearances in 1950–52. After two years in the military he was handed the starting job in 1955, but hit only .231. The relaxed and flexible Chiti became an excellent knuckleball catcher, but after improving his hitting with Kansas City in 1958–59, he batted just .201 in 1960 and was out of the majors by age 30. /(JCA)

Neil Chrisley [Barbra O'Neil] — 1931– . OF 1957–61 Senators, **Tigers**, Braves 302 g, .210, 16 hr, 64 rbi

Chrisley was a lefthanded power hitter who had 60 homers over his last three minor league seasons and hit .343 at Indianapolis in 1957. He was used sparingly in parts of five ML seasons. /(JCA)

Larry Christenson — 1953– . RHP 1973–83 **Phillies** 1403 ip, 83–71, 3.79. *3 LCS, 14 ip, 0–1, 7.53. 1 WS, .1 ip, 0–1, 108.00*

The Phillies' first draft selection in June 1972, the 6'4" Christenson won his ML debut in 1973 at age 19. He improved each year, and in 1977 went 19–6, winning 15 of his last 16. Hampered by injuries, he underwent three elbow operations and, in a 1979 charity bike-a-thon, broke his collarbone. He was knocked out in the first inning of Game Four of the 1980 WS, but won a divisional playoff game for the Phillies in strike-shortened 1981. He hit 11 career homers. /(JCA)

Mark Christman — 1913–1976. 3B-SS 1938–39, 43–49 Tigers, **Browns**, Senators 911 g, .253, 19 hr, 348 rbi. *1 WS, 6 g, .091, 1 rbi*

The older brother of NFL quarterback and TV football announcer Paul Christman, Mark was an ardent Cardinal fan who, spurned by Cardinal scouts, signed with Detroit but played most of his career with the Browns. A light hitter but a steady fielder, in his first year as a regular he led AL third basemen with a .972 fielding average in 1944. His career-high 83 RBI that year was more than twice his total for any other season. Sold to Washington in 1947, he played two seasons as the regular Senator shortstop. /(JCA)

Joe Christopher — 1935– . OF 1959–66 Pirates, **Mets**, Red Sox 638 g, .260, 29 hr, 173 rbi. *1 WS, 3 g, --*

The speedy and articulate Virgin Islander scored two runs without an at-bat as a pinch runner for the Pirates in the 1960 WS. An original Met, he had an outstanding 1964 season, hitting .300 with 16 HR and 76 RBI./(JCA)

Russ Christopher — 1917–1954. RHP 1942–48 **A's**, Indians 1000 ip, 54–64, 3.37. *1 WS, 0 ip, infinite*

The slim, 6'3" Christoper won in double figures three times, peaking with 14 victories for the 1944 A's. He pitched exclusively in relief in 1947–48, and his AL-leading 17 saves for Cleveland in his final year figured in the Indians' successful drive for the 1948 World Championship. His brother Lloyd played 16 ML games./(TJ)

Bubba Church [Emory Nicholas] — 1924– . RHP 1950–55 **Phillies**, Reds, Cubs 713 ip, 36–37, 4.10

In late July 1950, Church and Robin Roberts both pitched complete-game shutouts as the Whiz Kid Phillies swept a doubleheader from the Cubs. He was 8–6 as the Phils fought for their first pennant in 35 years but his season ended when he was struck in the face by a line drive off Ted Kluszewski's bat. In 1951 he bounced back with his top season, 15–11./(FK)

Nestor Chylak — 1922–1982. *Umpire* AL 1954–78 *3 LCS, 5 WS, 6 ASU*

Chylak, who "ate and lived umpiring," according to Dave Phillips, was an all-star among his peers. A fine teacher and technician, he set the standard for AL umps during much of his career. On June 14, 1974, unruly fans stormed the Cleveland field during the ninth inning of "Beer Night," when brew was available for 10 cents a cup. The game was tied 5–5 at the time, After several injuries, including a cut wrist for Chylak, peace was temporarily restored. But when another fan fight broke out near the pitcher's mound, Chylak declared visiting Texas the winner by forfeit./(RTM)

Al Cicotte (Bozo) — 1929–1982. RHP 1957–59, 61–62 Yankees, Senators, Tigers, Indians, **Cardinals**, Astros 260 ip, 10–13, 4.36

The grandnephew of Eddie Cicotte, Al spent three seasons with four AL clubs. Demoted to the International League in 1960, his 16–7 record with Syracuse earned him two more ML years. He was nicknamed "Bozo" after an ice cream he favored./(JCA)

Eddie Cicotte — 1884–1969. RHP 1905, 08–20 Tigers, Red Sox, **White Sox** 3224 ip, 208–149, 2.37. 20 wins: 17, 19–20 *2 WS, 45 ip, 2–3, 2.42*
☛ *Led League—w 17, 19. Led League—era 17.*

Had Eddie Cicotte not agreed to throw the 1919 World Series (and not been banned from baseball as a result), he would have been remembered as one of the game's greatest pitchers. He had a repertoire of deceptive pitches, and used pinpoint control and psychology.

In 1917 at age 33, Cicotte led the AL with 28 wins and a 1.53 ERA. He dropped to 12–19 in 1918, but led again in 1919 with a 29–7 mark. He walked few and fielded expertly, and the only time he "beat himself," he was paid $10,000 to do it. Though he took the bribe, he was not one of the disgruntled players at the core of the infamous "Black Sox." He was unhappy with his salary as his career wound down, and he wanted to buy a farm for security. "I did it for the wife and kiddies," he explained, but he had to work many years at Ford in Detroit before he could afford to retire./(JK)

Eddie Cicotte

Pete Cimino — 1942- . RHP 1965-68 Twins, **Angels** 161 ip, 5-8, 3.07

Cimino had only a blazing fastball when he struck out 20 in a minor league game. The one-pitch reliever worked to develop a curve and slurve (a slider-curve hybrid), but despite an excellent strikeout/innings-pitched ratio, he lasted just over two full ML seasons. /(JCA)

Gino Cimoli — 1929- . OF 1956-65 **Dodgers**, Cardinals, Pirates, Braves, A's, Orioles, Angels 969 g, .265, 44 hr, 321 rbi. *2 WS, 8 g, .250, 1 rbi*
☛ *All-Star—57.*

The strong-armed journeyman outfielder and opposite-field hitter had a career-high .293 BA for the Dodgers in 1957. Cimoli went to the Cardinals in December 1958 for Wally Moon and Phil Paine, but was traded to Pittsburgh after the 1959 season. A fourth outfielder for the Pirates, he was a valuable replacement, especially when Bob Skinner was hurt during the 1960 World Series. Cimoli's pinch-single in Game Seven sparked a five-run rally that preceded Mazeroski's dramatic Series-ending homer. Cimoli played regularly for the A's in 1962-63, and led the AL with 15 triples in 1962. /(ME)

Cincinnati Reds [aka Red Stockings, Redlegs] — 1882- . 7715-7537, .506. *American Association Champions 82 NL West Champions 70, 72-73, 75-76, 79 NL Champions 19, 39-40, 61, 70, 72, 75-76 World Champions 19, 40, 75-76*

The Red Stockings were charter members of the National League in 1876 but dropped out in 1881 because the NL banned beer sales at ballparks. They reappeared in the more liberal American Association in 1882, retaining only two players from the 1880 team, and captured the AA pennant on the strength of Will White's 40-win season and the best fielding in the league. They continued to contend in the AA until the franchise was switched to the NL for the 1890 season in an attempt to bolster the league's defense against the Players' League challenge. The club declined after that season and was sold by John T. Brush in 1902. He became famous later as the owner of the more lucrative Giants. The new owners were a group of city political bosses who named colleague August "Garry" Herrmann club president, a role he held until blindness forced him to retire in 1927. He was also the third member of the National Commission as long as that body existed. In 1905 Cy Seymour won the team's first batting title with a .377 average that still stands as the club record.

The Reds won their first NL pennant in 1919, only to have the Black Sox scandal taint their World Series victory. The team was built around Heinie Groh and Hall of Famer Edd Roush. A strong team, they were in contention through the end of Herrmann's tenure. Sidney Weil took over the club after Herrmann's resignation, but he was a victim of the Depression. Radio magnate Powel Crosley wanted to ensure the team would stay in town and bought the club in 1935, two years after Weil had had to turn over the club to the Central Trust Company, the bank that had held it for Weil after his financial collapse. Crosley was persuaded to buy by GM Larry McPhail, whom the bank had hired. McPhail's innovative style led to the first night game in 1935 and a thriving minor league system developed by Frank Lane. When McPhail resigned in mid-1936, Warren Giles took over. The club won back-to-back pennants in 1939-40 and beat Detroit in the 1940 World Series. Stars on the club included Hall of Famer Ernie Lombardi, 1939 MVP Bucky Walters, 1940 MVP Frank McCormick, Paul Derringer, and Johnny "Double No-Hit" Vander Meer, who had pulled off his famous feat in 1938. The team contended through the end of WWII, but then fell to the second division. A bright spot on the weak post-war teams was feared sidearm pitcher Ewell Blackwell, who became the only man to pitch in six consecutive All-Star Games.

Giles was named NL president in 1951 and was replaced as Reds GM by Gabe Paul, who built a slugging team featuring Ted Kluszewski. At about this time the club began to call itself the Redlegs, due to the association of "Reds" with "Communists" during the Senator Joe McCarthy years. The Redlegs almost won a tight three-team race in 1956, but finished third, two games behind the Dodgers. They tied the NL HR record with 221 that season and Birdie Tebbetts won Manager of the Year honors.

Bill DeWitt succeeded Paul after the Reds had sunk to a 67-87 record in 1960, and DeWitt did a masterly job, instantly rebuilding the team with a series of brilliant moves and trades. Led by MVP Frank Robinson and ace Joey Jay, the team won a surprise pennant in 1961 under the direction of manager Fred Hutchinson, who would tragically die of cancer during the 1964 race. The season was chronicled in *Pennant Race* by pitcher Jim Brosnan, who had written *The Long Season* about the 1959 campaign.

The Reds were often contenders through the rest

The 1972 Cincinnati Reds

of the decade. The team was purchased in 1966 by a group headed by Francis Dale after rumors of a move. DeWitt's reputation was tarnished by the ill-advised trade of Robinson to Baltimore in exchange for Milt Pappas, and DeWitt was replaced by Bob Howsam in 1967. Sparky Anderson was named manager in 1970 and immediately won the NL pennant. The decade of the "Big Red Machine" was at hand. Featuring Rookies of the Year Johnny Bench (1968), Pete Rose (1963), and Tommy Helms (1966), other superstars such as Tony Perez, Davey Concepcion, and Lee May, and the young arms of Gary Nolan, Don Gullett, and Wayne Simpson, the team dominated the NL with 102 wins. With the addition of George Foster (acquired in exchange for Frank Duffy), Joe Morgan, Jack Billingham, Tom Seaver, and Ken Griffey, the offensive powerhouse won six division titles in the 1970s, with four NL pennants and back-to-back World Championships in 1975–76. They averaged 95 wins a season in the decade, and only in 1971 did they finish below second place. Bench was named MVP in 1970 and 1972, Rose won in 1973, Morgan took consecutive awards in 1975–76, and Foster won in 1977 with league-leading totals of 52 HR and 149 RBI.

John McNamara replaced Anderson as manager in 1979, and the Reds lost the LCS. The aging team dropped to third in 1980, and although it had the best record in the NL in the strike-split 1981 season, second-place finishes in both halves left the club out of postseason play. The Reds collapsed to last place in 1982 and 1983, with the emergence of Mario Soto as the staff ace the only high point. Howsam, who had moved up to club president, returned to the GM role in 1983, and brought back Rose to manage the team at the end of 1984. That year, colorful Marge Schott, who made her money in used cars, assumed control of the team. The Reds went on to finish second four years in a row (1985–88). The team played 1989 under the cloud of controversy regarding Rose's gambling. /(JFC)

Galen Cisco — 1937– . RHP 1961–65, 67, 69 Red Sox, **Mets**, Royals 659 ip, 25–56, 4.56

Co-captain and fullback for Ohio State's 1957 national collegiate football champs, the curveballing Cisco had little success with Boston and was released on waivers to the 1962 Mets. In the longest game, by time, in ML history (the 7:23, 23-inning Mets-Giants marathon of 5/31/64), he worked the last nine innings, shutting out San Francisco the first eight, then yielding two runs to lose 8–6. In three-plus years with the Mets, he was 18–43. He later became a respected ML pitching coach. /(JCA)

Bill Cissell (Spider Bill) — 1904–1949. 2B-SS 1928–34, 37–38 **White Sox**, Indians, Red Sox, A's, Giants 956 g, .267, 29 hr, 423 rbi

Chicago's Charles Comiskey paid $123,000 for Bill Cissell, who later said, "The ballyhoo I got when Portland sold me for that sum was the greatest burden any player ever carried to the majors." Cissell had six hits in his first 11 ML at-bats in 1928, then struggled. A poor-fielding shortstop, he was moved to second base in 1930. One writer described the double-play combo of Luke Appling and Cissell as the best "Alphonse and Gaston" act in baseball. Cissell's misfortunes in Chicago ended with his 1932 trade to Cleveland. Without the pressure, he batted a career-high .315 that season. Years later he worked as a Comiskey Park maintenance man. He died destitute at age 45; his funeral expenses were paid by Charles Comiskey's grandson, Chuck. /(RL)

Bud Clancy — 1900–1968. 1B 1924–30, 32, 34 **White Sox**, Dodgers, Phillies 522 g, .281, 12 hr, 198 rbi

Clancy's place in the record book came through no effort of his own: he is one of three first basemen to play a full nine innings without a putout or assist (4/27/30). /(JK)

Jim Clancy — 1955– . RHP 1977– **Blue Jays**, Astros 2353 ip, 135–154, 4.16. *1 LCS, 1 ip, 0–1, 9.00* ☛ *All-Star—82.*

The only player to play for the Blue Jays in each of their first 11 seasons, Clancy was the club's record-holder in both wins and losses when he joined the Astros as a free agent before the 1989 season. Selected from Texas in the 1976 expansion draft, he was a consistent starter for the Blue Jays in their wretched early years and joined Dave Steib as a cornerstone of the starting rotation that helped Toronto to prominence in the AL East in the mid-1980s. Clancy enjoyed his best season in 1982, winning a career-high 16 games with a 3.71 ERA for a last-place club, and on September 28 that year he was three outs from a perfect game against Minnesota when he surrendered a broken-bat single and settled for a one-hit shutout. /(TF)

Allie Clark — 1923– . OF 1947–53 Yankees, **Indians**, A's, White Sox 358 g, .262, 32 hr, 149 rbi. *2 WS, 4 g, .200, 1 rbi*

Despite some impressive early credentials, Clark never won a full-time outfield spot. He finished second to Jackie Robinson in the 1947 International League batting race and hit .322 in spot duty in his first two big league seasons, with the Yankees and Indians. /(ME)

Bobby Clark — 1955– . OF 1979–85 **Angels**, Brewers 396 g, .239, 19 hr, 100 rbi. *2 LCS, 3 g, .000, 0 hr, 0 rbi*

Clark was the Texas League MVP in 1978 when he led in home runs and RBI. He failed to hit with the Angels, and was often used as a late-inning defensive replacement for Reggie Jackson. /(MC)

Bryan Clark — 1956– . LHP 1981– **Mariners**, Blue Jays, Indians, White Sox 505 ip, 18–23, 4.17

Clark spent seven years in the minors before sticking with Seattle for all of 1981. Generally unimpressive, from 1984–87 he split time between the Triple-A affiliates and parent clubs of three AL organizations, then signed with Minnesota for 1988. /(JCA)

Earl Clark — 1907–1938. OF 1927–34 **Braves**, Browns 292 g, .291, 4 hr, 81 rbi

Although he hit over .300 three times with the Braves, Clark had no home run power and never played more than 84 games in a season. He suffered a broken hand on Opening Day 1929, but on May 10 of that year he set the ML record for most outfield chances accepted in a nine-inning game with 12 putouts and one assist. /(NLM)

Jack Clark (Jack the Ripper) — 1955– . OF-1B-DH 1975– **Giants**, Cardinals, Yankees, Padres 1658 g, .271, 282 hr, 998 rbi. *2 LCS, 7 g, .364, 1 hr, 4 rbi. 1 WS, 7 g, .240, 4 rbi* ☛ *All-Star—78–79, 85, 87.*

In his first 13 seasons, spent in the NL, this injury-prone slugger appeared in 140 or more games only three times. However, from the time he became a regular in 1977, he has had slugging percentages over .400 every year and five times has slugged better than .500, including a league-leading .597 in 1987. In '87 he led the NL in walks with 136 (while getting 120 hits) and HR percentage while hitting 35 HR with 106 RBI and 93 runs scored before an ankle injury ended his season on September 9. His inactivity probably cost him the MVP and the Cardinals the World Championship.

Clark missed most of 1986 with injuries after being the hero of the 1985 LCS with a dramatic ninth-inning three-run homer off Tom Niedenfuer in Game Six. Clark came to St. Louis prior to the 1985 season in exchange for David Green, Gary Rajsich, Dave LaPoint, and Jose Uribe; Clark had made clear his wish to escape both the Giants and Candlestick Park. In his nine years with San Francisco, Clark established himself as a superb clutch hitter, leading the NL in game-winning RBI (18) in 1980 and tying for the lead (21) in 1982. He led NL outfielders in assists in 1981, but was switched to first base to reduce the risk of injury.

After his career 1987 season, Clark got into a contract squabble with the Cardinals and signed as a free agent with the Yankees, who already had Don Mattingly at first base. He hit .242, his lowest average in a full season, and had 93 RBI, mostly as a DH. He escaped the "Bronx Zoo" to San Diego in return for Stan Jefferson, Lance McCullers, and Jimmy Jones in a blatant salary dump by management, but had his worst season in 1989. /(TF)

Mel Clark — 1926– . OF 1951–55, 1957 **Phillies,** Tigers 215 g, .277, 3 hr, 63 rbi

A slap-hitting outfielder, Clark hit .335 playing part-time for the 1952 Phillies. A 1953 knee injury took something away from his stroke, and his average declined sharply until his final appearances with Detroit in 1957. /(JD)

Rickey Clark — 1946– . RHP 1967–69, 71–72 **Angels** 432 ip, 19–32, 3.38

The sinkerballer joined Bill Rigney's Angels in 1967, going 12–11 with a fine 2.59 ERA. He fell to 1–11 the following year and never again had a season with more than four wins. /(TJ)

Ron Clark — 1943– . 3B-SS-2B 1966–69, 71–72, 75 **Twins,** Pilots/Brewers, A's, Phillies 230 g, .189, 5 hr, 43 rbi

The slim Texan was a rodeo rider, a Golden Gloves boxer, and a fine-fielding third baseman. But he hit only .185 in 1968, the only ML season in which he played more than 100 games. /(JCA)

Stephen C. Clark, Jr. — 1882–1960. *Executive.*

The founder of the National Baseball Hall of Fame, Clark was an heir to the Singer sewing machine fortune. He financed the building of the Hall of Fame Museum and was its president from 1939 until his death. In 1935 when an old baseball, reputed to have been used by Abner Doubleday, was found in a trunk stored in an attic on a farm in Fly Creek, NY, near Cooperstown, Clark bought the ball and exhibited it with other relics in the Village Club in Cooperstown. The small exhibit drew so much attention the idea of a larger museum was born. In 1937 NL president Ford Frick suggested a Hall of Fame be added to the plans. Frick helped get the support of AL president Will Harridge and Commissioner Landis. /(NLM)

Terry Clark — 1960– . RHP 1988– **Angels** 105 ip, 6–8, 5.06

Clark finally made it to the majors in 1988, while the Angels were looking for a fifth starter, and went 6–6 with a 5.05 ERA. The arrival of Bert Blyleven and Jim Abbott in 1989 pushed Clark off the staff. /(JFC)

Tom Clark — 1941– . *Writer.*

Tom Clark's poetic output includes paeans to Bill Lee, Amos Otis, the St. Louis Browns, and, especially, Roberto Clemente. He has written more than twelve books of poems, three novels, and four books on baseball, including an examination of the short, unhappy career of Shuffin' Phil Douglas, *One More for the Shuffler.* Clark also edited the poetry section of *The Paris Review* for ten years. Born and raised in the Chicago area, he worked as a ballpark usher. /(SH)

Watty Clark [William Watson] — 1902–1972. LHP 1924, 27–37 Indians, **Dodgers,** Giants 1747 ip, 111–97, 3.66. 20 wins: 32

Clark peaked in 1932 with 20 wins for Brooklyn. He won in double figures five straight years (1928–32), but lost a NL-high 19 in 1929. Clark gave up as many or more hits as he had innings pitched in 11 of his 12 seasons. /(EW)

Will Clark (The Natural, Will the Thrill) — 1964– . 1B 1986– **Giants** 582 g, .304, 98 hr, 352 rbi. *2 LCS, 12 g, .489, 3 hr, 11 rbi. 1 WS, 4 g, .250*
☛ *Led League—rbi 88. All-Star—88–89.*

The most consistent NL slugger in the late 1980s, Clark was a member of the 1984 Olympic baseball team and was the second pick in the nation in the 1985 draft. He homered in his first pro at-bat with Fresno (Class A) and duplicated the feat in his first ML at-bat, facing Nolan Ryan in the Astrodome. In 1987 Clark tied a Giants record held by Willie Mays, Orlando Cepeda, and Willie McCovey by driving in runs in nine consecutive games. He led San Francisco to the NL West title with team highs of 35 HR, 91 RBI, and a .308 average while impressing with upper-deck smashes. He was the NL's starting All-Star first baseman in 1988 and 1989 and led the NL in '88 with 109 RBI and 100 walks. In 1989 he and Kevin Mitchell combined with Brett Butler and Rob Thompson to give the Giants the best top four of any lineup. Clark was the '89 LCS MVP, hitting .650 with two HR and 11 RBI. /(TF)

Boileryard Clarke [William Jones] (Noisy Bill) — 1868–1959. C-1B 1893–1905 Baltimore (NL), Boston (NL), **Senators,** Giants 950 g, .256, 21 hr, 431 rbi

Clarke shared catching duties with Wilbert Robinson on three consecutive first-place Baltimore (NL) teams (1894–96). In the American League's initial season, 1901, he was the Senators' first baseman. He later became the Princeton baseball coach. /(JK)

Fred Clarke (Cap) — 1872–1960. OF 1894–1911, 13–15 Louisville (NL), **Pirates** 2245 g, .315, 67 hr, 1015 rbi. *2 WS, 15 g, .245, 2 hr, 9 rbi.*
     Manager 1897–1915 Louisville (NL), **Pirates** 1602–1179, .576. First place: 01–03, 09 *2 WS, 7–8, .467*
☛ *Hall of Fame—1945.*

One of baseball's toughest competitors, a top hitter and daring baserunner, Clarke was the first successful boy manager. Discovered by Louisville owner Barney Dreyfuss in the minors, the lefthanded batter quickly dominated NL pitching to become one of the game's early stars. Clarke went 5-for-5 in his first game (6/30/1894), still a ML record. The leftfielder's playing style was compared to Ty Cobb's. Fearless and dynamic, he considered each season a war and each game a battle. In 1897 Clarke was made Louisville's manager. Despite the added responsibility, he batted a career-high .406.

After the 1899 season, Clarke was one of the 14 players who went to Pittsburgh when Dreyfuss virtually merged the Pirates and Colonels. With the best players from both teams, Clarke's powerhouse won 859 games in 1901–09 (.634 winning percentage). Clarke's strong leadership, potent bat, and a star-studded lineup accounted for three straight NL pennants, culminating with the first World Series in 1903, which the Pirates lost to the Boston Pilgrims (Red Sox).

In 1909 Clarke guided Pittsburgh to a club-record 110 wins and hit two homers against Detroit in the WS, which the Pirates won in seven games. That was Clarke's last great achievement. He had just completed four straight sub-.300 seasons as a hitter, after having hit over .300 ten times in his first 13 campaigns. Pushing sore, aging legs, Cap hit .324 in 1911, then virtually stopped playing, though he appeared in 12 games in 1913–15. After the 1915 season, he quit baseball and returned to his Kansas ranch.

     Clarke retired among the all-time leaders in batting average, runs scored, hits, triples, and stolen bases. He was Pittsburgh's most successful manager in both wins (1,422) and percentage (.595) and

Fred Clarke

ranked among the all-time club leaders in games, at-bats, hits, triples, and stolen bases. In 1945 the Hall of Fame Veterans Committee enshrined him at Cooperstown. His brother Josh spent five years in the ML. /(ME)

Horace Clarke (Hoss) — 1940– . 2B-SS-3B 1965–74 **Yankees,** Padres 1272 g, .256, 27 hr, 304 rbi

Clarke, a native of St. Croix, Virgin Islands, took over for Bobby Richardson on the Yankees in 1967 and became one of the league's more surehanded second basemen. His .990 fielding average led the AL at second base in 1967, and he set an AL record by leading in assists at second base six consecutive years, through 1972. He also led in putouts from 1968 through 1971. A durable switch-hitter, he played in at least 143 games every year from '67 to

1973, and led the AL in at-bats in 1969–70. He had 151 career stolen bases. Though he never batted higher than .285, he was a pesky hitter; in 1970 he broke up three no-hitters in the ninth inning, thwarting bids by Joe Niekro, Sonny Siebert, and Jim Rooker. /(JJM)

Nig Clarke [Jay Justin] — 1882–1949. C 1905–11, 19–20 **Indians**, Tigers, Browns, Phillies, Pirates 506 g, .254, 6 hr, 127 rbi

Clarke, one of the first Canadian players to have an extended stay in the majors, was a highly rated defensive catcher hampered by arm problems. The Tigers' Germany Schaefer exploited Clarke's short-coming in a tie game against Cleveland. Knowing the sore-armed catcher would have trouble throwing, Schaefer stole second, thinking the runner on third could score. When Clarke refused to throw, Schaefer "stole first base" and then, stealing second again, drew an errant throw from Clarke as the winning run scored. /(JK)

Tommy Clarke — 1888–1945. C 1909–18 **Reds**, Cubs 671 g, .265, 6 hr, 191 rbi

A native New Yorker who as a teenager played for George M. Cohan's semi-pro "Yankee Doodle Dandies," Clarke became a valued defensive catcher for the Reds. He was later a Giants coach under John McGraw and Bill Terry. /(JK)

John Clarkson — 1861–1909. RHP 1882, 84–94 Worcester (NL), Cubs, **Braves**, Cleveland (NL) 4536 ip, 326–177, 2.81. 20 wins: 85–92
☛ Led League—w 85, 87, 89. Led League—era 89. Led League—k 85–87, 89. Hall of Fame—1963.

Although never considered the premier pitcher of his day, Clarkson was highly regarded by teammates and opponents alike. He is still among the all-time leaders in wins, winning percentage, complete games, innings pitched, and several fielding categories.

Starting in an era of two-man rotations, Clarkson led the NL in wins, appearances, starts, complete games, innings, and strikeouts in 1885, 1887, and 1889; in shutouts in 1885 and 1889; and in strikeouts and ERA in 1889. As a result, the teams he pitched for during this period, the Chicago White Sox (later the Cubs) and the Boston Beaneaters (later the Braves), were consistently in contention, winning two pennants each. He accounted for 53 of the White Sox' 87 wins in 1885, and 49 of Boston's 83 victories in 1889. His win totals in those two years rank second and fourth on the all-time season list.

John Clarkson

On July 27, 1885, Clarkson hurled a no-hit, no-run game against the Providence Grays.

Manager Cap Anson proclaimed Clarkson "one of the greatest of pitchers," but complained about his ace's perpetual psychological demands, chiding that "he won't pitch if scolded." Clarkson was intelligent, sensitive, handsome, and generally subdued, but was not above certain acts of indiscretion on the field. In one game, he pitched a lemon instead of a ball to prove to the umpire that it was too dark to continue play. His contemporaries considered him a calculating, scientific pitcher who carefully analyzed every hitter's weaknesses. Peering out from deep-set dark eyes, his long, lean fingers cradling the ball, he had a slow, assured pace to his delivery, and he may well have dominated some hitters by intimidation alone.

The deal which sent Clarkson to Boston in 1888 rocked the baseball world, as he and teammate Mike "King" Kelly were sold outright to the Beaneaters for $10,000 apiece—an incredible sum at the time. After four years in Boston, a new manager, Frank Selee, traded Clarkson to also-ran Cleveland, where his talents faded. Along with pitching siblings Dad and Walter, John Clarkson shares third place in most career wins by brothers, behind the Niekros and Perrys (John and Dad both pitched for Boston in 1892). A business student before turning to pro ball, Clarkson purchased a cigar store in Cambridge upon retirement, and ran it until his death at age 47. He was inducted into the Hall of Fame 54 years later. /(AAs)

Walter Clarkson — 1878–1946. RHP 1904–08 **Yankees**, Indians 375 ip, 18–16, 3.17

The youngest of the pitching Clarkson brothers, Walter pitched for Harvard when the Ivy League school dominated college baseball. He was 9–4 with a 2.32 ERA for New York in 1906. /(JK)

Dain Clay (Ding-a-Ling) — 1919– . OF 1943–46 **Reds** 433 g, .258, 3 hr, 98 rbi

As players marched off to WWII, Clay moved from utility man to full-timer in the Reds' outfield. As his playing time increased, so did his defensive skills, and he showed some speed on the bases. /(EW)

Ken Clay — 1954– . RHP 1977–81 **Yankees**, Rangers, Mariners 354 ip, 10–24, 4.68. *1 LCS, 4 ip, 0.00. 2 WS, 6 ip, 6.00*

All but buried in the Yankee bullpen, the hard-throwing Clay starred in Game One of the 1978 AL LCS when he no-hit the Royals for 3–2/3 relief innings. New York sent Clay to Texas in a 1980 trade for Gaylord Perry. /(JCA)

Mark Clear — 1956– . RHP 1979–88 Angels, **Red Sox**, Brewers 797 ip, 71–49, 3.83. *1 LCS, 5.2 ip, 0–0, 4.76*
☛ *All-Star—79, 82.*

Clear's sweeping curveball was almost unhittable, but it didn't find the strike zone often enough to make him a dominating reliever. He still averaged more than one strikeout per inning over 10 ML seasons, and won 14 and saved 14 as the Red Sox' bullpen ace in 1982. /(SCL)

Doug Clemens — 1939– . OF 1960–68 Cardinals, **Cubs**, Phillies 452 g, .229, 12 hr, 88 rbi

A pinch-hitting specialist, Clemens went from the Cardinals to the Cubs as part of the Lou Brock deal in May 1964. He was platooned in centerfield and hit .279 in Chicago. After the Phillies acquired him for Wes Covington in 1966, he led the NL in pinch-hit at-bats in both 1966 and 1967. His career pinch-hit batting average of .229 matched his overall average. /(MC)

Roger Clemens (Rocket) — 1962– . RHP 1984- **Red Sox** 1285 ip, 95–45, 3.07. 20 wins: 86–87 *2 LCS, 30 ip, 1–1, 4.25. 1 WS, 12 ip, 0–0, 3.18*
☛ *Most Valuable Player—86. Led League—w 86–87. Led League—era 86. Led League—k 88. Cy Young Award—86–87. All-Star—86, 88.*

As a youngster, Clemens idolized all-time strikeout king Nolan Ryan, and in less than five full ML seasons he emerged as Ryan's rival as baseball's most overpowering pitcher. The physically imposing, 6'4" 220-lb Clemens has a confident attitude that borders on arrogance, impeccable mechanics, outstanding control, a good curveball, and a 95-mph fastball that can leave batters flailing helplessly. Clemens became only the fourth pitcher ever to win back-to-back Cy Young Awards, established a ML record with 20 strikeouts in a nine-inning game, and pitched 18 shutouts in his first 139 starts.

Originally drafted by the Mets out of high school, Clemens opted to pitch in college instead of signing, and in 1983 won the championship game of the College WS for the University of Texas. The Texas pitching staff included future major leaguers Greg Swindell, Calvin Schiraldi, and Bruce Ruffin. Drafted in the first round (19th overall) by the Red Sox that June, Clemens tore through Boston's minor league system. He fanned 36 batters in 29 innings at Class A Winter Haven and struck out 59 in 52 innings at Class AA New Britain before winning the Eastern League championship game with a three-hit shutout. In 1984, he began the season at Class AAA Pawtucket, struck out 50 in 39 innings, and was promoted to the ML in early May. On August 21, he fanned 15 Royals and walked none, and he finished the season 9–4. Shoulder troubles limited Clemens to a disappointing 15 starts in 1985, and he had surgery on his pitching shoulder on August 30.

At the start of 1986, Clemens's shoulder was still a question mark, but the 24-year-old responded with one of the finest pitching seasons in ML history. He won his first three starts and, on April 29, leaped into the national spotlight with 20 strikeouts in a 3–1 win over Seattle, breaking the record of 19 shared by Ryan, Steve Carlton, and Tom Seaver. In that game, Clemens tied an AL record with eight consecutive strikeouts and didn't walk a single batter. Red Sox manager John McNamara said afterwards, "I watched perfect games by Catfish Hunter and Mike Witt, but this was the most awesome pitching performance I've ever seen."

Clemens ran his record to 14–0 before losing to Toronto July 2, pitched three perfect innings to win the All-Star Game MVP award, and finished the season 24–4 with a 2.48 ERA. He won the AL Cy Young and MVP awards. In the postseason, however, he won only one of his four starts, and the Red Sox lost the WS in seven games.

Clemens skipped spring training in 1987 in a contract squabble, and was only 4–6 on June 12 that year, but went 16–3 the rest of the way to finish 20–9 with a league-leading seven shutouts and win his second consecutive Cy Young Award. In 1988, Clemens's 291 strikeouts were a Red Sox record, and he finished 18–12 with an AL-best eight shutouts. /(SCL)

Roberto Clemente (Bob) — 1934–1972. OF
1955–72 **Pirates** 2433 g, .317, 240 hr, 1305 rbi. *3 LCS,
12 g, .265, 1 hr, 7 rbi. 2 WS, 14 g, .362, 2 hr, 7 rbi*
☛ *Most Valuable Player—66. Led League—ba 61,
64–65, 67. All-Star—60–67, 69–72. Gold Glove—61–72.
Hall of Fame—1973.*

Roberto Clemente left his mark on baseball with a style of play rarely seen in modern ML competition. In a combination of brilliant scouting and luck, the Pirates claimed the Puerto Rican-born 20-year-old from the Dodgers' Montreal farm club for $4,000 in the 1954 minor league draft.

Clemente came to a club that had suffered through three straight 100-loss seasons and was the laughingstock of baseball. He was not an immediate superstar, although his brilliant fielding ability and rifle arm were apparent from the beginning. He would eventually earn 12 Gold Gloves as a right fielder and set a ML record by leading the NL in assists five times.

In 1960 the righthanded hitter began a streak of eight consecutive seasons in which he batted no less than .312. He made the first of his 14 All-Star appearances in the two 1960 games. That year, Pittsburgh fielded its best team since Clemente's arrival, winning the NL pennant. He hit safely in every game of the World Series against the Yankees, batting .310. In Game Seven, he kept an eighth-inning rally alive with a hustling infield single, setting up a go-ahead homer by Hal Smith. But Clemente never wore his 1960 Championship ring. He finished eighth in the NL MVP voting, though he'd led the Pirates with 94 RBI; feeling snubbed, he wore his 1961 All-Star ring instead.

Clemente won the first of four NL batting titles with a .351 mark in 1961. For the next several years, he was consistently brilliant. In the outfield,

Roberto Clemente

he would track down every ball in range, often making spectacular diving or leaping catches. He played caroms out of the tricky right field corner at Forbes Field faultlessly. On routine flies, he used the basket catch made famous by his contemporary, Willie Mays. At bat, Clemente seemed forever uncomfortable, always rolling his neck and stretching his back. Standing deep in the box, he would pounce on inside pitches, or wait and drive outside deliveries to right field. Playing in spacious Forbes Field reduced his home run totals. His baserunning style was marked by effort and determination, with arms and legs pumping and helmet often flying off.

Despite his all-out play, Clemente was unjustly considered a hypochondriac. When he hurt, he said so, an uncommon practice in his day. Despite a severe back injury in 1954, an arm injury in 1959, and an attack of malaria in 1965, the label stuck, even though he played 140 or more games in eight straight seasons, 1960–67.

Clemente won two more batting titles in 1964 (.339) and 1965 (.329). Long overdue recognition finally came in 1966; though the Pirates finished third, and Clemente did not lead the league in any major offensive category, his career-high 29 HR and 119 RBI helped him win the MVP award. In 1967 he captured his fourth batting crown with a .357 average, his best ever. By then, he was becoming the elder statesman on a young Pittsburgh team. Indisputably one of baseball's greatest players, he still did not receive a great deal of national media attention until 1971, when Pittsburgh met Baltimore in the World Series. Clemente played like a man possessed, chasing down fly balls, unleashing great throws at every opportunity, batting .414 with 12 hits and two home runs, one in Pittsburgh's climactic Game Seven victory, and winning the Series MVP award.

On September 30, 1972, Clemente drove a double off Met pitcher Jon Matlack at Three Rivers Stadium for his 3,000th career hit. His .312 average that year marked his 13th .300 season and he was at or near the top of every batting category in Pirate history.

On New Year's Eve of 1972, Clemente boarded a DC-7 loaded with relief supplies for earthquake victims in Managua, Nicaragua. Shortly after take-off, the plane crashed into the Atlantic Ocean, a mile off the Puerto Rican coast. There were no survivors. The five-year mandatory waiting period for Hall of Fame eligibility was waived and Clemente was inducted in 1973. The Pirates retired his uniform number 21. /(ME)

Jack Clements — 1864–1941. C 1884–1900 Philadelphia (UL), **Phillies**, Cardinals, Cleveland (NL), Braves 1157 g, .286, 77 hr, 672 rbi

Clements was a lefthanded-throwing catcher, a squat, powerful man who hit home runs when they were a rarity. He caught 105 games in 1892, and was the last lefthanded catcher to play regularly. Righthanded batters learned to duck when a runner broke for second; Clements simply fired away. /(JK)

Pat Clements — 1962– . LHP 1985– Angels, **Pirates**, Yankees 285 ip, 12–10, 3.89

Because lefthanded relievers with control are a valued commodity, Clements was one of the players the Pirates asked for when they sent John Candelaria and George Hendrick to the Angels in 1985. Cle-

ments, a rookie, was 5–0 when traded. He went 0–6 in 92 appearances for Pittsburgh before he was sent to the Yankees with Rick Rhoden after the 1986 season. /(JCA)

Verne Clemons (Fats) — 1892–1959. C 1916, 19–24 Browns, **Cardinals** 474 g, .286, 5 hr, 140 rbi

A specialist in handling spitball pitchers, Clemons called Spittin' Bill Doak the most effective hurler he ever caught. In 1921 the stout backstop hit .320 in 117 games for the Cardinals. /(NLM)

Donn Clendenon — 1935– . 1B 1961–72 **Pirates**, Expos, Mets, Cardinals 1362 g, .274, 159 hr, 682 rbi. *1 WS, 4 g, .357, 3 hr, 4 rbi*

Football's Cleveland Browns, basketball's Harlem Globetrotters, and baseball's Pittsburgh Pirates all offered contracts to 6′4″ Donn Clendenon. He chose the Pirates, and batted .302 for them in 80 games his rookie season (1962). In 1966 he hit 28 homers and drove in 98 runs, both career highs, while hitting .299. Clendenon twice topped NL batters in strikeouts. He led NL first basemen in errors three times, but he also paced them in double plays five times, and three times each in putouts and assists. The Expos took Clendenon in the October 1968 NL expansion draft, but dealt him to the Mets in June of 1969. Platooned with Ed Kranepool, Clendenon provided power that was critical to the team's surprising surge to a pennant. His home runs in Games Two, Four, and Five of the 1969 World Series meant the difference in each contest, and earned Clendenon the Series MVP award. He might never have played for the Mets had he not vetoed his trade from Montreal to Houston the previous January. /(TJ)

Cleveland Indians — 1901– . Team. 7061–6816, .509. *AL Champions 20, 48, 54 World Champions 20, 48*

As an American League charter franchise, the Cleveland Indians have a rich heritage overshadowed by a drought that began prior to the first expansion. First called the Blues, then the Bronchos, Cleveland became the Naps when Nap Lajoie was acquired in 1902. Pitching was an early and consistant club focal point. Addie Jones posted Hall of Fame credentials, including a perfect game during the heated 1908 pennant race. His career was tragically shortened by tuberculosis.

A new era dawned when Tris Speaker was acquired by the newly named Indians. After second place finishes in 1918 and 1919, Cleveland survived more tragedy to win its first pennant. Despite the loss of star shortstop Ray Chapman, killed by a Carl

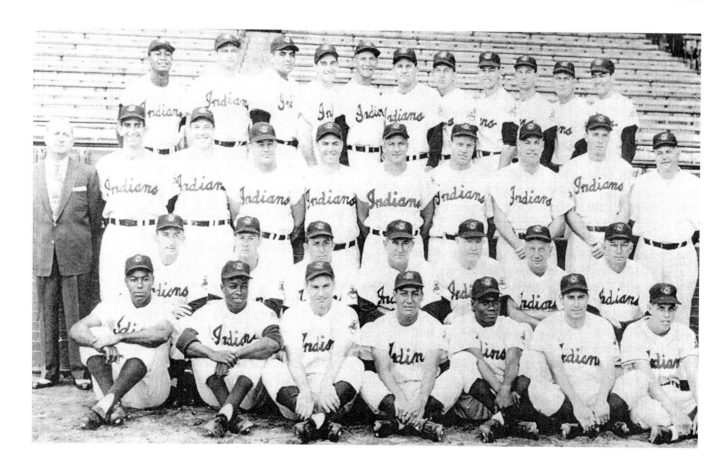

The 1954 Cleveland Indians

Mays pitch, the Indians outlasted the scandal-ridden White Sox and the Yankees to reach a memorable World Series featuring the first grand slam in Series history (Elmer Smith), first homer by a pitcher (30-game winner Jim Bagby), and the only unassisted triple play in championship annals (Bill Wambsganss). Cleveland topped Brooklyn five games to two.

The next 28 pennant-less years were highlighted by near-misses in 1921 and 1926 and the Crybabies incident of 1940. Four years earlier, Bob Feller burst on the scene to begin a legendary career. Teamed with pitchers Mel Harder and Johnny Allen, plus young shortstop Lou Boudreau, Cleveland was the team to beat in 1940. Still, discord between players and manager Ossie Vitt increased to the point that club members petitioned owner Alva Bradley to replace the unpopular skipper. Bradley refused, the Indians were labeled Crybabies, and Detroit rallied to the pennant when unknown Floyd Giebel beat Feller in the season's final weekend.

The golden age of Cleveland baseball dawned on June 21, 1946, when Bill Veeck purchased the club from Bradley. Veeck made Larry Doby the first black to play in the American League in 1947. In 1948 he brought Negro League great Satchel Paige to the big leagues. Led by MVP player-manager Boudreau, the 1948 Indians topped the AL in batting average, fielding average, ERA, and drew a record home attendance of over 2.6 million fans. They beat the Boston Red Sox in the first-ever AL pennant playoff, then turned back the Braves in the World Series, four games to two. Feller suffered both losses, despite a brilliant two-hitter in the first game. Cleveland remained a contender for the next decade.

Following three straight second-place finishes (1951–53) under new manager Al Lopez, Cleveland posted the winningest regular season in ML history (111) in 1954, then failed to win once in the World Series against the Giants. Further tragedy occurred in the late 1950s. Herb Score's brilliant early career was ruined by a line drive off Gil McDougal's bat and by subsequent arm trouble. A young, contending club built by Frank Lane for 1959 was devastated by the most controversial trade in club history. Lane sent young, handsome home run champ Rocky Colavito to Detroit for batting champ Harvey Kuenn. Thirty years of frustration followed. Underfinanced ownership barely kept the club afloat. Rumors of a move to cities like New Orleans and Seattle were constant. What success there was usually came on the pitching mound. Sam McDowell was the AL Sandy Koufax, but alcoholism kept him from greater success. Luis Tiant was AL ERA king in the year of the pitcher (1968). Gaylord Perry, acquired in a trade for McDowell, was Cleveland's first Cy Young Award winner (1972).

The Indians made Frank Robinson the majors' first black manager in 1974. Players came and went, the best demanding trades or seeking free agency rather than play for a non-contender with poor attendance in the ancient and cavernous stadium. As a renaissance in both Cleveland and baseball took shape in the late 1980s, financially solid ownership, in the person of brothers Richard and David Jacobs, took over in December 1986. /(ME)

Cleveland Stadium (The Mistake on the Lake) Cleveland Indians 1932- . LF-320, CF-400, RF-320

Currently the major league's largest stadium with a capacity of 77,797, Cleveland Stadium opened in 1932 for the Indians' Sunday and holiday games, while the remainder of their home schedule was played at League Park. By 1947 the entire schedule had been moved to this massive structure near the shore of Lake Erie. Originally called Lakefront and later Municipal Stadium, it has a circular, covered, double-decked grandstand that extends well beyond the foul poles before giving way to uncovered bleachers, which were originally 463' from home plate in right- and left-center fields. An inner fence was installed in April 1947, cutting the distance for a home run by over 40 feet, but to this date no ball has reached the centerfield bleachers. On September 12, 1954 the largest crowd in AL history (84,587) watched an Indians-Yankees game, but more recently poor Indians clubs and harsh winds from the nearby lake have often left the cavernous stadium depressingly empty. It is also home to the NFL's Cleveland Browns. /(SCL)

Reggie Cleveland — 1948- . RHP 1969-81 Cardinals, **Red Sox**, Rangers, Brewers 1809 ip, 105-106, 4.02. *1 LCS, 5 ip, 5.40. 1 WS, 7 ip, 0-1, 6.75*

This native Canadian was a durable starter and reliever who went 12-12 for St. Louis in 1971 to earn NL Rookie Pitcher of the Year honors. He won at least 10 games seven straight years, with 14 victories for the Cardinals in both 1972 and 1973. He was 46-41 in four-plus seasons with Boston. He was used mostly in relief with the Rangers and Brewers. /(EW)

Tex Clevenger [Truman Eugene] — 1932- . RHP 1954, 1956-62 Red Sox, **Senators**, Angels, Yankees 695 ip, 36-37, 4.18

Clevenger won a Boston roster spot after posting a 16-2 minor league record in 1953. He went to Washington, and was 9-9 in a league-leading 55 appearances in 1958. The Angels claimed Clevenger in the 1960 expansion draft, subsequently sending him and Bob Cerv to the Yankees in a trade for Ryne Duren. Clevenger closed his career with a 2-0 record and 2.84 ERA for the 1962 Yanks. /(TJ)

Stu Cliburn — 1956- . RHP 1984-85, 88 **Angels** 185 ip, 13-5, 3.11

Originally signed by Pittsburgh, Cliburn was picked up as a free agent by the Angels in 1982. He had a twin brother, Stan, who was an outfielder in the Angels' organization for six years. Stu relied upon a 90-mph fastball and a hard-breaking curve. He was named Angel "Rookie of the Year" in 1985, when he was 9-3 with six saves and a 2.09 ERA. /(EW)

Harlond Clift (Darkie) — 1912- . 3B 1934-45 **Browns**, Senators 1582 g, .272, 178 hr, 829 rbi
☛ *All-Star—37.*

In the years 1934-43, the St. Louis Browns' average season record was 62-90; in two of those seasons, they lost over 100 games. The rare good player on such a team is bound to go unrecognized. Harlond Clift was the most consistent power-hitting third baseman of his era, but was selected to the All-Star squad only once. When he hit 29 HR in 1937, it was a ML record for third basemen. He topped it the following year with 34 HR (third overall in the AL that season), and led the league's third basemen in HR four straight years, 1936-39. In his nine full seasons with the Browns he averaged 19 homers, 31 doubles, and 104 walks, hitting .300 twice and slugging .500 three times.

He was also one of the best fielders in the league; his 50 double plays and 405 assists in 1937 were records until Graig Nettles broke them in 1971, and Clift's 637 total chances in 1937 is still the second-best mark of this century. When he retired, his 309 double plays had broken Pie Traynor's career mark for third basemen.

Traded to the Senators in 1943, Clift missed the

Browns' one-shot championship the next year, and illness and injury ended his career in 1945. /(SH)

Ty Cline — 1939- . OF 1960–71 Indians, **Braves**, Cubs, Giants, Expos, Reds 892 g, .238, 6 hr, 125 rbi. *1 LCS,2 g, 1.000. 1 WS, 3 g, .333*

An All-American at Clemson, Cline spent virtually all of his ML career as a reserve outfielder and pinch hitter. He scored the Reds' winning runs (after pinch hitting) in both the first and third games of the 1970 LCS. /(RMu)

Gene Clines (Roadrunner) — 1946- . OF 1970–79 **Pirates**, Mets, Rangers, Cubs 870 g, .277, 5 hr, 187 rbi. *3 LCS, 5 g, .167, 1 hr, 1 rbi. 1 WS, 3 g, .091*

Clines batted .405 in his 31-game 1970 ML debut. A fourth outfielder for Pittsburgh, he was noted for his defensive skills. Besides batting .308 in 1971, "Road Runner" stole 15 bases. After hitting .334 in 107 contests in 1972, his hitting declined. The Cubs made him a coach in 1979. /(TJ)

Billy Clingman — 1869–1958. 3B-SS-2B 1890–91, 95–1901, 03 Cincinnati (PL), Cincinnati-Milwaukee (AA), Pirates, **Louisville (NL)**, Cubs, Senators, Indians 816 g, .246, 8 hr, 301 rbi

Clingman was considered the fastest infielder with the most accurate arm of the 1890s while with Louisville (NL). As a third baseman, Clingman led the NL in assists in 1896 and in fielding average in 1897. Moved to shortstop in 1898, he led AL shortstops in fielding average and assists in 1901. /(NLM)

Lu Clinton — 1937- . OF 1960–67 **Red Sox**, Angels, A's, Indians, Yankees 691 g, .247, 65 hr, 269 rbi

A good fielder with a strong and accurate throwing arm, Clinton could also be dangerous offensively. He had 52 extra-base hits for the Red Sox in both 1962 and 1963, including 22 HR (second on the club) in 1963. He had 77 RBI that year, but in four ensuing seasons with six clubs never again hit so productively. /(TJ)

Tony Cloninger — 1940- . RHP 1961–72 **Braves**, Reds, Cardinals 1768 ip, 113–97, 4.07. 20 wins: 65 *1 LCS, 5 ip, 3.60. 1 WS, 7 ip, 0–1, 7.36*

Raised on a North Carolina farm, the barrel-chested Cloninger usually got tougher as the game went on. He won 57 games in the 1964–66 seasons, peaking in 1965 with a 24–11 mark for Milwaukee. The $100,000 bonus baby was not only an effective, fireballing pitcher, but a dangerous batter as well. On July 3, 1966 against San Francisco, he hit two

grand slams in one game, the only man—no less the only pitcher—in NL history to do so. His nine RBI that day are a one-game ML record for a pitcher. After a shoulder muscle pull and eye problems caused by a virus dropped his 1967 record to 4–7, he was traded to Cincinnati. Though he had mixed success there, he contributed nine wins to the Reds' 1970 NL pennant. /(JCA)

David Clyde — 1955- . LHP 1973–75, 78–79 **Rangers**, Indians 416 ip, 18–33, 4.63

Rangers owner Bob Short drafted Clyde number one in 1973, signed him for a $125,000 bonus, and rushed him to the majors against the advice of scouts. Clyde started 39 games in two years but developed arm trouble. His best season was 8–11 in 1978 after a trade to the Indians. /(MC)

Otis Clymer (Grump) — 1880–1926. OF 1905–09, 13 Pirates, **Senators**, Cubs, Braves 385 g, .267, 2 hr, 98 rbi

Clymer hit .296 his rookie year, but persistent leg injuries hampered the switch-hitter's career. /(JK)

Andy Coakley — 1882–1963. RHP 1902–09, 1911 **A's**, Reds, Cubs, Yankees 1072 ip, 60–59, 2.36. 20 wins: 05 *1 WS, 9 ip, 0–1, 2.00*

Coakley is best remembered as Lou Gehrig's coach at Columbia University, where he directed the baseball team, 1915–51. Years before that, he came to the Philadelphia A's from Holy Cross, a natty collegian considered the "Beau Brummel" of baseball. He won 20 games in 1905 but, in his only World Series appearance, became one of Christy Mathewson's victims when the Giants' superstar threw three shutouts against the Athletics. Columbia's baseball team currently plays at Andy Coakley Field. /(JK)

Gil Coan — 1922- . OF 1946–56 **Senators**, Orioles, White Sox, Giants 918 g, .254, 39 hr, 278 rbi

As a rookie, Coan took on five-time AL stolen-base champ George Case in a Griffith Stadium foot race. "Gil Coan was very fast, but I beat him," Case said years later. "It was a darn good promotion and pulled a lot of people into the ballpark, including General Eisenhower." With 23 stolen bases in 1948, Coan finished second in the AL. In 1950 and 1951 he put together back-to-back .303 seasons. /(TJ)

Pacific Coast League Minor League 1903- .

The Pacific Coast League has operated continuously since 1903, making it the second-oldest extant minor league. The original six-team membership consisted of San Francisco, Los Angeles, Oakland, Sacramento, Portland, and Seattle. During its early years the PCL battled several outlaw leagues for fan support; by 1909 it had established itself as the predominant Western baseball organization, and remained so until the arrival of NL teams in 1958.

Thriving under strong local ownership, the PCL expanded to eight teams in 1919. A 200-game March-to-October schedule was the PCL norm, producing extraordinary season statistics such as Tony Lazzeri's 60 home runs and 222 RBI for Salt Lake City in 1925.

In the years following WWII, supported by minor league attendance records set in 1946–47 at San Francisco, Oakland, and Los Angeles during close pennant races, a strong movement developed to grant the PCL major league status. Open Classification, just a step below major league level, was obtained in 1952. However, the transfer of the Dodgers and Giants in 1958 robbed the PCL of its largest cities and ended its major league aspirations. /(DB)

Jim Coates — 1932– . RHP 1956, 59–63, 65–67 **Yankees**, Senators, Reds, Angels 683 ip, 43–22, 4.00. *3 WS, 13 ip, 0–1, 4.15*

"Coates," wrote Jim Bouton in *Ball Four* of his skeletal former teammate, "could pose as the illustration for an undertaker's sign. He has a personality to match . . . [and] was famous for throwing at people and then not getting into the fights that resulted." Regardless of Bouton's unflattering portrait, Coates was an effective pitcher for the Yankees in 1959–62, working both as a starter and reliever. He won 39 and lost only 15, with 15 saves. He benefited to an unusual extent from the strong offensive support the Yankees could offer. /(MC)

Ty Cobb [Tyrus Raymond] (The Georgia Peach) — 1886-1961. OF 1905-1926 **Tigers**, A's 3034 g, .367, 118 hr, 1961 rbi. *3 WS, 17 g, .354, 11 rbi.*
 Manager 1921-26 **Tigers** 479-444, .519
☛ *Most Valuable Player—11. Led League—ba 05-15, 17-19. Led League—hr 09. Led League—rbi 07-09, 11. Hall of Fame—1936.*

Cobb has the highest career batting average in baseball history. When he retired after the 1928 season, he held 90 major league records. But his skill as a hitter is almost overshadowed by his reputation as the fiercest competitor ever, a reputation he encouraged. He would ceremoniously pick out a prominent location in the dugout and start sharpen-

ing his spikes in full view of suddenly nervous opposing infielders.

One of the most vivid Cobb anecdotes is the half-true story of an interview that supposedly took place in the late 1950s. Cobb was asked how he would hit under "modern" conditions. Cobb answered, "Oh, I'd hit .310, .315." The interviewer was shocked. "But Mr. Cobb," he protested, "you hit over .400 three times! Why would you only hit .300 now?" Deadpan, Cobb replied, "Well, you have to remember. I'm 72 years old now." The other apocryphal stories about Cobb, a natural righthander who taught himself to hit lefthanded so he could be closer to first base, aren't as dubious. For instance: By mid-1925, he had finally had enough of reporters asking him about Babe Ruth's awesome home run prowess. Cobb, who had a split-handed grip that gave him more bat control but less power, had a well-known disdain for the long ball and the boisterous Babe, and told reporters that hitting home runs didn't take any special skill. To prove his point, he slid his hands down to the knob of the bat, Ruthian style, then hit three HR in that day's game against the Browns (5/5/25). To pound the point home, he hit two more the next day.

When the scrawny 18-year-old rookie joined the veteran Tigers in 1905, he was harassed regularly. Although the determined youngster doubled off Jack Chesbro in his first at-bat, he didn't hit well as a rookie. But in 1907 he became the youngest player ever to win a batting title. Cobb's own favorite moment came late in the 1907 season. The Tigers were only percentage points ahead over the Athletics for the league lead when the two teams met in Philadelphia on September 30. The A's took an 8–6 lead into the ninth, when Cobb smacked a two-run homer to tie the score. The two teams played 17 innings to a 9–9 tie, mathematically eliminating the A's and giving the Tigers their first pennant.

Cobb's batting title in 1907 was the first of 12, still a record, and first of nine in a row, also a record. He also established himself as a fine fielder. Cobb had 30 outfield assists in 1907, led the league in assists in 1908, and finished his career second all-time in assists and double plays among outfielders.

The Tigers took a third straight AL pennant in 1909, again stealing it from the A's, again with Cobb in the middle of things. In the first game of a three-game set against the A's in Detroit on August 24, Cobb's sharpened spikes opened up an ugly gash in third baseman Frank Baker's arm. Although the popular Baker finished the game, the Tigers swept the series to take first place and A's fans were

Ty Cobb, batting

incensed. The two teams met again in Philadelphia near the end of the season. Cobb had received telegraphed death threats that many, but not he, took seriously. Cobb got a police escort to and from the ballpark. Policemen ringed the field and plainclothesmen wandered the stands, but the only thing aimed at the hated Cobb was Philadelphia invective. The Tigers claimed their third pennant, and Cobb won his only Triple Crown, leading the league with 9 HR, 107 RBI, and a .377 average. The 1909 Series against the Pirates pitted AL batting champ Cobb against the NL's greatest star and batting champ, shortstop Honus Wagner. In the second game, after scoring the Tigers' first run on a steal of home, Cobb found himself on first. He yelled down at Wagner, "Watch out, Krauthead, I'm comin' down on the next pitch!" Sure enough, he took off. The 200-lb Wagner calmly took the throw and applied a none-too-gentle tag right in Cobb's mouth. The Tigers lost

their third straight Series, the first and only time a team has dropped three consecutive World Series.

It looked as if Cobb would win a fifth straight batting title in 1910, the year auto maker Chalmers decided to award the batting champ in each league with a new car. Cobb had a comfortable lead over the Indians' Nap Lajoie, but was sidelined the final game of the season. Lajoie was in St. Louis for a doubleheader, needing a perfect day to take the batting title. The Browns, like everyone else, wanted Lajoie to beat out the hated Cobb, and did all they could do to help Lajoie. In his first at-bat, Lajoie got a triple when his fly ball was "lost in the sun." Lajoie lined a clean single his next time up. Browns manager Jack O'Connor then ordered rookie third baseman Red Corrigan to play deep on the outfield grass, and the swift Lajoie exploited the alignment with six straight bunt singles. The final figures gave Cobb the title, .38415 to .38411, but Chalmers gave both players cars. O'Connor and Browns coach Henry Howell were later fired by the Browns. Ironically, later research revealed that record-keeping errors had denied Lajoie the title.

In 1911 Cobb set an AL record by hitting in 41 straight games, but Shoeless Joe Jackson was challenging Cobb for the batting title when the Tigers visited Jackson's Indians for a six-game set late in the season, the occasion of another apocryphal story. The young Jackson, batting over .400, was a great admirer of Cobb and tried hard to be friendly, but Cobb purposely ignored him. The slight supposedly flustered Jackson and affected his hitting. Cobb went on to win the title with a .420 average, while Jackson finished at .408. In 1912 Cobb was the unwitting catalyst to baseball's first strike. In a May 15 game against the Highlanders, Cobb's ears were burning from the continuous insults of a fan sitting behind the dugout. When Cobb could take no more, he charged into the stands and beat the fan senseless. Cobb was immediately suspended. The Tigers declared they would not play again until Cobb was reinstated. They were scheduled to play in Philadelphia the next day, and Tiger owner Frank Navin was notified he would be fined $5,000 if he didn't field a team. The players refused to play, so Navin and manager Hughie Jennings rounded up a group of amateurs to fill in. Needless to say, the ersatz Tigers were pounded 24–2. Cobb persuaded his teammates to go back before the next game. Jackson hit .395 that year, but Cobb ended up with his second straight .400 season, finishing at .410, which prompted the frustrated Jackson to publicly ponder just what it took to win a batting title.

Cobb's batting eye was certainly keen, but his baserunning won just as many games. Until Lou Brock half-a-century later, he was the career steal leader. He would steal second, then proceed directly to third as the throw came in behind him. A young catcher asked a veteran what to do when Cobb broke for second. "Throw to third," came the deadpan reply.

Cobb's batting reign finally ended in 1916, when Tris Speaker hit .386 to Cobb's .378, but Cobb won the next three years. In 1921 he was named player-manager of the Tigers, and responded with a career-high 12 HR. He got a taste of his own medicine in 1922, losing the batting title despite a .401 average when George Sisler batted .420.

Despite five straight winning seasons as manager, Cobb, followed a week later by Indians player-manager Speaker, suddenly retired after the 1926 season. The day after Christmas in 1926, the public found out why: Dutch Leonard, a disgruntled former player who had been released by both managers, accused Cobb and Speaker of fixing a game on September 24, 1919. Both stars, plus Cleveland outfielder Smokey Joe Wood, had allegedly agreed to let Detroit win the game to give the Tigers third place. Upon hearing the allegations, American League president Ban Johnson forced the two stars to quit. But Commissioner Kenesaw Landis cleared and reinstated both players when Leonard refused to leave California to testify. Cobb ended up in Philadelphia with Connie Mack, who defended the hated Cobb during the ordeal, and Cobb played two more years before retiring for good after a .328 season in 1928.

During his playing days, Cobb invested astutely in real estate, automobiles, and cotton, and bought a good-sized block of Coca-Cola stock at rock-bottom prices. By the time he retired, Coca-Cola had made Cobb one of the richest players in the game.

In 1936, despite an enduring reputation as the meanest player in the game, Cobb became the leading vote-getter among the first to be elected into the brand-new Hall of Fame. He received 222 of a possible 226 votes, seven ahead of Ruth and Wagner. Retirement didn't dull his competitive spirit, however. In 1941 Cobb beat Ruth in a well-publicized golf duel. In a 1947 old-timers game in Yankee Stadium, Cobb warned catcher Benny Bengough to move back since he hadn't swung a bat in almost 20 years. Bengough stepped back to avoid getting smacked by Cobb's unpracticed backswing. Cobb then laid a perfect bunt down in front of the plate, and easily beat the throw from a huffing and embarrassed Bengough.

The wealthy Cobb tried to clean up his image in his later years with philanthropy. In 1948 Cobb contributed $100,000 to a new hospital in his hometown of Royston, Georgia. He was the first witness in the 1951 congressional hearing on the reserve clause, testifying in favor of it. "Baseball," the fiery Cobb asserted, "is a sport. It's never been a business."/(SEW)

Gordon Cobbledick — 1899–1969. *Writer.*

A football player at Case University, Cobbledick became a baseball writer for the Cleveland *Plain Dealer* in 1928. After serving as a war correspondent, he was named sports editor in 1947. He also was a correspondent for *The Sporting News* until his retirement in 1964. He received the J.G. Taylor Spink Award in 1977./(NLM)

Jaime Cocanower — 1957– . RHP 1983–86 Brewers 366 ip, 16–25, 3.99

Cocanower was voted the California League's best pitching prospect after a stellar 1980 season but faded quickly after starting for the Brewers for most of 1984. His eight wins that year were a career high. /(ME)

Mickey Cochrane [Gordon Stanley] (Black Mike) — 1903–1962. C 1925–37 **A's**, Tigers 1482 g, .320, 119 hr, 832 rbi. *5 WS, 31 g, .245, 2 hr, 6 rbi.*
   Manager 1934–38 **Tigers** 413–297, .582. First place: 34–35 *2 WS, 7–6, .538*
☛ *Most Valuable Player—28, 34 . All-Star—34–35. Hall of Fame—1947.*

Cochrane's Hall of Fame plaque notes that he "compiled a notable record as a player and manager. The spark of the Athletics' championship teams of 1929–30–31, he had an average batting mark of .346 for those three years. Led Detroit to two league championships and a World Series title in 1935." Cochrane's lifetime .320 average is the highest of any ML catcher.

Cochrane demonstrated his leadership and versatility in his years at Boston University, where he was not only a quarterback, punter, and running back, but also at times the trainer and coach. Cochrane's competitive nature secured him the sobriquet "Black Mike." "Lose a one-to-nothing game," said teammate Doc Cramer, "and you didn't want to get into the clubhouse with Grove and Cochrane. You'd be ducking stools and gloves and bats and whatever else would fly." A natural leader, Mickey was also quick enough of foot to occasionally be placed in the leadoff spot, but more often he hit third in the order.

Cochrane joined the A's in 1925 and hit .330 that year, the first of his nine .300 seasons. On May 21, 1925, the lefthanded batter hit three home runs in a single game. That season was the first of his four campaigns as fielding leader among AL catchers. During his career, Cochrane twice led in errors, but led catchers six times in putouts and twice each in double plays and assists. He caught over 100 games in all but his final two seasons. Cochrane batted a career-best .357 in 1930, and reached career highs in homers (23), RBI (112), and runs scored (118) two years later. He hit for the cycle twice in his career (7/22/32, 8/2/33). He was named AL MVP in 1928 with Philadelphia and in 1934 with Detroit. Chosen as a player to two All-Star teams, he also managed the AL to victory in the 1935 contest.

Cochrane played in five World Series. In his first,

Mickey Cochrane

1929, he scored the tying run in Game Four as the A's overcame an 8–0 Cub lead with a 10-run seventh inning. The A's won the game en route to their first World Championship since 1913. In the

1930 WS, Cochrane hit an opening-game homer off Burleigh Grimes of the Cardinals, and a HR off Flint Rhem in Game Two. The A's won both contests. In 1935, on what he later called his "greatest day in baseball," Detroit's player-manager scored the run that beat the Cubs in the sixth and final Series game. Though he played in just 315 games over four seasons with the Tigers, Cochrane was chosen by Detroit fans in 1969 as the team's all-time catcher.

Black Mike's playing career ended abruptly on May 25, 1937, when his skull was fractured by a pitch from Yankee Bump Hadley. Cochrane, who had been the Tiger pilot since 1934, continued as manager until August 6, 1938. His .582 winning percentage (413–297) tops all who have spent at least one full season at the Detroit helm.

After WWII erupted, Cochrane was given a Navy commission to coach the Great Lakes Naval Base baseball team. In 1944, Great Lakes won 33 in a row, and beat the Cleveland Indians 17–4, to finish 48–2. Among his Great Lakes players were Tigers Barney McCosky, Schoolboy Rowe and Virgil Trucks, as well as John Mize, Billy Herman, and Gene Woodling. Following the 1944 season, the Navy assigned Lieutenant Commander Cochrane to the Pacific and replaced him at Great Lakes with Bob Feller. Cochrane eventually served as coach and GM for the A's, scout for the Yankees and Tigers, and VP of the Tigers. He and longtime batterymate Lefty Grove were elected to the Hall of Fame in 1947 by the BBWAA. Another Hall of Famer, Mickey Mantle, was named after Mickey Cochrane, his father's favorite player. /(TJ)

Phil Cockrell — 1898–1946. RHP-UMP Negro Leagues 1913–46 Hilldale, Bacharach Giants, Philadelphia Stars, Havana Red Sox, New York Lincoln Giants, Darby Daisies statistics not available

Cockrell began his career as a teenaged pitcher and eventually became a Negro National League umpire. During two years for which statistics are available, 1924–25, he won 25 games in leading Hilldale to Negro World Series matchups with the Kansas City Monarchs. He was the winning pitcher in the decisive sixth game in 1925. In the 1930s, Cockrell and Leon Day were Hilldale's only pitchers in a series of doubleheaders with the Brooklyn Bushwicks, an all-star team of major leaguers organized by Dizzy and Paul Dean. The major leaguers won only one of the 14 games. Cockrell was shot to death in Philadelphia in 1946. /(BP)

Chris Codiroli — 1958– . RHP 1982–88 A's, Indians 660 ip, 38–46, 4.80

Codiroli was Detroit's first pick in the 1978 June draft, but was plagued by elbow problems and released in 1981. Signed by the A's, he led Oakland with 12 wins as a rookie in 1983. Using a three-quarters and sometimes sidearm delivery, he worked painfully slowly, and was viewed as lacking confidence. He was demoted twice in 1984, but, working faster, came back in 1985 to go 14–14 and tie for the AL lead with 37 starts. His 1986 season was ended by elbow surgery, and, let go after 1987, he hooked on with Cleveland. /(JCA)

Dick Coffman — 1906–1972. RHP 1927–40, 45 Senators, Browns, Giants, Braves, Phillies 1460 ip, 72–95, 4.65. *2 WS, 6 ip, 12.00*

As a struggling starting pitcher for the lowly Browns, Coffman gained sudden recognition in August 1931 by pitching two 1–0 shutouts. He spent much of his later career in the bullpen, and was among the first to log over 300 games as a reliever. With the Giants, he led the NL in relief wins in both 1936 and 1937. His 51 appearances and 12 saves in 1938 were NL highs. Dick was a more successful big leaguer than brother George "Slick" Coffman. /(LRD)

Kevin Coffman — 1965– . RHP 1987–88 Braves 92 ip, 4–9, 5.46

Coffman was called up prematurely by the pitching-poor Braves and was extremely wild, averaging almost eight walks per nine innings in his first two years. He was traded to the Cubs with Kevin Blankenship for washed-up Jody Davis in September 1988. /(SFS)

Slick Coffman [George David] — 1910– . RHP 1937–40 Tigers, Browns 313 ip, 15–12, 5.60

Although Coffman had more self-confidence than stuff, in the cocky Alabaman's ML debut, he beat Lefty Grove 4–2. He was 7–5 as a Tiger rookie in 1937, but three straight seasons with ERAs over 6.00 followed. His brother, Dick, pitched 15 years in the majors. /(NLM)

Andy Cohen — 1904–1988. 2B 1926, 28–29 Giants 262 g, .281, 14 hr, 114 rbi.
 Manager 1960 Phillies 1–0, 1.000

When the Giants' John McGraw wanted a Jewish star and needed a second baseman to replace Rogers Hornsby, Cohen got the nod, but his .294 in 1929 couldn't compare with Hornsby. Cohen managed in the minors and coached for the Phillies, acting as manager for one game in 1960. Brother Syd pitched briefly for Washington and was the last AL pitcher to strike out Babe Ruth. /(NLM)

Rich Coggins — 1950- . OF 1972–76 **Orioles**, Expos, Yankees, White Sox 342 g, .265, 12 hr, 90 rbi. *2 LCS, 5 g, .200*

In 1973 the Orioles had the AL Rookie of the Year, Al Bumbry, and the runner-up, the short, slim, deceptively powerful Coggins, who hit .319 to Bumbry's .337. After a less impressive sophomore season and an 0-for-11 in the 1974 LCS, Coggins was traded with Dave McNally to Montreal for Ken Singleton and Mike Torrez. He developed a thyroid condition in the spring of 1975 and played his last ML season at age 25. /(JCA)

Jimmie Coker — 1936- . C 1958, 60–67 Phillies, Giants, **Reds** 233 g, .231, 16 hr, 70 rbi

This peppery third-string catcher, a rancher in Throckmorton, Texas, spent only two full seasons in the majors. Up with Cincinnati for all of 1965, Coker appeared in just 24 games. /(JCA)

Rocky Colavito [Rocco Domenico] (The Rock) — 1933- . OF 1955–68 **Indians**, Tigers, A's, Indians, White Sox, Dodgers, Yankees 1841 g, .266, 374 hr, 1159 rbi
☛ *Led League—hr 59. Led League—rbi 65. All-Star—59, 61, 62, 64–66.*

Few players captured the imagination of a town the way Rocky Colavito did Cleveland. The 6'3", boyishly handsome strongman from the Bronx had a charisma that made him the most memorable personality in Indians history; he was voted so in 1976. He reached 300 home runs faster than all but four players; he was 31 when he hit number 300.

Colavito came up with best buddy Herb Score in 1955, but stayed just five games. Called back to Cleveland in July 1956, he began a string of 11 straight seasons of more than 20 homers, averaging 32 a year. His numbers really soared when manager Joe Gordon convinced him to cut down his swing. Colavito made himself a complete player, a run-producing slugger and a right fielder with an arm comparable to that of Roberto Clemente. Colavito was prone to slumps, and the Cleveland fans would jump all over him. That's when one sportswriter first starting saying, "Don't knock the Rock."

In 1958 Colavito batted .303 with 41 homers and 113 RBI. In 1959 he became the first Indian to have two 40-HR seasons; his 42 tied him with Harmon Killebrew for the AL lead. That June 10, he hit four

Rocky Colavito

HR in consecutive at-bats in a game at Baltimore. Cleveland fans were stunned when GM Frank Lane sent him to Detroit for batting champion Harvey Kuenn the following April; Lane had actually had a clause in Colavito's 1959 contract that would have rewarded the slugger for hitting *fewer* than 40 homers. After a year of adjustment in Detroit in 1960 (he had only 87 RBI), Colavito had his greatest season, hitting .290 with 45 HR and 140 RBI.

Some still consider the Colavito-Kuenn trade highly responsible for the ensuing decades of baseball mediocrity in Cleveland. The error was corrected in 1965 when Colavito was re-acquired from Kansas City in a three-team deal by new Indians GM Gabe Paul. Colavito set a ML record by playing 162 errorless games in the outfield that year. He also led the league in walks (93) and RBI (108). In 1967 he accused Paul of forcing manager Joe Adcock to platoon him with Leon Wagner. He fell short of demanding a trade, but was sent to the White Sox. Though he played less than half his ML career with the Indians, when he left he was fifth on their all-time HR list (190). He had originally been signed as a pitcher-outfielder; he pitched one game for Cleveland in 1958, and beat the Tigers in relief for the Yankees in 1968, to record a career ERA of 0.00. The win with the Yankees, in which he hit a crucial home run, was the last win by a normally non-pitcher; since then, only Jose Oquendo, with a loss in 1988, has even had a decision. /(ME)

Nate Colbert — 1946- . 1B-OF 1966, 68-76 Astros, **Padres**, Tigers, Expos, A's 1004 g, .243, 173 hr, 520 rbi ☛ *All-Star—71-73.*

Colbert's name became synonymous with the young Padres. After coming through the St. Louis farm system and appearing with Houston, Colbert was San Diego's ninth selection in the 1968 expansion draft. A great fastball hitter with a strong, compact swing, Colbert devastated NL pitching, crashing 163 homers in his six seasons with San Diego. He led NL first basemen in assists in 1972 and 1973 and was an All-Star three times, 1971-73.

Colbert was the Padres' offense in 1972, driving in 111 of the 488 runs the club scored, and, for the second time, belting 38 homers, more than one-third of the Padres' total. On August 1, in Atlanta, he hit five homers in a doubleheader to tie the record set by Stan Musial, and drove in 13 runs, the most ever in a twin bill. Coincidentally, Colbert, a St. Louis native, recalls having been in the stands that day in 1954 when Musial hit the five homers.

Traded to Detroit in November 1974, back problems forced Colbert's retirement in 1976 at age 30. /(JCA)

Vince Colbert — 1945- . RHP 1970-72 **Indians** 249 ip, 9-14, 4.55

The Washington, D.C. native was Cleveland's only winning pitcher (7-6) with 10 or more starts in 1971. He was third on that staff with 50 total appearances, 40 in relief. Vince also excelled in track and basketball. /(ME)

Jim Colborn — 1946- . RHP 1969-78 Cubs, **Brewers**, Royals, Mariners 1597 ip, 83-88, 3.80. 20 wins: 73 ☛ *All-Star—73.*

In a 1966 College All-Star Game in the Netherlands, Colborn struck out 21. He attended the University of Edinburgh and was All-Scotland in basketball.

Success as a ML pitcher was harder to come by. As a young reliever in Chicago, Colborn found himself in Leo Durocher's doghouse and was shipped to Milwaukee. In 1973 he became the first Brewer to win 20 games. When three losing seasons ensued, Colborn went in a four-for-one trade to Kansas City for catcher Darrell Porter. On May 14, 1977, he tossed a 6-0 no-hitter against Texas, one of his 18 wins that year for the Royals. /(RMu)

Bert Cole — 1896-1975. LHP 1921-25, 27 **Tigers**, Indians, White Sox 605 ip, 28-32, 4.67

Scouted and signed out of the Pacific Coast League in 1920, Cole had his best year with the Tigers in 1923, 13-5. He later umpired in the PCL. /(NLM)

Dave Cole — 1930- . RHP 1950-55 **Braves**, Cubs, Phillies 237 ip, 6-18, 4.93

Good stuff and bad control kept Cole bouncing from ML bullpens to the minor leagues during his career. In 1954, the Cubs gave him 14 tries as a starter but he walked 62 in 84 innings en route to a 3-8 mark. /(FK)

King Cole [Leonard Leslie] — 1886-1916. RHP 1909-12, 14-15 **Cubs**, Pirates, Yankees 731 ip, 56-27, 3.12. 20 wins: 10 *1 WS, 8 ip, 3.38*

Cole's 20-4 record with the pennant-winning Cubs in 1910 gave him a league-leading .883 winning percentage. Ring Lardner gave King Cole literary immortality by writing about him in articles for *The Sporting News* which later emerged as the Alibi Ike stories. According to Lardner, Cole was a slow-thinking poker player who was threatened with a $50 fine by manager Frank Chance unless he quit spoiling poker games on train trips with his erratic playing. /(JK)

Bob Coleman — 1890-1959. C 1913-14, 16 **Pirates**, Indians 116 g, .241, 1 hr, 27 rbi.
Manager 1944-45 **Braves** 107-138, .437

After brief service as a big-league backstop with a good arm but no speed, Coleman served 37 years as a manager, 24 of them in the Three-I League, sending stars ranging from Hank Greenberg to Felix Mantilla to the majors. He managed the Boston Braves in 1944 and part of 1945. /(ME)

Ed Coleman — 1901-1964. OF 1932-36 **A's**, Browns 439 g, .285, 40 hr, 246 rbi

Coleman was batting .342 in his first month with the A's in 1932 when he broke his ankle. The left-handed hitter was slow, but showed occasional power. In his final season, he led the AL in pinch at-bats and pinch hits (20-for-62, .323). /(JK)

Gordy Coleman — 1934– . 1B 1959–67 Indians, **Reds** 773 g, .273, 98 hr, 387 rbi. *1 WS, 5 g, .250, 1 hr, 2 rbi*

A football player at Duke, the 6'3" 210-lb left-handed hitter won the Triple Crown and was league MVP with Mobile (Southern Association) in 1959. He became Cincinnati's regular first baseman in the early 1960s. In his first year in the lineup, he hit 26 HR to play a key role in the Reds drive to the 1961 NL pennant. In 1962 he hit 28 in his only other productive season. /(RMu)

Jerry Coleman — 1924– . 2B-SS 1949–57 Yankees 723 g, .263, 16 hr, 217 rbi. *6 WS, 26 g, .275, 9 rbi.* Manager 1980 **Padres** 73–89, .451
☛ *All-Star—50.*

The graceful Coleman led AL second basemen in fielding his rookie year and was an All-Star in his second season, averaging .282 over the two years. However, a 1951 injury diminished his skills, and he will never realize the prediction of Hall of Famer Frankie Frisch that Coleman would eventually join him there. After his retirement, Coleman became a broadcaster for the Yankees and Padres (with a one-year sabbatical to manage San Diego). As an announcer, he earned the nickname "Master of the Malaprop" with such gems as "he slides into second with a standup double." /(TJ)

Joe Coleman [Joseph Patrick] — 1922– . RHP 1942, 46–51, 53–55 **A's**, Orioles, Tigers 1134 ip, 52–76, 4.38
☛ *All-Star—48.*

A less successful pitcher than son Joseph Howard Coleman, the senior Coleman won 14 games for the 1948 A's and 13 for both the 1949 A's and 1954 Orioles. He hurled three scoreless innings in the 1948 All-Star Game, won 5–2 by the AL. Coleman was brought to the attention of A's owner-manager Connie Mack by Brother Gilbert, the man who had alerted Orioles' owner Jack Dunn to Babe Ruth. /(TJ)

Joe Coleman [Joseph Howard] — 1947– . RHP 1965–79 Senators, **Tigers**, Cubs, A's, Blue Jays, Giants, Pirates 2571 ip, 142–135, 3.69. 20 wins: 71, 73 *1 LCS, 9 ip, 1–0, 0.00*
☛ *All-Star—72.*

Coleman overcame a 9–32 minor league record to twice win 20 games in the big leagues. The first player chosen by the Senators in the initial 1965 free agent draft, he had his best years after going to

Detroit in an eight-player deal for Denny McLain in 1970. He won 20 games in 1971, 19 in 1972, and a career-high 23 in 1973. In Game Three of the 1972 LCS, he shut out Oakland 3–0, striking out an LCS-record 14 batters. After going 10–18 (5.55) in 1975, Coleman worked for six teams in four years, mostly out of the bullpen.

The son of Joseph Patrick Coleman, the two rank third in father-son combined wins, their 194 victories placing them behind the Bagbys and the Trouts. /(RMu)

John Coleman — 1863–1922. OF-RHP 1883–90 Phillies, **Philadelphia (AA)**, Pirates 629 g, .257, 6 hr, 80 rbi; 843 ip, 23–72, 4.68

As a 20-year-old rookie, Coleman pitched hapless Philadelphia (NL) to 12 of its 17 victories in 1883, but he also lost 48 games, still the ML record. After that season, he was used mostly in the outfield. /(FIC)

Ken Coleman — Unk.– . *Broadcaster.*

A native Bostonian, Coleman edged out Lindsey Nelson for his first pro sports job as the Cleveland Browns radio announcer in 1952 and joined the Indians in 1954. He replaced Curt Gowdy as the voice of his hometown Red Sox in 1966 and, after a four-year hiatus in Cincinnati, remained the Red Sox' radio play-by-play man through the 1980s. He called the 1967 WS for NBC-TV. /(SL)

Ray Coleman — 1922– . OF 1947–48, 50–52 **Browns**, A's, White Sox 559 g, .258, 20 hr, 199 rbi

Traded five times in five seasons (each time involving the Browns), Coleman hit .271 in 1950 and .280 in 1951 with 76 RBI. The Dodgers acquired Coleman, a fine defensive player, after the 1952 season as insurance for Duke Snider but stashed him at the AAA level. /(MC)

Rip Coleman (Walter) — 1931– . LHP 1955–57, 59–60 Yankees, **A's**, Orioles 247 ip, 7–25, 4.58. *1 WS, 1 ip, 0–0, 9.00*

After two years of long relief and spot starts with the Yankees, Coleman filled the same slot for Kansas City in 1957 and 1959, compiling a woeful 2–17 mark. /(NLM)

Vince Coleman — 1960– . OF 1985– **Cardinals** 754 g, .261, 9 hr, 178 rbi. *2 LCS, 10 g, .275, 5 rbi. 1 WS, 7 g, .143, 2 rbi*
☛ *Rookie of the Year—85. All-Star—88–89.*

Coleman has led a league in stolen bases in each of seven professional seasons. In 1983 he set the professional record for stolen bases with 145 while playing for Macon in the South Atlantic League. He won NL Rookie of the Year honors in 1985 with 110 stolen bases and 107 runs scored, and went on to become the first player in history to steal 100 bases in each of his first three major league seasons. In 1989 he set a record by stealing 51 consecutive bases without being caught. Coleman considers third base easier to steal than second, and in 1987 he stole second and third in the same inning 13 times. The switch-hitter serves as St. Louis's leadoff batter but has trouble with breaking balls, averaging 112 strike-outs per season. With steady improvement in left field, he moved among the yearly leaders in assists. /(FO)

Darnell Coles — 1962– . 3B-OF-SS 1983– **Mariners**, Tigers, Pirates 606 g, .247, 57 hr, 271 rbi

Coles was Southern California's High School Athlete of the Year in 1980 and turned down a football and baseball scholarship at UCLA to sign with Seattle as the sixth overall selection in the 1980 draft. Traded to Detroit, he was part of an all-20 HR infield in 1986 as the Tigers' third baseman. An erratic hitter and a defensive liability, he went to the Pittsburgh outfield in 1987 and tied a club record with a three-HR game (9/30). He was traded back to Seattle in mid-1988 and was a regular OF in 1989. /(ME)

Dave Collins — 1952– . OF-DH-1B 1975– Angels, Mariners, **Reds**, Yankees, Blue Jays, A's, Tigers 1602 g, .273, 32 hr, 370 rbi. *1 LCS, 3 g, .357, 1 rbi*

A versatile, slap-hitting speedster with good defensive skills, Collins emerged as a base-stealing threat in spot duty with the Angels. He became a Mariner in the expansion draft, but was peddled to Cincinnati a year later. He became a fair leadoff hitter, usually platooned. He stole a career-high 79 bases in his only season as an everyday player, 1980, and hit .300 twice for the Reds. He became a free agent after 1981 and signed with the Yankees, who were briefly infatuated with speed. Except for a big 1984 season with Toronto, when he led the AL with 15

triples while hitting .308, he was an unspectacular performer, mostly used for his speed on the bases and in the field, for the rest of his career. /(ME)

Eddie Collins [Edward Trowbridge Sr.](Cocky) — 1887–1951. 2B 1906–30 A's, **White Sox** 2826 g, .333, 47 hr, 1299 rbi. *6 WS, 34 g, .328, 11 rbi. Manager* 1925–26 **White Sox** 160–147, .521
☛ *Hall of Fame—1939.*

Eddie Collins was one of the most accomplished all-around ballplayers ever to play the game. They called Collins "Cocky," not because he was arrogant, but because he was filled with confidence based on sheer ability. Bill James wrote, "Collins sustained a remarkable level of performance for a remarkably long time. He was past thirty when the lively ball era began, yet he adapted to it and continued to be one of the best players in baseball every year . . .his was the most valuable career that any second baseman ever had."

Collins played for 25 years, 20 of them as a regular. He won no batting titles because he played during the same time as Ty Cobb, but did lead the AL in stolen bases four times and in runs scored three consecutive seasons, 1912–14. Collins batted .333 lifetime, and stole 743 bases. He had 3,311 hits (eighth all-time) and was a superlative fielder, leading second basemen in fielding average nine times. He was an adroit bunter, a slashing, lefthanded-batting hit-and-run man, and a brilliant baserunner. In the dugout or on the coaching lines, he was a canny, sign-stealing, intuitive strategist.

Collins's background was atypical of a player of the early 1900s. He starred as captain of Columbia University's baseball team. Barred from playing his senior year because he had disguised himself as "Eddie Sullivan" to play professionally (even getting into a few games with the Athletics), Collins was named Columbia's coach, and stayed to get his degree.

Collins was one of the key young players on Connie Mack's great Athletic teams of 1909–14 that won pennants in all but 1912. He was the premier player in Mack's "$100,000 Infield," with Jack Barry at shortstop, Stuffy McInnis at first base, and Frank Baker at third base, a unit valued for its finely meshed teamwork as well as the players' great individual skills. Collins later attributed this harmony on the field to the personal relationships off it, which continued past playing days. The "$100,000 Infield's" exceptional defense had a big payoff in the dead ball era, when teams scrapped for one run at a time.

When Connie Mack disbanded his long-reigning

Eddie Collins (l.), Pants Rowland

team in 1915, he sold Collins to the Chicago White Stockings. Collins starred in the 1917 World Series, hitting .409, and scoring a key run on one of his typical heads-up plays during a game-winning, Series-ending rally. Collins had maneuvered into a rundown between third and home to allow two other baserunners to get into scoring position. Seeing no one covering the plate, he wheeled past the catcher as he threw to third baseman Heinie Zimmerman, who unsuccessfully chased the fleet Collins home.

In 1918 Collins joined the Marines, but was back the next season on another pennant-winner, the infamous 1919 Chicago "Black Sox." As one of the "honest players," he was unforgiving of the eight who had sold out, yet described the team as the greatest on which he had played, winning despite hostility, feuds, and outright crookedness.

Collins continued to play season after season of superlative second base, always batting over .300. After the White Sox finished last in 1924, Collins was named manager. He led them for two seasons, winning more than he lost, but finished fifth both years. The White Sox judged that his days as an everyday infielder were ending, and released the $40,000-a-year player-manager.

Connie Mack invited his former star to return to his rebuilt Philadelphia A's. Collins played less and less, but took over more and more field duties from Mack. He was third-base coach and, unofficially, assistant manager, and turned down offers to manage other teams. The A's won three straight pennants (1929–31), with Collins pinch-hitting a few times in 1929 and '30. The promise of the Shibe brothers (the A's owners) and Mack that Collins would succeed old Connie (then 67) kept Collins on hand. Fortunately he didn't stay around long, since Mack didn't retire until age 88.

Instead, Collins's opportunity to run a team came with the Boston Red Sox. He and Tom Yawkey were alumni of the same prep school and became friends. The millionaire sportsman, on Collins's advice, purchased the Red Sox and brought Collins in as part-owner and GM. Collins began rebuilding a team that had never recovered from the sale of stars to the Yankees a decade earlier. Yawkey's money bought Joe Cronin from Washington to be player-manager, and pried loose stars Jimmie Foxx and Lefty Grove from the A's. Collins went on just one scouting trip for the Red Sox, to California, but came back with two extraordinary prospects, Bobby Doerr and Ted Williams.

Eddie Collins was elected to the Hall of Fame in 1939, the year Eddie, Jr. debuted with the Athletics as an outfielder. /(JK)

Hub Collins [George Hubbert] — 1864–1892. 2B-OF 1886–92 **Louisville (AA)**, Brooklyn (AA), Dodgers 680 g, .284, 11 hr, 242 rbi

Collins was the second baseman for successive Brooklyn pennant winners (American Association in 1889, NL in 1890). He led the AA in doubles (31) in 1888 and runs scored (148) in 1890, and stole 328 bases in his short career. Two seasons later, he died of typhoid fever. /(JK)

Jimmy Collins (Jaime) — Unk.- . OF 1978- Minor and Mexican Leagues

A light hitter in the Braves organization who never rose above Double-A, Collins joined Chihuahua (Mexican League) in 1978 and batted .350. Over the next decade, he played for six different Mexican League franchises, never falling below .302. His .438 mark in 1979 set a since-broken league record. He won another batting title with a .412 mark in 1984. /(MC)

Jimmy Collins — 1870-1943. 3B 1895-1908 Braves, Louisville (NL), **Red Sox**, A's 1728 g, .294, 64 hr, 982 rbi. *1 WS, 8 g, .250, 1 rbi.*
    Manager 1901-06 **Red Sox** 464-389, .544. First place: 03-04 *1 WS, 5-3, .625*
☛ *Led League—hr 1898. Hall of Fame—45.*

Until Pie Traynor came along in the 1920s, Jimmy Collins was universally considered baseball's greatest third baseman. Playing at the turn of the century, when the bunt was a big part of the game, Collins

Jimmy Collins with the Braves

was the best at fielding them. His 601 chances accepted at 3B in 1899 remain a National League record. He led his league's third basemen in putouts five times, assists four times, double plays twice, and still stands second all-time in career putouts at 3B.

Collins was also outstanding at the plate. He topped the .300 mark five times, with a high of .346 for Boston (NL) in 1897. In 1898, he won the NL home run crown with 15, drove in well over 100 runs for the second consecutive season, and scored more than 100 runs for the third of four times.

Collins was player-manager of the Red Sox in the American League's first six seasons, leading Boston to a victory over Pittsburgh in the initial World Series in 1903. The Red Sox repeated in 1904, but interleague feuding cancelled the WS. Relieved of the managerial reins in 1907, Collins was traded to the Athletics, and he left the majors after batting .217 in 1908. He played and managed in the minors through 1911 before retiring to his native Buffalo. Wiped out by the Depression, he became a Buffalo parks employee. His 1945 election to the Hall of Fame preceded Traynor's by three years, though Traynor had been eligible before Collins's induction. /(JK)

Jocko Collins [John P.] — 1905-86. *Scout.*

Collins was the basketball captain at St. Joseph's University in Philadelphia and remained active in basketball as well as baseball He was an NBA referee and NBA supervisor of officials, and a scout for the Philadelphia 76ers.

As a baseball scout, he worked for the Phillies for 27 years, and briefly for the Astros, Giants, Orioles, and Mets before his retirement in 1980. His discoveries included Del Ennis, Dallas Green, and Tommy Lasorda. /(FVP)

Joe Collins [born Joseph Kollonige] — 1922- . 1B-OF 1948-57 **Yankees** 908 g, .256, 86 hr, 329 rbi. *7 WS, 36 g, .163, 4 hr, 10 rbi*

Collins hit four World Series homers. The first won Game Two of the 1951 classic; the second put the Yanks ahead to stay in the 1953 opener; the other two led New York to victory in Game One of the 1955 Series. In the seventh game of the 1952 WS (which followed an 18-homer season for Collins), the first baseman lost Jackie Robinson's pop fly in the Ebbets Field sun, which Billy Martin recovered to catch in a famous game-saving play. /(TJ)

Pat Collins — 1896–1960. C 1919–24, 26–29 **Browns**, Yankees, Braves 541 g, .254, 33 hr, 168 rbi. *3 WS, 6 g, .500*

An often forgotten member of the mighty 1927 Yankees, Pat Collins was the dependable catcher who batted eighth in the "Murderer's Row" lineup./(JK)

Phil Collins (Fidgety Phil) — 1901–1948. RHP 1923, 1929–35 Cubs, **Phillies**, Cardinals 1324 ip, 80–85, 4.66

When Collins fidgeted on the mound, tugging his trousers and fingering the rosin bag, it was not a nervous affliction that delayed him; it was apprehension. Pitching in tiny Baker Bowl, he was backed by a team that was last in the league in fielding five of his six years with Philadelphia. Nonetheless, he achieved three winning seasons with them./(JK)

Ray Collins — 1887–1970. LHP 1909–15 **Red Sox** 1345 ip, 84–62, 2.51. *1 WS, 14 ip, 0–0, 1.88.* 20 wins: 14

A lefty with excellent control, Collins was 19–8 for the 1913 Red Sox and 20–13 the next year. Ty Cobb said Collins gave him as much trouble as any pitcher he ever faced, and, on occasion, Collins was said to have walked a batter intentionally to pitch to Cobb. Collins must have liked Detroit, for he had doubleheader complete games against the Tigers on September 22, 1914, winning 5–3 and 5–0. A graduate of the University of Vermont, he later returned there as baseball coach./(NLM)

Rip Collins [Harry Warren] — 1896–1968. RHP 1920–31 Yankees, Red Sox, **Tigers**, Browns 1712 ip, 108–82, 3.99. *1 WS, 2/3 ip, 0–0, 54.00*

Once described as a pitcher with a million dollars worth of talent and 25 cents worth of enthusiasm, Collins apparently played baseball only to support his real pleasures: hunting and fishing in the off-season, bright lights and parties during the season. He claimed to have become a beer drinker at age six, and his nickname came from a pre-Prohibition brand of whiskey. A four-sport star at Texas A & M, Collins won 14 games as a Yankee rookie in 1920, matched that figure with the Red Sox in 1922, and again with the Tigers in '24. He later became a law enforcement officer in Texas./(NLM)

Ripper Collins [James Anthony] — 1904–1970. 1B 1931–38, 41 **Cardinals**, Cubs, Pirates 1084 g, .296, 135 hr, 659 rbi. *3 WS, 13 g, .277, 4 rbi*
☛ *Led League—hr 34. All-Star—35–37.*

Though the 5'9" 165-lb Collins was small for a first baseman, he was the most dangerous slugger on the Cardinal Gas House Gang, hammering 35 HR for the NL title in 1934. He was a fun-maker off the field, but he was relentlessly serious on it. He broke up four no-hitters in late innings. A one-time coal miner from Altoona, PA, a strike freed Collins to try pro ball. He spent 30 years as a player, coach, minor league manager, and sporting goods rep. A facile talker, he became a broadcaster. He said he got his nickname when, as a boy, he once hit the team's only ball and snagged it on a fence nail, ripping its cover./(JK)

Shano Collins [John Francis] — 1885–1955. OF-1B 1910–25 **White Sox**, Red Sox 1798 g, .264, 22 hr, 705 rbi. *2 WS, 10 g, .270.*
    Manager 1931–32 Red Sox 73–136, .349

Collins was a versatile and cooperative team player. After making the White Sox in 1910, he was a disappointment at first base and was shifted to right field a few weeks into the season. By 1913 he had established himself as one of the AL's top defensive

Shano Collins

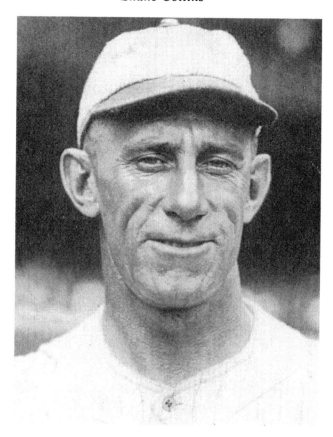

outfielders. He covered plenty of ground and had a strong arm. At the plate, his average suffered because of his tendency to overswing.

Collins was temporarily moved back to first base in 1915 when rookie Jacques Fournier proved to have an iron glove. When the White Sox captured the 1917 pennant on September 21, Collins delivered the game-winning hit. He was the team's senior player, platooned in right field with Nemo Leibold. Chicago won the World Series opener 2–1 thanks to Collins's 3-for-4 performance. He moved once more to 1B when Chick Gandil sat out the 1920 season. He finished his career as a regular outfielder with the talent-thin Red Sox of the early 1920s. His nickname, Shano, was a play on Sean, the Gaelic equivalent of John. /(RL)

Zip Collins [John Edgar] — 1892–1983. OF 1914–17, 21 **Pirates**, Braves, A's 286 g, .253, 2 hr, 63 rbi

Called "Zip" for his strong outfield throws, Collins's light hitting limited his ML career. A longtime minor league player and manager, he was active in efforts to establish a retirement home for former players. /(JK)

Jackie Collum — 1927– . LHP 1951–58, 62 Cardinals, **Reds**, Cubs, Dodgers, Twins, Indians 464 ip, 32–28, 4.15

Collum shut out the Cubs in his first ML game as a Cardinal rookie in 1951, and in 1956 he saved seven and won six out of the Cardinal bullpen. In between, he pitched nearly three full seasons for the Reds, winning 23 and losing 22. /(FK)

Nick Colosi — 1927– . *Umpire* NL 1968–82 *3 LCS 2 WS, 2 ASU*

Before turning to umpiring, Colosi was a maitre d' at the famous Copacabana night club in New York. His most famous call came in the 1975 WS. After much media hype on the legality of Red Sox pitcher Luis Tiant's hand movement as he came to a set position, Colosi called a balk (ironically, on Tiant's leg movement) in the fourth inning of the opening game. /(RTM)

Colt Stadium Houston Colt .45s 1962–64. LF-360, CF-420, RF-360

32,000-seat Colt Stadium housed the expansion Houston franchise until the Astrodome was completed in 1965, and was the site of two no-hitters. Renowned for its huge mosquitoes, it was located in what is now the Astrodome's north parking lot. /(SCL)

Bob Coluccio — 1951– . OF 1973–75, 77–78 **Brewers**, White Sox, Cardinals 370 g, .220, 26 hr, 114 rbi

Several athletes have been dubbed "The Italian Stallion," but Brewer broadcaster Merle Harmon labeled the 5'10" Coluccio "The Macaroni Pony." The speedy outfielder beat out Gorman Thomas for the Brewers' right-field job in 1973, but couldn't hit well enough to keep the position. /(RMu)

Earle Combs (The Kentucky Colonel) — 1899–1976. OF 1924–35 **Yankees** 1454 g, .325, 58 hr, 629 rbi. *4 WS, 16 g, .350, 1 hr, 9 rbi*
 Hall of Fame—1970.

A husky six-footer, the quiet leadoff man of the powerful 1927 Yankees covered Yankee Stadium's spacious center field, leading the league's centerfielders in putouts. Combs's specialty was the three-base hit; he had three in a 1927 game, led the AL in triples three times, and collected 154 in his career.

A cool, determined player, Combs was often overshadowed by his superstar teammates, but in nine seasons, he batted well over .300. In 1927 he

Earle Combs

hit .356, leading the AL with 231 hits (a team record until Don Mattingly broke it in 1986). He had a 29-game hitting streak in 1931.

The Kentucky Colonel's career came to an end in 1934 when, before the advent of warning tracks, he smashed into the wall at Sportsman's Park chasing a fly ball. His skull was fractured and his career virtually ended. After trying a comeback in 1935, and knowing that the Yankees would bring Joe DiMaggio up the next season, he accepted a coaching job. When DiMaggio arrived, Combs instructed him on the nuances of Yankee Stadium's outfield.

Combs left the Yankees during WWII. A good teacher, he returned to coach the Browns, Red Sox, and Phillies. He was inducted into the Hall of Fame in 1970 by the Veterans Committee./(JK)

Steve Comer — 1954– . RHP 1978–84 **Rangers**, Phillies, Indians 701 ip, 44–37, 4.13

Comer was said to have three pitching speeds—slow, slower, and reverse. Relying on his changeup, Steve led all righthanded pitchers with 17 wins in 1979. A sore shoulder curtailed Comer in 1980, but he fashioned one more good season in relief the following year. Steve was handicapped by having no other pitches to complement his change. He became pitching coach of the Indians in 1987./(ME)

Wayne Comer — 1944– . OF 1967–70, 72 Tigers, **Pilots/Brewers** 316 g, .229, 16 hr, 67 rbi. *1 WS, 1 g, 1.000*

The Virginian was the 25th player on the Tigers' 1968 championship squad. After the expansion draft, Comer took advantage of the friendly confines of Seattle's Sicks Stadium for 15 home runs and also stole 18 bases. A trade to Washington and a loss of power ended his career./(CC)

Charlie Comiskey (Commy, The Old Roman) — 1859–1931. 1B 1882–94 **St. Louis (AA)**, Chicago (PL), Reds 1385 g, .266, 29 hr, 883 rbi.
 Manager 1883, 85–94 **St. Louis (AA)**, Chicago (PL), Reds 824–533, .607. First place: 85–88
☞ *Hall of Fame—1939.*

Had the Black Sox scandal not exposed the pettiness that characterized most of Comiskey's later dealings, he might have been among the most respected elder statesmen of sport. Charles Comiskey was the son of a famous long-time Chicago alderman who represented the Irish ghettos of the near West Side. The boy rebelled against his father's plans to apprentice him to a plumber. Instead, he played semi-pro ball on the Chicago sandlots. In 1879 Comiskey hooked

Charlie Comiskey

up with baseball promoter Ted Sullivan, who taught him the art of playing first base. Until the 1880s, most first basemen started each play with a foot on the bag. Comiskey increased his range by playing off the bag, and his success popularized that style. As a player-manager for the St. Louis Browns of the American Association, Comiskey won four league titles (1885–1888).

Comiskey's greatest fame came not as a manager, but as a mogul. When Ban Johnson took over the fledgling Western League (formed November 21, 1893), few imagined that eight years later it would challenge the National League for baseball supremacy. Comiskey assisted Johnson by purchasing the Sioux City franchise, which he shifted to St. Paul, and in 1900, to Chicago, where it was christened the White Stockings. For the next 31 years "The Old Roman" was the driving force behind the White Sox, who won championships in 1901, 1906, 1917, and 1919.

Comiskey's own greed is considered to have been the real motivation for the "Black Sox" selling out to gamblers in 1919. When it was revealed that the players threw the Series for $10,000 because Comiskey had underpaid them for years, his sterling reputation was tarnished. Nonetheless, he was elected to the Hall of Fame in 1939, as an executive. /(RL)

Comiskey Park Chicago White Sox 1910- , American Giants (NAL)1941–50 LF-341, CF-401, RF-341

Comiskey Park stands on a piece of city landscape that once belonged to "Long" John Wentworth, Chicago's colorful mayor during the Civil War days. His South Side property later became the city dump before it was purchased by Charles Comiskey in 1909.

The ballpark constructed at 35th and Shields Avenue by the "Old Roman" has a troubled past and a questionable future. The so-called "curse" of Wentworth has nearly bankrupted several ownerships forced to deal with the old stadium's structural problems.

In 1910, construction workers rushed to finish the park before the scheduled unveiling on July 1. But a labor strike by the steel workers and the death of a carpenter who fell off a scaffold hours before the opener cast a pall over the festivities. Despite these setbacks, Comiskey Park opened for business on time, but the Sox lost the inaugural to the Browns 2–0.

The stadium was ideally suited for dead-ball-era play. Its spacious contours were influenced by pitcher Ed Walsh, who toured the major league parks with architect Zachary Taylor Davis. The thrifty Comiskey vetoed Davis's idea to build a cantilevered grandstand with ornate arches and cornices, and years later Comiskey Park suffered when compared to the great old stadiums of the past. But in the early years it was dubbed the "Baseball Capitol of the World," and the Cubs used it for the 1918 WS.

The changing nature of the game soon made Comiskey Park a relic. The long-ball hitting of Ruth, Gehrig, et al., during a time when the fans demanded high scores and prodigious home runs

Comiskey Park

from their heroes, was handicapped by a park the size of Comiskey. It wasn't until 1934, after Comiskey's death, that the ownership dealt with this problem. The plate was moved forward 14′ to accommodate power hitter Al Simmons, but he never cared much for Comiskey Park, and was gone a year later; the plate was then moved back to its original location. In 1949 a chickenwire fence was installed by Frank Lane, but it was the opposition and not the White Sox who profited from the smaller dimensions, so he removed it after only a few games.

Comiskey was the site of the first All-Star game in 1933; it was also the permanent site of the Negro Leagues' yearly East-West all-star game, 1933–50. The infield was a hazard in those years. Once Luke Appling tripped over a piece of metal protruding near second base. It was a copper kettle that had surfaced after five decades. Night games beginning in 1939 helped bolster sagging attendance. In 1950 a scoreboard was built in center field, replacing the ones situated on the left and right field walls. Ten years later Bill Veeck added a final touch by adding fireworks to the scoreboard's capabilities. In 1968 artificial turf was installed in the infield, but it was removed in 1976.

Maintaining the nation's oldest park was beyond Veeck's limited budget during his second period of ownership. He was forced to sell the team to Jerry Reinsdorf and Eddie Einhorn, who installed a new Diamond Vision board, luxury suites, wider aisles, and improved front office facilities. However, the masonry and the infrastructure reputedly remain inadequate. The state legislature has voted to appropriate funds for the construction of a new stadium for the Sox across the street from Comiskey Park. /(RL)

J. Louis Comiskey — 1885–1939. *Executive.*

The only son of Charles Comiskey, Lou was a shy and benevolent man who lived in the shadow of his illustrious father. He was appointed vice-president and treasurer of the White Sox in 1910. Two years later, he contracted scarlet fever and, for the rest of his life, had to maintain a hospital suite at St. Luke's in Chicago. Complicating his condition was his weight—300 lbs. In 1931, Charles Comiskey passed away, leaving the last-place White Sox to his son. Within a few years, Lou restored the club to respectability. He purchased Mule Haas, Al Simmons, and Jimmy Dykes from Philadelphia in 1932, and started the first White Sox farm system, which began yielding results by 1939. That year, Lou had

lights installed in Comiskey Park, but he did not live to see the first night game, passing away on July 18. /(RL)

Adam Comorosky — 1904–1951. OF 1926–35 **Pirates**, Reds 813 g, .285, 28 hr, 417 rbi

A gritty player from the Pennsylvania coal mines, Comorosky had two .300 seasons with Pittsburgh, where he teamed with the Waner brothers in the outfield for four seasons. /(JK)

Keith Comstock — 1955– . LHP 1984, 87– Twins, Giants, **Padres**, Mariners 97 ip, 3–3, 4.56

Comstock is a study in perseverance. Originally signed in 1976, he had a four-game stint with the Twins in 1984 but was released. He signed with the Yomiuri Giants in Japan to keep his career alive, but was 8–10 over two seasons and was released after 1986. He caught on with the Giants in 1987 and was traded to San Diego in the big deal that brought Kevin Mitchell to San Francisco. That season, his best in the majors, the reliever was 2–1 with a 4.61 ERA. /(WOR)

Dave Concepcion — 1948– . SS-2B-3B-1B 1970–88 **Reds** 2488 g, .267, 101 hr, 950 rbi. *5 LCS, 15 g, .351, 1 hr, 1 rbi. 4 WS, 20 g, .266, 1 hr, 12 rbi* ☛ *All-Star—73, 75–82. Gold Glove—74–77, 79.*

Concepcion came out of Venezuela to become one of baseball's greatest shortstops. Wearing number 13, the lithe infielder won the position in 1972 after sharing it with Woody Woodward for two seasons. In 1973, Concepcion was named captain of the Reds. The winner of five Gold Gloves, he also started five All-Star Games from 1973 to 1982, more than any other NL shortstop during that period. He responded to his eighth straight selection (ninth overall) in 1982 by winning the Game's MVP award, hitting a two-run homer as the NL won its 11th straight game.

In 1978 Concepcion became the first Cincinnati shortstop to bat .300 since Joe Tinker in 1913. Hampered by an elbow injury in 1980, Concepcion took advantage of the Astroturf at Riverfront Stadium and developed the one-hop throw to first base to reduce arm strain. The winner of the Roberto Clemente award as the top Latin American ballplayer in the majors in 1977, he led the NL with 14 game-winning RBI in 1981, when he was the Reds' MVP. In four World Series, Concepcion hit better than .300 three times and topped .400 in the 1975 and '79 LCS. He played over 100 games at shortstop

Dave Concepcion forces the Cubs' Gary Martin

12 straight years (1974–85) and in 14 of 15 seasons, with an injury cutting into his 1973 season. Replaced by Barry Larkin in 1986, Concepcion became a dependable handyman working at all four infield positions. Only Pete Rose is ahead of him in doubles (389), games, hits (2,326), and at-bats in Reds history, and only Joe Morgan has more Reds stolen bases than Concepcion's 321. Concepcion also ranks in the Reds' top five in runs, RBI, and total bases. On his retirement, he was only 44 games away from Larry Bowa's NL record for shortstops. /(ME)

Onix Concepcion [born Onix Cardona Cardona] — 1957– . SS-2B-3B 1980–85, 87 390 g, .239, 3 hr, 80 rbi. *2 LCS, 7 g, .000. 2 WS, 6 g, --*

Groomed as the successor to U.L. Washington at shortstop, Concepcion was hampered by injuries and was unable to capitalize on his defensive and running talents enough to compensate for his lack of power and mediocre batting average. /(FO)

David Cone — 1963– . RHP 1986– Royals, **Mets** 573 ip, 39–17, 3.11. 20 wins: 88 *1 LCS, 12 ip, 1–1, 4.50* ☛ *All-Star—88.*

Cone was acquired in one of the Mets' best deals; the most important player they gave up was injury-prone catcher Ed Hearn. Cone himself spent much of 1987 on the DL, but when arm problems shelved starter Rick Aguilera early in 1988, Cone replaced him. He won his last eight starts of the season and led the NL in winning percentage (.870), the sixth-best mark ever for a 20-game winner. Going 20–3 with a 2.22 ERA, he finished third in Cy Young award voting. He was third in wins and second in a close ERA race, with Joe Magrane sitting out his last start of the season to protect a 0.04 point lead. Cone also tied for the NL lead in balks with 10, in a season known for strict enforcement. He had an odd group of rooters known as the "Coneheads" after the old *Saturday Night Live* routine. They wore traffic cones or alien makeup like that worn on the TV show.

Cone was the focus of controversy in Game Two of the LCS. A ghostwritten column under his name in a New York paper following the first game said that Orel Hershiser had been lucky to shut out the Mets for eight innings and called loser Jay Howell a "high school pitcher." The Dodgers used this as a rallying point and drove Cone out after just two innings. However, he came back strong in Game Six, going the distance in a 5–1 five-hit victory.

Cone struggled in 1989, but managed a 14–8, 3.52 mark and led the Mets with seven complete games. /(SH)

Bunk Congalton — 1875-1937. OF 1902, 1905–07 Cubs, Indians, **Red Sox** 310 g, .290, 5 hr, 128 rbi

The Canadian-born outfielder's major league career was brief, but he starred in the minors, twice leading the Western Association in batting. Congalton died of a heart attack while watching Bob Feller pitch in Cleveland Stadium. /(JK)

Billy Conigliaro — 1947– . OF 1969–73 **Red Sox**, Brewers, A's 347 g, .256, 40 hr, 128 rbi. *1 LCS, 1 g, .000. 1 WS, 3 g, .000*

Tony's brother and Boston's top 1967 draft choice hit 18 homers in 1970. A year later, he accused Carl Yastrzemski of running the Red Sox, and claimed that cliques kept him from being a regular. Traded to Milwaukee that October, Conigliaro retired after 52 games with the Brewers, but resurfaced with the 1973 World Champion Oakland A's. /(TJ)

Tony Conigliaro — 1945– . OF 1964–67, 1969–71, 1975 **Red Sox**, Angels 876 g, .264, 166 hr, 516 rbi
☛ *Led League—hr 65. All-Star—67.*

Tony Conigliaro hit .290 with 24 home runs in 1964, but broke his arm in August; Tony Oliva won the AL Rookie of the Year award. When the 20-year-old Conigliaro hit 32 HR in 1965, he became the youngest home run leader in AL history. The hometown hero was enjoying another standout year in 1967 when, on August 18, he was struck by a Jack Hamilton fastball that broke his cheekbone and so damaged his eyesight that he missed the entire 1968 season. He returned in 1969 to win Comeback of the Year honors, and in 1970 hit 36 HR. But his vision was still impaired, and he left the majors in July 1971, returning for a short comeback try in 1975. Further tragedy befell Conigliaro at age 37, when he suffered a heart attack (while riding in a car with brother Billy) that left him severely incapacitated. /(TJ)

Jocko Conlan (John) — 1899– . OF 1934–35 **White Sox** 128 g, .264, 0 hr, 31 rbi.
Umpire NL 1941–65 *5 WS, 6 ASU*
☛ *Hall of Fame—74.*

Conlan had a brief career as an AL outfielder but was elected to baseball's Hall of Fame in 1974 as an umpire. His first stint of umpiring came by accident. When regular AL umpire Red Ormsby was overcome by heat during a 1935 Browns-White Sox game, Conlan, a Chicago reserve, filled in. The next year, he launched his new career as an ump.

He umpired in the NL for 25 years, starting in 1941. His trademarks were his quick grin, polka dot tie, and balloon chest protector. He was allowed to continue using the outside protector for five years after the NL adopted the inside protector for its umps because he was at risk from being hit in the throat by pitches.

The spunky Irishman had many run-ins with NL managers, particularly firebrands Leo Durocher and Frankie Frisch. In a 1955 game he was suffering from an attack of arthritis and found it difficult to bend to see low pitches. When he called a strike on Jackie Robinson on a pitch nearly in the dirt, "Robinson seemed so honestly shocked over the call," Conlan said, "I figured I must have missed it. I didn't want any more like that." Rather than make another mistake, he left the field. /(RTM)

Jocko Conlan

Gene Conley — 1930– . RHP 1952, 54–63 **Braves**, Phillies, Red Sox 1589 ip, 91–96, 3.82. *1 WS, 2 ip, 10.80*
☛ *All-Star—54–55, 59.*

During baseball's off-season, 6'9" Gene Conley played basketball for the Boston Celtics. He won 14 for Milwaukee and finished second in NL Rookie of the Year balloting in 1954. In the 1955 All-Star Game, Conley struck out Al Kaline, Mickey Vernon, and Al Rosen in the top of the 12th. Moments later, Stan Musial homered for the NL, making Conley the winning pitcher. He won a career-high 15 for the Red Sox in 1962. That year, in a New York traffic jam, Conley and infielder Pumpsie Green deserted their team bus. Green reported to the team hotel the next evening, but Conley remained AWOL nearly three days, unsuccessfully trying to fly to Israel. "I don't know why I did it," he later said. /(TJ)

Sarge Connally [George Walter] — 1898–1978. RHP 1921, 23–29, 31–34 **White Sox**, Indians 994 ip, 49–60, 4.30

Connally picked up his nickname from WWI service. In baseball, he saw action as both a starter and reliever in twelve ML campaigns. /(JK)

Bob Connery — 1879–1967. *Scout.*

Connery discovered Rogers Hornsby for the Cardinals in 1915, purchasing him from the Denison, Washington club for $600. He was head scout for the Yankees from 1918 to 1924, and was part-owner and president of the St. Paul American Association club from 1925 to 1935. He was involved in securing Earle Combs, Lefty Gomez, and Tony Lazzeri for the Yankees. /(FVP)

Ed Connolly — 1939– . LHP 1964, 67 **Red Sox**, Indians 130 ip, 6–12, 5.88

The son of Ed Connolly, a Red Sox catcher in 1929–32, Ed, Jr., made the majors in 1964, the year after his father's death. He went 4–11 for Boston that year with a 4.91 ERA, mostly as a starter. The fireballer lacked control, and after resurfacing briefly with the 1967 Indians he faded. /(WOR)

Joe Connolly — 1888–1943. OF 1913–16 **Braves** 412 g, .288, 14 hr, 157 rbi. *1 WS, 3 g, .111, 1 rbi*

Platooned against righthanded pitching, Connolly was the leading hitter (.306) for the 1914 "Miracle Braves." He later served in the Rhode Island State Legislature. /(JK)

Tom Connolly — 1870–1963. *Umpire* NL 1898–1900, **AL** 1901–31 *8 WS*
☛ *Hall of Fame—1953.*

Born in England, Tom Connolly didn't want to play baseball; when his family settled in Natick, MA, and he learned about the game, Connolly wanted to be an umpire. The 5'7" 135-lb Connolly worked local games until he was spotted by Tim Hurst, a legendary National League umpire. Hurst recommended Connolly to sportswriter Tim Murnane, who was running the Class B New England League. Murnane hired Connolly in 1894, and in 1898 Connolly moved up to the National League. When the NL failed to support him in a showdown with a player, Connolly resigned midway through the 1900 campaign. Although Connie Mack had never seen Connolly umpire, he had heard enough about him to recommend Ban Johnson hire him for the new American League. Three of the inaugural 1901 season's openers were rained out, so when the lone

game was played between Chicago and Cleveland, with Connolly its sole umpire, he could claim the distinction of having umpired the first AL game. He also umpired the first World Series in 1903.

Connolly earned a reputation for fearlessly ejecting hometown heroes when circumstances required. In his first AL season, he was challenged by Baltimore pitcher Joe McGinnity, who spit in his face. The league backed Connolly and suspended McGinnity. However, when Connolly failed to respond sufficiently after St. Louis outfielder Jesse Burkett punched a rival manager in the nose, he was reprimanded by Ban Johnson. Taking the hint, Connolly bounced ten players in his maiden season. After that, his reputation was enough to quell disturbances before they got out of hand. Ty Cobb said later that he learned to stop arguing when Tom's neck turned red. The last player Connolly tossed was Babe Ruth, in 1922. It was the last time Ruth was ejected. Ruth grew incensed by the taunts of a spectator, and started to climb into the stands. Connolly, nearly 100 pounds lighter and seven inches shorter than Ruth, blocked the Babe's path and scolded, "You should be ashamed of yourself," while escorting him off the field.

Connolly continued as an active umpire until 1931 when, at age 60, he became the chief of staff of American League umpires. He traveled the circuit evaluating and advising arbiters until he was 83. After retiring as Umpire-in-Chief, he served for many years on the Rules Committee. In 1953 Connolly and Bill Klem, his counterpart in the NL, became the first umpires named to the Hall of Fame. /(JK)

Roger Connor — 1857–1931. 1B-3B-2B-OF 1880–97 **Troy (NL)/Giants**, New York (PL), Phillies, Cardinals 1998 g, .318, 136 hr, 1078 rbi.
　　Manager 1896 **Cardinals** 9–37, .196
☛ *Led League—hr 90. Led League—rbi 89. Led League—ba 85 . Hall of Fame—1976.*

Connor's first major league team was the Troy Haymakers, when he was 23. Connor found a career and a wife in Troy when he went to a shirt factory where she worked; the long-torsoed Irishman had to be fitted with a special uniform and she took his measurements.

Connor was one of the greatest sluggers of the 19th century. His 136 career home runs stood as the record until Babe Ruth exceeded it in the lively ball era. A vivid image of the mustached Connor was written by veteran New York sportswriter Sam

Roger Connor

Crane, who claimed Connor was, "the best base runner I ever saw, excepting Bill Lange, and it behooved the baseman to give Roger a clear path. With his weight catapulting him, with speed and force, he slid feet first and, as he landed, could bob up, like a jack-in-the-box." Crane described Connor as a man with a tremendous reach and a good pair of hands who was exceedingly good on pickups, digging the ball out of the dirt. Although Roger

Connor could drive the ball for prodigious distances, his speed and line drives added up to triples and he is fifth on the all-time list with 233. His home runs could be awesome. He hit a magnificent shot in his first game with the Giants, in 1883, that caused jubilant patrons to pass the hat and buy a $500 gold watch in appreciation. He favored pitches down by his knees and would put his 220 pounds of farm-hardened muscle behind his hits.

After the Troy franchise moved to New York, Connor starred for the Giants until 1890, when he helped form the Players League and was its home run champion for its only season. His career continued after peace was made with the outlaws, alternating between the Giants, the Phillies, and the Cardinals until he retired from the ML after 1897. Back in his hometown of Waterbury he obtained a franchise in the tightly-knit Connecticut League, whose teams made one-day trolley jumps and slept at home every night. He hit .392 to lead his league in batting, his eye sharpened by spectacles that might have been laughed at in the big leagues. Later, he sold his Waterbury team and bought the franchise of the larger Springfield, MA entry. He played there until he was 46 in 1903, managing the team and saving himself, as owner, two salaries. He left baseball a prosperous man who could look back on his achievements in the earlier years of the game. He had six hits in six at-bats in an 1895 game against Jouett Meekin. He hit three home runs in succession in an 1888 game against Indianapolis and two home runs off Larry Corcoran in a game against Cap Anson's Chicago White Stockings when he was with Troy.

Roger Connor's case for the Hall of Fame election was argued strongly by Bill Klem, who held Connor in special esteem. In 1902, when Klem was breaking into professional umpiring in the Connecticut League, the young umpire gave several decisions against Connor's Springfield team. With the fans shouting for his blood, Klem was relieved when the huge playing manager of the home team put an encouraging arm across the young umpire's shoulders and assured everyone Klem had the right to call them as he saw them. /(JK)

Chuck Connors [Kevin] — 1921– . 1B 1949, 51 Dodgers, **Cubs** 67 g, .238, 2 hr, 18 rbi

The 6'7" Connors played pro basketball with the Boston Celtics after WWII before concentrating on baseball. In the Brooklyn organization he earned more applause for his spring training recitations of "Casey at the Bat" than for his hitting. He pinch-hit once for the Dodgers in 1949. The Cubs acquired him in 1951 and sent him to Los Angeles of the Pacific Coast League where he hit .321. A bit part in the Spencer Tracy—Katharine Hepburn movie "Pat and Mike" after the 1952 season convinced him to make acting his fulltime profession. In 1957 he landed the lead in the TV western series "The Rifleman," which aired through 1962. His second western series, "Branded," aired 1964–65. He has appeared in numerous movies and television dramas since, and won critical acclaim in the role of a slave owner in the television mini-series "Roots" (1977)./(MC)

Tim Conroy — 1960– . LHP 1978, 82–87 **A's**, Cardinals 467 ip, 18–32, 4.69

Conroy was Oakland's first pick in the 1978 June draft; Charley Finley brought the 18-year-old right to the majors, where he proved embarrassingly wild. Four years in Double-A and Class-A followed. He fought to control his 95-mph fastball and sharp-breaking curve, and returned to Oakland to go 7–10 in 1983. Back in the Pacific Coast League in 1985, he threw a seven-inning, 1–0 no-hitter against Tucson on May 14. He went to the Cardinals in the trade for Joaquin Andujar that December, but his flashes of brilliance were tempered by shoulder problems./(JCA)

Wid Conroy [William Edward] — 1877–1959. 3B-SS-OF 1901–11 Milwaukee (AL), Pirates, Yankees, Senators 1377 g, .248, 22 hr, 452 rbi

Conroy picked up the nickname "Widow" for his solicitous concern for younger boys on his sandlot team and was known as "Wid" all his long life in organized baseball. He began as a shortstop, replacing Honus Wagner with Paterson in the Atlantic League, but was struck by malarial fever and dropped from the team. In 1900 Connie Mack invited him to try out for the Western Association team he would field in Milwaukee and transfer to Philadelphia when the American League began as a major circuit; Conroy won the last spot on the roster.

Conroy was the first-string shortstop of the NL champion 1902 Pirates, but became a third baseman when he returned to the AL with the Highlanders (later the Yankees) in 1903. He led AL third basemen twice in total chances per game. His 22-year career in pro baseball ended as a Phillies coach in 1922./(JK)

Bob Considine — 1907–1975. *Writer.*

Author or co-author of 25 books and movie scripts, war correspondent, and syndicated columnist ("On the Line"), Considine wrote for the Hearst newspapers in Washington and New York, beginning in 1933. He was sports editor of the Washington *Herald* before writing for King Features. Among his books was a biography of Babe Ruth./(NLM)

Billy Consolo — 1934– . SS-2B-3B 1953–62 **Red Sox**, Senators/Twins, Phillies, Angels, A's 603 g, .221, 9 hr, 83 rbi

Consolo went directly to the Reds from high school after signing for $60,000 in 1953. His .270 in 1957 was 41 points better than he hit in any other season./(TJ)

Sandy Consuegra [Sandalio Simeon Castellon] — 1920– . RHP 1950–57 Senators, **White Sox**, Orioles, Giants 809 ip, 51–32, 3.37
☛ *All-Star—54.*

Consuegra's 16–3 record in 1954 produced an AL-best .842 winning percentage, and included a league-high eight relief wins (without a defeat). He pitched in the '54 All-Star Game, but yielded five earned runs on as many hits, retiring only one batter. The AL won despite him./(TJ)

Dennis Cook — 1962– . LHP 1988– Giants, **Phillies** 143 ip, 9–9, 3.59

After an impressive debut in 1988 (2–1, 2.86 in four games), Cook was part of the package sent to the Phillies in mid-1989 for Steve Bedrosian, and Cook immediately moved into their rotation./(JFC)

Doc Cook [Luther Almus] — 1886–1973. OF 1913–16 **Yankees** 286 g, .274, 3 hr, 75 rbi

The Yankees' regular right fielder in 1914–15, Cook had little extra-base power. His .283 was the best of any Yankee with over 100 games on the 1914 club, which was the worst-hitting team in the majors that year with a .229 team mark./(MG)

Dusty Cooke [Allen Lindsey] — 1907– . OF 1930–36, 38 Yankees, **Red Sox**, Reds 608 g, .280, 24 hr, 229 rbi. *Manager* 1948 **Phillies**, 6–5, .545

Once a high-priced Yankee prospect, Cooke was slowed by a broken collarbone and a fractured leg. He played satisfactorily but not up to expectations with the Red Sox. He later became the Phillies trainer, and, forgetting his station, was thrown out of a game for making remarks from the bench./(JK)

Duff Cooley [Dick Gordon] (Sir Richard) — 1873–1937. OF-1B 1893–1905 Cardinals, Phillies, Pirates, **Braves**, Tigers 1318 g, .294, 25 hr, 557 rbi

Cooley stood out among the rough types of turn-of-the-century baseball and was dubbed "Sir Richard" for his aristocratic manner. The lefthanded-hitting Texan played most in the outfield, but tried all positions except pitcher. When he retired, he had saved enough money to buy teams in Topeka and Salt Lake City, operating them profitably for many years. /(JK)

Danny Coombs — 1942– . LHP 1963–71 **Astros**, Padres 393 ip, 19–27, 4.08

A former Seton Hall basketball star, Coombs was initially unable to control his fastball-slider repertoire and was up and down with Houston for seven seasons. Sold to San Diego in 1970, he was 10–14 as a starter. /(MC)

Jack Coombs [John Wesley] (Colby Jack) — 1882–1957. RHP 1906–18, 20 **A's**, Dodgers, Tigers 2320 ip, 159–110, 2.78. 20 wins: 10–12 *3 WS, 53 ip, 5–0, 2.70.*
        Manager 1919 **Phillies** 18–44, .290
☛ *Led League—w 10–11.*

Colby Jack was signed by the Athletics off the campus of Colby College in Maine. On September 1, 1906, he pitched 24 innings to set an AL record tied only by his opponent that day, Boston's Joe Harris. Coombs's 13 shutouts in 1910 are an AL record. His 31 wins led the league that season, and he added three more victories in the World Series against the Cubs. Coombs was unbeaten in WS competition, winning another game in 1911 and one more for Wilbert Robinson's 1916 Brooklyn Dodgers. Coombs became a championship-winning coach at Duke University who sent many players to the majors. /(JK)

Jimmy Cooney (Scoops) — 1894– . SS 1917, 19, 24–28 Red Sox, Giants, Cardinals, **Cubs**, Phillies, Braves 448 g, .262, 2 hr, 150 rbi

Although he cracked 12 consecutive hits for Milwaukee of the American Association in 1923, the slick-fielding Cooney had trouble holding a ML job because of his weak bat. He made an unassisted triple play on May 30, 1927, for the Cubs against the Pirates. In the fourth inning he caught Paul Waner's liner, stepped on second to double Lloyd Waner, and tagged Clyde Barnhart coming down from first. He was the son of Jimmy Cooney, an

1890s NL shortstop, and his younger brother Johnny was a ML outfielder/pitcher for 20 years. /(BC)

Johnny Cooney — 1901– . OF-1B-LHP 1921–30, 1935–44 **Braves**, Dodgers, Yankees 1172 g, .286, 2 hr, 219 rbi; 795 ip, 34–44, 3.72

Johnny was the youngest of the "Cranston Cooneys," a Rhode Island ballplaying dynasty begun in the 1890s by James Joseph Cooney, whose four sons all played pro ball. Two brothers never got to the majors, but Johnny had two careers. As a pitcher who occasionally played first base or outfield, he had moderate success with the Braves in the 1920s. A sore arm forced him to give up pitching; after a four-year absence from the majors and an American Association batting title, he joined Casey Stengel's Dodgers in 1935. Cooney's best averages as a regular came with the Stengel-managed Braves, .318 in 1940 and .319 in 1941. Stengel later compared Cooney favorably to Joe DiMaggio as a fielder. /(JK)

Terry Cooney — 1933– . *Umpire* AL 1975–86 *2 LCS 1 WS, 1 ASU*

Ex-marine Cooney had some sensational confrontations with AL managers. In 1981 he endured a Billy Martin dirt attack (six kicks followed by a double handful fired at Cooney's mask) and in 1982 Earl Weaver attempted a punch, resulting in a week's suspension and $2,000 fine for Weaver. /(RTM)

Cecil Cooper — 1949– . 1B-DH 1971–1987 Red Sox, **Brewers** 1896 g, .298, 241 hr, 1125 rbi. *2 LCS, 8 g, .233, 5 rbi. 2 WS, 12 g, .191, 1 hr, 7 rbi*
☛ *Led League—rbi 80, 83. All-Star—79–80, 82–83, 85. Gold Glove—79–80.*

The smooth-fielding first baseman was one of the most consistent hitters of the late 1970s and early 1980s, always among the top batting and fielding leaders. But because he played at the same time as Rod Carew and George Brett, he never won a batting title.
    Cooper was haunted by Carl Yastrzemski. As a young player in Boston, Cooper was forced to DH, and played first base only on the odd occasions when Yaz played the outfield or was rested. At the end of the 1976 season, the Red Sox realized they'd be better off with a power hitter than with Cooper, perceived as a singles hitter, so they swapped the lefty Cooper to get the powerful George Scott back from the Brewers. Cooper flourished, batting over .300 his first seven years in Milwaukee. He finished

Cecil Cooper

second to Rod Carew in the All-Star balloting for first base in 1978, but when Carew got hurt, instead of Cooper taking his place, Yaz was brought in from the outfield to play first base.

Cooper had his best year in 1980. He led the league in RBI with 122 and hit a career-high .352, with 25 HR. But George Brett had his flirtation with .400 that year, finishing at .390 and spoiling Cooper's best shot at a batting title. Two years later, Cooper hit a career-high 32 HR and led Milwaukee to its comeback in the 1982 ALCS against the Angels. Down two games to none, the Brewers won three straight games at home, with Cooper singling in the tying and winning runs in the seventh inning of the final game. In 1983, he had his best power year, hitting .307, his last .300 season, with 30 HR and a league-leading and career-high 126 RBI./(SEW)

Claude Cooper — 1892–1974. OF 1913–17 Giants, Brooklyn (FL), Phillies 373 g, .260, 4 hr, 104 rbi. *1 WS, 2 g, --.*

Cooper parlayed a sensational Texas League season, after which he was hailed as "another Speaker," into an invitation to join the pennant-bound Giants in 1913. He was voted a full World Series share and showed perverse appreciation by jumping to the outlaw Federal League.

Cooper broke his leg as soon as the Federal League opened its 1914 season. When the Federal League dissolved, Cooper and Bill Bradley retained John M. Ward as an attorney. Ward won a suit for the players, whom he had dealt with earlier as general manager of the BrookFeds, for another "bonus" based on presumed World Series entitlements due had they not jumped legal contracts.

Reinstated, Cooper played two seasons with the Phillies, failing to hit even .200, and returned to Texas./(JK)

Mort Cooper — 1913–1958. RHP 1938–47, 49 **Cardinals**, Braves, Giants, Cubs 1841 ip, 128–75, 2.97. 20 wins: 42–44 *3 WS, 45 ip, 2–3, 3.00*
☛ *Most Valuable Player—42. Led League—w 42–43. Led League—era 42. All-Star—42–43, 46.*

Cooper, whose brother Walker was his catcher during the early 1940s, went 22–7 with 10 shutouts and a 1.77 ERA and was the NL MVP for the 1942 World Champion Cardinals. In 1943 he led the NL in victories (21) for the second straight year, and followed with a 22-win 1944 campaign. The fastballer, who occasionally chewed aspirin on the mound for relief from an aching arm, started and lost the 1942 and 1943 All-Star Games. St. Louis traded Cooper to the Braves in May 1945 after suspending him for leaving the club over a salary dispute. Mort and Walker teamed again in 1947, when the fading pitcher appeared in eight games with the Giants./(TJ)

Walker Cooper — 1915– . C 1940–57 **Cardinals**, Giants, Reds, Braves, Pirates, Cubs 1473 g, .285, 173 hr, 812 rbi. *3 WS, 16 g, .300, 6 rbi*
☛ *All-Star—42–44, 46–50.*

"He was just about the strongest man I've ever known," said Ewell Blackwell. Enos Slaughter called him "one of the best behind the plate," adding, "He was a great guy . . .very good-natured." Walker Cooper was a 6'3" 210-lb heavy hitter and practical joker who was named to every NL All-Star squad 1942–50 (there was no game in 1945). After three World Series with St. Louis (where he was older brother Mort's batterymate), Walker was sold to the

Walker Cooper

nor, would dive toward the bag as Cooper whipped a sidearm throw to third. Walter Schmidt caught him for most of his career with Pittsburgh and they knew each other so well that the battery wasted little time on signals. Cooper got a reputation as a fast worker.

A .239 lifetime batter, Cooper hit four homers in 1922, and hit .346 in 104 at-bats in 1924. /(JK)

Robert Coover — 1922– . *Writer.*

Novelist and playwright, and writer in residence at Brown University since 1979, Coover published *Universal Baseball Association, Inc., J. Henry Waugh, Prop.* in 1968. It depicts a statistics-obsessed loner compulsively playing a table baseball game and writing histories based on the results. /(NLM)

Wilbur Cooper

Giants in 1945. The Giants paid the then-princely sum of $175,000 while Cooper was still in the Navy. His best year was with the 1947 Giants, batting .305 with 122 RBI and contributing 35 of the club's 221 homers, a NL record. /(TJ)

Wilbur Cooper — 1892–1973. LHP 1912–26 **Pirates,** Cubs, Tigers 3480 ip, 216–178, 2.89. 20 wins: 20–22, 24 ☛ *Led League—w 21.*

Cooper won more games (202) than any other Pirate lefthander, at least 17 games a year from 1917 through 1924 with a career-high 24 in 1920 and a league-best 22 in 1921. The sinkerballer twice led the NL with 27 complete games, and led in two other seasons with 38 starts.

Cooper's fielding skills were exceptional, particularly his knack for picking runners off third base—seven in 1924 alone. His partner, Pie Tray-

Doug Corbett — 1952– . RHP 1980–87 Twins, **Angels**, Orioles 553 ip, 24–30, 3.32. *1 LCS, 7 ip, 1–0, 5.40*
☛ *All-Star—81.*

First signed by the Royals, Corbett was claimed by the Twins off Cincinnati's roster in the 1979 major league draft. In 1980, the sinkerballer set AL rookie records with 73 appearances and 23 saves. He saved 17 games with an AL-high 54 appearances in strike-shortened 1981. The Twins sent him to California in a 1982 trade for Tom Brunansky, but Corbett proved a disappointment. He spent parts of 1982 through 1985 in the minors, and did not record a save in 1983 or '85. His toughness was questioned; he would warn hitters, "Look out," when he'd accidentally let loose inside. He made a comeback of sorts in 1986, saving 10 for the AL West Champion Angels, and winning LCS Game Four. /(JCA)

Joe Corbett — 1875–1945. RHP 1895–97, 1904 Washington (NL), **Baltimore (NL)**, Cardinals 482 ip, 32–19, 3.42. 20 wins: 97

The brother of World Heavyweight Boxing Champion "Gentleman Jim," Corbett won 24 games for the 1897 Orioles and added two more in a Temple Cup sweep. Later, as baseball coach at Santa Clara University, his star player was Hal Chase. /(JK)

Ray Corbin — 1949– . RHP 1971–75 **Twins** 652 ip, 36–38, 3.84

Corbin had eight wins and 83 strikeouts in each of his first three ML seasons. He recorded 14 of his 17 saves in 1973, but after elbow surgery in 1975 never again pitched in the majors. /(RMu)

Larry Corcoran — 1859–1891. RHP 1880–87 **Cubs**, Giants, Washington (NL), Indianapolis (NL) 2392 ip, 177–90, 2.36. 20 wins: 80–84
☛ *Led League—w 81. Led League—era 82.*

Corcoran was one of the best pitchers of the 1880s, winning 170 games and losing only 84 from 1880 through 1884 for the Chicago NL team. He pitched three no-hitters. According to historian Lee Allen, Corcoran was the first pitcher to work out a set of signals with his catcher. He invariably carried a huge chew of tobacco in his mouth and when he chewed it shifted visibly. His regular catcher, Silver Flint, suggested that he signal his curve by shifting his chew, and the idea worked perfectly. Overwork, dissipation, and Bright's disease ended his career, and he was dead by the age of 32. His .663 winning percentage is eighth all-time. A brother, Mike, pitched one losing game for Chicago in 1884. /(BC)

Tim Corcoran — 1953– . 1B-OF 1977–81, 83–86 **Tigers**, Twins, Phillies, Mets 509 g, .270, 12 hr, 128 rbi

The lefthanded Corcoran led the AL with 10 pinch hits as a rookie in 1977. He batted .322 in five Tiger spring trainings, but only in 1978 and 1980 did he spend full seasons in Detroit. An extra outfielder and backup first baseman, he batted .341 for Philadelphia in 1984, but was released after dropping to .214 in 1985. /(JCA)

Tommy Corcoran — 1869–1960. SS 1890–1907 Pittsburgh (PL), Philadelphia (AA), Dodgers, **Reds**, Giants 2201 g, .257, 34 hr, 1135 rbi

Originally a barehanded fielder, Corcoran successfully made the transition to gloves and the 20th century. In Cincinnati he played shortstop alongside Bid McPhee, whose career was coming to an end, and Miller Huggins, who was just beginning. In his final season, with the Giants, the 18-year veteran spelled rookie Larry Doyle at second.

Corcoran survived two collapsed leagues (the Players' League and the American Association) in his first two seasons, caught on with Brooklyn, and

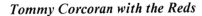

Tommy Corcoran with the Reds

was traded to Cincinnati in 1897. There he excelled for a decade as shortstop and team captain. In 1903, he set a still-standing ML record for SS with 14 assists in a nine-inning game. Corcoran ranks high on the lifetime lists for putouts, assists, and total chances. A skillful sign stealer, he once uprooted an electric signaling device the Phillies had buried in their third base coaching box (a binocular-equipped observer in the scoreboard passed along catcher's signs to aid Phillie batters). Corcoran later umpired in several leagues, including the Federal League. /(ADS)

Mike Corkins — 1946- . RHP 1969-74 **Padres** 459 ip, 19-28, 4.39

Taken from San Francisco by the Padres in the 1968 expansion draft, Corkins threw an Eastern League no-hitter in 1969, was called up, and on September 22 served up Willie Mays's 600th career home run. He was a lifetime .202 hitter with five HR in 119 at-bats. /(MC)

Pat Corrales — 1941- . C 1964-66, 68-73 Phillies, Cardinals, **Reds**, Padres 300 g, .216, 4 hr, 54 rbi. *1 WS, 1 g, .000.*
    Manager 1979-80, 82-87 Rangers, Phillies, **Indians** 572-634, .474

Corrales, a poor hitter, spent much of his career as the backup catcher to Johnny Bench in Cincinnati. On September 29, 1965, he became one of only four ML players to reach base twice on catcher's interference in the same game. He skippered the Rangers for two seasons and then the Phillies, who made him the only manager to be fired with his team in first place (7/18/83). Thirteen days later, Corrales replaced Mike Ferraro as the Indians' manager. In 1986, Corrales charged Oakland pitcher Dave Stewart and tried to kick him but was quickly decked by a Stewart right to the jaw. Corrales was fired by Cleveland during the 1987 All-Star break, with the last-place Indians on their way to their second 100-loss season in three years. /(JCA)

Ed Correa — 1966- . RHP 1985-87 White Sox, **Rangers** 283 ip, 16-19, 5.16

First signed out of Puerto Rico by the White Sox, Correa, at age 20, was the youngest player in the AL as a Rangers rookie in 1986. He went 12-14 with a team-high 189 strikeouts, but a severe shoulder injury ended his 1987 season in July. A Seventh Day Adventist, Correa balked at pitching on Friday nights or Saturday afternoons. /(JCA)

Vic Correll — 1946- . C 1972, 74-80 Red Sox, **Braves**, Reds 410 g, .229, 29 hr, 125 rbi

Correll, a South Carolina native, was a favorite with Atlanta fans and owner Ted Turner as a part-time catcher from 1974 through 1977. After a short minor league stint as a player-coach, he spent three seasons with Cincinnati as the backup to Johnny Bench. /(PB)

Frank Corridon (Fiddler) — 1880-1941. RHP 1904-05, 07-10 Cubs, **Phillies**, Cardinals 1216 ip, 70-68, 2.80

Corridon is one of several who claim to have originated the spitball. With the International League Providence Grays, Corridon discovered that a ball which had landed in a puddle and was wet on one side did odd things when he threw it. A teammate suggested he wet the ball during games, and Corridon went on to have a respectable ML career. /(JK)

Jim Corsi — 1961- . RHP 1988- **A's** 60 ip, 1-3, 2.56

Corsi became an effective middle reliever for the A's in 1989. /(SFS)

Bill Corum — 1894-1958. *Writer.*

A graduate of the University of Missouri and Columbia University journalism school, Corum was a major in the AEF in WWI. He joined the New York *Times* in 1920 and moved to the New York *Journal* in 1925 and the Detroit *Evening Times* in 1935. He was a columnist for the New York *Journal-American* at the time of his death in 1958. Well liked and respected among writers, he was named president of Churchill Downs race track in 1949. /(NLM)

Al Corwin [Elmer Nathan] — 1926- . RHP 1951-55 **Giants** 289 ip, 18-10, 3.98. *1 WS, 2 ip, 0-0, 0.00*

As a rookie he mopped up in Game Five of the 1951 WS after the Giants fell behind the Yankees 13-1. On September 4, 1953 the spot starter hit the second of three consecutive Giants home runs between Wes Westrum and Whitey Lockman. /(JK)

Pete Coscarart — 1931- . 2B-SS 1938-46 Dodgers, **Pirates** 864 g, .243, 28 hr, 269 rbi *1 WS, 3 g, .000* ☛ *All-Star—40.*

The brother of Braves' infielder Joe Coscarart was the outstanding rookie second baseman of 1939 and followed that season with an All-Star Game appearance the next year. As his hitting declined, Pete was replaced by Billy Herman in 1941 and then traded to Pittsburgh. He started at short for the 1942 Pirates and at second for the next three seasons. /(ME)

Howard Cosell — 1920- . *Broadcaster.*

Revolutionary in his work on ABC's boxing, "Wide World of Sports," and "Monday Night Football" telecasts, Howard Cosell was outspoken and opinionated, often insightful but annoyingly verbose. The overtly intelligent Cosell was never reverential toward the athletes he covered, but his shrill speaking style, incessant preaching, and overbearing manner were irritants that eventually got under the skin of his employers and co-workers, and much of his audience. He made no secret of his distate for baseball (he found it boring), and when he joined "Monday Night Baseball" in 1976 his lack of deep baseball knowledge was the subject of much criticism. When he retired from network television, he wrote a sports column for the New York *Daily News* through the late 1980s. /(SL)

Mike Cosgrove — 1951- . LHP 1972-76 **Astros** 275 ip, 12-11, 4.03

A hard-throwing reliever, Cosgrove was 7-3 for the Astros in 1974 and had five saves the next year, but when he switched to starting in '76, he developed arm trouble. /(MC)

John Costello — 1960- . RHP 1988- **Cardinals** 112 ip, 10-6, 2.65

Costello has been an effective set-up man in the Cardinals' bullpen, posting low ERAs. /(WOR)

Chuck Cottier [Charles Keith] — 1936- . 2B-SS-3B 1959-65, 68-69 Braves, Tigers, **Senators**, Angels 580 g, .220, 19 hr, 127 rbi.
 Manager 1984-86 **Mariners** 98-120

A good fielder but a weak hitter, Cottier had his best year at the plate with a .242 BA for the 1962 Senators. He tied a ML record that season with two doubles in one inning. The next year, he shocked Yankees' Hall of Famer Whitey Ford with two homers and four RBI in a game. As a manager, he once exhibited his temper by throwing bats and balls from the dugout after a call went against Seattle, finally uprooting first base and hurling it into the outfield. /(FK)

Henry Cotto — 1961- . OF 1984- Cubs, **Yankees**, Mariners 475 g, .258, 24 hr, 106 rbi. *1 LCS, 3 g, 1.000*

Cotto broke in with the Cubs as a defensive replacement for Gary Matthews, and in three seasons with the Yankees he shuttled between New York and Columbus (International League). He was traded to the Mariners along with Steve Trout for Lee Guetterman before the 1988 season, and hit .259 with 27 stolen bases for Seattle that year. /(TF)

Johnny Couch — 1891-1975. RHP 1917, 22-25 Tigers, Reds, **Phillies** 643 ip, 29-34, 4.63

In 1922, as a 31-year-old rookie with Cincinnati, Couch was a lucky 16-9. One writer stated, "If Couch allowed no runs, the Reds would make one. If he allowed five, his mates would make six." Couch's luck ran out; 1922 was his only winning season. /(AL)

Bill Coughlin — 1877-1943. 3B 1899, 1901-08 Washington (NL), Senators, **Tigers** 1050 g, .253, 15 hr, 380 rbi. *2 WS, 8 g, .214, 1 rbi*

Coughlin had a brief stay with Washington's NL club in 1899, and resurfaced there for the AL's inaugural 1901 season. Traded to Detroit in mid-1904, he captained the Tigers' first two pennant winners, 1907-08. Coughlin's best ML BA was .301 in 1902. /(JL)

Fritz Coumbe — 1889-1978. LHP 1914-21 Red Sox, Indians, Reds 761 ip, 38-38, 2.79

The slender junkballer won a career-high 13 with Cleveland in 1918. He played centerfield for the Reds in the major leagues' last triple-header (1920). /(ADS)

County Stadium Milwaukee Braves 1953-65, Milwaukee Brewers 1970- . LF-315, CF-402, RF-315

A publicly funded stadium built exclusively for baseball, County Stadium was also the first stadium built with lights included, rather than added at a later date. It opened for the Braves in 1953 with a capacity of 35,911, and the club drew a then NL-record 1.8 million fans after having drawn only 281,000 in Boston the season before. Now home to the Brewers, County Stadium has a natural grass field and extensive bleacher seating in left and center fields, as well as a reputation for the best bratwurst in the ML. Until recently, the Brewers' mascot, barrel-clad Bernie Brewer, would slide into a large beer stein in right-center field after each Brewer home run. /(SCL)

Clint Courtney (Scrap Iron) — 1927–1975. C 1951–61 Yankees, Browns/Orioles, White Sox, **Senators**, A's 946 g, .268, 38 hr, 313 rbi

The first catcher to wear glasses, Courtney was better known as a fearless battler. Obtained by the Browns at the request of manager Rogers Hornsby, Courtney was *TSN* AL Rookie of the Year in 1952 (.286, 5 HR, 50 RBI, 116 G). He twice batted over .300 as a platoon player. "Scrap Iron's" most famous baseball brawl came in 1953 when the Browns met the Yankees. Courtney and Phil Rizzuto collided at second base, and Billy Martin jumped on Courtney in a wild melee that nearly provoked a riot among the few fans at St. Louis. The incident produced a then-AL record $850 in fines. Courtney died on June 16, 1975 while manager of Richmond (International League), exactly two years to the day after he was hired for the position. /(ME)

Ernie Courtney — 1875–1920. 3B-1B-OF-SS 1902–03, 05–08 Braves, Orioles/Yankees, Tigers, **Phillies** 558 g, .245, 5 hr, 200 rbi

Reputed to have had the biggest hands in pro baseball, Courtney played every infield position. The lefthanded hitter enjoyed his best season in 1905 when he drove in 77 runs as the Phillies' regular third baseman. /(AL)

Henry Courtney — 1898–1954. LHP 1919–22 **Senators**, White Sox 444 ip, 22–26, 4.90

After service as a WWI ambulance driver, Courtney began pitching for New Haven of the Eastern League. The Senators paid $7,500 for his contract, and he threw three complete-game victories for them at the end of the 1919 season. /(NLM)

Harry Coveleski (The Giant Killer) — 1886–1950. LHP 1907–10, 14–18 Phillies, Reds, **Tigers** 1248 ip, 81–55, 2.39. 20 wins: 14–16

Thrust into the midst of a furious pennant race when he was called up by the Phillies in late September 1908, Coveleski defeated the contending Giants three times in five days, enabling the Cubs to win the flag. Coveleski earned a $50 bonus and the nickname "The Giant Killer." He slumped in 1909, was traded, and returned to the minors. Resurfacing with the Tigers in 1914, he put together three straight 20-win seasons while losing no more than 13.

Coveleski and three brothers (including Hall of Famer Stanley) came out of the Pennsylvania coal fields to play pro ball. /(JL)

Stan Coveleskie [born Stanislaus Kowalewski, aka Stan Coveleski] (Covey) — 1889–1984. RHP 1912, 16–28 A's, **Indians**, Senators, Yankees 3093 ip, 215–142, 2.88. 20 wins: 18–21, 25 *2 WS, 41 ip, 3–2, 1.74*
☛ *Led League—era 23, 25. Led League—k 20. Hall of Fame—1969.*

Coveleskie always said it was the spitball that made him a major-league pitcher. He had a three-hit shutout in his debut with the A's in 1912, but was returned to the minors for seasoning and learned the spitter while with Portland (PCL), shortly before being acquired by the Indians.

Despite the spitter's eccentricity, Coveleskie (as the name was spelled during his playing days) was a control pitcher who averaged one walk every 3.86 innings over fourteen years. His spitball broke three ways—down, out, and down and out—and he said

Stan Coveleskie

he always could control its movement by the placement of his fingers on the ball. It was his bread and butter pitch, although he sometimes went two or three innings without throwing it and had the usual fastball and curve to mix things up.

He was equally sparing with strikeouts (981 lifetime). Because of his control many batters swung at his first pitch. A number of times he got out of an inning with three pitches, and on one occasion he went seven innings when every pitch was a strike, a foul, or a hit. He claimed success in fanning Ruth and in reducing Cobb's effectiveness by feeding him fastballs inside.

Overall, he had 39 shutouts, a streak of 13 wins in 1925 when he was 36 years old, and six consecutive seasons pitching more than 276 innings. His best years were with Cleveland, particularly the championship year of 1920 when he won three splendid five-hitters against Brooklyn in the Series. He allowed a total of two runs and two walks, struck out eight, and had an ERA of 0.67. After two under-.500 seasons, Cleveland traded him to Washington for two nonentities. His .800 (20–5) winning percentage and 2.84 ERA led the AL as the 1925 Senators repeated as AL champions. He lost two, however, in the Series against the Pirates.

A quiet, modest man, Covey was the youngest and most successful of five ball-playing brothers. Harry, the "Giant Killer" of 1908, was the only other one to reach the majors. /(ADS)

Wes Covington — 1932– . OF 1956–66 Braves, White Sox, A's, **Phillies**, Cubs, Dodgers 1075 g, .279, 131 hr, 499 rbi. *3 WS, 15 g, .235, 5 rbi*

A notorious time-waster at the plate, Covington used an unorthodox batting stance. The lefthanded hitter, who never had more than 373 at-bats in a season, hit 21 homers for the World Champion 1957 Braves and 24 HR (while batting .330) in 90 games in 1958. Although not highly regarded as an outfielder, Covington made two outstanding catches in the 1957 WS. In 1961, he played for four ML teams. He had a .320 pinch-hitting average for the 1963 Phils, batting .303 overall. /(TJ)

Billy Cowan — 1938– . OF 1963–65, 67, 69–72 **Cubs**, Mets, Braves, Phillies, Yankees, Angels 493 g, .236, 40 hr, 125 rbi

The Mississippi native totaled 35 homers and 122 RBI playing for two Cub farm teams in 1962. His only ML season as a regular was 1964, when he hit .241 with 19 HR and 50 RBI as the Cub centerfielder. /(TJ)

Al Cowens — 1951– . OF 1974–86 **Royals**, Angels, Tigers, Mariners 1584 g, .270, 108 hr, 717 rbi. *3 LCS, 14 g, .200, 1 hr, 6 rbi*
☛ *Gold Glove—77.*

A journeyman hitter through most of his career, soft-spoken Cowens had his best year for the Royals in 1977, hitting .312 with 14 triples, 23 HR, and 112 RBI. He finished second to Rod Carew in the MVP voting. A good defensive outfielder with a strong arm, his only other season with a batting average over .277 was 1979, when he managed .295 despite missing three weeks when a pitch broke his jaw. In 1982 for the Mariners, he hit 20 home runs and in both 1982 and 1984 he drove in 78 runs, his second-best totals. /(NLM)

Joe Cowley — 1958– . RHP 1982, 84–87 Braves, **Yankees**, White Sox, Phillies 469 ip, 33–25, 4.20

Cowley set an AL record by striking out the first seven Texas Rangers batters to start a game (5/28/86), and he threw a no-hitter with seven walks at California in a 7–1 win (9/19/86). Cowley spent eight seasons in the minors before earning a starting spot with the Yankees in July 1984. He won eight straight decisions that year, finishing 9–2. He was traded to the White Sox after a 12–6 record in 1985, then to the Phillies for Gary Redus before the 1987 season. Cowley was a huge bust for the Phillies, going 0–4 with 17 walks, 21 hits and a 15.43 ERA in just 11-2/3 innings. He was sent down, pitched just as poorly, and was sent home in July. /(EG)

Billy Cox — 1919–1978. 3B-SS 1941, 46–55 Pirates, **Dodgers**, Orioles 1058 g, .262, 66 hr, 351 rbi. *3 WS, 15 g, .302, 1 hr, 6 rbi*

Cox is considered by many the greatest fielding third baseman prior to Brooks Robinson. After a brief ML fling in 1941 and four years of military service, Cox became the Pirates' starting shortstop in 1946 and hit .290 to lead the club. Despite his career-high 15 HR in 1947, Cox was traded with Preacher Roe and Gene Mauch to Brooklyn for 37-year-old Dixie Walker and pitchers Hal Gregg and Vic Lombardi. It was one of Pittsburgh's worst trades, and Branch Rickey's and the Dodgers' best. Cox held down third base in Brooklyn for seven seasons and three NL Championships. Casey Stengel said of him, "That ain't a third baseman. That's a f----g acrobat." He led the NL in fielding percentage in 1950 and '52. /(ME)

Bobby Cox — 1941– . 3B 1968–69 **Yankees** 220 g, .225, 9 hr, 58 rbi.
Manager 1978–85 Braves, **Blue Jays** 621–615, .502 First place: 85 *1 LCS, 3–4, .429*

Signed in 1959 for a $40,000 bonus, Cox spent seven years in the Dodger farm system and was Atlanta property before coming up to the Yankees. In 1968 he was the Topps rookie all-star third baseman despite hitting .229 with only seven HR. He lost his job to Bobby Murcer the next spring. After bad knees forced his retirement in 1971, he managed six years in the Yankee organization, was a New York coach in 1977, and managed the Braves from 1978 through 1981. He moved to the Blue Jays, winning *TSN* Manager of the Year honors when he led Toronto to their first division title in 1985. But Cox's strict platooning style allowed Royals manager Dick Howser to outmaneuver him in the LCS. After the season, Ted Turner lured Cox back to Atlanta as GM. /(MC)

Casey Cox — 1941– . RHP 1966–73 **Senators/ Rangers**, Yankees 761 ip, 39–42, 3.70

After three years as an effective reliever, 6'5" Casey Cox went 8–12 as a starter in 1970. Off to a 0–3 start in 1971, Cox asked Washington manager Ted Williams to return to the bullpen. He won five and saved seven, and Williams declared that "Casey might be the best righthanded relief pitcher in the league." Cox was out of the majors two years later. /(TJ)

Danny Cox (Coxie) — 1959– . RHP 1983–88 **Cardinals** 986 ip, 56–56, 3.40. *2 LCS, 23 ip, 2–1, .235. 2 WS, 26 ip, 1–2, 4.21*

Cox was a key ingredient in the Cardinals' 1985 pennant as he went 18–9 in just his second full season. Possessing only an average fastball, he relied heavily on a great change-up. He spent stretches on the disabled list in 1986, '87, most of 1988, and all of 1989 with bone chips, a broken foot, and tendinitis. /(FO)

Larry Cox — 1947– . C 1973–75, 77–82 Phillies, **Mariners**, Cubs, Rangers 348 g, .221, 12 hr, 85 rbi

In 1977 Cox was one of the original Mariners, serving as a backup catcher. Traded to the Cubs in 1978, he returned to Seattle in 1979 and spent two years as the regular catcher, hitting .215 and .202. /(NLM)

Ted Cox — 1955– . 3B-OF-DH 1977–81 Red Sox, **Indians**, Mariners, Blue Jays 272 g, .245, 10 hr, 79 rbi

The Red Sox drafted Cox number one in June 1973, ahead of Fred Lynn. He was the International League's MVP and all-star third baseman in 1977. After Boston called him up, Cox tied an AL record with four hits in his first full game in Baltimore on September 18. He extended the streak to six the next day against the Yankees, to set the mark for "most consecutive hits, start of career." When the season ended, he had hit .362 in 13 games. The following spring, Boston included Cox in a trade with Cleveland for Dennis Eckersley. Cox hit .233 in 1970 and never played regularly in the majors. /(EW)

Bob Coyne — 1898–1976. *Cartoonist.*

Before retiring in 1975 after a 47-year career, Coyne drew over 15,000 sports cartoons for several Boston newspapers. /(NLM)

Estel Crabtree (Crabby) — 1903–1967. OF 1929, 31–33, 41–44 **Reds**, Cardinals 489 g, .281, 13 hr, 142 rbi

An everyday outfielder with the Reds in 1931–32, Crabtree was buried in the St. Louis farm system after 1933. He came back up in 1941 as a 4-F wartime player, having lost a kidney due to an outfield collision. Crabtree was born in Crabtree, Ohio. /(JK)

Harry Craft — 1915– . OF 1937–42 **Reds** 566 g, .253, 44 hr, 267 rbi. *2 WS, 6 g, .083.*
Manager 1957–59, 61–64 A's, Reds, **Astros** 360–485, .426

In his day, it was said nobody played centerfield better than Harry Craft. His bat was adequate and he had fair power, but his glove and arm made him valuable on a Cincinnati team that won titles in 1939 and 1940 with stellar defense and superb pitching. Craft's disputed home run in the Polo Grounds in 1939 hastened the advent of foul pole screens. He managed a series of unsuccessful major league teams, including the expansion Houston Colt .45's, and never finished higher than seventh in seven seasons. /(JK)

Roger Craig — 1931– . RHP 1955–66 **Dodgers**, Giants, Cardinals, Reds, Phillies, Mets 1536 ip, 74–98, 3.83. *4 WS, 26 ip, 2–2, 6.49.*
Manager 1978–79, 85– Padres, **Giants** 423–404, .511. First place: 87, 89 *2 LCS, 7–5, .583. 1 WS, 0–4, .000*

In 1986 *Sports Illustrated* called Roger Craig "the acknowledged maestro of the split-fingered fastball."

In 1985 he taught the split-finger to the Astros' Mike Scott, who won the 1986 Cy Young award. Craig had previously managed the 1978–79 Padres and served as a scout and pitching coach, notably in Detroit, where he taught Jack Morris the split-finger. As a manager, Craig is noted for one-run tactics and for calling lots of pitchouts. He won the NL West title in 1987 and the NL pennant in 1989.

With the fledgling Mets in 1962–63, Craig became the first pitcher to lead the NL in losses two straight years (24 in 1962, 22 in 1963). He tied a league record in 1963 by dropping 18 straight decisions. Conversely, he tied for the NL lead with four shutouts for Los Angeles in 1959, and won two World Series games, one each with Brooklyn and St. Louis./(TJ)

Doc Cramer [Roger Maxwell] (Flit) — 1905– . OF 1929–48 A's, **Red Sox**, Senators, Tigers 2239 g, .296, 37 hr, 842 rbi *2 WS, 9 g, .387, 6 rbi*
☛ *All-Star—35, 37–40.*

Doc Cramer

An agile, swift centerfielder, Cramer led the AL in putouts in 1936 and 1938. He was considered to be one of the best judges of fly balls in the ML, and also owned an excellent arm. Offensively, he was a leadoff hitter who specialized in singles, topping the AL five times and tying for the lead in total hits (200) in 1940. Twice, he collected six hits in a game. In his career, he had 2,705 hits. He led the league in at-bats in seven different seasons, the ML record. At age 40, he was a hitting star for the Tigers in the 1945 WS, batting .379, scoring seven runs, and batting in four. Later, as a White Sox coach, he was credited with developing Nellie Fox as a hitter.

Cramer was a semi-pro pitcher when discovered by Cy Perkins and signed by the Athletics. Sent to Martinsburg of the Blue Ridge League in 1929, he was locked in a close race with Joe Vosmik for the league batting title. On the final day of the season, he pitched against Vosmik's team and walked his rival four times. Cramer's .404 won the title.

Cramer tied a ML record by going 6-for-6 in a nine-inning game, and is the only American Leaguer to do it twice (6/20/32 and 7/13/35). Towards the end of his career, he was frequently used as a pinch-hitter, and led the AL with nine pinch hits in 1947. Sent up six times for Birdie Tebbetts, Cramer came through four times, and when the Tigers traded Tebbetts to Boston, Cramer complained, "It's like tearing up my meal ticket. A game is not official until the announcement goes out 'Cramer for Tebbetts'."

Cramer gained medical knowledge before playing pro ball by observing a local doctor, and was therefore dubbed "Doc." Philadelphia sportswriter Jimmy Isaminger began calling him "Flit", after the insecticide, because the outfielder was death to fly balls./(NLM/JK)

Del Crandall — 1930- . C 1949–50, 53–66 **Braves,** Giants, Pirates, Indians 1573 g, .254, 179 hr, 657 rbi. *2 WS, 13 g, .227, 2 hr, 4 rbi.*
   Manager 1972–75, 83–84 **Brewers,** Mariners 364–469, .437
☛ *All-Star—53–56, 58–60, 62. Gold Glove—58–60, 62.*

"Crandall was a hell of a defensive catcher," Hank Aaron recalled. Joe Adcock said Crandall "couldn't hit with Campanella, but strictly as a catcher he was the best." Crandall replaced Walker Cooper as the Braves' regular catcher and captain and led NL backstops in fielding four times, winning four Gold Gloves. He appeared in eight All-Star games, homering in one; he also homered in both the 1957 and '58 WS, and three times collected over 20 HR in a season. After a shoulder problem sidelined him for most of 1961, Crandall batted a career-high .297 in 1962. Twenty years later, he managed Albuquerque (Pacific Coast League) to a remarkable 94–38 record, but in six years managing the Brewers and Mariners finished no higher than fifth. Crandall joined the White Sox broadcast team in 1985. /(TJ)

Doc Crandall [James Otis] — 1887–1951. RHP-2B 1908–16, 18 **Giants,** Cardinals, St. Louis (FL), Browns, Braves 1546 ip, 101–62, 2.92; 500 g, .285, 9 hr, 126 rbi. *20 wins: 15 3 WS, 10 ip, 1–0, 1.69*

Crandall was the first pitcher to be used consistently as a reliever. Damon Runyon nicknamed him "Doc," calling him "the physician of the pitching emergency." Crandall started often, but led the league in relief appearances five seasons in a row with the Giants. He led in relief victories from 1910 through 1912, during which time he went 45–16 overall, helping the Giants win three pennants in 1911–13. A nimble fielder despite his bulky frame, he filled in at infield positions. The .285 lifetime hitter also pinch hit often. When he was sent to the Cardinals in 1913, the displeasure in New York was so great that the Giants repurchased him after two games. But he wound up in St. Louis the following year, in the Federal League, spending more games at second base than on the mound. He led the Federal League in 1915 with 6 relief wins among his 21 victories. /(JK)

Cannonball Crane [Edward Nicholas] — 1862–1896. RHP-OF-C 1884–86, 88–93 **Boston (UA),** Providence (NL), Buffalo (NL), Washington (NL), Giants, New York (PL), Cincinnati-Milwaukee (AA), Reds, Dodgers 391 g, .238, 18 hr, 84 rbi; 1550 ip, 72–95, 3.99
☛ *Led League—era 91.*

As a rookie outfielder/catcher in 1884, Crane ranked second in the Union Association with 12 HR. By 1888 he had completed a transition to pitcher, and in 1891 led the American Association with a 2.45 ERA for Cincinnati/Milwaukee. Crane enjoyed only one winning season, and twice lost more than 20 games. He comitted suicide by drinking acid. /(FIC)

Sam Crane (Red) — 1894–1955. SS 1914–17, 20–22 A's, Senators, **Reds,** Dodgers 174 g, .208, 0 hr, 30 rbi

Crane was a light-hitting shortstop who continually impressed with brilliant play in the minors. He never won a permanent place until he was convicted of killing his girlfriend and her male companion in a hotel bar; he then secured a long-term position as SS on the prison team. /(JK)

Alfred R. Cratty — Unk.–Unk. *Writer.*

Cratty created the baseball and sporting department of the Pittsburgh *Chronicle-Telegraph* in 1885 and held that desk until he left in 1906 to enter medical school. He later returned to work for the Pittsburgh *Press.* He was an early correspondent for *The Sporting Life.* /(NLM)

Gavvy Cravath [Clifford Carlton] (Cactus) — 1881–1963. OF 1908–09, 12–20 Red Sox, White Sox, Senators, **Phillies** 1219 g, .287, 119 hr, 719 rbi. *1 WS, 5 g, .125, 1 rbi.*
   Manager 1919–20 **Phillies** 91–137, .399
☛ *Led League—hr 13–15, 17–19. Led League—rbi 13, 15.*

Cravath was the home run king of the deadball era. He set marks Babe Ruth would break soon after with the introduction of the lively ball. The tobacco-chewing, cussing bruiser was called "Cactus" for his prickly personality.
   Cravath was a sensation in the Pacific Coast League and the American Association. In between, he failed with the Red Sox, White Sox, and Senators. Given a second chance with the Phillies at age 31, he bloomed. In 1913 he led the NL with 19 HR and 128 RBI—35 more than runner-up Heinie Zimmerman. His league-high 179 hits gave him a .341 average, his career best. Over the next six years he won five more HR titles, with a high of 24 in 1915, when he repeated as RBI champ. That August 8, he tied a ML record with four doubles in a game. He won the 1919 NL HR crown with 12 in only 83 games.
   A gruff player, Cravath proved too easygoing as a manager, lasting just a season and a half at the Phillies helm. He frequently used himself off the

Gavvy Cravath with the Phillies

bench, and had a league-high 12 pinch hits in 1920. The California native became a justice of the peace in Laguna, but lost his job for being too easygoing./(JK)

Jerry Crawford — 1947– . *Umpire* NL 1977–87
3 LCS

A second-generation NL umpire, Jerry joined the NL staff in 1977, a year after his father, Shag Crawford, retired. Jerry's brother Joe umpired briefly in the minors before becoming an NBA referee./(RTM)

Jim Crawford (Catfish) — 1950– . LHP 1973, 1975–78 Astros, **Tigers** 432 ip, 15–28, 4.40

Crawford, most often used in relief, debuted with the 1973 Astros, saving six games. Traded to Detroit in a 1975 seven-player deal, he won a career-high seven games in 1977./(TJ)

Sam Crawford (Wahoo Sam) — 1880–1968. OF-1B 1899–1917 Reds, **Tigers** 2517 g, .309, 97 hr, 1525 rbi.
3 WS, 17 g, .243, 1 hr, 6 rbi
☛ *Led League—hr 01, 08. Led League—rbi 10, 14–15. Hall of Fame—1957.*

Crawford is most famous for hitting triples, 312 of them over a 19-year career, first on the all-time list. Second on the all-time triples list is Ty Cobb, who batted third in front of Crawford for the Tigers following the birth of the American League. The order is ironic because although the two were teammates, and often pulled off some uniquely synchronized double steals, the normally easy-going Crawford despised the fiery Cobb.

Crawford was nicknamed Wahoo Sam after his birthplace, Wahoo, Nebraska. A former barber, Crawford started out with the Cincinnati Reds in 1899 and hit a then-astounding total of 16 HR in 1901. In 1903 he jumped to the Tigers and led the American League in triples with 25. What is often forgotten about Crawford was his power to drive the ball over fences as well as between fielders; he hit 97 career HR, and at his retirement held the AL career record with 70. In 1908, Crawford led the AL in homers with seven, and so became the only player in baseball history to lead both leagues in homers.

Although they disliked each other, Cobb and Crawford worked closely together on the bases. Cobb, either by steals or by a triple, would often be standing at third when Crawford came to bat. Crawford was often walked. Crawford would jaunt easily to first and then, on cue from Cobb, switch into high gear and take off for second. At the same time, Cobb would break for home. "Sometimes they'd get him," Crawford would later recall, "sometimes they'd get me, and sometimes they wouldn't get either of us."

Once Cobb started winning batting titles regularly, fellow lefthanded hitter Crawford began to drive in more than 100 runs a season, leading the league three times in RBI in the 1910s. But, like Cobb, Crawford could find no success in the World Series. The duo's failures at the bat were the main reasons why the Tigers lost three straight Series in

Sam Crawford

1907, 1908, and 1909. Crawford's one shining World Series moment came in Game Five of the 1909 affair when he went 3-for-4 with a double and a homer, but the Tigers lost the game, 8–4, and the Series to Pittsburgh. Crawford ended his career 36 hits shy of 3,000 in 1917, then umpired in the Pacific Coast League for four years. /(SEW)

Shag Crawford — 1921– . *Umpire* NL 1956–75 *2 LCS 3 WS, 3 ASU*

Crawford caught briefly in the Phillies' organization, then umpired around the Philadelphia area to stay in the game. His slow, deliberate, strong calls and low crouch while touching the catcher's back with his hands characterized his umpiring style. One of

the founders of the ML Umpires' Association, Crawford was asked to work the 1975 WS by umpire supervisor Fred Fleig. Shag refused because it had been agreed that the Series would use a rotation system for umpires. According to Crawford, he was fired for his refusal. "They said they retired me," he said, "but in my personal opinion, they dumped me." /(RTM)

Steve Crawford — 1958– . RHP 1980–82, 84–87, 89 **Red Sox**, Royals 436 ip, 22–17, 3.98. *1 LCS, 2 ip, 1–0, 0.00. 1 WS, 4 ip, 1–0, 2.63*

A 6'5" 225-lb reliever with a menacing mustache but a straight fastball, Crawford won Game Five of the 1986 ALCS after escaping a bases-loaded, one-out jam in the bottom of the ninth, and won Game Two of the '86 WS in relief of Roger Clemens. /(SCL)

Willie Crawford — 1946– . OF 1964–77 **Dodgers**, Cardinals, Astros, A's 1210 g, .268, 86 hr, 419 rbi. *1 LCS, 2 g, .250, 0 hr, 1 rbi. 2 WS, 5 g, .375, 1 hr, 1 rbi*

Crawford never became the homegrown superstar the Dodgers anticipated when they signed him out of Los Angeles's Fremont High School for $100,000. In the majors at 17 and in the WS at 19, he struggled for consistency and eventually became a better-than-average player. In his best season, 1973, he hit .295, with 14 homers and 91 RBI. /(TG)

Robert Creamer — 1922– . *Writer.*

A senior editor at *Sports Illustrated* from 1954 to 1984, Creamer ghosted *Quality of Courage* for Mickey Mantle in 1964 and wrote *Jocko* with Jocko Conlan (1967), and *Rhubarb in the Catbird Seat* with Red Barber (1968). He was co-author of *The Yankees* (1979) and *Stengel: His Life and Times* (1984), and his 1974 book *Babe: The Legend Comes to Life* is considered the definitive biography of Babe Ruth. /(NLM)

Birdie Cree — 1882–1942. OF 1908–15 **Yankees** 742 g, .292, 11 hr, 332 rbi

The 5'6" 150-lb Cree spent three seasons as the regular leftfielder for the Highlanders (later called the Yankees), but ultimately spurned baseball in favor of banking. /(JK)

Keith Creel — 1959– . RHP 1982–83, 85, 87 **Royals**, Indians, Rangers 203 ip, 5–14, 5.60

A strong prospect after a 24–12 record his first two years in the Royals' organization, Creel never developed one potent, reliable pitch. His best opportunity came with pitching-poor Cleveland in 1985, but he lost his first five decisions. /(FO)

James Creighton — 1841–1862. RHP statistics not available

In baseball's early days, when pitchers were required to toss the ball underhand and stiff-armed (with the pitching wrist facing up), Creighton puzzled batters with the speed of his delivery, gained by a sly snap of the wrist. Believed to be baseball's first professional player and acclaimed in his obituary as "one of the best players in the Union," he starred for two Brooklyn clubs, Star and Excelsior, before his death at 21 of "an internal injury occasioned by strain while batting." /(FIC)

Creepy Crespi [Frank Angelo Joseph] — 1918– . 2B-SS 1938–42 **Cardinals** 264 g, .263, 4 hr, 88 rbi. *1 WS, 1 g, --*

This St. Louis native climbed quickly up the Cardinal ladder. Crespi was among the top-rated second basemen in 1941, his first successful major league season. Unfortunately, an army camp accident put a sudden end to his promising career. In 1943 he broke his left leg playing army baseball, then broke it again in another place when he crashed into a wall in a wheelchair race. /(EW)

Tim Crews — 1961– . RHP 1987– **Dodgers** 162 ip, 5–2, 3.05

Crews came to the Dodgers with Tim Leary from Milwaukee in exchange for Greg Brock. The reliever's 4–0, 3.14 record helped the 1988 Dodgers win their World Championship. /(JFC)

Jerry Crider — 1941– . RHP 1969–70 Twins, **White Sox** 119 ip, 5–7, 4.51

Crider, a junkballer, was a mediocre spot starter and long relief man for the pitching-thin 1970 White Sox. In one performance against the Red Sox, Crider allowed a game-winning home run off the bat of Vicente Romo, Boston's relief pitcher. It was the only homer of Romo's eight-year career. /(RL)

Lou Criger — 1872–1934. C 1896–1910, 1912 Cleveland (NL), Cardinals, **Red Sox**, Browns, Yankees 1012 g, .221, 11 hr, 342 rbi. *1 WS, 8 g, .231, 4 rbi*

Small and agile, light-hitting Lou Criger lasted 16 years in the majors because of his ability as a catcher. Beginning in 1896, he was the batterymate of Cy Young in Cleveland and St. Louis of the National League, and Boston in the American League. Criger caught most of Young's 511 victories; the two played together until Criger's December 1908 trade to the Browns. During the first World

Series, played in 1903 between the Boston Pilgrims (later the Red Sox) and Pirates, gamblers offered Criger a bribe to throw the games. Criger spurned it, and caught every inning of the eight games in the Boston victory. /(JK)

Chuck Crim — 1961– . RHP 1987– **Brewers** 357 ip, 22–21, 3.16

Crim was a last-minute, non-roster invitee to the Brewers' 1987 camp, but made the club with a 1.08 spring ERA. He was a set-up man and spot starter until becoming a closer, saving 12 games, after Dan Plesac hurt his elbow. Back in middle relief thereafter, he led the AL in appearances in 1988 and 1989. /(JCA)

Jack Crimian — 1926– . RHP 1951–52, 56–57 Cardinals, **A's**, Tigers 160 ip, 5–9, 6.36

Crimian was the International League MVP in 1955 when he went 19–6 for Toronto. He then failed in his only real major league shot, going 4–8 (5.51) for the 1956 A's. /(NLM)

Hughie Critz — 1900–1980. 2B 1924–35 **Reds**, Giants 1478 g, .268, 38 hr, 531 rbi. *1 WS, 5 g, .136*

The son of respected professor Colonel Critz of Mississippi A&M, 5'8" 147-lb Hughie, like his father, captained the school's baseball team. In his first game with the Reds Critz had two hits against Grover Alexander and hit .322 in 102 games as a rookie. Critz topped NL second basemen in fielding four times and double plays three times. /(JK)

Warren Cromartie — 1953– . OF-1B 1974, 76–83 **Expos** 1038 g, .280, 60 hr, 371 rbi. *1 LCS, 5 g, .167, 2 rbi*

Cromartie, Ellis Valentine, and Andre Dawson formed what Expos announcer Duke Snider termed "the best young outfield" he'd ever seen in 1977–79. Only Dawson really lived up to Snider's billing. Cromartie always hustled but was erratic, prone to long slumps, and was not a power hitter. Extremely popular in Montreal, he hit .304 in 1981 as the Expos won their only division title, then skidded to .254 in '82. After being platooned in '83, he signed with the Yomiuri Giants of the Japan Central League. A great success in Japan, he hit over 30 home runs in each of his first three seasons while compiling good batting averages. /(MC)

Ray Crone — 1931– . RHP 1954–58 **Braves**, Giants 546 ip, 30–30, 3.87

A control pitcher, Crone beat the Cubs five times in going 10–9 for the 1955 Braves. He went to the Giants with Bobby Thomson in a 1957 trade for Red Schoendienst, but a sore arm finished him in 1958. /(MC)

Joe Cronin — 1906–1984. SS 1928–1945 Pirates, Senators, **Red Sox** 2124 g, .301, 170 hr, 1424 rbi. *1 WS, 5 g, .318, 2 rbi.*
   Manager 33–47, Senators, **Red Sox** 1236–1055, .540. First place: 33, 46 *2 WS, 4–8, .333*
☛ *All-Star—33–35, 37–39, 41. Hall of Fame—1956.*

For 14 years, Joe Cronin's signature appeared on all the baseballs used in the American League. But a far more interesting tidbit about this former American League president is that he was once sold by his uncle-in-law—not his father-in-law, as is often reported. Cronin was one of baseball's "boy wonder" managers when he piloted the 1933 Senators to an AL pennant at the age of 27, a year younger than Washington's first "boy wonder," Bucky Harris, was when he took Washington to its first pennant in 1924. It is often forgotten that the gentlemanly Cronin was one of the premier shortstops of his day, and knocked in more than 100 runs in a season eight times. He was also Carl Hubbell's fifth consecutive

Joe Cronin with the Senators

Hall of Fame strikeout victim in the 1934 All-Star game.

A former bank clerk, Cronin came up as a slow and clumsy shortstop for Pittsburgh. The Pirates had Arky Vaughan at shortstop, and in 1928 Cronin was dealt to Washington, where he bloomed. In 1930, his second full season, he had career highs in batting average (.346) and RBI (126), and *TSN* named him player of the year (1930 was the year before the baseball writers started electing regular MVPs). In 1933, Cronin was named player-manager by Washington owner Clark Griffith, and Cronin responded by guiding the Senators to their final World Series appearance. The Giants beat Cronin's club in five games, but Cronin batted .318.

The following year, Griffith introduced his young manager to his niece, Mildred Robertson, then a club secretary. The two were married later that year. But at the end of the 1934 season, Griffith sold his new nephew to the Red Sox for $225,000, the highest amount paid for a single player (Boston's sale of Babe Ruth was actually only for $125,000, with the remaining $300,000 being a personal loan from Yankee owner Ruppert to Red Sox owner Harry Frazee). Griffith arranged, however, for Cronin to receive a five-year contract good for $50,000 per year.

Cronin loved hitting in Fenway Park. Three times he registered slugging percentages over .500, with a career-high .536 in 1938, the year he led the AL in doubles with 51. He hit a career-high 24 HR in 1940, the year he also led the league in putouts and assists. Despite hitting .311 with 16 HR and 95 RBI in 1941, he took himself out of the regular lineup in 1942 to make room for a youngster named Johnny Pesky. He still pinch hit, though, setting a major league record of five pinch homers in 1943, including two in one day—one each in two ends of a doubleheader.

In early 1945 Cronin broke his leg, ending his playing career for good. He took the Red Sox to the World Series the following year, losing to the Cardinals on Enos Slaughter's dash home in the seventh game. He moved into the Red Sox front office in 1948 for 11 years, during which time he was elected to the Hall of Fame. In 1959, he was chosen American League president by the owners, the first former player so honored. In his two terms as AL president, he presided over the league's expansion from eight to ten teams in 1960, then to 12 teams in 1969. In 1970, he fired two umpires for "incompetency" when he learned they were trying to form a union. In his final year as president, he blocked George Steinbrenner's attempt to hire Dick Williams as manager, but allowed the Tigers to sign Ralph Houk away from Steinbrenner's Yankees. /(SEW)

John Cronin — 1874–1929. RHP 1895, 98–99, 01–04 **Dodgers**, Pirates, Reds, Tigers, Baltimore (AL), Giants 923 ip, 43–57, 3.40

Cronin pitched half of a rare doubleheader shutout by the Dodgers in 1904 in his second tour with the club. He retired when his 2.70 ERA that year, slightly below the league average, brought him only a 12–23 record. /(TG)

Ed Crosby — 1949– . SS-2B-3B 1970, 72–76 **Cardinals**, Reds, Indians 297 g, .220, 0 hr, 44 rbi. *1 LCS, 3 g, .500, 0 hr, 0 rbi*

Light-hitting Crosby played 101 games as a Cardinal utility infielder in 1972, the only season in which he played in more than half of his team's games. His .217 batting average kept him on the bench. After a trade to the Angels in December 1976, he refused to report and was granted free agency. He signed with the A's but was released before the '77 season began. /(MC)

Frankie Crosetti (The Crow) — 1910– . SS-3B 1932–48 **Yankees** 1682 g, .245, 98 hr, 649 rbi. *7 WS, 29 g, .174, 1 hr, 11 rbi*
☛ *All-Star—36, 39.*

Anchoring the Yankee infield for most of his 17 seasons, Crosetti was always among the fielding leaders. In 1938 and 1939 he led AL shortstops in putouts and double plays. He topped the league with 27 stolen bases in 1938, and his 757 plate appearances that year set a ML record for a 154-game season. He led the AL in HBP eight times.

One of the game's great sign-stealers, he was also a master of the hidden ball trick. In his 17 playing years, Crosetti was a member of nine AL Champion teams and eight World Champions. After retiring in 1948, he was the Yankee third-base coach for 20 years, and participated in 15 more World Series. His continuous Yankee service was the longest in the team's history. /(EW)

Crosley Field Cincinnati Reds 1912–70. LF-328, CF-387, RF-366

The scene of baseball's first ML night game on May 24, 1935, Crosley Field opened in 1912 as Redland Field, but was renamed when Powell Crosley bought the Reds in 1934. Originally 360′ down each line and 420′ to center, the park was open almost a

Frankie Crosetti

decade before Pat Duncan hit the first over-the-fence home run, on June 2, 1921. In January 1937 the park virtually disappeared when a massive flood covered it with over 20′ of water, and Reds pitchers Lee Grissom and Gene Schott posed for a wire-service photo rowing a boat over the center field fence. A billboard behind the left field fence advertised "Hit this sign and win a Seibler suit," which the Reds' Wally Post did a record 11 times. Crosley Field was abandoned by the Reds for Riverfront Stadium. The city of Cincinnati impounded towed cars there before it was torn down and then reconstructed on a Reds fan's farm in nearby Kentucky. /(SCL)

Powell Crosley, Jr. — 1887–1961. *Executive*
At the urging of GM Larry MacPhail, Crosley, an inventor and manufacturer of autos, refrigerators and radios, bought the Reds in 1934 for $450,000

so the team would stay in Cincinnati. Redland Field, the home of the Reds from 1912 to 1970, was renamed Crosley Field in his honor./(NLM)

Lave Cross [Lafayette Napoleon] — 1866–1927. 3B-C-OF-SS-2B 1887–1907 Louisville (AA), Philadelphia (AA), Philadelphia (PL), Phillies, St. Louis (NL), Cleveland (NL), Cardinals, Dodgers, **A's**, Senators 2275 g, .292, 47 hr, 1345 rbi. *1 WS, 5 g, .105.*
    Manager 1899 **Cleveland (NL)**, 8–30, .211

Cross was a bowlegged wonder, cheered by Philadelphia fans in four different major leagues. He was primarily a catcher the first part of his career. When he switched to infield positions, he played them (until the rules were changed) using his catcher's mitt. With the Phillies on August 5, 1897, he set a still-standing ML record for most assists by a second baseman in a game, with 15 (12 innings).

Lave Cross

Cross left Philadelphia in 1898 to become the everyday third baseman for St. Louis (NL). For the first 38 games of 1899, he managed the Cleveland Spiders (NL), who compiled the worst record in ML history—20–134. He returned to Philadelphia as a member of the Athletics in 1901, the first AL season. From April 23, 1902 until May 8, 1905, he played in 447 consecutive games, all but one at third base. For seven straight seasons (1898–1904) he never batted below .290. Lave's brother, Amos, was a catcher for Louisville (AA) in 1885–87, and another brother, Frank, played one game for Cleveland (AL) in 1901./(JK)

Monte Cross — 1869–1934. SS 1892, 1894–1907 Baltimore (NL), Pirates, Cardinals, Phillies, **A's** 1681 g, .234, 31 hr, 621 rbi. *1 WS, 5 g, .176*

After stints with the Orioles, Pirates, and Cardinals, Cross became the Phillies' regular shortstop in 1898. Connie Mack, his former Pirate manager, lured Cross to the A's in the fledgling American League. Cross topped AL shortstops in putouts in 1902 and 1903. In the NL, he had led shortstops four times in putouts, twice in assists, and three times in errors./(TJ)

Frank Croucher (Dingle) — 1914–1980. SS-2B 1939–42 **Tigers**, Senators 296 g, .251, 7 hr, 86 rbi. *1 WS, 1 g, --*

A good fielder but a light hitter, Croucher missed the 1938 season with a broken leg but earned the Tigers' shortstop job in 1941 and hit a respectable .254. Traded to the Senators, he was out most of 1942 with a sore arm, then went into military service, ending his playing career./(NLM)

Buck Crouse [Clyde] — 1897–1983. C 1923–30 **White Sox** 470 g, .262, 8 hr, 160 rbi

The tobacco-chewing, drawling Crouse was a reliable backup for Hall of Fame catcher Ray Schalk. It was Crouse who said to the scholarly Moe Berg, "Moe, I don't care how many of those degrees you got, they ain't learned you to hit the curveball no better than me." In 1937, Crouse was International League MVP, leading Baltimore to the playoffs as player-manager./(DB)

General Crowder [Alvin] — 1899–1972. RHP 1926–36 **Senators**, Browns, Tigers 2344 ip, 167–115, 4.12. 20 wins: 28, 32–33 *3 WS, 26 ip, 1–2, 3.81*
☛ *Led League—w 32–33. All-Star—33.*

The 5'10" Crowder topped the AL in winning percentage for the Browns in 1928 (21–5, .808). In

1930 St. Louis traded him with Heinie Manush for Goose Goslin of the Senators. Crowder led the AL in wins with Washington in 1932 (26–13) and 1933 (24–15). Selected to play in the first All-Star Game in '33, he hurled three innings for the victorious AL. Pitching for the Tigers in Game Four of the 1935 World Series, Crowder beat the Cubs 2–1; Detroit took the Series in six games. His nickname came from General Enoch Crowder, originator of America's WWI draft lottery. /(TJ)

George Crowe — 1923– . 1B 1952–53, 55–61 **Braves, Reds,** Cardinals 702 g, .270, 81 hr, 299 rbi ☛ All-Star—58.

This Negro Leaguer played pro basketball as a center and forward for Dayton of the NBL before joining the Boston Braves. The 6'2" 210-lb left-handed batter supplied ten of Cincinnati's league record-tying 221 homers in 1956. As the Reds' regular first baseman, Crowe hit 31 HR in 1957, and was an All-Star in 1958. But Crowe was traded to St. Louis, where Stan Musial was manning first in 1959; Crowe, instead, led the NL with 17 pinch hits. /(TJ)

Terry Crowley — 1947– . DH-OF-1B 1969–83 **Orioles,** Reds, Braves, Expos 865 g, .250, 42 hr, 229 rbi. *3 LCS, 5 g, .250, 1 rbi. 3 WS, 8 g, .286, 2 rbi*

Crowley retired sixth all-time in both pinch hits (108) and pinch at-bats (419), with a .258 lifetime pinch average. The highlight of his career was a 9th-inning pinch grand slam against the Royals on August 8, 1982, giving the Orioles a 10–6 victory.

The lefthanded-hitting Crowley bounced between Baltimore and Rochester (International League) for his first five seasons, pinch hitting and filling in in the outfield. He moved increasingly to pinch hitting with the Reds in 1974. Back in Baltimore in 1977, Crowley hit .364 down the stretch. He pinch-hit .342 in 1978 and hit .317 in 1979. Crowley's best year, however, was 1980: 12 HR, 50 RBI, and a .288 average in 233 at-bats, including a .338 average with men in scoring position and a league-leading .297 pinch-hitting average. Crowley has worked as a major and minor league batting instructor. /(MC)

Walt Cruise — 1890–1975. OF 1914, 16–24 Cardinals, **Braves** 736 g, .277, 30 hr, 272 rbi

A journeyman major leaguer for parts of ten seasons, Cruise hit .346 in 108 games in 1921 and was the right fielder for the Braves in the 26-inning 1–1 tie played against Brooklyn on May 1, 1920. He scored the Boston run when his triple, his only hit in nine at-bats, was followed by Tony Boeckel's single. Cruise was married at home plate in Cincinnati between games of a double-header. He did not play in the nightcap. /(NLM)

James Crusinberry — 1879–1960. *Writer*

Crusinberry broke in with the Chicago *Chronicle* in 1903 and worked for newspapers in Chicago, St. Louis, and New York before a long stay with the Chicago *Daily News.* While working for the Chicago *Tribune* in 1920, he played a considerable part in bringing to light the facts about the fixed World Series of 1919. A charter member of the BBWAA, he was its president in 1929–30. He was later a radio sports commentator for CBS until his retirement in 1948. /(NLM)

Jimmie Crutchfield [John W.] — 1910– . OF Negro Leagues 1930–45 Birmingham Black Barons, Indianapolis ABC's, **Pittsburgh Crawfords,** Newark Eagles, Toledo Crawfords, Indianapolis Crawfords, Chicago American Giants, Cleveland Buckeyes 315 g, .266, 5 hr (inc.) ☛ All-Star—34–36, 41.

The 5'7" 150-lb righthanded-hitting Crutchfield was an excellent bat-handler, a fast runner, and a reliable outfielder. He batted .286 his rookie year for the 1930 Birmingham Black Barons, and in 1931 he moved to the Indianapolis ABC's and batted .330, believed to be his career high. When the financially troubled ABC's were unable to pay most of their players, Crutchfield jumped to the Pittsburgh Crawfords, with whom he stayed for five years, making the squad for the East-West all-star game three times. He played for the Newark Eagles in 1937, and though statistics are not available for his 1938–43 seasons, the hustling Crutchfield made the all-star team in 1941 as a member of the Chicago American Giants. /(JM)

Hector Cruz (Heity) — 1953– . OF-3B 1973, 75–82 **Cardinals,** Cubs, Giants, Reds 624 g, .225, 39 hr, 200 rbi. *1 LCS, 2 g, .200*

The younger brother of Jose and Tommy Cruz, who also wore Cardinal uniforms, Hector was signed out of Puerto Rico at age 17 and immediately heralded as the best of the three. In 1975 he was *TSN* Minor League Player of the Year, leading the American Association with 29 HR and 116 RBI. Converted from outfield to third base, he stuck with St. Louis in 1976 and led NL rookies with 13 HR and 71 RBI, but led NL third basemen with 26 errors. He never held another regular job. After bouncing around the NL, he played in Japan for Yomiuri in 1983. /(MC)

Jose Cruz — 1947– . OF-DH 1970–88 Cardinals, **Astros**, Yankees 2353 g, .284, 165 hr, 1077 rbi. *2 LCS, 11 g, .268, 6 rbi*
☛ *All-Star—80, 85.*

With quiet consistency and everyday play, Jose Cruz became one of the all-time Astro greats. Popular with Houston fans, he was one of three brothers to make the majors, along with Hector and Tommy. All three played in the St. Louis farm system, with Jose graduating to the Cardinals in 1970. He never blossomed alongside Lou Brock in the St. Louis outfield and was sold to Houston after the 1974 season. He became a fixture in the Astros' outfield and was their MVP in 1977, '80, '83, and '84. Hurt by the dimensions of the Astrodome and the fact that the ball doesn't carry well there, he led Houston in RBI seven times and in all Triple Crown catego-

Jose Cruz

ries in 1979 and '84 but received little recognition elsewhere.

Though he did not start on Opening Day in 1986 for the first time in a decade, Cruz was a key contributor to the Astros' division title, finishing second on the club in game-winning RBI. But he slumped badly in the LCS, a sharp contrast to his 1980 LCS performance which included a .400 average, four RBI, and eight walks. Few players appeared in more major league games without reaching the World Series than Cruz.

Cruz's reputation was dimmed by the effect of his home parks on his power stats; from 1975 through 1985, he had 80 HR on the road, but just 35 in the Astrodome. However, he hit .300 six times and stole as many as 44 bases (1977) while topping 30 steals in five years. And the lefthanded-hitting Puerto Rican had more games played, at-bats, hits, triples, and RBI than any player in Astros history. /(ME)

Julio Cruz — 1954– . 2B 1977–86 **Mariners**, White Sox 1156 g, .237, 23 hr, 279 rbi. *1 LCS, 4 g, .333*

Cruz was drafted by the expansion Mariners. A Gold Glove winner in 1978, he missed one-third of the next season with a torn ligament in his left thumb. Injuries also sidelined him for two months or more in '80 and '81, but he still stole more than 40 bases each year. With Willie Wilson, Cruz shares the AL record with 32 consecutive successful stolen base attempts. On June 7, 1981, he set an AL record for second basemen (and tied the ML record) with 18 total chances without an error in nine innings. The game went 11 innings and he handled one more chance to fall one short of the ML record. /(NLM)

Todd Cruz — 1955– . SS-3B 1978–80, 82–84 Phillies, Royals, Angels, White Sox, **Mariners**, Orioles 544 g, .220, 34 hr, 154 rbi. *1 LCS, 4 g, .133, 1 rbi. 1 WS, 5 g, .125*

Despite showing some home run power (16 homers in 1982), Cruz didn't hit enough to hold a regular ML job. A lower back injury and broken hand cost him the entire 1981 season. In 1982 and until they were both traded in mid-1983, he and unrelated Julio Cruz formed a "Cruz-and-Cruz" doubleplay combination for the Mariners. /(NLM)

Victor Cruz — 1957– . RHP 1978–81, 83 Blue Jays, **Indians**, Pirates, Rangers 271 ip, 18–23, 3.08

Cruz was Blue Jays Rookie of the Year and co-Rookie Pitcher of the Year in 1978 (7–3, 1.72, 9 saves). The pot-bellied righthander was then traded to Cleveland for infielders Alfredo Griffin and Phil Lansford. Continually fighting weight problems,

Cruz did not fulfill expectations in Cleveland and received little opportunity in Pittsburgh or Texas. /(ME)

Mike Cubbage (Cubbie) — 1950- . 3B-1B 1974-81 Rangers, **Twins**, Mets 703 g, .258, 34 hr, 251 rbi

After short trials with Texas, the bespectacled red-head went to Minnesota in a 1976 trade for Bert Blyleven. In 115 games at third base in 1978, Cubbage set a Twins fielding record (.971), batted a career-high .282, and hit for the cycle. He also filled in at first base, second base, and DH until 1980. Plagued by back miseries, Cubbage finished with the Mets as the NL's most active and successful pinch hitter in 1981 (12 for 44). He later became a manager in the Mets' farm system. /(MC)

Tony Cuccinello (Chick) — 1907- . 2B-3B 1930-40, 1942-45 Reds, **Dodgers**, Braves, Giants, White Sox 1704 g, .280, 94 hr, 884 rbi
☛ *All-Star—33, 38.*

As a rookie third baseman with Cincinnati, Cuccinello batted .312, and then spent nearly a decade as a regular at second base. He hit .300 four more times, and led NL second basemen in assists and double plays three times each. He pinch-hit for Carl Hubbell in the inaugural 1933 All-Star Game. "I'm the most surprised guy in baseball," said Cuccinello upon his release from the White Sox in January 1946, but with WWII over and younger players returning, Chicago cut the 38-year-old. He had finished the 1945 season at .308, one point behind NL leader Snuffy Stirnweiss's .309. Cuccinello did return to the Sox in 1957 as a coach under former teammate Al Lopez. Tony's younger brother, Al, spent one season with the Giants. /(TJ)

Mike Cuellar — 1937- . RHP 1959, 64-77 Reds, Cardinals, Astros, **Orioles**, Angels 2808 ip, 185-130, 3.14. 20 wins: 69-71, 74 *5 LCS, 44 ip, 2-2, 3.07. 3 WS, 41 ip, 2-2, 2.61*
☛ *Cy Young Award—69. All-Star—67, 71.*

Cuellar hurled a no-hitter for Cuban dictator Fulgencio Batista's Army team in 1955, at age 18. Allowed to sign with the Havana Sugar Kings of the International League two years later, he struck out seven straight batters in his very first game and had a 2.44 ERA.

Cuellar bounced from team to team in the high minors before he earned a promotion to the Cardinals and helped them win the 1964 pennant. He was on the World Series roster but did not get into a game. Back in the minors, Cuellar perfected a devastating palmball and was 9-1, 2.51 when dealt to Houston. In 1966, his first full year in the major leagues, Cuellar finished second in NL ERA, behind Sandy Koufax. He won a then-club-record 16 games in 1967, fanning 203. After the 1968 season, the Astros swapped Cuellar to Baltimore for Curt Blefary, at that point a highly regarded young power hitter.

Cuellar tied Denny McLain for AL Cy Young honors with a 23-11, 2.38 performance, then in the World Series was the only Oriole to beat the Mets. He led the AL with 24 wins and 21 complete games in 1970, capping the year by hitting a wind-blown grand slam off Jim Perry in the LCS against the Twins. Cuellar was 20-9 in 1971, as four Oriole starters won at least 20 that year. After winning 18 games in both 1972 and 1973, Cuellar enjoyed his last great season in 1974: 22-10, with a league-leading .688 winning percentage. At age 42 in 1979, two years after finishing up in the majors, Cuellar attempted a comeback, compiling a 7-6 record with three clubs in the Inter-American and Mexican Leagues. /(MC)

Leon Culberson — 1919- . OF 1943-48 **Red Sox**, Senators 370 g, .266, 14 hr, 131 rbi. *1 WS, 5 g, .222, 1 hr, 1 rbi*

Culberson had his highest BA in 1946 (.313) with the Red Sox. In that year's World Series, filling in for Dom DiMaggio, Culberson scooped up Harry Walker's single and threw it in to shortstop Johnny Pesky. When Pesky paused, Cardinal Enos Slaughter completed his dash home from first with the Series-winning run. /(TJ)

Tim Cullen — 1942- . 2B-SS 1966-72 **Senators**, White Sox, A's 700 g, .220, 9 hr, 134 rbi. *1 LCS, 2 g, .000*

On August 30, 1969 with the Senators, Cullen tied a ML record for second basemen by committing three errors in one inning. In 1970 he led AL second basemen with a .994 fielding percentage. The San Francisco native's best batting average came as a utility man in his last season, when he hit .261 across the bay in Oakland. /(TJ)

Roy Cullenbine — 1915- . OF-1B 1938-47 **Tigers**, Dodgers, Browns, Senators, Indians 1181 g, .276, 110 hr, 599 rbi. *2 WS, 12 g, .244, 6 rbi*
☛ *All-Star—41, 43.*

"Cullenbine wouldn't swing the bat," Bill Dewitt, a Browns official, later recalled. True, Cullenbine drew 852 walks in ten seasons, including an AL-leading 112 with Cleveland and Detroit in 1945. But he also swung well enough to twice bat .300, and hit 24 HR for the 1947 Tigers. Cullenbine was with three teams in 1942, ending up with the AL Champion Yankees. /(TJ)

Dick Culler — 1915-1964. SS-3B-2B 1936, 43-49 A's, White Sox, **Braves**, Cubs, Giants 472 g, .244, 2 hr, 99 rbi

An all-conference basketball player at High Point (NC) College, Culler became a good fielder but was a light hitter. His only service as a ML regular came with the Braves in 1945-46, when he also did his best hitting (.262, .255). /(NLM)

Nick Cullop [Henry Nicholas] (Tomato Face) — 1900-1978. OF 1926-27, 29-31 Yankees, Senators, Indians, Dodgers, **Reds** 173 g, .249, 11 hr, 67 rbi

Cullop was a good-fielding, power-hitting outfielder who set the minor league career record with 1857 RBI. In the best of his several ML trials, he hit eight homers in 104 games for Cincinnati in 1931; he also struck out 84 times to lead the league. He was *TSN* Minor League Manager of the Year in 1943 with Columbus and in 1947 with Milwaukee (both in the American Association). /(LRD)

Ray Culp — 1941- . RHP 1963-73 Phillies, Cubs, **Red Sox** 1897 ip, 122-101, 3.58
☛ *All-Star—63, 69.*

Culp signed with Philadelphia for $100,000 in 1959. As *TSN* NL Rookie Pitcher of the Year four years later, he led the Phillies with 14 victories, and posted a second 14-victory season in 1965. Often plagued by arm troubles, he slumped in 1966 and was traded to the Cubs. Dealt to Boston after one mediocre season, in 1968 he began using a palm ball and went 16-6, which included four straight shutouts. He won 17 games each of the next two seasons. On May 11, 1970, he struck out the first six batters he faced, tying the AL record. /(TJ)

George Culver — 1943- . RHP 1966-74 Indians, Reds, Cardinals, **Astros**, Dodgers, Phillies 788 ip, 48-49, 3.62

Signed by the Yankees, Culver struck out 18 in one of his first pro games. A starter with the Reds in 1968, he no-hit Philadelphia on July 29, walking five, to win 6-1. From 1970 on, he was a long reliever, and often led his club in appearances. Culver became a coach and manager in the Phillie system. /(MC)

John Cumberland — 1947- . LHP 1968-72, 74 Yankees, **Giants**, Cardinals, Angels 334 ip, 15-16, 3.82.
1 LCS, 3 ip, 0-1, 9.00

Cumberland came out of the Giants' bullpen in June 1971 to post a 9-6, 2.92 record as San Francisco's third starter in their drive to the division title. He was sold to St. Louis after starting 1972 0-4, and arm miseries ended his career. /(MC)

Candy Cummings [William Arthur] — 1848-1924. RHP 1872-77 **New York (NA)**, Baltimore (NA), Philadelphia (NA), Hartford (NA), Hartford (NL), Cincinnati (NL) *NA*: 124-72; *ML*: 372 ip, 21-22, 2.78
☛ *Hall of Fame—39.*

Cummings is generally credited with having invented the curveball. He maintained he came up with the idea as a 14-year-old in 1863 while watching the flight of clam shells he was throwing on a New England beach. Years of experimentation followed as he perfected the twisting pitch, and discovered that it worked best when thrown into the wind. He wore a kid glove on his pitching hand to prevent blisters, and once broke his wrist throwing the pitch. The 5'9" 120-lb Cummings felt he needed the advantage of the deceptive curveball because he was small even as an adult. His fame spread on the amateur diamond as he earned the nickname "Candy," a term of admiration.

Widely sought after by National Association clubs, Cummings performed for four different teams in as many years. In the NA, he never won fewer than 28 games a season. When the National League was formed in 1876, Cummings won 16 games for the Hartford Blues, and on September 9 he became the first major leaguer to pitch two complete games in one day. In 1877 he was appointed president of baseball's first minor league, the International Association, and performed as player-president. Pitching for Cincinnati (NL), he had lost his stuff and was soundly criticized by the press and fans.

The often conflicting testimony of 19th-century pitchers adds to the mystery surrounding the curveball's origin. One pitcher would claim to be the inventor, only to credit someone else years later. Because of Candy's 1908 article, "How I Pitched the First Curve," and the support of highly respected baseball writer Henry Chadwick, Cummings's claim has gained greatest backing. Another pitcher receiving support has been major leaguer Fred Goldsmith, who made the first recorded public demonstration of the curveball on August 16, 1870. Legend has it that Goldsmith, embittered at not receiving "official"

Candy Cummings with the Brooklyn Star

credit as the pitch's inventor, was found on his deathbed clutching a faded newspaper clipping of his demonstration. The heartbroken Goldsmith died in 1939—the year Cummings joined the Hall of Fame. /(DB)

Joseph Cummings — Unk.-Unk. *Writer.*

One of the first baseball writers to travel with a club, Cummings covered the Orioles of the 1890s for several Baltimore papers before succeeding Joe Flanner as editor of *The Sporting News*. /(NLM)

Bert Cunningham [Ellsworth Elmer] — 1865-1952. RHP 1887-91, 1895-1901 Brooklyn (AA), Baltimore (AA), Philadelphia (PL), Buffalo (PL), **Louisville (NL)**, Cubs 2727 ip, 142-167, 4.22. 20 wins: 88, 98

On August 20, 1890, Cunningham pitched two complete games for last-place Buffalo (Union Association), defeating Chicago 6-2 and 7-0. He went 28-15 as Louisville's top starter in 1898. /(JK)

Bill Cunningham — 1896-1960. *Writer.*

Cunningham, a popular radio commentator and after-dinner speaker throughout New England, served two 19-year hitches as a sportswriter and columnist in Boston. He was with the *Post* from 1922 to 1941, and then the *Herald* until 1960. /(NLM)

Bill Cunningham — 1895-1953. OF 1921-24 **Giants**, Braves 318 g, .286, 9 hr, 112 rbi. *2 WS, 8 g, .176, 3 rbi*

Cunningham was a gifted defensive centerfielder who patrolled the deep reaches of the Polo Grounds in the early 1920s. His acrobatic catch of Babe Ruth's 450-foot drive, after circling the Eddie Grant monument, saved Art Nehf's 1-0 shutout in Game Three of the 1923 WS. /(JK)

Bruce Cunningham — 1905-1984. RHP 1929-32 **Braves** 382 ip, 13-24, 4.64

Cunningham spent four mediocre seasons with the second-division Boston Braves. When a pinched nerve halted his pitching career, he became a homicide inspector, and later a private detective. /(JK)

George Cunningham — 1894-1972. RHP-OF 1916-19, 21 **Tigers** 162 g, .224, 1 hr, 13 rbi; 477 ip, 16-25, 3.13

As a young pitcher prone to shoulder trouble, Cunningham complained so much about the slump-ridden, injury-depleted Tiger outfield of 1918 that manager Hughie Jennings gave him the right-field job for three weeks. He did no better than the regulars. After his arm problems ended his pitching career in 1920, Cunningham worked on his hitting in the minors and returned to the Tigers as an outfielder for one game in 1921. /(MC)

Joe Cunningham — 1931- . 1B-OF 1954, 1956–66 Cardinals, White Sox, Senators 1141 g, .291, 64 hr, 436 rbi

☛ *All-Star—59.*

The articulate, lefthanded Cunningham hit three homers in his first two ML games. In his All-Star 1959 season, his .345 BA was second in the NL to Hank Aaron's .355. Describing Cunningham's 1962 season, when he led AL first basemen in fielding, Richard Lindberg wrote, "The balding first baseman made plays not seen since Joe Kuhel's time (1930s and '40s). . .after a game, Cunningham sat in a corner updating a little black book that he kept on each American League pitcher."/(TJ)

Mario Cuomo — 1932- . OF

Before entering law school and embarking on a political career, Cuomo played centerfield for the Class D Brunswick (Georgia) Pirates in 1952. He was hitting .353 when he injured his wrist in a collision with the outfield fence, and later spent two weeks in the hospital after being hit in the head with a pitch. He finished the season hitting .244 with one home run and 26 RBI in 81 games and retired from professional baseball. In 1976 Cuomo was elected Governor of New York, and in the late 1980s he was a proponent of bringing an expansion ML franchise to Buffalo./(SCL)

Nig Cuppy [George Joseph, born George Maceo Koppe] — 1869–1922. RHP 1892–1901 **Cleveland (NL)**, Cardinals, Braves, Red Sox 2284 ip, 162–98, 3.48. 20 wins: 92, 94–96

Cuppy and Cy Young provided a one-two punch that kept the Cleveland (NL) Spiders competitive during the mid-1890s. Cuppy was at his best as a rookie in 1892, going 28–13 (2.51). He was a 20-game winner again from 1894 through 1896, compiling a 75–43 record. He led the NL with three shutouts and eight relief wins in 1894. In those days, players who had dark skin were sometimes tagged with racist nicknames; Nig Cuppy may have been one./(AJA)

Clarence Currie — 1878–1941. RHP 1902–03 Reds, **Cardinals**, Cubs 364 ip, 14–23, 3.46

The Cardinals purchased Currie from the Reds in August of 1902, and he went 6–5 the rest of the season with the best ERA on the staff. In 1903 he struggled to 4–12 by mid-season and was sold to the Cubs./(FJO)

Cliff Curtis — 1883–1943. RHP 1909–13 **Braves**, Cubs, Phillies, Dodgers 745 ip, 28–61, 3.31

A starter with erratic control, Curtis began promisingly in his debut 1909 season, with a 1.41 ERA, eight complete games in nine starts, and the best winning percentage (.444) on the last-place Braves. The following year, he went 6–24./(MC)

Jack Curtis — 1937- . LHP 1961–63 **Cubs**, Braves, Indians 279 ip, 14–19, 4.84

Curtis finished third (behind Billy Williams and Joe Torre) in 1961 Rookie of the Year voting following his 10–13 season. Traded to Milwaukee for Bob Buhl the next year, Curtis finished with Cleveland in 1963./(TJ)

John Curtis — 1948- . LHP 1970–84 Red Sox, Cardinals, **Giants**, Padres, Angels 1641 ip, 89–97, 3.96

Curtis threw three no-hitters as a Clemson University freshman, and in the 1967 Pan American games he became the first U.S. pitcher to defeat Cuba. After going 11–8 and 13–13 for the Red Sox in 1972–73, he was traded to the Cardinals, who were in need of a lefthanded starter. He lasted another decade in the majors because of his adaptability; he started and worked in long and short relief, three times winning 10 games a season. While still active he worked as a sportswriter for the San Francisco *Examiner*./(FJO)

Robert W. Curtis — 1867–1939. *Writer.*

Curtis joined the sports department of the New York *Sun* in 1889 and was assigned to investigate the Brotherhood war and the Players' League. He scooped other reporters on the collapse of the league a year later. Before joining the *New York Times* in 1922, he worked for the *Recorder* and *Herald*./(NLM)

Guy Curtright — 1912- . OF 1943–46 **White Sox** 331 g, .276, 9 hr, 108 rbi

After earning his master's degree during a nine-year minor league apprenticeship, Curtright batted .291 and hit safely in 26 straight games as a rookie in 1943, his only season as a ML regular./(TJ)

George Cutshaw (Clancy) — 1887–1973. 2B 1912–23 **Dodgers**, Pirates, Tigers 1516 g, .265, 25 hr, 653 rbi. *1 WS, 5 g, .105, 2 rbi*

Cutshaw was voted the top defensive second baseman of 1910–20 by the Society for American Baseball Research. He led in putouts five times, assists four times, double plays twice, and fielding percentage three times. He batted cleanup and finished in the top ten in stolen bases seven years in a row (271 career). Cutshaw was tough to strike out, fanning only 10 times in 488 at-bats in 1920. /(CG)

Kiki Cuyler [Hazen Shirley] — 1899–1950. OF 1921–38 Pirates, **Cubs**, Reds, Dodgers 1879 g, .321, 127 hr, 1065 rbi. *3 WS, 16 g, .281, 2 hr, 12 rbi* ☛ *All-Star—34. Hall of Fame—1968.*

Curly-haired, hazel-eyed Kiki Cuyler played with competitive zeal, yet was admired amidst rough and tumble teammates for his gentlemanly qualities. He hit .300 ten times in his major league career. When the Pirates benched this superstar late in their 1927 pennant-winning year and kept him out of the World Series with the Yankees, the general public was mystified and Pittsburgh fans were outraged. When the 27-year-old Cuyler was traded for journeyman infielder Sparky Adams and rookie outfielder Pete Scott after the season, it created one of the mysteries of baseball history. That he became an even greater star for the Chicago Cubs removed suspicions that Cuyler's skills had lessened.

Cuyler, a hard-swinging batter who hit line drives to all fields and led the NL with 26 triples in 1925, had protested being moved from third to second in the lineup by Pirates first-year manager Donie Bush, who wanted Cuyler to replace Hall of Famer Max Carey, Pittsburgh's longtime number-two hitter (Carey had been traded the year before). Like Carey, Cuyler could steal bases. Carey had won ten titles; Cuyler would retire with four (and lead the NL twice in runs scored). However, where Carey was an adept bunter and sliced hits behind the runner, Cuyler swung from the heels, struck out more often than the average player of the era, and was not suited to bat second. Cuyler accepted his manager's decision but it rankled him. He chafed under Bush's expectations and batted below his usual level, dropping to .309 after seasons of .354, .357 and .321.

Cuyler, who ran the bases with abandon, was benched after he went into second base standing up in a risky effort to block a double play relay to first. When the baseman bobbled the ball, but managed to tag out Cuyler, Bush fumed that Cuyler would have been safe if he had slid. Cuyler had also angered Pittsburgh owner Barney Dreyfuss by winning a salary dispute before the season. When Lloyd Waner joined his brother Paul on the 1927 Pirates, the owner apparently feared the payroll impact of three superstar outfielders more than he appreciated

Kiki Cuyler

the distinction and success they could bring.

Cuyler had become a Pittsburgh favorite in 1925 when he finished a close second to triple crown winner Rogers Hornsby for MVP. He also became the hero of the World Series that year against Washington. Walter Johnson had won Game One 4–1 and shut out Pittsburgh 4–0 in Game Four. Johnson began the eighth inning of Game Seven with a 7–6 lead. Cuyler came to bat with the bases loaded and two out. He hit a tremendous drive to the right centerfield wall, clearing the bases with an apparent inside-the-park home run. However, the umpires ruled the ball had become entangled in a tarpaulin rolled up against the wall. Cuyler was given a ground rule double but the score was now 9–7 and the demoralized Senators were blanked in the top of the ninth.

Cuyler was called "Cuy" by his school teammates. It was while winning the MVP title of the Southern Association with Nashville in 1923 that he acquired the euphonious Kiki nickname. Fans heard the players shout for him to take the ball when he rushed in a short fly. The shortstop would yell, "Cuy," and the second baseman would echo the call. In the pressbox the writers turned this into "Kiki." Older fans wince to hear him called "Keekee."

Like Rogers Hornsby, whose batting style he copied, Cuyler didn't drink or smoke. After attending West Point during WWI, Cuyler returned home and married his high school sweetheart. He found a job in the Buick plant in Flint, Michigan, and switched to Chevrolet to play on the company's baseball team in the fast Detroit Industrial League. Soon the professional scouts found him. He kept his contacts with the automotive industry and between seasons served as athletic director for a 12,000-man program.

When a broken foot in 1932 and the passing of seasons slowed Cuyler, his final averages fell below his eventual lifetime .321 mark. He played his final years with second-division teams in Cincinnati and Brooklyn, serving as a playing coach. He returned to the Southern Association to manage and was called back to coach the Cubs early in the 1940s. He was a Boston Red Sox coach when he died suddenly, only 50 years old, before the 1950 season began. Cuyler was elected to the Baseball Hall of Fame by the Veterans Committee in 1968. /(JK)

Mike Cvengros — 1901–1970. LHP 1922–25, 27, 29 Giants, **White Sox**, Pirates, Cubs 552 ip, 25–40, 4.58. *1 WS, 2 ip, 0–0, 3.86*

This modestly talented pitcher of Slavic descent pitched one game for the 1922 World Championship Giants and, after bouncing back from the minors twice, collected losing World Series shares from the 1927 Pirates and 1929 Cubs. Cvengros was the victim of a three-run Babe Ruth homer in the 1927 WS. /(DB)

Cy Young Award

Commissioner Ford Frick pushed the idea of an MVP-type award for pitchers, and the BBWAA approved the idea in 1956. The Cy Young Memorial Award commemorated the career of baseball's all-time career victory leader, who had died the previous year. Part of Frick's rationale was that pitchers rarely won the MVP award, but in the award's inaugural season, Brooklyn's Don Newcombe won both. The NL and AL shared the award at first (also at Frick's insistence) rather than having separate winners in each league, but this was changed in 1967, two seasons after Frick's retirement. Sandy Koufax had won the award in three of the previous four seasons. The voting system originally had each writer voting for just one pitcher, but after Denny McLain and Mike Cuellar tied for the award in 1969, the rules were changed to allow each writer to cast weighted votes for first, second, and third. /(JFC)

John D'Acquisto — 1951- . RHP 1973-82 **Giants**, Cardinals, Padres, Expos, Angels, A's 780 ip, 34-51, 4.56

In 1974 *TSN* named D'Acquisto NL Rookie Pitcher of the Year when he went 12-14 with a 3.77 ERA for the fifth-place Giants, but he missed most of the next season after elbow surgery. Always wild, he was easier to hit afterwards, and was no longer a good starter. He tied an NL record with three wild pitches in the seventh inning on September 24, 1976. The San Diego native made a comeback with the Padres in 1978 by switching to the bullpen (10 saves, 2.13 ERA) but declined in subsequent years./(SH)

Lonnie Paul Dade — 1951- . OF-3B-DH 1975-80 Angels, **Indians**, Padres 439 g, .270, 10 hr, 107 rbi

A good-fielding third baseman in the minors, Dade played out his option with the Angels and became the Indians' regular leftfielder in 1977 (Buddy Bell was established at 3B). He hit a powerless .291 with 65 runs and 16 steals in 134 games. Traded to the Padres in June 1979 for Mike Hargrove, he moved back to 3B, but hit .189 in 1980 while sharing 3B with Luis Salazar, Tim Flannery, and Aurelio Rodriguez./(WOR)

Bill Dahlen (Bad Bill) — 1870-1950. SS-3B-OF 1891-1911 **Cubs**, Dodgers, Giants, Braves 2443 g, .274, 84 hr, 1233 rbi. *1 WS, 5 g, .000, 1 rbi.*
   Manager 1910-13 **Dodgers** 251-355, .414
☛ *Led League—rbi 1904.*

Dahlen played shortstop for a National League-record 20 years. His specialty was fielding, to which his NL-record 7,500 SS assists and ML-record 13,325 chances attest. Yet he lasted long enough to make 972 errors at SS, the most by a player at any position in a single league. He was also a consistent hitter with considerable power for the deadball era.

Dahlen broke in as a fleet-footed 21-year-old with the 1891 Chicago Colts (later the Cubs), playing third base and the outfield. By 1895 he was the everyday shortstop. Like many players of the era, he had his best season in 1894 (the year after pitchers were moved back), reaching personal highs of 15 HR, 107 RBI, and a .362 average. He set a record

from June 20 through August 6 with a 42-game hitting streak that Willie Keeler exceeded three years later. After failing to hit on August 7, he reeled off a 28-game streak, thus hitting in 70 of 71 games. Twice in his career, in 1896 and 1898, he tripled three times in a game, and in 1900 tripled twice in one inning.

Dahlen played for Brooklyn from 1899 through 1903, then achieved his lifelong dream of playing for the Giants when Brooklyn dealt him for pitcher John Cronin and shortstop Charlie Babb. It was one of the worst trades in Brooklyn history, as Cronin lasted one season, Babb two. Meanwhile, Dahlen led the NL with 80 RBI in 1904, and was the SS for the 1905 World Champion Giants. After a stint with the 1908-09 Braves, he returned to Brooklyn and managed the club for four seasons, never finishing higher than sixth. He was replaced by Wilbert Robinson in November of 1913./(AJA)

Babe Dahlgren [Ellsworth Tenney] — 1912- . 1B-3B 1935-46 Red Sox, **Yankees**, Braves, Cubs, Browns, Dodgers, Phillies, Pirates 1139 g, .261, 82 hr, 569 rbi. *1 WS, 4 g, .214, 1 hr, 2 rbi*

Dahlgren was the Red Sox' first baseman as a rookie in 1935, but was displaced in 1936 when Boston acquired Jimmie Foxx. He dropped to the minors, and in 1937 played third base for the championship Newark (International League) club. On May 2, 1939, he played first base for the Yankees in place of the ailing Lou Gehrig, whose consecutive-game string thus ended at 2,130. Dahlgren homered that day, and he remained the Yankee first baseman for two seasons. He saw regular action, mostly in the NL, through the end of WWII./(JK)

Bill Dailey — 1935- . RHP 1961-64 Indians, **Twins** 185 ip, 10-7, 2.76

Despite excellent minor league seasons and effective pitching in two brief trials with Cleveland, Dailey wasn't handed the stopper's role until 1963 with the Twins. In 66 games, he had six wins and 21 saves, with a 1.99 ERA. The next season he couldn't lift his arm without pain and his career was over./(MC)

Bill Dahlen

One Arm Daily [Hugh Ignatius, born Harry Criss] — 1857–Unk. RHP 1882–87 Buffalo (NL), Cleveland (NL), **Chicago-Pittsburgh (UA)**, Washington (UA), St. Louis (NL), Washington (NL), Cleveland (AA) 1415 ip, 73–89, 3.05. 20 wins: 83–84
☛ *Led League—k 84.*

Daily's nickname was an exaggeration of his physical handicap. Before the start of his major league career, he lost his left hand in a gun accident. He compensated by fashioning a pad covering his wrist; he would trap the ball between the pad and his good hand. He was able to play three games in the outfield, two at second base, and one at shortstop in his major league career, and he hit as high as .214 with six doubles in 1884.

Daily pitched well at times, especially in the beginning of his career. For the Cleveland Spiders (NL), the surly hurler threw a 1–0 no-hitter against Philadelphia on September 13, 1883. He was the first pitcher in ML history to toss consecutive one-hitters, striking out 19 in the first of the pair to tie a ML record that stood for over a century. This came in the Union Association, in that league's only year. At the end of the season, he had struck out 483, the second-best season total ever, although pitching conditions were to change greatly, and permanently, within a decade. His only winning seasons came in his first two years, as he went 15–14 and 23–19, fairly ordinary marks for the time. He went 28–30 for three UA teams in 1884 and was never again a good pitcher. He vanished from the scene after his last year in the majors. /(SFS)

Bruce Dal Canton — 1942– . RHP 1967–77 Pirates, **Royals**, Braves, White Sox 930 ip, 51–49, 3.68

Desperate for pitching, the Pirates in 1965 signed several mature semi-professionals who'd been by-passed by scouts when younger. One was Woody Fryman, 25; another was Dal Canton, 24. Both had settled down to teaching high school and coaching. Both had been passed over earlier because of control problems. Both jumped to the ML in their second year and became effective spot starters/long relievers. Dal Canton had a career-best 9–4 mark in 1970, helping Pittsburgh to a division title. He later returned to teaching as a pitching coach. /(MC)

Gene Dale — 1889–1958. RHP 1911–12, 15–16 Cardinals, **Reds** 442 ip, 21–28, 3.60

In 1915 Dale gave up the most walks of any pitcher in the NL but was 18–17 with a 2.46 ERA for the seventh-place Reds. The next year, after pitching less effectively early in the season, he was suspended by the Reds and left baseball. /(NLM)

Jerry Dale — 1933– . *Umpire* NL 1970–84 *3 LCS 1 WS, 2 ASU*

Dale was umpiring the sixth game of the 1977 WS when Reggie Jackson homered three times. A former pitcher in the Senators' organization, Dale was a NL umpire for 15 seasons before being dismissed, over his bitter objections, for "lack of mobility" resulting from a knee injury. Dale earned his Ph.D. from Pepperdine University. His masters thesis examined personality differences between 92 student umpires and active ML umpires. He began leading yearly photographic safaris to Kenya in 1972. /(RTM)

Arthur Daley — Unk.–1974. *Writer.*

A graduate of Fordham, Daley joined the *New York Times* in 1926. Ten years later he covered the Olympics in Berlin, the first *Times* sportswriter to get a foreign assignment. In 1942 he began 31 years as a columnist for the *Times*, and, in 1973, became the first sportswriter to win a Pulitzer Prize. Daley's books include *The Story of the Olympic Games* (with John Kieran) and *Times at Bat*. /(NLM)

Buddy Daley [Leavitt Leo] — 1932- . LHP 1955-64 Indians, **A's**, Yankees 967 ip, 60-64, 4.03. *2 WS, 1-0, 8 ip*
☛ *All-Star—59-60.*

This courageous southpaw was a natural righthander who contracted polio as a child. Though one arm was shorter than the other, Daley taught himself to throw lefthanded. A starter for the A's, he won 16 in both 1959 and '60, but mostly relieved with Cleveland and New York. Daley's specialties were a roundhouse curve and a knuckler. /(GDW)

Pete Daley — 1930- . C 1955-61 **Red Sox**, A's, Senators 391 g, .239, 18 hr, 120 rbi

Daley backed up defensive whiz Sammy White in Boston for five seasons, never getting 200 at-bats. He was taken by the "new" Washington Senators in the 1961 expansion draft, but lasted only one more season. /(JK)

Dom Dallessandro (Dim Dom) — 1913-1988. OF 1937, 40-44, 46-47 Red Sox, **Cubs** 746 g, .267, 22 hr, 303 rbi

Dom Dallesandro was a squat, colorful Cubs outfielder during WWII. The powerfully-built line-drive hitter batted .304 in 1944 but was called into the service in 1945 and missed the only Cubs pennant of the era. His nickname was short for "Diminutive Dominick," a reference to his 5'6" height. /(BC)

Abner Dalrymple — 1857-1939. OF 1878-88, 91 Milwaukee (NL), **Cubs**, Pirates, Cincinnati-Milwaukee (AA) 951 g, .288, 43 hr, 298 rbi
☛ *Led League—hr 1885.*

Dalrymple was the leadoff man for Cap Anson's Chicago White Stockings (later to become the Cubs), a team that won five National League pennants in seven seasons (1880-82, 85-86). In 1884 he hit 22 homers for the Chicago team that, benefiting from a short rightfield fence, amassed 140—a single-season club record that stood until the 1927 Yankees hit 158. Dalrymple led the NL in at-bats four times, in hits in 1880, and in homers, with 11, in 1885. He was credited with the 1878 batting crown until research in the 1960s dropped him to .354 while Providence's Paul Hines' average was elevated to .358. Dalrymple's four doubles in a game (7/3/1883) still tie him with many others for the ML record. /(JK)

Clay Dalrymple — 1936- . C 1960-71 **Phillies**, Orioles 1079 g, .233, 55 hr, 327 rbi. *1 WS, 2 g, 1.000*

Remembered mainly for his strong-armed defense, Dalrymple actually won the Phillies' regular catching job in 1960 with his bat, pinch-hitting 12-for-42, with an overall batting average of .272. Not a power threat, though a lefthanded dead pull hitter, Dalrymple had his best hitting year in 1962 (.276, 11 homers, and 54 RBI). He led NL catchers in assists in 1963, '65 and '67, and set a league record with 99 consecutive errorless games (and 628 chances) during 1966 and 1967. Traded to the Orioles in 1969, Dalrymple suffered a broken ankle in 1970, hastening his retirement. /(MC)

Dalton Gang

The Dalton Gang is the team of executives supporting Brewer GM Harry Dalton in the late 1970s and 1980s. They include: Walter Shannon, Senior Advisor, Baseball Operations; Bruce Manno, Assistant GM and Farm Director; Dee Fondy and Sal Bando, Special Assistants; Ray Poitevint, Vice President, International Baseball Operations; Dick Foster, Scouting Director; and Walter Youse, Eastern Scouting Supervisor. /(SOM)

Jack Dalton — 1885-Unk. OF 1910, 14-16 **Dodgers**, Buffalo (FL), Tigers 345 g, .286, 4 hr, 112 rbi

Dalton distinguished himself in his second ML game with four hits off Christy Mathewson (1910). He returned in 1914 to provide great fielding in an all-.300 Brooklyn outfield with Zack Wheat and Casey Stengel. /(TG)

Tom Daly [Thomas Peter] (Tido) — 1866-1939. 2B-C-3B 1887-96, 1898-1903 Cubs, Washington (NL), **Dodgers** 1564 g, .278, 49 hr, 811 rbi

Daly was the lone catcher on the Chicago club that made the world tour of 1888-89. Although he was considered a good receiver, his arm was suspect, and Chicago dealt him to Washington. He moved to the infield with Brooklyn and played mostly second base after 1892. He went on to manage in the high minor leagues and scout for the Indians and Yankees. /(JK)

Ray Dandridge (Hooks) — 1913- . 3B-2B-SS Negro Leagues 1933-49 Detroit Stars, Newark Dodgers, Newark Eagles, New York Cubans (NNL), Nashville Elite Giants statistics not available
☛ *Hall of Fame—1987.*

Ray Dandridge was a masterful third baseman, a stylist who could make all the plays. He was smooth and relaxed, with soft hands, a strong arm, and the versatility to excel at any infield position. "People would pay their way in to the game just to see him field," claimed Monte Irvin. Roy Campanella said, "I never saw anyone better as a fielder." Hoyt Wilhelm, who played against Dandridge in Cuba and with him in Minneapolis (American Association), asserted, "No matter how the ball was hit, he always made the throw so that he just did get the man at first." Others observed that a train could go through Dandridge's bowlegs, but that a baseball never did.

Dandridge started his pro career with the 1933 Detroit Stars and moved to the Negro National League's Newark Eagles, for whom he starred throughout the remainder of the 1930s. A spray hitter with good bat control, he seldom struck out, and skillfully executed the hit-and-run. In 1935, he hit .368. Looking for more money in 1939, he opted to play in Latin America. He went to Mexico in 1940, and spent most of the decade there. When he came back for a year in Newark in 1944, he batted .370, leading the NNL in hits, runs, and total bases. In 1945 he set a Mexican League record for hitting safely in the most consecutive games and managed his team to a pennant. In nine Mexican League seasons, he compiled a .343 average. Following the 1948 season, he returned to the States as player-manager of the New York Cubans.

During his time in the NNL, Dandridge registered a lifetime .355 average, and played in three East-West all-star games, hitting .545. He played winter ball in Mexico, Venezuela, Puerto Rico, and Cuba; in 11 seasons of Cuban Winter League action, he batted .282.

Soon after Jackie Robinson signed with the Brooklyn Dodgers, Bill Veeck contacted Dandridge about playing with the Cleveland Indians, but Dandridge refused to leave Mexico without a bonus. Later, in 1949, at age thirty-five, he was signed by the New York Giants and assigned to their Triple-A farm club at Minneapolis. He batted .363 his first year there, and won the league's MVP award in 1950, when he led Minneapolis to the league championship. Despite his achievements, the Giants would not promote him to the parent club.

While at Minneapolis, Dandridge provided advice and assistance to a young Willie Mays, who never forgot the help or the man. Returning to Cooperstown for Dandridge's induction into the Hall of Fame (he was elected by the Committee on Baseball Veterans in 1987), Mays stated, "Ray Dandridge helped me tremendously when I came through

Minneapolis. Sometimes you just can't overlook those things. Ray was a part of me when I was coming along." /(JR)

Dave Danforth (Dauntless Dave) — 1890–1970. LHP 1911–12, 16–19, 22–25 A's, **White Sox**, Browns 1186 ip, 71–66, 3.89. *1 WS, 1 ip, 0–0, 18.00*

Danforth was called Dauntless Dave because he pitched with a constantly pain-racked left arm. He used his large, strong hands to loosen the covers on baseballs, adding to the break on his curveball. In 1917 he recorded AL highs of 50 appearances, six relief wins, and nine saves for Chicago. He left the majors just in time to avoid involvement with the 1919 Black Sox, returning in 1922 for several strong seasons with the Browns. /(JK)

Dan Daniel [born Daniel Moskowitz] — 1890–1981. *Writer.*

Daniel, a raspy-voiced, round-shouldered hulk of a man, was still pecking out copy at the age of 91. Refused a byline early in his career because of his Jewish name, Moskowitz, Daniel made his first name do double duty from then on. The prodigious writer had long stints with *Baseball Magazine* and *The Sporting News* when they were the lone baseball publications. He also co-founded and edited *Ring Magazine*, covering boxing.

A resource of fact as well as acerbic opinion, Daniel conducted the "Ask Daniel" feature in the New York *World-Telegram* sports section at the peak of that paper's fame. /(JK)

Bennie Daniels — 1932– . RHP 1957–65 Pirates, **Senators** 997 ip, 45–76, 4.44

Daniels, a regular starter for the expansion Senators of the early 1960s, received little support, but was 12–11 for the last-place 1961 team. The next year he became the first pitcher to win a game at D.C. (now RFK) Stadium. /(FK)

Bert Daniels — 1882–1958. OF 1910–14 **Yankees**, Reds 523 g, .255, 5 hr, 130 rbi

An early itinerant college athlete, Daniels played football and baseball under his own name at Villanova, Notre Dame, and Bucknell while playing semi-pro and minor league ball under aliases. He led the AL in hit-by-pitch three times. New York led the AL in stolen bases in 1910 with 288; Daniels led the team with 41. /(CG)

Kal Daniels [Kalvoski] — 1963– . OF 1986- **Reds**, Dodgers 377 g, .302, 54 hr, 168 rbi

A young, fast power hitter, Daniels hit .334 with 26 HR and 26 stolen bases in 1987, despite missing a month on the DL, and in 1988 he led the NL in on-base percentage as the Reds' starting left fielder. Often temperamental, Daniels was suspended briefly in September 1988 for throwing a bat into the dugout. The erratic fielder missed most of 1989 with a variety of physical problems, and in midseason he was traded to the Dodgers with Lenny Harris for Tim Leary and Mariano Duncan. Only 25, he had his sixth knee operation near the end of the 1989 season./(ME)

Harry Danning (Harry The Horse) — 1911– . C 1933–42 **Giants** 890 g, .285, 57 hr, 397 rbi. *2 WS, 5 g, .214, 2 rbi*
☛ *All-Star—38–41.*

Danning, whose brother Ike caught two games for the 1928 Browns, backed up Gus Mancuso for the 1936 pennant-winning Giants, then took over as the regular for the 1937 NL Champions. He earned a reputation (and nickname) for durability. The Horse hit 46 homers and averaged .303 in the period 1937–40. Playing with injuries in the next two seasons, his hitting suffered. He retired after WWII military service./(MC)

Pat Darcy — 1950– . RHP 1974–76 **Reds** 187 ip, 14–8, 4.14. *1 WS, 4 ip, 0–1, 4.50*

Intermittent arm trouble caused the Astros to give up on Darcy after five years in their farm system. Dealt to the Reds, he was a one-year wonder, going 11–5 with a 3.57 ERA for the 1975 World Champions. The next year his arm problems returned and he was soon out of the majors./(MC)

Alvin Dark (Blackie) — 1922– . SS-3B 1946, 48–60 Braves, **Giants**, Cardinals, Cubs, Phillies 1828 g, .289, 126 hr, 757 rbi. *3 WS, 16 g, .323, 1 hr, 4 rbi.*
   Manager 1961–64, 66–71, 74–75, 77 **Giants**, A's, Indians, Padres 994–954, .510. First place: 62, 74–75 *2 LCS, 3–4, .429. 2 WS, 7–5, .583*
☛ *Rookie of the Year—48 . All-Star—51–52, 54.*

In 1969 fans chose Alvin Dark as the top shortstop in Giants' history. He won the 1948 Rookie of the Year award, hit .300 four times, led the NL in doubles once, led league shortstops three times each in putouts and double plays, and hit 20 or more home runs and scored over 100 runs twice each. Dark's single in the ninth inning of the third 1951 NL playoff game started the rally that culminated in Bobby Thomson's famous pennant-winning homer. As a manager, Dark won the 1962 NL pennant for

Alvin Dark

San Francisco and the 1974 World Championship with Oakland. While leading San Francisco, he once tore off a finger at the joint throwing a metal chair after a loss. After finding religion, his calmer personality enabled him to work two tours for A's owner Charlie Finley./(TJ)

Ron Darling — 1960– . RHP 1983– **Mets** 1392 ip, 87–55, 3.38. *2 LCS, 12 ip, 0–1, 7.50. 1 WS, 18 ip, 1–1, 1.53*
☛ *All-Star—85. Gold Glove—89.*

Darling, the Rangers' first pick in the June 1981 draft, came to the Mets with Walt Terrell in return for Lee Mazzilli in 1982. In his rookie 1984 season he went 12–9, quickly gaining a reputation for picking up hard-luck no-decisions, and was overshadowed by Dwight Gooden's amazing rookie year. Darling made the 1985 All-Star team and finished 16–6. He had perhaps his best start ever opening a crucial late-season series against the Cardinals, pitching nine shutout innings as the Mets won in the 11th inning on October 1. Earlier that year in his only ML relief appearance, he finished the Mets' 19-inning, 16–13 victory over the Braves by striking out Rick Camp at 3:55 am, the latest-ending game in baseball history.

The Hawaiian also led the NL in walks in 1985, with 114 in 248 innings, the second year in a row he topped 100. Some said he thought too much and was too much of a perfectionist. His control improved in 1986 (81 walks in 237 innings) and he posted a career-best 2.81 ERA as the Mets won the World Championship. He went 15–6, and the Mets were 27–8 in his starts. He was hit hard in his LCS start. Starting the World Series opener, he lost a 1–0 three-hitter on an unearned run. He came back to win Game Four with seven shutout innings. In the Mets' Game Seven victory, he was knocked out early.

Darling's worst season was 1987, when he posted a 4.29 ERA and missed September on the DL. The split-finger fastball artist came back in 1988, going 17–9 with a 3.25 ERA. In the LCS he took a no-decision in Game Three and lost Game Seven. He set a NLCS record for most runs allowed in a seven-game series (9). He struggled with his control through most of 1989.

Darling is an excellent fielder and has one of the best pick-off moves among righthanders. He is sometimes used as a pinch runner, and in 1989 he hit homers in two consecutive starts. His brother Eddie was in the Yankee system in 1981–82.

While at Yale, Darling faced St. John's pitcher Frank Viola in an NCAA playoff game, no-hitting them for 11 innings but losing in 1–0 in the 12th inning. It is the longest no-hitter in NCAA history. /(SH)

Bobby Darwin — 1943– . OF-DH-RHP 1962, 69, 71–77 Angels, Dodgers, **Twins**, Brewers, Red Sox, Cubs 646 g, .251, 83 hr, 328 rbi; 7 ip, 0–1, 10.29

Darwin signed with the Angels as a pitcher in 1962. That year with San Jose (California League) he struck out 202 and walked 149 in 153 innings. His control problems and disabling injuries contributed to his gradual switch to the outfield starting in 1966.

The Twins made Darwin their regular centerfielder in 1972, and although he showed good power over the next three seasons (22, 18, and 25 HR), he led the AL in strikeouts each year (145, 137, 127) and had fewer fielding chances than any other centerfielder. In 1974 he tied for fourth in HR and was fifth in RBI (94). Traded to Milwaukee in 1975 while hitting .219, he was never again a regular, and he finished his career with more strikeouts than hits. /(SH)

Danny Darwin — 1955– . RHP 1978– **Rangers**, Brewers, Astros 1750 ip, 100–105, 3.51

A Texan, Darwin went undrafted and was signed by the Rangers. Throwing in the 94-mph range, he fanned the first four Mariners he faced in his ML debut (9/24/78). In 1980 he went 13–4 (2.62) with eight saves but broke a knuckle on his right hand when aiding Mickey Rivers in a scuffle with fans outside Comiskey Park on June 4 and was disabled for three weeks. Moved into and out of the rotation, he was a .500 pitcher before his 1985 trade to Milwaukee. That year he went 8–18, despite a staff-best 3.80 ERA. He lost 10 consecutive games to set a Brewers record; it took a one-hitter against the Twins to halt the streak. Becoming more of a finesse pitcher, he was traded to Houston for their 1986 pennant drive and went 5–2. /(JCA)

Frank Dascoli — 1915– . *Umpire* NL 1948–62 *3 WS, 2 ASU*

Dascoli, a respected NL umpire for 15 years, effected a baseball oddity. On September 27, 1951 he cleared the Dodger bench after a disputed play. On the bench was Boston Celtics basketball star Bill Sharman, who was also a recently-recalled Dodger farmhand. Thus, Sharman became the only player ever kicked out of a ML game without ever appearing in one. In the off-season Dascoli was a Connecticut state trooper. /(RTM)

Jake Daubert — 1884–1924. 1B 1910–24 **Dodgers**, Reds 2014 g, .303, 56 hr, 722 rbi. *2 WS, 12 g, .217, 1 rbi* ☛ *Led League—ba 13–14.*

In his day, Daubert was the National League's best all-around first baseman. The lefthander was a two-time NL batting champion and steady .300 batter for ten years of the dead ball era. He escaped the Pennsylvania coal mines and the minor leagues in 1910, taking over first base for Brooklyn at age 26. He was a model of consistency, fielding within a .989-.994 range for 15 years, and was mobile enough to average 10.5 chances per game and take part in 1199 double plays. A chop hitter, he twice led the league in triples and had 165 lifetime. He also had a NL record 392 sacrifices, 4 in one 1914 game for another record.

Daubert was modest, polite, and colorless, though a tiger about money. WWI and competition with the Federal League raised salary levels generally, and Daubert's went from $5,000 to $9,000. Charles Ebbets probably guaranteed his 1916 Dodger pennant by extending Daubert's $9,000 another four years (and treating Zack Wheat and Nap Rucker liberally as well).

Jake Daubert

When the major leagues shortened the 1918 season and tried to prorate salaries, Daubert sued Ebbets for the unpaid balance ($2,150) and got most of it in a settlement. Furious at this, Ebbets traded him to Cincinnati in 1919 for the less-talented Tommy Griffith. Daubert helped lead the Reds to a pennant and a tarnished World Championship in the Black Sox WS.

Daubert benefited from the change to the lively ball. In 1922, at age 38, he had 205 hits for a .336 average, scored 114 runs, and hit 12 HR. Late in the 1924 season he became ill, and a month later died from complications after an appendectomy. /(ADS)

Rich Dauer — 1952- . 2B-3B 1976-85 **Orioles** 1140 g, .257, 43 hr, 372 RBI. *2 LCS, 8 g, .080, 1 rbi. 2 WS, 11 g, .250, 1 hr, 4 rbi*

After leading the International League with a .336 BA, Dauer replaced Bobby Grich at second base for the Orioles. He never hit up to expectations—.284 in 1980 was his best—but he seldom struck out and was a reliable fielder. His homer in the seventh game of the 1979 WS gave the Orioles a brief lead. He set

ML records in 1978 by playing 86 straight errorless games at second and handling 425 chances without an error. /(MC)

Darren Daulton — 1962- . C 1983, 85-89 **Phillies** 329 g, .206, 24 hr, 101 rbi

The Phillies traded away Bo Diaz and then Ozzie Virgil to make room for the Daulton–John Russell catching platoon, but injuries limited Daulton's playing time in 1984-85. A home-plate collision with Mike Heath ended his 1986 season in June. Thereafter, the resulting knee injury prevented him from crouching as low as other catchers. In 1987 the Phillies signed Lance Parrish, and Daulton remained the backup until 1989. /(SG)

Hooks Dauss [George August, born George August Daus] — 1889-1963. RHP 1912-26 **Tigers** 3391 ip, 221-183, 3.32. 20 wins: 15, 19, 23

Detroit's six long-term, one-team-only players is the most of any franchise; the first of them was Hooks (or Hookie) Dauss. A stocky righthander with nicknames deriving from his assortment of sharp-breaking curves, Dauss won 221 games in a fifteen-year career, the most for any pitcher while wearing a Tiger uniform. It is a record easily overlooked, for Dauss toiled mostly in the second division. Still, he achieved ten winning seasons and a winning percentage considerably better than his team's.

He was a friendly, good-natured fellow; some thought that with more aggression he might have won more games. Still, Hookie led the league in hit batsmen three times and is tenth on the lifetime list. /(ADS)

Dauvray Cup

In 1887 Giants shortstop Monte Ward's wife, actress Helen Dauvray, donated a cup that would be held by the winner of the yearly postseason series between the National League and American Association champions, a series which had been played (with one interruption) since 1882. The Cup would become the property of whichever team won it three times. However, the war between the leagues in 1891 resulted in an end to postseason play before any team had won three series. The Cup has been lost. /(SH)

Vic Davalillo — 1939- . OF 1963-74, 77-80 **Indians,** Angels, Cardinals, Pirates, A's, Dodgers 1458 g, .279, 36 hr, 329 rbi. *4 LCS, 8 g, .545, 1 rbi. 4 WS, 14 g, .200, 1 rbi*
☛ *All-Star—65. Gold Glove—64.*

Davalillo, whose older brother Yo-Yo played briefly for the Senators in 1953, started his pro career in 1958 as a pitcher. Called up to the Indians after only one full season as an outfielder, the Venezuelan missed two months in 1963 with a broken right wrist (hit with a pitch by Hank Aguirre) but still hit .292. He was Cleveland's regular centerfielder for the next four seasons. In 1964 the 5'7" 150-lb lefthander won a Gold Glove and led the league's outfielders in double plays (5) and finished third in stolen bases (21). In his All-Star year, 1965, his .301 BA was the third-best in the AL, he finished fifth in stolen bases (26), and he led outfielders in total chances per game. However, he lost much of his range in subsequent years, and he was a poor-percentage basestealer. He was also hindered by his lack of power and his impatience at the plate. The Indians experimented with him as a pinch hitter in 1966 and '67, but he was a poor 7-for-38 (.184) over that period.

After Davalillo bounced around for several years, the pinch-hitting experiment finally worked in St. Louis, where he led the NL in 1970 with 24 pinch hits and 73 pinch at-bats (.329). Traded to the Pirates with Nellie Briles for Matty Alou and George Brunet for 1971, he played outfield and pinch hit .333 for the World Champions. Pittsburgh's regular left fielder in 1972, he hit .318, but he slumped the next two seasons (.184, .174), although he hit .625 for the A's in the 1973 LCS. In Game Five, his RBI triple in the fourth (he scored when Jesus Alou singled) helped drive Doyle Alexander out of the game as Oakland clinched the series against the Orioles.

Davalillo went to the Mexican League early in 1974 and remained there until the Dodgers picked him up in August 1977 for their pennant drive (he hit .313). He became the first player to play for three different teams in the LCS, his only appearance being a crucial one. With the Phillies up 5–3 in Game Three, Davalillo beat out a drag bunt with two out in the ninth. He scored on Manny Mota's double, and the Dodgers rallied to win the game. They took the series the next day. Davalillo stayed with the Dodgers as a pinch hitter and reserve outfielder/first baseman for the next three seasons and retired with 95 pinch hits, which at that time tied him for sixth on the all-time list. /(SH)

Dave Davenport — 1890–1954. RHP 1914–19 Reds, St. Louis FL, **Browns** 1537 ip, 74–83, 2.93. 20 wins: 15
☛ *Led League—so 15.*

After ten games for the Reds in 1914, the 6'6" Davenport jumped to the Federal League. In 1915

he won 22 for the St. Louis Feds, led the league in games pitched, innings pitched, complete games, strikeouts, and shutouts, and pitched a no-hitter. When the FL folded, he joined the Browns, where Manager Fielder Jones called him the best pitching prospect he'd ever worked with. Although he had a couple of effective seasons with the Browns, including a 17–17 year in 1917, Davenport was out of the ML by 1920, the year his brother Claude pitched in one game for the Giants. /(NLM)

Jim Davenport (Peanut, Golden Glove) — 1933– . 3B-SS-2B 1958–70 **Giants** 1501 g, .258, 77 hr, 456 rbi. *1 WS, 7 g, .136, 1 rbi.*
Manager 1985 **Giants** 56–88, .389
☛ *All-Star—62. Gold Glove—62 .*

His first big league manager, Bill Rigney, called Jim Davenport "the greatest third baseman I ever saw—at least the only one I'd compare with Billy Cox." Davenport, who played every infield position as well as the outfield during his 13-year ML tenure, led NL third basemen in fielding three times and won a Gold Glove in 1962. Also in '62, Davenport reached career-high figures in batting (.297) and home runs (14) and played in an All-Star Game. In 1967 the 5'11" 180-lb Davenport played errorless ball in 65 straight games and averaged .370 as a pinch hitter. After many years as a Giants coach, he became their manager in 1985, 27 years after his ML playing debut in the team's first San Francisco game. Davenport relinquished the managerial reins before the season ended. In 1987 he became a Phillies coach. /(TJ)

L. Robert Davids — 1926– . *Writer.*

Bob Davids calls himself a statistorian. He is a longtime government employee, and his interest in the use of statistics in analyzing political and military history prepared him for baseball research. His digging turned up interesting sidelights on the game that appeared regularly in *The Sporting News* between 1951 and 1965. Davids began circulating his own newsletter, *Baseball Briefs*, and gathered a group of 16 like-minded individuals at Cooperstown on August 10, 1971, where they founded the Society for American Baseball Research. Davids was SABR's first president and served two later terms as well. /(NLM)

Mark Davidson — 1961– . OF 1986– **Twins** 271 g, .216, 3 hr, 31 rbi. *1 LCS, 1 g, --. 1 WS, 2 g, .000*

Davidson's best season came as an extra outfielder on the 1987 World Championship Twins. He hit

.267 and played errorlessly in the outfield. His father, Max, was a minor league outfielder from 1947 to 1954. /(SFS)

Satch Davidson (Dave) — 1936- . *Umpire* NL 1969-84 *2 LCS 2 WS*

Davidson, who was given the nickname Satch by schoolmates because he was a fan of that Bowery Boy, is an example mentioned by umpires who oppose instant replays on stadium TV. A replay in Cincinnati so excited one fan that he threw an unopened can of beer which struck Davidson. Two games as a catcher for Columbus (International League) were the extent of Davidson's pro playing career. /(RTM)

Ted Davidson — 1939- . LHP 1965-68 **Reds**, Braves 195 ip, 11-7, 3.69

Davidson was a stylish reliever with a good fastball who admitted to using a spitter now and then. He also had an excellent curveball, which he threw sidearm to lefthanded batters. In 1966 he made 54 appearances for the Reds. Prior to the 1967 season, he was at a bar when his estranged wife shot him in the stomach and chest with a .25 caliber pistol. He pitched only parts of two seasons after his recovery. /(RTM)

Alvin Davis — 1960- . 1B 1984- **Mariners** 881 g, .290, 131 hr, 530 rbi
☛ *Rookie of the Year—84. All-Star—84.*

The AL Rookie of the Year in 1984, Alvin Davis was the only Mariner to win a major award in the first dozen years of the franchise. In 1984 Davis set or tied franchise records for most RBI, game-winning RBI, walks, and intentional walks, as well as home runs by a rookie. Hitting most of his homers in the Kingdome, Davis is the Mariners' career home run leader, with a high of 29 in 1987. Davis is also the franchise leader in RBI (the Mariners' only player to have two 100-RBI seasons), total bases, extra-base hits, and walks. His sharp batting eye helps raise his on-base percentage almost 100 points above his batting average, making up for occasional fielding deficiencies and slow baserunning. /(TF)

Bob Davis — 1952- . C 1973, 75-81 **Padres**, Blue Jays, Angels 290 g, .197, 6 hr, 51 rbi

A backup catcher for five years in San Diego, Davis had a weak bat that kept him on the bench. In 1980 he appeared in 91 games for Toronto but hit only .216 with 19 RBI. /(MC)

Brock Davis [Bryshear Barnett] — 1943- . OF 1963-64, 66, 70-72 Astros, **Cubs**, Brewers 242 g, .260, 1 hr, 43 rbi

At age 19, Davis opened in centerfield for Houston, but he was soon in the minors, where he struggled for eight seasons. In 1971, he was platooned in the Cubs' outfield but hit a soft .256. Swapped to Milwaukee, he hit .318 in 85 games, 36 as a pinch hitter. /(MC)

Chili Davis [Charles Theodore] — 1960- . OF 1981- **Giants**, Angels 1186 g, .268, 144 hr, 601 rbi. *1 LCS, 6 g, .150*
☛ *All-Star—84, 86.*

The native of Kingston, Jamaica was another in the long line of outfielders developed by the Giants. The switch-hitter set a NL career record with three games in which he homered from both sides of the plate. Two of those games came in 1987, his best season, when he hit a career-high 24 HR. He signed with the Angels as a free agent after the season to escape Candlestick Park, which he hated. He had a career-high 93 RBI with California in 1988, but shattered the Angels team record for outfielders errors with a league-leading 19, fielding just .942. He did lead NL outfielders in assists in 1982, and when he led in errors in 1986, his nine errors tied the ML record for fewest errors by a league leader.

Davis's nickname was originally Chili Bowl, resulting from a bad haircut in his childhood. /(SH)

Curt Davis (Coonskin) — 1903-1965. RHP 1934-46 Phillies, Cubs, Cardinals, **Dodgers** 2325 ip, 158-131, 3.42. 20 wins: 39 *1 WS, 5 ip, 0-1, 5.06*
☛ *All-Star—36, 39.*

Curt Davis, a 6'2" 185-lb native of Greenfield, Missouri, pitched in a NL-leading 51 games, winning 19, as a Phillies rookie in 1934. Davis won 15 or more three additional times during his career: 1935 (16) for the Phillies, 1939 (22) for the Cardinals, and 1942 (15) for the Dodgers. Davis was named to the 1936 and 1939 NL All-Star teams; he surrendered three runs in 2/3 of an inning as Carl Hubbell's reliever in the 1936 game and did not play in the 1939 game. Davis was the Dodgers' starting and losing pitcher in the opening game of the 1941 World Series; the winner of that 3-2 contest was future Hall of Famer Red Ruffing. Davis was one of three players traded, along with cash, by the Cubs to the Cardinals for Dizzy Dean in 1938. /(TJ)

Dick Davis — 1953- . OF-DH 1977-82 **Brewers**, Phillies, Blue Jays, Pirates 403 g, .265, 27 hr, 141 rbi

Davis had his best season in part-time duty with the Brewers in 1979, when he had career highs in HR (12), runs (51), and RBI (41) while hitting .266. A terrible defensive liability, he was usually a DH until traded to the Phillies in 1981 for Randy Lerch. After his ML career, he became a star for Japan's Kintetsu Buffalos. He is a cousin of Enos Cabell. /(SFS)

Dixie Davis [Frank Talmadge] — 1890–1944. RHP 1912, 15, 18, 20–26 Cubs, White Sox, Phillies, **Browns** 1319 ip, 75–71, 3.97

After a decade of pitching in the minors, Davis became an effective pitcher for the Browns in 1920 with an 18–12 season. On August 9, 1921 he pitched a complete 19-inning game against the Senators, finally won by the Browns, 8–6. In the last nine innings, he did not allow a hit. Davis hit an inside-the-park home run in the 16th inning but was called out for failing to touch first base. /(NLM)

Eric Davis — 1962– . OF 1984– **Reds** 640 g, .275, 142 hr, 413 rbi
☛ *All-Star—87–89. Gold Glove—87–89.*

Davis seemed to have unlimited potential in 1987, when he hit .293 with 37 HR and 50 stolen bases and made numerous breathtaking catches in centerfield for the Reds. But he has also been prone to both strikeouts (at least 100 in each of his years as a regular) and nagging injuries. He has already hit three home runs in a game twice (9/10/86 and 5/3/87). /(ME)

George Davis — 1870–1940. SS-3B-OF 1890–1909 Cleveland (NL), **Giants**, White Sox 2377 g, .297, 73 hr, 1435 rbi.
    Manager 1895, 1900–01 **Giants** 108–139, .437
☛ *Led League—rbi 97 .*

Davis began his career as an outfielder in Cleveland, but was traded to the Giants in 1893 for future Hall of Famer Buck Ewing. Primarily a third baseman his first four years in New York, he became a full-time shortstop in 1897. He was the Giants' player-manager for part of 1895, and again from mid-1900 through 1901.

His anti-establishment stance in 1903 may have cost Davis consideration for the Hall of Fame. Davis was an outstanding hitter (he batted over .300 for nine consecutive seasons with the Giants), and an even better fielder, during a time when the National League was bitterly divided and corrupt. His problems began after the 1902 season, his first with the White Sox. Dissatisfied with Charles Comiskey's pay structure, Davis elected to jump back to the National League Giants. When peace was declared

George Davis

between the two warring leagues early in 1903, Davis was "awarded" to the White Sox, but he had other ideas. He sat out the season until John Brush, president of the National League, sanctioned an illegal scheme hatched by the Giants to regain Davis. After four games in a Giant uniform, Davis was served with an injunction. John Montgomery Ward, the famous baseball lawyer, represented Davis in court, and his efforts were supported by Brush, who filed a counter-suit to keep Davis in the NL. On July 15, 1903 the case was thrown out, and peace was restored in baseball. Years later, Ban Johnson punished Ward for his impertinence by seeing to it that he was not appointed NL president. As for Davis, he went on to play six more seasons with the White Sox, though he never again batted over .278. /(RL)

Glenn Davis — 1961– . 1B 1984– **Astros** 737 g, .264, 144 hr, 454 rbi. *1 LCS, 6 g, .269, 1 hr, 3 rbi*
☛ *All-Star—86, 89.*

Davis has been one of the NL's premier power hitters since his 1985 rookie season, despite playing half his games in the spacious Houston Astrodome where fly balls historically do not carry well. The strapping first baseman began the 1985 season in Tucson (Pacific Coast League), hitting .305 in 60 games there before being called up to Houston when

Terry Puhl was injured in June, and he hit 20 HR for the Astros, earning a spot on the *Topps* All-Rookie Team. 1986 was Davis's first full season in the ML, and the 25-year-old hit .265 with 32 doubles, 31 HR, and 101 RBI to finish second behind Mike Schmidt in the NL MVP voting as the Astros won the NL West. In the NLCS, he homered off Dwight Gooden in his first at bat to give the Astros a 1–0 win in Game One. Davis, a notorious streak hitter, added 27 HR in 1987 (including 3 in one game September 10) and 30 in 1988, and in 1989 became the first player in Astros history to hit 20 or more home runs in five consecutive seasons. As a child, he was adopted by the family of future ML pitcher Storm Davis. /(SCL)

Harry Davis (Jasper) — 1873–1947. 1B-OF-3B 1895–99, 1901–17 Giants, Pirates, Washington NL, **A's**, Indians 1757 g, .277, 74 hr, 952 rbi. *3 WS, 16 g, .246, 7 rbi.*
    Manager 1912 **Indians** 54–71, .432
☛ *Led League—hr 04–07. Led League—rbi 05–06.*

The gentlemanly Davis was an outstanding slugger for Connie Mack's Philadelphia teams in the early 20th century. In the A's 1911 WS victory over the Giants, he and Frank "Home Run" Baker each drove in five runs. Only Davis, Baker, Babe Ruth, and Ralph Kiner have led a ML in home runs four or more years in a row. Davis accomplished the feat 1904 through 1907 and also led in doubles in 1902, '05, and '07 and in RBI in '05 and '06. The native Philadelphian was named the A's first captain and managed whenever Connie Mack was absent. The highly regarded sign stealer remained with the team as a player or coach until 1927, except for 1912, when he became manager of Cleveland. His strict disciplinary tactics failed to help the Indians and he quit after 127 games with the team in sixth place. From 1913 to 1917 he made token appearances in the A's lineup. While still with the A's, he became a Philadelphia city councilman. /(ME/JK)

Jim Davis — 1924– . LHP 1954–57 **Cubs**, Cardinals, Giants 406 ip, 24–26, 4.01

A nephew of his contemporary, pitcher Marv Grissom, Davis was the best pitcher (11–7, 3.52) on the lowly 1954 Cubs. He never matched his freshman success. /(TJ)

Jody Davis — 1956– . C 1981– **Cubs**, Braves 1075 g, .246, 127 hr, 489 rbi. *1 LCS, 5 g, .389, 2 hr, 6 rbi*
☛ *All-Star—84, 86. Gold Glove—86.*

A fine catcher both offensively and defensively for the Cubs from 1981 to 1987, Davis became expend-

Harry Davis

able in 1988 when Damon Berryhill emerged as a capable ML player, and he was traded to the Braves on September 29 after hitting a career-low .230. Davis was originally drafted by the Mets, and he was traded to the Cardinals organization for Ray Searage after 1979. He played only 58 games in 1980 after losing 50 pounds while being treated for an ulcer, then was drafted by the Cubs following the season. As a rookie with Chicago in 1981, Davis grabbed the starting catching job by hitting .389 in May, but lost it the following spring to Keith Moreland before regaining it during the 1982 season. In 1983 Davis hit .271 with 24 HR and 84 RBI, and in 1984 he made the NL All-Star team for the first time as the Cubs won the NL East. Davis starred in the '84 NLCS, with seven hits in five games and home runs in Games Four and Five, but the Cubs lost the final three games to the Padres after taking a 2–0 series lead. He won a Gold Glove in 1986, throwing out 78 would-be basestealers, and hit 21 HR, but in 1987 his durability and consistency began to lapse. He had caught at least 138 games each of the previous four seasons, and had never gone on a ML disabled list, but in 1988 an early-season stint on the DL forced the promotion of Berryhill from the minors, and Davis would catch only 76 games. /(SCL)

Joel Davis — 1965– . RHP 1985–88 **White Sox** 248 ip, 8–14, 4.91

The White Sox made the 6'5" Davis their first pick and the 13th player chosen overall in the June 1983 draft. The Red Sox, with the 19th pick, took Roger Clemens. Davis was rushed from high school through the minors and arrived ill-prepared in the majors at age 20. Each year his ERA rose while his confidence dwindled. In his one brief shining ML moment, Davis was the winning pitcher on April 21, 1987, when the White Sox ended Milwaukee's 13-game winning streak to open the season. /(RL)

John Davis — 1963– . RHP 1987– Royals, **White Sox** 113 ip, 7–8, 4.84

The 6'7" 215-lb Chicago native came to the White Sox in the Floyd Bannister deal after going 5–2 with a 2.27 ERA in 1987. The reliever fell off to 2–5 with a 6.64 ERA in 1988 and pitched only briefly in 1989 before being sent back down. /(WOR)

Lefty Davis — 1875–1919. OF 1901–03, 07 Dodgers, **Pirates**, Yankees, Reds 348 g, .261, 3 hr, 110 rbi

Davis became the Pirate right fielder in 1901 when Honus Wagner moved to shortstop. A solid hitter with a strong arm, Davis never regained his form after he suffered a broken leg at the Pirates' Exposition Park in 1902. /(ME)

Mark Davis — 1960– . LHP 1980– Phillies, **Giants**, Padres 858 ip, 40–65, 3.76
☛ *Cy Young Award—89. All-Star—88–89.*

This stocky curveballer spent five seasons, split between the bullpen and the starting rotation, with the Giants before he blossomed as a relief stopper with the Padres in 1988. Originally signed by the Phillies, Davis was traded to the Giants with Mike Krukow for Joe Morgan and Al Holland before the 1983 season.

Davis was exclusively a starter in 1983 and was the Giants' Opening Day starter in 1984, but he spent almost all of 1985–86 in the bullpen, where he struck out over a batter an inning but saved only 11 games in two years. In a game against the Mets in 1985 he threw 23 straight curveballs.

Davis rejoined the Giants' rotation in 1987 before he was traded to San Diego in July, part of a seven-player deal that included Kevin Mitchell, Craig Lefferts, Dave Dravecky, and Chris Brown. Handed the stopper role for the first time in his career, Davis emerged as an overpowering reliever in 1988. He was the Padres' lone All-Star, posting 28 saves, a career-best 2.01 ERA, and 102 strikeouts in 98.1 innings. He won the NL Cy Young Award in 1989 with a 44-save season, posting a 1.85 ERA and striking out 92 batters in 92.2 innings. /(SCL)

Mike Davis — 1959– . OF-DH 1980– **A's**, Dodgers 963 g, .259, 91 hr, 371 rbi. *2 LCS, 5 g, .333. 1 WS, 4 g, .143, 1 hr, 2 rbi*

A speedy but unexceptional outfielder with a strong arm, Davis won Oakland's right field job in 1983 and batted .275 with 32 stolen bases. A first-ball, fastball hitter, he slumped to .230 in 1984 before adjusting in 1985, hitting .287 with 24 HR and 82 RBI. Just after the 1987 All-Star break, he kicked a dugout door in anger, injuring his knee, and fell into a prolonged slump. He signed as a free agent with the Dodgers for 1988, but failed to hit and lost his job. He found room in the lineup in the World Series as a DH, and his two-run homer in Game Five proved the winning margin as the Dodgers clinched their unlikely World Championship. In Game One, Davis pinch hit with two out in the ninth inning, drew a walk from the A's Dennis Eckersley, stole second, and scored on Kirk Gibson's dramatic game-winning homer. /(JCA)

Peaches Davis [Ray Thomas] — 1905– . RHP 1936–39 **Reds** 542 ip, 27–33, 3.87

Davis reached the ML at age thirty-one after developing an effective sinker. He split time between starting and relieving for the Reds, with a career-high 11 wins in 1937. /(NLM)

Piper Davis [Lorenzo] — 1917– . 1B-2B-SS-MGR Negro Leagues 1943–50 **Birmingham Black Barons** statistics not available
☛ *All-Star—46–48.*

Although he never played in the white major leagues, Davis teamed with future major leaguer Artie Wilson to form one of the outstanding double play combinations in Negro League ball. He hit a team-leading .353 and led the Negro National League in RBI as player-manager of the 1948 Birmingham Black Barons, leading them to the World Series. At Birmingham from 1948 to 1950, he managed Willie Mays. In 1951 Davis became the first black signed by the Red Sox. An outstanding all-around athlete, he also played basketball for the Harlem Globetrotters. /(BP)

Ron Davis — 1955– . RHP 1978–88 **Yankees**, Twins, Cubs, Dodgers, Giants 746 ip, 47–53, 4.05. *2 LCS, 7.1 ip, 0–0, 1.23. 1 WS, 2.1 ip, 0–0, 23.14*
☛ *All-Star—81.*

Davis never started a ML game, but was often outstanding in relief, especially as a set-up man for Rich Gossage with the Yankees. He had an AL rookie-record 14 relief wins in 1979, three seasons with 25 or more saves, and on May 4, 1981 he fanned eight consecutive Oakland batters. He also had little to offer besides a hard fastball, and was ineffective when it failed him. /(ME)

Spud Davis [Virgil Lawrence] — 1904–1984. C 1928–41, 44–45 Cardinals, **Phillies**, Reds, Pirates 1458 g, .308, 77 hr, 647 rbi. *1 WS, 2 g, 1.000, 1 rbi.*
    Manager 1946 **Pirates** 1–2, .333

Virgil Lawrence Davis batted .300 in 9 of his 16 seasons. In 1933 his .349 average was second in the NL to future Hall of Famer Chuck Klein's .368. Davis led NL catchers in assists in 1931, double plays in 1932, and total chances per game in 1934, years in which rival catchers included future Cooperstown enshrinees Gabby Hartnett and Al Lopez. Davis later backed up Ernie Lombardi at Cincinnati, and Lopez at Pittsburgh.

As a member of the 1935 Cardinals, Davis feuded with Dizzy Dean. Dean accused him of not hustling after a foul during a loss to Cincinnati, and insisted on a different catcher the next time out. Teammates sided with Davis, but manager Frankie Frisch complied with Dean's demand. Davis managed the Pirates briefly in 1946. /(TJ)

Storm Davis [George Earl] — 1961– . RHP 1982- **Orioles**, Padres, A's 1319 ip, 92–62, 3.86. *3 LCS, 19 ip, 0–1, 2.41. 2 WS, 13 ip, 1–2, 9.00*

Once a promising young starter for the Orioles (14–9, 3.12 as a 22-year-old in 1984), Davis seemed washed up with the Padres in 1987. He rallied in Oakland to win the AL Comeback Player of the Year award with a 16–7 record for the 1988 AL champions and was 19–7 (4.36) in 1989. He grew up with Astro Glenn Davis, who was raised by Storm's parents and adopted the family name. /(ME)

Tommy Davis — 1939– . OF-DH-3B 1959–76 **Dodgers**, Mets, White Sox, Pilots, Astros, A's, Cubs, Orioles, Angels, Royals 1999 g, .294, 153 hr, 1052 rbi. *3 LCS, 12 g, .295, 3 rbi. 2 WS, 8 g, .348, 2 rbi*
☛ *Led League—ba 62–63. Led League—rbi 62. All-Star—62–63.*

Tommy Davis

In 1981, Tommy Davis (then the Mariner batting coach) said, "They used to call me lazy or lackadaisical, but the lazier I felt the better I'd hit." Before playing pro ball, the 6'2" 195-lb Davis had been a high school basketball standout and teammate of future NBA great Lenny Wilkens. Jackie Robinson had helped convince Davis to sign a baseball pact with his hometown Brooklyn club in 1956. However, by the time Davis made the big leagues in 1959, the Dodgers had forsaken his borough for Los Angeles. Playing outfield and some third base, the line-drive hitter topped the NL in hits (230), and BA (.346) in 1962; his league-leading 153 RBI were the most in the NL in 25 years. The following year Davis won his fourth pro batting title (he'd captured crowns in the Midwest and Pacific Coast leagues), hitting .326. He was the first National Leaguer to capture successive batting crowns since Stan Musial (1950–52). He was the starting left fielder for the NL All-Stars in '62, and paced all hitters with a .400 average in the '63 World Series as the Dodgers swept the Yankees in four games.

Davis slipped to .275 in 1964, and a broken ankle in 1965 limited him to 17 games. He rebounded in 1966, enjoying the third of his six .300 ML seasons (.313), but when the Los Angeles-Baltimore World Series ended, the Dodgers sent Davis to the Mets in a trade for Ron Hunt. After one year in New York,

Davis went to the White Sox in a six-player deal that brought Tommie Agee to the Mets. From 1969 through 1972, Davis played with five teams, starting with the Seattle Pilots, who had taken him in the expansion draft. He landed in Baltimore in late '72, where he served primarily as DH for three seasons and in two LCS. Davis ended his playing days with the highest career pinch-hitting average (.320, 63-for-197) in baseball history. /(TJ)

Willie Davis — 1940- . OF 1960–76, 79 **Dodgers**, Expos, Cardinals, Rangers, Padres, Angels 2429 g, .279, 182 hr, 1053 rbi. *1 LCS, 2 g, .500. 3 WS, 15 g, .167, 3 rbi*
☛ *All-Star—71, 73. Gold Glove—71–73.*

Davis was named *TSN* Minor League Player of the Year in 1960, and was generally considered the fastest man in baseball. The Dodgers' regular centerfielder for 13 years, Davis ranks high in virtually every all-time Dodger offensive category. His 31-game hitting streak in 1969 was the longest in 24 years, and he later had another streak of 25 games. A three-time Gold Glove winner, Davis also twice led the NL in errors. He committed a WS-record three errors, all in the fifth inning of Game

Willie Davis

Two in 1966. In 1965, he set a WS record with three stolen bases in a game, and in '62, he and Maury Wills set a new NL record for stolen bases by two teammates with 136 (Wills had 104, Davis 32). Traded four times between December 1973 and October 1975, Davis played in Japan before a brief final tour as an Angel. /(TG)

Bill Dawley — 1958- . RHP 1983–88 **Astros**, White Sox, Cardinals, Phillies 462 ip, 27–30, 3.41
☛ *All-Star—83.*

Acquired from the Reds by Houston in 1983, Dawley was an All-Star as a rookie that year, saving 14 games. An imposing 6'4" 240-lb fastball-slider pitcher, he followed with a league-high 11 relief wins and a 1.93 ERA in 1984. But he suffered with tendinitis in 1985, was released the following spring, and spent each of the next three years with different clubs. /(JCA)

Andre Dawson (Hawk, Awesome) — 1954- . OF 1976- **Expos**, Cubs 1871 g, .281, 319 hr, 1131 rbi. *2 LCS, 10 g, .128, 3 rbi*
☛ *Rookie of the Year—77. Most Valuable Player—87. Led League—hr 87. Led League—rbi 87. All-Star—81–83, 87–89. Gold Glove—80–85, 87–88.*

After a decade of stardom with Montreal, Dawson reached new heights with the Cubs. A free-swinging righthanded batter susceptible to being hit by pitches, Dawson was a complete player with the Expos, outstanding at bat, in the field, and on the bases. Still, he was largely overshadowed by the popular Gary Carter. Dawson led NL outfielders in chances three straight seasons (1981–83), but the artificial surface at Olympic Stadium took its toll on his knees. By 1986 he was determined to play on grass. Despite the collusively-limited free agent market, he went to the Cubs by signing a blank contract, getting a 1987 salary far below market value ($500,000). Rejuvenated by natural grass and day baseball, and helped statistically by the move to the league's best offensive park after ten years in one of its worst, he turned in an MVP season in 1987, leading the NL with 49 HR and 137 RBI. He was the first player on a last-place team ever to win the MVP. /(ME)

James P. Dawson — 1896–1953. *Writer.*

Dawson began a 45-year career with the *New York Times* as a copy boy in 1908. Eight years later, he became boxing editor and covered boxing and baseball until his death during spring training in 1953. The annual award presented to the top rookie in the Yankees' training camp is named in his honor. /(NLM)

Andre Dawson

Joe Dawson — 1897–1978. RHP 1924, 27–29 Indians, **Pirates** 238 ip, 11–17, 4.15. *1 WS, 1 ip, 0.00*

Dawson led the Pirates with 24 relief appearances in 1928, garnering 7 of his 11 career victories./(ME)

Boots Day [Charles Frederick] — 1947– . OF 1969–74 Cardinals, Cubs, **Expos** 471 g, .256, 8 hr, 98 rbi

Sure-handed and quick, Day was one of the smaller modern players at 5'9", 160 lb. Platooned by the Expos, he hit .283 in 1971 and .275 two years later. He was 30-for-129 as a ML pinch hitter. After being sent down to the minors he tried unsuccessfully to make a comeback as a pitcher./(MC)

John B. Day — Unk.–Unk. *Executive.*

Founder of the New York Giants in the NL in 1883, Day began with the New York Mets of the American Association, with Jim Mutrie. He formed the Giants by bringing most of the Troy club to New York and won two pennants. A year after moving into the Polo Grounds site he lost most of his players to the Brotherhood's New York club in 1890 and went broke, holding various jobs with the NL thereafter./(NLM)

Leon Day — 1916– . RHP Negro Leagues 1934–50 Baltimore Black Sox, Brooklyn Eagles, **Newark Eagles,** Baltimore Elite Giants (NNL) statistics not available ☛ *All-Star—35, 37, 39, 42–43, 46.*

Day was the most outstanding pitcher in the Negro National League during the late 1930s and early 1940s. A heady pitcher, he was the Newark Eagles' ace. He had a sneaky fastball, which he delivered with a no-windup, sidearm motion and complemented with a good curve and change-of-pace to set impressive strikeout records.

Day was also a good hitter and baserunner. When not pitching, he often played second base or the outfield, or pinch-hit.

Day's best season was 1937, when, backed by the Eagles' "million-dollar infield," he was 13–0 in league play and batted .320. In 1940 he established the Puerto Rican record of 19 strikeouts while locked in an 18-inning marathon with spitballer Bill Byrd; the game was called with the score tied 1–1. He also played two winters in Cuba and one in Venezuela (going 12–1), and three summers in Mexico.

Day appeared in a record seven East-West all-star games from 1935 through 1946, winning his only decision and setting an all-star record by striking out a total of 14 batters. In the 1942 game, he struck out five of the seven he faced without giving up a hit. That year he set a Negro League record when he struck out 18 Baltimore batters in one game, including Roy Campanella three times. For post-season play, he was recruited by the Homestead Grays to oppose Satchel Paige in the Negro World Series; he struck out 12 batters in a 4–1 victory.

Day served in the army during WWII, was discharged in February 1946, and threw an Opening Day no-hitter against the Philadelphia Stars. He recorded a 9–4 record that year, led the league in strikeouts, and started two games in the Negro World Series, in which the Eagles defeated the Kansas City Monarchs.

After pitching for the 1949 champion Baltimore Elites, Day left to play in Canada in 1950. Then, well past his prime, he entered organized baseball, pitching for Toronto (International League) in 1951 and Scranton (Eastern League) in 1952 before returning to Canada, where he finished his career in 1955./(JR)

Ken Dayley — 1959- . LHP 1982- Braves, **Cardinals** 495 ip, 29-41, 3.63. *2 LCS, 10 ip, 0-0, 0.00. 2 WS, 10 ip, 1-0, 0.84*

Dayley used a snappy curve and fastball to become the Cardinals' top lefthanded reliever. He recovered from career-threatening ligament damage in his left elbow in 1986 to win a personal-best nine games in '87./(FJO)

Mike de la Hoz — 1939- . 3B-2B-SS 1960-69 Indians, **Braves**, Reds 494 g, .251, 25 hr, 115 rbi

A handy utility infielder, de la Hoz never had 200 at-bats in a season. The hustling Cuban pinch hit in 40% of his games. As a Milwaukee Brave on July 8, 1965, he hit a pinch-homer in the eighth inning, singled to tie the game in the ninth, and singled and scored in the 12th to give his club a 9-8 victory over the Astros./(RTM)

Don De Mola — 1952- . RHP 1974-75 **Expos** 156 ip, 5-7, 3.75

After he was signed and released by the Yankees, the Expos rediscovered De Mola pitching amateur ball in New York. He rose quickly to the majors, and worked 60 games in relief in 1975, but his arm blew out in 1976./(MC)

Charlie Deal — 1891-1979. 3B 1912-21 Tigers, Braves, St. Louis (FL), Browns, **Cubs** 850 g, .257, 11 hr, 318 rbi. *2 WS, 10 g, .152*

When regular Braves third baseman "Red" Smith broke his leg in one of the last regular-season games in 1914, Deal took over at third and helped Boston sweep the WS in four games. His $2,400 season salary was nearly matched by his $2,200 Series share. When the Braves denied him a $500 raise the next year, he jumped to the Federal League for $4,500 and a $3,000 bonus. From 1917 to 1921 he was the Cubs' regular third baseman./(BC)

Chubby Dean [Alfred Lovill] — 1916-1970. LHP-1B 1936-43 A's, Indians 533 g, .274, 3 hr, 128 rbi; 686 ip, 30-46, 5.08

Dean went right from Duke University -where his coach was former Philadelphia hurler Jack Coombs—to the Athletics. He played first base and pinch-hit often his first two seasons before Connie Mack, desperate for pitchers, put him on the mound. He was an unspectacular but useful starter, reliever, and pinch hitter for the A's and Indians. He went into the military in 1943 and never returned to ML baseball./(JK)

Dizzy Dean [Jay Hanna] — 1911-1974. RHP 1930, 32-41, 47 **Cardinals**, Cubs, Browns 1966 ip, 150-83, 3.03. 20 wins: 33-36 *2 WS, 34 ip, 2-2, 2.88* ☛ *Most Valuable Player—34. Led League—w 34-35. Led League—k 32-35. All-Star—34-37. Hall of Fame—1953.*

Dizzy Dean actually had only six full seasons in the majors, but no player packed more accomplishments, excitement, and shenanigans into a shorter time.

Dean was given his nickname by his sergeant in the army, where he picked up the basics of pitching. He was pitching for a semi-pro team in San Antonio when a manager in the Cardinals' farm system spotted him at a tryout camp. The Cardinals signed him, and he split 1930 between St. Joseph, Missouri, and Houston, rolling up a combined 25-10 minor league record before pitching a three-hitter for St. Louis on the last day of the season. Returned to Houston for the 1931 campaign, Dean struck out 303 batters on his way to 26 victories.

As a rookie in 1932, the 21-year-old Dean was joining the "Gas House Gang" World Champions. He won 18 and led the NL in strikeouts, shutouts, and innings pitched. He helped his own cause repeatedly with superb fielding, a .258 batting average, and fine speed on the bases. From 1933 to 1936 Dean absolutely dominated batters. During this stretch he won 102 games, led the league in complete games each year, and averaged 50 games and more than 300 innings per season. He was the unquestioned ace of the Cardinal staff and would often come in from the bullpen between starts. In 1933 he struck out 17 Cubs in a game, a major league record at that time.

During spring training in 1934, Dizzy proudly predicted that he and his brother Paul would win 45 games that season. The incredible prediction seemed ludicrous because Paul had never pitched a game in the majors. Yet Dizzy's boast proved conservative; he won 30 and Paul won 19. Dizzy led the league in wins, strikeouts, shutouts, and complete games, was second to Carl Hubbell for the ERA crown, and batted .246. He easily outdistanced Paul Waner for the MVP award. He capped off his spectacular year with two wins over the Tigers in the World Series, including a shutout in the seventh game.

The 1935 season proved a virtual carbon copy of 1934 as the Deans won 47. Dizzy slipped to 28 victories but still led the league in many pitching categories. This time he was edged out by Gabby Hartnett for MVP. Dean won 24 and saved 11 the next year and again narrowly missed the MVP award, losing to Carl Hubbell.

Dizzy Dean with the Browns

In 1937 Dean appeared headed for another 25-win season by the All-Star break. Exhausted from the toll of so many innings, he asked to sit out the All-Star Game but went at the urging of Cardinal owner Sam Breadon. As the starter for the NL, Dean suffered a broken toe when he was struck by an Earl Averill line drive. Dean tried to come back before it had fully healed, altering his pitching motion to favor the injured foot, but the change brought on bursitis in his valuable right arm.

Traded to the Cubs for three players and $185,000 just before the start of the 1938 season, he replaced his blazing fastball and dazzling curve with a changeup and slow curve. Dean was able to chip in a 7–1 mark with a 1.81 ERA in 13 games, helping Chicago to the NL pennant. Over the next three years Dean appeared in only 30 games. At age 30 he retired and became a broadcaster for the St. Louis Browns. In 1947, after frequent criticism of Browns hurlers all year, Dean took the mound himself three times. In the last game of the season he shut out the White Sox for four innings and got a base hit in his only at-bat.

Dean's meteoric pitching career provided ample reason to immortalize him. His bold and zany antics on and off the field have made him one of the most recognizable characters in American folklore. He loved to challenge and bait opposing players before and during games. He was a relentless braggart; fortunately he was as good as he said he was. He gambled and was pretty good at that too. Dean and Pepper Martin formed the core of the Gas House Gang. Whether in the dugout, clubhouse, or hotel, Dean and Martin could be expected to be up to some sort of prank. His popularity and colorful approach to the game continued unabated when he entered the radio broadcaster's booth. His malapropisms and blatant avoidance of the rules of grammar were legendary, and fans loved it. In 1950 he began doing baseball's Game of the Week on national television. He remained in sportscasting for more than 20 years. /(FO)

Paul Dean (Daffy) — 1913–1981. RHP 1934–41, 43 **Cardinals**, Giants, Browns 787 ip, 50–34, 3.75. *1 WS, 18 ip, 2–0, 1.00*

When Paul joined his famous brother Dizzy on the Cardinals' pitching staff, Dizzy predicted, "Me 'n Paul will win 45 games." They won 49, 19 by Paul, and put the Cards in the World Series, where they each won 2 more. During the September pennant drive, Dizzy shut out the Dodgers on three hits in the first game of a double-header; Paul pitched a no-hitter in the nightcap. "I wished I'da known Paul was goin' to pitch a no-hitter," Dizzy said. "I'da pitched one, too." Paul was dubbed "Daffy" by sportswriters but he was actually shy and rather serious. In 1935, he again won 19 for the Cardinals. The next year, he held out for more money. After signing, he tried to pitch too soon, hurt his arm, and never regained his form. /(FJO)

Tommy Dean — 1945– . SS 1967, 69–71 Dodgers, **Padres** 215 g, .180, 4 hr, 25 rbi

A high school basketball All-American, Dean signed with the Dodgers in 1964 for a $60,000 bonus. A reliable fielder, he was a poor hitter. In 101 games with the Padres in 1969, his most active ML season, he hit only .176. /()

Wayland Dean — 1902–1930. RHP 1924–27 **Giants**, Phillies, Cubs 446 ip, 24–36, 5.31

Wayland Dean was only 28 when he died of tuberculosis, two years after an arm problem halted his career. He was a fine batter and was 6-for-26 as a pinch hitter in 1926. /(JK)

Hank DeBerry — 1893–1951. C 1916–17, 22–30 Indians, **Dodgers** 648 g, .267, 11 hr, 234 rbi

After brief trials with the Indians, DeBerry had a great season in the Southern Association. Dodger scout Larry Sutton urged owner Charlie Ebbets to buy DeBerry and his batterymate, the almost 30-year-old Dazzy Vance. DeBerry's subsequent value was mostly as Vance's personal catcher. /(JK)

Dave DeBusschere — 1940– . RHP 1962–63 **White Sox** 102 ip, 3–4, 2.90

In his first summers as a White Sox minor league pitcher, DeBusschere was impressive, posting a 10–1 record with Savannah (Sally League) in 1962. In the winters, the 6′6″ Detroit native won fame as a dominating forward for the NBA's Detroit Pistons. The White Sox, who had given him a $75,000 signing bonus, were encouraged when he threw a ML shutout in 1963, but the Pistons upped the ante by naming him player-coach, at age 24 the youngest coach in NBA history. DeBusschere gave up baseball, going on to a Hall of Fame basketball career (1963–72). Disciplined, unselfish, and dedicated to defense, he was considered the ultimate team player, and was a catalyst on two New York Knicks World Championship teams. He wore number 22 during his entire pro career. He served one year as GM of the American Basketball Association Nets before becoming the ABA's commissioner. He later returned to the Knicks for a term as their GM. He was elected to the NBA Hall of Fame in 1982. /(DB)

Art Decatur — 1894–1966. RHP 1922–27 **Dodgers**, Phillies 549 ip, 23–34, 4.47

Usually a reliever, Decatur led the NL with seven relief wins for Brooklyn in 1924. Born in Ohio, he developed a fondness for Alabama while pitching in the minors and later became president of the Georgia-Alabama League. /(JK)

Doug DeCinces — 1950– . 3B 1973–87 **Orioles**, Angels, Cardinals 1649 g, .259, 237 hr, 879 rbi. *3 LCS, 16 g, .297, 1 hr, 6 rbi. 1 WS, 7 g, .200, 1 hr, 3 rbi* ☛ *All-Star—83.*

DeCinces had the impossible task of replacing Brooks Robinson at third base for the Orioles. Actually, his talents were similar to Robinson's. Slow afoot, DeCinces gained a reputation for good hands and as a clutch hitter. Battling back problems throughout his career, he became expendable with the arrival of Cal Ripken, Jr., who started his career at third base. Dealt to the Angels for 1982,

DeCinces responded with his best season, reaching career highs with 30 HR, 97 RBI, and a .301 average. He hit .316 in the LCS and won regard as the AL's best all-around third baseman. He averaged over 21 HR a season during his California career, which ended in late September of 1987 when he was traded to the Cardinals to make room for Jack Howell. DeCinces played only four games for St. Louis, which won the NL pennant, and went to Japan after being released following the season. /(ME)

Joe Decker — 1947– . RHP 1969–76, 79 Cubs, **Twins**, Mariners 710 ip, 36–44, 4.17

Decker threw hard but had streaks of wildness. In spring training, his own teammates sometimes refused to bat against him. He struggled unsuccessfully for four years to win a spot with the Cubs, then became a regular starter with the Twins in 1973 and 1974. After his 16–14 season in '74, he explained his success: "I try to tranquilize myself when I pitch. If I'm lethargic, I have better stuff." /(MC)

Jeff Dedmon — 1960– . RHP 1983–88 **Braves**, Indians 394 ip, 20–16, 3.84

Dedmon was drafted four times before signing with Atlanta. Throwing a sinker and adding a knuckle curve, he averaged 56 games a year as a long reliever in 1984–87, but lacked the control and consistency to be a stopper, and was traded to Cleveland in 1988. /(JCA)

Bill Deegan — 1935– . *Umpire* AL 1970–80 *3 LCS 1 WS, 1 ASU*

In 1977, Deegan was behind the plate for two AL no-hitters, a rare occurrence for any umpire. The year before, he was on the spot for an unusual play at Yankee Stadium when Red Sox first baseman Carl Yastrzemski lost his glove leaping for a high pickoff throw. The Yankees argued to invoke the rule that all runners advance two bases when a fielder throws his glove at a ball. Not so on two counts, ruled Deegan at first base. The glove did not touch the ball and the fielder's action was unintentional. /(RTM)

Rob Deer — 1960– . OF 1984– Giants, **Brewers** 624 g, .229, 121 hr, 339 rbi

A hacking, heavyset, righthanded slugger, Deer's prodigious home runs are matched by equally prodigious strikeout totals. He came up through the Giants minor league chain, winning three minor league home run crowns (one at each level), but also leading his league in strikeouts four times. Deer was with the Giants for all of 1985, but was traded to the Brewers after hitting only .185 with eight home runs in 78 games, and he won Milwaukee's right field job in 1986. He belted 33 HR in his first AL season, but also fanned a whopping 179 times, then set an AL record with 186 strikeouts the following season (breaking Pete Incaviglia's year-old mark by 1). He led the league again in 1988 with 153 strikeouts, hitting a career-high .252 as his home run output fell to 23. /(SCL)

Ivan DeJesus — 1953– . SS 1974–88 Dodgers, **Cubs**, Phillies, Cardinals, Yankees, Giants, Tigers 1371 g, .254, 21 hr, 324 rbi

Signed by the Dodgers in 1969 as a high school student in Puerto Rico, DeJesus got his break in 1977 when he was traded to the Cubs. Filling the gap left by Don Kessinger, he scored a league-high 104 runs in 1978, and in 1980 set a record for Cubs shortstops with 44 stolen bases. His poor attitude and unhappiness with the trade of friend and double-play partner Manny Trillo resulted in a disastrous 1981 season (.194); the Cubs made a splendid move by sending him to the Phillies for Larry Bowa and rookie Ryne Sandberg. In 1982, former Cub teammate Jody Davis accused DeJesus of intentionally allowing Latin opponents to slide in safely at second. In the 1983 World Series, DeJesus batted an anemic .125 and became the goat when his error in Game Three allowed Baltimore's winning run to score. /(DB)

Ed Delahanty (Big Ed) — 1867–1903. OF-IF 1888–1903 **Phillies**, Cleveland (PL), Senators 1834 g, .345, 100 hr, 1464 rbi
☛ Led League—ba 99, 02. Led League—hr 93. Led League—rbi 93, 96, 99. Hall of Fame—1945.

One of seven brothers from Cleveland, five of whom played ML baseball, Ed Delahanty was a premier 19th-century slugger. The 6'1" 190-lb righthander made his pro debut in 1887 with Mansfield of the Ohio State League, batting .355. The next year, he was at .408 after 21 games with Wheeling of the Tri-State League when the Phillies bought his contract for $1,500. He arrived in Philadelphia in time to play 74 games, mostly at second base, but hit only .228.

He jumped to the Players' League in 1890, but returned to the Phillies the next year. After a .306 year in 1892 with a league-leading 21 triples, he blossomed in 1893, narrowly missing the triple crown (.368, 19 HR, 146 RBI). The next year he hit

Ed Delahanty

.400, but he needed .408 in 1899 to win his first batting title. Delahanty collected six-hit games in 1890 and '94 and had ten consecutive hits in 1897. His four doubles in one game tied the record in 1899, and on July 13, 1896 he hit four home runs—the second man to do so—and a single in a losing cause at Chicago.

After switching to the new AL, he won a second batting title with the Senators (.376) in 1902. He also led in slugging average, a feat he'd accomplished three times in the NL. His disdain for training rules got him suspended in June 1903, and he left his club in Detroit to take a train to New York. At International Bridge near Niagara Falls, the conductor put him off the train for being drunk and disorderly. Staggering along the tracks in the dark, he fell through an open drawbridge and was swept over the falls to his death. /(AL)

Jim Delahanty — 1879–1953. 2B-3B-OF-1B 1901–02, 04–12, 14–15 Cubs, Giants, Braves, Reds, Browns, Senators, **Tigers**, Brooklyn (FL) 1186 g, .283, 18 hr, 489 rbi. *1 WS, 7 g, .346, 4 rbi*

Jim Delahanty, a versatile player, was one of five brothers who played major league ball, including Big Ed, a Hall of Famer. Jim had the next-best career, finishing in the Federal League and going to their outlaw minor, the New England Colonial League, in 1915 to lead the league in batting while managing Hartford to the championship. /(JK)

Bill DeLancey — 1901-1946. C 1932, 34-35, 40 Cardinals 219 g, .289, 19 hr, 85 rbi. *1 WS, 7 g, .172, 1 hr, 4 rbi*

Branch Rickey once gave DeLancey a place on his all-time team, even though the lefthanded-hitting catcher played in only 219 ML games. Thirty-one when he joined the Cardinals for a brief trial late in 1932, he returned in 1934 to platoon with Spud Davis for the World Champion "Gas House Gang," hitting .316 with 13 home runs and 40 RBI. He was particularly adept at handling the Cardinals' eccentric pitchers. In 1935, he slumped at the plate and appeared tired. At the end of the season he was discovered to be suffering from tuberculosis. He missed four years, then hit .222 in a comeback attempt in 1940. /(MC)

Art Delaney [born Arthur Helenius] (Swede) — 1895-1970. RHP 1924, 28-29 Cardinals, **Braves** 287 ip, 13-22, 4.26

After three strong years at Oakland of the Pacific Coast League, Delaney received a second ML trial with the Braves in 1928. Despite a fair 3.79 ERA, his record was 9-17. /(NLM)

Jose DeLeon [born Jose Chestaro] — 1960- . RHP 1983- **Pirates**, White Sox, Cardinals 1234 ip, 61-77, 3.70
☛ *Led League—k 89.*

A fireballing Dominican with a good forkball, DeLeon flirted with no-hitters in his second and third ML starts in 1983, carrying one into the seventh against the Padres, and the other into the ninth against the Mets. But he went 2-19 for Pittsburgh in 1985, leading the NL in losses—and received a raise. He was traded to the White Sox for Bobby Bonilla in 1986, went 11-12 in 1987, and was sent to the Cardinals for Lance Johnson and Ricky Horton. He eventually blossomed under Whitey Herzog, going 16-12, 3.05 in 1989 and leading the NL in strikeouts. /(RL)

Luis DeLeon — 1957- . RHP 1981-85, 87 Cardinals, **Padres**, Orioles 330 ip, 17-19, 3.14

Obtained as part of the deal that sent Ozzie Smith to the Cardinals, DeLeon gave the Padres two excellent seasons of relief until overwork caught up with him. In 1982 he was 9-5 with 15 saves in 61 appearances and the next year 6-6 with 13 saves. His strength was his control, as he walked only 43 batters in 223 innings during those seasons. /(MC)

Bobby Del Greco — 1933- . OF 1952, 56-58, 60-63, 65 Pirates, Cardinals, Cubs, Yankees, Phillies, **A's** 731 g, .229, 42 hr, 169 rbi

Plucked off the Pittsburgh sandlots, Bobby was part of the Pirates' youth parade in the early 1950s. Considered one of the top defensive outfielders of his era, the speedy Del Greco made a great catch for the Cardinals late in the 1956 season against the Braves that aided the Dodgers in winning the pennant. /(RM)

Wheezer Dell [William George] — 1887-1966. RHP 1912, 15-17 Cardinals, **Dodgers** 430 ip, 19-23, 2.55. *1 WS, 1 ip, 0.00*

Dell led the Dodgers in strikeouts as a rookie, but the acquisition of Rube Marquard and Larry Cheney limited him to a marginal role with the 1916 pennant winners. /(TG)

Ike Delock — 1929- . RHP 1952-53, 55-63 **Red Sox**, Orioles 1238 ip, 84-75, 4.03

Delock had several above-average seasons for the Red Sox in the 1950s. He led the AL with 11 relief wins in 1956 while tying for fourth with nine saves (then not an official statistic). In general, he was better coming out of the bullpen, compiling a 3.08 ERA lifetime in that role. But as his career went on, he was used less and less as a reliever. His record as a starting pitcher was 50-60. A 1962 knee injury hastened the end of his career. /(JFC)

Jim Delsing — 1925- . OF 1948-56, 60 White Sox, Yankees, Browns, **Tigers**, A's 822 g, .255, 40 hr, 286 rbi

The Browns' pinch-runner in 1951 for midget Eddie Gaedel, Delsing hit .300 several times in the minors and made the Northern League, Pacific Coast League, and American Association all-star teams. His top ML BA was .288 with the 1953 Tigers. His son Jim is a member of the PGA tour. /(RTM)

Joe DeMaestri (Oats) — 1928- . SS 1951-61 White Sox, Browns, **A's**, Yankees 1121 g, .236, 49 hr, 281 rbi. *1 WS, 4 g, .500*
☛ *All-Star—57.*

DeMaestri was drafted by the White Sox out of the Red Sox organization before being shuffled from Chicago to St. Louis, back to Chicago, and on to Philadelphia. He began a seven-year stretch as the Athletics' starting shortstop in 1953. On July 8, 1955 DeMaestri went 6-for-6. As a utility infielder finishing up with the Yankees, he roomed with Yogi Berra. /(RL)

Al Demaree — 1886-1962. RHP 1912-19 **Giants**, Phillies, Cubs, Braves 1424 ip, 80-72, 2.77. *1 WS, 4 ip, 0-1, 4.50*

Demaree was most effective early in the season, and 14 of his 80 career wins were shutouts. He was 13-4 for the Giant pennant winners in 1913 and 14-11 for the Phillies when they won the 1915 pennant. In 1916 he won 19, including both games of a September 20 doubleheader against the Phillies. Demaree later became a sports cartoonist, syndicated in over 200 newspapers. His work appeared in *The Sporting News* for over 30 years. /(NLM)

Frank Demaree [born Joseph Franklin Demaria] — 1910-1958. OF 1932-33, 35-44 **Cubs**, Giants, Braves, Cardinals, Browns 1155 g, .299, 72 hr, 591 rbi. *4 WS, 12 g, .214, 3 hr, 6 rbi*
☛ *All-Star—36-37.*

After hitting .272 in 1933 as the Cubs' centerfield replacement for injured Kiki Cuyler, who broke his leg in spring training, Demaree was sent to Los Angeles of the Pacific Coast League and responded with an MVP year (.383, 45 homers, 190 RBI, and 45 stolen bases in 186 games). Regaining the Cubs job in 1935, he had three consecutive excellent seasons, hitting .325, .350, and .324, with highs of 17 homers and 115 RBI in 1937. He was the starting centerfielder for the NL in the 1936 and 1937 All-Star games. In seven more ML seasons, he slipped to the status of journeyman reserve. /(ME)

Larry Demery — 1953- . RHP 1974-77 **Pirates** 445 ip, 29-23, 3.72. *2 WS, 3 ip, 21.00*

Son of Negro League outfielder/pitcher Artist Demery, Larry broke into the Pirate rotation a few days after turning 21. He was 7-5 (2.90) in 1975, mostly in long relief, and 10-7 (3.17) in 1976. A 1977 arm injury ended his career. /(MC)

Don Demeter — 1935- . OF-3B-1B 1956, 58-67 Dodgers, **Phillies**, Tigers, Red Sox, Indians 1109 g, .265, 163 hr, 563 rbi. *1 WS, 6 g, .250*

The slim, 6'4" righthanded slugger hit more than 20 HR each year from 1961 through 1964 and twice hit 3 homers in a game, with the Dodgers in 1959 and the Phillies in 1961. In his best offensive season, playing mostly third base for the '62 Phillies, Demeter batted .307 with 29 HR and 107 RBI. He set a ML record for outfielders with 266 consecutive errorless games, from September 1962 with the Phillies through July 1965 with the Tigers. /(AL)

Ray Demmitt — 1884-1956. OF 1909-10, 14-15, 17-19 Yankees, **Browns**, Tigers, White Sox 498 g, .257, 8 hr, 165 rbi

After graduating from the University of Illinois, Demmitt broke in with Ottawa in 1906 under the name of Ray. He was a regular in only three ML seasons; his best effort came in 1918, when he hit .281 with 61 RBI in 405 at-bats for the Browns. /(NLM)

Gene DeMontreville — 1874-1962. 2B-SS 1894-1904 Pirates, **Washington (NL)**, Baltimore (NL), Cubs, Dodgers, Braves, Senators, Browns 922 g, .306, 17 hr, 497 rbi

Eugene Napolean DeMontreville, the elegantly-named son of French parents, appeared in boxscores mostly as plain Gene Demont due to the space limitations of the typesetters. He finished his career with 228 stolen bases and was the master of the delayed steal. A younger brother, Lee, appeared briefly with the Cardinals. Ill health shortened DeMontreville's playing career. /(JK)

Bingo DeMoss [Elwood] — 1889-1965. 2B-SS-MGR Negro Leagues 1905-43 Topeka Giants, Kansas City Giants, **Chicago American Giants**, Indianapolis ABC's, Detroit Stars, Cleveland Giants, Chicago Brown Bombers, Brooklyn Brown Dodgers 462 g, .247, 4 hr (inc.)

DeMoss, a 6'2" 175-lb righthanded hitter and a smart, aggressive fielder, was considered the best second baseman of his day in Negro League baseball. He began as a shortstop in 1905 with the Topeka Giants, the first full-time black semi-pro team in the Midwest. After hurting his arm while pitching in an emergency, he moved to second base. DeMoss spent his prime years with the Chicago American Giants, and as a player-manager for the Indianapolis ABC's and Detroit Stars. From 1920 through 1930, he batted .247, including highs of .314 for the 1929 Detroit Stars and .292 for the 1920 Chicago American Giants.

DeMoss was a proficient bunter and hit-and-run man, making him an ideal second-place hitter. Jelly Gardner, who batted ahead of DeMoss on the American Giants, said of his teammate, "If he thought you'd be out trying to steal, he'd foul off the pitch if he couldn't hit it well. He could hit 'em anywhere he wanted to.

DeMoss retired as a player after 1930, but continued to manage through 1943. His last assignment was with the Brooklyn Brown Dodgers of the

United States Baseball League, a circuit organized by Branch Rickey to scout players for possible signing by the Brooklyn Dodgers. The league lasted only one full season, 1945./(JM)

Rick Dempsey — 1949- . C 1969- Twins, Yankees, **Orioles**, Indians, Dodgers 1635 g, .234, 90 hr, 435 rbi. *3 LCS, 11 g, .296, 4 rbi. 3 WS, 14 g, .308, 1 hr, 3 rbi*

A flaky individual but a take-charge catcher, Rick Dempsey's break came on June 15, 1976 when he went from the Yankees to the Orioles in a ten-player deal. When he left Baltimore, signing as a free agent with Cleveland in 1987, he had caught more games than anyone for the Orioles. His greatest moment came as MVP of the 1983 World Series. He had the game-winning RBI in Game Two and homered and doubled in the Game Five clincher, hitting .385 overall.

Dempsey led AL catchers in fielding in 1981 and 1983 and in assists in 1979. He sacrificed batting average for added power in his last years at Baltimore (1984–86). Expected to stabilize a young Cleveland club, Dempsey suffered on both offense and defense. His 1987 season was curtailed by a broken left thumb suffered in a home plate collision with Bo Jackson. Dempsey rebounded in a reserve role with the 1988 Dodgers./(ME)

Bill Denehy — 1946- . RHP 1967-68, 71 **Mets**, Senators, Tigers 105 ip, 1-10, 4.56

When Denehy led the rookie New York-Penn League in wins and shutouts, he was ranked as a top prospect. His tendency to surrender homers curtailed his success in the majors. He was traded with $100,000 to Washington for manager Gil Hodges in 1967./(MC)

Don Denkinger — 1936- . *Umpire* AL 1968, 77-87 *2 LCS 2 WS, 2 ASU*

Denkinger was at the center of the most controversial play of the 1985 WS. The Cardinals led in the Series 3–2 and led in the ninth inning of the sixth game, 1–0. Denkinger called the Royals' Jorge Orta safe at first on a grounder to the Cardinals' Jack Clark. TV replays showed pitcher Tod Worrell had beaten Orta to the bag. Kansas City went on to rally for two runs, averting elimination, and the next day they won the Series./(RTM)

Don Dennis — 1942- . RHP 1965-66 **Cardinals** 115 ip, 6-5, 3.69

Dennis's 1.47 ERA at Jacksonville in 1965 was his ticket to the majors. Brought in from the bullpen to protect a Cardinal lead in the ninth inning, the 6'2" fastballer served up a home run which tied the score. But when teammate Bill White homered in the Cardinals' next at-bat, it made a winner out of Dennis. Undaunted, he did not allow a run in his next nine appearances and finished the year at 2–3 with six saves. His efforts gained him St. Louis rookie-of-the-year honors./(RM)

Jerry Denny [born Jeremiah Dennis Eldridge] — 1859-1927. 3B 1881-91, 93-94 **Providence (NL)**, Cardinals, Indianapolis (NL), Giants, Cleveland (NL), Phillies, Louisville (NL) 1237 g, .260, 74 hr, 512 rbi

Denny set ML career records for third basemen that still stand: 4.2 total chances per game and 1.6 putouts per game. Though he also holds the NL career record for errors at third base (553), for five seasons he ranked first or second in fielding average. On October 24, 1884 Denny hit the only home run in the first post-season series (a forerunner of the World Series) to defeat the New York Metropolitans and win the game and the Series for the Providence Grays./(FIC)

John Denny — 1952- . RHP 1974-86 **Cardinals**, Indians, Phillies, Reds 2149 ip, 123-108, 3.58 *1 LCS, 6 ip, 0-1, 0.00. 1 WS, 13 ip, 1-1, 3.46*
☛ *Led League—w 83. Led League—era 76. Cy Young Award—83. All-Star—83.*

Denny had an excellent curve and changeup, but only an average fastball. Control was all-important for his success. He helped himself considerably with fine fielding and passable batting for a pitcher. A temperamental sort, he suffered from weak ankles throughout much of his career.

A hot and cold pitcher, he led the NL in ERA with the Cardinals in 1976 but was only 11–9 on the season. Two years later, he won 14, but when he fell off to 8 wins in 1979, St. Louis traded him to Cleveland. Late in 1982 the Indians dealt him to Philadelphia.

Denny had by far his best season in 1983 with the Phillies. His 19–6 mark gave him league highs in wins and percentage. His 2.45 ERA was his personal best. The Phillies won the pennant, and Denny received the Cy Young Award./(FJO)

Bucky Dent [Russell Earl] — 1951- . SS 1973-84 White Sox, **Yankees**, Rangers, Royals 1392 g, .247, 40 hr, 423 rbi. *3 LCS, 12 g, .200, 6 rbi. 2 WS, 12 g, .349, 9 rbi.* *Manager* 1989 **Yankees** 18-22, .450
☛ *All-Star—75, 80-81.*

In 1978 Dent was the unlikely hero in the playoff game against Boston when his short three-run homer over Fenway's Green Monster, off Mike Torrez, changed the course of the game as the Yankees went on to win 5–4. His fine play continued as he was named WS MVP as the Yankees won their second straight championship with Dent at shortstop.

Dent, a promising White Sox shortstop, came to the Yankees in a much-heralded deal in April 1977. He was touted as the final piece in the great Yankee team. Dent was a natural with his boyish good looks, the perfect foil for the Yankees' rough and abrasive identity. He became an instant idol with legions of adoring teenage girls to cheer him on. He remained popular even as his skills eroded; in 1982 he narrowly missed being voted starting All-Star shortstop while hitting .200 even as Robin Yount was tearing up the league en route to an MVP award. Dent played two years for Texas and finished his career in Kansas City in 1984. He constructed a baseball training school in Florida featuring a replica of the Green Monster, and replayed the feat with an obliging Mike Torrez at the opening of the field in 1989. Dent replaced Dallas Green as Yankee manager in August 1989. /(TJG)

Sam Dente (Blackie) — 1922– . SS-3B 1947–55 Red Sox, Browns, **Senators**, White Sox, Indians 745 g, .252, 4 hr, 214 rbi. *1 WS, 3 g, .000*

This modestly talented infielder joined the Senators' starting lineup in 1949, and hit a career-high .273. The slogan "We'll win plenty with Dente" circulated through the stands at Griffith Stadium early in the campaign when the team led the league, but the catchy rhyme became more famous than the player. After the 1951 season, Dente was relegated to a utility role with the White Sox and Indians. /(RL)

Bob Dernier — 1957– . OF 1980– Phillies, **Cubs** 904 g, .255, 23 hr, 152 rbi. *2 LCS, 6 g, .235, 1 hr, 1 rbi. 1 WS, 1 g, --*
☛ *Gold Glove—84.*

A leadoff man, Dernier set a Phillies' rookie record in 1982 with 42 stolen bases. But he showed little progress as a hitter, batted .231 in 1983, and tried unsuccessfully to learn to switch-hit. Traded to Chicago with Gary Matthews in 1984, he became the first Cubs outfielder to win a Gold Glove; a far-ranging centerfielder, he compensated for slow teammates Matthews in left and Keith Moreland in right. His 45 stolen bases in '84 were the most by a Cub in 77 years. Slowed by injuries in 1985–86, he eventually lost his job to Dave Martinez, and re-signed with the Phillies as a free agent for 1988. /(JCA)

Paul Derringer

Paul Derringer (Duke, 'Oom Paul) — 1906–1988. RHP 1931–45 Cardinals, **Reds**, Cubs 3645 ip, 223–212, 3.46. 20 wins: 35, 38–40 *4 WS, 53 ip, 2–4, 3.42*
☛ *All-Star—35, 38–42.*

Derringer won 40 games at Rochester in the International League and led them to two pennants in 1929 and 1930. He helped the Cardinals win the pennant with an 18–8 mark in 1931, but was traded to the Reds in 1933 for Leo Durocher. He started and won the first major league night game at Cincinnati in 1935. Hurling three consecutive 20-win seasons (1938–40) and going 25–7 in 1939, Derringer led the Reds to two successive pennants and the World Championship in 1940. He was the winning pitcher in the 1940 All-Star Game and had two one-hit games that same season.

Derringer led the league in winning percentage in 1931 and 1939, games lost in 1933, games started in 1936, 1938, and 1940, and complete games and innings pitched in 1938. He had 32 career shutouts, won ten 1–0 complete games, and had a 1.88 walk ratio. He was sold to the Cubs in 1943 and helped them capture the pennant in 1945. /(JE)

Gene Desautels (Red) — 1907– . C 1930–33, 37–43, 45–46 Tigers, **Red Sox**, Indians, A's 712 g, .233, 3 hr, 186 rbi

While playing at Holy Cross under coach Jack Berry, Desautels was a peppy, rah-rah catcher adept at encouraging and supporting young pitchers. He spent four seasons as a backup catcher for the Tigers and then returned to the minors for three seasons. He joined the Red Sox in 1937 and played regularly for four years. In 1938, his best season, he caught 108 games and hit .291. After the 1940 season, he was traded to the Indians and returned to his backup role. /(NLM)

Jim Deshaies — 1960– . LHP 1984– Yankees, **Astros** 738 ip, 49–36, 3.42

One of several promising young pitchers traded away by the impatient Yankees in the 1980s, Deshaies pitched a no-hitter for Nashville (Southern League) in 1984 before leading the International League in ERA at Columbus the same season, and became the 1,000th player ever to play for the Yankees that September. He was shelled in his two ML starts, however, then struggled at Columbus in 1985, and was traded to Houston for 40-year-old Joe Niekro in the last two weeks of the season.

Deshaies was 12–5, 3.25 as a rookie with the Astros in 1986, and on September 23 he set a ML record by striking out the first eight Dodgers he faced before journeyman Larry See popped out. As the Astros' fourth starter, however, he did not pitch in the LCS against the Mets. Deshaies struggled in 1987, but still posted an 11–6 record, and in 1988 he lowered his ERA to a career-best 3.00, while his record slipped to 11–14. /(SCL)

Jimmie DeShong — 1909– . RHP 1932, 34–39 A's, Yankees, **Senators** 873 ip, 47–44, 5.08

Notoriously wild, DeShong was a reliever for the 1934–35 Yankees before being dealt to Washington. He posted an 18–10 mark in 1936, but slumped in 1938, and was waived back to the Yankees early in 1939. He finished his career in the minors. /(MC)

Detroit Tigers — 1901– . Team. 7133–6613, .519. *AL East Champions 72, 84, 87 AL Champions 07–09, 34–35, 40, 45, 68, 84 World Champions 35, 45, 68, 84*

The Tigers rival any team in baseball for the distinction as most conservative. Authoritarian ownership through the years resisted change (night baseball, the hiring of black players and free agents) while fielding teams that have been generally re-

The 1935 Detroit Tigers

spectable, sometimes outstanding, rarely just bad. Detroit was a charter member of the American League in 1901. The city was at first an indifferent baseball town; AL president Ban Johnson considered moving the Detroit team to Pittsburgh in 1903. But the NL blocked the move at the same time it granted recognition to the American League. The automobile industry spurred growth in Detroit and support for the Tigers followed. That support has rarely slipped. Tiger baseball became big business under the ownership of Frank Navin (1907–35). The team won five pennants during that period, and its first World Series in 1935, shortly before Navin's death. Walter O. Briggs Sr., the new owner, enlarged the home stadium, Navin Field (dating to 1912) in 1938 to 56,000 seats and renamed it after himself.

In 1940, major league baseball Commissioner Landis awarded free agency to 91 Tigers players, ruling that general manager Jack Zeller had violated baseball's working agreement with the minor leagues by making secret deals with players on different teams in the same leagues. Forty-eight years later, an arbitrator freed Tigers star Kirk Gibson after finding the Tigers guilty of collusion in restricting the free agent market. Only the Cubs held out longer against night baseball than the Tigers, who added lights in 1948. Detroit signed no black players until after Briggs died in 1952 and his son, Walter Jr., succeeded him. Third baseman Ossie Virgil (June 6, 1958) was the first black to play for the Tigers. From 1951 to 1960, Detroit never finished better than 17 games out of first place. Briggs' heirs sold the team to his partners in 1960. John Fetzer and general manager Jim Campbell built strong teams based on pitching, defense, and left-handed power. In a key move, they hired Sparky Anderson to manage in mid-1979. Pizza magnate Tom Monaghan purchased the team in October 1983, and his new willingness to spend money helped Anderson acquire the right players to operate his incomparable platoon system. Anderson's tenure peaked with a World Series victory in 1984 over the San Diego Padres. /(KT)

Tom Dettore — 1947– . RHP 1973–76 Pirates, **Cubs** 179 ip, 8–11, 5.21

Dettore never spent a full season in the ML. In 1975, he was 5–4 as a reliever for the pitching-poor Cubs, but his 5.40 ERA showed his ineffectiveness in the bullpen. /(MC)

Mike Devereaux — 1963– . OF 1987– Dodgers, **Orioles** 171 g, .248, 8 hr, 52 rbi

Devereaux unexpectedly made the Dodgers with a hot spring training in 1987, but soon played himself back to the minors. He went to Baltimore after 1988 in the Eddie Murray deal and finally hit well at the major league level in 1989 as a part-time outfielder. A .300 hitter with power in the minors, in the majors he is more valuable for his speed. /(JFC)

Adrian Devine — 1951– . RHP 1973, 1975–80 **Braves**, Rangers 387 ip, 26–22, 4.21

Signed by Atlanta, swapped to Texas, returned to Atlanta, and traded back to Texas in some complicated deals, Devine rebounded after 1975 arm surgery and set a Ranger record with 15 saves in 1977. Arm trouble ultimately ended his career after 1980. /(MC)

Joe Devine — 1895–1951. *Scout.*

From 1923 to 1930 Devine was the Pirates scout on the West Coast, where he discovered Paul and Lloyd Waner, Joe Cronin, and Arky Vaughan. After managing in the Pacific Coast League for two years, he joined the Yankees' scouting staff, and discovered or purchased Joe DiMaggio, Billy Martin, and Jackie Jensen. /(FVP)

Art Devlin — 1879–1948. 3B 1904–13 **Giants**, Braves 1301 g, .269, 10 hr, 504 rbi. *1 WS, 5 g, .250, 1 rbi*

Famed sportswriter Grantland Rice named Devlin third baseman on his all-time Giants team. After

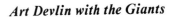

Art Devlin with the Giants

two minor league seasons at Newark, Devlin joined New York in 1904. In three of his eight Giant seasons, he led NL third basemen in assists; in 1908 he also led in putouts and fielding average. Alert and speedy, he had good range at third base (he ranks 15th all-time in chances per game) and stole more than 20 bases six times, tying for the league lead with 59 in 1905. Devlin's best batting average was .299 in 1906. He averaged only one HR per year but his first HR came in his first ML at bat, with the bases loaded. After finishing his NL career with two seasons in Boston, Devlin played four additional years in the minors. /(FIC)

Jim Devlin — 1849–1883. RHP-1B 1873–77 Philadelphia (NA), Chicago (NA), **Louisville (NL)** *NA*: 136 g, .275; 6–16; NL: 129 g, .293, 1 hr, 55 rbi; 1181 ip, 65–60, 1.89. 20 wins: 76–77
☛ *Led League—k 76.*

Devlin was the workhorse of the NL in its first two seasons, pitching nearly all of Louisville's games and logging 1,181 innings. Late in 1877, he was implicated with three teammates in throwing games that denied the Colonels what had seemed a sure pennant. He was expelled from baseball and died nearly destitute six years later. /(FIC)

Josh Devore — 1887–1954. OF 1908–14 **Giants**, Reds, Phillies, Braves 601 g, .277, 11 hr, 149 rbi

An expert bunter and baserunner who was adept at drawing walks, Devore was an effective leadoff man for the Giants' pennant-winners of 1911 and 1912. In a 21–12 win over the Braves (6/20/12), he stole four bases in one inning, reaching first twice in the ninth and stealing second and third each time. His spectacular catch of a fly ball in deep right center with two men on in Game Three of the 1912 WS preserved a 2–1 victory for the Giants. His last ML appearance was as a WS pinch hitter for the "Miracle Braves" of 1914. /(NLM)

Charlie Dexter — 1876–1934. OF-C-3B-1B 1896–1903 **Louisville (NL)**, Cubs, Braves 771 g, .261, 16 hr, 346 rbi

Dexter did everything but pitch, and six times stole over 20 bases. In 1898, his .314 BA was Louisville's second-highest, and his 44 stolen bases ranked fourth in the NL. /(FIC)

Lou Dials [Alonzo Odem] — 1904– . 1B-OF-MGR Negro Leagues 1925–46 Chicago American Giants, Memphis Red Sox, Detroit Stars, Hilldale, Columbus Blue Birds, Akron, New York Black Yankees, Cleveland Giants, Homestead Grays statistics not available
☛ *All-Star—36.*

An outstanding outfielder and first baseman, Dials broke in with one of Negro baseball's most powerful teams, the Chicago American Giants, in 1925. Unconfirmed statistics show Dials winning the 1931 Negro National League batting title with a .382 average for the Detroit Stars. Returning to Chicago, he was an all-star in 1936. With the Negro Leagues on shaky financial ground, Dials went to the North Mexican League, where he managed Torrion to two championships and continued to hit well over .300.

Had the Pacific Coast League owners had the strength to oppose Commissioner Landis, in 1943 Dials could have been the first black signed into organized ball. Dials and Chet Brewer were set to become members of the Los Angeles Angels (PCL) until Chicago Cubs owner Phil Wrigley vetoed the plan. They later were denied a chance by the Oakland owner as well, who said, "The other owners would crucify me if I let you play." Dials continued to barnstorm against white major leaguers until his retirement. He became a scout and an outstanding speaker on behalf of the Negro Leagues. /(DC)

Bo Diaz — 1953– . C 1977–89 Red Sox, Indians, Phillies, **Reds** 993 g, .255, 87 hr, 452 rbi. *1 LCS, 4 g, .154. 1 WS, 5 g, .333*
☛ *All-Star—81.*

Diaz had only one at-bat with the Red Sox in 1977 and played sporadically for Cleveland as the backup to Ron Hassey until an injury to Hassey made him the Indians' starting catcher early in 1981. He hit .356 with 25 RBI in the first half of that strike-interrupted season but sprained his wrist as the season resumed and missed the rest of the year. After he was traded to Philadelphia for 1982, his first NL season was his best, as he hit .288 with 18 HR and 85 RBI, but in 1984 he lost his job to Ozzie Virgil. Diaz became a starter again with the Reds in 1986–87, but hit only .219 in 92 games in 1988. In 1989, he shared the Reds' catching job with Jeff Reed. /(SG)

Carlos Diaz — 1958– . LHP 1982–86 Braves, Mets, **Dodgers** 258 ip, 13–6, 3.21. *1 LCS, 3 ip, 0–0, 3.00*

Diaz, who relied primarily upon a hard slider, was almost exclusively used as a set-up man. He was involved in a rare Hawaiian-for-Hawaiian trade when the Mets included him in the package to secure Sid Fernandez from the Dodgers. /(TG)

Mike Diaz (Rambo) — 1960– . 1B-OF-C 1983, 86- Cubs, **Pirates**, White Sox 293 g, .247, 31 hr, 102 rbi

The muscular Diaz could play first base, outfield, catcher, or third base, but always seemed best-suited for DH. He was popular and a good pinch hitter. His 12 HR in 1986 were second to teammate Barry Bonds among NL rookies. He tied a ML record with no putouts at first base in a nine-inning game on June 26, 1987./(ME)

Rob Dibble — 1964– . RHP 1988– **Reds** 158 ip, 11–6, 1.99

An extremely hard thrower with a phenomenal strikeout ratio, Dibble came into his own in the first half of 1989 as a set-up man for John Franco, although he injured his shoulder in a fight after hitting the Mets' Tim Teufel with a pitch./(SFS)

Leo Dickerman — 1896–1982. RHP 1923–25 Dodgers, **Cardinals** 436 ip, 19–27, 3.95

Dickerman, a 6'4" power pitcher, debuted at age 27 with the 1923 Dodgers. Traded to the Cards for veteran pitcher Bill Doak, Dickerman went 7–4 (2.84) in 1924. His 4–11 record and 5.58 ERA in 1925 meant the end of his ML career./(DQV)

Bill Dickey — 1907– . C 1928–43, 46 **Yankees** 1,789 g, .313, 202 hr, 1,209 rbi. *8 WS, 38 g, .255, 5 hr, 24 rbi*

☛ *All-Star—33–34, 36–43, 46. Hall of Fame—1954.*

The premier catcher of the late 1930s and early 1940s, the lefthanded-hitting Dickey was the soul of the Yankee dynasty bridging the Ruth, Gehrig and DiMaggio eras as a player, and the Mantle era as a coach. He was a keen handler of pitchers, especially the erratic Lefty Gomez, as quiet as his roommate, Gehrig, consistent, setting a major league record for catching 100 or more games in 13 straight seasons, and never played another game at another position. He was the first Yankee to find out about Gehrig's illness and was the only active player to play himself in the Gary Cooper movie "Pride of the Yankees." The Yankees retired his number 8, but ironically Dickey didn't wear that number at the start or the end of his Yankee days. When Dickey first came up, Benny Benbaugh wore number eight. When he came back to coach, Yogi Berra was wearing it.

Dickey's quiet demeanor off the field belied fiery behavior behind the plate. On July 4, 1932 he was suspended for 30 days and fined $1,000 for breaking the jaw of the Senators' Carl Reynolds with one punch, after a collision at home plate. In the 1934 All-Star Game, Dickey broke Carl Hubbell's strikeout string with a single. After six straight .300-plus seasons, Dickey dipped to .279 in 1935, but came back the next season with a fury. From 1936 to 1939, Dickey, who had never hit more than 14 homers in a season, belted 102 in four years. He had a career high of 29 in 1937, including grand slams on consecutive days, August 3 and 4. His batting average bloomed as well, with a career-high .362 in 1936, followed by a .332 mark in 1937.

Dickey continued his batting onslaught in the second game of the 1936 World Series against the crosstown Giants when he hit a two-run homer and knocked in five runs. On July 26, 1939 he slammed three straight homers against the Browns in a 14–1 win. In the four-game World Series sweep that year against the Reds, Dickey slammed two homers and drove in five runs, including the winning run in the bottom of the ninth in Game One. Dickey also

Bill Dickey

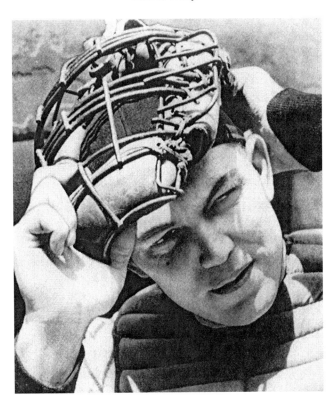

caught more World Series games than any catcher, 38.

Both Dickey's average and power dropped drastically in 1940 and 1941, totaling only 16 homers in two years. In 1942, Dickey caught only 82 games, and only 85 in 1943, but drove in the only two runs with a homer in the fifth and final game of the World Series against the Cardinals, avenging the Yankees' loss the year before. At the end of the season, at age 36, Dickey enlisted in the Navy. He came back for a final go-round in 1946, but appeared in only 54 games. Midway through the season, he took over the managerial reins from Joe McCarthy, who had gone to manage the Red Sox. He guided the Yankees to a 57–48 mark, but resigned right after the season. He came back as a coach under Casey Stengel from 1947 to 1957, passing along his knowledge to Berra. He scouted for the Yankees in 1959 before retiring. /(SEW)

George H. Dickinson — Unk.–1937. *Writer.*

Dickinson was sports editor of the New York *Herald* in its heyday, and his support in publicizing the Brotherhood helped get the Players' League off the ground in 1890. His knowledge of telegraphy helped him to a scoop when he picked up news of a big deal going over the wire in a hotel lobby. He was later managing editor of the New York *Evening Telegram.*/(NLM)

Emerson Dickman — 1914–1981. RHP 1936–41 **Red Sox** 349 ip, 22–15, 5.33

The two-sport star at Washington and Lee University was regularly ribbed for his resemblance to movie star Robert Taylor. His career in the Red Sox bullpen was curtailed by military service in WWII. He later coached at Princeton. /(NLM)

Johnny Dickshot [born John Oscar Dicksus] — 1910– . OF 1936–39, 44–45 Pirates, Giants, **White Sox** 322 g, .276, 7 hr, 116 rbi

A part-timer until 1945, Dickshot was Chicago's everyday left fielder that season; he batted .302, third-best in the AL, and finished fifth with 18 stolen bases./(TJ)

Jim Dickson — 1938– . RHP 1963–66 Astros, Red, A's 142 ip, 5–3, 4.36

Although Dickson came up briefly in 1963 with Houston, his first full season was 1965 with the A's. The hard thrower came out of the bullpen 68 times that summer to establish an AL rookie record. His 5.35 ERA in 1966 ended his ML career./(RTM)

Murry Dickson — 1916– . RHP 1939–40, 42–43, 46–59 Cardinals, **Pirates**, Phillies, A's, Yankees 3052 ip, 172–181, 3.66. 20 wins: 51 *3 WS, 19 ip, 0–1, 3.86* ☛ *All-Star—53.*

Since his six-pitch repertoire required much experimentation, Dickson came to be called "the Thomas Edison of the mound." He pitched in the 1943 WS while on furlough from the army. Topping the NL with a .714 winning percentage in 1946, his 15–6 record included the Cardinals' pennant-clinching playoff victory over Brooklyn. Sold to Pittsburgh in January 1949, Dickson had a career-high 20 wins in 1951. He led the league in losses three straight years (1952–54), losing 60 games over that span. Dickson received credit for the save in the 1953 All-Star Game. /(TJ)

Walt Dickson (Hickory) — 1878–1918. RHP 1910, 12–15 Giants, Braves, **Pittsburgh (FL)** 700 ip, 25–52, 3.60

Dickson had little success in either the National or Federal Leagues. He was 3–19 for the 1912 Braves and led the Feds with 21 losses for Pittsburgh in 1914. He led the Texas League in ERA (1.06) in 1916. /(ME)

Bob Didier — 1949– . C 1969–74 **Braves**, Tigers, Red Sox 247 g, .229, 0 hr, 51 rbi. *1 LCS, 3 g, .000*

The switch-hitting son of longtime baseball scout Mel Didier, Bob was named to the Topps ML rookie all-star team in 1969, when he hit .256 for Atlanta in his only season as a regular. He became an Oakland coach in 1984./(TJ)

Chuck Diering [Charles Edward Allen] — 1923– . OF 1947–52, 54–56 **Cardinals**, Giants, Orioles 752 g, .249, 14 hr, 141 rbi

Signed by his hometown Cardinals in 1941, Diering's most active year with St. Louis was 1949, when he hit .263 in 131 games. In December 1951, Diering and Max Lanier were traded to the Giants for Eddie Stanky. A late-inning defensive replacement in New York, Diering had only 23 at-bats in 1952. In 1954, Baltimore's first season, Diering was named the most valuable Oriole, batting .258. /(RTM)

Larry Dierker — 1946– . RHP 1964–77 **Astros**, Cardinals 2334 ip, 139–123, 3.30. 20 wins: 69 ☛ *All-Star—69, 71.*

Larry Dierker used his fastball, curveball, screwball, slider, and changeup to reach double figures in victories nine times, and in 1969 became the first Astro to win 20. Coveted by 18 ML teams, the 6'4" Hollywood, CA native signed with Houston and debuted on his 18th birthday. His 1967 campaign was shortened by military service, and in 1973 he suffered a shoulder injury. On July 9, 1976 Dierker no-hit the Expos; the Montreal manager was Karl Kuehl, who had signed him. "I didn't think I would ever do it," exclaimed Dierker upon finally pitching a no-hitter after four near-misses. He left the Astros in 1976 as their career leader in virtually every pitching department./(TJ)

Bill Dietrich (Bullfrog) — 1910–1978. RHP 1933–48 A's, Senators, **White Sox** 2004 ip, 108–128, 4.48

Though Dietrich was a Philadelphia product, the Athletics' Connie Mack waived him to Washington in 1936, believing he would never gain control. Unable to see without his glasses, Dietrich was a stubborn fireballer with streaks of wildness. He often hurt himself by getting frustrated by late-inning walks and hits, or by teammates' errors. He improved his control in his 10-plus seasons with the White Sox, but was never a strikeout pitcher, and rarely a winner. Yet on June 1, 1937 he no-hit the Browns, 8–0. Believing a seventh-inning error had been ruled a hit, he did not know what he had accomplished until his teammates mobbed him after the last out. He won a career-high 16 games in 1944 while losing 17, tops in the AL./(DB)

Dick Dietz (Mule) — 1941– . C 1966–73 **Giants**, Dodgers, Braves 646 g, .261, 66 hr, 301 rbi. *1 LCS, 4 g, .067*
☛ *All-Star—70.*

Signing for $90,000 in 1963, Dietz and his roommate, fellow bonus catcher Randy Hundley, became known as "The Gold Dust Twins." Called up late in 1966, he hit a 410-foot homer off Sandy Koufax. Playing just 56 games in 1967, he was named the Topps all-star rookie catcher, but didn't become a regular until 1970. That year, he peaked in every offensive category (.300, 22 HR, 107 RBI), and homered in the ninth inning of the All-Star Game. Beaned in mid-1971, Dietz played down the stretch in a tight race with L.A. with his head heavily bandaged. When the Giants clinched, Dietz grabbed a radio microphone to shout, "The Dodgers can go to hell!" Because of a clerical error, the Giants lost Dietz to the Dodgers in 1972, but he broke his finger in his first start for Los Angeles./(MC)

Dutch Dietz — 1912–1972. RHP 1940–43 **Pirates**, Phillies 295 ip, 14–16, 3.87

The reliever led Pittsburgh in winning percentage (.778, 7–2) and ERA (2.33) as a 29-year-old rookie in 1941. Dietz was the most active Pirate reliever in '41 and '42./(ME)

Martin Dihigo

Martin Dihigo — 1905–1971. 2B-RHP-OF-SS-3B-1B-C-MGR Negro Leagues 1923–36, 45 Cuban Stars (East), New York Cubans, Homestead Grays, Philadelphia Hilldale, Darby Daisies 405 g, .297, 62 hr (inc.); 218–106
☛ *Led League—hr 26 (ECL), 35 (NNL). All-Star—35, 45. Hall of Fame—1977.*

Martin Dihigo, a 6'3" 210-lb righthanded Cuban, was one of the most versatile players of all time. His incredible skills gained him the unique honor of being elected to the Mexican, Cuban, and American Halls of Fame. Endowed with great speed and an exceptionally strong arm, Dihigo was a star performer at every position.

Dihigo began his American career in 1923 at the age of 18, playing first base with the touring Cuban Stars. He played in America from 1923 until 1936. After 1936 he played his summer ball in Mexico, except in 1945 when he was the player-manager of the New York Cubans. He reportedly continued to play in the Mexican Leagues until the 1950s, although his statistics are available only through 1947.

Statistics documenting Dihigo's American career exist for 1923–31, 1935–36, and 1945. In those 12 years, Dihigo hit over .300 six times, including .325 in 1926 with a league-leading 11 home runs in 40 games, and .333 in 1935 with a league-leading 9 home runs in 42 games. His overall American statistics show a .295 career batting average and a 6–1 record as a pitcher in 1931.

Dihigo was primarily a pitcher in Latin America, where he was known for his blazing fastball. His Mexican League totals show a lifetime .317 batting average in 10 seasons (1937–44, 1946–47), including a league-leading .387 in 1938. He was 119–57 as a pitcher in Mexico, going 18–2 with a 0.90 ERA in 1938 and 22–7 with a league-leading 2.53 ERA in 1942. He threw the first no-hitter in Mexican League history, and also had no-hitters in Venezuela and Puerto Rico.

Dihigo played for 24 seasons in Cuba (1922–29, 1931–46). The record of his Cuban career is somewhat fragmentary, but for the years which are documented (1922–29, 1931, 1935–46), he hit over .300 nine times, finishing with a lifetime .291 batting average. As a pitcher he was 93–48 in 1935–46.

Statistics exist for one year of play in the Dominican Republic (1937), when Dihigo hit .351.

Combining his Dominican, American, Cuban and Mexican statistics results in a lifetime .302 batting average with 130 home runs (11 seasons worth of home run totals are missing) and a 218–106 (.673) pitching mark. Dihigo often showed his versatility in Negro League competition by playing all nine positions in the course of a single game.

Known for his warm, friendly personality, Dihigo was a national hero in his native Cuba, where he served as Minister of Sport in his later years. He was elected posthumously to the American baseball Hall of Fame in 1977. In a poll conducted in the early 1980s among ex-Negro League players and other experts on black baseball, Dihigo gathered votes as best all-time outfielder and third baseman, and was voted to the first team all-time black all-star team as a second baseman. /(JJM)

Steve Dillard — 1951– . 2B-3B-SS 1975–82 Red Sox, Tigers, **Cubs**, White Sox 438 g, .243, 13 hr, 102 rbi

A good-fielding utility man, Dillard never played more than 60 games at one position in a season. /(JFC)

Bob Dillinger — 1918– . 3B 1946–51 **Browns**, A's, Pirates, White Sox 753 g, .306, 10 hr, 213 rbi
☛ *All-Star—49.*

Dillinger led the AL in hits in 1948 and in stolen bases three consecutive years (1947–49). After batting .292 in 1951, Dillinger retired at age 33, claiming to have lost interest in the game. /(DQV)

Bill Dillman — 1945– . RHP 1967, 70 **Orioles**, Expos 155 ip, 7–12, 4.53

Dillman pitched five no-hit innings for Baltimore versus the A's in his ML debut, and won his first four decisions before the hitters caught up with his strictly fastball-curveball repertoire. /(MC)

Frank Dillon (Pop) — 1873–1931. 1B 1899–1902, 04 Pirates, Tigers, Orioles, **Dodgers** 312 g, .252, 1 hr, 116 rbi

On opening day of the AL's first season (4/25/01), Dillon led the Tigers to their first victory by becoming the first AL batter to hit four doubles in one game. Early in the 1902 season, he was sent to Los Angeles of the Pacific Coast League, where he became a hitting star. The adept hit-and-run man was captain of the Brooklyn Dodgers in 1904, then returned to Los Angeles to become player-manager for 11 seasons. In 2,175 minor league games, he averaged .295. /(TG)

Miguel Dilone [born Miguel Angel Reyes Reyes] — 1954– . OF 1974–85 Pirates, A's, **Indians**, White Sox, Expos, Padres 800 g, .265, 6 hr, 129 rbi

This free-swinging Dominican singles hitter stole 267 bases in his career, with a season-best 61 for the Indians in 1980, third in the AL. Dilone (pronounced de-lo-NAY) spent four seasons trying unsuccessfully to break into the Pirates' outfield. In 1977 he set a since-broken NL record for the most steals in a season without being caught, 12. He finally got some playing time with the A's in 1978, and he stole 50 bases, fourth in the AL. He was also caught stealing 23 times. Dilone hit just .229 that year and scored 34 runs in 258 at-bats. He was sold to the Cubs in mid-1979 and Cleveland bought him at the end of the season.

Dilone's stolen base percentage in 1980 was much better (61-for-79), and he had career highs in BA (.341, third in the AL) and runs (82), but walked only 28 times in 528 at-bats. He never again got as much playing time. /(WOR)

Dom DiMaggio (The Little Professor) — 1917– . OF 1940–42, 46–53 Red Sox 1,399 g, .298, 87 hr, 618 rbi.
1 WS, 7 g, .259, 3 rbi
☛ *All-Star—41–42, 46, 49–52.*

The youngest and smallest of the three DiMaggio brothers, the bespectacled centerfielder was a perennial All-Star with the Red Sox for 11 seasons, missing three years of his prime because of WWII. Twice DiMaggio, together with Ted Williams, was part of a .300-hitting outfield, once in his rookie year of 1940 with Doc Cramer in right field, and

*Dom DiMaggio with the San Francisco
Seals of the Pacific Coast League*

again 10 years later in 1950 with Al Zarilla in right. A slick fielder, fans used to yell that he played his own position as well as the slow-footed Williams's spot in left field. DiMaggio set the pace for consistency, hitting in 34 straight games in 1949, and another 27 straight in 1951, and scored more than 100 runs seven times. In the 1946 Series, he scored the deciding run in Game Five to give the Red Sox a 3–2 edge in the Series, eventually lost in seven games to the Cardinals on Enos Slaughter's dash for home. Twice DiMaggio led the league in at-bats from his leadoff spot, and twice in runs scored. He shared the outfield with brother Joe in three All-Star games, and drove him in with a single in the 1941 game./(SEW)

Joe DiMaggio (Joltin' Joe, The Yankee Clipper) — 1914- . OF 1936–42, 46–51 **Yankees** 1736 g, .325, 361 hr, 1537 rbi. *10 WS, 51 g, .271, 8 hr, 30 rbi* ☛ *Most Valuable Player—39, 41, 47. Led League—ba 39–40. Led League—hr 37, 48. Led League—rbi 41, 48. All-Star—36–42, 46–51. Hall of Fame—1955.*

During the centennial celebration of professional baseball, Joe DiMaggio was named the game's greatest living player. Since that 1969 assessment,

DiMaggio's legend has grown with the fans who made it. He remained a top-drawer celebrity almost 40 years after playing his final game.

The Yankee Clipper could do everything well. He may have been the best all-around player ever, with a generous dash of class added in. His natural talent became apparent in 1933 when he batted safely in 61 consecutive games playing for his hometown San Francisco Seals in the Pacific Coast League. Scouts flocked to see him, but they shied away when DiMaggio injured a knee. The Yankees' interest continued, however, and a deal was arranged in 1934 that allowed DiMaggio to play one more year with the Seals. He came to New York in 1936 and set AL rookie records for runs (132) and triples (15), besides hitting .323 with 29 HR and 125 RBI. He was an instant star.

DiMaggio was a beautiful hitter with a classic swing. He had an exceptionally wide stance that gave him a controlled short stride, strong wrists that generated enormous power, and the ability to wait until the last instant before lashing into a pitch. His 46 homers in 1937, including a ML-record 15 in July, remain a Yankee record for a righthanded hitter. What makes his HR total more impressive is that he played half his games at Yankee Stadium, then the toughest power park in baseball for righties. At the time left-centerfield, known as "Death Valley", extended 457 feet from the plate. DiMaggio also hit as high as .381 in 1939, and struck out only 369 times in his career while hitting 361 homers, a phenomenal ratio for a power hitter.

But DiMaggio was more than a hitter. He was a splendid defensive outfielder with a great throwing arm. He made tough plays look easy. He was graceful and free of theatrics, and he was positioned correctly all the time. He was studious. His positioning encompassed the batter, the pitcher, and the count. He was always alert to the game situation, and always threw to the correct base. He was virtually flawless in 1947, making one lone error on the year. And to his manager, Joe McCarthy, he was "the best base runner I ever saw." DiMaggio was the quiet, undemonstrative type McCarthy liked. He was introspective, sometimes stoic. But he was a leader all the same, steering the Yankees to nine World Championships.

DiMaggio had two major league careers, one before World War II and the other after it. In each year of the former (1936–42) he hit over .300 and exceeded 100 RBI. This was the time of his magical 56-game hitting streak. The "impossible" streak—traveling a dozen games beyond Wee Willie Keeler's 1897 consecutive-game record of 44 and 15

Joe DiMaggio, Senators third baseman Eddie Yost, umpire George McQuinn

games beyond what had been the modern record, George Sisler's 41-game string of 1922—began on May 15, 1941. It kept an entire nation enthralled through June and half of July, before two great plays by Cleveland third baseman Ken Keltner ended it on July 17. DiMaggio hit .407 during the streak and edged Boston's Ted Williams for the AL MVP award, even though Williams hit .406 that year.

The war took three prime years from DiMaggio's baseball life. His second career was beset by injuries and then eroding skills. But he was still DiMaggio. Boston claimed an easy pennant in 1946, but there would be no Red Sox dynasty. The Yankees were World Champions in 1947, 1949, 1950, and 1951. Even while playing most of 1948 with a painful heel injury, DiMaggio almost brought the Yankees home. The Yankees lost out to the Red Sox and Indians on the next-to-last day of the season, but DiMaggio led the league in home runs (39) and RBI (155).

DiMaggio's career seemed over in 1949. He was unable to stand on his sore heel without pain and, of course, was unable to play. One miraculous June morning, the pain was gone, and DiMaggio made a spectacular return. After missing the season's first 65 games, he led the Yankees to a three-game sweep of

the Red Sox at Fenway Park with four homers and nine RBI. His brother Dom, a Red Sox star, witnessed the display (another brother, Vince, also was a major leaguer).

Many experts consider Joe DiMaggio the best player in the history of the game. He is admired not only for his achievements but for his refusal to rest on his natural skills, working instead to constantly improve his play. He was responsible to himself, his teammates, and his fans. He had pride. He was more than an exceptional athlete; he was the consummate professional. /(MG)

Vince DiMaggio — 1912- . OF 1937–46 Braves, Reds, **Pirates**, Phillies, Giants 1110 g, .249, 125 hr, 584 rbi
☛ *All-Star—43–44.*

The oldest of the three DiMaggios, Vince was a good fielder and baserunner, but could not hit like Joe or Dom. Six times he led the league in striking out, and in 1938 set a ML record by fanning 134 times (a mark frequently surpassed since). He reached highs of 21 HR and 100 RBI for the Pirates in 1941, and hit four grand slams for the Phillies in 1945. He played in two All-Star Games and collected a homer, triple, and single in the 1943 contest. As a centerfielder, he led the NL in assists three times and putouts twice. Vince had a long minor league career, including four years as a player-manager. /(LRD)

Lou DiMuro — 1931-1982. *Umpire* AL 1963-80, 82 *3 LCS 2 WS, 4 ASU*

Affectionately called "Pops" by those who knew him, DiMuro was struck by a car and killed in Arlington, Texas, shortly after umpiring a twi-nite White Sox-Rangers game. He was beset by accidents throughout his career. In May 1979 the Yankees' Cliff Johnson crashed into him in a play at the plate and sidelined him for most of the season. Two years later he suffered a sprained back and severe bruises when he slipped and fell in the Milwaukee visitors' dugout during a rain delay. Ironically, his umpiring career began due to an injury; he had broken a finger while playing baseball in the Air Force and turned to umpiring to remain active. /(RTM)

Bill Dineen (Big Bill) — 1876-1955. RHP 1898-09 Washington NL, Braves, **Red Sox**, Browns 3074 ip, 171-177, 3.01. 20 wins: 00, 02-04 *1 WS, 35 ip, 3-1, 2.06.*
Umpire AL 1909-37 *8 WS, 1 ASU*

Dineen won 20 games for the 1900 Braves but really came into his own when he jumped to the Red Sox in 1902. He had three straight seasons of 21 or more wins. The hero of the 1903 WS, he won three of four decisions. Two of his victories, including the final game, were shutouts. In 1905, he pitched a no-hitter against the White Sox. Dineen went directly from pitching in the AL to umpiring in the league. During his 29 years as an AL umpire, he worked in 45 WS games. During the early 1930s, the AL gave a cash prize to the umpire with the lowest average time for his games. The winner was Dineen. /(RTM)

Frank DiPino — 1956- . LHP 1981- Brewers, **Astros**, Cubs, Cardinals 592 ip, 29-35, 3.69

DiPino threw a seven-inning, Eastern League no-hitter for Holyoke as a Milwaukee farmhand on June 8, 1980. Acquired in a 1982 trade for Don Sutton, DiPino led the Astros in saves in 1983 (20) and 1984 (14). He struggled with control in 1985, and, with Dave Smith's emergence as a closer, was dealt to the Cubs for Davey Lopes in 1986. He went 9-0 in 1989 as a middle reliever for the Cardinals. /(JCA)

Dizzy Dismukes [William] — 1890-1961. RHP-MGR Negro Leagues 1913-50 Philadelphia Giants, Brooklyn Royal Giants, Mohawk Giants, **Indianapolis ABC's,** Chicago American Giants, Dayton Marcos, Pittsburgh Keystones, Memphis Red Sox, St. Louis Stars, Cincinnati Dismukes, Detroit Wolves, Homestead Grays, Columbus Blue Birds, Birmingham Black Barons, Kansas City Monarchs 26-22 (inc.)

Dismukes had a 37-year career in Negro League baseball that spanned all aspects of the game. He began in 1913 as a submarine pitcher with the Philadelphia Giants and played until the early 1930s. He then spent 20 years as a coach, manager, team business manager, and, ultimately, secretary of the Negro National League. While overseas during WWI, he reputedly taught major leaguer Carl Mays how to pitch.

One of the top black pitchers of the 1910s, Dismukes pitched the Brooklyn Royal Giants to the Eastern Negro Championship in 1914, then started three times in the four-game Black World Series against the Chicago American Giants. The Royal Giants lost the series, but no record of Dismukes's efforts remain. His most productive years as a pitcher were spent with the Indianapolis ABC's. He appeared with them in three games of the 1916 Black World Series, starting two and going 1-1. He was 11-6 for the ABC's in 1920, the first year of his career. The five-time 20-game winner notched a creer-high 30 victories in 1961. From 1958 through 1964, he never worked fewer than 44 games or 263 innings a season. /(MC)

Art Ditmar — 1929- . RHP 1954-62 A's, **Yankees** 1268 ip, 72-77, 3.98. *3 WS, 11 ip, 0-2, 3.18*

After leading the AL with 22 losses with the 1956 A's, the rubber-armed Ditmar went to the Yankees in a nine-player deal. He won 28 games for the 1959-60 Yankees, then unexpectedly plummeted.

Manager Casey Stengel's decision to start Ditmar over ace Whitey Ford in Game One of the 1960 World Series has been second-guessed by many, since Ditmar retired only one batter while giving up three runs in the Pirates' 6-4 win. Deprived of the chance to pitch three times, Ford threw shutouts in the third and sixth games, but Pittsburgh triumphed in seven. Ditmar was bombed again in Game Five. When a Budweiser TV commercial of the mid-1980s incorporated the original radio broadcast of Game Seven, with announcer Chuck Thompson erroneously naming Ditmar instead of Ralph Terry as the pitcher off whom Bill Mazeroski hit his famous home run, Ditmar sued Anheuser-Busch for $500,000, saying his reputation was tarnished. /(RTM)

Jack Dittmer — 1928- . 2B 1952-57 **Braves**, Tigers 395 g, .232, 24 hr, 136 rbi

A hot lefthanded-hitting minor leaguer, Dittmer reached his ML peak batting .266 as the 1953 Braves' regular second baseman, but was a part-timer thereafter. /(RTM)

Ken Dixon — 1960- . RHP 1984-87 **Orioles** 482 ip, 26-28, 4.66

Dixon looked to have a long future with the Orioles after his 8-4 (3.67) rookie 1985 season. He had a 90-mph fastball and a major league curve. But after being hit hard in 1987, falling to 7-10 (6.43), he was dealt to Seattle for Mike Morgan in a trade of two disappointing righthanders. The Mariners were un-happy with Dixon's velocity when they released him in spring training of 1988. Dixon filed a grievance against the club, saying he was released after he hurt his shoulder that spring. The Mariners said Dixon was injured before joining them. /(JCA)

Rap Dixon [Herbert Albert] — 1902-1945. OF 1922-37 Harrisburg, Baltimore, Chicago, Darby, Pittsburgh, Philadelphia, Brooklyn, New York Cubans, Newark, Homestead, Washington statistics not available

Dixon was a slugging outfielder who played on many of the great Negro League teams of the 1920s and 1930s. He combined power, average, and speed to pose a triple threat. His range and fine throwing arm made him a top defensive outfielder. He played hard and was known as a ferocious slider.

In 1929 Dixon played with the Baltimore Black Sox, Negro American League champions. He batted .382 with seven home runs, and led the league with six triples. In 1930, taking part in the first game played between black teams in Yankee Stadium, Dixon launched three HR into the right field seats. In 1932, he became part of one of the finest black teams ever assembled, Gus Greenlee's barnstorming Pittsburgh Crawfords. Playing beside Hall of Famers Satchel Paige, Oscar Charleston, Judy Johnson, Josh Gibson, and Cool Papa Bell, Dixon held his own, batting .343 with 15 HR.

Dixon was selected to the inaugural East-West all-star game, in 1933, and in it stole a base, scored two runs, and had an RBI. He helped the Philadelphia Stars capture the Negro National League champion-ship in 1934. He hit .344 in 1935, his last year as a regular. In 26 games against white major leaguers, he compiled a .372 average. /(ETW)

Sonny Dixon [John Craig] — 1924- . RHP 1953-56 **Senators**, A's, Yankees 263 ip, 11-18, 4.17

Dixon, mainly a relief pitcher, led the AL in appearances (54) in a 1954 campaign split between Washington and Philadelphia. /(WOR)

Tom Dixon — 1955- . RHP 1977-79, 83 **Astros**, Expos 200 ip, 9-14, 4.33

Dixon debuted with a five-hitter over the Cardinals on August 6, 1977. He was 7-11 in 30 games for Houston in 1978, but erratic control shortened his ML stay. /(MC)

Bill Doak (Spittin' Bill) — 1891-1954. RHP 1912-24, 1927-29 Reds, **Cardinals**, Dodgers 2783 ip, 170-157, 2.98. 20 wins: 14, 20
☛ *Led League—era 14, 21.*

Doak joined St. Louis at age 22 and spent over 11 years as a dependable pitcher with generally lacklus-ter Cardinal teams. In his sophomore 1914 season, he went 20-6 with a NL-low 1.72 ERA, boosting the Cards to their best record up to that time. The spitballer's 20 wins in 1920 weren't enough to keep St. Louis from finishing fifth. The next year, Doak's .714 winning percentage (15-6) and 2.59 ERA led all NL hurlers. When Doak followed with losing seasons in 1922-23, Branch Rickey dealt the vet-eran to Brooklyn in mid-1924. Doak went 11-5 the remainder of that campaign, then voluntarily re-tired. He returned in 1927, and posted an 11-8 record with the Dodgers before fading and ending his career back with St. Louis in 1929. Doak remains among the Cardinals' top ten all-time in eight pitching categories, with his 32 shutouts rank-ing second only to Bob Gibson's 56. /(DQV)

Masayuki Dobashi — 1938- . P 1956-68 **Toei Flyers** 162-162, 2.64

Pitching for Tokyo's "other" team, the lackluster Toei Flyers, Dobashi never received the publicity accorded to stars of the crosstown rival Giants. That's how the shy and guarded hurler preferred it. A deadpan stoic on the mound, the five-time 20-game winner notched a career-high 30 victories in 1961. From 1958 through 1964, he never worked fewer than 44 games or 263 innings a season. /(MC)

John Dobbs — 1876-1934. OF 1901-05 Reds, Cubs, **Dodgers** 582 g, .263, 7 hr, 207 rbi

A strong-armed centerfielder with a weak bat, Dobbs had a short ML career. He managed 25 years in the minors, 23 in the Southern Association, and compiled a .563 winning percentage and six league championships. He was co-owner of the Charlotte team of the Piedmont League at his death. /(TG)

Chuck Dobson [Charles Thomas] — 1944– . RHP 1966–71, 73–75 A's, Angels 1258 ip, 74–69, 3.78

Kansas City scout Whitey Herzog had only to look in the A's backyard to find Dobson, a 6'4" fireballer. Dobson threw a Northwest League no-hitter his first pro season (1965), but was disabled much of his rookie 1966 season with a rotator cuff strain. He returned to win in double figures for five straight ML seasons. In 1970, Dobson led the AL with 40 starts, going 16–15. He was on his way to 20 wins in 1971 with a 15–5 record in August, but recurring shoulder problems cut short his season, and eventually ended his career. /(MC)

Joe Dobson (Burrhead) — 1917– . RHP 1939–43, 46–54 Indians, **Red Sox**, White Sox 2170 ip, 137–103, 3.62. *1 WS, 12.2 ip, 1–0, 0.00*
☛ *All-Star—48.*

The youngest of 14 children, Dobson grew up in the heart of the Depression dustbowl in Durrant, Texas. At the age of nine, he lost his thumb and left forefinger playing with a dynamite cap. He began his ML career with the Indians and was traded in December 1940 to Boston, where he had his best years. In 1947, he won a career-high 18, with a 2.95 ERA. Over the period 1941–50, with time out in 1944–45 for the military, Dobson was 106–72 for Boston. Traded to the White Sox in December 1950, Dobson turned in his final winning season in 1952 with a 14–10 mark. He finished his steady, unspectacular career with the Red Sox in 1954. /(RL)

Pat Dobson — 1942– . RHP 1967–77 Tigers, Padres, Orioles, Braves, **Yankees**, Indians 2120 ip, 122–129, 3.54. 20 wins: 71 *2 WS, 11 ip, 0–0, 3.97*
☛ *All-Star—72.*

Dobson used a big curveball to become one of the quartet of 20-game winners on the 1971 Orioles, when he went 20–8 with a 2.90 ERA in his first winning season in the majors. He signed with Detroit for a reported $35,000 bonus in 1959 and spent three years with the parent club, pitching mostly in relief. He was traded to the Padres in December 1969 with Dave Campbell for Joe Niekro and attracted the attention of the Orioles by going 14–15 as the ace for last-place San Diego.

Dobson's strong 1971 season earned him a start in Game Four of the World Series, but he gave up

10 hits in 5-1/3 innings, getting a no-decision in the loss, and was in the bullpen for the rest of the Series. Dobson's 2.65 ERA in 1972 was an improvement from his 20-win season, but he went 16–18 and tied for the AL lead in losses (only one member of the quartet, Jim Palmer, repeated as a 20-game winner). Traded to the Braves with Davey Johnson after the season, he was then sent to the Yankees in mid-1973 and in 1974 went 19–15 with a 3.07 ERA as the ace of second-place New York. After an off-year in 1975 (11–14, 4.07) he was traded to the Indians for Oscar Gamble and recovered with a 16–12, 3.48 season. But his 3–12, 6.16 record in 1977 ended his career. /(SFS)

Larry Doby — 1923– . OF 1947–59 **Indians**, White Sox, Tigers 1533 g, .283, 253 hr, 969 rbi. *2 WS, 10 g, .237, 1 hr, 2 rbi.*
Manager 1978 **White Sox** 37–50, .425
☛ *Led League—hr 52, 54. Led League—rbi 54. All-Star—49–55.*

In August 1947, four months after Jackie Robinson had broken the National League's color line, Larry Doby was signed for the Indians by Bill Veeck (whom he affectionately called his "godfather") and was the first black ballplayer in the American League. "The only difference [was] that Jackie Robinson got all of the publicity," Doby later recalled. "You didn't hear much about what I was going through because the media didn't want to repeat the same story." On the field, Doby noted, "I couldn't react to (prejudicial) situations from a physical standpoint. My reaction was to hit the ball as far as I could." Born in South Carolina, Doby grew up in New Jersey. He attended Long Island University and played in the Negro National League.

In 1948, his first full season, Doby hit 16 HR and contributed a .301 batting average to Cleveland's successful World Championship drive. He batted a team-leading .318 in the 1948 World Series, winning the fourth game with a 400-foot home run off Braves star Johnny Sain. Although he led league outfielders with 14 errors in 1948, he became a good enough fielder to be named by *TSN* as the top centerfielder in the majors in 1950, ahead of Joe DiMaggio and Duke Snider. In 1952 the lefthanded hitter led the AL with 32 HR, 104 runs, and a .541 slugging percentage. Doby topped AL batters in strikeouts two years running (111 in 1952 and 121 in '53).

He played in every All-Star Game from 1949 through 1954, hitting a key homer as a pinch-hitter

Larry Doby

in his last All-Star at-bat. In the Indians' 1954 record-setting 111-win season, his 32 HR and 126 RBI paced the league.

After his ML playing career, he played in Japan and coached for the Expos, Indians, and White Sox. He managed the White Sox for most of 1978; one of his catchers was his namesake, Cleveland native Larry Doby Johnson. /(TJ)

John Dodge — 1889–1916. 3B 1912–13 Phillies, **Reds** 127 g, .215, 4 hr, 48 rbi

Dodge was a fine-fielding third baseman whose hitting was too weak to keep him in the majors. He was playing for Mobile (Southern Association) against Nashville in June 1916 when he was hit in the face with a Tom Rogers pitch. He died the next night. /(JK)

Dodger Stadium [aka Chavez Ravine] Los Angeles Angels 1962–1965, Los Angeles Dodgers 1962– . LF-330, CF-400, RF-330

Built by Dodger owner Walter O'Malley in Chavez Ravine, overlooking downtown Los Angeles,

Dodger Stadium was the last baseball stadium constructed with team capital, and is one of the few modern stadiums to retain some of the atmosphere of smaller classic ballparks. Although it is large (56,000 capacity), Dodger Stadium was built exclusively for baseball, with the multi-decked grandstand extending along the foul lines to provide the best sight lines. The grandstand extends slightly beyond each foul pole before giving way to separate bleacher sections, called pavilions, in both left and right fields, distinctive for their unusual zigzag roofs. In the infield, Dodger Stadium offers some unique field-level box seats, which provide a dugout-level view of the game, and the infield dirt is a mixture of crushed brick and clay with an unusual reddish hue. The outfield fences are symmetrical, and the field is natural grass.

Originally, Dodger Stadium was home to both the Dodgers and the Angels, who called it Chavez Ravine to avoid publicizing their NL rivals, but the Angels moved to Anaheim in 1966, leaving the Dodgers as sole occupants. Deep power alleys (385') and substantial foul territory make Dodger Stadium a pitcher's park, and Dodger pitching staffs are routinely among the NL's best in ERA. In 1963 the unusually high mound was lowered five inches because it gave pitchers too much of an advantage. On September 9, 1965 Sandy Koufax pitched his then-record fourth no-hitter here, a 1–0 perfect game against the Cubs. Only two home runs have ever been hit completely out of the stadium, both by the Pirates' Willie Stargell.

Outside, Dodger Stadium is ringed with massive parking lots, reflecting its Southern California location, where all travel is done by freeway. The Dodgers routinely draw 40,000 fans to a game here, and were the first ML team ever to top three million in total attendance for one season. /(SCL)

Dodger Sym-Phony

The Brooklyn Dodgers, their fans, and their opponents were serenaded for more than twenty years by a small but faithful group of amateur ragtime musicians. Louis "Brother Lou" Soriano, the founder and conductor, played snare drum, Paddy Palma beat the bass drum with "Dodgers Sym-Phony Band" emblazoned on the drumhead, Phil Caccavale played trumpet, Al Alfano was the trombonist, and Pete Della Iacono was on cymbals. Della Iacono, later a deputy New York State boxing commissioner, said the group "moved up and down the aisles, but we always started in Section 8. I think they put us there because in the army, Section 8 was the classification for the guys who were crazy." The group mocked umpires with "Three Blind Mice" (in the days when only three umpires worked a game), played "Who's Sorry Now" or "The Worms Crawl In, the Worms Crawl Out" when opposing pitchers were knocked out, and, for each opposing player who made an out, provided a cymbal crash as he sat down. /(SH)

Bobby Doerr — 1918- . 2B 1937-44, 46-51 **Red Sox** 1865 g, .288, 223 hr, 1247 rbi. *1 WS, 6 g, .409, 1 hr, 3 rbi* ☛ *All-Star—41-44, 46-48, 50-51. Hall of Fame—1986.*

Owner Tom Yawkey had recently spent thousands of dollars to purchase established stars like Joe Cronin, Jimmy Foxx, and Lefty Grove in an effort to rebuild the forlorn Red Sox. But future Hall of Famer Bobby Doerr arrived as a 19-year-old rookie in 1937, having played pro ball since 1934. He was signed by Eddie Collins on the same scouting trip that netted Ted Williams. As the team's established second baseman in 1938, Doerr batted .289 and

never hit below .270 in his next 13 seasons with the Red Sox, his only ML team. In those years Doerr thrice topped .300 and led the league in slugging in 1944. Doerr played in eight All Star games. During his career his chief rivals in all-round second base play were the fading Charlie Gehringer of the Tigers and Joe Gordon of the Yankees.

Although generally ineffective at bat in All-Star play, Doerr was a tower of strength in his only World Series appearance. Returning from military service, Doerr helped the Red Sox land the 1946 pennant by batting .271 with 18 homers and 116 RBI. In the World Series that year, Doerr batted .406 with a homer and three RBI to pace the Red Sox in their losing seven-game struggle with the Cardinals.

Retiring after the 1951 season, Doerr later served the Red Sox as a coach and was still active as a coach with the 1980 Toronto Blue Jays. In 1986 Doerr was voted into the Hall of Fame by the Veterans Committee. /(DV)

Bobby Doerr making a force play

Ed Doheny — 1874-1916. LHP 1895-1903 **Giants**, Pirates 1393 ip, 75-83, 3.75

A Boston writer earned $100 in 1895 for tipping off Giants owner Andrew Freedman about Doheny, who was pitching for St. Albans, VT (Northern League). In seven seasons, Doheny was never a winner for New York, as the club only once finished higher than seventh. Traded to the Pirates in mid-season 1901, he overcame his control problems and went 16-4 for the 1902 pennant winners; his .800 winning percentage was the second-best in the NL. The Pirates repeated in 1903, and his 16-8, .667 mark was the fifth-best NL winning percentage./(NLM)

Cozy Dolan [Patrick Henry] — 1872-1907. OF-LHP 1895-96, 1900-06 **Braves**, Cubs, Dodgers, White Sox, Reds 830 g, .269, 10 hr, 315 rbi; 255 ip, 12-13, 4.44

Dolan was dropped to the minors after failing as a Braves pitcher in 1895-96, but resurfaced as an outfielder in 1900. He was sold back to Boston in 1905, and died of typhoid on a spring training trip in 1907, prompting the cancellation of the remainder of the Braves' camp./(JK)

Cozy Dolan [Albert J, born James Alberts] — 1889-1958. OF-3B 1909, 11-15, 22 Reds, Yankees, Phillies, Pirates, **Cardinals**, Giants 378 g, .252, 7 hr, 111 rbi

Dolan was a utility man who played most regularly in the outfield of the 1914-15 Cardinals. He was a Giants coach in 1924 when he was banned from baseball for game-fixing. New York outfielder Jimmy O'Connell accused him of instigating O'Connell's attempt to bribe Philadelphia shortstop Heinie Sand./(TJ)

Joe Dolan — 1873-1938. SS-2B-3B 1896-97, 1899-1901 Louisville (NL), **Phillies**, A's 323 g, .214, 6 hr, 122 rbi

Utility infielder Dolan played a career-high 108 games for both Philadelphia clubs in 1901, but hit only .203 and was gone from the ML the next year. He became a railroad flagman in Omaha./(JK)

Jiggs Donahue — 1879-1913. 1B-C 1900-02, 04-09 Pirates, Brewers, Browns, **White Sox**, Senators 813 g, .255, 5 hr, 327 rbi. *1 WS, 6 g, .333, 4 rbi*

Released by the Browns as a catcher in 1902, Donahue held the Chicago first base job for five seasons, three times leading the AL in fielding, 1905-1907. Though a notoriously poor hitter, Jiggs was one of only three White Sox starters to bat over

.250 for the 1906 World Champion "Hitless Wonders," and paced all batters with a .333 mark in the WS. In Detroit on May 31, 1908 the fancy fielder recorded 21 putouts in a nine-inning game. Donahue contracted syphilis, and died in 1913. He was survived by a brother, Pat, an AL catcher in the years 1908-10./(RL)

Red Donahue [Francis Rostell] — 1873-1913. RHP 1893, 1895-1906 Giants, Cardinals, **Phillies**, Browns, Indians, Tigers 2975 ip, 167-173, 3.61. 20 wins: 99, 01-02

Donahue led the NL in games, starts, and complete games for last-place St. Louis in 1897 and lost a league-high 33 games with a bloated 6.13 ERA. With the Phillies the next year he no-hit the Braves 5-0 on July 8 and then won 20 games three times between 1899 and 1902./(JK)

Tim Donahue — 1870-1902. C 1891, 95-1900, 02 Boston (AA), **Cubs**, Senators 466 g, .236, 2 hr, 163 rbi

Donahue, who played all but seven of his ML games with Chicago, led NL catchers with 16 double plays in 1898. However, his fielding throughout his career averaged 35 points lower than that of league leaders./(FIC)

Atley Donald (Swampy) — 1910- . RHP 1938-45 **Yankees** 932 ip, 65-33, 3.52. *2 WS, 7 ip, 0-1, 7.71*

Donald was the Yankees' number-four or -five starter for most of his career. He was blessed with the support of New York's tremendous offense and sparkling defense, but was also a good pitcher in his own right. His only losing record, 0-1, came in his two-game call-up in his first season, 1938. In 1939 he was 13-3 with a 3.71 ERA that was nearly a run lower than the league average. His 3.03 ERA in 1940 would have been the third-best in the AL had he been used enough to qualify. He continued to pitch effectively until 1945, when eye and elbow injuries ended his career.

In his only World Series start, Game Four of the 1941 WS, Donald took a no-decision, surrendering four runs in four innings. Nonetheless, the Yankees took a 3-1 Series lead when the Dodgers' Mickey Owen committed his famous passed ball in the ninth inning, allowing a Yankee rally to erupt. Donald took a loss in relief in Game Four of the 1942 Series as the Cardinals handed the Yankees their first losing World Series in 20 years./(SFS)

John Donaldson — 1943- . 2B 1966-70, 1974 A's, Pilots 405 g, .238, 4 hr, 86 rbi

Donaldson pushed Dick Green aside as the A's regular second baseman in 1967, batting a team-high .276 as a 160-lb cleanup hitter. Traded to the Pilots in June 1969, he returned in 1970 and finished as a reserve in Oakland./(MC)

John Donaldson — 1892-1970. LHP-OF Negro Leagues 1912-32 Tennessee Rats, All-Nations, Chicago American Giants, Indianapolis ABC's, Kansas City Monarchs, Detroit Stars, Brooklyn Royal Giants, Donaldson All-Stars, Los Angeles White Sox .248 (inc.)

In 1915, New York Giants manager John McGraw saw John Donaldson pitch for the All-Nations and remarked, "If Donaldson were a white man, or if the unwritten law of baseball didn't bar Negroes from the major leagues, I would give $50,000 for him and think I was getting a bargain." Donaldson had a sharp-breaking curveball, a lively fastball, and excellent control. He hit his peak with the All-Nations just before WWI. The club, founded in 1912 by J.L. Wilkinson and J.E. Gall, was composed of blacks, whites, Latins, Japanese, Hawaiians, and Native Americans. But it was more than a novelty—it was a competitive, successful team.

Donaldson was reported to have struck out more than 240 batters over a 12-game span in 1916. In one 18-inning game, he struck out 35; in a 12-inning contest, he fanned 27 more. He threw three consecutive no-hitters against semi-pro teams. He led the All-Nations to three victories in four games against that year's Black World Champions, the Indianapolis ABC's. In the fall, the All-Nations beat Rube Foster's Chicago American Giants two games out of three, with Donaldson earning both wins.

The All-Nations disbanded in 1918 when most of their quality players were drafted for WWI. Donaldson went to play for the Detroit Stars. Wilkinson regrouped his troops after the war, renamed them the Kansas City Monarchs, and entered the newly formed Negro National League. Donaldson rejoined the team as a centerfielder and pitcher. The solid rotation of Donaldson, Bullet Rogan, Jose Mendez and Rube Currie formed one of the most feared pitching staffs in the annals of black baseball.

After leaving the Monarchs in 1923, Donaldson formed the John Donaldson All-Stars and toured the Midwest against local and semi-pro teams. He went on to scout for the Chicago White Sox. /(LL)

Augie Donatelli — 1914-Unk. *Umpire* NL 1958-73 *5 WS*

Donatelli flew 18 missions as a tailgunner before being shot down over Europe. While a POW in a German Stalag, he began umpiring softball games. He reached the ML in 1958 and stayed for 24 years. Donatelli was one of the leaders in the formation of the Umpires' Association. He was the plate umpire in Game Four of the 1957 WS when the Braves' Nippy Jones insisted a called ball had really hit him in the foot. Jones proved his case by showing Donatelli the shoe polish on the baseball and was awarded first base./(RTM)

Mike Donlin (Turkey Mike) — 1878-1933. OF 1899-1906, 08, 11-12, 14 Cardinals, Orioles, Reds, **Giants**, Braves, Pirates 1050 g, .333, 51 hr, 543 rbi. *1 WS, 5 g, .316, 1 rbi*

Donlin became the idol of Giants fans after coming to New York in 1904. A superb hitter, he topped .300 ten times in 12 ML seasons. He hit .356 and scored a league-high 124 runs in 1905, then paced the Giants with six hits in their World Series victory over the Athletics. A broken leg limited him to 37 games in 1906, and he was a season-long holdout the next year. After another strong season in 1908 (.334, 106 RBI), Donlin left baseball for a fling at a vaudeville and movie career. Donlin again announced his retirement when Pittsburgh sold him to the Phillies in 1912, but returned as a pinch hitter with the Giants in 1914./(DQV)

Blix Donnelly [Sylvester Urban] — 1914-1976. RHP 1944-51 Cardinals, **Phillies**, Braves 692 ip, 27-36, 3.49. *1 WS, 6 ip, 1-0, 0.00*

The highlight of Donnelly's career came in his first major league season when he entered Game Two of the 1944 WS in the eighth inning and pitched four scoreless innings, striking out seven and getting the win when the Cardinals scored in the 11th. Sixty percent of his career appearances came in relief./(WOR)

Jim Donohue — 1938- . RHP 1961-62 Tigers, **Dodgers**, Twins 155 ip, 6-8, 4.29

Donohue was a Cardinal and Dodger farmhand before Detroit drafted him. Primarily a reliever, he was 5-7 with six saves as a rookie, and 1-1 in his second and final season./(TJ)

Pete Donohue — 1900-1988. RHP 1921-32 **Reds**, Giants, Indians, Red Sox 2112 ip, 134-118, 3.87. 20 wins: 23, 25, 26
☛ *Led League—w 26.*

Donohue, credited with perfecting the changeup, led the NL once each in wins, starts, complete games, and shutouts, and twice in innings. He beat the Phillies 20 consecutive times between 1921 and August 1925./(TJ)

Dick Donovan (Tricky Dick) — 1927- . RHP 1950–52, 1954–65 Braves, Tigers, **White Sox**, Senators, Indians 2017 ip, 122–99, 3.67. 20 wins: 62 *1 WS, 8 ip, 0–1, 5.40* ☛ *Led League—era 61.*

A late bloomer, the 6′3″ Donovan didn't win a game in four short ML trials with the Braves and Tigers. Traded to the White Sox in 1955, his mastery of the slider made him a 15-game winner. His .727 winning percentage (16–6) led the AL in 1957. With the expansion Senators, his 2.40 ERA was the league low in 1961, but Washington sent him to the Indians in an October trade for Jimmy Piersall. Donovan went 20–10 for Cleveland in 1962, his last winning season. /(DQV)

Patsy Donovan [Patrick Joseph] — 1865–1953. OF 1890–1904, 06–07 Braves, Dodgers, Louisville (AA), Washington (AA), Washington (NL), **Pirates**, Cardinals, Senators 1821 g, .300, 16 hr, 736 rbi.
   Manager 1897, 99, 1901–04, 06–08, 10–11 Pirates, Cardinals, Senators, **Dodgers**, Red Sox 683–878, .438

Born in County Cork, Ireland, Donovan joined the National League in 1890, the year the Players' League incursion created a player shortage. He was

Patsy Donovan

with Louisville and Washington of the American Association in that major league's final season, 1891. After a brief stint with Washington's NL entry in 1892, he starred with the Pirates for eight seasons, notching six consecutive .300 seasons and serving as player-manager in 1897 and 1899.

   Dealt to the Cardinals in 1900, Donovan was their player-manager in 1901–03. A good base-stealer, his 45 swipes in 1900 led the NL, and he stole 518 bases lifetime. Being traded to Washington of the American League in 1904 gave him the distinction of playing for three Washington clubs in three major leagues. In 1906–08 he managed the Dodgers, appearing in eight contests in '06 and '07. His last years at the helm came with the 1910–11 Boston Red Sox. Donovan was never on a pennant winner, and his best managerial effort was the 1910 Red Sox' 81 wins, good for fourth place. /(DQV)

Wild Bill Donovan [William Edward] — 1876–1923. RHP 1898–1912, 15–16, 18 Washington (NL), Dodgers, **Tigers**, Yankees 2967 ip, 186–139, 2.69. 20 wins: 01, 07 *3 WS, 50 ip, 1–4, 2.70.*
   Manager 1915–17, 21 **Yankees**, Phillies 251–310, .447
☛ *Led League—w 01.*

Donovan was durable, and needed to be; due to wildness, he threw more pitches than most hurlers. While he led the NL with 25 wins for Brooklyn in 1901, he also led with 152 walks. Wild Bill starred in both major leagues, jumping to Detroit in 1903. His best season (25–4, AL-high .862 winning percentage) turned the Tigers into pennant-winners in 1907, and they repeated in 1908 and '09. But Donovan's results in WS starts were poor, and he won only one of five decisions.

   After going 10–9 in 1911, Donovan continued his career in the minor leagues, as a pitcher, coach, and manager. He piloted the Yankees from 1915 to 1917, appearing in several games, and pitched two final games for Detroit in 1918. He also skippered the Phillies for part of 1921. He was killed in a train wreck while riding in a sleeper. As manager of his minor league team, he had claimed a lower berth. Above him slept the business manager, George Weiss, who was uninjured in the wreck, and who became a Hall of Famer as GM of the Yankees and Mets. /(JK)

Red Dooin [Charles Sebastian] — 1879–1952. C 1902–16 **Phillies**, Reds, Giants 1290 g, .240, 10 hr, 344 rbi.
   Manager 1910–14 **Phillies** 392–370, .514

Wild Bill Donovan (l.), Clark Griffith

Dooin was an outstanding defensive catcher for the Phillies during the first decade of the 20th century. Reportedly the first to use papier-mache shin guards, he wore them under his stockings. In 1908, he led all NL catchers in assists. That same year, he was offered a bribe to throw a series to the Giants; he reported it. Named the Phillies' player-manager in 1910, he suffered a broken ankle that season and a broken leg in 1911, ending his days as a regular. He shepherded the Phillies to second place in 1913. A fine singer, he performed with the Dumont Minstrels in Philadelphia. /(NLM)

Mickey Doolan — 1880-1951. SS 1905-16, 1918 **Phillies**, Baltimore (FL), Chicago (FL), Cubs, Giants, Dodgers 1728 g, .230, 15 hr, 554 rbi

Doolan, a dentist, served as Phillie captain and V.P. of the Players' Fraternity, a major leaguers' union. A regular shortstop for 11 seasons, he spent two years in the Federal League with Baltimore and Chicago. /(TJ)

John Dopson — 1963- . RHP 1985, 88- Expos, **Red Sox** 351 ip, 15-21, 3.79

Dopson went 3-11 in 1988 for the Expos despite a fine 3.04 ERA. Traded to the Red Sox after the season in the Spike Owen deal, he received better support and proved to be a good, if inconsistent, number-three starter. He had balk trouble in the American League. /(WOR)

Bill Doran — 1958- . 2B 1982- **Astros** 1056 g, .265, 63 hr, 372 rbi. *1 LCS, 6 g, .222, 1 hr, 3 rbi*

Doran led NL second basemen in assists in his rookie 1983 season and quickly established himself as one of the league's best both defensively and offensively. The pouty-lipped fan favorite proved a consistent offensive threat, with career highs of 16 HR (1987) and 42 steals (1986). His 92 runs in 1986, matching his personal best, helped the Astros win the division title. He had arm troubles in 1988, but nonetheless led NL second basemen in fielding. /(SH)

Harry Dorish (Fritz) — 1921- . RHP 1947-56 Red Sox, Browns, **White Sox**, Orioles 834 ip, 45-43, 3.83

One of the first relief specialists in the post-WWII era, Dorish recorded 44 lifetime saves. He led the league in 1952 with 11 saves for the 1952 White Sox. He bettered that in 1953, when he won 10 and saved 18, but Ellis Kinder led with 27. /(DQV)

Gus Dorner — 1876-1956. RHP 1902-03, 06-09 Indians, Reds, **Braves** 894 ip, 37-69, 3.33

Pitching for the Reds and Braves in 1906, Dorner had a decision in each of his 33 starts, and completed 30 of them; he still led the NL with 26 losses. He later managed in the minors. /(NLM)

Rich Dotson (Dot) — 1959- . RHP 1979- **White Sox**, Yankees 1828 ip, 111-109, 4.16. 20 wins: 83 *1 LCS, 5 ip, 0-1, 10.80*

At the 1977 winter meetings, the Angels sent Dotson, their first-round pick that June, to the White Sox in a headline-grabbing, six-player deal for Brian Downing. Dotson reached Chicago late in 1979, but was unimpressive until 1983, when he became the youngest White Sox pitcher in 70 years to record 20 victories; his 22-7 mark helped Chicago to a division title. Between the '83 and 1984 All-Star Games, he went 25-6. But he missed most of 1985 with a circulatory problem near his right shoulder that required surgery. He struggled back in 1986, did not miss a start, but lost a league-high 17 games with a 5.48 ERA. During the 1987 winter meetings, Chicago sent him to the Yankees for outfielder Dan Pasqua, whom they had long coveted. /(RL)

Abner Doubleday — 1819–1893

In 1905, a commission headed by Al Spalding wrongly credited Doubleday with inventing the game of baseball in in Cooperstown, New York in 1839. Doubleday was actually a cadet at West Point when he was alleged to have mapped out the first baseball diamond, and after graduating in 1842 he enjoyed a distinguished military career. He fought in Mexico as well as the Civil War, eventually becoming a major general.

The commission was convinced of Doubleday's role by the testimony of an elderly gentleman named Abner Graves, who claimed to be a childhood playmate of Doubleday's and present when the game was invented. Graves's story was later "verified" by the discovery of a rotting baseball among his personal effects. That ball became known as "The Doubleday Baseball" and remains on display at the Hall of Fame. Doubleday left behind numerous diaries and never claimed to have invented baseball, yet he remains one of the game's great mythological figures. The annual Hall of Fame Game is played each summer at Doubleday Field in Cooperstown. /(SCL)

Patsy Dougherty [Patrick Henry] — 1876–1940. OF 1902–11 Red Sox, Yankees, **White Sox** 1233 g, .284, 17 hr, 413 rbi. *2 WS, 14 g, .185, 2 hr, 6 rbi*

The brawling Irishman was the first player to hit two home runs in a World Series with a pair for the Red Sox in 1903. After Dougherty engaged in a fistfight with Highlanders Manager Clark Griffith, New York placed him on waivers. White Sox Manager Fielder Jones, who'd earlier discovered Dougherty as a semi-pro, claimed him to bolster the "Hitless Wonders," the 1906 Sox who won the World Championship. He led the AL in stolen bases in 1908 with 47. /(RL)

Phil Douglas (Shufflin' Phil, The Shuffler) — 1890–1952. RHP 1912, 14–15, 17–22 White Sox, Reds, Dodgers, Cubs, **Giants** 1708 ip, 93–93, 2.80

When he was sober and when his spitter was dancing, Douglas was one of the NL's better right-handers. His high point was two sterling Giant victories over the Yankees in the 1921 World Series. His low was banishment from baseball for life by Judge Landis. Befuddled first by a taxing drying-out

regimen and then by a relapse, and demoralized by a John McGraw tongue-lashing, Douglas had written a Cardinals outfielder about an ambiguous offer to quit the Giants in the heat of the 1922 pennant race in return for "an inducement." /(ADS)

Klondike Douglass [William Bigham] — 1872–1953. 1B-C-OF 1896–1904 Cardinals, **Phillies** 747 g, .274, 10 hr, 275 rbi

Douglass came to the majors in 1896 as the Cardinals' left fielder, but fielded only .894, low even for those days, and had poor range. He was primarily a catcher in 1897, and hit .329. He was the everyday first baseman for the Phillies in 1898, and hit .258 with 105 runs scored in his best season. Moved back and forth between catcher and 1B in subsequent seasons, he was never again an everyday player. /(JFC)

Taylor Douthit — 1901– . OF 1923–33 **Cardinals**, Reds, Cubs 1074 g, .291, 29 hr, 396 rbi. *3 WS, 13 g, .140, 1 hr, 3 rbi*

One of Branch Rickey's farm system products, Douthit joined the Cardinals in 1923 and spent nine seasons with St. Louis before finishing with the Reds and Cubs. A wide-ranging centerfielder, Douthit led NL outfielders in putouts three times, and twice in errors. He had little power (914 of his 1201 hits were singles) but he topped .300 three times. Over or near .300 in each of St. Louis' 1926, '28, and '30 pennant-winning seasons, he faltered in World Series play, going just 7-for-50. /(DQV)

Tommy Dowd [Thomas Jefferson] (Buttermilk Tommy) — 1869–1933. OF-2B 1891–99, 1901 Boston (AA), Washington (AA), Washington (NL), **St. Louis (NL) [Perfectos]**, Phillies, Cleveland (NL), Red Sox 1320 g, .271, 23 hr, 501 rbi.
Manager 1896–97 **St. Louis (NL)**, 30–63, .323

Dowd came up as a second baseman, but spent the heart of his career as the right fielder for the 1893–95 St. Louis Perfectos (NL). He managed St. Louis for the last 62 games of 1896, and was fired after a 6–25 start in 1897. He was dealt to the Phillies a few days later, only to be reacquired by St. Louis for the following season. /(AJA)

Tom Downey — 1884–1961. SS-2B-3B 1909–12, 14–15 **Reds**, Phillies, Cubs, Buffalo FL 651 g, .240, 7 hr, 188 rbi

Although he was a versatile infielder for four years in

the NL and two in the Federal League, his weak bat kept him from holding down a regular position. /(NLM)

Al Downing — 1941- . LHP 1961–77 **Yankees**, A's, Brewers, Dodgers 2268 ip, 123–107, 3.22 20 wins: 71 *1 LCS, 4 ip, 0–0, .000. 3 WS, 16 ip, 0–3, 6.06* ☛ *All-Star—67.*

Al Downing, who gave up Hank Aaron's record-breaking 715th homer, entered baseball loaded with potential. His fastball exploded and his curveball danced. Called by some "the black Sandy Koufax," he never lived up to that billing, partly because of control problems and inconsistency and later because of arm miseries, but for four seasons he was excellent.

Recalled from the minors to the Yankees for good in June 1963, Downing maintained a summer-long electric pace of low-hit games. The first black starting pitcher in club history allowed a scant 5.84 hits per nine innings and finished with a 13–5 record. In 1964 he led the league with 217 strikeouts. Downing in 1967 became a complete pitcher, cutting down on his walks, mastering a changeup and mixing up his pitches. He finished 14–10 with the ninth-place Yankees.

Pitching for the Dodgers in 1971, Downing reached the pinnacle, winning 20 games, including a league-leading five shutouts. /(MG)

Brian Downing — 1950- . OF-C-DH 1973- White Sox, **Angels** 2018 g, .266, 234 hr, 934 rbi. *3 LCS, 16 g, .197, 1 hr, 8 rbi* ☛ *All-Star—79.*

Downing transformed himself, through hard work, weight training (before it was common), and experimentation, from an inconsistent, weak-hitting catcher to a reliable clutch-hitting slugger who set the AL record for consecutive errorless games by an outfielder (244 games, from May 25, 1981 through July 21, 1983, second game).

Downing showed the intensity that would characterize his play throughout his career literally from the first pitch of his first game. Playing third base, he raced after a short foul pop-up that was apparently out of reach. He dived and caught it, but bruised his leg so severely that he was out for nearly six weeks. In his second day after coming back, he got his first ML hit, an inside-the-park HR off Mickey Lolich. In his first full season, 1974, Downing showed good power with 10 HR in 293 at-bats, but hit only .225. The White Sox' number-one catcher in 1975, he hit .240 with seven HR in 420 at-bats. Traded with two

pitchers to California after the 1977 season in return for Bobby Bonds, Rich Dotson, and Thad Bosley, he was their regular catcher for the next two seasons. In 1978 he set the club mark for fielding average by a catcher, .993. After the season he had bone chips removed from his right elbow. He made the All-Star team in 1979, hitting a career-high .326 with 12 HR and 75 RBI as the Angels won their first division title.

After missing most of 1980 with a broken ankle, he spent most of 1981 in the outfield and never caught again after that season. He began his errorless streak in the OF, but did not compile it at the expense of his aggressive style of play, which compensated for his below-average speed. His 330 errorless chances in 1982 set the AL mark for most chances in an errorless season. Downing hit 28 HR, 16 better than his previous high, and scored 109 runs while driving in 84. Manager Gene Mauch used him as both a leadoff hitter for his ability to get on base (86 walks), and as a cleanup hitter for his power and clutch hitting. The Angels won another division title, but once again Downing hit poorly in the LCS. He missed five weeks in 1983 with a broken left wrist, but otherwise continued his consistent production. Although he is a streaky hitter within each season, at the end of the year he has posted his usual 20 HR, 85 RBI and runs, and .275 BA. His career-high 95 RBI in 1986 helped the Angels to another division title, and although he hit only .222 in the LCS, he drove in seven runs to lead both teams. He utilized another of his talents, getting hit by a Calvin Schiraldi pitch with the bases loaded in the ninth inning of Game Four to send the contest into extra innings. His intense play and his unusually wide, open batting stance, as well as his clutch performance, finally gained him national notice. Angels owner Gene Autry earlier in the year had, as part of California's 25th anniversary, named Downing the left fielder on the franchise's all-time team.

Downing switched to DH in 1987 to lessen the wear on his body. He had his best season, reaching career highs with 29 HR, 110 runs, and 106 walks (tied for the AL lead). He spent three weeks on the DL near the start of the 1988 season and hit just .242, his lowest average since 1975, although he hit 25 HR in 484 at-bats. He recovered in 1989 and completed his domination of the Angels' all-time offense totals. He is first in home runs, RBI, runs, extra base hits, total bases, hits, doubles, games, and at-bats. He is in the top ten in most Angels' season records. /(SH)

Kelly Downs — 1960– . RHP 1986– **Giants** 525 ip, 33–30, 3.57. *2 LCS, 10 ip, 1–0, 2.70. 1 WS, 5 ip, 0–0, 7.71*

A tall control specialist, Downs spent six full seasons in the minors before finally reaching the Giants in 1986. He has been plagued by misfortune throughout his brief ML career. He posted a 2.75 ERA in 14 starts as a rookie in 1986 and was one of the Giants' top starters for most of 1987, but he was relegated to the bullpen when San Francisco acquired Rick Reuschel for its successful pennant drive. Downs rejoined the rotation in 1988 and was 13–9, 3.32 before spending the last month of the season on the DL with shoulder problems that plagued him through 1989. Originally with the Phillies organization, Downs was one of two pitchers traded to San Francisco for Al Oliver in 1984. His older brother, Dave, was 1–1 in four starts for the Phillies in 1972, including a 3–0 shutout against the Braves in his ML debut. /(SCL)

Billy Doyle — 1881–1939. *Scout.*

Doyle signed Branch Rickey out of Ohio Wesleyan University to play for the Texas League Dallas Steers. He later scouted for the Browns, Indians, and Phillies. He joined the Tigers in 1919 and stayed until his death in 1939. Eventual stars he scouted included Sad Sam Jones and Rick Ferrell. /(FVP)

Carl Doyle — 1912–1951. RHP 1935–36, 39–40 **A's**, Dodgers, Cardinals 223 ip, 6–15, 6.95

Doyle pitched five games for the 1939 Dodgers, one as a starter; it was the only shutout of his career. He suffered a broken arm in 1940, and later scouted for the Tigers. /(NLM)

Danny Doyle — 1917– . C 1943 **Red Sox** 13 g, .209, 0 hr, 6 rbi

Doyle played only 13 games for the Red Sox at catcher during WWII, but has been a full-time scout for Boston almost continuously since 1949. His signees and discoveries include Roger Clemens, Jim Lonborg, and Ellis Burks. /(FVP)

Hugh Doyle — 1876–1925. *Writer.*

Doyle was sports cartoonist for the Philadelphia *Press* for 25 years, then the *Ledger* until he retired in 1921. /(NLM)

Jack Doyle (Dirty Jack) — 1869–1958. 1B-C-OF-2B-SS-3B 1889–1905 Columbus (AA), Cleveland (NL), **Giants**, Baltimore (NL), Washington (NL), Cubs, Senators, Dodgers, Phillies, Yankees 1564 g, .301, 25 hr, 924 rbi.

Manager 1895, 98 **Giants**, Washington (NL) 51–55, .481.

Umpire NL 1911

Ireland native Jack Doyle is one of 20 major leaguers to have played 100 games at four different positions. He was also reputedly baseball's first pinch hitter, coming off the bench to single for the Giants in 1892. In five consecutive years, 1893 through 1897, and seven in all, he topped the .300 mark. He had three stints with the Giants, and from 1898 through 1900 was their starting first baseman. He was the second of three managers for the 1895 Giants, and the second of four with the 1898 Senators. /(AJA)

Larry Doyle (Laughing Larry) — 1886–1974. 2B 1907–20 **Giants**, Cubs 1765 g, .290, 74 hr, 793 rbi. *3 WS, 19 g, .237, 1 hr, 5 rbi*
☛ *Most Valuable Player—12. Led League—ba 15.*

Doyle was a nervous youngster in June 1907 when he took the wrong ferry across the Hudson River and arrived late for his first ML game. Giants manager John McGraw started the scrappy prospect at second base, a position unfamiliar to Doyle. The

Larry Doyle with the Giants

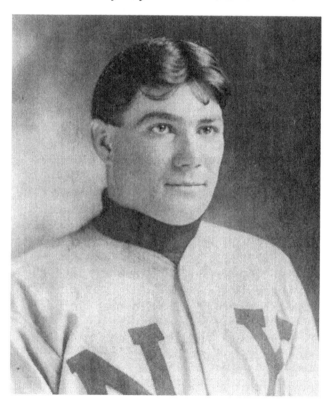

game was close, coming down to a crucial ninth-inning grounder which Doyle booted. Certain Mc-Graw would send him down, Doyle sheepishly confronted him, only to receive words of encouragement and, the following season, the Giants' captaincy. He became a five-time .300 hitter.

Doyle's hitting and solid defense helped New York to three straight pennants, starting in 1911, when he led the NL in triples and said, "It's great to be young and a Giant." He scored the famous "phantom" run that forestalled the Athletics' victory in the 1911 World Series. In the dusk of Game Five's 10th inning, Doyle came home on an outfield fly but did not touch the plate, umpire Bill Klem later admitted, saying he would have called Doyle out had the A's tried to tag him.

Doyle led the NL with 172 hits in 1909, and batted a high of .330 in 1912. He won the NL batting title in 1915 with a .320 mark and league highs of 189 hits and 40 doubles. He stole 297 career bases, swiping home 17 times. His eight errors tie him with Eddie Collins for most in total World Series at 2B. /(ASN)

Slow Joe Doyle [Judd Bruce] — 1881-1947. RHP 1906-10 **Yankees**, Reds 436 ip, 22-22, 2.85

When his team was at bat on hot days, Doyle would sometimes lie down on the tarpaulin and nap, but he earned his nickname by being one of the slowest workers ever to take the mound. In addition to stalling, he relied on a "drop" (a sinker), a "raise ball," and a spitter. Although he threw shutouts in his first two ML starts, 11 wins in 1907 was his career high. /(NLM)

Doug Drabek — 1962- . RHP 1986- **Yankees, Pirates** 771 ip, 47-39, 3.35

Drabek became a top pitching prospect with his strikeout ability. Despite a terrible first half (1-8) in 1987, he led the Pirates in starts and strikeouts and was NL Pitcher of the Month for August. He was acquired from the Yankees in the Rick Rhoden deal as part of Pittsburgh's rebuilding program. /(ME)

Moe Drabowsky — 1935- . RHP 1956-72 **Cubs**, Braves, Reds, A's, Orioles, Royals, Cardinals, White Sox 1641 ip, 88-105, 3.71. *2 WS, 10 ip, 1-0, 0.90*

Born in Ozanna, Poland, Drabowsky came to the U.S. with his parents in 1938, fleeing the Nazi invasion. He accepted a reported $50,000 bonus to sign with the Cubs after fanning 16 in a no-hitter for Trinity College of Hartford. Joining the Cubs' rotation immediately, Drabowsky managed a 2.47 ERA

as a rookie. Inclined to work inside, he led the NL with 10 hit batsmen in 1957, hitting a record four men on June 2, 1957. He finished second in the league with 170 strikeouts, going 13-15 for a seventh-place club. A sore arm cost Drabowsky his fastball in 1958, when he yielded Stan Musial's 3,000th hit. Drabowsky struggled, pitching for eight clubs in four years. The Orioles drafted him for 1966 and Drabowsky turned his career around with a 6-0, 2.81 record and seven saves for the 1966 World Champions. Relieving Dave McNally with one out and the bases loaded in the third inning of Game One of the World Series, Drabowsky gave up just one hit, no earned runs, and struck out 11 to earn the win as he finished the game. He had a WS-record six strikeouts in a row. He won his first 12 Baltimore decisions, achieving ERAs of 1.60 and 1.91 in '67 and '68. Doing it all, Drabowsky also batted .364, .350, and .286 in 1966-1968. Selected by the Royals in the 1969 expansion draft, Drabowsky led the AL with 11 relief wins, saving 11 with a 2.94 ERA in 52 games. He returned to Baltimore to post a 4-2 record down the stretch in 1970, climaxed with two more clutch relief performances in that World Series. He returned to Poland in 1987 as a baseball ambassador, helping the Poles form their first team for Olympic competition.

A well-known flake, he was once rolled to first base in a wheelchair after being hit by a pitch and specialized in bullpen pranks. /(MC)

Delos Drake — 1886-1965. OF 1911, 14-15 Tigers, St. Louis (FL) 331 g, .263, 5 hr, 119 rbi

Drake's efforts to break into the Detroit lineup were hampered by a broken leg in 1905. A consistent .300 hitter in the minors, he never rose above a utility role in the majors. He was a prize-winning trap shooter and worked as a cowboy. /(NLM)

Dick Drago — 1945- . RHP 1969-81 **Royals**, Red Sox, Angels, Mariners 1876 ip, 108-117, 3.62. *1 LCS, 5 ip, 0-0, 0.00. 1 WS, 4 ip, 0-1, 2.25*

Drago made the majors when he was picked by the Royals in the expansion draft, and he became the ace of their struggling staff. Improving with the rest of the team, he had his best season in 1971 (17-11, 3.01), but his record suffered when the team declined in 1972 (12-17 despite a 2.99 ERA). Boston acquired him for 1974, and in their AL championship season in 1975 he was their bullpen ace with 15 saves. He saved Games Two and Three as the Red Sox swept the A's in the ALCS, but lost Game Two of the World Series in the ninth inning on a Ken

Griffey double. His three scoreless innings of one-hit ball in Game Six kept Boston in the game, and they won on Carlton Fisk's famous homer in the 12th inning.

Traded to California for 1976 and then to Baltimore in mid-1977, he returned to the Red Sox for 1978 and had his last good season in 1979, going 10–6 with 13 saves./(SFS)

Dave Dravecky — 1956– . LHP 1982– **Padres**, Giants 1063 ip, 64–57, 3.13. *2 LCS, 21 ip, 1–1, 0.43. 1 WS, 5 ip, 0–0, 0.00*
☛ *All-Star—83.*

A consistently effective starter and occasional reliever for the Padres for over five seasons, Dravecky was traded to the Giants in mid-1987 in a seven-player swap that included Mark Davis, Kevin Mitchell, and Craig Lefferts. He was outstanding in the 1987 LCS, tossing a two-hit shutout in Game Two and running his LCS scoreless-inning string to a record-tying 16, but he made only seven starts in 1988 before going on the DL with what turned out to be a career- and life-threatening cancerous tumor in his pitching arm. He made a surprisingly successful comeback attempt in mid-1989, winning two games before his weakened arm snapped as he threw a pitch. He rebroke it during the Giants' LCS victory celebration./(ME)

John Drebinger — Unk.–Unk. *Writer*

A high school track star and son of a violinist in the Metropolitan Opera orchestra, Drebinger was the oldest writer traveling the baseball circuit when he retired at age 73. He began with the weekly Staten Island *Advance* and joined the *New York Times* in 1923. He covered every WS for the *Times* from 1929 to 1963. In 1973 he received the J.G. Taylor Spink Award from the Hall of Fame./(NLM)

Chuck Dressen [Charles Walter] — 1898–1966. 3B 1925–31 **Reds**, Giants 646 g, .272, 11 hr, 221 rbi.
Manager 1934–37, 51–53, 55–57, 60–61, 63–66 **Reds**, Dodgers, Senators, Braves, Tigers 1037–993, .511. First place: 52–53 *2 WS, 5–8, .385*

Dressen never doubted his own baseball savvy. "Hold them, boys," he often told his team. "I'll think of something." The 5'5" 146-lb extrovert took up diverse challenges: picking racetrack winners, quarterbacking George Halas's Decatur Staleys (forerunner of the Chicago Bears) and the Racine Legion of the early NFL, and playing eight years as a NL third baseman.

He is most famous as a ML manager. He managed successive pennant winners for the Dodg-

ers in 1952–53, but bucked owner Walter O'Malley's policy by asking for a multi-year contract. O'Malley replaced him with Walter Alston. Dressen spent a year at Oakland of the Pacific Coast League, then returned to the majors with the talentless Senators. Two seasons after leading Brooklyn to 105 victories, the same tactician took Washington to 101 losses. A second losing season and a poor 1957 start cost Dressen his job.

In 1960, he took over the Milwaukee Braves. Late in 1961, with the team in third place, he was summoned to the front office. Expecting photographers to record his signing of a new contract, he dressed in his best suit. Instead, he was told he was being let go.

Dressen managed Toronto in the minors the next season, then joined the Dodgers as a special scout in 1963. In June, he received his fourth ML command, with the ninth-place Tigers. He brought them in fifth and followed with two straight fourth-place finishes. On May 15, 1966 the 67-year-old Dressen managed his last victory. The next day he checked into a hospital. Twelve weeks later he died of a heart attack.

Dressen had a gambler's love for number 7 and wore it whenever he could. When the Dodgers acquired star Joe Medwick from St. Louis in 1940, he asked for 7, then worn by Dressen as a coach. Chuck agreed; the next day he went to his coach's box sporting his new number: 77. As usual, he'd "thought of something."/(JK)

Rob Dressler — 1954– . RHP 1975–76, 78–80 Giants, Cardinals, **Mariners** 390 ip, 11–23, 4.18

Dressler signed out of high school as San Francisco's first-round pick in the June 1972 draft. He had good control but was hit hard, going 3–10 with the 1976 Giants and 4–10 with the 1980 Mariners./(KC)

Karl Drews — 1920–1963. RHP 1946–49, 1951–54 Yankees, Browns, **Phillies**, Reds 827 ip, 44–53, 4.76. *1 WS, 3 ip, 3.00*

The 6'4" Drews came through the Yankee organization slowly, and was 6–6 for the 1947 world champs. When he unexpectedly won 14 for the Phillies in 1952, including five shutouts, his 2.72 ERA was by far his best. Brother Roy was a catcher in the Giants' organization./(RTM)

Dan Driessen — 1951– . 1B-3B-OF 1973–87 **Reds**, Expos, Giants, Astros, Cardinals 1732 g, .267, 153 hr, 763 rbi. *4 LCS, 13 g, .162, 2 rbi. 3 WS, 10 g, .276, 1 hr, 2 rbi*

Overshadowed on the star-studded "Big Red Machine," Driessen gave the Reds valuable versatility for his first four seasons. He hit a career-high .301 in his rookie season and then was Cincinnati's starting third baseman in 1974. Pete Rose moved to third base in 1975, but Driessen replaced Tony Perez at first base from 1977 to 1981, one of the longest tenures at first base in Reds history. The uncle of Gerald Perry, Driessen led NL first basemen in fielding three times. A smart, steady hitter, he led the NL with 93 walks in 1980 and generally walked more than he struck out.

In 1976, Driessen was the NL's first DH in the World Series. He hit .357, the only good average he had in post-season play. Traded in mid-1981, he wandered the league until his retirement, finishing his career filling in at first base for the 1987 NL champion Cardinals after first Jack Clark and then Cesar Cedeno were injured. /(ME)

John Drohan — 1890–1969. *Writer.*

Drohan retired in 1955 after covering baseball for the Boston *Traveler* from 1919. He was a frequent contributor to magazines and *The Sporting News.* /(NLM)

Walt Dropo (Moose) — 1923– . 1B 1949–61 Red Sox, **Tigers**, White Sox, Reds, Orioles 1288 g, .270, 152 hr, 704 rbi
☛ *Rookie of the Year—50. Led League—rbi 50. All-Star—50.*

The 6'5" 220-lb Moose, from Moosup, CT, was the embodiment of his era. He was the strong, silent type, slow afoot but a deadly power hitter. He hit 152 career home runs, but had only five stolen bases.

Dropo turned down an offer from football's Chicago Bears to sign with the Red Sox in 1947. He came up sensationally in 1950, starting on the All-Star team and winning AL Rookie of the Year honors with 34 homers, a .322 average, and a league-leading 144 RBI. Dropo's next best was 29 HR and 97 RBI two years later, but he never again had over 19 HR or hit over .281. In one brilliant stretch in July 1952, after being traded to Detroit, he collected 12 consecutive hits to tie a ML record. Included in the streak was a 7-for-7 performance in a doubleheader against Washington. /(RL)

Dick Drott (Hummer) — 1936–1985. RHP 1957–63 **Cubs**, Astros 688 ip, 27–46, 4.78

When Dick Drott won 15 games for the seventh-place Cubs in 1957, he seemed headed for stardom.

He was wild enough to lead the league in walks, but his fastball intimidated batters at first. Then, his career floundered because of arm problems and he passed to the expansion Houston team in the draft.

On April 27 of his rookie season, Drake was ejected from a game for borrowing a wheelchair from a crippled fan and wheeling fellow flake Moe Drabowsky to first base after Drabowsky was hit on the foot by a pitch. /(JK)

Louis Drucke — 1888–1955. RHP 1909–12 **Giants** 317 ip, 18–15, 2.90

Hailed as a wonder find by John McGraw when the Giants signed him out of TCU in 1909, Drucke was 12–10 in 1910. He struck out 151 in 215 innings but was wild. His career was cut short when he ruptured an arm muscle in a subway accident. /(NLM)

Cal Drummond — 1917–1970. *Umpire* AL 1960–69 *1 WS, 1 ASU*

Drummond was plagued with ill health late in his career. After brain surgery in 1969, he was working his way back to the majors when he died while umpiring a minor league game in 1970. He was a member of the umpiring crew that called a balk on Stu Miller during the 1961 All-Star Game at Candlestick Park when the little pitcher was blown off the mound by the wind. /(RTM)

Charles Dryden — 1869–1931. *Writer.*

A charter member of the BBWAA, Dryden's turns of phrase are often repeated. His assessment of the futile Senators, "Washington: first in war, first in peace, and last in the American League," is a classic. Of Ed Walsh, he wrote, "He's the only man who can strut standing still." He named Frank Chance "The Peerless Leader," Charles Comiskey "The Old Roman," Phil Douglas "Shuffin' Phil," and the 1906 White Sox "The Hitless Wonders." Dryden left grade school to work in a foundry before joining the San Francisco *Examiner* in the early 1890s. By 1893, he was sports editor of the San Francisco *Chronicle.* In 1900 he joined Hearst's New York *American.* When he began poking fun at Andrew Freedman, the Giants' owner barred him from the Polo Grounds. Dryden continued to write humorous accounts of games by perching on a telephone pole outside the park. After brief stints with the *Evening World* and Philadelphia *North American,* he joined the Chicago *Examiner* for what was then the highest salary of any baseball writer. He later worked for the *Herald Examiner* and *Tribune.* Dryden, who wrote all his copy in longhand until near the end of his career, retired in 1921 after a stroke left him paralyzed and nearly speechless. He was voted the J.G. Taylor Spink Award in 1965./(NLM)

Don Drysdale — 1936- . RHP 1956-68 **Dodgers**
3432 ip, 209-166, 2.95. 20 wins: 62, 65 *5 WS, 39 ip, 3-3, 2.95*
☛ *Led League—w 62. Cy Young Award—62. All-Star—59, 61-65, 67-68. Hall of Fame—1984.*

A tall, charismatic sidearmer, Drysdale combined an explosive fastball with great control to become one of baseball's premier power pitchers. His greatest personal achievement came in 1968, "the year of the pitcher." He logged six consecutive shutouts en route to a since-broken record 58.2 consecutive scoreless innings. He pitched his record-tying fifth

shutout on the day of the California presidential primary and was congratulated by Robert Kennedy in the speech he gave just before he was assassinated.

Drysdale's real glory days were earlier, when he was paired with Sandy Koufax as the most feared pitching duo of the 1960s. The Dodgers finished the regular season in first place in four out of five years from 1962 to 1966 without an overwhelming offense. The two staged a highly publicized joint holdout following their combined 49–20 record in 1965. They sought a three-year, $1.05 million contract to be divided evenly. Drysdale eventually signed for $110,000, quite a bit better than the $35,000 he made when he won 25 in 1962. He summed up his persepective in 1980: "When we played, World Series checks meant something. Now they just screw up your taxes."

Don Drysdale

Drysdale was a workhorse, leading the NL in games started every year from 1962 to 1965, as well as in innings pitched in 1962 and 1964. He never missed a start. He also led in shutouts in 1959. One of the best-hitting pitchers of his day, he led NL pitchers in homers four times, twice tying the NL record of seven. His career total of 29 ranks second to Warren Spahn's in NL history. In 1965 he hit .300 and slugged .508, pinch hit frequently, and achieved the rare feat of winning 20 and hitting .300 in the same year. In 1958 he slugged .591.

Drysdale's tenure spanned Dodger eras. He won 17 in their last year in Brooklyn, and pitched the team's first West Coast game (a loss at San Francisco). When he retired, he was the last Brooklyn player left on the Dodgers. He had the longest career played under a single manager—13 years with Walter Alston. When Drysdale came up, he played with Duke Snider and the "Boys of Summer." He retired from a staff that included Don Sutton, who pitched through the 1980s.

Knocking down hitters was a major tool in Drysdale's pitching repertoire. He set the 20th-century NL career record by hitting 154 batters, and led the NL in that category a record five times. His philosophy on the knockdown pitch was simple—"If one of our guys went down, I just doubled it. No confusion there. It didn't require a Rhodes scholar."

A fixture at All-Star time, Drysdale holds All-Star records with eight games pitched, five starts, 19.1 innings, and 19 strikeouts. He went 2–1, 1.40, allowing only 10 hits.

Drysdale was one of the most appealing Dodgers to the Hollywood entertainment community. He appeared on numerous TV shows including "You Bet Your Life," "The Donna Reed Show," and "The Brady Bunch." After his playing days, Drysdale became an announcer for the Angels and the White Sox before returning to the Dodgers. "Interviews were the hardest thing for me at first," he said. "I felt so damn funny asking players questions when I already knew the answers." /(TG)

Monk Dubiel [Walter John] — 1919–1969. RHP 1944–45, 48–52 Yankees, Phillies, **Cubs** 879 ip, 45–53, 3.87

Dubiel was a competent wartime Yankee pitcher, exempted from military service because of an eye problem. He went 13–13 as a rookie in 1944, 10–9 in 1945, then was demoted. Later toiling unspectacularly in the NL, he was hampered by a hip injury, an ear infection, and a chronic back ailment. /(JL)

Jean Dubuc (Chauncey) — 1888–1958. RHP 1908–09, 12–16, 1918–19 Reds, **Tigers**, Red Sox, Giants 1444 ip, 86–76, 3.04

Dubuc twice won 17 games for Detroit, and in 1919 led the NL with six relief victories. Used 93 times as a pinch hitter, he belted two homers during the dead ball season of 1913. His career ended when he was banned for life in connection with the Black Sox scandal. /(TJ)

Jim Duckworth — 1939– . RHP 1963–66 **Senators**, A's 267 ip, 7–25, 5.26

Pitching for Washington in a 1965 game, Duckworth struck out eight of the first nine Tigers he faced. Plagued by a fear of flying, he once went on the disabled list to seek help in overcoming it. /(RTM)

Clise Dudley — 1903– . RHP 1929–33 **Dodgers**, Phillies, Pirates 420 ip, 17–33, 5.03

Dudley hit the first major league pitch he saw over the Ebbets Field wall (4/27/29). He became a .333 pinch hitter. Unfortunately, he was a pitcher who was often pounded. In the one-third inning he worked in 1933, he allowed six hits and a walk for a 135.00 ERA. /(JK)

Hal Dues — 1954– . RHP 1977–78, 80 **Expos** 134 ip, 6–8, 3.09

Dues recorded a 2.36 ERA in his rookie 1978 season with Montreal, then had elbow surgery from which he could not recover. /(KC)

Jim Duffalo — 1935– . RHP 1961–65 **Giants**, Reds 298 ip, 15–8, 3.39

Duffalo twice recorded ERAs under 3.00 as a Giant reliever, but never appeared in over 35 games. He had a good fastball, and over his career averaged better than six strikeouts per nine innings. /(RTM)

Frank Duffy — 1946– . SS-3B-2B 1970–79 Reds, Giants, **Indians**, Red Sox 915 g, .232, 26 hr, 240 rbi. *1 LCS, 1G, .000*

The freckle-faced, sure-handed Duffy was Cleveland's starting shortstop from 1972 through 1977. A Stanford graduate drafted by Cincinnati, in May 1971 he went to the Giants with Vern Geishert for George Foster in a notoriously uneven trade, and that November he was dealt to the Indians with Gaylord Perry for Sam McDowell. He led AL shortstops in fielding in 1973 and 1976. /(JCA)

Hugh Duffy

Hugh Duffy — 1866–1954. OF 1888–1901, 04–06 Cubs, Chicago (PL), Boston (AA), **Braves**, Milwaukee (AL), Phillies 1736 g, .328, 103 hr, 1299 rbi.
 Manager 1901, 04–06, 10–11, 21–22 Milwaukee (AL), **Phillies**, White Sox, Red Sox 535–671, .444
☛ *Led League—ba 94. Led League—hr 94, 97. Led League—rbi 94 . Hall of Fame—1945.*

Owner of the highest single-season batting average in ML history (.438 in 1894), Duffy was one of the game's early stars. He was an outstanding outfielder for Boston in the 1890s, and later, as a Red Sox coach, was a tutor to the young Ted Williams.

Originally an infielder in the New England League, Duffy idolized Cap Anson and signed with Anson's Chicago White Stockings (later the Cubs) for the 1888 season despite being offered more money by the local Boston club. Only 5'7", Duffy replaced Billy Sunday, soon to be a world-famous evangelist, as Chicago's right fielder. Duffy was sold to Boston (American Association) after three seasons, and then became a Brave when the AA broke up. With Duffy now patrolling centerfield, he and right fielder Tommy McCarthy became known as the "Heavenly Twins."

Duffy hit over .300 in nine of his ten seasons in Boston, but 1894 was his best year by far. Not only did he hit .438, but he won baseball's first Triple Crown with 18 HR and 145 RBI as well. He also led the NL with 236 hits, 50 doubles, and a .679 slugging percentage. He never approached those numbers again, although he did win another home run crown in 1897. Duffy was not successful as a manager; in eight seasons, he finished over .500 only twice, never higher than fourth, and three times in the cellar. Still, as a Red Sox coach emeritus, he patiently indulged reporters' requests for tales of the good old days, while maintaining that his rookie pupil, Ted Williams, was the best hitter he had ever seen. In 1945 Duffy was elected to the Hall of Fame by the Veterans Committee. /(JK)

Joe Dugan (Jumping Joe) — 1897–1982. 3B-SS-2B 1917–29, 31 A's, Red Sox, **Yankees**, Braves, Tigers 1446 g, .280, 42 hr, 571 rbi. *5 WS, 25 g, .267, 1 hr, 8 rbi*

While he may have deserved it for his prowess afield, Joe Dugan earned his nickname for being AWOL from his first big league club as a youngster.

The tall, rangy infielder went directly from the campus of Holy Cross to the Athletics in 1917. A shortstop in his first three seasons, Dugan became one of the finest all-around third basemen of his era. After batting .194 and .195 in his first two seasons he found his stroke and developed into a timely hitter, reaching a high of .322 in 1920.

Best known for his six and one half years with the Yankees, Dugan was a key member of five pennant winners including the fabled 1927 World Champion "Murderer's Row."

Dugan's controversial trade from the Red Sox to the Yankees in late July 1922, during a heated pennant race, caused an uproar which helped to bring about a June 15 trading deadline the following year. /(JL)

Bill Duggleby (Frosty Bill) — 1874–1944. RHP 1898, 1901–07 **Phillies**, A's, Pirates 1732 ip, 92–104, 3.19

On April 21, 1898 Duggleby became the very first player to homer in his first ML at-bat, and remains the only man to accomplish the feat with a grand slam. Called Frosty Bill because he spurned the companionship of his teammates and dressed in a heavy black suit even in summer, Duggleby went 19–12 for the Phillies in 1901. When he and Nap

Lajoie jumped the team to join the Athletics of the second-year American League, they were both enjoined in a lawsuit. Unlike Lajoie, Duggleby jumped back to the Phillies after just two appearances with Connie Mack's Athletics. /(JK)

Tom Dukes — 1942- . RHP 1967–72 Astros, **Padres**, Orioles, Angels 216 ip, 5–16, 4.37. *1 WS, 4 ip, 0.00*

First signed by the Yankees, Dukes saved 10 of the 1970 Padres' 63 wins. He was 1–5 for the 1971 AL champion Orioles and went with them on their postseason tour of Japan. /(MC)

Bob Duliba (Ach) — 1935- . RHP 1959–60, 62–65, 67 Cardinals, **Dodgers**, Red Sox, A's 257 ip, 17–12, 3.47

Duliba's first ML hit helped seal his first ML victory, with St. Louis in 1960. The righthander with the musical nickname pitched solely in relief, at his best going 6–4 with nine saves with the 1964 Angels. /(JL)

George Dumont (Pea Soup) — 1895–1956. RHP 1915–19 **Senators**, Red Sox 347 ip, 10–23, 2.85

As a 19-year-old Washington rookie in 1915, Dumont threw successive two-hit shutouts and lost a 10-inning complete game to compile a 2–1 record. He never pitched that well again. In 1917, his only year as a regular starter, he was 5–14. /(NLM)

Dave Duncan — 1945- . C 1964, 67–76 **A's**, Indians, Orioles 929 g, .214, 109 hr, 341 rbi. *2 LCS, 4 g, .375, 2 rbi. 1 WS, 3 g, .200*
☛ *All-Star—71.*

Signed for a reported $65,000 bonus in 1963, Duncan hit for power, not average (46 HR, California League, 1966) and didn't win a job with the A's until they moved to Oakland in 1968. Batting just .126 in 1969, and often on Marine reserve duty, Duncan finally became a regular in 1971. After his military duty was over, Duncan grew his hair down his back. Following a career-high 19 HR (batting .218) for the A's in 1972, he was traded to Cleveland. After knee injuries forced his retirement, he became a continually-employed ML pitching coach. /(MC)

Frank Duncan — 1901–1973. C-OF-MGR Negro Leagues 1920–48 Chicago Giants, **Kansas City Monarchs**, New York Black Yankees, Pittsburgh Crawfords, Homestead Grays, New York Cubans, Chicago American Giants 517 g, .252 (inc.)
☛ *All-Star—38.*

Duncan was a top defensive catcher and a successful playing manager in the Negro Leagues. He was a hardnosed competitor who played on the great Kansas City Monarch teams of the 1920s and managed the Monarchs in the 1940s, guiding such stars as Satchel Paige, Josh Gibson, and Jackie Robinson. Kansas City teammate Newt Allen said Duncan was a "great receiver and thrower—one of the greatest," but "wasn't much of a hitter." He ran the bases with reckless abandon and earned a reputation as a hard-sliding competitor. /(PG)

Mariano Duncan — 1963- . SS-2B 1985–87, 89- **Dodgers**, Reds 421 g, .235, 23 hr, 108 rbi. *1 LCS, 5 g, .222, 1 rbi*

A surprise 1985 Opening Day starter at second base, Duncan took over at shortstop and placed third in the NL Rookie of the Year voting. But some criticism apparently shook his confidence and his batting average plummeted, leading to a demotion in 1987. He returned as a utility man in 1989 and went to the Reds in the Kal Daniels trade. /(TG)

Pat Duncan — 1893–1960. OF 1915, 19–24 Pirates, **Reds** 727 g, .307, 23 hr, 374 rbi. *1 WS, 8 g, .269, 8 rbi*

Duncan had three .300 seasons during his five-year tenure as Cincinnati's regular left fielder. In the fourth game of the tainted 1919 World Series, "Black Sox" conspirator Eddie Cicotte deliberately mishandled Duncan's grounder, beginning a game-winning rally for the Reds. /(TJ)

Vern Duncan — 1890–1954. OF 1913–15 Phillies, **Baltimore (FL)** 311 g, .279, 4 hr, 97 rbi

Duncan was the regular centerfielder for Baltimore in his, and the Federal League's, only two full seasons. /(TJ)

Sam Dungan — 1866–1939. OF 1892–94, 1900–01 **Cubs**, Louisville (NL), Senators 382 g, .301, 3 hr, 197 rbi

After a five-year absence from the National League, Dungan won the American League batting title in 1900, when the AL was still a minor league. He batted .320 as the Senators' right fielder in 1901, then retired. /(AJA)

Davey Dunkle (Edward) — 1872–1941. RHP 1897–99, 1903–04 Phillies, Washington (NL), White Sox, **Senators** 421 ip, 17–30, 5.02

After winning five of seven decisions for the 1897 Phillies, Dunkle lost his effectiveness. His 9–13 with a 4.16 ERA for the 1903 Senators was his best full season in the majors. /(BC)

Fred Dunlap (Sure Shot) — 1859–1902. 2B 1880–91 Cleveland (NL), St. Louis (UA)/Cardinals, Detroit (NL), Pirates, New York (PL), Washington (AA) 965 g, .292, 41 hr, 299 rbi (inc.)
☛ *Led League—hr 84. Led League—ba 84.*

In ten NL seasons, the slick-fielding Dunlap at various times led NL second basemen in all fielding categories and twice batted over .300. But his greatest year was 1884 when, playing for powerhouse St. Louis in the short-lived Union Association, he led UA second basemen in all five fielding categories while leading the league in BA (his .412 was 52 points above that of the next-best hitter), slugging (.621), runs (160), and HR (13). His 160 runs scored set a new ML record, and still rank fourteenth-best of all time. /(FIC)

Jack Dunn — 1872–1928. 3B-RHP-SS-OF 1897–1904 Dodgers, Phillies, Baltimore (AL), Giants 490 g, .245, 1 hr, 164 rbi; 1077 ip, 64–59, 4.11

Jack Dunn was a pitcher and infielder who won 23 games for the pennant-winning Dodgers in 1899. He managed Providence (Eastern League) to a pennant in 1905, then had his greatest success in Baltimore (Eastern League/International League) starting in 1907 where, as owner-manager, he built the most successful minor league franchise in history. After winning a pennant in 1908 he bought the team from his former manager Ned Hanlon. Known for his ability to size up young players, he never forgot a player or a play. He found and developed players like Lefty Grove, Babe Ruth, Joe Boley, Jack Bentley, Ernie Shore and sold them for $50,000 to $100,000. On the field the Orioles once posted a 27-game winning streak. In 1914 he fielded the greatest team in the minors. They were 15 games in front when competition from the crosstown Federal League team forced him to sell off his 12 top stars to the majors and temporarily move to Richmond. Starting in 1919, they won seven International League pennants in a row. Dunn declined an offer to manage the Braves in 1928, and that fall had a fatal heart attack while on horseback watching bird dog field trials. /(NLM)

Mike Dunne — 1962– . RHP 1987– Pirates, Mariners 433 ip, 23–27, 3.97

TSN NL Rookie Pitcher of the Year in 1987, Mike Dunne led the NL in winning percentage (.684), had the league's second-best ERA (3.03), and led all rookies in wins (13–6). He was the Cardinals' first draft choice in June 1984 and a member of the '84 U.S. Olympic baseball team. He went to Pittsburgh in the Tony Pena deal. /(ME)

Steve Dunning — 1949– . RHP 1970–74, 76–77 Indians, Rangers, Angels, Expos, A's 613 ip, 23–41, 4.57

Dunning, Stanford's MVP and *TSN* College Player of the Year in 1970, became Cleveland's first pick in that June's draft. He went right to the majors, but never met expectations. He even fooled Ted Williams, whose Senators Dunning one-hit on April 18, 1971. Williams said "he's going to be some pitcher some day." But Dunning went 8–14 in '71, and had little success with four other clubs. /(KC)

Shawon Dunston — 1963– . SS 1985– Cubs 612 g, .256, 44 hr, 224 rbi. *1 LCS, 5 g, .316*
☛ *All-Star—88.*

The Cubs made Dunston the first pick in the nation in the 1982 June draft after he batted .790 as a senior at Brooklyn's Thomas Jefferson High. A raw talent with a rifle arm, he was Chicago's Opening Day shortstop in 1985, but hit .194 before being sent down on May 15; he was obviously unprepared as a fielder, and made glaring baserunning mistakes. Some felt the Cubs had rushed the wild-swinging youngster. But Dunston was handed back his job when Larry Bowa was released in August. In 1986, he led NL shortstops in putouts, assists, double plays, errors, and home runs (17). He drew only 21 walks in more than 600 plate appearances. Injuries kept him out two months of 1987, but he was hitting .287 in mid-1988 and won an All-Star spot. He was pulled out of the last game before the break by manager Don Zimmer for reportedly missing three hit-and-run signs. /(JCA)

Ryne Duren (Blind Ryne) — 1929– . RHP 1954, 57–65 Orioles, A's, Yankees, Angels, Phillies, Reds, Senators 589 ip, 27–44, 3.83. *2 WS, 5 g, 13 ip, 1–1, 2.03*
☛ *All-Star—58–59, 61.*

Duren came to the Yankees in 1958 at age 29 with a blazing 95-mph fastball. He quickly became the most feared reliever in the league. "Blind Ryne," who had uncorrected vision of 20/70 and 20/200, would frighten hitters when he entered the game, squinting toward home through bottle-thick glasses. He enhanced the effect by intentionally throwing his first warm-up pitch back to the screen. Initially, it may not have always been planned; while in the minors his control was so erratic that he once hit the on-deck batter.

Duren's career peaked quickly. In 1958 he won

six and saved a league-high 20 games in just 44 appearances. He was often brilliant in New York's World Series victory over the Braves, going 1–1 (1.93) with a save. He saved 14 in 1959, at one point going 18 games—36 innings—without allowing a run. In those two seasons he allowed only 89 hits, fanning 183 in just 151 innings. But drinking did Duren in. Though he continued to record more strikeouts than innings, his downhill slide was swift, as his records show. His decline, despair, and hard-won recovery are chronicled in his autobiography, *The Comeback.* He retired with 57 career saves./(GDW)

Ed Durham (Bull) — 1907–1976. RHP 1929–33 **Red Sox**, White Sox 642 ip, 29–44, 4.45

The curveballing South Carolinian used good control to win a career-high 10 games for the White Sox in 1933. Illness ended his ML career the following spring./(JK)

Leon Durham (Bull) — 1957– . 1B-OF 1980-Cardinals, **Cubs**, Reds 1067 g, .277, 147 hr, 530 hr. *1 LCS, 5 g, .150, 2 hr, 4 rbi*
☛ *All-Star—82–83.*

A promising outfielder and first baseman with St. Louis, Durham was the bait that, with Ken Reitz, brought Bruce Sutter and a pennant to the Cardinals. Durham finished third in the 1982 NL batting race at .312 and became the Cubs' first 20-HR 20-steal player since 1911. He played outfield for the Cubs until replacing Bill Buckner at first base in 1984, when his career-high 96 RBI helped Chicago to a division title. Aided by Wrigley Field, but troubled by inside pitches, Durham joined the Cubs' all-time HR leaders but never fulfilled expectations. He was traded to his hometown Reds early in 1988 and missed most of the season with drug rehabilitation. He came back with the Cardinals in 1989 as a late-inning defensive replacement for Pedro Guerrero, but was again suspended for drug use./(ME)

Leo Durocher (The Lip) — 1905– . SS-2B 1925, 28–41, 43, 45 Yankees, Reds, **Cardinals**, Dodgers 1637 g, .247, 24 hr, 567 rbi. *2 WS, 11 g, .241.*
    Manager 1939–46, 48–55, 66–73 **Dodgers**, Giants, Cubs, Astros 2010-1710, .540. First place: 41, 51, 54
3 WS, 15 g, 7–8, .467
☛ *All-Star—36, 38, 40.*

Durocher had many adjectives applied to him during his colorful career, both kind and unkind. He was a brash, abrasive, hustling, light-hitting, slick-fielding, umpire-baiting bench jockey who was in

baseball for nearly five decades as a player, manager, coach, and commentator.

Durocher spent his first full major league season with the 1928 World Champion Yankees, and became New York's starting shortstop in 1929. He moved on to the Reds in 1930, and the Cardinals in 1933, becoming captain of the "Gashouse Gang" in 1934. His last season as a first-stringer came with the 1939 Dodgers. Never much of a hitter, he topped .260 only five times in 17 years, with a high of .286 in 1936. He became an All-Star mostly on the strength of his glovework; a flashy, acrobatic SS, he led the NL in fielding in '36 and 1938.

Durocher went on to a long, distinguished, and tumultuous career as a manager. He was player-manager of the Dodgers in 1939–41, 1943, and 1945, though he played only a few games in the latter three years. He guided the Dodgers to the NL pennant in 1941, and to second-place finishes in 1940, 1942, and 1946. Perhaps his finest moment as Dodger manager came in spring training of 1947 when he personally quashed a rebellion by players who were protesting the presence of Jackie Robinson.

Durocher's tenure in Brooklyn was marked by—among other things—feuds with GM Branch Rickey, who could not always tolerate Durocher's antics and managing style. Durocher lived life in the fast lane. He was a pro at the card table, and favored the horse track. Stories emerged that he was friendly with such characters as Bugsy Siegel. In 1945, he was indicted for assaulting a fan under the stands. His problems reached a peak in 1947, when he was suspended for the season for reputed association with gamblers. The Dodgers won the pennant with Burt Shotton at the helm instead.

Durocher returned in 1948, gave rookie Roy Campanella the catching job, and moved young Gil Hodges to first base. But the Dodgers fell to last place on July 7. Eight days later, Rickey fired Durocher and rehired Shotton, as the rival Giants fired their manager, Mel Ott, and hired Durocher. Durocher guided the Giants to a pennant in 1951, overtaking the Dodgers in a spectacular race and defeating them in the subsequent playoff, thanks to Bobby Thomson. In 1954, Durocher led New York to his only WS victory. After the 1955 season, he became a TV commentator.

Durocher returned to manage the Cubs from 1966 until late in 1972, and the Astros through 1973, finishing second several times. Toward the end, his players were aware that he was becoming

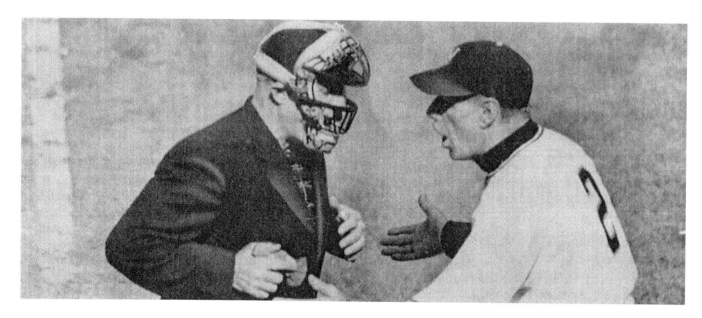

Leo Durocher, umpire Art Gore

senile; some were with Durocher for weeks before the manager knew who they were. He retired among the all-times leaders in games managed (3740), wins (2010), and losses (1710). His life story was told in his autobiography, *Nice Guys Finish Last*, co-written with Ed Linn. The phrase (or something to that effect) was one that had been attributed to Durocher in '47, referring to Ott, whose Giants had been losing. /(JJM)

Melvin Durslag — Unk.- . *Writer.*

After writing for Hearst newspapers for 26 years, Durslag was named executive sports editor of the Los Angeles *Herald Examiner* in 1964. His byline continued to appear in *TV Guide* and *The Sporting News*, and he was a Hearst syndicated columnist through the 1980s. /(NLM)

Cedric Durst — 1896–1971. OF-1B 1922–23, 26–30 Browns, **Yankees**, Red Sox 481 g, .244, 15 hr, 122 rbi. *2 WS, 5 g, .333, 1 hr, 2 rbi*

Durst's most important contribution to the Yankees came when they traded him and $50,000 to Boston for Red Ruffing early in the 1930 season. Durst had been a reserve outfielder on the great 1927 Yankees. Legend says that even the Yankee subs would have been stars for other teams. In truth, Durst had been only a utility player in three seasons with the Browns before coming to New York, and when the Red Sox played him regularly in 1930, he hit only .240, well below the AL average of .288. /(NLM)

Erv Dusak (Four Sack) — 1920- . OF-RHP 1941–42, 46–52 **Cardinals**, Pirates 413 g, .243, 24 hr, 106 rbi; 54 ip, 0–3, 5.33. *1 WS, 4 g, .250*

Tagged Four Sack after a game-winning homer early in his pro career, Dusak stuck with the 1946 World Championship Cardinals following WWII service. When his average dropped from .284 in 1947 to .209 in '48, Dusak became a pitcher, but he never won and never stayed a full season. /(MC)

Frank Dwyer — 1868–1943. RHP 1888–99 Cubs, Chicago (PL), Cincinnati-Milwaukee (AA), **Reds** 2810 ip, 176–152, 3.85. 20 wins: 1892, 96
  Manager 1902 **Tigers** 52–83, .385.
  Umpire 1889, 93–97, 99, 1901 NL, 1904 AL

Dwyer debuted with Cap Anson's powerhouse Chicago (NL) team, and in 1890 jumped to the Players' League, though he missed most of the season. He went 21–18 in 1892, toiling in the NL for St. Louis and Cincinnati. When the pitching mound was moved from 50' to 60'6" from the plate in 1893 and the league ERA ballooned, Dwyer survived the transition much better than many pitchers. He went 18–15 in '93, though his ERA rose from 2.98 to 4.13. Peaking in 1896, he compiled a 24–11 (3.15) mark. In 1899 he became a NL umpire, and, after managing the 1902 Tigers to seventh place, umpired in the AL in 1904. He later became the New York State Boxing Commissioner. /(AJA)

Jim Dwyer — 1950- . OF-DH-1B 1973- Cardinals, Expos, Mets, Cardinals, Giants, Red Sox, **Orioles** 1189 g, .257, 73 hr, 319 rbi. *1 LCS, 2 g, .250. 1 WS, 2 g, .375, 1 hr, 1 rbi*

After six years roaming the NL and two with the Red Sox, Dwyer found a home in Baltimore in 1981. A DH, extra outfielder, and lefthanded pinch hitter, he set the Orioles' career record for pinch homers. In his first World Series plate appearance, he homered off Philadelphia's John Denny for Baltimore's only run of Game One in 1983. /(JCA)

Jerry Dybzinski (Dybber) — 1955- . SS-3B-2B 1980-85 **Indians**, White Sox, Pirates 468 g, .234, 3 hr, 93 rbi. *1 LCS, 2 g, .250*

Dybzinski helped the AL West title-bound 1983 White Sox with clutch hitting and solid defense at shortstop, but committed a key baserunning gaffe in Chicago's Game Four LCS loss to Baltimore. Dybzinski was inserted in the lineup to replace regular shortstop Scott Fletcher, who was 0-for-7 in the Series at that point. With two on in the seventh inning of a scoreless tie at Comiskey Park, Dybzinski bunted into a force play. Julio Cruz followed with a sharp single to left, and lead runner Vance Law was held at third base. Dybzinski steamed around second with his head down before realizing third base was occupied. During the ensuing rundown, Law tried to score and was thrown out, effectively ending the rally; Baltimore won in the tenth inning.

Dybzinski, a Cleveland native, spent three seasons as an Indians utility man. /(ME)

Jim Dyck — 1922- . OF-3B 1951-56 **Browns/Orioles**, Indians, Reds 330 g, .246, 26 hr, 114 rbi

Dyck's all-around effective play for the Browns in 1952 earned him a spot on the ML rookie all-star team. He made a leaping catch at the left-field wall in Bobo Holloman's 1953 no-hitter against the A's, but played little after hitting .213 that season. /(RTM)

Duffy Dyer — 1945- . C 1968-81 **Mets**, Pirates, Expos, Tigers 722 g, .221, 30 hr, 173 rbi. *1 LCS, 1 g, --. 1 WS, 1 g, .000*

Dyer caught for the Arizona State 1965 and 1966 College World Series champs as a teammate of Reggie Jackson, Sal Bando, and Joe Keough. A poor hitter, he was a backup for Jerry Grote on the 1969 World Champion and 1973 NL champion Mets, and for Manny Sanguillen on the division-winning

1975 Pirates. Dyer caught a career-high 93 games for Pittsburgh in 1977. He later became a minor league manager and ML coach. /(MC)

Eddie Dyer — 1900-1964. LHP 1922-27 **Cardinals** 256 ip, 15-15, 4.75.
　　Manager 1946-50 **Cardinals** 446-325, .578. First place: 46 *1 WS, 4-3, .571*

Dyer, a genteel southerner, was a marginal pitcher for parts of six seasons with the Cardinals, becoming a manager in that organization after pitching just one inning in 1927. He managed nine minor league champions between 1928 and 1942, and was named *TSN* Minor League Manager of the Year for his leadership at Columbus (American Association) in 1942. Dyer headed the St. Louis farm operation while Billy Southworth took the Cardinals to three straight wartime pennants. When Southworth left to manage the Braves, Dyer replaced him, and won the 1946 pennant and the World Series against the Red Sox. Despite his successful debut, when the team finished second the next three seasons, Dyer's reputation as a gifted leader and developer of talent was not enough to quiet critics. After a fifth-place finish with a 78-75 record in 1950, Dyer was offered just a one-year contract extension; the Rice alumnus instead chose the business world in booming Houston. /(JK)

Jimmy Dygert (Sunny Jim) — 1884-1936. RHP 1905-10 **A's** 986 ip, 57-49, 2.65. 20 wins: 07

Dygert appeared with the pennant-winning Athletics of 1905 and 1910. He won 21 games in 1907, but poor control of his spitball (he walked a league-leading 97 in 1908) diminished his effectiveness. /(JK)

Jimmy Dykes — 1896-1976. 3B-2B-1B-SS 1918-39 **A's**, White Sox 2282 g, .280, 109 hr, 1071 rbi. *3 WS, 18 g, 1 hr, 11 rbi.*
　　Manager 1934-46, 51-54, 58-61 **White Sox**, A's, Orioles, Reds, Tigers, Indians 1407-1538, .478
☛ *All-Star—33* .

Jimmy Dykes averaged 125 games in 13 full seasons with the Athletics, but only once played the same position all year -second base in 1921. He had big, strong wrists from working as a pipefitter, and reputedly threw harder than any other non-pitcher in the game. He did everything but pitch and catch, prompting Connie Mack to call him his most valuable player. "Having one Dykes is like having five or six players and only one to feed, clothe, and pay," said Mack in 1929.

Jimmy Dykes

A Philadelphia native, Dykes was bought by the Athletics to take over second base in 1918 when regular Maury Shannon was drafted. Dykes played the season out before he too went into the army. Heavy-chested, heavy-legged, and wide in the rear, he returned in the spring of 1919 overweight and out of shape. He was sent down to play 2B with first baseman Ivy Griffin and shortstop Chick Galloway. In the fall they all joined the A's to stay.

In 1924, Dykes was given a Flint sedan for being named team MVP. He topped the .300 mark five times between '24 and 1930, and played third base in the 1929–31 World Series. In September of 1932, he was sold with Al Simmons and Mule Haas to the White Sox for $100,000. In the first All-Star Game, played at Comiskey Park in 1933, Dykes had two hits.

Dykes replaced Lew Fonseca as White Sox manager in 1934 and stayed until early in 1946. He was a player-manager until 1939. A chirping, joshing, noisy character and an accomplished bench jockey, he kept his calm in arguing with umpires as a player, but as a manager was frequently fined, and sometimes suspended, for letting loose volleys of strong language.

Dykes joined the Athletics as a coach in 1949, and was Mack's choice to manage the club in 1951.

After three poor finishes, he took over the Orioles in 1954, their first year in Baltimore after moving from St. Louis. He coached for the Reds, leading them for part of 1958, and managed the Tigers until August of 1960, when he was sent to the Indians for Joe Gordon in a rare trade of managers. He also coached the Braves and Kansas City A's. Gene Mauch broke Dykes's record of managing 21 years without winning a pennant. Dykes's highest finish was third place./(NLM)

Lenny Dykstra (Nails) — 1963- . OF 1985- **Mets**, Phillies 634 g, .268, 34 hr, 172 rbi. *2 LCS, 13 g, .351, 2 hr, 6 rbi. 1 WS, 7 g, .296, 2 hr, 3 rbi*

Dykstra is thought of as a speedy singles hitter, but after breaking in with a home run in his first game he went on to surprise with some of the most memorable homers in recent Mets history. In Game Three of the dramatic 1986 LCS, his two-run ninth-inning HR off Astros relief ace Dave Smith gave the Mets a 6–5 victory. He also starred in the Mets' clinching victory in Game Six. His pinch-triple leading off the ninth started a game-tying rally, and he drove in the last run in the three-run rally in the 16th inning that led to the Mets' 7–6 win. After New York lost the first two games of the World Series, Dykstra's leadoff HR in Game Three sparked them to a 7–1 victory, and he hit a two-run shot that went off Boston right fielder Dwight Evans's glove and over the wall in Game Four as the Mets evened the Series. Dykstra also hit .429 in the Mets' 1988 LCS loss to the Dodgers, including a three-run HR in Game Five.

Dykstra's rally-starting triple in the '86 LCS was more typical of what was expected of him. As the Mets' leadoff hitter against righthanded pitchers, he teamed with number-two hitter Wally Backman to ignite the Mets' offense. The pair's all-out style of play earned them the nickname "The Partners in Grime." Dykstra had career highs of 31 stolen bases, a .295 average, and 58 walks in '86. It was his ability to draw more walks than the Mets' former regular leadoff man, switch-hitter Mookie Wilson, that won Dykstra the larger part of the centerfield platoon. He also was a surer fielder than Wilson; Dykstra's diving, sliding catches made him a favorite of the fans, but he rarely took a chance that backfired. Dykstra had his most productive year in 1987 with career highs of 10 HR, 37 doubles, and 86 runs scored in 431 at-bats. He declined in 1988, and was traded to the Phillies in mid-1989 with Roger McDowell for Juan Samuel in a much-criticized move./(SH)

"The Hit Man"

Arnie Earley — 1933- . LHP 1960-67 **Red Sox**, Cubs, Astros 381 ip, 12-20, 4.48

The bespectacled Earley was often the set-up man for Dick Radatz with the 1962–65 Red Sox. In 1965 Earley made a career-high 57 appearances, but went 0-1 without a save. Seldom used for more than an inning, he was generally the first lefthander called in from the bullpen. /(PB)

Tom Earley (Chick) — 1917–1988. RHP 1938-42, 45 **Braves** 359 ip, 18-24, 3.78

Earley wanted a tryout with the Red Sox but settled for signing with the Braves. After pitching for them for parts of five seasons, he went into the military, where he damaged his arm irreparably, tearing ligaments playing first base. /(NLM)

Jake Early — 1915- . C 1939-43, 46-49 **Senators**, Browns 747 g, .241, 32 hr, 264 rbi
☛ *All-Star—43.*

While Early was the second-string catcher, he learned to handle the Senators' four knuckleballers by watching Rick Ferrell. When Ferrell spent a couple of years with the Browns, Early took over and he caught the entire 1943 game for the AL All-Stars. He was an exuberant chatterbox behind the plate, singing and doing mock pitch-by-pitch broadcasts to distract hitters. /(JK)

George Earnshaw (Moose) — 1900-1976. RHP 1928-36 **A's**, White Sox, Dodgers, Cardinals 1915 ip, 127-93, 4.38. 20 wins: 29-31 *3 WS, 63 ip, 4-3, 1.58*
☛ *Led League—w 29.*

Moose, a genial 6'4" 210-lb righthander from Swarthmore College, teamed with Lefty Grove on the Philadelphia A's to form the game's premier pitching duo for the years 1929–31 (79 wins by Grove, 67 by Earnshaw). He won a league-high 24 in 1929, but twice led the league in walks. A basic fastball and curveball pitcher, Earnshaw said, "I didn't fool around with those junk pitches." He won a Bronze Star as a WWII naval officer, then scouted and coached for the Phillies. /(TJ)

Mike Easler — 1950- . OF-DH 1973-77, 79-87 Astros, Angels, **Pirates**, Red Sox, Yankees, Phillies 1151 g, .293, 118 hr, 522 rbi. *1 LCS, 1 g, .000. 1 WS, 2 g, .000*

Mired in the minor leagues for a decade, Easler finally won a job with the Pirates in 1980, hitting .338 with 21 HR and 74 RBI (in 393 at-bats) after spending the previous season as their primary pinch hitter. Most effective against righthanded pitchers, he moved from the outfield to first base when traded to Boston for John Tudor in 1984 but his all-around poor defense made him a DH. He had career highs of 27 HR and 91 RBI. The lefthander was traded to the Yankees after the season for righthanded slugger Don Baylor, another DH, in an attempt to match the hitters to their most compatible ballparks. Successful in New York, Easler was traded, reacquired, and released within one year despite continuing to hit for average. /(ME)

Mal Eason (Kid) — 1879-1970. RHP 1900-03, 05-06 Cubs, Braves, Tigers, **Dodgers** 944 ip, 36-75, 3.39. *Umpire* NL 1901-02, 10-15

Eason posted his only winning record during his rookie season (1-0 in one start in 1900). Before hurting his arm in 1906, an injury that ultimately ended his career, Eason pitched a 2-0 no-hitter for the Dodgers against the Cardinals on July 20.

Eason became a Southern League umpire in 1910, then joined the National League. Eason's umpiring career lasted longer than his playing career, ending in 1922 in the Pacific Coast League. /(MA)

Luke Easter — 1915-1979. 1B 1949-54 **Indians** 491 g, .274, 93 hr, 340 rbi

The 6'4" 240-lb Negro League veteran was 34 when the Indians promoted him from the minors. In 1950, they thought so highly of the lefthanded hitter that they traded Mickey Vernon, a once and future AL batting champ, making Easter their everyday first baseman. He hit 28 home runs as a rookie; one, a 477-foot shot, is considered the longest ever hit at Cleveland Municipal Stadium. In 1952, he hit 31

Luke Easter

homers (his ML career high), one less than the AL leader, teammate Larry Doby; however, Easter's 7.1 HR percentage topped the AL. He continued playing Triple-A ball into his late forties. Working as a bank messenger in 1979, he was shot to death by holdup men. /(TJ)

Howard Easterling — Unk.–Unk. 3B-2B-SS Negro Leagues 1936–43, 46–49 Cincinnati Tigers, Chicago American Giants, **Homestead Grays**, New York Cubans statistics not available

Easterling was the third baseman for the 1940 through 1943 Negro National League pennant-winning Homestead Grays. A 5'9" 175-lb switch-hitter, he generally batted fifth behind power hitters Buck Leonard and Josh Gibson. He hit approximately .315 lifetime. In 1941, he went 6-for-10 in a doubleheader sweep as the Grays defeated the New York Cubans in the league championship series. He hit .333 in the 1942 Black World Series, and partial data on the 1943 BWS shows he batted .280. He started at third base for the East in the 1940, 1943, 1946, and 1949 all-star games, and at shortstop for

the West in 1937, compiling a .320 average. He led the 1949–50 Venezuelan Winter League in doubles (16) and home runs (nine) in closing out his career. /(MFK)

Jamie Easterly (The Rat) — 1953– . LHP 1974–79, 81–87 Braves, Brewers, **Indians** 613 ip, 23–33, 4.61

In nine full and four partial seasons in the majors, the 5'9", sneaky-fast Easterly managed 23 wins and 14 saves. After he posted his career-best 4–1 record in 1985, the long reliever re-signed with the Indians under a lucrative, two-year contract, but spent the bulk of that time disabled with shoulder problems. While on loan to the Expos organization on July 14, 1979, he threw a seven-inning perfect game for Denver (American Association). /(JCA)

Ted Easterly — 1885–1951. C-OF 1909–15 **Indians**, White Sox, Kansas City (FL) 704 g, .300, 7 hr, 261 rbi

A lefthanded-hitting catcher, Easterly had three AL years over .300 and led the league in pinch hits (13) in 1912 while playing for both Cleveland and Chicago. He jumped to the Federal League in 1914 and finished third in batting (.335). /(ME)

Rawley Eastwick — 1950– . RHP 1974–81 **Reds**, Cardinals, Yankees, Phillies, Royals, Cubs 526 ip, 28–27, 3.30. *3 LCS, 8 ip, 2–0, 5.87 1 WS, 8 ip, 2–0, 2.25*

Eastwick was a rookie sensation in 1975, tying for the NL lead with 22 saves, with a 2.60 ERA. He then won three and saved two in post-season play as the Reds became the '75 World Champions. The 6'3" fireballer saved a league-high 26 in 1976, which, with his 11 relief wins, earned him the NL Fireman of the Year award. After being traded to St. Louis during a 1977 salary dispute, Eastwick parlayed free agency into a $1.1 million five-year pact in 1978 with the Yankees. They shipped him to the Phillies that June 14. Eastwick set a NL fielding record for pitchers by going 274 consecutive error-less games. /(MC)

Ebbets Field Brooklyn Dodgers 1913–57. LF-348, CF-384, RF-297

Cramped but colorful Ebbets Field, in the Flatbush section of Brooklyn, was home to the Dodgers in their lean times and glory years, until the franchise was transplanted to Los Angeles. Built by Dodger owner Charlie Ebbets for the 1913 season, the widely anticipated park opened without a press box, and no one brought the key to the bleachers for the first game. Originally the double-decked grandstand stood only along the foul lines, leaving the left field

Ebbets Field

corner 419′ distant, and center 477′. The grandstand was extended to left and center in the 1930s, however, making the park a hitter's paradise. The left-field power alley was 351′ and center became a very comfortable 388′, made even shorter by the upper deck, which hung over the playing field. The right field wall was a sight in itself. A patchwork collection of local advertisements, a scoreboard, and a large black screen that was in play, it was 38′ high and abutted Bedford Avenue. The screen made up the top 19′, sending balls rebounding at unpredictable angles, while the wall itself was concave, angled in the middle. The large black scoreboard featured the famous Abe Stark "Hit sign, win suit" advertisement on the bottom, and a Schaefer beer ad on top which gave the official scorer's ruling on hits and errors by lighting up the appropriate letter (h or e).

Renowned for its laughable Dodgers in the 1920s and 1930s, Ebbets Field was also known for its vocal and boisterous fans. Hilda Chester would attend each game with her clanging cowbell, while the Dodgers Sym-Phony, a collection of musically inclined fans, played other instruments. In the 1940s, the Reds' Lonny Frey hit an inside-the-park home run when his drive to right hit the screen and fell straight down, coming to rest on top of the lower half of the wall, 19′ above the field. And on October 3, 1947 Cookie Lavagetto broke up Bill Bevens's World Series no-hit bid with two out in the ninth.

By 1957, however, Ebbets Field had grown too old to satisfy Dodger owner Walter O'Malley, and in 1958 Brooklyn's beloved Dodgers were in Los Angeles. Only 6,673 fans attended the final game, and the park was demolished in 1960. The Jackie Robinson apartment complex now stands on the site. /(SCL)

Charlie Ebbets — 1859–1925. Owner.
  Manager 1898 **Dodgers** 38–68, .358

Ebbets joined the Brooklyn club as a bookkeeper in 1883, gradually began buying shares in the team, and became president in 1898. He never played the game, but tried his hand at managing in 1898, finishing tenth. Ned Hanlon, the owner-manager of the Baltimore Orioles, bought some of the remaining Brooklyn stock after the '98 season, moved the best Baltimore players to Brooklyn, and won pennants in 1899 and 1900. However, when Hanlon wanted to move the team to Baltimore after the 1905 season, Ebbets bought him out.

Ebbets is sometimes credited with inventing the rain check and with suggesting that teams with the worst records should draft first, long before there was a draft. He had a deserved reputation for honesty and was popular in Brooklyn.

He financed the building of a new ball park for his team in 1912 by selling half of the club to the McKeever Brothers, contractors in Brooklyn. When the park was opened the next year, it was named Ebbets Field by a vote of sportswriters. Ebbets's Dodgers won pennants in 1916 and 1920. At the turn of the century, the prescient Ebbets was widely quoted when he said, "Baseball is in its infancy."/(NLM)

Dennis Eckersley (The Eck) — 1954– . RHP 1975- Indians, **Red Sox**, Cubs, A's 2742 ip, 165–138, 3.56. 20 wins: 78 *3 LCS, 17 ip, 0–1, 3.18. 2 WS, 3 ip, 0–1, 5.41*
☛ *All-Star—77, 82, 88.*

After an early career as a brash young flamethrower and a seven-year spell as a mediocre starter, The Eck was reborn in Oakland as a dominating bullpen stopper. In 1988, he led the AL with 45 saves, one shy of the ML record.

Eckersley broke into the ML with the Indians in 1975 as a cocky 20-year-old with shoulder-length hair and an explosive fastball. He fanned 200 batters in 1976, no-hit the Angels 1–0 on May 30, 1977 (part of a 22.1-inning hitless string), and was 20–8, 2.99 with the Red Sox in 1978. By 1980, however, his fastball had shortened, and he was 74–78 as a starter from 1980 to 1986.

Eckersley was traded to Oakland at the start of the 1987 season and was sent to the bullpen. He regained his effectiveness and fanned 113 batters in 116 innings. In 1988, he emerged as baseball's best reliever and he saved all four Oakland wins in the ALCS, but his season ended on a sour note when he

surrendered a two-out, two-run home run to a hobbling Kirk Gibson in the bottom of the ninth inning of Game One of the WS./(SCL)

William Eckert (Spike) — 1909–1971. Commissioner.

Eckert was a retired Air Force general, a supply officer who specialized in negotiating defense contracts. When he was elected commissioner in 1965, he knew nothing about baseball's inner workings and had not attended a game in ten years. At the time every baseball man nominated had too many enemies to gain enough votes. Eckert was quiet, bright, honest, and willing, but he was in a situation for which he had neither preparation nor aptitude. Lee McPhail was appointed administrator to help him, but Eckert became a symbol of executive futility. He incurred the public's ire by refusing to cancel games after the assassinations of Robert Kennedy and Martin Luther King and the owners' disdain because he refused to deal forcefully with substantive business issues. Anticipating a players' strike and having no confidence in Eckert's ability to handle the situation, the owners voted him out in early 1969 although he still had three years on his contract./(NLM)

Ox Eckhardt [Oscar George] — 1901–1951. OF 1932, 36 Braves, **Dodgers** 24 g, .192, 1 hr, 7 rbi

Eckhardt averaged .367 over 13 seasons lifetime as one of the greatest minor league hitters ever. The 6'1" 190-lb Texan led the Pacific Coast League in batting four times./(TJ)

Bruce Edwards (Bull) — 1923–1975. C 1946–52, 54–56 **Dodgers**, Cubs, Senators, Reds 591 g, .256, 39 hr, 241 rbi. *2 WS, 9 g, .241, 2 rbi*
☛ *All-Star—47, 51.*

A solid catcher with warning track power, Edwards hit .295 for Brooklyn in 1947 and led NL catchers that year in putouts and double plays. Following the season, the 5'8" 180-lb Bull hurt his arm throwing during an exhibition game against the inmates at Folsom Prison. His damaged arm and the emergence of Roy Campanella put him on the bench for the rest of his career./(RTM)

Dave Edwards — 1954– . OF 1978–82 **Twins**, Padres 321 g, .238, 14 hr, 73 rbi

Bigger than older brothers Mike and Marshall Edwards, Dave had the best arm and power of the three, but struck out almost as often as he got a hit./(MC)

Doc Edwards [Howard] — 1937– . C 1962–65, 70 Indians, **A's**, Yankees, Phillies 317 g, .238, 15 hr, 87 rbi. *Manager* 1987–89 **Indians** 173–207, .455

The ex-Navy medic applied solid defensive skills as a backup catcher in the bigs, followed by a career as a coach with the Phillies and Indians and as a minor league manager. Edwards's 1981 Charleston Charlies played Pawtucket in a 33-inning marathon, the longest game in professional history. He replaced Pat Corrales as the Indians' manager in July 1987 and was dismissed in September 1989. /(JCA)

Hank Edwards (Henry) — 1919–1988. OF 1941–43, 46–53 **Indians**, Cubs, Dodgers, Reds, White Sox, Browns 735 g, .280, 51 hr, 276 rbi

Edwards hit .301 and led the AL in triples (16) with the Indians in 1946. A series of injuries, the worst when he dislocated his shoulder landing on a fence while making a leaping catch, ended his days as a regular. /(ME)

Henry P. Edwards — 1873–1948. *Writer.*

An early dean of baseball writers, Edwards became sports editor of the Cleveland *Recorder* in 1898. In 1901 he joined the Cleveland *Plain Dealer*. He was credited with helping several sandlot players be discovered by ML teams, including Rube Marquard and Roger Peckinpaugh. In 1928 he organized the AL service bureau, which he managed from its beginning until 1942. One of the founders of the BBWAA, he served as secretary-treasurer for 15 years. /(NLM)

Jim Joe Edwards [James Corbette] — 1894–1965. LHP 1922–26, 28 **Indians**, White Sox, Reds 580 ip, 26–37, 4.41

Edwards was most productive in 1923, going 10–10 for Cleveland. With the White Sox three years later, three of his six wins were shutouts. /(TJ)

Johnny Edwards — 1938– . C 1961–74 **Reds**, Cardinals, Astros 1470 g, .242, 81 hr, 524 rbi. *2 WS, 4 g, .333, 2 rbi*
☛ *All-Star—63–65.*

Edwards was a durable, strong-armed, take-charge catcher whose intelligence matched his fine physical ability. A 6'4" 220-lb graduate of Ohio State, he set a ML season record for catcher's total chances (helped by a pitching staff of strikeout artists) with 1,221 in 1969, his first year with Houston. When he retired five years later, he held the NL career record for total chances by a catcher (9,745), since broken by Johnny Bench. Edwards won two Gold Gloves. As a rookie playing in the 1961 New York-Cincinnati World Series, he hit .364. He batted a career-high .281 for the 1964 Reds and had his best HR season in 1965 with 17. /(TJ)

Mike Edwards — 1952– . 2B 1977–80 Pirates, **A's** 317 g, .250, 2 hr, 49 rbi

Edwards won a regular job with Oakland in 1978, when he had a 17-game hitting streak. On August 8 of that year he set an AL record with two unassisted double plays in one game. He lost his job after leading the league in errors in both '78 and '79. Mike's twin, Marshall, and their younger brother, Dave, also played ML baseball. /(MC)

Dick Egan — 1884–1947. 2B-SS 1908–16 **Reds**, Dodgers, Braves 917 g, .249, 4 hr, 292 rbi

Egan hit over .250 only once in four years as the Reds' regular second baseman, but stole 141 bases, often teaming on double steals with Bob Bescher, who led the NL each year. /(JK)

Dick Egan — 1937– . LHP 1963–64, 66–67 **Tigers**, Angels, Dodgers 101 ip, 1–2, 5.15

In 1962, Egan led the Pacific Coast League in wins (17) and strikeouts (201) pitching for Hawaii. Used exclusively in relief in the ML, the southpaw picked up two saves. /(RTM)

Tom Egan — 1946– . C 1965–72, 74–75 **Angels**, White Sox 373 g, .200, 22 hr, 91 rbi

A high school All-American in baseball and football, the 6'4" Egan signed for $100,000 with California, and was converted from third base to catcher as a 19-year-old rookie in 1965. Egan allowed five passed balls in one game (7/28/70), then an AL record, but none the rest of the year. Always a backup, he had some power, but struck out once every three at-bats. In 1971, Egan was featured in a national ad campaign for life insurance that never mentioned that he played baseball. /(MC)

Wish Egan [Aloysius Jerome] — 1881–1951. RHP 1902, 05–06 Tigers, **Cardinals** 279 ip, 8–26, 3.83

Egan was 6–15, 3.58 as a starter for the Cardinals in 1905 before an arm injury ended his playing career. He signed on to scout for Detroit in 1910, and remained with the Tigers until 1950, sometimes doubling as a coach. His discoveries included Hal Newhouser, Dizzy Trout, and Hoot Evers, and it was at his insistence that the Tigers traded Barney McCosky for George Kell in 1946. /(FVP)

Howard Ehmke (Bob) — 1894-1959. RHP 1915-17, 19-30 Buffalo (FL), **Tigers**, Red Sox, A's 2820 ip, 166-166, 3.75. *1 WS, 12 ip, 1-0, 1.42.* 20 wins: 23

Ehmke broke in with the Federal League but was grabbed by Detroit when the Feds folded and twice won 17 games for them. Traded to the Red Sox in 1923, he pitched a no-hitter that would have been a one-hitter had not an Athletics' runner failed to touch first base on an apparent double. Four days later he pitched a one-hitter against the Yankees, the only hit being a ground ball that bounced off the third baseman's chest. Ehmke won 20 games for the Red Sox in '23 and 19 the next season. By 1929, he seemed nearly washed up, having won only seven games for the pennant-winning Athletics. It came as a shock when Connie Mack started him in the World Series opener against the Cubs. Mack reasoned that the sidearming Ehmke had the perfect mix of control and slow stuff to keep the predominantly righthand-hitting Cubs off balance, and gave Ehmke time off near the end of the season to personally scout the Cubs. Ehmke struck out a then-record 13 in pitching an eight-hit, 3-1 victory. /(NLM)

Howard Ehmke

Rube Ehrhardt [Welton Claude] — 1894-1980. RHP 1924-29 Dodgers, Reds 587 ip, 22-34, 4.15

Ehrhardt finessed batters with curves and change-ups, but manager Wilbert Robinson preferred big fastballers who overpowered hitters. Banished to the bullpen, Ehrhardt was called on so often that he twice led the NL in relief appearances and innings. /(JK)

Juan Eichelberger — 1953- . RHP 1978-83, 88 **Padres**, Indians, Braves 603 ip, 26-36, 4.10

The hard thrower with an unusual short-arm delivery had control problems, walking 273 while striking out 268 in the majors. Eichelberger was the staff ace of the last-place 1981 Padres, with eight victories. /(MC)

Mark Eichhorn — 1960- . RHP 1982, 86- **Blue Jays**, Braves 457 ip, 29-23, 3.19

Mark Eichhorn is a relief pitcher with a sidearm delivery who was the AL Rookie Pitcher of the Year in 1986, when he disdained the opportunity to pitch five meaningless extra innings at the end of the season in order to win the AL ERA title that went to Roger Clemens (whose ERA was 2.48 compared with Eichhorn's 1.72). As well as ERA, Eichhorn set Blue Jay rookie records for games, wins, saves, strikeouts and hit batters. In 1987 Eichhorn tied the AL record for appearances (89), being used mainly as a set-up man for fireballer Tom Henke. Eichhorn's effectiveness declined as he attempted to change his delivery so he wouldn't be so easy to steal on and as righthanded batters learned to lay off his wicked breaking ball. /(TF)

Dave Eilers — 1936- . RHP 1964-67 Braves, Mets, **Astros** 123 ip, 8-6, 4.45

Eilers's minor league record was 33-7 from 1963 to 1965. In the International League in 1964, he made 18 straight relief appearances without allowing a run. Used by Houston in 35 games in 1967, he went 6-4. /(RTM)

Eddie Einhorn — 1936- . *Executive.*

The colorful Einhorn was always in the midst of a controversy, be it the struggle to establish a United States Football League franchise in Chicago or answering his critics concerning the White Sox' new stadium. The former executive of CBS Sports began by selling hot dogs at Comiskey Park during the 1959 World Series. In 1981, former law school classmate Jerry Reinsdorf invited him to join the limited partnership which bought the club from Bill Veeck. Einhorn later founded Sportsvision, the Chicago cable outlet airing White Sox, Bulls, Sting, and Blackhawk games. He was instrumental in finalizing the six-year, multi-million-dollar pact between baseball and TV in 1981. In 1983, when the Chisox won the AL West division title, fans were treated to the sight of Einhorn jumping up and down in unabashed joy, wearing his Sox hat and warm-up jacket. /(RL)

Charles Einstein — 1926- . *Writer.*

A graduate of the University of Chicago and the son of radio comedian Harry (Parkyakarkas) Einstein, Charles Einstein worked for INS (1945–1953), San Francisco newspapers, and *Sport Magazine*, and edited the first wire-service news reports especially for television. In addition to novels, he has published four books with or about Willie Mays, and also co-authored books with Juan Marichal and Orlando Cepeda. /(NLM)

Jim Eisenreich — 1959- . OF-DH 1982–84, 87– Twins, **Royals** 308 g, .268, 16 hr, 111 rbi

Eisenreich vaulted through the minors to the Twins, but after a .303 beginning, he experienced Tourette's Syndrome, a nervous disorder that causes uncontrollable tics, sidelining him for most of 1982–84, and prompting an early retirement. His problems under control, he signed with the Royals in a comeback bid and batted .382 at Omaha (AAA) in 1987 after nearly three years away from pro ball. He joined Kansas City as a designated hitter and pinch hitter, better able to control himself when not in the field, but was able to play 64 games in the outfield in 1988. /(FO)

Harry Eisenstat — 1915- . LHP 1935–42 Dodgers, **Tigers**, Indians 479 ip, 25–27, 3.84

Primarily a reliever, the Brooklyn-born Eisenstat went 9–6 with the 1938 Tigers. Rather than return to baseball after 1942, Eisenstat felt it his patriotic duty to retain his defense plant job. /(TJ)

Kid Elberfeld (The Tabasco Kid) [Norman Arthur] — 1875–1944. SS-3B-2B 1898–99, 1901–11, 14 Phillies, Reds, Tigers, **Yankees**, Senators, Dodgers 1293 g, .271, 10 hr, 535 rbi.
   Manager 1908 **Yankees** 27–71, .276

The 5'5" Elberfeld played a fiery brand of baseball, challenging baserunners to slash him out of their way, living up to the title "The Tabasco Kid." His legs were badly scarred, and he grimly poured raw whiskey into spike wounds to cauterize them. He hit .310 as Detroit's shortstop his first full season, 1901, and was the Highlanders' everyday shortstop from mid-1903 through 1907. After a short, unsuccessful stint as New York's manager for part of 1908, he went back to playing full time the following year. He remained in baseball for decades, battling umpires and foes as a hotheaded minor league manager. /(JK)

Al Munro Elias — 1872–1939. *Statistician.*

In 1913 Al Elias and his brother Walter established their Bureau of Statistics. Their first production was scorecards featuring the latest team and individual statistics, which they peddled in saloons and other haunts of baseball fans. But newspapers refused to consider the use of their stats until three years later, when Elias sold their first weekly compilation of batting and pitching averages to the New York *Telegram*. Three years later the brothers were the official statisticians for the NL and International League. Other minor leagues soon signed up. In 1937 they took over publication of the *Little Red Book*, and for many years published the official *Green Book*, the NL's annual summary. /(NLM)

Hod Eller [Horace Owen] — 1894–1961. RHP 1917–21 **Reds** 863 ip, 61–40, 2.62. 20 wins: 19. *1 WS, 18 g, 2–0, 2.00*

Eller was an effective pitcher in his first four years with the Reds, peaking in the pennant-winning season of 1919, when he went 20–9 with a 2.39 ERA. That fall he threw a shutout in Game Five of the WS, with six consecutive strikeouts in the second and third innings, and a complete-game victory in the finale. But his WS achievements were tainted: the Reds' opponents were the infamous "Black Sox," bribed to throw the Series. /(JK)

Frank Ellerbe (The Governor) — 1895–1988. 3B-SS 1919–24 Senators, **Browns**, Indians 420 g, .268, 4 hr, 152 rbi

The last surviving member of the 1922 St. Louis Browns (the winningest team in the 52-year history of that franchise), The Governor from South Carolina was the only son of a state governor to play in the majors. /(WAB)

Hal Elliott (Ace) — 1899–1963. RHP 1929–32 **Phillies** 322 ip, 11–24, 6.95

Elliott led the NL in games pitched (48) as a starter and reliever for the last-place Phillies in 1930. The league as a whole batted a record .306 that year, and Elliott's ERA was 7.67. /(JK)

Jumbo Elliott [James Thomas] — 1900–1970. LHP 1923, 25, 27–34 Browns, Dodgers, **Phillies**, Braves 1206 ip, 63–74, 4.24
☛ *Led League—w 31.*

At one time the biggest man in the majors, Elliott stood 6'3" and his weight sometimes ballooned to 245. In 1931, he tied for the NL lead with 19 wins while pitching for the sixth-place Phillies. /(NLM)

Dock Ellis — 1945– . RHP 1968–79 **Pirates**, Yankees, A's, Rangers, Mets 2129 ip, 138–119, 3.45. *5 LCS, 30 ip, 2–2, 2.43. 2 WS, 6 ip, 0–2, 12.71*
☛ *All-Star—71.*

Flamboyant righthander Dock Ellis was among the most controversial players on the tempestuous Pirate teams of the early 1970s. An outspoken and political Afro-American, he antagonized the Pittsburgh front office by dressing colorfully and sometimes wearing his hair in curlers in the clubhouse. On June 12, 1970 in San Diego, he threw a no-hitter while under the influence of a hallucinogen, according to his autobiography (with Donald Hall) *Dock Ellis in the Country of Baseball*. And on May 1, 1974, in what he claimed was an attempt to rouse his teammates from lethargy, Ellis tied a major league record by bouncing baseballs off the first three Cincinnati batters he faced.

Ellis was 14–3 at the All-Star Break in 1971, but said he wouldn't start against the AL's Vida Blue in the All-Star Game because baseball would never start "two soul brothers" against each other. Ellis and Blue did start, and Ellis lost, the only loss for the NL between 1963 and 1982. He finished the season with a career-high 19 wins, and added another victory in Game Two of the NLCS against the Giants.

Ellis was traded to the Yankees with Willie Randolph and Ken Brett for Doc Medich after the 1975 season, and in 1976 he won Comeback Player of the Year honors with a 17–8, 3.19 record for the AL champions. He also won Game Three of the LCS against the Royals. In 1977, Ellis was traded to Oakland for Mike Torrez, then was sold to Texas six weeks later, and he finished the season 12–12. He retired after going 4–12 for the Rangers, Mets, and Pirates in 1979. /(TF)

John Ellis — 1948– . 1B-C-DH 1969–81 Yankees, **Indians**, Rangers 883 g, .262, 69 hr, 391 rbi

A competent hitter, the ungraceful 6'2" 225-lb Ellis played most regularly for the Indians in 1973–74, hitting career highs of 14 HR and 68 RBI in '73. He

came to Cleveland in the six-player 1972 deal that sent Graig Nettles to the Yankees. In May 1976 with Texas, Ellis suffered a broken leg, dislocated ankle, and torn ligaments sliding into second. He returned in 1977 to play part-time and, for a while, coach for the Rangers. /(TJ)

Rube Ellis [George William] — 1885–1938. OF 1909–12 **Cardinals** 555 g, .260, 14 hr, 199 rbi

Ellis stole 25 bases as the Cardinals' regular left fielder in 1910. Just before his death in 1938, he was an unsuccessful candidate for secretary of the Association of Professional Ball Players of America. /(WAB)

Sammy Ellis — 1941– . RHP 1962, 64–69 **Reds**, Angels, White Sox 1004 ip, 63–58, 4.15. 20 wins: 65
☛ *All-Star—65.*

Commenting on the 1965 season, when he went 22–10 for Cincinnati, Ellis said, "The Reds scored a lot of runs for me. I thought the year before was a better year (10–3) as far as being an asset to the team." In subsequent seasons, his blazing fastball and dancing knuckleball were weakened by arm problems. Ellis later became a Yankee pitching coach. /(RTM)

Dick Ellsworth — 1940– . LHP 1958, 60–71 **Cubs**, Phillies, Red Sox, Indians, Brewers 2156 ip, 115–137, 3.72. 20 wins: 63
☛ *All-Star—64.*

As a rookie, Dick Ellsworth paced NL pitchers in fielding. The lanky lefthander won 22 games for the 1963 Cubs. He lost 22, to lead the league and tie a Cub record, in 1966. Ellsworth twice led the NL in hits surrendered. He was tagged for 34 homers, most among NL hurlers, in 1964. Four years later, Ellsworth compiled a .696 (16–8) NL winning percentage. Like fellow big league hurlers Tom Seaver and Jim Maloney, Ellsworth attended Fresno (California) High School. /(TJ)

Don Elston — 1929– . RHP 1953, 57–64 **Cubs**, Dodgers 755 ip, 49–54, 3.69
☛ *All-Star—59.*

Hard-throwing Elston started 14 games for the Cubs in 1957 but switched to relief and became one of the NL's best. In 1958 he set a Cub record (since broken) with a league-leading 69 appearances. The following year, he and bullpen mate Bill Henry tied for the appearance lead with 65. Elston was picked for the 1959 NL All-Star team. In the eight seasons he relieved, Elston saved 63 games for Cub teams that seldom won very many games. "The most important asset of a reliever is his temperament," he said. "I wasn't too crazy about the term 'ice water in his veins,' but that is a good description."/(MC)

Bones Ely [Frederick] — 1863-1952 SS-OF 1884, 86, 90-02 Buffalo NL, Louisville AA, Syracuse AA, Dodgers, Cardinals, **Pirates**, A's, Senators 1341 g, .258, 24 hr, 585 rbi

Ely was the regular Pittsburgh shortstop from 1896 until early in 1901, when he was dismissed from the team for allegedly trying to persuade players to jump to the rival American League. His replacement was converted outfielder Honus Wagner. Half of Ely's career homers came in 1894./(ME)

Elysian Fields

This unenclosed field in Hoboken, New Jersey, was the site of the first organized baseball game June 19, 1846, when the New York Base Ball Club defeated Alexander Cartwright's New York Knickerbockers 23-1 in four innings./(SCL)

Red Embree [Charles Willard] — 1917- . RHP 1941-42, 44-49 **Indians**, Yankees, Browns 707 ip, 31-48, 3.72

The red-haired Embree pitched in 20 games for the Indians before retiring to become a farmer in 1943. He returned to lead the International League with 19 wins in '44, and rejoined the Tribe rotation to win eight games in each of 1946 and '47. His only winning record came with the 1948 Yankees, when he went 5-3 as a spot starter and reliever./(ME)

Bob Emslie — 1859-1953. RHP 1883-85 **Baltimore AA**, Philadelphia AA 792 ip, 44-44, 3.19.
    Umpire AA, NL 1890-24

Emslie's three-year ML pitching career was highlighted by his 32-17 season for Baltimore in 1884, a year of unusual records because talent was stretched thin with three major leagues operating. He became a ML umpire in 1890 and remained on the job for 35 years. Emslie was working the bases in the famous "Merkle Boner Game," but when he admitted he hadn't seen whether Merkle had touched second or not, fellow ump Hank O'Day was forced to make the call. According to a famous story, Emslie, irritated that Giants' manager John McGraw had called him a "blind robber," showed up at a Giants' practice with a rifle, placed a dime on the pitching mound, and then with a shot fired from behind home plate sent the coin spinning into the outfield. Reportedly, McGraw never again challenged his eyesight./(RTM)

Yutaka Enatsu — 1949- . LHP 1967-84 **Hanshin Tigers**, Hiroshima Carp, Seibu Lions 206-158, 2.49

Highly touted as a rookie fresh from high school, the sidearming Enatsu won 12 games for the Hanshin Tigers. He followed with 25 victories, a Japanese record 401 strikeouts, and a 2-1, 10-inning loss to the powerful Yomiuri Giants in the game that decided the 1968 pennant. In 1969 he pitched 34 consecutive shutout innings against Yomiuri for six of his 15 victories in a season shortened by elbow pain. He rebounded to go 21-14 in 1970 but was suspended for two weeks over alleged involvement with gamblers. When he again lost the game that meant the pennant, he became Japan's leading target of fan abuse and media criticism. He openly feuded with manager and fellow star pitcher Minoru Murayama over his workload.

Handicapped by arm trouble and a heart condition aggravated by chain-smoking, Enatsu still won 20 games in 1972 and 1973. Slumping the next two seasons, he was pronounced washed up at age 27. He scored a brilliant comeback following his trade to Hiroshima, becoming the first player to be named MVP in both Japanese major leagues. Working mainly in relief, he contributed a 9-5, 2.66 record to Hiroshima's 1979 championship.

Enatsu was the winningest and highest-paid active pitcher in Japan when he was released by the Seibu Lions in 1984 after a shoving match with the manager. In 1985, at age 36, he signed a minor league contract with the Milwaukee Brewers, hoping to make the major league team in spring training. He didn't, amid intense publicity. He refused a minor league assignment and returned to Japan./(MC)

Bob Engel — 1933- . *Umpire* NL 1965-87 *7 LCS 3 WS, 3 ASU*

Engel, a highly respected NL umpire, has worked more than a third of the NL LCS since their inauguation in 1969./(RTM)

Joe Engel — 1893-1969. RHP 1912-15, 17, 19-20 **Senators**, Reds, Indians 407 ip, 17-23, 3.38

Engel's ML pitching career was ordinary, but it launched him into a baseball role he filled joyously: minor league team owner. Starting in 1930, he was a one-man scouting system and his Chattanooga team (Southern Association) was the top farm club for the Senators. He became the most colorful baseball promoter of his time. He staged elephant hunts, hired a female pitcher to strike out Babe Ruth and Lou Gehrig in an exhibition game, and gave away bizarre and valuable gifts, all to pack people into his ball park. /(JK)

Clyde Engle (Hack) — 1884–1939. OF-1B-3B-2B 1909–16 Highlanders, **Red Sox**, Buffalo (FL), Indians 831 g, .265, 12 hr, 318 rbi. *1 WS, 3 g, .333, 2 rbi*

Engle, a run-of-the-mill utility man, was involved in one of the most celebrated plays in World Series history. Pinch hitting for the Red Sox in the tenth inning of the 1912 Series' final game, he lofted an easy fly ball which was muffed by Giants centerfielder Fred Snodgrass. Tris Speaker, getting a second chance after his foul pop fell uncaught, singled in Engle for the tying run. Boston then won it all on Larry Gardner's long outfield fly. /(JK)

Dave Engle — 1956– . C-OF-DH-1B 1981– **Twins**, Tigers, Expos 594 g, .262, 31 hr, 181 rbi
☛ *All-Star—84.*

Like brother-in-law Tom Brunansky, Engle was drafted by the Angels in 1978. He went to the Twins in the 1979 trade for Rod Carew, and hit the first official home run in the Metrodome (4/6/82). Converted from outfield to catcher for 1983, he batted .305, and in 1984 was the Twins' only All-Star. Never developing good catching skills, he became a reserve, and in 1987 was Montreal's top righthanded pinch hitter. /(JCA)

Gil English — 1909– . 3B-SS-2B 1931–32, 36–38, 44 Giants, Tigers, **Braves**, Dodgers 240 g, .245, 8 hr, 90 rbi

Reportedly the last player personally scouted by John McGraw, English was a strong-armed third baseman who kept up a steady stream of chatter. McGraw watched him for two weeks at Durham before signing him. Unfortunately, English could neither strong-arm nor chatter his way on base, and he never played a full season as a ML regular. /(NLM)

Woody English [Elwood George] — 1907– . SS-3B 1927–38 **Cubs**, Dodgers 1261 g, .286, 32 hr, 422 rbi. *2 WS, 9 g, .184, 1 rbi*
☛ *All-Star—33.*

English batted a career-best .335 in 1930 and was among the NL leaders in runs scored, triples, and walks. He hit .319 in 1931 while leading NL

shortstops in putouts, and paced NL third basemen in fielding (.973) in 1933. /(TJ)

Del Ennis — 1925– . OF 1946–59 **Phillies**, Cardinals, Reds, White Sox 1903 g, .284, 288 hr, 1284 rbi. *1 WS, 4 g, .143*
☛ *All-Star—46, 51, 55.*

The Philadelphia Irishman was the original *TSN* Rookie Award winner in 1946; he hit a career-high .313, and was among the NL top five in batting, HR, slugging percentage, and total bases. Ennis twice hit over .300 again, surpassed 30 HR twice, and knocked in more than 100 runs seven times, peaking with a NL-leading 126 RBI for the pennant-winning 1950 Phillies. That year Ennis set a team record by grounding into 25 double plays. He had three homers in one game (7/23/55) and was a no-hit spoiler three times in his career. In the Phillies' 100th anniversary year, 1983, Ennis was chosen for their "Centennial team." /(TJ)

James Enright — 1912–1982. *Writer.*

Enright covered baseball for the Chicago *Evening American* for 20 years, starting in 1944, and later for the Chicago *American* and Chicago *Today* before he retired in 1974. He was co-author of *Ernie Banks: Mr. Cub.* A tall man who weighed over 260 pounds, Enright was a basketball official in the Big Ten and worked several NCAA finals. He is a member of the Basketball Hall of Fame as an official. /(NLM)

Mike Epstein (Superjew) — 1943– . 1B 1966–74 Orioles, **Senators**, A's, Rangers, Angels .244, 130 hr, 380 rbi. *2 LCS, 7 g, .190, 1 hr, 1 rbi. 1 WS, 6 g, .000*

Epstein was dubbed Superjew by rival manager Rocky Bridges after he led the California League in batting and home runs in 1965, and was *The Sporting News* Minor League Player of the Year in 1966 when he won International League MVP honors at Rochester (.309, 29 HR, 102 RBI). The burly, lefthanded slugger arrived at spring training in 1967 as baseball's most-heralded prospect, but after the Orioles tried in vain to convert him to the outfield (they already had Boog Powell at first base), they demoted him to Rochester again. The outspoken Epstein refused to report, going home to California instead, and did not play again until the end of May, when he was traded to the Senators with Frank Bertaina for Pete Richert. Later that season, in his first at-bat against the Orioles, Epstein hit a grand slam.

Epstein was a capable power hitter in the ML, but

never hit quite well enough to offset his frequent strikeouts, poor defense, and big mouth. He hit .278 with 30 HR for the Senators in 1968, but slipped to .256 with 20 HR in 1970 and was one of four players traded to Oakland for Darold Knowles before the 1971 season. With the A's, Epstein hit .270 with 26 HR in 1972, but was 0-for-16 in the WS and was traded back to the Rangers (formerly the Senators) for relief pitcher Horacio Pina in November. He played only 27 games with Texas in 1973, then was traded to the Angels, and after hitting .161 in 18 games for California in 1974 Epstein was out of the ML for good. /(SCL)

Eddie Erautt [Joseph Michael] — 1924-1976. RHP 1947-51, 53 **Reds**, Cardinals 380 ip, 15-23, 4.86

Erautt, used mainly in long relief, and his older brother Joe (with the White Sox briefly in 1950-51) were trained as a battery by their father, a Saskatchewan semi-pro. /(MC)

Eric Erickson (The Swatting Swede) — 1892-1965. RHP 1914, 16, 18-22 Giants, Tigers. **Senators** 822 ip, 34-57, 3.85

Born in Sweden, Erickson was a semi-pro star whose bat was as feared as his fastball. He won 31 games in the Pacific Coast League in 1917, but never had a winning ML season. /(JK)

Paul Erickson (L'il Abner) — 1915- . RHP 1941-48 **Cubs**, Phillies, Giants 814 ip, 37-48, 3.86. *1 WS, 7 ip, 0-0, 3.86*

This 6'2" product of smalltown Zion, IL, was called "Li'l Abner" after Al Capp's hillbilly comic strip character. A fireballer who walked as many as he struck out, he both started and relieved. His most famous appearance was his pennant-clinching victory in relief for the Cubs in 1945. He entered the game with two on and two out, and a one-run lead. With the count 0-1, he threw a wild fastball from which Pittsburgh batter Tommy O'Brien ducked—but the ball hit the bat for a foul. Expecting another fastball, O'Brien looked at a sweeping curve for strike three. /(DB)

Roger Erickson — 1956- . RHP 1978-83 **Twins**, Yankees 799 ip, 35-53, 4.14

Erickson made the Twins after just one year in the minors and went 14-13 with a 3.96 ERA in 1978. It was his only winning season. /(JFC)

Dick Errickson (Lief) — 1914- . RHP 1938-42 **Braves**, Cubs 736 ip, 36-47, 3.85

A moderately successful pitcher with some poor Braves teams, Errickson peaked at 12-13 with a 3.16 ERA for the seventh-place 1940 club. It was said he was sometimes rattled by rival coaches who claimed he was tipping his pitches. /(NLM)

Carl Erskine (Oisk) — 1926- . RHP 1948-59 **Dodgers** 1719 ip, 122-78, 4.00. 20 wins: 53 *5 WS, 42 ip, 2-2, 5.83*
☛ *All-Star—54.*

Carl Erskine, who teamed with Don Newcombe to anchor the pitching staff for the powerful post-WWII Brooklyn teams, won 61% of his decisions in 12 years with the Dodgers. The 5'10" righthander injured his shoulder during his rookie season and pitched with pain most of his career. Because he couldn't throw a lot between starts, he never developed any specialty pitches. He remained a fastball/curveball/changeup pitcher who was able to change speeds on the curve. "Oisk" went 20-6 in 1953 to lead NL pitchers in winning percentage (.769). His 14 strikeouts as the winner of Game Three of the '53 WS set a Series record that stood for 14 years. He had two no-hitters: on June 19, 1952 against the Cubs, and on May 12, 1956 against the Giants. /(TJ)

Nick Esasky — 1960- . 1B-3B 1983- **Reds**, Red Sox 801 g, .251, 122 hr, 427 rbi

Esasky replaced Johnny Bench at third base for the Reds in 1983 and made the *Topps* all-rookie team with a .265 average and 12 HR. The strikeout-prone slugger was converted to first base full-time in 1987, and was traded to Boston with Rob Murphy for Todd Benzinger and Jeff Sellers before the 1989 season. /(ME)

Nino Escalera — 1929- . OF-1B 1954 **Reds** 73 g, .159, 0 hr, 3 rbi

Escalera was a scout for the Mets from 1966 to 1981 and for the Giants from 1982 to the present. His ML career consisted mostly of pinch hitting for the Reds in 1954. He discovered Jose Oquendo and Juan Berenguer. /(FVP)

Jimmy Esmond — 1889-1948. SS 1911-12, 14-15 Reds, Indianapolis FL, **Newark FL** 461 g, .264, 9 hr, 162 rbi

Esmond had a great arm and good range but frequent injuries and illnesses hampered him throughout his career. He played regularly in the Federal League's two seasons, and in 1914 led the FL in triples with 15. /(NLM)

Hector Espino — 1939- . 1B-OF 1960-84 Mexican Leagues

A symbol of Mexican pride, the slugging Espino declined offers from the Cardinals, Mets, and Padres while playing 25 seasons with San Luis de Potosi, Monterrey, and Tampico. He did play 32 games for Jacksonville (International League) in 1964, batting .300, but was offended by racial discrimination and swore he would never again play in the United States. He led the Mexican League in batting in 1964 and in 1966–68; in home runs in 1964 and 1972; and in RBI in 1962 and 1973. His Mexican League record of 46 HR, set in 1964, stood until 1986. He retired at age 45 with the career record for minor league home runs, 484. /(MC)

Nino Espinosa — 1953–1988. RHP 1974–81 **Mets**, Phillies, Blue Jays 821 ip, 44–55, 4.17

The Dominican was the ace of the miserable Mets of 1977–78. He beat the Phils 1–0 on a three-hitter, driving in the only run on September 14, 1977. Philadelphia traded for him in 1979, and he had a career-best 14–12. Bothered by arm trouble early in the Phillies' 1980 World Championship season, he returned to the minors, missing post-season play. /(MC)

Sammy Esposito — 1931– . 3B-SS-2B 1952, 55–63 **White Sox**, A's 560 g, .207, 8 hr, 73 rbi. *1 WS, 2 g, .000*

A career utility man from Chicago's South Side, Esposito was beloved by White Sox fans. On September 7, 1960, he started in place of Nellie Fox, ending Fox's consecutive-game streak at 798—a ML record for second basemen. When Esposito booted a cinch double play ball, an enraged fan, who had bet heavily on the game, charged onto the field and began punching the 5'9" infielder. /(DB)

Chuck Essegian — 1931– . OF 1958–63 Phillies, Cardinals, Dodgers, Orioles, A's, **Indians** 404 g, .255, 47 hr, 150 rbi. *1 WS, 4 g, .667, 2 hr, 2 rbi*

Essegian, a member of Stanford's 1952 Rose Bowl team, is one of two players to hit two pinch hit home runs in a World Series. In the 1959 WS, his sixth-inning pinch homer tied Game Two for Los Angeles and the Dodgers went on to win. With the Dodgers safely ahead in the sixth and final game, he batted for Duke Snider in the ninth inning and homered again. Essegian added a postscript by pinch-homering on Opening Day in 1960. /(RTM)

Jim Essian — 1951– . C 1973–84 Phillies, White Sox, A's, Mariners, Indians 709 g, .244, 33 hr, 206 rbi

Strong-armed Essian was the regular catcher for the White Sox in 1977, when he hit .273 with a good

batting eye and had career highs of 10 HR, 50 runs, and 44 RBI. Traded to the A's for 1978, he slumped to .223 and was never first-string again. /(WOR)

Bill Essick (Vinegar Bill) — 1881–1951. RHP 1906–07 Reds 61 ip, 2–3, 2.95

After a nine-game ML career with the Reds, Essick became a minor league owner and manager, leading Vernon to three consecutive Pacific Coast League pennants. As the PCL scout for the Yankees from 1926 to 1950, Essick signed Joe DiMaggio after other scouts had given up on him because of his leg injuries. His nickname was derived from his surname, which sounds like the German word for vinegar. /(FVP)

Bobby Estalella — 1911– . OF-3B 1935–36, 39, 41–45, 49 Senators, Browns, **A's** 680 g, .282, 44 hr, 308 rbi

The chunky native Cuban became a starter as a draft-exempt wartime player. He was suspended from 1946 to 1948 for trying to jump to the Mexican League and appeared in only eight more ML games. /(JK)

Chuck Estrada [Charles Leonard] — 1938– . RHP 1960–64, 66–67 **Orioles**, Cubs, Mets 764 ip, 50–44, 4.07 ☛ *Led League—w 60. All-Star—60.*

A hard thrower but often wild, Estrada was one of the brightest of several young Orioles pitchers who arrived in the ML about the same time. His 18 wins as a rookie topped the AL in 1960. He won 15 the next season but led only in walks. His 17 losses were the most in the AL in 1962. He never recovered from an elbow injury in 1963. After his retirement he found frequent employment as a pitching coach. /(CR)

Andy Etchebarren — 1942– . C 1962, 65–78 **Orioles**, Angels, Brewers 948 g, .235, 49 hr, 309 rbi. *5 LCS, 12 g, .2121, 1 hr, 4 rbi. 4 WS, 9 g, .074* ☛ *All-Star—66–67.*

Etchebarren became the Orioles' number-one catcher in 1966 when regular Dick Brown retired on account of a brain tumor. Etchebarren hit only .221 with 11 HR and 50 RBI while striking out 106 times in 412 at-bats, but the Orioles won the World Championship with him behind the plate. He caught every inning of their sweep of the Dodgers in the World Series as Jim Palmer, Wally Bunker, and Dave McNally tossed shutouts in the last three games. Known for his bushy eyebrows, Etchebarren was gradually supplanted by the better-hitting Elrod

Hendricks but remained with Baltimore as a back-up until 1975. Finishing his career with the Brewers, he later became a Milwaukee coach. /(SH)

Shinichi Eto — 1937- . OF 1959-76 **Chunichi Dragons**, Lotte Orions
☛ *Led League—ba 64-65, 71.*

An all-star Japanese left fielder, Eto hit between 20 and 30 home runs most seasons, collected 2,057 hits, and batted .300 for much of his career. He won batting titles in 1964 (.323) and 1965 (.336). Rebelling against Chunichi's team curfew in 1970, he threatened to retire if not traded. Shipped interleague to the Lotte Orions for 1971, he bested American teammate George Altman for his third batting crown—in somewhat tainted fashion. As Altman recalled, Eto, a righthanded batter, was an opposite-field hitter. With the title on the line, Nankai manager Katsuya Nomura positioned his infield so as to leave the right side open, and Eto went 4-for-4. Nomura had won the HR title over American Daryl Spencer through similar collusive measures six years earlier. /(MC)

Nick Etten — 1913- . 1B 1938-39, 41-47 A's, Phillies, **Yankees** 937 g, .277, 89 hr, 526 rbi. *1 WS, 5 g, .105, 2 rbi*
☛ *Led League—hr 44. Led League—rbi 45.*

Upon being dealt to the Yanks in 1943 after two seasons with the lowly Phillies, Etten exclaimed, "Imagine a man in that environment hearing that he had been sold to the Yankees!" The lefthanded batter thrived briefly in Yankee pinstripes, leading the AL with 22 HR and 97 bases on balls in 1944, and with 111 RBI the following year. /(TJ)

Al Evans — 1916-1979. C 1939-42, 44-51 **Senators**, Red Sox 704 g, .250, 13 hr, 211 rbi

Evans's defensive ability gradually won him more playing time with the Senators despite his largely unproductive bat. His best year was 1949, the only season in which he caught more than 100 games, when he hit .271 with 42 RBI. /(MC)

Barry Evans — 1956- . 3B-2B 1978-82 **Padres**, Yankees 224 g, .251, 2 hr, 41 rbi

After Evans led the Northwest League in hits and RBI in his 1977 pro debut, the Padres traded incumbent third baseman Doug Rader to make room for a budding star. But tantrums and injuries kept him from ever winning an everyday ML job. /(MC)

Billy Evans — 1884-1956. *Umpire* AL 1906-27 *6 WS*
☛ *Hall of Fame—1973.*

One of the foremost umpires in baseball history, Evans was refined and fastidious. He substituted diplomacy for belligerency during baseball's rowdier days. He began as a sportswriter but took up umpiring after he substituted for an absent arbiter in a game he was covering. He was only 22 when he was promoted from a Class C league to the AL, the youngest man ever to be employed as a ML umpire and the only one ever promoted all the way from Class C.

In his 22 years as an AL umpire, he achieved a reputation for fairness and unquestioned integrity. In Game Two of the 1909 WS, played in Pittsburgh, the Pirates' Dots Miller hit a low line drive along the foul line in the direction of temporary right-field bleachers that rested in part in fair territory. As the ball sailed over the stands the fans stood and obstructed the views of Evans and the other umpire, Bill Klem. Neither saw the ball land. Both marched to the outfield and Evans began questioning the bleacherites as to whether the ball was fair or foul. On their testimony Evans decided the ball had

Billy Evans

landed fair and skipped into the crowd. Miller, who had circled the bases, was sent back to second with a ground-rule double.

Although he was a diplomat, Evans once fought Ty Cobb under the grandstand after Cobb challenged Evans over two close out calls at the plate. Al Schacht, baseball's "Clown Prince," described the fight: "When the game ended they both went under the grandstand while the members of both teams became spectators. Billy posed like a real fighter while Ty stalked him like a Tiger and then suddenly hit him in the jaw. Down went Evans with Ty on top of him. With his knee on Evans' chest, Ty held Billy by the throat and tried to choke him. We finally got him off Billy and that was the end of the fight."

Evans continued his writing career, authoring many articles and a book: *Umpiring from the Inside.* From 1920 to 1927 he wrote a syndicated column, "Billy Evans Says." In later years Evans served as GM for Cleveland (1927–36) and Detroit (1947–51), farm director for Boston (1936–40), GM of the NFL's Cleveland Rams (1941), and president of the Southern Association (1942–46). In 1973 he was elected to baseball's Hall of Fame./(RTM)

Darrell Evans — 1947– . 3B-1B-DH 1969– Braves, **Giants**, Tigers 2687 g, .248, 414 hr, 1354 rbi. *2 LCS, 8 g, .296, 1 rbi. 1 WS, 5 g, .067, 1 rbi*
☛ *All-Star—73.*

During the early 1970s, Evans was considered to be the premier third baseman behind Mike Schmidt in the National League. The only player to hit 40 homers in each league, he is the oldest player to win a home run title, hitting 40 with the Tigers at the age of 38 in 1985.

Evans credits Ted Williams's book for teaching him how to hit; Eddie Mathews taught him how to pull. Originally drafted by the A's in 1968, Evans started wearing contact lenses in 1971 and started hitting for power regularly. Hitting third in front of Aaron, Evans saw plenty of good pitches and, in 1973, was one of a record three Braves players to crack 40 homers: Aaron had 40, Evans 41, and Davey Johnson had 43. Even though he preceded Aaron in the lineup, he led the league in walks with 124, and again the following year with 126. He finished his career 10th all-time in walks. Evans was on first base when Aaron hit number 715 on April 8, 1974. In June 1976, Evans was traded in a six-player deal to San Francisco. Although he was productive for seven years, Candlestick Park was not suited for his power. In 1983, he switched to first

Darrell Evans

base. On June 15, he hit three homers in a game. After the season, he signed on as a free agent with the Tigers.

The Tigers got immediate dividends when Evans hit a three-run homer Opening Day to spark the Tigers to a 35–5 start as they coasted to the American League pennant and World Series championship, despite Evans's 1-for-15 performance against the Padres. In 1985, he led the league in homers for the only time in his career to begin the most productive power phase of his career, hitting 29 homers in 1986 and 34 in 1987 at the age of 40. As a full-time DH in 1988, he managed 22 homers, but hit only .208, and was traded by the Tigers back to the Braves during the off-season. He saw considerable action in 1989 due to the demotion of third baseman Ron Gant and the season-ending injury of first baseman Gerald Perry, and continued to show good power while hitting for a low average. /(SEW)

Dwight Evans (Dewey) — 1951– . OF-DH 1972- **Red Sox** 2382 g, .273, 366 hr, 1283 rbi. *3 LCS, 14 g, .180, 1 hr, 6 rbi. 2 WS, 14 g. .300, 3 hr, 14 rbi*
☛ *Led League—hr 81. All-Star—78, 81, 87. Gold Glove—76, 78–79, 81–85.*

Dwight Evans

In the strike-shortened 1981 season, Evans suddenly arrived as a slugger. He hit .296, shared the AL HR title with 22, and led the league in what would become his specialty, bases on balls. Evans walked 85 times in 1981 (he had never drawn more than 69 walks before) and 112 in 1982, and led the AL twice more in '85 and '87 with 114 and 106. Along with his improved patience at the plate, Evans unveiled a new batting stance—a deeper crouch with his weight shifted drastically onto his back foot. The improvements were swift and dramatic. He hit .292 with 32 HR, 98 RBI, and 122 runs scored in 1982, and had a virtually identical season in 1984 (.295, 32 HR, 104 RBI, 121 runs scored). His average slumped in 1985–86, but he still slugged 55 HR and drew 211 walks over the two seasons, and in 1987, at the age of 35 and in his 16th ML season, Evans recorded career highs in batting average (.305), HR (34), and RBI (123).

The Red Sox shifted Evans to first base in July 1987. He never adjusted to the infield, and in mid-1988 he returned to right field, where his play declined appreciably. In mid-1989 he became Boston's regular DH. Still, Evans has retained his reputation as an outstanding clutch hitter, and his careful pitch selection makes him particularly dangerous batting with a 3–0 count (he has eight career HR in that situation). Only Carl Yastrzemski has played more games for the Boston Red Sox. /(SCL)

Jim Evans — 1946- . *Umpire* AL 1971-87 *4 LCS 3 WS, 1 ASU*

As a political science major at the University of Texas, Evans was a member of the debating team. He was the plate umpire in the longest AL game by time (8 hours, 6 minutes) in Chicago on May 8, 1984 (finished May 9), when the White Sox beat the Brewers 7–6. /(RTM)

Joe Evans (Doc) — 1895-1953. OF-3B 1915-25 **Indians**, Senators, Browns 732 g, .259, 3 hr, 209 rbi. *1 WS, 4 g, .308*

Converted from third base to the outfield in 1920, Evans alternated with left fielder Charlie Jamieson for Cleveland in that year's World Series, and had three hits in Game Six. He was a physician after leaving baseball. /(ME)

Roy Evans — 1874-1915. RHP 1897-99, 02-03 Cardinals, Louisville NL, Washington NL, Giants, **Dodgers**, Browns 614 ip, 28-42, 3.66

Evans pitched with only occasional success for six teams in five ML seasons. In 1902, in a season split

Evans had already become a regular in the Boston outfield when he was joined by sensational rookies Jim Rice and Fred Lynn in 1975. As the 1980s ended, Rice and Lynn were clearly at the ends of their careers, while Evans remained among the best in the game. Number 24 made his reputation as a strong-armed outfielder who froze baserunners in their tracks, and later blossomed into one of the AL's better hitters, averaging 28 HR per year after the age of 30.

After winning International League MVP honors at Louisville in 1972 (.300, 17 HR, 95 RBI), Evans joined the Red Sox for good in 1973 but hit only .223. His offensive contributions were unexciting for several seasons, but he excelled defensively. He mastered Fenway Park's tricky right-field corner and employed the strongest outfield throwing arm in the AL. His lunging catch in the 11th inning of Game Six of the 1975 WS robbed Joe Morgan of a Series-winning HR, started an inning-ending double play, and set the stage for Carlton Fisk's famous HR in the 12th. In 1976, he won the first of his eight Gold Gloves, fourth-best all-time among outfielders behind Willie Mays, Roberto Clemente, and Al Kaline.

between the Giants and Dodgers, he had his best ERA, 3.00, but led the NL in losses with 19./(BC)

Steve Evans — 1885–1943. OF 1908–15 Giants, **Cardinals**, Brooklyn (FL), Baltimore (FL) 978 g, .287, 32 hr, 466 rbi

Evans had his best year in 1914 with fifth place Brooklyn of the Federal League, finishing second in the league in batting (.348), homers (12), RBI (96), and doubles (41). One of baseball's funniest clowns, his antics got him traded to the Cardinals after just two games with the Giants in 1909./(WAB)

Bill Everett — 1868–1938. 1B-3B-OF 1895–1901 **Cubs**, Senators 698 g, .317, 11 hr, 341 rbi

An accomplished bunter and basestealer, Everett was a good leadoff man who topped 100 runs scored three times. His fielding, charitably described by one reporter as "always honest," was poor./(BC)

Hoot Evers [Walter Arthur] — 1921– . OF 1941, 46–56 **Tigers**, Red Sox, Giants, Orioles, Indians 1142 g, .278, 98 hr, 565 rbi
☛ *All-Star—48, 50.*

An outstanding prospect, Evers never achieved the stardom predicted for him. After his career was delayed four years by WWII, he returned as the Tigers' starting centerfielder in 1946, only to miss half the season with a broken ankle. He played his first full season in 1947, hitting .296, then hit over .300 three straight years. He peaked in 1950, making his second All-Star appearance, leading AL outfielders in fielding (.997), and hitting .323 with 21 homers, 103 RBI, and a league-leading 11 triples. He also hit for the cycle September 7. He slumped badly the next year. In 1952, as the Red Sox' left fielder while Ted Williams was in the military, a broken finger hampered Evers's batting grip and he never regained his stroke. A fine defensive player, Evers bounced from team to team until 1956 but never hit higher than .264./(JK)

Johnny Evers (The Trojan, The Crab) — 1883–1947. 2B 1902–1917, 22 **Cubs**, Braves, Phillies, White Sox 1783 g, .270, 12 hr, 538 rbi. *4 WS, 20 g, .316, 6 rbi.*
   Manager 1913, 21, 24 **Cubs**, White Sox 196–208, .485
☛ *Most Valuable Player—14 . Hall of Fame—1946.*

A Franklin P. Adams poem immortalized a snappy-fielding Cub infield that was primarily responsible for three straight NL pennants starting in 1906, and World Series victories in 1907 and 1908, with Evers its brainy center. The play that earned Evers

Johnny Evers

(rhymes with "beavers," not "feathers") his reputation as a quick-witted infielder came on September 23, 1908, in an afternoon at the Polo Grounds in the thick of a tight pennant race. Al Bridwell had singled in Mike McCormick from third with two out in the bottom of the ninth to give the Giants an apparent 2–1 victory. But Giants' rookie third baseman Fred Merkle, the runner at first base, didn't advance all the way to second on the play. As was the custom of the day, Merkle saw the run score, then turned and headed into the clubhouse. Evers, standing at second, called for the ball, and touched second for the force. Umpire Hank O'Day called Merkle out and declared the game a tie. When the two teams ended the season tied for the NL pennant, the game was replayed as a playoff, which the Cubs won.

The slightly-built but temperamental Evers was nicknamed "The Crab" for the way he sidled up to grounders. He joined the established Tinker and Chance full-time in 1903. Evers had identical .350 World Series averages in 1907 and 1908, knocking in the winning run in the fifth and final game. Ironically, 1910, the year Adams fashioned his poem, was the final season that the trio played together. Evers was hurt for most of 1911, and player-manager Chance had retired as a player to devote his full energies to managing. Evers and Tinker, despite their on-field teamwork, didn't speak to each other their final years together, the result of some imagined slight, and often traded punches in the clubhouse. Despite the fighting, Evers enjoyed his best season in 1912, when he hit a career high .341, and replaced Chance as manager in 1913. In February 1914, he was traded to Boston, where he formed another slick double-play combination with shortstop Rabbit Maranville. In the Miracle Braves sweep of the Athletics in the 1914 Series, Evers batted .438 and drove in the winning runs in the final 3–1 victory.

When Evers came back from Europe and WWI, he coached briefly for former enemy John McGraw on the Giants and was assistant manager for the Cubs in 1921. In 1923, he joined the crosstown White Sox as a coach, and managed the team in 1924. He entered the Hall of Fame six months before his death, and was the last surviving member of the double-play combo. /(SEW)

Bob Ewing (Long Bob) [George Lemuel] — 1873–1947. RHP 1902–12 **Reds**, Phillies, Cardinals 2301 ip, 128–118, 2.49. 20 wins: 05

A spitball pitcher, Ewing was a workhorse for the Reds in the century's first decade, topping 300 innings three times. He was 20–11 in 1905 and twice won 17. His 1907 ERA was 1.73. Traded to the Phillies in 1910, he pitched a two-hitter and two three-hitters while winning 16. /(NLM)

Buck Ewing [William] — 1859–1906. C-1B-OF-3B-2B-SS 1880–97 Troy (NL), **Giants**, New York (PL), Cleveland (NL), Reds 1315 g, .303, 70 hr, 733 rbi.
    Manager 1890, 95–1900 New York (PL), **Reds**, Giants 489–395, .553
☛ *Led League—hr 83 . Hall of Fame—1939.*

When the doors of the Baseball Hall of Fame were first opened, in 1939, Buck Ewing's plaque was ready to go up on the wall. Elected by the Committee on Baseball Veterans, Ewing had simply been baseball's best catcher and, according to his contemporaries, was unequaled as an all-around player in the 19th century. Until Mickey Cochrane, Bill Dickey, and Gabby Hartnett came along, Ewing was listed as the catcher on virtually everyone's all-time team.

A lifetime .303 hitter with a high of .344 in 1893,

Buck Ewing

Ewing was also a dead-ball-era NL home run champ, hitting 10 for New York in 1883. He topped the NL with 20 triples in 1884, and hit 15 triples four other times. In a June 9, 1883 game, he hit three triples. When stolen bases started being tallied, Ewing averaged 37 a season, with a high of 53 for the 1888 Giants.

Ewing played during a time when catchers did not catch every day. He never caught more than 97 games a season, and only once caught more than 80. He was said to have been a master at throwing out baserunners; he led NL catchers in assists three times in the 1880s, and in double plays twice. He spent few games behind the plate after 1890. Instead, he was stationed mostly in the outfield and at first base. He also pitched 47 innings.

Buck's brother John, a pitcher, compiled a 53–63 career record. He pitched for Buck in the 1890 Players' League, when Buck caught for and managed New York. John led the NL with a .724 winning percentage (21–8) and a 2.27 ERA as Buck's batterymate with the 1891 Giants. John then retired, and Buck went on to Cleveland in 1893. Buck returned to his hometown of Cincinnati as a first baseman-manager in 1895, and played one final game in 1897. Managing the Reds through 1899, he never finished higher than third. He piloted the Giants for part of 1900, and died six years later. /(JK)

Exhibition Stadium Toronto Blue Jays 1977–1989. LF-330, CF-400, RF-330

Exhibition Stadium was built for football in 1959 and was modified for the expansion Blue Jays. Home plate lay near the corner of one end zone, and the main seating areas, along each sideline of the football field, extended down the first-base line and behind the left-field fence. The best seats, both because they were the only roofed section and because they offered the best view of the game, were the left-field general admission seats, paradoxically the cheapest tickets. Originally there were no seats at all along what is now the third-base line (behind the end zone), and a number of seats in deep centerfield and down the right-field line were rarely sold due to poor sight lines. The artificial-turf playing field was contained by a temporary blue fence inside the permanent seating, and home runs to right field bounced across the unused portion of the football field. The Blue Jays' April 30, 1984 game was postponed due to heavy winds. The open end of the field faced Lake Ontario, and metal seats compounded the problems with cold weather. The discomfort led the team to move to the indoor Skydome in 1989. /(SCL)

Exposition Park — Pittsburgh Pirates 1891–1909, Pittsburgh (PL) 1890, Pittsburgh (FL) 1914–15

Home of the Pirates until Forbes Field was completed, Exposition Park twice had its roof ripped off by strong winds, in 1900 and 1901, and no ball ever cleared the original left and center field fences. Today, Three Rivers Stadium stands on the site. /(SCL)

Red Faber [Urban Clarence] — 1888-1976. RHP 1914-33 **White Sox** 4088 ip, 254-212, 3.15. 20 wins: 15, 20-22 *1 WS, 27 ip, 3-1, 2.33*
☛ *Led League—era 21-22. Hall of Fame—1964.*

Faber was a steady, even-tempered spitballer whose long life in the second division probably kept him from the select 300-win club. With Chicago's lineup decimated by the loss of the Black Sox stars, Faber endured 13 seasons in or below fifth place, and only three at .500 or above. His lifetime winning percentage of .545 was achieved mostly with teams below .500.

Faber acquired his spitter in 1911, after a sore arm ruined early tryouts with the Pirates. Sold to Des Moines (Western League), he had two sterling seasons, and was purchased by the White Sox for $3,500. The Sox and Giants scheduled a world tour after the 1913 season. Faber, who had not yet pitched an inning of major league ball, was loaned to the Giants when Christy Mathewson declined to take the trip. Faber won four exhibitions against his future teammates, and began his 20-year, one-team career in 1914.

He was the pitching star of the 1917 Series win over the Giants, missed most of 1918 in the Navy, and returned to help win the 1919 pennant with 11 victories. He was on the bench for the scandalous Series, however, with recurring arm trouble and the flu.

Faber's peak years were 1921 and 1922, when he won 25 and 21 games while the Sox were finishing seventh and fifth. He led the league in ERA and complete games both years. From 1914 through 1923, he had ten consecutive winning seasons. But he was not overpowering. His 1,471 strikeouts are far down the all-time list, yet he always claimed success against Ruth and Cobb. Like many spitballers, he threw the spitter sparingly, for contrast, and with a variety of motions. Always poised, the excellent control pitcher became increasingly sager. In his 4,087 innings, he allowed only 110 HR (one every 37 innings), and hit only 104 batters (one every 39).

His oddest statistical feats came as a batter. A .134 switch hitter, in 1915 he walked seven times in a row. Twice, he made the most of his rare on-base appearances by stealing home.

Faber served several seasons as a White Sox coach. After baseball, he worked until his eighties on a Cook County Highway Department survey team. /(ADS)

Roy Face — 1928- . (The Baron) RHP 1953, 55-69 **Pirates**, Tigers, Expos 1375 ip, 104-95, 3.48. *1 WS, 10 ip, 0-0, 5.23*

"Considered by many to be the best relief pitcher in history, [Face] confronted all types of jams in his career," wrote Edward Kiersh. "Relying mainly on a forkball, he squelched so many rallies in 1959, en route to his record winning percentage of .947 (18-1), that manager Danny Murtaugh tagged him Sam Spade." The shy, gutsy, 5'8" righthander was twice drafted by Branch Rickey, first for the Dodgers, then, in 1952, for Pittsburgh. Face recorded 96 career relief wins (fifth all-time), 193 saves (sixth), and holds the ML mark for most relief wins in a season, 18 (17 consecutive for another record). He owns the NL career records for most games finished (574) and most games pitched for one club (802, for Pittsburgh). Face led the NL three times each in saves and relief losses, and twice in appearances. He saved three games of the 1960 World Series. /(TJ)

Len Faedo — 1960- . SS 1980-84 **Twins** 174 g, .251, 5 hr, 52 rbi

Faedo seemed the heir apparent to the Twins' shortstop job despite a history of injuries in the minors. He was hitting .277 in 1983 when a leg injury put him out again. He came back overweight and played only 16 games in 1984. /(MC)

Bill Fahey — 1950- . C 1971-72, 74-77, 79-83 **Senators/Rangers**, Padres, Tigers 383 g, .241, 7 hr, 83 rbi

Always a backup catcher, Fahey saw his most action sharing duty with Gene Tenace for the Padres in 1979-80. In 1980 Fahey had career highs of 93 games and 22 RBI. The Detroit native then finished his career backing up Lance Parrish on the Tigers. The 1978 gap in his ML career came after he was called up by the Rangers but spent the rest of the season on the DL. /(SFS)

321

Red Faber

Roy Face

Ferris Fain (Burrhead) — 1921– . 1B 1947–55 **A's**,
White Sox, Tigers, Indians 1151 g, .290, 48 hr, 570 rbi
☛ *Led League—ba 51–52. All-Star—50–54.*

Ferris Fain won consecutive AL batting titles in
1951 (.344, when a broken foot held him to 117
games) and 1952 (.327). Although those were the
only two full seasons in which he hit .300, he also hit
.302 in 1954, when a knee injury limited him to 65
games and started the decline that cut off his career a
year later after just nine seasons. His career high in
HR was just 10 (1950), but he led the AL in doubles
in 1952. However, his greatest value lay in his
ability to get on base: his on-base percentage was
above .400 every year of his career, finishing at .425
lifetime. He walked 100 times in five seasons, and
was in the AL top five every season he was healthy;
only once did he strike out more than 37 times in a
season.

Fain was considered the best-fielding first baseman in the league until Vic Power came up.
Although he tied the AL record by leading in errors
five times, he was a daring, far-ranging fielder who

was the first first baseman to regularly field bunts on
the third base line. He holds the ML record for
double plays in a season with 194 in 1949; it broke
the previous record by 31 (his 192 in 1950 is
second). He set the since-tied AL record for double
plays in a nine-inning game (six on September 1,
1947 in the second game). He led the league four
times in assists and twice each in total chances per
game and double plays, and ranks third all-time
among first basemen in assists per game./(JFC)

Jim Fairey — 1944– . OF 1968–73 Dodgers, **Expos**
399 g, .235, 7 hr, 75 rbi

Despite his excellent arm, Fairey became typecast as
a lefthanded pinch hitter after smacking a pinch
homer for Los Angeles in 1968. Taken by the Expos
in the expansion draft, Fairey hit .254 lifetime in the
pinch, and led the NL with 55 pinch-hitting appearances in 1972./(MC)

Ferris Fain (sliding) and Roy Campanella in the 1951 All-Star Game

Ron Fairly — 1938– . 1B-OF-DH 1958–78 **Dodgers,** Expos, Cardinals, A's, Blue Jays, Angels 2442 g, .266, 215 hr, 1044 rbi. *4 WS, 20 g, .300, 2 hr, 6 rbi* ☛ *All-Star—73, 77.*

In a ML career that spanned 21 seasons, Fairly was a good hitter whose talents were sometimes overshadowed by a stunning lack of speed. When asked in his final season if he'd lost any speed, he replied, "There was nothing to lose." In both 1963 and 1967 he tied a ML record by having no triples in 150 or more games. A consistent hitter who hit at least 10 home runs 14 times, Fairly also walked often enough to post good-to-excellent on-base averages. DHing for the 1977 expansion Blue Jays, he hit a career-high 19 HR. Versatile enough to play the outfield despite his lumbering style, the steady Fairly was better suited to first base, leading NL first basemen in fielding in 1963. He took over at first base for the Dodgers in 1962, but surrendered the position to Gold Glover Wes Parker in 1966. Fairly returned to the outfield.

After several years of declining batting averages, Fairly was traded to the expansion Expos in 1969 in the deal that returned Maury Wills to Los Angeles. After he escaped the vastness of Dodger Stadium, Fairly's batting average and power rebounded. Starting in 1974 he was less of a full-time player; only with Toronto in 1977 did he play more than 110 games again. /(JFC)

Pete Falcone — 1953– . LHP 1975–84 Giants, Cardinals, **Mets,** Braves 1435 ip, 70–90, 4.07

The swarthy southpaw went 12–11 his rookie season with the Giants (1975), but lost to teammate John

Ron Fairly

Montefusco in Rookie Pitcher of the Year voting. Traded to the Cardinals for Ken Reitz, Falcone repeated as a 12-game winner in 1976. After two losing seasons with the Mets (1979–80), he was moved out of the rotation. He signed as a free agent in 1983 with Atlanta, whose skipper was Joe Torre—fellow Brooklynite and Falcone's manager in New York. /(TJ)

Bibb Falk (Jockey) — 1899– . OF 1920-31 **White Sox**, Indians 1354 g, .314, 69 hr, 785 rbi

The University of Texas southpaw was a versatile athlete, undefeated in three years of varsity pitching and an All-Conference tackle in football. He succeeded the banished Joe Jackson in left field at Comiskey Park, and gave the Sox nine strong seasons, averaging .315 and three times topping 90 RBI. Traded to Cleveland for catcher Chick Autry in 1929, he had three more .300-plus seasons, the last two as the AL's most productive pinch hitter.

From 1940 to 1967 (except for three years as an Air Force sergeant during WWII), he was the aggressive, witty, sharp-tongued baseball coach at his alma mater. His 468–176 record earned 20 Southwest Conference titles and two national championships.

His younger brother Chet pitched for the Browns. /(ADS)

Cy Falkenberg [Frederick Peter] — 1880–1961. RHP 1903, 05-11, 13-15, 17 Pirates, Senators, **Indians**, Indianapolis (FL), Newark (FL), Brooklyn (FL), A's 2275 ip, 131-123, 2.68. 20 wins: 13-14
☛ *Led League—k 15.*

The 6′5″ pitcher was already a veteran in 1913 when he reached his AL peak at 23–10 for Cleveland. Falkenberg was a prize recruit of the outlaw Federal League, jumping for a lucrative contract in 1914. He was worth the money, leading Indianapolis to the pennant by winning 25 and leading the league in games (49), starts (43), shutouts (9), innings pitched (377), and strikeouts (236). /(JK)

Joe Falls — 1928– . *Writer.*

Falls broke in as a copyboy for the Associated Press in 1946, then went on to cover baseball for three Detroit newspapers, the most recent being the *News.* Falls was a longtime *Sporting News* correspondent, and his writing reflects a sympathetic personality and a willingness to reveal his own emotions. /(NLM)

Cliff Fannin (Mule) — 1924–1966. RHP 1945-52 **Browns** 733 ip, 34-51, 4.85

Fannin pitched a shutout in his first ML start in 1946, beating the White Sox, 1–0. He is best remembered as the losing pitcher for the Browns in their 29–4 loss to the Red Sox on June 8, 1950, the most lopsided score in baseball history. /(WAB)

Frank Fanovich (Lefty) — 1922– . LHP 1949, 53 Reds, **A's** 105 ip, 0-5, 5.49

A New York City native and bullpen denizen, Fanovich failed to record a win or save in his two ML seasons. He lost his only start for the 1949 Reds, and two out of three for Jimmy Dykes's 1953 A's. /(TJ)

Carmen Fanzone — 1941– . 3B-1B-2B-OF 1970-74 Red Sox, **Cubs** 237 g, .224, 20 hr, 94 rbi

Fanzone reached the majors at age 29 after a largely undistinguished minor league career. From 1971 to 1974 he was an effective utility man with the Cubs, versatile and with good long-ball power. /(MC)

Ed Farmer — 1949- . RHP 1971–74, 77–83 Indians, Tigers, Phillies, Orioles, Brewers, Rangers, **White Sox**, A's 624 ip, 30–43, 4.30
☛ *All-Star—80.*

Farmer's best stint came as the bullpen ace of the White Sox; in the years 1979–81 he had 14, 30, and 10 saves. When he signed with the Phillies as a free agent following the 1981 season, Chicago picked Joel Skinner from the compensation pool. Farmer was property of the Yankees for three days during spring training in 1974 before being sold to the Phillies./(JFC)

Steve Farr — 1956- . RHP 1984- Indians, **Royals** 500 ip, 24–28, 3.67

After languishing over eight seasons in the minors, Farr capitalized on a trial with the Royals in 1985. Relying on a baffling slider and fine curveball, he eventually replaced Dan Quisenberry as the Royals' closer. In 1988 Farr saved 20 games and led Kansas City pitchers with a 2.50 ERA./(FO)

Dick Farrell (Turk) — 1934–1977. RHP 1956–69 **Phillies**, Dodgers, Astros 1704 ip, 106–111, 3.45
☛ *All-Star—58, 62, 64–65.*

The 6'4" 215-lb Farrell lost his major league debut as a starter in 1956, then relieved in his next 258 appearances. He overpowered hitters with his sinking fastball and led the NL with ten relief wins his rookie 1957 season with Philadelphia. In the 1958 All-Star Game, he struck out four of the seven batters he faced, including Ted Williams. Selected by Houston from Los Angeles in the 1961 expansion draft, Farrell became a starter and lost 20 for the original Colt .45s. Returned to the bullpen when the Phillies reacquired him in 1967, he again led the NL with ten relief wins. Farrell retired with 83 career saves. He worked on an offshore oil rig in Great Britain and was killed in a 1977 auto accident in Yarmouth, England./(AL)

Doc Farrell [Edward Stephen] — 1901–1966. SS-2B-3B 1925–30, 32–33, 35 Giants, **Braves**, Cardinals, Cubs, Yankees, Red Sox 591 g, .260, 10 hr, 213 rbi

The former captain of the University of Pennsylvania's baseball team played baseball in the summers and was a dentist in the off-season. He became a much-traveled utility player, with six ML teams in nine seasons. He hit a career-high .316 while playing three infield positions for the 1927 Giants and Braves. The next year the Braves gave him the shortstop job, the only season he played over 100 games at a single position. He hit .215./(JK)

Duke Farrell [Charles Andrew] — 1866–1925. C-3B 1888–1905 Cubs, Chicago (PL), Boston (AA), Pirates, Washington (NL), Giants, **Dodgers**, Red Sox 1563 g, .275, 51 hr, 912 rbi. *1 WS, 2 g, .000, 1 rbi*
☛ *Led League—hr 91. Led League—rbi 91.*

A versatile switch-hitter, Farrell broke in as a protege of Cap Anson, who discovered him as a semi-pro player while the White Stockings were barnstorming New England. With Boston of the American Association in 1891, Farrell had league highs of 12 HR and 110 RBI. He later led the NL in pinch hits three times, and pinch hit for the Boston Puritans (later Red Sox) in the first World Series in 1903. He was a Boston Brave scout until his death./(JK)

John Farrell — 1876–1921. 2B-OF 1901–05 Senators, **Cardinals** 541 g, .261, 4 hr, 141 rbi

Farrell's rookie 1901 season was his best offensively, as he batted .272, scored 100 runs, and stole 25 bases for the Senators. With the Cardinals, he led the league in assists at second base in 1902, and in double plays from 1902–04./(WAB)

John Farrell — 1962- . RHP 1987- **Indians** 487 ip, 28–25, 3.86

Farrell was the best the Indians' farm system had when he was called up to Cleveland on August 18, 1987, despite his 24–41 minor league mark. Eight days later he stopped Paul Molitor's hitting streak at 39 games. He turned out to be one of Cleveland's most pleasant surprises, finishing the year at 5–1 and following with a 14–10 record in 1988. Elbow problems cropped up toward the end of 1988 and he was less effective in 1989./(JCA)

Kerby Farrell — 1913–1975. 1B-LHP 1943, 45 Braves, **White Sox** 188 g, .262, 0 hr, 55 rbi; 23 ip, 0–1, 4.30.
    Manager 1957 **Indians** 76–77, .497

Farrell was a singles hitter who made it to the majors during the talent-poor WWII years. He succeeded Hall of Fame manager Al Lopez as the Indians' pilot in 1957 and Cleveland fell from second place to sixth./(JFC)

Bill Faul — 1940- . RHP 1962–66, 70 Tigers, **Cubs**, Giants 262 ip, 12–16, 4.71

The stocky righthander had an auspicious debut with two three-hit victories in his first three starts for the Tigers in 1963. Among his six triumphs for the 1965 Cubs, Faul tossed three shutouts. /(CC)

Charlie Faust [Charles Victor] (Victory) — 1880–1915. RHP 1911 **Giants** 2 ip, 0–0, 4.50

Giants manager John McGraw wrote, "I give Charlie Faust full credit for winning the pennant for me—the National League pennant of 1911." Faust had approached McGraw before the season and explained that a fortune teller told him if he pitched for the Giants, they would win the pennant. Faust became a good luck charm, traveling with the team and warming up to pitch every game. He hurled an inning against the last-place Dodgers on the final day, shutting them out on one hit. He also reached base by getting hit by a pitch, and was allowed to steal second and third, and score. "Who's loony now?" he asked teammates as the crowd cheered. Faust was committed to an institution in 1914. When he died in 1915, the Giants finished last. /(KT)

Federal League — 1914–1915. League.

Sure that the growing popularity of baseball could support a third major league, John T. Powers of Chicago brought together a group of entrepeneurs in 1913 and founded the Federal League. In its first year of existence the six-team circuit made no pretentions to major league status and respected major league contracts. Only a few faded major leaguers were in the league that season, although all six managers were former players of note, including Cy Young, who piloted Cleveland. Following the season, in which only one team folded, the owners ousted the cautious Powers and replaced him as president with James Gilmore, one of the Chicago owners.

The league expanded to eight teams and put franchises in Eastern cities for 1914, posing more direct competition to the major leagues. Some prominent players were signed, including Three Finger Brown and Joe Tinker. Officially, the FL was still respecting contracts, but as the majors began to play tough following some contract disputes with players who played the leagues against each other, open warfare erupted in the signing of players and in court. Walter Johnson almost signed with the upstart league, but Senators owner Clark Griffith convinced the AL to pay for Johnson's salary increase for the good of the league.

A close pennant race gave the FL fair attendance figures in most of its cities, but large financial losses were suffered due to extensive litigation. Even

though the Feds won most of the cases, the NL and AL continued to file suits in an attempt to drain the coffers of the Federal backers. In January 1915 the Federal League filed an antitrust suit against major league baseball, hoping for a ruling against the reserve clause that would give the FL protection against further such harassment. They chose to enter their case before Judge Kenesaw Mountain Landis, who was known for his hard line against monopolies. But Landis felt differently about baseball, and put off a decision. After a season of declining attendance despite having signed more stars and another close pennant race, talk of a "peace settlement" became common. The major leagues had also suffered, but were better able to sustain themselves.

That winter, the "peace treaty" was announced. The majors partially compensated the debt-ridden Federal League owners; the FL withdrew its lawsuit, still being sat on by Judge Landis; and FL owners Phil Ball and Charles Weeghman bought, respectively, the Browns and the Cubs. The grateful major leagues appointed Judge Landis to the new office of Commissioner five years later. /(SH)

Mike Felder (Tiny) — 1961– . OF 1985- **Brewers** 334 g, .240, 6 hr, 72 rbi

The 5'8", switch-hitting Felder won four straight minor league stolen-base titles (1982–85). The Brewers' left fielder at the start of 1986, he pulled a hamstring in May and was disabled and sent down. As Milwaukee's fourth outfielder in 1987, he stole 34 bases. /(JCA)

Harry Feldman — 1919–1962. RHP 1941-46 **Giants** 666 ip, 35–35, 3.80

A wartime pitcher, Feldman was the winner for his hometown Giants in the most lopsided victory in franchise history, 26–8 over the Dodgers (4/30/44). In 1946 Feldman jumped to the Mexican League, which was raiding major league rosters for experienced players. /(JK)

Gus Felix — 1895–1960. OF 1923-27 **Braves**, Dodgers 583 g, .274, 12 hr, 230 rbi

Strong, likable Felix led his team's outfielders three times in RBI, and twice in fielding. He peaked with the 1925 Braves, hitting .307. /(EC)

Bob Feller (Rapid Robert) — 1918- . RHP 1936-41,
45-56 **Indians** 3837 ip, 266-162, 3.25 20 wins: 39-41,
46-47, 51 *1 WS, 14 ip, 0-2, 5.02*
☛ *Led League—w 39-41, 46-47, 51. Led League—era
40. Led League—k 38-41, 46-48. All-Star—38-41,
46-48, 50. Hall of Fame—1962..*

The winningest pitcher in Cleveland Indians history,
in 1962 Feller became the first pitcher since charter
member Walter Johnson to be elected to the Hall of
Fame in his first year of eligibility. Though regarded
as the fastest pitcher of his day, he himself attributed
his strikeout records to his curve and slider. Blessed
with a strong arm and an encouraging father, young

*Bob Feller (r.) and Jim Hegan after
Feller's third no-hitter*

Feller pitched to a makeshift backstop on the family
farm near Van Meter, Iowa. Cleveland scout Cy
Slapnicka signed him for one dollar and an
autographed baseball.

His velocity became an immediate legend when
he struck out eight Cardinals in a three-inning
exhibition stint. He came up as a 17-year-old at the
end of 1936 and fanned 15 Browns in his first ML
start and 17 Athletics shortly thereafter. But he was
extremely wild. In 1938 he became a regular starter
for the Indians. He won 17 and led the AL in
strikeouts with 240. He also set a ML record with
208 walks. Although he led the AL in walks three
more times, his control progressively improved.
Meanwhile, he led the AL in both strikeouts and
wins from 1939 to 1941.

In 1940 he won his personal high with 27,
including an Opening Day no-hitter against the
White Sox. Yet the year was tarnished, first when
Cleveland veterans, including Feller, earned the
nickname Crybabies by asking Cleveland owner
Alva Bradley to replace stern manager Ossie Vitt.
Then Feller lost the season's climactic game and the
pennant to Tigers unknown Floyd Giebell, despite
pitching a three-hitter.

He lost nearly four seasons to the Navy during
WWII, earning eight battle stars. When he returned,
he was better than ever, rejoining a powerful pitching staff that would soon include Bob Lemon, Mike
Garcia, and Early Wynn. He won 26 games in 1946
and broke Rube Waddell's strikeout record with 348
(later research indicated Waddell may have fanned
349). He also threw his second no-hitter, against the
Yankees. All told, Feller threw three no-hitters and
12 one-hitters.

In 1948 he started to decline, although he led the
AL in strikeouts for the seventh and final time. He
salvaged his season with six straight wins down the
stretch to help the Indians to their first pennant in
28 years. He opened the WS against the Braves, but
lost 1-0 on a controversial call. He'd apparently
picked Boston's Phil Masi off second base, but the
Braves' catcher was called safe. Masi then scored the
game's only run when Tommy Holmes singled.

After two mediocre years, he bounced back with a
22-8 season in 1951 to lead the AL in wins for the
sixth time and in winning percentage for the only
time. He spent his final seasons as a highly effective
spot starter, but was not used in the 1954 WS.

One of the first of the modern businessman-
players, he was incorporated (Ro-Fel, Inc.) and
made nearly as much money from barnstorming
and endorsements as from playing. In 1957 his

number 19 was the first to be retired by the Indians. And in 1969 he was voted baseball's greatest living righthanded pitcher in ceremonies for professional baseball's centennial. Always outspoken, and a natural promoter, he remains a popular ambassador for baseball. /(ME)

Happy Felsch [Oscar Emil] — 1891-1964. OF 1915-20 **White Sox** 749 g, .293, 38 hr, 446 rbi. *2 WS, 14 g, .229, 1 hr, 6 rbi*

Broad and powerful, Felsch was a natural at playing the game. A superb centerfielder with exceptional range and a rifle arm, Felsch still shares the records for double plays by an outfielder in a season (15) and assists in a game (4). Warm, smiling, and amiable, he loved silly riddles, whiskey, ribald jokes, and playing baseball.

On the White Sox, the fun-loving Felsch gravitated to the more raucous members of the team, who included the ringleaders of the Black Sox conspiracy. Years later, Felsch told author Eliot Asinof, "There was so much crookedness around, you sort of fell into it. I was dumb, all right. We started out talking about all the big money we would take, like a bunch of kids pretending to be big shots. I never really believed it would happen . . . and the next thing we knew, we were all tied up in it." Once he agreed to the sinister plot, this simple man found himself in a situation he couldn't control. The gamblers had a hold on him. Through threats, they forced him to throw more games during the 1920 season.

When the Black Sox scandal came out and he was barred from baseball, he was just emerging as a top power hitter, with 14 home runs in 1920. /(DB)

John Felske — 1942- . C-1B 1968, 72-73 Cubs, **Brewers** 54 g, .135, 1 hr, 9 rbi.
Manager 1985-87 **Phillies** 190-194, .495

Felske came up with his hometown Cubs but never won a job in the majors. After Phillies GM Paul Owens decided to stop managing, he hired organization man Felske. Philadelphia finished second under Felske in 1986 but was 21-1/2 games behind the Mets. He was fired while at 29-32 in 1987 after another slow start by the Phillies. /(JFC)

Terry Felton — 1957- . RHP 1979-82 **Twins** 138 ip, 0-16, 5.53

Winless with three losses in brief appearances for the Twins from 1979 to 1981, Felton made 48 appearances in 1982 and went 0-13, setting ML records for most career losses without a victory and most consecutive losses from the beginning of career. He did collect three saves toward the end of 1982. /(MC)

Fenway Park Boston Red Sox 1912- , Boston Braves 1914-15. LF-315, CF-390, RF-302

Home of the Boston Red Sox since April 20, 1912, Fenway Park is one of baseball's last remaining classic ballparks, with a single-level grandstand, wildly asymmetrical fences intersecting at crazy angles, and extremely close seating that allows many fans to be nearer to home plate than any infielder. Built to conform to the surrounding streets near Boston's Kenmore Square, Fenway Park's wooden grandstand was converted to concrete and steel for the 1934 season by new owner Tom Yawkey, and the basic structure of the park has remained unchanged since. Its most distinctive feature is the Green Monster, a 37-foot-high wall that extends straight from the left field corner to almost dead centerfield. Once plastered with advertisements, it is now solid green, only 315' down the line (but rumored to be even shorter) and 379' to the intersection of the left and center field fences. From the plate, the wall seems to loom invitingly behind the shortstop, but while it does turn many routine fly balls into home runs, at the same time it knocks deep line drives back toward the infield for the longest singles in the majors. Outside, it runs along Lansdowne Street, and the 23' net atop it hangs over the sidewalk to protect pedestrians from falling baseballs, while inside it holds one of the major league's three remaining manually operated scoreboards. Originally, left field also included a 10' incline, known as Duffy's Cliff for Red Sox left fielder Duffy Lewis, but the hill was eliminated in the 1934 renovations.

The centerfield wall is 17' high and extends from the Monster to the right field bullpens, where it angles sharply toward the infield. The deepest part of the park, a triangle next to the Red Sox bullpen, is 420' from the plate. The bullpens were known as Williamsburg when they were added in 1940 to shorten the fences for young slugger Ted Williams, but are still 380' away in the right field power alley. The fence curves suddenly in toward the right-field foul pole (302'), creating another set of extremely tricky caroms. Balls hit down the line, if not cut off quickly, will hug the fence and roll all the way into right center for triples or even inside-the-park home runs. In this corner, the fence is the shortest in the ML, ranging from three to five feet high.

Like the playing field, the seating areas have

Fenway Park

changed little since 1934. The grandstand is still essentially a single deck, although some roof seats and luxury boxes have been added, and there is a massive bleacher section in center and right fields. Fenway Park has almost no foul territory, and fans along the left field line can literally reach into the outfield or hold conversations with obliging players. No ball has ever cleared the right field roof, but one red seat deep in the right field bleachers marks the landing spot of Ted Williams's longest home run here. Steel girders supporting the roof do create many obstructed-view seats, and several sections in deep right field do not even face home plate, but Fenway's seats are generally the best in the ML. Despite the park's small capacity (less than 34,000, lowest in the ML) and complete absence of parking facilities, the Red Sox frequently top two million in total attendance.

Fenway Park has hosted its share of memorable baseball moments. It was the scene of the AL's only two one-game playoffs, in 1948 and 1978, as well as what has been called the greatest WS game ever, Game Six in 1975. Carl Yastrzemski collected his 3,000th hit here, and Ted Williams homered in his final ML at-bat. On the lighter side, on May 17, 1947 a seagull dropped a three-pound fish on the Fenway Park mound during a game, leaving Browns' pitcher Ellis Kinder dumbfounded. /(SCL)

Alex Ferguson [James Alexander] — 1897–1976. RHP 1918, 21–29 Yankees, **Red Sox**, Senators, Phillies, Dodgers 1236 ip, 61–85, 4.91. *1 WS, 14 ip, 1–1, 3.21*

Forkball artist Ferguson had his winningest season for the seventh-place 1924 Red Sox, when he won 14 while losing a league-high 17. Traded twice in 1925, he joined the Senators in late August, went

5–1 down the stretch, and pitched well in the World Series. /(EW)

Bob Ferguson (Fighting Bob, Death to Flying Things) — 1845–1894. 2B-3B-SS 1871–84 New York (NA), Brooklyn (NA), Hartfords (NA), Hartford (NL), Cubs, **Troy (NL)**, Phillies, Pittsburgh (AA) *NA:* 259 g, .243, *ML:* 562 g, .271, 1 hr, 178 rbi (inc).

Manager 1871–84, 86–87 New York (NA), Brooklyn (NA), Hartfords (NA), Hartford (NL), Cubs, **Troy (NL)**, Phillies, Pittsburgh (AA), New York (AA) *NA:* not available; *ML:* 292–351, .454

One of the most outstanding and influential ballplayers of the 19th century, Ferguson first attracted national attention in 1870 when, as captain of the Brooklyn Atlantics, he drove in the tying run and scored the winning run as the Atlantics handed the Cincinnati Red Stockings their first loss in two years. An outstanding leader, he managed every team he played for from 1871 through 1884. Baseball's first switch-hitter, he was only ordinary with the bat but was considered an outstanding fielder (although the quaint nickname Death to Flying Things, signifying stellar play on fly balls, was first given to Atlantics teammate Jack Chapman). Ferguson's primary contribution to baseball was his forthright character and unquestioned honesty in a time when many baseball players had low morals and were often the pawns of gamblers. In 1872 he was elected president of the National Association of Professional Baseball Players and held that position for several years, leading the fight for honest baseball that resulted in the establishment of the National League in 1876. Quick-tempered and hot-headed, he became an umpire in his later years, and once broke a player's arm with a bat to finish an argument. /(BC)

George Ferguson — 1886–1943. RHP 1906–11 Giants, **Braves** 698 ip, 31–46, 3.34

Ferguson was 12–11 for the 1908 Braves but injured his arm. The next year he suffered through a 5–23 season, leading the NL in losses. /(NLM)

Joe Ferguson — 1946– . C-OF **Dodgers**, Cardinals, Astros, Angels 1013 g, .240, 122 hr, 445 rbi. *2 LCS, 6 g, .200, 2 rbi. 2 WS, 7 g, .200, 1 hr, 2 rbi*

Ferguson became the Dodgers' regular catcher in 1973 and set a ML catcher record by committing only three errors (700 or more chances), leading the league's catchers in fielding average and double plays. He hit .263 and reached career highs with 25 HR, 26 doubles, 88 RBI, 84 runs, and 87 walks (for an on-base percentage of .376), despite spending three weeks on the DL in the middle of the season. He also played 20 games in the outfield, and would continue to play both catcher and outfield throughout his career.

In 1974 Steve Yeager, better defensively, took over more of the catching duties. Ferguson hit 16 HR, but gained more attention for his playoff exploits, as the TV announcers were taken with the idea of a strong-armed catcher playing right field. Ferguson hit only .231 but drew five walks, scored three runs, and drove in two in the four-game series. In the World Series he hit a two-run homer off Vida Blue for what proved to be the winning margin in the Dodgers' only victory over the A's.

After spending the second half of 1975 on the DL and starting slowly in 1976, Ferguson was traded with two minor players to the Cardinals for Reggie Smith and was sent on to Houston after the season. As the Astros' primary catcher, Ferguson had another fine season (16 HR, 61 RBI, 85 walks) before the Dodgers reacquired him in July 1978 for Jeff Leonard and Rafael Landestoy. Ferguson helped Los Angeles to another NL pennant. In 1979, again splitting time between catching and the outfield, he hit 20 HR with 69 RBI in 122 games, but he finished his career as a part-timer. He ended the 1980s as a coach with the Dodgers. /(SH)

Chico Fernandez [Humberto Perez] — 1932– . SS 1956–63 Dodgers, Phillies, **Tigers**, Mets 856 g, .240, 40 hr, 259 rbi

Fernandez was a bright prospect who could not displace Pee Wee Reese at shortstop for the Dodgers, and the Phillies traded five players to get him for 1957. He was their regular shortstop for two seasons. After starting off adequately with the bat (.262 with 51 RBI in 1957), the native Cuban fell off over the next two seasons and saw limited time in 1959, hitting .211. The Tigers gave him the shortstop job in 1960, and although he led the AL in errors that season, he surprised in 1962 with 20 HR (half his career total). After starting 1963 with a .143 BA, he was traded to the Braves and then the Mets in just one day. The Mets traded him to the White Sox in 1964 for Charley Smith, but Fernandez didn't see any more major league action. /(WOR)

Frank Fernandez — 1943– . C-OF 1967–72 **Yankees**, A's, Senators, Cubs 285 g, .199, 39 hr, 116 rbi

A backup catcher his entire career, Fernandez never played in more than 94 games a year during his six seasons in the majors. His two best years were 1969 for the Yankees, when he hit a career-high .223 with

12 home runs, and 1970 for the A's, when he belted 15 homers.

Nanny Fernandez [Froilan] — 1918- . 3B-SS-OF 1942, 46-47, 50 **Braves**, Pirates 408 g, .248, 16 hr, 145 rbi

The dark, stocky Fernandez was of Castilian descent, his parents having left Spain for California shortly before his birth. He drove in 55 runs his first season but was not the same after losing three prime years to military service. /(JK)

Sid Fernandez (El Sid) — 1962- . LHP 1983- Dodgers, **Mets** 1033 ip, 69-45, 3.22. *2 LCS, 10 ip, 0-2, 8.10. 1 WS, 7 ip, 0-0, 1.35* ☛ *All-Star—86-87.*

A native Hawaiian who wears number 50 to honor his home state, Fernandez was given up on by the Dodgers because of his weight problems (despite two minor league no-hitters in 1982). Obtained by the Mets with infielder Ross Jones for Bob Bailor and Carlos Diaz, he blossomed in 1985, striking out 180 batters in 170 innings while going 9-9 with a 2.80 ERA. Fernandez has been inconsistent due to his widely fluctuating weight, which when high reduces his stamina. It has also caused him knee problems (which put him on the DL in August 1987) and makes him a poor fielder who's slow to cover first base.

Fernandez uses a herky-jerky motion, seemingly throwing the ball entirely with his arm after finishing his stride. It's hard for batters to pick up the ball coming out of his uniform, and his rising fastball is deceptive and effective. He led the NL in strikeouts per inning in 1985, and on July 14, 1989 he struck out 16 Braves (but lost, 3-2), setting a franchise record for lefthanders. At home games, fans in the right field upper deck post an "S" for each strikeout.

Fernandez's 16-6 record in 1986 helped the Mets to a pennant, but he didn't start in the World Series (after losing Game Four of the LCS 3-1 to Mike Scott) because manager Davey Johnson didn't want to use the lefthander in Fenway. But he had a 1.35 ERA out of the bullpen, and his 2-1/3 hitless innings in Game Seven, including four strikeouts, kept the Mets in the game after they had gone down by three runs early. New York rallied to win the Series.

Through the 1980s, Fernandez did not pitch to his potential for an entire season. He was bombed in Game Five of the 1988 LCS by the Dodgers and took the loss. /(SH)

Tony Fernandez — 1962- . SS 1983- **Blue Jays** 867 g, .292, 36 hr, 338 rbi. *2 LCS, 12 g, .341, 3 rbi* ☛ *All-Star—86-87, 89. Gold Glove—86-89.*

After becoming a regular with the Blue Jays midway into the 1984 season, Fernandez challenged Cal Ripken and Alan Trammell as the American League's best shortstop. A great defensive player, he led AL shortstops in putouts and fielding percentage in 1986. Rarely walking or striking out, Fernandez averaged around 600 at-bats per season. The speedy switch-hitter from San Pedro de Macoris, Dominican Republic, showed good extra-base power. His career average, close to .300, is nearly the same from both sides of the plate. He holds most Blue Jay records for switch-hitters. In 1986 he became the first Blue Jay to record a 200-hit season, and he set a major league record for most hits by a shortstop in this century, collecting 212 of his 213 hits at that position.

Fernandez showed toughness, playing with injuries. In one stretch he played in a Blue Jay-record 403 consecutive games. The elbow injury he sustained on a slide by Detroit's Bill Madlock with a week to go in the 1987 season was a turning point in the AL East pennant race, and the injury affected his play for the first half of the 1988 season. Fernandez was beaned by Cecilio Guante in April 1989 after hitting a grand slam earlier in the game. He returned to the Blue Jay lineup following reconstructive face surgery and hit a career-high 11 HR. /(TF)

Al Ferrara (The Bull) — 1939- . OF 1963, 65-71 **Dodgers**, Padres, Reds 574 g, .259, 51 hr, 198 rbi. *1 WS, 1 g, 1.000*

As a youngster, Ferrara appeared as a solo pianist at Carnegie Hall. Because of his muscular frame, a teammate once quipped, "He says he was a piano player, but more than likely he was a piano mover." Generally a fourth outfielder, with the Dodgers in a 1965 game against the Cubs, Ferrara broke up a Dick Ellsworth no-hitter with an eighth-inning, three-run pinch-homer. In 1967 he was Dodger of the Year, batting .277 with 16 homers. /(RM)

Don Ferrarese (Midget) — 1929- . LHP 1955-62 **Orioles**, Indians, White Sox, Phillies, Cardinals 507 ip, 19-36, 4.00

Like most little pitchers, the 5'9" 170-lb Midget struggled to make the majors. Used as a starter and reliever, he never won more than five games a season with his assortment of breaking balls. /(AL)

Mike Ferraro — 1944– . 3B 1966, 68–69, 72 **Brewers** 162 g, .232, 2 hr, 30 rbi.
Manager 1983, 86 **Indians**, Royals 76–98

Although he was voted the top Yankee farmhand in 1966, Ferraro did not gain a regular ML job until the Brewers handed him third base in 1972. He hit .255 with only two homers and the next year turned to coaching. As the Indians' manager in 1983, he left after 100 games with the team in seventh place. He was interim manager of the Royals in 1986./(MC)

Rick Ferrell — 1905– . C 1929–45, 47 **Browns**, Red Sox, Senators 1884 g, .281, 28 hr, 734 rbi
☛ *All-Star—33–38, 44. Hall of Fame—1984.*

A North Carolina farmboy and one of seven brothers, Rick Ferrell saved pennies to buy his first catcher's mitt for $1.50. Over 60 years later, the Veterans Committee elected him to the Hall of Fame. Although he played chiefly with second-division teams, Ferrell is always included among the greatest catchers of his age.

Blessed with a strong, durable physique and a placid yet determined personality, for 18 seasons Ferrell was a fine all-around receiver. In two stints each with the Browns and Senators, with three-plus years in Boston sandwiched between, he ultimately established the AL record with 1,805 games behind the plate.

At the plate, Ferrell had a fine eye and was remarkably selective. He coaxed 931 walks while fanning only 277 times, and achieved an impressive .433 career on-base percentage. Nineteen percent of his hits were doubles.

With St. Louis, he batted .290 over the years 1929–32, and caught the eye of Red Sox owner Tom Yawkey, who was trying to rebuild. Boston had had a .300-hitting catcher in only 1901 and 1919. In the years 1933–36, Ferrell broke Red Sox catchers' records in batting, doubles, HR, and RBI. His .302 average with the Red Sox is 12th on the club's all-time list. Rick's brother Wes joined him in Boston in 1934. Though a pitcher, Wes hit more career HR (38) than Rick (28). In June 1937, the brothers were packaged in a trade to Washington for Ben Chapman and Bobo Newsom.

Ferrell was back with the Browns in 1941–43. Then, during his second tour with Washington, he met the unprecedented challenge of handling four knuckleball pitchers in the starting rotation. In 1945 the Senators just missed the pennant, and their knuckle quartet amassed 60 wins.

Rick Ferrell with the Red Sox

After his playing days, Ferrell served as a Senators coach for four seasons. He followed with many years in the Tiger organization, as a coach, scout, GM, and, at over 80, executive consultant. In 1987 manager Sparky Anderson commented, "I hope I'm like Rick when I am his age!"/(EC)

Wes Ferrell — 1908–1976. RHP 1927–41 **Indians**, Red Sox, Senators, Yankees, Dodgers, Braves 2623 ip, 193–128, 4.04. 20 wins: 29–32, 35–36
☛ *Led League—w 35.*

"Wes was a marvelous character," recalled Bill Werber of teammate Wes Ferrell. "I've seen him, after being removed from a ball game, hit himself in the jaws with both fists and nearly knock himself out . . . jump in the air and crunch the face out of an expensive watch . . . tear card deck after card deck to pieces because he wasn't getting good hands. He hated to lose, at anything. He was a very determined competitor, the kind you like to have on your side."

Ferrell, an alumnus of Guilford College in his native North Carolina, set a ML record by posting 20 or more victories in each of his first four seasons (1929–32, with Cleveland). With Boston, the 6'2" righthander also won a league-high 25 games in 1935, and was 20–15 in 1936. On his way to a .601 career winning percentage, he led AL pitchers four times in complete games, and three times in innings pitched. In 1931 Ferrell won 13 consecutive decisions, and no-hit the Browns (4/29). Two years later, he was named to the original AL All-Star team.

Ferrell was one of the best-hitting pitchers baseball has known. He set records for most single-season HR (nine, in 1931) and career HR (38) by a pitcher, and averaged .280 lifetime. "I didn't see any big deal in being a good hitter as well as a good pitcher," said Ferrell, a two-time minor league batting champion as an outfielder after his ML playing days. "A lot of guys could do it if they tried."

Ferrell's older brother and sometime batterymate, Rick, is enshrined in Cooperstown. (A third Ferrell brother, George, had a 20-year minor league career.) Journalist Bob Broeg suggested that Wes, too, could have made the Hall of Fame if arm trouble (which changed him from a blinding fastballer into a curveball and off-speed specialist) hadn't curtailed his career. Broeg also wrote, "If . . .there was one major difference between [Wes and Rick] Ferrell, it was in their temperament. Wes was a prima donna and hotheaded. Rick, though he lost his cool occasionally, was . . . a soft-spoken team man." Wes's Cleveland manager, Roger Peckinpaugh, fined and suspended him for refusing to leave a 1932 game. His Bosox skipper, Joe Cronin, fined him for leaving a 1936 game without permission. Later, as a minor league manager, Ferrell was slapped with suspensions for belting an umpire, and removing his team from the field./(TJ)

Wes Ferrell with the Indians

Tom Ferrick — 1915– . RHP 1941–42, 46–52 A's, Indians, Browns, **Senators**, Browns, Yankees, Senators 674 ip, 40–40, 3.47. *1 WS, 1 ip, 1–0, 0.00*

A 6'2" 220-lb reliever, Ferrick saved 56 games in a career interrupted by three years of service in WWII. For the 1947 Senators, he led the AL with seven relief losses. In 1950 his nine relief wins topped the AL. Joining the Yankees that June, he was the man Casey Stengel turned to when the manager lost faith in bullpen ace Joe Page. On the way to the pennant, Ferrick won eight games and saved nine in just 30 appearances. Working one inning in relief, he won Game Three of New York's World Series sweep of the Phillies./(JJM)

Hobe Ferris [Albert Sayles] — 1877–1938. 2B-3B 1901–09 **Red Sox**, Browns 1286 g, .239, 39 hr, 550 rbi. *1 WS, 8 g, .290, 7 rbi*

A spirited competitor and skillful second baseman, Ferris was the hero of the final game of the first

World Series (1903), as he batted in all three Boston runs for the shutout victory over Pittsburgh. /(EW)

Boo Ferriss [David Meadow] — 1921- . RHP 1945-50 **Red Sox** 880 ip, 65-30, 3.64. 20 wins: 45-46 *1 WS, 13.1 ip, 1-0, 2.03*
☛ *All-Star—46.*

Just out of the military, in 1945 Ferriss was the sensation of the American League. The 6'2" 208-lb rookie went 21-10 and defeated all seven opponent clubs the first time he faced them. Supported by a powerful Red Sox lineup, he went 25-6, for a league-high .806 winning percentage, on the way to the 1946 pennant, and shut out St. Louis in World Series Game Three. A .250 lifetime hitter, he had 19 RBI in both 1945 and 1947, and was used 41 times as a lefthanded pinch hitter. Ferriss's career was cut short by asthma and arm trouble. He served as a coach for the Red Sox and at Delta State in Mississippi. /(EW)

Lou Fette — 1907-1981. RHP 1937-40, 45 **Braves,** Dodgers 691 ip, 41-40, 3.15. 20 wins: 37

Fette astounded the baseball world when he and fellow rookie teammate Jim Turner each won 20 games in 1937. More remarkable was that both of the Braves' "ancient rookies" topped 30 years of age. Fette was a quiet, hard-working, poised pitcher who shared the league lead in shutouts in 1937 with five, and led in 1939 with six. /(EW)

John Fetzer — 1901- . Owner.

As a developer of radio and TV stations, Fetzer's strength was in creating new concepts for packaging radio and television coverage of ML baseball after he became owner of the Tigers in 1962. He was a member of the ML executive council, and was active on expansion and planning committees. /(NLM)

Chick Fewster [Wilson Lloyd] — 1895-1945. 2B-OF-SS-3B 1917-27 **Yankees,** Red Sox, Indians, Dodgers 644 g, .258, 6 hr, 167 rbi. *1 WS, 4 g, .200, 1 hr, 2 rbi*

Despite an 11-year career, Fewster is chiefly remembered for one play: Brooklyn's "three-men-on-third" muddle of 1926 against the Braves. Actually, Fewster never made it to third. Babe Herman, whose base hit to right set things in motion, passed him between second and third, thereby becoming an automatic (second) out. With cautious Dazzy Vance clinging to third, Fewster's only option was to return to second. But, bemused by events, he fled into the

outfield, where he was tagged out to end the inning. /(ADS)

Mark Fidrych (The Bird) — 1954- . RHP 1976-80 **Tigers** 412 ip, 29-19, 3.10
☛ *Rookie of the Year—76. Led League—era 76.*

Fidrych had "a talent that was exceptional and an approach to his game that was both uninhibited and refreshing," said author Donald Honig, noting that Fidrych "talked to the ball, shook hands with his infielders after good plays, cavorted with the pure joy and unrestrained enthusiasm of a Little Leaguer." The 6'3" righthander with flowing, blond curls was the talk of baseball in 1976, starting and losing the All-Star Game, and going 19-9 for the Tigers with 24 complete games and a 2.34 ERA—both AL-bests. Arm trouble limited him to just ten ML wins after his Rookie of the Year showing. /(TJ)

Cecil Fielder (Big Daddy) — 1963- . DH-1B 1985- **Blue Jays** 220 g, .243, 31 hr, 84 rbi. *1 LCS, 3 g, .333*

Despite his name, Fielder reached the ML on the strength of his bat, not his glove. He hit .311 in a brief trial with the Blue Jays in 1985 and hit .269 with 14 HR in 1987, but was never more than a part-time player. Fielder was sold to Japan's Hanshin Tigers after the 1988 season. /(TF)

Ed Figueroa (Figgy, Eduardito) — 1948- . RHP 1974-81 Angels, **Yankees,** Rangers, A's 1309 ip, 80-67, 3.51. 20 wins: 78 *3 LCS, 17 ip, 0-2, 8.10. 2 WS, 15 ip, 0-2, 6.75*

After a solid 1975 season (2.91 ERA, fifth-best in the AL) with the last-place Angels, he was traded with Mickey Rivers to the Yankees for Bobby Bonds. He was the Yankee staff's biggest winner over three AL-championship seasons, winning 55 from 1976 to 1978. In 1978 Figueroa became the first native Puerto Rican to win 20 games in the majors (he had been close two years earlier, but a rainout on the last day of the season deprived him of his chance). After elbow surgery in 1979, he did not pitch effectively; leaving the majors, he continued pitching in Mexico. /(EW)

Tom Filer — 1956- . RHP 1985, 88- Blue Jays, **Brewers** 263 ip, 20-13, 4.27

After bouncing around the minors for seven years, Filer came up with the Blue Jays in mid-1985 and helped them to their only division title with a 7-0, 3.88 record. The starter spent all of 1986 on the DL

ROLLIE FINGERS F 335

but made it back to the majors with Milwaukee in 1988, going 5–8 with a 4.43 ERA. /(WOR)

Dana Fillingim — 1893–1961. RHP 1915, 18–23, 25 A's, **Braves**, Phillies 1076 ip, 43–73, 3.56

Righthander Fillingim was one of eight NL spitballers permitted to continue throwing the pitch after it was outlawed in 1920. He had two good years with the Braves of 1920–21, but thereafter was afflicted with a sore arm that led to rising ERAs. /(ADS)

Pete Filson — 1958– . LHP 1982–87 **Twins**, White Sox, Yankees 357 ip, 15–14, 4.01

First signed by the Yankees, Filson won his first 12 pro decisions, including seven-inning no-hitters in the 1979 Appalachian League and the 1980 South Atlantic League. Traded to the Twins in 1982, he proved to have only a mediocre major league fastball. Used mostly in long relief, he became known as an inconsistent, flaky lefthander who thought too much. The Yankees reacquired him in 1987. /(JCA)

Rollie Fingers [Roland Glen] — 1946– . RHP 1968–85 **A's**, Padres, Brewers 1701 ip, 114–118, 2.90. *5 LCS, 19 ip, 1–2, 3.72. 3 WS, 33 ip, 2–2, 1.35* ☛ *Most Valuable Player—81. Cy Young Award—81. All-Star—73–76, 78, 81–82.*

Almost as famous for his handlebar mustache as his pitching, the lanky righthander is the greatest relief artist in baseball, lasting 17 years and compiling the most career saves (341) and World Series saves (7).

Known for his control and durability, Fingers made it a point never to pitch more than two innings at a time in order to maintain his strength. Like many relievers, Fingers began his career as a starter. He began the 1969, 1970, and 1971 seasons as a starter, but finished all three seasons in the bullpen. In 1972 he finally became a full-time reliever, winning 11 games in relief and saving 21 to lead Oakland to its first-ever World Series appearance. In the decisive seventh game against the Reds, Fingers worked out of a bases-loaded, one-out jam in the eighth inning to preserve the 3–2 victory and the championship. He piled up another 22 saves with a 1.92 era in 1973 with two World Series saves, and led the AL in games in 1974 with 76.

In 1974 Fingers pitched the final two innings of the only four-pitcher no-hitter in baseball history as he, Vida Blue, Glenn Abbott, and Paul Lindblad combined to blank the California Angels 5–0. Fingers shone in the World Series that year, earning the victory in Game One, then saved Oakland's

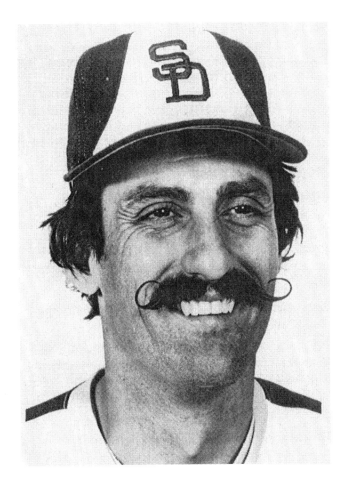

Rollie Fingers

other three victories over the Dodgers to win Series MVP honors. Fingers led the AL in appearances in 1975 with 75, but lost 11 games in relief in 1976.

Like many Oakland players, Fingers fled Charlie Finley, and signed on with San Diego as a free agent in 1977. He promptly led his new league in appearances with 78, and also led the league for the first time in saves with 35. He followed with 37 saves in 1978 to tie the then-ML record, even though he also lost 13 games in relief. He slumped to just 13 saves and a 4.50 ERA in 1979, then came up with a forkball to supplement his sinker and slider. In 1980 he saved 23 games and won 11 more games in relief.

After the season, San Diego believed Fingers, now 34, was past his prime and, in an 11-player deal, swapped Fingers and former Oakland teammate Gene Tenace to the Brewers. Fingers showed he still had plenty of arm left, though, leading the AL in saves with 28 with a 1.04 ERA and the 1981 Brewers to their first post-season appearance. Fingers figured in 55 percent of his team's victories, and won both the MVP and the Cy Young awards. He pitched much of the 1982 season in pain, saving 29 games, but missed the entire 1983 season.

At the age of 38, Fingers came back in 1984 to post a 1.96 ERA and compiled 23 saves for a team that won only 67 games. In 1985 age finally caught up to Fingers, who slumped to a 5.04 ERA, and he was released by the Brewers at the end of the year./(SEW)

Jim Finigan — 1928–1981. 3B-2B 1954–59 **A's,** Tigers, Giants, Orioles 512 g, .264, 19 hr, 168 rbi

Finigan had a banner rookie year in 1954. He led the league in double plays at third base, and his .302 batting average made him the last regular to hit over .300 for the Athletics in Philadelphia./(RM)

Herman Fink — 1911–1980. RHP 1935–37 **A's** 284 ip, 10–20, 5.22

A hefty North Carolina farmboy, Fink maximized his minimal salary by living on drugstore snacks and milkshakes on the road, pocketing most of his meal money. In the starting rotation only in 1936, Fink went 8–16./(NLM)

Charles O. Finley (Charley O) — 1918– . Owner.

One of the most flamboyant, innovative, and controversial baseball club owners ever, Finley began as a semi-pro first baseman-manager in Indiana. Near-fatal tuberculosis in 1946 ended his playing career but inspired him to found a life insurance empire. Outbid for the Kansas City A's in 1960 by Arnold Johnson, Finley acquired the team a few months later when Johnson died. The A's had been sending such stars as Roger Maris, Clete Boyer, and Ralph Terry to the Yankees in exchange for washed-up journeymen; Finley immediately suspended dealings with New York and, as his own general manager, soon established a knack for acquiring unheralded talent like Ed Charles and Jose Tartabull.

Finley's first of many feuds with players and managers commenced at the 1962 All-Star break when he ordered Manny Jimenez, who was leading the AL with a .350 average, to start hitting home runs. Manager Hank Bauer took Jimenez's side and was fired after the season. Jimenez slumped and was sent down in 1963. In mid-1967, Finley fined and suspended young pitcher Lew Krausse for "rowdyism," and publicly berated his players over an insignificant airplane incident. A near-mutiny by the players followed. Finley fired manager Alvin Dark,

then released Ken Harrelson, the team's best hitter, who had been quoted as saying that Finley was "a menace to baseball." Signed by the Red Sox, Harrelson helped them to the pennant, and won the AL RBI title the following year.

Finley had already established a reputation as a cantankerous buffoon by trading for sluggers Jim Gentile and Rocky Colavito, then building a bizarre "pennant porch" designed to increase their home run production. He later paraded a mule named Charley O about the field, into cocktail parties, and even through hotel lobbies. He relocated the A's Double-A franchise to Birmingham because he was born there. He introduced orange baseballs, ball girls, and a mechanical rabbit that gave baseballs to the umpires. He advocated night World Series games in an effort to boost fan interest.

Meanwhile, Finley signed Jim Hunter and dubbed him Catfish to give him press appeal, concocting a story set in Hunter's childhood to justify the nickname. Finley also signed Reggie Jackson, Sal Bando, Vida Blue, Bert Campaneris, and a host of others who became the nucleus of his Oakland dynasty. He shifted the club from Kansas City to Oakland after the 1967 season in a move he later acknowledged as his one big mistake. In a half-empty stadium, the A's were contenders during 1969 and 1970, then won five straight division titles in 1971–75 and World Championships in 1972–74.

Finley was named *TSN* Man of the Year for 1972, but continued having disputes with players. After Reggie Jackson hit 47 HR in 1969, Finley, during a prolonged contract dispute, threatened to send him back to the minors. Similar bitterness followed when Vida Blue won the Cy Young Award in his first full season, 1971. Both times, Commissioner Bowie Kuhn intervened to help bring about a resolution. In the 1973 World Series, Finley fired Mike Andrews after the reserve infielder committed two consecutive errors in the 12th inning of Oakland's Game Two loss to the Mets. Other A's and manager Dick Williams rallied to Andrews's defense. Kuhn forced Finley to reinstate the player. Williams resigned after winning the Series, and Finley replaced him with Alvin Dark.

Under Dark, the A's won another World Championship in 1974. But after the season, Catfish Hunter was declared a free agent by arbitrator Peter Seitz because Finley had failed to make contractually stipulated payments for Hunter into an insurance annuity fund. Even without Hunter, the A's easily won their division in 1975. In the spring of 1976, Finley traded Jackson to the Orioles. During the season, he tried to sell Joe Rudi and Rollie Fingers to the Red Sox and Vida Blue to the Yankees, and did sell Paul Lindblad to the Rangers. In desperate financial trouble because of low attendance, Finley claimed he needed the money to sign free agents and rebuild. Kuhn disagreed, voiding the sales of Rudi, Fingers, and Blue as not being "in the best interests of baseball." Kuhn later voided another sale of Blue, to the Reds. Meanwhile, major league players won the right to play out their options, and seven A's did so in 1976. Despite the uncompensated losses, Finley rebuilt, and the A's were en route to yet another division title in 1981 when he sold the club to the Levi-Strauss company. /(MC)

Chuck Finley — 1962- . LHP 1986- **Angels** 531 ip, 30-32, 3.58. *1 LCS, 2 ip, 0-0, 0.00*
☛ *All-Star—89.*

The 6'6" Finley pitched only 41 innings in the minors before joining the Angels as a reliever in 1986, and became a starter at the tail end of 1987. He was 9–15, 4.17 in 1988. In 1989 he harnessed his strikeout potential to go 16–9 with a 2.57 ERA as the Angels contended. /(ME)

Mickey Finn [Cornelius Francis Neal] — 1904-1933. 2B-3B 1930-33 **Dodgers**, Phillies 321 g, .262, 3 hr, 102 rbi

Finn was a scrapper from New York. While in the Pacific Coast League, he once punched out pitcher Duster Mails, who had thrown at Finn. As a Dodger, Finn drew a sneering comment from the Cubs' Rogers Hornsby and challenged him. Hornsby backed down, but his pugnacious teammate, Billy Jurges, got into the fight. Finn was traded to the Phillies, but died after complaining of stomach pains and undergoing an operation during the 1933 season. /(JK)

Happy Finneran [Joseph Ignatius] (Smokey Joe) — 1891-1942. RHP 1912-15, 18 Phillies, **Brooklyn (FL)**, Tigers, Yankees 570 ip, 27-34, 3.30

Finneran won 24 games in two seasons with the BrookFeds. Happy may have needed a change in demeanor in his later career as a funeral home director. /(JK)

Lou Finney — 1910-1966. OF-1B 1931, 33-42, 44-47 **A's**, Red Sox, Browns, Phillies 1270 g, .287, 31 hr, 494 rbi
☛ *All-Star—40.*

When Connie Mack broke up his champion Athletics, he hoped Finney would replace Al Simmons in the outfield and in the hearts of Philadelphia fans.

Lou did neither, but he provided 15 steady, dependable ML seasons. With Boston, he spelled strongman Jimmie Foxx at first base and, in 1939, collected a league-leading 13 pinch hits.

After managing in the low minors, he and his brother Hal, a reserve catcher for five seasons with the Pirates, ran a feed store in Alabama. /(JK)

Mike Fiore (Lefty) — 1944- . 1B-OF 1968-72 Orioles, **Royals**, Red Sox, Cardinals, Padres 254 g, .227, 13 hr, 50 rbi

Originally signed by the Mets, the Brooklynite was taken by the Orioles in the first-year draft. An excellent fielder, he had a good eye at the plate, and surprising power. /(EW)

Bill Fischer — 1891-1945. C 1913-17 Dodgers, Chicago (FL), Cubs, **Pirates** 412 g, .274, 10 hr, 115 rbi

The lefthanded-hitting Fischer struggled in the National League, but led the 1915 Federal League champion Chicago club by hitting .329 while sharing catching duties with Art Wilson. /(ME)

Bill Fischer — 1930- . RHP 1956-64 White Sox, Tigers, Senators, **A's**, Twins 831 ip, 45-58, 4.34

A former Marine drill instructor, Fischer established a ML record in 1962, pitching 84-1/3 consecutive innings for the A's without giving up a base on balls, surpassing Christy Mathewson's mark of 68. That season, Fischer walked only eight batters, covering 127-2/3 innings. He became a pitching coach for the Reds and Red Sox. /(RM)

Carl Fischer — 1905-1963. LHP 1930-35, 37 **Senators**, Browns, Tigers, White Sox, Indians 823 ip, 46-50, 4.63

The 6' 180-lb Fischer won 13 games for Walter Johnson's 1931 Senators, and was 11–15 for the 1933 Tigers. Among his batterymates were Hall of Famers Mickey Cochrane and Rick Ferrell. /(TJ)

Hank Fischer (Bulldog) — 1940- . RHP 1962-67 **Braves**, Reds, Red Sox 547 ip, 30-39, 4.23

Fischer was signed to a Braves contract in 1959 by John "Honey" Russell, his basketball coach at Seton Hall who doubled as a baseball scout. Bulldog had his best season in 1964, winning 11 for Milwaukee and recording all five of his career shutouts. /(RM)

Rube Fischer — 1916- . RHP 1941, 43-46 **Giants** 383 ip, 16-34, 5.10

Noted for his high, overhand delivery, the Giants considered the 6'4" Fischer a top prospect. His career all but ended in 1944 when he had an operation transplanting part of his shin bone to his spine. /(EW)

Mike Fischlin — 1955- . SS-2B-3B 1977-78, 80-87 Astros, **Indians**, Yankees, Braves 517 g, .220, 3 hr, 68 rbi

Fischlin hit a career-high .268 as Cleveland's regular shortstop in 1982 but spent the rest of his career as a journeyman utility infielder. In 1978 for the Astros, he tied an odd NL record by handling just one chance in two consecutive games at shortstop (June 18, 20). /(MM)

Bob Fishel — 1914-1988. *Executive.*

Fishel was Bill Veeck's publicity man at Cleveland and St. Louis, and was the man who signed midget Eddie Gaedel to a Browns contract. Later, he was promotion director for the Yankees for 20 years. At the time of his death, he was AL vice-president for public relations. An award named in his honor is given to the outstanding baseball publicist each year. /(NLM)

Bob Fisher — 1887-1963. SS-2B 1912-16, 18-19 **Dodgers**, Cubs, Reds, Cardinals 503 g, .276, 11 hr, 170 rbi

A regular shortstop in only two seasons, Fisher did not hit well enough to compensate for his errors and lack of range; in 1913 with Brooklyn, he led the NL with 52 errors. Bob's brother, Newt Fisher, was a longtime minor league catcher, manager, and umpire. /(JK)

Brian Fisher — 1962- . RHP 1985- Yankees, **Pirates** 544 ip, 32-31, 4.34

Fisher was a surprising relief star for the 1985 Yankees, leading AL rookies with 14 saves while posting a 2.38 ERA. He declined in effectiveness in 1986 and was traded to Pittsburgh. Becoming a starter in 1987 after 126 straight relief appearances, he proceeded to finish among the league leaders in complete games and shutouts. /(ME)

Chauncey Fisher (Peach) — 1872-1939. RHP 1893-94, 96-97, 1901 Cleveland (NL), **Reds**, Dodgers, Giants, Cardinals 436 ip, 21-27, 5.37

Chauncey was the older brother of Tom Fisher (1902 Tigers, 1904 Braves). He broke into the majors in 1893 with the Cleveland Spiders and tossed two complete-game losses. He was sent to Cincinnati in mid-1894. He finished the season with a dismal 2-10 record and an ERA of 7.76. He bounced back in 1896-97 for Cincinnati and Brooklyn, winning 19 games in the two years. He returned to the major leagues in 1901, when he

threw a game for the Giants and one for the Cardinals. He also pitched for the Chicago White Sox championship team of 1900, the year before they attained major league status. /(AJA)

Eddie Fisher — 1936- . RHP 1959-73 Giants, **White Sox**, Orioles, Indians, Angels, Cardinals 1538 ip, 85-70, 3.41

The 6'2" 200-lb University of Oklahoma graduate learned the knuckleball from Hoyt Wilhelm, and in 1965 the two teamed in the Chicago bullpen that set a record with 53 saves. That year Fisher led AL pitchers with 82 relief appearances and 15 relief wins, and saved 24, all career highs. He also pitched two shutout innings in the All-Star Game. Fisher again led the AL with 67 appearances in 1966, but he split the season between Chicago and Baltimore. Fisher had come to the White Sox in a 1961 trade that sent Billy Pierce and Don Larsen to San Francisco.

Fisher was known for his great Donald Duck impersonation. /(TJ)

Jack Fisher (Fat Jack) — 1919- . RHP 1959-69 Orioles, Giants, **Mets**, White Sox, Reds 1976 ip, 86-139, 4.06

With Baltimore in 1960, Fisher enjoyed his only winning season, going 12-11. That year he faced Ted Williams on September 28, allowing the Splendid Splinter to homer in his final ML at-bat. Almost a year later, on September 26, 1961, Fisher surrendered Roger Maris's 60th homer of the 1961 season. He pitched the Mets' first game at Shea Stadium (4/17/64), but was not involved in the decision as the Pirates won, 4-3. Fisher lost NL-highs of 24 in 1965 and 18 in 1967 for the Mets. /(RM)

Ray Fisher — 1887-1982. RHP 1910-17, 19-20 **Yankees**, Reds 1756 ip, 100-94, 2.82. *1 WS, 7.2 ip, 0-1, 2.35*

Fisher was a competent, consistent pitcher for the Yankees before the Babe Ruth era. The poised, studious righthander is best remembered as a college coach at Michigan University, and for the circumstances under which he left organized baseball. Fisher coached baseball (and, at first, freshman football, and young Gerald R. Ford) for 38 years, winning nine Big Ten championships.

He became the victim of the petulance and pettiness of Cincinnati owner Garry Herrman, and Commissioner Landis, often a capricious tyrant. Fisher, whose salary disputes had made him a target of the owners, asked to be released by the Reds so he could accept an offer from Michigan. Instead, he was blacklisted, dumped into the same group of suspended players as the Black Sox. Fisher was not accepted back into pro ball until late in life, becoming a spring training pitching instructor for the Braves in 1960, and the Tigers for 1963–65./(JK)

Carlton Fisk (Pudge) — 1947– . C 1969, 71- **Red Sox**, White Sox 2141 g, .271, 336 hr, 1166 rbi. *2 LCS, 7 g, .276, 2 rbi. 1 WS, 7 g, .240, 2 hr, 4 rbi*
☛ *Rookie of the Year—72. All-Star—72–74, 76–78, 80–82, 85. Gold Glove—72.*

One of the AL's premier catchers for almost two decades, Carlton Fisk overcame a series of serious injuries early in his career to establish himself as a marvel of durability at baseball's most taxing position. At the start of the 1989 season, Fisk's 1,838 games caught trailed only Bob Boone and Al Lopez in ML history, and his 282 HR as a catcher were exceeded only by Johnny Bench and Yogi Berra.

A true New Englander, Fisk was born in Vermont, attended the University of New Hampshire, and in January 1967 was the first-round draft choice of the Boston Red Sox, the fourth player chosen in the nation. When he arrived as Boston's full-time catcher in 1972, he already had a nickname (Pudge, from his childhood), and a trademark wad of tobacco that bulged inside one cheek. On the field, Fisk was an immediate star. He hit .293 with 22 HR and a league-leading nine triples in '72, won a Gold Glove, and became the first player ever to win the Rookie of the Year award unanimously. His average slipped to .246 in 1973 as he belted 26 more HR, and in 1974 he suffered the first major injury of his career, landing on the DL from June 28 until the end of the season with a broken collarbone. In 1975

Carlton Fisk (l.) with Boston, Roy Howell of the Blue Jays

Fisk reinjured himself in spring training and did not play until June, but he hit .331 in 79 games to help the Red Sox to the World Series.

Fisk found himself in the spotlight twice in the WS. In the 10th inning of Game Three, he collided with Ed Armbrister while chasing a bunt in front of home plate, but no interference was called, and the Reds rallied for the winning run. In Game Six, Fisk got his revenge, drilling a Pat Darcy pitch off the left-field foul pole for a 12th-inning, game-winning home run in what many consider the most dramatic game in WS history. Fisk's leaping gyrations down the first base line as he urged the ball to stay fair were recorded by NBC's television cameras, and placed the "reaction shot" into the vocabulary of baseball TV producers.

In 1977 Fisk hit .315 with 26 HR and 102 RBI and committed only four passed balls as he battled the Yankees' Thurman Munson for the distinction of being the AL's best catcher. Fisk started the All-Star Game in both 1977 and 1978, but the Yankees edged the Red Sox for the pennant and went on to win the WS each year. Injuries again curtailed Fisk's 1979 season (he played 91 games, mostly as a DH), and after a decent 1980 (.289, 18 HR) he stunned Boston fans by signing with the Chicago White Sox. The Red Sox' front office had blundered by failing to postmark his new contract in time, and Fisk became a free agent. With his change of Sox, Fisk flip-flopped his uniform number from 27 to 72, and in fairy-tale fashion, Chicago opened the 1981 season at Fenway Park. Playing against the Red Sox for the first time, Fisk hit a three-run, eighth-inning HR to win the game, 5–3.

In Chicago, Fisk has defied the aging process, accepting occasional assignments in the outfield, at first base, or as a DH, but playing most of his games at catcher. He hit .289 with 26 HR in 1983 to help the White Sox to their only AL West title, but hit only .176 in the ALCS as Chicago lost to Baltimore in four games. In 1984 he hit 21 HR but drove in only 43 runs, the fewest RBI ever for a player with 20 HR. Fisk hit only .238 in 1985, but recorded career bests in both HR (37) and RBI (107). Thirty-three of his 37 HR came as a catcher, eclipsing Lance Parrish's year-old AL record for the position. As a 40-year-old in 1988, he hit .277 with 19 HR in only 76 games. He missed much of the first half of 1989, but hit .293 with 13 HR and 68 RBI in 103 games. /(SCL)

Ed Fitz Gerald — 1924– . C 1948–59 Pirates, **Senators**, Indians 807 g, .260, 19 hr, 217 rbi

With the Senators in 1959, Fitz Gerald became the first ML player to hit into a triple play on Opening Day. In a 1953 game, the catcher turned a rare unassisted double play. He was one of seven brothers who barnstormed as the Traveling Fitz Gerald Basketball Team. /(RM)

Mike Fitzgerald — 1960– . C 1983– Mets, **Expos** 571 g, .241, 29 hr, 207 rbi

Fitzgerald homered off the Phillies' Tony Ghelfi in his first major league at-bat (9/13/83). As the Mets' starting catcher in 1984, he tied Jerry Grote's club record .995 fielding percentage and was named the Topps all-star rookie catcher. That December, the Mets sent him to the Expos with Hubie Brooks, Floyd Youmans, and Herm Winningham in the blockbuster trade for Gary Carter. Fitzgerald had trouble staying healthy as Carter's replacement in Montreal. He had shoulder and knee problems in 1985. He was batting a career-high .282 on August 1, 1986 when he broke a finger during a game at Shea Stadium—an injury that ended his season and bothered him for several years. /(JCA)

Al Fitzmorris — 1946– . RHP 1969–78 **Royals**, Indians, Angels 1277 ip, 77–59, 3.65

This switch-hitter began his career as an outfielder, and he hit a respectable .242 in the majors before the DH was introduced. The Royals took Fitzmorris from the White Sox in the expansion draft, and after four seasons of work as a reliever and spot starter, the good-fielding pitcher was sent down in 1973. Called back up in mid-season, he became a starter and went 8–3 with a 2.83 ERA. Fitzmorris was a reliable number-two starter for the next three seasons, winning 44 games as the Royals finally achieved respectability and won their first AL West title (1976). He was selected by the Blue Jays in the expansion draft after the 1976 season and was traded to the Indians for Alan Ashby and a minor leaguer. /(WOR)

Freddie Fitzsimmons (Fat Freddie) — 1901–1979. RHP 1925–43 **Giants**, Dodgers 3224 ip, 217–146, 3.51. 20 wins: 28 *3 WS, 25.2 ip, 0–3, 3.86.*
    Manager 1943–45 **Phillies** 102–179, .363

Fat Freddie Fitzsimmons "was from the old school," wrote Joe McGuff. "He knocked down line drives with his feet and legs, challenged batters and umpires and withstood the verbal explosions of John McGraw, the terrible-tempered manager of the New York Giants." The knuckle-curveballer led the NL with a .731 (19–7) winning percentage for the 1930 Giants. He again topped the league (and set a Dodger record) with an .889 (16–2) percentage in 1940.

Fred Fitzsimmons

As manager from mid-1943 to mid-1945, Fitzsimmons's Phillies were a flop. His *TSN* obit recalled that "he was one of the principals in the great tampering uproar in 1949 when he was a coach for the Giants and his old pal, Leo Durocher. The Braves claimed tampering, because the discussion of the Giants' job occurred while Fitzsimmons was still under contract to the Braves." Fitzsimmons and Durocher were fined by Commissioner Happy Chandler, who also suspended Fitzsimmons for a month. Fitzsimmons spent three years as GM of the National Football League Brooklyn Dodgers. /(TJ)

Max Flack — 1890-1975. OF 1914-25 Chicago (FL), **Cubs**, Cardinals 1411 g, .278, 35 hr, 391 rbi. *1 WS, 6 g, .263*

Flack's .974 lifetime fielding average was the best ever for a right fielder when he retired, and was only a point behind the record for all outfielders. He made it to the majors with the Chicago Whales of the Federal League in 1914-15, stealing 37 bases

each year. In 1915, when the Whales were league champions, that total ranked fourth in the league, and Flack's career-high .314 was fifth-best. The Cubs bought out the Whales after the FL folded. Flack spent the next six seasons as the Cubs' regular leadoff hitter, scoring 85 runs in 1920 for his personal NL high. He twice led NL outfielders in fielding, with very high averages for the time: .991 (1916) and .989 (1921).

When the Cubs lost the 1918 World Series, it was Flack's error in the third inning of the final game that let in the Red Sox' only two runs. Contrary to his record as listed in Macmillan's *Baseball Encyclopedia*, he did not have an RBI in the Series. /(SFS)

Ira Flagstead (Pete) — 1893-1940. OF 1917, 19-30 Tigers, **Red Sox**, Senators, Pirates 1218 g, .290, 40 hr, 450 rbi

A 5'9″ righthanded batter who hit for average more than power, Flagstead batted over .300 five times. A skillful fielder, he spent most of his career in centerfield, though the Tigers tried him at shortstop and second base in 1921. Flagstead holds the AL record, and is tied for the ML record for the most double plays started by an outfielder in a game, with three (4/19/26). /(EW)

Patsy Flaherty — 1876-1968. LHP-OF 1899-1900, 03-05, 07-08, 10-11 Louisville (NL), **Pirates**, White Sox, Braves, Phillies 1303 ip, 66-84, 3.10; 235 g, .197, 6 hr, 70 rbi. 20 wins: 04

Flaherty didn't stay long with any ML club, making seven moves in nine seasons. He lost a league-leading 25 games for the White Sox in 1903, giving up 338 hits. Chicago released him with a 1-2 record during the 1904 season. Picked up by the Pirates, he went 19-9, thus finishing 20-11 in his only winning season. Flaherty had dead ball era power and was sometimes used as a pinch hitter or in the outfield. /(JK)

Red Flaherty [John] — 1918- . *Umpire* AL 1953-73 *2 LCS 4 WS, 3 ASU*

An AL umpire for 21 years, Flaherty became involved in perhaps his most heated argument in Fenway Park in 1960 when he called Red Sox runner Don Buddin safe at the plate after the Tigers seemingly had caught him in a rundown. Flaherty ruled that the catcher had missed the tag. The Tigers countered that Buddin had run out of the baseline. Cal Hubbard, AL supervisor of umpires, happened to be in the stands that day. He supported Flaherty's call completely. /(RTM)

Vincent X. Flaherty — 1912–1977. *Writer.*

A nattily dressed night person, Flaherty worked for the Washington *Times-Herald* before going to the West Coast as a columnist for the Los Angeles *Examiner*. In the 1940s he was an early advocate of bringing a ML team to Los Angeles. /(NLM)

Mike Flanagan — 1951– . LHP 1975– **Orioles**, Blue Jays 2617 ip, 163–134, 3.89. *3 LCS, 16 ip, 2–1, 5.51. 2 WS, 19 ip, 1–1, 3.32*
☛ *Led League—w 79. Cy Young Award—79.*

After losing his first five major league decisions, Flanagan achieved a decade of dependable pitching. From 1977 to 1987, no AL pitcher started more games (334). His record was .500 or better each season from 1977 to 1984. His Cy Young season included the ML lead in wins (23–9). He tied for the league lead in shutouts, finished sixth in MVP voting, and was honored as Graduate of the Year by the Junior American Legion and Babe Ruth programs. He won the first game of the World Series, but lost Game Five when he was moved up in the rotation in a controversial move by manager Earl Weaver. Armed with a big-breaking curveball, an underrated fastball, and a great pickoff move, Flanagan suffered a severe knee injury in 1983 and a torn Achilles tendon in 1985. Struggling in Baltimore, Flanagan found new life after being acquired by Toronto during the 1987 stretch run. He had more wins (17) and innings pitched (208) against the Blue Jays than any other hurler. /(ME)

Joseph Flanner — Unk.–1924. *Writer.*

Flanner was editor of *The Sporting News* until he was named secretary to August Herrmann, chairman of the National Commission. He held his position until Judge Landis became baseball's first Commissioner in 1921. /(NLM)

Tim Flannery — 1957– . 2B-3B 1979–89 **Padres** 972 g, .255, 9 hr, 209 rbi. *1 LCS, 3 g, .500. 1 WS, 1 g, 1.000*

Flannery reached the Padres as a utility man in 1979, his second pro season. An intelligent and reliable player who made the most of limited ability, he was primarily a pinch hitter for the 1984 NL Champions; it was his grounder that eluded Cubs first baseman Leon Durham to start San Diego's winning rally in the deciding game of the LCS. Flannery batted .280 as a starter at second in 1985–86, but lost his job to Joey Cora in 1987, and Roberto Alomar in 1988. /(JCA)

Fred Fleig — 1908–1979. *Executive.*

Fleig broke into baseball in 1937 as business manager of a Cincinnati farm club for Warren Giles. He followed Giles into the NL and was secretary-treasurer of the league when he retired in 1978 after 28 years. /(NLM)

Bill Fleming [Leslie Fletchard] — 1913– . RHP 1940–44, 46 Red Sox, **Cubs** 442 ip, 16–21, 3.79

Effectively mixing his fastball and nice curve, the 6′ righthander won 18 at Hollywood and led the Pacific Coast League in strikeouts in 1940. But Fleming was a marginal wartime major leaguer, who in 1944 had a NL-high ten relief losses. /(EW)

Les Fleming (Moe) — 1915–1980. 1B 1939, 41–42, 45–47, 49 Tigers, **Indians**, Pirates 434 g, .277, 29 hr, 199 rbi

In his rookie 1942 season, Fleming hit .292 with 14 HR and 82 RBI as Cleveland's everyday first baseman, then took a job in a war-related industry. Expected to become a full-fledged star upon his return, he never matched his successful rookie year. /(EW)

Art Fletcher — 1885–1950. SS 1909–20, 22 **Giants**, Phillies 1529 g, .277, 32 hr, 675 rbi. *4 WS, 25 g, .191, 8 rbi.*
Manager 1923–26, 29 **Phillies**, Yankees 237–383, .382

Fletcher was John McGraw's shortstop for over a decade, providing the Giants with brilliant fielding, dependable hitting, and on-field leadership. A caustic, belligerent copy of McGraw during the game, off the field he was a non-profane, churchgoing family man. As the frustrated manager of four second-division Phillies teams, Fletcher's final gesture was the drawing of a caricature of umpire Bill Klem as a catfish, a comparison the jowly, heavy-lidded Klem loathed. Fletcher became Miller Huggins's assistant in 1927, and remained a Yankee coach until 1945. When Huggins died in 1929, Fletcher took over as interim manager, but refused all other offers to manage again. /(JK)

Elbie Fletcher — 1916– . 1B 1934–35, 37–43, 46–47, 49 Braves, **Pirates** 1415 g, .271, 79 hr, 616 rbi
☛ *All-Star—43.*

Line-drive-hitting, fancy-fielding, lefthanded Elbie Fletcher debuted with the 1934 Braves; he had attracted their attention by organizing a newspaper write-in campaign on his own behalf. Traded to Pittsburgh in June 1939, Fletcher batted .290 that

Art Fletcher

Elmer Flick — 1876–1971. OF 1898–1910 Phillies, A's, **Indians** 1484 g, .315, 47 hr, 756 rbi
☛ *Led League—rbi 00. Led League—ba 05. Hall of Fame—63.*

Largely unknown by modern fans, Flick was one of the great all-around performers at the turn of the century. In 1905 he won the AL batting title with a .306 average, the lowest mark to take the crown until Carl Yastrzemski's .301 in 1968. Flick narrowly missed the NL title in 1900, batting .378 to Honus Wagner's .381. After compiling a .344 lifetime average in the NL (1898–1901), Flick jumped to the Philadelphia Athletics, following Nap Lajoie, who'd gone a year earlier. When the Phillies obtained an injunction barring the jumpers from playing in Philadelphia, both Lajoie and Flick, an Ohioan, wound up in Cleveland.

Elmer Flick

year, had 104 RBI in 1940, drew the most walks in the NL in 1940 and 1941, and started in the 1943 All-Star Game. In 1944 Fletcher paced the Bainbridge, MD Naval Training Station team (which included ML veterans Dick Bartell and Buddy Blattner) in batting. /(TJ)

Scott Fletcher — 1958– . SS-2B-3B 1981– Cubs, White Sox, **Rangers** 997 g, .268, 17 hr, 302 rbi

Fletcher was considered a utility infielder by the Cubs, and was traded to the White Sox in 1983. Given the shortstop job in 1984, he batted .250 and played a solid defense. But with the arrival of Ozzie Guillen in 1985, Fletcher was left to shuttle around the infield, and was traded to Texas in November. He amazed skeptics in 1986 by putting together a 19-game July hitting streak, batting .300 for the season, and leading the Rangers with 34 doubles. He again topped Texas regulars in batting in 1987 (.287). /(RL)

In his first six seasons in Cleveland, Flick never batted below .297. The 5'6", lefthanded-hitting right fielder used a thick-handled bat, enabling him to get solid hits on inside pitches. On July 6, 1902, Flick became the first American Leaguer to hit three triples in one game, a feat he repeated in the NL. The speedster set a ML record by leading the AL in triples three consecutive seasons (1905–07). He also led the circuit in stolen bases twice (1904, 1906) and runs scored once (1906).

Following the 1907 season, Detroit manager Hughie Jennings offered Ty Cobb to Cleveland for Flick, but Cleveland declined the offer. The 21-year-old Cobb had just won his first batting title (.350), while the 31-year-old Flick managed .302. Cobb, however, was despised by his teammates. The likable Flick stayed in Cleveland. The rest of his career was plagued by a mysterious stomach ailment. He played just 99 more games over three seasons, but dragged down his lifetime average. Flick was elected to the Hall of Fame by the Veterans Committee in 1963. /(ME)

Curt Flood — 1938– . OF-3B 1956–69, 71 Reds, **Cardinals**, Senators 1759 g, .293, 85 hr, 636 rbi. *3 WS, 21 g, .221, 8 rbi*
☛ *All-Star—64, 66, 68. Gold Glove—63–69.*

Flood had a marvelous career that will always be marred by his misjudging of a fly ball in the seventh game of the 1968 World Series, and his suit against baseball that eventually led to free agency. The 5'9" Houston native played just eight games with Cincinnati before beginning his stellar 12-year stay with St. Louis in 1958. In 1964 he led the NL with 211 hits. He batted a career-high .335 in 1967.

In an act that Flood felt was "impersonal," the Cardinals traded him, Tim McCarver, Byron Browne, and Joe Hoerner to the Phillies on October 7, 1969, for slugger Dick Allen, Cookie Rojas, and Jerry Johnson. Flood balked at his trade to Philadelphia, which had a poor team and played its games in an old stadium, before usually belligerent fans in 1969. Flood fought the reserve clause. He first asked Commissioner Kuhn to declare him a free agent, and was denied. He filed suit on January 16, 1970, stating that baseball had violated the nation's antitrust laws. Even though he was making $90,000 at the time, Flood likened "being owned" to "being a slave 100 years ago." The case went to the Supreme Court, with former Supreme Court Justice Arthur Goldberg pressing his case. Goldberg agreed to work for expenses, which totaled nearly $200,000, before judgment was finally rendered. The Supreme Court

Curt Flood

upheld the District Court and Court of Appeals rulings favoring organized baseball.

Flood sat out 1970, but signed with the Senators in 1971 for $110,000. To get the rights to Flood, who was still bound by the reserve clause, Washington had to part with marginal players Greg Goossen, Jerry Terpko, and Gene Martin, none of whom would ever appear with Philadelphia. Flood played 13 games for Washington, hit a paltry .200, and retired in April. He later spent the 1978 season in the A's broadcasting booth with Bud Foster. /(WAB)

Jesse Flores — 1914- . RHP 1942-47, 50 Cubs, **A's**, Indians 973 ip, 44-59, 3.18

Released by the Cubs in 1942 because he had "nothing but a dink screwball," Flores pitched regularly for the A's in 1943-47. The Mexican's best game was an Opening Day two-hitter, which he lost 1-0. /(NLM)

Ben Flowers — 1927- . RHP 1951, 53, 55-56 **Red Sox**, Tigers, Cardinals, Phillies 168 ip, 3-7, 4.49

Flowers was a star athlete in the military during WWII, and had a brilliant minor league career. He set a since-surpassed AL record by relieving in eight consecutive Red Sox games in 1953. /(EW)

Jake Flowers [D'Arcy Raymond] — 1902-1962. 2B-SS-3B 1923, 26-34 Cardinals, **Dodgers**, Reds 583 g, .256, 16 hr, 201 rbi. *2 WS, 8 g, .071*

Flowers was a dangerous man to trade. When the Cardinals sent him to Brooklyn, his homer off Wee Willie Sherdel won his new team's first game against his former mates. Traded back to St. Louis, he homered off Brooklyn's Dazzy Vance the first time the clubs met. Sent back to Brooklyn, he hit a first-game homer off the Cardinals' Dizzy Dean. His ML career ended when a Paul Dean pitch broke his arm. *TSN* named him Minor League Manager of the Year in 1937. /(JK)

Doug Flynn — 1951- . 2B-SS-3B 1975-84 Reds, **Mets**, Rangers, Expos 1267 g, .238, 7 hr, 282 rbi. *1 LCS, 1 g, --*
☛ *Gold Glove—80.*

A weak hitter whose glove kept him in major league lineups for ten years, Flynn was one of four young Cincinnati players for whom the Mets traded Tom Seaver on June 15, 1977. /(CR)

Lee Fohl (Leo) — 1870-1965. C 1902-03 Pirates, **Reds** 5 g, .294, 0 hr, 3 rbi.
   Manager 1915-19, 21-26 **Indians**, Browns, Red Sox 713-792, .474

A catcher in only five ML games, Fohl was the owner and playing manager of Waterbury in the Eastern Association when the Indians hired him as manager in 1915. He finished second to the Red Sox by 2-1/2 games in 1918, but the next year, with the team in third place, he let his pitcher pitch to Babe Ruth instead of walking him. Ruth homered to win the game and Fohl was fired the next day. He was hired in 1921 by Bob Quinn to manage the Browns and came within one game of winning the 1922 pennant. George Sisler, the Browns' best player,

missed the entire 1923 season, but Fohl still had the club in third place when he was fired after 101 games. Quinn, then president of the Red Sox, hired him in 1924, but the Sox had sold off their best players and Fohl finished seventh once and last twice. /(NLM)

Hank Foiles — 1929- . C 1953, 55-64 Reds, Indians, **Pirates**, A's, Tigers, Orioles, Dodgers 608 g, .243, 46 hr, 166 rbi
☛ *All-Star—57.*

Foiles rode to the majors on the coattails of Herb Score, his Indianapolis batterymate in 1954. He batted .332 in the American Association that year. Foiles was a first-string ML catcher in only two seasons, including 1957, when he played a career-high 109 games and represented the last-place Pirates in the All-Star Game. /(ME)

Tom Foley — 1959- . SS-2B-3B 1983- Reds, Phillies, **Expos** 621 g, .254, 26 hr, 192 rbi

In high school, ambidextrous Tom Foley played shortstop righthanded and quarterback lefthanded. Unable to win an everyday job in the majors, his ability to play second, third, and short (though unspectacularly), and his value as a lefthanded pinch hitter got him into at least 100 games in four of his first six seasons. In spring training with the 1986 Phillies, he was knocked out cold sliding into a base on March 16 and had his wrist broken by a Roger McDowell pitch the next day, disabling him for more than a month. /(EW)

Tim Foli — 1950- . SS 1970-84 Mets, **Expos**, Giants, Pirates, Angels, Yankees 1677 g, .251, 25 hr, 499 rbi. *2 LCS, 8 g, .214, 4 rbi. 1 WS, 7 g, .333, 3 rbi*

The bespectacled Foli led NL shortstops in fielding as a Pirate in 1980, and AL shortstops as an Angel two years later. He paced NL shortstops twice each in double plays and total chances, and once in putouts. In 1982 his 14 walks set an AL record for the fewest received by a player in 150 or more games (broken by Ozzie Guillen three years later). Foli was the Mets' first draft pick in June 1968, and was traded with Ken Singleton and Mike Jorgensen to Montreal for Rusty Staub in 1972. The fiery Foli became the first Expo ever to hit for the cycle (4/21/76). He batted .333 in ten LCS and WS games for the World Champion 1979 Pirates. His older brother, Ernie, played minor league ball. Foli was a Ranger coach from 1985 to 1987. /(TJ)

Rich Folkers — 1946- . LHP 1970, 72–77 Mets, **Cardinals**, Padres, Brewers 422 ip, 19–23, 4.11

Folkers was best when used exclusively as a reliever, and his career year came with the 1974 Cardinals, when he went 6–2 with a 3.00 ERA. Traded to the Padres after the season in a three-way deal that also involved the Tigers, he became the subject of one of San Diego broadcaster Jerry Coleman's famous malaprops when Coleman reported that "Rich Folkers is throwing up in the bullpen." /(JFC)

Dee Fondy — 1924- . 1B 1951–58 **Cubs**, Pirates, Reds 967 g, .286, 69 hr, 373 rbi

The 6'3" lefthanded first baseman batted .376 to lead the Pacific Coast League in 1951, and thrice batted .300 in the majors. In July 1953, Fondy struck out six times in a Cubs' doubleheader, five times in one game. /(EW)

Lew Fonseca — 1899–1989. 1B-2B-OF 1921–25, 27–33 Reds, Phillies, **Indians**, White Sox 947 g, .316, 31 hr, 485 rbi.
    Manager 1932–34 **White Sox** 120–198, .377
☛ *Led League—ba 29* .

Though the 1929 AL batting champ had a distinguished playing career, his long-term contribution to baseball was pioneering the use of film to analyze and promote the game. Fonseca became interested in cameras while acting in "Slide, Kelly, Slide," a 1927 comedy starring Joe E. Brown. He used film to detect flaws in his players as manager of the Chicago White Sox (1932–34). Fonseca became director of promotions for both the AL and NL.

Versatile in the field and spectacular at the plate, Fonseca's only season as a regular at one position (first base with Cleveland) was 1929, and he responded by hitting .369. He topped the .300 mark six times, but had trouble staying healthy. He suffered a broken leg in 1928, and a broken arm in 1930. A torn ligament in his leg ended his career. /(ME)

Ray Fontenot — 1957- . LHP 1983–86 Yankees, **Cubs**, Twins 494 ip, 25–26, 4.03

Fontenot went 8–2 filling in for the injured Ron Guidry as a rookie on the 1983 Yankees, and the two Louisiana natives would often converse in French. The soft thrower was often injured himself, however, and never fulfilled the promise he had shown. /(ME)

Barry Foote — 1952- . C 1973–82 **Expos**, Phillies, Cubs, Yankees 687 g, .230, 57 hr, 230 rbi. *2 LCS, 3 g, .500. 1 WS, 1 g, .000*

Foote was Montreal's strong-armed starting catcher from his rookie 1974 season (when he recorded career highs of 60 RBI and .262) until 1977. On April 22, 1980, playing for the Cubs against the Cards, he had eight RBI, including a game-winning grand slam. Following his playing career he managed in the Yankee farm system. /(EW)

Forbes Field Pittsburgh Pirates 1909–1970. LF-365, CF-435, RF-300

Forbes Field was named for a British general of the French and Indian War, and most of its 35,000 seats were in a covered grandstand that extended from third base around home plate and into right field, while unfortunate fans in the upper left corner of the bleachers along the left field line could not see the batter. The park featured a huge foul territory behind home plate, an extremely hard infield, and spacious left and center fields contained by an ivy-covered brick wall. Lights were added in 1940, and during WWII a 32-foot-high Marine towered over the left field wall. Left field bullpens were added briefly to reduce the handicap facing Pirate sluggers Hank Greenberg and Ralph Kiner, and the area became known as both Greenberg Gardens and Kiner's Korner. No no-hitters were pitched at Forbes Field in 68 seasons, but it was the scene of Bill Mazeroski's Game Seven home run in the 1960 WS, and on May 25, 1935 Babe Ruth's final career home run was the first ball ever to clear the right field roof. The field is now the site of a University of Pittsburgh library and dorms, but home plate remains on display in its final location. /(SCL)

Dale Ford — 1942- . *Umpire* AL 1975–87 *2 LCS 1 WS*

Ford, who has also officiated basketball, was involved in two large controversies. During the 1981 season, he threatened to forfeit the second game of a White Sox-Angels doubleheader at Comiskey Park because of comments made by Chicago broadcaster Jimmy Piersall, which Ford said were inciting the 40,248 in attendance. In 1983 through union counsel Richie Phillips, Ford filed a lawsuit for an unspecified amount against Billy Martin for calling him "a stone liar" in an interview. /(RTM)

Dan Ford [Darnell Glenn, Sr.] (Disco Dan) — 1952- . OF-DH 1975–85 **Twins**, Angels, Orioles 1153 g, .270, 121 hr, 566 rbi. *2 LCS, 6 g, .273, 2 hr, 4 rbi. 1 WS, 5 g, .167, 1 hr, 1 rbi*

Unable to break into the A's outfield of Reggie Jackson, Joe Rudi, and Bill North, Ford was traded to the Twins after the 1974 season and immediately

Forbes Field

became a regular. His best season for Minnesota came in 1976, when he hit .267 with 20 HR, 86 RBI, 87 runs, and 17 steals. Traded to the Angels for 1979, he had his best season, with career highs of .290, 21 HR, 101 RBI, and 100 runs. He also homered in Games One and Two of the Angels' first LCS appearance, and batted .294 in the series.

Poor defensively, the right fielder led AL outfielders in errors in 1981 and was traded to the Orioles for Doug DeCinces. Ford was a semi-regular for two more years despite declining production. He came up lame after Game One of the 1983 LCS and had only one pinch-hit at-bat for the rest of the series. He played poorly in the World Series, but produced the winning run in Game Three when, with runners on first and third, Ivan DeJesus booted Ford's grounder.

Ford finished out his career with two more seasons as a Baltimore utility player. /(SFS)

Dave Ford — 1956- . RHP 1978-81 **Orioles** 155 ip, 5-6, 4.01

A solidly built, 6'4" Cleveland native, Ford threw a fastball, knuckle curve, changeup, and slider. In his ML debut, he shut out Chicago for 8-1/3 innings and won 1-0. Primarily a long reliever who'd get a

spot start, he appeared in a career-high 25 games in 1980. /(EW)

Hod Ford [Horace Hills] — 1897-1977. SS-2B 1919-33 Braves, Phillies, Dodgers, **Reds**, Cardinals 1446, .263, 16 hr, 494 rbi

Ford broke in with the Braves in 1919 while still attending Tufts University, foregoing his final year of college eligibility. A smooth fielder and timely hitter, he set the record (since broken) for double plays by a shortstop (128) with the Reds in 1928, as the team set a record for double plays (194) that lasted for 30 years. /(NLM)

Russ Ford — 1883-1960. RHP 1909-15 **Yankees**, Buffalo (FL) 1487 ip, 98-71, 2.59. 20 wins: 10-11, 14

While a semi-pro pitcher, Ford accidentally discovered that a scuffed baseball could be made to break sharply. He began intentionally doctoring the ball using emery paper, and disguised his pitches as spitballs, which were legal. The Canadian was brilliant as a New York rookie, going 26-6 in 1910. He followed with a 22-11 mark, but his effectiveness waned and chronic arm soreness developed. In 1912 he lost an AL-high 21. He had one resurgent season in 1914, leading the outlaw Federal League with a

.769 winning percentage (20–6). His brother Gene pitched seven games for the 1905 Tigers. /(JK)

Ted Ford — 1947– . OF 1970–73 Indians, **Rangers** 240 g, .219, 17 hr, 68 rbi

After failing to crack .200 in two trials with the Indians, Vietnam veteran Ford was installed as a regular in the Rangers' outfield in 1973. His 14 homers and 50 RBI did not make up for his .235 BA. /(MC)

Whitey Ford [Edward Charles] (The Chairman of the Board) — 1926– . LHP 1950, 1953–67 **Yankees** 3170 ip, 236–106, 2.75. 20 wins: 61, 63. *11 WS, 146 ip, 10–8, 2.71*

☛ *Led League—w 55, 61, 63. Led League—era 56, 58. Cy Young Award—61. All-Star—54–56, 58–61, 64. Hall of Fame—1974.*

They called Ford "The Chairman of the Board" for good reason. He was for more than a decade the star pitcher of a team that operated with corporate

Whitey Ford

efficiency, and his intelligence and confidence were on display whenever he was on the mound. In contrast to pitchers who dominated hitters with overpowering physical abilities, the 5'10" 180-lb lefthander controlled games with his mastery of the mental aspects of pitching and pinpoint control. Batters had to deal with his assortment of pitches: He mixed splendid changeups, marvelous curves, and a good fastball. He had one of the league's best pickoff moves, and he was an excellent fielder. And, like most successful businessmen, he was at his best when the pressure was greatest.

His most eye-catching statistics are his consistently low ERAs and his high winning percentage. In 11 of 16 seasons he was under a 3.00 ERA, and his worst was 3.24. His .690 winning percentage ranks third all-time and first among modern pitchers with 200 or more wins. Of course, he benefited from strong Yankee bat support, defense, and relief pitching, but his winning percentage was usually higher than the team's. He allowed an average of only 10.94 baserunners per nine innings and posted 45 career shutouts, including eight 1–0 victories.

After joining the Yankees in mid-season 1950, he won nine straight before a home run by Philadelphia's Sam Chapman gave him his only loss. In the WS, he pitched 8–2/3 innings without allowing an earned run to win the fourth game of a Yankee sweep. He spent 1951 and 1952 in the service, but returned to post 18–6 and 16–8 marks in 1953 and 1954.

His 18–7 record in 1955 tied him for most AL wins. He led in complete games (18) and was second in ERA (2.63). *TSN* named him to its annual ML all-star team. In the final month of the season, he pitched consecutive one-hitters. The following year he was even better, going 19–6, to lead the AL in winning percentage and ERA (2.47). Again he was named to the *TSN* all-star team. He won his second ERA crown in 1958 (2.01).

Through 1960, Yankee manager Casey Stengel limited Ford's starts, often resting him at least four days between appearances, and aiming him for more frequent use against better teams. In 1961 new manager Ralph Houk put him in a regular four-man rotation, and Ford led the AL in starts (39) and innings pitched (283) and earned the Cy Young Award with a 25–4 record, leading the ML in wins and percentage. Two years later, he again led in wins, percentage, starts, and innings pitched, with a 24–7 mark. At the time there was only a single Cy Young award for both leagues. Sandy Koufax won for 1963, but Ford was voted the top AL pitcher by

TSN. They opposed each other in both the first and fourth games of the '63 WS, with Koufax winning both times. In Game Four Ford lost a two-hitter on an unearned run.

The Yankees won 11 pennants in Ford's years with them. He ranks first all-time in WS wins (10), losses (8), games and games started (22), innings pitched, hits, bases on balls, and strikeouts. In the 1960, '61, and '62 Series, he pitched 33 consecutive scorelesss innings, breaking Babe Ruth's WS record of 29–2/3.

A fun-loving native New Yorker, Whitey formed a curious odd couple with Oklahoman Mickey Mantle. The two were a familiar duo in the Big Apple's nightclubs. They were inducted into the Hall of Fame together in 1974. /(FK)

Frank Foreman — 1863–1957. RHP 1884–85, 89–96, 1901–02 Chicago (UA), Kansas City (UA), Baltimore (AA), **Reds**, Washington (NL), Baltimore (NL), Giants, Red Sox, Baltimore (AL) 1726 ip, 97–93, 3.94. 20 wins: 89

Foreman won 23 games for Baltimore in 1889 and 97 over his 11-year ML career, throwing mostly fastballs. His main claim to fame was that he discovered future Hall of Fame lefthander Eddie Plank pitching at Gettysburg College. Foreman's brother, Brownie, pitched briefly in the ML. /(BC)

Mike Fornieles [Jose Miguel Torres] — 1932– . RHP 1952–63 Senators, White Sox, Orioles, **Red Sox**, Twins 1157 ip, 63–64, 3.96
☛ *All-Star—61.*

Fornieles had a spotty career as a starter/reliever, with a lifetime 18–31 record as a starter. But when the Cuban was used exclusively in relief by the Red Sox, he achieved success. In 1960 he went 10–5 and led the league with 14 saves (not then an official statistic) and an AL-record 70 appearances, and in 1961 he had a career-high 15 saves and made the All-Star team. /(SH)

Bob Forsch — 1950– . RHP 1974–88 **Cardinals**, Astros 2795 ip, 168–136, 3.76. 20 wins: 77. *3 LCS, 15 ip, 2–1, 3.52. 3 WS, 22 ip, 1–3, 7.36*

Only Hall of Famers Bob Gibson and Jesse Haines pitched more years or won more games for the Cardinals than Forsch. He won 20 games in 1977 and led the Cardinals staff in victories six times. Converted from a third baseman, he threw two no-hitters in the minors, then no-hit the Phillies in 1978 and the Expos in 1983. He and his brother, Ken, were the first brothers to toss ML no-hitters.

A power pitcher early in his career, Bob later

relied on a deliberate delivery, pinpoint control, and a changeup, mixed with a sinker and occasional fastball. He helped himself with his bat by becoming an excellent bunter with some home run power. He won *TSN*'s Silver Slugger Award in 1980 and 1987. /(FJO)

Ken Forsch — 1946– . RHP 1970–84, 86 **Astros**, Angels 2126 ip, 114–113, 3.37. *1 LCS, 8 ip 0–1, 4.15* ☛ *All-Star—76, 81.*

Ken Forsch and his brother Bob are the only brothers to hurl no-hitters (Ken's coming on April 7, 1979, against Atlanta) and only the third pair of brothers to win more than 100 games each. Ken coupled a forkball with his fastball to fashion a 16-year ML career. In 1976 he was named to the NL All-Star team as a reliever and finished the season with 19 saves for the Astros. In 1981 he was named to the AL team for his work as a starter with the Angels. /(FJO)

Terry Forster (Trees) — 1952– . LHP 1971–86 **White Sox**, Pirates, Dodgers, Braves, Angels 1105 ip, 54–65, 3.23. *2 LCS, 1 ip, 1–0, 0.00. 2 WS, 6 ip, 0–0, 0.00*

Forster was a phenom at 18, a glutton at 34. In between he notched 127 saves. Signed out of high school, he pitched just 10 games in A-ball in 1970, and was so impressive he made the White Sox the following April. In 1972 he broke a club record with 29 saves. In that last year before the DH rule, he batted .526; he was a .397 lifetime hitter. From 1971 to 1973 he hurled 138–1/3 innings without surrendering a home run. He was the AL Fireman of the Year in 1974, saving a league-high 24 games. His fastball was clocked at 94.9 mph that September 7, but by the next season he was on the shelf with a bad arm; most felt he had been overworked by manager Chuck Tanner. After going 2–12 in 1976, mostly as a starter, he was traded to Pittsburgh with Rich Gossage (whom Chicago had also made a starter) for Richie Zisk and Silvio Martinez.

In November of 1977, Forster became the first free agent ever signed by the Dodgers. He rebounded with 22 saves and a 1.94 ERA for the 1978 pennant winners, but had bone chips removed from his elbow after the World Series. He was sometimes effective from 1982 through 1986, constantly battling weight problems. His eating habits began attracting national attention. He was with the Braves when, in June 1985, *Late Night* host David Letterman made Forster a national celebrity by calling him "a fat tub of goo." /(RL)

Ray Fosse (Mule) — 1947– . C 1967–77, 79 **Indians**, A's, Indians, Mariners, Brewers 924 g, .256, 61 hr, 324 rbi. *3 LCS, 10 g, .200, 1 hr, 6 rbi. 2 WS, 12 g, .152, 1 hr, 1 rbi* ☛ *All-Star—70, 71. Gold Glove—70–71.*

Fosse was involved in one of the most celebrated plays in All-Star Game history. In 1970, his first season as a Cleveland regular, he established himself as one of baseball's best catchers, earning a spot on the All-Star team. With the score tied 4–4 in the 12th inning, Fosse blocked home plate with Pete Rose charging in. Rose barreled Fosse over to score the winning run. Never one to be stopped by injuries, Mule continued to play that year (though X-rays later revealed he had a fractured shoulder) until a broken index finger finally ended his season.

Fosse never again displayed the power and consistency he had shown in '70 (.307, 18 HR). He had been Cleveland's number-one pick in the first-ever June free agent draft (1965), chosen before Johnny Bench. Fosse was disabled five times in his career: while still in the minors in 1967; for most of 1969; for most of 1974 (hit by a pitch, pulled a side muscle, and then suffered a pinched nerve in his neck trying to break up a clubhouse fight); twice in 1976; and for all of 1978. And although it didn't put him on the DL, there was an odd incident in 1970: A cherry bomb thrown from the stands blew up by his foot, badly burning the arch of his foot and causing a shock. Always tough and determined, he stayed in the game, limping, was hit by a pitch, but played the next day.

Fosse, who had huge hands that were compared to ham hocks, was a Gold Glove winner in 1970 and 1971. He went on to catch for the 1973–75 pennant-winning A's, but the injuries took their toll and forced an early retirement. He later became an Oakland executive and broadcaster. /(ME)

Alan Foster — 1946– . RHP 1967–76 Dodgers, Indians, Angels, **Cardinals**, Padres 1026 ip, 48–63, 3.73

With Spokane of the Pacific Coast League in 1967, the Dodger bonus-baby pitched 1–0 no-hitters in consecutive appearances against Seattle and was tabbed "can't miss." After failure with the Dodgers and a trip to the AL, he had his most successful season with St. Louis in 1973 (13–9, 3.14). /(JCA)

Bill Foster [Willie] — 1904–1978. LHP-MGR Negro Leagues 1923–37 Memphis Red Sox, **Chicago American Giants**, Birmingham Black Barons, Homestead Grays, Kansas City Monarchs, Cole's American Giants 1544 ip, 150–70 ☛ *All-Star—33–34.*

Bill Foster—the younger half-brother of the Father of Negro Baseball, Rube Foster—was one of the finest lefthanded pitchers in Negro League history. He played most of his career with Rube's Chicago American Giants, and was an intelligent power pitcher with near-perfect control and a variety of pitches, all delivered with the same fluid motion. Occasionally, he would use a hesitation wind-up. Black all-star third baseman and manager Dave Malarcher once said, "Willie Foster's greatness was that he had this terrific speed and a great, fast-breaking curveball and a drop ball, and he was really a master of the change-of-pace. He could throw you a real fast one and then use the same motion and bring it up a little slower, and then a little slower yet. And then he'd use the same motion again, and Zzzz. He was really a great pitcher."

After a brief stay with the Memphis Red Sox in 1923, brother Rube enticed Willie to join his Chicago American Giants. For three years under Rube's tutelage, Willie learned the art of pitching. In 1926 he won 26 consecutive games, leading the Giants to the playoffs against the Kansas City Monarchs. He won the last two games 1–0 and 5–0 to win the league championship. In the Black World Series finale against the Bacharach Giants, he threw a 1–0 shutout.

In 1927 Foster posted a Negro League record of 18–3, and went 14–1 in the California Winter League. In a repeat BWS appearance against the Bacharach Giants, he won the opener 6–2, lost the fifth game (shortened to 6–1/2 innings due to darkness), lost the eighth game because of four fielding errors, and came back in the ninth game to win the championship.

After the 1929 season, Foster pitched a two-game series against an American League all-star team composed of players from the Tigers, Browns, Indians, and White Sox. He struggled in the first game, but followed with a shutout in the second contest, pitching eight innings of no-hit ball and striking out nine. Detroit slugger Charlie Gehringer told Foster after the series, "If I could paint you white I could get $150,000 for you right now."

Available box scores show Foster winning 11 of 21 confrontations with the legendary Satchel Paige. He also won six of seven games against white major leaguers. In 1933 he posted a complete-game victory in the first East-West all-star game, giving up seven hits and seven runs while striking out four. His last year in baseball was spent with a white semi-pro team in Elgin, IL, and a black team called the Washington Browns in Yakima, WA. He later

returned to his alma mater, Alcorn College, as baseball coach and dean of men. /(LL)

Eddie Foster (Kid) — 1888–1937. 3B-2B 1910, 12–23 Yankees, **Senators**, Red Sox, Browns 1498 g, .264, 6 hr, 446 rbi

The 5'6" Foster was widely regarded as the best hit-and-run man of his day. His clutch hitting deprived Eddie Plank of his last bid for a no-hitter. In Plank's final season, with the 1917 Browns, the 42-year-old pitcher had gone 8–2/3 innings without allowing Washington a hit. He walked a batter, and Foster doubled him home to end Plank's bid. /(JK)

George Foster — 1949– . OF 1969–86 Giants, **Reds**, Mets, White Sox 1977 g, .274, 348 hr, 1239 rbi. *4 LCS, 10 g, .242, 3 hr, 6 rbi. 3 WS, 13 g, .326, 6 rbi* ☛ *Most Valuable Player—77. Led League—hr 77–78. Led League—rbi 76–78. All-Star—76–79, 81.*

Foster excelled in track, football, and baseball at El Camino College in California, drawing the attention of the Giants, who made him their third pick in the January 1968 draft. It took seven seasons in the majors and minors, with two organizations, before Foster arrived with Cincinnati to stay. The 6'1" 180-lb outfielder soon became an important cog in the Big Red Machine of the 1970s.

Foster became a regular in 1975. A mediocre fielder at best, Foster had a strong but inaccurate arm. He was a better than average baserunner. But he made a name for himself as a powerful, productive hitter who had five of the best seasons of any player of his time. Foster's three consecutive RBI championships (1976–78) tied a ML record. In 1977, his MVP year, he hit .320 with 149 RBI and 124 runs and blasted 52 HR to become only the seventh NL player to hit 50 or more in a season. He hit three straight homers in a July 14 game that season, and his 31 road homers set the ML record for righthanded batters. In 1978 Foster again led the NL with 40 HR.

After eleven seasons and three World Series with Cincinnati, Foster was traded to the Mets in 1982. Signing him to a five-year contract worth over $10 million, the team's new owners, Nelson Doubleday and Fred Wilpon, showed their willingness to spend money to rebuild the Mets. He hit just 13 HR that year, 28 the next, and was considered a disappointment. Word got around among NL pitchers that he wouldn't lay off low curveballs, and he regularly struck out on curves in the dirt. Foster was released by the Mets in August of their World Championship 1986 season. The struggling veteran, hitting .227 at

George Foster

the time, claimed he was the victim of racism, but he failed to regain his stroke after the White Sox picked him up. He retired tied for tenth in career grand slams with 13. /(EW)

John B. Foster — 1863–1941. *Writer.*

Foster succeeded Henry Chadwick as editor of *Spalding's Guide* in 1908. He had been the state editor of the Cleveland *Press* until 1888. When the sports editor of the *Leader* became ill, Foster replaced him. In 1896 he moved to New York, where he worked for the *Evening Telegram* and *The Sun* and for the Consolidated Press Association. He served as sports editor of the *Telegram* for 15 years. He was secretary of the New York Giants from 1913 to 1919, then returned to *The Sun* until 1931. A member of the original rules committee, he was an authority on baseball rules, law, and administration. He was said to have answered more than 500,000 questions by mail on all phases of the game. /(NLM)

Pop Foster (Clarence) — 1878–1944. OF 1898–1901 **Giants**, Senators, White Sox 262 g, .281, 10 hr, 136 rbi

After a short ML career, Foster turned to coaching and physical education, where he achieved nationwide fame. He was director of athletics in army camps during WWI, physical director at Brooklyn Polytechnic Institute for five years, and in the physical education department at Princeton from 1924 until his death. /(BC)

Roy Foster — 1945– . OF 1970–72 **Indians** 337 g, .253, 45 hr, 118 rbi

A one-year wonder, Foster was second to Thurman Munson in 1970 AL Rookie of the Year voting, but was *TSN*'s AL Rookie Player of the Year (268, 23 HR, 60 RBI). He then played just two more mediocre seasons. /(ME)

Rube Foster [Andrew] — 1878–1930. RHP-MGR Negro Leagues 1902–26 Chicago Union Giants, Cuban Giants, Cuban X-Giants, Philadelphia Giants, Chicago Leland Giants, **Chicago American Giants** statistics not available
☞ *Hall of Fame—1981.*

Foster overcame childhood illness to become an outstanding pitcher, a shrewd manager, and the dominant executive in black baseball. As a 6'4" 200-lb teenager, he joined the Yellow Jackets, a traveling black team in Texas. John McGraw saw Foster during spring training of 1901 (or thereabouts) and wanted him and other blacks for his New York Giants. But, unable to use them, he instead asked Foster to tutor the Giants' pitchers. Christy Mathewson reportedly learned his "fadeaway" pitch (a screwball) from Foster.

Foster then joined the Chicago Union Giants, pitched a shutout in his first start, but soon lost his effectiveness. He regained his form while with a white semi-pro club in the Michigan State League, and defeated every team in the circuit. Because of his difficulties, he had become a keen student of the game, and a wily pitcher. By 1902 he was with the black Cuban Giants.

In 1903 Foster was the top black pitcher in the country. He pitched the Cuban X-Giants to the black championship, and was the winner in four of their five victories over the Philadelphia Giants in the Black World Series. The following year, he

Rube Foster

pitched the Philadelphia Giants to the title, and recorded both victories in a best-of-three series against the Cuban X-Giants.

It is difficult to distinguish fact from fiction in Foster's pitching career; he is credited with a 51–4 season early on. Documentation does exist for a 1904 no-hitter he tossed against the Camden, NJ team. He reportedly gained his nickname by defeating the Athletics' Rube Waddell in 1902, and is reputed to have fared well in duels with major league pitchers Chief Bender, Mordecai Brown, and Cy Young. Frank Chance called him "the most finished product I've ever seen in the pitcher's box," and Honus Wagner said he was "one of the greatest pitchers of all time . . .smartest pitcher I've ever seen . . ."

Foster began managing in 1907, when he guided the Chicago Leland Giants to a 110–10 record. Their record was 64–21–1 in 1908. In 1909 Foster challenged the Chicago Cubs to a series, which the Cubs won in three close games. Foster pitched the second game and took a 5–2 lead into the ninth inning, but lost 6–5. Mordecai Brown won the first and third contests. There is no record of any major league club coming forth to answer Foster's challenge in 1910, when his team went 123–6.

In 1911 Foster left the Lelands to form a partnership with Chicago businessman John C. Schorling. From this union came one of black baseball's strongest teams, the Chicago American Giants. They dominated both the Chicago semi-pro scene (regularly winning the championship) and national black baseball, capturing Negro League titles in 1914 and 1917 and sharing the 1915 championship with the New York Lincoln Stars. Competing against white major leaguers following the 1915 season, they won the California Winter League crown.

In the winter of 1919 Foster organized the first viable black major league, the Negro National League, which operated in the Midwest and the South from 1920 through 1931. He served as president of the new league until 1926, and ruled it completely. An Eastern counterpart was organized in 1923 and Black World Series between the two leagues were held from 1924 through 1927.

Foster continued to manage through 1925, and won the Negro National League's first three pennants (1920–22). He made use of psychology and speed, invented the bunt-and-run, and intimidated opponents. White major leaguers often attended his games to learn his tactics. Though he made few rules, he expected his players to follow them. He ran the games as he ran the NNL -in total control—and once hit a player across the head with his pipe for tripling after he was given the bunt sign.

Foster's last known public meeting was in 1926 with lifelong friends Ban Johnson and John Mc-Graw, through whom it is believed he was trying to schedule white major league teams to play his American Giants. Shortly thereafter he began to lose his mind, and spent his last four years in the Kankakee, Illinois State Hospital. /(MFK)

Rube Foster [George] — 1889–1976. RHP 1913–17 **Red Sox** 843 ip, 58–34, 2.35. *2 WS, 21 ip, 2–0, 1.71*

After Boston teammate Smoky Joe Wood taught him how to throw a fastball, the 5'7" Foster went 14–8 (1.65) in 1914 and 19–8 in 1915. He won two games and went 4-for-8 at the plate in the 1915 WS. Foster no-hit New York on June 21, 1916. /(EW)

Bob Fothergill (Fat) — 1897–1938. OF 1922–33
Tigers, White Sox, Red Sox 1105 g, .326, 36 hr, 582 rbi

Fothergill was an outstanding line-drive hitter more
famous for his girth than his hits. Charitably listed at
230, the 5′10″outfielder was sensitive about his size
and preferred Bob or Roy (his middle name) to Fat.
The stories were told in every dugout: Leo Durocher
once complained it was illegal to have two men in
the batter's box; during a crash fasting program,
Fothergill supposedly bit an umpire after a called
third strike; there were several accounts of his
shattering outfield fences in pursuit of fly balls. But
he could hit. In 1927, his top year, he batted .359
with 114 RBI for the Tigers. Eventually relegated to
pinch hitting, he led the AL with 19 in 1929. Of
those with more than 200 pinch-hit at-bats, only
Fothergill has posted a .300 career average. /(DB)

Steve Foucault — 1949– . RHP 1973–78 **Rangers**,
Tigers, Royals 496 ip, 35–36, 3.21

A catcher in the minors, Foucault switched to
pitching after suffering a knee injury. Hurling sidearm, overhand, and underhand, he was Texas's top
reliever from 1973 to 1975, recording all 12 Ranger
saves in 1974 and 52 lifetime. /(JCA)

Jack Fournier [Jacques Frank] — 1892–1973. 1B-OF
1912–18, 20–27 White Sox, Yankees, Cardinals,
Dodgers, Braves 1530 g, .313, 136, 859 rbi
☛ *Led League—hr 24.*

Purchased by the White Sox from the Red Sox in
1912, Fournier presented Clarence Rowland and a
half-dozen other managers with the dilemma of
what to do with this inept-fielding pure hitter.
Rowland solved that problem in 1916, a year after
Fournier had led the AL in slugging, by replacing
him at first base with the marginal Jack Ness.
Fournier hit .350 for the Yankees in limited duty in
1918 before they passed him off to the Cardinals.
Fournier led NL first basemen with 25 errors in
1920. After three productive years in St. Louis,
Fournier was dealt to Brooklyn on February 15,
1923. Fournier said he would quit the game rather
than leave St. Louis, but he ended his holdout and
reported to the Dodgers. Fournier had found his
spot, among an offensive unit that included Zack
Wheat, Milt Stock, and Zack Taylor. He turned in a
six-for-six performance on June 29 of that year, hit
.351, and made a league-high 21 errors. In 1924
Fournier led the NL with 27 HR, and in 1925 was
second to Rogers Hornsby with 130 RBI. /(RL)

Jack Fournier with the Braves

Dave Foutz (Scissors) — 1856–1897. RHP-1B-OF
1884–96 St. Louis (AA), Brooklyn (AA), **Dodgers** 1997 ip,
147–66, 2.84; 1135 g, .277, 32 hr, 547 rbi. 20 wins:
85–87
   Manager 1893–96 **Dodgers** 264–257, .507
☛ *Led League—w 86. Led League—era 86.*

Chris Von der Ahe, bumptious owner of the American Association St. Louis Browns, acquired Foutz
by buying the entire Bay City, MI franchise. Paired
with Bob Caruthers, the slender, 6′2″ Scissors
pitched the Browns to American Association championships from 1885 to 1887. Parisian Bob contributed 99 wins in those three seasons, Foutz 98. Foutz
won a league-leading 41 in 1886 (his third straight
year with an over-.700 winning percentage), in 504
innings, and recorded 11 shutouts. In 1887 Foutz
managed a mere 25 wins, but hit .357 in 65 games
as an outfielder and first baseman, positions he
played more frequently for the rest of his career.

Cashing in on his investment, Von der Ahe sold his ace righthanders to Brooklyn in 1888 for $13,500. With the hard-hitting Foutz at first base, Brooklyn won the 1889 Association championship, switched to the National League, and won another pennant in 1890. Foutz pitched more in 1892, recording his last 13 wins. In 1893 he became a playing manager, but in four years never moved the team higher than fifth.

As a pitcher, Foutz's .690 winning percentage is the second-highest career mark (tied with Whitey Ford) among retired pitchers, just behind the .692 of Bob Caruthers. /(ADS)

Art Fowler — 1922- . RHP 1954-57, 59, 61-64 **Reds**, Dodgers, Angels 1024 ip, 54-51, 4.03

As a 48-year-old player-coach on Billy Martin's 1970 Denver (American Association) team, Fowler saved 15 games and won 9, with a 1.59 ERA. He subsequently followed Martin as a pitching coach to several ML cities, including New York. Mostly a reliever during his playing days, Fowler won a career-high 12 games for the 1954 Reds. His brother, Jesse, pitched with the Cardinals 30 years before Art's ML debut. /(TJ)

Dick Fowler — 1921-1972. RHP 1941-42, 45-52 **A's** 1303 ip, 66-79, 4.11

Fowler anchored the Philadelphia Athletics' pitching staff in the late 1940s, but despite his splendid fastball and fine curve, he never had more than 15 wins. In 1945 he returned from the Canadian Army to no-hit St. Louis on September 9. Fowler was one of three A's pitchers to lose an AL-high 16 in 1946. /(EW)

Charlie Fox (Irish) — 1921- . C 1942 **Giants** 3 g, .429, 0 hr, 1 rbi.
    Manager 1970-74, 76, 83 **Giants**, Expos, Cubs 377-369, .505. First place: 71 *1 LCS, 1-3, .250*

Fox caught only three games for the Giants but began managing in their farm system at Class-D level and worked his way up to Triple-A. He served as a scout for the Giants and ML coach before replacing Clyde King as Giants manager early in the 1970 season. He led San Francisco to the Western Division championship the next year and was voted *TSN*'s ML Manager of the Year. A traditionalist with a fiery temper, Fox was later both GM and interim manager of the Expos and interim manager of the Cubs. /(BC)

Howie Fox — 1921-1955. RHP 1944-46, 48-52, 54 **Reds**, Phillies, Orioles 1108 ip, 43-72, 4.33

The 6'3" Fox attended the University of Oregon on a basketball scholarship for a year before signing with the Reds in 1943. His one winning season, 1950, came a year after his 6-19 mark made him the losingest pitcher in the majors. In December 1951 he was sent to the Phillies with Smoky Burgess in a seven-player deal. After pitching in the Texas League in 1955, he was stabbed to death while bouncing three young men from his tavern near San Antonio. /(NLM)

Nellie Fox [Jacob Nelson] — 1927-1975. 2B 1947-65 A's, **White Sox**, Astros 2367 g, .288, 35 hr, 790 rbi. *1 WS, 6 g, .375*
☛ *Most Valuable Player—59. All-Star—51-61, 63. Gold Glove—57, 59-60.*

The 5'10" 160-lb Fox was long one of the top AL second basemen. After an unimpressive 1948 rookie season, Fox was traded to the White Sox for catcher Joe Tipton. He became a vital member of the Go-Go Sox for 14 seasons, noted for his tobacco-chewing and aggressive play. He withstood injury and illness to establish a record for consecutive games at second base, playing 798 straight (August 7, 1956 through September 3, 1960). Teaming first

Nellie Fox

with Chico Carrasquel and then with Luis Aparicio, he gave the team strength up the middle. Hard work made him a reliable hitter (six .300-plus seasons) who rarely struck out. He led the AL in fewest strikeouts 11 times and he struck out only 216 times in 9232 career at-bats, the third-best percentage in ML history. In 1959, when the Sox won their first pennant in 40 years, he was AL MVP. The White Sox retired his uniform number, 2./(RL)

Pete Fox [Ervin] — 1909-1966. OF 1933-45 **Tigers**, Red Sox 1461 g, .298, 65 hr, 694 rbi. *3 WS, 14 g, .327, 6 rbi*

Fox was one of the AL's better outfielders, both offensively and defensively, and a mainstay of the strong Detroit teams of the mid-1930s. A semi-pro pitcher when the Tigers first spotted him, he was advised to concentrate on the outfield. Within three seasons, Fox had led the Texas League by hitting .357, and had arrived in Detroit. Always dangerous on the bases, he became a steady fielder with a good arm, and a good doubles hitter with occasional home run power. He hit over .300 each year from 1935 through 1937, had six doubles in the 1934 World Series, and was the top batter in the 1935 WS, getting ten hits (.385)./(EW)

Terry Fox — 1935- . RHP 1960-66 Braves, **Tigers**, Phillies 397 ip, 29-19, 2.99

A reliever with 59 career saves, Fox never had a losing ML season. He compiled a 1.41 ERA in 39 games for Detroit and surrendered Roger Maris's 58th homer in 1961. He recorded a 1.71 ERA in 1962./(TJ)

Bill Foxen — 1884-1937. LHP 1908-11 **Phillies**, Cubs 326 ip, 16-20, 2.56

Foxen's 7-7 as a rookie with the Phillies in 1908 turned out to be his best ML season. He annoyed umpires with his constant, open bickering during games./(NLM)

Jimmie Foxx (Double X, The Beast) — 1907-1967. 1B-3B-C 1925-42, 44-45 **A's**, Red Sox, Cubs, Phillies 2317 g, .325, 534 hr, 1921 rbi; 23 ip, 1-0, 1.59. *3 WS, 18 g, .344, 4 hr, 11 rbi*
☛ *Most Valuable Player—32-33, 38. Led League—ba 33, 38. Led League—hr 32-33, 35, 39. Led League—rbi 32-33, 38. All-Star—33-41. Hall of Fame—1951.*

One of the greatest power hitters in major league history, Foxx broke in as a catcher, won fame as a first baseman, and filled in elsewhere, including several turns on the mound.

Jimmie Foxx

Born at Sudlersville, MD, Foxx grew strong doing chores on his father's farm. At age ten, he had had enough of farm life, and tried to join the army. Rejected by the military, he turned to sports, especially his first love, track. He played high school baseball and was soon demonstrating the power which would make him famous. His power displays caught the attention of Frank "Home Run" Baker, who was managing Easton of the Eastern Shore League. After being invited for a tryout, Foxx soon became Baker's protege. Baker owed a favor to his old boss, Connie Mack, and recommended the youngster. Mack took the 17-year-old Foxx in 1925 and sat him next to him on the Athletics' bench for several seasons. Mack had the young Mickey Cochrane at catcher, so he converted Foxx to first base, where he became a regular in 1928.

Before long, Foxx was being called "the right-handed Babe Ruth." In virtually every AL park, there was a story to tell about a mighty Foxx homer. In Chicago, he hit a ball over the double-decked stands at Comiskey Park, clearing 34th Street. His gigantic clout in Cleveland won the 1935 All-Star Game. In Yankee Stadium, his blast high into the left field upper deck had enough power to break a seat. In St. Louis, his ninth inning blast in Game Five of the 1930 Series just about clinched it for the A's. In Detroit, he hit one of the longest balls ever, way up into the left field bleachers.

At bat, Foxx presented a menacing picture. A strong, powerful man, he held the bat at the end and stood fairly deep in the batter's box, using a wide stance and a full stride into the ball. As the pitch approached, his powerful arm muscles flexed visibly before he hit the ball. Like many sluggers, Foxx struck out often, and he led the AL seven times.

Perhaps more impressive than his homers was his record as an RBI man. Like Babe Ruth and Lou Gehrig, he drove in over 100 runs in 13 seasons. Also hitting for average, he won the Triple Crown in 1933 (.356, 48 HR, 163 RBI), one of three seasons he led the league in RBI; his best RBI mark was 175 in 1938, when he would have captured his second Triple Crown if not for Hank Greenberg's 58 HR. He was the HR champ four times despite competition from Ruth, Gehrig, Greenberg, and DiMaggio.

In 1932 Foxx hit 58 homers; he might have hit more than 60 if not for a spell in August when he suffered from an injured wrist. Five times he hit the right field screen in St. Louis; the screen was not there when Ruth hit 60 HR in 1927. Also in 1932, a screen that Ruth hadn't had to contend with was erected in left field in Cleveland. Reportedly, Foxx hit that at least three times.

Foxx never made big money with the financially troubled Athletics, and he had to be unloaded to Tom Yawkey's Boston Red Sox, where he was paid well. A good-natured and well-liked man, he became an immediate favorite. He also took a young slugger under his wing. "I truly loved Foxxie," said Ted Williams some 40 years later.

Foxx was sent to the Cubs in 1942. He retired in 1943, but came back to play a few games during WWII with the Cubs and Phillies. His exceptionally strong throwing arm even enabled him to pitch in nine games for the Phillies in 1945, including two starts. The BBWAA elected him to the Hall of Fame in 1951.

A friend to all, Double X was always picking up the check. He drank heavily, saw several business ventures fail, and what little money he had made in baseball disappeared. He managed in the minors, coached at Minneapolis (American Association), and took a turn in the Red Sox radio booth in 1946. In July 1967, at age 59, he choked to death on a piece of meat while dining with his brother. Foxx is still ninth on the all-time HR list (534), sixth in RBI (1921), and fourth in slugging percentage (.609). /(EW)

Joe Foy — 1943–1989. 3B 1966–72 **Red Sox**, Royals, Mets, Senators 716 g, .248, 58 hr, 298 rbi

Foy was *TSN* Minor League Player of the Year and International League MVP in 1965. A hustling infielder with fair home run power, he twice led AL third basemen in double plays while with Boston but also twice led them in errors. The World Champion Mets traded the promising Amos Otis to secure Foy as their regular third baseman in 1970, but his skills eroded prematurely, due in part to a substance abuse problem. /(JCA)

Paul Foytack — 1930– . RHP 1953, 55–64 **Tigers**, Angels 1498 ip, 86–87, 4.14

Though the strong-armed Foytack had control problems early on, he ultimately became a mainstay of the Tiger staff. From 1956 through 1959, he twice won 15, and twice 14. In '56 he led the AL with 142 walks, but also struck out a career-high 184. Traded to the Angels in mid-1963, Foytack set a ML record against the Indians on July 31 when he allowed four consecutive home runs to Woodie Held, Pedro Ramos, Tito Francona, and Larry Brown in one inning. /(JL)

Ken Frailing — 1948– . LHP 1972–76 White Sox, **Cubs** 218 ip, 10–16, 3.96

Frailing appeared briefly with the White Sox before going to the Cubs in a 1973 trade for Ron Santo. He was a reliever and spot starter for two seasons prior to a career-ending 1976 shoulder injury. /(JCA)

Earl Francis — 1936– . RHP 1960–65 **Pirates**, Cardinals 406 ip, 16–23, 3.77

Francis was born in Slab Fork, WV. His career was delayed four years by Air Force service. He won nine and was second to Bob Friend on the Pirates with 121 strikeouts in 1962, his best ML year. /(ME)

Ray Francis — 1893–1934. LHP 1922–23, 25
Senators, Tigers, Yankees, Red Sox 337 ip, 12–28, 4.65

In 1922 Francis went 7–18 for the sixth-place
Senators (including an 0–3 relief mark); his 4.28
ERA was the best of his career. /(JFC)

John Franco — 1960– . LHP 1984– **Reds** 528 ip,
42–30, 2.49
☛ *All-Star—86–87, 89.*

Franco only had one ERA below 4.00 in the minors,
but the hard-throwing Brooklyn native advanced to
the ML nonetheless, where he emerged as an overpowering bullpen stopper for the Reds. Originally
drafted by the Dodgers, Franco was traded to the
Reds with one other minor leaguer for Rafael
Landestoy in 1982. He debuted in 1984, posting a
2.64 ERA in 54 appearances for Cincinnati, and in
1985 Franco was the lefthanded set-up man for Ted
Power, leading the NL with 12 relief wins and saving
12 more games on his own. Franco has been the
Reds' lone closer since 1986, recording 29, 32, and
39 saves in 1986–88, and, thanks to the presence of
Rob Murphy and later Rob Dibble in the Reds
bullpen, seldom enters a game before the ninth
inning. In 1989 Franco enjoyed yet another outstanding season, although he tailed off in the second
half. /(SCL)

Julio Franco — 1961– . SS-2B 1982– Phillies,
Indians, Rangers 1064 g, .298, 58 hr, 524 rbi
☛ *All-Star—89.*

One of five players sent from Philadelphia to Cleveland for Von Hayes in 1982, Franco became one of
the best offensive middle infielders of the 1980s.
Some said the Dominican's immaturity made him a
divisive presence during his six years with the
Indians, but he was an easy target on losing teams
with his weak defense and flamboyant style. Hitting
from a distinctive knock-kneed stance with his bat
wrapped high behind his ear, he earned raves in
1985 when he drove in 90 runs, taking advantage of
a very high 244 opportunities with runners in
scoring position. Franco batted .303 or better in
1986–88, but the Indians continued to lose despite
high expectations (one national magazine picked
them to win the WS in 1987).

Franco led AL shortstops in errors in 1984 and
1985, but made fewer after his fielding percentage
was used against him in arbitration hearings. His
powerful bat only partly compensated for his lack of
range, and he gained a reputation of being unable to
make the big play defensively. On April 20, 1985,
he disappeared for two days in the Bronx, later
saying he had been ill at the home of a friend who
had no phone. On June 8, 1986, he left Cleveland

Stadium without permission just before a game after
fighting with his wife. "I would have let him go if he
had asked," said manager Pat Corrales, always a
Franco booster.

In May 1985 the Indians acquired shortstop
Johnnie LeMaster and asked Franco to move to
second base. Franco balked at taking the job from
his friend Tony Bernazard, and LeMaster was sent
packing three weeks later. Franco was finally moved
to second base in 1988 after Corrales was fired and
Bernazard was traded. Franco was traded to Texas
for Pete O'Brien, Jerry Browne, and Oddibe Mc-
Dowell before the 1989 season. He emerged as a
Rangers team leader and mentor to Rafael Palmeiro
and Ruben Sierra. Franco hit .316 with 92 RBI and
stole 21 bases in 24 attempts. /(JCA)

Terry Francona — 1959– . 1B-OF 1981– **Expos**,
Cubs, Reds, Indians 705 g, .274, 16 hr, 143 rbi. *1 LCS,
2 g, .000*

The son of long-time ML player Tito Francona,
Terry was *The Sporting News* College Player of the
Year at the U. of Arizona in 1980, and was the
Expos first-round draft pick in the 1980 free agent
draft. A line drive hitter with little power, Francona
played less than two seasons in the minors, and hit
.352 at Denver (American Association) in 1981 to
earn a promotion to Montreal. With the Expos, he
spent half of 1982 and half of 1984 on the DL, and
hit .267 in 1985 before being released. He played
single seasons with the Cubs and Reds in 1986–87,
then signed a minor league contract with the Indians
for 1988, and hit .311 after joining the parent club
in mid-season. /(SCL)

Tito Francona — 1933– . OF-1B 1956–70 Orioles,
White Sox, Tigers, **Indians**, Cardinals, Phillies, Braves,
A's, Brewers 1719 g, .272, 125 hr, 656 rbi

The standout mark in Francona's career is his .363
average in 1959. Platooned with Jimmy Piersall in
the outfield and Vic Power at first base, and often
used as a pinch hitter, the lefthanded batter did not
qualify for the batting title. He was later a full-time
starter in the outfield and at first base for the
Indians. He led the AL with 36 doubles in 1960.
After leaving Cleveland following the 1964 season,
Francona journeyed through baseball as a "supersub." He led the AL with 15 pinch hits in 1970. His
son Terry also played for the Indians, among
others. /(ME)

Fred Frankhouse — 1904– . RHP 1927–39
Cardinals, **Braves**, Dodgers 1888 ip, 106–97, 3.92
☛ *All-Star—34.*

Frankhouse won ten or more games each year from
1933 through 1937. In 1934, his All-Star year,
Frankhouse notched a career-high 17 victories for

the Braves. With Brooklyn in 1937, the curveballer outdueled Carl Hubbell to snap the latter's record 24-game winning streak. /(TJ)

Herman Franks — 1914- . C 1939-41, 47-49 Cardinals, **Dodgers**, Phillies, Giants 190 g, .199, 3 hr, 43 rbi. *1 WS, 1 g, .000.*
    Manager 1965-68, 77-79 **Giants**, Cubs 605-521, .537

A graduate of the University of Utah, Franks was a weak-hitting backup catcher for several NL teams. He scouted for the Giants for a dozen years, then became manager of their Salt Lake City club in 1961. He managed the Giants to four straight second-place finishes, 1965-68. He was also credited with straightening Willie Mays's financial affairs, which were a mess when Franks arrived in San Francisco. After leaving the Giants, he had a successful business career and formed a group that tried to buy the Yankees in 1972. He came out of retirement to manage the Cubs for three seasons beginning in 1977 as a favor to his friend, Cubs GM Bob Kennedy. /(NLM)

Chick Fraser [Charles Carrolton] — 1871-1940. RHP 1896-1909 Louisville (NL), Cleveland (NL), **Phillies**, A's, Braves, Reds, Cubs 3356 ip, 177-212, 3.68. 20 wins: 99, 01

Fraser was a hawk-nosed pitcher who threw a no-hitter in 1903 for the Phillies. He twice won 20 games, but he also led his league in walks three times. He became a coach with masterful control of the fungo bat. Fraser was the brother-in-law of Hall of Famer Fred Clarke; while with Louisville, the two had taken sisters as brides. They were reunited in Pittsburgh when Clarke signed Fraser as a scout. Fraser later scouted for the Dodgers and Yankees. /(JK)

Willie Fraser — 1964- . RHP 1986- **Angels** 467 ip, 26-30, 4.45

Fraser was the Angels' first-round selection in the June 1985 draft. He joined their starting rotation when Kirk McCaskill and John Candelaria were sidelined in 1987, and went 10-10 (3.92). His 5.41 ERA in 1988 was largely attributable to the 33 home runs he allowed -the most by any AL pitcher. The Yankees reached him for five HR that August 16, though California held on to win the game 15-6. On August 10, 1988, Fraser pitched a one-hitter against Seattle, winning 2-1. The one hit was a homer, by Alvin Davis. /(JCA)

Harry Frazee — 1881-1929. *Executive.*

The man who sold Babe Ruth to the Yankees for $100,000 and a $300,000 loan, Frazee was a theatrical producer who bought the World Champion Red Sox for $400,000 in 1917 and sold the last-place team for $1.5 million in 1923. Often when he needed money to cover his theatrical investments, he would sell off his best players, frequently to the Yankees. In the middle of the 1919 season, he sold pitcher Carl Mays, who had left the team, to New York. AL president Ban Johnson voided the deal, insisting Mays should have been suspended and not available for sale or trade. The Yankees went to court and won, causing a rift between club owners that was not healed until Johnson resigned nine years later. Meanwhile, Frazee had contributed Everett Scott and Herb Pennock to the budding Yankee dynasty. /(NLM)

George Frazier — 1954- . RHP 1978-87 Cardinals, **Yankees**, Indians, Cubs, Twins 676 ip, 35-43, 4.20. *2 LCS, 7 ip, 1-0, 2.45. 2 WS, 6 ip, 0-3, 11.12*

Frazier, who spent most of his career as a set-up reliever, is best known for tying the World Series record for losses with three for the Yankees in 1981. He also pitched in the 1984 LCS for the Cubs and the 1987 WS for the Twins. Frazier had a career-high eight saves for the 1983 Yankees. /(EG)

Vic Frazier — 1904-1977. RHP 1931-34, 37, 39 **White Sox**, Tigers, Braves 579 ip, 23-38, 5.77

Frazier's 1937 homesickness created a roster spot for Braves rookie Jim Turner. Turner responded with 20 wins, seven more than Frazier had collected in his top season (1931 with Chicago). /(TJ)

Johnny Frederick — 1902-1977. OF 1929-34 **Dodgers** 805 g, .308, 85 hr, 377 rbi

Frederick had a great rookie season in 1929, hitting .328, with 24 homers and a rookie record 52 doubles. Known for his extraordinary pinch hitting, in 1932 he connected for six pinch homers, breaking a 19-year-old record. /(WAB)

Roger Freed — 1946- . OF-1B 1970-72, 74, 76-79 Orioles, **Phillies**, Reds, Expos, Cardinals 344 g, .245, 22 hr, 109 rbi

The renowned minor league slugger hit 42 home runs for Denver (American Association) in 1976 but only 22 in parts of eight ML seasons. In 1971 with the Phillies, his only season as a ML regular, Freed hit .221. /(JCA)

Andrew Freedman — Unk.–1915. *Executive.*

Perhaps the most hated team owner in baseball history, Freedman owned the New York Giants from 1895 to 1902. He conspired unsuccessfully with John T. Brush in 1901 to create a trust in which all NL teams would be pooled and owned through shares held by the club owners. Upon his death, *The Sporting News* said, "He had an arbitrary disposition, a violent temper, and an ungovernable tongue in anger which was easily provoked and he was disposed to be arbitrary to the point of tyranny with subordinates." The Giants floundered during his regime and attendance dwindled. An influential Tammany Hall politician, he used his political clout to tie up possible sites where an AL team might play in New York until the peace treaty between the leagues in 1902. /(NLM)

Bill Freehan — 1941– . C-1B 1961, 63–76 **Tigers** 1774 g, .262, 200 hr, 758 rbi. *1 LCS, 3 g, .250, 1 hr, 3 rbi. 1 WS, 7 g, .083, 2 rbi*
☛ *All-Star—64–73, 75. Gold Glove—65–69.*

The Tigers signed Freehan, a University of Michigan baseball and football star, for a $100,000 bonus in 1961. Two years later the Detroit native became their regular catcher and held the position for 14 seasons.

Freehan showed signs of becoming the league's top catcher in 1964, his first and only season as a .300 hitter, and his first as an All-Star. That began a streak of ten straight years representing the AL, seven of those as a starter. After two seasons of hitting .234, the righthanded hitter matured in 1967, finishing third in MVP voting after leading the Tigers to within one game of the AL title. In 1968 the quiet leader reached career highs with 25 HR and 84 RBI, capping off the season by catching Tim McCarver's foul pop for the final out in Game Seven of the World Series triumph in St. Louis. A batter who crowded the plate, he was hit by pitches 24 times that year—then a league record—including three HBP in one game on August 16.

Freehan never matched his 1968 offensive stats, though he had a three home run game in Boston in August 1971. Freehan was outstanding behind the plate. The five-time Gold Glove recipient tied a record with 19 putouts in a 1965 contest. In 1968 he set an AL record for most putouts and chances in a year. When he retired, Freehan held the ML career marks for most chances, most putouts, and highest fielding average for a catcher. He is among the Detroit top ten in six offensive categories. He wrote *Behind the Mask,* a diary of the 1969 season. /(CC)

Bill Freehan

Buck Freeman [John Frank] — 1871–1949. OF-1B 1891, 98–1907 Washington (AA), Washington (NL), Braves, **Red Sox** 1126 g, .294, 82 hr, 713 rbi. *1 WS, 8 g, .281, 4 rbi*
☛ *Led League—hr 99, 03. Led League—rbi 02–03.*

This 5'11" 160-lb slugger preceded Babe Ruth by a generation, but could have been the prototype for the future home run champion. A lefthanded pitcher converted to the outfield because of his outstanding hitting, Freeman was one of the premier power hitters of baseball's dead-ball era.

In his first full ML season, 1899, Freeman hit 25 home runs for Washington to lead the National League. This total, only two fewer than Ned Williamson's record of 27 in 1884, was not surpassed until Ruth hit 29 in 1919. Moving to the Red Sox of the newly formed American League in 1901, he finished second in HR for two years before leading with 13 in 1903. (Freeman and Sam Crawford are the only players to have led both the AL and NL in home runs.) In both 1902 and 1903, Freeman was the AL leader in RBI.

Buck Freeman

Strong-armed but erratic in the field, Freeman was tried at first base, but was at his best in right field. His heavy hitting, especially in clutch situations, carried the Red Sox to two pennants (1903–04), and victory in the first modern World Series, in 1903. /(JL)

Hersh Freeman (Buster) — 1928– . RHP 1952–53, 55–58 **Red Sox, Reds,** Cubs 359 ip, 30–16, 3.74

Like many relievers, Freeman shone briefly, then faded. The big fireballer failed in three trials with the Red Sox but became a star in the Reds' bullpen. In 1956 he saved 18 and led the NL with 14 relief wins. That season he won three games within a 24-hour period, receiving credit for both victories in a twi-night doubleheader and then winning an afternoon game the next day. /(JK)

Marvin Freeman (Starvin' Marvin) — 1963– . RHP 1986, 88– **Phillies** 71 ip, 4–3, 5.22

The 6'6" 200-lb Freeman looked promising in his 1986 call-up, going 2–0 with a 2.25 ERA. He has pitched poorly at every level since then, although he

threw a 6–0 no-hitter against Richmond on July 28, 1988 for the Maine Guides (International League). He went on the DL early in 1989 with a strained right triceps muscle. /(JFC)

Gene Freese (Augie) — 1934– . 3B-2B 1955–66 **Pirates,** Cardinals, Phillies, White Sox, Reds, Astros 1115 g, .254, 115 hr, 432 rbi. *1 WS, 5 g, .063*

Rookie siblings Gene and George Freese teamed up on the 1955 Pirates and even battled for the same position. Both played third base, while Gene, seven years the junior, also played second base and turned in the better season (.253, 14 HR, 44 RBI). Shaky fielding offset his powerful bat. He played for five teams in four years (1958–61), and had his best season (.277, 26 HR, 87 RBI) for the 1961 NL Champion Reds. Freese lost everyday status after suffering a broken ankle in March 1962. He ranks among the all-time leaders with nine pinch homers, including two consecutive in April 1959. /(ME)

Jim Fregosi — 1942– . SS-3B-1B 1961–78 **Angels,** Mets, Rangers, Pirates 1902 g, .265, 151 hr, 706 rbi.
  Manager 1978–81, 86–87 **Angels,** White Sox 359–385, .483. First place: 79 *1 LCS, 1–3, .250*
☛ *All-Star—64, 66–70. Gold Glove—67* .

Fregosi was the premier power-hitting shortstop in the AL during the 1960s and the first and only star of the expansion California Angels in the late 1960s. During his playing days, he was known as a cheer-leader and was pegged as a future manager by many observers. In New York, however, Fregosi was simply the disappointing player the Mets received in the Nolan Ryan trade. Fregosi is one of the few players to hit for the cycle twice, once on July 28, 1964, and again on May 20, 1968. He had his best year in 1970, when he hit established career highs for homers (22), RBI (82), and runs (95) while hitting .278. He never regained his earlier form. After being sent to the Mets for four players, including Ryan, in December of 1971, Fregosi spent time with the Rangers and the Pirates. After 20 games with the Pirates in 1978, he was offered the manager's job with the Angels. In his first full season at the helm in 1979, he guided the Angels to the AL West title, the first pennant in their history. He later managed the White Sox in 1986–87. /(SEW)

Howard Freigau (Ty) — 1902–1932. 3B-SS-2B 1922–28 Cardinals, **Cubs,** Dodgers, Braves 579 g, .272, 15 hr, 226 rbi

Freigau was an early Big Ten basketball star at Ohio State. A utility man for the most part, he spent one year, 1926, as the Cubs' third baseman. /(JK)

Dave Freisleben — 1951- . RHP 1974-79 **Padres,**
Indians, Blue Jays 866 ip, 34-60, 4.29

Freisleben was the Padres' top pitching prospect
when he joined them in 1974 after compiling a
40-20 record in three minor league seasons.
Though he pitched well in his first few ML years, he
never had a winning record. He retired with 430
strikeouts and 430 walks. /(JCA)

Tony Freitas — 1908- . LHP 1932-36 A's, **Reds**
518 ip, 25-33, 4.48

The 5'8" southpaw had a 12-5 rookie year with the
A's in 1932. With the Reds on July 1, 1934, he lost
a thrilling 17-inning duel to Dizzy Dean of the
Cardinals. Freitas was the winningest lefthander in
minor league history, with 342 career victories,
mostly for Sacramento (Pacific Coast League), and
was selected by the Society of American Baseball
Research in 1984 as the all-time best minor league
pitcher. /(LRD)

Jim French — 1941- . C 1965-71 **Senators** 234 g,
.196, 5 hr, 51 rbi

French was a light-hitting backup catcher whose fine
batting eye and ability to throw out baserunners
weren't enough to keep him in the lineup. He was
hampered by a 1966 leg injury, and was most used
in 1969 and 1970, when he had more walks than
hits each season. A horse named after French
finished second in the 1971 Kentucky Derby and
Belmont Stakes. /(WOR)

Larry French — 1907- . LHP 1929-42 Pirates, **Cubs,**
Dodgers 3152 ip, 197-171, 3.44. *3 WS, 15 ip, 0-2, 3.00*
☛ *All-Star—40.*

In the 1930s, only Carl Hubbell worked more
innings than Larry French's 2,481. The rugged
lefthander appeared in more than 40 games seven
straight years, beginning with a league-high 47 in
1932. He led the NL in starts the next year, his
third straight as league leader in hits allowed. French
recorded 40 career shutouts, leading the NL in 1935
and 1936, his first two seasons with the Cubs. He
ignited Chicago's 21-game winning streak to capture
the 1935 NL pennant, winning five in that stretch.
He won 18 games three times, and lost 19 for the
1938 Cubs. French finished his career brilliantly,
leading the NL in winning percentage for the 1942
Dodgers (15-4, .789). He joined the Navy in 1943,
retiring in 1969 as a captain. /(ME)

Larry French

Walter French (Fitz) — 1899-1984. OF 1923, 25-29
A's 398 g, .303, 2 hr, 109 rbi. *1 WS, 1 g, .000*

An All-American halfback at West Point, French
left in 1922 to play with the Rochester Jeffersons of
the NFL. He tried baseball the next year, and spent
six seasons as a substitute outfielder and pinch
hitter/runner. In 1925 he played both football
(Pottsville Maroons) and baseball at the major
league level. /(LRD)

Benny Frey — 1906-1937. RHP 1929-36 **Reds,**
Cardinals 1160 ip, 57-82, 4.50

A sidearm pitcher with a sweeping motion that was
effective against righthanded hitters, Frey spent all
but one month (in 1932) of his ML career with the
Reds. He led the NL in losses (18) as a rookie in
1930. When the Reds sent him down to Nashville in
1937, the moody Frey refused to report and asked to
be put on the voluntarily retired list. He committed
suicide that November. /(JK)

Jim Frey — 1931- . *Manager* 1980-81, 84-86 Royals, **Cubs** 323-287, .530. First place: 80, 84 *2 LCS, 5-3, .625. 1 WS, 2-4, .333*

Frey led the Royals to the AL pennant in his first year as a major league manager, 1980, but was fired before the end of the 1981 season. His abilities as a judge of talent and as a leader were not questioned, but he was considered deficient in tactical judgment. Reappearing with the Cubs in 1984, he led them to a surprising division title, but they were upset by the Padres when Frey left his ace, Rick Sutcliffe, in Game Five a bit too long. The Cubs had won the first two games of the series. Again falling below .500 the following season, he was fired in mid-1986 but moved to the front office, replacing Dallas Green as GM. Frey's judgment of minor league talent and several astute trades were instrumental in Chicago's 1989 title. /(SH)

Lonny Frey [Linus Richard] (Junior) — 1910- . 2B-SS 1933-43, 46-48 Dodgers, Cubs, **Reds**, Yankees, Giants 1535 g, .269, 61 hr, 549 rbi. *3 WS, 8 g, .000, 1 rbi* ☛ *All-Star—39, 41, 43.*

Frey played in three All-Star Games and three World Series, and in 1939 batted .291 and scored 95 runs to help Cincinnati into the WS. Pitcher Bucky Walters remembered teammates Frey, Myers, and third baseman Bill Werber as "good, fast, smart ballplayers." Indeed, Frey was fast enough to lead the NL with 22 stolen bases for the Reds in 1940. Although he twice topped NL shortstops in errors, Frey led the league's second basemen twice each in fielding percentage and double plays. /(TJ)

Pepe Frias [Jesus] — 1948- . SS-2B-3B 1973-81 **Expos**, Braves, Rangers, Dodgers 723 g, .240, 1 hr, 108 rbi

One of the many latter-day shortstops from San Pedro de Macoris in the Dominican Republic, Frias was a light hitter but earned his pay with his glove. In 1978 he played 73 games at short and second without making an error. /(MC)

Barney Friberg [Augustaf Bernhardt] — 1899-1958. 3B-2B-OF-SS 1919-20, 22-33 Cubs, **Phillies**, Red Sox 1299 g, .281, 38 hr, 471 rbi

The versatile Friberg went from the Massachusetts sandlots to the Cubs before his twentieth birthday. A regular at second base, third base, and in right field, Friberg played every position during his career. The Phillies started to make him a pitcher during the early 1930s (he had pitched once in 1925), but

injuries to his teammates forced him to remain in the infield. /(JL)

Marion Fricano — 1923-1976. RHP 1952-55 **A's** 387 ip, 15-23, 4.32

Fricano made a promising 9-12, 3.88 ERA start as a 30-year-old rookie with the seventh-place A's in 1953. The next year, erratic control dropped him to 5-11 and 5.16. /(MC)

Ford Frick — 1895-1978. *Executive.* ☛ *Hall of Fame—1970.*

It was fitting that the ultimate tribute to Ford Frick was his election to the Hall of Fame. He was president of the National League when the shrine was proposed, and he gave the idea his fullest support.

Frick began his career as a midwestern sports writer and moved to New York with the Hearst papers. He pioneered the nightly radio sports report,

Ford Frick

giving scores and news. In 1934 he became NL public relations director and succeeded the ailing William Heydler as NL president the next year. In 1951 he replaced Happy Chandler as Commissioner as the owners sought a less stubbornly independent figure at the helm than Chandler or the untameable Judge Landis. Much-derided for his controversial decision to attach an asterisk to Roger Maris's record 61 HR in the new 162-game season in 1961 (Frick had been Babe Ruth's ghostwriter), he saw his resourceful administration and gentle guidance of the owners away from their instinct for self-destruction overshadowed by the asterisk issue. In Frick's wake have come General Eckert, Bowie Kuhn, and Peter Ueberroth, and a trend toward baseball as a billion-dollar business perhaps too willing to shed its old values, values the traditionalist Frick revered. /(JK)

Bob Friend (Warrior) — 1930- . RHP 1951-66 **Pirates**, Yankees, Mets 3611 ip, 197-230, 3.58. 20 wins: 58
1 WS, 6 ip, 0-2, 13.50
☛ *Led League—w 58. Led League—era 55. All-Star—56, 58, 60.*

In 15 seasons with Pittsburgh, Friend pitched on five last-place teams and is the only pitcher to have lost more than 200 (230) while winning fewer than 200 (197). In 1955 he became the first to lead a major league in ERA (2.83) while pitching for a last-place team. Friend twice topped the NL in hits allowed, and lost a league-high 19 in both 1959 and 1961. But he paced the NL in starts each season from 1956 through 1958, innings in 1956 and 1957, and tied with Warren Spahn for the NL lead with 22 wins in 1958. Friend shares the NL record with two All-Star Game victories (1956 and 1960), and lost the 1958 All-Star Game as a reliever. Friend lost Games Two and Six in the dramatic 1960 Yankee-Pirate World Series. A Purdue graduate, Friend served as Pittsburgh and NL player representative. /(TJ)

Owen Friend (Red) — 1927- . 2B-3B-SS 1949-50, 53, 55-56 **Browns**, Tigers, Indians, Red Sox, Cubs 208 g, .227, 13 hr, 76 rbi

Friend was a utility man whose early ability prompted comparison to Rogers Hornsby at the plate and Eddie Stanky in the field. He modeled himself after Joe Gordon. The result was still Owen Friend, and that was less than major league caliber. /(WAB)

Frankie Frisch (The Fordham Flash) — 1898-1973. 2B-3B 1919-37 Giants, **Cardinals** 2311 g, .316, 105 hr, 1244 rbi. *8 WS, 50 g, .294, 10 rbi.*
Manager 1933-38, 40-46, 49-51 Cardinals, **Pirates**, Cubs 1137-1078, .513. First place: 34 *1 WS, 4-3, .571*
☛ *Most Valuable Player—31 . All-Star—33-35. Hall of Fame—1947.*

Frisch graduated from Fordham University in 1919 after starring there in baseball, football, basketball, and track. He joined the Giants without playing a game in the minors. A natural athlete with great speed and dexterity, Frisch was tutored long and hard by manager John McGraw on batting and sliding technique. The youthful Frisch quickly became a favorite of McGraw, who named him team captain. He played second base, third base, and occasionally shortstop, wherever his talents were most needed. Although his first two seasons produced only modest offensive results, his fielding was superb and his speed spectacular. He also rarely struck out, an ability Frisch became legendary for. In 17 full seasons, only twice did he fan more than 18 times. From 1921 to 1926 Frisch averaged over 100 runs scored per season, never batted below .324, and stole bases with abandon. He was instrumental in four consecutive Giants pennants and batted .363 in those four World Series (1921–1924).

When the Giants faded in 1925 and 1926, McGraw vented much of his frustration on Frisch. After exactly 1,000 games as a Giant, Frankie was dealt to the Cardinals with pitcher Jimmy Ring for the dominant NL hitter of the 1920s, second baseman and manager Rogers Hornsby, who had had a falling-out with St. Louis owner Sam Breadon.

The extremely competitive, switch-hitting Frisch was saddled with the almost impossible task of making fans in St. Louis forget Hornsby, a man who had just won six straight batting titles with a six-season average of .397. As longtime St. Louis *Post-Dispatch* sportswriter Bob Broeg said, "Frisch didn't make them forget the Rajah, but he made them remember the Flash." In his first season in St. Louis, Frisch hit .337 and finished second in the MVP voting. He also had 641 assists and 1,059 chances at second base, season records which have endured, and he led the league in fielding average.

By the early 1930s, Branch Rickey's farm system had surrounded the veteran second baseman with hungry, talented youngsters, and the Gas House Gang was born. Frisch's zest for the game was contagious. He went on to bat .312 in a decade as a Cardinal and played on four more pennant winners.

Frankie Frisch

He batted over .300 thirteen times in his career. From 1933 to 1938 he managed the Cardinals. Ironically, Frisch was united with Rogers Hornsby in 1933 when Hornsby served as a pinch hitter and backup second baseman. Shortly after Frisch assumed the helm of the Cardinals in mid-season, Hornsby was released so he could accept the same position with the St. Louis Browns.

Frisch managed with the same fire with which he had played. He loved to argue with, show up, and humor umpires. He directed the 1934 Cardinals, one of the most raucous conglomerations of baseball characters, including the Dean brothers, Pepper

Martin, Leo Durocher, Joe Medwick, and Ripper Collins, to a World Championship. After he left the Cardinals, Frisch managed 10 more years with the Pirates and Cubs. He did radio play-by-play for the Boston Braves in 1939 and for the Giants in 1947 and was a Giants coach in 1948. /(FO)

Danny Frisella (Bear) — 1946-1977. RHP 1967-76 **Mets, Braves, Padres, Cardinals, Brewers** 611 ip, 34-40, 3.32

The swarthy forkballer won 8 and saved 12 with a 1.98 ERA for the Mets in 1971, his best year. He had 57 saves in his career, and was coming off a strong five-win, nine-save season with the Brewers when he was killed in a dune buggy accident on New Year's Day, 1977. /(JCA)

Doug Frobel — 1959- . OF 1982-85, 87- **Pirates,** Expos, Indians 268 g, .201, 20 hr, 58 rbi

Nurtured in the Pittsburgh farm system, Canadian-born Frobel proved unable to replace Dave Parker when handed the right field job in 1984. His long, looping swing produced homers in the minors, strikeouts in the majors. /(ME)

Sam Frock — 1882-1925. RHP 1907, 1909-11 **Braves, Pirates** 343 ip, 14-24, 3.23

Frock pitched in eight games for the 1909 World Champion Pirates and was eligible for but did not appear in the WS that year. Traded to the last-place Braves in 1910, he was 11-20. /(NLM)

Bruce Froemming — 1939- . *Umpire* NL 1971-87 *5 LCS 2 WS, 2 ASU*

In a 1986 *TSN* poll of its 26 correspondents, Froemming was voted the best all-around umpire in the NL and also the umpire with the quickest thumb. On September 2, 1972, the Cubs' Milt Pappas was one pitch away from a perfect game. The 3-2 pitch to the Padres' 27th batter was called a ball by Froemming. Pappas pitched his no-hitter, but sulked for years that the call cost him a perfect game. Froemming simply explained that he had to call it a ball or he would have no integrity. The rotund arbiter was behind the plate when Nolan Ryan pitched his record fifth no-hitter. /(RTM)

Todd Frohwirth — 1962- . RHP 1987- **Phillies** 86 ip, 3-2, 3.78

This 6'4" 195-lb reliever was 1-0 with a 0.00 ERA in his 10-game call-up in 1987, but has since suffered from wildness. /(SFS)

Art Fromme — 1883–1956. RHP 1906–15 Cardinals, **Reds,** Giants 1438 ip, 80–90, 2.90

After two consecutive 5–13 seasons for the Cardinals, Fromme was traded to the Reds and blossomed with a 19–13 mark and 1.90 ERA in 1909. Illness ruined his 1910 season, but he came back to win 16 in 1912. Early in 1913 he was traded to the Giants with Eddie Grant for Josh Devore, Red Ames, Heinie Groh, and $20,000. Although he was 20–11 for New York in 1913–14, he was regarded as a disappointment, and manager McGraw did not use him in the 1913 World Series. /(NLM)

Dave Frost — 1952– . RHP 1977–82 White Sox, **Angels,** Royals 550 ip, 33–37, 4.11. *1 LCS, 4 ip, 0–1, 18.69*

The 6'6" Frost went 16–10 with a staff-best 3.58 ERA for the 1979 AL West champion Angels. Elbow problems then made him less effective; he recorded ERAs of 5.31 and higher in each of his final three seasons. /(JCA)

Woodie Fryman — 1940– . LHP 1966–83 Pirates, Phillies, Tigers, **Expos,** Reds, Cubs 2411 ip, 141–155, 3.77. *2 LCS, 13 ip, 0–2, 6.08*
☛ *All-Star—68, 76.*

The Kentucky tobacco farmer didn't sign a pro contract until age 25. After only 12 minor league games, he started the 1966 season with Pittsburgh and hurled three consecutive shutouts. In his career, he threw four one-hitters. In 1972 he was 4–10 with the Phillies when he was sent to Detroit, where he went 10–3 to help the Tigers to a divisional title.

During his second stint with Montreal, he became a dependable reliever, racking up 24 wins and 46 saves in 1979–82. Modest and uncomplaining, Fryman pitched much of his career with severe arthritis in his elbow, yet stayed in the ML to age 43. /(JCA)

Tito Fuentes [Rigoberto Peat] — 1944– . 2B-SS-3B 1965–67, 69–78 **Giants,** Padres, Tigers, A's 1499 g, .268, 45 hr, 438 rbi. *1 LCS, 4 g, .313, 1 hr, 2 rbi*

The nimble Cuban was a flamboyant fielder who was often called a hot dog. Fuentes was San Francisco's regular second baseman in the early 1970s and set a NL record by committing just six errors (.993 fielding average) in 1973 after leading NL second basemen in errors the previous two seasons. A productive, punch-type switch-hitter, he drove in 78 runs for the Giants in 1973, and 83 for the Tigers in 1977 when he batted a career-high .309. On September 13, 1973, he was hit by three pitches in one game, a ML record. /(JCA)

Tomio Fujimura — Unk.–Unk. 1B-OF **Hanshin Tigers**
☛ *Led League—ba 49. Led League—hr 50.*

Fujimura was a Japanese slugger, a macho WWII veteran who disdained the use of a glove and refused the opportunity to switch teams for more money. He raised the single-season Japanese home run record from 25 to 45 in 1949. He also briefly held the national record for single-season batting average, hitting .362 in 1950. His career total of 224 HR was a Japanese record when he retired. /(MC)

Yutaka Fukumoto — 1947– . OF **Hankyu Braves**

Japanese baseball emphasizes power rather than speed; only 10 or 12 players steal more than 20 bases in any given year. Fukumoto, however, stole 106 bases in 1972, a Japanese record. His 95 stolen bases the following year have been the only serious challenge to the mark. At age 33, in 1979, he again led Japanese baseball in stolen bases, with 60. A centerfielder and leadoff hitter, he typically batted about .290. /(MC)

John Fulgham — 1956– . RHP 1979–80 **Cardinals** 231 ip, 14–12, 2.84

Fulgham's very promising career was cut short by a rotator cuff injury. He was 10–6 (2.53) as a rookie in 1979 but was plagued by the arm problem in 1980. All of his 14 ML wins were complete games. /(JCA)

Vern Fuller — 1944– . 2B-3B 1964, 66–70 **Indians** 325 g, .232, 14 hr, 65 rbi

Fuller was a steady fielder with a little power. He was mostly a backup, but played 102 games at second and hit .236 for Cleveland in 1969, his busiest season. Though a food connoisseur, the angular-featured infielder was always slender. /(JCA)

Curt Fullerton — 1898–1975. RHP 1921–25, 33 **Red Sox** 423 ip, 10–37, 5.11

Fullerton came down to Boston from his native Maine to struggle through six seasons with some of the worst Red Sox clubs ever assembled. He walked twice as many as he struck out. /(EW)

Hugh S. Fullerton, Jr. — 1904–1965. *Writer.*

A graduate of Princeton, Fullerton was on the New York sports desk of the Associated Press for his entire 38-year career. /(NLM)

Hugh S. Fullerton, Sr. — 1873-1935. *Writer.*

For the first 25 years of the 20th century, Fullerton was the best-known baseball writer in the country and a titan of the Chicago press box, along with Lardner, Sanborn, and Dryden. After graduating from Ohio State, he began in 1889 in Cincinnati. In 1896 he moved to the Chicago *Record* as baseball writer and then on to the *Tribune*. Fullerton was instrumental in exposing the Black Sox scandal in 1919. In the 1920s he moved to New York and was later editor of *Liberty Magazine* for six years. He also wrote for the Bell syndicate, the Columbus *Dispatch* and the Philadelphia *Inquirer*. He was one of the first to write stories on inside baseball for top mass-circulation magazines. Reportedly the first to use the slang word "dope" for baseball information, Fullerton also wrote fiction and a book on the science of baseball with Johnny Evers. One of the founders of the BBWAA, he was awarded the J.G. Taylor Spink Award in 1964. /(NLM)

Chick Fullis [Charles Philip] — 1904-1946. OF 1928-34, 36 **Giants**, Phillies, Cardinals 590 g, .295, 12 hr, 167 rbi. *1 WS, 3 g, .400*

In his only season as an everyday outfielder (Phillies, 1933), this speedy line-drive hitter had 200 hits to bat .309, and led the NL in at-bats and putouts. Briefly a member of the Cardinals' famed Gas House Gang, Fullis retired early due to eye trouble. /(JL)

Dave Fultz — 1875-1959. OF 1898-99, 1901-05 Phillies, Baltimore (NL), **A's**, Yankees 645 g, .271, 3 hr, 223 rbi

A Brown graduate with a law degree from Columbia, Fultz was a useful outfielder who led the AL in 1902 with 109 runs for Philadelphia. In 1903 he had the Highlanders' (Yankees) first extra-base hit. A practicing attorney, Fultz organized the Player's Fraternity in 1912. Ty Cobb and Christy Mathewson were among its officers, but it achieved little and folded in 1918. After service as a WWI aviator, Fultz became president of the International League. /(JK)

Frank Funk — 1935- . RHP 1960-63 **Indians**, Braves 248 ip, 20-17, 3.01

Funk was Cleveland's ace reliever in 1961, despite an AL-high 11 relief losses. He also won 11 and saved 11 that year. Funk became a minor league manager and ML coach. /(ME)

Liz Funk [Elias Calvin] — 1904-1968. OF 1929-30, 32-33 Yankees, **Tigers**, White Sox 273 g, .267, 6 hr, 105 rbi

Funk was a 5'8", lefthanded contact hitter. After a solid but unspectacular 1930 campaign with Detroit, he was sent down. In need of a leadoff hitter in 1932, the White Sox acquired him. They liked the centerfielder's speed and desire, but by 1933 they had better hitters. /(RL)

Carl Furillo (Skoonj, The Reading Rifle) — 1922- . OF 1946-60 **Dodgers** 1806 g, .299, 192 rbi, 1058 rbi. *7 WS, 40 g, .266, 2 hr, 13 rbi* ☛ *All-Star—52-53.*

Furillo was one of Roger Kahn's famed Boys of Summer. Kahn described him as The Hard Hat Who Sued Baseball. He sued the Dodgers in 1960 for dropping him while he was hurt. He was awarded $21,000 as a settlement. From then on, Furillo couldn't find a job in baseball. He contended

Carl Furillo

that he had been blackballed. Kahn found him years later, installing Otis elevators at the World Trade Center.

Furillo had his best season in 1953, when he hit .344 to win the NL batting title. A volatile and intense competitor, Skoonj (short for scungili, Italian for snail) broke his hand during a September brawl with Leo Durocher and the Giants, and missed most of the rest of the season. The Reading Rifle had a gun for an arm, and read the tricky, 40'-high right field wall in Ebbets Field masterfully. His career highlights include a miraculous catch of Johnny Mize's bid for a home run in Game Five of the 1952 World Series; a game-tying, ninth-inning homer in Game Six of the 1953 WS; and throwing Reds pitcher Mel Queen out at first on a 300' shot hit into the right field gap at Ebbets Field. /(WAB)

Fred Fussell (Moonlight Ace) — 1895–1966. LHP 1922–23, 28–29 Cubs, **Pirates** 295 ip, 14–17, 4.86

The 5'10" 156-lb lefthander had two unsuccessful trials in the majors. He was given his unusual nickname in 1933 after pitching the first International League twilight no-hitter. /(JK)

Frank Gabler (The Great Gabbo) — 1911–1967. RHP 1935–38 **Giants**, Braves, White Sox 376 ip, 16–23, 5.26. *1 WS, 5 ip, 0–0, 7.20*

The Great Gabbo was known for sounding off, and for fistfights on the mound with Tex Carleton. In the minors, his skull was fractured by a line drive. In 1936 Gabler boasted he'd win ten games. Eddie Brannick, the Giants' secretary, offered him a $100 suit if he won eight. Gabler helped his team to the NL pennant by winning nine, and collected on the bet./(NLM)

John Gabler (Gabe) — 1930– . RHP 1959–61 Yankees, **Senators** 164 ip, 7–12, 4.39

A fringe major leaguer, Gabler had brief stints with the Yankees and the expansion 1961 Senators. He failed to finish any of his 14 ML starting assignments./(DQV)

Ken Gables — 1919–1960. RHP 1945–47 **Pirates** 240 ip, 13–11, 4.69

Pittsburgh's youngest pitcher (26) in wartime 1945, the rookie was 11–7. Gables pitched in one final ML game in 1947 and worked in the Pacific Coast League, mostly with Sacramento, until 1954./(ME)

Len Gabrielson — 1940– . OF-1B 1960, 63–70 Braves, Cubs, Giants, Angels, **Dodgers** 708 g, .253, 37 hr, 315 rbi

Gabrielson got a $75,000 bonus to sign with the Braves in 1960. He had fair power but never won an everyday job. He played the most in 1965, when he hit a career-high .293 for the Cubs and Giants. He was a below-average outfielder. Used often as a pinch hitter, his best season in that role was 1969 (13-for-36) for the Dodgers. He is the son of Len Gabrielson, who played first base in five games for the 1939 Athletics./(WOR)

Eddie Gaedel — 1925–1961. PH 1951 **Browns** 1 g, --

The most publicized stunt in baseball history took place August 18, 1951, at Sportsman's Park in St. Louis, when, to the surprise of 18,369 fans, 3'7" 65-lb midget Eddie Gaedel emerged from a seven-foot

birthday cake between games of a Browns-Tigers doubleheader. Browns owner Bill Veeck concocted the idea to boost attendance, and to help celebrate the 50th anniversary of both the American League and the Falstaff Brewing Co., radio sponsor of the Browns.

Gaedel, a stage performer, was wearing a Browns uniform with the number 1/8, and little slippers turned up at the end like elf's shoes. In the bottom of the first, St. Louis manager Zach Taylor sent Gaedel to the plate to pinch hit for Frank Saucier. Veeck had instructed the diminutive Brownie to crouch low, and not swing his toy-like bat. Detroit skipper Red Rolfe protested Gaedel's presence, but Taylor produced a legitimate contract, filed with the AL and cleared by umpire Ed Hurley.

In his stance, Gaedel's strike zone measured 1-1/2 inches. Detroit pitcher Bob Cain walked the midget, throwing four straight balls. When Jim Delsing went in to run for him, the crowd gave Gaedel a standing ovation. The Browns lost, 6–2, despite Gaedel's instant offense. AL president Will Harridge was furious with Veeck's burlesque and unsuccessfully tried to strike Gaedel's name from the record books. Gaedel was paid $100 for his appearance, and was insured for $1 million by Veeck. In future years Veeck used him in a few other promotions./(RTM)

Gary Gaetti — 1958– . 3B 1981– **Twins** 1207 g, .259, 185 hr, 673 rbi. *1 LCS, 5 g, .300, 2 hr, 5 rbi. 1 WS, 7 g, .259, 1 hr, 4 rbi*
☛ *All-Star—89. Gold Glove—86–89.*

Gary Gaetti overcame a slow start to gain recognition as the AL's premier third baseman by 1988. The 1980 Midwest League home run champ, Gaetti became the 47th major leaguer to homer in his first big league at-bat, September 20, 1981 off Charlie Hough in Texas. In 1982 he replaced former co-Rookie of the Year John Castino at third for the Twins. An outstanding defensive player with multiple league leaderships in putouts, assists, and double plays, Gaetti's offense finally caught up in 1986 (.287, 34 HR, 108 RBI) and 1987 (31 HR, 109 RBI). In the 1987 LCS he became the first player ever to hit two home runs in his first two at-bats of postseason play. He was the LCS MVP, won his second straight Gold Glove, and set a Twins third base record with a .973 fielding average in 1987.

Gaetti gained notoriety in the 1989 All-Star Game when he displayed a religious slogan written on his batting gloves to the TV cameras during the pregame introductions. /(ME)

James A. Gaffney — Unk.–1932. *Executive.*

A successful New York contractor and politician with Tammany Hall connections, Gaffney was instrumental in putting together the 1914 Miracle Braves and bringing about a settlement of the Federal League war. He bought the Braves in 1911 and named John Montgomery Ward as president, but soon fired him and took over the operation himself. Gaffney set out to build a winner faster than his old friend Frank Farrell, the Yankees' owner. He hired George Stallings as manager and paid to keep Johnny Evers, the key man on the '14 team, from the Federal League. During the 1915 WS, Gaffney arranged a peace conference between the National Commission and the upstart Federal League. That fall he sold the Braves to a syndicate that included Harvard football coach Percy Haughton. /(NLM)

John Gaffney — Unk.–Unk. *Umpire* **NL, AA, PL** 1884–95

One of the first to be dubbed King of Umpires, Gaffney controlled the game through tact and diplomacy. At a time when umpires worked games alone, he popularized the technique of working behind the plate until a man reached base, then moving behind the pitcher. He also began the practice of calling a ball "fair" or "foul" at the point where it left the park, rather than where it was last seen. In 1888 he was the highest paid umpire in baseball, earning $2,500 a year plus expenses on the road. /(RTM)

Phil Gagliano — 1941– . 2B-3B-OF-1B 1963–74 **Cardinals,** Cubs, Red Sox, Reds 702 g, .238, 14 hr, 159 rbi. *1 LCS, 3 g, .000. 2 WS, 4 g, .000*

Gagliano was a solid utility player who spent his first seven-plus seasons with the Cardinals. He appeared in a career-high 122 games in 1965, hitting eight homers with 53 RBI. Developing into a top pinch hitter, he batted .354 in that role with the 1971–72 Red Sox, .366 for Cincinnati in 1973. He played with future St. Louis teammates Tim McCarver and Mike Shannon, and ML pitcher Jim Donahue, at Christian Brothers High School in Memphis, Ten-

nessee. His brother Ralph appeared in one game with the 1965 Indians. /(MC)

Greg Gagne — 1961– . SS 1983– **Twins** 717 g, .250, 47 hr, 216 rbi. *1 LCS, 5 g, .278, 2 hr, 3 rbi. 1 WS, 7 g, .200, 1 hr, 3 rbi*

Acquired from the Yankees in a 1982 deal for Roy Smalley, Gagne won Minnesota's shortstop job in 1985. He hit two inside-the-park homers in the Metrodome on October 4, 1986. Though he led AL shortstops with 26 errors that year, in 1987 he set a club shortstop record with 47 straight errorless games, and helped the Twins to their first World Championship. He hit solo homers in Games Three and Four of the LCS and in WS Game Four, and singled in the winning run in WS Game Seven. /(JCA)

Joe Gaines [Arnesta Joe] — 1936– . OF 1960–66 Reds, Orioles, **Astros** 362 g, .241, 21 hr, 95 rbi

The speedy Gaines enjoyed several .300 seasons in the minors, including a .315 year at Indianapolis (American Association) in 1961. Used mainly as a reserve in the majors, his top average was .286 with the 1963 Orioles. /(RTM)

Del Gainor (Sheriff) — 1886–1947. 1B 1909, 11–17, 19, 22 Tigers, **Red Sox,** Cardinals 546 g, .272, 14 hr, 185 rbi. *2 WS, 2 g, .500, 1 rbi*

Gainor's 14th-inning pinch single in Game Two of the 1916 World Series drove in Boston's winning run, ending the longest game in WS history and sealing Babe Ruth's first postseason pitching victory. /(JL)

Augie Galan — 1912– . OF 1934–49 **Cubs,** Dodgers, Reds, Giants, A's 1742 g, .287, 100 hr, 830 rbi. *3 WS, 10 g, .138, 2 rbi*
☛ *All-Star—36, 43–44.*

Galan was an injury-prone outfielder who had a good career despite the mishaps. He was the first everyday major leaguer to play an entire season without hitting into a double play, as well as the first to homer from both sides of the plate in the same contest (6/25/37). Having shattered his right elbow playing ball as a child, Galan had a deformed arm. He broke into the majors as a Cub infielder in 1934, and was a star outfielder by the following year, batting .314 and leading the league with 133 runs and 22 stolen bases to help Chicago to the pennant. In 646 at-bats, he did not hit into a single double play, although he did hit into a triple play. In 1936 Galan became the first Cub to homer in the All-Star Game.

After batting .304 for the Cubs in 1939, he broke his right knee in 1940. The Cubs gave up on Galan and his injuries, dealing him to the Dodgers in 1941. Two years later, he was back in the starting lineup, hitting over .300 each season from 1944 through 1947 before the years caught up with him. From 1945 on, he batted exclusively lefthanded. /(ARA)

Andres Galarraga (Big Cat) — 1961- . 1B 1985- **Expos** 585 g, .282, 77 hr, 313 rbi
☛ *Gold Glove—89.*

Andres Galarraga was signed by the Expos, at the recommendation of Felipe Alou, as a 17-year old power prodigy. Given the first-base job for 1986, he had a terrible spring training (.107, no extra base hits) and was assigned to platoon with Jason Thompson. The platoon ended quickly as Galarraga caught fire early in the regular season. The Venezuelan missed much of the 1986 season with a right knee injury and right rib cage pull, but gave better evidence of his skills in 1987 (.305, 13 HR, 90 RBI), finishing second in the NL in doubles. Capable of awesome power, Galarraga sacrificed some distance for batting average, but continued to post high strikeout numbers. He combined average and power in 1988, hitting .302 with 29 HR, leading in doubles (42) but also in strikeouts (153). He was nicknamed for his defensive quickness at first base. /(ME)

John W. Galbreath — 1898-1988. *Executive.*

A breeder of champion racehorses, Galbreath, with Bing Crosby and two other partners, bought the Pirates in 1946. He was president from 1950 to 1969, when his son succeeded him. The family sold the team in 1985. /(NLM)

Rich Gale — 1954- . RHP 1978-84 **Royals**, Giants, Reds, Red Sox 971 ip, 55-56, 4.53. *1 WS, 6 ip, 0-1, 4.26*

Gale was *TSN* Rookie Pitcher of the Year in 1978, with a 14-8, 3.09 record that remained his career best. His 13-9, 3.91 performance in 1980 was his only other winning season and helped the Royals to the AL pennant. He was hit hard by the Phillies in his two WS starts and lost the sixth and deciding game. /(SFS)

Denny Galehouse — 1911- . RHP 1934-44, 46-49 Indians, Red Sox, **Browns** 2003 ip, 109-118, 3.98. *1 WS, 18 ip, 1-1, 1.50*

During much of the 1944 campaign, Galehouse served the St. Louis Browns as a Sunday pitcher while working weekdays in an Akron, Ohio war plant. He relinquished his factory job late in the season. After posting several stretch drive victories, Galehouse beat Mort Cooper and the Cardinals in the 1944 World Series opener, but lost, 2-0, in a Game Five rematch. During his second stint with the Red Sox, Galehouse lost the 1948 pennant playoff game to Cleveland 8-3 as a surprise starter. It was his last major league decision. /(TJ)

Alan Gallagher (Dirty Al) — 1945- . 3B 1970-73 **Giants**, Angels 442 g, .263, 11 hr, 130 rbi. *1 LCS, 4 g, .100*

Gallagher's mother wanted many sons, but having just one, gave him all their names. Alan Mitchell Edward George Patrick Henry Gallagher, a self-proclaimed marginal player, lasted four seasons in the majors on sheer hustle. Dirty Al never looked good in a uniform. He was once the subject of a *New York Times Magazine* article on journeymen players. /(DQV)

Dave Gallagher — 1960- . OF 1987- Indians, **White Sox** 277 g, .273, 6 hr, 78 rbi

The White Sox signed Gallagher after the 1987 season, when he was released by the Mariners. He won the centerfield job in Chicago with his errorless fielding and a .303 average in 1988. /(WOR)

James Gallagher — 1904- . *Writer-Executive*

After twelve years as a baseball writer for the Chicago *American*, Gallagher moved to the front office of the Cubs as GM and later vice president in 1940. He spent 1957 heading an advertising and public relations agency with Bill Veeck, then joined the Phillies in 1958. He planned to retire in 1962, but was convinced to work part-time for Commissioner Ford Frick instead. He worked in the Commissioner's office until 1974. /(NLM)

Bert Gallia — 1891-1976. RHP 1912-20 **Senators**, Browns, Phillies 1277 ip, 65-58, 3.14

After winning 26 at Kansas City in the American Association, Gallia was bought by Washington for pitcher Jim Vaughn, outfielder Clarence Walker, and cash. Starting and relieving, he had seasons of 17-11 (1915) and 17-12 (1916). After the 1917 season he was traded to the Browns with $15,000 for Burt Shotton and Doc Lavan. /(NLM)

Paul Gallico — 1898-1976. *Writer.*

Gallico was the highest-paid sports editor in the country in the 1930s, earning $25,000 a year for the New York *Daily News* from 1923 to 1936. Then he asked for a $70-a-week city-desk job, which enabled him to turn to free-lance writing. He authored 41 books. As a columnist, he fought one round with Jack Dempsey and tried to catch Dizzy Dean's curveball so he could tell his readers what it was like. Gallico created the Golden Gloves boxing tournament. /(NLM)

Chick Galloway [Clarence Edward] — 1896–1969. SS 1919–28 **A's**, Tigers 1076 g, .264, 17 hr, 407 rbi

Galloway was the Athletics' everyday shortstop in 1921–26. His playing days ended when a pitch thrown by Haskell Billings in batting practice fractured his skull. A Presbyterian College (SC) grad, he returned to coach there, and later scouted for the Reds, A's, and Braves. /(NLM)

Pud Galvin [James Francis] (Gentle Jeems, The Little Steam Engine) — 1856–1902. RHP 1879–92 **Buffalo (NL)**, Pittsburgh (AA), Pirates, Pittsburgh (PL), Cardinals 5941 ip, 361–310, 2.87. 20 wins: 79–84, 86–89
   Manager 1885 **Buffalo (NL)** 8–22, .267
☛ *Hall of Fame—1965.*

A stocky pitcher with a blinding fastball, Pud Galvin racked up phenomenal totals in the early days of major league baseball. Galvin was 37–27 for Buffalo in 1879, his rookie season and the first of six straight 20-win campaigns. Though he never pitched for a club that finished better than third, Galvin became one of baseball's all-time winningest pitchers.

His best seasons came with Buffalo in 1883 and 1884. In the former, Galvin was 46–22 and led the NL in games (76), starts (75), complete games (72), innings pitched (656–1/3) and shutouts (5). His 1884 achievements (46–22, 12 shutouts) were overshadowed by Hoss Radbourn's 60 wins for Providence. Galvin had ended Radbourn's 18-game winning streak, and a 20-game Providence win streak, with a 2–0 victory on September 9. He threw three shutouts against Detroit between August 2 and August 8, including a no-hitter on August 4, becoming the second pitcher in ML history with two or more no-hitters. (He had no-hit Worcester in 1880.) His 396 strikeouts in 1884 were a career high, and one of the highest pre-1900 single season totals.

In 1885 Galvin jumped from Buffalo (NL) to Allegheny (American Association), the club that joined the NL in 1887 as Pittsburgh. From 1886 through 1889, Galvin notched another four straight 20-win seasons. Galvin jumped to the Players' League in 1890. He returned to the Pirates in 1891,

Pud Galvin

but was released during the following season. He finished his ML career in his native St. Louis.

Galvin retired as one of baseball's all-time leaders in wins (sixth), losses (second), complete games (639, second), innings pitched (second), and shutouts (57, tied for tenth). On July 21, 1892, Galvin faced Tim Keefe in the last battle of 300-game winners until Don Sutton met Phil Niekro in 1986. Galvin and Keefe met four times as 300-game winners from 1890 to 1892, the first such meetings in ML history.

Galvin died, penniless, in a Pittsburgh rooming house. Fan contributions paid for his burial. His brother, Lou, pitched two games for St. Paul (Union Association) in 1884. Pud was inducted into the Hall of Fame in 1965 by the Veterans Committee./(ME)

Oscar Gamble — 1949- . OF-DH 1969-85 Cubs, Phillies, Indians, **Yankees**, White Sox, Padres, Rangers 1584 g, .265, 200 hr, 666 rbi. *3 LCS, 8 g, .211, 2 rbi. 2 WS, 6 g, .214, 2 rbi*

Gamble was the Cubs' best prospect when he was traded to Philadelphia after the 1969 season with Dick Selma for Johnny Callison. His low batting average prevented him from winning a job in his three years with the Phillies, despite flashes of power. He had the last hit and the last RBI in Philadelphia's Connie Mack Stadium. Only after his trade to Cleveland for 1973 did the lefthanded batter finally blossom. As a platoon DH and occasional outfielder, he hit 20 HR in 390 at-bats.

After two more solid seasons, Gamble went to the Yankees for Pat Dobson in December 1975. He played right field, and helped New York to its first AL pennant in 12 years with 17 HR and 57 RBI in 340 at-bats. His wife, Juanita, sang the national anthem at Yankee Stadium several times that season, including once before a playoff game. However, the Yankee front office had her in tears when they forced Oscar to cut off his luxuriant Afro, the largest in baseball. It added more than four inches to his height and sometimes popped his batting helmet off.

Traded before the start of 1977 with LaMarr Hoyt, then a minor leaguer, and $200,000 for the White Sox' Bucky Dent, Gamble had his best season. He hit .297 with career highs of 31 HR, 83 RBI, 75 runs, and 22 doubles (in 408 at-bats), and the White Sox contended, improving to 90-72 from 64-97 the previous season. He opted for free agency after the season and signed a lucrative deal with San Diego. Slowed by minor injuries, he hit only seven HR and was traded to Texas after the season. He returned to the Yankees in August 1979 in a deal that also sent Mickey Rivers to the Rangers. Gamble was hitting .335 at the time of the trade, then caught fire. He hit .389 in his two months with the Yankees and finished with a career-high .358 mark that was by far the best in the league. But Gamble's 274 at-bats weren't close to qualifying him for the batting title. He spent the next five years in New York, finally accepting his career-long platoon role, and providing vital lefthanded power. He helped the

Yankees to their last two titles as they won their division in 1980 and took the AL pennant in the 1981 strike season. In that year's Eastern Division playoff, Gamble's two-run homer in the opener sparked New York to a 5-3 victory, and he also homered in the 7-3 clincher over Milwaukee. He hit .556 for the series, platooning with Lou Piniella at DH. In the LCS, he had only one hit, but walked five times in 11 plate appearances and scored the second run, after walking, of New York's 3-1 victory in the opener. Gamble finished with a return to the White Sox in 1985./(SH)

Chick Gandil [Charles Arnold] — 1888-1970. 1B 1910, 12-19 White Sox, **Senators**, Indians 1147 g, .277, 11 hr, 557 rbi. *2 WS, 14 g, .245, 10 rbi*

At age 17, Gandil ran away from home to play ball in the rough-and-tumble towns along the Arizona-Mexico border. He supplemented his income by boxing in the local heavyweight division, picking up $150 a fight. He joined the White Sox in 1910, lasted part of a year, and was sold to Washington, where he remained until 1916. Gandil made the acquaintance of Sport Sullivan, a sports gambler and bookie. Sullivan had rich and powerful friends, and his friendships with ballplayers like Gandil were crucial to a World Series fixing scheme he planned to pull off.

Gandil rejoined the White Sox in 1917 as their regular first baseman, but he was a malcontent, and was later considered to be the ringleader of the 1919 WS fix. His contacts with Sullivan, Abe Attell, and Billy Maharg paved the way for the 1920 scandal. In that 1919 Series, Gandil batted a paltry .233 but committed only one error. Gandil refused to play for Charles Comiskey in 1920, due to a salary dispute with the penurious owner. In 1921 he was banned from baseball by Commissioner Landis./(RL)

Bob Ganley — 1875-1945. OF 1905-09 Pirates, **Senators**, A's 572 g, .254, 2 hr, 123 rbi

Ganley's best season was 1907, when he hit .273 and had career highs of 73 runs and 40 stolen bases as the Senators' everyday right fielder, but he led AL outfielders in errors. His hitting declined thereafter, and when he hit .197 in 80 games with the Athletics in 1909, it ended his career./(JFC)

Ron Gant — 1965- . 3B-2B 1987- **Braves** 242 g, .236, 30 hr, 94 rbi

Gant became the Braves' starting second baseman at the age of 23 in 1988, replacing Damaso Garcia only two weeks into the season, and he enjoyed a solid year at the plate, leading all ML rookies in HR (19) and RBI (60) while batting .259. In the field, however, Gant was dreadful, letting ground ball after ground ball scoot through his legs as he led NL second baseman with 26 errors. The Braves shifted Gant to third base late in 1988, but it did little good, and he began the 1989 season in an awful batting slump, hitting below .200 into June. He was then sent down to the low minors to learn to play the outfield. /(SCL)

Jim Gantner (Gumby) — 1953- . 2B-3B 1976- **Brewers** 1472 g, .275, 44 hr, 478 rbi. *1 LCS, 5 g, .188, 2 rbi. 1 WS, 7 g, .333, 4 rbi*

Gantner is unheralded despite more than a decade of dependable performances that put him among the Brewers' all-time leaders in almost every offensive category. He became Milwaukee's starting second baseman in 1981 and has led the AL in chances at the position three times. He hit .282 with career highs in HR (11) and RBI (74) in 1983, and was the Brewers' MVP in 1984. He suffered a career-threatening knee injury in a 1989 collision with Yankee outfielder Marcus Lawton. /(ME)

John Ganzel — 1874–1959. 1B 1898, 1900–01, 03–04, 07–08 Pirates, Cubs, Giants, **Yankees**, Reds 747 g, .251, 18 hr, 336 rbi.
Manager 1908, 15 **Reds**, Brooklyn (FL) 90–99, .476

Ganzel led NL first basemen in putouts, fielding, and total chances per game in 1901 with the Giants, but hit a mere .215. He improved to career bests of .277, 71 RBI, and 61 runs with the Highlanders (later the Yankees) in 1903 and again led league first basemen in fielding and total chances per game. After another good year in 1904, when his six HR tied for fourth in the AL and the Highlanders lost the pennant on the last day of the season, he bought the Grand Rapids (Western League) club, and the next winter he paid the Highlanders (later the Yankees) $3,000 for his release so he could play for it. Returning to the majors in 1907, he led the NL with 19 triples for Cincinnati. He was player-manager for the 1908 Reds, and again led NL first base in fielding. While in the International League he was, at one time, the highest-paid minor league manager, earning $7,000 and a part of the profits.

John Ganzel was one of five brothers to play pro ball; one, Charlie, was a 14-year ML catcher. John's nephew, Charlie's son Babe Ganzel, played briefly for Washington in 1927–28. /(NLM)

Joe Garagiola

Joe Garagiola — 1926- . C 1946–54 **Cardinals**, Pirates, Cubs, Giants 676 g, .257, 42 hr, 255 rbi. *1 WS, 5 g, .316, 4 rbi*

The jokes in Garagiola's best-seller, *Baseball Is a Funny Game* (1960), helped foster his image as a marginal player. In truth, his career was no joke. Signed by the Cardinals' Branch Rickey for $500 off the sandlots of St. Louis, Garagiola (Yogi Berra's boyhood pal) began his pro baseball career at 16. After two years in the minors and two in the military, the catcher reported to the Cardinals in 1946. In the opening game of the '46 playoffs, Garagiola's three hits and two RBI helped the Cardinals to a 4–2 win over the Dodgers. In the World Series with Boston, he collected six hits, including four in Game Four.

In mid-June of 1950, Garagiola was hitting .347. During a game against the Dodgers, he laid down a bunt and raced to first. Brooklyn second baseman Jackie Robinson went to take the throw, but had trouble finding the bag with his foot. Garagiola, trying to avoid colliding with Robinson, broke stride and fell. He suffered a shoulder separation, caught only 30 games that year, and was traded to the Pirates in 1951. He played in a career-high 118 games and hit .273 for the last-place Pirates in 1952.

His broadcasting career began in 1955 with the Cardinals. In 1961 he began working for NBC's "Major League Baseball," where he continued until the end of 1988. In 1965 he replaced Mel Allen on Yankee broadcasts, then in 1969 moved to hosting NBC's daily "Today Show" until 1973. He remains a national celebrity known for one-liners, reminiscences of his days as a Pirate, and Yogi Berra anecdotes. His first book, *Baseball Is a Funny Game*, remains one of the best-selling baseball books ever. /(RTM)

Gene Garber — 1947- . RHP 1969-70, 72-88 Pirates, Royals, Phillies, **Braves** 1509 ip, 96-113, 3.34. *3 LCS, 9 ip, 1-3, 5.79*

Garber's corkscrew motion helped make him one of baseball's all-time leaders in saves, games pitched, and relief wins. He pitched in 249 games for Philadelphia, including a NL-high 71 in 1975, teaming with Tug McGraw for a great lefty-righty combination. Traded to the Braves on June 15, 1978 for Dick Ruthven, Gene set Atlanta records with 558 relief appearances and 141 saves. He also set club records with 56 games finished and 30 saves in 1982 as the Braves went to the playoffs and the bullpen won the Rolaids awards as the outstanding relief corps. The sidearmer ended Pete Rose's 44-game hit streak of 1978 with a memorable strikeout. A crafty pitcher relying on a change-up among a variety of pitches, Garber was unable to post consistently outstanding seasons, doing best in 1978, 1982 and 1986. /(ME)

Barbaro Garbey — 1956- . 1B-DH-OF-3B 1984-85, 88 **Tigers**, Rangers 196 g, .275, 11 hr, 81 rbi. *1 LCS, 3 g, .333. 1 WS, 4 g, .000*

A member of the Cuban national team, Garbey fled to the U.S. in the 1980 "Freedom Flotilla." While hitting .321 for Evansville (American Association) in 1983, he was suspended for a month during an investigation of charges that he had fixed games while in Cuba, but was exonerated. He was sus-

pended a second time in 1983 after threatening a heckling fan with a bat.

He joined the Tigers in 1984 and batted .287 for the World Champions. He was an aggressive, line-drive hitter, but could not play any position well. His temperamental behavior led to his November 1985 trade to the A's, with whom he never appeared. He played in Mexico before resurfacing with the Rangers in 1988. /(MC)

Chico Garcia — 1924- . 2B 1954 **Orioles** 39 g, .113, 0 hr, 5 rbi

Garcia's career was a microcosm of Mexican League history. The Pascual brothers were just beginning their effort to turn the Mexican League into a third major league when Garcia broke in with Mexico City. He and Vern Stephens were supposed to form the double play combo for San Luis Potosi in 1946, but Stephens reneged on his contract, returning instead to the majors. After Garcia hit over .300 there and with Puebla through 1948, he joined the Juarez franchise, jumping from the financially struggling Mexican League into the Arizona-Texas League for 1949. He led the league in runs, hits, triples, and batting (.377), then spent most of four years at Shreveport before finally teaming with Stephens in Baltimore.

Garcia enjoyed his best seasons after returning to Mexico with Monterrey in 1960-1965, averaging .351, .346, .342, and then .368 at age thirty-eight, plus a career-high 21 homers as he won his second batting title. He finished, still a .300 hitter, with Vera Cruz, Aguila, and the Mexico City Tigers, retiring at age 46. His career totals show a .306 average over 2,803 minor league games. /(MC)

Damaso Garcia — 1957- . 2B-SS 1978-86, 88- Yankees, **Blue Jays**, Braves, Expos 1032 g, .283, 36 hr, 323 rbi. *1 LCS, 7 g, .233, 1 rbi* ☛ *All-Star—84-85.*

A surly second baseman who rarely drew walks, Garcia was a good fielder when he hustled, but he was unwilling to dive for balls. Garcia hit above .300 in both 1982 and 1983, but later got into a power struggle with Toronto management, insisting he should be the leadoff batter. Toronto fans were particularly harsh with Garcia, especially after he burned his uniform in the clubhouse after one of his poorer performances.

After 29 games in two seasons for the Yankees, Garcia spent seven seasons with the Blue Jays, where he became the club's career leader in at-bats, hits, and stolen bases. In 1982 Garcia became the first Blue Jay to steal 50 bases in a season, and in 1986 he became the first player to collect 1,000 hits as a Blue Jay. Garcia's 21-game hitting streak in 1983 tied teammate Lloyd Moseby for the team record, and on June 27, 1986, he tied a ML record by hitting four doubles in a game against the Yankees. He was traded to Atlanta before the 1987 season, then was released after hitting only .117 in 21 games in 1988. He caught on with the Expos in 1989. /(TF)

Dave Garcia — 1920– . *Manager 1977–82 Angels, Indians 307–310, .498*

A minor league infielder for 20 years, Garcia never played in a ML game. After managing in the minors and coaching for the Padres, Indians, and Angels, he became California manager in July 1977 and held that position until May of the next season. He rejoined the Indians as a coach in 1979 and was named manager later that season. In four full seasons, he finished as high as fifth only once. Garcia was liked for his fairness and decency, but he was sometimes criticized for lacking the toughness to inspire his players. /(BC)

Kiko Garcia [Alfonso Rafael] — 1953– . SS-2B-3B 1976–85 *Orioles, Astros, Phillies 619 g, .239, 12 hr, 112 rbi. 1 LCS, 3 g, .273, 2 rbi. 1 WS, 6 g, .400, 6 rbi*

Garcia saw more and more action at shortstop with Baltimore from 1976 through 1979 as Mark Belanger's career began to wind down. He played 126 games for the '79 pennant winners, then tied or set three ALCS chances and assists records at shortstop. An unlikely hero in the Orioles' Game Three, 8–5 World Series victory over Pittsburgh, he went 4-for-4, driving in four runs—three with a bases-loaded triple. He had had only 24 RBI all season. Injuries sidelined him three times in 1980–82. He was a utility man for the 1983 pennant-winning Phillies, but did not play in the WS against his former Baltimore teammates. /(MC)

Mike Garcia (The Big Bear) — 1923–1986. RHP 1948–61 *Indians, White Sox, Senators 2175 ip, 142–97, 3.27. 20 wins: 51-52 1 WS, 5 ip, 0–1, 5.40*
☛ *Led League—era 54. All-Star—52–54.*

Garcia was part of the great Indian pitching staff that included Bob Feller, Early Wynn, and Bob Lemon. Signed in 1942, The Big Bear spent three years in the military. He went 14–5 in his rookie year (1949). The hard-throwing Californian of Mexican-Indian descent posted his second straight 20-win season in 1952, leading the AL in starts and hits

allowed, and tying for most shutouts (6). He again tied for the shutout lead (5) with an AL best 2.64 ERA in 1954 and was 19–8 as Cleveland set an AL record with 111 wins and ended the Yankees' pennant string at five. Garcia lost Game Three of the World Series in which Giants routed the Indians in four straight.

The championship season was Garcia's last good campaign. After three subpar years, he hurt his back in 1958. Cut and resigned, he won three final games in 1959. He left among the Indians' top ten all-time in wins, losses, games pitched, shutouts, winning percentage, and strikeouts. /(ME)

Pedro Garcia — 1950– . 2B 1973–77 **Brewers**, Tigers, Blue Jays *558 g, .220, 37 hr, 184 rbi*

As a rookie with the 1973 Brewers, Garcia tied for the AL lead with 32 doubles and was runner-up to Al Bumbry in AL Rookie of the Year voting. The native Puerto Rican hit just .199 as Milwaukee's everyday second baseman in 1974. /(DQV)

Rich Garcia — 1942– . *Umpire AL 1975–87 3 LCS 2 WS 1 ASU*

Garcia's common-sense approach put him in the wrong on the rules during his second ML season. When a pitch bounced in the dirt, hit A's catcher Tim Hosley in the throat, and lodged between his uniform and chest protector, Garcia called time and advanced runners on first and third one base. Actually rule 509-g states: "If the ball lodges in the catcher's mask, protector or uniform, it is a live ball and in play." Although he had grounds, A's manager Chick Tanner did not file a protest. /(RTM)

Danny Gardella — 1920– . OF-1B 1944–45, 50 **Giants**, Cardinals *169 g, .267, 24 hr, 85 rbi*

Gardella was a shipyard worker in 1944 when he joined the wartime Giants. He and brother Al, both lefthanded New Yorkers, were with the Giants in 1945 when 5'7" Danny hit 18 homers. Refusing the Giants' $4,500 contract offer in 1946, Gardella jumped to Vera Cruz of the Mexican League for $10,000. Suspended for five years by Commissioner Chandler along with the other Mexican League jumpers, Gardella sued baseball, claiming he had been bound only by the controversial reserve clause, not a contract. This celebrated antitrust case against baseball, Gardella v. Chandler, was dismissed by a district court in 1948, but Gardella's attorney, Frederic Johnson, won an appeal before the Second Circuit Court in 1949. Fearful of this significant threat to the reserve clause, baseball officials settled

Danny Gardella

out of court for $29,000 and lifted Gardella's suspension. Gardella joined the Cardinals in 1950 but was dropped after one at-bat. Nevertheless, his victory was the only successful challenge to baseball's reserve clause in the federal courts. Though his cause was much maligned by players and the press, his challenge was a stepping-stone to free agency./(DQV)

Ron Gardenhire — 1957– . SS-2B 1981–85 **Mets** 285 g, .232, 4 hr, 49 rbi

Gardenhire batted .240 as the Mets shortstop in 1982, but then was a utility man and shuttled between Triple-A and New York. A recurring hamstring injury in 1984–85 finished him with the Mets. The Twins made him a minor league manager after he played in their system./(JCA)

Billy Gardner (Shotgun) — 1927– . 2B-SS-3B 1954–63 Giants, **Orioles**, Senators/Twins, Yankees, Red Sox 1034 g, .237, 41 hr, 271 rbi. *1 WS, .000.*
　　Manager 1981–85, 87 **Twins**, Royals 330–417, .442

Ticketed to be the Royals' third-base coach in 1987, Gardner instead became the team's manager when terminally ill Dick Howser resigned during spring training. But Gardner was fired that August. He had piloted the Twins from May 1981 until June 1985, with a second-place finish in 1984. His pro playing career touched four decades (1945–71) and included ten ML seasons. He was Baltimore's regular second baseman from 1956 to 1959, and in 1957 he led the AL in doubles and at-bats. He was in Minnesota's original Opening Day lineup, and played briefly later that season for the powerful 1961 Yankees./(TJ)

Jelly Gardner [Floyd] — 1895– . OF-1B Negro Leagues 1919–33 Detroit Stars, **Chicago American Giants**, Homestead Grays, New York Lincoln Giants 567 g, .286, 1 hr (inc.)

Gardner was a 5'6″ 160-lb lefthanded line-drive hitter who batted leadoff for the powerful Chicago American Giant teams in the 1920s. An outstanding, far-ranging centerfielder, he was one of the era's fastest runners.
　　Gardner played his first full season with Chicago in 1920. He batted a career-high .367 in 1924 and .333 in 1926. The Giants won four pennants during Gardner's first seven-year tour with them (1920–26), and triumphed in the '26 Black World Series. Gardner played in all 11 games of the series, batted just .222, but stole three bases and scored eight runs.
　　Gardner went to the New York Lincoln Giants in 1927 after a salary dispute, but returned to Chicago in 1928 and batted .307 in 1929. He returned to his first team, the Detroit Stars, in 1931 and closed out his career with them./(JM)

Jim Gardner — 1874–1905. RHP 1895, 97–99, 1902 **Pirates**, Cubs 423 ip, 25–22, 3.85

Gardner had Pittsburgh's best winning percentage (.800, 8–2) in 1895, but only pitched in home games so he could attend law school. Most used in 1898, he was 10–13. Born in Pittsburgh, Gardner died there at age 30./(ME)

Larry Gardner — 1886–1976. 3B-2B 1908–24 **Red Sox**, Athletics, Indians 1922 g, .289, 27 hr, 929 rbi. *4 WS, 25 g, .198, 3 hr, 11 rbi*

Gardner was a steady third baseman and an above-average dead-ball era hitter. The lefthanded batter joined the Red Sox out of the University of Vermont in 1908, and was their regular third baseman from 1912 through 1917, including three World Championship seasons. Gardner's sacrifice fly in the tenth inning of the final game of the 1912 WS finished the Giants. In early 1918, the Red Sox sent him in a package to the A's for standout first baseman Stuffy McInnis. After a year in Philadelphia, Gardner joined Cleveland and his former teammate, manager Tris Speaker. He cashed another WS check with the Indians in 1920, and hit a career-high .319 in 1921. Gardner later returned to his alma mater as baseball coach and athletic director. /(EW)

Rob Gardner [Richard Frank] — 1944- . LHP 1965-68, 70-73 **Mets**, Cubs, Indians, Yankees, A's, Brewers 331 ip, 14-18, 4.35

Gardner's only good ML season came with the Yankees in 1972 (8-5, 3.06). He had a complex trade history. Originally sent to Oakland by the Yankees in April 1971 with Ron Klimkowski for Felipe Alou, he was reacquired by New York in May for Curt Blefary. The A's got him back after the 1972 season with Rich McKinney in return for Matty Alou and sold Gardner to Milwaukee in May 1973, but the deal was canceled and Gardner returned in July. /(SFS)

Wes Gardner — 1961- . RHP 1984- Mets, **Red Sox** 363 ip, 15-22, 4.83. *1 LCS, 5 ip, 0-0, 5.79*

Gardner led the International League in saves at Tidewater in 1984 and 1985, but couldn't earn a spot on the Mets' pitching staff. He was dealt to Boston with Calvin Schiraldi for Bob Ojeda. He pitched only one inning in 1986 before tearing cartilage in his right shoulder, but his 10 saves in 1987 led the Red Sox. In 1988 and 1989, he was used as an occasional starter. /(SCL)

Wayne Garland — 1950- . RHP 1973-81 Orioles, **Indians** 1040 ip, 55-66, 3.89. 20 wins: 76 *1 LCS, 0.2 ip, 0-0, 0.00*

After three years in the Baltimore bullpen, Garland became a starter in 1976 and went 20-7 with a 2.68 ERA, ranking third in the league in wins (and second in winning percentage with .741). He had played out his option, and he became a free agent after the season. After signing a lucrative long-term contract with the Indians, in 1977 Garland went 13-19 with a 3.59 ERA for fifth-place Cleveland, tying for the AL lead in losses. On May 5, 1978, he had to have surgery for a rotator cuff tear. He never had another winning season, and he is remembered whenever the supposed evils of free agency and long-term contracts are discussed. /(SH)

Mike Garman — 1949- . RHP 1969, 71-78 Red Sox, **Cardinals**, Cubs, Dodgers, Expos 434 ip, 22-27, 3.63. *1 LCS, 1.1 ip, 0-0, 0.00. 1 WS, 4 ip, 0-0, 0.00*

Boston's number-one pick in the June 1967 draft, the 6'3" Garman had an outstanding fastball and good curve. He pitched sparingly for the Red Sox but blossomed as a reliever with St. Louis. He saved 12 for the 1977 NL champion Dodgers, and 42 lifetime. Garman's father was in the Pirate farm system, brother Steve in the Giants'. /(EW)

Debs Garms — 1908-1984. OF-3B 1932-35, 37-41, 43-45 Browns, **Braves**, Pirates, Cardinals 1010 g, .293, 17 hr, 328 rbi. *2 WS, 4 g, .000* ☛ Led League—ba 40.

Slightly built Debs Garms, a lefthanded-hitting Texan, led the NL with a .355 batting average with Pittsburgh in 1940. Two years earlier, when he batted .315 for the Braves, Garms broke Johnny Vander Meer's string of 21-1/3 hitless innings, which included two consecutive no-hit games. At age 37, Garms was cut by the Cardinals after hitting .336 in 74 games in 1945. /(TJ)

Phil Garner (Scrap Iron) — 1949- . 2B-3B 1973-88 A's, Pirates, **Astros**, Dodgers, Giants 1845 g, .260, 109 hr, 839 rbi. *3 LCS, 9 g, .269, 1 hr, 3 rbi. 1 WS, 7 g, .500, 5 rbi* ☛ All-Star—76, 80-81.

A gritty infielder who got by as much on determination as talent, Garner established himself as a second baseman with the A's under manager Chuck Tanner. When Tanner moved to Pittsburgh, he promptly traded for Garner, who was used at third, then at second after the Pirates acquired Bill Madlock. In 1978 Garner tied a ML record with grand slams in consecutive games (September 14 and 15). An important member of the 1979 World Champion Pirates, he was sometimes called "the best number-eight hitter in baseball." His .500 batting average in the 1979 WS, with at least one hit in each of the seven games, underlined the contention. He was traded to Houston in mid-1981 for the younger Johnny Ray, and Garner, platooned at third base, helped the Astros win the NL Western Division in 1986. /(ME)

Ralph Garr (Roadrunner) — 1945- . OF 1968-80 **Braves**, White Sox, Angels 1317 g, .306, 75 hr, 408 rbi ☛ Led League—ba 74. All-Star—74.

A Grambling football star, Garr reached the Braves briefly in 1968 (his second pro season) and stole home for the first of 172 steals. Unable to crack the

Braves' talent-laden outfield, the lefthanded hitter spent 1969 and 1970 with Richmond (International League), winning back-to-back batting titles. Finally given a job in Atlanta in 1971, he batted .343, with 219 hits, 101 runs, and 30 stolen bases. In 1974 Garr's .353 took the NL batting crown, and he led the league with 214 hits and 17 triples. The free-swinging leadoff man repeated as triples leader in 1975, and hit .300 twice again with the White Sox (1976 and 1977). Among baseball insiders, Garr was known as much for his squeaky voice, Hank Aaron imitations, and nonstop comic monologues as for his bat. He later became a hitting and baserunning instructor. /(MC)

Scott Garrelts — 1961- . RHP 1982- **Giants** 758 ip, 56–41, 3.01. *2 LCS, 14 ip, 1–0, 5.65. 1 WS, 7 ip, 0–2, 9.82*
☛ *Led League—era 89. All-Star—85.*

The hard-throwing Garrelts was the best member of the Giants' bullpen from 1984 to 1988, leading the club in saves each year despite never posting more than 13. He was made a starter in 1989 as the Giants experimented with Mike LaCoss in relief; Garrelts led the NL in ERA (2.28) as the Giants won the division title. He was the Giants' first-round pick in the June 1979 free agent draft, and led the Midwest League in both strikeouts and walks in 1980. In 1985 he led the last-place Giants in both wins (9) and saves (13). /(SCL)

Wayne Garrett — 1947- . 3B-2B 1969–78 **Mets**, Expos, Cardinals 1092 g, .239, 61 hr, 340 rbi. *2 LCS, 8 g, .194, 1 hr, 4 rbi. 2 WS, 9 g, .161, 2 hr, 2 rbi*

The redheaded Garrett played mostly third base, and hit .385 for the Mets in the 1969 LCS. He led 1973 World Series players with 11 strikeouts (tying a seven-game Series futility record) and two HR. Brother Adrian spent small parts of eight seasons in the majors. After losing a game to the 1969 Mets, Cub Ron Santo—referring to rookie Garrett at second base, Ed Kranepool at first base, Al Weis at shortstop, and Bobby Pfeil at third base—remarked, "It's a shame losing to an infield like that . . . I wouldn't let that infield play in Tacoma." /(TJ)

Gil Garrido — 1941- . SS-2B-3B 1964, 68–72 Giants, **Braves** 334 g, .237, 1 hr, 51 rbi. *1 LCS, 3 g, .200*

The Panamanian was first called to the majors in 1961 at age 20, but, knowing no English, couldn't find Candlestick Park and was returned to the minors without getting to play. In the Pacific Coast League he set records at shortstop for fielding percentage and errorless games. He appeared briefly with the Giants, and eventually won a platoon job

with the Braves. Garrido never did master English, and finished in the Mexican League. /(MC)

Ned Garver — 1925- . RHP 1948–61 **Browns**, Tigers, A's, Angels 2477 ip, 129–157, 3.73. 20 wins: 51
☛ *All-Star—51.*

Garver became the only 20th century pitcher to win 20 games in a season for a team which lost 100 when he went 20–12 for the 1951 Browns. He led the AL in complete games (24) that season, as he had the previous year (22). His $25,000 contract in 1952 made him the highest-paid Brown in history. Garver had batted .407 in the Ohio State League in 1944, so it was no surprise when he batted .305 in 1951 to pace the Browns. He hit sixth on occasion, and had a .218 lifetime BA with seven HR. His zeal for hitting was arrested midway through his career when Early Wynn nearly beaned him. Garver lost a league-high 17 with St. Louis in 1949. He had very little trouble getting Mickey Mantle out, but found Vic Wertz a particular thorn in his side. /(WAB)

Steve Garvey (Senator) — 1948- . 1B-3B 1969–87 **Dodgers**, Padres 2332 g, .294, 272 hr, 1308 rbi. *5 LCS, 22 g, .356, 8 hr, 21 rbi. 5 WS, 28 g, .319, 1 hr, 6 rbi*
☛ *Most Valuable Player—74. All-Star—74–81, 84–85. Gold Glove—74–77.*

The most durable player of his era, Garvey played a NL-record 1,207 consecutive games. Originally a third baseman with a suspect arm, he became part of baseball's longest-running infield when he moved to first base. Ron Cey took over at third, and they flanked Davey Lopes and Bill Russell from 1973 to 1981.

Garvey projected his Mr. Clean image to the nation in a TV interview before the 1974 World Series when he explained that "I always try to act as though there is a little boy or a little girl around, and I try never to do anything that would give them a bad example." His nickname, Senator, referred to his post-baseball political aspirations.

Garvey exploded as a NL star in 1974. He was elected to the All-Star team as a write-in candidate that year, and was voted MVP of the game. He followed this up by winning the NL MVP award, capping a nearly perfect season for the man whose father used to drive the Dodgers' bus at Vero Beach during spring training.

Garvey's name would not be left off the All-Star ballot again, and he was elected as a starter the next six years. In 1978 he became the first player to receive more than four million All-Star votes, and he was named MVP of the game that year as well. In ten All-Star Games he hit .393, and his slugging

Steve Garvey

average of .955 is the highest of any player with more than 20 at-bats.

One of the great clutch players of his time, he retired with the NLCS career records for HR (8) and RBI (24) and was named LCS MVP in 1978 and 1984. He also hit .368 in the 1981 divisional series.

The winner of four Gold Gloves, Garvey retired with a .996 fielding average. In 1977 he hit a Los Angeles Dodgers-record 33 HR, the only time in a seven-year period when he failed to better .300 and 200 hits. With Cey, Reggie Smith, and Dusty Baker, Garvey was one of a record four Dodgers to hit 30 homers that year. He led the NL in hits twice and games played six times.

A tremendous Los Angeles favorite who had a junior high school named after him while still an active player, Garvey traumatized fans by signing with the Padres as a free agent in December 1982. On his first trip to Los Angeles as a Padre, he took out a full-page newspaper ad thanking fans for their past support. By the end of his career, lacking protection in the Padres' lineup, Garvey's unwillingness to take bases on balls and a parallel propensity for chasing bad pitches had taken their toll on his

yearly statistics. Following the expiration of his five-year contract with San Diego, he discussed returning to the Dodgers, but an arm injury caused him to retire.

Garvey's Mr. Clean image was tarnished two years after his retirement, when he admitted fathering the children of different women. He had earlier suffered the embarassment of a tell-all book by his ex-wife Cyndy. /(TG)

Jerry Garvin [Theodore Jared] — 1955– . LHP 1977–82 **Blue Jays** 607 ip, 20–41, 4.42

The 6'3" Garvin was taken by Toronto from Minnesota in the 1976 expansion draft. Going 10–18 in 1977 and picking off an unofficial record 22 baserunners, he was named to several all-rookie teams. A reliever after a 1979 arm injury, he set a club record with 61 appearances in 1980. /(EW)

Ned Garvin [Virgil Lee] — 1874–1908. RHP 1896, 99–1904 Phillies, Cubs, Brewers, White Sox, **Dodgers**, Yankees 1401 ip, 57–97, 2.72

Garvin had 13 shutouts among his 57 victories. With Chicago (NL) on September 22, 1899, Garvin allowed 13 hits, yet pitched a complete game shutout to beat the Braves 3–0. /(ARA)

Harry Gaspar — 1883–1940. RHP 1909–12 **Reds** 825 ip, 44–48, 2.69

Gaspar broke in with Duluth in 1905 and after playing with three other minor league teams was drafted by the Reds in 1908. He was released to Toronto in mid-1912 but refused to report and was suspended. Gaspar remained out of the game until 1914 when he joined Sioux City (Western League). He was named manager of Sioux City in mid-1915. He retired from the game in 1919. /(MA)

Pilo Gaspar [Miguel] — 1930– . C 1950–76 Minor and Mexican Leagues

Gaspar caught a record 2,291 minor league games. He hit 44 homers for Laredo (Rio Grande Valley League) in 1950–51, but had only 29 more in the 15 seasons that followed. Though Mexican-born, he didn't play professionally in Mexico until age 28. He batted as high as .330 with Vera Cruz, and caught regularly until age 44. /(MC)

Tommy Gastall — 1932–1956. C 1955–56 **Orioles** 52 g, .181, 0 hr, 4 rbi

Gastall followed in Harry Agganis's tragic footsteps as star quarterback at Boston College. Signed to a $40,000 bonus by the Orioles, he was used sparingly and died at the age of 24 on September 20, 1956 when he crashed while flying a light plane. /(SFS)

Clarence Gaston (Cito) — 1944- . OF 1967, 69-78 Braves, **Padres**, Pirates 1026 g, .256, 91 hr, 387 rbi.
　　Manager 1989- **Blue Jays** 77-49, .611. First place: 89
1 LCS, 1-4, .200
☛ *All-Star—70* .

San Diego took Gaston from the Braves in the 1968 expansion draft. In his 1970 All-Star season, he hit .318 with 29 HR and 93 RBI. The 6'3" Texan returned to Atlanta in 1975 as a backup and became a Blue Jays coach in 1982. Named Toronto's manager in mid-1989, he turned the team around and became the first black manager in post-season play./(TJ)

Milt Gaston [Nathaniel Milton] — 1896- . RHP 1924-34 Yankees, **Browns**, Senators, Red Sox, White Sox 2105 ip, 97-164, 4.55

A winner only in his first two seasons, Gaston led the league in losses with 18 for the Browns in 1926, and 20 with the Red Sox in 1930. He was one of the few players of his day to go straight to the majors. He threw a moving forkball that caused his catchers problems; it was rumored he was traded to Washington because Browns owner Phil Ball was tired of ducking his wild pitches. Milt's brother, Alex, was a ML catcher./(WAB)

Aubrey Gatewood — 1938- . RHP 1963-65, 70 **Angels**, Braves 178 ip, 8-9, 2.78

Gatewood debuted with the Angels, four-hit the Red Sox in his first ML start, and continued to look promising through 1965. Arm trouble sent him back to the minors, except for three games in 1970 with Atlanta./(MC)

Doc Gautreau [Walter Paul] — 1904-1970. 2B 1925-28 A's, **Braves** 261 g, .257, 0 hr, 52 rbi

Gautreau's fine career at Holy Cross made him a favorite in Boston. The 5'4" 129-lb backup second baseman spent a lifetime in organized ball as a scout and minor league manager./(JK)

Joe Gedeon — 1893-1941. 2B 1913-14, 16-20 Senators, Yankees, **Browns** 581 g, .244, 2 hr, 171 rbi

Gedeon was a fringe character in the 1919 Black Sox scandal. Not part of the principal activities, he was a light-hitting second baseman for the uninvolved Browns. He had, according to Commissioner Landis, "guilty knowledge" of the White Sox' intentions of throwing the Series. Banned from organized ball, Gedeon played independent West Coast baseball, causing a problem for other players who were forbidden to play in games when he appeared./(JK)

Rich Gedman — 1959- . C 1980- **Red Sox** 896 g, .260, 83 hr, 356 rbi. *2 LCS, 11 g, .357, 2 hr, 7 rbi. 1 WS, 7 g, .200, 1 hr, 1 rbi*
☛ *All-Star—85-86.*

Gedman was *TSN* AL Rookie Player of the Year in 1981 and by the age of 25 had become one of baseball's top catchers, but was plagued by injuries, holdouts, and inconsistency thereafter. With a wide-open, weight-back batting stance, Gedman hit 24 HR in 1984 and followed with career highs in average (.295) and RBI (80) in 1985 while throwing out nearly half of opposition basestealers. His average dipped to .258 in 1986, and in 1987 he remained unsigned until May 1, then hit only .205 before injuring his thumb in mid-July. In 1988 and 1989, he platooned with Rick Cerone./(SCL)

Lou Gehrig [born Ludwig Heinrich Gehrig] (Columbia Lou, The Iron Horse, Larrupin' Lou, Buster) — 1903-1941. 1B 1923-39 **Yankees** 2164 g, .340, 493 hr, 1990 rbi. *7 WS, 34 g, .361, 10 hr, 35 rbi*
☛ *Most Valuable Player—27, 36. Led League—ba 34. Led League—hr 31, 34, 36. Led League—rbi 27-28, 30-31, 34. All-Star—33-38. Hall of Fame—1939.*

Lou Gehrig was the greatest first baseman ever and a key component in the Yankee legend. He and Cy Young hold the last two "unbreakable" records; Gehrig's 2,130 consecutive games played has never been approached, and in fact the two longest such streaks since then, combined, don't even match his mark. Because he was also handsome, a native New Yorker, and eventually a tragic figure, he became as glamorous as a retiring "mama's boy" could be.

　　Born in a German neighborhood, Gehrig began his legendary career at Columbia University. Freshmen weren't eligible for varsity play, but in his sophomore season Gehrig set multiple school records, most notably season marks of seven HR, a .444 batting average, and a .937 slugging average. Also a pitcher, he still holds the Columbia record for strikeouts in a game, fanning 17 Williams batters in a game he lost. It is rumored that Columbia coach Andy Coakley, a former major leaguer, was paid $500 by the Yankees to convince the youngster to sign with the Yankees. By the way, although Gehrig did hit some prodigious shots at Columbia, he never hit one through a window in the athletic office in Low Library, as depicted in *The Pride of the Yankees*—nobody could.

Lou Gehrig

Gehrig played two seasons with Hartford of the Eastern League and debuted in the majors four days short of his 20th birthday. He had brief but successful stints with the Yankees in 1923 and 1924. He started his famous streak on May 31, 1925, pinch hitting for Pee Wee Wanninger. (Earlier that year, Wanninger had replaced Everett Scott at shortstop, breaking Scott's much-remarked-upon string of 1,307 consecutive games.) The next day, regular first baseman Wally Pipp sat out a game with a headache, and Gehrig started in his place. The team was in seventh place at the time, and Babe Ruth was sick, so some experimentation was in order. Hindsight makes it seem as though the rookie then monopolized the position, but in fact Gehrig's

position was still somewhat tenuous. He was pinch hit for three times that month, and didn't start on July 5, although he came into the game later. Gehrig had a good season, certainly, hitting .295 with 20 HR and 68 RBI in 126 games. But it was in 1927, when he was moved to the cleanup spot and had Bob Meusel protecting him in the order that became known as Murderer's Row, that Gehrig put up big numbers for the first time. He won the MVP award (then given by the league and not awarded to repeat winners) and led the AL with 175 RBI, 52 doubles, and 447 total bases. He finished behind Ruth with 47 HR, 149 runs, a .765 slugging average, and 109 walks. His .373 batting average also ranked second.

Gehrig was overshadowed by Ruth for as long as

Ruth was a Yankee. Gehrig was great, Gehrig was consistent, Gehrig was a role model—but Ruth was larger than life. However, it is Gehrig who owns the AL season record for RBI, with 184 in 1931, and who hit a ML-record 23 grand slams lifetime. Gehrig and Rocky Colavito are the only AL players to hit four homers in a nine-inning game, and Gehrig hit for the cycle twice; Ruth never did. He had at least 100 RBI and 100 runs every full season of his career, 13 straight years, and led the AL five times in RBI and four times in runs. In fact, he topped 150 RBI seven times, also a ML record, and is third all-time on the RBI list. His .632 slugging average also ranks third, and when he retired, only Ruth had hit more home runs.

Ruth pursued media attention and made great copy, but Gehrig led a quiet married life. For a while the two were friends, but a coolness developed between them, variously ascribed to Ruth making a pass at a female friend of Gehrig's or making a derogatory comment about Mom Gehrig, whom Lou always worshiped. Nonetheless, Ruth and Gehrig had a cordial professional relationship until Ruth left the team after the 1934 season. In 1931, the year they tied for the AL HR lead, Gehrig lost a home run passing Ruth on the bases.

Ruth and Gehrig carried the Yankees, but there were some years when they just weren't enough. Connie Mack's Athletics won three straight years, 1929–31, before the Yankees came back in 1932 for another World Championship. In the following seasons, it became clear that Ruth was fading. In their last year together, 1934, Gehrig won the Triple Crown with 49 HR, 165 RBI, and a .363 BA; in 1935 he dropped off to .329 with 30 HR and 119 RBI. He was also bothered more and more by lumbago; in 1934 he had suffered an attack on the field and had to be carried off. He was quite aware of his consecutive games streak, as were manager Joe McCarthy and the writers. The next day he was penciled in the lineup as the leadoff hitter, listed at shortstop. Hardly able to stand, he singled, and Red Rolfe pinch ran for him and finished the game at shortstop. He kept his string going through the years despite a broken thumb, a broken toe, back spasms, and lumbago, stoically, in fact proudly, playing through the pain.

The arrival of Joe DiMaggio in 1936 made enough of a difference that Gehrig had his last two great seasons in 1936 and 1937 as the Yankees won World Championships. The Giants managed something no other team had done since 1926: they won a World Series game from the Yankees. But Gehrig homered in close contests in Games Three and Four.

He was always a good World Series hitter, with 10 HR lifetime, including a record-setting four in the four-game 1928 WS.

The Yankees repeated in 1938, but Gehrig dropped below .300 for the first time since his rookie season. In 1939 he was obviously enfeebled, and on May 2 he took himself out of the lineup. He was hitting just .143, and was quite clumsy afield. Many players were afraid he would injure himself, but nobody would suggest that he sit down, not even manager McCarthy. Gehrig had to take the initiative himself. He never played again, and although, in his capacity as team captain, he continued to carry the lineup card out every day, eventually even that proved more than he could handle. He was diagnosed as having a rare, almost unknown, and incurable disease, amyotrophic lateral sclerosis, forever after known as Lou Gehrig's disease. It was not announced that he was doomed, although many suspected it and Gehrig knew. On July 4, 1939, Lou Gehrig Day was held at Yankee Stadium. It may be the most famous ceremony in baseball history, with Gehrig's assertion that "today, I consider myself the luckiest man on the face of the earth" an unforgettable statement. The waiting period for the new Hall of Fame was waived, and he was admitted the year it opened, in 1939. He spent his last two years of life working for New York Mayor Fiorello LaGuardia, and died on June 2, 1941./(SH)

Charlie Gehringer (The Mechanical Man) — 1903– . 2B 1924–42 **Tigers** 2323 g, .320, 184 hr, 1427 rbi. *3 WS, 20 g, .321, 1 hr, 7 rbi*
☛ *Most Valuable Player—37. Led League—ba 37. All-Star—1933–38. Hall of Fame—49.*

One of baseball's most surehanded second basemen and a dependable hitter, the taciturn and undemonstrative Gehringer was called The Mechanical Man. "You wind him up Opening Day and forget him," teammate Doc Cramer said. Detroit manager Mickey Cochrane explained, "Charlie says 'hello' on Opening Day, 'goodbye' on closing day, and in between hits .350." His silence and lack of color were legendary. During a game in the 1930s Detroit shortstop Bill Rogell captured a windblown pop fly well on the second-base side of the infield and accidentally spiked Gehringer. "I can catch those too," Gehringer said mildly and limped back to his position.

He covered second base in a smooth, seemingly effortless style. He had quick hands and rarely lost a ball he got his glove on. Gehringer led all AL second basemen in fielding percentage nine times, led or

Charlie Gehringer

In 1926 Gehringer became the Tigers' regular second baseman.

A reliable hitter with good power, he led the AL in batting in 1937 with a .371 mark. He was chosen MVP that season. He had more than 200 hits in seven different seasons and led the league in hits and runs scored in 1929 and 1934. He led once in triples and twice in doubles, ranking tenth all-time in two-base hits. Seven times he had more than 100 RBI. In 1929 he topped the AL in stolen bases. His controlled, lefthanded batting swing made him difficult to strike out. In 16 full seasons, his strikeouts ranged from 16 to 42.

Gehringer starred for Tigers pennant winners in 1934, 1935, and 1940. He slumped badly in 1941, then entered the Navy for three years. In 1949 he was elected to Baseball's Hall of Fame. From 1951 through 1953 he served as Detroit's GM and vice president, continuing in the latter position through 1959. At the time of baseball's centennial celebration in 1969, a special committee of baseball writers named him the game's greatest living second baseman. /(FS)

Phil Geier (Little Phil) — 1875–1967. OF-2B 1896–97, 1900–01, 04 Phillies, Reds, A's, Milwaukee (AL), **Braves** 349 g, .249, 2 hr, 102 rbi

Geier won the American Association batting championship in 1903, hitting .362 to earn a third ML trial. His .243 BA as a regular with the 1904 Braves sent him back down. /(BC)

Gary Geiger — 1937– . OF 1958–67, 69–70 Indians, **Red Sox**, Braves, Astros 954 g, .246, 77 hr, 283 rbi

After coming up through the Indians' system and playing in Cleveland in 1958, Geiger was traded to the Red Sox with the fading Vic Wertz in return for Jimmy Piersall. In 1959 Geiger played centerfield between the previous year's MVP, Jackie Jensen, and batting champ, Ted Williams. A lefthanded hitter playing in Fenway Park, Geiger was batting .302 in 1960 when he went down with a collapsed lung, missing the rest of the season. He hit 50 HR over the next three seasons, but never hit near .300 again. He did hit .385 in 1964, but in only five games; he missed most of the season due to illness that extended into 1965, when he also suffered a fractured skull. The Red Sox gave up on him, and comebacks with the Braves and Astros as a reserve outfielder and pinch hitter proved disappointing. /(SH)

tied for the lead in assists seven times, and had the most putouts three times. Baseball authority H.G. Salsinger wrote: "He lacks showmanship, but he has polish that no other second baseman, with the exception of the great Napoleon Lajoie, ever had. He has so well-schooled himself in the technique of his position that he makes the most difficult plays look easy."

Following one year at the University of Michigan, Gehringer was signed by the Tigers in 1924 on the recommendation of former Tigers star Bobby Veach. The legend persists that then-manager Ty Cobb doubted the slim youngster's ability to hit ML pitching. Cobb later said, "I knew Charlie would hit and I was so anxious to sign him that I didn't even take the time to change out of my uniform before rushing him into the front office to sign a contract."

Dave Geisel — 1955- . LHP 1978-79, 81-85 Cubs, **Blue Jays**, Mariners 208 ip, 5-5, 4.02

Geisel was a reliever with no outstanding pitch who was primarily used to get out lefthanded hitters. He had trouble staying healthy, broke an ankle in 1980 and a collarbone in 1981, and spent only one full season in the majors—1983 with Toronto (0-3, five saves). /(MC)

Harry Geisel — 1888-1966. *Umpire* AL 1925-42 *3 WS 2 ASU*

Geisel's complaints in 1937 about the slickness of new baseballs led to the ML adopting the special deglossing mud with which all balls are now rubbed before they go into play. On April 16, 1940, Geisel was behind the plate as Bob Feller blanked Chicago in the only Opening Day no-hitter. /(RTM)

Charley Gelbert — 1906-1967. SS-3B 1929-32, 35-37, 39-40 **Cardinals**, Reds, Tigers, Senators, Red Sox 876 g, .267, 17 hr, 350 rbi. *2 WS, 13 g, .300, 5 rbi*

A superb fielder with a lively bat, Gelbert was four years into a bright career with St. Louis when an off-season hunting accident nearly cost him his left leg. After sitting out two years, he returned to the majors in 1935 as a utility man. In 1931 Gelbert set records for shortstops in a seven-game World Series with 42 chances, 29 assists, 6 double plays, and a 1.000 fielding average. /(JL)

John Gelnar — 1943- . RHP 1964, 67, 69-71 Pirates, **Pilots/Brewers** 230 ip, 7-14, 4.19

In 1969 the expansion Pilots traded Lou Piniella, who won the Rookie of the Year award that season, to the expansion Royals for Gelnar and outfielder Steve Whitaker. Gelnar compiled a 3-10, 3.31 record starting and relieving. When the team moved to Milwaukee in 1970, he had his only winning season, going 4-3 with four saves. /(JFC)

Joe Genewich — 1897-1985. RHP 1922-30 **Braves**, Giants 1402 ip, 73-92, 4.29

Genewich was a $5-a-game sandlot pitcher with no college or minor league experience when the Braves signed him. As a rookie in early 1923, he outpitched the Giants' Jack Bentley, for whom John McGraw had just paid $65,000. Genewich had had limited success in five-plus Boston seasons (57-76) when McGraw traded four players for him in mid-1928. He went 11-4 the rest of the season, then faded. /(NLM)

Jim Gentile (Diamond Jim) — 1934- . 1B 1957-58, 60-66 Dodgers, **Orioles**, A's, Astros, Indians 936 g, .260, 179 hr, 549 rbi
☛ *All-Star—60-62.*

Since there was no room for a rookie first baseman on a team that already had Gil Hodges, Diamond Jim (so nicknamed by Roy Campanella, who considered the young lefthanded slugger a diamond in the rough) languished for eight years in the Dodger farm system. Finally traded to Baltimore, in 1961 the temperamental San Francisco native batted .302 with 46 HR and—on only 147 hits—a club record 141 RBI. His five '61 grand slams, including two straight in one game, set an AL record that stood until 1987. /(TJ)

Gary Gentry — 1946- . RHP 1969-75 **Mets**, Braves 903 ip, 46-49, 3.56. *1 LCS, 2 ip, 0-0, 9.00. 1 WS, 7 ip, 1-0, 0.00*

As a hard-throwing rookie, Gentry was an effective starter (13-12) for the 1969 Miracle Mets. With defensive help from Tommie Agee in centerfield, Gentry and Nolan Ryan combined to shut out Baltimore in Game Three of the '69 WS. His November 1972 trade to Atlanta was followed by a ruinous elbow injury. /(CR)

Rufe Gentry [James Rufus] — 1918- . RHP 1943-44, 46-48 **Tigers** 243 ip, 13-17, 4.37

Workhorse Gentry pitched 300 innings and won 20 games for Buffalo (International League) in 1943. For Detroit in 1944 he was 12-14, with an AL-high 108 walks. A holdout in 1945, he was placed on the voluntary retired list, but pitched ten innings for Detroit from 1946 to 1948. /(EW)

Wally Gerber (Spooks) — 1891-1951. SS 1914-15, 17-29 Pirates, **Browns**, Red Sox 1522 g, .257, 7 hr, 476 rbi

The Browns' aggressive everyday shortstop from 1919 through 1927, Gerber led AL shortstops in errors in 1919 and 1920, but settled down to lead in double plays four times. He had quick hands for everything, except (his teammates said) picking up the check, but when the Depression rolled around, Gerber, who had invested well, became a source of financial help for former teammates. /(JK)

Ken Gerhart — 1961- . OF 1986-88 **Orioles** 215 g, .221, 24 hr, 64 rbi

The injury-plagued Gerhart had his best year in 1987, reaching career highs with a .243 average, 14

HR, and 34 RBI before going on the DL in mid-August and missing the rest of the year. /(JFC)

Al Gerheauser (Lefty) — 1917–1972. LHP 1943–46, 48 **Phillies**, Pirates, Browns 643 ip, 25–50, 4.13

Gerheauser lost two of every three decisions as a wartime starter in Philadelphia and was mostly a reliever with Pittsburgh and St. Louis. Wildness was his primary handicap. /(EW)

Dick Gernert — 1928– . 1B-OF 1952–62 **Red Sox**, Cubs, Tigers, Reds, Astros 835 g, .254, 103 hr, 402 rbi. *1 WS, 4 g, .000*

Gernert was a power hitter out of Temple University. He hit 19 HR as a Boston rookie and 21 as a sophomore in the only years he was a regular. The off-season schoolteacher pinch hit four times for the Reds in the 1961 World Series. /(EW)

Cesar Geronimo — 1948– . OF 1969–83 Astros, **Reds**, Royals 1522 g, .258, 51 hr, 392 rbi. *5 LCS, 17 g, .095, 1 hr, 4 rbi. 3 WS, 18 g, .246, 2 hr, 7 rbi* ☛ *Gold Glove—74–77.*

Geronimo, the outstanding defensive centerfielder of five divisional champions and the 1975–76 World Champion Reds teams, was first signed by the Yankees, who briefly tried to make a pitcher out of him. The lefthanded Dominican made his ML debut with Houston, and went to Cincinnati in the November 1971 deal that also moved Joe Morgan to the Reds. Geronimo was the 3,000th strikeout victim of both Bob Gibson and Nolan Ryan. "I was just in the right place at the right time," he joked. /(TJ)

Doc Gessler [Harry Homer] — 1880–1924. OF-1B 1903–06, 08–11 Tigers, Dodgers, Cubs, Red Sox, **Senators** 880 g, .281, 14 hr, 363 rbi. *1 WS, 2 g, .000. Manager* 1914 **Pittsburgh (FL)** 6–12, .333

A fine batter but never a great outfielder, Gessler was known as the strong man of baseball for his feats of physical strength. One of three doctors in the 1906 World Series (with Doc White and Frank Owen), Gessler became a physician, graduating from Johns Hopkins Medical School. /(EW)

Al Gettel — 1917– . RHP 1945–49, 51, 55 **Yankees**, Indians, White Sox, Senators, Giants, Cardinals 734 ip, 38–45, 4.28

Gettel recorded a 2.97 ERA for the 1946 Yankees and won 11 games for the 1947 Indians. Later, with Oakland (Pacific Coast League), Gettel pitched and won a 22-inning marathon. /(TJ)

Gus Getz (Gee Gee) — 1889–1969. 3B-2B 1909–10, 14–18 Braves, **Dodgers**, Reds, Indians, Pirates 339 g, .238, 2 hr, 93 rbi. *1 WS, 1 g, .000*

A good glove man, Getz was the third baseman for the 1915 Dodgers. He played just seven games for the Reds in 1917, but one was the May 2, Fred Toney-Hippo Vaughn double no-hitter. He later managed and umpired in the minors. /(NLM)

Charlie Getzein (Pretzels) — 1864–1932. RHP 1884–92 **Detroit (NL)**, Indianapolis (NL), Braves, Cleveland (NL), Cardinals 2539 ip, 145–139, 3.46. 20 wins: 86–87, 90

Getzein was an outstanding pitcher of the 1880s. In 1886 he was 30–11 for the Detroit NL team. The following season, he was 29–13 and led the NL in winning percentage (.690) as Detroit won the pennant. In the 15-game postseason championship series between the NL winner and the American Association champion, he posted four wins. Getzein and catcher Charlie Ganzel became known as the Pretzel Battery because they both were of German extraction. /(BC)

Rube Geyer [Jacob Bowman] — 1885–1962. RHP 1910–13 **Cardinals** 412 ip, 17–26, 3.67

Geyer was a winner only in his rookie Cardinal season, going 9–6 in 1911. He was a minor league manager when his playing days ended. /(NLM)

Patsy Gharrity — 1892–1966. C-1B 1916–23, 29–30 **Senators** 679 g, .262, 20 hr, 249 rbi

A roommate and favorite catcher of Walter Johnson, Gharrity became a coach when Johnson managed the Senators and Indians. The versatile Gharrity also played first base and outfield. He hit .310 as Washington's regular catcher in 1921. /(JK)

A. Bartlett Giamatti (Bart) — 1938–1989. *Executive.*

Giamatti, a lifelong Red Sox fan, came to prominence as the president of Yale University, where his tough dealing with the college's union favorably impressed baseball's owners. Also appreciated was his devotion to baseball's tradition. Named president of the NL in December 1986, he gained attention for his 30-day suspension of Pete Rose in 1988 after Rose, the Reds' manager, shoved umpire Dave Pallone. After succeeding Peter Uebberoth as Commissioner in April 1989, Giamatti's most famous decision once again involved Rose, whom he suspended for life for gambling. A week later, Giamatti died of a massive heart attack.

Giamatti received his B.A. (English) and Ph.D. (Comparative Literature) from Yale and, after teaching at Princeton in 1964–66, returned to Yale in 1966. He became Yale's president in July 1978 and served for eight years. He wrote many books and articles on Renaissance literature as well as a number of baseball essays. /(SH)

Joe Giard (Peco) — 1898–1956. LHP 1925–27 **Browns**, Yankees 278 ip, 13–15, 5.96

As a rookie, Giard went 10–5 despite a 5.04 ERA and twice as many walks as strikeouts for the slugging 1925 Browns. He slipped to 3–10 (7.00) in 1926 and was traded to the Yankees. /(WAB)

Joe Gibbon — 1936– . LHP 1960–72 **Pirates**, Giants, Reds, Astros 1119 IP, 61–65, 3.52. *1 LCS, 0.1 ip, 0–0, 0.00. 1 WS, 3 ip, 0–0, 9.00*

A 6'4" University of Mississippi basketball All-American, Gibbon looked like the emerging star of Pittsburgh's staff in 1961 (13–10, 3.32). After an injury-plagued 1962, he bounced back in 1964 to go 10–7. He went to the Giants in a 1965 trade for Matty Alou, who then won the 1966 batting title. By 1968 Gibbon was solely a reliever. /(ME)

Jake Gibbs [Jerry Dean] — 1938– . C 1962–71 **Yankees** 538 g, .233, 25 hr, 146 rbi

This University of Mississippi All-American quarterback and third baseman was drafted by the AFL Oilers and the NFL Browns. A $105,000 Yankee bonus-baby, Gibbs was thought to be in the Dickey-Berra-Howard mold, but he had a weak bat and an injury-prone body, and spent most of his career as a platoon player. He returned to coach at Ole Miss. /(GDW)

Bob Gibson [Robert Louis, Jr.] — 1957– . RHP 1983–87 **Brewers**, Mets 270 ip, 12–18, 4.24

Gibson was a wild power pitcher with no effective breaking pitches. He was a middle reliever and sometimes starter except for the second half of 1985, when he bolstered a failing Rollie Fingers in Milwaukee's bullpen and finished 6–7 with 11 saves. /(JCA)

Bob Gibson (Hoot) — 1935– . RHP 1959–75 **Cardinals** 3885 ip, 251–174, 2.91. 20 wins: 65–66, 68–70 *3 WS, 81 ip, 7–2, 1.89*
☛ *Most Valuable Player—68. Led League—w 70. Led League—era 68. Led League—k 68. Cy Young Award—68, 70. All-Star—62, 65–70, 72. Gold Glove—65–73. Hall of Fame—1981.*

Bob Gibson getting his record 24th strikeout of the 1964 World Series

There have been few pitchers more intimidating or more dominating than Bob Gibson. His great physical stamina and tremendous concentration gave him an enormous edge enhanced by his willingness to pitch inside and sometimes hit batters. His 1968 season is one of the very best ever turned in by a pitcher, and his stellar World Series performances made him the toughest pitcher in the Fall Classic since Whitey Ford and brought him Hall of Fame election in 1981. With a blazing fastball, darting slider, good curve, and pinpoint control, from 1963 to 1972 Gibson averaged better than 19 wins per season. He struck out more than 200 batters nine times and led the NL four times in shutouts. In 1971 he no-hit the Pirates.

Two aspects of Gibson's career demand special mention. In 1968 he pitched 13 shutouts on his way to a 1.12 ERA, the second-lowest since 1893 in 300 innings. During one stretch Gibson allowed only two runs over 92 innings. His strikeouts to innings ratio approached 1.0, while he walked only 62 batters all season. At one point he won fifteen games in succession.

The second area in which Gibson proved phenomenal was World Series play. He won seven consecutive games and pitched eight straight complete games in World Series competition. Only Whitey Ford owns more World Series victories than Gibson, who is also second all-time in WS strikeouts. In the opening match of the 1968 classic, Gibson beat 30-game winner Denny McLain 4–0 and set a Series record by fanning 17 Tigers. His 35 total strikeouts in the 1968 WS were also a record. He won Game Four 10–1, but lost Game Seven 4–1, on two days' rest, to Mickey Lolich. Gibson lost a shutout in the seventh inning when Curt Flood uncharacteristically misjudged a routine fly ball.

Gibson won the clinchers in both the 1964 and 1967 Series. In Game Two of the 1964 Series against the Yankees, he lost 8–3 but kept it close until he was knocked out in the ninth inning. He won Game Five 5–2 in ten innings, taking a shutout into the ninth. Coming back on two days' rest for Game Seven, he won 7–5. In 27 innings, he had 31 strikeouts and a 3.00 ERA. In 1967 he beat Boston's Jose Santiago in the opener, 2–1, and in Game Four, 6–0, and bested Jim Lonborg 7–2 in the finale.

A sickly child who almost died, Gibson was found to have a heart murmur but went on to excel in basketball and baseball in high school. He accepted a basketball scholarship to Creighton University and was the first person inducted into the school's Sports Hall of Fame. In 1957 Bob agreed to sign with the Cardinals for $4,000 and reported to the Omaha farm club. After the baseball campaign was complete, he joined the Harlem Globetrotters for a season. His Omaha manager, Johnny Keane, had great confidence in him, but two trials with the Cardinals had produced a 6–11 record and not much of an impression on the St. Louis manager, Solly Hemus. However, when Keane replaced Hemus in 1961, he put Gibson in the starting rotation to stay. Gibson blossomed in 1963, going 18–9, as the Cardinals contended following the acquisition of fine-fielding shortstop Dick Groat.

Gibson retired as the winningest pitcher in

Cardinals history. He became the second pitcher in history to fan 3,000 batters and also hurled 56 shutouts. His incredible career was accomplished despite a fractured leg (1962), a severely strained elbow (1966), a broken leg (1967), and badly torn ligaments and knee surgery (1973). After struggling through the 1975 campaign on bad legs, Gibson decided in early September that it was time to retire when light-hitting Pete LaCock powered a grand-slam home run off him.

Gibson proved quickly and repeatedly there simply wasn't an element of the game he hadn't mastered. From 1965 to 1973 he won nine consecutive Gold Gloves for fielding excellence. He often helped his cause with the bat, laying down a successful bunt or hitting up the middle. He had 24 regular-season home runs plus a pair in World Series play. In 1970 he batted .303 and was occasionally employed as a pinch hitter.

After serving as former teammate Joe Torre's pitching coach with the Mets and Braves, Gibson returned to St. Louis as a baseball radio commentator and sports show host. /(FO)

Frank Gibson — 1890–1961. C 1913, 21–27 Tigers, **Braves** 468 g, .274, 8 hr, 146 rbi

A switch-hitting catcher and frequent pinch hitter, Gibson played pro ball for 21 years, mostly in the minors. He once held out with the Braves—not for more money, but for more work. /(NLM)

George Gibson (Moon) — 1880–1967. C 1905–18 **Pirates**, Giants 1213 g, .236, 15 hr, 345 rbi. *1 WS, 7 g, .240, 2 rbi.*
    Manager 1920–22, 1925, 1932–34 **Pirates**, Cubs 413–344, .546

For 11 years, Gibson was a full-time or platooned Pirate catcher. He set a Pittsburgh record with 1,113 games caught from 1905 through 1916. The burly Canadian was a surprisingly light hitter. Named Pirate manager by owner Barney Dreyfus in 1920, the team folded down the stretch in 1921 and Gibson quit in mid-1922. He was rehired by new owner Bill Benswanger ten years later, guided the Pirates to second-place finishes in 1932–33, but was fired after a slow start in 1934. Though he compiled a .546 career winning percentage, Gibson reputedly was unable to maintain discipline. /(ME)

Josh Gibson

Josh Gibson — 1911–1947. C-OF Negro Leagues
1930–46 Homestead Grays, Pittsburgh Crawfords 508 g,
.384, 142 hr (inc.)
☛ *Led League—ba 38, 42–43, 45. Led League—hr 32,
34, 36, 38–39, 42, 44–46. Hall of Fame—1972.*

The warm, fun-loving, well-liked Gibson was a 6'1"
215-lb catcher who was considered by many the
greatest Negro League player of all time and the best
hitter of his era.

Gibson's pro career began in 1930 at the age of
18. He was watching a game between the Homestead Grays and the Kansas City Monarchs, who
had brought along their new lighting system. It was
the first night baseball game played in Pittsburgh.
The lighting was poor, and Grays pitcher Smokey
Joe Williams and catcher Buck Ewing got their
signals crossed. Williams threw a fastball and split
Ewing's hand. Grays manager Judy Johnson, who
knew of Gibson's reputation as an outstanding semi-

pro player, recalled, "I called time and Josh was
sitting up there in the stands and I asked him if he
wanted to catch and he said 'yes sir,' so we had to
hold up the game while he went and put Buck
Ewing's uniform on. We signed him the next day."

Gibson played for the Grays in 1930–31, then
jumped to the Crawfords in 1932 and won three
home run titles (1932, 1934, and 1936). In '36 he
hit 20 HR in only 38 games. He batted .385 in
1933, and .457 in 1936. He began 1937 in the
Dominican Republic, where he hit .453. Returning
to the Grays in July, when the Dominican season
ended, he batted .435. He won the HR title in 1938
and 1939, and won his first batting title in '38 with a
.440 mark; he had just missed in '36 (.457) and '37
(.435).

Gibson joined Vera Cruz of the Mexican League
and hit .467 in an abbreviated 1940 season. In 1941
he batted .374 and led the league with 33 HR and
124 RBI in 94 games. He also won the Puerto Rican
Winter League batting title in '41 with a .480 mark,
and was named the league's MVP.

Gibson returned to the Homestead Grays in 1942
and led the league with 20 HR in only 42 games
while batting a league-high .452. On January 1,
1943, he suddenly fell into a coma that lasted for a
day. Doctors told him he had a brain tumor, but
Gibson refused to let them operate, fearing that
surgery would leave him a vegetable. He continued
to play, winning HR titles in 1944–46 and batting
crowns in 1943 and 1945.

On January 20, 1947, Gibson told his mother
that he was going to die that night. She laughed, but
told him to go to bed and that she would call a
doctor. With his family gathered around him, Gibson asked for his baseball trophies to be brought to
his bedside. He was laughing and talking when he
suddenly sat straight up, had a stroke, and died. He
was 35 years old.

Not only did Gibson hit home runs with amazing
frequency, he hit them astounding distances. He
blasted one in Monessen, PA, that was measured at
575'. *The Sporting News* of June 3, 1967, credits
him with a homer in a Negro League game at
Yankee Stadium that hit two feet from the top of the
wall circling the bleachers in centerfield, about 580'
from home plate. It was estimated that had the drive
had cleared the wall, it would have traveled 700'.
And, although it never has been conclusively verified, Jack Marshall, of the Chicago American Giants, claims that Gibson did smash a ball over the
stadium's triple deck next to the bullpen in left field,

the only fair ball ever hit out of the House That Ruth Built.

Regarding Gibson's defensive skills, Walter Johnson said he was as good as Bill Dickey. Roy Campanella called him "not only the greatest catcher, but the greatest ballplayer I ever saw." Cool Papa Bell said Gibson was merely a "good" catcher who had a strong arm, was a good handler of pitchers, but was poor on pop-ups. Jimmie Crutchfield, Gibson's teammate on the 1932–36 Crawfords, offered this assessment: "I can remember when he couldn't catch this building if you threw it at him . . .And I watched him develop into a very good defensive catcher. He was never given enough credit for his ability as a catcher."

In 13 complete seasons in the Negro Leagues, Gibson won nine HR titles and four batting crowns. His lifetime average of .384 was the highest in Negro League history. In a poll conducted in the early 1980s among experts on black baseball, Gibson was named the Negro Leagues' greatest catcher. He was elected to the Hall of Fame by the Committee on Negro Baseball Leagues in 1972. /(JM)

Kirk Gibson — 1957– . OF-DH 1979– **Tigers**, Dodgers 1114 g, .274, 184 hr, 603 rbi. *3 LCS, 15 g, .254, 2 hr, 12 rbi. 2 WS, 6 g, .368, 3 hr, 9 rbi*
☛ *Most Valuable Player—88.*

Coming to the Dodgers as a free agent in 1988, Gibson's intensity spurred the team to a World Championship highlighted by his dramatic game-winning home run in the Series opener. Kept out of the lineup by a leg injury, he pinch hit with two out in the bottom of the ninth with Mike Davis on base and the Dodgers down 4–3. Visibly wincing on each swing, he fouled off four pitches before he hit a slider out off A's relief ace Dennis Eckersley and limped around the bases. It was his only at-bat in the Series.

Gibson was also a hero in the LCS, with a 12th-inning solo shot to beat the Mets in Game Four. He hit a three-run homer in Los Angeles' 7–4 victory in Game Five and got the game-winning RBI in the clincher with a first-inning sacrifice fly. Not a good fielder, his approach was displayed in Game Three when, playing on a sloppy field, the gimpy Gibson made a crucial slipping, lunging catch in the mud despite nearly falling down three times in pursuit of the fly ball.

An All-America football flanker and baseball outfielder at Michigan State University, Gibson was Detroit's number-one pick in the June 1978 draft. His raw power and speed led Sparky Anderson to dub him "the next Mickey Mantle." Injuries restricted his progress until 1984, when he became the first Tiger ever to hit 20 home runs and steal 20 bases in the same season, the first with at least 10 doubles, triples, homers, and steals since Charlie Gehringer in 1930, and dominated postseason play. He was the MVP of the LCS, then led the Tigers with seven RBI and three steals in the World Series. He hit two homers and scored the winning run in the fifth, and final, game. In 1986 Gibson set a major league record with five consecutive game-winning RBI and was honored as AL Player of the Week three times. An extremely intense player, with awesome power resulting in several tape-measure home runs, Gibson's below-average defense resulted in a shift from right field to left in 1987. His home run and game-winning single at Toronto on September 27, 1987 enabled the Tigers to avoid a sweep, recover, and wrest the division title from the Blue Jays.

A year after his 1988 MVP award, injuries limited Gibson to 71 games and a .213 batting average. /(ME)

Norwood Gibson — 1877–1959. RHP 1903–06 **Red Sox** 609 ip, 34–32, 2.93

A 1901 Notre Dame graduate with a degree in chemistry, the spitballing Gibson was the number-four starting pitcher on both the 1903 and 1904 pennant-winning Red Sox. /(CG)

Paul Gibson — 1960– . LHP 1988– **Tigers** 224 ip, 8–10, 3.94

Both a starter and reliever, Gibson pitched well in his rookie season, going 4–2 with a 2.93 ERA, but experienced control problems in 1989. /(SFS)

Russ Gibson — 1939– . C 1967–72 **Red Sox**, Giants 264 g, .228, 8 hr, 78 rbi. *1 WS, 2 g, .000*

Gibson spent ten years in the minors, and in his first major league game, April 14, 1967, caught fellow rookie Billy Rohr as the latter came within one out of a no-hitter. Gibson caught the first game of that year's World Series. /(RMu)

Sam Gibson — 1899–1983. RHP 1926–28, 30, 32 **Tigers**, Yankees, Giants 594 ip, 32–38, 4.24

The sidearming Gibson was only moderately successful in the majors but was a legend in the Pacific Coast League. He had six 20-win seasons for San Francisco and won 307 minor league games, the last at age 47. /(JK)

Floyd Giebell — 1909– . RHP 1939–41 **Tigers** 68 ip, 3–1, 3.99

Giebell's meteoric career peaked on September 27,

1940, when he beat Cleveland ace Bob Feller and won the AL pennant for Detroit with a fine six-hitter that proved to be his last ML victory./(EW)

Paul Giel — 1932– . RHP 1954–55, 58–61 **Giants**, Pirates, Twins, A's 240 ip, 11–9, 5.39

Reliever Giel hurled for the original editions of both the San Francisco Giants (1958) and Minnesota Twins (1961). He later became the athletic director at his alma mater, the University of Minnesota, where he had been an All-American single-wing tailback./(TJ)

Billy Gilbert — 1876–1927. 2B-SS 1901–06, 08–09 Brewers, Baltimore (AL), **Giants**, Cardinals 850 g, .247, 5 hr, 237 rbi. *1 WS, 5 g, .235, 1 rbi*

Gilbert, a scrappy John McGraw-type player, was the keystone star of the Giants infield when they won pennants in 1904 and 1905. McGraw, managing Baltimore, had purchased Gilbert in 1902 to play shortstop. When McGraw took over the Giants in 1903, Gilbert came along and took charge of second base. Gilbert later managed in the minors and coached for the Boston Braves./(JK)

Charlie Gilbert — 1919–1983. OF 1940–43, 46–47 Dodgers, Cubs, **Phillies** 364 g, .229, 5 hr, 55 rbi

This injury-plagued, fleet outfielder had a weak bat, but nonetheless led the NL with 40 pinch at-bats for the Phillies in 1947. His father, Larry, was a Braves outfielder in 1914–15, and his brother, Tookie, was a Giants first baseman in 1950 and 1953./(EW)

Wally Gilbert — 1901–1958. 3B 1928–32 **Dodgers** 591 g, .269, 7 hr, 214 rbi

An adventurous third baseman, Gilbert led the NL in errors in 1930 and assists in 1931, when he got six hits in a game and went homerless in 552 AB./(TG)

Rod Gilbreath — 1952– . 2B-3B 1972–78 **Braves** 500 g, .248, 14 hr, 125 rbi

In seven years with the Braves Gilbreath performed as a utility infielder, mainly at second base. A light hitter, Gilbreath augmented his limited offensive ability by drawing 147 walks in his career./(DV)

Brian Giles — 1960– . 2B-SS 1981–83, 85–86 **Mets**, Brewers, White Sox 242 g, .228, 6 hr, 39 rbi

Giles was the Mets' regular second baseman in 1983 and hit .245 with 17 steals and 39 runs in 400 at-bats./(WOR)

George Giles — 1909– . 1B Negro Leagues 1927–38 Philadelphia Stars, Kansas City Monarchs, St. Louis Stars, Detroit Stars, Homestead Grays, Baltimore Elite Giants, Brooklyn Eagles, New York Black Yankees, Kansas City Royal Giants, Gilkerson Union Giants, Pittsburgh Crawfords, Satchel Paige All-Stars .312 (inc.) ☛ *All-Star—35.*

Giles was a superb Negro League first baseman and a lifetime .300 hitter. Black all-star Ted "Double Duty" Radcliffe called Giles "the best colored first baseman I ever saw . . ." Giles played for the St. Louis Stars, one of the Negro Leagues' greatest teams, from 1929 through 1931. In a 1930 eight-game series against major league all-stars, the Stars won six games against the pitching of Willis Hudlin, George Uhle, and Earl Whitehill. The Stars won the Negro National League pennant in 1930 and 1931. In the twilight of his career, Giles played for the Satchel Paige All-Stars. His final contribution to pro baseball was as manager of the 1935 Brooklyn Eagles./(LL)

Warren Giles — 1896–1979. *Executive.* ☛ *Hall of Fame—1979.*

Back home in Moline, Illinois, from the army in WWI, Giles went to a meeting about the future of the local Three-I League team, and was elected

Warren Giles

president of the club. After success with Moline, he moved to front-office positions in the St. Louis Cardinals' farm system, eventually becoming GM at Rochester, the Cardinals' top minor league club. In 1937 he took over as GM of the Cincinnati Reds; two years later, the team won the NL pennant and in 1940 they became World Champions. Giles was elected club president in 1948.

In 1951, during the owners' voting for a new Commissioner, Giles and Ford Frick stalemated through 17 ballots until Giles withdrew his name. The following year, he was elected president of the NL. During his 18-year tenure, the affable Giles presided over historic franchise shifts, including those of the Dodgers and Giants to the West Coast and the Boston Braves to Milwaukee and then Atlanta. New NL franchises were added with the Mets, Astros, Padres, and Expos. He was elected to the Hall of Fame in 1979. His son, Bill, is president and part owner of the Phillies. /(NLM)

Frank Gilhooley (Flash) — 1892–1959. OF 1911–19 Cardinals, **Yankees**, Red Sox 312 g, .271, 2 hr, 58 rbi

Gilhooley was a reserve outfielder who, in his one season as a regular (1918), led AL outfielders by participating in eight double plays, tying a Yankee record. /(EW)

George Gill — 1909– . RHP 1937–39 **Tigers**, Browns 395 ip, 24–26, 5.05

In May 1939, Gill was one of six Detroit players sent to the Browns in a trade for legendary hurler Bobo Newsom. He then went 1–12 for the worst Browns team in history (43–111). /(TJ)

Carden Gillenwater — 1918– . OF 1940, 43, 45–46, 48 Cardinals, Dodgers, **Braves**, Senators 335 g, .260, 11 hr, 114 rbi

Gillenwater was a glittering defensive outfielder with speed and a strong arm, but a disappointing bat. A regular only with the 1945 Braves, he hit a career-high .288, and in 1946 he tied a major league OF record with 12 putouts in a game. /(EW)

Bob Gillespie (Bunch) — 1918– . RHP 1944, 47–48, 50 Tigers, **White Sox**, Red Sox 202 ip, 5–13, 5.07

Purchased by the White Sox in 1947 after a strong year in the Texas League, Gillespie completed only 1 of 17 starts (5–8, 4.73). /(DB)

Ray Gillespie — Unk.–1979. *Writer.*

A sports writer for 55 years, Gillespie eventually carried BBWAA card No. 1, signifying seniority

among active writers. He was with the St. Louis *Star* until it folded in 1951 and he became associate editor of *The Sporting News*. His biggest scoop was the $5,000 fine and indefinite suspension of Babe Ruth by Yankees manager Miller Huggins in 1925. Friendly with the Pasqual brothers of Mexico, he scored many inside stories when they raided ML teams to stack their Mexican League in 1946. /(NLM)

Jim Gilliam (Junior) — 1928–1978. 2B-3B-OF 1953–66 Dodgers 1956 g, .265, 65 hr, 558 rbi *7 WS, 39 g, .211, 2 hr, 12 rbi*
☛ *Rookie of the Year—53. All-Star—56, 59.*

Nicknamed Junior as the youngest member of the Baltimore Elite Giants, Gilliam and shortstop Pee Wee Butts formed one of the great double play combos in Negro National League history during the 1940s. The Tennessean was named to the Negro NL East All-Star team three straight years (1948–50). Finally signed by the Dodgers and sent to Montreal, Gilliam twice led the International League in runs scored (117 in 1951, and 111 in 1952). He also led in fielding in 1952, convincing the Dodgers to shuttle Jackie Robinson between second base and third base and Gilliam between the infield and outfield to get him into the lineup.

As Dodger second baseman in 1953, Gilliam set a league rookie record with 100 walks, led the NL with 17 triples, scored a career-high 125 runs, and

Jim Gilliam

was named Rookie of the Year. He switch-hit homers in the 1953 World Series. In 1956, 1957, and 1959, Gilliam finished second to Willie Mays in stolen bases. He scored at least 100 runs in each of his first four seasons, and hit .300 for the only time in 1956.

Gilliam became a fan favorite in the Dodgers' first season in Los Angeles (1958) by leading the club in hits, doubles, steals, walks, and fielding. Switched to third base, he homered in the second 1959 All-Star Game. He retired after 1964 to become Los Angeles's third base coach, but he came out of retirement in 1965 to hit .280 for the World Champion Dodgers and join first baseman Wes Parker, second baseman Jim Lefebvre, and shortstop Maury Wills in the major leagues' first switch-hitting infield. He retired again and then returned once more to help the Dodgers repeat as NL champions in 1966. Gilliam coached until his sudden death of a brain hemorrhage just before the start of the 1978 World Series. The Dodgers retired his uniform number 19. /(MC)

James A. Gilmore — 1870–Unk. *Executive.*

A former coal company salesman, Gilmore was president of a company manufacturing ventilating machines when he organized and headed the Federal League. After two years of work and one year of operating the league, he received nothing in the settlement that ended the war with the National and American Leagues. /(NLM)

Joe Ginsberg [Myron Nathan] — 1926– . C 1948, 50–54, 56–62 **Tigers**, Indians, A's, Orioles, White Sox, Red Sox, Mets 695 g, .241, 20 hr, 182 rbi

The well-traveled Ginsberg was a second- or third-string catcher except for 1951–52 with Detroit. Yankee Vic Raschi wasn't amused when Ginsberg, a clubhouse comedian, homered to spoil his June 13, 1952 no-hit bid. He was the starting catcher in the Mets' first home game; as a result, his name has been in the "How to Score" section of Shea Stadium programs for over twenty years. /(EW)

Al Gionfriddo (The Little Italian) — 1922– . OF 1944–47 **Pirates**, Dodgers 228 g, .266, 2 hr, 58 rbi. *1 WS, 4 g, .000*

The 5'6" Gionfriddo pressed the best accomplishments of his career into the 1947 Dodger-Yankee World Series. In Game Four, he walked and scored on Cookie Lavagetto's two-run, ninth-inning single, the only hit off the Yankees' Bill Bevens. In Game Six, Gionfriddo went "back, back, back" (as called by announcer Red Barber) to make a crucial, one-handed catch of Joe DiMaggio's 415-foot shot. After the Series, neither Gionfriddo, Bevens, nor Lavagetto played another ML game. /(ME)

Dave Giusti — 1939– . RHP 1962, 64–77 Astros, Cardinals, **Pirates**, Cubs, A's 1717 ip, 100–93, 3.60. *5 LCS, 15 ip, 0–2, 6.60. 1 WS, 5.1 ip, 0–0, 0.00* ☛ *All-Star—73.*

Palmball master Dave Giusti ranks among the best relievers in Pirate history. He began as a starter, leading Houston with 15 wins in 1966 and 186 strikeouts in 1968. After one disappointing season with the Cardinals (1969), he was obtained by Pittsburgh GM Joe L. Brown in a four-player deal. Moved to the bullpen, Giusti led the NL with nine relief wins in 1970, and was named NL Fireman of the Year in 1971 when his 30 saves led the league. He became the first NL pitcher to appear in every game of a four-game LCS (1971), and notched a record three saves. One of the first consistent relief aces, he had four more double-figure save years for Pittsburgh, and in 1974 set the since-broken NL lifetime record for saves with 110. He finished out his career with the A's and Cubs in 1977, and retired with 145 saves. /(ME)

Dan Gladden — 1957– . OF 1983– Giants, **Twins** 731 g, .276, 43 hr, 256 rbi. *1 LCS, 5 g, .350, 5 rbi. 1 WS, 7 g, .290, 1 hr, 7 rbi*

Gladden was hitting .397 at Phoenix (Pacific Coast League) in 1984 when he was promoted to the Giants, and the speedy outfielder maintained his torrid pace in San Francisco, batting .351 with 31 stolen bases in 86 games as the Giants centerfielder. He earned spots on both the Topps and *Baseball Digest* all-rookie teams that year, but has hit no higher than .276 since. Traded to Minnesota before the 1987 season, Gladden was switched from centerfield to left, where he started regularly for the World Champion Twins. In the '87 WS, his grand slam off Bob Forsch broke open Game One. /(SCL)

Fred Gladding — 1936– . RHP 1961–73 **Tigers**, Astros 601 ip, 48–34, 3.13

A product of the majors' bullpen revolution, Gladding was groomed as a relief specialist. In his 13 years in the majors, he started only one game. He also managed only one hit in 63 career at-bats. But Gladding saved 109 games, and with the 1969 Astros the portly reliever's 29 saves led the National League. /(DV)

Fred Glade — 1876–1934. RHP 1902, 04–08 Cubs, Browns, Yankees 1072 ip, 52–68, 2.62

After a strong 18–15 rookie year with a 2.27 ERA, Glade, a durable Browns righthander with good control, plummeted to an AL-high 25 losses as St. Louis crashed to the cellar in 1905. He bounced back with winning seasons in the next two years./(FJO)

Jack Glasscock (Pebbly Jack) — 1859–1947. SS-2B 1879–95 **Cleveland (NL)**, Cincinnati (UA), St. Louis (NL) [Browns], Indianapolis (NL), Giants, St. Louis (NL) [Perfectos], Pirates, Louisville (NL), Washington (NL) 1736 g, .290, 27 hr, 752 rbi.
    Manager 1889 **Indianapolis (NL)** 34–33, .507
☛ *Led League—ba 1890* .

Glasscock was one of the National League's premier 19th-century shortstops. He was called "Pebbly Jack" for his habit of groundskeeping at his position, picking up and tossing away pebbles, which some baseball historians claim were imaginary. He played bare-handed, was one of the first to use a signal to inform his catcher which middle infielder would cover second on a steal, and was one of the first shortstops to back up throws to the second baseman. He managed Indianapolis for part of 1889, while leading the NL with 205 hits, and discovered 18-year-old farmboy Amos Rusie in the nearby countryside. In 1890 he replaced shortstop Monte Ward on the Giants when Ward led the defection of talent to the Players' League. Glasscock won the NL batting title that year, hitting .336, and had six singles in six at-bats on September 27. He topped the .300 mark five times./(JK)

Jack Glasscock

Tommy Glaviano (Harpo, The Rabbit) — 1923– . 3B-OF-2B 1949–53 **Cardinals**, Phillies 389 g, .257, 24 hr, 108 rbi

A favorite of Cardinal owner Sam Breadon, Glaviano was a wild dresser and clubhouse comedian. Errant throws kept the infielder from regular status. In a light rain at Ebbets Field on May 18, 1950, he made four errors at third base for the Cardinals. Three came on successive plays in the ninth inning, allowing the Dodgers to rally and win./(FJO)

Tom Glavine — 1966– . LHP 1987– **Braves** 432 ip, 23–29, 4.29

The Braves rushed Glavine to the majors, and he led the NL in losses in 1988, going 7–17 with a 4.56 ERA. He started 1989 as one of the hottest pitchers in the league, showing excellent control, but then dropped off in effectiveness later in the season.
    Glavine was the fourth pick of the NHL's Los Angeles Kings in the 1984 draft./(WOR)

Ralph Glaze — 1882–1968. RHP 1906–08 **Red Sox** 340 ip, 14–21, 2.89

A graduate of Dartmouth, Glaze was picked up by the Red Sox in 1906 from Savannah of the South Atlantic League for $300. Used as a part-time starter and sometimes-reliever, he was a strikeout artist. Glaze became baseball coach at Baylor, Drake, and the University of Southern California, where he also served as athletic director./(EW)

Whitey Glazner [Charles Franklin] — 1893– . RHP 1920–24 **Pirates**, Phillies 784 ip, 41–48, 4.21

Glazner turned in a brilliant rookie season (14–5, 2.77), then faltered and went to the Phillies in a 1923 deal that brought future Pirate star Lee Meadows to Pittsburgh./(ME)

Kid Gleason

Kid Gleason [William] — 1866–1933. 2B-RHP 1888–1908, 1912 Phillies, Cardinals, Baltimore NL, **Giants**, Tigers, White Sox 1966 g, .261, 15 hr, 823 rbi; 2389 ip, 134–134, 3.79. 20 wins: 90–91, 93
　　Manager 1919–23 **White Sox** 392–364, .519 *1 WS, 3–5, .375*

Best known today as the betrayed manager of the infamous Black Sox, Gleason was a star player of the 1890s. He began as a pitcher with the Phillies. After two losing seasons, he blossomed with a 38–17 mark in 1890 when desertions to the Players' League stripped the Phillies of their regular starters. He never approached that level again, although he twice more topped 20 wins. When the distance from the mound to the plate was increased in 1894, he lost his effectiveness.

A timely hitter and heady player, Gleason switched to second base, helping the Orioles win a

pennant in 1895. He was traded the next year to the Giants, where he was named team captain. According to some reports, he was the first to order an intentional base on balls as a way to bypass a strong hitter. In 1897 he had his best offensive year, hitting .319 with 106 RBI. He jumped to the AL in 1901, then returned to the Phillies in 1903 for four more years as the regular second baseman. He stole 328 career bases.

After retiring as a player, he served first as a coach, then as the manager of the White Sox. Nicknamed Kid in part because he was 5'7" but mostly for his enthusiasm, his heart was broken by his players' sellout of the 1919 WS. He continued as manager of the crippled team through 1923, then became a coach for Connie Mack in Philadelphia./(JK)

Jerry Don Gleaton — 1957– . LHP 1979–83, 84–85, 87-Rangers, Mariners, White Sox, **Royals** 258 ip, 10–18, 4.72

Gleaton was the Rangers' first-round draft pick in June of 1979, signed out of the University of Texas. After the 1980 season, he was included in an 11-player trade to Seattle that featured Rick Honeycutt and Richie Zisk. Gleaton was released by the White Sox before finding a home as a set-up man in the 1987 Royals bullpen./(NLM)

Jim Gleeson (Gee Gee) — 1912– . OF 1936, 39–42 Indians, **Cubs** Reds 392 g, .263, 16 hr, 154 rbi

Gleeson, a switch-hitter, hit .313 for the 1940 Cubs in his one solid season. He met Yogi Berra while in the Navy and coached under him with the Yankees in 1964. He also managed in the Yankee system and was a Brewers scouting supervisor./(NLM)

Marty Glickman — 1907– . *Broadcaster.*

An All-East football tailback at Syracuse University and a sprinter on the 1936 U.S. Olympic team, Glickman broadcast games from the Western Union ticker on WHN in New York before WWII, and broadcast a nightly re-creation of a New York game from 1940 to 1953. When night baseball took over and the Dodgers moved to Los Angeles, Glickman concentrated on New York pro football broadcasts./(NLM)

Al Glossop — 1912– . 2B-SS-3B 1939–40, 42–43, 46 Giants, Braves, **Phillies**, Dodgers, Cubs 309 g, .209, 15 hr, 86 rbi

The switch-hitting infielder was the Phillies' regular second baseman in 1942. Sold by the Dodgers to the Cubs in September 1943, he spent the 1944–45 seasons in the military and appeared in only four ML games after his return. /(EGM)

Bill Glynn — 1925- . 1B 1949, 52-54 Phillies, **Indians** 310 g, .249, 10 hr, 56 rbi

Glynn became Cleveland's first baseman when Luke Easter suffered a broken foot in 1953. He lost the job on June 1, 1954, when the Indians acquired Vic Wertz. However, in a July 5 game against Detroit, he hit three of his 10 ML home runs. /(ME)

Ed Glynn (The Flushing Flash) — 1953- . LHP 1975-83 Tigers, **Mets**, Indians 262 ip, 12-17, 4.12

A good strikeout pitcher, The Flushing Flash was a Shea Stadium hot dog vendor before Detroit signed him in 1971. Only one of the reliever's nine seasons was spent entirely in the majors (1980, with the Mets). /(JCA)

Larry Goetz — 1900-1962. *Umpire* NL 1936-57 *3 WS 2 ASU*

Goetz umpired in the NL for 22 years. A typical instance of his firm handling of dissenters came in 1956 when the Reds' Frank Robinson disputed a strike call longer than Goetz thought appropriate. The ump ordered the Giants' Steve Ridzik to pitch and called strike three while Robinson was still arguing. /(RTM)

Bill Gogolewski — 1947- . RHP 1970-75 **Senators/ Rangers**, Indians, White Sox 502 ip, 15-24, 4.02

Except for a pair of saves recorded with the 1975 White Sox, journeyman starter Gogolewski's decisions came with the moribund Senators and Rangers. His best year was 6-5 (2.76 ERA) in 1971 for Washington. /(DV)

Jim Golden — 1936- . RHP 1960-63 Dodgers, **Astros** 208 ip, 9-13, 4.54

A marginal pitcher with the 1960-61 Dodgers, Golden posted his best mark in a one-year stint with the expansion Houston Colt .45s in 1962. He went 7-11 and batted .222. /(DV)

Gordon Goldsberry — 1927- . 1B 1949-52 **White Sox**, Browns 217 g, .241, 6 hr, 56 rbi

The matinee idol Californian led the AL in pinch hits with 12 for the 1950 Chisox. He later became the Cubs' director of minor leagues and scouting. /(RL)

Peter Golenbock — 1946- . *Writer.*

In 1972 Golenbock was a lawyer with Prentice-Hall, checking reports, when he induced them to publish his book about the Yankees, *Dynasty.* In 1978 *The Bronx Zoo*, written with Sparky Lyle, sold 220,000 hardcover copies. His other baseball books include *Guidry*, with Ron Guidry, *Number 1*, with Billy Martin, and *Bums*, about the Brooklyn Dodgers. /(NLM)

Mike Goliat — 1925- . 2B 1949-52 **Phillies**, Browns 249 g, .225, 20 hr, 99 rbi. *1 WS, 4 g, .214, 1 rbi*

Despite never having played second base in the minors, Goliat started there for the 1950 NL Champion Whiz Kids. He struggled defensively, and his .234 average that year was his career best. /(JK)

Dave Goltz — 1949- . RHP 1972-83 **Twins**, Dodgers, Angels 2039 ip, 113-109, 3.69. 20 wins: 77 *1 LCS, 4 ip, 0-0, 7.36. 1 WS, 3 ip, 0-0, 5.40*
☛ *Led League—w 77.*

The 6'4" Goltz, the first native Minnesotan originally signed by the Twins to reach their major league roster, was throwing in his parents' backyard when he was discovered by a Twins scout in 1966. In his eight years with the Twins, Goltz became the fourth winningest pitcher in club history, never having a losing season. His ascent to the majors was thwarted by arm trouble and a stint in Vietnam. He rebounded for a combined 14-3 mark and a seven-inning no-hitter for Lynchburg (Carolina League) in 1971, his last full minor league season. Though a notoriously slow starter (he didn't win a game in April until 1979), he won 14 or more games five straight times (1975-79) for Minnesota. He peaked at 20-11 in 1977, tying for the AL lead in victories and starts, and one-hitting the powerful Red Sox on August 23.

Goltz opted for free agency and signed a six-year, multimillion contract with the Dodgers for 1980. He shut out the Giants twice that April, then struggled. Los Angeles released him in May 1982. He managed an 8-5 comeback with the '82 division champion Angels, but was finished by a torn rotator cuff in 1983. /(MC)

Lefty Gomez [Vernon Louis] (Goofy, The Gay Castillion) — 1908-1988. LHP 1930-43 **Yankees**, Senators 2503 ip, 189-102, 3.34. 20 wins: 31-32, 34, 37 *5 WS, 50 ip, 6-0, 2.86*
☛ *Led League—w 34, 37. Led League—era 34, 37. Led League—k 33-34, 37. All-Star—33-39. Hall of Fame—1972.*

Remembered mainly for his colorful personality, Lefty Gomez was also one of baseball's greatest winners, ranking third in Yankee history in regular-season wins with 189. His 6–0 World Series record gave him the most wins without a loss in World Series history. His three victories in All-Star Game competition (against one loss) also are a record.

Gomez's zaniness set him apart from the decorous Yankees of the 1930s. He once held up a World Series game, exasperating manager Joe McCarthy (as he did with some frequency), to watch an airplane pass by. Gomez got away with needling his buddy, Joe DiMaggio, because DiMaggio, like everyone else, enjoyed the Gomez wit, which produced such statements as: "I've got a new invention. It's a revolving bowl for tired goldfish."

The Yankees purchased Gomez from his hometown San Francisco Seals in 1929 for $35,000. Two years later he won 21 games for them. His smoking fastball belied his slender frame. He was a nail, with a whiplash arm and a high leg kick.

Lefty Gomez

Gomez and righthander Red Ruffing formed the lefty-righty pitching core for the great New York teams of the 1930s. In 1934 he led the league in seven major categories, including wins (26), ERA (2.33), and strikeouts (158), the pitching equivalent of the Triple Crown. He led the league again in the top three pitching categories in 1937.

Arm miseries hounded him throughout his career. As his fastball lost its effectiveness, Gomez moved from power pitcher to finesse pitcher. "I'm throwing as hard as I ever did," he quipped, "the ball's just not getting there as fast." Gomez fooled hitters and made a beautiful, slow curve work for him. He had a great comeback in 1941 (15–5) after a 3–3 mark in 1940, leading the league in winning percentage (.750).

Gomez threw a shutout in 1941 while issuing 11 walks, the most walks ever allowed in a shutout. And though a notoriously poor hitter, he produced the first RBI in All-Star history and singled home the winning run in the 1937 World Series clincher.

After pitching one game for Washington (he lost) in 1943, Gomez retired, later to hook up with the Wilson sporting goods company as a goodwill ambassador. He was asked on joining Wilson why he had left his last position. Gomez, who never took himself seriously, responded that he left because he couldn't "get the side out." /(MG)

Luis Gomez [born Luis Gomez Sanchez] — 1951– . SS-2B-3B 1974–81 **Twins**, Blue Jays, Braves 609 g, .210, 0 hr, 90 rbi

Born in Mexico and raised in Los Angeles, the 5'9" Gomez played freshman basketball at UCLA with Bill Walton. Gomez was a reserve in Minnesota before becoming Toronto's shortstop for 1978. He set an Atlanta record in 1980 with a .968 fielding percentage at shortstop and strung together 42 consecutive errorless games. But, batting .191, he lost his job to Rafael Ramirez. /(MC)

Preston Gomez — 1923– . 2B-SS 1944 **Senators** 8 g, .286, 0 hr, 2 rbi.
    Manager 1969–72, 74–75, 80 **Padres**, Astros, Cubs 346–529, .395

Gomez played eight games for the Senators in 1944 without having any minor league experience. He was sent down the following spring and did not return as a player. After a long minor league apprenticeship, the personable Cuban was named Padres manager in 1969 and remained until eleven games into the 1972 season. His 1974 Astro team finished fourth at 81–81, the only time a Gomez-managed team finished out of last place. Twice in his managerial career he pinch hit for pitchers who had no-hitters going, Clay Kirby (with the Padres) and Don Wilson (Astros). /(BC)

Ruben Gomez — 1927– . RHP 1953–60, 62, 67 **Giants**, Phillies, Indians, Twins 1454 ip, 76–86, 4.09. *1 WS, 7.1 ip, 1–0, 2.45*

Puerto Rican-born Ruben Gomez was an erratic starter, given to wildness, who went 17–9 for the 1954 World Champion Giants despite a league-leading 109 walks. Late in his rookie 1953 season, Gomez hit Carl Furillo with a pitch, and the Dodger outfielder went at Giant manager Leo Durocher, who the Dodgers accused of ordering beanballs. Furillo broke his hand in the ensuing melee, ending his season, while his .344 batting average stood to cop the NL crown.

The Braves' Joe Adcock had hit seven HR in nine games coming into a night game at Milwaukee on July 18, 1956. Gomez hit him on the wrist in his first at-bat and they exchanged remarks as Adcock went to first base. Adcock charged the mound; Gomez threw the ball, hitting him in the thigh, and then ran for the safety of the Giants' dugout. Gomez was fined $250. He also had a beanball war with Cardinals pitcher Sam Jones in 1957, and that July 16, Gomez put Frank Robinson in the hospital, hitting him in the head with a pitch. /(JK)

Jesse Gonder — 1936– . C 1960–67 Yankees, Reds, **Mets**, Braves, Pirates 395 g, .251, 26 hr, 94 rbi

The burly receiver was the 1962 Pacific Coast League batting champ and RBI leader. Defensive deficiencies and his lack of speed kept him a backup. Nearly 20 percent of his ML at-bats were as a pinch hitter. /(CR)

Hiroshi Gondo — 1940– . P 1961–64 **Chunichi Dragons**

Virtually a one-man staff, Gondo won 35 games and worked 429 innings as rookie for the Chunichi Dragons. But he was finished at age 24, the victim of a torn rotator cuff. Elder brother Masatochi pitched nearly 15 seasons for the Hanshin Tigers, but never with spectacular success. /(MC)

Mike Gonzales — 1890–1977. C 1912, 14–21, 24–29, 31–32 Braves, Reds, **Cardinals**, Giants, Cubs 1042 g, .253, 13 hr, 263 rbi. *1 WS, 2 g, .000.* Manager 1938, 40 **Cardinals** 9–13

Gonzales coined a standard phrase with his pithy assessment of the abilities of a player he scouted:

"Good field, no hit." That could also describe the playing career of the Cuban-born catcher. Although he played for five NL teams, he is most often associated with the Cardinals, for whom he served as regular catcher (1916–18 and 1924), longtime coach, and twice as interim manager. /(JK)

Pedro Gonzales — 1938– . 2B-3B 1963–67 Yankees, **Indians** 407 g, .244, 8 hr, 70 rbi. *1 WS, 1 g, .000*

One of the many ML infielders from San Pedro de Macoris, Dominican Republic, Gonzalez couldn't dislodge Bobby Richardson in New York and failed to hit enough to hold his job in Cleveland. He was suspended in 1965 for swinging his bat at pitcher Larry Sherry. /(ME)

Fernando Gonzalez — 1950– . 2B-3B 1972–74, 77–79 Pirates, Royals, Yankees, **Padres** 404 g, .235, 17 hr, 104 rbi

A lifetime .302 pinch hitter, the squat, hard-swinging Gonzalez was a utility infielder and outfielder until the Padres made him their second baseman for 1978–79. He opened the "Fernando Gonzalez Escuela de Beisbol" in his native Puerto Rico. /(JCA)

Julio Gonzalez [aka Julio Cesar Hernandez Hernandez] — 1959– . 2B-SS-3B 1977–83 **Astros**, Cardinals, Tigers 370 g, .235, 4 hr, 66 rbi

Signed out of Puerto Rico by the Cubs, Gonzalez went to Houston for Greg Gross in 1976. He was most active in his rookie 1977 season, hitting .245 as a shortstop and third baseman. /(MC)

Tony Gonzalez — 1936– . OF 1960–71 Reds, **Phillies**, Padres, Braves, Angels 1559 g, .286, 103 hr, 615 rbi. *1 LCS, 3 g, .357, 1 hr, 2 rbi*

Gonzalez spent his best years with the Phillies (mid-1960 through 1968). The Cuban led NL outfielders in fielding average three times, including 1962, when he had no errors in 276 chances. He was the first regular centerfielder ever to field 1.000, and only the third outfielder overall.

In 1967 Gonzalez's career-high .339 batting average was second in the NL and the majors. He was a reliable hitter for average, drew walks, and at times showed good power. He hit a career-high 20 HR in 1962 and in 1963 his career highs of 36 doubles and 12 triples tied for third and finished second in the NL, respectively.

Gonzalez was taken by the Padres in the expansion draft, but was traded to the Braves in June 1969 and helped them to their division title with a .294

average, 10 HR, and 50 RBI in 89 games for Atlanta. He homered off the Mets' Tom Seaver in Game One of the LCS but also made the final error of the Braves' blunder-filled eighth inning. With two out and the bases loaded, he let J.C. Martin's single get past him in centerfield and three runs scored to put the game out of reach. Gonzalez's .357 average in the series tied him with Hank Aaron to lead Braves batters, and his four runs scored tied him with Rico Carty. Gonzalez was sold to the Angels in mid-1970, and when he dropped to a career-low .245 average in 1971, it ended his major league career. /(JFC)

Johnny Gooch — 1897–1975. C 1921–30, 33 **Pirates**, Dodgers, Reds, Red Sox 815 g, .280, 7 hr, 293 rbi. *2 WS, 6 g, .000*

Gooch was a dependable switch-hitter and slick-fielding catcher for Pittsburgh from 1922 through 1927 who platooned first with Walter Schmidt and then with Earl Smith. He hit .329 as a rookie, and was part of a Pirate youth movement that made them a powerhouse in the 1920s. Gooch was later a successful minor league manager and a Pittsburgh coach in 1937–38. /(ME)

Wilbur Good (Lefty) — 1885–1963. OF 1905, 08–16, 18 Yankees, Indians, Braves, **Cubs**, Phillies, White Sox 750 g, .258, 9 hr, 187 rbi

An extra outfielder most of his career, the 5'6" Good was responsible for two events of some small significance in Cub history. On June 19, 1913, he hit the first pinch homer in Cub annals, and on August 18, 1915, he became the only Cub player to steal second, third, and home in the same inning. /(ARA)

Gladys Gooding — 1893–1963. Organist.

Larry MacPhail discovered Gladys Gooding at a hockey game at Madison Square Garden, where she played the organ for the New York Rangers and, later, the basketball Knickerbockers. He thought organ music might be a fine thing for Ebbets Field. Beginning in 1942, she was a favorite of Dodger fans and a celebrity in her own right until the team went west in 1958. She wrote the words and music for "Follow the Dodgers," the team's fight song even after the move to Los Angeles. /(NLM)

Dwight Gooden (Doc, Doctor K) — 1964– . RHP 1984– **Mets** 1291 ip, 100–39, 2.64. 20 wins: 85 *2 LCS, 35 ip, 0–1, 1.06. 1 WS, 9 ip, 0–2, 8.00*
☛ *Rookie of the Year—84. Led League—w 85. Led League—era 85. Led League—k 84–85. Cy Young Award—85. All-Star—84–86, 88.*

Gooden had a record-breaking Rookie of the Year season in 1984 after jumping straight to the majors from Lynchburg of the Class-A Carolina League. The Mets' number-one pick in the June 1982 draft (the fifth player taken) had led the league in wins, ERA, and strikeouts in 1983, fanning 300 in 191 innings, and Davey Johnson had sworn that wherever he was managing in 1984, he would have Gooden. But after he was named the Mets' manager, he discovered that GM Frank Cashen wanted to bring the 19-year-old Gooden along slowly; Cashen remembered the case of Tim Leary, once a hot Mets prospect, who blew out his arm in his 1981 debut on a cold, windy day at Wrigley after concealing pain. Gooden made his debut indoors, on April 7, in the Astrodome. He went on to set a ML rookie record with 276 strikeouts in only 218 innings. The strikeouts earned him the nickname Doctor K and a rooting section in the upper deck that hung out a red K for each strikeout during his starts. He tied the ML mark for strikeouts in two consecutive games, with 32 in starts on September 12 and 17, which, combined with his September 7 start, gave him a record 43 in three straight games. Going 17–9 with a 2.60 ERA, he instantly became the Mets' ace and made them overnight contenders. He was the youngest All-Star ever, and he and Fernando Valenzuela combined to strike out six consecutive batters, between them breaking Carl Hubbell's record.

Gooden reached new heights in 1985, winning the Cy Young award with the "pitcher's Triple Crown," leading the NL in wins (24–4), ERA (1.53), and strikeouts (268). His 16 complete games also led the league, and his rising fastball and snapping curve dominated NL hitters. Curveballs are referred to by ballplayers as "Uncle Charley," but Gooden's is called "Lord Charles." The shy but poised Gooden was the toast of New York; the only fault that could be found with him was that his big motion meant he had trouble holding runners close to first base. But the Mets, trying to protect their young superstar's future health, gave pitching coach Mel Stottlemyre the assignment of making Gooden less reliant on throwing hard. Perhaps it was that; perhaps it was hitters learning to lay off his rising fastball, which was often above the strike zone. Whatever it was, Gooden after 1985 was never the totally dominating strikeout king he had been. He went 4–0 in April 1986, but the question in every newspaper's sports section was "What's wrong with Gooden?" after he surrendered a home run to the first batter he faced that year, Pittsburgh's R.J. Reynolds. In contrast to his fine performance in the 1984 All-Star Game, in the 1986 game he gave up a two-run homer to Lou Whitaker and took the loss. No longer overpowering, he finished with 200 strikeouts in 250 innings, a 17–6 record, and a 2.84 ERA. The Mets won the World Championship, but Gooden went without a postseason win. He took a tough 1–0 loss in the LCS opener as the Astros' Mike Scott overwhelmed the Mets; the Astros' run came on a Glenn Davis home run. Gooden pitched masterfully in the Mets' Game Five victory, surrendering only one run in 10 innings in a matchup against Nolan Ryan; the Mets won in the 12th inning. It was the first time that Davey Johnson had ever let Gooden pitch beyond the ninth inning. Gooden set NLCS records for a seven-game series with 20 strikeouts and eight walks. He pitched less well in the World Series, and lost two games; he has rarely pitched well on three days' rest.

In 1987, following winter problems in his hometown Tampa that included a police beating of Gooden and his nephew Gary Sheffield, who would later be signed by the Brewers, Gooden went into a drug rehabilitation program just before the start of the season. He went 15–7 with a 3.21 ERA after coming back, but the club blamed his absence in the first two months for the Mets' narrow division title loss. In 1988 he declared that he wanted to be called Doc instead of Doctor K now that he was a different kind of pitcher. His 18–9, 3.19 record led the Mets to a division title, but he again lost the All-Star Game, tying the record for lifetime losses in the mid-summer classic. And again he pitched well in the LCS, but not well enough to win. He took no-decisions in the Mets' Game One victory and their 12th-inning loss in Game Four, giving up a game-tying solo homer to the Dodgers' Mike Scioscia in the ninth inning of the latter contest. He suffered his first injury in 1989, going down with a sore shoulder in the middle of the year, exactly the sort of injury the Mets had sought to prevent with their change of his pitching style. At the time, he was 9–4 with a 2.99 ERA and was the only consistently good starter in the Mets' rotation; his loss doomed the team's pennant hopes. He came back briefly in relief at the end of the season. /(SH)

Billy Goodman — 1926–1984. 2B-1B-3B-OF **Red Sox**, Orioles, White Sox, Astros 1623 g, .300, 19 hr, 591 rbi. *1 WS, 5 g, .231, 1 rbi*
☛ *Led League—ba 50. All-Star—49, 53.*

The versatile Goodman led the AL in batting with a .354 mark in 1950, one of five times he hit .300. He hit .290 or better 11 straight years (1948–58). But despite his steady hitting and versatile fielding, Goodman never quite achieved stardom.

Starting out as the regular first baseman for the powerful 1948 Red Sox, he led AL first basemen in total chances per game in 1948 and in fielding in 1949 while hitting .298. Because the lefthanded batter had no home run power and was capable at almost every position, he moved aside to accommodate the arrival of slugging first baseman Walt Dropo in 1950. Goodman won his batting championship that season while playing the outfield and all four infield positions. He took over as the regular at second base in 1952 after Bobby Doerr retired, and he led AL second basemen in total chances per game. He kept the job through 1956, finishing third in the AL in batting in 1953 (.313) and second in walks in 1955 (99). After leading the league's second basemen in errors in 1956 and starting out batting .063 in 1957, he was traded to the Orioles for Mike Fornieles. From then on, he played mainly third base, backing up George Kell for a year and then moving on to the White Sox in 1958. He was a dependable reserve on the White Sox' 1959 pennant-winners. /(WOR)

Ival Goodman (Goodie) — 1908–1984. OF 1935–44 **Reds**, Cubs 1107 g, .281, 95 hr, 525 rbi. *2 WS, 11 g, .295, 6 rbi*
☛ *All-Star—38–39.*

En route to the Cincinnati Reds Hall of Fame, Goodman led the NL in triples his first two seasons, set a since-broken Reds' season homer mark (30 in 1938), and played in two All-Star Games and World Series. In the 1939 Series opener, right fielder Goodman and centerfielder Harry Craft let Charlie Keller's fly ball drop between them for a triple; Keller soon scored the Yankees' winning run. /(TJ)

Ed Goodson — 1948– . 1B-3B 1970–77 **Giants**, Braves, Dodgers 515 g, .260, 30 hr, 170 rbi. *1 LCS, 1 g, .000. 1 WS, 1 g, .000*

Goodson's pure, lefthanded swing was at its best in 1973, his first full ML season. As the Giants' most-used third baseman he batted .302 with 12 homers in 102 games. With the Dodgers, he was almost exclusively a pinch hitter. /(JCA)

Danny Goodwin — 1953- . DH-1B 1975, 77-82 Angels, **Twins**, A's 252 g, .236, 13 hr, 81 rbi

Twice baseball's number-one draft pick, the intelligent catcher opted for pre-med studies in 1971, then accepted a six-figure bonus from the Angels upon graduation. However, he damaged his throwing arm early, and saw only limited ML action as a DH and first baseman. /(JCA)

Marv Goodwin — 1893-1925. RHP 1916-17, 19-22, 25 Senators, **Cardinals**, Reds 447 ip, 21-25, 3.30

Goodwin had just pitched his way back to the majors in 1925 when he died in an off-season plane crash on an Air Reserve training flight. Goodwin was one of the spitballers permitted to openly continue using the pitch after 1919. /(JK)

Don Gordon — 1959- . RHP 1986-88 Blue Jays, **Indians** 132 ip, 3-8, 4.72

Gordon came to Cleveland as part of the deal that sent Phil Niekro to the Blue Jays in August 1987. The reliever never got his ERA below 4.00 in the majors, but led the International League in ERA in 1985 with a 2.07 mark for Syracuse. /(JFC)

Joe Gordon (Flash) — 1915-1978. 2B 1938-43, 46-50 Yankees, Indians 1566 g, .268, 253 hr, 975 rbi. *6 WS, 29 g, .243, 4 hr, 16 rbi.*
   Manager 1958-61, 69 **Indians**, Tigers, A's, Royals 305-318, .490
☛ *Most Valuable Player—42 . All-Star—39-43, 46-49.*

The acrobatic Joe Gordon would be remembered for his defensive skills alone, but he was also a powerful and timely hitter. He holds the AL second basemen's records for career HR (246) and HR in a season (32 in 1948). The low-key, humorous player emerged from the Yankee system to take Tony Lazzeri's place. He hit for the cycle on September 8, 1940. In the 1941 World Series Gordon snuffed out Dodger rallies with his glove and went 7-for-14 with a .929 slugging average.

   In 1942 Gordon was the AL MVP, hitting .322 with 103 RBI. The eight-time All-Star missed two seasons for army service. He hit just .210 when he returned in 1946, and after exactly 1,000 games and 1,000 hits for the Yankees, was traded to Cleveland for Allie Reynolds. His hitting form returned, with career highs of 32 HR and 124 RBI in 1948, as he teamed with Lou Boudreau for a pennant and Gordon's sixth World Series.

   Gordon was named Cleveland manager in 1958 and the Indians finished second in 1959. In 1960 he was part of baseball's most unusual trade when the Indians and Tigers swapped managers, with Gordon and Jimmy Dykes trading places. Gordon managed the Kansas City A's for part of 1961, and the Kansas City Royals for all of their maiden 1969 season. /(JK)

Sid Gordon — 1917-1975. OF-3B 1941-43, 46-55 **Giants**, Braves, Pirates 1475 g, .283, 202 hr, 805 rbi
☛ *All-Star—48-49.*

Gordon became one of Manhattan's most popular players, after being born and raised in Brooklyn. A reliable outfielder who could play acceptably at third base, the stocky righthanded hitter hit .251 as a Giants rookie in 1943, then spent two years in the service. In 1947 the Giants broke the single-season home run record, and Gordon hit 13 of their 221. In 1948 he blossomed with 30 homers, 107 RBI, and a .299 batting average. He held out in the spring of 1949 but finally settled for $2,500 less than he'd asked for. After the season he was sent to the Braves in a multiplayer deal that brought Alvin Dark and Eddie Stanky to the Giants. A check for $2,500 from Giants owner Horace Stoneham underscored the esteem in which Gordon was held. /(FS)

Tom Gordon (Flash) — 1967- . RHP 1988- **Royals** 179 ip, 17-11, 3.78

A starter in the minors, Gordon came up to the Royals as a reliever. The 5'9" 160-lb flamethrower was 10-2 in July as a set-up man, with 78 strikeouts in 66 innings (twice as many strikeouts as hits allowed), when he was moved into the rotation. He finished the year 17-9. /(SFS)

George Gore (Piano Legs) — 1857-1933. OF 1879-92 **Cubs**, Giants, New York (PL), Cardinals 1310 g (1301 N/C), .301 (.303 N/C), 46 hr, 526 rbi (617 N/C)
☛ *Led League—ba 1880.*

Gore was signed by Chicago's Cap Anson after playing for a local New England team in an exhibition against the White Stockings (later the Cubs). In 1880, his second season, Gore won the NL batting crown with a .360 mark (Anson's .337 was second) and also led in slugging percentage (.463). Anson claimed that Gore was too much the playboy, however, and when Chicago lost the postseason championship series with St. Louis, the American Association pennant-winners, Gore was dispatched to the Gothams (later renamed the Giants).

   Gore led the NL in runs scored in 1881-82, and in walks three times. Scoring over 100 runs seven times, with a high of 150 (1886), he finished his career with 1,327 runs in 1,310 games. Gore, Harry Stovey, and Billy Hamilton are the only players

George Gore

(4,000 at-bats) with more runs scored than games. Gore set a ML record on June 25, 1881, when he had seven stolen bases in a game. On July 9, 1885, he hit two doubles and three triples to set a since-tied ML record of five extra-base hits in a game, and he went 6-for-6 on May 7, 1880. He was called Piano Legs for his bulging calf muscles. /(JK)

Tom Gorman — 1925- . RHP 1952-59 Yankees, **A's** 689 ip, 36-36, 3.77. *2 WS, 3.2 ip, 0-0, 2.45*

Gorman was about to be sent to the minors in 1952 when the Yankees gave him one more chance in relief against Washington. He responded by pitching nine innings of no-hit, no-run ball. Gorman went on to save 18 games for the A's in 1955, one behind the league leader. /(RTM)

Tom Gorman (Big Tom) — 1916-1986. LHP 1939 **Giants** 5 ip, 0-0, 7.20.
  Umpire NL 1951-76 *2 LCS 5 WS 5 ASU*

Gorman spent three years pitching in the Giants' organization before enlisting in the army in 1941. Upon his return in 1946, an arm injury curtailed his pitching career, and he turned to umpiring in 1947 in the New England League. He was promoted to

the NL in 1951 and quickly became one of its most respected arbiters. In the heat of the 1962 pennant race, Gorman discovered the San Francisco grounds-keepers had heavily watered the infield to slow down Dodger base-stealing star Maury Wills. Gorman held up the start of the game for an hour and a half until the basepaths dried out. In the 1968 WS, Gorman was behind the plate when Bob Gibson struck out 17 Tiger batters. After retiring as a field ump, Gorman served as a NL supervisor of umpires. The entertaining after-dinner speaker's autobiography, *Three and Two*, was published in 1979. /(RTM)

Tom Gorman [Thomas Patrick] — 1957- . LHP 1981-87 Expos, **Mets**, Phillies, Padres 214 ip, 12-10, 4.34

The 6'4" Gorman failed to become the ace reliever the Expos had hoped for. He developed a forkball, which kept him in the majors for three seasons as a Mets middle reliever. He went 6-0 (2.97) in 1984, but lost the good forkball in 1985 (4-4, 5.13). /(JCA)

Hank Gornicki [Frank Ted] — 1911- . RHP 1941-43, 46 Cardinals, Cubs, **Pirates** 285 ip, 15-19, 3.38

Gornicki pitched a shutout in his first major league start, but could not stick with a talented St. Louis club. He led the Pirates with a 2.57 ERA in 1942 and in appearances (42) in 1943. /(ME)

Johnny Gorsica [born John Gorczyca] — 1915- . RHP 1940-44, 46-47 **Tigers** 724 ip, 31-39, 4.18. *1 WS, 11 ip, 0-0, 0.79*

Gorsica started out playing first base, but made the Tigers in 1940 after just two seasons as a pitcher. Relying on an overhand sinkerball, he both started and relieved. Provided great relief work in 1940 WS, going 4.2 innings in Game Two, 6.2 innings in Game Six after starters were knocked out. Both games were losses, but he compiled a 0.79 ERA. /(NLM)

Johnny Goryl — 1933- . 2B-3B-SS 1957-59, 62-64 Cubs, **Twins** 276 g, .225, 16 hr, 48 rbi.
  Manager 1980-81 **Twins** 34-38, .472

The low-key Goryl spent 20 consecutive years with the Twins organization as a utility infielder, a minor league player and manager, a major league coach, and, finally, the Twins' manager when Gene Mauch resigned in August 1980. Replaced by Billy Gardner in 1981, Goryl became Cleveland's third base coach. /(JCA)

Jim Gosger — 1942– . OF-1B 1963, 65–71, 73–74 Red Sox, **A's**, Pilots, Mets, Expos 705 g, .226, 30 hr, 177 rbi

The hustling, lefthanded outfielder spent only three full seasons in the majors. Though he started the season as an original Seattle Pilot, he played in 10 games for the 1969 Mets, enough to earn a $100 World Series check. /(JCA)

Goose Goslin [Leon Allen] — 1900–1971. OF 1921–1938 **Senators**, Browns, Tigers 2287 g, .316, 248 hr, 1609 rbi. *5 WS, 32 g, .287, 7 hr, 18 rbi* ☛ *Led League—ba 28. Led League—rbi 24. Hall of Fame—1968.*

Although the sweet-hitting Goslin played for the usually mediocre Senators (in three separate tours) and Browns for much of his career, he managed to squeeze his way into five World Series, making the most of each appearance. In the 1924 Series, the Senators won their first and only world title, with Goslin batting .344 and contributing three HR and seven RBI. The following year he hit another three HR, although the Senators lost to Pittsburgh. After a subpar Series in 1933 back with the Senators, he drove in the winning run in Game Two of the 1934 Series for his new team, the Tigers, who lost to the Cardinals in seven games. The Tigers beat the Cubs in six games in 1935, thanks to Goslin's game-winning RBI single in the bottom of the ninth of the final game.

Clark Griffith almost didn't sign the powerful left fielder. When Griffith went to scout him in a Sally League game in South Carolina, Goslin managed to get hit on the head by a fly ball. But he also hit three HR in the game. Goslin's career was true to that good-hit, no-field pattern. Opposing players often described the arm-waving Goslin chasing a fly ball as a bird with wings flapping, giving further meaning to his nickname. As a young player, one defensive asset was a strong arm, but he ruined even that during one spring training with an ill-advised attempt to learn to put the shot.

Between 1924 and 1928, Goslin's lowest average was .334, yet his only batting title came in a rather unusual finish in 1928. He was tied with Heinie Manush on the last day of the season, and coincidentally, the Senators were playing Manush's Browns. Goslin went into his last at-bat leading Manush, but didn't want to bat for fear of making an out and losing the precarious lead. His teammates goaded him to bat. Goslin then tried to get himself thrown out of the game. He ended up with

Goose Goslin with the Browns

an infield hit and the batting title, having gone 7 for his final 15 to bat .379. Goslin would later join Manush in St. Louis for the 1930 through 1932 seasons.

Goslin was also responsible for the first fine levied against an umpire. In the 1935 fall classic, Goslin got into a heated discussion with Hall of Fame arbiter Bill Klem, during which Klem lost his temper and used what Goslin later described as "overripe language." Commissioner Landis then fined Klem, not Goslin.

Goslin spent his final years running a boat-rental concession in Bridgeton, New Jersey, his native state, and died just three days after his 1928 batting rival Manush. /(SEW)

Howie Goss — 1934– . OF 1962–63 Pirates, **Astros** 222 g, .216, 11 hr, 54 rbi

The 6'4″ outfielder showed power during his nine-year minor league career by hitting 172 home runs. With the 1963 Colt .45's, Goss managed nine HR in 133 games. /(RTM)

Goose Gossage [Richard Michael] — 1951– . RHP 1972–White Sox, Pirates, **Yankees**, Padres, Cubs, Giants 1636 ip, 113–98, 2.92. *4 LCS, 11 ip, 1–1, 4.91. 3 WS, 13.2 ip, 1–0, 2.63*
☛ *All-Star—75–78, 80–82, 84–85.*

Gossage was one of the most consistent relief pitchers ever, and is second on the all-time save list with 302 (entering 1989) and fourth in relief victories (101). The hard thrower had three mediocre seasons with the White Sox, but broke through in 1975, when he saved 26 games and won 9. The White Sox made him a starter in 1976, but Gossage went 9–17 and never started another game. The Pirates traded for him the following year, and he went 11–9 with 26 saves and a 1.62 ERA, his lowest for a full season. Gossage became a free agent and

Goose Gossage

signed with the Yankees, taking over the stopper role from the previous year's Cy Young winner, Sparky Lyle, as New York won its second straight World Championship. Gossage went 10–11 with 27 saves and pitched 134 innings, fourth-highest on the staff. He saved the AL East playoff game against the Red Sox, and was on the mound when New York clinched the pennant and World Championship.

Gossage's 1979 season was cut short following a clubhouse scuffle with Cliff Johnson, but he came back to save a career-high 33 games in 1980. He allowed George Brett's LCS-clinching home run in Game Three. Gossage was extremely effective during the strike-shortened 1981 season, allowing just 22 hits in 47 innings to go with 48 strikeouts and 20 saves. He saved all three wins over Milwaukee during the divisional playoffs and both Yankees wins over the Dodgers in the World Series. Following two more seasons in New York (30 saves in 1982, 13–5 with 22 saves in 1983), he signed with the Padres as a free agent and helped them reach the World Series in 1984. Gossage compiled 72 saves during his first three seasons with the Padres, but slumped in 1987 and 1988 (with Chicago Cubs) and was released. He signed with San Francisco for the 1989 season, was released, and signed with the Yankees./(EG)

Julio Gotay — 1939– . SS-2B-3B 1960–69 Cardinals, Pirates, Angels, **Astros** 389 g, .260, 6 hr, 70 rbi

This extremely superstitious native Puerto Rican, who feared touching the cross, had a ML career interrupted by several trips to the minors. In his only season as a regular, as the Cardinals' shortstop in 1962, Gotay hit .255./(RTM)

Jim Gott — 1959– . RHP 1982– **Blue Jays**, Giants, Pirates 749 ip, 35–48, 4.17

Gott is a pitcher with impressive stuff, but not always the greatest consistency. Drafted by the Blue Jays from the St. Louis organization, as a 22-year old rookie he won a 10-inning complete game 1–0 victory over the Detroit Tigers. In his three seasons in Toronto, Gott was shuttled between the bullpen and the starting rotation. In 1985 he was traded to San Francisco (for Gary Lavelle), where he learned the split-fingered fastball from manager Roger Craig and was used mainly as a starter. In 1987 Gott went to the Pirates in the late-season deal that sent Rick Reuschel and Don Robinson to the Giants. In Pittsburgh Gott emerged as the Pirates' late-inning stopper, but missed practically all of 1989 after being injured in the Pirates' opener. When trying to convince people that Dwight Gooden wasn't unhittable, Chili Davis remarked, "He ain't Gott, man." /(TF)

Curt Gowdy — 1919- . *Broadcaster.*

Smooth, steady, and always well-prepared, Curt Gowdy announced Super Bowls, Olympic Games, and NCAA basketball championships along with his record 12 World Series and two decades as host of television's "The American Sportsman." Gowdy joined Mel Allen on Yankee broadcasts in 1949. He became a New England institution as the radio voice of the Red Sox from 1951 to 1965. Gowdy left Boston to join the fledgling NBC "Game of the Week" on TV, and was baseball's lone national voice from 1966 to 1975, providing the play-by-play for every WS and All-Star Game in that span. He was named National Sportscaster of the Year three times, and in 1984 he was named to the writers and broadcasters wing of the Hall of Fame. /(SCL)

Hank Gowdy — 1889-1966. C 1910-17, 19-25, 29-30 Giants, **Braves** 1050 g, .270, 21 hr, 322 rbi. *3 WS, 14 g, .310, 1 hr, 4 rbi*

Gowdy joined the 1910 Giants at age 20, was dealt to the Braves in 1911, and spent the next twelve seasons in Boston. The 6'2" righthander was a starting catcher from 1914 through 1916 and batted .545 with a homer and three RBI to lead the "miracle" Braves to a 1914 World Series sweep over the Athletics. He caught the no-hitters of George Davis (9/9/1914) and Tom Hughes (6/16/1916). Gowdy was the first ML player to enlist for WWI and saw considerable action in France. After he returned in 1919, he shared Boston's catching duties before he was reacquired by the Giants in 1923. Gowdy was a goat in the Giants' 1924 WS loss to Washington; he tripped over his mask and missed a pop-up, which led to the Series-winning run. Dropped by the Giants in 1925, Gowdy returned to the Braves for limited duty in 1929-30. /(DQV)

Billy Grabarkewitz (Bulldog, Grabby) — 1946- . 3B-2B-SS 1969-75 **Dodgers**, Angels, Phillies, Cubs, A's 466 g, .236, 28 hr, 141 rbi
☛ *All-Star—70.*

The injury-prone Grabarkewitz was in the minors when he said, "I was X-rayed so often I glow in the dark." As a rookie, he led the 1970 Dodgers with 17 HR and 92 runs scored, and was named to the All-Star team. /(TG)

Johnny Grabowski (Nig) — 1900-1946. C 1924-29, 31 White Sox, **Yankees**, Tigers 296 g, .252, 3 hr, 86 rbi. *1 WS, 1 g, .000*

Grabowski shared catching duties with Pat Collins and Benny Bengough on the 1927 Yankees. He later became an umpire in the International League. /(JK)

Earl Grace — 1907-1980. C 1929, 31-37 Cubs, **Pirates**, Phillies 627 g, .263, 30 hr, 251 rbi

Grace was a platoon catcher at Pittsburgh in 1931-35. In 1932 he set NL records with 110 consecutive errorless games (400 chances) and fewest errors (one) in 100 or more games (114). /(ME)

Joe Grace — 1914-1969. OF 1938-41, 1946-47 **Browns**, Senators 484 g, .283, 20 hr, 172 rbi

The Browns first wanted the lefthanded line-drive hitter to catch, but manager Luke Sewell preferred Grace in the outfield. Grace hit .309 as a fourth outfielder in 1941. He spent 1942-45 in the Navy. /(WAB)

Mark Grace (Amazing Grace) — 1964- . 1B 1988- **Cubs** 276 g, .305, 20 hr, 136 rbi. *1 LCS, 5 g, .647, 1 hr, 8 rbi*

Only a 24th-round pick in the 1985 draft, Grace was the *TSN* NL Rookie of the Year in 1988, hitting .296 with seven HR and 57 RBI in 486 at-bats. However, he tied for the NL lead in errors by a first baseman. In 1989 he hit .314 and led the Cubs with 79 RBI, and led Chicago regulars in the LCS with 8 RBI and a .647 batting average. /(WOR)

Mike Grady — 1869-1943. C-1B-3B-OF 1894-1901, 1904-06 Phillies, **Cardinals**, Giants, Senators 919 g, .294, 35 hr, 459 rbi

Grady could not field any position well. Once, playing third base for the 1899 Giants, he bobbled a ground ball, overthrew first, and when the batter advanced all the way to third base, dropped the throw from the first baseman. As the runner headed home, Grady launched the ball over the catcher's head. /(AJA)

Bill Graham — 1884-1936. LHP 1908-10 **Browns** 348 ip, 14-29, 2.90

A hard-luck pitcher, Graham managed to compile a career 2.90 ERA, yet win less than a third of his decisions. In 1910 Graham was 0-8 with a poor 3.56 ERA for the last-place 47-107 Browns. /(WAB)

Kyle Graham (Skinny) — 1899–1973. RHP 1924–26, 29 **Braves**, Tigers 278 ip, 11–22, 5.02

Graham had just purchased a hot dog when called in to relieve for Detroit in a 1929 game against the A's. Told that Mickey Cochrane, Al Simmons, and Jimmie Foxx were coming to bat, Graham said, "Leave this hot dog alone. I'll be right back." /(NLM)

Alex Grammas — 1926– . SS-3B-2B 1954–63 **Cardinals**, Reds, Cubs 913 g, .247, 12 hr, 163 rbi
Manager 1969, 76–77 Pirates, **Brewers** 137–191, .418

The good-fielding Grammas barely hit enough to stay in the lineup, but was the Cardinals' everyday shortstop in 1954, 1955, and again in 1959. In between, he was a reserve with the Reds. His best average as a regular was .269 in 1959. He was the Pirate coach chosen to manage the last five games in 1969 after Larry Shepard was fired, and he piloted the Brewers to the basement in 1976 and 1977. He coached for Sparky Anderson in Cincinnati and Detroit. /(MC)

Jack Graney — 1886–1978. OF-LHP 1908, 10–22 **Indians** 1403 g, .250, 18 hr, 420 rbi; 3 ip, 0–0, 5.40. *1 WS, 3 g, .000*

The stocky, 5′9″ Graney, a sharp-eyed leadoff man, played his full 14-year career for Cleveland. The converted pitcher led the AL in doubles in 1916, and in walks in 1917 and 1919. When his playing days ended he became the first ex-major leaguer to move to the broadcasting booth. Graney became a popular Indians play-by-play announcer. /(JK)

Wayne Granger — 1944– . RHP 1968–76 Cardinals, **Reds**, Twins, Yankees, White Sox, Astros, Expos 640 ip, 35–35, 3.14. *1 LCS, 1 ip, 0–0, 0.00. 2 WS, 3 ip, 0–0, 13.50*

Teammates said that 6′2″ 165-lb Wayne Granger could "shower in a shotgun barrel." As a rookie Cardinals reliever in 1968, the sinkerballer recorded a 2.25 ERA. Swapped to the Reds with Bobby Tolan for Vada Pinson, in 1969 he went 9–6 (2.79) with 27 saves in a then-NL-record 90 appearances, winning his first of two straight Fireman of the Year awards. His 35 saves in 1970 set a since-broken NL mark. After yielding a grand slam to Orioles pitcher Dave McNally in Game Three of the '70 WS, Granger was never again as effective, though his 70 appearances in 1971 were again the NL high. He saved 19 games in 1972 for the Twins before arm trouble curtailed his effectiveness. He retired with 108 saves. /(MC)

Charles Grant (Chief Tokohama) — Unk.–1932. 2B Negro Leagues 1896–1910 Page Fence Giants, Columbia Giants, Cuban X Giants, Philadelphia Giants, New York Black Sox

When John McGraw took his Baltimore Orioles to Hot Springs, Arkansas for spring training in 1901, he saw that a bellboy at their hotel was a particularly fine second baseman. McGraw wanted to sign him for the Orioles, but Charles Grant was black. McGraw decided to sidestep the color line by composing an elaborate fiction that Grant, who was rather light-skinned, was Charlie Tokohama, a full-blooded Cherokee Indian. Grant went along with the ruse, and the sporting papers of the day were filled with news of McGraw's sensational new find. The plot was eventually exposed when Charles Comiskey, president of the Chicago White Sox, recognized Grant as the second baseman of the Columbia Giants, a Chicago-area black team.

McGraw dropped Grant from the Orioles' roster, and Chief Tokohama never played in the majors. No statistics survive from his 15 seasons in Negro baseball, though he was the starting second baseman for the black championship teams of 1903 and 1904, the Cuban X Giants and the Philadelphia Giants, respectively. Grant was killed in Cincinnati in a freak accident in July 1932 when a passing auto blew a tire and jumped the curb, striking him while he was relaxing in front of his apartment house. /(JJM)

Eddie Grant (Harvard Eddie) — 1883–1918. 3B-SS 1905, 07–15 Indians, **Phillies**, Reds, Giants 960 g, .249, 5 hr, 277 rbi. *1 WS, 2 g, .000*

Grant graduated from Harvard in 1905 and was given a tryout by Cleveland. He got three hits his first game, but was hitless the next day against Cy Young and was dropped to the minors. He reappeared with the 1907 Phillies, and took over as leadoff batter in 1908, leading the NL in at-bats in 1908 and 1909. Grant became a fine-fielding third baseman, fast on the bases and dependable in the clutch. After two-and-a-half seasons with the Giants, he retired in 1915 to practice law in New York City.

In World War I, he led a mission in the Argonne Forest offensive to rescue the "Lost Battalion" trapped behind German lines. When he met with machine gun fire, he became the only ML player killed in wartime action. A monument to his memory was placed in the Polo Grounds' deep centerfield, and each Memorial Day there was a wreath-laying ceremony at his plaque. /(JK)

Frank Grant — 1868–1937. 2B-SS Negro Leagues 1886–1903 Meriden (EL), Buffalo (IL), **Cuban X Giants**, Harrisburg (EL), Lansing, Colored Capital All-Americans, New York Gorhams, Philadelphia Giants statistics not available

The most accomplished black baseball player of the 19th century, Grant joined Buffalo (International League) in 1886 and became the first black to play on the same team in organized baseball for three consecutive seasons. With his extraordinary range and strong arm, he was compared favorably with the best second basemen of his era. One Buffalo writer asserted that Grant was the best all-around player Buffalo had ever seen; four future Hall of Famers had played in Buffalo prior to Grant. Though just 5'7" 155-lb, he had surprising power at the plate; one-fourth of his hits in the International League were for extra bases. He led his team and/or league in various offensive categories, including batting average, stolen bases, total bases, and home runs. During the 1887 season, he hit for the cycle in one game and stole home twice in another. By the late 1880s, black players were banished from organized baseball. Grant went on to play for such strong independent Negro teams as the Cuban X Giants, Big Gorhams, and Philadelphia Giants through 1903. /(JMa)

George Grant — 1903– . RHP 1923–25, 27–29, 31 Browns, **Indians**, Pirates 346 ip, 15–20, 5.64

Grant earned 10 of his 15 wins in 1928, when he led a weak Indians squad in winning percentage (.556) despite an ERA of 5.04. /(ME)

Mark Grant — 1963– . RHP 1984, 86– Giants, **Padres** 441 ip, 18–28, 4.12

The 10th player in the nation selected in the June 1981 free agent draft, Grant twice led his league in wins in the minors, and was Midwest League MVP at Clinton in 1982 (16–5, 2.36 ERA, 243 strikeouts). He has struggled both as a starter and in relief in the ML. /(ME)

Mudcat Grant [James Timothy] — 1935– . RHP 1958–71 **Indians**, Twins, Dodgers, Expos, Cardinals, A's, Pirates 2441 ip, 145–119, 3.63. 20 wins: 65 *1 LCS, 2 ip, 0–0, 0.00. 1 WS, 23 ip, 2–1, 2.74*
☛ *Led League—w 65. All-Star—65.*

Colorful Mudcat Grant was not only a 14-year ML pitcher, but a broadcaster and entertainer. He spent his first seven-plus seasons with the Indians, compiling a 67–63 record. He then reached his pinnacle with the 1965 pennant-winning Twins, leading the AL in victories and winning percentage (21–7, .750) and in shutouts (six). He defeated the Dodgers in the World Series opener 8–2, lost Game Four 7–2, and won Game Six 5–1, helping himself with a three-run homer. He worked mostly in relief after his trade to the Dodgers in November of 1967, and in 1969 recorded the expansion Expos' first win. With Oakland and Pittsburgh in 1970, he went 8–3 (1.87) with 24 saves. Sporting muttonchop sideburns, he was the lead singer of a group called "Mudcat and the Kittens." /(ME)

George Grantham (Boots) — 1900–1954. 2B-1B 1922–34 Cubs, **Pirates**, Reds, Giants 1444 g, .302, 105 hr, 712 rbi. *2 WS, 8 g, .231*

After driving in 160 runs for Tacoma (Western League) in 1922, Grantham became the Cubs' starting second baseman. He struck out more than any NL player in 1923 and 1924, but was the run producer Pittsburgh needed. In a major postseason deal in 1924, the Bucs sent Rabbit Maranville, Charlie Grimm, and Wilbur Cooper to the Cubs for Grantham, Vic Aldridge, and Al Niehaus. Some Pittsburgh fans criticized trading three popular players for an erratic fielder (Grantham) and two unknowns, but the trade paid off for the Pirates. Grantham, switched from second base to first base, batted a career-high .326 and dramatically reduced his strikeouts in 1925. Pittsburgh won the World Series, and the Cubs finished last. Grantham batted over .300 in each of his seven seasons with Pittsburgh, splitting time between first base and second base. /(ME)

Mickey Grasso [Newton Michael] — 1920–1975. C 1946, 50–55 Giants, **Senators**, Indians 322 g, .226, 5 hr, 87 rbi. *1 WS, 1 g, --*

Nicknamed Mickey because of his remarkable resemblance to Hall of Fame catcher Mickey Cochrane, Grasso homered for Trenton in 1941 in his first at-bat in organized baseball. A former WWII prisoner of the Germans in North Africa, he batted .287 as a part-time catcher with the Senators in 1950. /(RM)

Stephen O. Grauley (Sog) — 1879–1958. *Writer.*

In nearly 60 years with the Philadelphia *Inquirer*, Grauley covered Connie Mack's Athletics from their inception until after Mack's retirement. At the 1951 A's home opener, Mack chose Grauley as his box-seat companion for the first Athletics game without Mack as manager. Sog (his initials) played on the first baseball team fielded by Temple University, in the 1890s. As a sportswriter, he was known for his factual and accurate writing in an age of flamboyant phrasing. He became sports editor of the *Inquirer* in 1924. He was a charter member of the BBWAA. /(NLM)

Dolly Gray [William] — 1878–1956. LHP 1909–11 **Senators** 568 ip, 15–51, 3.52

Nicknamed for "Goodbye, Dolly Gray," a popular Spanish-American War ballad, Gray had a record worse than that of his doormat team. He lost a one-hitter when, after a two-out error, he walked seven straight on 3–2 counts. /(JK)

Gary Gray — 1952– . 1B-DH 1977–82 Rangers, Indians, **Mariners** 211 g, .240, 24 hr, 71 rbi

In his one full ML season, Gray had 13 HR — 10 by June 1 — in 69 games for the 1981 Mariners. In 12 minor league seasons, including many in the Mexican League, he never hit below .300. /(JCA)

John Gray (Mitty) — 1927– . RHP 1954–55, 57–58 **A's**, Indians, Phillies 169 ip, 4–18, 6.18

Gray had the top ERA (2.72) in the American Association with Indianapolis in 1956. Pitching for Cleveland in 1957, he hurled his only shutout, for his final ML victory. /(RTM)

Pete Gray — 1917– . OF 1945 **Browns** .218, 0 hr, 13 rbi

Despite losing his right arm in a childhood truck accident, Gray became a major league ballplayer. The naturally righthanded youngster learned to throw and bat from the opposite side. Batting with one arm, Gray sprayed line drives around the field. On the basepaths, he displayed speed and daring, and fielding was a study in agility and dexterity. After catching a fly ball, Gray would tuck his thinly padded glove under his stump, roll the ball across his chest, and throw, all in one fluid motion.

Gray was a semi-pro star in the coal towns of his native Pennsylvania and with the famed Brooklyn Bushwicks. He entered pro ball in 1942 with Three Rivers (Canadian-American League) and hit .381 in 42 games. In the Southern Association in 1943, Gray hit .289 in a full season with Memphis. He won national attention in 1944 when he batted .333 for Memphis, hit five HR, tied a league record by stealing 68 bases, and was named the Southern Association's MVP. This outstanding showing earned Gray a spot with the 1945 St. Louis Browns.

Even with the quality of major league play at an all-time low due to the WWII player shortage, Gray was overmatched. But he was capable of remarkable performances. In a doubleheader at Yankee Stadium in May, Gray had four hits, scored twice, drove in two, and handled nine chances in the outfield. When baseball returned to full strength in 1946, the Browns sent Gray down. He continued to play in the minors and barnstorm with exhibition teams until the early 1950s. Gray retired to his hometown of Nanticoke, PA, and became a recluse. /(JL)

Sam Gray (Sad Sam) — 1897–1953. RHP 1924–33 A's, Browns 1951 ip, 112–115, 4.20. 20 wins: 28

Gray once started off a game for the 1926 Athletics by throwing 15 straight balls. He eventually won the game with a two-hitter, 3–1. In 1925 a series of misfortunes kept him from an outstanding record. He won his first eight, but a pitched ball broke his right thumb. Later that season, his wife died suddenly. He still finished 16–8. Two years later, Gray went a career-best 20–12 for the Browns. The eccentric curveballer led the AL with 37 starts, 305 innings, and four shutouts in 1929, and with 37 starts and 24 losses in 1931. /(WAB)

Ted Gray — 1924– . LHP 1946, 48–55 **Tigers**, White Sox, Indians, Yankees, Orioles 1134 ip, 59–74, 4.37
☛ *All-Star—50.*

Signed off the Detroit sandlots, Gray was a hard-throwing star in WWII service ball. In the majors, the forkballer was hindered by chronic blisters and he held his ERA below 4.00 only once in nine seasons. After eight seasons with the Tigers, he appeared with four different teams in 1955. /(JK)

Harry M. Grayson — 1894–1968. *Writer.*

Grayson retired in 1964 after 30 years as sports editor of *NEA*. It was said of him that he never went to bed; he was one of the few nightlifers who could outlast Casey Stengel. His book, *They Played the Game*, was published in 1944. /(NLM)

Eli Grba — 1934– . RHP 1959–63 Yankees, **Angels** 536 ip, 28–33, 4.48

On Opening Day, 1961, the bespectacled Grba defeated Baltimore in the first game ever played by the expansion Angels. The ex-Yankee reliever used a good fastball to win 19 games for the Angels in two years, 17 as a starter. /(RTM)

Dallas Green — 1934– . RHP 1960–67 **Phillies,** Senators, Mets 562 ip, 20–22, 4.26.
Manager 1979–81, 89 **Phillies,** Yankees 225–195, .536. First place: 80 *1 LCS, 3–2, .600. 1 WS, 4–2, .667*

After a pitching career in which he recorded all his ML decisions for the Phillies, Dallas Green managed two Phillies farm clubs, served as an assistant director and director of their minor league system, and managed the parent club for over two years. In 1980 the 6'5" 245-lb Green guided the Phillies to their first World Championship since 1915. "I express my thoughts," he said. "I'm a screamer, a yeller and a cusser. I never hold back." At the 1981 press conference marking his appointment as the Cubs' GM, Green remarked, "I'm no Messiah, but I'll guarantee no one will ever outwork us. When I hire someone he better work at it or hear from me." In 1984 the Cubs won the NL East title, their first championship in nearly 40 years, based largely on strong years from former Phillies Gary Mathews, Bob Dernier, and MVP Ryne Sandberg. Green resigned after a 1987 last-place finish, but his rebuilding of the Chicago farm system paid off with a pennant in 1989.

Hired by George Steinbrenner to manage the Yankees in 1989, Green rebuilt the team with GM Syd Thrift but was fired before the end of the season for referring to Steinbrenner as Manager George. /(TJ)

Danny Green — 1876–1914. OF 1898–1905 Cubs, **White Sox** 923 g, .293, 29 hr, 422 rbi

Green was a foolhardy baserunner and a .304 hitter for the Chicago Colts (Cubs) in 1898–1901. When American League raiders offered lucrative contracts to unhappy National League stars, Charles Comiskey landed Green, who became the White Sox right fielder in 1902. In 1906, with Green's throwing arm burning out, Comiskey let him manage half the club in split-squad spring training. Green had his players roller-skating, believing it was better than jogging, but his training ideas did not please Comiskey. After Green's spring squad lost most of its games, Green was outrighted to the American Association. He died in 1914 of complications from a beaning. /(RL)

David Green — 1960– . OF-1B 1981–85, 87 **Cardinals,** Giants 489 g, .268, 31 hr, 180 rbi. *1 LCS, 2 g, 1.000. 1 WS, 7 g, .200*

Green was a highly touted young talent, showing speed, power, and excellent defensive ability. He hit .283 in 76 games in 1982 and .284 with 34 stolen bases in 1983. The Giants obtained him with Jose Uribe, Dave LaPoint, and Gary Rajsich for Jack Clark, and hoped he would be a capable successor to Clark at first base. He wasn't. Personal problems, including fear for his family in strife-torn Nicaragua, led to his decline. After flings in the Mexican and Japanese leagues (1986–87), a glimmer of his potential shone again in September 1987. The Cardinals recalled him during their successful pennant drive to substitute for the injured Clark, and Green hit .267 and slugged .500 in limited action. /(FO)

Dick Green — 1941– . 2B 1963–74 **A's** 1288 g, .240, 80 hr, 422 rbi. *4 LCS, 17 g, .162, 1 rbi. 3 WS, 19 g, .149, 2 RBI*

Green was a superb-fielding, light-hitting second baseman, whose glove work was a key to Oakland's three straight World Championships (1972–74) and a highlight of the 1974 WS. In the clincher, he was the pivot man in an exciting eighth-inning double play that preserved the A's 3–2 victory over the Dodgers. The Iowan led AL second basemen in fielding in 1969 (.986). Usually a second baseman during his 12 years in Kansas City and Oakland, Green played every infield position and even caught two games. He had some power, reaching double figures in homers four times. His best year offensively was 1969, when he hit .275, with career highs of 64 RBI and 43 extra-base hits. /(TJ)

Freddie Green — 1933– . LHP 1959–62, 64 **Pirates,** Senators 142 ip, 9–7, 3.48. *1 WS, 4 ip, 0–0, 22.50*

Out of nowhere, Green became the ace lefthander in the 1960 Pirate bullpen (8–4, three saves) and even hit two HR. But he lost his battle with his control problems and never notched another win or save. /(ME)

Gene Green — 1933–1981. OF-C 1957–63 **Cardinals,** Orioles, Senators, Indians, Reds 408 g, .267, 46 hr, 160 rbi

Overlooked by the scouts, the strong-armed outfielder had to ask for a tryout in 1952. Green took up catching, but sat on the bench most of his short career. "If baseball ever adopted the two platoon system," he once quipped, "I'd get $50,000: 25 for hitting, and 25 for sitting." /(WAB)

Lenny Green — 1934– . OF 1957–68 Orioles, **Senators/Twins,** Angels, Red Sox, Tigers 1136 g, .267, 47 hr, 253 rbi

Twice in his career, Green was traded to a club against which his team was playing its next game.

The Twins' everyday centerfielder in their first two seasons, Green had a 24-game hitting streak in 1961, a club record until Ken Landreaux broke it in 1980. /(RTM)

Pumpsie Green [Elijah Jerry] — 1933– . 2B-SS 1959–63 **Red Sox, Mets** 344 g, .246, 13 hr, 74 rbi

In 1959 Pumpsie became the first black player on the Red Sox, the major leagues' last integrated team. The switch-hitter's brother, Cornell Green, was a Dallas Cowboys defensive back. /(RMu)

Hank Greenberg (Hammerin' Hank) — 1911–1986. 1B-OF 1930, 33–41, 45–47 **Tigers, Pirates** 1394 g, .313, 331 hr, 1276 rbi. *4 WS, 23 g, .318, 5 hr, 22 rbi* ☛ *Most Valuable Player—35, 40. Led League—hr 35, 38, 40, 46. Led League—rbi 35, 37, 40, 46. All-Star—37–40. Hall of Fame—1956.*

Although he missed time through injuries, military service, and early retirement, Greenberg still ranks as one of the most fearsome sluggers in baseball history. The powerful righthander played only the equivalent of nine-and-a-half seasons, yet produced outstanding career totals as well as exceptional season marks.

A native New Yorker, Greenberg was the son of Rumanian-born Jewish immigrants who owned a successful cloth-shrinking plant. Hank graduated from James Monroe High School in the Bronx, then attended New York University on an athletic scholarship for one semester before beginning his professional baseball career. The 6'4" 215-lb Greenberg's athletic success stemmed from size, strength, and hard work, more than native talent. His high school coach explained: "Hank was so big for his age and so awkward that he became painfully self-conscious. The fear of being made to look foolish drove him to practice constantly and, as a result, to overcome his handicaps."

Greenberg tried out for the New York Giants but Giants Manager John McGraw, although constantly on the lookout for a Jewish star to attract New York's large Jewish population and impressed by Greenberg's powerful hitting, decided Hank was too clumsy and uncoordinated to help the Giants. Hank turned down a lucrative offer from the Yankees, realizing there would be little chance of making the ML with Lou Gehrig on first for the Bombers. He also rejected overtures from the Senators, who had Joe Judge. In January 1930 he signed with the Tigers.

After several minor league stops, he was called up to the Tigers in 1933. Still awkward in the field,

Hank Greenberg

though quick on his feet, he showed line-drive power, with 33 doubles, 12 homers, and a .301 batting average. In 1934 he cracked a league-leading 63 doubles and batted .339 with 26 homers and 139 RBI as the Tigers won the AL pennant. In the WS loss to the Gashouse Gang Cardinals, he hit .321 but struck out nine times.

The Tigers repeated as AL champs in 1935, spurred by Greenberg's league-topping 36 homers and 170 RBI. He was named AL MVP. He suffered a broken wrist in the second game of the WS and watched from the sideline as the Tigers defeated the Cubs. Off to an excellent start in 1936, with 16 RBI in 12 games, he broke the same wrist in a collision at first base and missed the rest of the season, amid speculation that his career was over.

Instead, he rebounded with 183 RBI in 1937, the third-highest total ever. He also hit 40 homers and batted .337. The next season he made a determined assault on Babe Ruth's 60 home run record. With five games to go, he had 58, to tie Jimmie Foxx's record for righthanded hitters, but he was unable to add to that total. He set a record for most multi-homer games in a season, with eleven.

In 1940, Greenberg shifted from his hard-won first base position to left field to enable the Tigers to find a regular lineup spot for hard-hitting but poor-fielding Rudy York. The result was a Detroit pennant, breaking the Yankees' streak of four straight pennants. Many credited Greenberg's willingness and ability to learn a completely new position as the key factor in Detroit's success. He hit .340 and led the AL in doubles (50), home runs (41), and RBI (150), and earned his second MVP award.

Greenberg, then a bachelor, was one of the first major leaguers inducted into the service, entering 19 games into the 1941 season. He was discharged from the army on December 5, 1941, two days before the Japanese attack on Pearl Harbor. He immediately enlisted as an officer candidate in the Air Corps. Hank served with distinction in the Far East until his discharge in mid-1945. He returned with a bang, with a home run in his first game. His grand slam on the final day of the season won the pennant for the Tigers. In the WS win over the Cubs, he hit two more homers and batted in seven runs.

He led the AL in homers (44) and RBI (127) again in 1946, but a salary dispute developed with the Tigers during the season. Rather than raise his salary, Detroit waived him out of the AL to Pittsburgh. Greenberg deeply resented learning of the deal from the radio rather than being informed in advance of the public announcement. The Pirates coaxed him into playing the 1947 season with a complicated contract that netted him between $100,000 and $145,000, making him the NL's first $100,000 player. A bullpen was built in front of Forbes Field's distant left field wall and fans quickly labeled it "Greenberg Gardens." Although he hit a disappointing .249, he contributed 25 home runs and served as a gate instructor. More important, he served as hitting instructor and advisor to his protege and friend, young Ralph Kiner. When Greenberg retired after the 1947 season, the left field bullpen became known as "Kiner's Korner."

In 1948 Cleveland owner Bill Veeck hired Greenberg as farm system director. He became general manager in 1950 and built the team that derailed the Yankees' string of pennants in 1954. Unable to purchase stock in the Indians, he moved to the White Sox as part owner and vice president as that

team won the 1959 pennant. He retired from baseball in 1963 to become a successful investment banker. /(FS)

Joe Greene [James Elbert] — 1911- .C-1B-OF Negro Leagues 1932-48 Atlanta Black Crackers, **Kansas City Monarchs**, Cleveland Buckeyes statistics not available

Greene caught for the perennial Negro American League champion Kansas City Monarchs from 1939 through 1947. Strong pitching was a Monarch trademark; Greene handled some of the best, including Satchel Paige. His career opened with the Atlanta Black Crackers, and ended there with a NAL title series in 1938, canceled after the Memphis Red Sox won two games. He was the starting catcher for the West in the 1940 and 1942 East-West all-star games, and in the Monarchs' 1942 Black World Series triumph he batted .444 with a home run and eight RBI. He was decorated for combat service in WWII. In 1947 he hit a long home run off Bob Feller in an exhibition game. In his last three years in the NAL, Greene batted .293. /(MFK)

Kent Greenfield — 1902-1978. RHP 1924-29 **Giants**, Braves, Dodgers 775 ip, 41-48, 4.54

Greenfield, a rangy curveballer, pitched creditably for the Giants in 1925-26 before being traded to the Braves. Hampered by recurring control problems, he was less effective from then on. /(FS)

Jim Greengrass — 1927- . OF 1952-56 **Reds**, Phillies 504 g, .269, 69 hr, 282 rbi

The husky righthanded hitter joined the Reds in September 1952, more than eight years after his pro debut. He had 100 RBI his first full season, 27 HR his second, then faded, hampered by phlebitis. /(AL)

Gus Greenlee [William Augustus] — 1897-1952. *Executive.*

The owner of the Pittsburgh Crawfords, 1931-38, in 1933 Greenlee organized the National Negro Association, commonly known as the second Negro National League, into which it evolved. He served as its president with absolute power, awarding the first pennant to his own Crawfords. This claim was disputed by the Chicago American Giants, since the schedule had not been completed. The circuit survived until being absorbed by the Negro American League in 1949. Greenlee also initiated the East-West all-star game in 1933. The Negro Leagues' showcase event, it annually drew crowds approaching 50,000 to Comiskey Field.

In addition to the Crawfords, he also owned his

own ballpark, a famous nightclub (the Crawford Bar & Grill), and a stable of boxers including light-heavyweight champion John Henry Lewis. Greenlee was a power in black Pittsburgh's racketeering and politics. /(MFK)

Tom Greenwade — 1904–1986. *Scout.*

A scout for the Browns and Dodgers before beginning a 40-year stint with the Yankees in 1945, Greenwade gave Dodger owner Branch Rickey favorable reports on Jackie Robinson and Roy Campanella, and signed Mickey Mantle and Bobby Murcer for the Yankees. /(FVP)

Mike Greenwell — 1963– . OF 1985– **Red Sox**
476 g, .320, 59 hr, 315 rbi. *2 LCS, 6 g, .250, 1 hr, 3 rbi.
1 WS, 4 g, .000*
☛ *All-Star—88–89.*

The heir to Ted Williams, Carl Yastrzemski, and Jim Rice in left field for the Boston Red Sox, Greenwell rapidly established himself as one of baseball's best hitters. With a smooth lefthanded batting stroke modeled after George Brett's, he finished third in the 1987 AL Rookie of the Year voting (behind Mark McGwire and Kevin Seitzer) and in 1988 beat out Jim Rice for the leftfield job, hitting .325 with 22 HR, 119 RBI, and only 38 strikeouts. His first three ML hits were home runs, the first a 13th-inning game-winner at Toronto September 25, 1985. /(SCL)

Eric Gregg — 1951– . *Umpire* NL 1977– *2 LCS 1 ASU*

The roly-poly Gregg gained off-season recognition with a TV sports show on "Evening Magazine." He was perhaps the only ump ever to call interference on himself. In 1978 he bumped Cardinal catcher Ted Simmons in the act of throwing and subsequently nullified a Dodgers double steal. /(RTM)

Hal Gregg — 1921– . RHP 1943–50, 52 **Dodgers**,
Pirates, Giants 827 IP, 40–48, 4.54. *1 WS, 12.2 ip, 0–1,
3.55*

Gregg led the NL in walks in 1944 and 1945, and walked 11 batters in one 15-inning game (6/15/44). He went 18–13 (3.47) to lead Dodger pitchers in '45, but a sore arm held him to just 13 more victories. /(ME)

Tommy Gregg — 1963– . OF-1B 1987– Pirates,
Braves 137 g, .250, 7 hr, 30 rbi

Gregg led the Eastern League in batting in 1987 with a .371 mark. When Pirates GM Syd Thrift sent him

to the Braves as the player to be named later in return for Ken Oberkfell in September 1988, it contributed to Thrift's firing in the off-season. Gregg started 1989 as one of the Braves' hottest hitters, but was disabled early. When he returned, he was moved to first base part-time to replace Gerald Perry, who was out for the rest of the year. /(JFC)

Vean Gregg [Sylveanus Augustus] — 1885–1964. LHP
1911–16, 18, 25 **Indians**, Red Sox, A's, Senators 1392 ip,
91–63, 2.70. 20 wins: 11–13
☛ *Led League—era 11.*

Gregg had a great 1910 season in the Pacific Coast League, throwing 14 shutouts. He continued his success in his rookie season with the Indians in 1911, going 23–7 to lead the AL with a .767 winning percentage and a 1.81 ERA. The powerful left-hander followed with two more 20-win seasons before suffering a sore arm which reduced his effectiveness. Traded to the Red Sox in mid-1914, he never again had a successful ML season, though he was a big winner after he returned to the minors. Younger brother Dave had a one-inning ML pitching career with Cleveland in 1913. /(JK)

Paul Gregory (Pop) — 1908– . RHP 1932–33 **White
Sox** 221 ip, 9–14, 4.72

Gregory bore an uncanny resemblance to and copied the delivery of White Sox ace Ted Lyons. He became Lyons' protege and constant companion. After pitching well late in 1932, he was slated to be Chicago's third starter in 1933, but reported overweight and was ineffective. /(RL)

Bill Greif — 1950– . RHP 1971–76 Astros, **Padres**,
Cardinals 716 ip, 31–67, 4.41

As a starter for the last-place 1972–74 Padres, 6'4" Bill Greif suffered through records of 5–16, 10–17, and 9–19. He was traded from St. Louis to Montreal in 1976, but was released without appearing in a game. /(MC)

Ed Gremminger (Battleship) — 1874–1942. 3B 1895,
1902–04 Cleveland (NL), **Braves**, Tigers 383 g, .251, 7 hr,
165 rbi

Playing for the Braves, Gremminger led NL third basemen in putouts and fielding in 1902 and in putouts, assists, and double plays in 1903; those were his only years as a regular, despite respectable hitting. He managed in the minors from 1908 to 1912. /(NLM)

Zane Grey — 1875–1939. *Writer.*

A star outfielder while studying dentistry at the University of Pennsylvania, Grey was signed by Ed Barrow for Wheeling in the Interstate League in 1895. He got as far as Toronto of the Eastern League in 1899 before beginning his dental practice in New York. His brother, Romer, played briefly with the Pirates. Grey wrote 86 books, mostly westerns, but three were baseball novels: *The Short-stop, The Redheaded Outfield,* and *The Young Pitcher.* /(NLM)

Bobby Grich — 1949– . 2B 1970–86 Orioles, **Angels** 2008 g, .266, 224 hr, 864 rbi. *5 LCS, 24 g, .182, 3 hr, 9 rbi* ☛ *Led League—hr 81. All-Star—72, 74, 76, 79–80, 82. Gold Glove—73–76.*

An excellent fielder with a surprisingly powerful bat, Grich was one of the AL's best all-around second basemen for over 15 seasons with the Orioles and Angels, earning All-Star recognition six times. The 6'2" 180-lb Grich was big for a middle infielder, but as a converted minor league shortstop he had plenty of range in the field, and he generated considerable power with a strong-wristed righthanded batting stroke.

Grich was *TSN* Minor League Player of the Year at Rochester (International League) in 1971, hitting .336 with 32 HR and leading the league's shortstops in fielding, and as a 23-year old rookie with the Orioles in 1972, he played shortstop for the AL in the All-Star Game, finishing the season at .278 with 12 HR. Grich moved to second base full-time in 1973 and promptly set a ML record for that position with a .995 fielding percentage, and from 1973–76 he reached double figures in home runs and stolen bases each year while hitting near .260.

Grich became a free agent after the 1976 season and signed with the Angels for 1977, only to spend most of the year on the DL. He then had a miserable year offensively in 1978, but rebounded in 1979 to hit .294 with career highs in HR (30) and RBI (101) as the Angels won the AL West. In the strike-shortened 1981 season, Grich was one of four AL players to tie for the league home run title with 22, and also led the league with a .543 slugging percentage while batting a career-high .304. In the field, Grich had lost some range, but was still sure-handed, and in 1985 he regained his ML fielding record (which had been broken by Rob Wilfong in 1980) with a .997 percentage, committing only two errors at second base all season.

Bobby Grich

Grich played in the ALCS five times, yet never reached the WS. He came closest in his final ML season (1986), when the Angels blew a 5–2 lead to the Red Sox in the ninth inning of Game Five, then lost Games Six and Seven as well. Grich is second behind Brian Downing on the Angels all-time home run list. /(SCL)

Bill Grieve — 1900–1979. *Umpire* AL 1938–55 *3 WS 2 ASU*

Grieve was known for two things among AL players: his many little fears and phobias, and for showing favoritism to the Yankees. Although the latter charge was without merit, some players called him the Number One Yankee Fan. /(RTM)

Tom Grieve — 1948– . OF-DH 1970, 72–79 **Senators/Rangers**, Mets, Cardinals 670 g, .249, 65 hr, 254 rbi

Grieve has spent almost all of his two-plus decades in professional baseball with the Senators-Rangers organization. He played two errorless seasons (1973–74) in the Rangers' outfield in limited duty, and saw his most activity in 1976 as a DH, reaching career highs of 20 HR, 23 doubles, 81 RBI, and 57 runs while batting .255. In December 1977 he went to the Mets in a four-team deal that netted Texas Jon Matlack, and one year later he was dealt to St. Louis for Pete Falcone. The Cardinals released him in May and he finished the season with the Rangers' Triple-A Tucson club, then joined the Texas front-office in 1980. In 1984, at age 36, he became the youngest GM in the ML. /(JFC)

Ken Griffey, Jr. — 1967– . OF 1989– **Mariners** 127 g, .264, 16 hr, 61 rbi

Griffey was off to a Rookie of the Year season in 1989 before injury ended his season right after the All-Star break. He and his father, Ken Sr., are the first father-son duo to play in the majors at the same time. /(JFC)

Ken Griffey, Sr. — 1950– . OF-1B 1973– **Reds**, Yankees, Braves 2000 g, .297, 147 hr, 824 rbi. *3 LCS, 9 g, .313, 6 rbi. 2 WS, 11 g, .186, 5 rbi*
☛ *All-Star—76–77, 80.*

An unsung star of the 1975–81 Reds, Ken Griffey hit .307 in nine years in his first stint with Cincinnati and challenged for the NL batting title in 1976 and 1977. The right fielder was a heads-up, all-around player, but was most proficient at the plate. Hailing from Donora, Pennsylvania, like Stan Musial, the lefthanded Griffey's career slumped after he moved to the Yankees in a 1981 transaction. Used in a platoon role at first base and in the outfield, Griffey's entire game suffered. Injuries also slowed him, but Ken was rejuvenated upon joining the Braves. Rejoining the Reds in 1989, he and his son, Ken Jr., made history as the first father and son to play in the major leagues at the same time. /(ME)

Alfredo Griffin — 1957– . SS 1976– Indians, **Blue Jays**, A's, Dodgers 1603 g, .253, 23 hr, 452 rbi. *1 LCS, 7 g, .160, 3 rbi. 1 WS, 5 g, .188*
☛ *All-Star—84. Gold Glove—85.*

Griffin was co-winner of the 1979 AL Rookie of the Year award, along with Minnesota's John Castino. As a steady, everyday shortstop, he spent six years with the Blue Jays, playing in 392 consecutive games. Griffin was traded after the 1984 season to Oakland, where, despite his reluctance to draw walks and a tendency to be overaggressive on the basepaths, he began to harness the offensive promise he showed in 1980 when he set an AL record for most triples by a switch-hitter with a league-leading 15. After establishing personal bests in most offensive categories with the Athletics, Griffin was traded to the Dodgers for Bob Welch prior to the 1988

season in a move that helped both teams to league championships. A Dwight Gooden fastball broke his hand in May 1988, and he was disabled for much of 1988 and 1989. /(TF)

Doug Griffin — 1947– . 2B 1970–77 Angels, **Red Sox** 632 g, .245, 7 hr, 165 rbi. *1 WS, 1 g, .000*
☛ *Gold Glove—72.*

Tony Conigliaro went to the Angels in a 1971 deal that brought this Pacific Coast League All-Star to Boston. The injury-plagued 1972 Gold Glove second baseman was beaned by a Nolan Ryan fastball on April 30, 1974. /(RMu)

Mike Griffin — 1865–1908. OF 1887–98 Baltimore (AA), Philadelphia (PL), **Dodgers** 1511 g, .299, 41 hr, 625 rbi.
Manager 1898 **Dodgers** 1–3, .250

In 1887, playing centerfield for Baltimore of the American Association, Griffin stole 94 bases to set a ML rookie record that stood until Vince Coleman stole 110 in 1985. In 1889 he led the AA in runs scored. He led the NL in doubles in 1891, his first season in CF for the Brooklyn Bridegrooms (later called the Dodgers), where he remained through 1898. He retired with 473 stolen bases. /(AJA)

Mike Griffin — 1957– . RHP 1979–82, 87 Yankees, Cubs, Padres, **Orioles** 199 ip, 7–15, 4.44

Texas traded the 6′4″ Griffin to the Yankees with Dave Righetti in a 1978, 10-player deal. Griffin was New York's best rookie in the spring of 1980, then went 2–4 and was sent down. He pitched for seven organizations without a full or winning season in the majors. /(MC)

Tom Griffin — 1948– . RHP 1969–82 **Astros**, Padres, Angels, Giants, Pirates 1493 ip, 77–94, 4.07

Griffin struggled through three minor league seasons before going 11–10 for Houston in 1969, winning *TSN* NL Rookie Pitcher of the Year honors. He struck out 200 batters in 188 innings. On April 19, 1970, he one-hit the Padres, but slipped to 3–13 and spent time in Triple-A. He battled back from arm trouble and worked mostly out of the Astros bullpen until late in 1973. On May 7, 1974, he one-hit the Pirates en route to a career-best 14–10 mark. A good-hitting pitcher, he managed 10 HR in 405 career at-bats. /(MC)

Griffith Stadium Washington Senators 1911–61. LF-388, CF-421, RF-320

Built for Clark Griffith's Senators when National Park burned down during spring training in 1911, the original concrete and steel grandstand took only 18 days to construct, but when the double-decked stands were extended from the bases to the foul poles in 1920, the roofs of the new sections were considerably higher than the originals, giving the stadium a makeshift appearance. While Griffith Stadium's left field fence was usually over 380′ away, right field was never more than 330', but it was guarded by a 30′ wall that extended all the way to the centerfield bleachers, jutting in dramatically in deep right-center to allow for a large tree on the outside. It was the AL's lowest-capacity park (27,410) for many years, and the president traditionally threw out the first ball each Opening Day. It was demolished in 1965 and is now the site of Howard University Hospital. /(SCL)

Clark Griffith (The Old Fox) — 1869–1955. RHP 1891, 93–1907, 09–10, 12–14 St. Louis (AA), Boston (AA), **Cubs**, White Sox, Yankees, Reds, Senators 3386 ip, 240–141, 3.31. 20 wins: 94–99, 01
Manager 1901–20 White Sox, Yankees, Reds, **Senators** 1491–1367, .522 First place: 01
☛ *Led League—era 98. Hall of Fame—1946.*

A native of the prairie, Griffith was a professional trapper at age ten, emulating his father, a commercial hunter. When the Griffiths relocated to Bloomington, IL, young Clark discovered organized baseball. He signed his first pro contract in 1888 with Milwaukee of the Western League, and jumped to the American Association, pitching for both St. Louis and Boston in 1891 before the league collapsed.

In 1893 Griffith assembled a 30–18 record for the Oakland Oaks (Pacific Coast League). When the Oaks' owners, in mid-season, did not come up with back pay owed the players, Griffith organized his

Griffith Stadium

teammates to strike. Needing employment, several of them, including Griffith, audaciously found work as itinerant vaudevillians in San Francisco's Barbary Coast district. When the owners found enough money, the greasepaint was abandoned and the season was completed.

Griffith was signed by Cap Anson for his NL Chicago Colts (later Cubs) in 1893. Griffith's eight years in Chicago were the high point of his playing career, and Anson's tutelage added a dimension to his ambitious personality. The Old Fox earned his nickname by utilizing a six-pitch arsenal, including the screwball (which he claimed to have invented), a silencing quick-pitch delivery, and the ruse of hiding the ball in the plane of his body before delivering. Griffith scuffed, scratched, cut, and spit upon nearly every pitch without hesitation, yet when the call came to make these tactics illegal in 1920, Griffith led that bandwagon. Young Clark claimed it was bad luck to pitch a shutout, and avoided doing so until 1897.

Griffith served as vice president of the League Protective Players' Association, and in 1900, he led the members in baseball's first universal strike. The players wanted the minimum salary raised to $3,000 and their uniforms paid for by the owners. Honorable demands aside, The Old Fox had the ulterior motive of helping old friend Ban Johnson establish his rival American League. He contrived to get every player to pledge not to sign a new contract without LPPA approval. This tactic crippled NL owners. Griffith persuaded 39 NL stars to jump to the AL; for his efforts, he was rewarded with the player/managership of the new Chicago franchise in 1901 and 1902, before moving on to the same duties with the newborn New York Highlanders (later Yankees) from 1903 to 1908. A tremendous animosity grew between Griffith and the New York owners. Oddly enough, the NL took him back with open arms to manage the Cincinnati Reds from 1909 to 1911. But when Johnson convinced him to rebuild the ailing franchise in Washington, Griffith had a home for life.

Placing himself in debt (a position from which he never strayed far), Griffith purchased control of the lackluster Senators over the years 1912–20. His financial ills forever kept him at odds with his players. It was probably an economic motivation that brought about a change in his racial views. As early as 1911, with the Reds, Griffith began signing Cuban ballplayers, the first to do so. The often-broke Griffith sometimes combined sentimentality with a nose for box-office attractions. During the

Clark Griffith

Depression, Griffith sold star outfielder Goose Goslin to Detroit, asserting he could no longer afford him. But when the aging Goslin was released by the Tigers some years later, Griffith found a spot for him on the Senators' roster. War hero Bert Shepard had potential as a pitcher, but lost a leg in combat. Griffith signed him anyway. Wartime blackout restrictions did not prevent him from obtaining government approval to hold more night games than other franchises in order to provide more "R-and-R" for the dayworkers of the Washington bureaucracy. The ex-vaudevillian always knew what drew a crowd. In 1946 he installed the first device to record pitch speed (borrowed from the U.S. Army) so that visiting flamethrower Bob Feller could give the fans a pre-game thrill.

Griffith's major strategic contribution to the game was the development of the relief pitcher. While in New York, he yielded to the pressures from his Tammany Hall owners and pitched his two premier starters, Jack Chesbro and Jack Powell, a staggering 845 combined innings in 1904. In 1905 both were markedly less effective, and completed many fewer games. The Old Fox finished many games for them personally, making a career-high 18 relief appearances that season. Along with John McGraw, Griffith revolutionized baseball with his reliance on the bullpen. He subsequently developed the first great relievers, Allan Russell and Fred Marberry. He turned relief strategy into a weapon against Mc-Graw's Giants in the 1924 World Series. In Game Seven, Griffith sent in a succession of relief pitchers that led McGraw, committed to the lefty-righty percentages, to remove star first baseman Bill Terry from the game. When Griffith finished up with the great Walter Johnson, the Senators went on to win the Series with a 12-inning triumph. /(ASN)

Tommy Griffith — 1889-1967. OF 1913-25 Braves, Reds, **Dodgers**, Cubs 1401 g, .280, 52 hr, 619 rbi. *1 WS, 7 g, .190, 3 rbi*

Griffith was a swift right fielder with one of the best arms in the NL. He was consistently in double figures in assists and topped 20 three times. A favorite with Dodger fans from 1919 to 1924, he was an occasional .300 hitter. His best all-around year was 1921, when he hit .312 with a dozen homers and drove in 71 runs for Brooklyn. /(TG)

Art Griggs — 1883-1938. 1B-OF-2B 1909-12, 14-15, 18 **Browns**, Indians, Brooklyn (FL), Tigers 442 g, .277, 5 hr, 152 rbi

Griggs was a football star at Kansas University and the University of Pittsburgh. In his baseball career, he was a steady hitter who played on 15 clubs in ten leagues throughout a 27-year pro career. In his best ML performance, he hit .364 in 28 games with Detroit in 1918. He was also a respected minor league manager. /(WAB)

Hal Griggs — 1928- . RHP 1956-59 **Senators** 347 ip, 6-26, 5.50

Griggs was a 21-year-old bellhop in a Miami hotel when the owner of a minor league team invited him to try out. He once lost 18 straight in the minors, and he fared poorly with Washington. /(RTM)

Steve Grilli — 1949- . RHP 1975-77, 79 **Tigers**, Blue Jays 148 ip, 4-3, 4.51

The slender Grilli was the righthanded complement to John Hiller in the Detroit bullpen of 1976. Control problems limited his effectiveness, and he was sold to Toronto in 1978. /(CC)

J. Ed Grillo — 1870-1920. *Writer.*

One of the most famous sportswriters of his time, Grillo was a sports editor in Cincinnati in the 1890s, where he became a confidant of Ban Johnson. When the American Association was reorganized in 1904, he became league president. He returned to sports writing a few years later with the Washington *Post*, and was with the Washington *Star* when he retired in 1917. /(NLM)

Bob Grim — 1930- . RHP 1954-60, 62 **Yankees**, A's, Indians, Reds, Cardinals 760 ip, 61-41, 3.61. 20 wins: 54 *2 WS, 11 ip, 0-2, 4.91*
☛ *Rookie of the Year—54. All-Star—57.*

In 1954 Grim became the first Yankee rookie since Russ Ford in 1910 to win 20 games. He won a league-leading eight in relief to compile the only 20-win season ever of fewer than 200 innings (199). Coupled with his blazing fastball was a biting slider which damaged his arm and reduced his ability in subsequent years. In the 1955 WS he saved Game One, but in Game Five he gave up three Dodger homers to lose his only WS start.

Grim's arm troubles forced him solely into relief by 1957, when he led AL relievers with 12 wins, eight losses, and 19 saves. In Game Four of the '57 WS, he relieved Tommy Byrne in the bottom of the tenth after Byrne had hit Milwaukee's Nippy Jones with a pitch. Grim surrendered a double that tied the game, and then gave up a home run to Eddie Mathews. Grim was generally mediocre after leaving New York in 1958. /(GDW)

Burleigh Grimes (Ol' Stubblebeard) — 1893-1985. RHP 1916-34 Pirates, **Dodgers**, Giants, Braves, Cardinals, Cubs, Yankees 4180 ip, 270-212, 3.53. 20 wins: 20-21, 23-24, 28 *4 WS, 56.2 ip, 3-4, 4.29.*
*Manager 1937-38 **Dodgers** 130-171, .432*
☛ *Led League—w 21, 28. Led League—k 21. Hall of Fame—1964.*

Burleigh Grimes was the last legal spitball pitcher in the majors. In a 19-year career that ended in 1934, he often faked the spitter to keep batters guessing.

Grimes never shaved on days he pitched, because the slippery elm he chewed to increase saliva irri-

Burleigh Grimes

developing a winner were undermined when new boss Larry McPhail brought shortstop Leo Durocher to the team. Grimes and Durocher were both battlers, but Durocher was brash and charming, while Grimes was simply pugnacious. Grimes was also frustrated when McPhail signed Babe Ruth as a first base coach and batting practice attraction. Ruth would belt ball after ball over the screen into Bedford Avenue, but his attention span would lapse in the first base coaching box. By 1939 Burleigh and the Babe were gone. Durocher began his managerial career and a new era came to Brooklyn.

A decade of minor league managing followed for Grimes, during which he never ceased his aggressive baseball behavior. Although he was a genial companion off the field, he raged at every close decision against his team. He was suspended in 1940 while managing Grand Rapids (Michigan State League) for an altercation with an umpire. He died of cancer at age 92, twenty-one years after the Veterans Committee selected him for Cooperstown. /(JK)

Oscar Grimes — 1915- . 3B-2B-1B-3B 1938–46 Indians, **Yankees**, A's 602 g, .256, 18 hr, 200 rbi

After parts of five seasons as a Cleveland utility infielder, Grimes was handed the third base job for the Yankees in 1944. He made three errors in one game in 1944 and led AL third basemen with 31 errors in 1945. His father, Ray Grimes, was a NL first baseman in the 1920s. /(MG)

Ray Grimes — 1893–1953. 1B 1920–24, 26 Red Sox, **Cubs**, Phillies 433 g, .329, 27 hr, 263 rbi

Ray Grimes was a Cub hero of the early 1920s whose twin brother Roy had a brief trial with the Giants, and whose son Oscar was a ML infielder. Ray had two fine seasons for the Cubs in 1921 and 1922, batting .321 and .354 (second in the NL). During one stretch in 1922, he drove in at least one run for 17 consecutive games, a ML record. A slipped disc in June 1923 shortened his promising career. /(ARA)

Charlie Grimm (Jolly Cholly) — 1898–1983. 1B 1916, 18–36 A's, Cardinals, Pirates, **Cubs** 2164 g, .290, 79 hr, 1078 rbi. *2 WS, 9 g, .364, 1 hr, 5 rbi.*
Manager 1932–38, 44–49, 52–56, 60 **Cubs**, Braves 1287–1069, .546 First place: 32, 35, 45 *3 WS, 5–12, .294*

Jolly Cholly was an ebullient, fun-loving fellow who frolicked through 20 seasons as a player. He was also a tolerant manager who could coax career-best performances from mediocre players and gave free rein to his stars.

tated his skin. His growth of stubble added to his ominous mound presence and led to his nickname, Ol' Stubblebeard. The belligerent pitcher never permitted a batter to dig in at the plate. It was said Grimes's idea of an intentional pass was four pitches at the batter's head.

During the 1920s, Grimes was a standout, twice leading the league in victories and five times topping the 20-win mark. He was durable, leading the league four times in starts and three times in innings pitched. After five straight winning seasons for Brooklyn, his 19 losses in 1925 topped the NL. Following a 12–13 mark in 1926, he was traded to the Giants and was 19–8 in his one season for New York. He peaked as a 25-game winner for Pittsburgh in 1928.

Grimes carried his cantankerous ways with him as manager of the Dodgers, though the team was rarely in a game long enough to make battling tactics pay off. He took over a bedraggled club that had frustrated Casey Stengel in 1937. His chances of

Charlie Grimm

Grimm was the most skillful first baseman of his era. He won nine fielding titles wearing a small mitt and ranging wide of the bag. He broke in with the Athletics in 1916 and won his first regular job with the 1920 Pirates. In Pittsburgh, he teamed with fellow free spirits Rabbit Maranville and Cotton Tierney, to the despair of owner Barney Dreyfuss. The vaudeville team of Gallagher and Shean had a patter song which Grimm, a lefthanded banjo player, appropriated. Once, Grimm snared a sharp grounder, and instead of simply stepping on first, threw the ball to Cotton, shouting, "Have we got him, Mr. Tierney?" "Absolutely, Mr. Grimm," came the rejoinder as the ball was thrown back to Charlie for the putout. Grimm had a 23-game hitting streak in 1923.

Grimm and Maranville were traded to the Cubs after the 1924 season, and continued their fun-loving ways. In 1932, his eighth year as Chicago's first baseman, Grimm became manager of a Cub team that had responded badly to Rogers Hornsby's stern direction, and captured the pennant with a 14-

game September winning streak. They won again in 1935, but in mid-1938 Grimm resigned, saying he couldn't relate to or control his players. Gabby Hartnett stepped in, and the team rallied to the pennant while Grimm called the games from the broadcasting booth.

Grimm gave up sportscasting in 1941 to return as a Cubs coach, and then had what he described as the most fun of his career, managing Milwaukee of the American Association for Bill Veeck. After three successful seasons, Grimm was back at the helm in Wrigley Field. In 1945 his Cubs won another pennant, one which would have to last Cub fans for decades.

After being relieved as manager in 1949, Grimm moved to the front office, but in 1950 he returned to the minors, again leading Milwaukee to win the Little World Series. Braves owner Lou Perini invited him to manage in Boston in 1952, and when Perini shifted the franchise to Milwaukee the next year, the established local hero, Charlie Grimm, went along to manage. He remained for over three seasons, twice finishing second.

Grimm had a final fling leading the Cubs in 1960, but, after 17 games, swapped jobs with broadcaster Lou Boudreau. He stayed with the Cubs in various front office jobs another 15 seasons. After his death, his widow was allowed to scatter his ashes over Wrigley Field. /(JK)

Ross Grimsley — 1950- . LHP 1971-80, 82 Reds, Orioles, Expos, Indians 2039 ip, 124-99, 3.81. 20 wins: 78 *3 LCS, 18 ip, 1-1, 3.50. 1 WS, 7 ip, 2-1, 2.57* ☛ *All-Star—78.*

Although his pitching speeds ranged from slow to slower, Grimsley was effective for the powerful Reds of 1971-75. He was named lefthander on the *Baseball Digest* 1971 All-Star Rookie team, pitched a two-hitter in Game Four of the 1972 NLCS, and won a pair in the WS. Handsome, with wild, curly hair and piercing green eyes, he was also a free spirit. His refusal to conform to the Reds' short-hair policy helped hasten a trade to Baltimore. The son of Ross Sr., who pitched briefly in the ML, Grimsley signed with Montreal as a free agent in 1978. That year he became the Expos' first 20-game winner and was named Montreal Player of the Year and Tennessee's top pro athlete. /(ME)

Dan Griner (Rusty) — 1888-1950. RHP 1912-16, 18 Cardinals, Dodgers 674 ip, 28-55, 3.49

Griner never had a winning major league season; with the 1913 Cardinals, he topped the NL with 22 losses. Back with St. Paul (American Association) in 1919, relying on his "mudball," he did not allow an earned run in winning three complete games in the playoffs against Vernon (Pacific Coast League). /(NLM)

Lee Grissom (Lefty) — 1907- . LHP 1934-41 **Reds**, Yankees, Dodgers, Phillies 702 ip, 29-48, 3.89. *1 WS, 1.1 ip, 0-0, 0.00*
☛ *All-Star—37.*

The loss of the brother of ML pitcher Marv Grissom might have cost the 1938 Reds a pennant. He had won 12 in 1937 and was counted to contribute again, but early in '38 he tried to steal a base, broke his ankle, and was out for the season. When Grissom returned in 1939 to win nine, Cincinnati won the pennant by 4-1/2 games. /(JK)

Marv Grissom — 1918- . RHP 1946, 49, 52-59 **Giants**, Tigers, White Sox, Red Sox, Cardinals 810 ip, 47-45, 3.41. *1 WS, 3 ip, 1-0, 0.00*
☛ *All-Star—54.*

The 6'3" 190-lb Grissom was 12-10 in 1952, his first full season in the majors. He starred as a reliever for the Giants from mid-1953 to 1958, winning 10 games and saving 19 in 1954, and also winning the first game of the WS that year. He registered his career-low ERA of 1.56 in 1956. He served as the A's pitching coach after his retirement as an active player. His brother Lee pitched in the majors from 1934 to 1941. /(JJM)

Dick Groat — 1930- . SS 1952, 55-67 **Pirates**, Cardinals, Phillies, Giants 1929 g, .286, 39 hr, 707 rbi. *2 WS, 14 g, .204, 3 rbi*
☛ *Most Valuable Player—60. All-Star—59-60, 62-64.*

Groat was an All-American basketball player at Duke and averaged 12 points per game with the Fort Wayne Pistons in the NBL (52-53). However, it was at shortstop in double play combinations with Bill Mazeroski and later with Julian Javier that Groat excelled. A natural athlete, he never played minor league ball. The slick ball-handler was at or near the top of the league each year in assists, putouts, and double plays.

Groat was the complete ballplayer. He batted over .300 four times, and in 1960, Phillies manager Gene Mauch said, "He holds the Pirates together," as Pittsburgh won a World Championship over the Yankees. Traded to St. Louis, he solved the Cardinals' shortstop problem (there had been a different regular shortstop every year since 1956). With Groat, the Cardinals finished second in 1963

Dick Groat

and were World Champions the following season. /(FO)

Heinie Groh — 1889-1968. 3B-2B 1912-27 Giants, **Reds**, Pirates 1676 g, .292, 26 hr, 566 rbi. *5 WS, 21 g, .264, 4 rbi.*
  Manager 1918 **Reds** 7-3, .700

Famous for his unique "bottle bat," with a non-tapered barrel and thin handle, the 5'8" 158-lb third baseman was an outstanding leadoff man. He deftly dropped bunts from his peculiar wide-open stance, used his keen eye and short stature to draw walks, and kept his BA in the .280-.320 range. He had played only 31 games for the Giants when he was traded to Cincinnati, where he starred for eight seasons. He hit for the cycle on July 5, 1915. After a bitter holdout in 1921, he signed in June only on the promise that he would be traded. He was immediately swapped to New York but Commissioner Landis canceled the deal. In December, the Giants finally reacquired him and the still-peppery Groh helped them win three straight pennants. His older brother Lew played two games for the A's in 1919 as a 36-year-old rookie. /(JK)

Heinie Groh

Steve Gromek — 1920– . RHP 1941–57 **Indians**, Tigers 2065 ip, 123–108, 3.41. *1 WS, 9 ip, 1–0, 1.00*

Gromek had pitched mostly in relief for the 1948 Indians, going 9–3 (2.84), but started the pivotal fourth game of the '48 World Series against the Braves, and threw a complete-game, 2–1 victory. The picture of Gromek hugging teammate Larry Doby, who had homered, is a landmark in the annals of baseball's battle to integrate successfully. Gromek relied on a fastball, change, and knuckle-curve. He played his first two pro seasons as an infielder, but made it to Cleveland in his first year pitching, 1941, by going 14–2 in the Michigan State League. He led the Indians with a 19–9 record in 1945. Traded to Detroit in 1943, the native of Hamtramck (just a few miles from Tiger Stadium) led the 1954 Tigers with 18 wins. /(ME)

Bob Groom — 1884–1948. RHP 1909–18 **Senators**, St. Louis (FL), Browns, Indians 2336 ip, 120–150, 3.10. 20 wins: 12

From June 19 through September 25, 1909, Washington rookie Bob Groom set a since-tied major league record by losing 19 consecutive games. He finished the season at 7–26, tying the AL mark for losses. A wild fireballer, he also led the league with 105 walks for the 42–110 Senators. He finally found success in 1912, going 24–13. Jumping to the Federal League in 1914, he did atypically poorly for a ML veteran, losing 20 games. As a St. Louis Brown, Groom no-hit the White Sox in the second game of a May 6, 1917 doubleheader, a day after teammate Ernest Koob had no-hit them. While Chicago went on to win the pennant, Koob went 6–14, and Groom's 8–19 tied him for the league lead in losses. /(NLM)

Don Gross — 1931– . LHP 1955–60 **Reds**, Pirates 398 ip, 20–22, 3.73

Gross became a lefthanded pitcher through an accident. As a seven-year-old he caught his right arm in his mother's washing machine wringer. He learned to throw lefthanded while his arm mended but in everything else he remained righthanded. /(BC)

Greg Gross — 1952– . OF 1973– Astros, Cubs, **Phillies** 1809 g, .287, 7 hr, 308 rbi. *2 LCS, 8 g, .333, 1 rbi. 2 WS, 6 g, .000*

An excellent contact hitter who rarely struck out, Gross had at least 39 pinch-hit at-bats in each of his nine seasons in Philadelphia, and through 1988 was the third leading pinch hitter in ML history, with 136 hits. He hit .314 for Houston in 1974 to win *The Sporting News* NL Rookie Player of the Year honors, but it would be his only ML season as a full-time starter, as his weak arm, little speed, and no power came to be seen as liabilities. He still got over 400 AB in two more seasons in Houston, and after a 1979 trade sent him from the Cubs to the Phillies, Gross became a pinch hit specialist. He returned to Houston in 1989. /(SG)

Kevin Gross — 1961– . RHP 1983–89 **Phillies**, Expos 1306 ip, 71–78, 3.95
☛ *All-Star—88.*

Plagued by back troubles most of his career, the 6'5" Gross pitched most of 1987 with a herniated disc. He was suspended for 10 days in August when he was caught using sandpaper to scuff the ball on the mound. He started fast in 1988, earning a spot on the All-Star team, but slumped to 12–14 by the end of the year. Gross was traded to Montreal for Floyd Youmans and Jeff Parrett before the 1989 season. /(SG)

Milt Gross — 1912–1973. *Writer.*

Gross was a humorist and humanist whose column, "Speaking Out," appeared in the New York *Post* and other papers for 24 years. He was one of the first to interview athletes and write about them as people with human emotions and frailties. Gross wrote numerous magazine articles and books on boxing and golf, and a baseball book, *Yankee Doodles.*/(NLM)

Wayne Gross — 1952– . 3B-1B 1976–86 **A's**, Orioles .233, 121 hr, 396 rbi. *1 LCS, 3 g, .000*
☛ *All-Star—77.*

A stocky lefthanded hitter with good power and little speed, Gross was the A's starting third baseman as a rookie in 1977, and with 22 HR was the last-place club's lone representative at the All-Star Game that year. He hit only .233, though, and began the 1978 season at Vancouver (Pacific Coast League) before rejoining the A's for good after 17 games. Gross played regularly with Oakland, either at third or first, until he was traded to the Orioles for Tim Stoddard after the 1983 season. He hit .216 as Baltimore's third baseman in 1984, and matched his rookie year and career-high HR output with 22./(SCL)

Jerry Grote — 1941– . C-3B 1963–64, 66–78, 81 Astros, **Mets**, Dodgers, Royals. 1421 g, .252, 39 hr, 404 rbi. *4 WS, 15 g, .240, 1 rbi. 4 LCS, 11 g, .194, 3 rbi*
☛ *All-Star—68, 74.*

Success came, but not easily or early for Jerry Grote. After hitting .181 in 100 games for the 1964 Colt .45s (later the Astros), he returned to the minors. The Mets purchased his contract, but in his first two years in New York Grote hit poorly, was mediocre behind the plate, and blamed it on the umpires, manager, and teammates. Manager Wes Westrum said, "If he ever learns to control himself, he might become the best catcher in baseball." Grote learned, becoming a key ingredient on Met teams for a dozen years. Lou Brock once said that Grote was the toughest catcher in the league to steal against. Grote was behind the plate on his birthday when the Mets won their first pennant in 1969. He caught every inning of the 1969 and 1973 LCS and WS, setting three WS fielding records in 1973. Though he played only 61 games with the Dodgers, he appeared with them in the 1977 and 1978 WS. The Royals, short of catching, lured him out of retirement in 1981./(FJO)

Johnny Groth — 1926– . OF 1946–60 **Tigers**, Browns, White Sox, Senators, A's 1248 g, .279, 60 hr, 486 rbi

Time, Collier's, The Saturday Evening Post, and *Life* all tabbed Groth for superstardom in 1949 after he hit .340 with 30 home runs for Buffalo (International League) in 1948. He hit .293 as the Tigers' regular centerfielder, and in 1950 hit .306 with 12 homers and 85 RBI, at one point banging eight consecutive hits. Groth played 10 more seasons, but never equaled his 1950 totals. /(JK)

Lefty Grove [Robert Moses] (Mose) — 1900–1975. LHP 1925–41 **A's**, Red Sox 3941 ip, 300–140, 3.06. 20 wins: 27–33, 35 *3 WS, 51 ip, 4–2, 1.75*
☛ *Most Valuable Player—31. Led League—w 28, 30–31, 33. Led League—era 26, 29–32, 35–36, 38–39. Led League—k 25–31. All-Star—33, 35–39. Hall of Fame—1947.*

Lefty Grove had a blazing fastball and a temper to match. By the time he had pitched 17 seasons, eking out a 300th win in his last appearance, both were gone. He arrived with a reputation for wrath, and led the American League in strikeouts seven consecutive years, victories four times (including 31 wins in 1931), ERA nine times (no one else ever did more than five), and winning percentage five times. Grove also led in shredded uniforms, kicked buckets, ripped-apart lockers, and alienated teammates.

Grove tested the saintly patience of Connie Mack, a placid patriarch who won his last three pennants mostly by handing Grove the ball. Eventually, Grove gained control over himself and the ball. As a rookie, he led the league in walks as well as strikeouts. Later, he learned to win with pinpoint control and guile. Connie Mack explained, "Groves was a thrower until after we sold him to Boston and he hurt his arm. Then he learned to pitch."

Mack called his star "Groves," for that's how Lefty's name appeared in box scores while pitching for Baltimore in the International League. He arrived there in the midst of a string of seven consecutive pennants, and Baltimore was not required to sell its stars to the majors. Grove was 25 before he could reach the Athletics, after Mack paid $100,600 for him, topping the flat $100,000 the Yankees had paid the Red Sox for Babe Ruth.

The nine seasons Grove pitched for Philadelphia were his best. The team won three pennants, but crowds dwindled, tiring of victory and pinched by the ongoing Depression. Grove was sold to the suddenly rich Red Sox, whose new owner, Tom Yawkey, was buying up star players. Though Grove had led the league with 24 wins in 1933, his first year with Boston, 1934, was a sore-armed struggle.

Lefty Grove

He bounced back in 1935 with his final 20-victory season, but won by craftily working hitters.

Grove had largely overcome his uneasiness with strangers. He came, with a limited education, from a hard life in the bituminous hills of western Maryland. It took him time to adjust to being a national celebrity. When he had a rubber stamp made with his facsimile autograph, so as to accommodate as many fans as possible, he was branded an illiterate who couldn't write his name. If there was one thing he could write, it was his signature; it appeared on a string of lucrative contracts, first with Mack, then topped by Yawkey.

Grove went home between seasons to the hard-scrabble town of Lonaconing, MD, and opened a bowling alley that became the social center of the region. He retired to become a genial townsman, his hair turning white, weight added to his 6'3" frame. He would smile when reminded of stories of his once-terrible temper. He'd shake his head when someone spoke of the game he lost while trying for an AL record-breaking 17th consecutive victory in

1931. The A's failed to get him a run, and, after the game's only hit (a bloop single), a substitute out-fielder misjudged an ordinary line drive, and the winning run scored. In later years, Grove would have forgiven the player who misjudged the ball, if he could have remembered his name. He never forgot, or forgave, star fielder Al Simmons, who had taken the day off to visit a doctor. Despite missing that record, Grove left behind a bevy of honors, including a batting record: he fanned 593 times, the most ever by a pitcher. His ultimate honor came with his 1947 induction into Cooperstown. /(JK)

Orval Grove — 1919– . RHP 1940–49 **White Sox** 1177 ip, 63–73, 3.78

Grove was one of the first pitchers to come out of the White Sox farm system, established in 1939. Invited to camp in 1943 with a $1 contract, having missed most of 1942 following knee surgery, he made the club and was given his first start in June. He then set a White Sox season record by winning his first nine decisions. On July 8, he took a no-hitter into the ninth inning against the Yankees. With one out, Joe Gordon broke it up with a double to left that was fair by inches. Grove ended the year at 15–9, but proved a winner only during the war years. /(RL)

Johnny Grubb — 1948– . OF-DH 1972–87 **Padres**, Indians, Rangers, Tigers 1424 g, .278, 99 hr, 475 rbi. *2 LCS, 5 g, .455, 2 rbi. 1 WS, 4 g, .333* ☛ *All-Star—74.*

Naturally a righthanded batter, Grubb learned to hit lefthanded by emulating his hero, Mickey Mantle. He batted .311 as a Padres rookie in 1973, and in 1975 set a then-club record of 36 doubles. His 21-game hitting streak with Texas tied for the longest in the AL in 1979. He had nine stints on the DL; in 1981 surgeons removed a rib to relieve a circulatory problem. He became a key Tiger DH, extra out-fielder, and pinch hitter. His 11th-inning double won Game Two of the 1984 LCS. /(JCA)

Frank Grube (Hans) — 1905–1945. C 1931–36, 41 **White Sox**, Browns 394 g, .244, 1 hr, 107 rbi

When Moe Berg held out in 1931, White Sox scouts combed the minors for another catcher, coming up with Grube. In 1932 Chicago acquired Charlie Berry, who had beaten out Grube for the first-string catching job at Lafayette College and did so again with the White Sox. On the football field, Grube succeeded Berry as star end at Lafayette College and then followed him into the NFL for a season (1928) before turning to baseball. /(RL)

John Gruber — Unk.–1932. *Writer.*

The official scorer for the Pittsburgh Pirates for 40 years until the early 1930s, Gruber was honored with a plaque put up in the Forbes Field press box in 1933. /(NLM)

Kelly Gruber — 1962– . 3B 1984– **Blue Jays** 538 g, .263, 52 hr, 208 rbi. *1 LCS, 5 g, .294, 1 rbi*
☛ *All-Star—89.*

Gruber emerged in 1988 as a key player for the Blue Jays, hitting .278 with 16 home runs and 81 RBI. Primarily a third baseman, he made appearances at second base and shortstop and in the outfield as well. Gruber was acquired by Toronto from Cleveland in the major league draft, which required him to spend time on the Blue Jays' bench during the 1984 season before being sent to the minors. In 1986 Gruber was expected to take the third base job from the aging platoon of Rance Mulliniks and Garth Iorg, but he had a disappointing season after minor injuries and was used mainly as a utility player. When Mulliniks was injured in the first inning of the 1988 home opener, Gruber took over for him in dramatic fashion, with a 4-for-6 game featuring two home runs and an RBI double. He became the full-time third baseman, showed promise of becoming a fine all-around player, and was named to the 1989 AL All-Star team. /(TF)

Joe Grzenda — 1937– . LHP 1961, 64, 66–67, 69–72 Tigers, A's, Mets, Twins, **Senators**, Cardinals 308 ip, 14–13, 4.01. *1 LCS, 0.2 ip, 0–0, 0.00*

A reliever in all but three of his ML appearances, Grzenda, a nervous chain-smoker, was known as Shaky Joe. He threw the last pitch for the Senators in 1971 before the fans swarmed the field and the team (sans Grzenda) moved to Texas. /(JL)

Cecilio Guante — 1960– . RHP 1982– **Pirates**, Yankees, Rangers 548 ip, 27–31, 3.35

The hard-throwing, injury-prone Dominican led the 1985 Pirates in appearances and games finished. The tall, slender pitcher was a career reliever, delivering from all angles, but throwing more than pitching. /(ME)

Mark Gubicza — 1962– . RHP 1984– **Royals** 1313 ip, 84–67, 3.51. *1 LCS, 8 ip, 1–0, 3.24*
☛ *All-Star—88–89.*

Gubicza fired a 93-mph fastball and 90-mph slider, but wildness was his early nemesis. Equipped with better control and an improved changeup and slider, he was the ace of the Royals' staff in 1988. /(FO)

Mike Guerra [Fermin Romero] — 1912– . C 1937, 44–51 Senators, A's, Red Sox 565 g, .242, 9 hr, 168 rbi

Guerra was one of 10 Latins signed by Joe Cambria to play for the Senators during WWII. His best years, though, came with the 1949 and 1950 Athletics. He managed his hometown Havana club in the Florida International League and scouted for the Tigers. /(NLM)

Mario Guerrero — 1949– . SS-2B 1973–80 Red Sox, Cardinals, Angels, **A's** 697 g, .257, 7 hr, 170 rbi

In his only season of everyday play, this error-prone Dominican hit .275 but drew only 15 walks in 505 at-bats, scoring just 27 runs. /(SH)

Pedro Guerrero — 1956– . OF-3B-1B 1978– **Dodgers**, Cardinals 1242 g, .308, 193 hr, 732 rbi. *3 LCS, 15 g, .196, 1 hr, 8 rbi. 1 WS, 6 g, .333, 2 hr, 7 rbi*
☛ *All-Star—81, 83, 85, 87, 89.*

Writer Bill James called Guerrero "the best hitter God has made in a long time." Originally signed as a free agent by the Indians, Guerrero was virtually stolen by the Dodgers after his first pro season, acquired in exchange for pitching flop Bruce Ellingsen. He first hit the limelight when his five RBIs in the final game of the 1981 World Series gave him a piece of the first three-way Series MVP award. In 1982 he became the first Dodger to hit 30 HR and steal 20 bases in a season, and he did it again the following year.

In 1985 Guerrero tied a major league record with 15 HR in June, en route to tying the Los Angeles record of 33. He also reached base 14 consecutive times that year, two shy of Ted Williams's record, and led the league in both slugging and on-base percentage.

Although an aggressive baserunner, he is considered a poor slider; he ruptured a tendon sliding in spring training and missed most of the 1986 season. His basestealing was subsequently curtailed. His .338 BA in 1987 was the highest for a Dodger since Tommy Davis's .348 in 1962 and earned him UPI's Comeback of the Year award.

Dodger management appeared to believe him

capable of any athletic feat, and they thought nothing of shifting him to third base in mid-career, and in and out as the need arose. Although he gained a reputation for being shaky at third, statistics show that he was about as good as anyone in the league at getting to the ball. In the minors he made all-star teams at both first base and third base, and he broke into the Dodger lineup as a replacement for the injured Davey Lopes at second base. Guerrero was traded to the Cardinals for pitcher John Tudor during the 1988 season and missed out on the Dodgers' World Championship that fall. /(TG)

Lee Guetterman — 1958- . LHP 1984- **Mariners, Yankees** 337 ip, 17-15, 4.30

The 6'8" Guetterman is the third-tallest player in major league history. Showing a pattern of near-invincibility in the beginning of the season but inconsistency the rest of the time, the reliever won his first five games for the Mariners in 1987 and was 8-1 at the All-Star break, but finished 11-4 with a 3.81 ERA. In 1989 he set the Yankee record for scoreless innings from the start of a season with 29, but was hit hard for much of June and July before regaining his touch. /(TF)

Ron Guidry (Gator, Louisiana Lightning, The Ragin' Cajun) — 1950- . LHP 1975-88 **Yankees** 2392 ip, 170-91, 3.29. 20 wins: 78, 83, 85 *3 LCS, 22 ip, 2-1, 4.03. 3 WS, 32 ip, 3-1, 1.69*
☛ *Led League—w 78, 85. Led League—era 78-79.. Cy Young Award—78. All-Star—78-79, 82-83. Gold Glove—82-86.*

Although Guidry won over 20 games three times in his career, he is remembered for having one of the greatest single seasons ever. He was 25-3 with a 1.74 ERA in 1978, won the Cy Young Award unanimously, and finished second to Boston's Jim Rice in AL MVP voting. Guidry set club records that year in strikeouts (248) and consecutive wins at the start of a season (13). He called his Yankee-record 18 strikeouts against California on June 17 of that season "perhaps my greatest single thrill." He started the AL East playoff game on October 2, 1978 against Boston and won 5-4 in what was "probably the most tension-packed game I ever played in." Guidry was named *TSN* Player of the Year and Man of the Year and the Associated Press's Male Athlete of the Year, and he made every all-star team. His nine shutouts tied Babe Ruth's AL record for a lefthander.

During the 1970s, Yankee management made a policy of acquiring pitchers through trades and free agent signings. As a result, Guidry did not find a regular place in the Yankee rotation until 1977, when he was 26 years old. Even then, there were those who felt that the 5'11" 160-lb lefty was too small to pitch effectively and last in the major leagues. Guidry dispelled the notion by going 16-7 that year and perfecting the wicked slider that became his bread and butter pitch. He went on to lead the majors in victories from 1977 through 1987 with 168, posting records of 18-8 (1979), 21-9 (1983), and 22-6 (1985). He is fourth on the all-time Yankee victory list (170), second in strikeouts (1,778), sixth in games and innings, and tied for sixth in shutouts (26). Guidry compiled a 5-2 postseason record, 3-1 in World Series play.

Guidry's success and durability were attributable in part to the fact that he was an outstanding athlete. He won five straight Gold Glove awards (1982–1986) and was twice used briefly in the outfield.

Guidry was slow to recover from elbow surgery following the 1988 season, and he started 1989 on the disabled list before beginning a rehabilitation assignment in June at Triple-A. When he didn't impress the Yankee management with his performance at Columbus, he retired from baseball on July 12, 1989.

Guidry was a good amateur drummer who kept a trap set at Yankee Stadium and once played with the Beach Boys during a postgame concert. /(EG/ CR)

Ozzie Guillen [born Oswaldo Jose Guillen Barrios] — 1964- . SS 1985- **White Sox** 769 g, .263, 6 hr, 224 rbi
☛ *Rookie of the Year—85. All-Star—88.*

The White Sox drew criticism for trading LaMarr Hoyt to the Padres in December of 1984 in a seven-player deal that yielded them prospect Ozzie Guillen. But the highly rated, 21-year-old Venezuelan shortstop easily outdistanced Milwaukee's Ted Higuera to capture 1985 AL Rookie of the Year honors. Guillen committed just 12 errors to lead AL shortstops in fielding and set a record for White Sox shortstops. His .273 batting average was higher than expected. He was right when he predicted he would drive in the winning run in Tom Seaver's first attempt to win his 300th game that August 4. While his bubbly, gregarious personality became interpreted by opponents as hot-dogging, by 1988 he established himself as an All-Star. /(RL)

Don Gullett — 1951- . LHP 1970-78 **Reds**, Yankees 1391 ip, 109-50, 3.11. *6 LCS, 41 ip, 2-3, 3.98. 5 WS, 52 ip, 2-2, 3.61*

Hailed by Sparky Anderson as a sure Hall of Famer and the next Sandy Koufax, this Kentucky farm boy was a vital part of the Big Red Machine in the early 1970s. The 19-year-old rookie flamethrower struck out six Mets in a row on August 23, 1970 (2nd game), tying a relief record, and Willie Stargell said Gullett "throws nothing but wall-to-wall heat." Moved into the rotation in 1971, Gullett went 16-6 (2.64) and led the NL in winning percentage (.727). He usually had a high winning percentage; from 1973 through 1976 he was 61-26. He was named to *TSN*'s postseason all-star team in 1974.

Gullett signed with the Yankees as a free agent for 1977 and went 14-4 to help New York to a World Championship, but it would be his last good season. Persistent shoulder problems, perhaps caused by his pitching motion, led to rotator cuff damage that ended his career. /(KC)

Bill Gullickson — 1959- . RHP 1979-87 **Expos**, Reds, Yankees 1644 ip, 101-86, 3.61. *1 LCS, 14 ip, 0-2, 2.51*

Gullickson was the second player taken in the June 1977 draft, and his 10-5, 3.00 record in 1980 earned him *TSN* NL Rookie Pitcher of the Year honors. He finished second (behind Steve Howe) in the NL Rookie of the Year voting. In 1981 he helped the Expos to their only division title with a 7-9, 2.81 record and beat the Phillies 3-1 in Game Two of the divisional playoff necessitated by the split-season format used after the players' strike. In the LCS, he lost Games One and Four to the Dodgers when Montreal could muster only one run each game for him.

With the exception of the strike season, the consistent Gullickson was in double figures in wins every season from his rookie year on. Acquired by the Reds for 1986, he went 15-12. The Yankees traded Dennis Rasmussen to get Gullickson, in the last year of his contract, for their 1987 pennant drive, but he was unhappy with the atmosphere in the Bronx and accepted a $2 million offer to pitch in Japan the following season.

In an April 10, 1982 game, Gullickson tied the modern ML record with six wild pitches. /(JFC)

Harry Gumbert (Gunboat) — 1909- . RHP 1935-44, 46-50 **Giants**, Cardinals, Reds, Pirates 2157 ip, 143-113, 3.68. *3 WS, 4 ip, 0-0, 27.00*

The 6'2" 185-lb Gumbert began his fifteen-year career as a starter. He reached double figures in wins from 1936 to 1941 and again in 1943-1944, including an 11-3 mark in 1936 and an 18-11 record in 1939. He spent 1945 in the military and by 1947 was strictly a reliever, totaling 48 saves over his career.

Gumbert appeared in WS for the Giants in 1936 and 1937 and the Cardinals in 1942. He pitched in a total of six games, allowing 12 hits and five walks with a 27.00 ERA.

Gumbert led the NL in games pitched in 1948 (61), relief wins in 1947 (10) and 1948 (10), relief loses in '47 (10) and '48 (8), and saves in '48 (17). /(JJM)

Dave Gumpert — 1958- . RHP 1982-83, 85-87 Tigers, **Cubs**, Royals 136 ip, 3-2, 4.31

A Michigan native who grew up idolizing Detroit's Al Kaline, Gumpert was signed by the Tigers in 1980. At his peak, he recorded a 2.64 ERA relieving in 26 games in 1983 and was voted the Detroit Sports Broadcasters Association's Rookie of the Year. /(JCA)

Randy Gumpert — 1918- . RHP 1936-38, 1946-52 A's, Yankees, **White Sox**, Red Sox, Senators 1053 ip, 51-59, 4.17
☛ *All-Star—51.*

As a teenager, Gumpert threw batting practice for the A's at Shibe Park for two years before signing in 1936 for $300 a month. He was 11-3 (2.31) at his best in 1946 for the Yankees, for whom he became a scout. /(NLM)

Larry Gura — 1947- . LHP 1970-85 Cubs, Yankees, **Royals** 2046 ip, 126-97, 3.76. *4 LCS, 28 ip, 2-2, 4.18. 1 WS, 12.1 ip, 0-0, 2.19*
☛ *All-Star—80.*

An All-American at Arizona State, in 1968 Gura pitched two no-hitters in the National Baseball Congress tournament. Drafted by the Cubs, he saw limited ML duty from 1970 to 1973 and was then dealt to Texas and sold to the Yankees. In New York, Gura posted a 12-9 record over two seasons, but new manager Billy Martin didn't like him and sent him to the Royals for catcher Fran Healy. Healy played only 74 games for the Yankees, while Gura blossomed as a crafty starter with the Royals, going 88-49 from 1976 through 1982. He was the Royals' Pitcher of the Year in 1978 (16-4, 2.72), won 18 in both 1980 and 1982, and was on four Royals division winners. The fine-fielding Gura went through both 1980 and 1981 without an error. He was known as a fitness fanatic who pursued a strict diet and conditioning regimen. In 1983 he slumped to a league-leading 18 losses. Gura finished where he had started, pitching briefly with the Cubs in 1985. /(DQV)

Frankie Gustine — 1920- . 2B-3B-SS 1939-50 **Pirates**, Cubs, Browns 1261 g, .265, 38 hr, 480 rbi ☛ *All-Star—46-48.*

Gustine was signed by Pie Traynor as a 16-year-old prospect and was 19 when he joined the Pirates as a third baseman in Traynor's last season as manager. With his mentor gone, Gustine was shifted between second base and shortstop. His progress was also hindered by a chronic double hernia and assorted injuries. Finally, in 1947, he returned to Traynor's old position and led NL third basemen in putouts, assists, errors, and double plays while he had his best season offensively (.297, nine HR, 67 RBI, 102 runs). He was an All-Star at second base in 1946 and at third base in 1947-48. /(JK)

Bill Guthrie — Unk.-1950. *Umpire* NL, **AL** 1913-15, 22, 28-32

Guthrie was one of the few umpires to work in both the National and American leagues. On the last day of the 1928 season, Goose Goslin, knowing he could lock up the AL batting title by avoiding his final at-bat, attempted to get himself thrown out of the game by constantly arguing Guthrie's calls. The umpire understood Goslin's intent and refused to be ruffled. The frustrated Goslin swung away and got a hit. /(RTM)

Cesar Gutierrez (Cocoa) — 1943- . SS 1967, 69-71 Giants, **Tigers** 223 g, .235, 0 hr, 26 rbi

The quintessential "good field, no hit" shortstop, Gutierrez nevertheless made baseball history with his bat. In the second game of a June 21, 1970 doubleheader, he had six singles and a double in seven at-bats in a 12-inning game to set the AL record (and tie the ML mark) for hits in a game without making an out. But 1970 was the Venezuelan's only season as a regular; he hit a career-high .243 and led AL shortstops in errors. /(SH)

Jackie Gutierrez — 1960- . SS-2B 1983-88 **Red Sox**, Orioles, Phillies 356 g, .237, 4 hr, 63 rbi

Gutierrez hit a career-high .263 as the Red Sox' rookie shortstop in 1984, but set ML records for the fewest assists and total chances by a shortstop in a full season. He hit only .218 the following year, lost his job back to Glenn Hoffman, and was traded to

Baltimore. His father and brother competed in track and field in, respectively, the 1936 and 1964 Olympics. /(SCL)

Don Gutteridge — 1912- . 2B-3B 1936-40, 1942-48. Cardinals, **Browns**, Red Sox, Pirates 1151 g, .256, 39 hr, 391 rbi. *2 WS, 9 g, .192, 1 rbi.* *Manager* 1969-70 **White Sox** 109-172, .388

The high point of Gutteridge's career came on his second day as a Cardinal, in 1936. In a doubleheader in Ebbets Field, the rookie got six hits, including an inside-the-park HR, and stole home twice. One of 70 players to play for both the Cardinals and Browns, Gutteridge was a pepperpot second baseman on the Browns' lone pennant-winner in 1944. On June 30, 1944, Gutteridge took part in five double plays in one game, setting a since-surpassed AL second basemen's record. Coaching for the White Sox when Al Lopez retired on May 4, 1969, Gutteridge replaced him and stayed at the helm until he was fired in September 1970. /(WAB)

Joe Guyon — 1892-1971. OF *Minor Leagues.*

A Chippewa Indian, Guyon was Jim Thorpe's football teammate at Carlisle and later an All-America at Georgia Tech (named as a tackle even though he was a triple-threat halfback). He played professional football from 1919 through 1926, often in the same backfield with Thorpe. He was named to both the National College Football Hall of Fame and the Pro Football Hall of Fame. But he preferred baseball and hit .329 over twelve summers, mostly with Atlanta (Southern Association) and Louisville (American Association) in the high minors. He stole 203 bases for his career, with a high of 45 in 1921 for Atlanta. Four times he scored over 100 runs, including 152 in 1925, his best year overall. He hit .363 that year, with 38 doubles, 17 triples, and 106 RBI, all full-season career highs. His football career and his hopes of making the ML in baseball were both ended by a knee injury sustained when he ran into an outfield fence in May 1928. /(MC)

Jose Guzman — 1963- . RHP 1985-88 **Rangers** 620 ip, 37-44, 4.21

Guzman has shown flashes of great talent in four ML seasons, but it has been tempered by injuries and poor pitching. He was 14-14 in 1987 and fanned 157 batters in 206.2 innings in 1988. Arm trouble caused him to miss all of 1989. /(ME)

Tony Gwynn — 1960- . OF 1982- **Padres** 1060 g, .332, 45 hr, 416 rbi. *1 LCS, 5 g, .368, 3 rbi. 1 WS, 5 g, .263*

☛ *Led League—ba 84, 87–89. All-Star—84–89. Gold Glove—86–89.*

By 1988 Tony Gwynn had established himself as the outstanding average hitter in the National League. San Diego's third-round choice in the June 1981 draft, Gwynn quickly moved to the majors after a batting title and Most Valuable Player honors at Walla Walla (Rookie Northwest League). Despite a broken left wrist in 1982, Gwynn's batting prowess improved at the big league level. He became the first Padre to reach 200 hits and captured the first batting title for the frachise in 1984. Gwynn was voted into the All-Star Game, finished third in the NL MVP voting, and delivered the game-winning RBI in the fifth game of the Championship Series that sent San Diego to its first World Series. Tony also earned the first of three Padres MVP awards. The wrist injury hampered Gwynn in 1985, but he led the NL in hits the following two years. His 1987 season was the greatest offensive show in Padres history. His .370 batting average was the best in the NL since Stan Musial's .376 in 1948. He became San Diego's career leader in batting average and was among the all-time club leaders in runs scored, hits and doubles. He added another title in 1988 despite a terrible first half, coming on to win with a .313 mark that is the lowest ever to lead the NL. Originally a deficient outfielder, Gwynn improved to Gold Glove quality in 1986. A tough batter to strike out, Gwynn tied a record with five stolen bases on September 20, 1986 in Houston. He was also part of the first trio to hit consecutive home runs to start a major league game, in 1987. Tony was also a draft choice of the San Diego Clippers of the National Basketball Association. His brother Chris played with the Dodgers. /(ME)

Bert Haas — 1914- . 1B-3B-OF 1937-38, 42-43, 46-49, 51 Dodgers, **Reds**, Phillies, Giants, White Sox 723 g, .264, 22 hr, 263 rbi
☛ *All-Star—47.*

When Haas arrived in the majors with Brooklyn, he pinch-hit four days in a row, collecting a single and three doubles. Haas served in Italy during WWII. Aggressive and hard-hitting, he hit a career-high .286 in 1947./(EW)

Moose Haas [Bryan Edmund] — 1956- . RHP 1976-87 **Brewers**, A's 1655 ip, 100-83, 4.01. *1 LCS, 7 ip, 1-0, 4.91. 1 WS, 7 ip, 0-0, 7.36*

Finesse pitcher Haas employed pinpoint control in 1980 to go 16-15 with a 3.11 ERA. In the 1981 strike season, he was 11-7, but lost his two starts in the divisional playoff as the Brewers lost to the Yankees. He had better luck in 1982, defeating the Angels 9-5 in Game Four of the LCS, although he was hit hard in two appearances in the World Series. His best season came in 1983 as his 13-3 mark gave him a league-leading .814 winning percentage. The A's gave up four players to get Haas for 1986, but after a 7-2 start, arm trouble ended his season and, eventually, his career. On April 12, 1978 he set a Brewers record with 14 strikeouts against the Yankees./(WOR)

Mule Haas [George William] — 1903-1974. OF-1B 1925, 28-38 Pirates, **A's**, White Sox 1168 g, .292, 43 hr, 496 rbi. *3 WS, 18 g, .161, 2 hr, 9 rbi*

Haas had a great outfield tutor in Tris Speaker with the Athletics in 1928. He adopted Speaker's style of playing shallow, loping back to catch fly balls over his shoulder or dashing in for shoetop grabs. He learned bench jockeying from another master, Eddie Rommel. Haas, Al Simmons, and Jimmy Dykes were sold to the White Sox for $100,000 in 1932./(JK)

John Habyan — 1964- . RHP 1985- **Orioles** 160 ip, 9-10, 4.61

Pitching for Charlotte (Southern League) on May 13, 1985, Habyan no-hit Columbus in a 6-0

victory. He went from the Instructional League to Baltimore that September. In spending most of 1987 with the Orioles, he posted a 6-7 record./(JCA)

Stan Hack (Smiling Stan, Stanislaus) — 1909-1979. 3B 1932-47 **Cubs** 1938 g, .301, 57 hr, 642 rbi. *4 WS, 18 g, .348, 5 rbi.*
   Manager 1954-56, 58 **Cubs**, Cardinals 199-272, .423
☛ *All-Star—38-39, 41, 43.*

Genial Stan Hack, with his famous smile, was one of the most popular players of his day. He batted .352 in 1931, his first year in pro ball, and William Veeck personally went to Sacramento to sign him to a Cubs contract. By 1934 Hack was a fixture at third base in Wrigley Field. He exhibited a smooth, easy style, twice leading the NL in fielding and assists, and five times in putouts. At bat, he slashed singles and doubles, rarely swinging for the fences. He topped the 100 mark in runs scored seven times (six consecutive), had league-high stolen base totals in 1938 and 1939, and league-high hit totals in 1940 and 1941.

Hack retired in 1943, in part because he didn't get along with Cubs manager Jimmy Wilson. When Wilson was fired early in 1944, Charlie Grimm returned and coaxed Hack out of retirement. In 1945 Hack hit a career-high .323 in helping the Cubs to a pennant for a fourth time. When he finished playing in 1947, he had tied the then-record for most years as a NL third baseman (16). He began managing the Cubs in 1954, in three years never finishing higher than sixth. He coached for the Cardinals, and managed in the minors until 1966.

An opposing player once said that Hack "has more friends than Leo Durocher has enemies." Hack was known to party in his early career, and reportedly was often carried home by drinking partner Pat Malone. Bill Veeck turned Hack's captivating smile into a promotion; he once walked the Wrigley bleachers selling an item featuring a grinning picture of Hack on the back of a mirror, with the slogan, "Smile with Stan Hack." The fans began shining the mirrors into opposing batters' eyes, which prompted the umpires to confiscate the gimmicks and threaten to forfeit the game./(DB)

Stan Hack

Warren Hacker — 1924– . RHP 1948–58, 61 **Cubs**, Reds, Phillies, White Sox 1283 ip, 62–89, 4.21

As a boy, Hacker wanted to be a coal miner like his father, who insisted he pursue baseball instead. Hacker followed a 15–9, 2.58 1952 season with a league-leading 19 defeats in 1953, and had three more losing seasons with poor Cub teams. The righthander relied mostly on knucklers and sinkers. He came within two outs of a no-hitter versus the Braves on May 21, 1955. /(AA)

Harvey Haddix (The Kitten) — 1925– . LHP 1952–65 Cardinals, Phillies, Reds, **Pirates**, Orioles 2235 ip, 136–113, 3.63. 20 wins: 53 *1 WS, 7 ip, 2–0, 2.45* ☛ *All-Star—53–55. Gold Glove—58–60.*

Haddix will always be remembered for his performance on the night of May 26, 1959. Though he didn't feel well, he took his turn against Lew Burdette and the Braves. Haddix retired 36 consecutive batters, pitching 12 perfect innings, but his Pirate teammates didn't score. In the 13th, Milwaukee's leadoff batter, Felix Mantilla, reached first on

third baseman Don Hoak's error and was then sacrificed to second. The tiring Haddix intentionally walked Hank Aaron, and Joe Adcock followed with a home run. Adcock passed Aaron on the basepath (making the final score 1–0), but the no-hitter and the game were lost. Haddix's 12–2/3-inning, one-hit complete game was the majors' longest ever.

Haddix led the American Association in ERA, wins, strikeouts, and complete games in 1950. After serving in the military in 1951, and pitching briefly in 1952, the wiry southpaw had a brilliant 20–9 rookie season with the Cardinals, leading the NL with six shutouts. Basically a .500 pitcher after his sophomore season, Haddix went to the Pirates from Cincinnati with Hoak and Smoky Burgess in a seven-player deal. He was in the spotlight in the 1960 World Series. After winning Game Five as a starter, he relieved in Game Seven and won when Bill Mazeroski hit his famous homer. Nicknamed "the Kitten" at St. Louis for his resemblance to Harry "the Cat" Brecheen, Haddix finished as an effective reliever for the Orioles. He later served as pitching coach for several big league clubs. /(ME)

George Haddock (Gentleman George) — 1866–1926. RHP-OF 1888–94 Washington (NL), Buffalo (PL), Boston (AA), **Dodgers**, Phillies 1580 ip, 95–87, 4.07. 20 wins: 91–92
☛ *Led League—w 91.*

In 1891, a year after losing a league-high 26 games for Buffalo (Players' League), Haddock snapped back to lead Boston (American Association) to a pennant with 34 wins, tying Baltimore's Sadie McMahon for the league lead. /(FIC)

Bump Hadley [Irving Darius] — 1904–1963. RHP 1926–41 **Senators**, White Sox, Browns, Yankees, Giants, A's 2945 ip, 161–165, 4.25. *3 WS, 3 g, 2–1, 4.15*

The chunky curveballer was 14–6 as a rookie (1927), but generally had mediocre records with the Senators. Things got worse with the second-division Browns; in 1932, he led the AL with 21 losses. In 1932 and 1933 he led the league in walks, and retired third on the all-time walks list. After being traded to the powerful Yankees, he achieved consistent success and played on four straight pennant winners (1936–39). Hadley fractured Mickey Cochrane's skull with a pitch in 1937, ending the great catcher's career. Bump came by his nickname as a child when his short, heavy build was likened to that of a children's book character, Bumpus. /(JK)

Mickey Haefner — 1912– . LHP 1943–50 **Senators**, White Sox, Braves 1467 ip, 78–91, 3.50

Haefner was one of the Senators' four wartime knuckleballers, whose butterfly pitches brought out the best in Hall of Fame catcher Rick Ferrell and 1943 All-Star catcher Jake Early. In 1945, the chunky lefthander won 16, his ML high, but had losing records from 1947 on. /(JK)

Chick Hafey [Charles James] — 1903–1973. OF 1924–35, 37 **Cardinals**, Reds 1283 g, .317, 164 hr, 833 rbi. *4 WS, 23 g, .205, 2 rbi*
☛ *Led League—ba 31. All-Star—33. Hall of Fame—1971.*

One of the hardest-hitting righthanded batters in the game, Hafey had his best years with the Cardinals. It is difficult to assess how great Hafey might have been if not for his ill health, poor eyesight, and constant salary disputes. Hafey had a chronic sinus condition that required several operations and affected his vision. After beanings in 1926, a doctor advised him to wear glasses, and since his eyesight would vary from day to day, he used three different pairs. He became one of the first bespectacled outfielders.

Chick Hafey

Hafey was known for his rifle arm and his line drives. He started as a pitcher, but switched to everyday play under Branch Rickey. He was regarded by many as the second-best righthanded hitter of his day, behind Rogers Hornsby. A quiet man, he was somewhat overshadowed by the more colorful individuals who played on the Cardinals' championship teams of the 1920s and early 1930s.

In 1929 Hafey tied a National League record with ten successive hits. After batting .336 in 1930, he held out for $15,000, reporting ten days late to spring training. He eventually signed for $12,500, but Rickey fined him $2,100 for not being in playing shape. Hafey responded by winning the 1931 batting title with a .349 mark. He then demanded $17,000 for 1932, including a return of the $2,100. Rickey offered him $13,000, a raise of just $500. Incensed, Hafey drove home to California and waited until April 11, when he found out he had been traded to the Reds for Bennie Frey, Harvey Hendrick, and $50,000; Rickey had Joe Medwick waiting in the wings.

Hafey was happy to join the Reds, who paid him $15,000, though they were a last-place club. Battling the flu and his sinus condition, Hafey played just 84 games, but hit .344. In 1933 he hit .303, making the first All-Star team (and getting the first hit in All-Star history, a single in the second inning), but his health was not good. His last campaign as an everyday player was 1934. He hurt his shoulder in 1935, but on May 24, played in the first-ever regular season night game. The evening's dampness aggravated his sinuses. He saw the future of night baseball, and realized his career was ending. He retired, sitting out the rest of 1935 and all of 1936, but attempted a comeback in '37, playing in 89 games. He then quit for good, at the age of 34. He was elected to the Hall of Fame 34 years later by the Veterans Committee. /(WB)

Rip Hagerman (Zeriah) — 1888-1930. RHP 1909, 14-16 Cubs, **Indians** 431 ip, 19-33, 3.09

A minor league whiz (30–17 with Topeka of the Western Association in 1908), the fastballer was too wild for consistent ML success, averaging nearly five walks per nine innings. /(ME)

Joe Hague — 1944- . 1B-OF 1968-73 **Cardinals**, Reds 430 g, .239, 40 hr, 163 rbi. *1 LCS, 3 g, .000. 1 WS, 3g, .000*

Hague peaked in 1970, hitting .271. Traded to the Reds for Bernie Carbo in 1972 after publicly blaming Cardinal president Gussie Busch for the team's demise, he batted .270 lifetime (24-for-89) as a lefthanded pinch hitter. /(WAB)

Don Hahn — 1948- . OF 1969-75 Expos, **Mets**, Phillies, Cardinals, Padres 454 g, .236, 7 hr, 74 rbi. *1 LCS, 5 g, .235, 1 rbi. 1 WS, 7 g, .241, 2 rbi*

Hahn alternated in centerfield with an aging Willie Mays on the 1973 pennant-winning Mets. /(FSt)

Ed Hahn — 1875-1941. OF 1905-10 Yankees, **White Sox** 553 g, .237, 1 hr, 122 rbi. *1 WS, 6 g, .273*

Hahn's keen eye and speed made him a valuable leadoff man for the White Sox during their "Hitless Wonders" years. He still holds the AL season records, set in 1907, for fewest putouts (182) and fewest chances (206) for a full-time outfielder. /(DBing)

Noodles Hahn [Frank] — 1879-1960. LHP 1899-1906 **Reds**, Yankees 2012 ip, 129-92, 2.55. 20 wins: 99, 01-03

At the turn of the century, Noodles was Cincinnati's best pitcher. A splendid 23–7 in his rookie season, he was the only lefthander until Steve Carlton to win 20 games for an eighth-place team. He also led the league in strikeouts. He no-hit the Phillies in 1900, completed 41 games in 42 1901 starts, a year in which he fanned 19 Bostons, and he achieved his fourth 20-win record in five seasons in 1903. In 1905 his arm gave out. Over his career he had 210 complete games in 229 starts, threw 25 shutouts, and issued only 379 walks, about 1.7 per nine innings. After baseball he was a Cincinnati meat inspector and stayed in good physical condition by working out afternoons with the Reds until he was 67. /(ADS)

Hinkey Haines [Henry Luther] — 1898-1979. OF 1923 **Yankees** 28 g, .160, 0 hr, 3 rbi. *1 WS, 2 g, .000*

Haines was a member of both the Yankees' first World Championship team (1923) and the first NFL championship team of the New York Giants (1927). The exciting running back from Penn State was the darling of Giants fans. /(MG)

Jesse Haines (Pop) — 1893-1978. RHP 1918, 20-37 Reds, **Cardinals** 3208 ip, 210-158, 3.64. 20 wins: 23, 27, 28 *4 WS, 32 ip, 3-1, 1.67*
☛ *Hall of Fame—1970.*

Haines pitched more years (18) in a Cardinals uniform than anyone in history, and only Bob Gibson won more games for the club. Although originally signed by the Tigers, he played his entire ML career, except one game, with St. Louis. In 1920, with the Cardinals desperately short of starting pitching, field manager and president Branch Rickey coaxed the team directors into borrowing $10,000 to buy the 26-year-old Haines from Kansas City (American Association), where he'd gone 21–5 in 1919. He immediately became the St. Louis workhorse, throwing more than 300 innings in his first year.

Jesse Haines

Haines had a blazing fastball and acquired a knuckleball that extended his career. He learned it from Eddie Rommell, who had been very successful with the pitch for the Athletics. Haines actually gripped the ball with his knuckles, rather than the fingertips, as do most knuckleball pitchers. This allowed him to fire his knuckler with more speed than most.

A pleasant and kind fellow off the field, Haines couldn't stand defeat and was known to lose his temper at teammates when poor defense cost him a game. He won 20 games for the first time in 1923 but stumbled to an 8–19 record the next year. One of his eight wins was a 5–0 no-hitter against Boston on July 17, making him the first Cardinal pitcher to throw a no-hitter since 1876.

The Cardinals won the 1926 pennant as Haines went 13–4. In the WS, he shut out the Yankees 4–0

in Game Three, hitting a two-run homer to help his own cause. He started the seventh game and allowed only two runs through six innings. But he'd developed a blister from throwing his knuckler and in the seventh inning he loaded the bases with two out. In came Grover Alexander to strike out New York's Tony Lazzeri for one of the great moments in Series history. Haines received credit for the win that made the Cardinals World Champions, but Alexander was the hero. In the movie *The Winning Team*, with Ronald Reagan as Alexander, Haines was played by Bob Lemon.

The 1927 season was Haines's finest, as he rolled up 24 victories and led the NL with six shutouts and 25 complete games. He followed with a 20–8 season in 1928, as the Cardinals won their second pennant. He pitched for three more pennant-winners: 1930, 1931, and 1934. In WS play he was 3–1, with a 1.67 ERA.

As he put on years and saw his hair thin, Haines picked up the nickname "Pop." The label accurately described his fatherly treatment of younger players. His knuckleball remained intimidating, and he continued as an effective reliever and spot starter past his forty-fourth birthday. He served as the Dodgers' pitching coach in 1938. In 1970 the Veterans Committee named him to the Hall of Fame. /(FJO)

Jerry Hairston (Popeye) — 1952– . OF-DH-1B 1973–77, 81–89 **White Sox**, Pirates 859 g, .258, 30 hr, 205 rbi. *1 LCS, 2 g, .000*

Jerry's father, Sam Hairston, was the first American-born black player signed by the White Sox; he caught two games in 1951. Working for Chicago as a scout in 1970, Sam signed his son. Jerry proved adequate at the plate, but his outfielding was suspect. After four unproductive seasons, he was sold to Pittsburgh in 1977, then drifted to Mexico. Reacquired by Chicago late in 1981, Hairston led the AL in pinch at-bats each year from 1982 to 1985, and in pinch hits in 1983–85. On April 15, 1983, his two-out, ninth-inning pinch hit ended a perfect-game bid by Detroit's Milt Wilcox. Hairston switch-hit, but was stronger from the left side. When released in 1988, his 93 career pinch hits put him in a tie for 12th all-time; he came back in 1989 to get his 94th pinch hit. His brother John played briefly for the 1969 Cubs. /(RL)

George Halas (Papa Bear) — 1895–1983. OF 1919 **Yankees** 12 g, .091, 0 hr, 0 rbi

Although Halas played only 12 games with the Yankees—six in the outfield—the myth persists that he was Babe Ruth's predecessor as Yankee rightfielder. Ruth actually replaced Sammy Vick in 1920. Soon after Halas's demotion that season, he helped establish the National Football League. For over 60 years, he operated the Chicago Bears, playing end through 1929, and coaching through 1968. He is a member of the Pro Football Hall of Fame. /(MG)

Bob Hale — 1933– . 1B 1955–61 **Orioles**, Indians, Yankees 376 g, .273, 2 hr, 89 rbi

Hale was called up after his three hits led the Orioles' Piedmont League team to an upset of the parent club in an exhibition game. His 19 pinch hits (an Indian record) and 63 pinch at-bats in 1960 led the AL. 40% of his ML at-bats came as a pinch hitter. /(RTM)

John Hale — 1953– . OF-DH 1974–79 **Dodgers**, Mariners 359 g, .201, 14 hr, 72 rbi

Hale had four hits in four at-bats in 1974; one drove in the winning run to clinch the NL West title for Los Angeles. /(EW)

Odell Hale (Bad News, Chief) — 1908–1980. 2B-3B 1931, 33–41 **Indians**, Red Sox, Giants 1062 g, .289, 73 hr, 573 rbi

Hale was named Bad News by enemy pitchers. A good RBI man, twice exceeding 100 in a season, he hit for the cycle on July 12, 1958. He made the most errors among AL second basemen in 1934 and third basemen in 1935, but he led third basemen in assists in 1935 and 1936. One peculiar assist in 1935 came when the Red Sox loaded the bases against the Indians. Joe Cronin hit a line drive that conked Indians third baseman Hale in the head. Deflected to the shortstop on the fly, the ball was relayed to second base and on to first for a triple play. /(EW)

Sammy Hale — 1896–1974. 3B-OF 1920–21 23–30 Tigers, **A's**, Browns 883 g, .302, 30 hr, 392 rbi

As a Tiger rookie in 1920, Hale led the AL with 17 pinch hits in 52 at-bats, but he failed to stick, and the A's bought him from Portland for $75,000 in 1923. At Philadelphia, he played third base whenever Jimmy Dykes was playing another position. Hale was a smart fielder reputed to have the smallest hands in the game. /(NLM)

Ed Halicki — 1950– . RHP 1974–80 **Giants**, Angels 1063 ip, 55–66, 3.62

The 6'7" Halicki ascended quickly through the Giants system, and in his sophomore ML season,

no-hit the Mets 6–0 (8/24/75). He won a career-high 16 in 1977, and in May 1979, he pitched back-to-back two-hitters. /(EW)

Albert Hall — 1958– . OF 1981– **Braves** 375 g, .251, 5 hr, 53 rbi

The switch-hitting, 155-lb Hall was a four-time minor league basestealing champion who stole 100 bases in the Carolina League in 1980. He was a 10-year veteran of the Braves organization in 1987 when he finally had a 200 at-bat season with Atlanta, hitting .284 in a part-time role. That September 23 he became the first Atlanta Brave ever to hit for the cycle. /(JCA)

Bob Hall — 1923–1983. RHP 1949–50, 53 **Braves**, Pirates 276 ip, 9–18, 5.40

Hall's best season was as a rookie reliever with the 1949 Braves (6–4, 4.36). Born in the Pittsburgh suburb of Swissvale, Hall finished his ML career with the Pirates, his arm having been ruined in a 21-inning stint in a Pacific Coast League game. /(ME)

Charley Hall [born Carlos Clolo] (Sea Lion) — 1885–1943. RHP 1906–07, 09–13, 16, 18 Reds, **Red Sox**, Cardinals, Tigers 911 ip, 53–45, 3.08. *1 WS, 11 ip, 3.38*

Among the first pitchers to specialize in relief, Hall started only 81 games in 188 appearances. He led the AL with six relief wins for Boston in both 1910 and 1912. /(EW)

Dick Hall — 1930– . RHP-OF 1952–57, 59–71 Pirates, A's, **Orioles**, Phillies 669 g, .210, 4 hr, 56 rbi; 1259 ip, 93–75, 3.32. *2 LCS, 5 ip, 2–0, 0.00. 3 WS, 3 ip, 0–1, 0.00*

A Little All-American football end at Swarthmore College, the 6'6" Hall went straight to the Pirate outfield after signing for a substantial bonus. When he failed to hit well, he switched to pitching. Hall struggled with his new craft in the minors and missed the 1958 season with hepatitis, before emerging to lead the Pacific Coast League in wins, winning percentage, and ERA in 1959. After marginal success as a ML starter, he became one of the top relievers of the 1960s, exhibiting exceptional control despite an awkward-looking herky-jerky motion. In his last 462 ML innings, he unintentionally walked only 23 batters. He led the AL in relief wins in 1970. /(ME)

Donald Hall — 1928– . *Writer.*

A prolific writer of poetry and children's fiction, and professor of English at the University of Michigan from 1957 to 1976, Hall wrote *Fathers Playing Catch with Sons* (1985) and *Dock Ellis in the Country of Baseball* (1976)./(NLM)

Drew Hall — 1963- . LHP 1986- **Cubs**, Rangers 137 ip, 5-5, 5.26

The hard-throwing Hall, the third player in the nation selected in the June 1984 draft, has been hampered by control problems. He was traded to the Rangers with Rafael Palmiero and Jamie Moyer for Mitch Williams and five other players after the 1988 season./(SFS)

Halsey Hall — 1899-1978. *Writer-Broadcaster*

"Mr. Baseball" in Minneapolis, Hall was a sportswriter and broadcaster in the Twin Cities for 45 years. His first radio work was covering the Dempsey-Gibbons fight in 1923. After 35 years with the Minneapolis *Star*, he left in 1961 to become a full-time member of the Twins' broadcasting team until his retirement in 1972. A chain smoker of cigars, he was doing a Twins game one day when some ashes ignited a pile of papers. His coat was soon in flames, but he shed it without missing a play. Fans sent him an asbestos jacket./(NLM)

Irv Hall — 1918- . 2B-SS 1943-46 A's 508 g, .261, 0 hr, 168 rbi

Despite 40 errors as a wartime rookie shortstop, Hall was known as a heads-up fielder. He became a player-manager in the Browns' and A's farm systems./(EW)

Jimmie Hall — 1938- . OF 1963-70 **Twins**, Angels, Indians, Yankees, Cubs, Braves 968 g, .254, 121 hr, 391 rbi. *1 WS, 2 g, .143*
☛ *All-Star—64-65.*

Hall's career-high 33 HR in his rookie season ranked fourth in the AL in 1963. The Twins' centerfielder by default, he didn't cover enough ground but gave Minnesota a powerful outfield trio when he played with Bob Allison and Harmon Killebrew or Tony Oliva. His best year came in the Twins' 1965 AL championship season, when he reached career highs in BA (.285), RBI (86), steals (14), and doubles (25). After dropping to .239 in 1966, he was traded to the Angels, for whom he had one more decent season before declining. He played for five teams in his last three seasons./(SFS)

Marc Hall — 1887-1915. RHP 1910, 13-14 Browns, **Tigers** 302 ip, 15-25, 3.25

Hall won 10 games for the 1913 Tigers and had a 2.69 ERA the following season until rheumatism and Bright's disease ended his career. He died less than a year later./(NLM)

Mel Hall — 1960- . OF 1981- Cubs, **Indians**, Yankees 845 g, .278, 88 hr, 408 rbi

After hitting 17 HR in his first full season in 1983 for the Cubs, Hall was traded in mid-1984 in the deal that brought Rick Sutcliffe and a division title to Chicago. He was hitting a career-high .318 in 1985 when he broke his collarbone running into an outfield wall. He rebounded to hit 18 HR in both 1986 and 1987, but dropped off to 6 HR in 1988. The Yankees traded Joel Skinner for Hall shortly after Dave Winfield's back problem became known in spring training of 1989, but Hall slumped, was injured, and found himself in part-time duty as a DH and left fielder on his return to the lineup, the Yankees having acquired Jesse Barfield in the interim./(SFS)

Tom Hall (The Blade) — 1947- . LHP 1968-77 Twins, **Reds**, Mets, Royals 853 ip, 52-33, 3.27. *5 LCS, 14 ip, 1-1, 6.28. 1 WS, 8 ip, 0-0, 0.00*

The 6' 150-lb frame that earned him the sobriquet The Blade didn't stop Hall from being one of the hardest throwers in the majors (he averaged nearly a strikeout per inning). Used for starting and relief by Twins teams that won divisional championships in 1969 and 1970 (Hall lost his Game Two start in the 1970 LCS), he came into his own after being acquired by the Reds for the 1972 season. Getting plenty of work in the deep bullpen employed by manager Sparky "Captain Hook" Anderson, Hall was 10-1 with eight saves (3-0 in seven spot starts) for the NL champs. He won Game Two of the LCS after entering in the fifth inning with two out and two runners on and a two-ball, no-strike count on the Pirates' Willie Stargell. Hall fanned Stargell on a called third strike and finished the game, allowing only one run. He also contributed three innings of scoreless, one-hit relief in Game Five to keep the Reds in the game for their ninth-inning, come-from-behind, pennant-clinching victory. He continued his fine work in the World Series, saving Game Six and throwing 8-1/3 scoreless innings overall in the Reds' losing effort against the A's. After two more solid seasons with Cincinnati, Hall was dealt to the Mets early in 1975 and then was picked up by the Royals in May 1976 as Kansas City went on to win its first division title. /(SH)

Bill Hallahan (Wild Bill) — 1902–1981. LHP 1925–26, 29–38 **Cardinals**, Reds, Phillies 1740 ip, 102–94, 4.03. *4 WS, 40 ip, 3–1, 1.36*
☛ *Led League—w 31. Led League—k 30–31. All-Star—33.*

Hallahan was not called Wild Bill because of his temperament, but because his fastball produced league-leading totals in walks (1930–31, '33), and strikeouts (1930–31). Until Dizzy Dean emerged, he was the star of the Cardinal staff, and he led them to pennants in 1930–31. He threw two WS shutouts. The NL's starting pitcher for the first All-Star Game in 1933, Wild Bill lived up to his name. After walking five batters, he was lifted in the third inning and was the losing pitcher. /(JK)

Bill Haller — 1935– . *Umpire AL 1961, 63–82 4 WS*

Haller was "an umpire's umpire," according to fellow ump Dave Phillips. One of the last to wear an outside chest protector, Haller was assistant supervisor of AL umpires in 1983–85, but was fired, he believes, because of his refusal to work a game during the 1984 umpires' strike. His brother Tom was a ML catcher. /(RTM)

Tom Haller — 1937– . C 1961–72 **Giants**, Dodgers, Tigers 1294 g, .257, 134 hr, 504 rbi. *1 LCS, 1 g, .000. 1 WS, 4 g, .286, 1 hr, 3 rbi*
☛ *All-Star—66–68.*

After a career at quarterback for the University of Illinois, the 6'4" Haller signed with the Giants in 1958. In their pennant-winning 1962 season, he hit 18 HR as a platoon catcher. He was San Francisco's first-string receiver in the years 1964–67, and hit 27 HR in 1966. He went to the Dodgers in a 1968 trade for Ron Hunt and Nate Oliver, the first trade between the two clubs since 1956. In a ML first, on July 14, 1972, Tom was the Tiger catcher while his brother, Bill, umpired behind the plate. The durable Haller caught all 23 innings of a May 31, 1964 Mets-Giants game, and set the NL record for most double plays by a catcher in a season (23, in 1968). After serving as a Giant coach from 1977 to 1979, he was their vice president of baseball operations from mid-1981 until September 1986. /(RTM)

Jack Hallet — 1913–1982. RHP 1940–43, 46, 48 Cubs, **Pirates**, Giants 277 ip, 12–16, 4.05

A borderline major leaguer for five of his six seasons, Hallet's best season was 1946 with the Pirates when he struck out 64 in 115 innings with a 3.29 ERA. /(ME)

Bill Hallman — 1876–1950. OF 1901, 03, 06–07 **Milwaukee (AL)**, White Sox, Pirates 319 g, .235, 3 hr, 86 rbi

Hallman was the first outfielder to lead the American League in errors, committing 26 for Milwaukee in 1901, the AL's initial season. He was never again a major league regular, but had a long minor league career. /(NLM)

Bill Hallman — 1867–1920. 2B-3B-SS-OF-C 1888–98, 1901–03 **Phillies**, Philadelphia (PL), Philadelphia (AA), Cardinals, Dodgers, Indians 1503 g, .272, 20 hr, 769 rbi. *Manager* 1897 **Cardinals** 13–46, .220

This 5'8" Pittsburgh native played every position during his 14-year major league carer, although he was primarily a second baseman. He batted over .300 for four straight seasons in the mid-1890s and had three stints with the Phillies. /(AL)

Billy Hamilton (Sliding Billy) — 1866–1940. OF 1888–1901 Kansas City (AA), **Phillies**, Braves 1593 g, .344, 40 hr, 736 rbi
☛ *Led League—ba 91, 93. Hall of Fame—1961.*

One of only three players in ML history with more runs scored than games played, Hamilton was perhaps the best player of the 1890s. Seven times a stolen-base champion, he combined raw speed, daring baserunning, patience at the plate, and a .344 career average (sixth-best all-time) to become the game's first great leadoff hitter. In a period when stolen bases were also credited when baserunners gained more bases than a batter earned on a hit, Hamilton compiled phenomenal stolen base totals.

After 35 games with Kansas City in 1888, Hamilton won a starting spot the next year and hit .301 with a league-leading 117 stolen bases. He would not fall below .300 again until his final ML season. In 1890 Hamilton brought his head-first slides to the NL's Phillies, where he led the league with 102 steals in 1890 and 115 in 1891, the year he won his first batting title with a .340 mark. Following an off-year in 1892, he moved from left field to center in 1893 and hit .380 to edge teammate Sam Thompson for his second batting championship.

Sliding Billy continued his record-setting basepath feats in 1894 with the help of his fellow Phillies, who hit a ML-record .343 as a team that year. Playing in 131 of his club's 132 games, Hamilton scored 196 runs, by far the best ML season total ever. He accomplished this by leading

Billy Hamilton

the league in walks (126) and stolen bases (99), including 7 steals in one game on August 31. He also strung together a 36-game hitting streak, the sixth-longest in NL history, and had career highs of 87 RBI, 223 hits, 15 triples, 25 doubles, and a .399 batting average. After leading the league once again in runs, walks, and stolen bases in 1895, he was traded to the Braves for third baseman Billy Nash. In Boston, he continued to terrorize opposing infields, leading the NL in stolen bases twice more in 1896 and 1898. But knee and leg injuries in 1898 and 1899 finally began to slow him down, and he retired after hitting only .287 in 1901.

In addition to his lofty batting average, Hamilton finished his career with a .455 on-base percentage, 1,187 walks, 1,692 runs scored, and 937 stolen bases. He was elected to the Hall of Fame by the Veterans' Committee in 1961. /(AJA)

Dave Hamilton — 1947– . LHP 1972–80 **A's**, White Sox, Cardinals, Pirates 704 ip, 39–41, 3.85. *1 LCS, 0 ip, 0–0, 0.00. 1 WS, 1 ip, 0–0, 27.00*

Hamilton was the fifth starter on the A's teams that won three consecutive World Championships, 1972–74. Traded to the White Sox with Chet

Lemon for Stan Bahnsen and Skip Pitlock in June 1975, he was used almost exclusively in relief. In 1976 he was made the stopper of the bullpen, collecting 10 saves while Chicago made an ill-advised attempt to convert Goose Gossage into a starter. /(SH)

Earl Hamilton — 1891–1968. LHP 1911–24 **Browns**, Tigers, Pirates, Phillies 2343 ip, 116–147, 3.16

The 5'8" 160-lb Hamilton no-hit the Tigers 5–1 on August 30, 1912, and used his good changeup to become the Browns' leading winner from 1912 to 1914. After going 0–9 in 1917, he was sold to the Pirates. He completed all six of his starts for a perfect 6–0 (0.83) record in 1918 before military service shortened his season. Two years later he and the Giants' Rube Benton matched shutouts for 16 innings before New York prevailed in the 17th. Hamilton later owned the St. Joseph's franchise in the Western League. /(NLM)

Jack Hamilton (Hairbreadth Harry) — 1938– . RHP 1962–69 Phillies, Tigers, **Mets**, Angels, Indians, White Sox 612 ip, 32–40, 4.53

Hamilton led the NL in walks in his rookie 1962 season and was 7–12 as a starter. His 1.95 ERA in 15 relief appearances showed promise, so he saw most of his subsequent action out of the bullpen. After spending most of 1965 on the DL with the Tigers, he was sold to the Mets for 1966 and had a career-high 13 saves. That May 4, he pitched an 8–0 one-hitter against the Cardinals; the only hit was a third-inning single by the opposing pitcher, Ray Sadecki. Traded to the Angels in mid-1967, he returned to starting and went 9–6, 3.25 for them the rest of the way. It was his best season, but it was marred in August when he hit Tony Conigliaro in the face with a pitch, nearly blinding him and curtailing a great career. /(SFS)

Jeff Hamilton — 1964– . 3B 1986– **Dodgers** 368 g, .237, 23 hr, 109 rbi. *1 LCS, 7 g, .217, 1 rbi. 1 WS, 5 g, .105*

Hamilton had his best season for the 1988 World Champion Dodgers, reaching career highs with a .236 average, six HR, and 33 RBI but spending all of August on the DL. /(WOR)

Steve Hamilton (Hambone) — 1935– . LHP 1961–72 Indians, Senators, **Yankees**, White Sox, Giants, Cubs 664 ip, 40–31, 3.05. *1 LCS, 1 ip, 9.00. 2 WS, 3 ip, 3.00*

An important Yankee reliever who had played pro basketball with the Minneapolis Lakers, the 6'6" Hamilton threw a nasty slider with a three-quarter sidearm motion that froze lefthanded hitters. He saved the sixth game of the 1964 World Series. In 1965, he recorded a 1.39 ERA in 46 games, and in 1968 saved a career-high 11. Late in his career he added a blooper pitch, thrown with a hesitation delivery, fashioned after Rip Sewell's "Eephus" ball. Hamilton called it the "Folly Floater," and it helped extend his career. He recorded 42 ML saves./(GDW)

Ken Hamlin — 1935- . SS-2B 1957, 59–62, 65–66 Pirates, A's, Angels, **Senators** 468 g, .241, 11 hr, 89 rbi

A product of Western Michigan University, Hamlin was a fine fielder with good speed and a strong arm. His best offensive year came in 1965, when he hit .273 for the Senators./(RTM)

Luke Hamlin (Hot Potato) — 1906–1978. RHP 1933–34, 37–42, 44 Tigers, **Dodgers**, Pirates, A's 1405 ip, 73–76, 3.77. 20 wins: 39

Hamlin got his nickname because he juggled the ball while getting ready to pitch. Hamlin led the NL with 36 starts and won 20 in 1939, but Dodger manager Leo Durocher subsequently became disenchanted with the pitcher's inability to hold leads. Once, when Durocher saw an old political campaign poster for the Abe Lincoln-Hannibal Hamlin ticket, he commented, "It proves Lincoln was a great man; he could win even with Hamlin."/(JK)

Atlee Hammaker — 1958- . LHP 1981- Royals, **Giants** 980 ip, 55–57, 3.54. *2 LCS, 9 ip, 0–1, 7.00. 1 WS, 2 ip, 0–0, 15.43*
☛ *Led League—era 83. All-Star—83.*

One of three pitchers acquired from the Royals for an aging Vida Blue in 1982, Hammaker seemed headed for stardom in 1983 when he made the NL All-Star team, led the league in ERA (2.25) and fanned 14 Astros on September 11, but has been plagued by arm woes ever since. Hammaker's troubles seemed to begin in the 1983 All-Star Game. He entered in the third inning and retired only two batters, surrendering a home run to Jim Rice, a grand slam to Fred Lynn, and seven runs altogether as the NL lost for the first time since 1971. He went on the DL for a month later in '83, and had surgery twice in 1984, once on his shoulder and once on his elbow, limiting him to only six starts. He then missed all of 1986 recovering from a second shoulder operation. Since 1988, Hammaker has been used more often in relief than as a starter./(SCL)

Granny Hamner [Granville] — 1927- . SS-2B-3B-RHP 1944–59, 62 **Phillies**, Indians, A's 1531 g, .262, 104 hr, 708 rbi. *1 WS, 4 g, .429*
☛ *All-Star—52–54.*

An All-Star at shortstop and second base, Hamner was 17 when he made his ML debut in 1944. He stuck for good in 1949. Hamner played a key role on the 1950 pennant-winning club and hit well in the four-game WS loss to the Yankees. Regarded as one of the NL's best clutch hitters, Hamner rapped 30 or more doubles four times. He was also a superb relay man with a very strong arm. He took brief turns on the mound in 1956–57. When his career as an infielder ended after his trade to Cleveland in 1959, he joined the A's as a minor league manager and honed his knuckleball sufficiently to pitch three AL games in relief for Kansas City in 1962. Granny's brother, Garvin (Wes) Hamner, played infield with the Phillies in 1945./(AL)

Ralph Hamner (Bruz) — 1916- . RHP 1946–49 White Sox, **Cubs** 220 ip, 8–20, 4.58

Hamner started and relieved for both Chicago clubs, but never had a winning season. His most active season was 1948 with the Cubs when he went 5–9, allowing nearly a hit an inning and walking more batters than he struck out./(JFC)

Garry Hancock — 1954- . OF-DH-1B 1978, 80–84 **Red Sox**, A's 273 g, .247, 12 hr, 64 rbi

Drafted six times while in school, Hancock finally signed with Cleveland in 1976. After being traded to Boston, he won the International League batting championship for Pawtucket in 1979, but he never cracked the Red Sox all-star outfield of Jim Rice, Fred Lynn, and Dwight Evans./(RMu)

Rich Hand — 1948- . RHP 1970–73 **Indians**, Rangers, Angels 488 ip, 24–39, 4.00

A standout college pitcher at the University of Puget Sound, Hand signed with the Indians in 1969 and jumped into the Cleveland rotation after less than a season in the minors. He was 8–19 in a year and a half and gained a reputation for being hard to coach. He was returned to the minors, then swapped to the Rangers. In 1972, he was 10–14 with a 3.32 ERA for Texas but developed a sore arm and was through at 26./(MC)

Lee Handley (Jeep) — 1913–1970. 3B-2B 1936–41, 44–47 Reds, **Pirates**, Phillies 968 g, .269, 15 hr, 297 rbi

Handley was a rookie Pirate regular at second base in 1937, and a full- or part-time third baseman from 1938 through 1941, tying for the NL lead in steals (17) in 1939. The flashy 5'7" infielder suffered a serious beaning in 1939 and was hurt in an auto accident after the 1941 season. He recovered and platooned at third base for Pittsburgh in 1945–46. Brother Gene was an A's infielder, 1946–47./(ME)

Bill Hands — 1940– . RHP 1965–75 Giants, **Cubs**, Twins, Rangers 1951 ip, 111–110, 3.35. 20 wins: 69

In the Cubs clubhouse, Hands was the undisputed chess champion. He also had some fine years as a pitcher. In 1968 he was 16–10. Hands won 20 games and led the staff with a 2.49 ERA when the Cubs contended in 1969. Hands was the stopper, halting several losing streaks to keep the Cubs in the race against the Mets.

He was 18–15 in 1970, but back ailments and muscle spasms in his pitching arm limited his effectiveness in later years. His finest outing came August 3, 1972, when he one-hit the Expos. A .078 lifetime hitter, Hands set a ML record by fanning in 14 straight official at-bats in 1968./(AA)

Fred Haney (Pudge) — 1898–1977. 3B-2B 1922–27, 29 **Tigers**, Red Sox, Cubs, Cardinals 622 g, .275, 8 hr, 228 rbi.
    Manager 1939–41, 53–59 Browns, Pirates, **Braves** 629–757, .454. First place: 57, 58 *2 WS, 7–7, .500*

Following a career spent mostly as a Tiger third baseman and a long stint in Triple-A, Haney began managing at Toledo (American Association) in 1936. He was elevated to the Browns in 1939, but guided them to a club-record 111 losses. Replaced early in 1941, he went back to Toledo. He turned to broadcasting games for Hollywood (Pacific Coast League) in 1943–48, then managed the club to two pennants in four seasons. That success earned him the job in Pittsburgh, where he finished last three years in a row (1953–55). Taking over the Braves in June 1956, he led them to a world championship in 1957 and a pennant in 1958. Despite finishing second in 1959, he was fired. He was called a conservative manager and was once hung in effigy by Milwaukee fans during a pennant-winning campaign. He later broadcast NBC-TV's Game of the Week, and served as GM of the expansion Los Angeles Angels./(ME)

Larry Haney — 1942– . C 1966–70, 72–78 Orioles, Pilots, **A's**, Cardinals, Brewers 480 g, .215, 12 hr, 73 rbi.
1 WS, 2 g, --

Although he hit a game-winning two-run homer in his first ML game, Haney's weak bat kept him from being more than a reserve catcher throughout his career. With the division-winning A's in 1974, he played in 76 games but hit just .165. Two years later, in his most active season, he batted .226 in 88 games./(MC)

Ned Hanlon — 1857–1937. OF 1880–92 Cleveland (NL), **Detroit (NL)**, Pirates, Pittsburgh (PL), Baltimore (NL) 1267 g, .260, 30 hr, 406 rbi.
    Manager 1889–1907 Pirates, Pittsburgh (PL), **Dodgers**, Reds 1315–1165, .530. First place: 1894–96, 99, 1900

Hanlon had a longer and more illustrious career as a manager than as a player. Though never much of a hitter, he was the centerfielder for the National League Detroit club from 1881 through 1888. In

Ned Hanlon

1889 he went to the Pirates, and by season's end he was their manager. In 1890 he was one of the discontented players that formed the Players' League, but when the league folded he was taken back by the Pirates. He lasted for 78 games as their manager, and took over the Baltimore Orioles in 1892. There he remained through 1898.

In Baltimore, Hanlon put together one of the most famous 19th-century teams. They finished first in 1894–96, becoming known for their temperament, aggressive tactics, and heads-up play. Hanlon was partially responsible for the widespread use of the hit-and-run, fielders covering each other on plays, and the full-time use of a groundskeeper. His cunning rubbed off on such future managers as John McGraw, Hughie Jennings, Wilbert Robinson, Kid Gleason, and Miller Huggins. He was such an autocrat that Orioles owner Harry Vonderhorst wore a button that said "Ask Hanlon."

With owners having a hand in more than one club, it was decided in 1899 that Hanlon and his top players go to the Brooklyn Superbas (later known as the Dodgers), which had more drawing power; Baltimore folded after the season. In Brooklyn, Hanlon led his team to two consecutive pennants in 1899 and 1900. Let go after a last-place finish in 1905, he was picked up by Cincinnati, which placed sixth in Hanlon's two final years as a ML manager./(AJA)

Bill Hanna — 1862–1930. *Writer.*

A baseball writer in New York for 42 years, Hanna graduated from Lafayette in 1878 and began his career with the Kansas City *Star*. In 1888, he moved to New York with the *Herald*, spent many years with the *Sun*, and then returned to the *Herald* in 1920. One of the best-informed writers of his time, Hanna disliked slang and jargon. He wrote in simple, terse, but well-chosen and informative phrases, and helped make sportswriting a respected profession./(NLM)

Preston Hanna — 1954– . RHP 1975–82 **Braves, A's** 436 ip, 17–25, 4.62

The Braves' top draft choice (and 11th in the nation) in 1972, Hanna never blossomed due to injuries and an inability to control his knuckle curve. He was 7–13 in 1978, his only year as a regular starter./(MC)

Jim Hannan — 1940– . RHP 1962–71 **Senators,** Tigers, Brewers 822 ip, 41–48, 3.88

Notre Dame graduate Hannan's 254 strikeouts (in only 196 innings) in his first pro season led the New York-Penn League in 1961, but he was always plagued by control problems. Taken from the Red Sox organization by the Senators in the second expansion draft, his best year was 1968, when he went 10–6 for the 65–96 Washington team. The lifetime .091 hitter struck out in 13 consecutive at-bats in 1968, an AL record. Hannan was a player representative, and his master's thesis on the Major League pension plan was used by Marvin Miller to acquaint himself with baseball's benefit system. Hannan became a stockbroker in the Washington area./(CG)

Andy Hansen (Swede) — 1924– . RHP 1944–45, 47–53 **Giants,** Phillies 618 ip, 23–30, 4.22

This thin, 6'3" blond sinkerballer was generally used in middle relief. He had a career-high 100 innings in 1948, coming out of the Giants' bullpen 27 times and going 5–3 with a 2.97 ERA./(RTM)

Ron Hansen — 1938– . SS-3B-2B 1958–72 **Orioles, White Sox,** Senators, Yankees, Royals 1384 g, .234, 106 hr, 501 rbi

☛ *Rookie of the Year—60. All-Star—60.*

The uncommonly tall (6'3") shortstop missed the 1957 season with a slipped disc, and went 0-for-19 in his 1958 Orioles debut. He returned to Baltimore in 1960, and his career-high 22 HR and 86 RBI won him AL Rookie of the Year honors. He led AL shortstops in double plays in 1961, spent six months of 1962 in the Marines due to the Cuban Missile Crisis, re-injured his back, and was traded to the White Sox in a January 1963 deal for Luis Aparicio. Hansen led the league twice more in double plays and four times in assists. On August 29, 1965 he tied an AL record with 18 chances in the first game of a doubleheader, and added 10 more in the second for a total of 28, setting another record. Out again with back problems in 1966, he was swapped to the Senators in a 1968 deal for Tim Cullen. Hansen turned the majors' first unassisted triple play in 41 years on July 30, 1968 against the Indians. He was then shipped back to the White Sox for Cullen, making them the only two players to be traded for one another twice in the same season. Hansen finished his career as a utility man, and became a coach and minor league manager./(MC)

Erik Hanson — 1965– . RHP 1988- **Mariners** 155 ip, 11–8, 3.19

Hanson was the Mariners' top pitching prospect at the start of 1989 after going 2–3 with a 3.24 ERA in a September call-up the year before. He was 9–5 with a 3.18 ERA—the lowest for a Seattle starter that year—but missed almost half of 1989 on the DL. He pitched a 5–0 no-hitter for Calgary (Pacific Coast League) against Las Vegas on August 21, 1988 (seven innings). /(SFS)

Mel Harder (Chief, Wimpy) — 1909– . RHP 1928–47
Indians 3426 ip, 223–186, 3.80. 20 wins: 34–35
Manager 1961 **Indians** 0–1, .000
☛ *All-Star—34–37.*

Only Bob Feller won more games for the Indians than Mel Harder, who spent 36 years with the club as a pitcher and coach. His 582 appearances and 186 losses set Cleveland records. Only Walter Johnson and Ted Lyons pitched more seasons with one club than Harder's 20 with Cleveland. Harder pitched the first game ever in Cleveland Municipal Stadium, losing 1–0 to Philadelphia's Lefty Grove on July 31, 1932.

Nearsighted, Harder wore thick glasses. Joe DiMaggio said that he gave him more trouble than just about any pitcher, wasting his fine curveball outside, then coming in tight with the fastball. Harder held DiMaggio to a .180 average against him lifetime, and struck him out three times in a 1940 game.

By today's rules, Harder would have been the ERA leader in 1933, when he posted a 2.95 mark. But he was a .500 pitcher until 1934, when he went 20–12. He followed with a 22–11 season, but came down with bursitis in his shoulder and a sore elbow. He nevertheless won an average of 15 games a season from 1936 through 1940. He was released late in 1941, but was given another chance after having elbow surgery. Though he won 47 more games over the next six seasons, he did not regain his old form.

Harder is the only pitcher to work 10 or more All-Star innings without allowing an earned run. Though overshadowed by Carl Hubbell, he won the 1934 All-Star Game, finishing it with five shutout innings. Using today's standards, he would have been awarded saves in the 1935 and 1937 contests.

Harder became one of the first coaches to be exclusively a pitching coach, and lasted through 12 Cleveland managers. Under Harder, seven different Indians won 20 games, for a total of 17 times. Two others led the AL in wins with fewer than 20. He was credited with changing Bob Lemon from a poor-hitting infielder to a Hall of Fame pitcher. He

Mel Harder

left Cleveland in 1964, going on to coach for the Mets, Cubs, Reds, and Royals through 1969. /(ME)

Jim Hardin — 1943– . RHP 1967–72 **Orioles,** **Yankees, Braves** 751 ip, 43–32, 3.18

Originally signed by the Mets, Hardin was drafted by Baltimore and went 18–13 (2.51) in 1968, his second ML year. He failed to win more than six in any of his remaining four seasons. /(JCA)

Carroll Hardy — 1933- . OF 1958–64, 67 Indians, **Red Sox**, Astros, Twins 433 g, .225, 17 hr, 113 rbi

Hardy was the only man ever to pinch hit for Ted Williams; after Williams fouled a pitch off his foot in a 1960 game, Hardy finished the at-bat. A reserve for most of his ML baseball career, he saw the most action in 1962 (362 at-bats for the Red Sox) but hit only .215. He was also a defensive back with the NFL's San Francisco 49ers in 1955./(JCA)

Larry Hardy — 1948- . RHP 1974–76 **Padres**, Astros 127 ip, 9–4, 5.24

As a rookie in 1974, Hardy worked 76 games (second in the NL only to Mike Marshall) in going 9–4 for the last-place Padres. Arm trouble finished the sinker-slider pitcher's career./(MC)

Steve Hargan — 1942- . RHP 1965–72, 74–77 **Indians**, Rangers, Blue Jays, Braves 1632 ip, 87–107, 3.92
☛ *All-Star—67.*

Hargan had a roller coaster career. He was an All-Star in 1967, his second full season with Cleveland (14–13, 2.62, six shutouts). After elbow surgery in 1968, he struggled until 1970, when he bounced back to go 11–3 (2.90). In the three seasons that followed, he went 1–16 and spent more than a year in the minors. He again rebounded, posting a 12–9 mark with the Rangers in 1974./(JCA)

Alan Hargesheimer — 1956- . RHP 1980–81, 83, 86 **Giants**, Cubs, Royals 111 ip, 5–9, 4.70

A sub-.500 pitcher in the minors, the strong right-hander was capable of working a lot of innings. The starter was most active with the 1980 Giants, going 4–6 with a 4.32 ERA./(FO)

Bubbles Hargrave [Eugene Franklin] — 1892–1969. C 1913–15, 21–28, 30 Cubs, **Reds**, Yankees 852 g, .310, 29 hr, 376 rbi
☛ *Led League—ba 26.*

When Hargrave hit .353 in 1926, he became the first full-time catcher to lead his league in batting; only Ernie Lombardi ever matched the feat. It was the first time that decade that Rogers Hornsby, who slumped to .317 that year, didn't win the crown. Hargrave had only 326 at-bats, but at the time the percentage title qualification was 100 games; Hargrave caught 93 games, but pinch-hitting appearances brought his total to 105 games. The primitive state of catchers' protective gear made it fairly common for first-string catchers to play fewer than 100 games. It wasn't until 1951 that the require-

ment was changed to 400 at-bats, but the statistical record book *Total Baseball* doesn't list him as the league leader in 1926.

Hargrave hit .300 six straight years (1922–27). His best season was 1923, when he caught the most games of his career (109) and reached personal highs in HR (10), RBI (78), runs (54), and doubles (23) while batting .333. He had failed his first major league trial, hitting .207 in parts of three seasons with the Cubs. He was the Reds' primary catcher in the years he was a .300 hitter, and in 1924 he led NL receivers in double plays. His last season was spent as a backup catcher for the Yankees. His younger brother was Pinky Hargrave./(JFC)

Pinky Hargrave (William) — 1896–1942. C 1923–26, 28–33 Senators, Browns, **Tigers**, Braves 650 g, .278, 39 hr, 265 rbi

Not as good a hitter as his older brother Bubbles, Pinky batted righthanded in his first four ML seasons, switch-hit from 1928 to 1932, and batted only lefthanded in 1933. His flaming red hair inspired his nickname and his defensive ability earned him ten years as a ML catcher, mostly as a backup./(JK)

Charlie Hargreaves — 1896–1979. C 1923–30 **Dodgers**, Pirates 421 g, .270, 4 hr, 139 rbi

Though Hargreaves only once caught as many as 70 games for the Dodgers, Brooklyn fans liked him enough to pelt Phillies outfielder George Harper with soda bottles for colliding with him./(TG)

Mike Hargrove [Dudley Michael] (The Human Rain Delay, Grover) — 1949- . 1B-OF 1974–85 **Rangers**, Padres, Indians 1559 g, .290, 79 hr, 659 rbi
☛ *Rookie of the Year—74. All-Star—75.*

Nicknamed The Human Rain Delay for his deliberate preparation in the batter's box as he analyzed each situation, the lefthanded Hargrove ranks 16th in career on-base percentage and twice led the AL in walks. He was named 1974 AL Rookie of the Year, hitting a career-high .323 with the Rangers. He led AL first basemen in assists twice and errors three times. Traded to the Padres in 1979, he slumped to .192 in 52 games and was waived back to the AL, hitting .325 in 100 games for the Indians. He followed with two more .300 seasons, but slowly lost his job to Pat Tabler. Hargrove became a minor league manager for the Indians./(MC)

Isao Harimoto — 1935- . OF 1959–81 **Toei Flyers/ Niitaku Home Flyers/Nippon Ham Fighters**, Yomiuri Giants, Lotte Orions .319 (inc)
☛ *Led League—ba 67–68.*

Considered the greatest ballplayer ever to emerge from Korea, Harimoto retired with a Japanese baseball record 3,085 hits and the second highest lifetime batting average in Japanese history. He hit between 23 and 30 home runs a season until late in his career.

Several times, Harimoto attracted tentative interest from American teams who hoped that, as a Korean (though of Japanese ancestry), Harimoto would not feel bound to remain in Japan. After the 1968 season and a second batting title, he qualified for free agency, an option Japanese players rarely exercise. Though he did not declare interest in signing with other teams, he did threaten to retire if not given a 10-year bonus by the Toei Flyers, who were not financially sound. The San Francisco Giants and Los Angeles Dodgers were rumored to be ready to make offers when Harimoto finally accepted more than double the Flyers' initial offer. This episode, a drinking problem, and alleged lack of hustle made Harimoto a leading target of fan abuse for the rest of his career. /(MC)

Mike Harkey — 1966- . RHP 1988- **Cubs** 35 ip, 0–3, 2.60

The fourth pick overall in the June 1987 draft, Harkey was the Cubs' best pitching prospect coming off his 1988 call-up when he was 0–3 but had a 2.60 ERA. However, in Spring Training in 1989 he had lost more than 10 mph off his fastball, and was sent down. /(WOR)

Tim Harkness — 1937- . 1B 1961–64 Dodgers, **Mets** 259 g, .235, 14 hr, 61 rbi

After signing a pro hockey contract with the Montreal Canadiens organization, this Quebec native opted to play baseball. Harkness unseated Marv Throneberry as the Mets' first baseman in 1963, only to be replaced shortly thereafter by bonus baby Ed Kranepool. /(CR)

Dick Harley — 1872–1952. OF 1897–1903 **Cardinals**, Cleveland (NL), Reds, Tigers, Cubs 740 g, .262, 10 hr, 236 rbi

Georgetown University graduate Harley was a journeyman outfielder for seven ML seasons. Later he became a highly respected college baseball coach at Pitt, Penn State, and Villanova. /(BC)

Larry Harlow — 1951- . OF 1975, 77–81 **Orioles**, Angels 449 g, .248, 12 hr, 72 rbi. *1 LCS, 3 g, .125, 1 rbi*

In his first (and only) season as a regular, Harlow had just 26 RBI for the 1978 Orioles, and was traded to California. In a ninth-inning rally in 1979 ALCS Game Three, Harlow doubled off Baltimore's Don Stanhouse to drive in Brian Downing for the Angels' first-ever playoff victory. /(JCA)

Bob Harmon (Hickory Bob) — 1887–1961. RHP 1909–16, 18 **Cardinals**, Pirates 2054 ip, 107–133, 3.33. 20 wins: 11

Bought by the Cardinals after pitching a no-hitter for Shreveport (Texas League) early in 1909, Harmon hurled a 16-inning victory over the Phillies that year. After winning 23 games in 1911 and 18 in 1912, he lost his effectiveness and was traded to Pittsburgh. /(NLM)

Chuck Harmon — 1926- . 3B-OF-1B 1954–57 **Reds**, Cardinals, Phillies 289 g, .238, 7 hr, 59 rbi

Harmon hit over .300 five consecutive years in the minors but never approached such numbers in the majors. As a star basketball player at the University of Toledo, he led the school to the 1943 NIT finals. /(RTM)

Terry Harmon — 1944- . 2B-SS-3B 1967, 69–77 **Phillies** 547 g, .233, 4 hr, 72 rbi. *1 LCS, 1 g, --*

The versatile infielder set a NL record when he successfully accepted 18 chances at second base in a game (6/12/71). He was also the Phillies' player representative and a regular member of their winter basketball team. /(JCA)

Brian Harper — 1959- . OF-C-DH 1979, 81- Angels, Pirates, Cardinals, Tigers, A's, **Twins** 393 g, .282, 22 hr, 127 rbi. *1 LCS, 1 g, .000. 1 WS, 4 g, .250, 1 rbi*

After wandering through six organizations in eleven years (he was 7-for-26 as a pinch-hitter for the NL-champion 1985 Cardinals), Harper finally found a home in 1988 platooning at catcher for the Twins. He hit .295 in 166 at-bats, his most playing time to that point at the major league level, and earned more playing time. He responded by hitting .325 in 1989 as the Twins' primary catcher, with career highs of eight HR and 57 RBI. /(JFC)

George Harper — 1892–1978. OF 1916–18, 22–29 Tigers, Reds, **Phillies**, Giants, Cardinals, Braves 1073 g, .303, 91 hr, 528 rbi. *1 WS, 3 g, .111*

A good hitter with decent power, Harper hit three home runs in the first game of a September 20, 1928 doubleheader. After 11 ML seasons he continued in the minors during the Depression and was still a player-manager at the age of 44. /(JK)

Harry Harper — 1895–1963. LHP 1913–21, 23 **Senators**, Red Sox, Yankees, Dodgers 1256 ip, 57–76, 2.87. *1 WS, 1 ip, 0–0, 20.25*

Harper spent seven years with the luckless Senators, with a 6–21 record in 1919 to lead the AL in losses. He later made a fortune as a New Jersey industrialist./(JK)

Jack Harper [Charles William] — 1878–1950. RHP 1899–1906 Cleveland (NL), Cardinals, Browns, **Reds**, Cubs 1207 ip, 79–63, 3.58. *20 wins: 01, 04*

Called up for his first major league start at age 21, Harper halted the National League-record 24-game losing streak of the 1899 Cleveland Spiders by winning 5–4. When the NL was cut from twelve teams to eight in 1900, he was transferred to the Cardinals, for whom he went 23–13 in 1901, finishing second in the NL in wins and winning percentage. After two more average years, he again won 23 (losing 9) with a career-low 2.37 ERA for the Reds and was third in the NL in wins and winning percentage. After missing most of 1906 with a finger injury and bone chips in his elbow, he was traded to the Cubs in October. A holdout the following year ended his major league career./(NLM)

Terry Harper — 1955– . OF 1980–87 **Braves**, Tigers, Pirates 540 g, .253, 36 hr, 180 rbi. *1 LCS, 1 g, .000*

A Georgia native signed by the Braves as a pitcher in 1973, Harper was made an everyday player in 1976, but it was 1983 before he spent a full season in Atlanta. In July of 1982 he dislocated his left shoulder while standing by the plate and enthusiastically waving a runner home. In his one solid season, 1985, he hit 17 HR. He played in Japan after his 1987 release by Pittsburgh./(JCA)

Tommy Harper — 1940– . OF-3B 1962–76 **Reds**, Indians, Pilots/Brewers, Red Sox, Angels, A's, Orioles 1810 g, .257, 146 hr, 567 rbi. *1 LCS, 1 g, .000* ☛ *All-Star—70.*

Blending speed and power, Harper became only the fifth member of the "30–30 Club," hitting 31 HR and stealing 38 bases for the 1970 Brewers. As a young, highly touted outfielder with the Reds in 1965, he hit 18 homers and led the NL with 126 runs scored. After a disappointing 1967 season (.217), he was traded to Cleveland, where he continued to slump in a platoon role. Rescued by the Seattle Pilots in the 1968 expansion draft, he led the

ML with 73 stolen bases in 1969, the highest AL total since Ty Cobb's 96 in 1915.

Although he preferred the outfield, Harper played mostly at third base (and 82 games at second base) for the Pilots and Brewers. Traded to Boston before the 1972 season, he returned to the outfield. In 1973 he was the Red Sox' MVP, hitting 17 HR, scoring 71 runs, and stealing an AL-high 54 bases./(JCA)

Toby Harrah [Colbert Dale] — 1948– . 3B-SS-2B 1969, 71–86 **Senators/Rangers**, Indians, Yankees 2155 g, .264, 195 hr, 919 rbi ☛ *All-Star—72, 75–76, 82.*

Harrah was a power-hitting infielder who spent most of his 17-year career on second-division teams. He was the Senators' primary shortstop in their last season of existence and remained there for the franchise's first five seasons in Texas. Coming up straight from Double-A ball in 1971, he was overmatched at first, hitting .230 and slugging .290. He improved as a batter and fielder in 1972 after spending the winter studying with Chico Carrasquel in South America. Harrah hit .259 with 10 HR despite missing time with an appendectomy and a shoulder injury; the injury forced him out of the All-Star Game.

He came into his own in 1974, hitting 21 HR with 74 RBI and 79 runs. It was the first of his five 20-HR seasons. He also showed range in the field, leading AL shortstops in putouts and tying in errors. Manager Billy Martin said, "I don't know how a guy could cover more ground, and he also has that great arm." In 1975 Harrah improved further, hitting .293 and drawing 98 walks while driving in a career-high 93 runs. It was the first of his .400 on-base percentage seasons; his .406 was fourth in the AL. *TSN* named him the shortstop on its postseason AL all-star team. In 1976 he had his best year defensively, leading AL shortstops in putouts and total chances per game (and errors). He also established the first of his two odd fielding records, accepting no chances at shortstop in a June 25 doubleheader. On September 17 the following year, he set another record by playing 17 innings at third base without recording an assist.

Harrah's best year offensively came in 1977, when he was moved to third base after Bert Campaneris was signed as a free agent. Harrah led the AL with 109 walks and hit 27 HR, both career highs, and stole 27 bases. He and Bump Wills hit back-to-back inside-the-park home runs at Yankee Stadium, only the second time that was ever accomplished. In 1978 he stole a career-high 31 bases but slumped to .229. He moved back to shortstop at mid-season as Campaneris hit .186.

After the season Harrah was traded to the Indians for Buddy Bell and he replaced Bell at third base. Although the Rangers often had losing records, they had contended in 1974, 1977, and 1978. In Cleveland, Harrah's talents were buried on a perennial sixth-place finisher that dropped another notch when the expansion Blue Jays finally improved. In his five years with the Indians, Harrah scored 100 runs twice (his career high, in 1980 and 1982). In his only .300 season, .304 in 1982, he also hit 25 HR and finished second in the AL with a .400 on-base percentage. He led AL third basemen in fielding in 1983. At third, he almost always guarded the line, which cut down on his range; he maintained that it was more important to cut off potential doubles than singles. He played in 476 consecutive games before a Dennis Martinez pitch sidelined him with a broken hand in April 1983.

The Yankees acquired Harrah in a five-player deal in February 1984. By the end of spring training, Graig Nettles had been traded to San Diego for panning the club's planned third-base platoon, and Harrah was not only faced with the pressure of replacing the popular Nettles, but was also blamed for causing his departure. He slumped horribly, lost the job to rookie Mike Pagliarulo, and hit just .217. After the season he was traded back to the Rangers for Billy Sample and a minor league pitcher. Happy to be back in Texas, he was the regular second baseman (Buddy Bell was at 3B) and rebounded to .270. Drawing a career-high 113 walks (second in the majors), he finished third in the AL with a .437 on-base average, behind Wade Boggs and George Brett. He retired after hitting .218 in 1986. /(SH)

Ray Harrell (Cowboy) — 1912–1984. RHP 1935, 37–40, 45 **Cardinals**, Cubs, Phillies, Pirates, Giants 330 ip, 9–20, 5.70

Harrell was unimpressive in a 1935 trial with St. Louis, but Branch Rickey, trying to bolster a sagging Cardinal pitching staff, gave him another shot in 1937 as a reliever and spot starter. Hit hard, Harrell was sold to the Cubs after the 1938 season. /(FJO)

Bud Harrelson [Derrel McKinley] — 1944– . SS-2B 1965–80 **Mets**, Phillies, Rangers 1533 g, .236, 7 hr, 267 rbi. *2 LCS, 8 g, .172, 5 rbi. 2 WS, 12 g, .220, 1 rbi* ☛ *All-Star—70–71. Gold Glove—71.*

Harrelson grew up in California wanting to play for the Giants, who rejected him as too small. He signed with the Mets, and on September 16, 1966, stole home in the ninth to cost the Giants a key game in a pennant race they lost by one and a half games. That same week, he stole home to beat the Pirates, who finished two out. After a .108 debut in 1965, he learned to switch-hit.

Between recurring back problems and weekend duty in the National Guard Reserve, he missed considerable playing time, but when he was in the lineup, he sparked the Mets. His excellent fielding kept him in the lineup no matter what his average, but he also contributed with his speed on the basepaths and by drawing more than his share of walks. His best year was 1970, when he reached career highs in five offensive categories and tied the since-broken NL shortstop record of 54 consecutive errorless games (6/24–8/19). In 1971 he won a Gold Glove and led the Mets with 28 stolen bases. Harrelson is second on the Mets' all-time list in games and at-bats (to Ed Kranepool) and triples, and ranks high in hits, runs, and stolen bases. He became a minor league manager and ML coach for the Mets. Pete Rose is still booed in Shea Stadium for his hard collision with Harrelson while trying to break up a double play in the 1973 New York–Cincinnati LCS. Released after 1977, Harrelson turned to softball, but was picked up by the Phillies on their way to the division title. /(MC)

Ken Harrelson (Hawk) — 1941– . 1B-OF 1963–71 A's, Senators, Red Sox, Indians 900 g, .239, 131 hr, 421 rbi. *1 WS, 4 g, .077, 1 rbi* ☛ *All-Star—68.*

The big and powerful Harrelson was baseball's 1960s flower child. He wore his blond hair long and sported Nehru jackets, beads, bell bottoms, and no socks. Catcher Duke Sims dubbed him "Hawk" for his aquiline nose, and he had that emblazoned on the back of his uniform. A careless-fielding power hitter, he hit 23 homers for Kansas City in 1965. Late in 1967, Harrelson was quoted as saying, "Charlie Finley is a menace to baseball." The angered A's owner released him. Seven teams approached Harrelson; the Red Sox, in the thick of a pennant race, won him with a $73,000 bonus, and Harrelson helped them to the '67 pennant. In 1968, he hit 35 homers and led the AL with 109 RBI. Boston fans picketed Fenway Park early in 1969 when Harrelson was traded to Cleveland. He missed most of 1970 with a broken leg and played grudgingly for the Indians until 1971, when he quit to become a pro golfer, something he had threatened for years. When that failed, he became an outspoken broadcaster, and, for 1986, was the White Sox' much-criticized GM. /(JCA)

Will Harridge — 1883-1971. *Executive.*
☛ *Hall of Fame—1972.*

As a Wabash Railroad ticket agent, Harridge handled travel arrangements for the AL until Ban Johnson hired him as his private secretary, a position he held from 1911 to 1927. When Johnson resigned as AL president, Harridge became league secretary. When Johnson's successor, E.S. Barnard, died in 1931, Harridge became the third AL president.

Softspoken, reserved, and iron-willed, he remained for 28 years. He avoided the spotlight, preferring to handle league matters discreetly behind closed doors. He always said his most difficult moment came in 1931 when he fined Yankees catcher Bill Dickey $1,000 and suspended him for 30 days during a hot pennant race. Dickey had slugged White Sox outfielder Carl Reynolds and broke his jaw in an unprovoked attack.

Will Harridge

Although Harridge advocated the establishment of an annual All-Star Game, which began in 1933, he generally supported the status quo in baseball. He originally opposed night baseball. He was persuaded during WWII that night games enabled more families to attend games, and he became a supporter of baseball under lights. After retiring as league president in 1958, he served as chairman of the board until his death in 1971. In 1972, he was elected to the Hall of Fame./(NLM)

Bill Harrington — 1927- . RHP 1953, 55-56 **A's** 116 ip, 5-5, 5.03

After two innings with the 1953 Philadelphia Athletics, Harrington moved with the franchise to Kansas City. The wild reliever compiled records of 3-3 and 2-2 with the lowly 1955-56 clubs./(FK)

Bill Harris — 1900-1965. RHP 1923-24, 31-34, 38 Reds, **Pirates**, Red Sox 434 ip, 24-22, 3.92

From 1921 to 1945, Harris won 257 minor league games, including two no-hitters for Buffalo in 1936. The righthander had one decent ML season (10-9, 3.64) for the 1932 Pirates./(ME)

Bob Harris [Robert Ned] — 1916-1976. OF 1941-43, 46 **Tigers** 262 g, .259, 16 hr, 81 rbi

A good hitter and a decent fielder, Harris did well enough at the plate and in the outfield with Buffalo to earn a promotion to Detroit. He played most in 1942 and 1943 before entering military service./(EW)

Bob Harris [Robert Arthur] — 1916- . RHP 1938-42 Tigers, **Browns**, A's 646 ip, 30-52, 4.96

A fur trapper in Nebraska between seasons, Harris pitched valiantly for poor Browns' and A's teams before leaving for army service, 1943-45. Released by the Athletics upon his return, he demanded compensation for this shoddy treatment, and settled for an undisclosed sum with Connie Mack./(JK/EW)

Bucky Harris [Stanley Raymond] — 1896-1977. 2B 1919-29, 31 **Senators**, Tigers 1264 g, .274, 9 hr, 506 rbi. *2 WS, 14 g, .232, 2 hr, 7 rbi.*
Manager 1924-43, 47-48, 50-56 **Senators**, Tigers, Red Sox, Phillies, Yankees 2159-2219, .493. *3 WS, 11-10, .523*
☛ *Hall of Fame—1975.*

"First in war, first in peace, and last in the American League," ran the old saw about Washington, but in

Bucky Harris

1924 the perennial AL tail-ender Senators were World Champions. In his first season at the helm was 27-year-old Bucky Harris, the youngest regular ML manager and the team's second baseman. Washington's rugged "Boy Manager" led by example and earned the respect of such veterans as Walter Johnson, Sam Rice, and Roger Peckinpaugh.

In the 1924 World Series against the Giants, Harris batted .333 and hit two home runs. He also set records for chances accepted, double plays, and putouts in the exciting seven-game affair. His base hit in the eighth inning of the deciding contest tied the score, and the Senators rallied in the twelfth to clinch Washington's one and only World Championship. It was in that contest that Harris the manager won acclaim. His strategy of replacing righthanded starter Curly Ogden with lefthander George Mogridge after only two batters forced the Giants' hard-hitting Bill Terry out of the lineup.

Harris learned baseball in the mining region of northeastern Pennsylvania. After leaving school at 13, he worked in a local colliery. Hughie Jennings,

another future Hall of Famer from Harris's home town of Pittston, arranged for the scrappy youngster's first job in pro ball, in 1915. Harris reached the majors in 1919.

An exceptional fielder, he topped AL second basemen in putouts four times and in double plays a record five straight times (1921–25). An adequate hitter with base stealing ability, Harris had a knack for being hit by pitches. An outstanding basketball player, he played professionally with local Pennsylvania teams during the off-season, until concerned Washington officials ordered him to cease.

Under Harris, the Senators repeated as AL champs in 1925, but lost a hard-fought seven-game Series to the Pirates. After suffering his first losing season in 1928, he was traded to, and named manager of, the Tigers. Except for a few appearances at second base, Harris was a bench manager from then on. He spent five unsuccessful seasons directing the Tigers, one with the Red Sox, and then eight more with the Senators, never finishing higher than fourth. Despite the many losing campaigns, Harris was regarded as a knowledgeable manager and was extremely popular with his players. His patient, gentlemanly manner inspired such loyalty that when the Phillies fired Harris in mid-1943, his players threatened to strike.

Between ML jobs, Harris managed in the International and Pacific Coast leagues. In 1947, he led the Yankees to a World Series victory, and was named *TSN* Manager of the Year. He was dropped abruptly a year later after a 94–60 third-place finish. Though he managed for another seven years, Harris never again landed in the first division.

Harris also served as assistant GM of the Red Sox and scouted for the White Sox. Named a special assignment scout with the expansion Washington Senators in 1963, he finished where he had begun his ML career a half century earlier. Harris, the youngest man to lead a major league team to a World Series victory, was elected, as a manager, to the Hall of Fame in 1975 by the Veterans Committee. /(JL)

Charlie Harris (Bubba) — 1926– . RHP 1948–49, 51 **A's**, Indians 186 ip, 6–3, 4.84

Harris came out of the bullpen 45 times as a rookie for the 1948 A's and went 5–2 with five saves. /(RTM)

Dave Harris (Sheriff) — 1900-1973. OF 1925, 28, 30-34 Braves, White Sox, **Senators** 542 g, .281, 32 hr, 247, rbi. *1 WS, 3 g, .000*

Never a regular, Harris hit .310 as a pinch hitter. On August 5, 1932, with the Senators trailing Detroit 13-0 and two outs in the ninth inning, Harris's pinch single ruined Tommy Bridges's perfect game./(NLM)

Gail Harris — 1931- . 1B 1955-60 Giants, **Tigers** 437 g, .240, 51 hr, 190 rbi

Harris was a power hitter but lacked consistency. In 1958 for the Tigers, his best season, he had 20 home runs and 83 RBI but led AL first basemen in errors./(BC)

Greg Harris — 1955- . RHP 1981- Mets, Reds, Expos, Padres, **Rangers**, Phillies 791 ip, 35-45, 3.52. *1 LCS, 2 ip, 0-0, 31.50. 1 WS, 5 ip, 0-0, 0.00*

The curveballing, ambidextrous Harris bounced around the NL before landing with the 1984 NL champion Padres. Roughed up by the Cubs in the playoff opener, he allowed a NLCS-record six earned runs in one inning. He came into his own after his 1985 sale to Texas, leading AL relievers with 111 strikeouts and posting a 2.47 ERA. He went 10-8 (2.83) with a staff-high 20 saves in 1986, but in 1987 he both started and relieved, went 5-10 without a save, and was released. He had missed some games that season after injuring his elbow flicking sunflower seeds to a friend in the stands./(JCA)

Greg Harris [Greg Wade] — 1963- . RHP 1988- **Padres** 153 ip, 10-9, 2.47

Harris has one of the best curves in the league and will use it repeatedly. In 1989 he established himself as the number-two man out of the Padres' bullpen./(SFS)

Joe Harris (Moon) — 1891-1959. 1B-OF 1914, 17, 19, 22-28 Yankees, Indians, **Red Sox**, Senators, Pirates, Dodgers 971 g, .317, 47 hr, 517 rbi. *2 WS, 11 g, .350, 3 hr, 7 rbi*

Harris batted over .300 each of his full seasons except his last. A starting outfielder for the Red Sox in 1922-23 before moving to first base in 1924, Harris was traded to Washington in 1925 and hit .323 to help the Senators to the pennant. He batted .440 with three HR in the seven-game WS loss to Pittsburgh./(ME)

Joe Harris — 1882-1966. RHP 1905-07 **Red Sox** 317 ip, 3-30, 3.35

In 1906, the luckless Harris compiled one of the worst records ever by a ML hurler. His 2-21 record for the error-prone last-place Red Sox included 14 straight losses and eight shutouts pitched against him. He set an AL record going the route in a 24-inning loss to Philadelphia's Jack Coombs (4-1, on September 1). Boston-area native Harris suffered again in 1907, going 0-7./(EW)

Lum Harris [Chalmer Luman] — 1915- . RHP 1941-44, 46-47 **A's**, Senators 820 ip, 35-63, 4.16. *Manager* 1961, 64-65, 68-72 Orioles, Astros, **Braves** 466-488, .488. First place: 69 *1 LCS, 0-3, .000*

Harris had a good fastball and a fair knuckler, but he pitched for poor A's clubs. His 21 losses (including 13 straight) in 1943 were the most in the AL. In the most successful of his years as manager of the Braves, he led Atlanta to the 1969 NL West title. The Mets swept the LCS./(EW)

Mark Harris — 1922- . *Writer.*

A novelist, playwright, and English professor at San Francisco State, Purdue, and Arizona State, Harris is known among baseball fans for his series of novels about Dizzy Dean-esque flake Henry Wiggen: *The Southpaw* (1953), *Bang the Drum Slowly* (1956), *A Ticket for a Seamstitch* (1959), and *It Looked Like Forever* (1979). Harris also did the screenplay for the Robert De Niro film of *Bang the Drum Slowly*, considered by many critics to be among the best baseball movies ever./(NLM)

Mickey Harris — 1917-1971. LHP 1940-41, 46-52 **Red Sox**, Senators, Indians 1050 ip, 59-71, 4.18. *1 WS, 10 ip, 0-2, 3.72*
☛ *All-Star—46.*

Harris's 17-9 record in 1946 (after four years in the army) contributed to a Red Sox pennant. Though plagued by arm problems most of his career, his 53 relief appearances and 15 saves for the 1950 Senators led the AL./(EW)

Spence Harris — 1900-1982. OF 1925-26, 29-30 **White Sox**, Senators, A's 164 g, .249, 3 hr, 46 rbi

Harris was unimpressive in several trials in the majors but had a long and productive career in the minors (1921-48), setting all-time minor league career records for hits (3,617), runs (2,287), doubles (743), and total bases (5,434)./(LRD)

Vic Harris — 1905-1978. OF-MGR Negro Leagues 1923-50 Cleveland Tate Stars, Toledo Tigers, Chicago American Giants, **Homestead Grays**, Detroit Stars, Pittsburgh Crawfords, Cleveland Browns, Baltimore Elite Giants, Birmingham Black Barons statistics not available ☛ *All-Star—38, 42-43, 47.*

Unlike many Negro League players who flitted from team to team, Harris spent most of his career (23 of 28 years) with one club—the Homestead Grays—as a strong-hitting outfielder and manager. He started playing as a 17-year-old with the Cleveland Tate Stars, and settled in with the Grays during their strong independent years. He was an aggressive baserunner and could "undress an infielder, cut the uniform right off his back," according to one contemporary.

Harris managed the Grays during their years in league play, from 1936 through 1948, winning nine consecutive pennants (1937-45) and two Black World Series titles (1943 and 1944). In 1938, when the Grays dominated the league and won the first half with an .813 winning percentage, Harris reportedly hit .380. In the waning days of the Negro Leagues, he coached for the Baltimore Elite Giants in 1949 and managed the Birmingham Black Barons in 1950. /(BP)

Vic Harris — 1950- . 2B-OF-3B-SS 1972-78, 80 **Rangers**, Cubs, Cardinals, Giants, Brewers 579 g, .217, 13 hr, 121 rbi

Harris batted .249 with eight homers for Texas in 1973, his only season as a regular. Because he switch-hit and could play the infield and the outfield, he was a valuable utility man. /(JCA)

Chuck Harrison (Charles William) — 1941- . 1B 1965-69, 71 **Astros**, Royals 328 g, .238, 17 hr, 126 rbi

The Texas Tech linebacker was a tenacious first baseman who could hit home runs in the minors (40 at San Antonio in 1964). He was Houston's regular first baseman only for 1966, as he had trouble hitting the curveball. /(JCA)

Roric Harrison — 1946- . RHP 1972-75, 78 Orioles, **Braves**, Indians, Twins 590 ip, 30-35, 4.24

Harrison was the property of nine organizations. He led the International League with 15 wins in 1971, but a wrenched knee in the playoffs cost him a promotion to the Orioles. He underwent several knee operations, the first in 1969. At his best, he went 11-8 for the 1973 Braves. /(MC)

Slim Harriss [William Jennings Bryan] — 1896-1963. RHP 1920-28 **A's**, Red Sox 1750 ip, 95-135, 4.25

Slim was a 6'6" 180-lb, hard-throwing Texan. Pitching for the A's against the White Sox, he gave up singles to the first 2 hitters, then retired 27 in a row. While teammate Eddie Rommel was winning an AL-high 27 games in 1922, Harriss was losing a league-high 20. His only winning season was 1925 (19-12). He again led the AL in losses in 1927, with 21 for the Red Sox. /(NLM)

Earl Harrist (Irish) — 1919- . RHP 1945, 47-48, 52-53 Reds, **White Sox**, Senators, Browns, Tigers 384 ip, 12-28, 4.34

On July 5, 1947 Harrist faced pinch hitter Larry Doby, the AL's first black player, in Doby's first ML appearance, and struck him out. The mediocre reliever won that game, but only 11 others. /(JK)

Jack Harshman — 1927- . LHP-1B, 1948, 50, 52, 54-60 Giants, **White Sox**, Orioles, Red Sox, Indians 258 g, .179, 21 hr, 65 rbi; 1169 ip, 69-65, 3.50

Harshman began his pro career as a slugging first baseman, leading the Southern Association in HR (47) and RBI (141) in 1951; he went on to hit 21 ML homers. In 1952 he began the transition to the mound. Harshman set the White Sox team record for strikeouts in a single game with 16 at Boston on July 25, 1954. /(EW)

Bill Hart — 1865-1936. RHP-OF 1886-87, 92, 95-98, 1901 Philadelphia (AA), Dodgers, Pirates, **Cardinals**, Indians 229 g, .207, 4 hr, 66 rbi; 1582 ip, 66-120, 4.65

In 1896, pitching for the Cardinals, Hart led the NL in losses with 29, but he won over 250 minor league games. He pitched for 25 seasons in the ML and minors, beginning and ending with Chattanooga of the Southern Association. When he retired as a player in 1910 after winning his last start, he turned to umpiring. /(BC)

Jim Ray Hart — 1941- . 3B-OF-DH 1963-74 **Giants**, Yankees 1125 g, .278, 170 hr, 578 rbi. *1 LCS, 3 g, .000* ☛ *All-Star—66.*

Bob Gibson welcomed Jim Ray to the big leagues in 1963 by breaking his shoulder blade with a fast ball in the back. A few days after Hart's return, he was beaned by Curt Simmons and missed the rest of the season. But in 1964, his first full year, the stocky strongman proved he wasn't gun-shy with a San Francisco-rookie record 31 homers. Until a 1969 shoulder injury made him a part-timer, he averaged

28 homers a season. On September 8, 1970 he hit for the cycle and tied a ML record with six RBI in one inning. Although the former North Carolina cotton picker was so quiet it was said a soft chuckle was a whole conversation for him, he was vocal about his hatred of playing third base: it was "just too damn close to the hitters." /(JCA)

Chuck Hartenstein (Twiggy) — 1942– . RHP 1965–70, 77 **Cubs**, Pirates, Cardinals, Red Sox, Blue Jays 297 ip, 17–19, 4.52

A sinkerballing reliever, the slender Hartenstein was nicknamed Twiggy by teammate Billy Williams. At his best as a rookie with the 1967 Cubs, he was 9–5 with ten saves. Hartenstein became a ML pitching coach with Cleveland and Milwaukee. /(AA)

Grover Hartley (Slick) — 1888–1964. C 1911–17, 24–27, 29–30, 34 Giants, **St. Louis (FL)**, Browns, Red Sox, Indians 569 g, .268, 3 hr, 144 rbi

The well-traveled catcher was a master with young pitchers. Hartley's only year as a regular came in 1915 with St. Louis of the Federal League. He was a minor league manager and a coach with the Browns and Pirates. /(EW)

Fred Hartman (Dutch) — 1868–1938. 3B 1894, 1897–99, 1901–02 Pirates, Cardinals, **Giants**, White Sox 580 g, .278, 10 hr, 332 rbi

After two-plus National League seasons, Hartman played for Chicago in 1900, when the American League was a minor league. When the AL became a major league in 1901, Hartman batted .309 as the third baseman on the league's first pennant-winner. /(AJA)

Harry Hartman — Unk.–Unk. *Broadcaster.*

A Cincinnati sports broadcaster and Reds' P.A. announcer in the 1930s, Hartman was voted the most popular ML sports announcer in a 1933 *Sporting News* poll. Supposedly, he was the first to call a home run with "Going, going, gone!" /(NLM)

Gabby Hartnett [Charles Leo] — 1900–1972. C 1922–41 **Cubs**, Giants 1990 g, .297, 236 hr, 1179 rbi. *4 WS, 16 g, .241, 2 hr, 3 rbi.*
   Manager 1938–40 **Cubs** 203–176, .536. *1 WS, 0–4, .000*
☛ *Most Valuable Player—35. All-Star—33–38. Hall of Fame—1955.*

Hartnett was the oldest of 14 children. His father Fred was a semi-pro catcher who had an exceptional

Gabby Hartnett

throwing arm. Millville, MA, oldtimers still talk about "the Hartnett arm"—Fred's, four of his sons', and three of his five daughters' who barnstormed with a women's team.

Gabby broke his arm as a child. It didn't knit properly, and his mother insisted he carry a pail of stones or sand wherever he went, to exercise it. His father held backyard baseball clinics for four sons, all of whom played amateur or semi-pro ball. Chickie, a catcher, once signed a pro contract, but was homesick and returned to Millville before ever playing. Gabby completed eight years of schooling, went to work in the U.S. Rubber shop, and caught for the plant nine and any other team his father could get him on. He spent a year and a half at a junior college, and in 1921 signed with the Eastern League's Worcester Boosters. He batted .264, and was purchased by Chicago for $2,500. As a shy rookie, his reticent personality led to his ironic nickname.

Hartnett became Chicago's catcher by 1924, batting .299, and in 1925 hit 24 HR, though he struck out 77 times to lead the NL. In 1929, his arm went mysteriously dead in spring training, where he had reported with his new bride, Martha. Nothing helped the arm, and during a Cubs' series in Boston, he went to see his mother in Woonsocket, RI, after the games. She predicted that his arm would be better as soon as his pregnant wife delivered their child. Hartnett caught just one game that season. Junior was born December 4, and within two weeks, Gabby's arm soreness was gone.

Hartnett followed in 1930 with his best season ever, hitting .339 with career highs of 37 HR and 122 RBI. An All-Star six straight years, in the 1934 game he was the catcher when Carl Hubbell fanned Ruth, Gehrig, Foxx, Simmons, and Cronin in succession. He was named NL MVP in 1935, batting .344 (third in the league), topping NL catchers in assists, double plays, and fielding average, and led the Cubs to the pennant.

His finest day came on September 28, 1938. He had become the Cubs' manager in mid-season, and had his team within a half game of the first-place Pirates. With darkness and haze rapidly enveloping Wrigley Field in the ninth, and the score 5–5, two out, no one on, down 0–2 in the count, Hartnett slammed his "Homer in the Gloamin'." Three days later, the Cubs clinched the pennant.

Hartnett managed the Cubs to fifth place in 1940, was fired, and hit .300 as a 40-year-old catcher/pinch hitter for the Giants in 1941. He retired as a player, having four times led NL catchers in putouts, six times in assists, and seven in double plays. Though he topped the league in errors three of his first four seasons, he later led in fielding average six years, including a record-tying four straight from 1934–37.

After an often hectic five seasons managing in the minors, Hartnett quit baseball after 1946, opening a recreation center and bowling alley in Lincolnwood, IL. He sold it in 1964 to join Kansas City as a coach, scout, and troubleshooter for two years, but relations with manager Alvin Dark were not good, and Hartnett was dropped.

Joe McCarthy, who saw much of Mickey Cochrane and managed both Bill Dickey and Hartnett, called Gabby "The Perfect Catcher." He is widely considered the greatest NL catcher before Johnny Bench. His 20 years and 1,790 games behind the plate put him among the all-time leaders in service, and he is among the Cubs' all-time top ten in nine offensive categories. The BBWAA inducted him into Cooperstown in 1955. /(JK)

Topsy Hartsel [Tully Frederick] — 1874–1944. OF 1898–1911 Louisville (NL), Reds, Cubs, **A's** 1354 g, .276, 30 hr, 341 rbi. *2 WS, 6 g, .273*

The 5'5" Hartsel used his size to work pitchers for walks, five times leading the league. The lefthanded leadoff man played for four pennant winners in his ten seasons with the Athletics. The dependable leftfielder led the AL in stolen bases and runs scored in 1902. /(JK)

Roy Hartsfield — 1925– . 2B 1950–52 **Braves** 265 g, .273, 13 hr, 59 rbi. *Manager* 1977–79 **Blue Jays** 166–318, .343

A competent second baseman whose playing career was curtailed by injuries, Hartsfield became the first-ever manager of the Toronto Blue Jays, directing them to three consecutive last-place finishes in 1977–79. /(FS)

Clint Hartung (Floppy, The Hondo Hurricane) — 1922– . RHP-OF 1947–52 **Giants** 511 ip, 29–29, 5.02; 196 g, .238, 14 hr, 43 rbi, *1 WS, 2 g, .000*

Hartung is a baseball metaphor for a player with apparently unlimited talent who is never able to harness it. The 6'5", 210-lb Hondo, Texas, native joined the Giants with a fabulous record as a pitcher and hitter while on WWII service teams against ML-caliber competition. Contemporary cynics said he should "not bother playing, just get ready for the Hall of Fame," and he struggled for six unproductive seasons. He lacked the control to be an effective pitcher, and he struck out too much to play regularly. /(FS)

Paul Hartzell (Tall Paul) — 1953– . RHP 1976–80, 84 **Angels**, Twins, Orioles, Brewers 703 ip, 27–39, 3.90

After just one season of Class A ball, the 6'5" flame-thrower went 7–4 (2.77) with the Angels in 1976, but followed with two losing seasons. One of four players dealt to Minnesota for Rod Carew in 1979, Hartzell went 6–10 that season and returned to the minors. /(JCA)

Roy Hartzell — 1881–1961. OF-3B-SS-2B 1906–16 Browns, **Yankees** 1288 g, .252, 12 hr, 397 rbi

The lefthanded hitter shuttled among second base, third base, shortstop, and outfield each season. His 595 at-bats for the Browns led the AL in 1909, and his 91 RBI for New York in 1911 were the most by a player in the Yankees' first 13 years. /(FS)

Bryan Harvey — 1963– . RHP 1987- **Angels** 136 ip, 10–8, 2.58

Harvey was named *TSN* Rookie Pitcher of the Year for 1988 when he had 17 saves and a 2.13 ERA to establish himself as the ace of the Angels' bullpen. /(WOR)

Doug Harvey — 1930– . *Umpire* NL 1962–87 *6 LCS 4 WS 5 ASU*

One of the most respected umpires of his time, Harvey says of his profession: "Umpires are necessary evils. That's just the nature of the beast. For years people have looked on umpiring as a job they could get any postman to do." He first got the urge to become an umpire while watching Don Larsen's perfect game in the 1956 WS on TV. In a 1978 game, Harvey collected three scuffed baseballs, then ejected Dodger pitcher Don Sutton for apparently doctoring the balls. The league decided not to penalize Sutton after he threatened to sue the NL if he was suspended. /(RTM)

Ernie Harwell — 1918– . *Broadcaster.*

A talented writer and accomplished lyricist and composer outside the broadcast booth, Harwell has been the immensely popular voice of the Tigers for almost three decades. In 1934, as a 16-year-old Georgia high school student, Harwell became *The Sporting News*'s Atlanta correspondent. His work would eventually appear in *Collier's*, *Reader's Digest*, and *The Saturday Evening Post*, but he chose to make his living as a broadcaster.

Harwell was broadcasting for the Atlanta Crackers when his work caught the attention of Dodgers owner Branch Rickey, and Rickey traded minor league catcher Cliff Dapper to the Crackers to bring Harwell to Brooklyn in 1948. He later worked briefly with the Giants and Orioles before settling in Detroit in 1960. Harwell originally worked on both TV and radio, but after 1965 his endearing, friendly voice was heard exclusively on radio. His 1955 baseball essay, "A Game for All America," is displayed in baseball's Hall of Fame. /(SL)

Tufie Hashem — Unk.–1968. *Scout.*

Hashem began his baseball career as GM of Mexicali in 1949, and began scouting for the Cardinals in 1954 when he steered Ruben Amaro their way. He also worked briefly for the Pirates and Angels, and made numerous scouting trips to Mexico and Latin America, but his most prominent discoveries were American-born players like Jay Johnstone, Rudy May, Doug Griffin, and Roy White. /(FVP)

Mickey Haslin — 1910– . SS-2B-3B 1933–38 **Phillies**, Braves, Giants 318 g, .272, 9 hr, 109 rbi

Haslin was a 5'8" utility infielder who led the Phillies in pinch hits in 1934. In the first ML night game (5/24/35), Haslin drove in Philadelphia's only run in a 2–1 loss at Cincinnati. /(GEB)

Buddy Hassett — 1911– . 1B-OF 1936–42 **Dodgers**, Braves, Yankees 929 g, .292, 12 hr, 343 rbi. *1 WS, 3 g, .333, 2 rbi*

The steady-hitting first baseman was stuck in the Yankee farm system while Lou Gehrig was in his prime. Sold to Brooklyn, Hassett hit .310 his rookie year. Gehrig retired, and the Yankees traded top prospect Tommy Holmes to the Braves in 1942 to retrieve Hassett. His appearance with the Yankees in the 1942 WS, before entering the military, marked the end of his career. /(JK)

Ron Hassey (Babe) — 1953– . C-DH 1978- **Indians**, Cubs, Yankees, White Sox, A's 1046 g, .272, 65 hr, 402 rbi. *2 LCS, 6 g, .537, 1 hr, 4 rbi. 1 WS, 5 g, .250, 1 rbi*

The good-hitting, burly Hassey was Cleveland's primary catcher from mid-1979 to 1984. He led all major league catchers by batting .318 in 1980. A decent defensive catcher, he caught Len Barker's perfect game in 1981. The lefthanded hitter was proficient as a pinch hitter and was a strong finisher. He was traded between Chicago and New York four times from 1984 to 1986. Bad knees limited him, especially on defense. He was a backup on championship A's teams in 1988 and 1989. /(ME)

Andy Hassler — 1951– . LHP 1971, 73–85 **Angels**, Royals, Red Sox, Mets, Pirates, Cardinals 1123 ip, 44–71, 3.83. *3 LCS, 16 ip, 0–2, 4.60*

The 6'5" Hassler recorded a pair of one-hitters, one with the 1974 Angels, the other with the 1977 Royals. In 1975–76, Hassler lost an Angel-record 17 straight decisions. /(EW)

Bob Hasty — 1896–1972. RHP 1919–24 **A's** 752 ip, 29–53, 4.65

Before improving his fielding, Hasty was in danger of being bunted out of baseball. The finesse pitcher never had an ERA below 4.25. /(NLM)

Billy Hatcher — 1960– . OF 1984- Cubs, **Astros**, Pirates 609 g, .263, 30 hr, 212 rbi. *1 LCS, 6 g, .280, 1 hr, 2 rbi*

The Astros left fielder was ejected from a September 1, 1987 game against Chicago when the barrel of his bat split, revealing it had been corked. Hatcher claimed he had no idea the bat had been doctored, that he had borrowed it from pitcher Dave Smith, who had used it only during batting practice. Hatcher received a 10-day suspension. That year, the year of the rabbit ball, was the most successful of Hatcher's first four (.296, 11 HR, 63 RBI). His 53 stolen bases ranked third in the NL. A catalyst on Houston's 1986 division-winner, Hatcher hit a dramatic, 14th-inning home run to tie Game Six of the LCS at 4–4; it took 16 innings for the Mets to win the game, clinching the pennant. /(JCA)

Mickey Hatcher — 1955– . OF-3B-1B 1979– Dodgers, **Twins** 1044 g, .283, 38 hr, 362 rbi. *1 LCS, 6 g, .238, 3 rbi. 1 WS, 5 g, .368, 2 hr, 5 rbi*

This clubhouse comic and team energizer sometimes wears a batting helmet with a propeller on it. He became the nation's darling with his 1988 postseason play. After hitting only one HR all year, he homered in the first inning of the first and final WS games and made the finest defensive plays of the Series. An enthusiastic, hustling player, he would have been WS MVP but for Orel Hershiser. Hatcher spent six seasons with the Twins as an effective utility player, then was released during the spring of 1987 before signing with the Dodgers. /(TG)

Fred Hatfield — 1925– . 3B-2B-SS 1950–58 Red Sox, **Tigers**, White Sox, Indians, Reds. 722 g, .242, 25 hr, 165 rbi

In only two seasons did the versatile utility infielder play 100 games at any one position. Hatfield was twice involved in trades involving future Hall of Famers, first George Kell and later Early Wynn. He was a direct descendant of the Hatfields who feuded with the McCoys. /(GEB)

Joe Hatten — 1916–1988. LHP 1946–52 **Dodgers**, Cubs 1087 ip, 65–49, 3.87. *2 WS, 11 ip, 8.44*

After four years in the minors and several in the service, Hatten reached the majors at the age of twenty-nine. The Dodger starting pitcher in Jackie Robinson's first ML game in 1947, Hatten went on to a career-best 17–8 that year. /(EGM)

Lou Hatter — 1920–1988. *Writer.*

Hatter was a baseball writer for 40 years for the Baltimore *Sun*, and covered the Orioles from 1954 until he retired in 1984. /(NLM)

Grady Hatton — 1922– . 3B-2B 1946–56, 60 **Reds**, White Sox, Red Sox, Cardinals, Orioles, Cubs 1312 g, .254, 91 hr, 533 rbi.
    Manager 1966–68 **Astros** 164–221, .426
☛ *All-Star—52* .

Hatton jumped straight to the Reds from military service in 1946, hitting .271 with 14 HR and 69 RBI. He followed in 1947 with 16 HR, 77 RBI, 91 runs, and a .281 average, but tailed off thereafter. He managed the Oklahoma City 89ers to two pennants in three years and then managed the Astros from 1966 to 1968. He finished eighth, ninth, and last, despite the presence of Rusty Staub, Jim Wynn, Bob Watson, Nate Colbert, Mike Cuellar, Larry Dierker, Don Wilson, Doug Rader, and Joe Morgan (whom he tried to turn into an outfielder). /(MC)

Arnold Hauser (Pee Wee) — 1888–1966. SS 1910–13, 15 **Cardinals**, Chicago (FL) 433 g, .238, 6 hr, 137 rbi

Called "The Midget" by Cardinal manager Roger Bresnahan, the 5'7" Hauser was actually a half-inch taller than his double-play partner, Miller Huggins. /(JK)

Joe Hauser (Unser Choe) — 1899– . 1B 1922–24, 26, 28–29 **A's**, Indians 629 g, .284, 79 hr, 356 rbi

The lefthanded-hitting Hauser batted .323 as a rookie in 1922, and in 1924 led the A's with 27 HR (second to Ruth) and 115 RBI. He broke his kneecap in 1925, missing the entire season. Following his ML career, he became a minor league slugger. He is the only player in professional ball to twice hit 60 home runs in a season, with 63 for Baltimore (International League) in 1930 and 69 for Minneapolis (American Association) in 1933. /(LRD)

Tom Hausman — 1953– . RHP 1975–76, 78–82 Brewers, **Mets**, Braves 441 ip, 15–23, 3.79

Chronic back problems and ulcers headed a long list of maladies that sidelined Hausman year after year. In 1980, his healthiest season, he appeared in 55 Met games, mostly in middle relief. /(JCA)

Clem Hausmann — 1919–1972. RHP 1944–45, 49 **Red Sox**, A's 263 ip, 9–14, 4.21

The slim Texan used an effective curveball in a brief ML career during WWII. /(EW)

George Hausmann — 1916- . 2B 1944-45, 49 Giants 301 g, .268, 3 hr, 78 rbi

At 5'5" 145-lb, Hausmann was the Giants' regular second baseman during the last years of WWII. He was suspended for jumping to the outlaw Mexican League in 1946. After the suspension was lifted, he played a few games in 1949. /(FS)

Brad Havens — 1959- . LHP 1981-83, 85- **Twins**, Orioles, Dodgers, Indians, Tigers 591 ip, 24-37, 4.81

After leading the Twins' 1982 pitching staff in starts (32) and strikeouts (129), Havens was their Opening Day pitcher in 1983, but he was twice sent down, and finished with an 8.18 ERA. The International League strikeout leader in 1984 and 1985, he returned to the majors as a middle reliever. /(JCA)

Andy Hawkins — 1960- . RHP 1982- **Padres**, Yankees 1311 ip, 75-73, 4.00. *1 LCS, 4 ip, 0-0, 0.00. 1 WS, 12 ip, 1-1, 0.75*

The Padres' first pick in the 1978 June draft, Hawkins showed few signs of living up to expectations until the 1984 postseason, when he allowed just one earned run in 15.2 innings of relief and was the winner in San Diego's only World Series victory. In 1985 he picked up where he had left off, becoming the first NL pitcher in 26 years to win his first 11 decisions, breaking the Padres' record for consecutive wins by a starter. Hampered in the second half by a circulatory problem in his left index finger (caused by throwing the slider), he finished the season at 18-8. He recovered from 1987 shoulder problems to go 14-11 (3.35) in 1988. Signed by the Yankees after the season to a big free agent contract, he became their number-one pitcher and had another hot streak in the middle of the season after a bad start. /(JCA)

Wynn Hawkins (Hawk) — 1936- . RHP 1960-62 Indians 203 ip, 12-13, 4.17

The 6'3" Hawkins came out of Baldwin-Wallace University as their all-time leading basketball scorer. On June 17, 1960 he surrendered Ted Williams's 500th home run. He later served the Indians as a scout and as their traveling secretary. /(RTM)

Pink Hawley [Emerson P.] — 1872-1938. RHP 1892-01 Cardinals, **Pirates**, Reds, Giants, Milwaukee (AL) 3012 ip, 168-177, 3.96. 20 wins: 95, 96, 98

After suffering a NL-high 26 losses with St. Louis in 1894, Hawley rebounded for the Pirates in 1895 with a 32-21 year, including a league-leading 444

innings pitched. He topped 300 innings in five other seasons. /(ME)

Ben Hayes — 1957- . RHP 1982-83 **Reds** 115 ip, 6-6, 4.70

The inconsistent reliever had a 1.97 ERA in 26 appearances in 1982. The next year he allowed only one earned run in 18 appearances during June and July, but collapsed to finish 4-6, 6.49, and never appeared again in the ML. /(JCA)

Frankie Hayes (Blimp) — 1914-1955. C 1933-34, 36-47 **A's**, Browns, Indians, White Sox, Red Sox 1364 g, .259, 119 hr, 628 rbi
☛ *All-Star—39-41, 44, 46.*

Hayes was a highly-regarded defensive catcher and a five-time All-Star. He led the AL three times in total chances per game, twice each in fielding, putouts, double plays, and errors, and once in assists. His 29 double plays in 1945 is the second-highest total ever for a catcher. When he caught 155 games in 1944, he set a still-standing AL record.

He failed in his first trial in the majors, batting just .226 in 1934, but he came back up in 1936 to spend six seasons as the Athletics' primary catcher. His best offensive season was 1939, when he hit .283 and had career highs of 20 HR and 83 RBI; he hit a career-high .308 in 1940 (with 61 walks in 465 at-bats). On July 25, 1936 he tied the major league record with four doubles in a game. /(WOR)

Jackie Hayes [Minter Carney] — 1906-1983 2B-3B-SS 1927-40 Senators, **White Sox** 1091 g, .265, 20 hr, 493 rbi

Joe Cronin called second baseman Hayes "the best double play artist in the league." Hayes and shortstop Luke Appling formed a fine double play combination while Hayes was the White Sox' regular at second base for much of 1932-37. In 1937 Hayes's 115 double plays led AL second basemen. He had career highs of 84 RBI in 1936, and .328 average in 1938. /(EW)

Von Hayes — 1958- . OF-1B 1981-89 Indians, **Phillies** 1195 g, .274, 122 hr, 573 rbi. *1 LCS, 2 g, .000. 1 WS, 4 g, .000*
☛ *All-Star—89.*

Tall and reed-thin, with great speed and deceptive strength, Hayes is a natural outfielder, but has spent much of his playing time at first base. The Indians touted him as their best prospect in a decade, and he made his ML debut after only one season in the minors. His first full ML season, 1982, produced a .250 average, 14 HR, 82 RBI, and 32 stolen bases.

The Phillies were sufficiently impressed to send five players, including Julio Franco, to Cleveland in exchange for Hayes. Hayes never lived up to the "five-for-one" expectations he faced in 1983, but in 1984 he hit .292 with 16 HR and 46 stolen bases, and on June 11, 1985 he homered twice in the first inning against the Mets, a ML first. Faced with a surplus of outfielders, the Phillies switched Hayes to first base in 1986, and he hit .305 with 19 HR, 98 RBI, and 24 steals, leading the NL in doubles and tying for the lead in runs scored. He made the All-Star team in 1989, hit a career-high 26 HR, and was second in the NL with 101 walks./(SG)

Joe Haynes — 1917–1967. RHP 1939–52 Senators, **White Sox** 1581 ip, 76–82, .401

Haynes sandwiched eight years with the White Sox between two stints with the Senators. He was Chicago's ace reliever in 1942 (8–5, 2.62, six saves), leading the AL with 40 appearances. His best season came as a starter in 1947 (14–6, 2.42). Haynes was married to Thelma Griffith, adopted daughter of Washington owner Clark Griffith, who brought Joe back home in a December 1948 trade with Cleveland. Haynes later became a Senators coach, GM, and vice president, moving with the franchise to Minnesota./(GB)

Ray Hayworth — 1904– . C 1926, 29–39, 42, 44–45 **Tigers**, Dodgers, Giants, Browns 698 g, .265, 5 hr, 238 rbi. *1 WS, 1 g, --*

A fine defensive catcher but only an ordinary hitter, Hayworth lost his job as the regular Tiger backstop in 1934 when Mickey Cochrane became player-manager. Hayworth was Cochrane's sub as Detroit won pennants in 1934 and 1935 and continued as a backup for the remainder of his career. His brother Red caught for the Browns during WWII./(JK)

Bob Hazle (Hurricane) — 1930– . OF 1955, 57–58 Reds, **Braves**, Tigers 110 g, .310, 9 hr, 37 rbi

A lefthanded streak hitter, Hazle was called up by the Braves when outfielder Bill Bruton was injured in July 1957. Red hot, he batted .403 in 41 games and helped Milwaukee win the pennant./(NLM)

Ed Head — 1918–1980. RHP 1940, 42–44, 46 **Dodgers** 465 ip, 27–23, 3.48

After spending the 1945 season in the military, he no-hit the Braves at Ebbets Field on April 23, 1946. Shortly thereafter, Head suffered a career-ending arm injury./(EGM)

Fran Healy — 1946– . C 1969, 71–78 **Royals**, Giants, Yankees 470 g, .250, 20 hr, 141 rbi

The son of 1930s NL catcher Francis Healy, Fran was regarded as a potential star in 1974, when he hit .252 for the Royals with 53 RBI. Unusually fast for a catcher, he had 16 stolen bases that season, the most by a ML catcher in 37 years. He caught both of Steve Busby's no-hitters. His career sank with a shoulder injury in 1975. Traded to the Yankees, he backed up Thurman Munson and was a valuable mediator in the Reggie Jackson-Billy Martin feuds of 1977–78. He later became a broadcaster for a NY cable sports network./(MC)

Bunny Hearn [Bunn] — 1891–1959. LHP 1910–11, 13, 15, 18, 20 Cardinals, Giants, **Pittsburgh (FL)**, Braves 400 ip, 13–24, 3.56

Hearn never earned more than a temporary spot on a ML roster, but he was baseball coach at the University of North Carolina for 27 years./(ME)

Jim Hearn — 1921– . RHP 1947–59 Cardinals, **Giants**, Phillies 1703 ip, 109–89, 3.81 *1 WS, 8 ip, 1–0, 1.04* ☛ *Led League—era 50. All-Star—52.*

After a promising 12–7 rookie year with the Cardinals in 1947, Hearn went into a tailspin, engendered in part by a chronic lack of confidence. The Giants were able to purchase him cheaply in July of 1950. He was 0–1 with a 10.00 ERA when he arrived in New York, but for the remainder of the season he went 11–3 and brought his ERA down to a league-leading 2.49. His five shutouts tied for the league lead. The next season, he was 17–9 as the third starter on the staff behind aces Sal Maglie and Larry Jansen, as the Giants swept to the "miracle" pennant of 1951. Hearn was a sinkerball pitcher. Although he had fairly good control, his walks often outnumbered his strikeouts, but he was excellent at throwing double play pitches./(FS)

Jeff Heath — 1915–1975. OF 1936–49 **Indians**, Senators, Browns, Braves 1383 g, .293, 194 hr, 887 rbi ☛ *All-Star—41, 43.*

Heath twice led the AL in triples, and averaged 18 HR and over 81 RBI in ten seasons as a regular. He hit a career-high .343 in 1938, his first year as Cleveland's everyday left fielder. In Bob Feller's 1940 Opening Day no-hitter, Heath scored the game's only run. In 1947 with the Browns he hit career highs of 27 HR and 87 RBI. Bought by the 1948 pennant-bound Boston Braves, Heath responded with a .319 average and 20 HR, but in the final week of the season, he broke his leg sliding and missed the WS against the Indians. Heath remains among Cleveland's top ten in triples, HR, and slugging percentage. /(GEB)

Mike Heath — 1955- . C-OF 1978- Yankees, **A's**, Cardinals, Tigers 1153 g, .252, 78 hr, 419 rbi. *2 LCS, 6 g, .308, 1 hr, 2 rbi. 1 WS, 1 g, --*

Heath was the A's starting catcher in the early 1980s, but the veteran righthander has been a part-time player and valuable reserve for most of his career, and has played every position but pitcher in the ML. Heath was a shortstop when signed by the Yankees in 1973, and did not begin catching until 1976. Two years later, at the age of 23, he caught one inning in Game Five of the WS after the Yankees had called him up in the latter half of the season. Heath was traded to the Rangers in the deal that made Dave Righetti a Yankee in November 1978, and was still in the minors when the Rangers traded him to Oakland. He became Oakland's starting catcher in strike-shortened 1981, and caught over 100 games in both 1984 and 1985, hitting exactly .250 with 13 HR each year. After 65 games with the Cardinals in 1986, Heath returned to the AL with the Tigers, where he has shared the catching chores with Matt Nokes. /(SCL)

Jeff Heathcock — 1959- . RHP 1983, 85, 87-88 Astros 158 ip, 9-9, 3.76

A 6'4" sinkerballer, Heathcock was one of the Astros' most highly regarded prospects when, while with Tucson (Pacific Coast League) in April 1984, he tore up his right knee while covering first base. He missed the rest of that season, and through 1988 was shuttled between Tucson and Houston. /(JCA)

Cliff Heathcote — 1898-1939. OF-1B 1918-32 Cardinals, **Cubs**, Reds, Phillies 1415 g, .275, 42 hr, 448 rbi. *1 WS, 2g, .000*

Heathcote was part of an unusual trade on May 30, 1922. Swapped from the Cardinals to the Cubs between games of a doubleheader for outfielder Max Flack, he and Flack were hitless in the morning but collected hits with their new teams that afternoon as the Cubs took a pair. On August 25, 1922 the lefthanded-hitting Heathcote was 5-for-5 with four RBI and five runs scored in the major leagues' biggest slugfest ever: Cubs 26, Phillies 23. Usually a regular through 1926, he hit a career-high .313 in 82 games in 1929 as the Cubs won the pennant. /(AA)

Neal Heaton — 1960- . LHP 1982- **Indians**, Twins, Expos, Pirates 1223 ip, 61-83, 4.46

Heaton was the pearl of a Cleveland farm system that produced little in the early 1980s. He went 11-7 as a rookie in 1983, but was having his third straight losing season when traded to Minnesota for John Butcher in 1986. The move proved folly for Cleveland that winter when they released Butcher, and the Twins sent Heaton to Montreal in a deal for Jeff Reardon. Heaton was 10-4 at the 1987 All-Star break, then skidded to finish 13-10. Reardon's 31 saves helped the Twins to the World Championship. /(JCA)

Dave Heaverlo — 1950- . RHP 1975-81 **Giants**, A's, Mariners 539 ip, 26-26, 3.41

A jokester who shaved his head and insisted on keeping his non-roster number 60 as a rookie, Heaverlo relieved in all his 356 ML appearances. After he went 5-1 (2.55) in 1977, the Giants sent him to Oakland with six other players, plus $390,000, for Vida Blue. He earned 19 saves in two years with the A's. /(JCA)

Wally Hebert (Preacher) — 1907- . LHP 1931-33, 43 Browns, Pirates 484 ip, 21-36, 4.63

The sidearmer insisted his name be pronounced "Ay-bare." After three poor seasons with the Browns, he reemerged during WWII to go 10-11, 2.98 for the 1943 Pirates. /(JK)

Richie Hebner — 1947- . 3B-1B 1968-85 **Pirates**, Phillies, Mets, Tigers, Cubs 1908 g, .276, 203 hr, 1890 rbi. *8 LCS, 26 g, .284, 3 hr, 12 rbi. 1 WS, 3 g, .167, 1 hr, 3 rbi*

An off-season gravedigger at a cemetery run by his father, Hebner signed for $40,000 and made the Pirates two seasons later despite losing playing time to military reserve duty. He led NL rookies with a .301 average in 1969, and hit a career-high 25 HR for Pittsburgh in 1973. After seven years and five division championships as the Pirate third baseman, Hebner played out his option, and spent two seasons at first base helping the Phillies win NL East titles in 1977 and 1978. Ousted by the 1979 arrival of free agent Pete Rose, he led the Mets with 79 RBI that season, was swapped to the Tigers, and had a career-high 82 RBI in only 104 games in 1980. After a second tour with the Pirates, he became the top pinch hitter for the division-winning 1984 Cubs. He set the ML record for most times on the losing club in the LCS (7) and the NL record for most LCS played in (8). /(MC)

Guy Hecker (Blond Guy) — 1856–1938. RHP-1B-OF 1882–90 **Louisville (AA)**, Pirates 709 g, .284, 19 hr, 102 rbi; 2906 ip, 177–150, 2.92.
   Manager 1890 **Pirates** 23–113, .169
☛ *Led League—ba 86. Led League—era 84. Led League—w 84. Led League—k 84 .*

Hecker is the only pitcher ever to win a ML batting title. A hard thrower (when the regulation pitching distance was 50 feet), he often played first base or outfield for his mediocre Louisville team when he wasn't pitching. Appearing in only 84 of the Colonels' 136 games in 1886, he hit .342 to top Pete Browning by .002 and lead the league. In a game against Baltimore that year, he went 6-for-7, a record for pitchers; his seven runs scored in that game is still a record for any player. Three of his hits that day were inside-the-park home runs; this was the first three-homer game by a pitcher and the only three-homer game for any player in the American Association's ten-year existence as a major league. Hecker also won 27 games for sixth-place Louisville that year, but by then he was on the downgrade, each year slipping farther from his phenomenal 52–20 season of 1884, when he completed 72 games in 73 starts, pitched 670.2 innings, had 385 strikeouts, and compiled an estimated ERA of 1.80, all league-leading statistics. /(ADS)

Mike Hedlund (Red) — 1946– . RHP 1965, 68–72 Indians, **Royals** 466 ip, 25–24, 3.55

Hedlund signed with Cleveland for a significant bonus after throwing a no-hitter in the 1963 Connie Mack World Series. In 1969 he went to Kansas City in the expansion draft. He was 15–8, 2.71 in 1971 but spent the rest of his career fighting a sore arm. /(MC)

Danny Heep — 1957– . OF-1B 1979– Astros, **Mets**, Dodgers, Red Sox 828 g, .259, 30 hr, 218 rbi. *3 LCS, 13 g, .167, 1 rbi. 2 WS, 8 g, .158, 2 rbi*

Heep was an extra lefthanded bat when the Astros sent him to the Mets for pitcher Mike Scott in December 1982. His four pinch-hit home runs in 1983 led the majors and set a Mets record. Heep was the top pinch hitter (9-for-30) for the 1986 World Champion Mets. He had career highs of 320 at-bats, 49 RBI, and a .300 batting average in 1989 for the Red Sox when they lost several outfielders to injury. /(JCA)

Bob Heffner (Butch) — 1938– . RHP 1963–66, 68 **Red Sox**, Indians, Angels 353 ip, 11–21, 4.51

On June 28, 1963 with Boston, Heffner became only the second ML pitcher to record three putouts in an inning. /(GEB)

Don Heffner (Jeep) — 1911– . 2B-SS-3B 1934–44 Yankees, **Browns**, A's, Tigers 743 g, .241, 6 hr, 248 rbi.
   Manager 66 **Reds** 37–46, .446

Although he played 11 years as a ML infielder, Heffner's proudest moment came as a 19-year-old minor leaguer. He pitched for an all-star team of ML players against the Baltimore Black Sox, a top Negro team, and beat star pitcher Pud Flornoy 1–0 in a five-inning game. After several seasons as a Yankee utility man, he was a regular with the Browns for four years before WWII. /(JK)

Jim Hegan (Shanty) — 1920–1984. C 1941–42, 46–50 **Indians**, Tigers, Phillies, Giants, Cubs 1666 g, .228, 92 hr, 525 rbi. *2 WS, 10 g, .188, 1 hr, 5 rbi*
☛ *All-Star—47, 49–52.*

This superb defensive catcher spent more than a decade as a Cleveland regular, catching 20-game winners Feller, Lemon, Wynn, Garcia, Score, and Bearden. Although he hit 14 home runs in both 1948 and 1950, he never had a batting average

Jim Hegan

higher than .249. But Cleveland fans never booed the likable Hegan, no matter how low his average dropped. As Bill Dickey commented, "When you can catch like Hegan, you don't have to hit." Lithe, quick, and graceful, the durable Hegan was artful on pop-ups and balls in the dirt and was respected by baserunners. He received much of the credit for Cleveland's pitching success; fellow catcher Joe Tipton said, "Hitters who strike out against the Indians cuss Hegan." Hegan caught no-hitters by Don Black (7/10/1947), Bob Lemon (6/30/1948), and Bob Feller (7/1/1951). His catching was a key to the Indians' 1948 and 1954 pennants. When he retired in 1960, his 1,629 games caught was seventh on the all-time list. Mike Hegan is his son./(JCA)

Mike Hegan — 1942– . 1B-OF-DH 1964, 66–67, 69–77 Yankees, **Pilots/Brewers**, A's 965 g, .242, 53 hr, 229 rbi. *2 LCS, 4 g, .000. 2 WS, 9 g, .167*
☛ *All-Star—69.*

Hegan grew up shagging flies with dad Jim at Cleveland's Municipal Stadium, and came up only four years after his father's last season. Although in only five games with the 1964 Yankees, he appeared in the WS that year. In 1969 the strapping left-hander led Seattle with a .292 mark. A popular, all-out player, Hegan took pride in his defense; he set a ML record by playing 178 consecutive errorless games at first base from 1970 to 1973. He retired to become a Milwaukee broadcaster./(JCA)

Jack Heidemann — 1949– . SS-3B-2B 1969–72, 74–77 **Indians**, Cardinals, Mets, Brewers 426 g, .211, 9 hr, 75 rbi

Cleveland's first-round draft pick in 1967, Heidemann became the Indian shortstop in 1970 at age 20, but hit only .211. In two separate mishaps the next year, he suffered a concussion and a knee injury. After that he was limited to a utility role./(JCA)

Emmet Heidrick (Snags) — 1876–1916. OF 1898–1904, 08 Cleveland (NL), Cardinals, **Browns** 757 g, .300, 16 hr, 342 rbi

Heidrick was transferred from Cleveland to St. Louis after 1898 by Frank and Stanley Robison, who owned both teams. He stole 55 bases for the Cardinals in 1899, and in 1901 hit a career-high .339 as part of their all-.300 outfield./(WAB)

Harry Heilmann (Slug) — 1894–1951. OF-1B 1914, 16–30, 32 **Tigers**, Reds 2146 g, .342, 183 hr, 1551 rbi
☛ *Led League—ba 21, 23, 25, 27. Hall of Fame—52.*

Heilmann was a 6'1" 200-lb righthanded hitter who captured four American League batting titles in 15 seasons with the Tigers. Heilmann is among Detroit's all-time leaders in every major hitting category. He was working as a bookkeeper when he was offered his first baseball job. In 1913 he hit .305 for Portland (Northwest League) and was purchased by the Tigers for $1,500. He first joined Detroit in 1914, but stayed from 1916 through 1929, with only two gaps; he missed half of 1918 while on a Navy submarine, and several weeks of 1922 with a broken collarbone.

Harry Heilmann

A fair outfielder, Heilmann was moved to first base for 1919 and 1920 and led the AL in errors at that position both seasons. During the 1920s, he was a part of .300-hitting Tiger outfields in seven seasons. Joining him, at various times, were Hall of Famers Ty Cobb and Heinie Manush, and Detroit stars Bobby Veach and Bob Fothergill. Disgruntled pitcher Dutch Leonard wrote to Heilmann in December 1926, telling him of the two letters Leonard had sent to Ban Johnson implicating Joe Wood and Ty Cobb in betting on games. Heilmann showed the letter to Tigers owner Frank Navin and the story came out into the open.

Heilmann was involved in many close batting races. In 1921, he topped Ty Cobb by five points by hitting .394 with a league-high 237 hits. His .403 mark in 1923 bested Babe Ruth's .393. In 1925 he caught and passed Tris Speaker with a few games to go; he refused to come out of the lineup, and won the title, .393 to .389. He trailed Al Simmons by one point going into the last day of the 1927 season; in a doubleheader at Cleveland, he had four hits in the first game, and three in the second, finishing at .398—six points above Simmons.

Arthritis in his wrists began bothering Heilmann in 1929. He was sold to the Reds after the '29 season, but was unable to play in 1931. He came back as a player-coach in 1932, appearing in 15 games. Popular with fans and players, with a keen sense of humor and a trove of stories, he was the radio voice of the Tigers for 17 years. During WWII, he traveled to the Middle East as part of a baseball group entertaining troops. He died of lung cancer at age 56 in 1951, and was elected to the Hall of Fame the following year. /(NLM)

Fred Heimach (Lefty) — 1901-1973. LHP 1920-26, 28-33 **A's**, Red Sox, Yankees, Dodgers 1289 ip, 62-69, 4.46

Heimach helped himself. His fielding skill made him a "fifth infielder," and his .236 lifetime average included 52 pinch-hit appearances in which he hit .385. When a broken ankle finished him in 1933, he had run up a string of errorless games that went back to 1926, covering 171 chances. /(JK)

Don Heinkel — 1959- . RHP 1988- **Tigers**, Cardinals 63 ip, 1-1, 4.74

When Heinkel finally made the majors in 1988 with the Tigers as a relief pitcher, his season was interrupted for a month and a half by injury. Released at the end of the season, he was picked up by the Cardinals and was used as a starter in 1989 to fill in on their injury-prone staff. /(JFC)

Ken Heintzelman — 1915- . LHP 1937-42, 46-52 Pirates, **Phillies** 1502 ip, 77-98, 3.93. *1 WS, 8 ip, 1.17*

Twelve years after his ML debut, Heintzelman had sudden success in 1949 (17-10, 3.02) with a NL-high five shutouts and a nine-game winning streak for the Phillies. His son Tom was an infielder for the Cardinals and Giants in the 1970s. /(ME)

Bob Heise — 1947- . SS-2B-3B 1967-77 Mets, Giants, **Brewers**, Cardinals, Angels, Red Sox, Royals 499 g, .247, 1 hr, 86 rbi

Heise was a utility man his entire career. He hit .323 in his first call-up, a 62 at-bat stint, but never again hit higher than .268 in more than 10 at-bats and hit as low as .204. /(SFS)

Woodie Held [Woodson George] — 1932- . SS-OF-2B-3B 1954, 57-69 Yankees, A's, **Indians**, Senators, Orioles, Angels, White Sox 1390 g, .240, 179 hr, 559 rbi

As an outfielder with Kansas City in 1957, his rookie year, Held hit 20 HR. He was Cleveland's starting shortstop from 1959 through 1962. He hit a career-high 29 homers in 1959 and averaged 21 a year in six seasons with the Indians. He struck out often, nearly once in every four at-bats. Though easy-going off the field, he was notorious for his tantrums after striking out. A versatile and reliable fielder, he remained a valuable utility man after his days as a regular. /(JCA)

Al Helfer — 1912-1975. *Broadcaster.*

In 1935, while playing first base for Washington & Jefferson University, Helfer was offered a contract by Connie Mack, but he was set on a career in radio. During his career, he traveled five million miles and broadcast more Rose Bowl and WS games than anyone before or since. He worked on local broadcast teams in Pittsburgh, Cincinnati, Brooklyn, New York, and Oakland, and in 1950 began calling the Mutual Network's Game of the Day. He was also a television announcer on non-sports shows. "Red Barber and I were the first play-by-play team," he once claimed. "Before that, one man would do the first half of the game and then disappear. We interacted during the entire game." /(NLM)

Tommy Helms — 1941- . 2B-3B-SS-DH 1964-77 **Reds**, Astros, Pirates, Red Sox 1435 g, .269, 34 hr, 477 rbi. *1 LCS, 3 g, .273. 1 WS, 5 g, .222.*
Manager 1988- **Reds** 26-36, .419
☛ *Rookie of the Year—66. All-Star—67-68. Gold Glove—70-71.*

The NL Rookie of the Year in 1966 as a third baseman, Helms became one of the best second basemen of the 1960s. The excellent fielder led the NL in fielding percentage and double plays three times. Noted more as a hit-and-run man than a power hitter, he hit the first HR by a Red at Riverfront Stadium. Helms went to Houston with Lee May in the blockbuster November 1971 trade that brought Joe Morgan, Jack Billingham, and Cesar Geronimo to Cincinnati.

A longtime Reds coach, Helms filled in for manager Pete Rose during Rose's 30-day suspension in 1988 and replaced him after Rose was banned in 1989. /(GEB)

Roland Hemond (Rollie) — 1929- . *Executive.*

After a successful career as director of the Angels' farm system, 1961-70, developing such players as Clyde Wright and Jim Spencer, Hemond was hired in 1971 as director of player personnel by the White Sox (and later became GM) to reverse their fortunes. At the winter meetings that year, he moved 16 players within 18 hours. Chuck Tanner was brought in to manage, and the team won 23 more games than in 1970. Hemond traded for Dick Allen, who became the AL MVP in 1972. Richie Zisk, Rich Dotson, Rudy Law, and Bob James were just a few of his other productive acquisitions. Hemond was the architect of the 1983 Division Champions, for which he won UPI's Executive of the Year award. /(RL)

Charlie Hemphill (Eagle Eye) — 1876-1953. OF 1899, 1901-04, 06-11 Cleveland (NL), Cardinals, Red Sox, Indians, **Browns**, Yankees 1242 g, .271, 22 hr, 421 rbi

Hemphill was with the Cleveland Spiders when the best members of that team were transferred to St. Louis in 1899 by owners who controlled both teams at once. He managed the Yankees briefly when Hal Chase was ill, and later was a playing manager at Atlanta. His brother, Frank, played briefly for the White Sox and Senators. /(NLM)

Harry Hempstead — 1869-1938. *Executive.*

The son-in-law of John T. Brush, Hempstead took over the Giants in 1912 when Brush died, and ran the club until 1919, winning three pennants. He then sold the team to Charles A. Stoneham. /(NLM)

Rollie Hemsley [Ralston Burdett] — 1907-1972. C 1928-44, 46-47 Pirates, Cubs, Reds, **Browns**, Indians, Yankees, Phillies 1593 g, .262, 31 hr, 555 rbi. *1 WS, 3 g, .000*

Hemsley drank himself off four clubs before whipping alcoholism with the help of Alcoholics Anonymous. Early on, his speed was above average for a catcher. Platooned in Pittsburgh, he was traded to the Cubs in 1931 to back up Gabby Hartnett, and then to the Reds in 1933. Waived to the Browns in 1933, he became a top AL receiver, hitting .309 in 1934. Despite a .222 batting average in 1937, Cleveland traded three players to get him, and he handled the bulk of the Indians' catching chores in 1939 after an injury to Frank Pytlak. He caught Bob Feller's 1940 Opening Day no-hitter, and drove in the game's only run with a triple. He became a backup after his December 1941 sale to the Reds. Hemsley was *TSN* Minor League Manager of the Year in 1950 and 1963. /(ME)

Solly Hemus — 1923- . SS-2B-3B 1949-59 **Cardinals**, Phillies 969 g, .273, 51 hr, 263 rbi.
Manager 1959-61 **Cardinals** 190-192, .497

A consistent performer with a good eye at the plate, Hemus led the NL three times in HBP. Aided by 20 HBP and 96 walks in 1952, Hemus scored 105 runs to tie teammate Stan Musial for the NL lead. The regular Cardinals shortstop from 1951 through 1953, in 1954 Hemus batted a career-high .302.

Since 1959 there have been only five ML playing managers: Pete Rose, Frank Robinson, Joe Torre, Don Kessinger, and Hemus. As the Cardinals skipper in 1959, he played 24 games, mostly pinch hitting, as St. Louis finished seventh. In 1960 he managed the team to third place. With the Cardinals in sixth place midway through the 1961 season, Hemus was replaced. He later coached for the Mets and Indians. /(RTM)

Dave Henderson — 1958- . OF 1981- **Mariners**, Red Sox, Giants, A's 1078 g, .260, 127 hr, 474 rbi. *3 LCS, 14 g, .273, 3 hr, 9 rbi. 3 WS, 16 g, .345, 4 hr, 10 rbi*

The Red Sox acquired Henderson for their 1986 stretch run. He hit a two-out, two-run homer for Boston in the top of the ninth inning of Game Five of the 1986 LCS with the California Angels one strike away from their first World Series appearance. The game was won on Henderson's sacrifice fly in the 11th inning and also featured a home run by

Bobby Grich that popped out of Henderson's glove and over the outfield wall.

Traded to the Giants on September 1, 1987 to make room for rookie Ellis Burks, Henderson helped the Giants to a division title and then signed as a free agent with Oakland that winter. The centerfielder posted career-high totals of 24 homers, 38 doubles, 100 runs, 94 RBI, and a .304 batting average, (.051 above his previous career average) for the AL champion 1988 A's. In the 1989 WS, he hit home runs in consecutive innings in Game Three after just missing one in the first inning (a double off the railing).

Henderson was the Mariners' first pick in the 1977 free-agent draft. At the time of his trade to Boston, Henderson was Seattle's career leader in home runs and was tied for the team lead in extra-base hits. He is the nephew of Joe Henderson, a pitcher with the White Sox and Reds in the 1970s. /(TF)

Ken Henderson — 1946– . OF 1965–80 **Giants**, White Sox, Braves, Rangers, Mets, Reds, Cubs 1444 g, .257, 122 hr, 576 rbi. *1 LCS, 4 g, .313, 2 rbi*

Touted at 19 as Willie Mays's successor, Henderson was a regular in only four of his eight years with the Giants. He hit a career-high .294 with 17 home runs and 20 stolen bases as San Francisco's left fielder in 1970, but his average dropped the next two years and he was traded to the White Sox. Henderson was shocked by the trade, but recovered to hit .292 with 20 HR and 95 RBI for Chicago in 1974. /(FS)

Rickey Henderson (The Man of Steal, Style Dog) — 1957– . OF 1979– **A's**, Yankees 1472 g, .290, 138 hr, 561 rbi. *2 LCS, 8 g, .385, 2 hr, 6 rbi. 1 WS, 4 g, .474, 1 hr, 3 rbi*
☛ *All-Star—80, 82–88. Gold Glove—81.*

Baseball's most brilliant leadoff man came to quick prominence. The speedy switch-hitter set the AL season steal record with 100 in 1980, his second ML season. Responding to the leadership of manager Billy Martin (1980–82), Henderson's remarkable 130 steals in 1982 broke Lou Brock's ML record. The Martin-Henderson combination was reunited following a December 5, 1984 trade that sent Stan Javier and Jay Howell, Jose Rijo, Eric Plunk and Tim Birtsas to Oakland for Henderson and pitcher Bert Bradley. He returned to the A's in 1989, while in the last year of his contract, in return for Eric Plunk, Greg Cadaret, and Luis Polonia. The MVP of the 1989 LCS, he set a LCS (and postseason) record with eight steals and tied the LCS record for

Rickey Henderson

runs with eight. He hit .400, had a .609 on-base average, and led both teams with five RBI in the five-game series. He then hit .474 in the WS and led off Game Three with a HR as the A's swept the Giants.

In 1985 Henderson became the first AL player ever with a 20 homer-50 steal season (24, 80), a feat he repeated in 1986. He broke Bobby Bonds's career record for leadoff home runs (35) in 1989. Henderson has led the AL three times in runs scored, tied for the lead once, and scored 100 runs in nine seasons. His 146 runs scored in 1985 were the most in the majors since 1949 and his average of over a run scored per game was the best since 1939. Though teammate Don Mattingly won the 1985 AL MVP Award, Henderson may have been more valuable, scoring on 56 of Mattingly's 145 RBI. Rickey was a close second in the 1981 MVP voting, but a distant third in 1985.

A Gold Glove winner in 1981, Henderson moved from left field to centerfield in 1985, returning to left, which he preferred, in 1988. He became notorious for his snatch catch on easy fly balls, swatting his glove from over his head to his side. Henderson's 1985 achievements came despite missing the first 15 games of the season with a sprained ankle. Hamstring injuries (his "hammies," as he called them) slowed Henderson in 1987 and 1988. Already possessing the all-time stolen base records for the Yankees and the Oakland A's, Henderson seems certain to top Lou Brock's all-time career stolen base record. He had nearly twice as many steals as Brock over a comparable number of games. Henderson chose number 24 after his idol, Willie Mays. The ultimate leadoff hitter led the AL in steals in each of his first eight seasons with over 100 games played (1980–86, '88). His three singles in the 1982 All-Star game tied a record. /(ME)

Steve Henderson (Hendu) — 1952– . OF-DH 1977–88 **Mets**, Cubs, Mariners, A's, Astros 1085 g, .280, 68 hr, 428 rbi

Henderson was one of four young players the Reds traded to the Mets for Tom Seaver on June 15, 1977. Though he played in only 99 games that year, he led the last-place Mets with 65 RBI and lost by one vote to Andre Dawson in Rookie-of-the-Year balloting. His nine triples in 1978 tied a club record, and his .306 average in 1979 and .290 in 1980 led the Mets. Traded to the Cubs for Dave Kingman in 1981, he had one more solid season, hitting .294 with 32 doubles for the 1983 Mariners. /(JCA)

Bob Hendley — 1939– . LHP 1961–67 **Braves**, Giants, Cubs, Mets 879 ip, 48–52, 3.97

On September 9, 1965 Hendley one-hit the Dodgers for the Cubs, but opposing pitcher Sandy Koufax threw a perfect game for a 1–0 Dodger victory. Five days later, the two hurlers met again and Hendley pitched a four-hitter to beat Koufax, 2–1. /(RTM)

George Hendrick (Silent George) — 1949– . OF-1B 1971–88 A's, Indians, Padres, **Cardinals**, Pirates, Angels 2048 g, .278, 267 hr, 1111 rbi. *3 LCS, 11 g, .188, 2 rbi. 2 WS, 12 g, .256, 5 rbi*
☛ *All-Star—74–75, 80, 83.*

Hendrick gave credit to Joe Rudi for enabling him to become a complete player in Oakland. Hendrick had an easy style that seemed too casual to some, but he averaged 22 homers annually in four campaigns with Cleveland. Traded to San Diego, he responded with a .311 season. Hendrick blossomed with the Cardinals, reaching the .300 plateau three times while driving in over 100 twice. Although Silent George had long refused to speak to the press, he was well-liked by his teammates and the fans in St. Louis. He was a very capable right fielder and

later assumed duties at first base when Keith Hernandez was dealt. *TSN* awarded Hendrick Silver Slugger Awards at each position. /(FO)

Harvey Hendrick (Gink) — 1897–1941. 1B-OF-3B 1923–25, 27–34 Yankees, Indians, **Dodgers**, Reds, Cardinals, Cubs, Phillies 922 g, .308, 48 hr, 413 rbi. *1 WS, 1 g, .000*

The 6'2" Vanderbilt graduate played every position but catcher and pitcher. In his one full season at a single position, Hendrick led the NL with 18 errors and 147 double plays at first base for the 1931 Reds. He was traded frequently, as most teams found his poor defense outweighed his .300 bat. /(JK)

Ellie Hendricks [Elrod Jerome] — 1940– . C 1968–79 **Orioles**, Cubs, Yankees 711 g, .220, 62 hr, 230 rbi. *5 LCS, 10 g, .333, 1 hr, 5 rbi. 4 WS, 14 g, .238, 1 hr, 5 rbi*

Hendricks became famous in Game One of the 1970 World Series for a defensive play that he didn't really make. Attempting to tag out Bernie Carbo of the Reds in the sixth inning after Ty Cline hit a chopper in front of the plate, Hendricks collided with umpire Ken Burkhart while "tagging" Carbo with his mitt and holding the ball in his throwing hand. The bowled-over Burkhart couldn't see the play and called Carbo out. Hendricks had hit the game-tying HR in the previous inning. The next day, his two-run double in the fifth inning drove in the winning runs; he had four RBI in the Series.

The ever-smiling Hendricks was a favorite of Earl Weaver's for his steady fielding and because left-handed-hitting catchers were hard to come by. Twice Baltimore traded and reacquired him. Hendricks had back-to-back 12 HR seasons in 1969–70 while platooning with Andy Etchebarren, but never started more than 95 games in a season. The native Virgin Islander did lead AL catchers in fielding in 1969. His .250 average in 1971 was a career high. He spent much of the 1980s as the Orioles' bullpen coach. /(SH)

Jack Hendricks — 1875–1943. OF 1902–03 Giants, Cubs, **Senators** 42 g, .207, 0 hr, 4 rbi.
Manager 1918, 24–29 Cardinals, **Reds** 520–528, .496

After an undistinguished ML trial as an outfielder, Hendricks began managing in the minors in 1906. Beginning in 1910, he won three straight pennants with Denver in the Western League, then managed at Indianapolis in the American Association for four years. When Miller Huggins was fired by the Cardinals, Hendricks signed a two-year contract to replace him, finished last in 1918, and resigned to become athletic director for the Knights of Columbus. He went to France in 1919, then spent five more years as manager at Indianapolis. When Reds manager Pat Moran died in March of 1924, Hendricks took over the Cincinnati job. He finished second, only two games behind the Cardinals in 1926. Educated as a lawyer at North Christian University, he never practiced. /(NLM)

Claude Hendrix — 1889–1944. RHP 1911–20 Pirates, Chicago (FL), **Cubs** 2371 ip, 143–117, 2.65. 20 wins: 12, 14 *1 WS, 1 ip, 0.00*
Led League—w 14.

A 24-game-winner for the Pirates in 1912, Hendrix's best season came with the Chicago Whales of the Federal League in 1914, when he went 29–11 with a 1.69 ERA and led the league in wins, appearances, and complete games. He also batted .322 that season and was a lifetime .241 hitter, with 13 HR and 97 RBI. On May 15, 1915 he pitched a 10–0 no-hitter over Pittsburgh (FL). Following the Federal League's demise, Hendrix went to the Cubs in 1916. His 19–7 record tied for the league lead in winning percentage (.727) in 1918 and helped the Cubs capture the pennant. Hendrix's career ended under suspicious circumstances in February of 1921. The Cubs released him for having allegedly bet against his teammates in a game he was scheduled to pitch the previous August, but in which he was replaced at the last moment by Grover Alexander. /(AA)

Tim Hendryx — 1891–1957. OF 1911–12, 15–18, 20–21 Indians, **Yankees**, Browns, Red Sox 414 g, .276, 6 hr, 191 rbi

A depleted 1917 Yankee outfield afforded Hendryx his first regular major league job. Another OF spot opened up with the 1920 Red Sox when Babe Ruth was sold to New York, and Hendryx, filling in, batted .328. /(MG)

Tom Henke (The Terminator) — 1957– . RHP 1982- Rangers, **Blue Jays** 442 ip, 27–22, 2.81. *2 LCS, 9 ip, 2–0, 3.00*
All-Star—87.

One of the most overpowering relievers of the late 1980s, Henke combined a 95-mph fastball with an effective forkball to average more than a strikeout per inning. After appearing in 41 games over three seasons for the Rangers, Henke was selected by the Blue Jays as compensation when Texas signed free agent Cliff Johnson. He pitched impressively at Syracuse (International League) before being called up to Toronto on July 28, 1985. In his first month, Henke recorded eight saves; prior to 1985, the most saves by a Blue Jay reliever in an entire season was 11. Henke converted 13 of his 15 opportunities into saves in 1985, and by the time of the 1985 LCS, "The Ballad of Tom Henke" was being played over loudspeakers outside Exhibition Stadium.

In 1986 Henke's 27 saves set a new Blue Jay record, which he broke in 1987 with a league-leading 34. In 1987 Henke allowed fewer hits (5.9) and recorded more strikeouts (12.3) per nine innings than any other AL pitcher. /(TF)

Weldon Henley — 1880–1960. RHP 1903–05, 07 **A's**, Dodgers 32–43, 2.94

Henley pitched for Connie Mack's Athletics shortly after the turn of the century, posting his only winning record (12–9) in his first season. One of Henley's four victories in the 1905 season was a 6–0 no-hitter against the Browns on July 22. /(MA)

Butch Henline [Walter John] — 1894–1957. C-OF 1921–31 Giants, **Phillies**, Dodgers, White Sox 740 g, .291, 40 hr, 268 rbi.
Umpire NL 1945–48

The Phillies were roundly criticized for trading .300 hitter Irish Meusel to the Giants for an unproven rookie, but Henline became Philadelphia's most-used catcher from 1922 to 1926. In 1922 he batted a career-high .316 and led NL receivers in fielding. /(GB)

Mike Henneman — 1961– . RHP 1987- **Tigers** 278 ip, 31–13, 2.85. *1 LCS, 5 ip, 1–0, 10.80*
All-Star—89.

When Detroit reliever Guillermo Hernandez faltered in 1987, 6'4" rookie Mike Henneman took up the slack, going 11–3 with seven saves. He scored two wins and a save in the last four meetings with Toronto as the Tigers overtook the Blue Jays for the division title. *TSN* named Henneman AL Rookie Pitcher of the Year. He recorded 10 saves in the first month of the 1988 season before his arm tightened up. Disabled for a time, he finished at 9–6 (1.87) with 22 saves. He was 11–4 with a 3.70 ERA in 1989. /(JCA)

Phil Hennigan — 1946- . RHP 1969-73 **Indians**, Mets 281 ip, 17-14, 4.26

Hennigan's progress was delayed by a year in Vietnam, where he won a medal for valor. From 1970 through 1972, he posted winning records in relief for losing Cleveland clubs, and led the staff with 14 saves in 1971./(ME)

Pete Henning — 1887-1939. RHP 1914-15 **Kansas City (FL)** 345 ip, 14-28, 3.83

Henning's only major league experience came in the Federal League, where he went 6-12 and 8-16 and led the league in relief losses with 11 in 1914./(SFS)

Tommy Henrich (Old Reliable) — 1913- . OF-1B 1937-42, 46-50 **Yankees** 1284 g, .282, 183 hr, 795 rbi. *4 WS, 21 g, .262, 4 hr, 8 rbi*
☛ *All-Star—42, 47-50.*

Along with Joe DiMaggio and Charlie Keller, Henrich formed one of baseball's most acclaimed outfields for the Yankees before and after WWII. Commissioner Landis ruled Henrich a free agent in April 1937 after he had been illegally hidden in the Indians' farm system, and he signed with the Yankees, hitting .320 as a part-timer. He helped the team to six pennants, and although he played in only four WS because of injury and military service, he was a key figure in two of the most famous Series games. In 1941, he was the man whose third strike skipped past Mickey Owen, leading to a legendary Yankee rally. In 1949 he homered off Don Newcombe in the ninth inning of the first game to give Allie Reynolds a 1-0 victory.

An excellent fielder, Henrich lived up to his "Old Reliable" nickname with his bat, hitting 22 homers in 1938 and 31 in 1941. After the war, he had his greatest season statistically in 1948, leading the AL in triples and runs scored, and batting .308 with 25 homers and 100 RBI. But he was probably more valuable in 1949, when his consistent clutch hitting helped keep the injury-racked Yankees in the pennant race. In 115 games, he hit 24 homers, batted in 85, and scored 90. He finished sixth in the MVP voting./(MC)

Bill Henry — 1927- . LHP 1952-55, 58-69 Red Sox, Cubs, **Reds**, Giants, Pirates, Astros 913 ip, 46-50, 3.26. *1 WS, 2.1 ip, 0-0, 19.29*
☛ *All-Star—60.*

Henry blossomed as an outstanding lefthanded reliever in 1959, when he led NL pitchers with 65 appearances. In 1961, his 16 saves were instrumen-tal in helping the Reds win the National League pennant. He had five straight seasons in double figures in saves and retired with 90./(GB)

Dutch Henry [Frank John] — 1902-1968. LHP 1921-24, 27-30 Browns, Dodgers, **Giants**, White Sox 646 ip, 27-43, 4.39

The slender curveballer, primarily a reliever, had his career year for the 1927 Giants, with an 11-6 record and a league-high six wins out of the bullpen. Henry was handicapped by poor control./(FS)

Dwayne Henry — 1962- . RHP 1984- **Rangers**, Braves 78 ip, 3-6, 5.33

Henry looked promising in his 1985 call-up, when he was 2-2 with three saves and a 2.57 ERA. But after his 1986 season was interrupted by injury, he never had an ERA below 4.66 at any level./(SFS)

John Henry (Bull) — 1889-1941. C-1B 1910-18 **Senators**, Braves 683 g, .207, 2 hr, 171 rbi

Henry was Walter Johnson's catcher during the pitcher's peak years. A smart baseball man, this Amherst alumnus subsequently coached at Cornell before becoming a minor league umpire./(JK)

Roy Henshaw — 1911- . LHP 1933, 35-38, 42-44 **Cubs**, Dodgers, Cardinals, Tigers 742 ip, 33-40, 4.16

Henshaw's best record was 13-5 for the Cubs in his second year. In 1937 he went from Brooklyn to the Cardinals in the trade for Leo Durocher./(GEB)

Ron Herbel — 1938- . RHP 1963-71 **Giants**, Padres, Mets, Braves 894 ip, 42-37, 3.82

The powerfully-built Herbel was a part-time starter who won a career-high 12 games with the 1965 Giants. Hampered by arm problems, he pitched mostly in long relief, leading the NL in 1970 with 76 appearances and nine relief wins for the Padres and Mets. He was the worst-hitting pitcher ever (minimum 100 at-bats), batting a mere .029 (6-for-206)./(FS)

Ray Herbert — 1929- . RHP 1950-51, 53-55, 58-66 Tigers, A's, White Sox, Phillies 1881 ip, 104-107, 4.01. 20 wins: 62
☛ *All-Star—62.*

In his tenth ML season, with the White Sox in 1962, the durable Herbert went 20-9 for a league-leading .690 winning percentage. Though he dropped to 13-10 in 1963, his seven shutouts led the AL. Herbert gave up Carl Yastrzemski's first base hit, in 1961, and holds Kansas City Athletic records for most innings, most earned runs, and most games lost. /(GB)

Babe Herman [Floyd Caves] — 1903–1987. OF-1B 1926–37, 45 **Dodgers**, Reds, Cubs, Pirates, Tigers 1552 g, .324, 181 hr, 997 rbi

As the lefthanded-batting Herman put it, "I wasn't the world's greatest fielder, as a lot of stories will attest, but I was always a pretty fair country hitter." Having led the NL in errors in consecutive seasons

Babe Herman

(at first base in 1927, outfield in 1928), Herman often had to deny having once been hit on the head by a fly ball.

Only he and Bob Meusel have hit for the cycle three times. The .393 batting average (second to Bill Terry's .401), 416 total bases, 241 hits, and 143 runs he amassed in 1930 still stand as Dodger records. He also reached a high of 35 HR in 1930, and, with the Reds in 1932, led the NL with 19 triples. On July 10, 1935 at Cincinnati, he hit the first home run in a night game. The "headless horseman of Ebbets Field," as Dazzy Vance called Herman, once "tripled" into a double play (Herman got a double on the play), as three Dodgers wound up on third base, leading to the greatest of all the "Daffiness Boys" quips: "The Dodgers have three men on base." "Oh yeah, which base?"/(TG)

Billy Herman [William Jennings Bryan] (Bryan) — 1909– . 2B-3B 1931–47 **Cubs**, Dodgers, Braves, Pirates 1922 g, .304, 47 hr, 839 rbi. *4 WS, 18 g, .242, 1 hr, 7 rbi.*
  Manager 1947, 64–66 Pirates, **Red Sox** 189–274, .408
☛ *All-Star—34–43. Hall of Fame—75.*

Herman was the finest National League second baseman of the 1930s and early 1940s. He batted more than .300 eight times in his 15-year career, and scored at least 100 runs five times. His top years came as a Cub. In 1935 he led the NL with 227 hits and 57 doubles, and reached career highs with a .341 average and 113 runs scored. His 18 triples in 1939 led the league.

A starter at 2B from 1932 to 1943, in several seasons he played in every one of his team's games. He tied the NL record at 2B for most years leading in putouts (seven). He led the NL in 2B assists three times, errors four times, and fielding average three times. On June 28, 1933 he tied the ML record for most 2B putouts in a doubleheader (16), and tied the NL record for most 2B putouts in a game (11); an acknowledged master at playing the hitters, that season he set the NL season record for putouts (466). He appeared in 10 All-Star games, batting .433 (13-for-30). A member of three Cubs pennant-winners, he led all participants in the 1935 World Series with six RBI. After a slow start in 1941, he was traded to the Dodgers for two mediocrities and $65,000, supposedly because Cub manager Jimmie Wilson saw Herman as a threat to his job.

Kirby Higbe, a teammate in Chicago and Brooklyn, said that Herman "stood out at second base over any other second baseman I ever saw . . . he was the greatest hit-and-run man in baseball then or now." Leo Durocher agreed, saying Herman was

Billy Herman

". . . universally accepted as the classic number-two hitter . . . an absolute master at hitting behind the runner."

Herman managed extensively in the minors, coached for the Dodgers, Braves, Red Sox, Angels, and Padres, and also scouted. He managed the 1947 Pirates for all but the last game of the season; winning the season finale under replacement Bill Burwell, they moved into a tie for seventh place. Herman took over the Red Sox in October 1964 and lasted through 146 games of 1966, never finishing higher than eighth. /(JJM)

Gene Hermanski — 1920– . OF 1943, 46–53 Dodgers, Cubs, Pirates 739 g, .272, 46 hr, 259 rbi. *2 WS, 11 g, .219, 3 rbi*

Hermanski batted .295 for the 1948–50 Dodgers, but his fielding deficiencies kept him from being a regular outfielder. In 1948 he hit a career-high 15

home runs—three coming in consecutive at-bats in an August 5 game. /(JJM)

Enzo Hernandez — 1949– . SS 1971–78 **Padres**, Dodgers 714 g, .224, 2 hr, 113 rbi

Acquired from the Orioles, Hernandez was installed as a Padres regular in 1971 and led NL shortstops with 33 errors. He had only 12 RBI in 549 times at bat. More or less the regular through 1976, he improved his defense but never hit well. Only in 1976 did his RBI outnumber his stolen bases (24 to 12). /(MC)

Jackie Hernandez — 1940– . SS-3B 1965–73 Angels, Twins, **Royals**, Pirates 618 g, .208, 12 hr, 121 rbi. *1 LCS, 4 g, .231, 1 rbi. 1 WS, 7 g, .222, 1 rbi*

Originally signed as a catcher, the Cuban native was converted to shortstop. In 1965, he was voted the best-throwing shortstop in the Pacific Coast League. In the 1971 WS, Hernandez fielded flawlessly for the Pirates. /(RTM)

Keith Hernandez (Mex) — 1953- . 1B 1974-
Cardinals, Mets 2045 g, .298, 161 hr, 1063 rbi. *3 LCS, 16 g, .281, 1 hr, 9 rbi. 2 WS, 14 g, .245, 1 hr, 12 rbi*
☛ *Most Valuable Player—79. Led League—ba 79. All-Star—79-80, 84, 86-87. Gold Glove—78-88.*

Hernandez was indisputably the best-fielding first baseman of his time, winning eleven straight Gold Gloves and setting major league records for most seasons leading league first basemen in double plays (six) and lifetime assists by a first baseman. He revived Ferris Fain's practice of charging to the third base line on bunts and made the technique his own; trying for the force in such situations is usually a risky proposition, but Hernandez's judgment was rarely wrong. His great range helped him lead NL first basemen in assists five times, putouts four times, and fielding average twice. Twice he tied for

Keith Hernandez

the lead in errors with 13; it is the lowest total ever to lead the NL, and he never made more errors than that in a season.

Hernandez led the NL in batting in 1979 with the Cardinals, winning the only shared MVP award in history that year (Willie Stargell was the other recipient) as well as *TSN* NL Player of the Year. He also had career highs with 48 doubles and 116 runs, both league-leading totals, and 105 RBI. His .344 BA, also a career high, marked the first time he had hit .300; he went on to top .300 five other times. But while with the Cardinals, he had a reputation as a carefree, unintense player. Manager Whitey Herzog traded him to the last-place Mets for journeyman relief pitcher Neil Allen in mid-1983 after becoming convinced that Hernandez was using drugs. When Herzog defended the trade by hinting as much, Hernandez threatened a libel suit, but the 1985 Pittsburgh drug trials revealed it was true.

With the Mets, it seemed that Hernandez was trying to live down his old reputation. From the first day, he was the team's most intense player. Usually the Mets' number-three hitter, he became a great clutch hitter who worked the count and fouled off pitches until he got the offering he wanted. In the short lifetime of the game-winning RBI as an official statistic, he set ML records for most in a season (24 in 1985) and most lifetime (129). Always selective, he led the NL with 94 walks in 1986. His on-base percentage was above .400 seven times during his career, and he led the league in 1979 and 1980. His clubhouse leadership was acknowledged in 1987, when he was named the team captain. It was his last good season. After missing much of 1988 (hamstring troubles) and 1989 (knee problems), he was released. /(SH)

Ramon Hernandez — 1940- . LHP 1967-68, 71-77 Braves, Cubs, **Pirates**, Red Sox 430 ip, 23-15, 3.03. *3 LCS, 8 ip, 0-1, 3.24*

First signed in 1959, the sidearming screwballer peaked with the Pirates, teaming with righthander Dave Giusti to give Pittsburgh an exceptional bullpen from 1972-75. The Puerto Rican-born reliever was brilliant in 1972 (5-0, 1.67, 14 saves). /(ME)

Willie Hernandez [Guillermo Villanueva] — 1954- . LHP 1977- Cubs, Phillies, **Tigers** 1045 ip, 70-63, 3.38. *2 LCS, 4 ip, 0-0, 4.08. 2 WS, 9 ip, 0-0, 0.96*
☛ *Most Valuable Player—84. Cy Young Award—84. All-Star—84-86.*

Willie Hernandez was a fine, but unsung, reliever until 1984. He had been among the NL leaders in appearances with the Cubs in 1982 and the Cubs and Phillies in 1983. Traded to Detroit March 24, 1984, Hernandez quickly became manager Sparky Anderson's stopper. His phenomenal season (9–3, 1.92, 32 saves in 33 chances, 80 games, 112 strikeouts in 140 innings) earned both the MVP and Cy Young awards. He appeared in every non-complete postseason game for Detroit, with three saves in as many chances. In 1985 he became the first Tiger with back-to-back 30-save seasons, but he lost 10 games and gradually fell into disfavor with the fans. Stating a preference to be called Guillermo (his given first name), the mustachioed screwballer took a back seat to Mike Henneman in Detroit's bullpen in 1987 and 1988. /(ME)

Larry Herndon — 1953– . OF-DH 1974, 76–88 Cardinals, Giants, **Tigers** 1537 g, .273, 107 hr, 550 rbi. *2 LCS, 5 g, .286, 1 hr, 3 rbi. 1 WS, 5 g, .333, 1 hr, 3 rbi*

Herndon was *TSN* NL Rookie Player of the Year as the Giants' centerfielder in 1976, hitting .288 in 337 at-bats. His batting average fell as his playing time increased in San Francisco, and he was traded to the Tigers after the 1981 season. In cozy Tiger Stadium Herndon found his home run stroke, belting a career-high 23 (including three in one game May 18) in 1982 and 20 more in 1983. In 1987, platooning against lefthanded pitchers, he hit a career-high .324. /(SCL)

Eddie Herr — 1872–1943. *Scout.*

Herr was a minor league pitcher and manager who joined the Cardinals as a scout in 1913, and also scouted for the Tigers, Yankees, and Indians. He secured Bill Doak for the Cardinals and Bill Dickey for the Yankees, and unsuccessfully tried to get Carl Hubbell a tryout with the Tigers. /(FVP)

Tom Herr — 1956– . 2B 1979– **Cardinals**, Twins 1262 g, .275, 22 hr, 493 rbi. *3 LCS, 16 g, .262, 1 hr, 9 rbi. 3 WS, 21 g, .190, 1 hr, 6 rbi*
☛ *All-Star—85.*

Herr took over as St. Louis's second baseman in 1980. With Ozzie Smith, he formed one of the best double play combinations in baseball, three times leading the NL in twin killings. He made only six errors at second base in 1984, nine in 1986, and seven in 1987. Not known for power, the selective switch-hitter did not get his first home run until his 337th major league game. Nonetheless, his speed and ability to make contact made him an excellent third-place hitter, especially in Busch Stadium with its distant fences and Astroturf. In 1981 and 1982 he did not go hitless more than two games in a row

and in 1985 and 1986 he led Cardinals batters in RBI. He drove in 110 runs in 1983, becoming only the seventh second baseman in history to reach the century mark.

Herr was traded to the Twins for Tom Brunansky early in the 1988 season and was a disappointment for Minnesota. They traded him to the Phillies for Shane Rawley after the season. /(FO)

Pancho Herrera — 1934– . 1B-2B-3B 1958, 60–61 Phillies 300 g, .271, 31 hr, 128 rbi

In 1960 the 6'3" 220-lb Cuban set a NL record for a 154-game season by striking out 136 times. He led NL first basemen in assists and tied for the lead in errors that year. /(GEB)

Art Herring (Sandy) — 1907– . RHP 1929–34, 39, 44–47 **Tigers**, Dodgers, White Sox, Pirates 698 ip, 34–38, 4.32

The wiry, 5'7" Herring was at his best in relief. After his first ML tour, he slipped back to the minors. He resurfaced with Brooklyn at age 37, during the war-caused player shortage, to have his best seasons. /(EW)

Ed Herrmann — 1946– . C 1967, 69–78 **White Sox**, Yankees, Angels, Astros, Expos 922 g, .240, 80 hr, 320 rbi
☛ *All-Star—74.*

Herrmann was a hard working White Sox catcher in the early 1970s, gutsy in blocking the plate and knocking down Wilbur Wood's knuckleballs. Thanks mainly to Wood, Herrmann led the AL in passed balls four times. Although his batting averages were generally low, he had some power. In 1970, when he hit a career-high .283 with 19 homers in 96 games, he spent his bench time during home games in the bullpen helping restore a 1929 Ford. After infrequent Chicago victories, he'd delight fans by riding the smoking "Big White Machine" around the park. His grandfather Marty pitched for the Dodgers in 1918. /(DB)

Garry Herrmann [August] — 1859–1931. *Executive.*

Herrmann was president of the Cincinnati Reds from 1902 until illness forced his retirement in 1927. He began as a printer's devil and acquired the nickname "Garibaldi," later shortened to "Garry," but rose to a position of prominence through Cincinnati ward politics. In addition to his duties as Reds president, Herrmann served as president of the National Commission, the governing body of major league baseball, from its creation in 1903 until 1920. Sometimes called "The Father of the World

Series," he was influential in reestablishing the event in 1905 after the Giants had refused to participate in 1904. /(BC)

Mike Hershberger — 1939- . OF 1961–71 White Sox, **A's**, Brewers 1150 g, .252, 26 hr, 344 rbi

Quick and strong-armed, Hershberger was called up to the White Sox in late 1961 and hit .309 down the stretch. Once he became a regular, however, his hitting tailed off. His .279 in 1963 was his career best for any season as a regular. Despite his so-so bat, his defensive ability kept him in the majors for eleven seasons. He led AL outfielders with 17 assists in 1967. /(MC)

Willard Hershberger — 1910–1940. C 1938–40 **Reds** 160 g, .316, 0 hr, 70 rbi. *1 WS, 3 g, .500*

Hershberger's suicide during the 1940 season ended a frustrated career. A farmhand in the player-rich Yankee system, he shared a catching future with Buddy Rosar, judged the better defensive player. Bill Dickey was the Yankee catcher, a lefthanded hitter. Both Hershberger and Rosar were righthanded, and Rosar was chosen as Dickey's backup. Hershberger was sold to Cincinnati, and had to settle in behind another future Hall of Fame catcher, Ernie Lombardi. /(JK)

Orel Hershiser (Bulldog) — 1958- . RHP 1983- **Dodgers** 1457 ip, 98–64, 2.69. 20 wins: 88 *2 LCS, 40 ip, 2–0, 2.03. 1 WS, 18 ip, 2–0, 1.00* ☛ *Led League—w 88. Cy Young Award—88. All-Star—87–89. Gold Glove—88.*

No pitcher ever finished a season the way Hershiser finished 1988. After pitching five consecutive shut-outs, the sinkerballer broke former Dodger Don Drysdale's record 58-inning scoreless streak by one with a ten-inning scoreless, no-decision effort in his final start of the season at San Diego. With his eight shutout innings in the LCS opener against the Mets, he went 67 innings without being scored upon. He picked up a save against the Mets in Game Four the day after a start, finished the Mets off with a shutout in Game Seven, and followed with another against the A's in the WS en route to becoming the first NL player to win the MVP in both postseason series. In the one WS game he batted in (Game Two), he went 3-for-3 with two doubles, a run, and an RBI while surrendering only three hits, all to Dave Parker.

Hershiser averaged 15 wins a season in the four years prior to 1988, and was 19–3, 2.03 in 1985, including an 11–0, 1.08 record at Dodger Stadium.

In 1989 lack of support left him with a 15–15 record despite a 2.31 ERA, second-best in the NL.

Nicknamed Bulldog by Dodger manager Tom Lasorda, the devoutly religious Hershiser has said, "You don't have to be a wimp to be a Christian." He played defense and left wing for the Philadelphia Flyers' Junior A hockey team. He is the fourth in his family to bear the name Orel, and his son is the fifth. /(TG)

Buck Herzog [Charles Lincoln] — 1885–1953. 2B-3B-SS 1908–20 **Giants**, Braves, Reds, Cubs 1493 g, .259, 20 hr, 445 rbi. *4 WS, 25 g, .245, 6 rbi.* *Manager* 1914–16 **Reds** 165–226, .422

Giants manager John McGraw traded away the aggressive Herzog three times. The second trade, in 1913, came after Herzog played third base on three straight Giants pennant winners and hit .400 in the 1912 WS. McGraw brought Herzog back a third time, and in 1917, Herzog was on another New York pennant-winner, this time playing second base. The much-traveled University of Maryland graduate found an appropriate second career as the general athletic passenger agent for the B&O Railroad. /(JK)

Whitey Herzog [Dorrel Norman Elvert] (The White Rat) — 1931- . OF 1956–63 Senators, A's, **Orioles**, Tigers 634 g, .257, 25 hr, 172 rbi. *Manager* 1973, 75- Rangers, Royals, **Cardinals** 1248–1078, .537. First place: 76–78, 82, 85, 87 *6 LCS, 16–14, .533. 3 WS, 10–11, .476*

Affectionately called The White Rat, Herzog has earned respect in baseball for his superb managerial skills. He has had five division winners and one World Champion (the 1982 Cardinals). Herzog was named Manager of the Year in 1976 by UPI, and in 1982 by *TSN* and UPI. He was also voted Manager of the Year by the BBWAA in 1985 for leading St. Louis to the NL pennant. In 1981 and 1982, when he was also GM, the UPI named him Executive of the Year as well. He is one of 37 managers to collect over 1,000 victories. Columnist Larry King says, "Every game is like a chess match with Whitey, and other managers must feel like they are playing against 10 guys when they go up against him."

Signed by the Yankees out of high school, Herzog reported to McAlester in the Sooner State League in 1949. It was there that sportscaster Bill Speith nicknamed the chunky spray hitter Whitey for his light-colored hair. As a member of the Athletics in 1960, Herzog hit into an all-Cuban triple play

Whitey Herzog

against Washington. The Senators involved were pitcher Camilio Pascual, first baseman Julio Becquer, and shortstop Jose Valdivelso. /(RTM)

Joe Hesketh (Fungo) — 1959- . LHP 1984- **Expos** 433 ip, 28-19, 3.37

Teammates dubbed Hesketh Fungo because his 6'2" 170-lb build reminded them of the long, thin bat. The American Association Pitcher of the Year for 1984 (12-3), in his ML debut that August he was called for a balk before ever throwing a pitch. He was 10-5 in 1985 before fracturing his shin in a collision with Dodger catcher Mike Scioscia, and in 1986 he underwent surgery for an impinged shoulder nerve. He returned to Montreal as a reliever late in 1987. /(JCA)

Otto Hess — 1878-1926. LHP-OF 1902, 04-08, 12-15 **Indians**, Braves 1418 ip, 70-90, 2.98; 279 g, .215, 5 hr, 58 rbi. 20 wins: 06

Hess was born in Berne, Switzerland, and reached the majors after serving with the army in the Philippines. He was unhittable at times, erratic at

others, and had a reputation for having one bad inning in each game. He had one big season, going 20-17 for Cleveland in 1906. /(NLM)

Johnny Hetki — 1922- . RHP 1945-48, 50, 52-54 **Reds**, Browns, Pirates 525 ip, 18-26, 4.39

After spending parts of five seasons with the Reds, in 1951 Hetki went 19-10 for Toronto (International League). He was the relief ace of the 1953-54 last-place Pirates. /(ME)

Ed Heusser (The Wild Elk of the Wasatch) — 1900-1956. RHP 1935-36, 38, 40, 43-46, 48 Cardinals, Phillies, A's, **Reds** 1087 ip, 56-57, 3.69
☛ Led League—era 44.

The Utah native was generally a reliever until 1944 when, as a Reds' starter, he led the NL with a 2.38 ERA. A switch hitter, it was said Heusser could also throw with either arm, and may have in the minors. /(EW)

Joe Heving — 1900-1970. RHP 1930-31, 33-34, 37-45 Giants, White Sox, **Indians**, Red Sox, Braves 1038 ip, 76-48, 3.90

The brother of catcher Johnnie Heving, Joe was a sinkerballer who led his league three times in relief wins and twice in relief losses. In 1944 he was the only grandfather playing ML baseball, but still topped the AL with 63 appearances for Cleveland, and had a career-best 1.96 ERA. Heving finished in 1945 with 63 lifetime saves. /(GEB)

Johnnie Heving — 1896-1968. C 1920, 24-25, 28-32 Browns, **Red Sox**, A's 398 g, .265, 1 hr, 89 rbi. *1 WS, 1 g, .000*

Heving was winding up his major league career as a non-power hitting backup catcher as his younger brother Joe, a ML reliever, was breaking in with the Giants. /(EW)

John A. Heydler — 1869-1956. *Executive. Umpire* 1895-98 NL

Heydler was a government printer in Washington in the 1880s. His interest in baseball led him into umpiring and later sportswriting. He became secretary to NL president Harry Pulliam and became interim president after Pulliam's suicide. He became secretary-treasurer under president John K. Tener, and succeeded Tener as NL president in 1918. Heydler was not very energetic in investigating scandal or in opposing league owners, but he was innovative in his thinking. He supported the selection of Judge Kenesaw Landis as Commissioner of

Baseball in 1920, helped establish the Baseball Hall of Fame, and proposed the designated hitter as early as 1929. After resigning as president in 1934, he served as NL chairman of the board until his death. /(NLM)

Jack Hiatt — 1942- . C-1B 1964-72 Angels, **Giants**, Expos, Cubs, Astros 483 g, .251, 22 hr, 154 rbi

A second-string catcher and fill-in first baseman with the Giants in 1968, Hiatt figured in Don Drysdale's record scoreless inning streak. When Dick Dietz flied out after being refused first base despite being hit by a pitch with the bases loaded, Hiatt followed by popping up for the last out of Drysdale's fifth straight shutout. /(GEB)

Kevin Hickey — 1956- . LHP 1981-83, 89 **White Sox**, Orioles 192 ip, 7-11, 3.38

Hickey was a softball pitcher signed out of a public tryout by the White Sox in 1978. Arm trouble interrupted his career after three years, but he made a successful comeback with the 1989 Orioles. His herky-jerky motion made him effective in both long and short relief. /(RL)

Jim Hickman — 1937- . OF-1B-3B 1962-74 Mets, Dodgers, **Cubs**, Cardinals 1421 g, .252, 159 hr, 560 rbi
☛ All-Star—70.

This original New York Met was both the first member of the franchise to hit for the cycle (8/7/63) and the first to hit three home runs in a game (9/3/65). During his first seven ML seasons Hickman was considered a clumsy outfielder whose occasional power insufficiently compensated for frequent strikeouts. The Cubs acquired him from the Dodgers in 1968, and he batted a paltry .223. On August 1, 1969, he was down to .216 on the first-place Cubs. While his teammates faltered in the stretch, Hickman came off the bench to hit .301 for August, with 10 HR and 25 RBI. He kept hitting well the next year with a .315 average, 32 HR, 115 RBI, and 13 game-winning hits. In the 1970 All-Star Game, his 12th-inning single drove in Pete Rose for the game-winning run. He was slowed in ensuing years by various ailments. /(AA)

Piano Legs Hickman (Charles) — 1876-1934. 1B-OF-2B-3B Braves, Giants, Red Sox, **Indians**, Tigers, Senators, White Sox 1,080 g, .301, 59 hr, 614 rbi

An early slugger, Hickman was the first player to lead a league while playing for two teams (Boston and Cleveland) with 194 in 1902. That year, he approached a triple crown season when he was second in the AL home runs (11) and RBI (110), and

third in BA (.363). On June 30, 1902 Nap Lajoie, Hickman, and Bill Bradley became the first trio to hit consecutive home runs in this century. With the 1900 Giants, he set an NL record for errors by a third baseman with 91, after which he was usually stationed in the outfield or at first base. His nickname described his massive limbs which supported his 5'9" 215-lb frame. /(ME)

Kirby Higbe [Walter Kirby] — 1915-1985. RHP 1937-43, 46-50 Cubs, Phillies, **Dodgers**, Pirates, Giants 1952 ip, 118-101, 3.69. 20 wins: 41 *1 WS, 4 ip, 0-0, 7.36*
☛ Led League—w 41. Led League—k 40. All-Star—40, 46.

The title of Higbe's autobiography, *The High Hard One*, describes his pitching style. He led the NL in walks four times (1939-41 and '47). He also led with 137 strikeouts in 1940. After he went 14-19 for the last-place Phillies in 1940, both the Giants and Dodgers were after the young flamethrower. Brooklyn's Larry MacPhail snatched Higbe by giving the financially troubled Phillies $100,000 and three players in return. Higbe was worth the price, joining teammate Whit Wyatt atop the NL with 22 wins in 1941 and leading the league with 48 games and 39 starts for the NL champs.

Higbe was ambivalent concerning the addition of Jackie Robinson to the Dodgers. Higbe had spent many hours throwing rocks at blacks while growing up in South Carolina, and he believed in segregation, telling Branch Rickey he preferred not to have to play with a "negruh." But Higbe's competitive nature made him respect the fiery Robinson. He didn't have to worry about Robinson for long; he was traded to Pittsburgh on May 3, 1947. /(ME)

Dennis Higgins — 1939- . RHP 1966-72 White Sox, **Senators**, Indians, Cardinals 410 ip, 22-23, 3.42

Higgins had a herky-jerky motion and a live fastball, and was among the AL's best relievers during his two years with the Senators. In 1968 he was 4-4 with 13 saves, and he finished third in the 1969 Fireman of the Year balloting with a 10-9 record and 16 saves. /(JCA)

Pinky Higgins [Michael Franklin] — 1909-1969. 3B 1930, 33-44, 46 A's, Red Sox, **Tigers** 1802 g, .292, 141 hr, 1075 rbi. *2 WS, 14 g, .271, 1 hr, 8 rbi.*
 Manager 1955-62 **Red Sox** 543-541, .501
☛ All-Star—34, 36, 44.

Signed out of the University of Texas, for a dozen years Higgins was a hard-hitting, steady-fielding third baseman. Especially dangerous with men on base, he twice drove in 106 runs. Higgins set a ML record when he hit safely in 12 consecutive at-bats in 1938. He hit .333 in the 1940 World Series with the Tigers and handled a record ten chances at third base in Game Four. After playing in all seven games of the 1946 WS with the Red Sox, Higgins retired.

A low-key approach and patience with young players made Higgins a popular manager in the minors and later with the Red Sox. In 1955, his first of eight seasons managing Boston, he was named *TSN* Manager of the Year. His best showings were third-place finishes in 1957–58. Higgins also served as Red Sox vice president and GM, and later was an Astro scout. /(JL)

Andy High (Handy Andy) — 1897–1981. 3B-2B-SS 1922–34 **Dodgers**, Braves, Cardinals, Reds, Phillies 1314 g, .284, 44 hr, 482 rbi. *3 WS, 9 g, .294, 1 rbi*

The best of the three lefthanded-hitting High brothers played in the daffier days of Wilbert Robinson's Dodgers and was dubbed "Handy Andy" for his competent versatility. The Cards used him mostly at third base, and he was with them for pennants in 1928, '30, and '31. In only three seasons did he appear in over 100 games at a single position. /(JK)

Hugh High (Bunny, Lefty) — 1887–1962. OF 1913–18 Tigers, **Yankees** 504 g, .250, 3 hr, 123 rbi

Oldest of the three High brothers, Hugh couldn't break into the Tiger outfield of Cobb, Sam Crawford, and Bob Veach. He was a regular with the Yankees for three years. /(JK)

Dick Higham — 1851–1905. OF 1871–76, 78, 80 New York (NA), Lord Baltimores (NA), Chicago (NA), **Hartford (NL)**, Providence (NL), Troy (NL) *NA: 239 g, .288; ML: 130 g, .323, 1 hr, 64 rbi.*
Umpire NL 1881–82

Higham was the only ML umpire ever dismissed for cheating. When he was a hard-hitting outfielder in the National Association and early NL, the English-born Higham was the subject of rumors that his play was not always on the level. Even though he led the NL in doubles in 1876 and 1878 and in runs scored in '78, his reputation for shady dealings curtailed his ML career. Nevertheless, the NL hired him as an umpire after his playing days ended, apparently because he had sometimes umpired in the NA. In 1882 William Thompson, the mayor of Detroit and president of the Wolverines baseball team, became convinced that Higham was consistently calling close decisions against Detroit. Thompson hired a private detective who turned up a letter that Higham had mailed to a well-known gambler in which he

outlined a simple telegram code on how and when to bet. "Buy all the lumber you can!" meant bet on Detroit. No telegram meant bet against them. Thompson and the other owners confronted Higham and he was banished from baseball. Reportedly, the crooked ump went back to Chicago and became a bookkeeper. /(RTM)

Ted Higuera — 1958– . LHP 1985– **Brewers** 1085 ip, 78–44, 3.28. 20 wins: 86
☛ *All-Star—86.*

Signed by the Brewers after a great year at Juarez in the Mexican League (league leader in wins, complete games, innings pitched and strikeouts), Higuera posted the best rookie record in the Milwaukee club's history (15–8), finished second in Rookie of the Year balloting, and was *TSN* AL Rookie Pitcher of the Year in 1985. The following season, Higuera became Milwaukee's first 20-game winner of the 1980s (and the first Mexican-born 20-game winner, beating Fernando Valenzuela by a matter of days) and finished second in the Cy Young Award voting. His 240 strikeouts in 1987 were the most by any Milwaukee pitcher, surpassing Tony Cloninger's 211 with the 1965 Braves. /(ME)

George Hildebrand — 1878–1960. OF 1902 **Dodgers** 11 g, .220, 0 hr, 5 rbi.
Umpire AL 1912–34 4 WS

Some historians credit Hildebrand with inventing the spitball. Supposedly, while playing catch as a minor league outfielder in 1902, he discovered what a ball dampened by dew on the grass could do. Subsequently, he taught the pitch to Elmer Stricklett, who taught it to Ed Walsh. Of all his calls in 23 years as a ML umpire, the most controversial came in Game Two of the 1922 WS between the Giants and Yankees when he stopped play because of darkness in the 10th inning of a 3–3 tie. He was criticized at the time by many who believed the game could have been continued for several more innings. Commissioner Landis, sensitive to WS scandal two years after the Black Sox, turned the game receipts over to charity. /(RTM)

Oral Hildebrand — 1907–1977. RHP 1931–40 **Indians**, Browns, Yankees 1430 ip, 83–78, 4.35. *1 WS, 4 ip, 0–0, 0.00*
☛ *All-Star—33.*

The rangy righthander was a star basketball player at Butler University before turning to baseball. His best season, (16–11, 3.76) in 1933 with the Indians, earned him a spot on the AL's first All-Star Game roster./(ME)

Tom Hilgendorf — 1942– . LHP 1969–70, 72–75 Cardinals, **Indians**, Phillies 313 ip, 19–14, 3.04

After a decade spent mostly in the minors, the father of six led the Indians 1973 bullpen with six saves in 48 appearances. In 1975 with Philadelphia, the forkballer had his best and last ML season, 7–3 with a 2.13 ERA./(JCA)

Carmen Hill (Specs, Bunker) — 1895– . RHP 1915–16, 18–19, 22, 26–30 **Pirates**, Giants, Cardinals 787 ip, 49–33, 3.44. 20 wins: 27 *1 WS, 6 ip, 4.50*

In 1915 Hill and Lee Meadows were the first two pitchers to wear glasses in the majors. After winning 22 for Pittsburgh in 1927, Hill started Game Four of the WS against the Yankees and gave up the home run that Babe Ruth is shown hitting on the Ruth 20-cent stamp issued in 1983./(NLM)

Donnie Hill — 1960– . 2B-SS-3B 1983–88 **A's**, White Sox 551 g, .257, 22 hr, 174 rbi

The A's had optioned the ambidextrous, switch-hitting Hill to Triple-A in spring training of 1985 when Tony Phillips broke his foot. Hill took Phillips's second base job and, changing from a pull hitter to a spray hitter, improved his average from .230 in 1984 to a career-high .285. His 1987 season with the White Sox was marred by conjunctivitis, caused by his contact lenses./(JCA)

Hunter Hill — 1879–1959. 3B 1903–05 Browns, **Senators** 325 g, .216, 1 hr, 80 rbi

Hill missed the first month of the 1904 season with the mumps and led AL third basemen in errors. Traded by the Browns that July, he batted .197 for the 38–113 Senators. He spent 20 years in the Texas League, managing Houston and umpiring./(NLM)

Jesse Hill — 1907– . OF 1935–37 Yankees, **Senators**, A's 295 g, .289, 6 hr, 108 rbi

Hill was an Olympic hopeful in track and a football star at the University of Southern California. The fleet fielder hit a pinch homer in his first pro game./(JK)

Ken Hill — 1965– . RHP 1988– **Cardinals** 211 ip, 7–16, 3.89

Despite only one winning record and one ERA below 4.50 in seven stops before 1989, St. Louis called up Hill when their staff was stricken with multiple injuries. After a good start, he found himself overmatched, and finished 7–15, 3.80./(WOR)

Marc Hill — 1952– . C 1973–86 Cardinals, **Giants**, Mariners, White Sox 737 g, .223, 34 hr, 198 rbi

A sound defensive catcher, the solidly built Hill served as a backup nearly all of his 14 ML seasons. His only time as a regular came with the Giants in 1977–78, when he hit .250 and .243./(FS)

Pete Hill [J. Preston] — 1880–1951. OF-2B-MGR Negro Leagues 1904–25 Philadelphia Giants, Leland Giants, Chicago American Giants, Detroit Stars, Philadelphia Madison Stars, Cleveland Tate Stars, Milwaukee Bears, Baltimore Black Sox statistics not available

Hill was one of the outstanding players in Negro League history. He was a lefthanded line-drive batter who hit to all fields, and an excellent defensive outfielder with great range and a strong accurate arm.

Hill was the cornerstone of three of the most talented teams in the pioneer years of black baseball. From 1904 through 1907, he was the star left fielder for Sol White's powerhouse Philadelphia Giants. Rube Foster took over as manager of Frank Leland's Giants in 1907, reorganized the team, and brought Hill to the club for his leadership ability. For three seasons beginning in 1908, Hill was Foster's field general. The 1910 Leland Giants posted a 123–6 record, including 21 shutouts against the best talent in the Midwest. In 1911, Foster formed a new team, the Chicago American Giants, consisting mostly of former Leland players. He made Hill the team captain the following year.

Hill was always his team's premier slugger. In 1911, as an American Giant, only once in 116 games did he fail to get a hit. He accomplished this feat against pitchers of the Tri-State League and against many white major leaguers, including Nap Rucker, Eddie Plank, Chief Bender, and Mordecai Brown. Cum Posey, owner of the Homestead Grays, called Hill "the most consistent hitter of his time. While a lefthanded batter, he hit both lefthanders and righthanders equally well. He was the backbone, year in and year out, of great ball clubs."

When Foster organized the Detroit Stars in 1919, he asked Hill to become the team's player-manager. At the age of 41 in 1921, Hill led the Stars in batting with a .388 average. He went on to play with the Madison Stars of Philadelphia, the Cleveland Tate Bears, and the Milwaukee Bears. He also played in

Cuba, compiling a .307 average in six seasons. He led the Cuban Winter League with a .365 average for Habana in '10–11. His final position in pro baseball was as the business manager of the 1924–25 Baltimore Black Sox. /(LL)

Shawn Hillegas — 1964– . RHP 1987– Dodgers, White Sox 274 ip, 17–20, 4.13

Hillegas (pronounced HILL-uh-gus) pitched well after joining the White Sox in a September 1988 trade, going 3–2 with a 3.15 ERA. But he pitched so badly at the start of 1989 that he was relegated to the bullpen. /(JFC)

Chuck Hiller (Iron Hands) — 1934– . 2B 1961–68 Giants, Mets, Phillies, Pirates 704 g, .243, 20 hr, 152 rbi. *1 WS, 7 g, .269, 1 hr, 5 rbi*

Iron Hands Hiller led NL second basemen with 29 errors playing for the 1962 NL champion Giants. He was the first NL player to hit a World Series grand slam, connecting off Marshall Bridges in the seventh inning of San Francisco's 7–3, Game Four victory over the Yankees. Later used extensively as a pinch hitter by the Mets, he led the NL with 15 pinch hits in 1966. /(CR)

Frank Hiller — 1920–1987. RHP 1946, 48–53 Yankees, **Cubs**, Reds, Giants 533 ip, 30–32, 4.42

The top pitcher in Lafayette College history, going 22–2, Hiller was a hot prospect in the Yankee farm system before he hurt his arm. After surgery, he became the forgotten man in the New York bullpen. Sold to the Cubs in 1950, he was 12–5 with the help of a forkball he'd learned from former major leaguer Joe Bush. /(BC)

John Hiller — 1943– . LHP 1965–70, 72–80 **Tigers** 1241 ip, 87–76, 2.83. *1 LCS, 3 ip, 1–0, 0.00. 1 WS, 2 ip, 0–0, 13.50*
☛ *All-Star—74.*

Hiller nearly died when he suffered a massive stroke in 1971, but after a miraculous recovery he was pitching again for the Tigers by the end of 1972. He posted 38 saves in 1973 to set a ML record and win Comeback Player of the Year and Fireman of the Year honors. He was also 10–5 with a 1.44 ERA and led the AL with 65 appearances.

After a moderately successful career as a reliever and occasional starter (he tied a since-broken ML record for consecutive strikeouts from the start of a game with six on August 6, 1968) Hiller missed all of 1971 after being stricken. He came back as a batting-practice pitcher in June 1972 and returned

to action a month later, helping Detroit to the division title and winning Game Four of the LCS. Hiller set some more relief marks in 1974, the year after his save record, when his 17–14 record (13 saves) tied both the AL mark for relief wins and the ML standard for relief losses. The Canadian had several more seasons as the ace of the Tigers' bullpen and retired with a club-record 125 saves. /(JFC)

Dave Hillman — 1927– . RHP 1955–62 **Cubs**, Red Sox, Reds, Mets 624 ip, 21–37, 3.87

Hillman and the Cubs defeated the Dodgers 12–2 on September 26, 1959, forcing Los Angeles into the pennant playoff in which they beat the Braves. /(AA)

Hilltop Park New York Yankees 1903–12, New York Giants 1911. LF-365, CF-542, RF-400

Hilltop Park's single-decked wooden grandstand provided a scenic view of the nearby Hudson River and New Jersey Palisades from behind home plate. Its upper-Manhattan site is now occupied by Columbia-Presbyterian Hospital. /(SCL)

Dave Hilton — 1950– . 3B-2B 1972–75 **Padres** 161 g, .213, 6 hr, 33 rbi

Hilton was San Diego's Opening Day third baseman in both 1973 and '74, but his weak bat sent him back to Hawaii both times. After four games in 1975, he was stricken with hepatitis and never again appeared in a ML game. /(JCA)

Bill Hinchman — 1883–1963. OF 1905–09, 15–18, 20 Reds, Indians, **Pirates** 908 g, .261, 20 hr, 369 rbi

Hinchman failed to hit as a regular Cleveland outfielder (1907–09) but won a second chance at the majors by setting American Association records for hits, doubles, and total bases at Columbus in 1914. In both 1915 and '16 he topped .300 for the Pirates. A broken leg in 1917 ended his productivity. As a Pittsburgh scout, he discovered Arky Vaughan, Lloyd Waner, and Billy Cox, among others. His brother Harry played briefly with Cleveland in 1907. /(ME)

Paul Hines — 1852–1935. OF-1B-2B-3B-SS 1872–91 Washington (NA), Chicago (NA/NL), **Providence (NL)**, Washington (NL), Indianapolis (NL), Pirates, Braves, Washington (AA) *NA: 178 g, .302; ML: 1481 g, .301, 56 hr, 631 rbi*
☛ *Led League—ba 78. Led League—hr 78. Led League—rbi 78.*

With Providence in 1878, Hines's career-high .358 average, four HR, and 50 RBI in 62 games were enough to earn him baseball's first triple crown. He hit over .300 eleven times. Rarely ranked among the leaders in fielding, he was famous for his running outfield catches. One such catch in 1878 began a triple play. Boston runners on first and third took off on a short fly over the shortstop's head which seemed a sure hit. Hines charged in from centerfield to make a spectacular shoestring catch, ran to third base to double off one runner, then threw to second base to catch the other and complete the triple play. Some of the game's participants later argued that both runners had rounded third before Hines tagged the base, thereby giving him an unassisted triple play. But newspaper accounts agree that Hines's contribution was two putouts and an assist. /(FIC)

Chuck Hinton [Charles Edward] — 1934- . OF-1B 1961-71 Senators, **Indians**, Angels 1353 g, .264, 113 hr, 443 rbi
☛ All-Star—64.

Grabbed from Baltimore by Washington in the 1960 expansion draft, the graceful Hinton became a regular outfielder and infield fill-in for the Senators. He had an excellent 1962 season (.310, 17 HR, 75 RBI, 28 steals) and was an All-Star in 1964. Traded to Cleveland for Woody Held and Bob Chance, Hinton played six years for the Indians, interrupted by one disappointing season (.195) with California in 1968. Nominally an outfielder/first baseman, the versatile Hinton played every defensive position during his ML career. /(JCA)

Rich Hinton — 1947- . LHP 1971-72, 75-76, 78-79 **White Sox**, Yankees, Rangers, Reds, Mariners 250 ip, 8-17, 4.86

This native Tucsonan and University of Arizona product pitched three Triple-A seasons in front of his hometown fans while he was a White Sox farmhand. Traded five times, he never won or saved more than two games in any ML year. /(JCA)

Al Hirshberg — 1910-1973. *Writer.*

The author of the Jim Piersall biography, *Fear Strikes Out*, Hirshberg also wrote books about Carl Yastrzemski, Frank Howard, and Bob Cousy. A Boston University graduate, he worked for the Boston *Post* and *Herald* before becoming a book and magazine writer. /(NLM)

Larry Hisle — 1947- . OF-DH 1968-71, 73-82 Phillies, **Twins**, Brewers 1197 g, .273, 166 hr, 674 rbi
☛ Led League—rbi 77. All-Star—77-78.

Hisle, a soft-spoken orphan, was recruited for Ohio State University by the governor of Ohio, and signed with the Phillies while still enrolled. Despite tying the then-ML rookie record by striking out 152 times, Hisle was a Topps Rookie All-Star (.266, 20 HR) in 1969 even though he was still weak from a 1968 hepatitis infection. He had an abysmal sophomore season, batting .205 and fanning once every three at-bats. Traded and returned to the minors, he resurfaced with Minnesota in 1973 and blossomed. Fleet afoot, with a strong arm and excellent power, he became a top run producer in five seasons as a Twins regular, culminating in 1977 with a league-leading 119 RBI (.302, 28 HR). He didn't get along with parsimonious Twins owner Calvin Griffith; as a free agent, Hisle signed a $3.2 million package with Milwaukee in 1978 and delivered 34 homers and 115 RBI to finish third in the AL MVP balloting. Brewer manager George Bamberger called him "the kind of player kids should look up to" and "without a doubt one of the nicest men I've ever known." In April 1979, Hisle tore his rotator cuff making a throw and played just 79 games in four more ML seasons. /(JCA)

Billy Hitchcock — 1916- . 3B-2B-SS 1942, 46-53 Tigers, Senators, Browns, Red Sox, **A's** 703 g, .243, 5 hr, 257 rbi.
Manager 1960, 62-63, 66-67 Tigers, **Orioles**, Braves 274-261, .512

Hitchcock was the Tigers' primary shortstop in his first season, but spent 1943-45 in the Army Air Force, receiving the Bronze Medal for his service in the Pacific. The only team for which he played more than a hundred games in a season was the Athletics, in 1950 (second base) and 1952 (third base); he led AL third basemen in errors in 1952. He later managed, finishing highest with the fourth-place 1963 Orioles. He was also a coach and a scout, and was president of the Southern Association from 1971 to 1980. His brother, Jim, played briefly with the Braves in 1938. /(NLM/MA)

Lloyd Hittle (Red) — 1924- . LHP 1949-50 **Senators** 152 ip, 7-11, 4.43

Casey Stengel's redheaded ace at Oakland (Pacific Coast League), Hittle earned five of his seven ML victories against the White Sox. /(JK)

Myril Hoag — 1908–1971. OF 1931–32, 34–42, 44–45 **Yankees**, Browns, White Sox, Indians 1020 g, .271, 28 hr, 401 rbi. *3 WS, 8 g, .320, 1 hr, 3 rbi*

Journeyman Hoag served as a reserve on four Yankee pennant-winners. He had extremely small feet which required special shoes, and somehow supported a 5′11″ 180-lb body. In a career-high 129 games as the 1939 Browns' right fielder, Hoag hit .295 with 10 HR. /(JK)

Don Hoak (Tiger) — 1928–1969. 3B 1954–64 Dodgers, Cubs, Reds, **Pirates**, Phillies 1263 g, .265, 89 hr, 498 rbi. *2 WS, 10 g, .231, 3 rbi*
☛ *All-Star—57.*

Hoak was an outspoken, brawling firebrand, the spiritual leader of the 1960 World Champion Pirates. A pro boxer as a teenager, he lost seven straight knockouts before giving it up. He carried his pugnacity to the ballfield. He broke in sharing third base in Brooklyn with Billy Cox and Jackie Robinson. As a Cub on May 2, 1956, he set a NL record by striking out six times in a game (17 innings). In 1957, he led the NL with 39 doubles for the Reds and earned an All-Star Game berth in the Cincinnati ballot-box-stuffing incident. Traded to Pittsburgh, he led the Pirates in walks in 1959–61, and paced the 1960 championship team with 97 runs scored.

In a Braves-Reds game on April 21, 1957, Hoak was on second and Gus Bell was on first when Wally Post grounded to shortstop. Hoak fielded the ball himself, flipping it to a stunned Johnny Logan at short. Hoak was out for getting hit by a batted ball, but the Reds still had two on and Post was credited with a single. The third such incident involving the Reds that season, it moved league presidents Warren Giles and Will Harridge to jointly announce a rule change that declared both the runner and the batter out if the runner intentionally interfered with a batted ball, with no runners allowed to advance.

Hoak later managed in the Pittsburgh system. He died of a heart attack chasing his brother-in-law's stolen car on October 9, 1969, the day Danny Murtaugh was rehired as Pirates manager—a position Hoak had openly sought. /(ME)

Ed Hobaugh — 1934– . RHP 1961–63 **Senators** 212 ip, 9–10, 4.34

The captain of the 1954 Big Ten champion Michigan State baseball team had his most active ML season as a rookie seven years later. He was 7–9 for the last-place Senators. /(RTM)

Glen Hobbie — 1936– . RHP 1957–64 **Cubs**, Cardinals 1263 ip, 62–81, 4.20

The Cub ace from 1958 to 1960, Hobbie peaked in 1959, going 16–13. Included was a 1–0 one-hitter over the Cardinals April 22 in which Stan Musial spoiled a perfect game by doubling with two out in the seventh. Hobbie's 20 losses in 1960 led the league. A strained shoulder in 1961 ended his effectiveness. /(AA)

Dick Hoblitzell — 1888–1962. 1B 1908–18 **Reds**, Red Sox 1317 g, .278, 27 hr, 619 rbi. *2 WS, 10 g, .273, 3 rbi*

A consistent first baseman for the Reds, Hoblitzell was sold to the Red Sox in the middle of 1914 and assigned to room with rookie pitcher Babe Ruth. A starter for Boston's World Champions in 1915 and '16, he retired two years later at the age of 29 to practice dentistry. He later returned to baseball as a minor league manager and umpire. /(JK)

Butch Hobson [Clell Lavern] — 1951– . 3B-DH 1975–82 **Red Sox**, Angels, Yankees 738 g, .248, 98 hr, 397 rbi

The former University of Alabama football star's all-out play caused him many injuries throughout his baseball career. He became a Red Sox regular in 1977, setting team records for third basemen with 30 home runs and 112 RBI. His 43 errors in 1978 were the most by any AL fielder, and his .899 fielding average was the first below .900 by a regular in 62 years. The hard-nosed slugger suffered through elbow problems and, after a trade to California in 1981, a shoulder separation. He played 30 games for the Yankees in 1982 before being sent down to Columbus (International League). /(JCA)

Oris Hockett — 1909–1969. OF 1938–39, 41–45 Dodgers, **Indians**, White Sox 551 g, .276, 13 hr, 214 rbi

After failing in a trial with Brooklyn, Hockett won a second ML chance with strong years at Nashville (Southern Association). He played regularly for four wartime years, with a top mark of .293 for the White Sox in 1945. /(ME)

Johnny Hodapp — 1905–1980. 2B-3B 1925–33 Indians, White Sox, Red Sox 787 g, .311, 28 hr, 429 rbi

As Cleveland's starting second baseman, Hodapp hit .300 four straight seasons, climaxing with .354 in 1930, when he led the AL in hits (225) and doubles (51), batted in 121 runs and scored 111. He also topped AL second basemen in putouts. A knee injury the next season hampered him on both offense and defense, shattered his confidence, and finally ended his career. /(ME)

Shovel Hodge [Clarence Clement] — 1893–1967.
RHP 1920–22 **White Sox** 301 ip, 14–15, 5.17

Hodge stood 6′4″ and was dubbed Shovel for his big feet. In his September 6, 1920 debut, he held the Tigers hitless for 7–1/3 innings. When the Black Sox scandal decimated Chicago's pitching staff in 1921, Hodge proved an inadequate replacement. /(RL)

Gil Hodges [born Gilbert Ray Hodge] — 1924–1972.
1B-OF-C-3B 1943, 47–63 **Dodgers**, Mets 2071 g, .273, 370 hr, 1274 rbi. *7 WS, 39 g, .267, 5 hr, 21 rbi.*
   Manager 1963–71 **Senators**, Mets 660–754, .467.
1 LCS, 3–0, 1.000. 1 WS, 4–1, .800
☛ *All-Star—49–55, 57. Gold Glove—57–59 .*

Known as the "Miracle Worker" when he piloted the 1969 Mets to the World Championship, Hodges was a slugging, eight-time All-Star first baseman. A dead-pull hitter who always looked for the inside pitch, Hodges was a model of consistency, collecting over 100 RBI for seven consecutive years (1949–55) and hitting 20 or more HR 11 straight seasons (1949–59). His lifetime 14 grand slams established the NL mark, since eclipsed by Willie McCovey (18) and Hank Aaron (16).

Hodges was nineteen when he played third base for one game with the Dodgers in late 1943. He struck out twice and walked, then joined the Marines. He returned in 1947 as a catcher, but with the emergence of Roy Campanella, he was moved to first base. Manager Leo Durocher said, "With my catching set, I put a first baseman's glove on our other rookie catcher, Gil Hodges, and told him to have some fun. Three days later, I looked up and, wow, I was looking at the best first baseman I'd seen since Dolf Camilli."

Hodges was the Dodgers' Lou Gehrig—big, strong, and gentle. The three-time Gold Glove winner played first base gracefully. His hands were so large that teammates joked he didn't even need a glove. His quick footwork provoked the allegation that he rarely had his foot on the bag for his putouts.

On August 31, 1950 against the Braves, Hodges hit four homers. His 40 HR in 1951 were second only to Ralph Kiner's 42, but he struck out a league-high 99 times. He reached career highs in 1954, hitting .304 with 42 HR and 130 RBI (second to Ted Kluszewski's 49 and 141). During the 1952 WS loss to the Yankees, Hodges went a dreadful 0-for-21, and prayers were said for the beloved Dodger in

Gil Hodges

churches all across Brooklyn. In the following year's Series he hit .364. Hodges homered in each of his last four World Series, his shots winning 1956's Game One and 1959's Game Four for the Dodgers.

Ending his playing career with the Mets, Hodges hit the first homer in their history, on April 11, 1962 at St. Louis. Though he began 1963 with the Mets, he was sent to Washington for Jimmy Piersall, and took over as manager of the struggling Senators, who were 14–26 under Mickey Vernon. In five seasons, the best Hodges could do was a sixth-place finish in 1967.

Hodges was traded back to the Mets as manager in exchange for pitcher Bill Denehy and cash. His 1968 club finished ninth, but the following season, Hodges took the Mets to the pennant, skillfully platooning at five positions. The Mets swept the Braves in the LCS, then took the WS from Baltimore in five games. Hodges managed the Mets to two third-place finishes in 1970 and '71. He died suddenly of a heart attack after a spring training golf game on April 2, 1972, two days before his 48th birthday. The Mets retired his number 14. /(RTM)

Ron Hodges — 1949– . C 1973–84 **Mets** 666 g, .240, 19 hr, 147 rbi. *1 WS, 1 g, --*

No relation to the great Gil Hodges, Ron roomed with Gil Hodges, Jr., in the minor leagues. A reliable backup catcher and lefthanded pinch hitter, Ron's patience at the plate allowed him to draw enough walks to make him more effective than his BA indicated. He caught a career-high 96 games in 1983. /(JCA)

Russ Hodges — 1910–1971. *Broadcaster.*

When Bobby Thomson stunned the Dodgers with his "Shot Heard 'Round the World" to win the 1951 NL playoff series, Russ Hodges delivered what has become the most famous call in ML history, repeatedly crying "The Giants win the pennant! The Giants win the pennant!" as bedlam reigned in the Polo Grounds. Raised in Kentucky, Hodges broadcast for the White Sox, Cubs, Reds, Senators, and Yankees before settling for two decades as the voice of the Giants. He would salute each Giants home run with his trademark "Bye, bye baby!" and was heard on New York's WMCA and San Francisco's KSFO until his sudden death of a heart attack in 1971. /(SCL)

Ralph Hodgin — 1916– . OF-3B 1939, 43–44, 46–48 Braves, **White Sox** 530 g, .285, 4 hr, 188 rbi

Hodgin batted .314 for the 1943 White Sox, but became one of the few players to bat .300 as a rookie but never repeat the feat. On April 21, 1947 he suffered a concussion when a fastball from Tiger ace Hal Newhouser glanced off his skull. After that he lost his aggressiveness at the plate. /(RL)

Billy Hoeft — 1932– . LHP 1952–66 **Tigers**, Red Sox, Orioles, Giants, Braves, Cubs 1847 ip, 97–101, 3.94. 20 wins: 56
☛ *All-Star—55.*

Hoeft was a mainstay in the Tigers starting rotation in the 1950s, then embarked on a second career as an itinerant lefthanded reliever, changing teams six times between 1959 and 1966. He spent most of his rookie season in the Detroit bullpen, then struggled as a starter in 1953–54, winning only 16 games over the two seasons. In 1955 Hoeft was still only Detroit's third starter in terms of starts and innings, but he led the AL with seven shutouts on his way to a 16–7, 2.99 record and a spot on the AL All-Star team. In 1956 Hoeft became the first Tiger left-hander since Hal Newhouser to win 20 games, posting a 20–14 mark, but after mediocre seasons in 1957–58, Hoeft returned to the bullpen for the balance of his career.

He was traded to the Red Sox for Ted Lepcio and Dave Sisler in May, 1959, then shipped to Baltimore for Jack Harshman six weeks later. Hoeft enjoyed his best seasons in relief with the Orioles, recording a 2.02 ERA in 1961 and four wins plus seven saves in 1962, then was traded to the Giants and later to the Braves, spending single seasons with each club. On July 14, 1957 Hoeft hit two of his three career home runs. /(SCL)

Joe Hoerner — 1936– . LHP 1963–64, 66–77 Astros, **Cardinals**, Phillies, Braves, Royals, Rangers, Reds 563 ip, 39–34, 2.99. *2 WS, 5 ip, 0–1, 8.44*
☛ *All-Star—70.*

A clubhouse prankster and top short reliever, Hoerner blossomed after a weak heart forced him to switch to a less taxing sidearm delivery. His highest ERA in the years 1966–71 was 2.89. He recorded career bests of 17 saves and a 1.47 ERA for the Cardinals in 1968; on June 1, he tied a NL record for consecutive strikeouts by a relief pitcher, with six. In 1969 Hoerner was involved in the celebrated Curt Flood trade. Though Flood did not report to the Phillies, Hoerner did, and led the NL with nine relief wins in 1970. He retired with 99 career saves, and Hank Aaron never got a hit off him in 22 career at-bats. /(JCA)

Frank Hoerst (Lefty) — 1917– . LHP 1940–42, 46–47 **Phillies** 348 ip, 10–33, 5.17

Hoerst went 3–10 in 1941, but two of the victories came over the pennant-winning Dodgers. In 1944 he broke an ankle while coaching a high school basket-ball team. /(NLM)

Fred Hoey — 1885-1932. *Broadcaster.*

In 1926 the president of the Yankee Radio Network decided that every major sporting event in New England should be broadcast by a recognized authority. Hoey, who saw his first baseball game in the 1897 Temple Cup Series, worked all Boston home games until he died. During winters he held an executive position at the Boston Garden. In 1931 Fenway Park fans honored him with a special day. /(NLM)

Bill Hoffer — 1870-1959. RHP 1895-99, 1901 **Baltimore (NL)**, Pirates, Indians 1254 ip, 91-47, 3.75. 20 wins: 1895-97

Baltimore's Bill Hoffer led the National League with winning percentages of .811 (30-7) in 1895 and .781 (25-7) in 1896. When the American League was recognized as a major league in 1901, Hoffer became the AL's first pitcher; he issued the first walk, got the first strikeout, and was tagged with the first loss as Cleveland dropped an 8-2 decision to Chicago on April 24, 1901. He won just three games in that, his final ML season. /(ME)

Danny Hoffman — 1880-1922. OF 1903-11 A's, Yankees, **Browns** 828 g, .256, 13 hr, 235 rbi. *1 WS, 1 g, .000*

The lefthanded-hitting Hoffman was considered a top A's prospect in 1904 when a pitch from Boston southpaw Jesse Tannehill hit him in the eye. He never recovered enough vision to stand in against lefthanded pitching. He was the American League's 1905 stolen-base champ, with 46, and stole 185 bases in his career. /(NLM)

Glenn Hoffman — 1958- . SS-3B 1980-87 **Red Sox**, Dodgers 718 g, .244, 22 hr, 207 rbi

After hitting .285 in 114 games as a rookie third baseman in 1980, Hoffman was shifted to shortstop in 1981 when the Red Sox acquired Carney Lansford. He started at shortstop in Boston in 1982-83 and again in 1985, but he spent almost all of 1986 on the DL and didn't make the Red Sox' postseason roster. /(SCL)

Guy Hoffman — 1956- . LHP 1979-80, 83, 86-88 **White Sox**, Cubs, Reds, Rangers 339 ip, 17-17, 4.25

Just 5'9", Hoffman was not drafted after college but was signed by the White Sox in 1978 while playing in a Peoria, IL weekend league. He went 8-0 in the minors, was promoted to Chicago in less than a

year, and was 0-5 as a rookie reliever. After spending much of 1981-85 in Triple-A, he went 6-2 for the 1986 Cubs and, despite elbow problems, produced a 9-10 mark for the 1987 Reds. /(JCA)

Bobby Hofman — 1925- . 2B-1B-3B-C 1949, 52-57 **Giants** 341 g, .248, 32 hr, 101 rbi

Hofman, the nephew of Circus Solly Hofman, had nine career pinch HR. A useful utility infielder who even made 26 appearances at catcher, he continued to show versatility later when, as a coach for budget-minded Charles O. Finley, he doubled as the Oakland A's traveling secretary. /(RTM)

Solly Hofman [Arthur Frederick] (Circus Solly) — 1894-1956. OF-2B-1B-SS 1903-16 Pirates, **Cubs**, Brooklyn (FL), Buffalo (FL), Yankees 1194 g, .269, 19 hr, 495 rbi. *3 WS, 16 g, .298, 8 rbi*

Hofman was the slick centerfielder and general handyman for the four Cub pennant-winners of 1906-08 and 1910. His teammates called him Circus Solly because of his many "circus" catches in the outfield. Hofman was a timely hitter and good baserunner. His best season was 1910 when he hit .325 and had 86 RBI.

In the "Merkle Boner" game of 1908 against the Giants, it was Hofman who retrieved Al Bridwell's single and called to second baseman Johnny Evers that Merkle had failed to touch second. His throw from the outfield sailed over Evers' head but was eventually retrieved for the forceout that ended the game in a tie. The Cubs won the makeup game and the pennant. According to baseball historian Paddy Keough, a friend of Hofman, the throw got past Evers because Circus Solly could not resist clowning, even on that crucial play, and threw a curveball to Evers. /(BC)

Fred Hofmann (Bootnose) — 1894-1964. C 1919-25, 27-28 **Yankees**, Red Sox 378 g, .247, 7 hr, 93 rbi. *1 WS, 2 g, .000*

Hofmann's 36 years in organized baseball started as the Yankees' backup catcher at the beginning of their dynasty. He was a pennant-winning minor league manager and coached 12 years for the Browns. When the team moved to Baltimore, he went along as a scout. /(JK)

Shanty Hogan [James Francis] — 1906-1967. C 1925-37 Braves, **Giants**, Senators 989 g, .295, 61 hr, 474 rbi

Nicknamed for his physical resemblance to a small hut, the 6'1" 240-lb Hogan was an excellent target behind the plate as well as a solid hitter. Traded to the Giants with Jimmy Welsh for Rogers Hornsby in January 1928, Hogan hit .333, the first of four consecutive .300 seasons, and was one of seven Giants regulars to hit .300 that year. Sold back to the Braves for the 1933 season, he shook off public criticism of his weight to record 120 consecutive errorless games, 18 shy of the NL record for catchers. /(JK)

Bill Hogg (Buffalo Bill) — 1880-1909. RHP 1905-08 **Yankees** 730 ip, 37-50, 3.06

The Highlanders' number-three or number-four starter for his entire stay in the majors, Hogg was wild with above-average ERAs. He had two winning records, 14-13 in 1906 and 10-8 in 1907. /(JFC)

Brad Hogg — 1888-1935. RHP 1911-12, 15, 18-19 Braves, Cubs, **Phillies** 448 ip, 20-29, 3.70

Seven years after his first of three short major league trials, Hogg won 13 games for the 1918 Phillies, tying for the staff high. A graduate of Mercer University, Hogg was a lawyer. /(NLM)

Chief Hogsett [Elon Chester] — 1903- . LHP 1929-38, 44 **Tigers**, Browns, Senators 1222 ip, 63-87, 5.02. *2 WS, 8 ip, 0-0, 1.08*

Dubbed with the nickname accorded anyone with Indian ancestry, the half-Cherokee was a successful reliever for the Tigers during the early 1930s, twice leading the AL in relief wins (1932, 1935). His work helped Detroit to pennants in 1934 and '35. He left the majors after 1938 and pitched six years of AAA ball before being recalled by the Tigers for a brief wartime stint. /(JK)

Bobby Hogue — 1921- . RHP 1948-52 **Braves**, Browns, Yankees 327 ip, 18-16, 3.97. *1 WS, 3 ip, 0-0, 0.00*

Hogue compiled an 8-2 record as a relief pitcher for the pennant-winning 1948 Boston Braves. He saw no action in the World Series that year, but he did appear twice for the Yankees in the 1951 Series. /(FK)

Cal Hogue — 1927- . RHP 1952-54 **Pirates** 114 ip, 2-10, 4.91

From 1945 to 1953, Hogue pitched for 10 different teams in 10 different leagues, only once winning as many as 10 games. In three trials with Pittsburgh, he walked almost twice as many batters as he struck out. /(ME)

Ken Holcombe — 1918- . RHP 1945, 48, 50-53 Yankees, Reds, **White Sox**, Browns, Red Sox 375 ip, 18-32, 3.98

Holcombe showed promise as a reliever with the Yankees in 1945 but bursitis sent him back to the minors. He reemerged as the White Sox' fourth starter in the 1950s and posted an 11-12 mark in 1951. The bursitis reappeared the next season and eventually ended his career. /(RL)

Fred Holdsworth — 1952- . RHP 1972-74, 76-78, 80 Tigers, **Orioles**, Expos, Brewers 183 ip, 7-10, 4.38

Control artist Holdsworth was an effective relief pitcher in a partial season for Baltimore in 1976, winning four and saving two with a 2.03 ERA. /(MC)

Walter Holke (Union Man) — 1892-1954. 1B 1914, 16-25 Giants, **Braves**, Phillies, Reds 1212 g, .287, 24 hr, 487 rbi. *1 WS, 6 g, .286, 1 rbi*

A sure-handed first baseman with a reliable bat, Holke played most of his career with losing teams. In the Braves' 26-inning tie with Brooklyn in 1920, he made 42 putouts at first base. Though he played at a time when players often tried to intimidate umpires with aggressive arguing, the mild-mannered Holke played 11 ML seasons without being thrown out of a game and stretched his record to 20 pro seasons before he was given the boot as a manager in the Three-Eye League. /(JK)

Al Holland — 1952- . LHP 1977, 79-87 Pirates, **Giants**, Phillies, Angels, Yankees 646 ip, 34-30, 2.98. *1 LCS, 3 ip, 0-0, 0.00. 1 WS, 4 ip, 0-0, 0.00.* ☛ *All-Star—84.*

"Gimme the ball!" is what Al Holland wants his epitaph to say. A career reliever with an excellent fastball, he finished his rookie season with a 1.76 ERA and seven saves for the Giants in 1980, but was always part of a bullpen-by-committee in San Francisco.

Traded with Joe Morgan to the Phillies for Mark Davis and Mike Krukow, Holland became their stopper in 1983. His 25 saves plus two more in the postseason helped them to the World Series, where they lost to the Orioles. He saved a career-high 29 games in 1984, but also lost 10, as his ERA jumped to 3.39 and his fastball grew more hittable. He would notch only five more saves before being released by the Yankees early in 1987. /(SG)

Bill Holland — 1901–Unk. RHP-MGR Negro Leagues 1920–41 Detroit Stars, Chicago American Giants, New York Lincoln Giants, Brooklyn Royal Giants, **New York Black Yankees**, Philadelphia Stars statistics not available ☛ *All-Star—39.*

Holland was the mainstay of the New York Black Yankees' pitching staff in the 1930s. Of his 22 years in baseball, 18 were spent in New York. He was the first black pitcher to pitch in Yankee Stadium when he beat the Baltimore Elite Giants before a crowd of 15,000 in 1930.

The 5'8" 175-lb Holland joined his first pro team, the Detroit Stars, in 1920. In 1922 he led the league with 16 wins. Hall of Famer Cool Papa Bell ranked Holland with Satchel Paige, Smokey Joe Williams, and Bullet Joe Rogan as the best pitchers in the Negro Leagues. Though he relied mainly on the fastball, he also expertly mixed in a curve, a drop, a changeup, and an occasional emery ball. /(PG)

Ed Holley — 1899–1986. RHP 1928, 32–34 Cubs, **Phillies**, Pirates 548 ip, 25–40, 4.40

Holley led the 1932–33 Phillies pitching staff in starts and complete games and won a club-high 13 in 1933. He was sold to Pittsburgh after a 1–8 start in 1934. /(ME)

Bug Holliday [James Wear] — 1867–1910. OF 1889–98 Cincinnati (AA), **Reds** 929 g, .316, 65 hr, 617 rbi. *Umpire* NL 1903
☛ *Led League—hr 1889, 92 .*

Holliday tied for the 1889 American Association home run title, with 19, while batting .343 as a rookie for Cincinnati. From 1890 to 1894 he was the Reds' centerfielder, and in 1892 he captured the National League HR crown, with 13. His last season as a regular, '94, was his finest, as he again hit 13 HR, batted a career-high .383 and drove in 119 runs. He returned to the NL as an umpire in 1903. /(AJA)

Al Hollingsworth (Boots) — 1908– . LHP 1935–40, 42–46 Reds, Phillies, Dodgers, Senators, **Browns**, White Sox 1520 ip, 70–104, 3.99. *1 WS, 4 ip, 0–0, 2.25*

Hollingsworth split 11 seasons between starting and relieving, never winning more than a dozen games. On May 28, 1938 he hit a grand slam off the Cardinals' Lon Warneke. He later became a minor league manager and served two stints as a Cardinals coach. /(WAB)

Charlie Hollocher — 1896–1940. SS 1918–24 **Cubs** 760 g, .304, 14 hr, 241 rbi. *1 WS, 6 g, .190*

When healthy, Hollocher was a first-rate shortstop. He took part in two triple plays and twice led the league in fielding average. The lefthanded hitter batted second and seldom struck out. He led the NL with 161 hits and 509 at-bats as a rookie in 1918, and his .340 in 1922 was the highest mark for a shortstop since Honus Wagner's .354 in 1908. He never fulfilled his great promise due to recurrent illness, and committed suicide at age 44. /(ADS)

Bobo Holloman [Alva Lee] — 1925–1987. RHP 1953 **Browns** 65 ip, 3–7, 5.23

Holloman was the third pitcher in major league history, after Charlie Jones and Ted Breitenstein, to throw a no-hitter in his first start. After he had bounced around the Cubs' farm system, Holloman's contract was purchased by the lowly St. Louis Browns prior to the 1953 season. His early appearances with them, all in relief, yielded an ERA close to 9.00. Undaunted, the confident Holloman pestered manager Marty Marion to give him a chance as a starter. He took the mound in that capacity for the first time on the rainy night of May 6, 1953 before a hometown crowd of 2,473 and no-hit the Athletics 6–0. The 29-year-old rookie embellished his performance with three RBI and his only two hits in the majors. He never pitched another complete game in his major league career, which was over before the end of 1953.

Holloman was a colorful personality who stopped at the foul line each time he pitched to scratch the initials of his wife and son in the dirt. Brown's owner Bill Veeck said of him, "He had charm and he had humor and he had unlimited confidence in himself." /(CR)

Ken Holloway [born Kenneth Eugene Hollaway] — 1897–1968. RHP 1922–30 **Tigers**, Indians, Yankees 1160 ip, 64–52, 4.40

"As a handler of men, Ty Cobb is cruel, autocratic, and entirely without sympathy," said Holloway, a Tiger curveballer. "Cobb made his pitchers throw a beanball. One day I ignored his order to throw at Joe Judge. Even though I got Judge to pop up, it cost me a hundred dollar fine." Holloway's best seasons were 1924 (14–6), when his nine relief wins led the AL, and 1925 (13–4). /(NLM)

Wattie Holm [Roscoe Albert] — 1901–1950 OF-3B-C 1924–29, 32 **Cardinals** 436 g, .275, 6 hr, 174 rbi. *2 WS, 8 g, .136, 2 rbi*

Holm was signed as a schoolboy by the Cardinals. Normally an outfielder, he eventually played every position during his pro career. One of his three home runs in 1928 was a pinch hit grand slam. /(JL)

Brian Holman — 1965– . RHP 1988– **Expos**, Mariners 132 ip, 5–10, 3.61

One of several Expos rookies in 1988 who had a losing record despite pitching well, Holman was traded to the Mariners in May 1989 and moved into the Mariners' rotation. /(SFS)

Scott Holman — 1958– . RHP 1980, 82–83 **Mets** 134 ip, 3–8, 3.34

The muscular Californian was a power pitcher with chronic shoulder problems. He was 1–7 in 35 appearances for the Mets in 1983, his only complete ML season. /(JCA)

Ducky Holmes [James William] — 1869–1932. OF 1895–99, 1901–05 Louisville (NL), Giants, Cardinals, **Baltimore (NL)**, Tigers, Senators, White Sox 932 g, .282, 17 hr, 374 rbi

The chunky Iowan insulted a Jewish club owner with an ethnic slur, leading to a lengthy clash between NL owners. One of his suspensions, for verbal abuse of an umpire, is cited as the start of the feud between AL founders Ban Johnson and Charles Comiskey. A fine hitter and basestealer, he once played for four teams in two years because he was such a troublemaker. /(DB)

Tommy Holmes (Kelly) — 1917– . OF 1942–52 **Braves**, Dodgers 1320 g, .302, 88 hr, 581 rbi. *2 WS, 9 g, .185, 1 rbi.*
  Manager 1951–52 **Braves** 61–69, .469
☛ *Led League—hr 45.*

Braves right fielder Holmes hit safely in a 20th-century NL record 37 straight games, from June 6 through July 8 of his 1945 *TSN* MVP season. That year, he hit .352 with 117 RBI, 125 runs, and 15 stolen bases, and had league highs of 47 doubles, 224 hits, a .577 slugging average, and 28 HR; he is the only player ever to lead a league in home runs and fewest strikeouts (9) in the same season. But these totals were all career highs, and though he batted over .300 in his next three seasons, he never

again managed more than nine homers or 79 RBI. Appointed the Braves' manager in mid-1951, Holmes was fired early in 1952, finishing up as a Dodger pinch hitter. When Pete Rose broke his hitting-streak record in 1978, a tearful Holmes thanked him "for making people remember me." /(MC)

Tommy Holmes — 1904–1975. *Writer.*

Holmes, who was handicapped by the loss of an arm as a youth, became one of the foremost baseball writers in the country. He covered the Dodgers for over 30 years, starting with the Brooklyn *Eagle* in 1926 and later moving to the New York *Herald-Tribune*. He was president of the BBWAA in 1947 and wrote several books, including *The Dodgers*. He was given the J.G. Taylor Spink Award in 1979. /(NLM)

Jim Holt — 1944– . OF-1B 1968–76 **Twins**, A's 707 g, .265, 19 hr, 177 rbi. *3 LCS, 8 g, .125. 1 WS, 4 g, .667, 2 rbi*

After hitting .266 and .259 as a platoon player for Minnesota in 1970–71, Vietnam veteran Holt was sent down to the Pacific Coast League. Recalled in '73, he hit .297 and knocked 11 homers in 132 games. When he slumped the next year, he was traded to the A's. At Oakland he was mainly a pinch hitter, leading the AL in pinch at-bats and hits in 1975. /(MC)

Brian Holton — 1959– . RHP 1985– **Dodgers**, Orioles 313 ip, 18–16, 3.45. *1 LCS, 4 ip, 0–0, 2.25. 1 WS, 2 ip, 0–0, 0.00*

Curveballer Holton spent nine seasons in the minors, including six at Albuquerque (Pacific Coast League), before finally reaching the ML, and found his niche as a middle-inning reliever in the Dodgers' 1988 World Championship season. He saved Game Five of the NLCS against the Mets and pitched two scoreless innings in the World Series opener, helping the Dodgers to stay close in the game won by Kirk Gibson's famous ninth-inning pinch homer. The Dodgers quickly converted his newly-established value and traded him to the Orioles that winter in the Eddie Murray deal. /(TG)

Jerome Holtzman — 1926– . *Writer.*

Senior baseball writer and columnist for the Chicago *Sun-Times* and a weekly contributor the *The Sporting News* for many years, Holtzman has written more than 100 articles for other publications. He is baseball advisor for the *Encyclopaedia Britannica* and sports editor for the *Britannica Yearbook*. For the *Official Baseball Guide*, Holtzman writes a 25,000-word review of the year, intended as a historical record. His books include *No Cheering in the Press Box*, *Three and Two* (a biography of umpire Tom Gorman), and *Fielder's Choice*, an anthology of baseball fiction. /(NLM)

Ken Holtzman — 1945- . LHP 1965-79 **Cubs**, A's, Orioles, Yankees 2867 ip, 174-150, 3.49. 20 wins: 73
4 LCS, 35 ip, 2-3, 2.06. 3 WS, 35 ip, 4-1, 2.55
☛ *All-Star—72, 73.*

Holtzman was christened "The New Koufax" as a 20-year-old rookie in 1966, and Cubs fans hoped their hard-throwing, Jewish lefthander would rival the achievements of the retiring Dodger ace. Holtzman never did, of course, but he did pitch two no-hitters with the Cubs and was an excellent ML starter for over a decade, helping the A's to three consecutive World Championships in 1972–74. He had outstanding control as well as a lively fastball, and he preferred inducing batters to hit the ball into outs rather than simply trying to overpower them.

Holtzman brought the Koufax comparisons upon himself on September 25, 1966, when he squared off against the Hall of Famer for the first and only time. Holtzman was on his way to an 11–16 rookie season while Koufax was in the final weeks of his career, and on that day Holtzman took a no-hitter into the ninth inning before settling for a 2–1 win. He was a perfect 9–0 in 1967, but spent most of the season in military service. He was a disappointing 11–14, 3.35 in 1968. Still only 23 in 1969, Holtzman was 17–13 for the second-place Cubs and tossed six shutouts, including a 3–0 no-hitter against the Braves August 19. Less than two years later he pitched a second no-hitter, beating the Reds 1–0 on June 3, 1971, but finished the season 9–15, 4.48 and was traded to the A's for outfielder Rick Monday.

Joining a rotation that already included Catfish Hunter, Blue Moon Odom, and Vida Blue, Holtzman helped Oakland over the top in 1972, going 19–11, 2.51 as the A's won the first of three consecutive WS. In 1973 he was 21–13, 2.97, won Game Three of the LCS 2–1 with an 11-inning complete game, and won Game Seven of the WS against the Mets. And in 1974 he was 19–17, 3.07, tossed a shutout in the LCS, and won Game Four of the WS. He won 18 games in 1975, but lost twice in the LCS as Oakland was swept by Boston, and in 1976 he was traded with Reggie Jackson to the Orioles for Don Baylor, Mike Torrez, and Paul Mitchell. He lasted less than half a season in

Baltimore before being traded to the Yankees in a 10-player blockbuster that brought Rudy May, Tippy Martinez, Scott McGregor, and Rick Dempsey to the Orioles in exchange for Doyle Alexander, Elrod Hendricks, and Grant Jackson. In 1978 the Yankees dealt him back to the Cubs for reliever Ron Davis. /(SCL)

John Holway — 1929- . *Writer.*

A graduate of the University of Iowa and Georgetown, Holway has worked for the U.S. Information Agency since 1956. A historian of black baseball, he wrote *Voices of the Great Black Baseball Leagues* (1975). /(NLM)

Rick Honeycutt — 1954- . LHP 1977- Mariners, Rangers, **Dodgers**, A's 1858 ip, 95-125, 3.76. *4 LCS, 7 ip, 1-0, 16.19. 2 WS, 6 ip, 1-0, 3.00*
☛ *Led League—era 83. All-Star—80, 83.*

Honeycutt began his roller-coaster ML career as a bright young prospect for the Mariners, then was traded to the Rangers in an 11-player deal before the 1981 season. He collapsed from 11–6, 3.30 in 1981 to 5–17, 5.27 in 1982, but won the AL Comeback of the Year award in 1983, leading the AL in ERA even though he finished the season with the NL Dodgers. A control pitcher, Honeycutt enjoyed three solid seasons in Los Angeles before beginning the 1987 season 2–12 and being traded to Oakland for Tim Belcher. He reestablished himself as a set-up man in the A's bullpen, and in 1988 he won Game One of the LCS and Game Two of the WS in relief.

Honeycutt was an All-American first baseman at the University of Tennessee, and hit .301 in his first pro season while playing first base and shortstop in addition to pitching. In 1980 he was ejected from a game when an umpire found a tack inside a bandage on his finger. /(TG)

Donald Honig — 1931- . *Writer.*

Novelist Honig is among the most prolific factual baseball book writers ever. His publications include: *Baseball When the Grass Was Real* (1975), *Baseball Between the Lines* (1976), *Man in the Dugout* (1977), *The Last Great Season* (1979), *October Heroes* (1979), *Image of Their Greatness* (1979), and *100 Greatest Baseball Players of All Time* (1980). In the 1980s, he has focused on coffee table–style illustrated histories, producing over a dozen. /(NLM)

Jim Honochick — 1917- . *Umpire* AL 1949-73
1 LCS 6 WS 5 ASU

A sore arm caused Honochick to turn from being a
minor league outfielder to umpiring in 1946. The
highlight of his 25 ML seasons, he claims, was
working behind the plate in the Seventh Game of
the 1955 WS when Brooklyn's Johnny Podres beat
the Yankees, 2-0. Honochick gained fame in the
1980s for his myopic self-portrayal in a Miller Lite
beer commercial with Boog Powell. /(RTM)

Don Hood — 1949- . LHP 1973-80, 82-83 Orioles,
Indians, Yankees, Cardinals, Royals 847 ip, 34-35, 3.79

Hood was Baltimore's number-one draft selection in
June 1969. He allowed just one HR in 57 innings in
1974. Both a starter and reliever, he worked a
career-high 155 innings with Cleveland in
1978. /(JCA)

Jay Hook [James Wesley] — 1936- . RHP 1957-64
Reds, Mets 752 ip, 29-62, 5.23

A bonus player signed by the Reds out of Northwestern, he seemed to be hitting his stride until
mumps laid him low in 1960. Ineffective the next
year, he was acquired by the expansion Mets in
1962 and pitched the first game won by the team
(after they'd lost their first nine). After receiving his
masters degree in thermodynamics, he retired at
twenty-eight to take a job with Chrysler. /(JK)

Harry Hooper — 1887-1974. OF 1909-25 **Red Sox**,
White Sox 2308 g, .281, 75 hr, 817 rbi. *4 WS, 24 g, .293,
2 hr, 6 rbi*
☞ *Hall of Fame—1971.*

Hooper prided himself on being a college man of
high ideals during an era when most ballplayers
weren't, and he nearly became a civil engineer
before the lure of big money led him to sign with the
Red Sox for $2,850 in 1909. Extremely popular
with teammates, fans, and even opponents, he was
the right fielder in the fabled "Million Dollar
Outfield" with Tris Speaker and Duffy Lewis. He
taught himself to play the difficult sun field and
invented the famous rump slide to snare short flies
and stop with his body those he could not reach. His
strong, accurate arm accounted for 150 of the trio's
455 assists. Hooper never led the American League
in any of the important offensive categories, but he
did compile a valuable .403 on-base average as the
Red Sox leadoff hitter from 1909 to 1920, and

Harry Hooper

became the Red Sox' all-time leader in triples with
130 and in stolen bases with 300. He went on to
collect 2,466 hits over 17 seasons.

The strongly religious Hooper was reputed to
have prayed for a Boston victory in the final game of
the 1912 Series and to have attributed to divine
intervention his bare-handed, game-saving catch off
Larry Doyle which prevented victory by the Giants.
Years later at an old-timers' game, Doyle was asked
if he remembered Hooper and replied, "How in hell
can I ever forget him!" In 1915 Hooper became the
first player to hit two homers in a single World
Series game.

Recalling his years with the Red Sox, Hooper told
Lawrence Ritter that it was he who convinced
manager Ed Barrow to move young Babe Ruth to
the outfield on the days when Ruth was not pitching
in order to exploit Ruth's crowd appeal and ability
as a slugger. That was in 1919, shortly before owner
Harry Frazee sold off his best players, including
Ruth, for cash. Disgusted by the sales, Hooper held

out for a salary of $15,000. Frazee dealt Hooper for cash and two reserve outfielders to the Chicago White Sox, whose owner, Charlie Comiskey, hoped that the acquisition of a big-name player would restore credibility to his franchise, which had been shattered by the Black Sox scandal. The unhappy Hooper threatened to retire, but finally joined the White Sox for a salary of $13,250 which he told Comiskey he would accept as a goodwill gesture toward the new club. Five years later, when the White Sox had seemingly righted themselves with an influx of young talent, Comiskey reduced Hooper's salary to a stingy $7,000.

Hooper retired to enter the booming real estate market. He later coached baseball at Princeton and was the postmaster of Capitola, California. In 1971 Hooper was elected to the Hall of Fame by the Veterans Committee. /(CR)

Bob Hoopere — 1922-80. RHP 1950-55 **A's**, Indians, Reds 621 ip, 40-41, 4.80

Canadian-born Hoopere won 15 games as a rookie with the last-place 1950 Philadelphia Athletics, who won only 52 games that year. After one more good season in 1951 (12-10), Hoopere developed arm trouble. He spent two more seasons with the A's before becoming a relatively obscure member of the great 1954 Cleveland pitching staff. /(MA)

Burt Hooton (Happy) — 1950- . RHP 1971-85 Cubs, **Dodgers**, Rangers 2651 ip, 151-136, 3.38. *3 LCS, 21 ip, 2-0, 3.00 3 WS, 32 ip, 3-3, 3.69* ☛ *All-Star—81.*

Hooton acquired the ironic nickname Happy from Tommy Lasorda for never looking the part. After going 35-3 for the University of Texas, he signed with the Cubs for $50,000 in 1971 and went straight to Tacoma, where his 19-strikeout game tied a 66-year-old Pacific Coast League record. In his first three ML games, in September of that year, he held opposing hitters to a .111 average and struck out 15 in one game. The following April 16, he no-hit the Phillies in his fourth ML start. His performance steadily declined with the Cubs, but he responded to a 1975 trade to the Dodgers by winning his final 12 decisions, finishing 18-9. His unusual knuckle curve made him a mainstay of baseball's best rotation through nine seasons and three pennants. He peaked at 19-10 in 1978. During the prolonged 1981 postseason he went 4-1 with a 0.82 ERA and defeated the Yankees in the final game of the WS. /(TG)

Joe Hoover — 1915-1965. SS 1943-45 **Tigers** 338 g, .243, 5 hr, 84 rbi. *1 WS, 1 g, .333*

Hoover was the Tigers shortstop in 1943-45 while all three Detroit shortstops from 1942—Billy Hitchcock, Johnny Lipon, and Murray Franklin -were in the military. His last ML appearance came in Game Six of the 1945 World Series. Hoover drove a run in during that game, which Detroit won 8-7 in extra innings. /(JCA)

Gail Hopkins — 1943- . 1B 1968-74 **White Sox**, Royals, Dodgers 514 g, .266, 25 hr, 145 rbi

Signed as a catcher, the stocky contact hitter mostly played first base and pinch hit during his seven ML seasons, then pursued a medical career. The left-handed hitter was tough to strike out, fanning only 83 times in 1,219 at-bats (6.8%). /(JCA)

Johnny Hopp (Cotney, Hippity) — 1916- . OF-1B 1939-52 **Cardinals**, Braves, Pirates, Dodgers, Yankees, Tigers 1393 g, .296, 46 hr, 458 rbi. *5 WS, 16 g, .160* ☛ *All-Star—46.*

Hopp's cotton-colored hair led to the nickname Cotney, used by friends and teammates; the press preferred the alliterative Hippity. He played with abandon typical of the Cardinals Gashouse Gang, diving into bases head first as Pepper Martin had before him. 1941 was Hopp's first season as a regular, when he subbed at first base for an injured Johnny Mize. Hopp was so successful (.303) that St. Louis traded Mize to the Giants. Hopp hit .336 as the 1944 World Champion Cardinals' centerfielder, leading NL outfielders with a .997 fielding percentage. He batted a career-high .339 in 1950 with Pittsburgh and the Yankeees. /(JK)

Tsuneo Horiuchi (Bad Boy Taro) — 1948- . P 1966-81 **Yomiuri Giants**

One of the Yomiuri Giants' top pitchers throughout the late 1960s and 1970s, Horiuchi became better known for his mouth and flamboyance than for his arm. Winning 12 consecutive games as an 18-year-old rookie, he proclaimed himself a superstar, refused to bow respectfully to elder players, argued with management, goofed off in exhibition games, spat while on television, and shamefully let his cap fall off during his follow-through. He went on to taunt rivals and discuss their shortcomings with uncommon candor throughout his career. He pitched his way back into the good graces of Japanese fans in a disastrous 1971 postseason series against the Baltimore Orioles as one Japanese pitcher with whom the Orioles had trouble./(MC)

Joe Horlen [Joel Edward] — 1937- . RHP 1961-72 **White Sox**, A's 2001 ip, 116-117, 3.11. *1 LCS, 0 ip, 0-1, 1 WS, 1 ip, 0-0, 6.75*
☛ *Led League—era 67. All-Star—67.*

Tobacco made Horlen sick. The cure was a wad of Kleenex; Horlen swirled the stuff around in his mouth the day he no-hit the Tigers, September 10, 1967. Four years earlier, against Washington on July 29, 1963, he had carried a no-hitter into the ninth. With one out, Chuck Hinton dribbled a single into center, and with two out, Don Lock drilled a hanging curve to the outer reaches of RFK Stadium. The memory of that game seemed to cast a pall on "Hard Luck Horlen," who posted a 1.88 ERA the next season, but had to settle for a 13–9 record. His glory year was 1967, but even a 19–7 record with the AL's highest winning percentage (.731) and lowest ERA (2.06) did not translate into a Cy Young award. The honor went to Jim Lonborg (22–9, 3.16) of the pennant-winning Red Sox./(RL)

Bob Horner — 1957- . 3B-1B 1978-86, 88 **Braves**, Cardinals 1020 g, .277, 218 hr, 685 rbi. *1 LCS, 3 g, .091*
☛ *Rookie of the Year—78. All-Star—82.*

Bob Horner went straight from Arizona State University to Atlanta's starting line-up with impressive but ultimately disappointing results. He was a second baseman on *TSN*'s College All-America team in 1977 and 1978, signed for a $175,000 bonus with the Braves, hit a home run in his first major league game, and won Rookie of the Year honors. A steady home run hitter, Horner fought weight and injury problems. Slow, with poor range, he moved from third to first in 1985. A dead-pull streak hitter and slow starter, Horner played for the Yakult Swallows of Japan in 1987 after playing out his option with the Braves. He was signed by the Cardinals in 1988 to replace their departed slugger Jack Clark. Horner tied a major league record with a four-home run game in 1986./(ME)

Rogers Hornsby (Rajah) — 1896-1963. 2B-SS 1915-37 **Cardinals**, Giants, Braves, Cubs, Browns 2259 g, .358, 301 hr, 1584 rbi. *2 WS, 12 g, .245, 5 rbi.*
    Manager 1925-26, 28, 30-37, 52-53 Cardinals, Braves, Cubs, **Browns**, Reds 680-798, .460. *1 WS, 4-3, .571*
☛ *Most Valuable Player—25, 29. Led League—ba 20-25, 28. Led League—hr 22, 25. Led League—rbi 20-22, 25. Hall of Fame—1942.*

Baseball's greatest righthanded hitter always stood in the far back corner of the batter's box and strode into the pitch with a perfectly level swing. Catchers frequently called low and away against him, but his diagonal stride brought those pitches comfortably within reach. High and inside, he said, was hardest to hit, because his move edged him so close to the pitch. Often he simply leaned away, and umpires who respected his judgment of the strike zone would call a ball.

At the plate, Hornsby was imperturbable. He never argued with umpires, and was never thrown out of a game. He hit line drives to all fields, and was swift down to first and going for extra bases. His power was formidable; he led his league four times in doubles, once in triples, and twice in home runs, and his 289 HR as a second baseman are an all-time record. He hit safely in 33 consecutive games in 1922. Only thirteen players have amassed more than his 1,011 extra-base hits, and just six have topped his .577 career slugging average. Only Ty Cobb exceeded his .358 lifetime batting average, and no modern player (four did it before 1900) ever hit higher than his .424 in 1924. Since he could hit them all, he feared no pitcher. He disdained golf, he once explained, because when he hit a ball, he wanted someone else to chase it.

Hornsby came to the Cardinals as a shortstop, but was tried at third, and even in the outfield. By 1920 he was settled at second. No disgrace in the field, he led the NL in various categories, ending with a .957 career fielding average. As a shortstop in 1917 he tied a ML record with 14 assists in a game. He was known for the difficulty he had with pop flies, due to a balance problem when going back and looking up.

Outwardly, Hornsby was clearly made in the heroic mold. Handsome, dimpled, rosy-cheeked, forthright, professional, spirited, and motivated, he had the statistics to prove his preeminence. When Sam Breadon traded him to the Giants in 1926, following his first MVP year and at the height of his popularity as a World Series-winning player-manager, St. Louis rocked in a hurricane of protest. But

Rogers Hornsby

it, too. He received $100,000 even though every club in the league had to ante up to pay for it.

In New York, Hornsby had grudging admiration for manager John McGraw, and served as deputy manager in his absence. He won few friends among the players, however, and had no admiration at all for the management. Owner Charles Stoneham and his subordinates suffered the rough edge of Hornsby's tongue in public, and Stoneham was so angry that he took a fraction of the hero's value from the Braves to get rid of him after one season.

Boston liked him, and his .387 average, but could not refuse the Cubs' offer of $200,000 and five players in a trade after the 1928 season. The Rajah won his second MVP award in 1929 (.380, 39 HR, 149 RBI, and a league-leading 156 runs scored) as the Cubs took their first pennant since 1918. Hornsby was cool, distant, and professional with everyone, though still outspoken. A broken leg kept him out of action in 1930, and shortly before season's end he replaced Joe McCarthy as manager.

He led the Cubs to third place in 1931, batting .331, but was fired in mid-1932. A heel spur had kept him from playing much, but the club was doing well. Again, it was front-office trouble that got him ousted. Gambling on horses, a lifelong compulsion, had him in debt. Even scoldings by Commissioner Landis were received in chill silence or were bluntly rebuffed. Under Charlie Grimm, the club clinched the pennant, and its smoldering dislike for Hornsby ignited when the team did not vote him a World Series share.

Hornsby played out his career as a pinch hitter, hitting .300 for both St. Louis teams. He then managed the Browns and a succession of minor league teams. Bill Veeck brought him back in 1952 to manage the Browns again, and Gabe Paul gave him a shot with Cincinnati. In 1961 he scouted for the about-to-be New York Mets, and then he coached for them in 1962. Through it all, he never changed. He didn't smoke or drink, not even coffee. To preserve his unparalleled batting eye, he refused to read or go to the movies. He was an old-time lobby-sitter, and would talk endlessly about hitting to anyone who wanted to learn, though he never understood why ordinary players didn't become Hornsbys by heeding his instructions. /(ADS)

Rick Horton — 1959– . LHP 1984– **Cardinals**, White Sox, Dodgers 631 ip, 31–26, 3.68. *3 LCS, 10 ip, 0–0, 2.61. 2 WS, 7 ip, 0–0, 6.43*

In four years with the Cardinals, Horton was successful in long and short relief and starting. The soft

Breadon had had a bellyful of Hornsby. The other side of the man was a barbed-wire personality, cold, contentious, and brutally frank. He had a big problem dealing with authority. Owners and front-office men invariably saw him at his most belligerent. His hazel eyes locking into theirs, he told them to get out of his clubhouse, stop harassing his players, mind their own business, and leave him alone or get someone else to do the job.

For Breadon, already infuriated by his employee's verbal abuse, the last straw was a contract dispute. Hornsby wanted three years at $50,000 each. Breadon, always nervous about money, offered one year, lost patience with the impasse, and dealt him away for Frank Frisch and Jimmy Ring, a better trade for St. Louis than it first seemed. The Rajah then added insult to injury by pushing Breadon for top dollar for the 1,167 shares of Cardinal stock he had acquired at Branch Rickey's departure. He got thrower was best at working the corners and holding runners. His speed made him valuable as a pinch runner. /(FO)

Tony Horton — 1944– . 1B 1964–70 Red Sox, **Indians** 636 g, .268, 76 hr, 297 rbi

After hitting .278 with 27 HR and 93 RBI in 1969, the career of this promising hitter ended at age 25 the following year when a batting slump and booing fans led to such emotional distress that he had to be hospitalized. Horton hit three homers for Cleveland on May 24, 1970, but was reportedly upset because the Indians lost when he failed to hit a fourth. /(JCA)

Willie Horton — 1942– . OF-DH 1963–80 **Tigers**, Rangers, Indians, A's, Blue Jays, Mariners 2028 g, .273, 325 hr, 1163 rbi. *1 LCS, 5 g, .100. 1 WS, 7 g, .304, 1 hr, 3 rbi*
☛ *All-Star—65, 68, 70, 73.*

A short, squat, but immensely strong righthanded slugger, Horton battled weight problems throughout his ML career but was always one of the AL's most dangerous long-ball threats, hitting two home runs in a game 30 different times. He was the Tigers left fielder from 1965 to 1974, then became a designated hitter as he added both years and pounds, and in his final four ML seasons he played for six different AL clubs.

Horton stood barely 5'11", and early in his career he often reported to spring training weighing 220–230 lbs., where he would attempt to shed 20 lbs. to reach his playing weight. He was an All-Star in his first full ML season (1965), hitting .273 with 29 HR and 104 RBI, and hit 27 HR with 100 RBI the following year. An ankle problem hampered him in 1967, but he recovered from off-season surgery to hit .285 with 36 HR in 1968 as the Tigers captured the AL pennant. In the WS, he showed a surprisingly strong throwing arm, nailing Cardinals speedster Lou Brock at home plate on a key play in Game Five on the way to a seven-game Detroit victory. And in 1969 three of his 28 HR were grand slams.

Horton's home run production tailed off considerably from 1970 to 1974, but he hit .305 in 1970 and a career-high .316 in 1973. Then, in 1975, he became Detroit's full-time designated hitter and belted 25 HR. The Tigers traded Horton to Texas for Steve Foucault at the beginning of the 1977 season, and the Rangers shipped him to Cleveland with aborted phenom David Clyde for Tom Buskey and John Lowenstein before 1978. Horton was the DH for the Indians, A's, and Blue Jays at various times in 1978, then signed with the Mariners as a

free agent and played all 162 games in 1979, slugging 29 HR with 106 RBI. He retired after the 1980 season, fourth on the Tigers all-time home run list. /(SCL)

Al Horwits — 1903–Unk. *Writer.*

Horwits went from high school in 1920 to the baseball beat for the Philadelphia *Public Ledger*. His biggest scoop came in 1933, when he broke the story of the A's stars being sold three weeks before the official announcement. The *Public Ledger* folded in 1942, and Horwits worked for the Athletics for a few years. In 1945 he was president of the BBWAA. Later he worked in Hollywood as a publicist for Universal Pictures. /(NLM)

Dave Hostetler — 1956– . 1B-DH 1981–84, 88 Expos, **Rangers**, Pirates 255 g, .229, 37 hr, 124 rbi

Hostetler hit .232 with 22 HR and 67 RBI as the Rangers' primary first baseman in 1982, but struck out 113 times in 418 at-bats and saw less playing time thereafter. /(WOR)

Byron Houck — 1891–1969. RHP 1912–14, 18 **A's**, Brooklyn (FL), Browns 531 ip, 26–24, 3.30

With the Athletics, Houck was sometimes unbeatable, and sometimes walked virtually every batter he faced. He led the AL with eight relief wins in 1913, earning $2,100, and jumped to the Federal League in 1914. /(NLM)

Charlie Hough — 1948– . RHP 1970– Dodgers, **Rangers** 2888 ip, 174–157, 3.60. *3 LCS, 6 ip, 0–0, 5.68. 3 WS, 12 ip, 0–0, 4.38*
☛ *All-Star—86.*

Almost exclusively a reliever with the Dodgers, Charlie Hough became one of the greatest starting pitchers in Texas Rangers history. The knuckleballer led Texas in wins, complete games, and innings pitched each year from 1982 to 1987, winning a higher percentage of his club's victories than any other major league hurler those six years, and became the club's all-time leader in strikeouts, games pitched, wins, losses, innings pitched, and walks. In 1987 Charlie became the oldest pitcher in American League history to lead the league in starts and innings pitched, achieving career highs in wins, strikeouts, starts and innings at age 39. He also helped the Rangers set a major league record with 73 passed balls, contributing to 65 of them.

Originally signed as a third baseman, Hough learned the knuckler from Los Angeles scout Goldie Hold, with help from Hoyt Wilhelm, Jim Brewer, and Tom Lasorda. A middle-innings reliever with the Dodgers, Hough led the NL with 12 relief wins in 1976. He started just once from 1970 to 1978. /(ME)

Frank Hough — Unk.-1913. *Writer.*

Hough was a baseball writer for the Philadelphia *Inquirer* when Connie Mack arrived to launch the A's in 1901, and was one of two newspapermen given 25 percent of the team to help get it started. He later sold his interest in the club to Mack and became sporting editor of the *Inquirer.* /(NLM)

Ralph Houk (Major) — 1919- . C 1947-54 **Yankees** 91 g, .272, 0 hr, 20 rbi. *2 WS, 2 g, .500.*
    Manager 1961-63, 66-78, 81-84 **Yankees**, Tigers, Red Sox 1619-1531, .514. First place: 61-63 *3 WS, 8-8, .500*

After WWII combat duty, Houk debuted with the 1947 Yankees, hitting .272 in 41 games, before the arrival of Yogi Berra sent Houk back to the minors. He played only 50 more games in seven seasons as Berra's back-up. Following three years managing Denver (American Association) and three as a Yankee coach, he replaced Casey Stengel as Yankee manager in 1961, winning World Championships his first two seasons and adding a pennant in 1963. Kicked upstairs after the Dodgers swept the '63 WS, Houk served as Yankee vice president and general manager until May 1966. During that time, critical mistakes were made, notably keeping declining veterans until their trade value dissipated. Back on the field, Houk managed the Yankees (1966–73), the Tigers (1974–78), and the Red Sox (1981–84). After 20 years of managing, he stood tenth in games, wins, and losses, with a .514 winning percentage. A player favorite, Houk was never fired. Houk was named a Twins' vice president in November 1986, and his advice helped build the Twins' 1987 World Champions. /(MC)

Frank House [Henry Franklin] (Pig) — 1930- . C 1950-51, 54-61 **Tigers**, A's, Reds 653 g, .248, 47 hr, 235 rbi

This bonus baby was the Tigers' most active catcher from 1954 to 1957. The chunky, lefthanded-hitting Alabaman peaked in 1955 with 15 HR and 53 RBI in 102 games. He earned his nickname as a baby, when his family used to say he was "big as a house" and he twisted "big" into "pig." /(CC)

Tom House — 1947- . LHP 1971-78 **Braves**, Red Sox, Mariners 536 ip, 29-23, 3.79

The bespectacled reliever led Atlanta with 11 saves in both 1974 and '75. An extra in several movies and TV shows, House had his biggest moment in the spotlight on April 8, 1974, when he caught Hank Aaron's 715th home run in Atlanta's bullpen. He became the Rangers' pitching coach in 1985 and gained notoriety for having his pitchers throw footballs as a training routine. /(JCA)

Paul Householder — 1958- . OF 1980-87 **Reds**, Cardinals, Brewers, Astros 466 g, .236, 29 hr, 144 rbi

A switch-hitter with power in the minors who was said to have had all the tools, Householder was continually expected to blossom, but never did. With the Reds in 1983, his .991 fielding percentage led all NL outfielders. When Milwaukee's Robin Yount had surgery in September 1985, Householder, given a last chance to play every day, hit eight homers for the month. /(JCA)

Houston Astros [aka Colt .45s] — 1962- . Team. 2167-2306, .484. *NL West Champions 80, 86*

The Astros gave their name to Astroturf, the plastic grass that came into baseball because the real thing died indoors. It was a new problem, for the Astrodome was the first domed baseball park (opened in 1965), an attempt to avoid the Texas heat. The stadium was the brainchild of Astros owner Roy Hofheinz, who had a Texan's sense of size and spectacle.

    The club was originally to be in the proposed Continental League, an operation forestalled by the major leagues with the old tactic of offering the soundest owners new ML franchises. Unlike the Mets, the Astros (then called the Colt .45s) immediately went with youth under the direction of GM Paul Richards, a master talent evaluator. Products of the Astros' farm system in the 1960s included Joe Morgan and Rusty Staub. The strategy didn't make them instant contenders, like the AL's Angels, but it kept them above the Mets. The club reached the .500 level in the first year of divisional play, 1969, and contended off and on through the 1970s, which featured Cesar Cedeno, called "The New Willie Mays" by manager Leo Durocher. The arrival of overpowering pitcher J.R. Richard in 1976 made the team even stronger. He suffered a career-ending stroke in 1980, but the club went on to its first division title that year, led by franchise favorite Jose Cruz, the reacquired Morgan, and 20-game-winner

The 1980 Houston Astros

Joe Niekro. They finished in a tie with the Dodgers but won the one-game playoff. The team won the second half of the 1981 strike-split season, but this time the Dodgers prevailed in postseason play. Led by Cy Young winner and split-finger fastballer Mike Scott, the Astros captured another division title in 1986, but lost to the Mets in a storied LCS that featured Scott's MVP performance in a losing cause, Nolan Ryan's nine innings of two-hit, 12-strikeout pitching to a no-decision in Game Five as the Astros lost in 12 innings, and the climactic Game Six, a 16-inning topsy-turvy marathon won by New York. /(WOR)

Art Houtteman (Hard Luck) — 1927- . RHP 1945–50, 52–57 **Tigers**, Indians, Orioles 1555 ip, 87–91, 4.14. *1 WS, 2 ip, 0–0, 4.50*
☛ *All-Star—50.*

Signed off the Detroit sandlots, Houtteman first appeared with the Tigers at 17. A fast learner with a sharp curve and deceptive sinker, he came back from a 2–16 season in 1948 to win 15 in 1949. He suffered a fractured skull that year but recovered to win 19 games in 1950. After a year in the army, and the death of his baby in a car crash, he struggled to

an 8–20 record in 1952. Traded to Cleveland, he was 15–7 for the 1954 pennant-winners. /(JCA)

Steve Hovley — 1944- . OF 1969–73 **Pilots/ Brewers**, A's, Royals 436 g, .258, 8 hr, 88 rbi

The free-spirited Stanford graduate once quipped, "Billy Graham is a cracker." Hovley debuted with the one-year Pilots in 1969. Starting the season with a crewcut, he wouldn't cut his hair, not wanting to discriminate against any particular hairs. A line-drive hitter with good speed, Hovley was generally a fourth outfielder and led the AL in pinch-hit appearances with Kansas City in 1972. /(JCA)

Bruce Howard — 1943- . RHP 1963–68 **White Sox**, Orioles, Senators 528 ip, 26–31, 3.18

Because of roster limits, the White Sox had to decide which of two young pitchers to keep at the beginning of the 1963 season. They squared off in an intra-squad game. Howard won and remained with the team, becoming a spot starter from 1965 to 1967. He used a slip pitch and sinker effectively, but was troubled by wildness and eventually left the majors. The other young pitcher, after being released by the Sox, signed with the Tigers. His name was Denny McLain. /(RL)

Del Howard (George) — 1877–1956. OF-1B-2B
Pirates, Braves, **Cubs** 536 g, .263, 6 hr, 193 rbi. *2 WS, 3 g, .167*

Howard played regularly for the Pirates and Braves before coming to the Cubs in 1907. Although he could not break into the strong Chicago lineup, he was a useful backup on the 1907 and '08 championship teams. His younger brother Ivan played in the AL from 1914 to 1917. /(BC)

Elston Howard — 1929–1980. C-OF 1955–68
Yankees, Red Sox 1605 g, .274, 167 hr, 762 rbi. *10 WS, 54 g, .246, 5 hr, 19 rbi*
☛ *Most Valuable Player—63. All-Star—57–65. Gold Glove—63–64.*

The Yankees' first black player, Howard was forced to play the outfield through much of his first five seasons because Yogi Berra was behind the plate. By 1960, Howard was the starting catcher and Berra was more often in the field. Howard was an exceptional defensive catcher; his .993 career fielding average is one of the highest ever, and he pioneered

Elston Howard

the use of a hinged catcher's mitt that led to the modern one-handed catching techniques. He was also highly regarded as a handler of pitchers. He was named to the AL All-Star team nine consecutive years.

Howard was a strong hitter, three times topping .300, with a high of .348 in 1961. He hit from an exaggerated spread stance when he came up, which he modified later in his career. He was AL MVP in 1963, as much for his leadership as for his .287 BA, 28 homers, and 85 RBI. He led the Yankees to their fourth straight pennant in a year when Maris and Mantle were often out with injuries.

After playing in nine WS with the Yankees, he was traded to the Red Sox in August of 1967 and helped Boston to that season's pennant. In 1969, he returned to the Yankees, where he served as a coach for eleven years. Howard and Pee Wee Reese share the record for playing on the most WS losers. /(GDW)

Frank Howard (The Capital Punisher, Hondo) —
1936– OF-1B 1958–73 Dodgers, **Senators**,
Rangers, Tigers 1902 g, .273, 382 hr, 1119 rbi. *1 WS, 3 g, .300, 1 hr, 1 rbi.*
    Manager 1981, 83 Padres, **Mets** 93–133, .412
☛ *Rookie of the Year—60. Led League—hr 68, 70. Led League—rbi 70. All-Star—68–71.*

The 6'8" 275-lb Howard captured NL Rookie of the Year honors in 1960 with the Dodgers, batting .268 with 23 HR and 77 RBI in 117 games. He hit 31 HR in 1962, but was traded to Washington in a December 1964 deal that brought Claude Osteen to Los Angeles. The Senators' behemoth slugger went on a rampage in May 1968, hitting a ML record 10 HR in 20 at-bats over a stretch of six consecutive games. He finished the year with 44 HR, leading the AL. He hit a career-high 48 in 1969, but Harmon Killebrew beat him by one. Howard recaptured the HR crown (44) and added the RBI title (126) in 1970. In 1974 he went to Japan to play for Taiheiyo, but he hurt his back striking out in his first game and never played again.

A warm and upbeat character, Howard coached for the Brewers and was the Padres' manager for the 1981 season. A coach with the Mets, he took over as interim manager for 116 games in 1983 when George Bamberger resigned. He began coaching first base for the Mariners in 1987.

A college All-American at Ohio State in both baseball and basketball, Howard still holds two Madison Square Garden Holiday Festival Tournament rebounding records. /(RTM)

Frank Howard

Wilbur Howard — 1947– . OF 1973–78 Brewers, **Astros** 466 g, .250, 6 hr, 71 rbi

Howard spent his first year in the minors as a pitcher, but reached the ML as a good defensive outfielder and pinch hitter. In by far his busiest season (121 games, Houston, 1975), he hit .283 with 32 steals and 67 runs. /(JCA)

Art Howe — 1946– . 3B-2B-1B 1974–82, 84–85 Pirates, **Astros**, Cardinals 891 g, .260, 43 hr, 293 rbi. *2 LCS, 6 g, .188, 2 rbi.*
Manager 1989– **Astros** 86–76, .531

A handyman in the Astros' infield from 1977 to 1982, Howe's .432 average in May 1981 earned NL Player of the Month honors. He hit a career-high .296 that year. After five years as a Rangers coach, Howe was named the Astros manager for 1989. /(FJO)

Irwin M. Howe — 1866–1934. *Statistician.*

After 20 years as a printing salesman, Howe began compiling and distributing baseball records. In 1911 he formed the Howe News Bureau and became official statistician for the American League and many minor leagues. He designed the official scoring blank still in use. /(NLM)

Steve Howe — 1958– . LHP 1980–83, 85, 87 **Dodgers**, Twins, Rangers 379 ip, 29–31, 2.70. *1 LCS, 2 ip, 0–0, 0.00. 1 WS, 7 ip, 1–0, 3.86*
☛ *Rookie of the Year—80. All-Star—82.*

Howe broke Joe Black's club rookie record for saves with 17 for the 1980 Dodgers. The hard-throwing reliever enjoyed four sparkling seasons in Los Angeles, concluding with 18 saves and a 1.44 ERA in 1983. Howe unraveled quickly, however, when he admitted using cocaine during games the previous year, and after he failed drug tests, Commissioner Bowie Kuhn suspended him for the 1984 season to protect the "image of baseball." Comeback attempts in 1985 and 1987 failed as Howe kept reverting to drug use, but in 1989 he claimed once again to have finally beaten his addiction and announced plans to return to the ML in 1990. /(TG)

Dixie Howell [Millard] — 1920–1960. RHP 1940, 49, 55–58 Indians, Reds, **White Sox** 226 ip, 19–15, 3.78

Howell labored in the minors for 18 years before earning a spot in the White Sox bullpen in 1955 at age 35. In three years of short relief, he won 19 and saved 19. /(RL)

Dixie Howell [Homer Elliott] — 1919– . C 1947, 49–53, 55–56 Pirates, **Reds**, Dodgers 340 g, .246, 12 hr, 93 rbi

After performing part-time duty behind the plate for the 1947 Pirates and for the Reds, Howell closed out his career in Brooklyn as a seldom-seen backup to the great Roy Campanella. /(FK)

Harry Howell (Handsome Harry) — 1876–1956. RHP 1898–1910 Dodgers, Baltimore (NL), Baltimore (AL)/ Yankees, **Browns** 2568 ip, 131–146, 2.74

An early spitballer, Howell was the workhorse of the 1904–08 Browns pitching staff, averaging 308 innings and 15 wins a season. In three of those years, his ERA was 1.98 or less. He lost his job as a

Browns scout when he tried to pressure the St. Louis official scorer to give an extra hit to Cleveland's Nap Lajoie on the last day of the 1910 season. Lajoie and Ty Cobb were in a tight race for the batting title; Lajoie had eight hits against the Browns that day, but Cobb took the title by a point. Howell became a minor league umpire. /(NLM)

Jack Howell — 1961- . 3B-OF 1985- **Angels** 542 g, .241, 68 hr, 218 rbi. *1 LCS, 2 g, .000*

The Angels released veteran third baseman Doug DeCinces late in 1987 to give a position to left-handed-hitting Jack Howell, who had spent that season playing third, second, and the outfield and had hit 23 HR. One of those homers was a broken-bat shot in Yankee Stadium that confirmed for many that the 1987 ball was juiced up. Bothered by a thumb injury for much of 1988, Howell put up only mediocre numbers (.254, 16 HR, 63 RBI)./(JCA)

Jay Howell — 1955- . RHP 1980- Reds, Cubs, **Yankees**, A's, Dodgers 579 ip, 39–36, 3.58. *1 LCS, 0.2 ip, 0–1, 27.00. 1 WS, 3 ip, 0–1, 3.38*
☛ *All-Star—85, 87, 89.*

Howell was one of the hardest-throwing relief pitchers of the 1980s, despite an up-and-down career. He led the AL in strikeouts per inning in 1984 with the Yankees and became the stopper for the A's and the Dodgers. He had his best season in 1989 (5–3, 1.58 ERA, 28 saves). In between, he endured horrible collapses, with ERAs above 5.00 in both 1983 and 1987. He was the losing pitcher in the 1987 All-Star Game.

Howell achieved national notoriety with the Dodgers in the 1988 LCS against the Mets. In Game Three, played in a cold rain, he was ejected for having pine tar on his glove. He was suspended: at first for the next three LCS games, but ultimately, after an appeal, for two. He had already lost Game One in the ninth inning on the first run he had surrendered since August 11. In the World Series, his inconsistency continued; he surrendered a game-losing ninth-inning homer to the A's Mark McGwire in Game Three, but came back the next day to save Game Four with 2–1/3 innings of scoreless relief. /(TG)

Ken Howell — 1960- . RHP 1984- **Dodgers**, Phillies 303 ip, 18–29, 4.04. *1 LCS, 2 ip, 0–0, 0.00*

One of the hardest throwers in baseball, Howell once struck out 14 consecutive batters in winter ball. He enjoyed uncharacteristically good control when he

came up in 1984, but reverted to form in subsequent years. He was traded from the Dodgers to the Orioles in the Eddie Murray deal December 4, 1988, then was dealt to the Phillies in a package for Phil Bradley four days later. Made a starter, he went 12–12 with a 3.44 ERA for last-place Philadelphia and was the ace of their rotation. /(TG)

Roy Howell — 1953- . 3B 1974–84 Rangers, **Blue Jays**, Brewers 1112 g, .261, 80 hr, 454 rbi. *1 LCS, 1 g, .000. 1 WS, 4 g, .000*
☛ *All-Star—78.*

Drafted from the Rangers in 1977, the red-haired Howell became a local star for the brand-new expansion Blue Jays. In September of that year, he had a team-record nine RBI as Toronto thrashed the Yankees 19–3 at Yankee Stadium. He held team career records in hits, total bases, RBI, and strike-outs when he left as a free agent to sign with Milwaukee in 1981. /(TF)

Bill Howerton (Hopalong) — 1921- . OF 1949–52 **Cardinals**, Pirates, Giants 247 g, .274, 22 hr, 106 rbi

Wild horses couldn't keep Howerton from a professional baseball career. The California cowboy overcame a severe ankle injury in a childhood riding accident to be named to *TSN*'s 1950 All-Rookie team, hitting .281 with 10 HR and 59 RBI. /(JL)

Dan Howley (Dapper Dan) — 1885–1944. C 1913 **Phillies** 26 g, .125, 0 hr, 2 rbi.
Manager 1927–32 **Browns**, Reds 397–524, .431

Howley broke in as a catcher with Indianapolis of the American Association in 1906 and appeared briefly with the Phillies in 1913. He managed at Montreal for four years, then moved to Toronto (International League), where he won a pennant in 1918. He was a coach for the Tigers in 1919 and 1921–22. He returned to Toronto, and in 1926 won a pennant to break Baltimore's streak of seven straight flags. A combative manager known for his ability to develop young pitchers, he managed the Browns and Reds for three seasons each. In 1928 he brought the Browns in third, his best ML finish. /(NLM)

Dick Howser — 1937–1987. SS-2B 1961–68 A's, **Indians**, Yankees 789 g, .248, 16 hr, 165 rbi.
Manager 1978, 80–86 Yankees, **Royals** 507–425, .544. First place: 80–81, 84–85 *3 LCS, 4–9, .308. 1 WS, 4–3, .571*
☛ *All-Star—61.*

A feisty, quick infielder with good bat, Howser later became respected as a successful manager, but died tragically on the heels of his greatest personal triumph: leading the Royals to the 1985 World Championship.

The 5'8" 155-lb Howser signed with the Athletics for a reported $21,000 bonus and had two outstanding seasons. In 1961 he hit .280, stole 37 bases, scored 108 runs, and was named *TSN* AL Rookie of the Year. He also led AL shortstops in putouts and errors. His only other year as a regular was 1964, when he hit .258 with 101 runs and 20 steals.

Howser won an AL East title for the Yankees his first full year as manager (1980), but was sacked by George Steinbrenner when the Yankees lost the LCS. He returned to the majors in late 1981 to lead the Royals to the AL West title. He won the division again in 1984 and the WS in 1985. But two days after he managed the AL to an All-Star Game victory in 1986, it was discovered that he had a brain tumor. He retired during spring training of 1987 and succumbed shortly afterward. /(JM)

Dummy Hoy [William Ellsworth] — 1862–1961. OF 1888–99, 1901–02 **Washington (NL)**, Buffalo (PL), St. Louis (AA), Reds, Louisville (NL), White Sox 1798 g, .288, 40 hr, 726 rbi

Hoy was the reason umpires adopted hand signals to go along with the vocal calls of "out," "safe," and "strike." The 5'4" 148-lb outfielder was a deaf-mute, but he overcame adversity to have the greatest career of any seriously handicapped player, accumulating 2,054 hits. He hit .300 three times and scored 100 runs eight times. He also stole 30 or more bases in his first twelve ML seasons, and totaled 597 in an era when runners were credited with stolen bases for taking an "extra base" (going from first to third on a single, for example). Hoy led the NL with 82 steals in his first season and set NL rookie records for games, at-bats, hits, singles, and walks. He walked frequently, leading his league with 119 in 1891 and 86 in 1901. His on-base average topped .400 four times. In the field, the centerfielder led NL outfielders in putouts and total chances per game in 1897. On June 19, 1889, he threw out three runners at the plate in one game—one of only three players ever to do that.

Hoy, one of 29 players to play in four major leagues, was a regular until his last season. He began with perennially bad Washington, jumped to the Players' League for its one season (1890), and had his first experience with a winning team playing for the Browns (AA) in 1891. When the AA folded, he was returned to Washington, but the Ohio native

Dummy Hoy with Washington of the NL

joined Cincinnati for 1894. After two seasons with the feeble Louisville franchise, he left the majors for the new Chicago White Sox of the American League. He remained with the team in 1901, the AL's first major league season. He closed out his major league career with one last season in Cincinnati in 1902, but hung on for another year with Los Angeles (Pacific Coast League), playing all of the team's 211 games and stealing 46 bases at the age of 42. He lived longer than any major league player before him, which earned him the honor of throwing out the first ball of Game Three of the 1961 World Series, at Cincinnati, at the age of 99. /(WOR)

LaMarr Hoyt [Dewey LaMarr] — 1955– . RHP 1979–86 **White Sox**, Padres 1311 ip, 98–68, 3.99. 20 wins: 83 *1 LCS, 9 ip, 1–0, 1.00*
☛ *Led League—w 82–83. Cy Young Award—83. All-Star—85.*

Hoyt was an unknown pitcher struggling in the Yankee farm system sent to the White Sox along with Oscar Gamble and Bob Polinsky on April 5, 1976. In return the Yanks received Bucky Dent. The deal was roundly criticized in Chicago, but it ultimately paid dividends. Hoyt began his ML career in 1980 in Chicago's bullpen. In 1982 he was put into the rotation with startling success. He won his first nine decisions to equal a White Sox record set by Lefty Williams in 1917 and Orval Grove in 1943, and finished 19–15, leading the AL in wins. As a starter, his already sharp control became almost unbelievable; he walked only 48 batters in 239.2 innings.

As good as he'd been, Hoyt improved in every way to lead Chicago to the AL West title in 1983. He was 15–2 after the All-Star break, en route to a landslide Cy Young Award. Hoyt walked just 31 batters that year, four of which were intentional. The total was just three more than Cy Young's record of 28, set in 1904. His 24 victories paced the AL for the second year in a row, and in the ALCS he tossed a five-hitter against Baltimore in the opener to claim Chicago's only win.

Hoyt faltered along with the rest of the White Sox team in 1984. He did fire a one-hitter against the Yankees on May 2 in Comiskey Park, allowing only a scratch single to Don Mattingly. Hoyt gave up 31 homers in 1984, second-highest in the league, and after the season he was traded to San Diego with two minor leaguers for Tim Lollar, Ozzie Guillen, Bill Long, and Luis Salazar.

Hoyt was 16–8 in his first season with the Padres, and started the 1985 All-Star Game for the NL. By 1986, however, a lingering drug problem came to light, and he was suspended by Commissioner Peter Uebberoth for one year in 1987. Hoyt was invited to try out for the White Sox in 1988 following his 45-day stay in prison, but he was arrested again after law-enforcement officials uncovered a cache of marijuana and cocaine in his Columbia, South Carolina apartment. He began his second prison term on February 21, 1988./(NLM)

Waite Hoyt (Schoolboy) — 1899–1984. RHP 1918–38 Giants, Red Sox, **Yankees**, Tigers, A's, Dodgers, Pirates 3763 ip, 237–182, 3.59. 20 wins: 27–28 *7 WS, 84 ip, 6–4, 1.83*
☛ *Led League—w 27. Led League—era 27. Hall of Fame—1969.*

Hoyt was a mainstay on the pitching staff of the great Yankee teams of the 1920s. The righthander pitched for New York from 1921 to early 1930 and had a record of 157–98 in pinstripes. He was 23–7 in 1928 and also led the AL with eight saves. In 1927 he was 22–7, and he won 19 in 1921 and '22. In 1927 he led the AL in wins (22), ERA (2.63), and winning percentage (.759). He reached double figures in wins from 1921 to 1931 and in 1934. He

Waite Hoyt

spent the last seven years of his career in the NL, which he led in relief wins in 1934 (7) and 1935 (5).

Hoyt appeared in seven WS (1921–23, '26–28 with the Yankees and 1931 with the A's). He was 2–0 in 1928, and 2–1 in 1921, tying Christy Mathewson's record with a 0.00 ERA in three games started. He ranks high in numerous WS lifetime categories, including wins (6 for fifth), losses (4 for seventh), strikeouts (49 for eighth), games (12 for seventh), and innings pitched (84 for fifth). In 1941 Hoyt moved to the broadcast booth. He was the voice of the Reds until his retirement in 1965. He was elected to the Hall of Fame in 1969. /(JM)

Al Hrabosky (The Mad Hungarian) — 1949– . LHP 1970–82 **Cardinals**, Royals, Braves 721 ip, 64–35, 3.11. *1 LCS, 3 ip, 0–0, 3.00*

A blazing fastball, used 90 percent of the time, made Hrabosky one of the most effective relievers of the 1970s. The chunky southpaw's nickname, The Mad Hungarian, came from his nationality, Fu Manchu mustache and long hair, and angry stomping to the back of the mound to psych himself up. He was *TSN* NL Fireman of the Year in 1975 with St. Louis (13–3, 1.67, 22 saves). When he wasn't selected to the All-Star team in 1974, St. Louis fans rallied behind him, honoring him with a "We Hlove Hrabosky Hbanner Hday." Traded in December 1977 to the Royals for reliever Mark Littell, in 1979 he signed a multi-million-dollar contract with the Braves via free agency, but recorded only 7 of his lifetime 97 saves with Atlanta. He became a Cardinal broadcaster. /(FJO)

Kent Hrbek (Herbie) — 1960– . 1B-DH 1981- **Twins** 1156 g, .290, 201 hr, 724 rbi. *1 LCS, 5 g, .150, 1 hr, 1 rbi. 1 WS, 7 g, .208, 1 hr, 6 rbi*
☛ *All-Star—82.*

Born in Minneapolis, Minnesota, Kent Hrbek was an instant fan favorite when he joined the Twins in 1982, following a .379 batting average in the California League, best among all pro hitters in 1981. He hit the first home run in the Hubert H. Humphrey Metrodome on April 3, 1982 in an exhibition game against the Phillies. He was second to Cal Ripken, Jr. in the 1982 AL Rookie of the Year vote. The Twin MVP in 1984, Hrbek was the senior member (Minnesota service) on the 1987 World Champion Twins. Kent made the final putouts in the game that clinched the Western Division and in the final games of the LCS and World Series. He hit the 14th grand slam in World Series history in Game Six. He set club records with 20 homers in

the Metrodome and a .996 fielding percentage in 1987. With batting championship skills, the burly, sometimes overweight Hrbek sacrificed some batting average for power, but also exhibited improved discipline at the plate through his career. /(ME)

Cal Hubbard [Robert] — 1900–1977. *Umpire* AL 1937–51 *4 WS 3 ASU*
☛ *Hall of Fame—1976.*

The only man to be elected to the baseball, college football, and pro football halls of fame, Hubbard was a huge man, 6'3" and 250 lbs. At little Centenary and Geneva colleges, he won nationwide fame as a bone-crushing tackle. In his professional football career, he played end and linebacker in addition to tackle for the 1927 champion New York Giants and the 1929–31 Green Bay Packers champions. He was named at tackle on the first three official All-NFL teams, 1931–33.

He began umpiring minor league games during the summers while he was playing pro football, and

Cal Hubbard

the year after he retired from the gridiron, he became an AL umpire. In 1944, Hubbard gained notoriety as the first umpire to eject a pitcher (the Browns' Nels Potter) for throwing a spitball. Hubbard's imposing size and keen eyesight made him one of the best at his trade. He was once examined at the Boston Optical Lab and was found to have 20–10 vision, the strongest ever recorded—even better than Ted Williams.

Ironically, a hunting accident in 1951 affected the sight in his left eye and led to his retirement from the field. He served as supervisor of AL umpires for 15 years. He was elected to the Baseball Hall of Fame in 1976, the year before his death. /(RTM)

Glenn Hubbard — 1957– . 2B 1979–89 **Braves**, A's 1354 g, .244, 70 hr, 448 rbi. *1 LCS, 3 g, .222, 1 rbi. 1 WS, 4 g, .250*
☛ *All-Star—83.*

Hubbard led NL second basemen in double plays three times and assists twice, but his offensive skills gradually eroded from their 1983 peak (.263, 12 HR, 70 RBI) and his range in the field shrank as well. An aggressive, fearless player, he started at second base for Oakland's 1988 AL Champions after spending 10 seasons with Atlanta. /(ME)

Bill Hubbell — 1897–1980. RHP 1919–25 Giants, **Phillies**, Dodgers 931 ip, 40–63, 4.68

Hubbell was the cause of a baseball rules change. With the Phillies in 1925, he walked a batter intentionally by throwing four times to first base, as there was no rule against it. When he did it again several weeks later, league president John Heydler threatened to suspend him. The following year the rule was changed, requiring that the pitches be made to the catcher. /(NLM)

Carl Hubbell (King Carl, The Meal Ticket) — 1903–1988. LHP 1928–43 **Giants** 3589 ip, 253–154, 2.97. 20 wins: 33–37 *3 WS, 50 ip, 4–2, 1.79*
☛ *Most Valuable Player—33, 36. Led League—w 33, 36–37. Led League—k 37. Led League—era 33–34, 36. All-Star—33–38, 40–42. Hall of Fame—1947.*

Carl Hubbell

With his slow, cartwheel-like delivery of the screwball, the lefthander off the Oklahoma oil fields recorded five consecutive 20-win seasons for the Giants and helped propel his team to World Series competition in 1933, 1936, and 1937. He was the only peacetime pitcher ever to win two MVP awards (Hal Newhouser won two during the talent-poor years of WWII) and was a true workhorse; in 1934, while winning 21 games, pitching 313 innings, and leading the league with a 2.30 ERA, Hubbell also paced NL hurlers with eight saves. With his gaunt, smiling face, big, floppy ears, and an arm permanently turned completely around from the strain of tens of thousands of screwballs, King Carl appeared unlikely to strike fear in the hearts of opposing batters.

Hubbell was obtained by Detroit from Oklahoma

City (Western League) in 1925, but performed unspectacularly in their farm system. Manager Ty Cobb wouldn't let him throw his screwball in spring training trials, and Hubbell was outrighted to Beaumont (Texas League) in 1928. That season, a Giants' scout convinced John McGraw to acquire him. McGraw encouraged his young southpaw to utilize his best pitch at will, and Hubbell went 10–6 after his promotion in 1928. The following May 8, he no-hit the Pirates. In sixteen years with New York, he had only one losing record (11–12 in 1940) and established himself as the premier NL pitcher of his era, though he was never as colorful as his archrival, Dizzy Dean.

Hubbell's preeminence shone through most strikingly in 1933 and 1936, his MVP seasons. In '33, he led the AL with 23 wins, a 1.66 ERA, ten shutouts, and 308.2 IP. Typical of his performance was a July 2 game against the powerful Cardinals. Through eighteen innings, he controlled his singular pitch so masterfully as not to allow a walk, while striking out 12. In his two WS starts that year against the Senators, Hubbell pitched 20 innings, striking out 15, and did not allow an earned run.

The feat that Hubbell will always be remembered for took place in New York's Polo Grounds, in the second ML All-Star Game, July 10, 1934. Matched against his crosstown rival, Lefty Gomez, Hubbell allowed a single to Charley Gehringer, then walked Heinie Manush. Babe Ruth went down on five pitches, taking a screwball for a called third strike. Next, Lou Gehrig, in his prime, struck out swinging on four pitches. The baserunners pulled off a double steal, but could not break the southpaw's concentration. Jimmie Foxx fanned on three screwballs to end the first-inning threat. Handed a one-run lead, in the second, Hubbell continued his amazing streak, striking out Al Simmons and Joe Cronin. Bill Dickey managed a sharp single to center, but Hubbell came back to strike out Gomez, going on to complete three scoreless innings and establishing the All-Star record of six strikeouts.

Over the course of the 1936–37 seasons, Hubbell accomplished another incredible achievement. On July 17, 1936, with a record of 10–6, he began a streak of 16 consecutive wins through the end of the season, then picked up with eight victories to open 1937, establishing the ML record of 24 consecutive wins. His 26 victories, .813 winning percentage, and 2.31 ERA in '36 led the NL, and his 1937 numbers, 22 wins, .733, and 159 strikeouts, did the same.

After undergoing elbow surgery following the 1938 campaign, Hubbell won 11 games a season,

1939–42. He retired from play in 1943, and was named the Giants' director of minor league operations. He joined the immortals of Cooperstown in 1947, and worked for the Giants until 1977, when a stroke relegated him to part-time scouting duties. The Giants retired his number 11. /(AAs)

Ken Hubbs — 1941–1964. 2B 1961–63 **Cubs** 324 g, .247, 14 hr, 98 rbi
☛ *Rookie of the Year—62. Gold Glove—62.*

The 1962 NL Rookie of the Year set a ML record with 78 consecutive errorless games. He handled 418 chances over that stretch, also a record. "Hubbs of the Cubs" was the first rookie to win a Gold Glove, and also set a NL rookie record with 661 at-bats. Hubbs died in February 1964, when a private plane he was piloting crashed in Utah. /(DS)

Clarence Huber (Gilly) — 1897–1965. 3B 1920–21, 25–26 Tigers, **Phillies** 254 g, .263, 6 hr, 93 rbi

Huber broke in with Mexia in the West Texas League in 1915, and spent most of his career in the Texas League and Southern Association. He saw the most major league action with the 1925–26 Phillies, hitting a career-high .284 in '25 but dropping off to .245 in '26. /(NLM)

Hubert H. Humphrey Metrodome (The Homer Dome) Minnesota Twins 1982– . LF-343, CF-408, RF-327

Located just east of downtown Minneapolis, the Metrodome features a distinctive air-supported fiberglass roof, a 23′ canvas fence in right field, and the liveliest artificial turf in the ML. It was dubbed the Homer Dome in its inaugural season when 191 home runs were hit there, but with the addition of air conditioning in 1984 and the gradual raising of the fences (left field is now 13′ high), it has become a largely neutral home run park. The white roof, which makes it difficult to see fly balls, collapsed during the fall of 1982, but was quickly reinflated. And on May 4, 1984 Dave Kingman was awarded a double when his towering infield pop-up hit the roof and never came down. The Twins thrive on the support of an often deafening crowd in the Metrodome, and were 56–25 at home in 1987 (85–77 overall) before becoming the World Champions with the worst regular-season record when they swept four home WS games against the Cardinals. The Metrodome also houses football's Minnesota Vikings. /(SCL)

Rex Hudler — 1960- . 2B-SS 1984-86, 88- Yankees, Orioles, **Expos** 212 g, .247, 10 hr, 28 rbi

After bouncing around for ten years, Hudler won a platoon job at second base and shortstop with the 1988 Expos and reached new highs in every category, hitting .273 and stealing 29 bases. /(WOR)

Willis Hudlin (Ace, Hud) — 1906- . RHP 1926-40, 44 **Indians**, Senators, Browns, Giants 2613 ip, 158-156, 4.41

Hudlin and his sidearm sinker accounted for the seventh-most wins (157) and third-most losses (151) in Indian history. His work was overshadowed by teammates Mel Harder and Bob Feller, the only pitchers to work more games for Cleveland than Hudlin's 475. For three years, 1927-29, he was Cleveland's Yankee-killer, with 14 wins against New York. The scholarly-looking Hudlin was a Detroit coach, 1957-59. /(ME)

Charles Hudson — 1959- . RHP 1983- **Phillies**, Yankees, Tigers 1008 ip, 50-60, 4.14. *1 LCS, 9 ip, 1-0, 2.00. 1 WS, 8 ip, 0-2, 8.64*

Hudson made an immediate impact when the Phillies brought him up from Triple-A in June 1983. Inserted into the starting rotation, he posted an 8-8 record in 26 starts. He took a no-hitter into the ninth inning on July 20 against Houston before Craig Reynolds broke it up with a one-out bloop single. Hudson helped the Phillies reach the World Series by defeating the Dodgers in Game Three of the LCS. But he lost two games during the Series to the Orioles, never lasting through the fifth inning and tying a five-game Series record by allowing four home runs. He never reached .500 again with the Phillies and was traded to New York in 1987, where he won his first six decisions. A month-long slump led to a brief demotion to Columbus, but he recovered to finish 11-7 in 16 starts and 19 relief appearances. After a 6-6 1988 season, the Yankees traded him to Detroit. /(EG)

Johnny Hudson (Mr. Chips) — 1912-1970. 2B-SS-3B 1936-41, 45 **Dodgers**, Cubs, Giants 426 g, .242, 4 hr, 96 rbi

Hudson became a favorite in Brooklyn for his clutch hitting. Later a Giant scout, he remained on their staff from 1945 until his death. /(JK)

Sid Hudson — 1915- . RHP 1940-42, 46-54 **Senators**, Red Sox 2181 ip, 104-152, 4.28
☛ *All-Star—41-42.*

The 6'4" Hudson jumped to the Senators after two years in the Florida State League, going 24-4 in the latter. His best major league mark was 17-16 as a rookie in 1940, and he pitched an inning in the 1941 All-Star Game. After military service (1943-45), Hudson resumed his place in the Senators' rotation, tying for the AL lead with 17 losses in 1949. A good-hitting pitcher, he batted .220 lifetime, .308 in 1947. Active until age 39, he became a longtime pitching coach, instructor, and scout. /(MC)

Frank Huelsman — 1874-1959. OF 1897, 1904-05 Cardinals, White Sox, Tigers, Browns, **Senators** 240 g, .258, 5 hr, 97 rbi

Huelsman played for three other AL teams in 1904 before landing a regular position for the Senators, but after hitting .271 for Washington in 1905 he returned to the minors. He was a star in the minor leagues, compiling a .342 batting mark over nearly 20 years and winning five batting crowns and six RBI titles. /(BC)

Phil Huffman — 1958- . RHP 1979 **Blue Jays** 173 ip, 6-18, 5.77

In 1979 the pitching-poor Blue Jays rushed the 21-year-old into their starting rotation after only 34 games in the minors. He led the AL in losses (18) in a one-season career highlighted by a one-hitter against Oakland. /(TF)

Miller Huggins (Hug, The Mighty Mite) — 1879-1929. 2B-3B 1904-16 Reds, **Cardinals** 1585 g, .265, 9 hr, 318 rbi.
 Manager 1913-1929 Cardinals, **Yankees** 1413-1134, .555. First place: 21-23, 26-28 *6 WS, 18-15, .545*
☛ *Hall of Fame—1964.*

The smart, scrawny 5'6" Huggins was a first-rate second baseman before he became famous for managing the Yankees to their first six pennants and three World Championships. He was fast and sure-handed afield; his record is dotted with games in which he handled 15 chances, or figured in three double plays. He led the league in putouts, assists, double plays, and fielding once each, and twice in errors. The Mighty Mite was the ideal leadoff man, a switch-hitter who coaxed 1,002 career walks (four times leading the league) and stole some 50 bases a season (though stolen bases were not tabulated during his six early years with Cincinnati). Not a long-ball hitter, he did have three triples in a game in 1904.

  The Cardinals acquired Huggins in 1910. By 1913 he was player-manager, and by 1917 had retired to the bench. He prodded two third-place

Miller Huggins

finishes out of his nondescript team, and guided a green and awkward Rogers Hornsby through his first ML seasons. Holder of a law degree (though he never practiced) and a shrewd investor in the stock market, Huggins was businessman enough to think he could buy the St. Louis club. His bid rebuffed, he resigned. Ban Johnson, the opportunistic president of the American League, promptly urged Jacob Ruppert, the Yankees' principal owner, to grab Huggins. The manager's record was not distinguished, but he was a sound baseball man, and Johnson was happy to help steal him from the NL.

Together with imperious Ed Barrow, the GM, Huggins developed the slugging Yankee teams that ended the dead-ball era forever. A mediocre lot when he arrived, they were among the all-time greats at his death. They were a bunch of carousers

and bad actors until an appalling slump in 1925 and the $5,000 fine and nine-day suspension of Babe Ruth. With Ruppert's backing, Huggins brought his unruly crew to heel, and established himself as boss, beginning the club's tradition of Yankee pride. Though history recalls the pillage of Harry Frazee's Red Sox as the making of the Yankees, Gehrig, Earle Combs, and Tony Lazzeri were discovered elsewhere, and others (Bob Meusel and Herb Pennock, for example) blossomed under Huggins's encouragement and handling. When he died of erysipelas in 1929, at age 50, judgment was nearly universal that Huggins was in a managerial class by himself. A plaque in his honor was placed in Yankee Stadium's centerfield in 1932. /(ADS)

Dick Hughes — 1938- . RHP 1966–68 **Cardinals** 307 ip, 20–9, 2.79. *2 WS, 9 ip, 0–1, 4.82*

When Bob Gibson suffered a broken ankle with the pennant-bound 1967 Cardinals, Hughes, a 29-year-old rookie, made up for the loss by going 16–6 for a league-leading .727 winning percentage. Arm trouble ended his short career. /(FJO)

Jim Hughes — 1951- . RHP 1974–77 **Twins** 441 ip, 25–30, 4.31

Hughes's only winning season was 1975, when he was 16–14 with a 3.82 ERA. He pitched a seven-inning perfect game for Lynchburg in the Carolina League against Rocky Mount on July 30, 1972. /(SFS)

Jim Hughes [James Jay] — 1874–1924. RHP 1898–99, 1901–02 Baltimore (NL), **Dodgers** 1097 ip, 83–41, 3.00. 20 wins: 98–99
☛ *Led League—w 99.*

Hughes gained fame in 1897 when he shut out the famous Baltimore Orioles on three hits during a West Coast exhibition. Orioles Manager Ned Hanlon hired him and brought him east, where he had four excellent seasons, including a league-leading 28–6 mark with the 1899 Dodgers. Preferring to play in California, he joined the Pacific Coast League in 1903 and pitched there until a back injury ended his career. His older brother Mickey won 25 games for the 1888 Brooklyn team. /(BC)

Long Tom Hughes — 1878–1956. RHP 1900–09, 11–13 Cubs, Orioles, Red Sox, Yankees, **Senators** 2644 ip, 131–174, 3.09. 20 wins: 03 *1 WS, 2 ip, 0–1, 9.00*

Nicknamed for his height, a then-impressive 6'1", Hughes completed 32 starts as a Cubs rookie while striking out 225, the third-best NL rookie total ever.

He jumped to the AL the following year, and helped the Red Sox to the first World Series with a 20–7, 2.57 mark as their third starter in 1903, behind Cy Young and Bill Dineen. He was the only Boston pitcher besides Young and Dineen to appear in the WS, losing Game Three. /(JK)

Roy Hughes (Jeep, Sage) — 1911– . 2B-3B-SS 1935–39, 44–46 **Indians**, Browns, Phillies, Cubs 762 g, .273, 5 hr, 205 rbi. *1 WS, 6 g, .294, 3 rbi*

A much-used utility infielder, in 1936 Hughes hit a career-high .295 as Cleveland's regular second baseman. Nicknamed Jeep because of his speed, Hughes was the Cubs shortstop in the 1945 World Series. /(DS)

Sammy Hughes — 1910–1981. 2B Negro Leagues 1930–46 Louisville White Sox, Washington Pilots, Nashville Elite Giants, Columbus Elite Giants, Washington Elite Giants, **Baltimore Elite Giants** statistics not available

Generally considered black baseball's premier second baseman, Hughes was a crack defensive player with wide range and a strong arm. The 6'3" 190-lb righthanded batter was a solid contact hitter and a proficient hit-and-run man who had occasional power. His good baserunning and tough, intelligent style of play made him a complete ballplayer.

A native of Louisville, KY, Hughes began his pro career with the local black White Sox in 1930. After spending 1932 with the Washington Pilots, he joined the Elite Giants in 1933. With the exception of 1941, which he spent in Mexico, Hughes stayed with the Elites until his retirement.

From 1930 through 1937, Hughes batted .333. In the 1937 Denver Post Baseball Tournament, he batted .379. In 10 exhibition games with white major leaguers, he collected 16 hits for a .390 average.

Hughes started the 1934 and 1935 East-West all-star games for the West, and the 1936, 1938, and 1939 contests for the East. He batted .263 (5-for-19) in his five all-star appearances.

Two things eluded Hughes. The first was a Negro League championship. The closest he came was 1936, when his Washington Elite Giants won the NNL first-half crown and faced the second-half winners, the Pittsburgh Crawfords. The league championship series was canceled after one game. The Giants won that contest, 2–0.

The second thing to elude Hughes was an opportunity to enter organized baseball. In 1943, Hughes and Roy Campanella were to receive tryouts with the Pittsburgh Pirates, but the opportunity never materialized. Along with Larry Doby, Monte Irvin, Sam Jethroe, and others who eventually made the major leagues, Hughes was promoted by Negro League sportswriters as a candidate for the integration of baseball. By the time Branch Rickey tabbed Jackie Robinson, Hughes was long past his prime. /(MFK)

Tom Hughes — 1884–1961. RHP 1906–07, 09–10, 14–18 Yankees, **Braves** 863 ip, 55–39, 2.56

On August 30, 1910 Hughes didn't allow Cleveland a hit or a walk for 9 innings, but lost 5–0 in the 11th. He resurfaced for the Braves in 1914 and won 16 games in both 1915 and 1916, leading the NL in relief wins each year. On June 16, 1916 he pitched a second no-hitter, winning 2–0 over Pittsburgh and striking out Honus Wagner to end the game. /(JK)

Tommy Hughes — 1919– . RHP 1941–42, 46–48 **Phillies**, Reds 688 ip, 31–56, 3.92

Hughes was the fireballing ace of two of the worst teams in Phillies history (1941–42). On June 3, 1941 he one-hit the Cubs, retiring the first 21 batters. /(JL)

Jim Hughey (Cold Water Jim) — 1869–1945. RHP 1891, 93, 96–1900 Cincinnati-Milwaukee (AA), Cubs, Pirates, **Cardinals**, Cleveland (NL) 1007 ip, 29–80, 4.87

After going 7–24 with the last-place Cardinals of 1898, Hughey led the NL in losses with a 4–30 mark for the incredible Cleveland Spiders of 1899, generally considered the worst team ever in the NL. His nickname referred to his hometown, Coldwater, Michigan. /(BC)

Tex Hughson [Cecil Carlton] — 1916– . RHP 1941–44, 46–49 **Red Sox** 1376 ip, 96–54, 2.94. 20 wins: 42, 46 *1 WS, 14 ip, 0–1, 3.14* ☛ *Led League—w 42. Led League—k 42. All-Star—42–44.*

The Texan was a fastballer with a sharp curve. Going 22–6 in 1942, he led the AL in wins, complete games (22), innings (281), and strikeouts (113). He again led in complete games (20) in 1943, and his .783 winning percentage (18–5) in 1944 was the AL's best. After spending 1945 in the military, Hughson returned in good form, going 20–11 in 1946. Arm problems prematurely ended his successful career. /(EW)

Mark Huismann — 1958– . RHP 1983– **Royals,** Mariners, Indians, Tigers, Orioles 288 ip, 12–11, 4.31. *1 LCS, 3 ip, 0–0, 10.13*

A career reliever, Huismann won the Allie Reynolds Award as the top pitcher in the American Association with 34 saves and a 2.04 ERA at Omaha in 1985. He was traded to Seattle in May 1986 and then to Cleveland a year later, and was released by the Indians in the spring of 1988 before signing a minor league contract with the Tigers. /(SCL)

William Hulbert — 1832–1882. *Executive.*

A Chicago businessman who owned the Chicago White Stockings of the National Association, Hulbert induced several stars from eastern teams, including Philadelphia's Cap Anson and Boston's Al Spalding, to jump to his team for the 1876 season. The NA was a weak league, beset by gamblers, failing franchises, and rowdy and drunken behavior among players. Hulbert avoided any action by the

William Hulbert

NA over his pirating of players by convening several responsible team owners and founding the National League. Although Hartford owner Morgan Bulkeley was the figurehead president in the NL's first year, Hulbert was actually in charge. In 1877, he officially took over as president. He introduced regular schedules (and expelled New York and Philadelphia for failing to fulfill theirs), banned alcoholic beverages from ball parks, and worked to eliminate gambling on games. In 1877, when the Louisville club began to fritter away a 3–1/2 game lead in August, Hulbert supported an investigation that uncovered evidence of game-fixing. Four players were banned for life. When Hulbert died in 1882, he left a league firmly established. /(NLM)

Tim Hulett — 1960– . 3B-2B 1983–87 **White Sox** 373 g, .239, 29 hr, 108 rbi

A brash, hard-nosed player in the old mold, Hulett was not afraid of anyone. In one game Hulett was berated by Tom Seaver for making an error at second base. Unintimidated, Hulett blasted Seaver in no uncertain terms. He played regularly at second and third with the White Sox in 1985–86, hitting 17 HR in '86, but he slumped in June 1987 and lost his job. /(RL)

Rudy Hulswitt — 1877–1950. SS 1899, 1902–04, 08–10 Louisville (NL), **Phillies**, Reds, Cardinals 644 g, .253, 3 hr, 203 rbi

In his first full ML season, 1902, Hulswitt hit .272 for the Phillies and led NL shortstops in putouts. The next season was his best, as he had career highs in games (138), doubles (22), and RBI (58) and again led in putouts. However, he set the post-1900 National League record by making 81 errors. A bad shoulder ended his playing days. He had a long managing career in the minors and scouted for the Red Sox and Braves. /(NLM)

Tom Hume — 1953– . RHP 1977–87 **Reds**, Phillies 1086 ip, 57–71, 3.85. *1 LCS, 4 ip, 0–1, 6.75* ☛ *All-Star—82.*

In 1980, his first season exclusively as a reliever, the mild-looking, bespectacled Hume was named co-winner (with Rollie Fingers) of the NL Fireman of the Year Award (9–10, 2.56, 78 games, 25 saves). That off-season, he and Reds teammate Bill Bonham and their wives were trapped in a Las Vegas hotel fire and had to be rescued from the roof.

Hume's nine relief wins in 1981 led the NL. Forced out for two months of the 1982 season after he injured his knee by catching his foot in a turf seam in Montreal, he never again recorded more than nine saves in a season, and was generally reduced to the role of set-up man. Hume's first ML hit was a home run. In 183 more at-bats, he never hit another. /(JCA)

John Hummel (Silent John) — 1883-1959. 2B-OF-1B 1905-15, 18 **Dodgers**, Yankees 1161 g, .254, 29 hr, 394 rbi

Hummel spent 12 seasons in the majors, two of them as the Dodgers' starting second baseman. He led NL second basemen in fielding both years (.965 and .972). Hummel also led the league in strikeouts (81) in 1910. Hummel's career in organized baseball spanned 24 years. After his playing career in the majors, Hummel coached in the minors. Hummel managed minor league teams in Saskatoon, Binghamton, Harrisburg, Scranton, and Wheeling, and finished his career managing Springfield in 1927. /(MA)

Terry Humphrey — 1949- . C 1971-79 Expos, Tigers, **Angels** 415 g, .211, 6 hr, 85 rbi

Hitting was not Humphrey's strong point. A smart, 6'3" catcher with a rifle arm, he suffered several injuries with Montreal and Detroit, but was California's regular receiver in 1977, before Brian Downing's arrival. /(EW)

Bob Humphreys — 1935- . RHP 1962-70 Tigers, Cardinals, Cubs, **Senators**, Brewers 566 ip, 27-21, 3.36. *1 WS, 1 ip, 0-0, 0.00*

Noted for his "side-saddle" delivery, reliever Humphreys joined the pennant-winning Cardinals in 1964 in time to contribute two wins and two saves down the stretch. The next year, he was part of an unusual Cubs staff that also included submariner Ted Abernathy and sidearmer Bill Faul. He pitched well for the Senators in the late 1960s but made frequent brief trips to the minors to correct his mechanics. /(MC)

Bert Humphries — 1880-1945. RHP 1910-15 Phillies, Reds, **Cubs** 798 ip, 50-43, 2.79

Already 30 years old when he broke into the majors, Humphries had one outstanding season, leading the

NL with an .800 winning percentage (16-4) for the 1913 Cubs. /(AA)

John Humphries — 1915-1965. RHP 1938-46 Indians, **White Sox**, Phillies 1002 ip, 52-63, 3.78

The smoke-throwing righthander from the University of North Carolina went 20-7 for New Orleans in 1937, including a no-hitter. He jumped to Cleveland in 1938, leading the AL with 45 appearances and eight relief wins as the Indians' Rookie of the Year. All four of Humphries's 1941 White Sox victories were shutouts. /(EW)

Randy Hundley — 1942- . C 1964-77 Giants, **Cubs**, Twins, Padres 1061 g, .236, 82 hr, 381 rbi
☛ *All-Star—69. Gold Glove—67.*

In December 1965 the Cubs made one of their best deals of the decade, acquiring two unproven players, Hundley and pitcher Bill Hands, from the Giants for Don Landrum, Lindy McDaniel, and Jim Rittwage. Hands became a 20-game winner, and Hundley turned out to be the best Cub catcher since Gabby Hartnett.

In the years 1966-69, Hundley caught nearly every Cub game. He set a ML record with 160 games behind the plate (147 complete) in 1968, and became the first player in history to catch 150 or more games for three consecutive years (1967-69). This iron man accomplishment stems in part from his own stamina, but was also a result of manager Leo Durocher's reluctance to play the second-stringers. When he won the Gold Glove in 1967, he committed just four errors for a NL record. Hundley popularized a new hinged glove that permitted a one-handed catching style, protecting his throwing hand. His arm was strong and accurate, he called pitches well, and hit with power. When the Cubs made their unsuccessful run for the flag in 1969, Hundley's fielding and 18 HR were key contributions, but he was thoroughly worn out by season's end.

The effects of overwork began to show the following April when Hundley injured his left knee and missed more than half the season. The right knee popped in 1971, limiting his action to nine games. Never the same after that, he drifted to the Twins in 1973, the Padres in 1974, and returned to finish with 15 games for the Cubs in 1976-77. /(AA)

Bill Hunnefield (Wild Bill) — 1899–1976. SS-2B-3B 1926–31 **White Sox**, Indians, Braves, Giants 511 g, .272, 9 hr, 144 rbi

An off-season accountant, Hunnefield often reported late to spring training because it coincided with tax season. An infielder with an erratic arm, he twice played on the winning side in no-hitters (Ted Lyons, 1926, and Wes Ferrell, 1931) and made a total of four errors in the two games. /(DB)

Ken Hunt — 1934– . OF 1959–64 Yankees, **Angels**, Senators 310 g, .226, 33 hr, 111 rbi

Hunt came up as a slick fielder, but was unable to crack the powerful Yankee lineup. His only year as a regular came with the 1961 expansion Angels. He hit .255 with 25 HR and 84 RBI, but struck out 120 times in 479 at-bats and led AL outfielders in errors. He played only 13 games in 1962 due to an arm injury and military service; from then on he never reached .200. /(SFS)

Ron Hunt (Zeke) — 1941– . 2B-3B 1963–74 Mets, Dodgers, Giants, **Expos**, Cardinals 1483 g, .273, 39 hr, 370 rbi
☛ *All-Star—64, 66.*

Hunt once said, "Some people give their bodies to science; I give mine to baseball." He retired with three major league records for HBP: most times in a career (243); in a season (50, 1971); and in a game (three, tied). For seven straight years he led the NL in HBP. He had other ways to get on, as two .300 seasons and good walk totals showed. He set Expo team records for fewest strikeouts in a season (19, 1973) and fewest times hitting into double plays (one, 1971). Though he played on the early, horrid Met teams, he was heartbroken when he was traded to the Dodgers in November 1966. After retiring, Hunt went into ranching outside St. Louis. /(FJO)

Billy Hunter — 1928– . SS-2B 1953–58 **Browns/ Orioles**, Yankees, A's, Indians 630 g, .219, 16 hr, 144 rbi.
Manager 1977–78 **Rangers** 147–108, .576
☛ *All-Star—53 .*

A flashy fielder, Hunter was an All-Star as a Browns rookie. He was hitting .252 at the time, but finished the season at .219. As the Orioles' third base coach, he was renowned for his frenetic, arm-wheeling "Go!" signal. /(WAB)

Catfish Hunter [James Augustus] — 1946– . RHP 1965–79 **A's**, Yankees 3448 ip, 224–266, 3.26. 20 wins: 71–75 *6 LCS, 69 ip, 4–3, 3.25. 6 WS, 63 ip, 5–3, 3.29*
☛ *Led League—w 74–75. Led League—era 74. Cy Young Award—74. All-Star—66–67, 70, 72–76. Hall of Fame—1987.*

Nicknamed Catfish for effect by A's owner Charles O. Finley when Hunter was signed for $75,000, other stories about the origin of the humble North Carolina farmboy's moniker are apocryphal. He was 26–2 with five no-hitters in high school, but nearly lost his chance to play pro ball when he suffered a foot wound in a hunting accident. He missed the 1964 season due to surgery, and made the A's in 1965. From then until 1977, Hunter didn't miss a start. Named to the All-Star team for the first of eight times in 1966, he first participated in '67, yielding only one run in five innings, but lost. On May 8, 1968 against Minnesota, he pitched the AL's first regular-season perfect game in 46 years. (Charlie Robertson in 1922 was the last; Don Larsen's came in the World Series in 1956.) Hunter received a $5,000 raise on the spot from Finley.

In 1970, his first season over .500 (18–14), Hunter tied for the AL lead with 40 starts. He then won 21 games each season from 1971 to 1973; his .750 winning percentage (21–7) in 1972 and .808 (21–5) in 1973 led the AL. In 1974 he won the Cy Young Award; his 25 wins tied him with Fergie Jenkins for the AL lead, and his 2.49 ERA stood alone at the top. In each of those four seasons, Oakland won their division, and three times were World Champions. Hunter was 4–0 with one save in seven A's WS appearances.

Hunter was declared a free agent for 1975 by arbitrator Peter Seitz when Finley failed to pay $50,000, half of Hunter's salary, to a life-insurance fund. Hunter signed with the Yankees for $3.5 million, by far the largest amount ever paid a player to that point, inspiring others, especially A's stars, to seek free agency. In 1975, his first season in New York, Catfish went 23–14, tying with Jim Palmer for the league lead in wins and topping the AL in complete games and innings pitched. However, he took the loss in the '75 All-Star Game. He helped the Yankees to three straight pennants (1976–78) despite declining effectiveness due to arm strain and diabetes. After going 2–9 in 1979, Hunter retired at age 33. Though continuing to assist the Yankees in spring training, his priorities remained on his farm in Hertford, NC.

✗ Walk totals not spectaguler

Catfish Hunter

A good hitting pitcher, Hunter batted .350 in 1971 (36-for-103) and .226 lifetime, with six home runs. He holds Oakland's all-time top spots in wins (161), starts (340), innings (2,456), shutouts (31), and strikeouts (1,520). His World Series marks in five categories rank him among the top ten in history. Soft-spoken and humble, with a dose of country charm, Catfish was inducted into the Hall of Fame in 1987. /(MC)

Willard Hunter — 1934– . LHP 1962, 64 Dodgers, **Mets** 114 ip, 4–9, 5.68

Hunter contributed a 1–6 record to the worst team in ML history, the 1962, 40–120 Mets. Hunter was 3–3 as a reliever in 41 games in '64, but overwork blew out his arm. /(MC)

Huntington Avenue Grounds Boston Red Sox 1901–11. LF-440, CF-635, RF-280

A huge field that hosted circuses and carnivals, the Huntington Avenue Grounds were the site of the first World Series game, October 1, 1903, and are now part of Northeastern University. /(SCL)

Steve Huntz — 1945– . SS-3B-2B 1967, 69–71, 75 Cardinals, **Padres**, White Sox 237 g, .206, 16 hr, 60 rbi

The Cardinals drafted Huntz from the Orioles' organization in December 1964 after he showed fine fielding skills in his first pro season, but he broke a leg in spring training and missed all of 1965. His only significant ML action came with the Padres in their sophomore season, 1970, when he had career highs of .219, 11 HR, and 54 runs. /(WOR)

Tom Hurd (Whitey) — 1924–1982. RHP 1954–56 **Red Sox** 186 ip, 13–10, 3.96

Hurd spent seven years in the White Sox system before reaching the majors with the Red Sox. The first team he beat was the White Sox. In 1955 he led the AL with eight relief wins. /(NLM)

Clint Hurdle — 1957– . OF-1B 1977–83, 85–87 **Royals**, Reds, Mets, Cardinals 515 g, .259, 32 hr, 193 rbi. *2 LCS, 7 g, .300, 1 rbi. 1 WS, 4 g, .417*

A Royals number-one draft pick, Hurdle was American Association Rookie of the Year and MVP in 1977 but never reached the ML stardom many predicted for him. As the regular right fielder for the 1980 Royals pennant winners, he hit .294, with 10 homers and 60 RBI. A back injury put him out most of the next season, and he never regained his batting stroke. A positive clubhouse attitude and a willingness to play anywhere, even catch, extended his career. /(FJO)

Ed Hurley — 1910–1969. *Umpire AL 1947–65 4 WS 3 ASU*

The plate umpire at one of baseball's most bizarre moments, Hurley called four straight balls in 1951 when the Browns sent 3'7" midget Eddie Gaedel to bat. When Hurley was retired by the AL in 1965 because of age, he fought the action in court but lost. /(RTM)

Bruce Hurst — 1958– . LHP 1980– **Red Sox**, Padres 1704 ip, 103–84, 4.01. *2 LCS, 28 ip, 1–2, 2.57. 1 WS, 23 ip, 2–0, 1.96*
☛ *All-Star—87.*

Keeping righthanded sluggers at bay with a mix of slow breaking pitches and a sneaky fastball, Hurst was a rare lefthander who excelled at Fenway Park. He was 33–9 there from 1986 to 1988, and his 56 Fenway wins are second only to Mel Parnell's among lefthanders. His pickoff move to first base is a weapon as well (he caught 15 baserunners in 1984), but he has never excelled consistently over a full season. Hurst had a 2.99 ERA in 1986, a year in which he spent six midsummer weeks on the DL with a pulled groin, and 1984 (3.92) and 1988 (3.62) are the only other years in Boston his ERA was below 4.00. He baffled the Mets in the 1986 WS, winning Game One 1–0 and Game Four 4–2, prompting Darryl Strawberry to remark, "Clemens is tough, but he's no Hurst." He had been voted WS MVP before the Mets rallied to win Game Six with three runs in the bottom of the 10th, and the award was given to Ray Knight when the Mets won Game Seven as well. Hurst became baseball's most coveted free agent after a career-best 18–6 record in 1988, and he accepted less money from the Padres than the Red Sox had offered so he could pitch in San Diego, closer to his Utah roots. He went 15–11 with a career-best 2.69 ERA in 1989. /(SCL)

Don Hurst — 1905–1952. 1B-OF 1928–34 **Phillies**, Cubs 905 g, .298, 115 hr, 610 rbi
☛ *Led League—rbi 32.*

This strong lefthanded hitter came into the majors when offense was at its peak. In four of his first five years with the Phillies, he batted over .300. In 1932, his best all-around season, he hit .339 with 24 HR, and led the NL with 143 RBI. Traded to the Cubs during the 1934 season, he failed to hit, and his ML career ended. /(AL)

Tim Hurst — 1865–1915. *Umpire* **NL**, AL 1891–97, 00–09
  Manager 1898 **Cardinals** 39–111, .260

Pugnacious Tim Hurst had a reputation for settling arguments over disputed calls by striking arguing players on their heads with his mask or his fists. In 1897 an irate fan tossed a beer stein at Hurst. The umpire threw it back, hit the wrong fan, and was fined $100 and dismissed by the NL. Hired to manage the Cardinals, he took them to a last-place finish while reputedly leading the league in umpire-baiting. After another stormy five years as a NL ump, Hurst joined the AL. In one game, after an argument with New York manager Clark Griffith, he followed Griffith to the dugout and knocked him cold. On August 4, 1909, he spit in the eye of Athletics second baseman Eddie Collins, ending an argument and igniting a riot. Hurst was fired by the AL, after which he became a boxing referee./(RTM)

Hy Hurwitz — 1910–1966. *Writer.*

Hurwitz was a baseball writer for the Boston *Globe* for 40 years and secretary-treasurer of the BBWAA for eight years until his death./(NLM)

Ted Husing — 1901–1961. *Broadcaster.*

Husing was a top radio personality for 30 years. In 1924, he won an announcing audition that had 600 competitors. Three years later he joined CBS, doing all sports, including several WS. His rapid delivery was once measured at 400 words-per-minute. A colorful, outspoken, sometimes imaginative announcer, Husing was banned from Harvard's football games for calling the play of their All-America quarterback "putrid." Three years later he was temporarily suspended from doing the 1934 WS by Judge Landis for allegedly second-guessing the umpires in previous broadcasts. Husing left CBS in 1946 to become one of the first disc jockeys./(NLM)

Bert Husting (Pete) — 1878–1948. RHP 1900–02 Pirates, **Milwaukee AL**, Red Sox, A's 437 ip, 24–21, 4.16

A fullback in the same University of Wisconsin backfield with the legendary Pat O'Dea, Husting pitched his college team to the 1898 Western Conference championship. After a strong 14–5 with the 1902 A's, he left baseball to pursue a law career./(BC)

Johnny Hutchings — 1916–1963. RHP 1940–42, 44–46 Reds, **Braves** 471 ip, 12–18, 3.96. *1 WS, 1 ip, 9.00*

The tireless, 6'2" 250-lb Hutchings made a career-high 57 appearances in 1945. Following his ML days, he pitched, coached, and managed in Indianapolis from 1946 through 1960./(JK)

Bill Hutchinson (Wild Bill) — 1859–1926. RHP 1889–95, 97 **Cubs**, Cardinals 3066 ip, 182–158, 3.59. 20 wins: 90–92
☛ *Led League—w 90–92. Led League—k 92.*

Yale grad Hutchinson played weekend ball as a hobby and from there went straight to the majors. Pitching for average Cubs teams, he led NL hurlers three straight years in wins, complete games, and innings pitched, despite competition from Amos Rusie, Cy Young, and Kid Gleason. His worst ERA in that stretch was 2.81, but he was out of the ML four years later./(JK)

Fred Hutchinson (Moose, The Bear, The Great Stone Face) — 1919–1964. RHP 1939–41, 46–53 **Tigers** 1464 ip, 95–71, 3.73. *1 WS, 1 ip, 0–0, 9.00.*
    Manager 1952–54, 56–64 Tigers, Cardinals, **Reds** 830–827, .501. First place: 61 *1 WS, 1–4, .200*

One writer said Hutchinson looked like a man who had just lost an argument to an umpire—something Hutchinson often did. He was hot-tempered, given to tossing furniture about the clubhouse and smashing light bulbs after frustrating defeats. But he was extremely well-liked as a player, and as a manager, commanded love and veneration from his players.

Hutchinson was an aggressive, relentless, and smart pitcher, but did not have overwhelming speed. His career with Detroit was interrupted by four years

Fred Hutchinson

in the Navy, but he returned in 1946 and had five consecutive winning campaigns, averaging 15 victories a season. A lifetime .263 hitter, he was used 91 times in the pinch, with four home runs—one of them his last hit, in 1953. For several years he was the AL player representative.

Hutchinson replaced Red Rolfe as Detroit manager in mid-1952. He left after the 1954 season because the Tigers would not give him more than a one-year contract. From 1956 through 1958, he managed the Cardinals. Cincinnati's Frank Lane explained why he hired Hutchinson in 1959: "When I was general manager of the White Sox and Hutch was at Detroit, I went looking for him in Chicago one night to talk about something. I found him in a hotel room with several players, explaining the cutoff play on a blackboard. He was the first manager I ever knew who believed in night school. That impressed me."

Hutchinson won one pennant with the Reds, in 1961, but lost the World Series to the Yankees. He battled cancer until he was forced to resign in August of 1964. Named as a coach for the '64 All-Star Game, he moved with great effort and pain, but would not miss it. The Reds went on to finish second. When Hutchinson died at age 45 that November 12, he was voted Most Courageous Athlete and was honored by several chapters of the Baseball Writers Association with fundraising events for cancer research. /(NLM)

Ira Hutchinson — 1910–1973. RHP 1933, 37–41, 44–45 White Sox, **Braves**, Dodgers, Cardinals 611 ip, 34–33, 3.76

In 1933 Hutchinson was shelled in his lone appearance for his hometown White Sox, but he found a home in the NL four years later, pitching capably in relief for seven seasons. /(JK)

Tom Hutton — 1946– . 1B-OF 1966, 69, 72–81 Dodgers, **Phillies**, Blue Jays, Expos 952 g, .248, 22 hr, 186 rbi. *2 LCS, 4 g, .000*

This slick-fielding lefthanded first baseman and fill-in outfielder excelled as a late-inning defensive replacement. He hit .700 against Tom Seaver and batted .269 lifetime as a pinch hitter. He had three game-winning pinch homers during his career with the Phillies. The brother-in-law of pitcher Dick Ruthven, he was a guitar player who played professionally in Las Vegas. Hutton later became a ML broadcaster. /(AL)

Dick Hyde — 1928– . RHP 1955, 57–61 **Senators**, Orioles 298 ip, 17–14, 3.56

The bespectacled, submariner was the AL's top reliever in 1958. He led in relief wins (10) and saved 18 to account for 46% of the last-place Senators' victories. His 1.75 ERA was Washington's best since Walter Johnson's 1.49 in 1919. Back problems the next season ended his effectiveness. /(MC)

Iron Man Inao [Kasuhisa] — 1938- . P 1956–1969
Nishitetsu Lions 276-137, 1.98
☛ *Rookie of the Year—56 Sawamura Award 57–58, 61, 63.*

With a 276–137 lifetime record, and a career ERA of 1.98, Iron Man Inao is widely regarded as the greatest of all Japanese pitchers. He broke in with a 21–6 record and 1.06 ERA at age 18, pacing the Lions to their second pennant and first Japan Championship as both ace starter and top clutch reliever. Inao earned his nickname Iron Man two years later, as the Lions made it four pennants in five years and three Japan Championships in a row. Either starting or relieving in all the Lions' last nine regular-season games to put them into the Japan Series, Inao then started five of seven games against the Yomiuri Giants. He lost once as a starter and once in relief as the Giants took a 3–0 lead.

Pitching the last six innings of the fourth game, Inao homered in the 10th to keep the Lions alive. He then tossed three complete-game victories in a row, including a 26-inning scoreless streak, to beat the Giants in the greatest comeback in baseball history, Japanese or American. After his sensational debut, Inao posted records of 35–6, 33–10, 30–15, 20–7, 42–14, 25–18, and 28–16. His ERA climbed above 1.69 only once in his first five years, and never topped 2.54 in any year he pitched more than half a dozen games. Most incredibly, Inao appeared in 61, 68, 72, 75, 39, 78, 57, and 74 games over his first eight years, working 262, 374, 373, 402, 243, 404, 321, and 386 innings. In the seven years following his rookie season, Inao never completed fewer than 19 games. Not since the pitching distance was increased to 60′ 6″ has any American pitcher handled a comparable workload. Inao struck out 182, 288, 334, 321, 179, 353, 228, and 226 batters during his eight-year streak of dominance, totals even more impressive considering that Japanese batting styles then stressed contact over power. A complete player, he often kept himself in close games with excellent hitting and fielding, as well as his arm. The arm gave out in 1964. Appearing in only two games, Inao came back to handle a more normal workload in 1965 and 1966, averaging "only" 200 innings with ERAs of 2.38 and 1.79, in a "mere" 38 and 54 games, many in relief. Retiring as an active player three years later when only 31, Inao managed the Lions to five straight second-division finishes, 1970–74./(MC)

Pete Incaviglia (Inky) — 1964- . OF-DH 1986-
Rangers 541 g, .252, 100 hr, 303 rbi

Incaviglia is one of the few players to jump directly from college ball—he was *Baseball America*'s NCAA Player of the Year at Oklahoma State in 1985—to the ML. His slugging prowess has been offset by defensive failings and enormous strikeout totals. He was the Expos' first- round draft choice in June 1985, but refused to sign until a trade with Texas had been negotiated. In 1986, he tied the Rangers' single-season home run record with 30 as a rookie, but he also struck out 185 times, four shy of Barry Bonds's ML record. In three ML seasons through 1988, Incaviglia had 506 strikeouts and 377 hits. Injuries slowed him in 1989./(ME)

Jeff Innis — 1962- . RHP 1987- **Mets** 84 ip, 1-3, 2.88

Despite pitching well in his call-ups, Innis was stuck behind fellow submarine reliever Terry Leach until Leach was traded to the Royals in mid-1989./(JFC)

International League — 1883- . *Minor League.*

The International League, the oldest minor league in existence, was founded in 1883 as the Interstate League, either the second or the fourth minor league formed, depending on the definition. It was reorganized as the Eastern League in 1884 and took the name International League in 1913. Usually one of the strongest minor leagues, it has boasted some legendary teams. The Baltimore Orioles of the 1910s and 1920s, owned by Jack Dunn, developed such stars as Babe Ruth (who hit only one HR in his short time in the minors), Lefty Grove, Max Bishop, and George Earnshaw. They won seven straight pennants (1919–25) by keeping many of those stars for years after they were ready for the majors. Minor league teams were still mostly independent then, not tightly controlled by major league teams. The late 1930s Newark Bears, referred to as the Yankee B-team, featured future stars Joe Gordon and Charlie Keller. Clubs in Toronto and Montreal justified the International name, and it was in Montreal, where Branch Rickey judged that racial prejudice would be less of a problem than in the States, that Jackie Robinson made his organized-baseball debut in 1946.

In 1988 the International League combined with the American Association in the "Triple-A Alliance", playing interleague games and a postseason series. /(SFS)

Dane Iorg — 1950– . OF-1B 1977–86 **Phillies, Cardinals,** Royals, Padres 743 g, .276, 14 hr, 216 rbi. *2 LCS, 6 g, .500, 1 rbi. 2 WS, 7 g, .526, 3 rbi*

A contact hitter without power or speed, Iorg excelled in the post-season. He hit .529 as the Cardinals' designated hitter in the 1982 WS and won Game Six of the 1985 WS for the Royals with a two-run pinch single in the bottom of the ninth against the Cardinals. Garth Iorg is his brother. /(FJO)

Garth Iorg — 1954– . 3B-2B 1978, 80–87 **Blue Jays** 931 g, .258, 20 hr, 238 rbi. *1 LCS, 7 g, .133*

Iorg was a solid utility player who spent most of his career as the righthanded half of a third-base platoon with Rance Mulliniks. He was most recognizable for his strange batting stance, on the toes of his front foot and leaning back toward the catcher as the ball was being pitched.

Selected by the Blue Jays from the Yankee organization in the 1976 expansion draft, Iorg spent his entire nine-season ML career with the Blue Jays. In his final ML plate appearance, Iorg made Toronto's last out of the 1987 season when a hit would have tied the Blue Jays with Detroit for the AL East title. At the time of his retirement, Iorg was the Blue Jay career leader in pinch hits. Usually a singles hitter, Iorg hit well enough (with batting stats aided by judicious platooning) to have the highest batting average (.313) on the Blue Jays in their division-winning 1985 season, along with a .469 slugging percentage. Garth is the brother of Dane Iorg. /(TF)

Monte Irvin — 1919– . OF-1B 1949–56 **Giants,** Cubs 764 g, .293, 99 hr, 443 rbi. *2 WS, 10 g, .394, 4 rbi* ☛ *Led League—rbi 51. Hall of Fame—1973.*

After baseball's color line was broken in 1947, Monte Irvin was one of the first black players signed

Monte Irvin with the Newark Eagles

by the Giants. He could run, throw, field, hit, and hit with power, all brilliantly. He earned 16 letters and all-state honors in four sports at East Orange (NJ) High School. His outstanding athletic career was almost prematurely ended in 1938 when he scratched his hand in a basketball game; the resulting infection kept him near death for seven weeks. He recovered and returned to the Orange Triangles, a semi-pro team that he had joined in 1932. He began playing for the Newark Eagles on weekends under the name "Jimmy Nelson" to protect his amateur standing, a practice he continued while attending Lincoln University.

Irvin became one of the brightest stars in the Negro Leagues, playing in four East-West all-star games. After hitting league highs of .422 in 1940 and .396 in 1941, he won the triple crown in Mexico with a .398 average and 30 home runs in 68 games. Many Negro League owners felt Irvin was the best-qualified candidate to break the major league color line, but Irvin was drafted in 1942 and spent the next three years in the army.

Upon his return from the service, Irvin was tentatively contacted by the Dodgers' Branch Rickey, but felt he needed to play himself back into shape. He earned MVP honors in the 1945–46 Puerto Rican Winter League. He then led the Negro National League in RBI and hit .389, taking the Eagles to a victory over the Kansas City Monarchs in the 1946 Negro World Series. Irvin hit .462, slammed three HR, and scored the winning run in the seventh game. He was ready for the majors, but Rickey did not want to pay Eagles owner Effa Manley for the rights to Irvin's contract. Irvin remained with the Eagles and proceeded to lead the NNL in HR and RBI.

After Irvin spent the 1948–49 winter in Cuba, Rickey relinquished his claim, and the New York Giants paid Manley $5,000 for Irvin's contract. Assigned to Jersey City (International League), he batted .373. He debuted with the Giants on July 27, 1949 as a pinch hitter. Back with Jersey City in 1950, he was called up after hitting .510 with 10 HR in 18 games. He batted .299 for the Giants that season, playing first base and the outfield. In 1951 Irvin emerged as a star, hitting .312 with 24 HR, leading the National League with 121 RBI, and finishing third in MVP balloting. He hit .458 in the 1951 World Series and stole home off Yankee pitcher Allie Reynolds in the second game.

During an exhibition game in April 1952, Irvin broke his ankle sliding into third. He reinjured the leg in August 1953 and never regained his earlier form. He was sent down in mid-1955, and spent his final ML season with the Cubs. He scouted for the Mets in 1967–68, then joined the Commissioner's office as a public relations representative. The Committee on Negro Baseball Leagues elected him to the Hall of Fame in 1973; he later became a member of that body and of the Hall of Fame Committee on Baseball Veterans. /(JR)

Charlie Irwin — 1869–1925. 3B-SS-2B-OF 1893–1902 Cubs, **Reds**, Dodgers 989 g, .267, 16 hr, 488 rbi

A sure-handed fielder and one of the fastest third basemen of his day, Irwin was always among the 1890s' NL defensive leaders. He showed a flash of power in 1894, with eight home runs for Chicago. /(DAS)

James C. Isaminger — 1881–1946. *Writer.*

The rotund Isaminger broke in with the Cincinnati *Times-Herald*. In 1905, he was recommended by Ban Johnson for a job with the Philadelphia *North American*, where he remained until the paper was sold in 1925. He moved to the *Inquirer*, where he remained until his death. Isaminger was credited with investigative reporting second only to Hugh Fullerton in exposing the Black Sox of 1919. His columns "Under the Spotlight" and "Tips from the Sporting Ticker" were widely read, as were his reports in *The Sporting News*. He edited the Reach Guides from 1928 until they were discontinued just before WWII. President of the BBWAA in 1946, Isaminger was voted the J.G. Taylor Spink Award in 1974. /(NLM)

Frank Isbell (Bald Eagle) — 1875–1941. 1B-2B-OF-3B 1898, 1901–09 Cubs, **White Sox** 1119 g, .250, 13 hr, 455 rbi. *1 WS, 6 g, .308, 4 rbi*

The leading hitter (.279) on the 1906 "Hitless Wonder" White Sox, Isbell was a versatile player who at one time or another played every position, including pitcher (4–7, 3.59). He joined the White Sox as a first baseman in 1900, the year before the AL declared itself a major league. Totally bald, he was upset when the team picture was taken without caps. The next year he led the new major league in stolen bases (52). When his hitting declined, he moved to second base, where he played when the weak-hitting White Sox won the World Championship in '06. Ironically, Isbell set several WS offensive records that still stand: most hits, two consecutive games (7); and most doubles and extra base hits in a game (4). He also held the record for most errors in a WS by a second baseman until 1981, when Davey Lopes took that dubious distinction. /(DB)

Mike Ivie (Poison Ivie) — 1952– . 1B-3B-DH-C 1971, 74–83 **Padres**, Giants, Astros, Tigers 857 g, .269, 81 hr, 411 rbi

Padres manager John McNamara said Ivie, San Diego's number-one draft choice in 1970, "was born to catch." But Ivie hated catching and preferred first base; the Padres tried him at third base too, including 61 games there in 1975. When he was moved again to third base in 1977, he jumped the team for several days. It looked as though he would live up to his promise as a hitter in 1976, when he hit .291 with 70 RBI in 405 at-bats. But San Diego tired of his attitude and traded him in February 1978 for Derrel Thomas.

Ivie hit a career-high .308 for the Giants in 1978 when he backed up the aging Willie McCovey at first base. Ivie showed little range but was a useful pinch hitter. He went 12-for-31 in the pinch and tied a major league record with two pinch grand slams that season. That performance won him more playing time in 1979, and he had career highs of 27 HR and 89 RBI in 402 at-bats. He also had a clause written into his contract specifying that he would not have to catch.

His power vanished in 1980 (four HR in 286 at-bats) and Ivie once again wore out his welcome. He was traded to Houston in April 1981 for Jeff Leonard and Dave Bergman, and his career petered out thereafter. Rick Monday summed it up best when he said, "Mike Ivie is a forty-million-dollar airport with a thirty-dollar control tower." /(JFC)

Jerry Izenberg — 1930– . *Writer.*

A graduate of Rutgers, Izenberg joined the Newark *Star-Ledger* in 1963 and is a columnist for the Newhouse syndicate. He has published several collections of columns and essays and has written and produced over 30 television shows, including documentaries on manager Johnny Keane, the New York Mets, and Roberto Clemente. /(NLM)

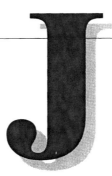

Ray Jablonski (Jabbo). — 1926–1985. 3B-OF-1B
1953–60 **Cardinals**, Reds, Giants, A's 808 g, .268, 83 hr,
438 rbi
☛ *All-Star—54.*

In the mid-1950s, the Cardinals had a group known
as the Polish Falcons; Ray Jablonski, Rip Repulski,
and Steve Bilko. Jablonski debuted as the Cards'
regular third baseman in 1953, hitting 21 HR and
collecting 112 RBI. He developed an exuberant
following, with a large section of Sportsmans Park
frequently yelling, "Go-Go Jabbo." An All-Star in
1954, Jablonski peaked at the plate, hitting .296,
but his league-high 34 errors at 3B and .925 FA
(worst in the AL for regulars at all positions) made
him expendable. Traded to the Reds, he was replaced in St. Louis by rookie Ken Boyer. Jablonski's
glove kept him from further success. /(RTM)

Jack Murphy Stadium San Diego Padres 1969– .
LF-329, CF-405, RF-329

An attractive modern facility with natural grass and
good sight lines, Jack Murphy Stadium opened as
San Diego Stadium in 1967, and did not have a
tenant until the Padres were created in the NL's
1969 expansion. Renamed in 1981, the stadium was
originally three-sided, open in right field with only a
small bleacher section there, as opposed to five
seating levels around the rest of the field. The right-
field bleachers were recently expanded, however,
enclosing the field fully and bringing the capacity up
to its current 59,022. The Padres share the stadium
with the NFL's San Diego Chargers. /(SCL)

Fred Jacklitsch — 1876–1937. C-1B-2B 1900–05,
07–10, 14–15, 17 **Phillies**, Dodgers, Yankees, Baltimore
(FL), Braves 490 g, .243, 5 hr, 153 rbi

Except for 1914, when he jumped to Baltimore of
the Federal League, this native Brooklynite spent his
ML career as a second-string catcher, filling in a few
times in the outfield and at every infield
position. /(AL)

Bill Jackowski (Jack) — 1914– . *Umpire* NL 1952–68
3 WS 3 ASU

Jackowski was the plate umpire on September 18,
1968 when the Cardinals' Ray Washburn pitched a
no-hitter against the Giants the day after San
Francisco's Gaylord Perry no-hit St. Louis, the first
consecutive game no-hitters in history. It was the
second no-hitter called by Jackowski that season,
making him one of ten umpires to have worked the
plate for two no-hitters in one season. /(RTM)

Al Jackson — 1935– . LHP 1959–69 Pirates, **Mets**,
Cardinals, Reds 1389 ip, 67–99, 3.98

Former Reds outfielder Vada Pinson described this
5'10" Texan as "Very competitive, small, big
heart—he knew how to pitch. He fought you every
kind of way to help beat you." Although Jackson
went 8–20 for the fledgling Mets in both 1962 and
1965, the gutty southpaw threw all four of the Mets'
shutouts in 1962. His 43 career victories were a pre-
Seaver Met high. Jackson went 9–4 with the World
Champion '67 Cards but did not appear in the
World Series. /(RTM)

Bo Jackson [Vincent Edward] — 1962– . OF 1986-
Royals 400 g, .244, 81 hr, 235 rbi
☛ *All-Star—89.*

After winning the Heisman Trophy and *TSN* College Football Player of the Year in 1985, Jackson
opted to sign with the Royals instead of Tampa Bay
in the NFL. He joined the Royals after just 53
games in the minors and, while showing speed and
power, he struck out frequently and displayed questionable defense.

After showing improvement in 1987 with 22 HR
despite 158 strikeouts, Bo announced his plan to
play football in the off-season with the Raiders as "a
hobby," a move initially not appreciated by Kansas
City players or fans. In 1988 Jackson slammed 25
homers and stole 27 bases but still struck out 146
times. However, in 1989 he finally raised his batting
average, to .256, hit 32 HR with 105 RBI, and used
his speed and strong arm to become one of the most
exciting left fielders in baseball. /(FO)

Danny Jackson — 1962– . LHP 1983– **Royals**, Reds 1089 ip, 66–68, 3.66. *1 LCS, 10 ip, 1–0, 0.00. 1 WS, 16 ip, 1–1, 1.69*
☛ Led League—w 88.

Jackson was a member of a cast of talented pitchers the Royals developed in the early 1980s. After some early successes, Danny fought through an 18-loss season in 1987. The Royals, desperate for a short-stop, dealt him to the Reds for Kurt Stillwell.

In 1988 Jackson dominated NL hitters with a moving fastball and wicked slider on his way to a league-leading 23 victories. He finished second in the Cy Young balloting only because of Orel Hershiser's record-setting scoreless innings streak. Injuries limited him to a 6–11, 5.60 record in only 20 starts in 1989. /(FO)

Darrell Jackson — 1956– . LHP 1978–82 **Twins** 411 ip, 20–27, 4.38

This Arizona State product started 15 games for Minnesota in his first pro year (1978). He was 9–9 (3.87) in 1980; then, chemical dependency and shoulder problems cut short his career. /(JCA)

Darrin Jackson — 1963– . OF 1985, 87–88 **Cubs** 112 g, .270, 6 hr, 20 rbi

Jackson saw the most action in 1988, hitting .266 with six HR in 188 at-bats. /(SFS)

Grant Jackson (Buck) — 1942– . LHP 1965–82 Phillies, Orioles, Yankees, **Pirates**, Expos, Royals 1359 ip, 86–75, 3.46. *4 LCS, 9 ip, 2–0, 3.12. 3 WS, 9 ip, 1–0, 2.00*
☛ All-Star—69.

Jackson, a quality reliever for much of his 18-year career, got his greatest attention as a member of Pittsburgh's World Champion "Family" in 1979. The number-two man in the bullpen behind Kent Tekulve, Jackson went 8–5 with a career-high 14 saves and finished third in the NL in appearances, behind teammates Tekulve and Enrique Romo. Jackson gave up no runs and only two hits in his six postseason appearances in '79, winning Game One of the LCS and the World Series clincher as the Pirates completed their dramatic seven-game comeback. He was only the sixth black pitcher to win a WS game.

Jackson didn't have a winning record in six seasons for the Phillies at the start of his career. An attempt to use him as a starter looked promising in 1969 (14–18, 3.34) but fell apart in 1970 (3–15, 5.28, plus two relief wins). Traded to the Orioles for 1971, he became an important member of the

Orioles' bullpen-by-committee arrangement and never again had a losing season. In 1973 he was 8–0, tied for sixth all-time for most wins in a season without a loss, and won Game Four of the LCS over the A's. Traded to the Yankees in the 10-player June 1976 deal that brought Rick Dempsey, Rudy May, and Scott McGregor to Baltimore, Jackson was the only new Yankee who didn't disappoint, going 6–0 the rest of the way to help New York to its first AL pennant in 12 years. /(WOR)

Jim Jackson — 1877–1955. OF 1901–02, 05–06 Orioles, Giants, **Indians** 347 g, .236, 4 hr, 132 rbi

Jackson followed manager John McGraw from the original Orioles to the Giants in 1902 but was released after hitting .182. In Cleveland he served under another Hall of Famer, Nap Lajoie, then played and managed in the minors until 1917. /(ME)

Joe Jackson (Shoeless Joe) — 1887–1951. OF 1908–1920 A's, **Indians**, White Sox 1330 g, .356, 54 hr, 785 rbi. *2 WS, 14 g, .345, 1 hr, 8 rbi*

Jackson was supremely gifted in his baseball ability and supremely limited in his ability to deal with real life. He could hit, run, and throw with the best but he lacked education, judgment, and character. When his limitations overcame his gifts, it was a tragedy of both baseball and American life.

Joe was an illiterate son of the cotton-town South, ignorant of city ways, easy to ridicule for everything but his baseball talent. The Athletics, his first ML team, turned him sullen and ineffective with their cruel, mocking humor. Manager Connie Mack gave up on him and shipped him to Cleveland for a mediocre outfielder, Bris Lord.

His Cleveland teammates accepted Jackson as he was and treated him well. He responded with the great years of his career. A graceful natural hitter (supposedly Babe Ruth patterned his batting stance on Jackson's), he hit for power in an age of slap hitters, yet kept his BA near the top. In 1911, his first full season, he hit .408, then followed with .395, .373, and a mere .338 in 1914. He was unerring in the field, had a powerful and accurate arm, and ran the bases with savvy.

Money troubles forced Cleveland to trade him to the White Sox in 1915 for three undistinguished players and $31,500. He hit less well for the Sox but still reigned as the star of the powerful team Comiskey had assembled. He contributed an uncharacteristically low .301 to the championship 1917 Sox but hit .351 with 96 RBI for the 1919 pennant winners. In 1920, he had one of his greatest seasons (.392, 12

Shoeless Joe Jackson

HR, 121 RBI), but everything crashed with the revelation of the Black Sox scandal.

Friends pointed to his .375 WS average as evidence that he'd played on the square, but Jackson had undoubtedly accepted the promise of $5,000 to fix the games. Banned from baseball for life, he returned to his small South Carolina town, started a dry-cleaning business, and prospered. Occasionally he swung "Black Betsy," his famous bat, in sandlot and outlaw games. In time, he retrieved some of his dignity if not the glory. Locally, he was warmly regarded at his death. /(ADS)

Joe S. Jackson — Unk.-Unk. *Writer.*

Jackson was the founder of the BBWAA and its first and only president from 1907 to 1919. He became sports editor of the Detroit *Free Press* in 1901. In 1910, he joined the Washington *Post* as sports editor, remaining for three years. /(NLM)

Larry Jackson (Hot Potato) — 1931- . RHP 1955-68 **Cardinals**, Cubs, Phillies 3262 ip, 194-183, 3.40. 20 wins: 64
☛ *Led League—w 64. All-Star—57-58, 60, 63.*

In his second year of pro ball, Jackson dominated the California League, striking out 351 batters while posting a 28-4 record. A reliever early on with the Cardinals, the strong-armed workhorse averaged 259 innings over his last ten campaigns while winning 13 or more each of his final 12 years. After leading the NL with 38 starts and 282 innings in 1960, Jackson suffered a broken jaw in spring training of 1961 when hit by Duke Snider's shattered bat. He recovered, winning 11 of his last 12 decisions and the St. Louis baseball writers' Comeback of the Year Award. In October 1962, Jackson and Lindy McDaniel were traded to the Cubs in a complicated three-team deal. Jackson pitched nearly 300 innings in 1964 and won a league-high 24 games, accounting for almost one third of the Cubs' victories. Rather than report to the expansion Expos in 1969, Jackson returned to his native Idaho, becoming a sportswriter and state legislator. /(FJO)

Mike Jackson — 1964- . RHP 1986- Phillies, Mariners 321 ip, 13-21, 3.36

In parts of two seasons with the Phillies, Jackson was 3-10 with a 4.12 ERA, mainly in relief. After being traded to Seattle along with Glenn Wilson in exchange for Phil Bradley, he emerged as a fine reliever. In his first season with the Mariners, Jackson had the lowest ERA on the club. /(TF)

Randy Jackson [Ransom Joseph] (Handsome Ransom) — 1926- . 3B 1950-59 **Cubs**, Dodgers, Indians 955 g, .261, 103 hr, 415 rbi. *1 WS, 3 g, .000*
☛ *All-Star—54-55.*

A Texas Christian University football player, Jackson played in the 1945 and '46 Cotton Bowls. He hit 19, 19, and 21 homers in 1953-55 with the Cubs. In 1955 he led NL third basemen in double plays. The Dodgers traded Walt Moryn, Don Hoak, and Russ Meyer to the Cubs for Jackson and pitcher Don Elston in expectation that the slugger would succeed Jackie Robinson at third base, but after a serious knee injury in 1957, Jackson never again played regularly. /(MC)

Reggie Jackson (Mr. October) — 1946– . OF-DH
1967–1987 **A's**, Orioles, Yankees, Angels 2820 g, .262,
563 hr, 1702 rbi. *11 LCS, 45 g, .227, 6 hrs, 20 rbi. 5 WS,
27 g, .357, 10 hr, 24 rbi*
☛ *Most Valuable Player—73. Led League—hr 73, 75, 80,
83. Led League—rbi 73. All-Star—69, 71–75, 77–84.*

Jackson became the first player to have a candy bar
named after him, predicting that this would happen
if he played in New York. Reggie could talk and
Reggie could hit: a sportswriter's dream. The peak
of his career came in a boisterous five-year stint with
the Yankees, which he began by asserting that he
was "the straw that stirred the drink," a statement
that drew the ire of new teammate Thurman Munson and manager Billy Martin. But the outspoken,
flamboyant, muscular outfielder was a winner wherever he went.

In 21 seasons, Jackson played on 11 divisional
winners, six pennant winners, and five World Champions. He has a .357 lifetime World Series average,
nearly 100 points above his lifetime regular-season
average, and the best career World Series slugging
average at .755. His total of 563 HR was sixth all-time when he retired. His 2,597 strikeouts, however,
are first all-time.

If the Mets had been wiser, Jackson actually
would have started his career in New York after
playing at Arizona State. But the Mets selected a
catcher, Steve Chilcott, with the first pick in the
1967 amatuer draft, and the A's got Jackson. Joe
DiMaggio was a batting instructor with the A's in
those years, and tried unsuccessfully to get the
youngster to cut down his swing to reduce his
strikeouts. In 1968 Jackson came close to setting an
all-time strikeout mark, fanning 171 times. In 1969
he set career highs in HR with 47, RBI with 118,
slugging average at .608, runs with 123, and walks
with 114, leading the league in the last two catego-

Reggie Jackson

ries. He also led the league in strikeouts for the second of four straight years with 142.

His success in 1969 was haunted by what could have been. In a weekend series in June in Boston, he had 15 RBI in 14 at-bats, including 10 with two homers on Saturday the 15th. On July 2, he hit three HR in Oakland against Seattle. By July 29, he had 40 HR and was 23 games ahead of Ruth's 1927 pace. He then stopped hitting. The slump lasted throughout the 1970 season and practically until the All-Star game in Detroit in 1971, where his mammoth blast over the right-field roof at Tiger Stadium would have left the stadium completely had it not struck a light tower. He made the 1971 All-Star squad only because of an injury to Tony Oliva.

Jackson was as aggressive on the bases and in the field as he was at the plate. In the 1972 LCS against Detroit, he twisted his knee sliding home, and he was forced to watch the World Series in street clothes. He came back with a vengeance in 1973. He won the MVP award with a .293 average and league-leading figures in HR (32), RBI (117), runs (99), and slugging average (.531). In the World Series against the Mets, Jackson was helpless in the three night games, getting only one hit in 10 at-bats. During the day, however, he was 8-for-17. In Game Six, he drove in two runs with a double, then scored the third Oakland run in the A's 3–1 victory over Tom Seaver. He hit his first Series homer in the third inning of the seventh game, a two-run shot that proved to be the difference in the clincher, and led the right-field bleachers in cheers throughout the game. He was named the Series MVP.

Jackson sometimes revealed surprising humility. He once admitted that he'd settle for being "one half the player Willie Mays is." Modest or not, he led the A's to their third straight world title in 1974. But regular clashes with owner Charlie Finley in 1975 prompted Jackson to seek greener pastures. Finley swapped him to Baltimore in 1976, where he led the league in slugging for the third time. But the pull of the New York media circus was strong to Jackson, and in 1977 he set up his permanent press conference in the Bronx. There were continual fights and headlines, but also the first World Championships in Yankee Stadium in over a decade.

Game Six of the 1977 Series was Jackson's shining moment. He had already homered in each of the previous two games. In the fourth inning, he hit a two-run shot into the right-field seats on Burt Hooton's first pitch to him to give the Yankees a 4–3 lead. The following inning, he hit Elias Sosa's first offering into an identical location for another

two runs and a 7–3 lead. In the eighth, when he knocked the first pitch he saw from Charlie Hough into the bleachers, he became the first player besides Babe Ruth to homer three times in a Series game, and the first ever to hit five home runs in one Series.

Jackson's dugout fights with Martin and the clash of personalities with owner George Steinbrenner drove him to California in 1982, where he led the league in HR with 39 and the Angels to a division title. He also led the league in strikeouts, with 156, for the first time in 11 years. His final years with the Angels were spent in the pursuit of Mickey Mantle's career home run total of 536, which he finally surpassed in 1986. He ended his career back in Oakland in 1987. He announced his intentions to retire before the season began, which created a grand farewell tour. /(SEW)

Ron Jackson — 1953- . 1B-3B 1975-84 **Angels**, Twins, Tigers, Orioles 926 g, .259, 56 hr, 342 rbi. *1 LCS, 1 g, 1.000*

One of thirteen children, Jackson was a third baseman/handyman through 1978. Traded to Minnesota, he was the Twins' regular first baseman for 2-1/2 years, hitting 14 home runs in 1979. /(JCA)

Roy Lee Jackson — 1954- . RHP 1977-86 Mets, **Blue Jays**, Padres, Twins 559 ip, 28-34, 3.77

Toronto obtained Jackson from the Mets in a trade for Bob Bailor, the Blue Jays' first pick in the expansion draft, and Jackson became a competent reliever for a poor team. With fairly modest accomplishments, Jackson was able to make entries in the Blue Jay record book that would stand until the emergence of Tom Henke. Jackson's 10 saves in 1984 tied the Blue Jay single-season high at that time, and his 30 career saves had him one behind club leader Joey McLaughlin at the time of Jackson's release. In May 1984, Jackson set a club record for wins in a month with six, all in relief. /(TF)

Sonny Jackson [Roland Thomas] — 1944- . SS-OF 1963-74 Astros, **Braves** 936 g, .251, 7 hr, 162 rbi. *1 LCS, 1 g, --*

Jackson was a 150-lb lefthanded batter who hit .292 and stole a post-1900 NL rookie record 49 bases in 1966. He and Joe Morgan were supposed to be Houston's double-play combo of the future, but Jackson hit just .237 his sophomore season and was traded to Atlanta. There he had injury problems, and never played more than 97 games at shortstop. He spent the 1971 season in the outfield. /(PB)

Travis Jackson (Stonewall) — 1903–1987. SS-3B
1922–36 **Giants** 1656 g, .291, 135 hr, 929 rbi. *4 WS, 19 g,
.149, 4 rbi*
☛ *Hall of Fame—1982.*

Jackson was the first of John McGraw's final generation of great rookies. Succeeding Dave Bancroft at
shortstop in 1924, the 5'10" 160-lb Arkansan was
soon joined by Bill Terry, Freddie Lindstrom, and
Mel Ott as key players on Giant pennant winners of
the 1930s. Jackson was a strong-armed SS with good
range, as indicated by rankings in the top dozen for
lifetime per-game putouts, assists, and chances. He
led NL shortstops with 58 errors as a rookie in 1924,
but twice led in fielding average, twice in double
plays, and four times in assists. In 1934, with knee
injuries lessening his mobility, he played his last
season at SS, leading the NL with 43 errors. He
moved to third base for his last two seasons.

Though generally batting around the sixth spot in
the Giants' lineup, he was a keen bunter and a
consistent righthanded hitter who had the measure
of the short Polo Grounds fences. He batted over
.300 six times, peaking at .339 in 1930. His 21 HR
in 1929 were a career high, as were his 101 RBI in
1934. After his playing days, he coached for the
Giants and managed a dozen minor league
clubs. /(ADS)

Elmer Jacobs — 1892–1958. RHP 1914, 16–20,
24–25, 27 Phillies, **Pirates**, Cardinals, Cubs, White Sox
1189 ip, 50–81, 3.55

Jacobs had one winning year, going 9–6 in 1918,
having been swapped from Pittsburgh to the Phillies
in July for former 20-game winner Erskine Mayer.
Never an overpowering pitcher, he walked more
than he struck out. /(DAS)

Spook Jacobs [Forrest Vandergrift] — 1925– . 2B
1954–56 **A's**, Pirates 188 g, .247, 0 hr, 33 rbi

After years of minor league apprenticeship, the frail
infielder was the regular A's second baseman in
1954, but his good glove couldn't compensate for
his light bat. He later produced baseball card and
autograph shows. /(JK)

Travis Jackson

Baby Doll Jacobson [William Chester] (Jake) — 1890–1977. OF 1915, 17, 19–27 Tigers, **Browns**, Red Sox, Indians, A's 1472 g, .311, 84 hr, 819 rbi

At Mobile (Southern League) in 1912, the grandstand band played "Oh, You Beautiful Doll" after Jacobson's Opening Day homer, and the next day's paper captioned his photo, "Baby Doll." After a decade in the minors, he spent 1917 in the majors, served a year in the military, and returned as a Browns' regular at 28. The best of Jacobson's ML career was contained in seven straight years over .300 (1919–25), five of them with Ken Williams and Jack Tobin flanking him in the Browns' best-remembered outfield. A burly righthander who swung a light bat, he hit well for average, if not for power. For all his heft (at 6'3" and 215-lb, he was the league's biggest man), he was also a capable fielder. At one time he held 13 fielding marks; his 484 putouts in 1924 stood as a record for 24 years. In 1927 he played seven consecutive games for the Red Sox without a putout or assist. /(ADS)

Beany Jacobson [Albert L.] — 1881–1933. LHP 1904–07 **Senators**, Browns, Red Sox 612 ip, 25–47, 3.19

Jumped all the way from Decatur of the Three-I League to the majors in 1904, Jacobson went 6–23 for the Senators despite a respectable 3.55 ERA. /(BC)

Merwin Jacobson (Jake) — 1894–1978. OF 1915–16, 26–27 Giants, Cubs, **Dodgers** 133 g, .230, 0 hr, 24 rbi

Jacobson, a great minor league hitter, played on seven straight International League Baltimore Oriole championship teams (1919–25). He hit .404 to lead the league in batting in 1920. He made the equivalent of major league wages and pocketed postseason shares with the independently owned team. His few major league opportunities came before he reached his peak and after he had passed it. /(JK)

Brook Jacoby (Jake) — 1959– . 3B 1981, 83–Braves, **Indians** 914 g, .273, 98 hr, 390 rbi
☛ All-Star—86.

In one of the worst trades in Atlanta history, Jacoby, Brett Butler, and Rick Behenna were sent to Cleveland for Len Barker in 1983. Jacoby had spent five years in the Braves system, hitting with power. He quickly became the Indians' hardy, everyday third baseman. An exceedingly quiet, unaggressive player, he proved a calm and sure-handed fielder, good on

fielding the bunt and going to his left, but hesitant to dive for a ball. A poor baserunner and a streaky hitter, he peaked in 1987 (the year of the rabbit ball) when he cut way down on his strikeouts. He batted .300 but managed just 69 RBI; 27 of his 32 homers were solo shots, and he hit just .225 with runners in scoring position. /(JCA)

Sig Jakucki [Sigmund] (Jack) — 1909–1979. RHP 1936, 44–45 **Browns** 411 ip, 25–22, 3.79. *1 WS, 3 ip, 0–1, 9.00*

After an unsuccessful stint in 1936, Jakucki resurfaced during WWII and clinched the Browns' only pennant with a 5–2 win over the Yankees on the last day of the 1944 season. His heavy drinking resulted in his suspension the following year. /(WAB)

Bill James (Big Bill) — 1887–1942. RHP 1911–12, 14–19 Indians, Browns, **Tigers**, Red Sox, White Sox 1180 ip, 65–71, 3.20. *1 WS, 4.2 ip, 0–0, 5.79*

Big Bill's nickname reflected his 6'4" frame and differentiated him from the contemporary Braves pitcher of the same name. James went 15–14, 2.85 for the Browns in 1914 and earned a spot on an AL all-star squad that barnstormed the country in a 32-game series against NL stars. He was sold to the White Sox in August 1919, just in time for the tainted World Series. He made his final ML appearance in the deciding game, relieving intentional loser Lefty Williams with only one out in the first inning and the White Sox already trailing 4–0. /(JK)

Bill James (Seattle Bill) — 1892–1971. RHP 1913–15, 19 **Braves** 542 ip, 37–21, 2.28. 20 wins: 14 *1 WS, 11 ip, 2–0, 0.00*

James was brilliant for one season, helping pitch the 1914 Miracle Braves to a World Championship with 26–7 record and 1.90 ERA. In the WS he shut out the Giants 1–0 on two hits in Game Two and won Game Three in relief. He won only five games in 1916, entered the military for WWI, and got no decision in his one postwar appearance. /(JK)

Bill James — 1949– . *Writer.*

A former high school English teacher in Kansas, Bill James delved into the study of baseball statistics, publishing a series of "baseball abstracts" each season from 1977 through 1988 and *The Bill James Historical Baseball Abstract* in 1985. One of the primary developers of modern sabermetrics, he is largely responsible for the newfound popularity of statistical analyses of baseball questions. His writing is accessible and often acerbic. James is also a contributing editor to *Inside Sports*. /(NLM)

Bob James — 1958- . RHP 1978-79, 82-87 Expos, Tigers, **White Sox** 407 ip, 24-26, 3.80

An intimidating 6'4" 230-lb power pitcher, James was the Expos' first-round pick in the 1976 June draft. After saving 10 games for Montreal in 1984 (his first full ML season), he was traded to the White Sox and earned a club-record 32 saves in 1985. But he essentially ended his 1986 season, and his career, that August 4 by tearing a muscle in his pitching arm. Disabled for more than two months of 1987, the bearded reliever could not regain his 92-mph fastball and was released. He recorded 73 career saves. /(JCA)

Charlie James — 1937- . OF 1960-65 **Cardinals**, Reds 510 g, .255, 29 hr, 172 rbi. *1 WS, 3 g, .000*

The Texas League rookie of the year in his first pro season (1958) and an International League all-star the following year, James was a platoon player with the Cardinals, splitting leftfield duty with Stan Musial in 1963. /(MC)

Chris James — 1962- . OF-3B 1986- **Phillies**, Padres 413 g, .256, 50 hr, 190 rbi

James was a promising young hitter with great speed before he missed most of the 1986 season with a broken ankle. He rebounded in 1987 to hit .293 with 17 HR while playing only part-time in the crowded Phillies outfield. As a starter in 1988, he tried to hit home runs, and his average fell 50 points. He played third base when Mike Schmidt went on the DL for rotator cuff surgery and was announced as Schmidt's successor when the Hall of Famer retired in 1989, but he was traded to San Diego within a month. His brother Craig was a running back for the New England Patriots. /(SG)

Dion James — 1962- . OF 1983-85, 87- Brewers, **Braves**, Indians 557 g, .285, 19 hr, 165 rbi

James was the Brewers' Rookie of the Year in 1984, when he won the centerfield job and batted .295. The following spring he twice dislocated his right shoulder diving for fly balls. After spending 1986 in the minors, James (Milwaukee's first-round pick in 1980) was traded for Brad Komminsk (Atlanta's top pick in 1979). The slap-hitter switched from a straight-up stance to an open crouch, giving him new power; he hit .312 with 37 doubles and 10 HR in 1987. On April 13 against the Mets, his routine fly ball hit a dove and fell uncaught. James was a

major disappointment in Atlanta's dismal 1988 season and was criticized for erratic fielding. He was traded to the Indians in mid-1989 for Oddibe McDowell, the Rangers' number-one pick in 1984. /(JCA)

Jeff James (Jesse) — 1941- . RHP 1968-69 **Phillies** 147 ip, 6-6, 4.51

James earned a spot with the Phillies after winning 11 straight for their San Diego (Pacific Coast League) farm club in 1967. The highlight of his brief ML career was a four-hit shutout of Chicago in July of his rookie season. /(AL)

Johnny James — 1933- . RHP 1958, 60-61 Yankees, **Angels** 119 ip, 5-3, 4.76

A career reliever, James earned a spot with the Yankees in 1960 by pitching part of a team no-hitter in spring training. He contributed a 5-1 mark to the pennant winners but was dropped from the roster before the WS. /(MC)

Charlie Jamieson (Chuck, Jamie, Hawk) — 1893-1969. OF-LHP 1915-32 Senators, A's, **Indians** 1779 g, .303, 18 hr, 550 rbi; 48 ip, 2-1, 6.19. *1 WS, 6 g, .333, 1 rbi*

Jamieson was a late bloomer. He had been in the majors for four years before Cleveland manager Tris Speaker bamboozled Connie Mack into adding him to an already unbalanced 1919 trade in the Indians' favor. From 1920 to 1931, he owned left field at League Park. Jamieson started as a pitcher, and he took to the mound in five of his ML seasons. By the time he reached Cleveland, he was clearly a superbly athletic outfielder and a swift, hard-hitting leadoff man. He had nine full seasons over .300, including .359 in 1924. In 1923, he had a 23-game hitting streak and led the AL with 222 hits and 644 at-bats. Defensively, he made spectacular diving catches and powerful, accurate throws. In 1928 his 22 outfield assists were tops, and in a 17-day span he started two triple plays. Jamieson was a frequent MVP candidate, though never a winner. /(ADS)

Gerry Janeski — 1946- . RHP 1970-72 **White Sox**, Senators/Rangers 281 ip, 11-23, 4.71

Janeski tied for the International League lead with 15 wins at Louisville in 1969. When the White Sox traded Gary Peters and Don Pavletich to the Red Sox for Syd O'Brien and pitcher Billy Farmer that December, Janeski replaced Farmer when the latter was discovered to have a sore arm. Farmer was

10–17 for the White Sox in 1970, earning Chicago Rookie of the Year honors. Local sportswriters dubbed him The Wheat Germ Kid because his locker resembled a health food store. /(RL)

Vic Janowicz (Crash) — 1930– . C-3B 1953–54 **Pirates** 83 g, .214, 2 hr, 10 rbi

From Ohio State, the 1950 Heisman Trophy winner was the first to ever play ML baseball. One of several bonus baby busts for Pittsburgh in the 1950s, Janowicz returned to the NFL Redskins after 1954, but his career was tragically ended by a 1956 car accident. /(ME)

Larry Jansen — 1920– . RHP 1947–54, 56 **Giants** 1765 ip, 122–89, 3.58. 20 wins: 47, 51. *1 WS, 10 ip, 0–2, 6.30*
☛ *Led League—w 51. All-Star—50–51.*

The lantern-jawed Jansen was nearing his 27th birthday when he arrived in the NL, but for five seasons he was one of the league's best righthanders. After being purchased from the Pacific Coast League, he had a magnificent rookie year in 1947, going 21–5 and leading the league in winning percentage. He threw an outstanding overhand curve and a good fastball, and had excellent control. After one of his ten consecutive complete-game wins, Giants catcher Walker Cooper commented, "I don't believe he missed the target (catcher's mitt) by more than two inches all day." He won 18 in 1948 and 19 in 1950, while tying for the league lead with five shutouts. In 1951, the mild-mannered Jansen combined with Sal Maglie as the Giants' one-two pitching punch in winning the "miracle" pennant. They tied for the league lead in victories with 23 each.

Later, as pitching coach for the Giants, he helped develop Juan Marichal and Gaylord Perry. /(FS)

Hal Janvrin (Childe Harold) — 1892–1962. SS-2B-1B-3B-OF 1911, 13–17, 19–22 **Red Sox**, Senators, Cardinals, Dodgers 756 g, .232, 6 hr, 210 rbi. *2 WS, 6 g, .208, 1 rbi*

A teenager when he joined his hometown Red Sox in 1911, Childe Harold was nicknamed for the hero of Byron's epic poem. Janvrin demonstrated versatility but never held a steady job at any one position. /(JK)

Jarry Park (Le Parc Jarry) Montreal Expos 1969–76. LF-340, CF-420, RF-340

Cozy but often cool Jarry Park, site of the first ML games played outside the United States, had a capacity of 28,000 and featured hearty fans and ML baseball's first bilingual public address announcements. Home runs to right field occasionally landed in an adjacent public swimming pool. /(SCL)

Pat Jarvis — 1941– . RHP 1966–73 **Braves**, Expos 1284 ip, 85–73, 3.58. *1 LCS, 4 ip, 0–1, 12.46*

Hard-nosed Pat Jarvis was the Braves' number-three starter behind Phil Niekro and Ron Reed in the late 1960s. He won between 13 and 16 games a year from 1967 to 1970 and had just one losing ML season (1971, 6–14). In the 1969 LCS, Jarvis started and lost the final game to the Mets. He was a rodeo rider before playing baseball. /(PB)

Ray Jarvis — 1946– . RHP 1969–70 **Red Sox** 116 ip, 5–7, 4.64

Signed by Boston out of the Cape Cod summer league, the sinkerballing native of Providence pitched in two ML seasons before succumbing to arm injuries. Jarvis tied a ML record by striking out five times in a nine-inning game. /(RMu)

Larry Jaster — 1944– . LHP 1965–70, 72 **Cardinals**, Expos, Braves 597 ip, 35–33, 3.65. *2 WS, 0.1 ip, 0–0, 81.00*

Called up to the Cardinals late in 1965, Jaster threw three complete-game victories in three starts. In 1966 he threw five shutouts, all against the pennant-bound Dodgers, to set a major league record for most consecutive shutouts won from one club in a season. He finished the year with a career-high 11 victories.

Relieving in the third inning of Game Six of the 1968 World Series, Jaster pitched to three batters without retiring any, surrendering a grand slam to Jim Northrup, as the Tigers scored a Series-record 10 runs. He threw the first ML pitch in Canada, pitching for the Expos in their 1969 home opener. /(FJO)

Al Javery (Bear Tracks) — 1918–1977. RHP 1940–46 **Braves** 1143 ip, 53–74, 3.80
☛ *All-Star—43–44.*

A wartime workhorse for the Braves (he was deferred for varicose veins), Javery had four straight seasons with double-figure wins and earned spots on two All-Star teams, but had only one winning record (17–16 in 1943). /(JK)

Julian Javier (Hoolie, The Phantom) — 1936- . 2B-3B
1960-72 **Cardinals**, Reds 1622 g, .257, 78 hr, 506 rbi.
4 WS, 19 g, .333, 1 hr, 7 rbi
☛ *All-Star—63, 68.*

The Dominican Javier was dealt from the Pirate
farm system to the Cardinals in a May 1960 trade
for popular pitcher Vinegar Bend Mizell. His range
and speed quickly enabled him to establish himself
as the everyday second baseman for a dozen seasons
in St. Louis. In 1963, Javier and teammates Ken
Boyer, Dick Groat, and Bill White made up an all-
Cardinal starting All-Star infield. Javier was so good
covering ground, pivoting on the double plays, and
going back for pop-ups that GM Bing Devine
proclaimed him better defensively than Frankie
Frisch, Rogers Hornsby, or Red Schoendienst.

Javier hit .360 in the 1967 WS against Boston,
including a three-run homer in Game Seven to help
Bob Gibson win his third Series game and bring the
World Championship to St. Louis. He is the father
of Stan Javier. /(FJO)

Stan Javier — 1965- . OF 1984, 86- Yankees, A's
384 g, .236, 5 hr, 80 rbi. *2 LCS, 3 g, .333, 1 rbi. 1 WS, 3 g,
.500, 2 rbi*

Javier was part of the package Oakland received for
Rickey Henderson in December 1984. He became a
semi-regular in the A's 1988 AL pennant-winning
season after they became dissatisfied with Luis
Polonia's fielding. Javier hit .257 with 20 steals and
49 runs in 397 at-bats. In Game Five of the 1988
World Series, he drove in the only two runs the A's
scored against Orel Hershiser in the whole
Series. /(WOR)

Joey Jay — 1935- . RHP 1953-55, 57-66 Braves,
Reds 1546 ip, 99-91, 3.77. 20 wins: 61-62 *1 WS, 9 ip,
1-1, 5.59*
☛ *Led League—w 61. All-Star—61.*

Late in 1953 at the age of eighteen, Jay hurled a
three-hit shutout for the Braves to beat the Reds in
his first ML start. A $20,000 bonus baby, Jay was
the first graduate of the Little League program to
reach the majors. Ironically, he had been the subject
of a petition attempting to bar him from Little
League at age twelve because of his advanced size.
While in the majors, he wrote an article entitled
"Don't Trap Your Son in Little League Madness."

But Jay didn't blossom with Milwaukee, who still
had Warren Spahn and Lew Burdette winning 20 a
year. He went 7-5 (2.14) in 1958, but missed the
World Series with a broken finger. Traded to Cincinnati in December 1960, he flourished, in 1961 tying

Spahn for the league lead in wins (21) and shutouts
(4), and beating the Yankees in Game Two of the
WS. He won 21 again in 1962, but dropped to 7-18
the following year and was finished by 1966. /(RTM)

Hal Jeffcoat — 1924- . OF-LHP 1948-59 **Cubs**,
Reds, Cardinals 918 g, .248, 26 hr, 188 rbi; 697 ip, 39-37,
4.22

One of a family of pro ballplayers (older brother
George pitched in the NL), fast, smooth-fielding Hal
Jeffcoat broke in with the 1948 Cubs as an outfielder. His light hitting forced him into a backup
role by 1950, and he converted to pitching in 1954
to utilize his strong arm. He became a top reliever,
making 50 appearances (2.95 ERA) in 1955 and,
after his trade to the Reds, went 8-2 in
1956. /(DAS)

Mike Jeffcoat — 1959- . LHP 1983-85, 87, 87 **Indians**,
Giants, Rangers 287 ip, 15-16, 4.01

Jeffcoat spent one full season in the majors, as a long
reliever for the 1984 Indians (5-2, 2.99). He saw
little ML action after his 1985 trade to the
Giants. /(JCA)

Gregg Jefferies — 1967- . 2B-3B 1987- **Mets** 176 g,
.271, 18 hr, 75 rbi. *1 LCS, 7 g, .333, 1 rbi*

Jefferies was the Mets' first-round pick in the 1985
June draft and was a minor league MVP each of his
first three seasons. He had an outstanding late-
season call-up in 1988, hitting .321 with six HR in
109 at-bats, and Mets manager Davey Johnson
deliberately held him out of some games so that he
would qualify for Rookie of the Year in 1989.
Jefferies pushed the slumping, injured Howard
Johnson off third base for the LCS and hit well, but
his inability to bunt may have cost the Mets Game
Five. In Game Seven he made a crucial error in the
Dodgers' five-run second inning, completely muffing
an easy double play ball.

Jefferies was given the second base job from the
start of the 1989 season, but went through a horrible
slump in the first two months, showing very little
selectivity at the plate. Manager Johnson stuck with
him, and he eventually came around, hitting .258 in
1989. Johnson, a Gold Glove second baseman in his
playing days, also worked with him on turning the
double play.

The intense scrutiny of Jefferies extended to his
father's training regimen for him while he was
growing up, which included unusual exercises such
as building strength by swinging a bat
underwater. /(JFC)

Jesse Jefferson — 1949- . RHP 1973-81 Orioles, White Sox, **Blue Jays**, Pirates, Angels 1086 ip, 39-81, 4.81

The hard-throwing but often wild Jefferson had his only winning season (6–5) as an Oriole rookie in 1973. The 24th pick of the Blue Jays in the 1976 expansion draft, he was an abysmal 22–56 in four years in Toronto. Jefferson's two-hitter against the Mariners on July 27, 1980 demonstrated that he could be a brilliant pitcher at times. There were other times when he was terrible. He set a Blue Jay franchise record with nine walks in a game against Baltimore on June 18, 1977, and he allowed 10 earned runs (with four homers) against Chicago on April 11, 1978. Jefferson's best full season came in 1977, when he went 9–17 with a 4.31 ERA. /(TF/JCA)

Stan Jefferson — 1962- . OF 1986- Mets, **Padres**, Yankees, Orioles 224 g, .218, 14 hr, 57 rbi

This native New Yorker was the Mets' first-round pick in the June 1983 draft. Sent to San Diego in the Kevin McReynolds-Kevin Mitchell deal after the 1986 season, Jefferson was a regular in the Padres' outfield in 1987, although he spent much of the first half on the DL. He stole 34 bases but hit just .230, although that remained a career high. /(SFS)

Steve Jeltz — 1959- . SS 1983- **Phillies** 653 g, .213, 5 hr, 120 rbi

Jeltz beat out Luis Aguayo for the Phillies' starting shortstop job in 1986 but hit only .219. The Phillies signed Dickie Thon for 1989, and Jeltz and Thon shared the job. Jeltz hit three homers in a 17-game span after hitting one in six previous seasons and became the first Phillie ever to homer from both sides of the plate in one game. /(SG)

Fats Jenkins [Clarence] — 1898-1968. OF-MGR Negro Leagues 1920-40 New York Lincoln Giants, Harrisburg Giants, Bacharach Giants, Baltimore Black Sox, **New York Black Yankees**, Philadelphia Stars, Brooklyn Eagles, Brooklyn Royal Giants statistics not available

Fats Jenkins was a wiry, 5'7" outfielder who inherited his nickname from a plump older brother. A great all-around athlete who played professional basketball with the Renaissance team, he was a good hitter and a fast runner.

Statistics documenting Jenkins's career are sketchy; none exist for his first four years (1920–23).

He batted .319 in 1924 and .307 in 1925 for the Harrisburg Giants, and .358 for the 1929 Atlantic City Bacharachs. He played in the 1933 and 1935 East-West all-star games. At the age of 37, Jenkins hit .305 for the 1935 Brooklyn Eagles and stole nine bases in 42 games to lead the league.

Though his name is most often linked with the New York Black Yankees, virtually no recorded statistics remain of Jenkins's years with them. Fragmentary evidence gives him a lifetime average of .319 in the Negro Leagues, while black-baseball historian James Riley credits him with a .331 mark. His last job in black baseball was as manager of the 1940 Brooklyn Royal Giants. /(JM)

Ferguson Jenkins — 1943- . RHP 1965-1983 Phillies, **Cubs**, Rangers, Red Sox 4500 ip, 284-226, 3.34. 20 wins: 67-72, 74
Led League—w 71, 74. Led League—k 69. Cy Young Award—71. All-Star—67, 71.

Jenkins never received the fame his accomplishments warrant. He racked up 284 victories, had six consecutive 20-win seasons paired with 200-plus strikeouts, pitched more than 300 innings five times, and is high on the all-time strikeout list with 3,192. He never pitched on a pennant winner, though, and was usually on teams that were known more for hitting than pitching.

When the Cubs acquired Jenkins midway through the 1966 season, manager Leo Durocher converted the hard-throwing 6'5" 200-lb righthander into a starter. Beginning in 1967 and continuing through 1972, Jenkins won at least 20 games every year. He set a modern Cubs record with 236 strikeouts in 1967, then raised the record each of the next three seasons to 260, 273, and 274. In the 15-inning 1967 All-Star game, Jenkins equaled Carl Hubbell's 1934 strikeout numbers, fanning six in three innings, but he gave up a sixth-inning homer to Brooks Robinson that tied the score at 1–1. He gave up another homer, to Harmon Killebrew, in his only other All-Star appearance (1971). He led the NL in 1971 with a 24–13 record with 263 strikeouts, a 2.77 ERA, and 30 complete games to win the Cy Young award. He also hit .243 with six homers.

After failing to win 20 games in 1973, and because of Ron Santo's diminishing skills at third base, the Cubs traded Jenkins to the Texas Rangers for Bill Madlock. In his first start in a Ranger uniform, he shut out the World Champion A's on one hit. He led the AL with a 25–12 record, the seventh and last time he would win 20 games. He fell to 17–18 in 1975 and was traded to Boston. He

Ferguson Jenkins

Hughie Jennings (Ee-Yah) — 1869–1928. SS-1B-2B 1891–1903, 07–09, 12, 18 Louisville (AA)/(NL), **Baltimore (NL)**, Dodgers, Phillies, Tigers 1285 g, .312, 18 hr, 840 rbi.
Manager 1907–20 **Tigers** 1131–972, .538. First place: 07–09 *3 WS, 4–12, .250*
☛ *Hall of Fame—1945.*

One of baseball's most colorful and best-loved characters, Jennings rose from breaker boy in the Pennsylvania anthracite fields to the Hall of Fame. The redheaded, freckled firebrand wore a major league uniform for more than three decades as a player, coach, and manager. He also earned a law degree and built a successful off-season legal practice. Jennings's best years came as captain of the powerful, brawling Baltimore Orioles, National League champions in three straight years, 1894–96 and winners of the 1897 Temple Cup. Operating within and outside the rules, Jennings and teammates John McGraw, Willie Keeler, Joe Kelley, and Wilbert Robinson were the scourge of opponents and umpires. During his five full seasons in Baltimore, Jennings never batted below .328 and achieved a high of .398 in 1896, the ML record for shortstops. In addition, he stole as many as 70 bases in a season and was the leader in fielding average and putouts three times each.

His hitting declined in later years, and a sore arm forced a move back to first base, but Jennings's superior skills as a strategist and field leader kept him steadily employed. He played for pennant winners in Brooklyn in 1899 and 1900, and later captained the Phillies before embarking on a managing career in the minors. Purchased by the Tigers in 1907, Jennings guided the team to pennants in his first three years at the helm. The Tigers lost all three World Series, however, and never again won a pennant under Jennings, who remained on the job through 1920. From the third base coaching box, the hyperactive skipper prodded his charges, among them the young Ty Cobb, and taunted the opposition with shouts, whistles, and gyrations. His piercing yell of "Ee-Yah" became a trademark. Upon leaving the Tigers, Jennings was signed by former Oriole teammate John McGraw as a coach and assistant manager with the Giants. In the role of right-hand man, Jennings was a part of four consecutive pennant-winning clubs (1921–24).

Though durable, Jennings suffered an incredible string of mishaps on and off the field. He was often hit by pitches; a then-record 49 times in 1896 alone. Two skull fractures, one the result of an accidental dive into an empty swimming pool, slowed but did

was going to Fenway Park with high expectations for 1976, joining a Red Sox team that had come within one win of a world title the previous year. But the fire had gone out of Jenkins's arm. He could not win more games than he lost. By late 1977, Red Sox manager Don Zimmer was fed up with Jenkins's inconsistency and banished him to the bullpen. On September 18 in Baltimore, Brooks Robinson Night, Jenkins supposedly fell asleep (Jenkins said he simply had his feet up in the cart) in the bullpen and had to be woken up to warm up. Zimmer was livid, and Jenkins didn't pitch again in a Boston uniform. At the end of the year, Jenkins headed back to Texas, where he partially regained his form and won 18 games. Jenkins was reacquired by the Cubs in 1982 and led the club in innings pitched and ERA with a 14–15 record at the age of 38. /(SEW)

Hughie Jennings

not stop him. A nervous breakdown after the 1925 season, however, brought his baseball days to an end. He was elected to the Hall of Fame in 1945./(JL)

Jackie Jensen — 1927–1982. OF 1950–61 Yankees, Senators, **Red Sox** 1,438 g, .279, 199 hr, 929 rbi. *1 WS, 1 g, .000*
☛ *Most Valuable Player—58. All-Star—52, 55, 58. Gold Glove—59.*

The blond Golden Boy, a product of the Yankee farm system of the 1940s, was heralded as DiMaggio's heir as a rookie in 1950. But he hit only .171 in 45 games, and Mickey Mantle assumed that role the following year. Jensen, freed from the pressures of following a legend, enjoyed a solid, if less productive

than predicted, career up the coast in Boston. Jensen played just 11 years, his career cut short by a fear of flying. Ted Williams called his right-field partner the best outfielder he ever saw. A steady RBI man, Jensen drove in 100 or more runs five of his seven years with the Red Sox and led the league three times with 116 in 1955, 122 in 1958, and 112 in 1959. He hit over .300 only once, in 1956, a season highlighted on August 2, when he drove in nine runs. Although the speedy Jensen led the league in stolen bases with 22 in 1954 and in triples with 11 in 1956, he also had a proclivity for grounding into double plays, hitting into 185 over his career (once every 28 at-bats)./(SEW)

Woody Jensen [Forrest Docenus] — 1907– . OF 1931–39 **Pirates** 738 g, .285, 26 hr, 235 rbi

In the mid-1930s, Jensen teamed with Paul and Lloyd Waner in the Pittsburgh outfield. He was called Woody as a play on Forrest, and because (from Bremerton, Washington) he once played in the Timber League. The lefthanded hitter rarely walked and set a ML record with 696 at-bats in 1936, batting leadoff with Lloyd dropping to second./(ME)

John Jeter (The Jet) — 1944– . OF 1969–74 Pirates, **Padres**, White Sox, Indians 336 g, .244, 18 hr, 69 rbi. *1 LCS, 3 g, .000*

The speedy Jeter spent his first two seasons as a late-inning defensive substitute for Willie Stargell in the Pirates' outfield. He couldn't produce consistently when given more playing time by the Padres in 1972 (.221) and the White Sox in 1973 (.240)./(SFS)

Sam Jethroe (Jet) — 1922– . C-OF Negro Leagues 1942–49 Cincinnati Buckeyes, Cleveland Buckeyes statistics not available; ML: OF 1950–52, 54 **Braves**, Pirates 442 g, .261, 49 hr, 181 rbi
☛ *Rookie of the Year—50.*

After stealing 89 bases in the International League in 1949, Jethroe became the first black to play for the Braves. The twenty-eight-year-old switch-hitter was the 1950 NL Rookie of the Year, hitting .273 with 18 HR, 100 runs scored, and a major league-leading 35 stolen bases. His numbers were virtually identical in 1951 and he again won the major league stolen base title with 35. The centerfielder slumped to .232 in 1952, struck out 112 times, fielded poorly (leading NL outfielders in errors for the third straight season, and reportedly had vision trouble (his 28 steals was second in the NL and the majors). Amid rumors he was older than listed, he spent 1953 in Toledo, batting .307. Acquired by Pittsburgh, he played just two games for the Pirates. He spent five more seasons with Toronto (International League).

But Jethroe's best years had been spent in the Negro Leagues with the Cleveland Buckeyes, for whom he batted .342 in six seasons. He was selected to the Negro Leagues' East-West all-star game four times. He is the only player to have hit a ball over the 472-foot leftfield fence at Toledo's Swayne Field and into the coal piles of the Red Man Tobacco Factory. In the spring of 1945, he was selected with Jackie Robinson and Marvin Williams for an unsuccessful tryout with the Red Sox. Boston coach Hugh Duffy said, "There is no doubt about it that they are ballplayers. They look good to me." Robinson said that at that tryout, Jethroe "looked like a gazelle in the outfield." But the Red Sox would be the last major league team to integrate, while Jethroe went on to star for their crosstown rivals. /(LL/ME)

Houston Jimenez [Alfonso] — 1957- . SS-2B
1983-84, 87-88 **Twins**, Pirates, Indians 158 g, .185, 0 hr, 29 rbi

Jimenez spent much of his career in the Mexican League. He saw the most major league action with the 1984 Twins, hitting a ML-career-high .201 in 298 at-bats. He received his nickname as a child after a television Western character. /(WOR)

Manny Jimenez — 1938- . OF 1962-64, 66-69 **A's**, Pirates, Cubs 429 g, .272, 26 hr, 144 rbi

Jimenez looked promising when he hit .301 with 11 HR and 69 RBI in his rookie 1962 season. But he lost his power in reduced playing time in 1963 and, regaining it in 1964, saw his BA plummet to .225. He resurfaced with the Pirates, leading the NL in pinch hits in 1967 and in pinch at-bats the following year, when he went 10-for-53 in that role. He hit .303 overall that year by going 10-for-13 in his only non-pinch at-bats. /(JFC)

Tommy John — 1943- . LHP 1963-74, 76-89
Indians, White Sox, **Dodgers**, Yankees, Angels, A's
4707 ip, 288-231, 3.34. 20 wins: 77, 79-80 *5 LCS, 48 ip, 4-1, 2.08. 3 WS, 34 ip, 2-1, 2.67*
☛ *All-Star—68, 78-80.*

A sinkerballer with impeccable control, John's major league career spanned 26 seasons and seven U.S. presidents, both ML records. In mid-career, he

Tommy John

made history by becoming the game's first "right-handed southpaw" when he had a tendon transplanted from his right forearm to his left elbow to remedy a tear that threatened to drive him from baseball.

After breaking in with the Indians, John became an effective starter for the mediocre White Sox from 1965 to 1971, leading the AL in shutouts in 1966 and 1967. He was traded to the Dodgers for Dick Allen before the 1972 season, and in 1973 he led the NL in winning percentage with a 16–9 record. John seemed to be embarking on his best season in 1974, posting a 13–3 mark before injuring his pitching elbow in July.

Dr. Frank Jobe performed the revolutionary surgery that saved John's career, and it was amazingly successful. The soft-throwing John joked that he told Jobe to "put in a Koufax fastball. He did, but it was Mrs. Koufax's." He underwent rehabilitation for a year and a half, missing the entire 1975 season, and his 10–10 record in 1976 earned him the Comeback Player of the Year Award. He then won

20 games in three of the next four seasons. John was 20–7 for the Dodgers in 1977 and 17–10 in '78, helping them to the World Series each year. But the Dodgers lost to the Yankees both times. John then signed with the Yankees as a free agent before the 1979 season and won 21 and 22 games in his first two seasons in New York.

John was traded to the Angels for Dennis Rasmussen late in the 1982 season and was released in 1985 at the age of forty-two, but after a brief stint with Oakland he returned to the Yankees in 1986 and led the club in innings pitched as a 44-year-old in 1987. He often explained his unusual durability by pointing out that his pitching arm was much younger than his chronological age.

John's excellent sinker induced numerous ground balls and double plays throughout his career, and he was usually a fine fielder himself, setting club records with errorless seasons for both the Dodgers and White Sox. On July 27, 1988, however, John tied a ML record by committing three errors on one play. In the fourth inning against the Brewers, John muffed a ground ball for one error and threw wildly past first base for a second. Then, inexplicably, he intercepted the throw home from right field and threw wildly past the catcher.

He was released by the Yankees early in the 1989 season. /(TG)

Adam Johnson (Tex) — 1888–1972. RHP 1914–15, 18 Red Sox, **Chicago (FL)**, Baltimore (FL), Cardinals 450 ip, 23–30, 2.92

Johnson was 4–9, 3.08 with the Red Sox, earning $400 a month in his rookie 1914 season, when he was traded to the Indians. He jumped to the Chicago Whales of the Federal League and went 9–5, 1.58 the rest of the way to lead the FL in ERA. It was his only successful season. His son Adam Jr. pitched briefly for the 1941 Athletics. /(NLM)

Alex Johnson — 1942– . OF 1964–76 Phillies, Cardinals, **Reds**, Angels, Indians, Rangers, Yankees, Tigers 1322 g, .288, 78 hr, 525 rbi
☛ Led League—ba 70. All-Star—70.

No one could quite figure how to motivate Johnson, a surly yet talented hitter with a great arm who never achieved popularity despite his skills. He is best remembered for edging the popular Carl Yastrzemski in the AL batting race in 1970, .3289 to .3286. Known as an aggressive contact hitter who didn't strike out much and who hated to walk or talk, Johnson admitted that he never gave 100% and never hustled. He once told a reporter, "I'm just

paid to hit." As a result of this lackadaisical attitude, he spent time with eight different teams in his 13-year career. Called the fastest righthanded hitter from home plate to first, Johnson had his first success with the Reds in the late 1960s, hitting over .300 both seasons he spent in Cincinnati. His fine play in 1970 was quickly forgotten the next season when Angels manager Lefty Phillips suspended him for being "a bad influence." After leaving California, he never again hit .300. /(SEW)

Ban Johnson [Byron Bancroft] — 1864–1931. *Executive*

The American League is Johnson's gift to baseball. Others were present at the creation, but it was Johnson's driving force, shrewd business sense, rigorous standards, and lively imagination that made the league a success.

He gave form and definition to the emerging role of baseball executive. After studying law but falling short of a degree at Marietta (Ohio) College, he became sports editor for the Cincinnati *Commercial-Gazette*. After Johnson's friend Charlie Comiskey was fired as Reds manager after the 1894 season, they took over the faltering Western League, with Ban as president. It soon became known as the best-run circuit in baseball. A name change (to the American League) in 1900, combined with a series of swift, opportunistic maneuvers, outflanked the established NL, and by 1901 Johnson's league claimed major status. After some fine-tuning of franchises, the AL achieved the structure it held until 1954. In 1903 the NL was forced to accept its parity and agree to a World Series between league champions.

As boss, Johnson found no task too large or too small to merit his attention. He located millionaires to bankroll his teams, came down hard on rowdies and roughhousing on the field, appointed managers, arranged trades, and apportioned players. He arranged schedules to spread travel costs equitably, interpreted rules, levied fines and suspensions, issued statistics, and even recruited William Howard Taft as the first president to throw out an Opening Day ball. One of his most important contributions was to enforce respect for umpires as symbols of baseball's integrity.

He did it all with little grace and no humor. Johnson was hot-tempered, bullheaded, imperious, and uncompromising, not unlike many other tycoons of his time. But he was successful. His owners voted him $25,000 a year and his presidency for life.

During his term on the National Commission (the triumvirate, including the AL and NL presidents,

Ban Johnson

that ruled ML baseball from 1903 until 1920), he was thought of as baseball's czar, but his downfall was inevitable. New AL owners were less willing to accept his high-handed decisions affecting their investments. Old friends were angered. Comiskey had once said, "Ban Johnson IS the American League!" But when he lost pitcher Jack Quinn to the Yankees on a Johnson ruling, the White Sox owner thundered: "I made you, and by God I'll break you!"

Indirectly, he did. The Black Sox scandal caused the abolition of the National Commission and the establishment of Judge Landis as Commissioner of Baseball. Johnson's era had ended. He remained AL president, but Landis limited his duties, curtailed his power, and ultimately humiliated him. After promoting an investigation concerning charges that Ty Cobb and Tris Speaker had been involved in gambling fixes in 1919, he was persuaded to resign on October 17, 1927./(ADS)

Bart Johnson [Clair Barth] — 1950- . RHP 1969–74, 76–77 **White Sox** 810 ip, 43–51, 3.95

Dogged by injuries throughout his career (he missed all of the 1975 season with an ailing back), the 6'5″ power pitcher had two good seasons. In 1971 he went 12–10, with 14 saves, and in 1974 he was 10–4 with a 2.73 ERA. He hit .329 in 50 games as an outfielder with Appleton (Midwest League) in 1972./(JCA)

Billy Johnson (Bull) — 1918- . 3B 1943, 46–53 **Yankees**, Cardinals 964 g, .271, 61 hr, 487 rbi. *4 WS, 18 g, .237, 5 rbi*
☛ *All-Star—47.*

Johnson caught manager Joe McCarthy's attention in the Yankees' wartime 1943 Asbury Park, New Jersey, training camp by taking infield practice while it was snowing. Johnson took over the Yankee third base job from Red Rolfe that season and had a great rookie year, hitting .280 with 94 RBI (third in the league) and leading AL third basemen in putouts, assists, and double plays. His bases-loaded triple in the eighth inning of Game Three of the 1943 WS overcame a 2–1 deficit to win the game. He spent 1944–45 in the military and had an off-year in 1946, but came back strong in 1947 to tie for fourth in the AL with 95 RBI. He set a record for a seven-game Series that fall with three triples; his four overall tied the lifetime WS record. He also led the Yankees with eight runs in the '47 Series, twice as many as runner-up Joe DiMaggio.

In 1948 he hit a career-high .294 with 12 HR while leading AL third basemen in total chances per game, but dropped off in overall production. The arrival of Casey Stengel in 1949 cut into his playing time and his effectiveness, as Stengel platooned him with Bobby Brown, used him as a defensive replacement, and played him at first base. When Gil McDougald arrived in 1951, Johnson was traded in May to the Cardinals for Don Bollweg and $15,000. In his last full-time season, he led NL third basemen in fielding and hit a career-high 14 HR./(SH)

Bob Johnson [Robert Lee] (Indian Bob) — 1906- . OF-1B-2B-3B 1933–45 **A's**, Senators, Red Sox 1863 g, .296, 288 hr, 1283 rbi
☛ *All-Star—35, 38–40, 42–44.*

Indian Bob, half Cherokee, had speed and power. When the Athletics sold Al Simmons after the 1932 season and Lou Finney, tabbed as his replacement in left field, didn't measure up, Johnson won the job. An A's regular for a decade, Johnson hit .307 with a

Bob Johnson [Robert Wallace] — 1936– . SS-2B-3B-1B 1960–70 A's, Senators, **Orioles**, Mets, Reds, Braves, Cardinals 874 g, .272, 44 hr, 230 rbi

This versatile infielder only once appeared in more than 100 games in a season: in 1962, when he had career highs of 112 HR, 58 runs, and 43 RBI for the Senators. He led his league in pinch hits three times (1964, 1967, and 1969). In the years 1967–1969 he played with six teams, two each season, returning finally to the A's, with whom he had begun his career. /(JFC)

Bob Johnson [Robert Dale] — 1943– . RHP 1969–74, 77 Mets, Royals, **Pirates**, Indians, Braves 692 ip, 28–34, 3.48. *2 LCS, 14 ip, 1–0, 1.29. 1 WS, 5 ip, 0–1, 9.00*

In his one season with Kansas City (1970), 6'4" Bob Johnson struck out 206, the third-highest total ever for a rookie and a Royal record. He was second to Bert Blyleven in *TSN* AL Rookie Pitcher of the Year voting. Johnson went 9–10 with a 3.45 ERA for the World Champion 1971 Pirates. When Nellie Briles pulled a hamstring warming up for Game Three of the LCS, Johnson was his emergency replacement and pitched five-hit ball for eight innings, surrendering only an unearned run and winning a 2–1 duel against the Giants' Juan Marichal. He lost his Game Two World Series start, however, giving up four runs in 3–1/3 innings.

Johnson followed up his triumph with his best season in 1972 (4–4, 2.96), relieving more, as the Pirates won the division title, and in 1973 had his only winning record (4–2), coming almost exclusively out of the bullpen. /(SFS)

Chappie Johnson [George] — 1875–Unk. C-1B-MGR Negro Leagues 1896–1921 Page Fence Giants, Columbia Giants, Chicago Union Giants, Brooklyn Royal Giants, Leland Giants, Philadelphia Giants, Chicago Giants, St. Louis Giants, Dayton Chappies, Custer's Baseball Club of Columbus, Philadelphia Royal Giants, Norfolk Stars statistics not available

Johnson was one of the best black catchers during the two decades before the Negro National League was formed. He also played first base, starting his career there with the Columbia Giants of Chicago in 1896. As he developed as a catcher, he became known not only as an excellent handler of pitchers but also as a coach. He reportedly was hired by the white St. Paul club of the American Association to work with young catchers for several years in the early 1900s. He later became a highly successful manager. /(BP)

Indian Bob Johnson

career-high 34 HR his second year and batted a peak .338 in 1939. For seven straight seasons, he drove in over 100 runs. He had a 26-game hitting streak in 1934. On June 16, 1934 Johnson went six-for-six with two homers and two doubles, and on August 29, 1937 he set a ML record with six RBI in one inning on a grand slam and a double. He got the only hit in three one-hitters, once with a home run off Lefty Gomez in 1937. But Johnson was one of the few players to have serious difficulties with Connie Mack; he felt he was underpaid, and eventually demanded to be traded. He went to the Senators in 1943, and then to the Red Sox, where he hit .324 in 1944, his seventh and final All-Star season. He then spent five more seasons in the minors. Brother Roy played from 1929–38 with four major league teams. /(NLM)

Chief Johnson [George Howard] — 1886–1922. RHP 1913–15 Reds, **Kansas City (FL)** 688 ip, 41–43, 2.95

Johnson was a Winnebago Indian from Nebraska who went to the Carlisle Indian School in Pennsylvania. He was earning $3,200 a year with the Reds in 1914 when he jumped to Kansas City of the Federal League. Johnson's best season came in his last, 1915, as he went 18–17 with a 2.75 ERA in the Federal League, beefing up his record with a 4–0 mark in relief. /(NLM)

Cliff Johnson [Clifford, Jr.] (Heathcliff) — 1947– . DH-1B-C-OF 1972–86 Astros, Yankees, Indians, Cubs, A's, **Blue Jays**, Rangers 1369 g, .258, 196 hr, 699 rbi. *4 LCS, 15 g, .317, 1 hr, 4 rbi. 2 WS, 4 g, .000*

A powerful righthanded slugger whose bat often sailed across the infield as he swung at pitches and missed, Johnson holds the ML record for pinch home runs with 20, including an Astro-record 5 in his first full season. Without the designated hitter rule, Johnson struggled in the NL, never settling at a defensive position and leading the ML in passed balls in 1976 in only 66 games at catcher. Traded to the Yankees on June 15, 1977, Heathcliff blasted three home runs against the Blue Jays 15 days later, including two in the 8th inning. In 1979 he broke the thumb of teammate and Yankee bullpen ace Rich Gossage in a locker room scuffle and was traded to Cleveland. After 1980 the smart, patient hitter was primarily a DH. /(TF)

Connie Johnson [Clifford] — 1922– . RHP 1953, 55–58 White Sox, **Orioles** 716 ip, 40–39, 3.44

Johnson led the 1957 Orioles starters in wins (14), innings pitched (242), and ERA (3.20). He teamed with George Zuverink to match the one-hitter thrown by Chicago's Jack Harshman, but the Orioles lost 1–0. /(FK)

Darrell Johnson — 1928– . C 1952, 57–58, 60–62 Browns, White Sox, **Yankees**, Cardinals, Phillies, Reds, Orioles 134 g, .234, 2 hr, 28 rbi. *1 WS, 2 g, .500.*
Manager 1974–80, 82 Red Sox, **Mariners**, Rangers 472–590, .444. First place: 75 *1 LCS, 3–0, 1.000. 1 WS, 3–4, .429*

Johnson spent six seasons in the major leagues as a reserve catcher with seven different teams, developing the patience and perspective needed to manage. After success in the Red Sox farm system, he was named Boston manager in 1974. The following season the Sox won the pennant and took the WS to seven games before losing. Fired in July 1976,

Johnson became manager of the expansion Mariners in 1977 and piloted them through their first three and a half seasons. /(BC)

Dave Johnson — 1948– . RHP 1974–75, 77–78 Orioles, **Twins** 108 ip, 4–10, 4.64

Groomed as a reliever by the Orioles, Johnson broke his wrist in a 1975 motorcycle accident but became the "original" Mariner when Seattle purchased him (9/29/1976). Sold to the Twins, he made 30 appearances in 1977. /(EW)

Davey Johnson — 1943– . 2B-1B-3B 1965–75, 77–78 **Orioles**, Braves, Phillies, Cubs 1435 g, .261, 136 hr, 609 rbi. *4 LCS, 10 g, .289, 2 hr, 6 rbi. 4 WS, 21 g, .192, 6 rbi.*
   Manager 1984– **Mets** 575–395, .593. First place: 86, 88 *2 LCS, 7–6, .538. 1 WS, 4–3, .571*
☛ *All-Star—68–70, 73. Gold Glove—69–71 .*

Johnson was a three-time Gold Glove winner for the Orioles at second base (1969–71) and a good enough fielder to play 43 games at shortstop, filling in for Mark Belanger. But he is known as a home run hitter and as a manager. In 1973 his 43 HR, one behind the NL leader, set the ML record for second basemen as the Braves became the only team ever to have three 40-HR men: Johnson, Hank Aaron, and Darrell Evans. Johnson hit .270 that year, with career highs of 99 RBI, 84 runs, and 81 walks, and was *TSN*'s NL Comeback Player of the Year.

   The Orioles had traded him because manager Earl Weaver felt that Johnson had lost too much range afield by bulking up for power; Bobby Grich took over the job. Prior to that Johnson had led AL second basemen in putouts (1970), double plays (1971), fielding (1972), and errors (1966, his rookie season). Even before his surprising power in 1973, he'd been a useful hitter, finishing fourth in the AL in doubles in 1967 and third in 1969. That year, when the Orioles lost to the Miracle Mets in the World Series, Johnson's fly ball to Cleon Jones was the final out. He had better luck in 1970, hitting two homers in the LCS as Baltimore swept the Twins. His best offensive figures for Baltimore came in 1971, when he hit .282 with 18 HR and 72 RBI. After he dropped off to .221 with five HR in 1972, he was traded to Atlanta with Pat Dobson, Roric Harrison, and Johnny Oates for Earl Williams and a throw-in. Besides his record-setting power performance, Johnson tied for the NL lead in double plays by a second baseman, but he also led in errors and couldn't cover as much ground as he once had. He split 1974 between first and second and fell off to

Davey Johnson

.251 with 15 HR, and after one pinch at-bat in 1975 he signed with the Yomiuri Giants for two years. In Japan, he became the only player to be a teammate of both Hank Aaron and Sadaharu Oh. He was a disappointment in his first year overseas (.197, 13 HR), but he improved to .275 with 26 HR in 1976.

Johnson made it back to the majors with the division-winning 1977 Phillies as a utility man and pinch hitter (9-for-26), hitting .321 with eight HR in 156 at-bats. In 1978 he tied a ML record with two pinch grand slams. But although he hit .333 in the pinch, his overall average dropped to .232.

Johnson began his managerial career in 1979. He won pennants in each of his three seasons in the minors and advanced quickly through the Mets' system, jumping over more experienced managerial candidates. Mets GM Frank Cashen had been the GM at Baltimore during Johnson's time there. Johnson, who earned a mathematics degree from Trinity (Texas) University, gained immediate atten-

tion for his use of computers to compile player data. His attention to batter-pitcher matchups for platooning and in-game switches was learned from Earl Weaver. Johnson's strategy also owes much to his former manager. He dislikes the bunt and manages according to the credos of "pitching and three-run homers" and "play for one run, lose by one run." Johnson took over a team that hadn't won a pennant since 1973 but was ready to win after being rebuilt from the minors up by Cashen and the Mets' new owners. Johnson went on to become the first NL manager to win at least 90 games in each of his first five seasons, winning the World Championship in 1986 and the NL East in 1988 and finishing second in the other years. /(SH)

Deron Johnson — 1938– . 1B-3B-DH-OF 1960–62, 64–76 Yankees, A's, **Reds**, Braves, Phillies, Brewers, Red Sox, White Sox 1765 g, .244, 245 hr, 923 rbi. *1 LCS, 4 g, .100. 1 WS, 6 g, .300*
☛ *Led League—rbi 65.*

Johnson was a muscular, strikeout-prone, right-handed slugger who didn't play regularly in the ML until his ninth professional season, but still hit 245 home runs in the ML after belting 162 in the minors. He was dubbed "another Mickey Mantle" by the overreactive New York press after hitting .329 with 24 HR and 78 RBI in only 63 games in the lowly Nebraska State League in 1956, but he played only 19 games for the Yankees before being traded to the A's in 1961. He was purchased by the Reds after spending most of 1962 in the military, and in 1963 he led the Pacific Coast League with 33 HR at San Diego.

Johnson hit 21 HR for the Reds in 1964, and no longer tried to pull every pitch over the left-field fence, although he still struck out often. In 1965 he led the NL with 130 RBI while batting .287 with 32 HR, and he added 24 HR in 1966. Defensively, Johnson was bouncing from first base to third base to the outfield, rarely remaining at one position for more than a season. The Braves traded three players to get Johnson after the 1967 season, but sold him to Philadelphia after he hit only .208 in 1968, and with the Phillies he tied a ML record with home runs in four consecutive at-bats, July 10 and 11, 1971. After Johnson's average dipped again to .213 in 1972, the Phillies traded him to the A's for a single minor leaguer, and he spent 1973–76 shuttling around the AL as a designated hitter and occasional first baseman. /(SCL)

Don Johnson (Pep) — 1911– . 2B-3B 1943–48 **Cubs** 511 g, .273, 8 hr, 175 rbi. *1 WS, 7 g, .172*

Don was born in Chicago the winter before his father, shortstop Ernie Johnson, debuted with the White Sox. Pep, a journeyman minor leaguer, joined the Cubs in 1943 at age thirty-one, became a regular at second base in 1944, and hit a high of .302 for the 1945 pennant winners. /(DAS)

Don Johnson — 1926– . RHP 1947, 50–52, 54–55, 58 Yankees, Browns, **Senators**, White Sox, Orioles, Giants 631 ip, 27–38, 4.78

Johnson contributed a 4–3 mark to the Yankees' 1947 pennant winners but was not used in the WS. Bouncing between the majors and minors for the next decade, he had his best season with the 1954 White Sox, going 8–7 with a 3.13 ERA. /(MC)

Earl Johnson (Lefty) — 1919– . LHP 1940–41, 46–51 **Red Sox**, Tigers 546 ip, 410–32, 4.30. *1 WS, 3 ip, 1–0, 2.70*

The "smiling Swedish southpaw" spent two seasons with the Red Sox before enlisting in the Army right after Pearl Harbor. He returned with a Silver Star, Bronze Star, and a cluster for heroism earned during the Battle of the Bulge. Back to the baseball wars, Johnson won the opening game of the 1946 WS in relief and in 1948 won an AL-high nine out of the bullpen. His brother Chet pitched briefly with the Browns in 1946. /(JK)

Ernie Johnson — 1888–1952. SS-2B 1912, 15–18, 21–25 **White Sox**, St. Louis (FL), Browns, Yankees 809 g, .265, 19 hr, 256 rbi. *1 WS, 2 g, --*

Johnson was given the White Sox' starting shortstop job in 1921 when Swede Risberg was banned for fixing the 1919 WS. He hit .295 that year, but clumsy fielding and a 1923 salary holdout prompted his sale to the Yankees. His son Don was a Cubs second baseman. /(RL)

Ernie Johnson — 1924– . RHP 1950, 52–59 **Braves**, Orioles 575 ip, 40–23, 3.27. *1 WS, 7 ip, 0–1, 1.29*

A Braves reliever for eight of his nine ML seasons, Johnson pitched well in the 1957 WS but lost Game Six when he surrendered a solo home run to the Yankees' Hank Bauer. Johnson has been with the Braves organization more than forty years and has been a fulltime broadcaster since 1966. /(FK)

Grant Johnson (Home Run) — 1874–Unk. SS-2B-MGR Negro Leagues 1894–1921 Page Fence Giants, Columbia Giants, Brooklyn Royal Giants, Cuban X-Giants, Philadelphia Giants, New York Lincoln Giants, Lincoln Stars, Pittsburgh Colored Stars, Pittsburgh Stars of Buffalo statistics not available

Dubbed "Home Run" for his power hitting during the turn-of-the-century dead-ball era, the right-handed-hitting Johnson was one of the pioneers of black baseball. His first team, the Page Fence Giants, which he formed with fellow pioneer Bud Fowler, played for a time in a white league in Michigan. Johnson moved on to play for what was regarded as the best black team of the early 1900s, the 1906 Philadelphia Giants, managed by Hall of Famer Rube Foster. Foster then took Johnson and five other players with him to form the Chicago American Giants of 1910, which Foster said was his best team ever. Playing in Cuba that winter, Johnson hit .412 against top competition that included the Detroit Tigers with Ty Cobb. In five years in the Cuban Winter League, he batted .319 in 156 games.

A star shortstop, Johnson moved to second base with the New York Lincoln Giants in 1912 to make room for future Hall of Fame SS John Henry Lloyd. Johnson finished his career as a playing manager in Buffalo, retiring at the age of fifty-eight. /(PG)

Hank Johnson — 1906–1982. RHP 1925–36, 39 **Yankees**, Red Sox, A's, Reds 1066 ip, 63–56, 4.75

A starter and reliever during a career hampered by illness, Johnson had several victorious seasons as a Yankee; in 1928 he was 4–0 against the Athletics' Lefty Grove (14–9 overall), and in 1930 he led the AL with nine relief wins. /(EW)

Harold Johnson (Speed) — 1884–Unk. *Writer*

The editor of *Who's Who in Major League Baseball* in 1933, Johnson had begun his career with the Columbus (Ohio) *Citizen* in 1906. For the next ten years, he covered the Cubs and White Sox for the Chicago *Record-Herald*. After a year as sports editor for NEA in Cleveland, he returned to Chicago with the *Evening American* from 1919 to 1932. /(NLM)

Howard Johnson (HoJo) — 1960– . 3B-SS Tigers, **Mets** 869 g, .258, 136 hr, 422 rbi. *2 LCS, 8 g, .050. 2 WS, 3 g, .000*
☛ *All-Star—89.*

When finally given a chance to play regularly, Johnson established himself as one of the most well-rounded hitters in the game. In 1987 he and Darryl Strawberry became the first teammates to both hit

30 HR and steal 30 bases, and Johnson's 36 HR set a NL record for a switch-hitter.

Johnson's first full season came with the World Champion 1984 Tigers. He hit 12 HR with 50 RBI in 355 at-bats, but manager Sparky Anderson chose to use Dave Bergman, Marty Castillo, and Tom Brookens in the postseason rather than Johnson, who got only one pinch at-bat in the World Series. Detroit's disbelief in his potential led them to trade him to the Mets that December for Walt Terrell. In New York Johnson found himself in a platoon with Ray Knight. His ability to play shortstop, although without much range, got him in the lineup sometimes; manager Davey Johnson was quite willing to stack his lineup offensively at the cost of weaker defense. But it wasn't until after Knight left as a free agent that Johnson played every day, staving off the challenge of the promising Dave Magadan.

Usually hitting sixth or seventh, Johnson was easy to pitch around in 1987, but still hit .265 with 36 HR (fifth in the league) and 99 RBI. Opposing managers, especially Whitey Herzog of the rival Cardinals, repeatedly had Johnson's bat confiscated to check for cork. Eventually Herzog realized that Johnson's power was for real; two years later he suggested that Johnson's arms should be checked instead. Johnson fell off to 24 HR and 23 steals in 1988, playing the second half of the season with a sore right shoulder; he hit very poorly in the LCS. Over the winter, he was the center of many trade rumors, with hot rookie Gregg Jefferies supposedly ready to take over third base. The Mets were glad they kept him. At the All-Star break, Davey Johnson said, "the Mets' season [was] a Howard Johnson highlight film." HoJo moved to third in the lineup but continued to draw walks, showing both that he was a patient hitter and that NL pitchers would rather pitch to anybody else, even Darryl Strawberry. Johnson finished with career highs of 101 RBI (tied for fourth in the NL), 104 runs (tied for the NL lead), and 41 steals (tied for third) while batting .287 with 36 HR (second in the NL). He was only the third player ever to have two 30–30 seasons in HR and steals.

A dead fastball hitter in his first few seasons, Johnson used a high-tech reflex program to learn to wait better. But his ability to hit even the best fastballs gave him many clutch late-inning home runs against opponents' ace relievers, who tend to be fireballers. A favorite victim is the Cardinals' Todd Worrell, who surrendered five home runs lifetime to Johnson before Whitey Herzog finally wouldn't let Worrell pitch to Johnson in vital situations.

Johnson's major weakness is his fielding. He has a strong but erratic arm, and his range is generally poor. Davey Johnson tends to use him at shortstop when fly-ball pitchers are on the mound, with Sid Fernandez being the best example. Johnson sometimes seems not to know all the duties of a shortstop and has been known to forget to take throws from the outfield. However, he does have a third baseman's reflexes and can leap well for liners over his head. /(SH)

Jerry Johnson — 1943– . RHP 1968–77 Phillies, Cardinals, **Giants**, Indians, Astros, Padres, Blue Jays 770 ip, 48–51, 4.31. *1 LCS, 1 ip, 0–0, 13.50*

Originally a third baseman in the Mets' system, Johnson's longest ML stint without a trip to the minors was 1970–73. With the division-winning 1971 Giants, he led NL relievers with 12 wins and 9 losses and recorded 18 saves. He retired with 41 lifetime saves. /(JCA)

Jing Johnson [Russell Conwell] — 1894–1950. RHP 1916–17, 19, 27–28 **A's** 539 ip, 24–37, 3.35

A research chemist out of Ursinus (PA) College, where he later served as athletic director, Johnson was 9–12 for the A's in 1917 and 9–15 in 1919, serving in the military in between. He also coached at Bucknell and Lehigh. /(NLM)

Joe Johnson — 1961– . RHP 1985–87 **Braves**, Blue Jays 327 ip, 20–18, 4.48

Johnson won 13 games as a starting pitcher in 1986 while spending time with the Braves and Blue Jays. He failed to make the Blue Jays out of spring training in 1987, but he joined them later in the season and posted a 3–5 record and 5.13 ERA. Selected by the Angels in the December 1987 major league draft, he spent the 1988 season with California's Triple-A team at Edmonton. /(TF)

John Henry Johnson — 1956– . LHP 1978–81, 83–84, 86–87 A's, **Rangers**, Red Sox, Brewers 603 ip, 26–33, 3.89

After coming from the Giants to Oakland in a seven-for-one trade for Vida Blue in 1978, the rookie Johnson went 11–10 to lead the A's in wins. Possessing a fine fastball and little else, he was 2–8 the following June when he was sent to the Rangers. He played out his ML career in middle relief. Pitching for Hawaii (Pacific Coast League) on May 2, 1985, he no-hit Calgary. /(JCA)

Judy Johnson [William Julius] — 1899–1989. 3B Negro Leagues 1921–38 Hilldale, Homestead Grays, Darby Daisies, Pittsburgh Crawfords 615 g, 19 hr (inc.) ☛ *All-Star—33, 36. Hall of Fame—1975.*

Connie Mack once told Judy Johnson, "If you were

a white boy you could name your own price." Johnson was considered the Negro Leagues' top third baseman in the 1920s and 1930s. Because of his defensive abilities, he was known as "the black Pie Traynor."

When Johnson was a child growing up in Wilmington, DE, his father set up a "fitness center" for the neighborhood children, complete with barbells, monkey bars, and the like. "My Daddy liked physical fitness and wanted me to be a prizefighter," Johnson recalled. He was exposed to baseball at an early age, serving as batboy for his father's local team. He realized then that his "greatest ambition was to play baseball." He quite school after tenth grade and went to work on the New Jersey docks during WWI.

After the war, Johnson caught on with the Chester Giants, playing on weekends. He then signed a pro contract with the Atlantic City Bacharach Giants, who paid him $5 per game. In 1919, he played for the semi-pro Madison Stars of Philadelphia, which served as a sort of minor league team for the Hilldale club. Hilldale purchased Johnson for $100 in 1920, and in 1921 gave him $150 a month to be their starting third baseman. While with Hilldale, Johnson acquired the nickname Judy, because he resembled a Chicago American Giants player, Judy Gans.

Hilldale won a championship in 1921 and played in the first two Negro League World Series, in 1924 and 1925, winning the latter. In the 1924 NLWS, lost to the Kansas City Monarchs, Johnson led both teams in hitting (.341) and had five doubles, a triple, and a home run. Hilldale and Kansas City met again in the 1925 NLWS, and though Johnson batted just .250, he singled and later scored the winning run in the tenth inning of a 1–1 tie in Game Three. Hilldale won, five games to one.

By the mid-1920s, Johnson had established himself as a top third baseman and a dangerous clutch hitter, with a career average of over .300. Hall of Famer John Henry Lloyd had great influence on him. Said Johnson of Lloyd, "He's the man I give the credit for polishing me; he taught me how to play third base." Johnson was not a particularly fast runner, but he meticulously studied opposing pitchers and took every advantage on the basepaths. He often stole third base. He played winters in Florida or Cuba (where he compiled a .334 average in six seasons) but never again set foot on a boat after his return voyage from Cuba in 1931.

In 1929, his final season with Hilldale, Johnson batted .401—believed to have been his career high. The Eastern Colored League folded in 1930 as a result of the Depression, and Johnson joined the

Judy Johnson

Homestead Grays as a player-coach. One night, when the Grays' catcher was injured during a game, Johnson pulled from the stands and signed 18-year-old catcher Josh Gibson, who became a Hall of Famer.

Johnson returned to Hilldale (which had become the Darby Daisies) in 1931 and remained there until mid-1932, when he jumped to the Pittsburgh Crawfords. The Crawfords' lineup, which included Gibson and fellow Hall of Famers Cool Papa Bell and Oscar Charleston, was often compared to the New York Yankees' "Murderers Row." He played in his last NLWS in 1935 when the Crawfords faced the New York Cubans. He got a clutch hit in the ninth inning of the sixth game, with the bases loaded, the score tied 6–6, and the Crawfords behind three games to two in the series. His sharp single down the first base line won the game for them and they went on to win the series the next day.

After baseball's color barrier was broken, Johnson scouted and coached for the Philadelphia Athletics. He worked for the Phillies from 1959 to 1973 and helped sign Richia Allen. In 1975 he was elected to the Hall of Fame by the Committee on Negro Baseball Leagues. /(TB)

Ken Johnson [Kenneth Wandersee] (Hooks) — 1923 – . LHP 1947–52 Cardinals, **Phillies**, Tigers 269 ip, 12–14, 4.58

The rangy Johnson's wildness impeded his career, though he had flashes of brilliance; he pitched a one-hitter for the Cardinals in his first ML start. Traded to the Phillies in April 1950, Johnson went 4–1 on the way to the pennant. /(AL)

Ken Johnson — 1933 – . RHP 1958–70 A's, Reds, **Astros**, **Braves**, Yankees, Cubs, Expos 1737 ip, 91–106, 3.46. *1 WS, 0.2 ip, 0–0, 0.00*

Johnson was the ultimate hard-luck pitcher: He pitched a no-hitter against the Reds on April 24, 1964 but lost 1–0 on two walks and two errors. He first gained notice when he was acquired by the Reds in July 1961 and went 6–2 for them (6–6 on the season) as they won a surprise pennant. He had his first winning season in 1965 when he was traded to the Braves in May; he finished at 16–10, 3.42, and followed up with 14–8 and 13–9 seasons before falling below .500 for the rest of his career. /(WOR)

Lamar Johnson — 1950 – . 1B-DH 1974–82 **White Sox**, Rangers 792 g, .287, 64 hr, 381 rbi

A 6′2″ offensive player who hit for power and average, as he ballooned to 232 pounds Johnson's speed, fielding, and numbers suffered. He batted .309 for the 1979 White Sox, including a 19-game hitting streak. A choir singer, in 1977 he sang "The Star Spangled Banner" before a Chicago game, then had two homers and a double, the White Sox' only hits in their 2–1 victory. /(EW)

Lou Johnson (Slick, Sweet Lou) — 1934 – . OF 1960–62, 65–69 Cubs, Angels, Braves, **Dodgers**, Indians 677 g, .258, 48 hr, 232 rbi. *2 WS, 11 g, .286, 2 hr, 4 rbi*

Johnson spent almost a decade in the minors and failed to stick after brief stints with the Cubs, Angels, and Braves. The Dodgers acquired him from Detroit in exchange for Larry Sherry before the 1964 season, and in their 1965 World Series victory he hit two homers, including the winning shot in the clincher. In the 1966 Series against the Orioles, Johnson's .267 average led the otherwise baffled Los Angeles offense, and his one run scored was half the Dodgers' total. He was the Dodgers' regular left fielder in 1965–67 and one of the few power sources the team had. In 1965 his 12 HR tied for the team lead, and he was second on the club in 1966 (17) and 1967 (11). A broken leg in 1967 reduced his playing time, and he was traded after the season. He split 1968 between the Cubs and the Indians in his last season as a regular. /(JFC)

Randy Johnson — 1963 – . RHP 1988 – Expos, **Mariners** 187 ip, 10–13, 3.34

The tallest major leaguer ever, 6′10″ 225-lb, hard-throwing Randy Johnson had an excellent September stint with the Expos in 1988, going 3–0 with a 2.42 ERA in four starts. But he started poorly in 1989 and ascribed it to being rattled by taunts about his size; he was moved to relief and then sent down. One of the three pitchers sent to Seattle in May 1989 for Mark Langston, he went 7–9 with a 4.40 in the Mariner rotation, showing below-average control. /(JFC)

Roy Johnson — 1903–1973. OF 1929–38 Tigers, **Red Sox**, Yankees, Braves 1153 g, .296, 58 hr, 556 rbi. *1 WS, 2 g, .000.*
　　Manager 1944 **Cubs** 0–1, .000

Roy and his brother, the A's "Indian Bob" Johnson, were part-Indian, from Oklahoma. A strong-armed outfielder, Roy twice led the league in assists and twice in errors; as a Tiger rookie in 1929, he set the still-standing AL record of 31 outfield errors. Also in 1929, he led the league with 640 at-bats and tied for the top spot with 45 doubles. He led the AL with 19 triples for the 1931 Tigers and often finished among the league leaders in stolen bases. A four-time .300 hitter, he became a genuine team leader. Johnson, Smead Jolley, and Earl Averill formed one of the all-time great-hitting minor league outfields with the Pacific Coast League San Francisco Seals. /(EW)

Si Johnson — 1900–1985. RHP 1928–43, 46–47 **Reds**, Cardinals, Phillies, Braves 2281 ip, 101–165, 4.09

Pitching almost exclusively for second-division clubs, Johnson won only 101 games in 17 seasons. He led the NL in losses twice and in 1933 lost 12 straight for the last-place Reds. He spent 1944–45 in the Navy, avoiding two more last-place finishes by the Phillies. /(JK)

Steamboat Johnson [Harry] — Unk.-1951. *Umpire* NL 1914

Although he umpired only one year in the ML, Johnson became famous for his work in the minors, including 28 years in the Southern Association. Fittingly, he was behind the plate for the longest Southern Association game, a 23-inning tie between Atlanta and Chattanooga in 1919. Johnson, who received his nickname for a voice that "resembled the blast of a Mississippi River side-wheeler," published a book about umpiring called *Standing the Gaff* in 1935./(RTM)

Syl Johnson — 1900-1984. RHP 1922-40 Tigers, Cardinals, Reds, **Phillies** 2165 ip, 112-117, 4.06. *3 WS, 16 ip, 0-1, 4.50*

Syl Johnson's injury-plagued career extended for 19 unspectacular seasons as a starter and workhorse reliever. At various times, line drives broke his cheekbone, ribs, big toe, and three fingers on his pitching hand. He did have six consecutive healthy seasons, in which time he compiled almost half his career wins and appeared in three Cardinals World Series./(JK)

Tim Johnson — 1949- . SS-2B-3B 1973-79 **Brewers**, Blue Jays 516 g, .223, 0 hr, 84 rbi

The light-hitting motorcycle enthusiast was given the Brewers shortstop job in 1973 but hit only .213. He was primarily a utility player for the remainder of his ML career./(JCA)

Tom Johnson — 1951- . RHP 1974-78 **Twins** 273 ip, 23-14, 3.39

After three undistinguished seasons, Johnson emerged as the Twins' bullpen ace in 1977, with 15 saves and a ML-high 16 relief wins. But his 71 appearances took their toll, and Johnson vanished after an ineffective 1978 season./(JCA)

Wallace Johnson (Wally) — 1956- . 1B-2B 1981-84, 86-**Expos**, Giants 381 g, .263, 4 hr, 54 rbi

With the exception of seven games in 1983 with the Giants, Johnson has spent his entire ML career with Montreal. He came up as a second baseman and has played first base in recent years, but he is primarily a pinch hitter. He led the NL in pinch hits in 1987 (17-for-61, .279) and 1988 (22-for-64, .344), and in pinch at-bats in '89./(SFS)

Walter Johnson (The Big Train, Barney) — 1887-1946. RHP 1907-27 **Senators** 5923 ip, 416-279, 2.17. 20 wins: 10-19, 24-25 *2 WS, 50 ip, 3-3, 2.34.*

Manager 1929-35 **Senators**, Indians 530-432, .551
☛ *Most Valuable Player—13, 24 . Led League—w 13-16, 18, 24. Led League—k 10, 12-19, 21, 23-24. Hall of Fame—1936.*

Ty Cobb is supposed to have said that his greatest embarrassment was batting against Walter Johnson on a dark day in Washington. An uncommonly mellow acknowledgment of human frailty by cranky Ty, it was surely God's truth about gentle Walter. In an era lacking electronic speed guns, Johnson was generally thought to throw the fastest ball in the game. A 6'1" righthander with long arms, he threw his hummer with an easy sidearm motion. Contemporaries recalled his pitches as nearly invisible, arriving with a "swoosh" and smashing into the catcher's mitt like a thunderclap. In 21 seasons with the Washington Senators (10 in the second division), Johnson won 416 games. Only Cy Young won more (and only Young and Pud Galvin lost more). There was no pitching category in which he did not excel. In 1914, for example, he led the AL in wins, games, starts, complete games, innings, strikeouts, and shutouts. He eventually amassed 110 shutouts, the most ever. His 38 1-0 wins are, by far, an all-time record.

Among his accomplishments were 16 straight wins (1912); a string of 56 scoreless innings, and a 36-7 (1.09) mark in 1913; five wins, three of them shutouts, in nine days (1908); 66 triumphs over Detroit, the most for any AL pitcher against any one team; 200 victories in eight seasons, 300 in 14. He had his disappointments: 65 of his losses were by shutouts, 26 of them by 1-0 scores (both records); he lost six of eight duels with formidable Red Sox lefty Babe Ruth; and for all of Ty Cobb's dark-day embarrassments, he batted .335 in 67 games against Johnson.

Forgetting the numbers, what pleased people most was that Johnson combined extraordinary baseball talent with a wholly admirable character. In a rowdy game, he was mild, modest, decent, friendly, and forbearing. Across the nation, beyond the confines of baseball, he personified values that Americans respected. He persisted into the lively ball era and the Jazz Age with his old-fashioned, almost Lincolnesque virtues intact. Sportswriters rarely found him less than chivalric and dubbed him "Sir Walter" and the "White Knight."

He was Kansas-born of a farm family which ventured West to try its luck in the California oil

Walter Johnson

fields. When Washington got him, he was going on twenty, and burning up a semi-pro league in southwestern Idaho. The story has, variously, a fan, a traveling liquor salesman, or an old-time umpire writing east about the young phenom, but only purse-poor Washington and its manager, Joe Cantillon, acted in time. Already interested in a fleet Western Association outfielder named Clyde Milan, Cantillon sent an injured catcher west to scout the pair. He corralled them both; Johnson signed for a $100 bonus, train fare, and a big league salary of $350 a month.

He was not an overnight success. The fastball was undeniable, but he was susceptible to the bunt and to the confusions of inexperience and an eighth-place club. After going 13–25 his third season (1909), he turned things around and became the AL's premier pitcher. For the Senators he was both starter and relief ace. Ultimately, he was 40–30 in relief, with 34 saves. The legend grew with him. He acquired nicknames deriving from the machinery that best exemplified the overwhelming speed of his fastball: "Barney," for Oldfield, the mile-a-minute auto racer; and "Big Train," for America's impressive, highballing railroads. Still, the image of the kindly fellow prevailed; one who, comfortably ahead in a late inning, might ease up to allow a weak batter or an old friend a hit; who never blamed teammates for losses, however grievously they erred; who never drank, cussed, or argued with umpires; who never deliberately threw at hitters, although his long career contributed to his setting the ML career mark with 206 hit batsmen. Cobb said he'd move up in the box and crowd the plate knowing he would never get a brush-back pitch from Sir Walter.

Johnson's control was exemplary. His catchers swore by him. In 802 games, he gave up a mere 1,405 walks, less than one every 4.1 innings. But he had wild streaks and still has a piece of the AL record for wild pitches in one season (21).

As the years wore on, Johnson became a Washington landmark. He was tempted during the Federal League uproar, and actually signed with the Chicago Whales, but revoked the contract when penny-pinching Clark Griffith made an emergency trip to Kansas to up the ante and restore him to his pedestal. Finally, in 1924, with the shrewdest trades of his life, Griffith put together Washington's first pennant winner. Going 23–7 at age thirty-seven, Johnson was finally in a World Series. His performance against the Giants in the seventh game is one of baseball's favorite stories. Appearing in relief, two days after pitching a complete game, he held the Giants scoreless for four innings until Early McNeely's 12th-inning grounder deflected off a pebble, over Freddie Lindstrom's head, allowing Washington's winning run to score. In 1925, with another 20 wins from Johnson, the Senators repeated. This time, after winning two from the Pirates, Johnson lost Game Seven. Rain and Roger Peckinpaugh's errors helped, but he was rapped for 15 hits and deserved the 9–7 loss.

When his glorious career wound down, Johnson tried his hand at managing: Newark for a season, Washington (1929–32), and Cleveland (1933–35). His .551 winning percentage was respectable, but the manager never measured up to the player. He was considered too easygoing. But he was among the select group admitted to the Hall of Fame when it first opened. /(ADS)

Doc Johnston [Wheeler Roger] — 1887–1961. 1B
1909, 12–16, 18–22 Reds, **Indians**, Pirates, A's 1055 g,
.263, 14 hr, 379 rbi. *1 WS, 5 g, .273*

When Doc's Indians met younger brother Jimmy's
Dodgers in the 1920 World Series, Doc outhit his
sibling, though Jimmy finished with the higher
career mark. In 1919, Doc had nine consecutive hits
in a four-game stretch. /(JL)

Jimmy Johnston — 1889–1967. 3B-OF-2B-SS-1B
1911, 14, 16–26 White Sox, Cubs, **Dodgers**, Braves,
Giants 1377 g, .294, 22 hr, 410 rbi. *2 WS, 7 g, .250*

No star, Johnston was a hustler who would play
anywhere and always to the outer limits of his
abilities. He was well-traveled in the minors, hiring
on with seven clubs in four leagues before finding a
home in 1916 with Brooklyn, where he was a fan
favorite for a decade. Essentially an outfielder, he
finally played the most games at third, a significant
number at second and short, and 49 at first. He was
a solid righthanded hitter, even in the dead-ball
days, and eventually achieved .325 averages in the
two years (1921 and 1923) when he had 203 hits. In
a 1922 game, he hit for the cycle. The Dodgers used
him in the leadoff spot, as he could wait out a
pitcher, run the bases cleverly, and steal. In 1920 he
and brother Doc, of the Indians, were the first family
pair to face each other in a World Series (beating the
Meusels by a year). After his playing days, the
Tennessean coached the Dodgers and managed a
number of minor league teams. /(ADS)

James Johnstone — Unk.–Unk. *Umpire* AL, **NL**, FL
1902–12, 14–25

Johnstone, who umpired in three different major
leagues, angered the Giants with some of his calls in
a 1906 game. The next day, August 7, he was denied
entry to the ballpark. Bob Emslie, the second
umpire, refused to start the game without him, and
the game was forfeited to the Cubs as one of their
record 116 wins. /(RTM)

Jay Johnstone — 1945– . OF 1966–85 Angels, White
Sox, A's, **Phillies**, Yankees, Padres, Dodgers, Cubs
1748 g, .267, 102 hr, 531 rbi. *4 LCS, 8 g, .471, 2 rbi.
2 WS, 5 g, .667, 1 hr, 3 rbi*

Johnstone earned a deserved reputation as a flake
who kept his teammates entertained with his uninhibited clubhouse antics, but he was also a fine
lefthanded hitter who managed to last 20 seasons in
the ML despite playing over 130 games only once
(1969 with the Angels). He was originally a speedy,
switch-hitting centerfielder, but abandoned hitting
from the right side after his rookie season. Only two
years after hitting a career-high 16 HR for the White
Sox in 1971, Johnstone was released outright and
his career seemed doomed. He came back with the
Phillies, however, and in the 1976 LCS he was
phenomenal in a losing effort. He was seven-for-nine
in the series, but the Reds swept the Phillies in three.
Johnstone starred again in the 1981 WS for the
Dodgers, belting a pinch two-run HR as Los Angeles
came back from a 6–3 deficit to win Game Four
8–7. After finishing his career as a reserve outfielder
and pinch hitter, Johnstone became a baseball
broadcaster. /(SCL)

Smead Jolley (Smudge) — 1902– . OF-C 1930–33
White Sox, **Red Sox** 473 g, .305, 46 hr, 313 rbi

The 6'3" Jolley had over 100 RBI in two of his four
ML seasons, but his fielding was subject to ridicule.
However, the story about a line drive going through
his legs, bouncing off the wall and again threading
his wickets, then him throwing wildly, adding up to
three errors, is undocumented. His fielding lapses
were tolerated in the minors, where he led his league
in batting six times. /(LRD)

Dave Jolly (Gabby) — 1924–1963. RHP 1953–57
Braves 291 ip, 16–14, 3.77

Jolly had horrible control, walking 6.1 batters per
nine innings pitched. In 1954, his best season, he
won 11 and saved 10 with a 2.43 ERA out of the
Braves' bullpen. /(FK)

Barry Jones — 1963– . RHP 1986– **Pirates**, White
Sox 193 ip, 11–13, 3.40

Jones was traded to the White Sox for Dave LaPoint
in August 1988 and was effective the rest of the
season as Bobby Thigpen's set-up man. He slumped
in 1989. /(WOR)

Bob Jones (Ducky) — 1889–1964. 3B 1917–25 **Tigers** 853 g, .265, 7 hr, 316 rbi

Jones hit .303 with 72 RBI as the Tigers' third baseman in 1921, easily his best season. After nine underproductive years in Detroit he returned to the Pacific Coast League, where he had starred before reaching the majors. /(JK)

Bobby Jones — 1949– . OF-DH-1B 1974–77, 81, 83–86 **Rangers**, Angels 314 g, .221, 20 hr, 86 rbi

Jones was 34 years old when he finally spent a full season in the majors, as an extra lefthanded bat with the 1984 Rangers. First signed by the Washington Senators in 1967, he became deaf in one ear during 14 months of combat in Vietnam. A standout hitter year after year in Triple-A, he left to play in Japan for 1979 and 1980. Two of his 17 ML doubles came in the 12-run 15th inning of a July 3, 1983 game between Texas and Oakland. /(JCA)

Charley Jones [born Benjamin Wesley Rippay] (Long Charley) — 1850–Unk. OF 1875–80, 83–88 Keokuk (NA), Reds, Cubs, Braves, **Cincinnati (AA)**, New York (AA), Kansas City (AA) *NA*: 12 g, .250; *ML*: 882 g, .299, 55 hr, 219 rbi (inc)
☛ *Led League—hr 79. Led League—rbi 79.*

Jones was an outstanding but often controversial slugger during the 1870s and 1880s. With Cincinnati from 1876 to 1878, he became the Reds' most popular player but was sometimes criticized in the press for carousing. In 1877, he caused a furor by signing a contract with the Cubs when he believed that his Cincinnati team was about to fold. After two games with Chicago, he returned to the still-struggling Reds. However, in 1879 he was able to sign a three-year contract with Boston. He led the NL in home runs (9) and RBI (62) in 1879 for the Braves. The next year he became the first player to hit two homers in one inning (6/10/80). But after the 1880 season he was suspended by the club and blacklisted for refusing to play. He countered that he had not been paid and sued for his salary. A jury sided with the club and Jones stayed out of baseball until 1883 when the blacklisting was lifted and he signed with Cincinnati of the American Association. In 1884, he became the third man to hit three triples in one game. /(BC)

Charlie Jones (Casey) — 1876–1947. OF 1901, 05–08 Red Sox, **Senators**, Browns 478 g, .233, 5 hr, 143 rbi

Jones was a smart, strong-armed outfielder and an adept basestealer who collected 84 stolen bases in three seasons as a Senators regular. He was replaced in Washington's outfield by Clyde Milan, who remained for 15 years. Jones lasted one more year after his 1907 trade to the Browns. /(NLM)

Cleon Jones — 1942– . OF 1963, 65–76 **Mets**, White Sox 1213 g, .281, 93 hr, 524 rbi. *2 LCS, 8 g, .353, 1 hr, 7 rbi. 2 WS, 12 g, .234, 1 hr, 1 rbi*
☛ *All-Star—69.*

Jones was a major ingredient in the 1969 Mets' World Championship. His career-high .340 average was third in the NL, the highest a Met has ever finished in that category. He led the Mets with 10 game-winning RBI (not an official statistic at the time) and established personal bests with 92 runs and 75 RBI as one of the few offensive forces on a team that did it with pitching and mirrors. At the start of the year he was 26 years old, but he was the oldest regular on the team.

Jones figures especially prominently in Mets history as a pivotal figure in the turning points of the 1969 and 1973 seasons. In 1969, manager Gil Hodges removed Jones from left field after Jones had not hustled after a hit during the first game of a doubleheader on July 30 against the Astros; it signaled to the players that Hodges would accept only 100% effort and helped the Mets take themselves more seriously in their suprising pennant contention. In 1973, it was a fielding play that Jones did make that suggested that another miracle season was in the making. The evening Willie Mays announced that he would retire at the end of the season, September 20, the Mets were in the middle of a three-game series with the first-place Pirates. With the game tied 3–3 in the ninth inning, the Pirates had Richie Zisk on at first when Dave Augustine hit what seemed to be a certain home run. But the ball hit the top of the fence and bounced back into Jones's glove. Jones threw a strike to third baseman Wayne Garrett, whose relay caught Zisk at the plate. The Mets won in the thirteenth inning, and took over first place the next day. /(SH)

Cowboy Jones (Albert, Bronco) — 1874–1958. LHP 1898–01 Cleveland NL, **Cardinals** 526 ip, 25–34, 3.61

Jones was a second-line Cleveland Spiders pitcher in 1898 but good enough to be switched to the Cardinals in 1899 when owner Frank Robison, who owned both clubs, stripped the Cleveland roster in a vain attempt to build a St. Louis powerhouse. In 1900, Jones's only year of regular starting, he was 13–19. /(BC)

Dalton Jones — 1943– . 2B-3B-1B 1964–72 **Red Sox**, Tigers, Rangers 907 g, .235, 41 hr, 237 rbi. *1 WS, 6 g, .389, 1 rbi*

Jones was a utility infielder, but he contributed several key hits to the Red Sox' "Impossible Dream" pennant of 1967. On September 18, in the heat of a tight four-team race, he hit a game-winning tenth-inning homer at Tiger Stadium. The left-handed batter led the AL with 13 pinch hits that season. He started at third base in four games of the World Series and batted .389 (7-for-18). A .261 lifetime pinch hitter, he got more than one third of his ML at-bats off the bench. Dalton hit a grand slam for Detroit on July 9, 1970 but passed Don Wert between first and second base, making it a single. /(PB)

Davy Jones (Kangaroo) — 1880–1972. OF 1901–04, 06–15 Milwaukee (AL), Browns, Cubs, **Tigers**, White Sox, Pittsburgh (FL) 1085 g, .270, 9 hr, 289 rbi. *3 WS, 15 g, .265, 1 hr, 2 rbi*

Davy Jones was the third or fourth outfielder, with Ty Cobb and Sam Crawford, during the Tigers' years of early AL dominance. A speedy leadoff man, he was sure-handed afield and a settling influence on the volatile Cobb and the sometimes surly Crawford. /(JK)

Doug Jones — 1957– . RHP 1982, 86– Brewers, **Indians** 276 ip, 17–19, 2.67
☛ *All-Star—88–89.*

Jones had spent seven years in the Milwaukee organization and was recovering from shoulder problems when the Indians gave him a chance in 1985 at Double-A. There he took on an austere attitude and learned a new pitch, the circle change, which behaves like a screwball. With it he became a 30-year-old rookie with the 1987 Indians. In 1988 he was among baseball's elite relievers, setting a ML mark by recording saves in 15 consecutive appearances and breaking the Indians record for saves in a season. /(JCA)

Fielder Jones — 1874–1934. OF 1896–08, 14–15 Dodgers, White Sox, St. Louis (FL) 1794 g, .285, 22 hr, 632 rbi. *1 WS, 6 g, .095.*
    Manager 1904–08, 14–18 **White Sox**, St. Louis (FL), Browns 685–582, .541. First place: 06 *1 WS, 4–2, .667*

Prophetically named, Jones became an outstanding centerfielder (first AL outfielder to execute an unassisted double play) as well as a top-notch slap-hitter who six times batted over .300. However, he's most

Fielder Jones with the St. Louis Terriers of the Federal League

remembered as the manager of the 1906 White Sox, the "Hitless Wonders." Jones led this group of powder-puff hitters to a surprise AL pennant and then won the only all-Chicago World Series from the favored Cubs. When he threatened to quit, he drew a $10,000 contract from miserly White Sox owner Charles Comiskey. The sullen-faced Jones brought the Sox to within a few games of the pennant in each of his other four years as their manager.

A stern taskmaster, Jones routinely suspended players for drinking, being out of shape, or making bonehead plays, but he was also an early champion of players' rights and often argued with Comiskey on their behalf. He would charge in from his centerfield position to berate umpires and was often banished from games for kicking and swearing. An innovative tactician, he is credited with inventing the "motion infield" and was one of the first to position his outfielders according to the hitter.

He quit the White Sox after a controversy. He lost the final game of the 1908 season and the pennant when he started a weary Doc White in place of a rested Frank Smith. Personal motives may have been involved: Jones and Smith despised each other. Coaxed back to baseball by a fat Federal League contract in 1914, he guided a last-place St. Louis team to within a percentage point of the pennant the next year. Named manager of the Browns, he had three also-ran finishes with them. /(DB)

Gordon Jones — 1930- . RHP 1954-62, 64-65 **Cardinals**, Giants, Orioles, A's, Astros 378 ip, 15-18, 4.16

Jones was 4-4 with two shutouts and a 2.00 ERA after his 1954 call-up by the Cardinals. He was traded with Red Schoendienst in one of GM Frank Lane's many unpopular trades, a six-for-three deal with the Giants. Jones later scouted for the Yankees. /(FO)

Jake Jones — 1920- . 1B 1941-42, 46-48 White Sox, **Red Sox** 224 g, .229, 23 hr, 117 rbi

Jones played briefly with the White Sox before entering WWII and returned to play a full season only once, hitting .237 with 19 HR and 96 RBI for the White Sox and Red Sox in 1947. /(FS)

Jeff Jones — 1956- . RHP 1980-84 **A's** 205 ip, 9-9, 3.96. *1 LCS, 2 ip, 0-0, 4.50*

The 6'3" reliever was unscored upon in his first seven ML games and peaked with Billy Martin's AL West champion A's in 1981 (4-1, 3.39). He then suffered arm problems and his ERA ballooned to over 5.00. /(JCA)

Jimmy Jones — 1964- . RHP 1986- **Padres**, Yankees 391 ip, 22-22, 4.04

The third choice overall in the 1982 June draft (two picks before Dwight Gooden), Jones suffered injuries in three of five unspectacular minor league seasons. San Diego's choice seemed vindicated when he one-hit the Astros in his ML debut (9/21/86), but the inconsistent Jones endured the tirades of impatient manager Larry Bowa in 1987 and fell to 9-14 in 1988. Sent to the Yankees in the Jack Clark trade, he didn't make the team in the spring and appeared in only 11 games, with a 5.25 ERA. /(JCA)

Lynn Jones — 1953- . OF 1979-86 **Tigers**, Royals 527 g, .252, 7 hr, 91 rbi. *2 LCS, 8 g, .200. 1 WS, 5 g, .667*

A career backup player (he had trouble hitting the curveball), Jones proved most valuable to the 1985 World Champion Kansas City Royals as a late-inning defensive replacement for left fielder Lonnie "Skates" Smith. In the 1985 World Series, he doubled and tripled in two pinch-hitting appearances. His brother Darryl was a DH-outfielder for the 1979 Yankees. /(JCA)

Mack Jones (Mack the Knife) — 1938- . OF 1961-63, 65-71 **Braves**, Reds, Expos 1002 g, .252, 133 hr, 415 rbi

Jones broke in with four hits in his first game, tying the post-1900 NL mark. He hit 31 HR in his first full season (1965), finishing third in the NL in home run percentage. He teamed that year with Hank Aaron, Eddie Mathews, Joe Torre, Felipe Alou, and Gene Oliver as the Braves set a NL record with six 20-HR men in one season. When the Braves moved to Jones's native Atlanta in 1966 he hit 23 HR despite a shoulder injury, but his power gradually dropped off until 1969. Playing for the expansion Expos in cozy Jarry Park, he hit 22 HR and batted a career-high .270, and on April 14 he hit the first ML home run in Canada off Nelson Briles. /(JFC)

Mike Jones — 1959- . LHP 1980-81, 84-85 **Royals** 226 ip, 11-10, 4.42. *1 LCS, 1 ip, 0-0, 6.75*

Undisciplined and wild in the minors, Jones sparkled with a 6-3 mark after a mid-season call-up by the Royals in 1981. He fought back from a fractured neck sustained in an 1981 auto accident but never completely recovered his velocity. /(FJO)

Nippy Jones [Vernal Leroy] — 1925- . 1B-2B 1946-52, 57 **Cardinals**, Phillies, Braves 412 g, .267, 25 hr, 209 rbi. *2 WS, 4 g, .000*

In his final ML appearance of a career plagued by back problems, Jones batted in the bottom of the 10th inning of Game Four of the 1957 WS, with his Braves trailing the Yankees 5-4. After appearing to have avoided a wild Tommy Byrne pitch, Jones successfully argued that the pitch had struck his foot by pointing to a polish smudge on the ball. He took first base and the Braves rallied for three runs to win the game. /(FJO)

Odell Jones — 1953- . RHP 1975, 77-79, 81, 83-84, 86, 88 Pirates, Mariners, **Rangers**, Orioles, Brewers 549 ip, 24-35, 4.42

A fastball alone wasn't enough to keep Jones in the ML. He had brief success with the 1983 Rangers in relief (10 saves) by adding a submarine motion to his normal overhand delivery. /(ME)

Oscar Jones (Flip Flap) — 1879-1946. RHP 1903-05 **Dodgers** 875 ip, 45-46, 3.20. 20 wins: 03

A 20-game winner as a rookie, Jones flip-flopped his record to 17-25 in his sophomore year to lead the NL in losses, even though he lowered his ERA from 2.94 to 2.75. He threw 324 innings with 31 complete games in 1903 and 377 innings with 38 complete games the next year, all among the highest figures for post-1900 pitchers. /(BC)

Percy Jones — 1899-1979. RHP 1920-22, 25-30 **Cubs**, Braves, Pirates 1028 ip, 53-57, 4.33

Jones pitched mostly in relief for his nine ML seasons, with a top year of 12-7 for the 1926 Cubs. In 1928, he was the talk of the baseball world when he reportedly inherited $500,000. Three years later, while on the Columbus Redbirds roster, he fell from a third-story window and broke his back. He spent the rest of his life in a wheelchair. /(BC)

Randy Jones — 1950- . LHP 1973-82 **Padres**, Mets 1931 ip, 100-123, 3.42. 20 wins: 75-76

☛ Led League—w 76. Led League—era 75. Cy Young Award—76. All-Star—75-76.

A poised, fast-working control pitcher and a master of the slider and sinker, Jones won the 1976 NL Cy Young Award, going 22-14 for the Padres with league highs in wins, starts, complete games, and innings. That year, he tied Christy Mathewson's NL record of 68 innings without issuing a walk and became the first NL pitcher since WWII to win 20 and not strike out 100. With a 20-12 record and an ERA title (2.24) the previous season, Jones finished second to Tom Seaver in Cy Young voting, making him only the second pitcher to be runner-up one year and win the award the next (Mike Marshall was the other). He tied for most losses in the NL in 1974, when he went 8-22, and his 1975 performance won him *TSN*'s NL Comeback Player of the Year Award. He stopped the AL in the ninth inning of the 1975 All-Star Game and was the starter and winner in the 1976 contest. The owner of two one-hitters, Jones established a Padre record by hurling three consecutive shutouts in May 1980. He was often injured and generally ineffective after his trade to the Mets following the 1980 season, and he had trouble winning at Shea Stadium even in periods when he was pitching well on the road.

Jones established the ML season record for most chances accepted by a pitcher without an error (112 in 1976), tied ML pitchers' records for highest season fielding percentage (1.000, 1976) and most

assists in an inning (3, 9/28/75), and tied the NL pitchers' season record for the most double plays (12, 1976). /(EW)

Rick Jones [Thomas Frederick] — 1955- . LHP 1976-78 **Red Sox**, Mariners 158 ip, 6-9, 4.04

The 1975 Carolina League Pitcher of the Year (13-3), the 6'5" Jones came up with the Red Sox, was drafted by the expansion Mariners, and had a short and unimpressive ML stay. His father and brother both played minor league ball. /(MC)

Ron Jones — 1964- . OF 1988- **Phillies** 45 g, .290, 10 hr, 30 rbi

Jones showed power beyond any of his minor league numbers when the Phillies called him up in 1988; he hit eight homers in 124 at-bats. However, he spent most of 1989 on the DL. /(JFC)

Ruppert Jones — 1955- . OF 1976-87 Royals, **Mariners**, Yankees, Padres, Tigers, Angels 1331 g, .250, 147 hr, 579 rbi

Seattle made Jones the first player selected in the 1976 expansion draft, which created the Mariners and Blue Jays. A lefthanded hitter with good speed early in his career, Jones hit 24 home runs in Seattle's inaugural season and 21 in 1979, then was traded away to become an extra outfielder and spare bat for several other teams. With the Angels in 1985, he slugged 21 home runs in only 389 at-bats. Jones holds the Mariner record for most runs scored in a season (109 in 1979) and is tied for club records for runs and walks in a single game. Against Detroit on May 16, 1978, Jones tied a major league record for most putouts by an outfielder in an extra-inning game. Jones was a favorite with Seattle fans, and after being traded he was still greeted with cries of "Rupe! Rupe!" when he visited the Kingdome. /(TF)

Sad Sam Jones (Horsewhips Sam) — 1892-1966. RHP 1914-35 Indians, Red Sox, **Yankees**, Browns, Senators, White Sox 3883 ip, 229-217, 3.84. *4 WS, 22 ip, 0-2, 2.05*

Sad Sam's 22 consecutive seasons pitching in one league (the American) is a ML record shared with Herb Pennock, Early Wynn, Red Ruffing, and Steve Carlton. The native Ohioan was sent from Cleveland to the Red Sox in a 1916 trade for Tris Speaker, who was in his prime. In 1918, Jones's first season in a starting rotation, he went 16-5 (league-best .762 winning percentage). He won 23 games for the fifth-place 1921 Red Sox, with a league-high five shut-outs. But his finest season may have been 1923, when he was 21–8 as the Yankees' ace, hurling a September 4 no-hitter against the Athletics and leading New York to their first World Championship. His relief work in the final game of the Series clinched it for the Yanks.

Bill McGeehan of the New York *Herald-Tribune* dubbed him Sad Sam because, to him, Jones looked downcast on the field. Jones told Lawrence Ritter that the reason he looked downcast was because, "I would always wear my cap down real low over my eyes. And the sportswriters were more used to fellows like Waite Hoyt, who'd always wear their caps way up so they wouldn't miss any pretty girls." Jones' sharp-breaking curve also earned him the name Horsewhips Sam. Like most pitchers of his day, Jones relieved as well as started, and his eight saves in 1922 led the AL. He lost a league-high 21 in 1925 as the Yanks dropped to seventh. Waived from St. Louis to Washington in 1927, Jones rebounded to top the 1928 Senators' staff with a 17–7 record. His 15–7 finish in 1930 marked his last outstanding season. /(EW)

Sam Jones (Toothpick Sam, Sad Sam, Red) — 1925–1971. RHP 1951–52, 55–64 Indians, Cubs, Cardinals, **Giants**, Tigers, Orioles 1643 ip, 102–101, 3.59. 20 wins: 59
☛ *Led League—w 59. Led League—k 55–56, 58. Led League—era 59. All-Star—55, 59.*

Known as Red in the Negro leagues for his reddish complexion, in the majors Jones became Sad Sam, after the original Sad Sam Jones, and Toothpick Sam for the toothpick he always chewed on the mound. Jones pitched the Cleveland Buckeyes to the Negro World Series in 1947. He signed with the Cleveland Indians in 1950 but never got a chance in the rotation of Bob Feller, Bob Lemon, Early Wynn, and Mike Garcia, spending most of five years in the minors. Swapped to the Cubs in a deal for Ralph Kiner, on May 12, 1955 Jones no-hit Pittsburgh, walking seven in the process. He led the NL in losses (20), strikeouts, and walks (185, while allowing only 175 hits). He repeated as strikeout and walk leader in 1956, and again in 1958 after his trade to the Cardinals. With the Giants in 1959, he was both a leading starter and most effective reliever in a tight race. On June 30 of that year, at Los Angeles, a bobble by Giant shortstop Andre Rodgers was scored a single, depriving Jones of a second no-hitter; he got it instead on September 26, though it

was a rain-shortened, seven-inning one against St. Louis. His 21 wins in 1959 led the NL, as did his 2.83 ERA and 109 walks. After an 18–14 1960 season, Jones was hampered by arm trouble, winning 12 more over four seasons.

Recalled Hobie Landrith, who caught Jones with the Cubs, Cards, and Giants, "You've never seen a curveball until you've seen Sam Jones's curveball. If you were a righthanded hitter that ball was a good four feet behind you. It took a little courage to stay in there because he was wild and he could throw a fastball very hard. He wasn't very expressive, he wasn't the gregarious type (but) he injected humor." /(MC)

Sheldon Jones (Available) — 1922– . RHP 1946–53 Giants, Braves, Cubs 920 ip, 54–57, 3.96. *1 WS, 4 ip, 0–0, 2.08*

Jones' nickname, Available, came from a character in the Li'l Abner comic strip, but it suited the hard-throwing righthander during his days with the Giants. He both started and relieved on a regular basis from 1948 to 1951. He was most effective in 1948, when he went 16–8, with five saves, but for the four-year period, he started 88 games and relieved in 90 others. /(FS)

Sherman Jones (Roadblock) — 1935– . RHP 1960–62 Giants, **Reds**, Mets 110 ip, 2–6, 4.73. *1 WS, 1 ip, 0–0, 0.00*

Hard-throwing but wild, the 6'4" Jones was one of a record eight pitchers used by the Reds against the Yankees in the fifth and final game of the 1961 World Series. The Mets' starter in their first-ever home game (4/13/62), he was 0–4 that year before recurring arm problems finished him. /(MC)

Slim Jones [Stuart] — 1913–1938. LHP Negro Leagues 1933–38 Baltimore, Philadelphia statistics not available
☛ *All-Star—34–35.*

Jones was the 6'6" 185-lb ace of the Negro National League's Philadelphia Stars. His blistering fastball consistently put him among NNL leaders in strikeouts. His league-high 11 victories helped the Stars capture the 1934 NNL championship. He was the starting pitcher for the East in the all-star games of 1934 and 1935. Duels between Jones and Satchel Paige at Yankee Stadium were a major attraction during the 1930s. Jones's career was ended by arm trouble in 1938. He died later that year. /(ETW)

Tom Jones — 1877–1923. 1B-2B 1902, 04–10 Baltimore (AL), **Browns**, Tigers 1058 g, .251, 3 hr, 336 rbi. *1 WS, 7 g, .250, 2 rbi*

Outstanding fielding and clever baserunning made Jones a regular for seven seasons. His 22 putouts at first base in a nine-inning 1906 Browns game set a longstanding AL record. Jones homered just three times in 3,847 at-bats, one of the ten worst HR percentages in ML history. /(JL)

Tracy Jones — 1961– . OF 1986– **Reds**, Expos, Giants, Tigers 339 g, .280, 18 hr, 116 rbi

Comparisons were quickly drawn between the aggressive, solid-hitting, high-strung Jones and his manager in Cincinnati, Pete Rose. "I like aggressiveness," Rose said in 1987, "but Tracy has to learn to control his . . .He has to learn you don't have to swing at the first pitch every time . . .He never quits moving . . .He gets just enough of a lead so he has to dive back into first and get his uniform dirty. Then his night is complete." Often injured, and unable to find a permanent place in the Reds' talent-laden outfield, the outspoken Jones was traded to Montreal in 1988. /(JCA)

Willie Jones (Puddin' Head) — 1925–1983. 3B 1947–61 **Phillies**, Indians, Reds 1691 g, .258, 190 hr, 812 rbi. *1 WS, 4 g, .286*
☛ *All-Star—50–51.*

Signed off the sandlots of South Carolina, the 6′2″ 205-lb Jones became the Phillies' regular at third base in 1949 and remained there for a decade. As a rookie, he tied a major league record with four straight doubles in a game at Boston (4/20/1949) and, for the only time in his career, led NL third basemen in errors. In five seasons the durable Jones had the league's best fielding percentage, and his seven years leading the NL in putouts at 3B tied a record. A dependable hitter with power, he had a career-high 25 HR as a key member of the 1950 pennant-winning "Whiz Kids." He stands in Philadelphia's all-time top ten in six offensive categories, and his six career Phillie grand slams ties him for second behind Mike Schmidt. Traded to Cleveland in 1959, he ended with Cincinnati in 1961. /(AL)

Bubber Jonnard [Clarence James] — 1897–1977. C 1920, 22, 26–27, 29, 35 White Sox, Pirates, **Phillies**, Cardinals 103 g, .230, 0 hr, 20 rbi

Bubber and his twin brother, Claude, formed a rare brother battery in Nashville in 1920–21, but neither one enjoyed much ML success. After spreading 103

ML games over six seasons and 15 years, Jonnard worked as a scout and coach for the Giants for almost 20 years and later scouted for the Kansas City A's, the Orioles, and the Mets. He landed Ken Singleton and Ed Kranepool for the Mets. /(FVP)

Claude Jonnard — 1897–1959. RHP 1921–24, 26, 29 **Giants**, Browns, Cubs 349 ip, 14–12, 3.79. *2 WS, 2 ip, 0–0, 0.00*

A slender, curveballing reliever, Jonnard led the NL in saves in 1922 and 1923 and tied Giant teammate Rosy Ryan for the league lead in appearances (45) in 1923. With those two in the bullpen, New York won pennants from 1922 through 1924. An .056 lifetime hitter, the Tennesseean's twin brother was Clarence "Bubber" Jonnard. /(FS)

Eddie Joost — 1916– . SS-2B-3B 1936–37, 39–43, 45, 47–55 Reds, Braves, **A's**, Red Sox 1574 g, .239, 134 hr, 601 rbi. *1 WS, 7 g, .200, 2 rbi.*
    Manager 1954 **A's** 51–103, .331
☛ *All-Star—49, 52.*

Joost became the Reds' regular shortstop in 1941 and committed 45 errors. After his 45 errors in '42 led the league, he was traded to the Braves. There, Joost suffered further ignominy in 1943, setting a record by hitting just .185, the lowest batting average ever for a player with 400 or more at-bats. He then retired voluntarily but gained a second life with the Athletics beginning in 1947. Though his hitting improved, he found a better way to reach base: walking. From 1947 through 1952, he walked more than 100 times a season, twice gaining more walks than hits. He was an All-Star in 1949 (reaching highs of 23 HR and 81 RBI), and again in '52, after having led AL shortstops in putouts four times to tie the league record. Joost was the A's manager in 1954 but led his untalented crew to a last-place finish. /(EW)

Lou Jorda — 1893–1964. *Umpire* NL 1927–31, 40–52 *2 WS 2 ASU*

Jorda was immortalized in the famous Norman Rockwell painting which appeared on the April 23, 1949 cover of *The Saturday Evening Post*, depicting three umpires and two managers. Beans Reardon is flanked by Larry Goetz and Jorda, who is standing behind Reardon's left shoulder and staring into a rainy sky. Two years later, Jorda was the home plate umpire as Bobby Thomson hit the three-run homer in the playoff to win the 1951 pennant for the Giants. /(RTM)

Buck Jordan [Baxter Byerly] — 1907– . 1B-3B 1927, 29, 31–38 Giants, Senators, **Braves**, Reds, Phillies 811 g, .299, 17 hr, 281 rbi

A reliable contact hitter, Jordan compiled high averages in the minors, but his way to the majors was blocked by first basemen with more powerful bats. Finally a regular with the Braves in the mid-1930s, he twice topped .300, with a career-high .323 in 1936, and twice had eight hits in a doubleheader (8/25/35 and 6/26/38)./(JK)

Jimmy Jordan (Lord) — 1908–1957. 2B-SS-3B 1933–36 **Dodgers** 376 g, .257, 4 hr, 118 rbi

Jordan won the Central League batting crown in 1928 and was the Sally League MVP in 1930. Originally in the Cardinal chain, he was sold to the Dodgers and became a much-used utility infielder./(EW)

Pat Jordan — 1941– . *Writer.*

A minor league player for four years, an auto racer, and an English teacher, Jordan is a contributor to *Sports Illustrated* and published the book *A False Spring* in 1975./(NLM)

Ricky Jordan [Paul Scott] — 1965– . 1B 1988- **Phillies** 213 g, .293, 23 hr, 118 rbi

Philadelphia's first-round pick in the June 1983 draft, Jordan was called up in mid-1988 when Von Hayes went on the DL. He won the first base job (with Hayes moving to the outfield on his return) by hitting .308 with 11 HR in 273 at-bats. In his first full season as the Phillies' regular first baseman, he hit .285 with 12 HR and 75 RBI despite an injury early in the season./(SH)

Tim Jordan — 1879–1949. 1B 1901, 03, 06–10 Senators, Yankees, **Dodgers** 540 g, .261, 32 hr, 232 rbi
☛ *Led League—hr 06, 08.*

The popular Jordan was one of the few players to live up to the Brooklyn team's nickname, Superbas. A feared lefthanded slugger, he led the NL with 12 HR in 1906 and 1908, but ailing knees forced his premature retirement./(JL)

Arndt Jorgens — 1905–1980. C 1929–39 **Yankees** 306 g, .238, 4 hr, 89 rbi

The Norwegian-born Jorgens filled in especially well when Bill Dickey was supended in 1932. His brother Orville pitched for the Phillies./(EW)

Orville Jorgens — 1908– . RHP 1935–37 **Phillies** 496 ip, 21–27, 4.70

Unlike older brother Arndt, Orville was born in the U.S. Obtained by the Phillies after winning 14 for Galveston (Texas League) in 1934, he led the NL with 53 appearances as a rookie in '35, going 10–15 for a seventh-place team./(AL)

Mike Jorgensen — 1948– . 1B-OF 1968, 70–85 Mets, **Expos**, A's, Rangers, Braves, Cardinals 1633 g, .243, 95 hr, 426 rbi. *1 LCS, 2 g, .000. 1 WS, 2 g, .000* ☛ *Gold Glove—73.*

Jorgensen was always an asset due to fine defensive skills (he won a Gold Glove at first base in 1973), a team-first attitude, and an ability to draw walks, despite being a modest batsman. Originally a Met, he was traded to Montreal in 1972 with Tim Foli and Ken Singleton for Rusty Staub. He had career highs of 18 HR and 144 games as the Expos' first baseman in 1975. Mostly a lefthanded pinch hitter and defensive replacement in later years, after appearing in the 1985 WS with the Cardinals he became a manager in their farm system./(FJO)

Spider Jorgensen [John Donald] — 1919– . 3B-OF 1947–51 **Dodgers**, Giants 267 g, .266, 9 hr, 107 rbi. *2 WS, 11 g, .194, 3 rbi*

As a rookie in 1947, the wiry Jorgensen was the Dodgers' clutch third baseman. He bruised his throwing arm by hunting that winter, injured it further in spring training, and his career collapsed./(EW)

Rick Joseph [Ricardo Emelino] — 1940–1979. 3B-1B-OF 1964, 67–70 A's, **Phillies** 270 g, .243, 13 hr, 65 rbi

A strong, 6'1″ 190-lb Dominican, Joseph was mostly a Phillies fill-in. When the team, beset by injuries, won nine in a row in mid-1969, Joseph batted .368 with 12 RBI. That year, he hit safely in 16 straight games. Joseph died at age 39 of a kidney ailment./(AL)

Duane Josephson (Josie) — 1942– . C-1B 1965–72 **White Sox**, Red Sox 470 g, .258, 23 hr, 164 rbi
☛ *All-Star—68.*

A Southern League All-Star and Pacific Coast League MVP, Josephson had the reputation of being injury-prone, though his bruises resulted from his hard-nosed play. The White Sox' regular catcher in 1968, a heart problem forced his retirement./(EW)

Addie Joss [Adrian] — 1880–1911. RHP 1902–1910
Indians 2336 ip, 160–97, 1.88. 20 wins: 05–08
☛ *Led League—w 07. Led League—era 04, 08. Hall of Fame—1978.*

Contemporaries of 6'3″ Addie Joss admired him as much as almost anyone who ever put on a major league uniform. His untimely death from an attack of tubercular meningitis in April 1911 shocked the baseball world; Cleveland's opener in Detroit was

Addie Joss

postponed due to funeral services in Toledo. So well thought of was Joss that the top AL players of the day formed an all-star team to play the Indians for the benefit of his widow.

After winning 25 games in his second pro season at Toledo (Western Association), Joss pitched a one-hitter in his 1902 debut. He led the AL with five shutouts that season, and he won at least 20 games each year from 1905 through 1908. His career-high 27 victories in 1907 tied him for the AL lead with Chicago's Doc White. Joss used a good fastball and an exceptional curve to five times record ERAs of 1.83 or less. His 1908 league-leading ERA of 1.16 is the eighth-lowest ever. On October 2, 1908 Joss and Chicago's 40-game winner, Big Ed Walsh, squared off in one of the game's most memorable pitching duels. Cleveland, Chicago, and Detroit (who ultimately prevailed) were locked in a pennant race, adding to the tension of the contest. Walsh tossed a four-hitter, striking out 15 and allowing only one run. Joss, however, was even better, setting down 27 straight for a perfect game. Two years later, he no-hit the White Sox again.

Perhaps most remarkable of Joss's feats was his completion of 234 of his 260 starts. In his final season he was plagued by arm injuries, making just 13 appearances. His lifetime 1.88 ERA ranks second all-time to Ed Walsh's 1.82. Joss pitched only nine years; it was his ERA that convinced the Veterans Committee to bend the 10-year career minimum rule and let him into the Hall of Fame. /(EW)

Bill Joyce (Scrappy Bill) — 1865–1941. 3B-1B
1890–92, 94–98 Brooklyn (PL), Boston (AA), Dodgers, Washington (NL), **Giants** 905 g, .294, 71 hr, 607 rbi.
Manager 1896–98 **Giants** 177–122, .592
☛ *Led League—hr 96 .*

Scrappy Bill Joyce bounced from team to team in the 1890s, intimidating opponents with his ready fists and pitchers with his potent blue-tipped bat. After three undistinguished seasons in three different leagues, Joyce sat out 1893 in a contract dispute but returned with Washington in 1894 to hit a career-high .355, the first of four consecutive .300 seasons. Joyce's 17 home runs in both '94 and '95 were one shy of the league lead, but he won the HR crown in 1896, edging Ed Delahanty 14–13. He hit three homers in one game August 20, 1894, hit for the cycle May 30, 1896, and set a ML record with four triples in a game May 18, 1897. He was also partly responsible for the term "Texas Leaguer"—a shallow pop fly that falls for a hit—when he and fellow

Texas League alumnus Arthur Sunday debuted in Toledo with back-to-back bloopers. /(JK)

Wally Joyner (Wally World) — 1962– . 1B 1986- **Angels** 620 g, .288, 85 hr, 381 rbi. *1 LCS, 3 g, .455, 1 hr, 2 rbi*

A baby-faced lefthanded hitter, Joyner replaced Rod Carew as the Angels' first baseman in 1986. He became the first rookie to start an All-Star Game since fan balloting returned in 1970 and finished a close second to Jose Canseco in AL Rookie of the Year balloting. After a brilliant first half, he struggled during the second half and missed four games of the LCS with a staph infection. In 1987 Joyner was California's MVP, set a club record for HR by a first baseman (34), and became the ninth player in ML history with back-to-back 100-RBI seasons as a rookie and sophomore. His power declined in 1988 (13 HR), as the ball was deadened, but he still managed 85 RBI. After a slow start in 1989 he finished with 16 HR and 79 RBI while batting .282. /(ME)

Oscar Judd (Lefty, Ossie) — 1908– . LHP 1941-48 Red Sox, **Phillies** 771 ip, 40-51, 3.90
☞ *All-Star—43.*

The Canadian-born Judd was a hard worker and a good hitter (.262 lifetime) and pinch hitter. Towards the end of his career he was afflicted with a sore arm. He was 11-6 (2.90) at his best for the 1943 Red Sox. /(EW)

Joe Judge — 1894-1963. 1B 1915-34 **Senators**, Dodgers, Red Sox 2170 g, .298, 71 hr, 1034 rbi. *2 WS, 14 g, .286, 1 hr, 4 rbi*

Agile and diminutive, Judge set fielding standards for first basemen with graceful sure-handedness. He played from the dead-ball era to the rabbit-ball era of the 1920s and 1930s and led or tied AL first basemen in fielding six times, still an AL record. He compiled a brilliant lifetime fielding average of .993, an AL record that stood for more than 30 years. At his retirement, he also held AL career first base marks for games, putouts, double plays, and total chances, and his 131 double plays in 1922 set a since-broken AL season record.

A lefthanded thrower and hitter, his batting average topped .300 in nine full seasons. Judge was a perennial Washington favorite who, in 1924, with Bucky Harris at second base, Ossie Bluege at third base, and MVP Roger Peckinpaugh at shortstop, formed a defensive unit which is thought by many to be the best ever assembled. Judge was the baseball

coach at Georgetown from 1937 to 1958, except for 1945–46, when he helped coach the Senators. /(JK)

Walt Judnich — 1917-1971. OF-1B 1940-42, 46-49 **Browns**, Indians, Pirates 790 g, .281, 90 hr, 420 rbi. *1 WS, 4 g, .077, 1 rbi*

While advancing through the Yankee farm system, the 6'1", nervously charged outfielder reminded scouts of Joe DiMaggio. Judnich's problem was the Yankees already had DiMaggio in centerfield; that was solved by Judnich's sale to the Browns. While never "another DiMaggio," he led AL outfielders in fielding three times and had an arm like DiMaggio's. A lefthanded power hitter who debuted in 1940 with 24 HR, he lost three prime years to military service. /(JK)

Howie Judson — 1926– . RHP 1948-54 **White Sox**, Reds 615 ip, 17-37, 4.29

A courageous man, Judson pitched his final seasons knowing he might be going blind from a retina infection. Though he never had a winning season, he was a highly respected hurler. /(EW)

Billy Jurges — 1908– . SS-3B 1931-47 **Cubs**, Giants 1816 g, .258, 43 hr, 656 rbi. *3 WS, 13 g, .156, 2 rbi.*
Manager 1959-60 **Red Sox** 78-83, .484
☞ *All-Star—37, 39-40.*

After attending Richmond Hill High School in Brooklyn, where Phil Rizzuto went a decade later, the fiery Jurges came up to the Chicago Cubs in 1931. His fine defensive skills prompted the Cubs to move Woody English from shortstop to third base, despite Jurges's .201 batting average. Jurges and second baseman Billy Herman, a fellow rookie and former Louisville teammate, became the league's premier double-play combination and teamed in three World Series during the 1930s. Jurges went on to patrol National League infields for 17 seasons, four times leading the league's shortstops in fielding percentage. An adequate hitter, Jurges once rapped nine consecutive hits, one shy of the NL record.

Jurges's solid, steady career started off with a bang. On July 6, 1932 Violet Valli (dubbed Violet Popovitch Heindel Valli by Cubs player/manager Charlie Grimm) called Jurges on the telephone, then entered his hotel room with a gun to attempt suicide. Jurges intervened and took a bullet in the hand and another through the ribs. This episode may have served as the prototype for *The Natural*, rather than the shooting of Eddie Waitkus by a crazed female fan in 1949. Although Jurges wound up missing only three weeks of action, the contending Cubs signed ex-Yankee shortstop Mark Koenig, who hit .353 for them. Because the Cubs voted Koenig a one half Series share, they were ridden by the Yankees that year's World Series, highlighted by Ruth's "called" home run.

Although Jurges was an unexceptional Red Sox manager for parts of two seasons, 1959–60, his tenure is worth noting. Under Jurges, infielder Pumpsie Green ended the Red Sox' status as the only team in the majors without a black player. /(JC/CR)

Al Jurisich — 1921–1981. RHP 1944–47 **Cardinals**, Phillies 388 ip, 15–22, 4.24. *1 WS, 0.2 ip, 0–0, 27.00*

Effective as a rookie spot-starter and long reliever for the 1944 champion Cardinals, the Louisianan lost his job to returning veterans after WWII ended. Injuries curtailed Jurisich's time with the Phillies. /(MC)

Skip Jutze [Alfred Henry] — 1946– . C 1972–77 Cardinals, **Astros**, Mariners 254 g, .215, 3 hr, 51 rbi

Good defense kept this poor-hitting backup catcher in the majors. In his most active season, he caught 86 games for the 1973 Astros, batting .223. He hit his three career homers with the Mariners in 1977, his final year. /(JCA)

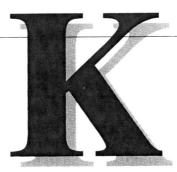

Jim Kaat (Kitty) — 1938– . LHP 1959–83 **Senators/ Twins**, White Sox, Phillies, Yankees, Cardinals 4528 ip, 283–237, 3.45. 20 wins: 66, 74–75 *2 LCS, 8 ip, 0–1, 4.50. 2 WS, 17 ip, 1–2, 3.78*
☛ *Led League—w 66. All-Star—62, 66, 75. Gold Glove—62–77.*

The square-shouldered, 6'4" Kaat is one of a handful of major leaguers to play in four decades. His 25 years of pitching was a major league record. The last active original Washington Senator, Kaat moved like a cat around the mound, winning 16 consecutive Gold Gloves. He won 18 games for the AL champion Twins in 1965, then had his best season in 1966, going 25–13 and leading the league with 41 starts, 19 complete games, and 304 innings. That year only one Cy Young trophy was awarded for both leagues, to the Dodgers' Sandy Koufax, but *TSN* selected Kaat as AL Pitcher of the Year.

Following five more seasons with victories in double figures, Kaat was 10–2 in 1972 when he sprained his left wrist and missed the remainder of the season. He was 11–12 in August 1973 (including a one-hitter at California on July 1) when, thinking Kaat's best days were behind him, the Twins sold him to the White Sox. In Chicago, Kaat was reunited with his former Minnesota pitching coach and mentor, Johnny Sain. In his two full seasons in the Chicago stable, Kaat won 41 games, often using a quick-pitch delivery.

Despite his 20–14 record with over 300 innings pitched in 1975, Kaat, age thirty-seven, was sent to the Phillies in a trade for Alan Bannister, Dick Ruthven, and Roy Thomas, the oldest of whom was twenty-four. In his first tour of duty in the NL, Kaat was 26–30 in three seasons. In May 1979, he was sold to the Yankees and, for the first time, relieved in more games than he started. He spent most of his final four ML years working out of the bullpen, and pitched in relief in four games of the 1982 World Series for St. Louis against Milwaukee.

A good all-around athlete, Kaat also hit 16 homers in his career, with a .185 lifetime batting average. He stands as the Twins' all-time winningest pitcher, with 189 victories. After retiring as a player, he was the Reds' pitching coach in 1986. He has also worked as a TV announcer for the Yankees. /(RM)

Clifford Kachline — 1922– . *Writer.*

An associate editor of *The Sporting News*, Kachline edited the *Spink Baseball Guide* and *Dope Book* for 20 years until 1967. He was the historian at the Hall of Fame from 1969 to 1982, when he became the first full-time executive director of SABR. He retired in 1985. /(NLM)

Harold Kaese — 1909–1975. *Writer.*

Kaese began as sport editor for the Boston *Transcript* after graduating from Tufts University. He was a sportswriter and columnist for the Boston *Globe* for 32 years until his 1973 retirement. In 1976 he was given the J.G. Taylor Spink Award (admittance to the Writers Wing of the Hall of Fame). /(NLM)

Oscar Kahan — 1910–1981. *Writer.*

A 1930 graduate of the University of Missouri, Kahan broke in with the St. Louis *Star-Times*, then went to the Associated Press, where he gained a reputation for accurate and authoritative writing. He became assistant managing editor of *The Sporting News* and remained for 32 years, specializing in developing news of the minor leagues. /(NLM)

George Kahler (Krum) — 1889–1924. RHP 1910–14 **Indians** 627 ip, 32–41, 3.17

The hard-throwing Kahler led the AL in walks (121) and went 12–19 in 1912, his only season as a regular ML starter. /(ME)

Roger Kahn — 1927– . *Writer.*

A premier baseball essayist, the Brooklyn-born Kahn at twenty-five began covering the Dodgers for the New York *Herald Tribune*. He later wrote for *Sports Illustrated* and *Newsweek*. His 1972 best-seller, *The Boys of Summer*, an account of the great Brooklyn teams of the 1950s, is a recognized classic. It was followed by *Season in the Sun* (1977) and *The Seventh Game* (1982). Kahn bought the Utica club in the New York-Penn League and in 1985 wrote

Jim Kaat

Good Enough to Dream based on that experience. Kahn and Pete Rose wrote *Pete Rose: My Story* in 1989. /(NLM)

Mike Kahoe — 1873–1949. C, 1895, 99–1905, 07–09 Reds, Cubs, **Browns**, Phillies, Senators 410 g, .212, 4 hr, 105 rbi

One of the first catchers to wear shin guards, Kahoe joined the Browns in their inaugural season (1902) and won the starting job from Joe Sugden the following year. He promptly gave it back by hitting .189. /(WAB)

Don Kaiser (Tiger) — 1935– . RHP 1955–57 **Cubs** 240 ip, 6–15, 4.15

Kaiser was one of many young players hurt by the rule of the 1950s that forced bonus signees to rust on the ML roster instead of playing in the minors. He won 49 of 50 high school games, including seven no-hitters and two perfect games. In his first start with the Cubs he pitched a two-hitter, but his lack of seasoning made him generally ineffective. /(BC)

Ken Kaiser — 1945– . *Umpire* AL 1977–87 *2 LCS 1 WS*

Voted the Most Colorful Umpire in the AL in a 1986 *TSN* poll, Kaiser is a former bar bouncer and pro wrestler. In the ring he wore a black hood, carried an ax, and was billed as "The Hatchet Man." In 1981, when Billy Martin was suspended but still telephoning instructions to the dugout, Kaiser took the phone from a player's hand, said, "You're disconnected, Billy!" and ripped the instrument from the dugout wall. He was a strict enforcer of the balk rule even before the leagues toughened enforcement in 1988. He was behind the plate for Gaylord Perry's 300th win on May 6, 1982. /(RTM)

George Kaiserling — 1893–1918. RHP 1914–15 Indianapolis (FL), **Newark (FL)** 537 ip, 30–23, 2.68

Kaiserling spent his ML career in the Federal League, winning 17 games for league champion Indianapolis in 1914 after pitching in the same city's American Association franchise in 1913. When the league collapsed he was sold to the Tigers, spent two years in the minors, and died in March 1918. /(JK)

Al Kaline (Mr. Tiger) — 1934– . OF 1953–74 **Tigers** 2834 g, .297, 399 hr, 1583 rbi. *1 LCS, 5 g, .263, 1 hr, 1 rbi. 1 WS, 7 g, .379, 2 hr, 8 rbi*
☛ *Led League—ba 55. All-Star—55–67, 71, 74. Hall of Fame—1980.*

Al Kaline is Mr. Tiger, not only because he played in more games as a Tiger than anyone else and hit more home runs than any Tiger, but also because he gave his Detroit teammates and fans his classiest best in baseball skill, leadership, and determination each inning he played.

Kaline was born into a sports-minded family that included a father and two uncles who played semi-pro baseball. Though smaller than most boys his age and somewhat shy, he became a top-notch player by sheer practice and playing time. He enrolled in several organized leagues each season, being transported from field to field by family members. Young Al possessed a great arm, developed solid hitting skills, and had great infielder quickness.

Scout Ed Katalinas signed Kaline ($35,000 bonus) right off the Baltimore sandlots and Al never played one inning in the minor leagues. On June 25, 1953, his first game, he played right field for the first time in his life. He was used sparingly by Manager Fred Hutchinson, usually as a pinch runner. His first homer came off Dave Hoskins (Cleveland) and he

Al Kaline

singled off Satchel Paige before that first season ended.

In his rookie year of 1954 Kaline hit a modest .276 with four HR and was part of an outfield corps that included Don Lund, Bob Nieman, Bill Tuttle and highly touted Jim Delsing. By 1959 all of these phenom outfielders were gone in favor of Charlie Maxwell, Harvey Kuenn, and Kaline. Kaline's second career homer in 1954 was a grand slam, making him the second youngest ever to have hit one. (Eddie Onslow of the 1912 Tigers was the youngest until Boston's Tony Conigliaro moved him back in 1964.) Red Sox legend Ted Williams told Kaline to build his wrist strength up over the winter by squeezing baseballs as hard as he could. Though the slender rookie's glove was never in doubt, his power was. Those doubts were laid to rest early in 1955 as Kaline hit in 23 of his first 24 games, including seven home runs—three at Kansas City in one game (his only three-homer game), two in one inning. Ending at .340, 27 HR, 102 RBI, and 121 runs, he was the youngest AL batting champ, shading the immortal Ty Cobb for the honor. It was the only time he would amass 200 hits in a season. He finished second in MVP voting, just 17 points behind Yogi Berra.

As a perennial All-Star, Kaline homered off Lew Burdette (1959) and Bob Buhl (1960) while hitting .324 in All-Star 16 games. In 1962 Kaline was having a fantastic year (.336, 13 HR, 38 RBI) when on May 26 he fractured his right collarbone diving for the last-out catch in a 2–1 Hank Aguirre win at New York. Two months later he reentered the race with a game-winning, two-run single in a 4–3 Aguirre win. In a mere 100 games that year he hit 29 HRs with 94 RBI. Proportionately, had he played the entire season, he would have eclipsed 30 homers and possibly 40 for the only time in his career. That injury certainly cost him the opportunity to later become the first American Leaguer to collect 400 homers and 3,000 hits in a career. Various injuries removed Kaline from some 200 games during his 15 "prime" years. In 1963 Kaline again finished second to a Yankee catcher, Elson Howard, in the MVP balloting.

After missing a third of the 1968 season, Kaline was fit into manager Mayo Smith's World Series lineup by playing centerfielder Mickey Stanley at shortstop. In the seventh inning of Game Five, the bases were full and the Tigers were down 3–2 in score and 3–1 in games. Kaline singled home two runs to win the game and ignite Detroit's comeback for the World Championship.

Kaline made playing right field into an art form. He won 10 Gold Gloves in 11 years (1957–59, 61–67). All comparisons to his glove work eventually fell short because he was so graceful and quick. Never a wasted motion, never a wrong decision. Kaline has said, "When I first came up to the Tigers I was scared stiff, but I had desire. Desire is something you must have to make it in the majors. I was never satisfied with just average." Though he was not spectacular, he was as close to perfect as a player could be. All of his baseball skills were impeccably honed: hitting for power and average, speed, throwing, and fielding judgment.

Always a Detroit hero, Al Kaline joined the Tiger broadcasting crew after his retirement from the field. /(RT)

Rudy Kallio — 1892–1979. RHP 1918–19, 25 **Tigers**, Red Sox 222 ip, 9–18, 4.17

Kallio failed both his ML trials, but the native Oregonian found a home in the Pacific Coast League, winning 211 games in 20 seasons. /(JK)

Willie Kamm — 1900–1988. 3B 1923–35 White Sox, Indians 1692 g, .281, 29 hr, 826 rbi

After two years of stopgap at third base, for the 1923 season, the White Sox found Willie Kamm to replace the banished Buck Weaver. He cost them $100,000, then the highest price ever paid for a rookie. Kamm never had Weaver's flair, but he was a more polished third baseman. He had exceptional hands and good instincts, and got his throws away quickly. He led his league in fielding eight times in a 13-year career. He was also adept at the hidden-ball play, claiming success once or twice a season. Kamm attributed his high number of fielding chances to canny White Sox pitchers Ted Lyons and Red Faber; Lyons's low curves and Faber's spitballs induced hitters to top the ball, often to third. Kamm was not as successful as a hitter, although he had a reputation for coming through in the clutch. In 1931 he was sent to Cleveland for first baseman Lew Fonseca. In 1936–37 he managed the San Francisco Missions (Pacific Coast League). Although his highest baseball salary was $13,500, he retired in comfort, having survived the 1929 crash to make a substantial gain in the stock market./(ADS)

Alex Kampouris — 1912– . 2B 1934–39, 41–43 Reds, Giants, Dodgers, Senators 708 g, .243, 45 hr, 284 rbi

The Chicago Hellenic Society, hungering for a countryman to honor in 1937, assembled at Wrigley Field one day to salute the Reds' second baseman. Kampouris was given a car and extolled before the game, then proceeded to commit three errors in one inning. Kampouris hit .316 in 16 games for the Dodgers in 1941, but never hit better than .249 in any other season./(JK)

Masanichi Kaneda (Golden Arm, Emperor) — 1930– . LHP 1951–70 Kokutetsu Swallows, Yomiuri Giants, Lotte Orions 400 wins, 2.24 (inc). 20 wins: 1950–64

Kaneda, a fastballer born of Korean parents, won at least 20 games in Japan each year from 1950 through 1964, twice winning 30. While going 30–17 in 1963, he refused to pitch without three days' rest, causing a national uproar as the first pitcher to violate the ironman "Code of the Samurai." In 1964, he became the first Japanese star to play out his option and switch teams, leaving Kokutetsu for Yomiuri. There, he immediately rejected strict and strenuous team discipline, choosing to train himself, inciting another uproar./(MC)

Rod Kanehl (Hot Rod) — 1934– . 2B-OF-3B 1962–64 Mets 340 g, .241, 6 hr, 47 rbi

The Mets picked up Kanehl, who spent eight years in the Yankee farm system, in the minor league draft. Manager Casey Stengel remembered the hustling utility man who vaulted a fence to catch a fly ball in the Yankees' 1954 instructional camp. The fan favorite hit the Mets' first grand slam on July 6, 1962, in the first Met victory witnessed by owner Joan Payson./(SH)

Kansas City Athletics — 1955–1967. Team. 829–1222, .404

The Athletics had operated in Philadelphia for 54 years, but attendance and better Phillies teams prompted the shift to Kansas City, which had not seen major league baseball since the Federal League (1914–15). Blues Stadium was expanded and renamed Municipal Stadium to accommodate the Athletics. Their maiden year in Missouri produced a sixth-place finish under manager Lou Boudreau, the highest the Athletics would ever place in Kansas City. In 13 seasons they compiled an unenviable 829–1,222 record under ten managers.

In 1960 insurance and real estate magnate Charlie Finley purchased controlling interest in the club. He took a strong role in the daily operations of the club, often usurping his manager's function. Finley tried numerous promotions, moved the fences in and out, fired managers and broadcasters yearly, and traded players in an attempt to produce a winner and maintain fan interest. After a 13th consecutive losing season in Kansas City, Finley moved the Athletics to Oakland without realizing the great baseball potential the Royals would later discover./(FO)

Kansas City Royals — 1969– . Team. 1922–1734, .526. *AL West Champions 76–78, 80, 84–85 AL Champions 80, 85 World Champions 85*

In 1968 Ewing Kauffman purchased an AL expansion franchise that took the field the following year as the Kansas City Royals. In 1971, only their third season, the Royals finished second. Never has an expansion team fared so well so quickly. Three factors contributed to the rapid and sustained success. First, their farm system quickly produced a number of stars, including George Brett, Willie Wilson, and Frank White, and pitchers Paul Splittorff, Steve Busby, Dennis Leonard, and Dan Quisenberry. Second, the Royals' front office made

The 1977 Kansas City Royals

several trades that brought pivotal players to Kansas City, such as Hal McRae, Amos Otis, Freddie Patek, John Mayberry, and Cookie Rojas. And finally, the team employed highly competent field bosses like Jack McKeon, Whitey Herzog, Jim Frey, and Dick Howser, who molded youth and veterans into winning combinations. In their first twenty campaigns, the Royals won a World Championship (1985), two AL pennants, six AL Western Division titles, and had seven second-place finishes. They lost three straight bitterly contested LCS to the Yankees from 1976 to 1978 before finally reaching the WS with a sweep of the Yankees in the 1980 playoffs. /(FJO)

Erv Kantlehner — 1892- . LHP 1914-16 **Pirates**, Phillies 399 ip, 13-29, 2.84

Kantlehner struck out 253 batters for Victoria (Northwestern League) in 1913. Despite a 2.26 ERA in 1915, he was 5-12 for Pittsburgh; in 8 of those 12 losses, Pittsburgh was shut out. /(ME)

Ed Karger (Loose) — 1883-1957. LHP 1906-11 Pirates, **Cardinals**, Reds, Red Sox 1088 ip, 48-67, 2.79

Karger's most successful season was with the Red Sox in 1910, when he was 11-7 with a relatively high 3.19 ERA. Before that he compiled losing records despite better ERAs for second-division Cardinals teams. /(WOR)

Ron Karkovice — 1963- . C 1986- **White Sox** 193 g, .204, 12 hr, 53 rbi

The White Sox' first draft pick in 1982 hit four HR in 97 at-bats in his 1986 call-up. The strong-armed catcher was handed Carlton Fisk's job in 1987 but hit just .071 in 39 games, struck out 40 times in 85 at-bats, and was sent down. Under new batting coach Walt Hriniak, he improved to .264 in 1989, although at the expense of his power. Karkovice has been used as a pinch runner, unusual for a catcher. /(SFS)

Andy Karl [Anton Andrew] — 1914- . RHP 1943-47 Red Sox, **Phillies**, Braves 422 ip, 19-23, 3.51

Though lackluster in Louisville (American Association) in 1942 in his sixth season in the Red Sox farm system, Karl made the ML with the 1943 Red Sox because of the WWII player shortage. His 67 appearances and 15 saves for the 1945 Phillies were NL highs. /(AL)

Benn Karr (Baldy) — 1893–1968. RHP 1920–22, 25–27 **Red Sox**, Indians 780 ip, 35–48, 4.60

Handy Benn Karr both started and relieved; a .245 batter, he also pinch-hit 79 times. With Boston he had AL highs of six relief losses in 1920 and five relief wins in 1921./(JK)

Max Kase — 1898–1974. *Writer*

Kase was sports editor and columnist ("Brief Kase") for the New York *Journal American* from 1938 until the paper folded in 1966. He won the Pulitzer Prize in 1950 for exposing the college basketball scandal. Kase's career began in 1917 with International News Service. He was sports editor of the Havana *Telegram* and Boston *American* before moving to New York, where he also operated two restaurants./(NLM)

Eddie Kasko — 1932– . SS-3B-2B 1957–66 Cardinals, **Reds**, Astros, Red Sox 1077 g, .264, 22 hr, 261 rbi. *1 WS, 5 g, .318, 1 rbi.*
   Manager 1970–73 **Red Sox** 346–295, .540
☛ *All-Star—61 .*

Kasko, a reliable ML infielder for ten years, was named the NL All-Star shortstop in 1961 when the Reds won the pennant. The year before, he set career highs by hitting .292 with 51 RBI. With Houston in 1964, he led NL shortstops in fielding percentage. He was known as a laid-back practical joker who could keep a clubhouse loose. After managing for three years in the International League, he led the Red Sox for four seasons. Although he brought them in third twice and second twice, his soft-spoken, unflappable approach was deemed too placid by the front office./(BC)

Ed Katalinas — Unk.–1988. *Scout.*

Katalinas was a member of the Detroit Tigers organization for over four decades, joining as a part-time scout in 1940 and rising to scouting director in 1956 and scouting coordinator in 1975. He first spotted Al Kaline as a Baltimore grade-school player, and signed him in 1953 just after his high-school graduation. In 1963 Katalinas's recommendation brought Denny McLain from the White Sox on waivers when Chicago failed to protect him, and he also helped sign Ray Oyler and Jim Northrup./(FVP)

John Katoll (Big Jack) — 1872–1955. RHP 1898–1902 Cubs, **White Sox**, Baltimore (AL) 361 ip, 17–22, 3.22

The 6′4″ 200-lb Big Jack won 16 games, including six shutouts, for the 1900 White Sox when the AL was still a minor league. On August 21, 1901 he threw a baseball at umpire Jack Haskell, instigating a brawl in which Haskell's lip was split by Chicago shortstop Frank Shugart. Both Katoll and Shugart were arrested and then suspended./(RL)

Ray Katt — 1927– . C 1952–59 **Giants**, Cardinals 417 g, .232, 32 hr, 120 rbi

A sound catcher but a weak hitter, Katt was a regular only once, for the 1955 Giants. He set the NL record with four passed balls in one inning on September 10, 1954; knuckleballer Hoyt Wilhelm was the pitcher./(FS)

Benny Kauff — 1890–1961. OF 1912, 14–20 Yankees, Indianapolis (FL), Brooklyn (FL), **Giants** 859 g, .311, 49 hr, 454 rbi. *1 WS, 6 g, 2 hr, 5 rbi*
☛ *Led League—ba 14–15.*

"The Ty Cobb of the Federal League" led the FL in batting and stolen bases in both its seasons. When it disbanded, Kauff was the plum picked by John McGraw for the Giants. In 1917 the lefthander batted .308 and hit two HR in the World Series. Kauff began running with a suspect crowd, and in 1920 was ruled ineligible for major league play by Commissioner Landis, not for throwing games, but for being implicated in a stolen car ring. Kauff was cleared of criminal charges in court, but his entreaties for readmission to baseball failed./(JK)

Tony Kaufmann — 1900–1982. RHP 1921–31, 35 Cubs, Phillies, Cardinals, Giants 1086 ip, 64–62, 4.18

Pitching for the Cubs in the early 1920s, Kaufmann was tutored by Grover Alexander. He was 14–10 in 1923 and 16–11 the next year, his best seasons. A good hitter, his two home runs on the Fourth of July, 1925 made him one of a handful of pitchers to homer twice in one game. From 1938 to 1961 he worked for the Cardinals as a minor league manager, ML coach, and scout./(BC)

Marty Kavanagh — 1891–1960. 2B-1B-OF 1914–18 Tigers, Indians, Cardinals 369 g, .249, 10 hr, 122 rbi

The Tigers starting second baseman as a rookie, Kavanagh lost his job to Ralph Young in 1915 but remained a handy backup, playing every position except pitcher and catcher. After leading the AL with 10 pinch hits in 1915 he was given 46 pinch at-bats in 1916, but hit only .152./(JK)

Tetsuharu Kawakami (The God of Batting) — Unk.-Unk. 1B 1938-39, 46-58 **Yomiuri Giants** .313 (inc)

For many years, Kawakami had the highest lifetime average in Japanese baseball history. He was the first Japanese to hit 20 home runs in a season, and his .377 average in 1950 set a single-season Japanese record. The icy and aloof Kawakami attributed his success to winters spent in Zen meditation at remote mountain temples, and to a distinctive red bat.

Kawakami became the Yomiuri Giants' manager in 1961 and promptly released longtime batting rival Wally Yonamine, a Nisei. He built an all-Japanese team that won 11 pennants and nine consecutive championships (1965–73) in 14 years. When Yomiuri beat the 1968 National League champion St. Louis Cardinals twice in three games on a goodwill tour, Kawakami argued that his club was the best in baseball. Irritated, the Cardinals came back to pummel Yomiuri seven games in a row. After a period of humility, Kawakami proclaimed superiority to the visiting American League champion Baltimore Orioles in the fall of 1971. In 11 confrontations, the Orioles scored eight convincing wins and three ties./(MC)

Eddie Kazak [born Edward Tkaczuk] — 1920- . 3B 1948-52 **Cardinals**, Reds 218 g, .273, 11 hr, 71 rbi

Kazak hit .304 with occasional power as a Cardinal rookie in 1949, but was injured and lost his third base job to Tommy Glaviano. Relegated to pinch hitting, he led the NL with 42 pinch at-bats in 1950./(MC)

Ted Kazanski — 1934- . 2B-SS-3B 1953-58 **Phillies** 417 g, .217, 14 hr, 116 rbi

One of the most highly rated schoolboy players of his time, this rangy infielder was given a reported $100,000 bonus to sign with the Phillies and debuted at nineteen. Only in 1956 did he play in over 100 games, batting just .211, and he was through by the age of twenty-four./(AL)

Steve Kealey — 1947- . RHP 1968-73 Angels, **White Sox** 214 ip, 8-5, 4.28

Kealey was an undistinguished reliever who was most active with the 1971 White Sox, going 2-2 with six saves and a 3.86 ERA./(SFS)

Johnny Keane — 1911-1967. *Manager* 1961-66 Cardinals, Yankees 398-350, .532. First place: 64 *1 WS, 4-3, .571*

After 31 years in the Cardinals organization, Keane replaced Solly Hemus as manager midway through 1961. He led St. Louis to a World Championship in 1964 but, upset that friend and GM Bing Devine had been fired, resigned to manage the Yankees in 1965 in an arrangement made months prior to beating New York in the Series.

He took over a deteriorating Yankee team that finished below .500 for the first time since 1925. He was fired the next season after a 4–16 start./(FJO)

Bob Kearney (Sarge) — 1956- . C 1979, 81-87 Giants, A's, **Mariners** 479 g, .233, 27 hr, 133 rbi

Kearney was a take-charge guy and a good enough defensive catcher to entice the Mariners to trade relief ace Bill Caudill for him. He never hit well enough in Seattle to secure the starting catching job./(TF)

Ray Keating — 1891-1963. RHP 1912-16, 18-19 **Yankees**, Braves 751 ip, 30-51, 3.29

Keating was one of the pitchers allowed to continue throwing the spitball after it was banned in 1919. The amnesty did Keating no good, as he was dropped by the Braves before the 1920 season. He kept throwing his pet pitch in the Pacific Coast League, using it successfully until he retired in 1932./(JK)

Cactus Keck [Frank Joseph] — 1899-1981. RHP 1922-23 **Reds** 218 ip, 10-12, 3.51

Sidearmer Keck got his nickname by pitching in the West Texas League after WWI, after having served in the army as an underage volunteer./(JK)

Harry Keck — 1897-Unk. *Writer.*

Keck at fifteen had his first byline, with the Philadelphia *Evening Times* in 1912. Two years later, he moved to Pittsburgh with the *Post*. He became sports editor for the Pittsburgh *Gazette-Times* in 1919, then for the Baltimore *American* from 1923 to 1925 before beginning a stay at the Pittsburgh *Sun-Telegraph* from 1927 to 1960./(NLM)

Bob Keefe — 1882-1964. RHP 1907, 1911-12 Yankees, **Reds** 361 ip, 16-21, 3.14

The closest Keefe came to a winning season was 12–13 in 1911 for the sixth-place Reds./(JFC)

Dave Keefe — 1897–1978. RHP 1917, 19–22 **A's**, Indians 354 ip, 9–17, 4.15

Keefe is credited with originating the forkball, which came naturally to him—he lost the middle finger on his pitching hand in a childhood accident. In his one respectable year, with the Athletics in 1920, he was 6–7 (2.97), with half his wins coming in relief. He continued in the minors until 1932, when he went to Philadelphia's Shibe Park to pitch batting practice for the exercise; he stayed for 19 years, 7 as a coach, and he pitched batting practice for the AL at nine All-Star games. In 1950 he became the Athletics' traveling secretary. /(NLM)

Tim Keefe (Sir Timothy) — 1857–1933. RHP 1880–93 Troy (NL), New York (AA), **Giants**, New York (PL), Phillies 5072 ip, 344–225, 2.62. 20 wins: 83–89, 92
☛ *Led League—w 88. Led League—era 80, 85, 88. Hall of Fame—1964.*

Keefe was one of the iron-armed marvels of 19th-century baseball. He flourished in the days of two- or four-man pitching staffs, and threw mostly from 50', although his rookie year was the last at 45' and his final one the first at 60'6". Scarcely a season went by without an impressive, league-leading performance in one statistical category or another. In 1880, though pitching only 12 games for Troy (NY), he had an ERA of 0.86. In 1883, when the franchise collapsed and was moved to New York as Jim Mutrie's Metropolitans, he pitched 68 complete games in 68 starts for a total of 619 innings, won 41 and struck out 361. On July 4, he won a doubleheader against Columbus (OH), throwing a one-hitter in the morning game, a two-hitter after lunch. Two years later, John B. Day, who owned both the Mets and the Giants, shifted Keefe and manager Mutrie to the National League team. Keefe's colleagues were Buck Ewing, Monte Ward, and Roger Conner, as well as his Troy pitching mate, Mickey Welch.

Shoulder-high overhand pitching was now permitted and coming into vogue. Keefe had his doubts about the effectiveness of full overhand pitching, but was strong for fundamentals, first of all control. He threw a fastball, curve, and a change-up. In 1886 Keefe had 62 complete games and won 42, his career high, although 1888, when the Giants achieved their first pennant, was his finest season. He led the league in seven categories: 51 complete games, 35 victories (for a winning percentage of .745), a 1.74 ERA, 333 strikeouts, eight shutouts, and the fewest average hits per nine innings (6.55).

Tim Keefe

Nineteen of his wins were consecutive, a record that would stand for 24 years. In postseason play he scored four more over the St. Louis Browns of the American Association. Keefe even designed and sold to the Giants their famous "funeral" uniforms of that year, all-black with "New York" in white letters across the shirt front.

His 1889 contract paid him $4,500, more than any other Giant. Yet for all his star status, Keefe fought actively for ballplayers' welfare. He helped his brother-in-law Monte Ward to establish the Players League and served as secretary for the Brotherhood. He protested player salary ceilings and was among those who won court tests of the reserve clause. He was a quiet, gentle man. In 1887 he had a nervous breakdown after skulling a batter with a fastball.

With the collapse of the Brotherhood, he signed with the Phillies for his final three years, enjoying an outfield of Ed Delahanty, Billy Hamilton, and Sam Thompson behind him. Finished as a player after 1893, he umpired in the National League for two years, then left the game for the real-estate business and occasional coaching duties at Harvard, Princeton, and Tufts. /(ADS)

Bob Keegan (Smiley) — 1920- . RHP 1953–58 **White Sox** 645 ip, 40–36, 3.66
☛ *All-Star—54.*

After years as a Yankee farmhand battling injuries and criticism of his unorthodox delivery, Keegan made it to the ML as a 32-year-old rookie with the White Sox in 1953. In 1954 he was 12–3 by mid-season and was named to the All-Star team. A knee injury handicapped his next two seasons, but in 1957 he came back to win ten games, including a no-hitter. Keegan credited a slowed delivery for his renewed success. He was called Smiley because, according to Billy Pierce, "it always looked like he was smiling, even when he wasn't."/(DB)

Willie Keeler (Wee Willie) — 1872–1923. OF 1892–1910 Giants, Dodgers, Baltimore (NL), **Yankees** 2124 g, .345, 34 hr, 810 rbi
☛ *Led League—ba 97–98. Hall of Fame—1939.*

Wee Willie had a catchy nickname, extraordinary statistics, membership on one of the game's great teams, and a formula for success that became baseball's classic axiom. A two-time batting champion as the Baltimore Orioles' right fielder, Keeler advised simply, "Keep your eye on the ball and hit 'em where they ain't."

Keeler arrived from Binghamton (Eastern League) as a hard-hitting lefthanded third baseman in 1892, the last year pitchers threw from 50 feet. But it was not until Ned Hanlon acquired him for Baltimore in 1894 that he blossomed into an excellent outfielder. The 5'4-1/2" 140-lb Keeler was Hanlon's leadoff man through nine glorious years in Baltimore and Brooklyn, five as pennant winners, three in second place. He was a consistent contributor to those successes, batting .378 over the nine-year period and averaging 215 hits and 134 runs. While there was a surge of high-average hitting as pitchers adjusted to the new 60'6" distance to the plate, Keeler hit .355 or better until 1902 and did not drop below .300 until 1907.

In 1897, at age twenty-five, Wee Willie enjoyed his finest season. He batted .432, the third-highest mark in ML history, and led the league with 243 hits in only 128 games. He also hit safely in 44 consecutive games, an NL record since equaled by only Pete Rose.

Although the native Brooklynite jumped to the New York Highlanders in 1903, becoming one of few to play for three New York teams, he is best remembered for his years in Baltimore. His contemporaries recognized him as one of the game's great

Willie Keeler

bat handlers, a precise bunter, and place hitter as well as a master of the "Baltimore chop" off the hardened dirt in front of home plate. He choked his short bat almost halfway up, and with a quick wrist snap would punch the ball over the infielders' heads. He was extremely fast down the line and worked the hit-and-run expertly with teammate John McGraw. Aggressive and opportunistic, Keeler remained cheerful and friendly, without a trace of McGraw's unpleasant anger. A bachelor who prospered in real estate when his playing days ended, he was elected to the Hall of Fame in 1939./(ADS)

Vic Keen — 1899–1976. RHP 1918, 21–27 A's, **Cubs**, Cardinals 748 ip, 42–44, 4.11. *1 WS, 1 ip, 0–0, 0.00*

When he pitched at the University of Maryland, 15 teams offered Keen contracts. He was never more than a journeyman ML pitcher, with a top season of 15–14 in 1924 for the Cubs, but his ten wins two years later helped the Cardinals win their first pennant./(BC)

Sid C. Keener — 1888–Unk. *Writer.*

Director of the Hall of Fame from 1952 to 1963, Keener started as a copyboy with the St. Louis *Star* in 1902. He saw his first byline with the St. Louis *Times* in 1907. After a year in Chicago, he returned to the *Times* as assistant sports editor and succeeded Harry Neily as sports editor in 1914. He rejoined the *Star* in 1929 and continued as sports editor when the *Star* and *Times* merged. /(NLM)

Bill Keister (Wagon Tongue) — 1874–1924. SS-2B-OF-3B 1896, 98–1903 **Baltimore (NL)**, Braves, Cardinals, Baltimore (AL), Senators, Phillies 621 g, .312, 18 hr, 400 rbi

Keister holds the record for the lowest season fielding average for a shortstop in 100 or more games with a butterfingered .861 for Baltimore of the AL in 1901. In 114 games he made 97 errors. From 1898 through 1903 he hit .300 or better each season (and each with a different team), but even batting .320 in '03 could not keep him in the majors. /(BC)

Mike Kekich — 1945– . LHP 1965, 68–75, 77 Dodgers, **Yankees**, Indians, Rangers, Mariners 861 ip, 39–51, 4.59

Occasionally brilliant but more often erratic, Kekich was a hard-throwing lefthander who is best remembered for swapping families with Yankees teammate Fritz Peterson. He came up with the Dodgers but couldn't crack their tough staff, and he spent his most active years with the Yankees. He was 10–9, 4.08 for New York in 1971 and 10–13, 3.70 in 1972. His American career was ended by a shoulder injury in 1977, though he later pitched in Mexico and Japan. /(JJM)

Charles Kelchner (Pop) — Unk.–1958. *Scout.*

Kelchner was a professor of languages and athletic director at Albright College, and a scout for the A's, Browns, and Cardinals, working for the last for 40 years. He signed Joe Medwick and Rip Collins. /(FVP)

George Kell — 1922– . 3B 1943–57 A's, **Tigers**, Red Sox, White Sox, Orioles 1795 g, .306, 78 hr, 870 rbi
☛ *Led League—ba 49. All-Star—47–54, 56–57. Hall of Fame—1983.*

Easily the best player to emerge during the WWII player shortage, Kell remained the AL's premier third baseman long after the war had ended, and eventually earned a spot in the Hall of Fame.

George Kell

After two seasons as the Athletics' third baseman, Kell was traded to Detroit for Barney McCosky in May 1946 and became a perennial All-Star. He finished the 1946 season at .322, his first of eight consecutive .300 seasons. He missed 57 games in 1948 due to injuries. He first suffered a broken wrist when hit by a Vic Raschi pitch, and then several weeks later a Joe DiMaggio line drive fractured his jaw.

In 1949, Kell won his only batting title, and in the process denied Ted Williams his third triple crown. Williams had led the batting race until the final week of the season, but Kell came back from an injury to have a hot streak. When Williams went hitless in the season finale, Kell snatched the title, .3429 to .3428. Kell hit .340 the following year, leading the AL with 218 hits and 56 doubles, but lost the batting title to

Boston's Billy Goodman. After leading the league in hits and doubles once again in 1951, Kell was sent to Boston in June 1952 as part of a nine-man deal that included Dizzy Trout, Hoot Evers, Walt Dropo, and Johnny Pesky. His brother, Skeeter, played for the Athletics that season.

George Kell was as gifted in the field as he was at the plate, leading AL third baseman seven times in fielding and four times each in assists and total chances/game. After concluding his career as Baltimore's third baseman, he was succeeded there by Brooks Robinson. Kell became a Tigers play-by-play man and was inducted into the Hall of Fame by the Veterans Committee in 1983. /(JK)

Hal Kelleher — 1913- . RHP 1935-38 **Phillies** 135 ip, 4-9, 5.95

Kelleher shut out the Reds 1-0 in his September 17, 1935 debut for his hometown Phillies. He only won three more games after that. /(JK)

Mick Kelleher — 1947- . SS-3B-2B 1972-82 Cardinals, Astros, **Cubs**, Tigers, Angels 622 g, .213, 0 hr, 65 rbi

Kelleher was a good-fielding shortstop who saw the most action when acquired by the Cubs for 1976, stepping into Don Kessinger's shoes. He hit .228 in 124 games and thereafter was a utility infielder. /(SFS)

Charlie Keller (King Kong) — 1916- . OF 1939-43, 45-52 **Yankees**, Tigers 1170 g, .286, 189 hr, 760 rbi. *4 WS, 19 g, .306, 5 hr, 18 rbi* ☛ *All-Star—40-41, 43, 46-47.*

Keller's black, bushy brows and muscular body inspired his alliterative nickname. The talent-laden Yankees kept the lefthanded slugger in Newark (International League) the season after he was the league batting champion and *TSN* Minor League Player of the Year for 1937. A place was made for him in 1939, and he hit .334 with the first of six Yankee pennant winners for which he would play. He was a five-time All-Star and reached highs of 33 HR and 122 RBI in 1941. He led the AL in walks with 106 in both 1940 and 1943. Keller's career was interrupted for maritime service in WWII. He had chronic back problems which eventually relegated him to pinch hitting, and he led the league in that department (9-for-38) in 1951, his final full season. Keller coached for the Yankees before retiring to rural Maryland to run a horse farm. His brother Hal caught briefly for the Senators and spent over 20 years as a front-office man for the Senators, Rangers,

and Mariners. His son, Charlie Jr., led the Eastern League in hitting with a .349 average before being sidelined by the same congenital back problem that had plagued his father. /(JK)

Dick Kelley — 1940- . LHP 1964-69, 71 **Braves**, Padres 520 ip, 18-30, 3.39

Kelley's only winning record came with the 1966 Braves when he went 7-5 with a 3.22 ERA, mostly as a starter. /(SFS)

Harry Kelley — 1906-1958. RHP 1925-26, 36-39 Senators, **A's** 676 ip, 42-47, 4.86

Breaking in with the Senators at nineteen, Kelley spent a decade in the minors before the A's brought him back in 1936. His 21 losses in 1937 led the AL. He won 265 games in the minors. /(JK)

Joe Kelley — 1871-1943. OF-1B 1891-1908 Braves, Pirates, **Baltimore (NL)**, Dodgers, Reds 1845 g, .317, 65 hr, 1194 rbi.
  Manager 1902-05, 08 **Reds**, Braves 337-321, .512
☛ *Hall of Fame—71.*

A turn-of-the-century star, Kelley was an outfielder for the Baltimore Orioles dynasty in the 1890s, and a player-manager in the first decade of the 20th century. A 19-year-old rookie for Boston and Pittsburgh in 1891, Kelley bounced to Baltimore by the end of 1892 and was starting in center field in 1893. Switched to left in 1894, Kelley had his best season as the Orioles won the first of four consecutive league championships. He hit .393 with 167 runs scored, the second-best run total in NL history, but also only the second-best that season, as Philadelphia's Billy Hamilton scored an amazing 196 times. Kelley went a perfect 9-for-9 in a September 3 doubleheader that year, including a ML-record-tying four doubles in one game. From 1895 to 1897, his average never dipped below .364.

After the 1898 season, Kelley moved to the Brooklyn Dodgers along with manager Ned Hanlon and Orioles stars Dan McGann, Hughie Jennings, Willie Keeler, Jim Hughes, and Doc McJames. The Dodgers won pennants in 1899 and 1900. Kelley moved to first base in 1901 and returned to the Orioles, now in the fledgling AL, in 1902. With the club headed for a last-place finish, he left in mid-season to become Cincinnati's player-manager. By 1906, Kelley's average had crashed to .228 and the Reds let him go, but he resurfaced for a final season, managing the Braves to a sixth-place finish in 1908 while batting .259. The Veterans Committee elected him to the Hall of Fame in 1971. /(AJA)

Joe Kelley

Tom Kelley — 1944- . RHP 1964-67, 71-73 Indians, **Braves** 408 ip, 20-22, 3.75

Kelley was given a chance with Cleveland after going 16-3 for Portland (Pacific Coast League) in 1965, including a no-hitter against Spokane on May 29. Back in the minors by 1967, he had shoulder surgery but returned with the Braves in 1971 to post a 9-5 (2.96) mark. /(PB)

Alex Kellner — 1924- . LHP 1948-59 **A's**, Reds, Cardinals 1849 ip, 101-112, 4.41. 20 wins: 49
☛ *All-Star—49.*

Noted for his roundhouse, off-speed curve, Kellner was 20-12 as a rookie in 1949 despite walking 129 batters while fanning only 94. He led the AL with 20 losses the next year and tied for the 1951 loss lead (14) as the A's plummeted into the second division. He never again won more than 12. Like longtime teammate and pal Bobby Shantz, Kellner worked

hard at hitting and fielding to help his cause, batting .215 lifetime. He remained with the A's (joined briefly in 1952-53 by brother Walt, a pitcher) until waived to the Reds in mid-1958. His 7-3 record, 2.30 ERA, and .282 average the rest of the way helped his former A's manager Jimmy Dykes keep the Reds in distant contention. Kellner was swapped to the Cardinals after the season, and recurring shoulder trouble ended his career. /(MC)

Win Kellum [Winford Ansley] — 1876-1951. LHP 1901, 04-05 Red Sox, **Reds,** Cardinals 347 ip, 20-16, 3.19

Kellum went 15-10, 2.60 for the third-place 1904 Reds and was then sold to the Cardinals. /(WOR)

Bob Kelly — 1927- . RHP 1951-53, 58 **Cubs**, Reds, Indians 362 ip, 12-18, 4.50

Kelly posted his only winning record (7-4) as a rookie and occasional starter with the last-place Cubs in 1951. /(FK)

George Kelly (Highpockets) — 1895-1984. 1B-2B 1915-17, 19-30, 32 **Giants**, Pirates, Reds, Cubs, Dodgers 1622 g, .297, 148 hr, 1020 rbi. *4 WS, 26 g, .248, 1 hr, 10 rbi*
☛ *Led League—hr 21. Led League—rbi 20, 24. Hall of Fame—1973.*

Kelly flourished in an era of weak first basemen in the National League. Though his credentials for entry into the Hall of Fame may be marginal, he had respectable talents afield and at bat, and he joined Frank Frisch, Dave Bancroft, and Heinie Groh in what many consider the best Giant infield of all time.

A nephew of outfielder Bill Lange, one of Cap Anson's Colts (later the Cubs) of the 1890s, and a brother of Ren Kelly, who pitched one game with the 1923 A's, George was shuffled about for five years before becoming the Giants' regular first baseman in 1920. Tall for his time (6'4"), he was nicknamed Highpockets and Long George by the press; to his teammates he was Kell, a reserved and even-tempered fellow.

Kelly excelled in the field, setting single-season marks for putouts, assists, double plays, and total chances, in part because shortstop Bancroft was also setting marks for assists. A righthander, he had a powerful and accurate arm. In 1921 against the Yankees, he made a brilliant first-to-third throw to nip Aaron Ward for a game-ending, Series-winning double play. He was John McGraw's preferred cutoff man, dashing into the outfield on long hits to handle the relay. Despite his size, he played a creditable second base for most of 1925, when

George Kelly as a coach

McGraw wanted Kelly's bat in the lineup while trying young Bill Terry at first base. He even won his only game as a pitcher, beating the Phillies and Joe Oeschger in five innings of relief.

He batted over .300 for six consecutive seasons (1921–26) and was intermittently impressive as a long-ball hitter. Twice he hit three home runs in one game, the splurge in 1924 accounting for all eight Giant runs, the National League record for most RBIs in a game while batting in all the club's runs. The same year, he set another NL record by hitting seven homers in six games, with at least one in each. He also knocked in 100 or more runs four years in a row, capped by a league- and career-high 136 in 1924. Even so, his lifetime slugging average was an unspectacular .452. This evidently did not worry his manager. Over the years, McGraw said, the placid, reliable Kelly made more important hits than any player he ever had.

Displaced by Terry in 1927, Kelly was traded to

the Reds for Edd Roush. Released in 1930, he returned briefly to the majors with the Cubs and Dodgers when Charlie Grimm and Del Bissonette were injured. When his playing days were over, he coached the Reds and Braves for 11 years and scouted for several teams. /(ADS)

Joe Kelly — 1886–1977. OF 1914, 16–19 Pirates, Cubs, **Braves** 376 g, .224, 6 hr, 117 rbi

Kelly was the everyday centerfielder for the 1914 Pirates, hitting .222 with career highs of 48 RBI, 47 runs, 21 steals, and 19 doubles, but he was a poor fielder. In his next-most-active season, 1917, he led NL outfielders in errors while again hitting .222. /(SFS)

John Kelly (Honest John, Diamond John, Kick) — 1856–1926. C 1879 **Syracuse NL**, Troy NL 16 g, .155, 0 hr, 2 rbi.
   Manager 1887 **Louisville** 76–60, .559.
   Umpire **AA**, NL, PL 1882–88, 90, 97

Kelly, a robust 6-footer, became an umpire because of his weak hitting and proneness to injuries. He worked in both the NL and American Association in 1884 and was requested by the owners of the AA Browns and Union Association Maroons when they agreed to play a seven-game series at the end of the season. The following year he was selected to umpire the "world championship" series between Chicago of the NL and St. Louis of the AA. In 1887 he managed the Louisville Eclipse of the AA, where he introduced the "Hurrah Plan" with the players sprinting to and from their positions, even in practice. At the end of the season he umpired his third world championship series. Eventually, he was dismissed from umpiring as "unjustly severe." He turned first to refereeing boxing and worked three championship bouts. He later opened a gambling house in New York. /(RTM)

King Kelly [Michael Joseph] — 1857–1894. OF-C 1878–93 Reds, **Cubs (NL)**, Braves, Boston (PL), Cincinnati-Milwaukee (AA), Boston (AA), Giants 1463 g, .307, 69 hr, 794 rbi.
   Manager 1890–91 **Boston (PL)**, Cincinnati-Milwaukee (AA) 124–105, .541
   ☛ *Led League—ba 84, 86 . Hall of Fame—1945.*

Kelly, who played every position, was one of the greatest players of his era. Beginning his career with the Reds in 1878, he soon was given the title King of Baseball, and became the number one idol of the nation. Joining Chicago in 1880, Kelly sparked Cap Anson's team to five NL titles. He performed on

King Kelly

eight pennant winners in 16 seasons and hit .300 or better eight times. His .354 in 1884 and .388 in 1886 led the NL. He led the league three times each in doubles and runs scored, and he is one of ten NL players to have scored a league-record six runs in one game. Kelly won renown for his daring baserunning, stealing at least 50 bases for four successive years, with a high of 84 for the Braves in 1887. He once stole six bases in one game. His sensational baserunning and sliding led fans to cheer him on, yelling, "Slide, Kelly, slide!"

After Kelly was traded to the Braves for a record $10,000 in one of the biggest deals in baseball's early history, Chicago fans were so upset they boycotted their team, except when Boston played there. Joining the Players' League in 1890 as Boston's player-manager, Kelly's team captured the league championship by posting an 81–48 record.

After serving as player-manager for Cincinnati-Milwaukee of the American Association for part of 1891, Kelly returned to Boston and helped the Braves win titles in 1891 and 1892. He played a few games for the Giants in 1893, then drifted to the minors, managing Allentown in the Pennsylvania State League and Yonkers in the Eastern League.

Imaginative and quick-thinking, Kelly was credited by Cap Anson with devising the hit-and-run play, although this is disputed. He studied the rules and found ways to get around them, causing the league to make changes. Colorful both on and off the field, Kelly acted with flair and was admired and adored by fans. He wore the finest tailored clothes and the most current styles. American billboards featured the handsome, happy-go-lucky Irishman as the nation's best-dressed man. Kelly supplemented his income with off-season stage appearances and wrote *Play Ball*. Following his retirement from baseball, he opened a saloon in New York. In 1894, en route to Boston to appear at the Palace Theater, he died of pneumonia at age thirty-six. /(JE)

Ray Kelly — 1914–1988. *Writer.*

Kelly spent 50 years with the Philadelphia *Bulletin*, beginning at sisteen as a copyboy. For the last few years he formed a rare father-and-son combination, covering the Phillies with Ray W. Kelly of the Camden (New Jersey) *Post*. Kelly was a semi-pro soccer player in the 1930s who once covered a game in which he scored the winning goal. In his story for the *Bulletin* he gave credit for the goal to another player. Following his retirement he wrote for a weekly paper and did publicity for Philadelphia Park racetrack. /(NLM)

Roberto Kelly — 1964– . OF 1985- **Yankees** 198 g, .291, 11 hr, 62 rbi

This speedy Panamanian won the Yankee's centerfield job in 1989 after Claudell Washington wasn't signed and hit a surprising .302 with 35 steals. /(WOR)

Tom Kelly — 1950– . 1B 1975 **Twins** 49 g, .181, 1 hr, 11 rbi.
    Manager 1986- **Twins** 268–241, .527

Longtime Twins organization man Kelly was the surprise choice to manage the club at the end of 1986. His low-key style helped him lead the underdog club to a World Championship in 1987 despite an 85–77 mark. Improving to 91–71 in 1988, the Twins finished second. /(SFS)

Bill Kelso — 1940– . RHP 1964, 66–68 **Angels**, Reds 201 ip, 12–5, 3.13

Kelso spent four years catching in the minors before converting to pitcher. His best effort was a 5–3, 11-save season for the 1967 Angels. /(RM)

Ken Keltner — 1916– . 3B 1937–44, 46–50 **Indians**, Red Sox 1526 g, .276, 163 hr, 852 rbi. *1 WS, 6 g, .095* ☞ *All-Star—40–44, 46, 48.*

Keltner earned recognition as Cleveland's all-time greatest third baseman for his 11 seasons there. A timely hitter, the seven-time All-Star was a fabulous fielder known for going to his right. He ended Joe DiMaggio's record hit streak at 56 on July 17, 1941 before a then-record night crowd (67,468) in Cleveland. Keltner made two stops of DiMaggio line drives, one a brilliant backhanded stab. On October 4, 1948, in the first playoff in AL history, Keltner's single, double, and three-run homer helped the Indians defeat the Red Sox at Fenway Park. That season, Keltner reached career highs of 31 HR (third in the AL) and 119 RBI (sixth). When he left Cleveland, he was among the club's all-time leaders in games played, doubles, HR, RBI, and hits. /(ME)

Russ Kemmerer (Rusty, Dutch) — 1931– . RHP 1954–55, 57–63 Red Sox, **Senators**, White Sox, Astros 1067 ip, 43–59, 4.46

Hard-throwing Kemmerer was 5–3 down the stretch for the Red Sox as a rookie in 1954. He was swapped to the Senators in 1957, spending three losing seasons in their rotation, and he finished as a long reliever with the Colt .45s (later the Astros). /(MC)

Steve Kemp — 1954– . OF 1977–86, 88 **Tigers**, White Sox, Yankees, Pirates, Rangers 1168 g, .278, 130 hr, 634 rbi ☞ *All-Star—79.*

A highly touted hitter while at the University of Southern California, Kemp was the first player chosen in the nation in the January 1976 draft. After only one season in the minors he was the Tigers' starting left fielder in 1977. He had a looping, lefthanded batting stroke and was neither fast nor graceful in the field, but he made the AL All-Star team in 1979 when he hit .318 with 26 HR and 105 RBI. Kemp was traded to the White Sox for outfielder Chet Lemon after the 1981 season and spent only one season in Chicago before signing with the Yankees as a free agent. His batting average wilted to .241 under the pressure of high expectations in New York, and after the 1984 season he was

traded with Tim Foli to the Pirates for Dale Berra and Jay Buhner. Battling vision problems, he hit only three home runs in 105 games with Pittsburgh in 1985–86 before retiring. /(SCL)

Fred Kendall — 1949– . C 1969–80 **Padres**, Indians, Red Sox 877 g, .234, 31 hr, 244 rbi

Kendall became a San Diego favorite as their regular catcher for much of 1972–76 and was named Most Valuable Padre in 1973 when he hit a career-high .282. Randy Jones credited Kendall with much of his success, and Kendall caught all of Jones's league-leading 22 victories in 1976. The last original Padre when sent to the Indians in December 1976, he returned as a backup in 1979. /(JCA)

Bill Kennedy (Lefty) — 1921–83. LHP 1948–53, 56–57 Indians, **Browns**, White Sox, Red Sox, Reds 465 ip, 15–28, 4.71

Kennedy struck out 456 for Rocky Mount in the Western Carolinas League in 1946. He went 8–8 his rookie year with Cleveland and St. Louis, but wildness dogged his career. As a White Sox reliever in 1952, he led the AL with 47 appearances, but his record was otherwise undistinguished. /(BC)

Bob Kennedy — 1920– . OF-3B 1939–42, 46–57 White Sox, **Indians**, Orioles, Tigers, Dodgers 1483 g, .254, 63 hr, 514 rbi. *1 WS, 3 g, .500, 1 rbi.* *Manager* 1963–65, 68 **Cubs**, A's 264–278, .487

Blessed with a strong, accurate throwing arm, Bob Kennedy was one of the first rookie prospects to come out of the newly developed White Sox farm system. The night before he signed in 1937, he was working as a popcorn vendor at Comiskey Park for the Louis-Braddock boxing match. He moved into the starting lineup in 1940, but he committed a league-leading 33 errors at third base. After missing three seasons in military service, he returned to play mostly outfield. Dealt to the Indians in June 1948, he batted .301 the rest of the way and became a member of the last World Championship Indians team. He hit a career-high .291 as their right fielder in 1950.

Kennedy managed the Cubs from 1963 to early 1965, never finishing higher than seventh, and the A's in their first year in Oakland (1968). In subsequent years he was the GM of the Cubs and Astros. His son, Terry, became a star catcher. /(RL)

Brickyard Kennedy [William P.] (Roaring Bill) — 1867–1915. RHP 1892–1903 **Brooklyn (NL)**, Giants, Pirates 3021 ip, 184–160, 3.96. 20 wins: 93–94, 99–1900 *1 WS, 7 ip, 0–1, 5.14*

A prototype of all the Daffy Dodgers to come, Roaring Bill, who conversed at the top of his lungs, was a lovable, eccentric illiterate. He once left the team, misdirected by a policeman who thought Bill wanted to go home to Ohio, rather than find his way from Brooklyn to the Polo Grounds. His restaurant misadventures became legendary, as he always waited until a teammate ordered, then asked for the same, though he wasn't always sure what he was getting. Once, when he reached the hotel dining room as the others were leaving, he asked, "Did you have a good dinner?" Told by one departing diner he had, Bill said to the waiter, "I'll have what he had." Later he complained to the player who had bequeathed him his dinner selection, "It was all right, except for that newfangled dessert." Bill had encountered his first charlotte russe, served in a cardboard cone. "It was that Charley Ross, the waiter called it, the crust was so tough I could hardly eat it."

Kennedy was a winner his first four years with Brooklyn and went 26–20 in 1893. After three losing seasons, he rebounded to go 22–8 in 1899 and 20–13 in 1900. As a spot starter with the Pirates, he pitched in the first World Series in 1903. Up 3–1 in games, Pittsburgh pitted Kennedy against Boston's Cy Young. They matched zeros for five innings until Pittsburgh fell apart, making four errors, losing 11–2. It was Kennedy's last game. Boston won the next three to become World Champions. /(JK)

John Kennedy — 1941– . 3B-SS-2B 1962–67, 69–74 Senators, Dodgers, Yankees, Pilots/Brewers, **Red Sox** 856 g, .225, 32 hr, 185 rbi. *2 WS, 6 g, .167*

Kennedy was the model good-field, no-hit utility infielder. He pinch-homered in his first major league at-bat, for the Senators on September 5, 1962. He shared the birthdate of May 29 with President John F. Kennedy. /(BC)

Junior Kennedy — 1950– . 2B-SS-3B 1974, 78–83 **Reds**, Cubs 447 g, .248, 4 hr, 95 rbi

After ten years in the minors, Kennedy filled in as Cincinnati's second baseman in 1978–79 while Joe Morgan was hurt. After Morgan signed with Houston as a free agent, Kennedy lost the second base job in 1980 to Ron Oester. His brother Jim was a Cardinal infielder in 1970. /(JCA)

Monte Kennedy (Lefty) — 1922– . LHP 1946–53 Giants 961 ip, 42–55, 3.84. *1 WS, 3 ip, 0–0, 6.00*

Kennedy came to the Giants in 1946 after three years in the army. Wildness curtailed his effectiveness and he led the NL in walks his rookie year. He won a career-high 12 in 1949. /(JK)

Terry Kennedy — 1956– . C 1978– Cardinals, Padres, Orioles, Giants 1315 g, .264, 108 hr, 589 hr. *2 LCS, 10 g, .206, 1 rbi. 2 WS, 9 g, .194, 1 hr, 5 rbi* ☛ *All-Star—81, 83, 85, 87.*

Kennedy was stuck behind catcher Ted Simmons at St. Louis until the 11-player deal on December 8, 1980 that sent Kennedy to San Diego and brought Rollie Fingers, briefly, to the Cardinals. From 1981 to 1987, only Gary Carter (940) caught more major league games than Kennedy (934). Terry was San Diego's MVP in 1982, tying Johnny Bench's catchers' record of 40 doubles. Kennedy had 42 doubles overall and led all catchers with 64 extra-base hits. He lost his job to Benito Santiago late in 1986 but set a Padres record by batting .478 as a pinch hitter. Traded to Baltimore for 1987, Kennedy became the second catcher to start All-Star games for both leagues and set club records in starts (135) and total games (142) as a catcher. The strikeout-prone, 6′4″ 224-lb lefthanded batter never produced the power expected to go with his size. A prime target for basestealers due to a suspect throwing arm, Kennedy compensated with great knowledge of hitters and ability to handle pitchers.

Terry and his father, Bob Kennedy, are one of only four father-son duos to both play in the World Series. Acquired by the Giants in 1989 while his father was a Giants executive, Terry helped them to the NL pennant. /(ME)

Vern Kennedy [Lloyd Vernon] — 1907– . RHP 1934–45 **White Sox**, Tigers, Browns, Senators, Indians, Phillies, Reds 2026 ip, 104–132, 4.67. 20 wins: 36 ☛ *All-Star—36, 38.*

Vern Kennedy pitched a no-hitter for Chicago against Cleveland in his first full season in 1935. He followed with a 21–9 record in 1936, but he led the league with 147 walks. A sore arm slowed him down after 1937, and in 1939 with Detroit he lost an AL-high 20 games. /(JK)

Jerry Kenney — 1945- . 3B-SS 1967, 69-73 **Yankees**, Indians 465 g, .237, 7 hr, 103 rbi

Kenney, a tall, slender (6'1" 170-lb) lefthanded-hitting third baseman, was part of the trade that brought Graig Nettles to the Yankees in 1973. He was the Yankee third baseman from 1969 to 1971, and had career highs in 1971 with a .262 average, 56 walks, and 50 runs, in 325 at-bats. /(JM)

Joe Keough — 1946- . OF 1968-73 A's, **Royals**, White Sox 332 g, .246, 9 hr, 81 rbi

Keough played semi-pro ball in Canada before signing with Oakland in 1966, the last year in the majors for his brother Marty. Joe homered in his first ML at-bat but rarely thereafter. In 1971 he hit .248 in 110 games for the Royals in his best season. /(FJO)

Marty Keough — 1935- . OF-1B 1956-66 Red Sox, Indians, Senators, **Reds**, Braves, Cubs 841 g, .242, 43 hr, 176 rbi

Marty, older brother of outfielder Joe Keough, spent his 11 ML seasons as a part-timer. In 1962, his first year in Cincinnati, he hit a personal-best .278 with seven HR in 111 games. His son Matt pitched for Oakland. /(BC)

Matt Keough — 1955- . RHP 1977-83, 85-86 **A's**, Yankees, Cardinals, Cubs, Astros 1190 ip, 58-84, 4.17. *1 LCS, 8 ip, 0-1, 1.08*
☛ *All-Star—78.*

Signed as an infielder, Keough was heralded by A's owner Charley Finley as Sal Bando's successor at third base. But when Keough hit .210 in Double-A in 1976, Finley put him on the mound. He joined Oakland a year later, and as a sophomore in 1978 was the A's only All-Star. He remained in the rotation on Finley's orders in 1979 despite a 2-17 record; he lost his first 14 decisions to tie the ML record for most consecutive losses at the start of a season. But his 16-13 mark in 1980 won him AL Comeback Player of the Year honors. He slumped to 11-18 (5.72) in 1982, tying for the AL lead in losses. Nursing a sore arm, he bounced around before landing in Japan, where his father, major leaguer Marty Keough, had played in 1968. His uncle, Joe Keough, spent most of his six-year career with the A's. /(MC)

Kurt Kepshire — 1959- . RHP 1984-86 **Cardinals** 270 ip, 16-15, 4.16

After a promising rookie season, Kepshire became very inconsistent, with excellent control and velocity one game and neither the next. He was so unpredictable the Cardinals left him off their 1985 postseason roster despite his 10-9 record. /(FJO)

Charlie Kerfeld — 1963- . RHP 1985-87 **Astros** 168 ip, 15-6, 3.70. *1 LCS, 4 ip, 0-1, 2.25*

Kerfeld was a breath of fresh air as an enthusiastic, wisecracking, and obese 6'6" righthander who won 11 games and saved seven for the 1986 NL West champion Astros. But his weight problems forced him back to the minors after a horrendous start in 1987, and elbow trouble has put his pitching career in jeopardy. /(ME)

Jim Kern (Emu) — 1949- . RHP 1974-86 **Indians**, Rangers, Reds, White Sox, Phillies, Brewers 793 ip, 53-57, 3.33
☛ *All-Star—77-79.*

The eccentric, intelligent 6'5" prankster was nicknamed Emu because he looked and acted like a big bird. Kern and Sparky Lyle, in the Rangers' bullpen for two seasons, were known as Craziness, Inc. for their antics and off-the-field misadventures. Kern was hit in the mouth with a throw from his catcher while watching a foul ball in Texas in August 1980. He fell backward off the mound, suffering a concussion. The temporary amnesia he reportedly suffered may have been the result of an opportunistic sense of humor.

His overpowering fastball and lunatic reputation made him an intimidating short reliever; he averaged 8.6 strikeouts per nine innings, 1976-79, when he won 41 games and saved 75. Though he lost an AL-high 10 in relief for Cleveland in 1977, he turned it around in 1979 with Texas, where he was 13-5 with 29 saves and a 1.57 ERA, earning him Fireman of the Year cohonors with Mike Marshall. That was his last effective season, as he injured his elbow in 1980. Unhappy in Cincinnati, Kern forced the Reds to trade him in 1982 by regrowing his scraggly beard, breaking the Reds' unwritten "no facial hair" rule. /(BC)

Buddy Kerr [John Joseph] — 1922- . SS 1943-51 **Giants**, Braves 1067 g, .249, 31 hr, 333 rbi
☛ *All-Star—48.*

Kerr was a slick, wide-ranging shortstop for the otherwise lumbering Giants of the 1940s. Although a less-than-average hitter, he led NL shortstops in assists, putouts, and double plays in 1945, and he had a top .982 fielding average in 1946. When the

Giants hit a NL record 221 home runs in 1947, Kerr's contribution was a mere 7, though he managed a career-high .287 batting average. /(BC)

Dickey Kerr — 1893–1963 . LHP 1919–21, 25 **White Sox** 811 ip, 53–34, 3.84. 20 wins: 20 *1 WS, 19 ip, 2–0, 1.42*

Kerr was the one honest starter employed by the White Sox in the scandalous 1919 World Series. He won his two starts against the Reds, one by shutout, while the corrupt star pitchers, Ed Cicotte and Lefty Williams, each dumped their first two assignments. Kerr was 21–9 in 1920 and, after the guilty players were purged, went 19–17 for the demoralized, seventh-place 1921 White Sox. Denied a $500 raise, he decided to pitch for independent teams rather than for tightfisted Charley Comiskey.

Kerr had a long career as a minor league manager. He converted the 19-year-old Stan Musial from a pitcher to an outfielder. The Kerrs befriended the Musials, whose first son was born while Dickey Kerr drove through red lights to get Lil Musial to the hospital; the boy was named Richard in his honor. When Stan achieved stardom with the Cardinals, the Musials repaid the Kerrs' kindness by giving them a house in Houston. /(JK)

John Kerr — 1898–1980. 2B-SS 1923–24, 29–34 Tigers, **White Sox**, Senators 471 g, .266, 6 hr, 145 rbi. *1 WS, 1 g, .000*

A native of San Francisco, Kerr was a favorite in the Pacific Coast League. He was the White Sox regular second baseman in 1929 and 1931. With Washington, Kerr was the roommate and inseparable companion of Moe Berg. /(JK)

Joe Kerrigan — 1954– . RHP 1976–78, 80 **Expos**, Orioles 219 ip, 8–12, 3.90

As a rookie in 1976, Kerrigan won both games of a doubleheader against St. Louis, his only two wins that season. The 6'5" forkballer shared Montreal bullpen duties with Don Stanhouse in 1977, making 66 appearances and saving 11. The two were then shipped to Baltimore. Kerrigan returned as the Expos' bullpen coach in 1983. His brother Tom was a catcher in the Phillies organization in the 1960s. /(MC)

Don Kessinger — 1942– . SS 1964–79 **Cubs**, Cardinals, White Sox 2078 g, .252, 14 hr, 527 rbi.
Manager 1979 **White Sox** 46–60, .434
☛ *All-Star—68–72, 74 .*

Kessinger accepted a $25,000 bonus to sign out of the University of Mississippi. With Ernie Banks, Glenn Beckert, and Ron Santo, he gave Chicago an all-star infield. Though he led the NL in errors in his first season as a regular (1965), Kessinger quickly established himself as an outstanding fielder, leading league shortstops in putouts three years, assists four years, double plays four years, and fielding average once. He played 54 straight errorless games in 1969, then the record for shortstops, and started for the NL in five All-Star games. He was a pesky, reliable hitter, with a top average of .274 in 1966 and 1972. On July 17, 1970 he went 6-for-6 in a 10-inning game. The clean-living Kessinger served as player-manager for the White Sox in 1979. /(BC)

Jimmy Key — 1961– . LHP 1984– **Blue Jays** 1115 ip, 74–49, 3.36. *2 LCS, 15 ip, 1–1, 4.91*
☛ *Led League—era 87. All-Star—85.*

Key bounced back from 1988 arm trouble but could not reestablish himself as one of the AL's top lefthanders in 1989. When Key began with the Blue Jays in 1984, the franchise had never enjoyed good lefthanded pitching. Key set a club rookie record for saves (10), as well as a club mark for appearances with 63. In 1985 Key joined the starting rotation and became the first lefthanded starter to win a game for Toronto since 1980 (a 614-game dry spell) on his way to a 14–6 record with a 3.00 ERA. On May 22, 1986 Key threw a one-hitter against the White Sox (the only hit a fifth-inning single by Ozzie Guillen). In 1987 Key was the AL ERA leader (2.76) while tying the Blue Jay record with 17 wins. In his eight defeats, his teammates scored only 12 runs, and he had seven no-decisions in which he held the opposition to two runs or less. Key's most heartbreaking loss was a 1–0 defeat in the final game of the 1987 season in Detroit, with the division championship on the line. He is the Blue Jays' career leader in ERA and ranks third in wins, strikeouts, and shutouts. /(TF)

John Kibler — 1929– . *Umpire NL 1963–86 5 LCS 4 WS 4 ASU*

A 24-year veteran umpire, Kibler seldom made a mistake. One of those rare occasions came on June 16, 1986, his final season, when, as crew chief, he called a rainy Pirates-Cardinals game without waiting the stipulated amount of time. NL president Chub Feeney upheld the protest. /(RTM)

Leo Kiely — 1929–1984. LHP 1951, 54–56, 58–60 **Red Sox**, A's 523 ip, 26–27, 3.37

After a 7–7 rookie half season with Boston in 1951, Kiely went into the army. Returning in 1954, he was demoted to the bullpen. Kiely led Pacific Coast League relievers in 1957, going 21–6, and saved 12 for the Red Sox in 1958. /(JK)

John Kieran — 1882–1981. *Writer.*

The son of the first president of Hunter College, Kieran had the mind of a college professor and the voice of a New York taxi driver. An amateur naturalist, he was an expert in several subjects on the radio program *Information, Please* for ten years beginning in 1938. He started his newspaper career in 1915, writing at space rates for the sports section of *The New York Times*, then moved to the *Herald Tribune* in 1922. After two years with the Hearst papers (1925–26), he returned to the *Times* to begin the paper's first bylined sports column, "Sports of the Times," starting January 1, 1927. In 1943, he went to the New York *Sun* and wrote a general column. His columns often included bits of poetry. Among his books are *Not Under Oath*, *The Story of the Olympics* (with Arthur Daley), and *The Natural History of New York*. He received the J.G. Taylor Spink Award from the Hall of Fame in 1973. /(NLM)

Pete Kilduff — 1893–1930. 2B-SS-3B 1917–1921 Giants, Cubs, **Dodgers** 428 g, .270, 4 hr, 159 rbi. *1 WS, 7 g, .095*

Kilduff would unknowingly tip off Dodger teammate Burleigh Grimes's spitter by tossing dirt into his glove. He was also one of the baserunners erased by Bill Wambsganss's unassisted triple play in the 1920 Brooklyn-Cleveland WS. /(JK)

Paul Kilgus — 1962– . LHP 1987– **Rangers**, Cubs 438 ip, 20–32, 4.23. *1 LCS, 3 ip, 0–0, 0.00*

After two losing seasons in which he showed glimmers of talent (three shutouts in 1988) but had control problems, Kilgus went to the Cubs in the Rafael Palmiero-Mitch Williams trade and struggled, going 6–10 with a 4.39 ERA. /(JFC)

Mike Kilkenny — 1945– . LHP 1969–73 **Tigers**, A's, Padres, Indians 410 ip, 23–18, 4.44

Kilkenny signed off the Toronto sandlots, choosing baseball over hockey. He was voted Tiger Rookie of the Year in 1969, with eight wins and four shutouts,

but was inconsistent after that. He was traded three times between May 9 and June 11, 1972. /(CC)

Harmon Killebrew (Killer) — 1936– . 1B-3B-OF-DH 1954–1975 **Senators/Twins**, Royals 2435 g, .256, 573 hr, 1584 rbi. *2 LCS, 6 g, .211, 2 hr, 4 rbi. 1 WS, 7 g, .286, 1 hr, 2 rbi*
☛ *Most Valuable Player—69. Led League—hr 59, 62–64, 67, 69. Led League—rbi 62, 69, 71. All-Star—59, 61, 63–71. Hall of Fame—1984.*

In the mid-1960s, it wasn't Aaron or Mays or Mantle but Harmon Killebrew who seemed to have the best shot at Ruth's lifetime homer record. At the end of 1967, the 31-year-old Killer, a nickname that contradicted his gentle nature, had hit 380 home runs, more than Ruth had at the same age. But in 1968 he was out much of the year with an injury, and after 1970 his enormous power dissipated quickly. Killebrew finished fifth in HR all-time, and third in home run frequency, and left behind a legacy of pure power.

Killebrew was the Senators' first "bonus baby" in 1954, signing a week before his 18th birthday on the recommendation of a U.S. Senator from his home state of Idaho. He shuttled between the majors and minors for five years before finally getting a legitimate shot. He made the starting lineup for good in 1959 when second baseman Pete Runnels got spiked and Killebrew came through with two HR. He finished the season with a league-leading 42, the first of eight times he would top 40.

Throughout his career, Killebrew changed positions frequently. He came up as a second baseman, was soon moved to third, then to left field for a few seasons, over to first base for a while, then back to third, back to first, and finally off the field altogether to DH. He would often shift between two positions in the same game. But Killer never groused and his lack of a permanent defensive spot never seemed to affect his power. In 1962, the second year after the original Senators moved to Minnesota and became the Twins, Killebrew hit a ball completely over the left-field roof at massive Tiger Stadium. On May 2, 1964 he was the fourth straight Twin to homer in the eleventh inning against the Angels to tie a ML record. On June 3, 1967 against the Angels, Killebrew rifled a three-run shot six rows into Metropolitan Stadium's upper deck in left field, shattering two seats. The shot was estimated to have gone 530 feet. The splintered seats were painted orange and never sold again. The next day he hit another shot to

Harmon Killebrew

almost the same spot, the ball pounding off the upper deck facing.

All-Star games brought out the best and worst in Killebrew. He homered in three contests. His first came in the first game in 1961 and provided the AL with its first run in an eventual 5–4 loss. In the 1965 game, his sixth-inning two-run homer in front of his home fans tied the game at 5–5 in another one-run AL loss. In 1968, he overstretched for a throw for an error that led to the only run of the game. The stretch also caused him to pull his hamstring, and he was out for the rest of the season, effectively ruining his chance to catch Ruth. In the homer-rich contest at Tiger Stadium in 1971, his two-run shot in the sixth provided the eventual winning runs in a 6–5 AL victory to snap an eight-game AL slide.

Killebrew, who never drank and was never thrown out of a game, came back from his All-Star hamstring injury to have his best season in 1969. He had career highs with 49 HR and 140 RBI and was selected the AL MVP. He hit another 41 HR in 1970 but saw his home run total slide to only 28 in

1971, although he did lead the league in RBI with 114. His home run totals slid further to 26 in 1972, to 5 in an injury-plagued 1973, and to 13 in 1974. The press reported acrimony between Killebrew and Twins owner Cal Griffith when Killer was released after the 1974 season, which Killebrew denied. But it was obvious that his eroding skills could no longer help Minnesota. He signed on with Kansas City for a final season in 1975. After retirement, he became a Twins broadcaster. He was elected to the Hall of Fame in 1984. /(SEW)

Bill Killefer (Reindeer Bill) — 1887–1960. C 1909–21 Browns, **Phillies**, Cubs 1035 g, .238, 4 hr, 240 rbi. *2 WS, 7 g, .111, 2 rbi.*
   Manager 1921–25, 30–33 **Cubs**, Browns 523–623, .456

Bill Killefer was Grover Alexander's batterymate, first with the Phillies and then with the Cubs, to whom the two were traded in 1917. He became the Cubs' manager during the 1921 season, led them until 1925, and managed the Browns in 1930–33.

In nine years he had just one first-division finish, when the Cubs came in fourth in 1923. Killefer fared better in developing catchers, bringing Bob O'Farrell and Gabby Hartnett to stardom with the Cubs. Bill was the younger brother of utility player Red Killefer. /(JK)

Red Killefer [Wade] (Lollypop) — 1884–1958. OF-2B 1907–10, 14–16 Tigers, Senators, **Reds**, Giants 467 g, .248, 3 hr, 116 rbi

Journeyman brother of catcher Bill Killefer, Red played every infield position during his career. He was a regular only once, in the outfield of the 1915 Reds. He had a long and successful career managing in the Pacific Coast League. /(JK)

Frank Killen (Lefty) — 1870–1939. LHP 1891–1900 Cincinnati-Milwaukee (AA), Washington (NL), **Pirates**, Braves, Cubs 2511 ip, 161–124, 3.78. 20 wins: 1892–93, 96
☛ *Led League—w 1893.*

Pittsburgh workhorse Killen won 34 games in 1893, his first year with the Pirates. Connie Mack, Killen's manager and batterymate, said the primary reason the Pirates did not win the 1895 pennant was that Killen was injured. The hurler came back strong in 1896, leading the NL in games, starts, complete games, and innings pitched, and winning 29 games in his last big season. A lifetime .241 hitter, he had 11 home runs in 998 at-bats. /(ME)

Ed Killian (Twilight Ed) — 1876–1928. LHP 1903–10 Indians, **Tigers** 1598 ip, 102–78, 2.38. 20 wins: 05, 07
2 WS, 6 ip, 0–0, 4.26

A hero in Detroit when he won both games of a doubleheader against Boston to clinch the 1907 pennant, Killian was the hardest pitcher to homer against in ML history. Pitching in the dead-ball era, he allowed only nine HR in his career—one every 178 innings—and once went almost four full seasons (1,001 innings) without surrendering one. Acquired by Detroit after one season in Cleveland, Killian won 23 games in his second year as a Tiger, and in 1907 wents 25–13 with a 1.78 ERA and .320 batting average. /(JK)

Matt Kilroy (Matches) — 1866–1940. LHP-OF 1886–94, 98 **Baltimore (AA)**, Boston (PL), Cincinnati-Milwaukee (AA), Washington (NL), Louisville (NL), Cubs 330 g, .222, 1 hr, 66 rbi, 2436 ip, 142–134, 3.47. 20 wins: 86–87, 89
☛ *Led League—w 87. Led League—k 86.*

Although Kilroy lost an American Association-high 34 games as a rookie in 1886, he also led last-place Baltimore with 29 wins and struck out 513 batters (in 583 IP) for a ML record that has never been equaled. In 1887, though striking out "only" 217, Kilroy led the AA with 46 wins to boost Baltimore to third place. Younger brother Mike joined him to pitch one game in 1888 and later appeared with the Phillies. /(FIC)

Newt Kimball — 1915– . RHP 1937–38, 40–43 Cubs, **Dodgers**, Cardinals, Phillies 235 ip, 11–9, 3.78

Blond, broad-shouldered Newt Kimball went 9–3 in four part-time seasons for the Dodgers. Sold to the Cardinals in 1940, he was returned to Brooklyn after pitching two games when Commissioner Landis voided the transaction due to a mishandling of the waiver process. /(JK)

Henry Kimbro — 1912–Unk. OF-MGR Negro Leagues 1937–50 Washington Elite Giants, Homestead Grays, **Baltimore Elite Giants**, New York Black Yankees statistics not available
☛ *All-Star—41, 43–44, 46–47.*

A good all-around ballplayer, Kimbro hit for consistently high averages and was noted for his defensive ability and baserunning. At various times in the 1940s he led the league in runs scored, doubles, and triples. He batted .371 in 1946 and .363 in 1947, finishing third each season. He appeared in six East-West all-star games. Playing for Havana in the Cuban Winter League during the 1947–48 season, he won the batting crown with a .346 average, and set a league record with 104 hits. /(BP)

Chad Kimsey [Clyde Elias] — 1905–1942. RHP 1929–33, 36 **Browns**, White Sox, Tigers 509 ip, 24–29, 5.07

This burly, 6'3" reliever had strong arms and hands from milking cows. With the Browns, Kimsey's five relief losses in 1929, and seven in 1930, were AL highs. The lifetime .282 batter was sometimes used to pinch-hit. /(JK)

Jerry Kindall (Slim) — 1935– . 2B-SS 1956–58, 60–65 **Cubs**, Indians, Twins 742 g, .213, 44 hr, 198 rbi

After three seasons below .170, Kindall tried switch-hitting to win the Cubs' second base job, but he was traded to Cleveland when Ken Hubbs arrived. He was the Twins' 2B for most of their AL Championship 1965 season, but he hit only .196 and was released before the WS. /(MC)

Ellis Kinder (Old Folks) — 1914–1968. RHP 1946–57
Browns, **Red Sox**, Cardinals, White Sox 1479 ip, 102–71,
3.43. 20 wins: 49

Old Folks Kinder didn't pitch in the majors until he
was over thirty, but he went on to an occasionally
spectacular 12-year career. After two ordinary years
with the Browns, he was traded to the Red Sox
following the 1947 season. In 1949 he was a
sensational starter, going 23–6 with league highs of
six shutouts and a .793 winning percentage. With
the Red Sox and Yankees tied before the last game
of the season, Kinder vowed to win if given three
runs. He left after eight innings, trailing 1–0, and
New York bombed his relief to take the game 5–4
and win the pennant. He became a top reliever in
1951, saving 14 and winning 10 out of the bullpen,
both top AL marks. In 1953 he made a then-record
69 appearances, again leading in relief wins (10) and
saves (27). He retired with 102 career saves./(BC)

Ralph Kiner — 1922– . OF-1B 1946–1955 **Pirates**,
Cubs, Indians 1472 g, .279, 369 hr, 1015 rbi
☛ *Led League—hr 46–52. Led League—rbi 49. All-
Star—48–53. Hall of Fame—1975..*

Kiner was baseball's greatest home run hitter during
the years after WWII. Although his career was
curtailed by a bad back, the powerful righthanded
slugger had a ratio of homers to at-bats exceeded
only by Babe Ruth.

Signed by the Pirates for an $8,000 bonus, Kiner
hit 27 home runs in two minor league seasons before
the war. Following military service (1943–45), he
became Pittsburgh's starting left fielder in 1946.
Despite starting slowly, he hit 23 homers to tie the
club record and lead the NL, the lowest total to lead
the league since 1921. Kiner was the Pirates' first
home run champion since 1906, and home attendance rose to its highest level since the pennant year
of 1927 even though the team tumbled to seventh
place.

In 1947, the Pirates obtained Hank Greenberg,
the '46 AL home run champ, and tailored Forbes
Field to the two righthanded power hitters. A double
bullpen, 30 feet wide by 200 feet long, significantly
cut the distances in left field. "Greenberg Gardens"
(later "Kiner's Korner") reduced the left-field line
from 365 to 335 feet and the left-center power alley
from 406 to 355 feet. The two sluggers became
roommates and Kiner credited Greenberg with his
continued success. Greenberg managed only 25
homers in his final season, but Kiner blasted 51 to
tie Johnny Mize for the NL lead. Finishing strong,
he set a ML record with eight homers in four games

Ralph Kiner

from September 10 to 12. His batting average
jumped to a career-high .313 and he led the NL with
a slugging percentage of .639.

Meanwhile, attendance boomed at Forbes Field
despite the Pirates' poor record. Fans would stay in
the stands until Kiner had his final at-bat, then file
for the exits. More than five million fans paid to
watch losing Pirates teams from 1947 to 1950.

In 1948, Kiner again tied Mize for the NL homer
championship, hitting 40. The following year, a
stretch drive of 16 September homers brought him
to 54, only two shy of Hack Wilson's NL record. He
also became the first player to hit 50 homers twice in
the NL. His 47 home runs in 1950 established a
league record of 102 in two consecutive seasons, and
he was named *TSN* Player of the Year.

Kiner was sometimes mistakenly labeled a poor
outfielder. He lacked speed, but he was sure-handed

and had an accurate (but weak) arm. He led the NL in HR in 1951 and 1952 to run his streak to seven consecutive titles, but the Pirates around him were in shambles. His back problems were also beginning to plague him. On June 3, 1953 he was traded to the Cubs in a famous "we finished last with you, we can finish last without you" deal. In Chicago, Kiner teamed in the outfield with the equally slow and powerful Hank Sauer, with whom he had shared the NL home run title the year before. Before the 1955 season, Cleveland GM Greenberg acquired him for the Indians. He hit 18 homers for the Tribe in his final season. Only thirty-three when his bad back ended his career, Kiner retired having hit a home run in every 14.1 at-bats.

After his retirement, he served briefly as GM of the San Diego Padres in the Pacific Coast League, then launched a broadcasting career. Since 1962, he has done play-by-play for the Mets. In 1975 Kiner was named to Baseball's Hall of Fame. /(ME)

Clyde King — 1925- . RHP 1944-45, 47-48, 51-53 **Dodgers**, Reds 496 ip, 32-25, 4.14.
Manager 1969-70, 1974-75, 82 **Giants**, Braves, Yankees 235-231, .504

King was a righthanded reliever who started only 21 of the 200 games in which he appeared. He was the star of the Dodger bullpen in 1951, going 14-7 with six saves and leading the NL in relief wins (13). King managed three major league teams: the Giants in 1969-1970, the Braves in 1974-1975, and the Yankees in 1982. His best managerial record was 90-72 with the Giants in 1969, good for second place in the AL West. After his dismissal as Yankees manager, he remained part of owner George Steinbrenner's brain trust through the 1980s. /(JJM)

Eric King — 1964- . RHP 1986- **Tigers**, White Sox 482 ip, 30-24, 3.79. *1 LCS, 5 ip, 0-0, 1.69*

Acquired from the Giants in a six-man 1985 trade, King was Tiger Rookie of the Year in 1986 when he replaced injured starter Dan Petry and went 11-4 (6-0 at Tiger Stadium). He moved to the bullpen when Petry returned in 1987, saving nine games for Detroit's AL East Champions. Traded to the White Sox for 1989, he returned to starting and was 9-10 with a 3.39 ERA. /(JCA)

Hal King — 1944- . C 1967-68, 70-74 Astros, **Braves**, Rangers, Reds 322 g, .214, 24 hr, 82 rbi. *1 LCS, 3 g, .500*

Never a regular, King saw the most action when he platooned with Bob Tillman in 1970. King had career highs in batting (.260), HR (11), and RBI (30) that year. Over the course of his career, he struck out more often than he got a hit. /(WOR)

Jim King — 1932- . OF 1955-58, 61-67 Cubs, Cardinals, Giants, **Senators**, White Sox, Indians 1125 g, .240, 117 hr, 401 rbi

A steady, strong-armed right fielder for a decade, the lefthanded-hitting King had home run power, though he seldom topped .250 in batting average. He had personal highs of 24 HR and 62 RBI for the 1963 Senators. /(BC)

Joe King — 1909-1979. *Writer.*

A sportswriter and columnist ("Clouting 'Em") for 40 years with the New York *Telegram* and its successors, King left in 1969 to become an assistant managing editor in Ridgewood, New Jersey. A longtime correspondent for *The Sporting News*, he wrote eleven books, including *Batboy of the Giants*. /(NLM)

Lee King — 1892-1967. OF 1916-22 Pirates, **Giants**, Phillies 411 g, .247, 15 hr, 144 rbi. *1 WS, 2 g, 1.000, 1 rbi*

John McGraw waived King, a substitute outfielder, to the Phillies in 1921 but reacquired him in 1922. As a late-inning replacement in the final game of the '22 WS, King singled home the insurance run that wrapped up a 5-3 win and a four-game sweep for the Giants over the Yankees. /(JK)

Nellie King — 1928- . RHP 1954-57 **Pirates** 173 ip, 7-5, 3.58

The 6'6" King displayed uncanny control in the minors. He was effective out of the Pirate bullpen before a sore arm forced an early retirement. /(JL)

Silver King [born Charles Frederick Koenig] — 1868-1938. RHP 1886-93, 96-97 Kansas City (NL), **St. Louis (AA)**, Chicago (PL), Pirates, Giants, Reds, Washington (NL) 3191 ip, 206-152, 3.18. 20 wins: 87-90, 92
☛ *Led League—w 88, 90. Led League—era 88, 90.*

Before he was twenty-one, King had helped pitch St. Louis to two AA pennants (1887 and 1888) and recorded the first two of four consecutive seasons in which he would win more than 30 games. His finest—and busiest—year was 1888, when he led the AA with personal bests in complete games (64), innings pitched (586), wins (45), shutouts (6), and ERA (1.64). His 258 strikeouts in 1888, also a personal high, were second best in the AA.

This fastball pitcher played as Silver King: "King" from the translation of the German, "Koenig;" "Silver" for a thatch of hair that resembled burnished silver. Wide-shouldered, with long, pow-

Silver King with Chicago of the Players' League

erful arms and tremendous hands, King is credited with being the first to use a sidearm delivery. He mixed fastballs, curves, and changes, using just one motion, disdaining a windup. /(JK/FIC)

Mike Kingery — 1961- . OF 1986- Royals, **Mariners** 270 g, .256, 15 hr, 81 rbi

Six-and-a-half seasons in the minors as a non-drafted free agent earned Mike Kingery spot duty in the outfield for the 1986 Royals, and he hit safely in each of his first nine games. He was traded (with Scott Bankhead and Steve Shields) to Seattle for Danny Tartabull after the season. In 1987, his first full major league season, Kingery hit .280 and played excellent, hustling defense, leading Mariner outfielders in assists with 15. His average fell off to .203 in 1988, however, and a crowd of young, talented, Seattle outfielders pushed him back to the minors. /(TF)

Brian Kingman — 1954- . RHP 1979–83 **A's**, Giants 551 ip, 23–45, 4.13. *1 LCS, 0.1 ip, 0–0, 81.00*

Despite Kingman's leading the AL in losses in 1980 with his 8–20 mark for Oakland, his 3.84 ERA showed enough capability to keep him in the majors. But he was a combined 7–18 in 1981–82, his last full seasons. /(BC)

Dave Kingman (Kong, Sky, Big Bird) — 1948- . OF-1B-3B-DH 1971–86 Giants, **Mets**, Padres, Angels, Yankees, Cubs, A's 1941 g, .236, 442 hr, 1210 rbi. *1 LCS, 4 g, .111*
☛ *Led League—hr 79, 82. All-Star—76, 79–80.*

Kingman could hit baseballs great distances, but disdained defense, the fans, and sportswriters—female writers in particular. He was a pitcher at USC before coach Rod Dedeaux converted him to the outfield. He played mostly third base and first base with the Giants, pitching in a couple of games, played outfield and first base with the Mets and Cubs, and became a DH in the American League.

Kong's tremendous home runs (he retired 20th on the all-time list) and sweeping strikeouts (he led the NL three times), after which he'd sometimes fall in a 6'6" tangle of arms and legs, brought him unwanted attention. People admired his strength, laughed at his awkwardness. In 1979 he tied a ML record for HR in two consecutive games (five), and most times hitting three or more HR in a game in one season (two). On the other hand, in 1982 he tied a ML record by striking out five times in a nine-inning game.

Kingman was a smart and, at one time, fast baserunner, and he had a lightning-quick swing with a home run uppercut. He shortened his stroke while with the Cubs in 1979 (in the "friendly confines" of Wrigley Field) and set career marks in batting average (.288) and home runs (a league-high 48). He led the NL in HR with 37 for the 1982 Mets but batted just .204. His average dropped to .198 in 1983; with Oakland in 1984, his 35 homers, career-high 118 RBI, and .268 average won him AL Comeback Player of the Year honors. Kingman's unpredictable, often antisocial behavior and one-dimensional game got him traded often; he tied a modern record by playing with four different clubs during the 1977 season. While with Oakland in 1985, he sent a rat to a female sportswriter. In 1986, though he had just come off a 35-HR season, the free agent found no takers. /(KT)

Dennis Kinney — 1952- . LHP 1978-82 Indians, **Padres**, Tigers, A's 155 ip, 4-9, 4.53

In 1980, his only full major league season, Kinney relieved in 50 games for the Padres, recording his four career wins. /(BC)

Walt Kinney — 1893-1971. LHP 1918-20, 23 Red Sox, **A's** 291 ip, 11-20, 3.59

Kinney had poor control and went 9-15 while walking 91 in 202 innings in his most active season, 1919 with the Athletics. /(JFC)

Richard Kinsella (Sinister Dick) — 1862-1939. *Scout.*

Never a player, Kinsella was a Springfield, Illinois businessman and a powerful local Democrat. He was friends with Giants manager John McGraw and steered Fred Merkle, Rube Marquard, and Ross Youngs to New York. /(FVP)

W.P. Kinsella — Unk.- . *Writer.*

A Canadian English professor at the University of Calgary, Kinsella's baseball fiction includes *Shoeless Joe* (1982), and *The Iowa Baseball Confederacy* (1985), fantasies that show imagination and a fan's love for the game. *Shoeless Joe* was the basis for the hit movie *Field of Dreams* (1989). /(NLM)

Sachio Kinugasa — 1947- . 3B 1964- **Hiroshima Toyo Carp**

Kinugasa made headlines wherever people follow baseball on June 13, 1987 when he played in his 2,131st consecutive game to break the record held for 48 years by New York Yankees great Lou Gehrig. A few weeks later, Kinugasa became the third Japanese player to crack 500 career home runs, following Sadaharu Oh and Katsuya Nomura. At long last he became a fan favorite, overcoming years of abuse endured because his father was a black American soldier. Kinugasa struck out often, in contrast to most Japanese players, and did not hit for a high average. Some typical Kinugasa seasons were 30 HR, 72 RBI, and .271 for Hiroshima's 1979 pennant winners, and 20 HR, 57 RBI, and .278 for the 1981 winners. /(MC)

Fred Kipp — 1931- . LHP 1957-60 **Dodgers**, Yankees 113 ip, 6-7, 5.08

Kipp's only full year was 1958, when he appeared in 40 games for the Dodgers, 31 in relief, and went 6-6 with a 5.01 ERA. /(BC)

Bob Kipper — 1964- . LHP 1985- Angels, **Pirates** 401 ip, 17-30, 4.49

Born with spondylitis (inflamation of the vertebrae), Kipper was California's first choice in the June 1982 draft. The youthful-looking, inconsistent lefthander was California League Pitcher of the Year in 1984 and jumped up to the Angels in 1985. He suffered from shoulder trouble in 1986. /(ME)

Clay Kirby — 1948- . RHP 1969-76 **Padres**, Reds, Expos 1549 ip, 75-104, 3.83

Saddled with little support at San Diego, Kirby lost 20 games (the league high) as a rookie in 1969, and 18 in 1973, but registered a fine 15-13 (231 strikeouts) with the last-place Padres in 1971. He was 12-9 and 10-6 with the heavy-hitting Reds in 1974 and 1975.

On July 21, 1970 manager Preston Gomez of the Padres pinch hit for Kirby in the eighth inning of a game against the Mets in which he had not allowed a hit, but was losing 1-0. On September 4, 1974 Kirby was in the Reds' dugout when the Astros' Don Wilson was losing a no-hitter 2-1 after eight innings. Kirby's teammate Don Gullett asked what the odds were that Gomez, managing the Astros, would pinch hit for Wilson; Kirby replied, "I guarantee he will." He was right. /(BC)

Jay Kirke [Judson Fabian] — 1888-1968. OF-1B-3B 1910-15, 18 Tigers, Braves, **Indians**, Giants 320 g, .301, 7 hr, 148 rbi

Kirke was legendary as an eccentric who lived for his base hits. His fearsome hitting offset his poor defense, about which he was unconcerned. The despair of four ML teams who tried to fit him into their lineups, Kirke collected over 3,000 hits in his 1906-35 minor league career. /(JK)

Willie Kirkland (Boom Boom) — 1934- . OF 1958-66 **Giants**, **Indians**, Orioles, Senators 1149 g, .240, 148 hr, 509 rbi

Though he possessed power, a strong arm, and defensive skill, Kirkland never fully capitalized on his talent. A starting outfielder for three years with both the Giants (1958-60) and the Indians (1961-63), the lefthanded slugger amassed 91 HR in 1959-62. In 1961 he hit three straight homers on July 9 off Chicago's Cal McLish (all on two-strike pitches), then walked and sacrificed in two more plate appearances. Following the All-Star break, he homered in his first official at-bat against the Twins, tying the major league record with four consecutive home runs. That season Kirkland led the Indians with 27 HR and 95 RBI and tied for the AL lead in double plays by an outfielder. He had led NL outfielders in double plays in 1958. Kirkland later played in Japan, hitting .241 with 126 HR for Hanshin, 1968–73. Unlike many former ML players in Japan, Kirkland adjusted well, learning to speak Japanese, and married a Japanese woman. /(ME)

Ed Kirkpatrick (Spanky) — 1944– . OF-C-1B 1962–77 Angels, **Royals**, Pirates, Rangers, Brewers 1311 g, .238, 85 hr, 424 rbi. *2 LCS, 5 g, .000*

Popular Ed Kirkpatrick earned his keep with versatility and occasional power. Debuting at age seventeen, he spent seven years up and down with the Angels before he was traded in 1968 to Kansas City, where he played more or less regularly for five seasons. Most productive in his first two years with the Royals, he had 14 HR in 1969. As Kansas City's regular catcher (a position he preferred not to play) in 1970, he hit 18 HR with 62 RBI. A 1981 car accident left Kirkpatrick in a wheelchair. /(BC)

Don Kirkwood — 1950– . RHP 1974–78 **Angels**, White Sox, Blue Jays 374 ip, 18–23, 4.37

Twins Don and Ron Kirkwood signed with the Angels in 1972, but only Don reached the majors. He was 6–5 with seven saves as a rookie in 1975, his best year. Arm trouble ended his career prematurely. /(MC)

Bruce Kison (Buster) — 1950– . RHP 1971–85 **Pirates**, Angels, Red Sox 1809 ip, 115–88, 3.66. *5 LCS, 29 ip, 4–0, 1.21 2 WS, 6 ip, 1–1, 5.40*

Slender, 6'4", baby-faced Bruce Kison gained quick notoriety in Game Four of the 1971 World Series, the first night game in Series history. The rookie Pirate relieved Luke Walker in the first inning with two out and three runs in. He hit a Series record three batters but allowed the Orioles only one hit in 6-1/3 innings to win 4–3. The injury-prone pitcher became known both for brushback pitches and quality stretch-run performances. He tied a record with four wins in LCS play. /(ME)

Frank Kitson — 1872–1930. LHP 1898–1907 Baltimore (NL), **Dodgers**, Tigers, Senators, Yankees 2215 ip, 128–118, 3.17. 20 wins: 99

Kitson was a top lefthander at the turn of the century, winning 22 games for Baltimore in 1899 and 19 for Brooklyn in both 1901 and 1902. He jumped to the AL in 1903 but was less successful.

Friends blamed overwork; from 1899 through 1903 he never pitched fewer than 253 innings. /(BC)

Ron Kittle — 1958– . OF-DH 1982– **White Sox**, Yankees, Indians 721 g, .241, 156 hr, 407 rbi. *1 LCS, 3 g, .286*
☛ *Rookie of the Year—83. All-Star—83.*

This strongboy from nearby Gary, Indiana, was an instant hit in Chicago. Kittle had been released by the Dodger organization after a spinal fusion operation in 1978 and was working in iron construction when invited to Comiskey Park for a tryout. His combined output for two minor league seasons, 1981 and 1982, was 90 homers. As the White Sox left fielder in 1983, he batted .254 with 35 HR and 100 RBI, combining with Greg Luzinski to form the most potent HR duo in club history. He played in the All-Star Game and the LCS, and he won AL Rookie of the Year honors. But he also struck out a league-high 150 times. In 1984 his average dropped to .215, and his 32 HR did not compensate for his failure to advance runners and hit in the clutch. He was hampered by a shoulder injury in 1985 and was batting .213 in 1986 when he was traded to the Yankees. He hit 12 HR in 159 at-bats in 1987, spent 40 days on the disabled list, and was released. The Indians picked him up in 1988, and he returned to the White Sox for 1989 but spent much of the season on the DL after a good start. /(RL)

Malachi Kittredge — 1869–1928. C 1890–99, 1901–06 **Cubs**, Louisville (NL), Washington (NL), Braves, Senators, Indians 1215 g, .219, 17 hr, 390 rbi

Kittredge caught for the Chicago NL team through most of the 1890s. Although he was a poor hitter, he was steady and reliable behind the plate and an accurate thrower. In 1904 he was made manager of the hapless Washington Senators, but after the team led off the season at 1–16, he relinquished the reins to Patsy Donovan. /(BC)

Billy Klaus — 1928– . SS-3B 1952–53, 55–63 Braves, **Red Sox**, Orioles, Senators, Phillies 821 g, .249, 40 hr, 250 rbi

After seven years in the minors, Klaus hit a career-high .283 with 7 HR as the Red Sox' rookie shortstop in 1955. His brother Bobby played briefly with the Reds and Giants. /(JK)

Bobby Klaus — 1937– . 2B-3B-SS 1964–65 Reds, **Mets** 215 g, .208, 6 hr, 29 rbi

The younger brother of Billy Klaus briefly replaced Pete Rose at second base for the Reds in 1964. A utility infielder good at turning the double play, he hit .244 as a Met later that season, but just .191 in 119 games the next. /(KT)

Chuck Klein — 1904-1958. OF 1928-44 **Phillies**, Cubs, Pirates 1753 g, .320, 300 hr, 1201 rbi. *1 WS, 5 g, .333, 1 hr, 2 rbi*
☛ *Most Valuable Player—32. Led League—ba 33. Led League—hr 29, 31-33. Led League—rbi 31, 33. All-Star—33-34. Hall of Fame—1980.*

One of the most prodigious sluggers of the late 1920s and early 1930s, Chuck Klein was a star from the day he joined the Phillies in July 1928. The short right-field fence at Baker Bowl (280 feet) contributed

Chuck Klein

to the lefthanded-hitting Klein's slugging records and high batting average. He collected more than 200 hits for five straight seasons (1929–33), leading the NL the last two. With 250 hits in 1930, he batted .386 but still finished third in the league behind Bill Terry (.401) and Babe Herman (.393). It was a hitter's year, but Klein's average was 83 points above the league mark.

Klein led the league in total bases for four consecutive years (1930–33), leading in doubles in two of them and HR in three. He led in runs scored three straight years, powered six HR in four straight games in 1929, and twice hit five in three games. Unlike most sluggers, he was a competent baserunner, topping the circuit in 1932 with 20 steals and hitting 15 triples. His league-leading numbers of outfield assists in 1930 (44, a modern NL record), 1932, and 1933 were largely a product of his skill at fielding the strange caroms off the corrugated tin wall at Baker Bowl.

The NL MVP in 1932, Klein won the Triple Crown in 1933 (28 HR, 120 RBI, .368), though Carl Hubbell took MVP honors. During his first six years, Klein hit 191 HR and collected 1,209 hits, 699 runs, and 727 RBI. Traded to the Cubs for the 1934 season, Klein was a disappointment in Chicago by his previous standards. Many Baker Bowl home runs turned into long outs at Wrigley Field. Even so, he hit 20 and 21 HR in two seasons and batted .301 and .293. The Phillies reacquired him in May 1936, and Klein had his greatest game when he smashed four homers in a 10-inning contest on July 10. Klein was elected to the Hall of Fame by the Veterans Committee in 1980. /(AA)

Lou Klein — 1918-1976. 2B-SS 1943, 45-46, 49, 51 **Cardinals**, Indians, A's 305 g, .259, 16 hr, 101 rbi. *1 WS, 5 g, .136.*
*Manager 1961-62, 65 **Cubs** 65-83, .439*

Klein unexpectedly fought his way into the Cardinal lineup in 1943, playing every inning of every game, batting .287. After losing almost two years to WWII, he returned to lose second base in a three-way battle with Red Schoendienst and Emil Verban. Disgusted, he jumped to the Mexican League, was barred from organized baseball, and later signed to play in the outlaw Quebec Provincial League. Before playing an inning in Canada, he was reinstated in 1949 and became the first jumper to return to the big leagues. But he still couldn't beat Schoendienst out of a job. Klein was one of the Cubs' "College of Coaches," managing in 1961–62, and again, by himself, for most of 1965./(MC)

Ted Kleinhans — 1899–1985. LHP 1934, 36–38 Phillies, **Reds**, Yankees 143 ip, 4–9, 5.27

After a career spent largely in the minors, Kleinhans found his niche in baseball as the coach for Syracuse, his alma mater, and later was that city's commissioner of parks and recreation./(JK)

Red Kleinow [John Peter] — 1879–1929. C 1904–11 **Yankees**, Red Sox, Phillies 584 g, .213, 3 hr, 135 rbi

In 1904 the Highlanders (later the Yankees) came within one pitch of winning their first pennant. Forty-one-game winner Jack Chesbro sailed a spitball well over Kleinow's head which was ruled a wild pitch, but Kleinow took criticism for failing to catch it./(JK) R

Bill Klem (The Old Arbitrator) — 1874–1951. *Umpire 1905–40 NL 18 WS 2 ASU*
☛ *Hall of Fame—1953.*

Generally regarded as the greatest umpire in the game's history, Klem umpired exclusively behind the plate his first 16 years because of his acknowledged superiority in calling balls and strikes. As a plate umpire, he pioneered the inside chest protector. Until Klem, all plate umpires wore the outside protector, commonly called the "balloon." Klem said the inside protector gave him a better look at the pitch because he could move in closer behind the catcher. He took a catcher's protector, added shoulder pads, and wore it under his shirt instead of outside. Since he was the dean of NL umpires, the senior circuit adopted the inside protector years before the AL.

Klem worked a record 18 WS, a total of 104 games, including five straight assignments from 1911 to 1915. His first WS was 1908 (Cubs-Tigers) and his last 1940 (Reds-Tigers). Klem also umpired the first All-Star Game in 1933. In 36 years, he was behind the plate for five no-hitters, the last being Paul Dean's over Brooklyn (9/21/34). He even officiated a race around the bases between Hans Lobert and a horse in 1914 at Oxnard, California. He declared the horse the winner by a nose.

Among the many memorable games Klem umpired was Opening Day at the Polo Grounds in 1907. A winter storm left piles of snow around the field. In the eighth inning, with New York leading the Phillies 3–0, spectators began bombarding the visting Phillies, umpires, and each other with snow-

Bill Klem

balls. Klem forfeited the game to Philadelphia because it was up to the home team to keep order.

He could be stubborn. He reportedly once started to call a runner out at the plate, then signaled safe when a ball rolled loose. The catcher showed him he still held the ball; the loose ball had apparently fallen from one of Klem's pockets. He refused to change his call.

He adored the nickname The Old Arbitrator but despised being called Catfish. In Lawrence Ritter's *The Glory of Their Times*, Chief Meyers said, "All you had to do was call him Catfish and out of the game you'd go. Maybe it was because he had rather prominent lips, and when he'd call a ball or a strike he'd let fly a rather fine spray from his mouth. Sort of gave the general impression of a catfish, you know."

Early in Klem's career, Giants manager John

McGraw threatened to get him fired. Klem replied: "Mr. Manager, if it's possible for you to take my job away from me, I don't want it." His integrity helped secure the reputation of umpires as honest and impartial. He brought dignity to the game, along with competence and pride. Shortly before he died, he described the last game he ever worked. "I walked away from the beefing ballplayer, saying to myself, 'I'm almost certain Herman tagged him.' Then it came to me and I almost wept. For the first time in my career, I only 'thought' a man was tagged." Klem retired that afternoon.

He always maintained, "I never called one wrong," though in later years he would place his hand over his heart and add, "from here." After his retirement, he served as Chief of NL Umpires until his death. Klem was elected to the Hall of Fame in 1953./(RTM)

Ed Klepfer (Big Ed) — 1888-1950. RHP 1911, 13, 15-17, 19 Yankees, White Sox, **Indians** 448 ip, 22-17, 2.81

Spitballer Klepfer went to Cleveland in the 1915 deal that sent Joe Jackson to Chicago and was 14-4, 2.37 with the 1917 Indians. He spent 1918 in the military and apparently lost his stuff afterward. His career .048 batting average is the second-worst ever for a pitcher with at least 100 at-bats./(ME)

Eddie Klieman (Babe) — 1918-1979. RHP 1943-50 **Indians**, Senators, White Sox, A's 542 ip, 26-28, 3.49. *1 WS, 0 ip, 0-0, infinite*

Klieman pitched well despite fits of wildness as a part-time starter for Cleveland in 1944-45, but he was gradually forced to the bullpen, and then the minors, by veterans returning from WWII. He came back in 1947 to lead the AL with 17 saves and 58 appearances and posted a 2.60 ERA for the 1948 World Champion Indians./(MC)

Lou Klimchock — 1939- . 3B-2B-1B A's, Braves, Senators, Mets, **Indians** 318 g, .232, 13 hr, 69 rbi

Klimchock won two minor league batting titles, but his indifferent defense kept him on the bench in the ML. In 1969 with the Indians, he hit .287 in a career-high 90 games./(JCA)

Ron Klimkowski — 1945- . RHP 1969-72 **Yankees**, A's 188 ip, 8-12, 2.92

After leading the International League with 15 wins and a 2.18 ERA in 1969, the junkball specialist pitched in 45 games for the Yankees in 1970, mostly in middle relief, going 6-7 (2.66)./(JCA)

Bob Kline (Junior) — 1909- . RHP 1930-34 **Red Sox**, A's, Senators 441 ip, 30-28, 5.05

Alternating a fastball with a sinker he learned from roommate Wilcy Moore, Kline won 11 games for the hapless 1932 Red Sox. In 1934, he led the AL in relief wins (7) despite a 7.21 ERA./(JK)

Ron Kline — 1932- . RHP 1952, 55-70 Pirates, Cardinals, Angels, Tigers, **Senators**, Twins, Giants, Red Sox, Braves 2077 ip, 114-144, 3.75

A starter the first half of his career, Kline was converted to relief and collected 108 saves. As a Pirate starter, his 18 losses in 1956 and 16 in 1958 were NL highs. In 1965 he led the AL with 29 saves and was second with 74 appearances, giving him the single-season Senator club records for saves, games pitched, and games finished. Returning to the Pirates in 1968, Kline had 12 relief wins (10 in succession) to lead the NL.

Kline had one of the most peculiar pitching rituals in baseball, touching his cap, belt, and shirt before each pitch. One of the poorer-hitting pitchers in the game, Kline managed only a lifetime .092 average./(JLE)

Steve Kline — 1947- . RHP 1970-74, 77 **Yankees**, Indians, Braves 749 ip, 43-45, 3.27

Kline, a control pitcher, had a banner year in 1972, going 16-9 for the Yankees with a 2.40 ERA. After injuring his arm the next year, he went to Cleveland in the 1974 deal that brought Chris Chambliss to the Yankees./(JCA)

Johnny Kling (Noisy) — 1875-1947. C 1900-08, 10-13 **Cubs**, Braves, Reds 1260 g, .272, 20 hr, 513 rbi. *4 WS, 21 g, .185, 3 rbi.* *Manager* 1912 **Braves** 52-101, .340

The catcher of Frank Chance's great Cub teams of 1906-10, Kling was the NL's premier defensive catcher and a capable hitter. Batterymate Ed Reulbach called him "one of the greatest catchers who ever wore a mask." In the years 1902-08, Kling led the league in fielding four times, putouts six, assists twice, and double plays once. On June 21, 1907, he threw out all four Cardinal runners who attempted to steal second base. In the WS that fall, Kling nabbed seven Tigers in 14 tries, with Ty Cobb unable to steal a single base. In the winter of 1908-09, Kling won the world pocket billiard championship and decided to forsake the baseball diamond for the pool table. Defeated in his attempt to retain the title, he rejoined the Cubs in 1910 but

Johnny Kling

was a part-timer thereafter. His brother Bill pitched briefly in the NL during the 1890s./(ARA)

Bob Klinger — 1908-1977. RHP 1938-43, 46-47 **Pirates**, Red Sox 1090 ip, 66-61, 3.68. *1 WS, 0.2 ip, 0-1, 13.50*

The Pirates' leading winner in 1939, when he went 14-17 and led the NL in losses, Klinger returned from WWII Navy duty to lead the AL with nine saves for the 1946 Red Sox. He was the pitcher

when Enos Slaughter made his fabled mad dash home to win Game Seven of the '46 WS./(ME)

Johnny Klippstein — 1927- . RHP 1950-67 **Cubs**, Reds, Dodgers, Indians, Senators, Phillies, Twins, Tigers 1967 ip, 101-118, 4.24. *2 WS, 5 ip, 0-0, 0.00*

Klippstein was sometimes called "the wild man of Borneo" because of his frequent control troubles. The journeyman was used in both starting and relief assignments in his early days, but in 1958 was made almost exclusively a reliever by Dodger manager Walter Alston. Though he never won more than 12 games in a season, there was always a team willing to take him. With the Indians for one season, he had a league-leading 14 saves in 1960. Five years later, teaming in the Minnesota bullpen with ace Al Worthington, Klippstein went 9-3 with five saves to help the Twins to their first pennant. He finished with 66 career saves. He is the son-in-law of former pitcher Emil "Dutch" Leonard./(ARA)

Fred Klobedanz — 1871-1940. LHP 1896-99, 1902 **Braves** 702 ip, 53-25, 4.12. 20 wins: 97

Although Boston fans said Klobedanz "was as hard to hit as he was to pronounce," he profited from the fact that the 1897-98 NL-champion Braves had by far the league's best run-scoring machine. In 1897 he went 26-7 and led the NL in winning percentage. The next year he was 19-10. But in both seasons, his ERA was higher than the league average, he gave up more hits than innings pitched, and he walked many more than he struck out. When the Braves' hitters tailed off in 1899, he ceased to win./(BC)

Ted Kluszewski (Klu) — 1924-1988. 1B 1947-61 **Reds**, Pirates, White Sox, Angels 1718 g, .298, 279 hr, 1028 rbi. *1 WS, 6 g, .391, 3 hr, 10 rbi*
☛ *Led League—hr 54. Led League—rbi 54. All-Star—53-56.*

The sleeveless Cincinnati uniforms of the 1950s were made to allow Kluszewski's bulging muscles room to move, but he was more than a slugger. The former University of Indiana football star hit with marked consistency and awesome power and fielded his position smoothly. He led the NL with 49 homers and 141 RBI in 1954 and averaged 43 HRs and 116 RBIs from 1953 to 1956. He also hit .300 seven times. In 1955 he led in hits (192) and set a modern NL record by scoring runs in 17 straight games. Starting in 1951, he topped NL first basemen in fielding five straight years, a ML record. Injuries eventually cut into his skills, and he spent his last

Ted Kluszewski

five seasons pinch-hitting nearly as often as he started, but with the White Sox in the six-game 1959 WS, he banged three homers and drove in 10 runs. /(ME)

Mickey Klutts [Gene Ellis] — 1954– . 3B-SS-2B 1976–83 Yankees, **A's**, Blue Jays 199 g, .241, 14 hr, 59 rbi. *1 LCS, 3 g, .429*

Klutts was disabled at least ten times; he suffered one injury when he ran into a tarp. In 1981 with Oakland, the round-faced infielder hit five homers in just 15 games. /(JCA)

Clyde Kluttz — 1917–1979. C 1942–48, 51–52 **Braves**, Giants, Cardinals, Pirates, Browns, Senators 656 g, .268, 19 hr, 212 rbi

A journeyman ML catcher for nine seasons, Kluttz spent 42 years in professional baseball. As a scout for the Yankees, he convinced free agent Catfish Hunter to sign with New York. Later, Kluttz served as Baltimore's Director of Player Development. /(JCA)

Otto Knabe [Franz Otto] (Dutch) — 1884–1961. 2B 1905, 07–16 Pirates, **Phillies**, Baltimore (FL), Cubs 1285 g, .247, 8 hr, 364 rbi.
    Manager 1914–15 **Baltimore (FL)** 131–177, .425

With Knabe on one side of second base and shortstop Mickey Doolan on the other, opposing baserunners entered this territory at considerable physical risk. The roughhousing second baseman jumped the Phillies to become a player-manager in the Federal League. /(JL)

Chris Knapp [Robert Christian] — 1953– . RHP 1975–80 White Sox, **Angels** 603 ip, 36–32, 5.00. *1 LCS, 2 ip, 0–1, 7.71*

Knapp was 12–7 after his promotion to the White Sox in 1977, then was traded to the Angels. He jumped the club for three weeks in mid-1978 over a contract dispute but finished 14–8. Knapp slipped on a wet Yankee Stadium mound in May 1979, rupturing a disc, and was through after a 2–11 record in 1980. /(MC)

Bob Knepper — 1954– . LHP 1976– Giants, **Astros** 2663 ip, 143–152, 3.64. *1 LCS, 15 ip, 0–0, 3.52* ☛ *All-Star—81.*

Knepper stepped into San Francisco's starting rotation, replacing injured John Montefusco, in 1977. The following year, Knepper led NL lefthanders in ERA, led the entire league in shutouts, and won a career-high 17 games. Two straight off-years resulted in a trade to Houston for Enos Cabell, where Knepper became the winningest lefthander in Astros history. He was the NL Comeback Player of the Year in 1981 (9–5, 2.18), finishing second to Nolan Ryan in the ERA race. From 1984 to 1986 Knepper was one of the NL's best lefties. His 17 wins in 1986 tied the Houston record for lefthanders. He also tied teammate Mike Scott for the league lead with five shutouts. Knepper took leads to the ninth inning in Games Three and Six of the 1986 LCS, but New York rallied to win both, and the series. Knepper dipped to a league-high 17 losses in 1987, but in 1988 a great start propelled him to a 14–5, 3.14 record. He returned to the Giants in 1989 after a terrible start and finished 7–12, 5.13. /(ME)

Lou Knerr [Wallace Luther] — 1921–1980. RHP 1945–47 **A's**, Senators 287 ip, 8–27, 5.04

Knerr managed records of only 5–11 and 3–16 in his two years with the Athletics; in 1946 he was one of three last-place A's pitchers to lose a league-high 16. He finished his career in 1949 in the outlaw Quebec Provincial League, filling in for Mexican League jumpers who had returned to the majors after their suspensions were lifted in mid-season. /(MC)

Elmer Knetzer (Baron) — 1885–1975. RHP 1909–12, 14–17 **Dodgers**, Pittsburgh (FL), Braves, Reds 1267 ip, 68–69, 3.15

Knetzer played a long time as a journeyman pitcher, compiling his best record with the Pittsburgh Federal League club in 1914 (19–11) after missing the entire 1913 season as a holdout. He continued pitching after leaving the majors and finished his career with Springfield of the Mid-Atlantic League in 1934 at the age of forty-nine. /(MA)

Bill Knickerbocker (Knick) — 1911–1963. SS-2B 1933–42 **Indians**, Browns, Yankees, White Sox, A's 907 g, .276, 28 hr, 368 rbi

Knickerbocker was Cleveland's regular shortstop from 1934–36, and though he hit well (.317 in '34), he had difficulties in the field. /(RL)

Jack Knight [Elmer Russell] — 1895–1976. RHP 1922, 25–27 Cardinals, **Phillies**, Braves 255 ip, 10–18, 6.85

On a personal eight-game losing streak in his last full ML season, Knight came on in relief against the Giants on June 24, 1926. He hit his only two career homers, in innings five and six, but Philadelphia still lost to New York 12–7. /(AL)

John Knight (Schoolboy) — 1885–1965. SS-3B-1B-2B 1905–07, 09–13 A's, Red Sox, **Yankees**, Senators 767 g, .239, 14 hr, 270 rbi

Signed out of high school, this native of Philadelphia was nineteen when he found himself in the Athletics' 1905 Opening Day lineup because shortstop Monte Cross broke a hand. Knight was hitting .400 in mid-June but finished the season at .203. Eager to win a pennant in 1907, Connie Mack traded Knight to the Red Sox for veteran third baseman Jimmy Collins. Mack later said Knight was the only young player he ever regretted letting go. /(NLM)

Ray Knight — 1952– . 3B-1B 1974, 77–88 **Reds**, Astros, Mets, Orioles, Tigers 1495 g, .271, 84 hr, 595 rbi. *2 LCS, 9 g, .211, 2 rbi. 1 WS, 7 g, .391, 1 hr, 5 rbi* ☛ *All-Star—80, 82.*

The man who replaced Pete Rose as Cincinnati's third baseman in 1979 later became the first World Series MVP to join a new team the next season. After three seasons at Cincinnati, Knight was traded to Houston, making way for another Cincinnati legend, Johnny Bench. Knight saw extensive duty at first base for the Astros before going to the Mets, for

three minor leaguers, in 1984. After a poor 1985 season, New York coach Bill Robinson changed Knight's batting stance from a crouching to a straight-up position. Ray earned Comeback Player of the Year honors for his 1986 season (.298, 11 HR, 76 RBI) while platooning with Howard Johnson. Knight hit the decisive homer in the Game Seven of the World Series after scoring the winning run in Game Six on Mookie Wilson's grounder through Bill Buckner's legs. Knight had nearly been the goat of Game Six for his fielding miscues, but the Mets' win wiped that out. Following a contract dispute, Knight went to Baltimore as a free agent in 1987, allowing Johnson to emerge as a star on the Mets. Knight is married to golf star Nancy Lopez, and caddied for her briefly after his retirement. /(ME)

Bobby Knoop — 1938– . 2B-3B 1964–72 **Angels**, White Sox, Royals 1153 g, .236, 56 hr, 331 rbi ☛ *All-Star—66. Gold Glove—66–68.*

A superlative second baseman, Knoop (pronounced "Kuh-NOP") won three Gold Gloves and was voted the Angels' Owner's Trophy for "inspirational leadership, sportsmanship and professional ability" four times. Called "the Nureyev of second base" by sportswriters, the acrobatic introvert established an AL second base record with 12 putouts in a nine-inning game (8/60/66). Knoop and his roommate, shortstop Jim Fregosi, turned an AL-record six double plays in a May 1, 1966 game. Usually a poor hitter, he hit 17 home runs in 1966, including a home run and double in the same inning (April 30). He became an Angel coach in 1979. /(JCA)

Jack Knott [John Henry] — 1907–1981. RHP 1933–42, 46 **Browns**, White Sox, A's 1557 ip, 82–103, 4.97

In eleven ML seasons, Knott only once pitched for a team that reached the first division, the fourth-place White Sox of 1939. Playing during a high-scoring era, he never finished with an ERA under 4.15 but still produced winning records in five seasons. /(JK)

Darold Knowles — 1941– . LHP 1965–80 Orioles, Phillies, **Senators**, A's, Cubs, Rangers, Expos, Cardinals 1092 ip, 66–74, 3.12. *1 LCS, 1/3 ip, 0–0, 0.00. 1 WS, 6 ip, 0–0, 0.00* ☛ *All-Star—69.*

The fast-working reliever earned 143 career saves. In his rookie year, while Knowles was saving 13 for the Phillies, manager Gene Mauch said, "He's got the courage of a daylight burglar." Pitching for the last-place Senators in 1970, he lost a ML-record 14 in relief yet saved 27 with a 2.04 ERA. In 54 games with Oakland in 1972 he registered a superb 1.36 ERA. He became the only pitcher ever to appear in all seven games of a World Series, saving two in Oakland's victory over the Mets in 1973. On his retirement, he was tied for 13th in career saves. /(JCA)

Mark Knudson — 1960- . RHP 1985- Astros, **Brewers** 273 ip, 13–17, 4.32

Despite unimpressive minor league credentials, Knudson pitched in the ML briefly each season from 1985 to 1988, and 1989 was the first time he began the season on a ML roster. He was 11–8, 3.40 with Denver (American Association) in '88. /(ME)

Kevin Kobel — 1953- . LHP 1973–74, 76, 78–80 Brewers, **Mets** 475 ip, 18–34, 3.88

Kobel debuted with Milwaukee before his 20th birthday. He pitched one full season, going 6–14 in 1974, before arm trouble forced him to the minors for most of 1975 through 1977. Given a second chance by the Mets, he pitched respectably in 1978–79. /(JCA)

Alan Koch — 1938- . RHP 1963–64 Tigers, **Senators** 128 ip, 4–11, 5.41

A flamethrower who also swung a mean bat (.286), Koch lacked control and returned to the minors after spending most of 1964 in the Senators' starting rotation. /(MC)

Len Koenecke — 1904–1935. OF 1932, 34–35 Giants, **Dodgers** 265 g, .297, 22 hr, 114 rbi

Koenecke hit .320 with 14 HR for Brooklyn in 1934. Dismissed by Casey Stengel for erratic play and behavior in September 1935, Koenecke chartered a plane home. A fight broke out on board the small plane, supposedly after the drunken Koenecke made improper advances to the pilot and copilot. Koenecke was hit on the head with a fire extinguisher by the copilot and killed. /(TG)

Mark Koenig — 1902- . SS-3B-2B 1925–36 **Yankees**, Tigers, Cubs, Reds, Giants 1162 g, .279, 28 hr, 443 rbi. *5 WS, 20 g, .237, 5 rbi*

In 1926 Koenig and Tony Lazzeri became the Yankees' double play combination. Switch-hitter Koenig batted second. He had a shaky rookie year afield with a league-leading 52 errors during the season and 4 more in the 1926 World Series, one of which opened the door to the Cardinals' winning rally in Game Seven. He batted .500 in the 1927

Series, and in 1928 again led the AL in errors, but hit a career-high .319. In 1929 Leo Durocher played more games at shortstop than he did, and the following year, Koenig was traded to Detroit, where he played some short, some second, and pitched unsuccessfully. Released to the San Francisco Missions (Pacific Coast League) in 1932, he was called up by the Cubs in August when Billy Jurges was shot, hit .353 in a 33-game dash for the pennant, and was awarded an ungenerous one half Series share. The Cubs' WS opponents were his old teammates, the Yankees, who reacted hotly to this supposed mistreatment. Some accounts say that Ruth's "called shot" HR was an indirect result, with Ruth razzing Cubs pitcher Root. With Cincinnati in 1934, old-timers Koenig and Jim Bottomley refused to fly on road trips, taking the train instead. /(ADS)

Jack Kofoed — 1894–Unk. *Writer.*

Kofoed was one of America's most prolific magazine writers, contributing articles and fiction to 200 magazines. He did movie and radio writing as well. He began in 1912 with the Philadelphia *Ledger and Record*, then moved to New York, where he was a columnist for the *Post* from 1924 to 1933. He later was a feature columnist for the Miami *Herald*. /(NLM)

Dick Kokos [born Richard Jerome Kokoszka] — 1928–1986. OF 1948–50, 53–54 **Browns/ Orioles** 475 g, .263, 59 hr, 223 rbi

As a Browns rookie at twenty, Kokos showed power, but his play was erratic. In 1949 he led AL outfielders in assists and double plays, hit 23 HR, but struck out a league-high 91 times. He led the AL in errors in 1950, and was returned to the minors, reappearing as a platoon player in '53. He was able to throw from the outfield to home plate while on his knees. /(MC)

Don Kolloway (Butch, Cab, The Blue Island Flash) — 1918- . 2B-1B 1940–43, 46–53 **White Sox**, Tigers, A's 1079 g, .271, 29 hr, 393 rbi

Brought up to the White Sox in 1940, the infielder from Chicago's South Side moved into the second base spot in 1942. A line drive hitter with exceptional speed, Kolloway led the league in doubles that year and is one of only a handful of AL players to steal second, third, and home in one game (6/28/41 vs. Cleveland). /(RL)

Ray Kolp (Jockey) — 1894–1967. RHP 1921–24, 27–34 Browns, **Reds** 1688 ip, 79–95, 4.08

After a 14–4 sophomore season with the 1922 Browns, who lost the pennant to the Yankees by one game, Kolp had just one more year over .500. He was nicknamed Jockey for his ability to badger opponents with a salty tongue and loud mouth. /(ADS)

Brad Komminsk — 1961– . OF 1983–87, 89 **Braves**, Brewers, Indians 298 g, .219, 20 hr, 95 rbi

Komminsk was the Braves' greatest disappointment of the 1980s. A first-round pick in June 1979, he homered in his first pro at-bat and reached double figures in homers for four consecutive minor league seasons. But he hit just .227 with four HR in spending all of 1985 with Atlanta. The Braves gave up on him in 1987, sending him to Milwaukee for Dion James. He resurfaced with the 1989 Indians, hitting .237 but driving in 33 runs in 198 at-bats. /(JCA)

Ed Konetchy (Big Ed) — 1885–1947. 1B 1907–21 **Cardinals**, Pirates, Pittsburgh (FL), Braves, Dodgers, Phillies 2083 g, .281, 74 hr, 992 rbi. *1 WS, 7 g, .174, 2 rbi*

Konetchy began playing first base for the Cardinals in 1907, had a 20-game hitting streak in 1910, and in 1911 led the NL with 38 doubles. He was one of very few players to hit a ball out of old Robinson Field in St. Louis. Sent to the Pirates in a December 1913 trade, in 1915 he jumped to Pittsburgh of the Federal League. With the Dodgers in 1919, Konetchy became the third of eight NL players to collect a record ten consecutive hits. He also played the entire major-league-record 26-inning game in 1920 between the Dodgers and Braves. Batting over .300 four times, Konetchy compiled 100 or more hits in 14 consecutive seasons and broke up four no-hitters. After his ML days, he played with Fort Worth (Texas League) in 1922–27, batting .345 with 41 HR in 1925. /(JLE)

Doug Konieczny — 1951– . RHP 1973–75, 77 **Astros** 221 ip, 7–18, 4.93

Konieczny struck out a Southern League-leading 222 for Columbus in 1973. He was 6–13 in 1975, his only full year in the Astros' rotation, but suffered arm trouble throughout his career. /(MC)

Jim Konstanty [Casimir James] — 1917–1976. RHP 1944, 46, 48–56 Reds, Braves, **Phillies**, Yankees, Cardinals 945 ip, 66–48, 3.46. *1 WS 15 ip, 0–1, 2.40*
☛ *Most Valuable Player—50. All-Star—50.*

Ed Konetchy

Jim Konstanty

An all-around athlete from Syracuse University, Konstanty had brief trials with the Reds and Braves before finally developing a palmball and sticking with the Phillies in 1949, at age thirty-two. In 1950 he led Philadelphia to the pennant with 16 wins and 22 saves (both NL highs) in a then-record 74 appearances, all NL highs. He was the first relief pitcher to win the MVP award. After having relieved in 133 straight games for the Phillies, he started Game One of the 1950 WS and lost to the Yankees 1–0. Konstanty dropped a league-high 10 out of the bullpen in 1951, started 19 games in 1953, and saved 11 for the 1955 pennant-winning Yankees, but he never again approached the success of his MVP season. /(AL)

Ernie Koob — 1893–1941. LHP 1915–17, 19 **Browns** 500 ip, 23–30, 3.13

In 1916 Koob pitched a 17-inning scoreless tie against the Red Sox, losing a win when he failed to touch third while rounding the bases in the 15th inning. The next year, he won a 1–0 no-hitter against the White Sox. /(JK)

Cal Koonce — 1940– . RHP 1962–71 **Cubs**, Mets, Red Sox 970 ip, 47–49, 3.78

In mid-season of 1962, Cub rookie Koonce looked like a new Cy Young with a 9–1 mark. He finished the year 10–10 and never again reached double figures in wins. /(ARA)

Jerry Koosman — 1943– . LHP 1967–85 **Mets**, Twins, White Sox, Phillies 3839 ip, 222–209, 3.36. 20 wins: 76, 79 *3 LCS, 14 ip, 1–0, 6.43 2 WS, 26 ip, 3–0, 2.39*
☛ *All-Star—68–69.*

Known for his control throughout his career, Koosman led the International League in strikeouts in 1967, and in 1968 emerged as the Mets' lefthanded ace. He was NL Rookie Pitcher of the Year and

Jerry Koosman

runner-up to Johnny Bench for Rookie of the Year. He broke club records with 19 wins, seven shutouts, and a 2.08 ERA (all set by Tom Seaver the year before). All are still Met rookie records. He also fanned 62 times (in 91 at-bats), the most by a NL pitcher since 1900.

Seaver and Koosman became one of the league's top righty/lefty starting combos. As a sophomore, Koosman was 17–9 for the 1969 World Champions, and he beat Baltimore twice in the Series. He overcame arm problems in 1971 and was a hard-luck 14–15 (2.84) for the '73 pennant winners. Peaking in 1976, he recorded a 21–10 mark. But in 1977, Seaver was traded to the Reds, the Mets deteriorated, and Koosman went 8–20 to tie Phil Niekro for the league lead in losses. Koosman left the Mets as runner-up to Seaver or all-time club leader in ten pitching categories. Sent to the Twins in a December 1978 trade for Jesse Orosco, Koosman rebounded for a 20–13 record in 1979. In the strike-shortened 1981 season, his 13 losses for the Twins and White Sox were enough to tie for the AL lead. Recurring arm and shoulder trouble ended his career after two seasons with the Phillies. /(MC)

Larry Kopf [William Lorenz] — 1890–1986. SS-2B 1913–17, 19–23 Indians, A's, **Reds**, Braves 850 g, .249, 5 hr, 266 rbi. *1 WS, 8 g, .222, 2 rbi*

Kopf never hit .300 at any professional level, but on May 2, 1917 his 10th-inning single off Hippo Vaughn broke up the double no-hit duel between Vaughn and Fred Toney. Kopf came around to score the game's only run on Jim Thorpe's scratch single. Brother Wally Kopf played two games at third for the Giants. /(LRD)

Howie Koplitz — 1938– . RHP 1961–62, 64–66 Tigers, **Senators** 175 ip, 9–7, 4.21

The Tigers promoted Koplitz after his 23–3 performance with a no-hitter for Birmingham (Southern Association) in 1961. He won his first seven big league decisions, spanning 1961–65, but injured his shoulder in 1966. /(KT)

Joe Koppe [born Joseph Kopchia] — 1930– . SS-2B 1958–65 Braves, Phillies, **Angels** 578 g, .236, 19 hr, 141 rbi

In his rookie 1959 season, Koppe showed good range at shortstop and hit .261 with seven HR, seven triples, and 68 runs. They were to be career highs; he missed much of the next season with a wrist injury and never hit as well afterward. Traded to the expansion Angels in May 1961, he was their regular shortstop for two seasons, before he lost the job to Jim Fregosi in 1963. Koppe spent the rest of his career as a utility infielder. /(SFS)

Leonard Koppett — 1923– . *Writer.*

Born in Moscow, Russia, Koppett came to the United States at age five and grew up one block from Yankee Stadium. His sportswriting career began with the New York *Herald-Tribune* in 1948. In 1954, he moved to the *Post* and in 1963 the *Times.* In 1975, Koppett left daily sportswriting to live in Palo Alto, California. In addition to many magazine articles, he wrote *Thinking Man's Guide to Baseball* in 1967. /(NLM)

Andy Kosco — 1941– . OF-1B 1965–74 Twins, Yankees, **Dodgers**, Brewers, Angels, Red Sox, Reds 658 g, .236, 73 hr, 267 rbi. *1 LCS, 3 g, .300*

Originally a Tiger bonus baby, the slugging outfielder played for seven other ML teams in ten years, usually as a part-timer. In 1969, his best year, he led the Dodgers with 19 homers and 74 RBI. He hit .300 for the Reds in the '73 NLCS. /(JCA)

Dave Koslo [born George Bernard Koslowski] — 1920–1975. LHP 1941–42, 46–55 **Giants**, Orioles, Braves 1591 ip, 92–107, 3.68. *1 WS, 15 ip, 1–1, 3.00*
☛ *Led League—era 49.*

After spending 1943–45 in the military, Koslo returned to the Giants in '46 to lead the NL with 19 losses, 35 starts, and 251 hits allowed. In 1949, he became the only pitcher to lead the league in ERA (2.50) without recording a shutout. Kelso beat the Yankees, 5–1, in the 1951 World Series opener, but lost the sixth and final game 4–3. /(RMu)

Sandy Koufax — 1935– . LHP 1955–66 **Dodgers** 2324, 165–87, 2.76. 20 wins: 63, 65–66 *4 WS, 57 ip, 4–3, 0.95*
☛ *Most Valuable Player—63. Led League—w 63, 65–66. Led League—era 62–66. Led League—k 61, 63, 65–66. Cy Young Award—63, 65–66. All-Star—61–66. Hall of Fame—1972.*

Koufax packed a Hall of Fame career into the final six of his dozen ML seasons. He was always a hard thrower, but control problems hobbled him during his early years. A Brooklyn high school baseball and basketball star, Koufax played both sports as a freshman at the University of Cincinnati, then signed a bonus contract with the Dodgers. Under the rules of the time, the club was forced to keep the 19-year-old on its ML roster.

Used little while the team was in Brooklyn,

Sandy Koufax

Koufax began to show flashes of brilliance once the Dodgers reached the West Coast. He was 11–11 in 1958 and tied the then-ML strikeout mark with 18 against the Giants on August 31, 1959. That season he lost a 1–0 game to the White Sox in the WS. Although only 8–13 in 1960, he struck out 197 batters in 175 innings.

Whether it was following the advice of part-time Dodger catcher Norm Sherry to ease up on his speed to achieve control or simply the maturing of a pitcher with great stuff, almost overnight Koufax became overpowering. In 1961, he went 18–13 and led the NL in strikeouts with 269. Between 1961 and 1966, he led the NL in wins and shutouts three times each, complete games twice, and strikeouts four times. His 382 strikeouts in 1965 set a new ML record. He led in ERA a record five consecutive years, with his best mark 1.73 in his final year. He pitched a no-hitter each season from 1962 to 1965, with the last a 1–0 perfect game against the Cubs on September 9, 1965. He led the Dodgers to pennants in 1963, 1965, and 1966, and won the NL Cy

Young Award each year. His 25–5 mark in 1963 also won him the MVP. Koufax and Don Drysdale formed one of baseball's all-time great lefty-righty duos. They held out as a "package" in 1966, forcing the Dodgers to meet their terms.

Koufax achieved success despite physical problems. A mysterious circulatory ailment in his pitching arm cost him half a season in 1962. Another arm injury in 1964 shortly led to an arthritic pitching elbow. After a 27–9 record in 1966, he retired at age thirty-one rather than risk crippling his arm. Five years later he became the youngest man to be elected to the Baseball Hall of Fame and only the sixth to achieve the honor in his first year of eligibility. /(JL)

Lou Koupal — 1898–1961. RHP 1925–26, 28–30, 37 Pirates, **Dodgers**, Phillies, Browns 335 ip, 10–21, 5.58

Koupal was not an overpowering pitcher, and he became accustomed to working with runners on base. He left the majors in 1930 and resurfaced at age thirty-eight with the pitching-poor 1937 Browns, going 4–9 with six complete games. /(FJO)

Ernie Koy (Chief) — 1909– . OF 1938–42 **Dodgers**, Cardinals, Reds, Phillies 556 g, .279, 36 hr, 260 rbi

Chief Koy, of Indian ancestry, was a powerfully built righthanded hitter with blazing speed. A Dodger regular in 1938 and 1939, he homered in his first ML at-bat (4/19/38). A son, Ernie Jr., played for the pro football Giants, 1965–70. /(LAW)

Masayaki Koyama — Unk.–Unk. P 1952–75 **Hanshin Tigers**

Koyama enjoyed the longest career of any Japanese pitcher by combining bull's-eye control with a baffling variety of motions, ranging from straight over-the-top to deep submarine. He "could throw strikes blindfolded," said Daryl Spencer. Nonetheless, Koyama walked Spencer four times on 16 consecutive balls in late 1965 to ensure that Katsuya Nomura, and not the American Spencer, would win the home run title. /(MC)

Al Kozar — 1922– . 2B 1948–50 **Senators**, White Sox 285 g, .254, 6 hr, 94 rbi

Kozar was the everyday second baseman of the Senators in his first season and hit .250 with 25 doubles. Batting just .200 in May 1950, he was a throw-in in a deal with the White Sox but was blocked by Nellie Fox's presence. /(SFS)

Joe Krakauskas — 1915–1960. LHP 1937–42, 46 **Senators**, Indians 583 ip, 26–36, 4.53

Among the few Quebecers to make the majors, Krakauskas was 11–17 at his most active, with the 1939 Senators. Traded to Cleveland for Ben Chapman after the 1940 season, he couldn't break into the deep Indians' rotation. /(MC)

Jack Kralick — 1935– . LHP 1959–67 Senators/ Twins, **Indians** 1218 ip, 67–65, 3.56
☛ *All-Star—64.*

On August 26, 1962, pitching for Minnesota, Kralick no-hit the Athletics 1–0, retiring the first 25 batters. Traded to Cleveland for Jim Perry the following year, he recorded a career-high 14 wins. /(JCA)

Jack Kramer — 1918– . RHP 1939–41, 43–51 **Browns**, Red Sox, Giants, Yankees 1637 ip, 95–103, 4.24. *1 WS, 11 ip, 1–0, 0.00*

Flunking in four shots with the Browns due to poor control, Kramer got a fifth chance, thanks to the WWII player shortage. He went 17–13 (2.49) for the 1944 pennant winners, adding a complete game victory in Game Three of the WS against the Cardinals. Traded to the Red Sox after 1947, he enjoyed an 18–5 season in '48, with an AL-best .783 winning percentage. Though he pitched with both pennant-winners in 1951, the Yankees and Giants, he didn't last to the Series with either. /(MC)

Randy Kramer — 1960– . RHP 1988– **Pirates** 121 ip, 6–11, 4.08

Kramer struggled with his control when moved into the Pirates' rotation in 1989. /(SFS)

Ed Kranepool (Krane) — 1944– . 1B-OF 1962–79 **Mets** 1853 g, .261, 118 hr, 614 rbi. *2 LCS, 4 g, .286, 3 rbi. 2 WS, 5 g, .143, 1 hr, 1 rbi*
☛ *All-Star—65.*

Kranepool signed with the Mets out of James Madison High in the Bronx for $85,000. Asked why the 6'3″, lefthanded first baseman was being kept on the bench in 1962, manager Casey Stengel replied, "Listen. He's only seventeen and he runs like he's thirty." When, by nineteen, Kranepool hadn't developed as expected, a New York newspaper headline asked, "Is Ed Kranepool Over the Hill?" He endured such taunts but later enjoyed glory. After six years, including the 1969 World Championship season, as the Mets' most regular first baseman, in 1970 hefty number 7 was sent to the minors, and considered retiring. But in 1971, he hit .280 with career highs in HR, RBI, and runs scored, and led the league with a .998 fielding average. He flowered as a pinch hitter late in his career, batting a ML-record .486 in 1974 (with a league-leading 17 pinch hits) and hit .396 in the role from 1974 through 1978. Kranepool played in each of the Mets' first 18 seasons, retiring as the all-time club leader in eight offensive categories. He made money away from baseball as a stockbroker and restaurateur. /(KT)

Gene Krapp (Rubber, Rubber Arm) — 1887–1923. RHP 1911–12, 14–15 Indians, **Buffalo (FL)** 757 ip, 38–47, 3.23

Krapp led AL pitchers with 136 walks (in 215 innings) in his rookie 1911 season, but was the third-hardest to hit and went 13–9. His control worsened in 1912 (42 BB in 59 innings) and he was out of the majors until coming back in the Federal League, going 14–14 and 9–19 for the BufFeds. /(JFC)

Harry Krause (Hal) — 1887–1940. LHP 1908–12 **A's**, Indians 525 ip, 37–26, 2.50
☛ *Led League—era 09.*

Krause won his first ten starts as a rookie in 1909; six of the ten wins were shutouts, and four of those were 1–0. He finished the season 18–8 with an AL-best 1.39 ERA, the ninth-best AL ERA ever and a record low for AL rookies. He still had to scrape for work on a staff that featured Jack Coombs and Hall of Famers Chief Bender and Eddie Plank, and he was 6–6 and 12–8 the following two seasons as the Athletics won consecutive World Championships. He didn't pitch in either WS. Krause was sent to the minors with a sore arm in 1912 and found a home in the Pacific Coast League, winning 249 games there in 16 seasons. Overall, he won 337 games in his professional career. /(NLM)

Lew Krausse [Lewis Bernard, Jr.] — 1943– . RHP 1961, 64–74 **A's**, Brewers, Red Sox, Cardinals, Braves 1284 ip, 68–91, 4.00

Krausse was signed by his father, an A's scout and a former Philadelphia Athletics pitcher, for a $125,000 bonus in 1961. Just days out of high school, the raw youngster was immediately brought to Kansas City by A's owner Charlie Finley. Krausse shut out the Angels in his first pro start, but after 12 ML games he was sent to the minors for seasoning. Krausse wasn't a ML winner until 1966 (14–9, 2.99). Known as a rowdy playboy, he was a leading figure in the "war" between Finley and his players in 1967, and his record dropped to 7–17. /(JCA)

Ken Kravec — 1951– . LHP 1975–82 **White Sox**, Cubs 859 ip, 43–56, 4.46

Kravec led White Sox pitchers in strikeouts from 1977 to 1979. He was 15–13 in 1979, his best season. Back problems reduced his effectiveness from 1980 through the end of his career. /(JCA)

Danny Kravitz (Dusty, Beak) — 1930– . C 1956–60 **Pirates**, A's 215 g, .236, 10 hr, 54 rbi

A lefthanded-hitting defensive specialist, Kravitz was a third-string catcher with the Pirates and, in 1960, the A's. His first ML homer came with the bases filled to seal a 6–5 Pirate win in 1956. /(JL)

Mike Kreevich (Iron Mike) — 1908– . OF-3B 1931, 35–45 Cubs, **White Sox**, A's, Browns, Senators 1238 g, .283, 45 hr, 514 rbi. *1 WS, 6 g, .231*
☛ *All-Star—38.*

There were two outstanding AL rookies in 1936. Joe DiMaggio was the other. Kreevich, originally signed by the Cubs, quietly hit .307 for the White Sox that year. His 16 triples in 1937 were the league high. He was a consistent .300 hitter early on, with stellar defensive work in centerfield. Thanks to his powerful throwing arm, he led NL outfielders with 18 assists in 1939. But after a two-year slump at the plate, Kreevich was sent to the A's in a December 1941 deal for Wally Moses. Kreevich was only the second player in history to ground into four double plays in a game, on August 4, 1939 against the Senators. /(RL)

Ray Kremer [Remy Peter] (Wiz) — 1893–1965. RHP 1924–33 **Pirates** 1954 ip, 143–85, 3.76. 20 wins: 26, 30 *2 WS, 26 ip, 2–2, 3.12*
☛ *Led League—w 26, 30. Led League—era 26–27.*

An immediate success in 1924, Kremer went 18–10 for Pittsburgh, tying for the NL lead with 41 appearances and four shutouts. He later tied for the league high in wins with 20 in both 1926 and 1930, led the NL in ERA in 1926 and '27, and in starts (38), innings (276) and hits (366) in 1930. A two-fisted drinker, Kremer was known to tear up a Pullman car and throw his teammates' shoes out the

window en route to the next city. But he had 15 or more wins for seven straight years. After pitching a complete game victory in Game Six of the 1925 WS, he returned to defeat the Senators in the clincher with four innings of relief work. /(NLM)

Wayne Krenchicki (Chick) — 1954– . 3B-1B-2B-SS 1979–86 Orioles, **Reds**, Tigers, Expos 550 g, .266, 15 hr, 124 rbi

A strong defensive player trained at three infield positions in the Orioles organization, the lefthanded-hitting Krenchicki never was a front-liner because he couldn't handle lefthanded pitching. He batted just .188 lifetime against lefties, with no extra-base hits. /(JCA)

Red Kress [Ralph] — 1907–1962. SS-3B-1B-OF-2B 1927–36, 38–40, 46 **Browns**, White Sox, Senators, Tigers, Giants 1391 g, .286, 89 hr, 799 rbi

Ebullient Red Kress led AL shortstops in fielding in 1929, but in errors in 1930. The Browns moved him off SS so Jim Levey could move in; Levey, in turn, led the league in errors. The next season, St. Louis traded Kress (after three seasons of hitting over .300 with over 100 RBI a year) to the White Sox, who were unveiling Luke Appling at SS. Kress therefore adapted to whatever position he had to, even pitching, to the detriment of his batting average. The Senators got him next and he competed with Joe Cronin, who was not only the shortstop but the manager; Cronin released Kress. After he spent 1937 in Minneapolis (American Association), hitting .330 and leading shortstops in total chances, the Browns reacquired him. Played at short, he responded by hitting .302 and leading the league in fielding. Traded to Detroit in 1939, he broke his leg during the season. In 1940, the pennant-bound Tigers released the hard-luck Kress. He loved baseball enough to quit after coaching for the hapless 1962 Mets. That November, his heart gave out. /(JK)

Lou Kretlow — 1923– . RHP 1946, 48–56 Tigers, **Browns/Orioles**, White Sox, A's 785 ip, 27–47, 4.87

The Tigers gave Kretlow a $35,000 bonus to sign in January 1946, but he never managed more than a half-dozen wins in any of his ten ML seasons. /(FK)

Frank Kreutzer — 1939– . LHP 1962–66, 69 White Sox, **Senators** 210 ip, 8–18, 4.40

First signed by the Red Sox, Villanova's Kreutzer was in and out of the Senator rotation from 1964 to 1966, struggling with control. He then spent two disappointing years with hometown Buffalo (International League)./(MC)

Paul Krichell — 1882–1957. C 1911–12 **Browns** 85 g, .222, 0 hr, 16 rbi

Krichell had fewer than 250 ML at-bats as a reserve catcher with the Browns, but he became one of the greatest scouts in ML history. After coaching for the Red Sox in 1919, Krichell was hired by Ed Barrow to scout for the Yankees in 1920 and remained with them until his death in 1957. He was director of scouting and chief scout beginning in 1946. He discovered Yankee Hall of Famers Lou Gehrig and Whitey Ford, as well as standouts like Tony Lazzeri, Mark Koenig, and Vic Raschi./(FVP)

Howie Krist (Spud) — 1916– . RHP 1937–38, 41–43, 46 **Cardinals** 444 ip, 37–11, 3.32. *1 WS, 0 ip, 0–0, --*

Krist's 10–0 record in 1941, his first full season, is the third-best undefeated season ever. Usually a reliever, he threw three shutouts in 1943, but arm trouble and a two-year army hitch ended his effectiveness./(FJO)

Gary Kroll — 1941– . RHP 1964–66, 69 Phillies, **Mets**, Astros, Indians 159 ip, 6–7, 4.24

A fireballing giant with a deceptive motion, Kroll pitched two no-hitters in the minors and once struck out 309 batters in a season. As a nervous ML rookie, however, he committed a league-leading four balks in just 24 innings./(JL)

Bill Krueger — 1958– . LHP 1983– **A's**, Dodgers, Brewers 541 ip, 30–33, 4.44

A 6'5" basketball player at Portland (Oregon) University, Krueger did not begin pitching until his junior year. He joined the A's rotation in 1983 and was 6–5 on June 25 when he strained a forearm muscle; scouts said he lost his best stuff with the injury. Traded to the Dodgers in 1987, he threw a seven-inning no-hitter for Albuquerque (Pacific Coast League) against Phoenix that August 14./(JCA)

Ernie Krueger — 1890–1976. C 1913, 15, 17–21, 25 Indians, Yankees, Giants, **Dodgers**, Reds 318 g, .263, 11 hr, 93 rbi. *1 WS, 4 g, .167*

A backup receiver, the native of Illinois had better than average speed and power. He appeared with Brooklyn in the 1920 WS against Cleveland./(EM)

Otto Krueger [Arthur William] (Oom Paul) — 1876–1961. SS-3B-OF 1899–1905 Cleveland (NL), **Cardinals**, Pirates, Phillies 507 g, .251, 5 hr, 196 rbi

Krueger was a regular infielder for two years with the Cardinals before being traded in 1903 to the pennant-winning Pirates, where he was used as a utility man. He missed the 1903 World Series, the first between the NL and AL, because he was in the hospital after being beaned in a late-season game against his former Cardinal teammates./(BC)

Art Kruger — 1881–1949. OF 1907, 10, 14–15 Reds, Indians, Braves, **Kansas City (FL)** 365 g, .232, 6 hr, 115 rbi

Kruger failed to hit in the National and American leagues and was earning $275 a month with Los Angeles (Pacific Coast League) when he joined the Kansas City Packers of the newly formed Federal League to have his only respectable season in 1914./(NLM)

John Kruk — 1961– . 1B-OF 1986– **Padres**, Phillies 492 g, .290, 41 hr, 217 rbi

The 5'10" 195-lb Kruk looks quite unathletic but hit over .300 his first two seasons. His best season was 1987, when he hit .313 with 20 HR, 91 RBI, and 18 stolen bases. He slumped to .241 in 1988 but rebounded to .300 in 1989 and was traded to the Phillies in mid-season./(WOR)

Mike Krukow — 1952– . RHP 1976– Cubs, Phillies, Giants 2190 ip, 124–117, 3.90. 20 wins: 86 *1 LCS, 9 ip, 1–0, 2.00*
☛ *All-Star—86.*

After nine seasons as a consistent but unspectacular starter, Krukow starred for the Giants in 1986, recording career bests in wins (20), ERA (3.05), and strikeouts (178) and finishing third in the NL Cy Young balloting. Prior to 1986 the 6'5" curveballer rarely completed games and had never won more than 13 games despite making regular starts for whichever team he played for. In 1987–89 he was hampered by injuries, winning only 16 games. Krukow's 20 wins in 1986 were the most by a Giants pitcher since Ron Bryant won 24 in 1973./(SCL)

Dick Kryhoski — 1925– . 1B 1949–55 Yankees, Tigers, **Browns/Orioles**, A's 569 g, .265, 45 hr, 231 rbi

Kryhoski and Roy Sievers shared first base for the Browns in 1953, the last year of the team's existence. Kryhoski was involved in baseball's biggest trade ever, a 17-player, two-part 1954 deal between the Orioles and Yankees./(RM)

Tony Kubek — 1936- . SS-OF 1957-65 **Yankees** 1092 g, .266, 57 hr, 373 rbi. *6 WS, 37 g, .240 2 hr, 10 rbi* ☛ *Rookie of the Year—57. All-Star—58, 59, 61.*

Kubek was the AL Rookie of the Year in 1957, hitting .297 and showing amazing versatility as he spent substantial time in the outfield, at shortstop, and at third base, with brief early stints at second base and first base as well. He displaced Gil McDougald and became the Yankees' regular shortstop in 1958. For eight seasons he and second baseman Bobby Richardson formed one of baseball's best double-play combinations. In 1961, Kubek cracked 38 doubles (a Yankees record for shortstops), and in his first at-bat after returning from the army late in 1962, he delivered a three-run home run. Kubek appeared in six WS with the Yankees. Playing in his hometown of Milwaukee, he hit a pair of homers in Game Three of the 1957 Series against the Braves. And in Game Seven of the 1960 WS he was victimized by one of the most famous bad hops in history. An apparently tailor-made double-play ball skipped up and hit Kubek in the throat, prolonging a five-run eighth-inning Pittsburgh rally that set the stage for Bill Mazeroski's Series-winning home run in the bottom of the ninth. A dangerous neck and back condition forced Kubek to retire at the age of twenty-nine, but he quickly became one of television's most successful baseball announcers. Kubek remained extremely friendly, popular, and respected long after his playing days ended. /(MG)

Ted Kubiak — 1942- . 2B-SS-3B 1967-76 **A's,** Brewers, Cardinals, Rangers, Padres 977 g, .231, 13 hr, 202 rbi. *2 LCS, 7 g, .333, 1 rbi. 2 WS, 8 g, .167*

Kubiak four times led his minor league in putouts, assists, and double plays at shortstop, prompting A's owner Charles O. Finley to shift All-Star shortstop Bert Campaneris to the outfield. After Campaneris balked, Kubiak was traded to the Brewers before the 1970 season. He returned to Oakland to become their infield reserve for three World Championships (1972-74). /(MC)

Johnny Kucab (Yats) — 1919-1977. RHP 1950-52 **A's** 152 ip, 5-5, 4.44

Kucab made just three starts in his 59 major league appearances, but one, on the final day of the 1950 season, was his first win, and Connie Mack's last game as a ML manager. /(LAW)

Jack Kucek [John Andrew] — 1953- . RHP 1974-80 **White Sox,** Phillies, Blue Jays 206 ip, 7-16, 5.10

A 90-mph fastball vaulted the articulate speech major to the majors for nine games in his first pro season but couldn't keep him there. Impressive minor league ERAs and a 1978 Iowa no-hitter won him yearly trials with the White Sox from 1974 to 1979. /(JCA)

Johnny Kucks — 1933- . RHP 1955-60 **Yankees,** A's 938 ip, 54-56, 4.10. *4 WS, 19 ip, 1-0, 1.89*

A 6'3" sidearmer, Kucks had a sensational sophomore year in 1956, going 18-9 for the Yankees with a spectacular, three-hit shutout of the Dodgers in Game Seven of the World Series. He never had another winning season. /(GW)

Harvey Kuenn — 1930-1988. OF-SS-3B 1952-66 **Tigers,** Indians, Giants, Cubs, Phillies 1833 g, .303, 87 hr, 671 rbi. *1 WS, 4 g, .083.*
    Manager 1975, 82-83 **Brewers** 160-118, .576. First place: 82 *1 LCS, 3-2, .600. 1 WS, 3-4, .429* ☛ *Rookie of the Year—53. Led League—ba 59. All-Star—53-60.*

The unassuming, broad-faced Tiger bonus baby reached the majors in his first pro season after just 63 games in the low minors. En route to the 1953

Harvey Kuenn

Rookie of the Year Award, Kuenn hit .308 with a league-leading 209 hits, setting a ML rookie record with 679 at-bats and an AL rookie record with 167 singles. Smooth and consistent, Kuenn was Detroit's shortstop from 1953 to 1957 and then switched to the outfield. A line-drive hitter, he led the AL in hits four times and won the league batting title in 1959 with a .353 mark. Traded to Cleveland the next year for home run champion Rocky Colavito, he was booed by Indian fans who blamed him for Colavito's departure. Nevertheless, Kuenn hit .308. He spent the remainder of his playing career in the NL and retired after the 1966 season with 2,092 hits.

Made a Brewer coach in 1972, the native of Milwaukee overcame heart and stomach surgery and the amputation of his right leg below the knee. In June 1982 he took over as manager of the fifth-place Brewers. He took the team, known as "Harvey's Wallbangers" for their heavy hitting, to the 1982 World Series, where they lost in seven games to St. Louis. Kuenn was named Manager of the Year./(JCA)

Joe Kuhel — 1906-1984. 1B 1930-47 **Senators**, White Sox 2105 g, .277, 131 hr, 1049 rbi. *1 WS, 5 g, .150, 1 rbi.*
   Manager 1948-49 **Senators** 106-201, .345

The Comiskeys took a lot of heat for trading away colorful Zeke Bonura in 1938, but the deal brought the AL's best-fielding first baseman to the White Sox for the worst. Whatever Joe Kuhel lacked in flamboyance, he made up for with his steady, reliable defense. In time, Chicago fans accepted him.

Kuhel moved into the Senators' lineup in 1931. In the pennant year of 1933, he enjoyed his finest season, hitting .322 and leading AL first basemen in putouts. He never batted that high with Chicago, but he did hit 27 HR in 1940 (by far his most) and continued to excel with the glove. In a July 20, 1941 doubleheader against the Athletics, he recorded 17 putouts in the first game, and 23 in the second, eclipsing a 35-year-old record held by Hal Chase. He was a fearless player, who once took on Eldon Auker and the entire Browns team after being skulled by a high hard one. Kuhel managed the Senators to seventh- and eighth-place finishes in 1948 and 1949./(RL)

Bowie Kuhn — 1926- . *Executive*

As baseball's Commissioner from 1969 to 1984, Kuhn presided over the sport's period of greatest affluence but also, paradoxically, one of its most strife-ridden eras. With the major leagues threatened by a players' strike before the 1969 season and with

the office of the Commissioner vacant after the firing of General Eckert in December 1968, the owners hired Kuhn, a lawyer for the National League and a favorite of Dodgers owner Walter O'Malley. In the style that he would use throughout his three terms, Kuhn verbally placated the owners and then gave in to all the Players Association demands. He dealt with the controversial Curt Flood case at the end of the year, denying Flood's request to overturn the reserve clause and, more specifically, allow Flood to circumvent a trade that had sent him from the contending Cardinals to the cellar-dwelling Phillies.

Kuhn went on to withstand a spring training strike in 1972 that cut into the start of the season, and he forced the owners to abandon a pre-season lockout in 1976 following a pro-player decision by

Bowie Kuhn

an independent arbitrator in the Messersmith-Mc-Nally challenge to the reserve clause. Kuhn had advised against the use of an arbitrator in the case, his law background perhaps leading him to realize what shaky ground the owners were on. Kuhn forestalled a player strike in 1980, but was unable to prevent the mid-season strike of 1981, when the owners stood firm in an ultimately unsuccessful rear-guard action against free agency.

Despite his frequent, albeit forced, accomodations of player demands, Kuhn was perceived as a tool of the owners and as overmatched by the head of the Players Association, Marvin Miller. Kuhn regularly chided the players for their demands, called them overpaid, and preached of the potential evils of free agency, all stances pleasing to his employers, the owners. But Kuhn's officious, pompous manner gained him enemies beyond the ranks of the players. His handling of an investigation of Cubs manager Leo Durocher ended in personal, although largely private, embarrassment. Writer Red Smith excoriated Kuhn in many columns, producing such bon mots during the 1981 strike as "this strike wouldn't have happened if Bowie Kuhn were alive today" and "an empty car pulled up and Bowie Kuhn got out." Kuhn also feuded with A's owner Charlie Finley, who referred to Kuhn as a "village idiot" and then apologized for the offense to village idiots. Kuhn vetoed some of Finley's innovations, and in 1973 he prevented Finley from vindictively placing second baseman Mike Andrews on the DL during the World Series following a costly error. Their biggest clash came when Kuhn voided the sales, and lopsided trades involving cash, of A's stars Vida Blue, Joe Rudi, and others. The players were going to leave Oakland as free agents to escape Finley's tyrannical ownership, and Finley was trying to get some value for them. Many owners in the past had sold off their stars; Connie Mack, who had guided the A's for a half-century, was famous for breaking up his great teams. But Kuhn ruled that Finley's deals were not "in the best interests of baseball." Kuhn also suspended Yankees owner George Steinbrenner for a year after he was convicted of perjury and making illegal contributions to the election campaign of Richard Nixon, and suspended Braves owner Ted Turner for tampering.

Kuhn may ultimately be remembered for the spectacular growth of baseball in the 1970s and 1980s, a period that began with expansion in 1969, the same year Kuhn became Commissioner. Attendance in 1980 was more than triple what it had been in 1968, and television revenue was up more than $10 million dollars in the same period. But the eagerness of baseball to bow to the demands of network TV resulted in concessions criticized by purists. The most notable of these concessions was night baseball during the World Series. The first such game, in 1971, found Kuhn attending bareheaded and coatless despite the cold weather, with the cameras frequently focusing on him in an attempt to deny the effects of the temperature./(WOR)

Duane Kuiper — 1950– . 2B 1974–85 **Indians**, Giants 1057 g, .271, 1 hr, 263 rbi

An outstanding fielder who twice led AL second basemen in fielding percentage, Kuiper's disciplined hitting style made him a fine spoiler: three times (against Andy Hassler, Nolan Ryan, and Ron Guidry), he was the only man to get a hit. On August 29, 1977 after 1,381 ML at-bats without a home run, he finally popped one, off Steve Stone. In his remaining 1,997 plate appearances, the lean infielder managed (intentionally, he contends) to not hit another one. The clowning Kuiper took a warped pride in his accomplishment, saying: "One is better than none, but any more than that and people start expecting them."/(JCA)

Won Kuk Lee (Ernesto) — Unk.– . P, Minor and Mexican Leagues

A Korean, Kuk Lee was signed in 1964 by the San Francisco Giants organization, who also signed Masanori Murakami that year. He pitched ambidextrously, earning brief looks in spring training. After the Giants released him, he concentrated on pitching righthanded, changed his name to Ernesto, married a Mexican woman, grew a handlebar mustache, and, playing into the 1980s, won more than 150 Mexican League games./(MC)

Bill Kunkel — 1936–1985. RHP 1961–63 **A's**, Yankees 142 ip, 6–6, 4.29.
Umpire AL 1968–85 *4 LCS 2 WS 2 ASU*

Kunkel had a brief fling as a ML reliever. His most active year was 1961, when he appeared in 58 games for the A's. He turned to umpiring and reached the ML in 1968. It was Kunkel who discovered pitcher Rick Honeycutt doctoring the baseball with a tack wedged inside a Band-Aid on his right hand. "I grabbed his hand and got stuck," Kunkel explained. Honeycutt received a 10-day suspension. During 1984 spring training, Kunkel's son Jeff, a member of the Rangers, brought the lineup card to the plate the only time father and son have appeared in the same ML game as umpire and player. Kunkel was also a college basketball referee for 20 years./(RTM)

Jeff Kunkel — 1962- . SS-2B-3B-OF 1984- **Rangers** 238 g, .241, 15 hr, 55 rbi

Kunkel is the son of Bill Kunkel, whose umpiring career overlapped the first season of Jeff's ML career. Jeff was the third pick in the nation in the June 1983 draft, but his offense was too weak for a regular job and he became a utility man. /(JFC)

Whitey Kurowski [George John] — 1918- . 3B-SS-2B 1941-49 **Cardinals** 916 g, .286, 106 hr, 529 rbi. *4 WS, 23 g, .253, 1 hr, 9 rbi*
☛ *All-Star—43-44, 46.*

A stocky, thick-legged infielder with surprising speed, Kurowski overcame childhood osteomyelitis (which made his right arm shorter than his left) to become one of the finest third basemen of the 1940s. Kurowski led the NL three times in putouts, twice in fielding average, and once each in assists and double plays. He displayed power, hitting 20 or more home runs in three different seasons. His ninth-inning homer off Yankee pitcher Red Ruffing in Game Five of the 1942 World Series broke a 2-2 tie to clinch the championship for the Cardinals.

Kurowski reached career highs of 27 HR and 104 RBI in 1947, his last season playing regularly, and batted over .300 three times (1945-47). An arm injury in 1948 and an elbow injury in 1949 combined to end his career. /(LAW)

Emil Kush — 1916-1969. RHP 1941-42, 46-49 **Cubs** 346 ip, 21-12, 3.48

Kush "had a natural sidearm sinker and a pretty good curve," according to Cubs manager Charlie Grimm, who recommended Chicago sign him after he tried out on a whim. He pitched mostly in relief and was 9-2 in 1946 and 8-3 the next year before arm trouble and an operation curtailed his career. Considered something of a jinxed pitcher, he often spoke of a 1948 incident. With the Cubs leading by two runs in the ninth with two out and two on, his centerfielder knocked himself cold crashing into the wall pursuing a fly ball. Before another outfielder recovered the ball, the batter circled the bases for a game-winning homer. /(BC)

Craig Kusick — 1948- . 1B-DH 1973-79 **Twins**, Blue Jays 497 g, .235, 46 hr, 171 rbi

A brawny long-ball hitter and a slow, deficient fielder, Kusick split his time among first base, DH, and pinch hitter. He saw the most action in 1977, when he posted career highs of 12 homers and 45 RBI in 115 games. /(JCA)

Randy Kutcher — 1960- . OF-SS 1986- **Giants**, Red Sox 181 g, .227, 9 hr, 35 rbi

Alaskan-born Kutcher saw the most action in 1986, when he hit .237 in 71 games as a utility man for the Giants. He went to the Red Sox after the 1987 as the player to be named later in return for Dave Henderson. /(SFS)

Marty Kutyna — 1932- . RHP 1959-62 A's, **Senators** 290 ip, 14-16, 3.88

Kutyna was 14-10 for Portland (Pacific Coast League) as a starter in 1959, then allowed no earned runs in his four-game debut as an Athletics reliever. He appeared in at least 50 games in each of his three remaining seasons. /(MC)

Bob Kuzava (Sarge) — 1923- . LHP 1946-47, 49-55, 57 Indians, White Sox, Senators, **Yankees**, Orioles, Phillies, Pirates, Cardinals 862 ip, 49-44, 4.05. *3 WS, 4 ip, 0-0, 2.08*

Kuzava rose to sergeant during WWII, then tried unsuccessfully to crack the Indians rotation. Traded to the White Sox, he went 10-6 as a rookie in 1949. By mid-1951, he was a Yankee spot starter and long reliever, going 11-7. In the final game of the '51 WS, he retired the Giants with the bases loaded to record a save, and in Game Seven of the '52 Series, set down the last eight Dodgers for another. The latter performance was especially notable; lefthanders weren't supposed to be able to beat the Dodgers, who featured a righthanded lineup with the exception of Duke Snider, especially not in Ebbets Field. But manager Casey Stengel played his hunch and proved correct.

In a rare 1953 start, he lost a no-hitter against the White Sox with one out in the ninth. /(MC)

Chet Laabs — 1912–1983. OF 1937–47 Tigers, Browns, A's 950 g, .262, 117 hr, 509 rbi. *1 WS, 5 g, .200* ☛ *All-Star—43.*

The stocky Laabs was a wartime hero for the St. Louis Browns when they won their only pennant in 1944. Used sparingly all season, he had only three home runs before he hit two against the Yankees on the season's last day to win the pennant-clinching game.

Laabs had good power, finishing second in the AL in 1942 with 27 HR. He had a knack for timely hits, leading the AL in pinch hits in 1940. But he was strikeout prone and led the AL (105) in 1943. In 1938, when Cleveland's Bob Feller struck out 18 Tigers, Laabs was a five-time victim. /(JK)

Clem Labine — 1926– . RHP 1950–62 Dodgers, Tigers, Pirates, Mets 1079 ip, 77–56, 3.63. *5 WS, 31 ip, 2–2, 3.16* ☛ *All-Star—56–57.*

The free-spirited sinkerballer was one of baseball's premier relievers in the 1950s. The durable Labine helped the Dodgers to four pennants in Brooklyn and another in Los Angeles. Labine was 13–5 in a NL-leading 60 appearances for the 1955 World Champions and led the league in saves the next two seasons. He retired Dodger-killer Stan Musial 49 consecutive times. After leaving the Dodgers, Labine pitched for the Pirates in the 1960 WS.

Two of Labine's brightest moments came in the unaccustomed role of a starter, a 10–0 victory over the Giants in the second game of the 1951 NL playoff and a 1–0 10-inning shutout of the Yankees in Game Six of the 1956 WS. Although never a threat at bat, Labine's three hits in 1955 were all home runs. /(LAW)

Coco Laboy [Jose Alberto] — 1939– . 3B 1969–73 Expos 420 g, .233, 28 hr, 166 rbi

As a 29-year-old rookie, Laboy led the Expos with 83 RBI in the team's inaugural season. After a second-year slump (.199), the popular Puerto Rican was relegated to the bench. /(LAW)

Bob Lacey — 1953– . LHP 1977–81, 83–84 A's, Indians, Rangers, Angels, Giants 451 ip, 20–29, 3.67

The 6'5" Lacey debuted with Oakland in 1977 and worked 33 innings before allowing an earned run. In 1978 he led the American League with 74 appearances. He was used only 47 times by manager Billy Martin in 1980 but recorded a 2.93 ERA. On the last day of the '80 season, he was given his first ML start, pitched a complete-game shutout, and apparently ruined his arm. He bounced around, was often disabled, and was never again consistent. /(MC)

Candy LaChance [George Joseph] — 1870–1932. 1B 1893–99, 1901–05 Dodgers, Baltimore NL, Indians, Red Sox; 1263 g, .280, 39 HR, 690 RBI. *1 WS, 8 g, .222*

A bull-like man who prided himself on his strength, LaChance belied his nickname with a sour disposition. He once challenged Rube Waddell to a wrestling match before a game. After an hour, Waddell pinned him, then went out and pitched a shutout while LaChance recuperated on the bench. /(JK)

Marcel Lachemann — 1941– . RHP 1969–71 A's 101 ip, 7–4, 3.45

A pitching star at the University of Southern California, in the majors Lachemann was used exclusively in relief. His brother Rene was a ML player, coach, and manager. /(LAW)

Pete LaCock — 1952– . 1B-OF 1972–80 Cubs, Royals 715 g, .257, 27 hr, 224 rbi. *3 LCS, 6 g, .333, 1 rbi. 1 WS, 1 g, --*

The son of TV game-show host Peter Marshall, LaCock was the American Association MVP in 1974 (.327, 23 HR, 91 RBI). The 6'2" lefthander hit .364 in the 1978 LCS. He left the majors in 1981 to play in Japan. /(TL)

Frank LaCorte — 1951– . RHP 1975–84 Braves, Astros, Angels 490 ip, 23–44, 5.01. *1 LCS, 3 ip, 1–1, 3.00*

This curveballer had chronic arm trouble, spending parts of four seasons and all of one (1985) on the disabled list. A starter with Atlanta, he was demoted after going 1–8 in 1977. Traded to the Astros in

1979, he became a reliever, and he excelled in 1980. He was 5–0 with eight saves and a 0.90 ERA at the All-Star break, but tendinitis in his shoulder (which eventually ended his career) caused a second-half slump; he finished 8–5, with 11 saves and a 2.82 ERA. /(MC)

Mike LaCoss (Buffy) — 1956– . RHP 1978– Reds, Astros, Royals, **Giants** 1615 ip, 91–94, 3.93. *3 LCS, 8 ip, 0–1, 5.63. 1 WS, 4 ip, 0–0, 6.23* ☛ *All-Star—79.*

A resilient, versatile finesse pitcher, LaCoss was waived by the Reds after 1981 and released by the Royals after 1985 before making the Giants staff as a nonroster invitee to spring training in 1986. He led San Francisco's 1987 NL West champions with 13 wins, and after an injury-plagued 1988, began the 1989 season as the Giants' bullpen stopper. The success of Craig Lefferts in relief and injuries to many starters moved LaCoss into the rotation; he finished 10–10 with a 3.17 ERA as the Giants won the NL pennant.

LaCoss enjoyed his best season at age twenty-three, going 14–9 with the NL West champion Reds in 1979 and pitching in the All-Star Game. But by 1983 he was a struggling reliever and occasional starter with the Astros, and he posted a 5.09 ERA in 1985. In 1985 he hit his only two ML home runs in consecutive at-bats. /(SCL)

Lee Lacy — 1948– . OF-2B 1972–87 Dodgers, Braves, **Pirates**, Orioles 1523 g, .286, 91 hr, 458 rbi. *3 LCS, 4 g, .333. 4 WS, 13 g, .231, 3 rbi*

Lee Lacy was a utility man for years before getting steady outfield play. A dependable pinch-hitter, Lacy hit five pinch home runs in 1978, including a ML record-tying three in a row. The free swinger was a fair number-two batter with his speed and hitting prowess. He was briefly the starting second baseman of the 1973 Dodgers until Davey Lopes took over. Full-time duty seemed to beckon in 1976, after a trade to Atlanta, but Lacy was dealt back to Los Angeles in June. He went to Pittsburgh as a free agent in 1979. The righthander batted .304 in six seasons with Pirates, with extensive playing time from 1982 to 1984. The final year included a NL-high .996 fielding percentage in the outfield. Defensively, his speed and strong arm were his best assets. /(ME)

Pete Ladd (Bigfoot) — 1956– . RHP 1979, 82–86 Astros, **Brewers**, Mariners 287 ip, 17–23, 4.14. *1 LCS, 3 ip, 0–0, 0.00. 1 WS, 1 ip, 0–0, 0.00*

Ladd was a one-year phenom. A hard-throwing

sinker-slider pitcher with a herky-jerky motion, he was an intimidating presence with his long hair, beard, and 6′3″ 240-lb physique. He saved 25 games for the 1983 Brewers, replacing the injured Rollie Fingers, but was hit hard in 1984 (5.24 ERA). By the end of 1985 he was back in the minors. In the 1982 LCS, he saved two games and was runner-up in the series MVP voting. /(JCA)

Doyle Lade (Porky) — 1921– . RHP 1946–50 **Cubs** 537 ip, 25–29, 4.39

The corpulent Cub was 11–10 as a rookie in 1947 but never won more than five or had an ERA under 4.00 after that. A switch-hitter in his first two seasons, he had a lifetime .220 BA and was considered a good-hitting pitcher. /(AA)

Ed Lafitte (Doc) — 1886–1971. RHP 1909, 11–12, 14–15 Tigers, **Brooklyn (FL)**, Buffalo (FL) 647 ip, 35–36, 3.34

After an 11–8 season with the 1911 Tigers, Lafitte told manager Hugh Jennings that he wanted to leave early the following season to resume dental school. Jennings told him if he left early to keep on going. Lafitte did. He became a dentist, but also pitched in the Federal League. With the Brooklyn Tip-Tops, he pitched the Feds' first no-hitter, defeating Kansas City 6–2 on September 19, 1914 (walking seven), and went 16–16 with a 2.63 ERA but led the league in walks (127 in 291 innings). /(NLM)

Lerrin LaGrow — 1948– . RHP 1970, 72–80 **Tigers**, Cardinals, White Sox, Dodgers, Phillies 779 ip, 34–55, 4.11. *1 LCS, 1 ip, 0–0, 0.00*

LaGrow earned his first call-up to the majors by being named Southern League Player of the Year in 1970. In his only two seasons as a starting pitcher, he went 8–19 (1974) and 7–14 (1975), prompting the Tigers to give up on him. After returning to the AL with the White Sox in 1977, he was the ace of their bullpen for two seasons; he finished third in the AL with 25 saves in '77. /(WOR)

Joe Lahoud (Duck) — 1947– . OF-DH 1968–78 **Red Sox**, Brewers, Angels, Rangers, Royals; 791 g, .223, 65 hr, 218 rbi. *1 LCS, 1 g, .000*

Lahoud was rushed to the Red Sox from Class A in 1968 to replace the injured Tony Conigliaro in right field, but had trouble hitting curves. Although he surpassed the league BA only once (in 1974 with .271) in 11 seasons of platooning, his power produced seasons of 14, 12, and 13 homers in 1971–74. He hit three in one game for the Red Sox on June 11, 1969. /(MC)

Jeff Lahti — 1956- . RHP 1982–86 **Cardinals** 286 ip, 17–11, 3.12. *1 LCS, 2 ip, 1–0, 0.00. 2 WS, 5 ip, 0–0, 11.81*

With the pennant-bound 1985 Cardinals, Lahti was brilliant with 19 saves and a 1.84 ERA. He retired 27 consecutive batters during one stretch, and he was the winner in Game Five of the LCS. Recurring shoulder damage ended his career. /(FO)

Nap Lajoie (Larry) — 1874–1959. 2B-1B-SS 1896–16 Phillies, A's, **Indians** 2475 g, .339, 82 hr, 1599 rbi.
  Manager 1905–09 **Indians** 397–330, .546
☛ *Led League—ba 01, 04–05. Led League—hr 01. Led League—rbi 98, 01, 04 . Hall of Fame—1937.*

One of the most powerful and consistent right-handed hitters of the dead-ball era, Lajoie is often rated the greatest second baseman in baseball history. Handsome, graceful, talented, and popular with both fans and teammates, he was an important figure in the launching of the AL and the survival of the Cleveland franchise. In 1937, he became the sixth player elected to the Hall of Fame.

Lajoie joined the NL Phillies during the 1896 season and played first base in 39 games. The following year he became a regular, hit .363, and led the NL in slugging percentage (.578). He moved to second base in 1898 and led the league in RBI (127) and doubles (40).

In 1901 he jumped across town to the new AL Athletics of Connie Mack, giving the fledgling league instant credibility. Although the young AL was not yet on a par with the established NL, Lajoie's batting marks were nevertheless exceptional. He led in hits (229), doubles (48), home runs (14), runs scored (145), and RBI (125). His .422 batting average still stands as a league record.

The next year the Phillies obtained an injunction forbidding Lajoie from playing in Pennsylvania. As a defense against unpredictable court proceedings, AL president Ban Johnson transferred Lajoie's contract to Cleveland, where his arrival instantly invigorated a moribund franchise.

Although Lajoie led the AL in batting twice more, hitting .355 in 1903 and .381 in 1904, the race he lost to Ty Cobb in 1910 is a piece of baseball legend. The 1910 batting title was hotly contested, with a Chalmers automobile to go to the leading batter. Most of the baseball world rooted for the popular Lajoie and against the hotheaded Cobb, who had won the three previous titles. On the final day of the season, Lajoie bunted for seven infield

Nap Lajoie

hits and swung for a triple in a doubleheader at St. Louis. St. Louis manager Jack O'Connor was ultimately fired when it was revealed that he had ordered his third baseman to play deep against Lajoie. Lajoie finished second by a point despite the machinations but received an auto anyway. Later historical research by *The Sporting News* revealed Lajoie's .384 average actually should have won the title. Cobb's official average of .385 was inflated because one of his games was inadvertently counted twice. In a dispute that rose to the highest baseball levels, Commissioner Bowie Kuhn ruled in 1981 that the mistake would not be corrected.

Playing in the dead-ball era, Lajoie was not a home run hitter. He was, however, a powerful, righthanded pull hitter and his smashes down the left-field foul line were legendary. His 648 doubles rank tenth all-time and he hit ten or more triples in seven seasons. He finished his career with 3,251 hits. In the field, the 6'1"195-lb Lajoie was known for his grace despite being considerably bigger than most infielders of his day. He had excellent speed and good hands.

He managed the Cleveland team from 1905 to 1909 and during that time the club was called the Naps in his honor. He stepped down voluntarily because he believed his managing duties were hurting his play and ultimately hurting the team. His only sub-.300 batting marks (until his final three seasons) came while he was the Cleveland manager./(JM)

Eddie Lake — 1916- . SS-2B 1939-41, 43-50 Cardinals, Red Sox, **Tigers** 835 g, .231, 39 hr, 193 rbi

Although a weak bat kept him in a utility role most of his career, Lake had a knack for drawing walks and topped 100 in each of the three years he played regularly, 1945-47. He led AL shortstops in assists and double plays in '45 for the Red Sox and scored 105 runs for the 1946 Tigers./(LAW)

Joe Lake — 1881-1950. RHP 1908-13 Yankees, **Browns**, Tigers 1318 ip, 62-90, 2.85

Lake lost a league-leading 22 games for the 1908 Highlanders with a high 3.17 ERA (third-worst in the league). His ERA fell to 1.88 in 1909 and he was 14-11. He was 15-9 lifetime in relief./(WAB)

Steve Lake — 1957- . C 1983- Cubs, **Cardinals**, Phillies 325 g, .239, 11 hr, 76 rbi. *1 LCS, 1 g, 1.000. 1 WS, 3 g, .333, 1 rbi*

Lake played in the Orioles, Brewers, and Astro systems before joining the Cubs. Well-liked for his team-first attitude, he was excellent at gunning down runners. He was a boon to the NL champion 1987 Cardinals, filling in for the injured Tony Pena./(FO)

Al Lakeman (Moose) 1918-1976. C 1942-49, 54 **Reds**, Phillies, Braves, Tigers 239 g, .203, 15 hr, 66 rbi

Lakeman was a backup catcher for parts of nine ML seasons but never caught even half of his team's games. In 76 games for the 1945 Reds, he hit a career-high .256. Later, he managed in the minors for ten years, nine in the second division./(MC)

Jack Lamabe — 1936- . RHP 1962-68 Pirates, **Red Sox**, Astros, White Sox, Mets, Cardinals, Cubs 711 ip, 33-41, 4.24. *1 WS, 3 ip, 0-1, 6.75*

Lamabe was successful in his first two seasons, going 7-4, 3.15, with six saves for the 1963 Red Sox. A conversion to starting failed, however, and he bounced around the majors for the rest of his career. He was acquired by the Cardinals in July 1967 and made eight appearances in August without allowing a run, helping St. Louis to the NL pennant. He lost Game Six of the World Series as the Cardinals used eight pitchers that day, tying the record./(SFS)

Al LaMacchia — 1921- . RHP 1943, 45-46 **Browns**, Senators 31 ip, 2-2, 6.46

LaMacchia was 15-2 for San Antonio (Texas League) in 1942 but appeared in only 16 ML games, mostly as a wartime reliever. He scouted briefly for the Phillies before working for the Braves from 1961 to 1975. He has been with the Blue Jays since their inception in 1977. His signees and discoveries include Rick Mahler and Bruce Benedict./(FVP)

Ray Lamanno — 1919- . C 1941-42, 46-48 **Reds** 442 g, .252, 18 hr, 150 rbi
☛ *All-Star—46.*

In 1942 Lamanno replaced his boyhood idol and fellow native Oaklander Ernie Lombardi as the Reds' starting catcher and hit .264 with 12 home runs. He lost the next three seasons to WWII./(JK)

Bill Lamar (Good Time Bill) — 1897-1970. OF 1917-21, 24-27 Yankees, Red Sox, Dodgers, **A's** 550 g, .310, 19 hr, 245 rbi. *1 WS, 3 g, .000*

As Lamar's nickname indicates, he often tested his managers' patience. Two years after he hit .356 for the A's they traded him to Washington. When he refused to report without a raise, he was suspended for the season and never again played in the majors./(JK)

Wayne LaMaster — 1907- . LHP 1937-38 **Phillies**, Dodgers 295 ip, 19-27, 5.82

LaMaster was drafted by the Phillies after two winning seasons in the American Association. Although he led the NL with 19 defeats as a rookie in 1937, he won 15 for the seventh-place Phillies. In August of his poor second season, he was traded to the Dodgers, who used him in three games and then sent him back to the minors./(AL)

Ray Lamb — 1944- . RHP 1969-73 Dodgers, **Indians** 424 ip, 20-23, 3.54

This high-kicking curveballer was overshadowed at the University of Southern California by teammate Tom Seaver. Signed by the Dodgers in 1966, Lamb was a Hollywood movie extra in the off-season. Though generally used in relief, he started 30 games for Cleveland in 1971-72./(ME)

Dennis Lamp — 1952- . RHP 1977- **Cubs**, White Sox, Blue Jays, A's, Red Sox 1605 ip, 86-87, 3.81. *2 LCS, 11 ip, 0-0, 0.00*

A jack-of-all-trades, Lamp was an effective starter early in his career, led the White Sox in saves in 1983, and has pitched middle-relief almost exclusively since 1985. He joined the Cubs' rotation in 1978 and pitched a one-hitter against San Diego June 9, finishing 7-15 with a 3.29 ERA. After a rocky 1980, in 1981 Lamp was traded to the White Sox; his 2.41 ERA was third-best in the AL. He also settled for a second one-hitter when Robin Yount led off the ninth inning with a double on August 25. Lamp was pitching in relief as well as starting for the White Sox, and in 1983 he saved 15 games for the AL West champions, then signed with the Blue Jays. At the time, the White Sox were entitled to compensation for losing a Type A free agent, and they selected the Mets' Tom Seaver from the compensation pool in a move that stunned New York fans. In 1985 Lamp went 11-0 in relief for the Blue Jays, but his ERA swelled to 5.05 in 1986. He made the Red Sox' pitching staff as a non-roster invitee to spring training in 1988./(SCL)

Les Lancaster — 1962- . RHP 1987- **Cubs** 291 ip, 16-11, 3.68. *1 LCS, 6 ip, 1-1, 6.35*

Lancaster started 18 games as a rookie for the Cubs in 1987 but was dispatched to the bullpen the following year. He played a vital role in the Cubs' 1989 NL East championship, saving eight games with a 1.36 ERA (4-2) behind stopper Mitch Williams. He won Game Two of the LCS against the Giants 9-5 with four innings of relief, although he gave up three runs. He came into the seventh inning of Game Three with a runner on, the Cubs winning 4-3, and a 1-0 count on Robby Thompson, who had homered off him the previous day. Thinking the count was 2-0, he threw another ball, then grooved what he thought was a 3-0 fastball; Thompson hit another HR, and the Giants won 5-4./(SCL)

Stan Landes — 1923- . *Umpire* NL 1955-72 *3 WS 2 ASU*

Landes was the first president of the Umpires'

Association but states his union efforts were not the cause of his firing in 1972. His weight had ballooned to 360 pounds (before he lost 75 on a crash diet). He was also deeply in debt, which made him a potential target for gamblers./(RTM)

Rafael Landestoy — 1953- . 2B-SS 1977-84 Dodgers, **Astros**, Reds 596 g, .237, 4 hr, 83 rbi. *2 LCS, 7 g, .182, 2 rbi. 1 WS, 1 g, .000*

Signed out of the Dominican Republic as an outfielder, the speedy Landestoy became a utility man in the majors. In his best season, he hit .270 for the Astros as their regular second baseman for most of 1979. He followed in 1980 with 23 stolen bases, again in a utility role./(MC)

Bill Landis — 1942- . LHP 1963, 67-69 A's, **Red Sox** 170 ip, 9-8, 4.46

Despite a record of 40-69 over six minor league seasons, Landis joined the 1967 World Champion Red Sox and went 1-0 in 18 appearances. The reliever missed the World Series due to an army commitment./(PB)

Jim Landis — 1934- . OF 1957-67 **White Sox**, A's, Indians, Astros, Tigers, Red Sox 1346 g, .247, 93 hr, 467 rbi. *1 WS, 6 g, .292, 1 rbi* ☛ *All-Star—62. Gold Glove—60-64.*

The swift, graceful fielder was the White Sox' center fielder for 8 of his 11 seasons. In 1959 Landis scored six runs in the six-game WS for the "Go-Go Sox." Although his batting average was usually low, as a regular he averaged 67 walks a season, showed occasional power, and had 14 or more stolen bases six straight times in a nonrunning era. By far his best year was 1961, when he hit .283 with 22 HR and 85 RBI, all career highs. His .989 fielding average at retirement was second all-time among outfielders./(CC)

Kenesaw Mountain Landis — 1866-1944. *Executive.* ☛ *Hall of Fame—1939.*

Landis was granted absolute power over the game as commissioner in 1920 after the Black Sox scandal had tainted the game. He exercised his authority tyrannically until his death in 1944, with no recourse from his decisions available or public criticism of them permitted. Although he was harsh and narrow-minded, and often arbitrary and inconsistent, he persuaded most Americans that the integrity of the national pastime had been restored.

Landis was a judge in an Illinois federal district court when he came to the attention of baseball's

Judge Landis

years as commissioner he banished 15 players, including the eight Black Sox, and at one time had 53 players ineligible. Though he did not treat his victims equally or, in some cases, fairly, the numerous bribe offers, thrown games, and betting plots that arose showed baseball's corruption to be far deeper than once believed, and his no-mercy stance was accepted, if not applauded.

Landis was opposed to the development of farm systems and made free agents of numerous players he decreed to have been "covered up" in the minor leagues, but he was unable to eradicate the practice, which preserved many of the faltering leagues. He loved the World Series, conducted it personally, and was constantly photographed at games with his chin on the railing of a front row box. He was also a strong supporter of both the Hall of Fame and the All-Star Game, pushing hard to continue the midsummer exhibitions during WWII. Landis was inducted to the Hall of Fame himself in 1939, and no commissioner since has enjoyed such power. /(ADS)

Ken Landreaux — 1954– . OF 1977–87 Angels, Twins, **Dodgers** 1264 g, .268, 91 hr, 479 rbi. *3 LCS, 14 g, .238, 3 rbi. 1 WS, 5 g, .167*
☛ *All-Star—80.*

Landreaux was *TSN* Minor League Player of the Year in 1977 with a .359 average at Salt Lake City (Pacific Coast League) and broke in with the Angels late that year. He threw out three baserunners from the outfield in his first ML game. He was traded to the Twins when the Angels acquired Rod Carew before the 1979 season, and in 1980 he set a Minnesota record with a 31-game hitting streak, the longest in the AL since Dom DiMaggio's 34 in 1949. He also tied a ML record with three triples in one game that July 3. Landreaux was traded to the Dodgers for three prospects in 1981 and was their starting centerfielder through 1985. He enjoyed his best season in 1983 (.281, 17 HR, 66 RBI), and in the strike-shortened 1981 season he did not make a single error. /(TG)

Hobie Landrith [Hobert Neal] — 1930– . C 1950–63 Reds, Cubs, Cardinals, **Giants**, Mets, Orioles, Senators 772 g, .233, 34 hr, 203 rbi

Landrith is perhaps best known as the Mets' first pick in the expansion draft; manager Casey Stengel explained the choice by saying, "You gotta have a

establishment during the Federal League's antitrust suit, which was heard in his court. A Federal League victory would have destroyed baseball's unique monopoly status, and Landis won the owners' gratitude by stalling his decision until the Feds had collapsed and their suit was withdrawn. The three-man National Commission, which had ruled baseball since 1903 under the leadership of Ban Johnson, had been weakened by owner disputes and grievances, and collapsed in the aftermath of the Series scandal. Judge Landis was the first and only choice for commissioner.

Named after a Civil War battle, young Kenesaw was meagerly educated and minimally trained for the law. Still, his craggy face, shock of white hair, and flamboyant style were captivating. In his first catcher or you're gonna have a lot of passed balls." Landrith had been a backup for the Reds (1950–55) but was traded after the 1955 season, when he had missed time with a broken collarbone. He was a regular for a weak Cubs team in 1956 and hit .221 while leading the league's catchers in errors. As a regular on the 1959 Giants, he had his best season, hitting .251 with 29 RBI and 30 runs in 283 at-bats. /(JFC)

Bill Landrum — 1957– . RHP 1986– Reds, Cubs, **Pirates** 172 ip, 6–5, 3.51

Landrum bounced around for a decade before catching fire with the Pirates in 1989. Picked up in desperation to replace injured bullpen stopper Jim Gott, Landrum had a 0.21 ERA in his first 28 appearances. He finished the year with 26 saves and a 1.67 ERA. His father, Joe Landrum, pitched for the Dodgers in 1950 and 1952. /(WOR)

Don Landrum — 1936– . OF 1957, 60–66 Phillies, Cardinals, **Cubs**, Giants 456 g, .234, 12 hr, 75 rbi

A lefthanded hitter with outstanding speed but not much else, Landrum hit .282 in a platoon role for the 1962 Cubs. Half of his career homers came in 1965 when the Cubs used him regularly in centerfield. /(LAW)

Tito Landrum — 1954– . OF 1980–88 **Cardinals**, Orioles, Dodgers 607 g, .249, 13 hr, 111 rbi. *2 LCS, .333, 1 hr, 1 rbi. 2 WS, 10 g, .360, 1 hr, 1 rbi*

Landrum's surprising 10th-inning home run off Britt Burns in Game Four of the 1983 LCS broke up a scoreless tie and clinched the series for the Orioles. A utility player always in top physical condition, Tito batted .391 and .333 as a pinch hitter in 1984–85. With the 1985 Cardinals he batted .429 in the LCS and .360 in the WS, with a HR in Game Four. /(FO)

F.C. Lane [Ferdinand] — 1885–Unk. *Writer.*

A biologist trained at Boston University and MIT, Lane wrote extensively about baseball. He was editor of *Baseball Magazine* for 27 years. /(NLM)

Frank Lane (Trader Frank, Frantic Frank, The Wheeler Dealer) — 1896–Unk. *Executive.*

Lane played a little minor league ball and was a minor league executive and president of the American Association, but gained fame as general manager of the White Sox, Cardinals, and Indians. He traded stars like Red Schoendienst, Rocky Colavito, and Roger Maris with abandon. Cardinal owner Gussie Busch blocked Lane's attempted trade of Stan Musial. Lane became business manager of the Athletics in 1961 and later scouted for the Orioles and Brewers. /(FJO)

Al Lang — Unk.–Unk

A Pittsburgh laundry owner and Florida real estate investor, Lang was the mayor of St. Petersburg when he persuaded the Yankees to come there for spring training in 1925, three years after the Boston Braves had made it their headquarters. Since then, Florida has remained the center of spring training activity. /(NLM)

Jack Lang — 1921– . *Writer.*

The secretary of the BBWAA makes the phone call to notify players when they are named MVP or Cy Young Award winner or have been elected to the Hall of Fame. Since 1966 that has been Jack Lang's pleasure, first as secretary-treasurer of the writers' organization and, since 1988, as executive secretary.

Lang made his debut on the baseball beat in 1946 covering the Dodgers for the Long Island *Press*. When the Dodgers left town, he switched to the Yankees. Out of that came his first book, *The Fighting Southpaw* (1962), with Whitey Ford. That year the Mets were born and Lang covered them for the *Press* until that paper closed in 1977, then for the New York *Daily News* until he left in 1987 to join *SportsTicker* as a contributing editor and columnist. He received the J.G. Taylor Spink Award in 1986. Lang also wrote *Baseball Basics for Teenagers* (1981) and *The New York Mets: 25 Years of Baseball Magic* (1986). /(NLM)

Bill Lange (Little Eva) — 1871–1950. OF 1893–99 **Cubs** 811 g, .330, 40 hr, 578 rbi

Later described by A.H. Spink, founder and editor of *The Sporting News*, as "Ty Cobb enlarged, fully as great in speed, batting skill and base running," the legendary Chicago outfielder quit baseball at his peak to wed the daughter of a San Francisco real estate magnate, who forbade her to marry a ball-player. The exceptionally popular Lange set the Cub season batting record with .389 in 1895 (still unbroken) and had a string of six consecutive .300 seasons when he quit. He was famous as a reveler while with the Cubs, but he also discovered Frank Chance and recommended him to the team. Fables grew around his career. For many years he was credited as the last player before Maury Wills to steal 100 bases in a season, but later research reduced his 1896 total to 84. The next season Lange led the NL with 73. His

Bill Lange

but fanned 13 against New York on September 20, 1910. He compiled a .500 record over the next two years but was released in mid-1913./(RL)

Rick Langford — 1952- . RHP 1976-86 Pirates, **A's** 1491 ip, 73-106, 4.01. *1 LCS, 7 ip, 1-0, 1.23*

Langford, who had tied for the AL lead with 19 losses in 1977, had his first of two winning seasons when Billy Martin arrived in Oakland in 1980. Langford went 19-12 that year with league highs of 290 innings pitched and 28 complete games—22 of them consecutive, setting an A's record. In 1981 he again led the AL in complete games (18) and won the clincher in the AL Western Division playoffs. He was a fast-working finesse pitcher and an excellent fielder; his first major league error (10/2/80) broke a streak of 230 consecutive chances accepted—an AL record for pitchers. When he developed elbow trouble in 1983 after leading the A's in innings and complete games a fourth straight year, many—but not Langford—blamed Martin for having overworked his starters. Langford struggled to come back through the last four years of a six-year contract and went 1-10 (7.36) in a final try in 1986./(JCA)

Mark Langston — 1960- . LHP 1984- **Mariners,** Expos 1374 ip, 86-76, 3.80
☛ *Led League—k 84, 86-87. All-Star—87. Gold Glove—87-88.*

One of the most overpowering lefthanders of his day, Mark Langston ended the 1989 season with the likelihood of becoming the highest-paid pitcher of all time. Traded to contending Montreal for three pitching prospects during the 1989 season by a Seattle club that feared losing him to free agency, Langston quickly established that he could strike out batters in either league.

Langston was *TSN* AL Rookie Pitcher of the Year in 1984, the fourth rookie to lead the league in strikeouts, and he set a Mariners record with 17 wins. Injuries hampered him in 1985 and kept him below 200 strikeouts for the only time in the 1980s. But he came back to lead the AL in strikeouts in 1986 and 1987. In 1987 Langston set a new Mariner record with 19 wins and became the first Mariner to win a Gold Glove. He set team season records for innings, complete games, strikeouts, and shutouts. On May 10, 1988 Langston broke his own team record by striking out 16 Blue Jays. Langston complements a blazing fastball with an effective assortment of other pitches./(TF)

defense was so sensational that a story grew up that he once crashed through a wooden outfield fence making a catch. Again, later research has restored the boards (though the catch was remarkable, according to eyewitnesses). A huge man for his time, the 6'1" 190-lb Lange refused all comeback offers once he left the game, although the marriage for which he quit the game ended in divorce./(ARA)

Dick Lange — 1948- . RHP 1972-75 **Angels** 277 ip, 9-15, 4.46

Lange was a star in the Angel farm system: 13-0 in 14 starts for Idaho Falls in 1970 and the top ERA in the Pacific Coast League in 1972. He was never consistent in four ML seasons./(MC)

Frank Lange (Seagan, Bill) — 1883-1945. RHP 1910-13 **White Sox** 498 ip, 28-25, 2.96

The Chicago press labeled Lange "Bill" after the popular Chicago NL outfielder of the 19th century. The White Sox curveballer battled arm problems

Hal Lanier — 1942– . SS-2B-3B 1964–73 **Giants,** Yankees 1196 g, .228, 8 hr, 273 rbi. *1 LCS, 1 g, .000.*
   Manager 1986–88 **Astros** 254–232, .523. First place: 86 *1 LCS, 2–4, .333*

Signed for a $50,000 bonus, Lanier made a successful ML debut, batting a career-high .274 and gaining a spot on the 1964 Topps All-Star Rookie team. A serious beaning in 1965 left him with epilepsy, and he never hit above .233 again. He spent seven seasons as a Giants regular, moving from second base to shortstop, and finally to third base. In 1968 Lanier led all NL shortstops in putouts and fielding average. After his playing days, he managed in the minors and coached in the majors. In 1986, as the rookie manager of the Astros, he led Houston to the NL West title and was named Manager of the Year. His father, Max, was an NL pitching star. /(LAW)

Max Lanier — 1915– . LHP 1938–46, 49–53 **Cardinals,** Giants, Browns 1618 ip, 108–82, 3.01. *3 WS, 32 ip, 2–1, 1.71*
   All-Star—43–44.

Although he became a lefthander only because he broke his right arm twice as a child, Lanier was the top-winning southpaw for three consecutive Cardinal pennant winners, 1942–44. He was 6–0 in 1946, then jumped to the Mexican League, causing his suspension from organized baseball. He was reinstated in 1949 and won 11 games for the Cardinals in both 1950 and '51. Lanier's son Hal became a major league player, coach, and manager. /(LAW)

Ernest J. Lanigan — 1873–1962. *Writer*

Shortly after *The Sporting News* was launched, 15-year-old Lanigan went to work for his uncles, the Spink brothers. He worked for the New York *Press* until 1911, when he became secretary of the International League under Ed Barrow. He served stints as baseball editor for the Cleveland *Leader*, business manager of several Cardinals farm teams, and press information director for the International League. His frail health was a factor in his frequent job changes. In 1946, he was named curator of the Hall of Fame and later served as its historian.

   Lanigan is a titan of baseball record keeping. He was among the first to advocate the formation of the BBWAA and published *The Baseball Cyclopedia* in 1922, an early model for today's *The Baseball Encyclopedia* and *Total Baseball*. He was instrumental in making the RBI an official statistic and the unofficial lists he compiled for years are a valuable resource. Called Figure Filbert by Damon Runyon, he once confided: "I really don't care much about baseball, or looking at ball games, major or minor. All my interest in baseball is in its statistics." /(NLM)

Johnny Lanning (Tobacco Chewin' Johnny) — 1910– . RHP 1936–43, 45–47 Braves, **Pirates** 1071 ip, 58–60, 3.58

Lanning gained attention in his first ML year when he defeated the Cardinals, Cubs, and Giants in succession in September 1936, when the three teams were fighting for the pennant. Although a consistent pitcher for eleven ML seasons, he never met the expectations he raised as a rookie. His brother Tom pitched three games for the Phillies in 1938. /(ME)

Carney Lansford — 1957– . 3B-1B 1978– Angels, Red Sox, **A's** 1588 g, .294, 141 hr, 748 rbi. *3 LCS, 11 g, .333, 1 hr, 9 rbi. 2 WS, 9 g, .294, 1 hr, 5 rbi*
   Led League—ba 81.

An often-overlooked outstanding natural hitter, Lansford was the Angels Rookie of the Year in 1978, third in the overall AL vote. Traded to Boston in December 1980, in 1981 Lansford became the first righthanded hitter since 1970 to lead the AL in hitting (.336). He went to Oakland in December 1982 in a deal for Tony Armas. A superb fielder despite a lack of range, Carney appeared headed to first base until the emergence of Mark McGwire. Slowed by wrist and ankle injuries in 1983 and a broken right wrist in 1985, the streaky Lansford was healthy over the next four years and was usually the leadoff or number-two hitter. He stole a career-high 29 bases in 1988 and was second in the AL with a .336 batting average as Oakland won AL pennants both years. He is Oakland's all-time leading hitter (.296) entering the 1990 season and among its all-time leaders in runs, hits, doubles, and slugging percentage. A quietly intense player, Lansford became recognized as a team leader on the Athletics.
   Carney's younger brother Joe played 25 games for the Padres in 1982–83. /(ME)

Paul LaPalme (Lefty) — 1923– . LHP 1951–57 **Pirates,** Cardinals, Reds, White Sox 616 ip, 24–45, 4.42

LaPalme pitched a shutout in his first ML game but suffered for much of his career with some of baseball's worst teams, the 1952–54 Pirates. The knuckleballer led the NL with eight wild pitches in '54. Despite his wildness, he had seven saves for the White Sox in 1957. /(ME)

Dave LaPoint — 1959– . LHP 1980– Brewers, Cardinals, Giants, Tigers, Padres, White Sox, Pirates, Yankees 1324 ip, 73–75, 3.96. *1 WS, 8 ip, 0–0, 3.24*

LaPoint joined the Cardinals in a blockbuster deal that sent Ted Simmons and Rollie Fingers to Milwaukee. A finesse pitcher with good control who relied on making batters hit his pitch, LaPoint had three winning years with the Cardinals. Then, in a series of rapid moves, he played for seven teams between 1985 and 1989. Popular with his team-mates for his good humor and upbeat attitude, LaPoint was the White Sox' best starter in 1988 until he was acquired for the stretch run by the Pirates that August. The following winter he signed with the Yankees as a free agent, but missed most of 1989 on the DL. /(FO)

Frank LaPorte (Pot) — 1880–1939. 2B-3B-OF 1905–15 **Yankees**, Red Sox, Browns, Senators, Indianapolis (FL), Newark (FL) 1193 g, .281, 14 hr, 560 rbi
☛ *Led League—rbi 14.*

LaPorte was a quiet player who split most of his seasons among several positions. In 1911 he batted a career-high .314 with 37 doubles and 82 as the Browns' second baseman, leading AL second base-men in assists, double plays, and errors. He was pushed out by Del Pratt in 1912 and sold to the Senators. He could hit line drives as hard as any AL player when he jumped to the Federal League, which he led with 107 RBI in 1914 while batting .311 for the first-place Indianapolis Hoosiers in 1914. He bowed out after a 1915 season in which his average dropped to .253, although he did lead league second basemen in putouts, assists, and double plays. /(NLM)

Jack Lapp — 1884–1920. C 1908–16 **A's**, White Sox 565 g, 5 hr, 166 rbi. *4 WS, 5 g, .235, 1 rbi*

Lapp was a platooned or backup catcher on four Philadelphia A's pennant winners in five seasons (1910–11, 13–14). In 1911 he was the top-hitting AL catcher, with a .353 mark in 68 games. He died of pneumonia at age thirty-five. /(NLM)

John Lardner — 1912–1960. *Writer.*

One of Ring Lardner's four sons, John continued the family tradition of superb sports journalism and is best remembered for his weekly column in *News-week*, where he observed with wry humor events in the sports world. He also served as TV critic for *The New Yorker* and was drama critic for the New York daily *The Star*. /(JK)

Ring Lardner — 1885–1933. *Writer.*

Ring Lardner was regarded as unusual when he made the switch from writing baseball humor to being the prolific author of witty essays and short stories. No writer had ever examined baseball as a source for serious literary material until Lardner did it with his stories about Jack Keefe, the prototype of all eccentric rookies, in *You Know Me, Al*. Lardner based his fictional character and the events of his baseball stories on his experiences covering the Chicago teams for the *Tribune*, and his series "Pullman Tales" delighted readers of *The Sporting News*. He eventually gave up beat coverage, confin-ing his reporting to the coverage of annual events such as the World Series. His sardonic outlook is best exemplified by a comment directed at overly inquisitive children. "Shut up, I explained," he wrote.

Lardner suspected the White Sox of throwing the 1919 World Series from the start and walked through the team's train car during the Series singing a self-penned ditty, "I'm Forever Blowing Ball-games," to the tune of "I'm Forever Blowing Bubbles," a popular song of the day. /(JK)

Roy Largent — 1879–1943. *Scout.*

Roy and his wife, Bessie, formed a unique husband-and-wife scouting tandem for the White Sox from 1924 to 1939. Roy was totally deaf, and Bessie would read his lips, serve as his ears, and drive the car on scouting trips. She eventually became a shrewd judge of talent herself. The Largents discov-ered over 100 eventual ML players, including Luke Appling, Zeke Bonura, and Lon Warneke. /(FVP)

Norm Larker — 1930– . 1B-OF 1958–63 **Dodgers**, Astros, Braves, Giants 667 g, .275, 32 hr, 271 rbi. *1 WS, 6 g, .188*
☛ *All-Star—60.*

The hustling lefthander, who overcame the loss of a kidney, was considered as a fine fielder but an ordinary hitter until 1960. Suddenly, his line drives fell in, and he finished with a .323 batting average, within one hit of the NL batting crown won by Dick Groat. He never came close to matching his '60 season and was out of the majors three years later. /(LAW)

Barry Larkin — 1964– . SS 1986– **Reds** 414 g, .289, 31 hr, 154 rbi
☛ *All-Star—88–89.*

Like many of his companions on the 1984 U.S. Olympic baseball team, Larkin sped to the majors.

The Reds made the native Cincinnatian their first pick in the June 1985 draft; 14 months later, they made him their shortstop. Larkin gave them a leadoff hitter with good power for a middle infielder. He homered on Opening Day of 1987 but was hampered by a hyperextended knee for the first half of the year. In 1988 he became an All-Star and led the Reds with a .296 batting average. Larkin was hitting .340 at the All-Star break in 1989, but tore ligaments in his elbow during an outfield-to-home relay contest the day before the All-Star Game. When he returned in September he could only pinch hit./(JCA)

Gene Larkin — 1962- . DH-1B 1987- **Twins** 370 g, .267, 18 hr, 144 rbi. *1 LCS, 1 g, 1.000, 1 rbi. 1 WS, 5 g, .000*

Larkin surpassed all of Lou Gehrig's school batting records as a switch-hitting third baseman at Columbia, and never hit below .302 in the minors. The line-drive hitter splits his time between DH and first base, where he backs up Kent Hrbek. Larkin was hit by 15 pitches in 1988 to lead the AL./(SCL)

Dave LaRoche — 1948- . LHP 1970-83 **Angels**, Twins, Cubs, Indians, Yankees 1049 ip, 65-58, 3.53. *1 LCS, 1 ip, 0-0, 6.75. 1 WS, 1 ip, 0-0, 0.00* ☛ *All-Star—76-77.*

LaRoche gained notoriety for his blooper pitch, called the LaLob. Almost exclusively a reliever (he lost all six decisions in his 15 career starts), he saved 126 games lifetime. His best season was 1978, when he saved 25 while going 10-9 with a 2.81 ERA for the Angels. He had five other seasons in double figures in saves./(SFS)

Don Larsen — 1929- . RHP 1953-65, 67 Browns/ Orioles, **Yankees**, A's, White Sox, Giants, Astros, Cubs 1548 ip, 81-91, 3.78 *5 WS, 36 ip, 4-2, 2.75*

Though he had a mediocre career record, Larsen was immortalized by his World Series perfect game of October 8, 1956. He had gone 11-5 for the Yankees that year and, after being knocked out in the second inning of Game Two, started Game Five. He set down 27 Dodgers in a row, outdueling Sal Maglie and winning 2-0 for the first no-hitter in Series history. The last batter Larsen faced was Dale Mitchell, who was declared out by umpire Babe Pinelli on a called third strike. Mitchell and others, including Mickey Mantle in centerfield, thought the ball a bit outside, but mayhem had erupted and catcher Yogi Berra had jumped into Larsen's arms before Mitchell could argue.

Before joining the Yankees, Larsen had a 3-21

Don Larsen

record for the 1954 Orioles to lead the AL in losses. But two of his wins came against New York, who took him as part of an 18-player deal that winter. One early morning in spring training of 1956, Larsen, who had a reputation as a partier, crashed his car into a telephone pole, prompting manager Casey Stengel to say, "He was probably mailing a letter." But he was a capable pitcher who, like Yankee teammate Bob Turley, adopted a no-windup delivery. His 11 wins in 1956 were his season high. He went 1-10 with the A's in 1960 and bounced around before receiving his last ML chance with the Cubs in 1967. He was the last active former St. Louis Brown. A lifetime .242 batter, he had 14 career home runs and was used 66 times as a pinch hitter./(GDW)

Dan Larson — 1954- . RHP 1976-82 **Astros**, Phillies, Cubs 324 ip, 10-25, 4.39

Larson went 5-8 and 1-7 for the Astros and then was traded before 1978 to the Phillies. He was then included in a package with Keith Moreland and Dickie Noles to get Mike Krukow from the Cubs. /(JFC)

Tony LaRussa — 1944- . 2B-SS 1963, 68-71, 73 A's, Braves, Cubs 132 g, .199, 0 hr, 7 rbi.
Manager 1979- **White Sox**, A's 752-683, .524. First place: 83, 88 *2 LCS, 5-3, .625. 2 WS, 5-4, .556*

LaRussa had managed less than two full seasons in the minors when he replaced Don Kessinger as the White Sox manager on August 2, 1979 at the age of thirty-four. Extremely bright and articulate, LaRussa led the White Sox to the AL West title with a ML-high 99 wins in 1983, winning several Manager of the Year awards. The White Sox stumbled in 1984-85, however, and after a 26-38 start in 1986 LaRussa was fired June 19, only to sign as the manager of the A's three weeks later. He managed the A's to third place finishes in 1986 and 1987, then took them to the WS in 1988, where they lost to the Dodgers in five games. As a player, LaRussa made his ML debut with the Kansas City A's at the age of eighteen, but spent most of his career in the minors, where he played until 1977. LaRussa received a law degree from Florida State in 1978, making him the fifth lawyer/manager in baseball history. The other four are in the Hall of Fame /(SCL)

Frank Lary (Mule, The Yankee Killer) — 1930- . RHP 1954-65 **Tigers**, Mets, Braves, White Sox 2162 ip, 128-116, 3.49 20 wins: 56, 61
☛ *Led League—w 56. All-Star—60-61. Gold Glove—61.*

Frank Lary and older brother Al, a Cubs pitcher, both debuted in 1954. Al's major league career was short, but in 1956, the fireballing Frank emerged as the ace of a strong Tiger staff, leading the American League with 21 wins. He was especially tough on the perennial pennant-winning Yankees, going 5-1 against them in 1956 and 7-0 in 1958—the first time since 1916 that New York had been beaten seven times in one season by one pitcher. Lary defeated them five times in a row in 1959, making it 13 wins in 14 decisions. Lifetime against the Yankees, Lary was 27-13. His best season was 1961, when he was 23-9, threw a one-hitter, and led the league with 22 complete games. In his three All-Star appearances, he didn't allow an earned run. He developed a sore arm in 1962 and changed teams four times during 1964 and 1965. As late as the 1970s, while coaching and scouting for various organizations, he was trying to convince teams he could pitch again. /(MC)

Lyn Lary (Broadway) — 1906-1973. SS-3B 1929-40 **Yankees**, Red Sox, Senators, Browns, Indians, Dodgers, Cardinals 1302 g, .269, 38 hr, 526 rbi

In 1928 the Yankees paid Oakland (Pacific Coast League) the then-exorbitant sum of $125,000 for their sensational double-play combo, Lyn Lary and Jimmy Reese. Shortstop Lary was a Yankee until May 1934. In 1931 Lary had 107 RBI, the most ever by a Yankee shortstop, and was one of six Yankees to score 100 runs. He also cost Lou Gehrig that season's home run title when, incorrectly thinking a ball Gehrig hit out had been caught, Lary left the basepath and was passed by Gehrig, who was declared out. Playing for the 1936 Browns, Lary led the AL with 37 stolen bases. /(MG)

Fred Lasher (Whip) — 1941- . RHP 1963, 67-71 Twins, **Tigers**, Indians, Angels 202 ip, 11-13, 3.88. *1 WS, 2 ip, 0-0, 0.00*

This sidearming reliever appeared in 34 games for the 1968 World Champion Tigers and a career-high 55 for Detroit and Cleveland in 1970. /(FK)

Bill Laskey — 1957- . RHP 1982-86, 88 **Giants**, Expos, Indians 745 ip, 42-53, 4.14

A soft-throwing righthander with excellent control, Laskey made the Topps and *Baseball Digest* All-Rookie teams as a starting pitcher in 1983, going 13-12, 3.14 for the Giants. His ERA rose and his strikeout total fell each year until 1986, when he was sent to the bullpen, and he spent all of 1987 working in relief for the Tigers AAA Toledo club. In 1988, Laskey posted a 5.18 ERA in 17 relief appearances with the Indians and was released August 21. /(SCL)

Tommy Lasorda — 1927- . LHP 1954-56 Dodgers, A's 26 ip, 0-4, 6.48.
Manager 1976- **Dodgers** 1099-957, .535. First place: 77-78, 81, 83, 85, 88 *6 LCS, 16-14, .533. 4 WS, 12-11, .522*

"My heart bleeds Dodger blue," Lasorda has claimed, during his 35-plus years in the Dodger organization. He looked like a promising pitcher on June 1, 1948 when, in a 15-inning game for the Schenectady Blue Jays (Canadian-American League, Class C), he struck out 25 Amsterdam Rugmakers, setting a since-broken pro record. He even drove in the winning run with a single. In his next two starts, he struck out 15 and 13, gaining the attention of the Dodgers, who signed him for their Montreal club. Lasorda compiled a 98-49 record in nine years with Montreal of the International

Tommy Lasorda

infield of Steve Garvey, Davey Lopes, Bill Russell, and Ron Cey that he had helped assemble in the minor leagues, and he reacquired catcher Joe Ferguson, another of his proteges, to alternate with Steve Yeager. In 1977–78, he became the first NL manager to win pennants his first two seasons, but the Dodgers lost the WS to the Yankees in six games each time. After the 1981 player strike, Lasorda's Dodgers defeated the Astros in the divisional playoff; beat the Expos in the LCS on Rick Monday's two-out, ninth-inning homer; and then crushed the Yankees with a power display in the World Series. Lasorda managed the Dodgers to division titles in 1983 and 1985, but lost both times in the LCS. In 1988, he shared NL Manager of the Year honors with the Pirates Jim Leyland and took the Dodgers to an upset win over the Mets in the LCS and a shocking WS upset of the A's. A media favorite, Lasorda is noted for his good humor and his love of Italian cooking. /(MC)

Arlie Latham [Walter Arlington] (The Freshest Man on Earth) — 1859–1952. 3B 1880, 83–96, 99, 1909 Buffalo (NL), **St. Louis (AA)**, Chicago (PL), Reds, Cardinals, Washington (NL), Giants 1627 g, .269, 27 hr, 398 rbi (inc.).
    Manager 1896 **Cardinals** 0–2, .000

The impish Latham laughed his way through baseball. A dandy third baseman and leadoff hitter for the St. Louis Browns of the then-major league American Association when they won four straight pennants in the 1880s, he scored 100 or more runs nine times, leading the AA in 1886 (152). In 1888 he led with 109 stolen bases under the more liberal scoring rules of the time.

He was equally famous for his comedy in the coach's box, taunting rivals while amusing the crowd with his antics. He was probably the first clown in baseball to develop an act and certainly the first to be hired exclusively as a baseline coach, by John McGraw of the Giants.

Eventually he and his wife moved to England, returning only when WWII seemed imminent. The Giants made a place for him as an attendant in the press box, where the still spry Latham amused writers with his witty observations and reminiscences. /(JK)

Barry Latman (Shoulders) — 1936– . RHP 1957–67 White Sox, **Indians**, Angels, Astros 1219 ip, 59–68, 3.91 ☛ *All-Star–61*.

The broad-shouldered, hard-throwing Latman was considered an outstanding prospect, yet his only successful year was 1961, when he went 13–5 for

League, the Dodgers' top farm club, 1950–1955 and 1958–1960. His best records were 17–8 in 1953 and 18–6 in 1958, when he led the league in victories, complete games, and shutouts. Lasorda helped Montreal to the International League championship five times. He received only two brief trials with the Dodgers, and on May 5, 1955 he tied a ML record with three wild pitches in one inning. Lasorda was demoted in 1955 to make room for bonus baby Sandy Koufax, then sold to Kansas City in 1956, but couldn't stick with the Athletics or Yankees either. Stuck in the high minors, Lasorda moved to Los Angeles a year before the Dodgers did, with the Angels of the Pacific Coast League.

After his second stint in Montreal, Lasorda became a Dodger scout in 1961 and then a minor league manager in 1965. He won five pennants and finished second twice and third once through 1972, with only one record below .500.

Promoted to the Dodgers as a coach, Lasorda served as Walter Alston's understudy until September 29, 1976, when Alston retired. He inherited the

Cleveland and was named to the AL All-Star squad for the second game. /(ME)

Charlie Lau — 1933–1984. C 1956, 58–67 Tigers, Braves, **Orioles**, A's 527 g, .255, 16 hr, 140 rbi

Except for catching Warren Spahn's 1961 no-hitter, Lau's playing career was relatively uneventful; he gained his notoriety as the most respected batting coach of his time. He was a lifetime .180 hitter until 1962, when he radically changed his batting style to win a job with the Orioles. He adopted a contact hitter's stance, straight out of the 19th century: feet wide apart, bat held almost parallel to the ground. He had two hits in an inning he entered as a pinch hitter on June 23 and doubled four times in a game on July 13, 1962, tying a ML record. His average jumped to .294. Slow afoot, with a weak arm, he caught less and pinch hit more each season. After 1966 arm surgery, he only pinch hit. At a team party in August 1966, he saved MVP Frank Robinson from drowning after a swimming pool accident.

Lau taught his hitting technique to the Orioles, A's, Royals, Yankees, and White Sox. His book *How to Hit .300* supplanted Ted Williams's *The Science of Hitting* as the "Bible of Batting." Most of the Royals adopted his spray-hitting style: Hal McRae, George Brett, Amos Otis, and Willie Wilson all used the Lau approach during their most successful seasons. In 1983 Lau voluntarily gave up his spot on the White Sox coaching staff to enable scout Loren Babe, who was dying of lung cancer, to qualify for his ten-year pension. Babe died in February 1984. Lau died from cancer of the colon in March. /(MC)

Billy Lauder — 1874–1933. 3B 1898–99, 1901–03 **Phillies**, A's, Giants 483 g, .261, 6 hr, 254 rbi

A steady third baseman but an average runner, Lauder had his best year with the 1899 Phillies, when he had career highs of 90 RBI and 74 runs while hitting .268. /(DAS)

Tim Laudner — 1958– . C 1981– **Twins** 734 g, .224, 77 hr, 263 rbi. *1 LCS, 5 g, .071, 2 rbi. 1 WS, 7 g, .318, 1 hr, 4 rbi*
☛ *All-Star—88.*

Laudner was the Southern League MVP in 1981, hitting .284 with 42 HR at Orlando to earn a September promotion to the Twins. He was the Twins starting catcher in 1982, then shared with job with Dave Engle and Mark Salas until 1987 when he became the starter once again. A strong righthanded

batter, Laudner hit only .191 in 1987, but he made the AL All-Star Team in 1988 with a .251 average and 13 HR and doubled in his only at-bat in the All-Star Game. /(SCL)

France Laux — Unk.–Unk. *Broadcaster.*

A pioneer sports announcer in St. Louis, Laux worked most World Series and All-Star games between 1929 and 1939, when he moved to WABC in New York. /(NLM)

George Lauzerique — 1947– . RHP 1967–70 **A's**, Brewers 113 ip, 4–8, 5.00

Lauzerique never had a winning season in his short ML career, suffering from control problems. The native Cuban was 13–4, 2.30 in 1967 for a Birmingham (Southern League) team that included Reggie Jackson, Joe Rudi, and Rollie Fingers. On July 6 that year, he pitched a seven-inning perfect game. /(WOR)

Cookie Lavagetto [Harry Arthur] — 1912– . 3B-2B 1934–41, 46–47 Pirates, **Dodgers** 1043 g, .269, 40 hr, 486 rbi. *2 WS, 8 g, .118, 3 rbi.*
    Manager 1957–61 **Senators/Twins 276–393, .413**
☛ *All-Star—38–41.*

A dependable regular, Cookie Lavagetto's moment of fame came in Game Four of the 1947 World Series. Yankee pitcher Bill Bevens had walked two batters in the ninth inning but was one out away from a no-hitter when Lavagetto pinch hit a game-winning double off the right-field wall, beating Bevens 2–1. /(JK)

Mike LaValliere (Spanky) — 1960– . C 1984- Phillies, Cardinals, **Pirates** 437 g, .269, 8 hr, 142 rbi
☛ *Gold Glove—87.*

LaValliere helped make the trade of Pittsburgh favorite Tony Pena look good with a .300 bat and Gold Glove fielding in 1987. He excelled in throwing out potential basestealers and earned a starting spot on the 1986 Cardinals, starting a club rookie record 108 games behind the plate. Signed as a third baseman by the Phillies, the squat LaValliere moved to catcher in 1982. He was MVP in the 1976 Babe Ruth World Series. /(ME)

Doc Lavan [John Leonard] — 1890–1952. SS 1913–24 Browns, A's, Senators, **Cardinals** 1162 g, .245, 7 hr, 377 rbi

A light-hitting shortstop, Lavan was error-prone, booting the ball for both St. Louis teams. He made 75 errors in 1915 for the Browns and later twice led

NL shortstops in miscues while with the Cardinals. /(JK)

Gary Lavelle — 1949- . LHP 1974-85, 87 **Giants**, Blue Jays, A's 1086 ip, 80-77, 2.93. *1 LCS, 0 ip, 0-0. 0.00*
☛ *All-Star—77, 83.*

Lavelle's 136 career saves ranked him third among lefthanded relievers on his retirement. He spent 7-1/2 seasons in the minors before being called up by the Giants in mid-1974, but he remained a fixture in San Francisco for the next decade. In 11 seasons with the Giants, his ERA only once was above 3.42. In 1977 he set team records for games (73) and saves (20), and by 1984 he was the Giants' all-time leader in those categories (breaking Christy Mathewson's games mark). Lavelle led NL relievers with 13 wins in 1978. Greg Minton took over as the Giants' main closer in 1980, and in 1983 he and Lavelle became the NL's first relief duo to each post at least 20 saves in a season.

Lavelle was traded to Toronto for Jim Gott and two minor leaguers before the 1985 season and led the AL East champions with 69 appearances that season. Chronic elbow problems forced him to sit out the 1986 season. Toronto released him in early 1987, and an attempted comeback with the A's failed. /(TF)

Jimmy Lavender — 1884-1960. RHP 1912-17 **Cubs**, Phillies 1207 ip, 62-76, 3.09

Lavender was a spitballer who won ten or more games in five seasons. His two career highlights came against the Giants. On July 8, 1912 he won the game that ended Rube Marquard's record 19-game winning streak, and on August 31, 1915 he hurled a 2-0 no-hitter against New York. /(ARA)

Rudy Law (Lawman) — 1956- . OF 1978, 80, 82-86 Dodgers, **White Sox**, Royals 749 g, .271, 18 hr, 198 rbi. *1 LCS, 4 g, .389*

Law set a since-surpassed Los Angeles Dodger rookie record by stealing 40 bases in 1980 but, failing to hit in the second half, was returned to the minors. The White Sox acquired him in 1982 and made him their leadoff man. In 1983 he was the catalyst in Chicago's division championship; he led AL outfielders in fielding average and eclipsed Luis Aparicio's club stolen base record, with 77. He was forced to give up his uniform 11 in 1984 when it was retired in honor of Aparicio. Signed as a free agent by the Royals in 1986, he injured a knee and soon left the majors. /(RL)

Vance Law — 1956- . 3B-2B-SS-1B 1980- Pirates, **White Sox**, Expos, Cubs 1138 g, .257, 71 hr, 433 rbi. *1 LCS, 2 g, .000*
☛ *All-Star—88.*

The son of Vern Law, Vance was drafted by Pittsburgh in 1978, traded to the White Sox in March 1982 and became Chicago's everyday third baseman in 1983. On May 8 and 9, 1984 against the Brewers, he played all 25 innings of the longest game in AL history, establishing the AL record for the longest errorless game by a third baseman. He erupted with 17 homers in 1984 but then was traded to Montreal for Bob James. Manager Buck Rodgers made good use of Law's talents in 1985-87, even using him as a relief pitcher six times. Law signed with the Cubs as a free agent for 1988, had a productive first half, and made the NL All-Star team. A bad back limited him in 1989, and he struck out in all three of his LCS at-bats. /(RL)

Vern Law (Deacon) — 1930- . RHP 1950-51, 54-67 Pirates 2672 ip, 162-147, 3.77. 20 wins: 60 *1 WS, 18 ip, 2-0, 3.44*
☛ *Cy Young Award—60. All-Star—60.*

Law was largely responsible for the Pirates' World Championship in 1960, when he captured the Cy Young Award with a 20-9 record and a league-high 18 complete games. Despite nursing a late-season sprained ankle, he won the first and fourth games of the Series and had a no-decision in the famed seventh game, won by the Pirates on Bill Mazeroski's ninth-inning homer.

Idaho Senator Herman Welker recommended favorite son Law to former classmate Bing Crosby, part owner of the Pirates. Signed by the Pirates in 1948, Law, a control pitcher with a classic, straight-up motion, reached Pittsburgh in 1950 but spent 1952 and 1953 in the military. He and Bob Friend anchored a young pitching staff on last-place teams in 1954, 1955, and 1957. But both blossomed in 1958 and the Pirates rose to second place. Though Friend slumped in 1959, Law went 18-9.

After reaching the top in 1960, Law missed most of 1961 with a torn rotator muscle. Pitching in pain throughout 1962, he rebounded to go 10-7, but more physical problems in 1963 forced him on to the voluntary retired list. He made a surprising comeback in 1964 (12-13, 3.61) and in 1965, at age thirty-five, led the Pirates with 17 wins and a 2.15 ERA. He was honored with the Lou Gehrig Memorial Award as comeback player of the year. After more injuries his last two years, he retired among Pittsburgh's all-time pitching leaders. Vern and his wife, VaNita, had six children: Veldon, Veryl,

Vern Law

Vaughn, Varlin, VaLynda, and major league infielder Vance. /(ME)

Tom Lawless — 1956- . 2B-3B 1982, 84- Reds, **Cardinals**, Blue Jays 328 g, .210, 2 hr, 23 rbi. *1 LCS, 3 g, .333. 2 WS, 4 g, .100, 1 hr, 3 rbi*

Lawless was the unlikely hero of Game Four of the 1987 World Series. With the Twins and Cardinals tied 1–1 in the fourth inning, he hit a three-run homer off Frank Viola as the Cardinals went on to win 7–2. The speedy utility man was playing only because third baseman Terry Pendleton's rib injury hindered his righthanded hitting. Lawless had had only two hits in 25 at-bats the entire season (.080), and at that point in his career he had one HR in 215 at-bats and hadn't homered in the last three years. /(JFC)

Brooks Lawrence (Bull) — 1925- . RHP 1954-60 Cardinals, **Reds** 1041 ip, 69-62, 4.25

As a 29-year-old rookie seasoned in the Negro National League, Lawrence went 15–6, starting and relieving for the 1954 Cardinals. Hit hard in 1955, he was demoted to Oakland (Pacific Coast League), where he earned a second chance by going 5–1 down the stretch. Acquired by the Reds, he opened 1956 with 13 straight victories, among them two two-hitters. He finished 19–10, then went 16–13 in 1957. He won only eight games in 1958 and seven in 1959, when he threw a third two-hitter. /(MC)

Earl Lawson — Unk.-Unk. *Writer.*

President of the BBWAA in 1976 and longtime correspondent for *The Sporting News*, Lawson covered the Reds for 34 years for the Cincinnati *Star* and *Post*. He retired in 1984 and received the J.G. Taylor Spink Award in 1985. /(NLM)

Roxie Lawson [Alfred Voyle] — 1906–1977. RHP 1930-31, 33, 35-40 Indians, **Tigers**, Browns 852 ip, 47-39, 5.37

After three ML trials with ERAs over 6.00, Lawson had three wins for the 1935 World Champion Tigers, including a shutout over Lefty Grove. In 1937 he managed 18 wins with a whopping 5.26 ERA. /(JK)

Bill Laxton — 1948- . LHP 1970-71, 74, 76-77 Phillies, **Padres**, Tigers, Mariners, Indians 244 ip, 3-10, 4.72

Laxton's only winning record came when the wild reliever was 3–2 for the 1977 expansion Mariners. He had a 7-inning, 2–1 no-hit win on August 25, 1967 for Clinton (Midwest League). /(SFS)

Johnny Lazor — 1912- . OF 1943-46 **Red Sox** 223 g, .263, 6 hr, 62 rbi

Lazor played centerfield for the Red Sox while Dom DiMaggio was in the military. He hit .310 in 1945 but was out of work the next year. /(JK)

Jack Lazorko — 1956– . RHP 1984–88 Brewers, Mariners, Tigers, **Angels** 222 ip, 5–8, 4.22

Drafted five times before signing with the Astros, Lazorko relieved his way through seven organizations and temporarily filled gaps in a few major league bullpens. Given a chance to start by the disappointing 1987 Angels, the 31-year-old recorded all five of his ML wins. /(JCA)

Tony Lazzeri (Poosh 'Em Up) — 1903–1946. 2B-3B-SS 1926–39 **Yankees**, Cubs, Dodgers, Giants 1739 g, .292, 178 hr, 1191 rbi. *7 WS, 32 g, .262, 4 hr, 19 rbi* ☛ *All-Star—33.*

Lazzeri was a prominent member of the 1927 Yankees' "Murderers' Row" lineup and the second baseman on five World Championship Yankee clubs. He had seven 100-RBI seasons and four times hit as many as 18 home runs. His excellent glove, driving leadership, and superior baseball instincts made him the hero of Italian-Americans, as their first superstar. He was known as "the quiet man of the Yankees." Though an epileptic, he never had an on-the-field seizure in his 12 Yankee seasons.

Playing for Salt Lake City (Pacific Coast League) in 1925, assisted by the altitude and a 200-game schedule, Lazzeri set since-broken pro baseball records for HR (60) and RBI (222) and a still-standing record for runs (202). The following year, he played 155 games for New York. With two out and the bases loaded in the seventh inning, he struck out against Grover Cleveland Alexander in the Game Seven of the 1926 World Series, won by the Cardinals 3–2. The famous incident damaged Lazzeri's reputation as a clutch hitter. Yet Miller Huggins, his manager, said: "Anyone can strike out, but ballplayers like Lazzeri come along once in a generation."

From 1927 through 1930, and again in 1932, Lazzeri batted .300 or better; his .354 in 1929 put him among the league leaders. On May 24, 1936 he became the first major leaguer to hit two grand slams in one game and set a still-standing AL record with 11 RBI. /(MG)

Charlie Lea — 1956– . RHP 1980–84, 87–88 **Expos**, Twins 923 ip, 62–48, 3.54 ☛ *All-Star—84.*

An excellent young starter for the Expos for several seasons, Lea was the NL's starting and winning pitcher in the 1984 All-Star Game, then saw his career ruined by arm problems that forced him to miss the entire 1985 and 1986 seasons. He began

Tony Lazzeri

the 1980 season at Memphis (Southern League) for the third consecutive year, but after a 9–0, 0.84 start he was in Montreal by mid-season, where he went 7–5. Lea won only five games in the strike-shortened 1981 season, but one of them was a 4–0 no-hitter against the Giants May 10, and in 1982 he cracked double figures in wins for the first time in his pro career, finishing 12–10. In 1983 Lea won a career-high 16 games, and in 1984 he was 15–10, 2.89 to earn his All-Star Game start but was hurt shortly thereafter. He could not pitch at all in 1985 or 1986. Lea spent most of 1987 rehabilitating in the minors and endured one dreadful inning with the Expos before his comeback as a starter for the Twins in 1988, finishing 7–7 with a 4.85 ERA. /(SCL)

Freddy Leach — 1897–1981. OF 1923–32 **Phillies**, Giants, Braves 991 g, .307, 72 hr, 509 rbi

Leach was a railroad telegrapher playing for town baseball teams in the Ozarks in 1922 when he decided to try professional baseball. After leading the Missouri Valley League in hitting (.383) in his first year, he finished the season with George Stallings's independent Rochester team in the International League, and by 1923 he was with the Phillies. The stocky, thick-eyebrowed Leach bounced up and down between the majors and minors for several years before establishing himself as a steady-hitting, strong-armed outfielder with the Phillies. In 1927 he led NL outfielders in assists. The Giants traded Lefty O'Doul and cash for Leach's contract in October 1928. The deal was widely regarded as a mistake by Giants manager John McGraw when O'Doul hit .398, 108 points higher than Leach, to win the 1929 NL batting title, but McGraw announced he was satisfied that Leach was more versatile and far better defensively. Leach contributed two .300-plus seasons before retiring. /(JK)

Rick Leach — 1957– . OF-1B 1981– Tigers, **Blue Jays**, Rangers 721 g, .265, 16 hr, 167 rbi

Leach was a star quarterback at the University of Michigan from 1976 to 1978 and was a local hero when he signed with the Tigers rather than play pro football. After several seasons as a utility outfielder with Detroit, Leach was released and picked up by Toronto, where he was a star in the minors and a role player with the Blue Jays. Although his role was limited to that of backup outfielder and lefthanded bat off the bench, Leach demonstrated the psychological makeup that made him a winner in football, diving for balls a faster outfielder would have caught easily or a lazier outfielder would have let drop. /(TF)

Terry Leach — 1954– . RHP 1981–82, 85– **Mets**, Royals 461 ip, 29-15, 3.28. *1 LCS, 5 ip, 0–0, 0.00*

This control pitcher uses a low sidearm motion. Bending to his right as he throws, he scrapes his padded right knee on the mound. Leach had a career season (11–1) in 1987, when numerous injuries to the Mets staff gave him more chances to

pitch. After three straight wins in relief, he became a starter and won another seven in a row, for a Met-record 10 consecutive wins from the beginning of the season.

Leach set another record in his first stint with the Mets. His 10-inning, 1–0 one-hitter against the Phillies on October 1, 1982 is the only extra-inning one-hitter in club history. His NL career record as a starter is 11–2 with a 2.82 ERA, but the Mets' rotation was so deep that he only saw emergency work in that role. He was a valuable long-relief man on two pennant winners. In 1989 he was traded to Kansas City. /(SH)

Tommy Leach — 1877–1969. OF-3B-SS 1898–1915, 18 Louisville (NL), **Pirates**, Cubs, Reds 2155 g, .269, 62 hr, 810 rbi. *2 WS, 15 g, .293, 9 rbi*
☛ *Led League—hr 02.*

A 5'6" speedster, Leach was Pittsburgh's third baseman in the first World Series, played in 1903 against the Red Sox. He specialized in triples and hit four in the '03 WS—two in one game—to set still-

Tommy Leach

standing Series records. Of his 62 major league home runs, 49 were inside the park; none of his seven 1903 homers were hit over the fence. He led the National League with six home runs in 1902 and twice topped the league in runs scored—with Pittsburgh in 1909 and with Chicago in 1913. /(JK)

League Park Cincinnati Reds 1894–1901. LF-253

In 1895 the Reds created the first "batter's eye" by painting the centerfield wall black, making it easier to see incoming pitches. Erected on the site of Cincinnati's original League Park, which saw its grandstand collapse on Opening Day 1884, killing one spectator, the second League Park burned down in 1901 and was rebuilt as Crosley Field. /(SCL)

League Park Cleveland (NL) 1891–99, Cleveland Indians 1901–32, 34–46. LF-375, CF-420, RF-290

Converted to baseball's fourth concrete-and-steel park in 1910, Cleveland's League Park never had lights, and after 1932 the Indians played many of their home games at the colossal new Municipal Stadium. The scene of Bill Wambsganss's unassisted triple play in the 1920 WS, League Park had its stands torn down in 1950 and it is now a public park. /(SCL)

Luis Leal — 1957– . RHP 1980–85 **Blue Jays** 947 ip, 51–58, 4.14

The chunky starter from Venezuela showed flashes of brilliance for the Blue Jays within a mediocre career. Leal was erratic, with a five-game winning streak in 1983 that was followed by a four-game losing streak the same season. On June 2, 1980 Leal gave up an AL-record five consecutive hits to start a game. On August 15, 1984 in a doubleheader with Cleveland, Leal was allowed to stay in the game to give up a team-record 10 runs (all earned). At the time of his release, Leal ranked behind only Jim Clancy and Dave Stieb as Blue Jays' career leader in starts, innings, wins, losses, strikeouts, and walks. /(TF)

Tim Leary — 1958– . RHP 1981, 83– Mets, Brewers, **Dodgers**, Reds 831 ip, 45–56, 3.77. *1 LCS, 4 ip, 0–1, 6.23. 1 WS, 7 ip, 0–0, 1.35*

One of several successful reclamation projects of Dodgers pitching coach Ron Perranoski, Leary posted a 17–11, 2.91 record for the World Champion Dodgers in 1988 after winning a total of 20 games in six previous ML seasons. Leary was a college All-American at UCLA and was the second pick overall in the June 1979 free-agent draft, and in 1980 he was Texas League MVP, leading the league

in wins and shutouts for Jackson. Leary made the Mets in 1981, only to be injured in his first start on a cold April day at Wrigley Field, then missed all of 1982 with an injured nerve. He moved to Milwaukee in a six-player, four-team trade in 1985 and was 12–12 for the Brewers in 1986 before being traded to Los Angeles with Tim Crews for slugger Greg Brock. Leary started and lost Game Six of the 1988 LCS for the Dodgers, but he pitched well out of the bullpen in the World Series. After the season he received the NL Comeback Player of the Year Award. He was traded to the Reds in mid-1989. /(TG)

Bevo LeBourveau [DeWitt Wiley] — 1894–1947. OF 1919–22, 29 **Phillies**, A's 280 g, .275, 11 hr, 69 rbi

LeBourveau was the scourge of American Association pitching, twice winning the batting championship, and he hit .349 in 1,584 minor league games. His hitting skills resisted transfer to the majors, and he never had a 100-game season. /(JK)

Bill Lee (Spaceman) — 1946– . LHP 1969–82 **Red Sox**, Expos 1945 ip, 119–90, 3.62 *1 LCS, 1 ip, 0–0, 0.00. 1 WS, 14 ip, 0–0, 3.14*
☛ *All-Star—73.*

Lee's colorful personality sometimes overshadowed his excellent pitching. He earned his Spaceman nickname when, on his first view of Fenway's left field wall, he asked, "Do they leave it there during games?" Always willing to speak his mind, he led a Red Sox revolt against manager Don Zimmer (whom he called "the gerbil"); criticized domed stadiums, artificial turf, and the designated hitter rule; and admitted to marijuana use, but only "sprinkled on cereal." He ultimately left the ML when he walked off the Expos in protest of the release of friend Rodney Scott. He was the victim of freak accidents, including one where he was nearly killed by a taxi that ran him down while he was jogging. In between the oddities, he was a fine control pitcher who won 17 games three straight seasons for Boston (1973–75) and 16 for the Expos in 1979. /(MC)

Bill Lee [William Crutchfield] (Big Bill, General) — 1909–1977. RHP 1934–47 **Cubs**, Phillies, Braves 2864 ip, 169–157, 3.54. 20 wins: 35, 38 *2 WS, 21 ip, 0–2, 2.95*
☛ *Led League—w 38. Led League—era 38. All-Star—38–39.*

General Lee was a 6'3" Louisianan whose extremely high leg kick deceived batters and gave his fastball added speed. He was buried in the Cardinals system despite a 71–31 record over four seasons. Branch

Rickey made a choice between Paul Dean and Lee in 1934, bringing Dean to the majors and selling Lee to the Cubs. Lee shut out the Phillies in his first ML start (5/7/34). In his sophomore season, 1935, he led the NL with a .769 winning percentage (20–6), recorded five victories during the Cubs' 21-game winning streak, and won the pennant clincher.

Lee was positively intimidating in 1938, helping the Cubs to another World Series by leading the league with 22 wins, a .710 winning percentage, a 2.66 ERA, 37 starts, and nine shutouts. During one period he reeled off 32 consecutive scoreless innings and yielded only one run in 47 innings; the lone run was driven in by a pitcher and prevented Lee from hurling five straight shutouts. In September he racked up a streak of 37–1/3 scoreless innings, which included a flawless relief job between four shutouts.

Lee lost his touch in 1940. His eyes began to fail, and he had trouble seeing his catcher's signals. The high point of his 8–14 season in 1941 came on May 7, when he hit two home runs in a game. With the help of eyeglasses, he went 13–13 in 1942, then bounced from team to team, twice winning 10 games. After he retired, he underwent delicate surgery for two detached retinas and eventually lost his sight. /(DB)

Bob Lee (Moose, Horse) — 1937– . RHP 1964–68 **Angels**, Dodgers, Reds 492 ip, 25–23, 2.71

Lee was the ace of the Angels' bullpen for three years, finishing fifth in the AL with 19 saves his rookie year (1964) and fourth with 23 in 1965 (before the save was an official statistic). His 1.51 ERA in 1964 was the second-lowest ever in the AL for a rookie. He faded after being traded to the NL following the 1966 season. /(JFC)

Cliff Lee — 1896–1980. OF-1B 1919–26 Pirates, **Phillies**, Reds, Indians 521 g, .300, 38 hr, 216 rbi

Cliff's bat earned him one season (1923) as an outfield regular with the cellar-dwelling Phillies, but essentially he was a utility man who had catching, outfield, and first base skills. /(ADS)

Don Lee (Moose) — 1934– . RHP 1957–58, 60–66 Tigers, Senators/Twins, **Angels**, Astros, Cubs 828 ip, 40–44, 3.61

The son of 16-year veteran Thornton Lee, Don was an occasional starter who won a career-high 11 games in 1962, 8 for the expansion Angels. /(FK)

Hal Lee (Sheriff) — 1905– . OF 1930–36 Dodgers, Phillies, **Braves** 752 g, .275, 33 hr, 323 rbi

Discovered as a college star for the University of Mississippi, Lee was a graceful fielder who twice hit .303. Yet he never lived up to early promise, reportedly because he lacked ambition. /(JK)

Leron Lee — 1948– . OF 1969–76. Cardinals, **Padres**, Indians, Dodgers 614 g, .250, 31 hr, 152 rbi

A top high school football player, Lee refused numerous scholarship offers to sign with the Cardinals for an estimated $50,000. His only good year came with the Padres in 1972 when he batted .300 in 101 games, only the second Padre ever to hit that mark. /(BC)

Manny Lee — 1965– . 2B-SS 1985– **Blue Jays** 370 g, .265, 7 hr, 90 rbi. *2 LCS, 2 g, .250*

Lee's natural position is shortstop, but at Toronto he found himself behind fellow San Pedro de Macoris, Dominican Republic native Tony Fernandez. In 1988, between the departure of Damaso Garcia and the ascendance of Nelson Liriano, Lee was the Blue Jays' primary second baseman, and hit a career-high .291. /(SFS)

Mark Lee — 1953– . RHP 1978–81 **Padres**, Pirates 176 ip, 7–8, 3.63

Lee's only winning record came in his rookie 1978 season, when the 6'4" 225-lb reliever went 5–1 with a 3.28 ERA. /(WOR)

Thornton Lee (Lefty) — 1906– . LHP 1933–48 Indians, **White Sox**, Giants 2331 ip, 117–124, 3.56. 20 wins: 41

☛ *Led League—era 41. All-Star—41.*

Lee reached the major leagues in 1933 at age twenty-seven and struggled for four years with Cleveland. His fortunes changed when White Sox manager Jimmy Dykes saw something in the left-hander and obtained him in a three-way deal. Relying on fine control and a sinking fastball, he blossomed under the tutelage of coach Muddy Ruel and became one of baseball's top lefthanders from 1937 to 1941. But little offensive support left him on the losing end of many close decisions. In 1941 he had a great year, leading the league with 30 complete games and a 2.37 ERA, and collecting a $2,500 bonus for winning more than 20. Three years of misery followed; he broke his arm and underwent two bone chip removals and a neck operation. He bounced back in 1945, going 15–12, and was still pitching at age forty-two, nine years before his son, pitcher Don Lee, broke in with the

Tigers. Ted Williams homered off both of them, the only man to hit a HR off a father and son. /(DB)

Watty Lee [Wyatt Arnold] — 1879-1936. OF-LHP 1901-04 **Senators**, Pirates 235 g, .242, 4 hr, 70 rbi; 549 ip, 30-37, 4.29

Lee divided his playing time between the mound, where he was 16–16 as a rookie, and the outfield, where he hit .256 as a regular the next year. /(JK)

Sam Leever (The Goshen Schoolmaster) — 1871-1953. RHP 1898-1910 **Pirates** 2661 ip, 193-101, 2.47. 20 wins: 99, 03, 06 *1 WS, 10 ip, 0-2, 6.30*
☛ *Led League—era 03.*

A righthander of quiet ways, sober temperament, and sharp-breaking curveball, Leever was a mainstay of the Pirate pitching staff during the heyday of Honus Wagner. Born in Goshen, Ohio, and a former teacher (hence his nickname), Leever was not colorful, just consistent, posting 11 consecutive winning seasons. In 1903, his best year, he led the NL in winning percentage (.781), ERA (2.06) and shutouts (7). Two of his 25 wins came in a string of six consecutive shutouts, still the ML record. Near the end of that season he injured his shoulder while trapshooting, a second sport at which he excelled. As a result he had a sore arm during the 1903 WS and lost twice to the Red Sox. His lifetime winning percentage of .656 is third (after Christy Mathewson and Sal Maglie) among NL pitchers in the 20th century and tenth all-time. /(ADS)

Jim Lefebvre (Frenchy) — 1943- . 2B-3B 1965-72 **Dodgers** 922 g, .251, 74 hr, 404 rbi. *2 WS, 7 g, .273, 1 hr, 1 rbi.*
    Manager 1989- **Mariners** 73-89, .451

Part of the Dodgers' switch-hitting infield of the mid-1960s with Jim Gilliam, Maury Wills, and Wes Parker, Lefebvre homered from both sides of the plate in one game on May 7, 1966. His 12 HR as a rookie in 1965 was the lowest total to lead a pennant winner since 1947, and he homered off Dave McNally in the 1966 WS opener, providing one of the two runs the Dodgers would score all series in a four-game sweep by the Orioles. He played in Japan in 1973–76 and later coached the Dodgers, Giants, and A's. He was named the Mariners' manager in the winter of 1988 after gaining respect as the batting coach of the AL champion A's. /(TG)

Joe Lefebvre — 1956- . OF-3B 1980-84, 86 Yankees, **Padres**, Phillies 447 g, .258, 31 hr, 130 rbi. *2 LCS, 3 g, .000. 1 WS, 3 g, .200, 2 rbi*

Lefebvre (pronounced "luh-FAY") was a promising power hitter who homered in his first two major league games for the Yankees, tying a record. After being traded to the Padres, he was unsuccessfully converted to third base (and even caught some games). On September 13, 1982 he had six hits in a 16-inning game.

Lefebvre seemed finally ready to fulfill his promise after hitting .310 following a May 1983 trade to the Phillies, finishing at .306 for the year with eight HR and 20 doubles in 278 at-bats and helping Philadelphia win the NL pennant. But he was felled by back trouble in June 1984 and missed all of 1985 too; a comeback attempt in 1986 failed. /(SFS)

Craig Lefferts — 1957- . LHP 1983- Cubs, **Padres**, Giants 683 ip, 32-39, 3.00. *3 LCS, 7 ip, 2-0, 1.29. 2 WS, 9 ip, 0-0, 1.04*

A career reliever, the German-born Lefferts was a set-up man for six years before emerging as the Giants' closer in the first half of 1989. After Steve Bedrosian was acquired, the two shared the role. Lefferts pitched 10 shutout innings in the 1984 postseason for the Padres, winning the final two games of the LCS and saving San Diego's lone victory in the WS, and in 1986 led the ML with 83 appearances (breaking Rollie Fingers's Padres record). He was traded to San Francisco in the seven-player, July 4, 1987 deal that also involved Kevin Mitchell and Mark Davis. /(SCL)

Ron LeFlore — 1948- . OF 1974-82 **Tigers**, Expos 1099 g, .288, 59 hr, 353 rbi
☛ *All-Star—76.*

Ron LeFlore first played baseball while serving a 5- to-15-year sentence for armed robbery. The native of Detroit, who first claimed to have been born in 1952, then 1950, and finally admitted to 1948, was discovered when Tiger manager Billy Martin visited Jackson State Prison. Signed to a contract in July 1973, he made the majors a year later and was made Detroit's regular centerfielder by manager Ralph Houk to take advantage of LeFlore's blinding speed. Possibly the fastest man in baseball during his prime, he hit .316 with 93 runs and 58 stolen bases in 1976 despite a season-halting leg injury late in the year. He had a 30-game hitting streak, the longest in the AL in 27 years. He added power with 16 HR in 1977 and was the first Tiger since Al Kaline, 22 years earlier, to get more than 200 hits. LeFlore also led AL righthanded batters with a .325 average after a slow start that saw him hitting .230 at the end of May. His life story was published in *Breakout*, later made into the movie *One in a Million.*

In his best season, 1978, he led the AL with 126 runs and 68 stolen bases, had a career-high 62 RBI despite being a leadoff batter, and hit in 27 straight games. After reaching a new personal high of 78 steals in 1979, also hitting .300 with 100 runs scored, he was sent to Montreal in a salary dispute. He led the NL with 97 steals but dropped to .257 with four HR. He retired after two part-time seasons with the White Sox. /(SH)

Ken Lehman — 1928- . LHP 1952, 56–58, 61 Dodgers, **Orioles**, Phillies 265 ip, 14–10, 3.91. *1 WS, 2 ip, 0–0, 0.00*

As a rookie, Lehman mopped up in the Dodgers' Game Two loss in the 1952 WS. An ineffective reliever in Brooklyn, he was sold to Baltimore in 1957 and had his best season, 8–3 with six saves and a 2.52 ERA. /(FK)

Paul Lehner — 1920–1967. OF 1946–52 **Browns**, A's, White Sox, Indians, Red Sox 540 g, .257, 22 hr, 197 rbi

Lehner was an average outfielder with a weak bat for the Browns during his first four ML seasons. Suddenly, after a trade to Philadelphia in 1950, he hit .309 with nine homers, far beyond his previous highs. Believing Lehner had hit his stride, the White Sox insisted he be included in the three-team deal that brought Minnie Minoso to Chicago. Lehner's batting average sank and he was out of the majors by 1952. /(RL)

Nemo Leibold [Harry Loran] — 1892–1977. OF 1913–25 Indians, **White Sox**, Red Sox, Senators 1258 g, .266, 4 hr, 283 rbi. *4 WS, 13 g, .161, 2 rbi*

The 5'7" 157-lb Leibold, nicknamed for the comic strip character Little Nemo, hit only four homers in 13 ML seasons but played on four pennant winners. He was a reliable fielder and a pesky hitter, particularly when platooned against righthanded pitchers. As a longtime minor league manager, he was notoriously bellicose. In 1946 he was suspended for the season after a shoving match with a minor league umpire. When he was reinstated before the end of the season, several umpires quit in protest. /(JK)

Charlie Leibrandt — 1956- . LHP 1979–82, 84– Reds, **Royals** 1573 ip, 92–78, 3.77. *3 LCS, 24 ip, 1–3, 3.80. 1 WS, 16 ip, 0–1, 2.76*

The Leibrandt for Bob Tufts deal remains one of the Royals' best trades. While Tufts never pitched

another game, Charlie established himself as the paradigm of reliability in the Kansas City rotation. Not equipped with one outstanding pitch, he mastered the talent of painting the edge of the strike zone while never coming down the center. Overshadowed by Saberhagen and Gubicza, he posted the most Royals victories from 1985 to 1988. /(FJO)

Lefty Leifield [Albert Peter] — 1883–1970. LHP 1905–13, 18–20 **Pirates**, Cubs, Browns 1838 ip, 124–96, 2.47. 20 wins: 07 *1 WS, 4 ip, 0–1, 11.25*

Leifield was an outstanding starter for the Pirates until a sore arm all but ended his career at age twenty-eight. He won 20 games in 1907 and 19 for the 1909 pennant winners. He threw three one-hitters, but in one, he got his team's only hit and lost to the Cubs' Three Finger Brown. /(JK)

Dave Leiper — 1962- . LHP 1984, 86- **A's**, Padres 190 ip, 9–4, 3.94

The Padres took Leiper from Oakland in a 1987 trade for Storm Davis. Leiper recorded a 2.17 ERA in 35 games of middle relief for San Diego in 1988. /(JCA)

Al Leiter — 1965- . LHP 1987- **Yankees**, Blue Jays 114 ip, 7–8, 4.92

The Yankees' second-round pick in the June 1984 draft, Leiter came up in 1987 hailed as the trade-decimated farm system's best pitching talent. Put into the rotation in 1988, he was frequently unable to pitch due to a recurring blister. Traded to Toronto early in the 1989 season for Jesse Barfield, he went on the DL with tendinitis shortly thereafter. His brothers Kurt and Mark pitched in the Orioles organization. /(WOR)

Larry LeJeune [Sheldon Aldenbert] — 1885–1952. OF 1911, 15 Dodgers, **Pirates** 24 g, .167, 4 rbi

On October 12, 1910, Field Day in Cincinnati, LeJeune threw a baseball a record 426 feet 9 inches. Although he never hit well in the ML, he was a five-time minor league batting champion. /(ME)

Jack Lelivelt — 1885–1941. OF 1909–14 **Senators**, Yankees, Indians 381 g, .301, 2 hr, 126 rbi

Lelivelt was a bulky, slow-footed outfielder who became an outstanding minor league manager. He compiled a .331 minor league batting average from 1906 through 1925, the last five seasons as a playing manager. Over 21 seasons, his teams won 1861 games for a .564 percentage, including three Pacific Coast League titles. /(JK)

Dave Lemanczyk (Tarzan) — 1950- . RHP 1973-80 Tigers, **Blue Jays**, Angels 920 ip, 37-63, 4.62
☛ *All-Star—79.*

Lemanczyk was a workhorse starter for the Blue Jays in their expansion years. His 13 wins in 1977 tied a record for a first-year expansion team. A dozen seasons later, Lemanczyk remained on the franchise record books for his 1977 totals for wild pitches, hits, and runs allowed. On April 24, 1979 against the Rangers, Lemanczyk threw the Blue Jays' first one-hitter, on his way to an All-Star selection and a career-best 3.71 ERA. After his playing career, Lemanczyk became a player agent, and became engaged in acrimonious litigation with Dave Stieb. /(TF)

Denny Lemaster — 1939- . LHP 1962-72 **Braves**, Astros, Expos 1788 ip, 90-105, 3.58
☛ *All-Star—67.*

Lemaster seemed on the brink of stardom through most of his 11-season ML career but never quite fulfilled his early promise. Signed by the Braves for a $60,000 bonus in 1958, the hard-throwing lefty fanned 11 straight batters for Jacksonville in 1959 and led the Texas League in strikeouts the next year. After going 10-4 in half a season at Louisville and apparently overcoming his early control problems, he joined the Braves' rotation in mid-season. He struck out 190 with a 3.04 era in 1963 and went 17-11 in 1964. The next year he developed a sore arm which bothered him intermittently through the rest of his career. Traded to Houston in 1968, he continued to show flashes of brilliance and record excellent strikeout totals until his arm problems ended his effectiveness in 1971. /(MC)

Johnnie LeMaster — 1954- . SS 1975-85, 87 **Giants**, Indians, Pirates, A's 1039 g, .222, 22 hr, 229 rbi

LeMaster was the 43rd player to hit a home run in his first ML at-bat, but he hit very little after that. As the Giants' regular shortstop from 1978 through 1985, the slender infielder was a sometimes competent fielder. /(FS)

Dick LeMay (Lefty) — 1938- . LHP 1961-63 **Giants**, Cubs 108 ip, 3-8, 4.17

Known for his weird, leg-kicking, arm-flailing, hip-swiveling, shoulder-dipping windup, LeMay depended on his screwball. Recommended to the Giants by famed screwballer Carl Hubbell, LeMay

enjoyed strong International and Pacific Coast league years after leaving the majors. /(BC)

Bob Lemon — 1920- . RHP-3B 1941-42, 46-58 **Indians** 615 g, .232, 37 hr, 147 rbi; 2850 ip, 207-128, 3.23. 20 wins: 48-50, 52-54, 56 *2 WS, 30 ip, 2-2, 3.94.*
 Manager 1970-72, 77-79, 81-82 **Royals**, White Sox, Yankees 432-401, .519. First place: 78, 81 *2 LCS, 6-1, .857. 2 WS, 6-6, .500*
☛ *Led League—w 50, 54-55. Led League—k 50. All-Star—48-54. Hall of Fame—1976.*

The easygoing Lemon learned to pitch in the major leagues and went on to become one of the most successful righthanders of the post-WWII period. He was enshrined in the Hall of Fame in 1976. In two trials as a third baseman before the war he failed to stick with the Indians because of his mediocre hitting. He showed a strong arm in the field, but his throws had a natural sinking effect. Upon his return to Cleveland after three years in the Navy, he turned to pitching at age twenty-six.

Bob Lemon

Although bothered by wildness, he showed enough promise in his first season on the mound (2.49 ERA in 94 innings) to continue the experiment. In 1947 he was 11–5 and became the Indians' second most effective starter behind Hall of Famer Bob Feller.

Cleveland won the 1948 pennant, as Feller, Lemon, and rookie Gene Bearden combined for 59 wins. Lemon, at 20–14, led the AL in shutouts (10), complete games (20), and innings pitched (294). On June 30, he threw a no-hitter to top the Tigers 2–0. In the World Series, he picked up two wins (1.65 ERA) as the Indians defeated the Braves.

Lemon became the leader of the outstanding Indians pitching staffs of the 1950s that also included Feller, Early Wynn, Mike Garcia, and later Herb Score. In a remarkably consistent nine-year stretch (1948–56), Lemon won 20 or more games seven times. He missed the magic number only in 1951 with 17 victories and 1955 when his 18 wins topped the league. A workhorse, he led in complete games five times and innings pitched four. *TSN* named him the Outstanding AL Pitcher three times (1948, 50, 54).

The 1954 Indians set an AL record with 111 victories (in 154 games) as Lemon led the pitching staff with a 23–7 mark. He opened the World Series against the Giants and took a 2–2 tie into the tenth inning before giving up a three-run home run to pinch hitter Dusty Rhodes. When the Indians lost the next two, manager Al Lopez brought Lemon back on two days' rest, but he was shelled early as the Giants swept the Series.

Lemon's money pitch was his sinking fastball. He led the AL in strikeouts with 170 in 1950, but he was most effective when opposing batters were beating the ball into the dirt. Always slightly wild, his season bases on balls and strikeout marks were usually similar, as were his career bases totals of 1,251 walks and 1,277 strikeouts.

Lemon was considered to be one of the best-hitting pitchers of his time and was often used as a pinch hitter, totaling 31 hits in 109 pinch-hit appearances (.284). His 37 home runs lifetime is just one behind Wes Ferrell's record for pitchers, and his 7 HR in 1949 ties him for second on the pitchers' season list.

After leaving the majors, Lemon pitched briefly in the Pacific Coast League, then turned to scouting, coaching, and managing. In 1966 *TSN* named him Minor League Manager of the Year when his Seattle team won the PCL championship. From 1970–72 he managed the Kansas City Royals, with a 1971

second place the team's best mark, earning him Manager of the Year honors. He took over the Chicago White Sox in 1977, managing another mediocre team to a strong finish, and again won Manager of the Year. But Lemon was replaced the next season with the team in fifth place.

A few weeks later, Lemon began a bewildering series of ups and downs with the New York Yankees. First, he succeeded fiery Billy Martin as skipper of the third-place Yankees. The team responded to his relaxed leadership and finished the regular schedule tied with the Red Sox for the division title. New York won the one-game playoff on Bucky Dent's home run. After taking the LCS, Lemon's Yankees went on to a World Series win over the Dodgers.

Midway through the 1979 season, Martin replaced him as Yankee manager. In 1981, when the player strike split the season into two parts, Gene Michael managed the Yankees to a first-half division lead, but when the team faltered in the second half after the strike, Lemon returned as manager. He took the Yankees to victory in the divisional playoff between the Yankees and second-half winner Milwaukee and then a three-game sweep of Oakland in the LCS. The Yankees lost the World Series to the Dodgers in six games. When New York started slowly in 1982, Lemon was again replaced as manager, this time by Michael. /(BC)

Chet Lemon — 1955– . OF 1975– White Sox, **Tigers** 1884 g, .274, 210 hr, 852 rbi. *2 LCS, 8 g, .161, 2 hr, 4 rbi. 1 WS, 5 g, .294, 1 rbi*
☛ *All-Star—78–79, 84.*

Lemon first signed with the A's but was acquired by the White Sox in a June 1975 trade for Stan Bahnsen. A third baseman in the minors, he became Chicago's center fielder in 1976. He made a hustling, aggressive style of play his trademark, with headfirst slides into first base and his willingness to be hit by a pitch. Getting great jumps on the ball, he broke two AL records in 1977: most chances for an outfielder (524) and most putouts (512). From 1978 through 1981, he batted .304, with a high of .318 in 1979, when he tied for the AL lead with 44 doubles.

After the '81 season, Lemon was traded to Detroit for Steve Kemp. Leaving spacious Comiskey Park for smaller Tiger Stadium, his home run production went up, but his average dipped. He matured as a player, becoming a smarter baserunner and a key contributor to Detroit's perennially strong teams. /(RL)

Jim Lemon — 1928- . OF-1B 1950, 53-63 Indians, **Senators/Twins**, Phillies, White Sox 1010 g, .262, 164 hr, 529 rbi.

Manager 1968 **Senators** 65-96, .404

☛ *All-Star—60 .*

Combining power, speed, and an exceptional arm, Lemon joined the Indians in 1950 but lost 1951 and 1952 to the Korean War. Sold to the Senators in May 1954, in 1956 he hit 27 home runs and led the AL in triples and in double plays by an outfielder. That August 31 he became the first Senator to hit three consecutive home runs. Lemon led the AL in strikeouts three years in a row (1956–58); his 138 strikeouts in 1956 (in a 154-game season) set a record. On September 5, 1959 he tied two ML records by hitting two homers and driving in six runs in one inning. He had 100 RBI in both 1959 and 1960. In 1960 he chased Mickey Mantle and Roger Maris for the AL home run crown, losing to Mantle 40 to 38. Slowed by injuries in 1961 and 1962, he attempted a comeback as a first baseman with the Phillies in 1963. He coached for the Twins from 1965 to 1967 and managed the Senators to their usual last-place finish in 1968. Replaced by Ted Williams for 1969, he remained in baseball as a batting coach, mainly with the Twins./(MC)

Mark Lemongello — 1955- . RHP 1976-79 Astros, Blue Jays 537 ip, 22-38, 4.06

After breaking in impressively with Houston late in the 1976 season with a 3-1 record and a 2.79 ERA, Lemongello slipped once he was placed in the regular rotation. His trade to Toronto brought catcher Alan Ashby to the Astros./(BC)

Don Lenhardt — 1922- . OF-1B-3B 1950-54 **Browns**, White Sox, Tigers, Orioles 481 g, .271, 61 hr, 239 rbi

Footsie (because of his narrow shoe size) was a rangy power hitter whose slow drawl matched his running speed. Despite 22 home runs as a rookie, he was dealt five times in five years, including the nine-player swap that sent George Kell to the Red Sox. A broken leg in 1954 ended his career./(BC)

Ed Lennox (Eggie) — 1885-1939. 3B 1906, 09-10, 12, 14-15 Phillies, **Dodgers**, Cubs, Pittsburgh (FL) 448 g, .274, 18 hr, 185 rbi

A journeyman infielder, Lennox led NL third basemen in fielding average in 1909 as a Dodger rookie. He hit best in the Federal League. His 1914 totals (.312, 11 HR, 84 RBI) were all career highs./(JK)

Eddie Leon — 1946- . SS-2B 1968-75 **Indians**, White Sox, Yankees 601 g, .236, 24 hr, 159 rbi

Leon was a college baseball All-American at the University of Arizona in 1966 with a .378 batting average and 74 RBIs, but he showed little hitting ability in his eight-year ML career./(BC)

Max Leon — 1950- . RHP 1973-78 **Braves** 311 ip, 14-18, 3.70

Leon began pitching professionally in his native Mexico, joining the Braves organization in 1973 after a 17-7 season at Jalisco. A starter in Mexico, he was used mainly in long relief once he reached the majors. After suffering arm trouble, he returned to Mexico and again became a consistent winner, including an 18-2 record in 1983-84./(MC)

Buck Leonard [Walter Fenner] — 1907- . 1B-OF Negro Leagues 1933-50 Brooklyn Royal Giants, Homestead Grays statistics not available

☛ *Hall of Fame—1972.*

Leonard is the only Negro League first baseman enshrined in Cooperstown. A lefthanded power hitter, he teamed with legendary slugger Josh Gibson to lead the Homestead Grays to nine consecutive Negro National League championships from 1937 through 1945. The duo was dubbed the "Thunder Twins" by the black press. Leonard was called a black Lou Gehrig, Gibson a black Babe Ruth. While Gibson slugged tape measure home runs, the pull-hitting Leonard, who feasted on fastballs, demonstrated his smooth, powerful stroke by hitting line drives off and over the walls. Leonard was equally smooth and consistent at first base. His sure-handed glove work was compared with that of Hal Chase and George Sisler. He was a smart fielder who always made the right play. Dependable and respected by his teammates, he was a steadying influence on the Grays.

Leonard began his career in 1933 with the semi-pro Elks and Black Swans in his native Rocky Mount, NC, after he lost his job due to the Depression. After being picked up by the Portsmouth, VA Firefighters, he was soon signed by the Baltimore Stars. When the Stars broke up later that season, he finished with the Brooklyn Royal Giants. The next spring, he was recruited by former Homestead ace Smokey Joe Williams for Cum Posey's Grays. For the next 17 years, Leonard was the Grays' first baseman.

Beginning in 1942, when Leonard hit 42 HR, the Grays appeared in four consecutive Black World

Buck Leonard

Series and won championships in 1943–44. Leonard tied Gibson for the '44 HR title, and in the BWS he batted .500. He hit .375 in 1945, finishing behind Gibson in the HR race. Leonard tied for the HR lead and won his third batting title with a .395 mark in 1948. Under Leonard's inspirational leadership, the Grays won their 10th pennant that year and a record third BWS.

Years before Branch Rickey brought Jackie Robinson to the Dodgers, Senators owner Clark Griffith approached Leonard and Gibson about playing in the majors. But Griffith backed down,

deciding not to disturb the status quo. When the color line was finally broken, Bill Veeck contacted Leonard about playing in the majors, but the veteran felt he was too old. He said he "didn't want to embarrass anyone or hurt the chances of those who might follow." His only appearance in organized ball came at age forty-six, in 1953, when he played 10 games for Portsmouth (Piedmont League) and batted .333.

Leonard compiled a lifetime .341 average in the Negro National League and a .382 mark in exhibitions against major leaguers. He made a record 12 appearances in the annual East-West all-star game, hitting .317 with an all-star record three HR.

After the Grays disbanded, Leonard played in Mexico from 1951 to 1955. He liked the warm climate, having spent winters on the diamonds of Cuba, Puerto Rico, and Venezuela. In 1962 he helped organize the Rocky Mount (Carolina League) club and served as its vice-president. Leonard and Gibson were inducted into the Hall of Fame by the Committee on Negro Baseball Leagues in 1972. /(JR)

Dennis Leonard — 1951– . RHP 1974–83, 85–86 **Royals** 2187 ip, 144–106, 3.69. 20 wins: 77–78, 80 *4 LCS, 31 ip, 2–3, 4.31. 1 WS, 11 ip, 1–1, 6.75* ☛ *Led League—w 77.*

The redhead was the Royals' Pitcher of the Year in 1975, 1977, and 1979. He employed a hard fastball, curve, and slider to average 18 wins a year, 1975–80. His philosophy: "Win or lose, take something out of a game that will help me next time." In 1982 he missed half the season after suffering a broken finger from a line drive. Torn knee ligaments cost him nearly all of the next three seasons. In 1986 Leonard returned to honor the final year of his contract. He made the starting rotation, and though his record was only 8–13, he pitched several strong games in the first half of the season, including two shutouts. Before coming to the Royals, he hurled two no-hitters in the minors. /(FO)

Dutch Leonard [Emil] — 1909–1983. RHP 1933–36, 38–53 Dodgers, **Senators**, Phillies, Cubs 3218 ip, 191–181, 3.25. 20 wins: 39

Emil "Dutch" Leonard was one of the first pitchers to rely heavily on the knuckleball. Pitching almost exclusively for losing teams during his 20 years in the ML, he nevertheless won 191 games. His success with what was until then considered a trick pitch inspired a whole generation of knuckleball specialists, including Hoyt Wilhelm.

After his 14–11 year with the Dodgers in 1934, a sore arm threatened Leonard's career. Eventually he was sent to Atlanta of the Southern Association where, with the help of the knuckleball, he posted two strong seasons. He returned to the majors with Washington in 1938 and the next year enjoyed a 20–8 year with the sixth-place Senators.

Although Leonard occasionally mixed in a fastball or slip pitch to keep hitters off-balance, the knuckler was his primary out pitch. He had exceptional control of all his pitches, averaging only 2.06 walks per nine innings pitched.

After an 18–13 season in 1941, Leonard missed almost all the next year with a broken ankle, but he came back to post double-digit win totals for the Senators through 1946, including a 17–7 mark in 1945. An oddity that season, aside from Washington's uncharacteristic second-place finish, was that three other regular Senator hurlers—Roger Wolff, Mickey Haefner, and Johnny Niggeling—were knuckleballers.

Leonard was sold to the Phillies after the 1946 season and was traded with Monk Dubiel to the Cubs for Eddie Waitkus and Hank Borowy two years later. Though he had always been a starting pitcher, he became an outstanding reliever with the Cubs. He once cited as one of his greatest thrills a game in which he was called in against the powerful Dodgers to protect a one-run lead in the ninth inning with the bases loaded and no outs. He retired Jackie Robinson, Gil Hodges, and Roy Campanella without a run scoring. /(BC)

Hub Leonard (Dutch) — 1892–1952. LHP 1913–21, 24–25 **Red Sox**, Tigers 2190 ip, 139–112, 2.77. *2 WS, 2–0, 1.00*
☛ *Led League—era 14.*

Hub was a sterling lefthander in the days of Red Sox greatness, although he never achieved a 20-win season. He threw two no-hitters and his 1.01 ERA in 1914 is the all-time top mark. In 1927, then a successful California grape grower, he made public two letters implicating Ty Cobb, Tris Speaker, and himself in a possibly fixed game in 1919. Other than resentment of his two former managers, his motive was unclear. When he refused to leave California to press his case, the two Hall of Famers were exonerated by Judge Landis. /(ADS)

Jeffrey Leonard (Hac-Man) — 1955– . OF-DH 1977-Dodgers, Astros, **Giants**, Brewers, Mariners 1281 g, .268, 134 hr, 648 rbi. *2 LCS, 10 g, .310, 4 hr, 5 rbi*
☛ *All-Star—87, 89.*

Called Hac-Man for his aggressiveness at the plate and Penitentiary Face for his perpetual scowl, Leonard escaped the streets of Philadelphia to become a dangerous, free-swinging ML hitter. He led all minor leaguers with a .365 average at Albuquerque (Pacific Coast League) in 1978 and was *TSN* NL Rookie Player of the Year when he hit .290 with 23 steals for the Astros in 1979. Traded to the Giants with Dave Bergman for Mike Ivie in late 1981, the sullen-looking slugger injured his hand diving for a ball in 1982 but rebounded with 21 HR in both 1983 and 1984, and his .302 average in 1984 was a career high. A sizzling start in 1987 (he was hitting .374 on May 27) earned Leonard an All-Star appearance, and in the 1987 LCS he became only the third player in postseason history to win the MVP award while his team lost the series. Leonard hit home runs in each of the first four games, taunting the Cardinals with his slow, deliberate "one-flap-down" trot, with one arm held against his side and the other arm extended. He hit .417 for the series. He was traded to Milwaukee for Ernest Riles in June 1988, and after the season signed as a free agent with Seattle, where he resurrected his career. A foot injury confined him to DHing, but he nonetheless reached career highs with 24 HR and 93 RBI. /(SCL)

Joe Leonard — 1894–1920. 3B-2B-1B 1914, 16–17, 19–20 Pirates, Indians, **Senators** 269 g, .226, 2 hr, 61 rbi

Utility man Leonard of the Senators fell ill in Boston early in 1920 and was sent back to Washington, where he died of a ruptured appendix. /(JK)

Dave Leonhard — 1942– . RHP 1967–72 **Orioles** 337 ip, 16–14, 3.15. *2 WS, 18 ip, 0–0, 3.00*

A perpetual prospect, college-trained Leonhard (degree in history from Johns Hopkins) used good control of his slow ball to teeter just short of the brink of blossoming. Seven wins in 1968 and again in '69 were his best marks. /(BC)

Ted Lepcio — 1930– . 2B-3B-SS 1952–61 **Red Sox**, Tigers, Phillies, White Sox, Twins 729 g, .245, 69 hr, 251 rbi

Although his 1960 manager, Eddie Sawyer, labeled him "the worst player I ever saw," Lepcio was a competent utility man with occasional power (15 home runs in 1956) for ten ML seasons. A bonus baby out of Seton Hall College, he reportedly signed for $60,000. /(BC)

Don Leppert — 1931- . C 1961-64, Pirates, **Senators** 190 g, .229, 15 hr, 59 rbi

The burly backup catcher, known as a handy man in a brawl, became the 20th player to hit a home run in his first ML at-bat (June 18, 1961). At Wabash College, he starred with the shotput and discus. /(BC)

Randy Lerch — 1954- . LHP 1975-86 **Phillies**, Brewers, Expos, Giants 1100 ip, 60-64, 4.52. *1 LCS, 5 ip, 0-0, 5.06*

Known nearly as well for his hitting as for his pitching, Lerch had a lifetime batting average of .206, with 56 base hits. In 1978 his three home runs led all NL pitchers. Two of those came in a crucial September 30 game against the Pirates to help edge the Phillies past Pittsburgh for the division crown.

He started the fourth and final game of the 1978 LCS, but was tagged for three runs and seven hits in 5-1/3 innings, as the Phillies lost to the Dodgers. The 6'5" lefthander enjoyed three seasons in double-figure wins but was less effective after breaking a bone in his wrist in 1979. /(BC)

Walt Lerian (Peck) — 1903-1929. C 1928-29 **Phillies** 201 g, .246, 9 hr, 50 rbi

The Phillies' starting catcher in 1929, Lerian was killed during the off-season when he was struck by an out-of-control automobile that ran up onto the sidewalk. /(JK)

Barry Lersch — 1944- . RHP 1969-74 **Phillies**, Cardinals 570 ip, 18-32, 3.82

Blond, fun-loving Lersch featured a good curve with excellent control and added a knuckleball late in his career. In 1971, he suffered through a personal 11-game losing streak, one less than the Phillie record. /(BC)

Sam Leslie (Sambo) — 1905-1979. 1B 1929-38 **Giants**, Dodgers 822 g, .304, 36 hr, 389 rbi. *2 WS, 5 g, .500*

Leslie was a solid hitter but mediocre fielder, leading one writer to comment: "He could hit if you woke him up at two in the morning but couldn't field if you played him at two in the afternoon." A top pinch hitter with the Giants (22 for 72 in 1932), he was traded to the Dodgers for Lefty O'Doul and Watty Clark in 1933. After four years as a regular, he was sold back to the Giants, where his pinch hitting contributed to pennants in 1936 and 1937. /(FS)

Walt Leverenz (Tiny) — 1887-1973. LHP 1913-15 **Browns** 323 ip, 7-31, 3.15

Leverenz had two dismal seasons for the Browns, going 6-17 as a rookie in 1913 and 1-12 in 1914. His downfall was the base on balls; he averaged almost five walks and only three strikeouts a game. /(WAB)

Dixie Leverett [Gorham Vance] — 1894-1957. RHP 1922-24, 26, 29 **White Sox**, Braves 638 ip, 29-34, 4.50

Leverett was impressive as 1922 White Sox rookie, going 13-10 with four shutouts. When he reported to camp 10 pounds overweight in 1925, he was sent down. He shed the weight but couldn't do the job after making the club in 1926. /(RL)

Jim Levey — 1906-1970. SS 1930-33 **Browns** 440 g, .230, 11 hr, 140 rbi

Discovered while playing for the Marines, Levey made 147 errors in three years as the Browns' regular shortstop, hitting .280 in 1932 but under .210 in all his other seasons. In 1934 he joined Pittsburgh of the NFL and played three seasons at halfback. /(JK)

Dutch Levsen [Emil Henry] — 1898-1972. RHP 1923-28 **Indians** 404 ip, 21-26, 4.17

Levsen registered 16 of his 21 major league wins in 1926. That August 28, he became the last pitcher to record complete game victories in both ends of a doubleheader, as he tossed a pair of four-hitters against the Red Sox. /(ME)

Allen Lewis — 1916- . *Writer.*

Lewis was with the Philadelphia *Evening Ledger* before starting 33 years as a baseball writer for the *Inquirer* in 1946. For 16 years he wrote a weekly column on baseball and was a *Sporting News* correspondent. He covered 24 WS and was a member of the scoring-rules committee from 1958 to 1972. Lewis wrote *This Date in Philadelphia Phillies History* and *Phillies Pictorial History*. He received the J.G. Taylor Spink Award in 1981. /(NLM)

Buddy Lewis [John Kelly] — 1916- . 3B-OF 1935-41, 45-47, 49 **Senators** 1349 g, .297, 71 hr, 607 rbi
☛ *All-Star—38, 47.*

One of several stars who lost the peak years of their careers to military service, Lewis joined the Senators for eight games as an 18-year-old in 1935. The next season, when second baseman Buddy Myer was injured, the Washington infield was reshuffled and Lewis took over at third base. Myer was the defending AL batting champ, but Lewis hit a very respectable .291 and scored 100 runs. Myer became Lewis's mentor and the veteran's nickname was given to the youngster.

In the years before WWII, Lewis hit over .300 three times and scored 100 or more runs four times, with a high of 122 in 1938. He led the AL in triples (16) in 1939. In 1940 he moved to right field, allowing longtime Senator shortstop Cecil Travis, who was slowing down, to move to third. After returning from the service, he hit .333 at the end of the 1945 season and .292 in 1946. He had an off-year in 1947, then missed all of 1948 with an injury. When he could not regain his earlier form in a 1949 comeback bid, he retired. /(MC)

Duffy Lewis [George Edward] — 1888-1979. OF 1910-17, 19-21 **Red Sox**, Yankees, Senators 1459 g, .284, 38 hr, 793 rbi. *3 WS, 18 g, .284, 1 hr, 8 rbi*

Lewis was the left fielder in the famous Red Sox outfield that included Tris Speaker and Harry Hooper. He became so adept at fielding along the steep incline in front of Fenway Park's left-field fence that it became known as "Duffy's Cliff." Despite being one of the few players apparently liked by Ty Cobb, Lewis's fondest memories included throwing out Cobb as he attempted to stretch hits. At bat, he was a reliable line-drive hitter and good RBI man, with a personal high of 109 in 1912. In 1914 he became the first ML player to pinch hit for Babe Ruth, then a Red Sox rookie pitcher. The next season, he saw Ruth's first homer; in 1935, as traveling secretary for the Braves, a post he held for 30 years, he saw Ruth's last. /(EC)

Johnny Lewis — 1939- . OF 1964-67 Cardinals, **Mets** 266 g, .227, 22 hr, 74 hr

Shy and quiet, Lewis played in a shell, never realizing the stardom predicted for him. His career highlight came on June 14, 1965 when he homered leading off the 10th inning at Crosley Field to break up Jim Maloney's no-hitter and win the game 1-0 for the Mets. That was his only year as a regular; he hit .245 with 15 HR, 45 RBI, and 64 runs. /(BC)

Phil Lewis — 1883-1959. SS 1905-08 **Dodgers** 508 g, .242, 4 hr, 130 rbi

The 6' 195-lb Lewis was big for a turn-of-the-century shortstop, yet he was no slugger, and in four years as Brooklyn's shortstop was found lacking

defensively. He later became a logger in the Adirondacks. /(JK)

Ted Lewis (Parson, The Pitching Professor) — 1872-1936. RHP 1896-1901 **Braves**, Red Sox 1405 ip, 94-64, 3.53. 20 wins: 97-98

Born in Wales, Lewis signed with the Boston Nationals in 1896 after graduating from Williams College. He won 21 games that season and went 26-8 in 1897, both pennant-winning years for Boston. On June 22, 1898 he won a marathon game in relief and did not walk a batter in 13-2/3 innings. He continued his education during the off-season and coached baseball at Harvard, 1897-1901. After the 1901 season, he retired from baseball to teach full-time at Columbia and later at Williams. He became a prominent educator, eventually serving as president of Massachusetts State College, 1926-27, and the University of New Hampshire from 1927 until his death. /(LRD)

Jim Leyland — 1944- . *Manager* 1986- **Pirates** 303-343, .469

Leyland won Manager of the Year honors for leading the Pirates to a surprising second-place finish in 1988. A patient teacher, he worked well with Pittsburgh's young stars. /(JFC)

Sixto Lezcano — 1953- . OF 1974-85 **Brewers**, Cardinals, Padres, Phillies, Pirates 1291 g, .271, 148 hr, 591 rbi. *1 LCS, 4 g, .308, 1 hr, 2 rbi. 1 WS, 4 g, .125* ☛ *Gold Glove—79.*

Lezcano led both leagues in outfielder assists, with the Brewers in 1978 and the Padres in 1983. Erratic at bat, Lezcano had his best year in 1979 with the Brewers when he hit .321, with 28 homers (10 in August) and 101 RBI. /(MC)

Al Libke (Big Al) — 1918- . OF 1945-46 **Reds** 254 g, .268, 9 hr, 95 rbi

Libke was a top prospect during WWII when he hit .309 and won several games as a pitcher in the Pacific Coast League. He started in right field for the Reds for two seasons but couldn't hold his job when the talent supply improved after the war. /(JK)

Don Liddle (Little) — 1925- . LHP 1953-56 Braves, Giants, Cardinals 428 ip, 28-18, 3.75. *1 WS, 7 ip, 1-0 1.29*

The 160-lb lefthander was inevitably Little Liddle. Traded to the Giants as part of the Braves' deal for Johnny Antonelli and Bobby Thomson, he started and won the final game of the 1954 World Series four-game sweep of the Indians. /(BC)

Fred Lieb — 1888–1980. *Writer.*

Lieb was working as a clerk for the Norfolk & Western Railroad in 1909 when he began submitting biographies of players to *Baseball Magazine*. That led to a job with the Philadelphia News Bureau, and in 1911 he moved to New York, joined the new Base Ball Writers Association, and held honorary card No. 1. During the next 20 years he worked for the New York *Sun, Evening Telegraph,* and *Post.* In 1931 the cigar- and pipe-smoking Lieb took a team to Japan for a profitable tour. That and other profitable investments allowed him to retire in 1934. The following year Taylor Spink induced him to write a regular column and the most important obituaries for *The Sporting News,* which he did from his home in St. Petersburg, Florida, for 35 years. He also did a weekly Hot Stove League column for the St. Petersburg *Times.* His books include the classic *Baseball As I Have Known It; Connie Mack, Grand Old Man of Baseball;* and team histories of the Tigers, Red Sox, Cardinals, Pirates, Orioles, and Phillies. He received the J.G. Taylor Spink Award from the Hall of Fame in 1972. /(NLM)

Hank Lieber — 1911– . OF 1933–42 **Giants,** Cubs 813 g, .288, 101 hr, 518 rbi. *2 WS, 5 g, .235, 2 rbi* ☛ *All-Star—38, 40–41.*

Leiber was a 6'1-1/2" 205-lb, righthanded outfielder who was a starter with the Giants in 1935, '36, and '38 and the Cubs in 1939–1940. He hit over .300 three times (.331 in 1935, .310 in '39 and .302 in '40). His best year was 1935 when he had 203 hits, 22 home runs, 110 runs scored, 107 RBI, and a career-high .331 batting average. In 1942 he had a complete-game loss as a pitcher. /(JM)

Glenn Liebhardt (Sandy) — 1883–1956. RHP 1906–09 **Indians** 613 ip, 36–35, 2.17

Liebhardt had two solid seasons, going 18–14 (2.05) for Cleveland in 1907 and 15–16 (2.20) in 1908. His son of the same name pitched briefly for the A's and Browns in the 1930s. /(WAB)

Derek Lilliquist — 1966– . LHP 1989– **Braves** 166 ip, 8–10, 3.97

Lilliquist was the sixth selection nationwide in the June 1987 draft. He was one of several young Braves pitchers to do well at the start of 1989 and showed good control. /(JFC)

Bob Lillis (Flea) — 1930– . SS-2B-3B 1958–67 Dodgers, Cardinals, **Astros** 817 g, .236, 3 hr, 137 rbi. *Manager* 1982–85 **Astros** 276–261, .514

A native of Los Angeles, Lillis signed with Brooklyn in 1951 and appeared to be ready to replace Pee Wee Reese at shortstop in 1958, the year the Dodgers moved to Los Angeles. After injuries delayed his debut, he batted .391 in 20 games in 1958, but he lost the shortstop job to rookie Maury Wills in 1959. He was swapped to the Cardinals in mid-1961, drafted by the expansion Colt .45s that winter, and was the team's MVP in its inaugural season. He batted a career-high .268 in 1964 and remained a Houston regular until 1966. A scout and instructor in the Astros organization from 1968 to 1972, he joined their major league coaching staff in 1973 and replaced Bill Virdon as manager on August 10, 1982. Leading the Astros to third place in 1983, Lillis finished second in NL Manager of the Year voting. After an 83–79 record in 1985, he was replaced by Hal Lanier. /(MC)

Lou Limmer — 1925– . 1B 1951, 54 **A's** 209 g, .202, 19 hr, 62 rbi

Limmer suffered a broken neck in 1948 but led the American Association in home runs and RBI the next year. Despite outstanding minor league stats, he failed two ML trials because of his low batting average and indifferent fielding. /(BC)

Rufino Linares — 1955– . OF 1981–82, 84–85 **Braves,** Angels 207 g, .270, 11 hr, 63 rbi

One of many Dominicans from the little town of San Pedro de Macoris to reach the majors, Linares hit .298 in 1982. But that winter a devastating broken ankle while playing winter ball kept him out for a year and took away his speed. /(BC)

Carl Lind — 1904–1946. 2B-SS 1927–30 **Indians** 256 g, .272, 1 hr, 74 rbi

As a rookie in 1928, Lind batted .294 with a league-high 650 at-bats and led the Indians with 42 doubles and 102 runs scored. After a postseason illness, he was never again a regular. /(ME)

Jose Lind — 1964– . 2B 1987– **Pirates** 342 g, .255, 4 hr, 108 rbi

The acrobatic Lind is famous for his ability to jump over any teammate from a standing start. In his first full season in 1988 he quickly established himself as one of the best-fielding second basemen in the league and just missed leading NL second basemen in fielding average and putouts. The Pirates traded Johnny Ray near the end of the 1987 season to make room for Lind, who hit .322 in his call-up. In 1988 he hit .262, stole 15 bases, and scored 82 runs.

Lind is a cousin of Onix Concepcion and has a brother, Orlando, who pitches in the Pirates system./(SFS)

Vive Lindaman [Vivian Alexander] — 1877-1927. LHP 1906-09 **Braves** 904 ip, 36-60, 2.92

Lindaman kept in shape by walking 17 miles a day as a mail carrier. He shut out Brooklyn 1-0 in his first ML start on April 14, 1906. Despite throwing 32 complete games (third in the league) as a rookie, he finished 12-23; his Braves teammates were shut out in eight of his losses./(NLM)

Paul Lindblad — 1941- . LHP 1965-78 **A's**, Senators, Rangers, Yankees 1214 ip, 68-63, 3.28. *1 LCS, 5 ip, 0-0, 0.00. 1 WS, 6 ip, 1-0, 4.76*

Lindblad was a useful AL lefthander for 14 seasons, working mainly in middle relief. Although he never won more than nine games in a single season, he had 64 career saves in addition to his 68 wins (61 in relief). He received credit for the win in the Athletics' third-game, 11-inning World Series victory in '73 by working two scoreless innings. A strong fielder, he set a record by going from 1966 through 1974 (385 appearances) without making a single error./(BC)

Johnny Lindell — 1916-1986. OF-1B-RHP 1941-50, 53-54 **Yankees**, Cardinals, Pirates, Phillies 854 g, .273, 72 hr, 405 rbi; 252 ip, 8-18, 4.47. *3 WS, 12 g, .324, 7 rbi*

Johnny Lindell made the transition from a pitcher to an outfielder in the major leagues, then battled back to the majors again as a pitcher near the end of his career. After signing with the Yankees while at the University of Southern California, he posted outstanding minor league pitching marks, including 23-4 at Newark in 1941. He was called up to the majors at the end of that season and spent '42 on the Yankee staff. He threw a knuckleball and curve, but Yankee manager Joe McCarthy did not believe he had a major league fastball and switched him to the outfield in 1943. In his best season, 1944, he hit .300 with 18 home runs and 103 RBI. After WWII ended, he was used mostly as a reserve. All told, he played on three pennant winners (1943, '47, '49).

Sold to the Cardinals in May 1950, he managed only a .186 batting average. At the end of the season, he was sold again, this time to Hollywood of the PCL, where manager Fred Haney put him back

on the pitching mound. In 1952 he posted a 24-9 pitching record, batted fourth, and occasionally played the outfield. He was easily the league MVP. At age thirty-six he returned to the majors, pitching for the Pirates and Phillies in 1953 for a combined 6-17 mark. He had trouble putting his knuckleball over (his 139 bases on balls led the league) and hitters sat on his fastball./(BC)

Jim Lindsey — 1898-1963. RHP 1922, 24, 29-34, 37 Indians, **Cardinals**, Reds, Dodgers 431 ip, 21-20, 4.70. *2 WS, 8 ip, 0-0, 3.38*

After a couple of awful trials with Cleveland, Lindsey became the Cardinals' most-used reliever in 1930-31. During those two pennant-winning seasons, he won 9 and saved 12. His 2.77 ERA in '31 led the staff./(FJO)

Freddie Lindstrom (Lindy) — 1905-1981. 3B-OF-2B 1924-36 **Giants**, Pirates, Cubs, Dodgers 1438 g, .311, 103 hr, 779 rbi. *2 WS, 11 g, .289, 4 rbi*
☛ *Hall of Fame—76.*

Lindstrom joined the Giants in 1924 and that fall became the youngest player (18 years, 10 months, 13 days) to appear in a World Series. In Game Five, he had four hits against Washington's Walter Johnson, but Lindstrom is best remembered for his part in the seventh and deciding game. In the bottom of the 12th, Earl McNeely's grounder took a wild hop (blamed on a pebble) over third baseman Lindstrom's head, allowing the Series-winning run to score.

Lindstrom hit .300 or better in seven of his 13 ML seasons. In 1928 he batted .358 with a league-leading 231 hits; he had 231 hits again in 1930, reaching career highs of .379 and 22 home runs. He drove in more than 100 runs in both seasons.

He was never outstanding at 3B, and when he suffered back problems in 1931, Lindstrom was moved to the outfield. Bill Terry was made Giants manager in 1932 when John McGraw retired. Lindstrom was bitter that he was not the choice and asked Terry to trade him. He was obliged in a three-team deal that sent him to Pittsburgh that December. But 1933 was his last year as a regular. In 1935 he helped the Cubs to a pennant by filling in at 3B and in the OF. He retired while with Brooklyn in 1936. He finally got his chance to manage, in the minors, from 1940 through 1942, and he coached at Northwestern University in the early 1950s. His son, Charlie, caught one game with the 1958 White Sox. Despite being an everyday player in only seven seasons, Lindstrom was elected to the Hall of Fame

Freddie Lindstrom

by the Committee on Baseball Veterans in 1976. /(JJM)

Dick Lines — 1938– . LHP 1966–67 **Senators** 169 ip, 7–7, 2.83

A native of Quebec, Canada, Lines relieved in 53 and 54 games for the 1966–67 Senators, winning seven, losing seven, and saving six. /(FK)

Ed Linke — 1911– . RHP 1933–38 **Senators**, Browns 449 ip, 22–22, 5.61

In 1935 a line drive by the Yankees' Jesse Hill rebounded off Linke's head to catcher Jack Redmond on the fly, and Ben Chapman was caught off second base for a rally-killing double play. Linke was hospitalized for three days but returned to win his next eight starts. /(JK)

Larry Lintz — 1949– . SS-2B-3B 1973–78 **Expos**, Cardinals, A's, Indians 350 g, .227, 0 hr, 27 rbi

In 1976 Lintz's stat line included 21 runs scored, 31 stolen bases, and one official at-bat. For his career,

nearly a third of his appearances were as a pinch runner. He stole 128 bases, but he couldn't steal first. /(BC)

Phil Linz (Supersub, Mr. Laffs) — 1939– . SS-2B-3B-OF 1962–68 **Yankees**, Phillies, Mets 519 g, .235, 11 hr, 96 rbi. *2 WS, 10 g, .235, 2 hr, 2 rbi*

In spring training of 1962, rookies Phil Linz and Tom Tresh battled for the Yankee shortstop job. Linz was a feisty singles hitter, but the more powerful Tresh won the contest, and thereafter Linz filled in capably at three infield positions. The humorous Linz was the protagonist in the famed "Harmonica Incident" of late August 1964. The third-place Yankees, who had just lost four straight in Chicago, were in the team bus, stuck in traffic. Linz began playing "Mary Had a Little Lamb" on his harmonica, enraging manager Yogi Berra. A ruckus ensued. The event may have galvanized the successful stretch run for a pennant, but the publicity sealed Berra's dismissal after the season. /(GDW)

Frank Linzy — 1940- . RHP 1963, 1965-74 **Giants**, Cardinals, Brewers, Phillies 516 g, 817 ip, 62-57, 2.85

Sinkerball specialist Linzy totaled 111 saves in 11 ML seasons. In 1965, he was named *TSN* NL Rookie Pitcher of the Year when he won 9 and saved 21 (his top total) for the Giants. The stocky righthander led the NL in relief wins with 14 in 1969, adding 11 saves. Traded (for relief pitcher Jerry Johnson) in 1970, he appeared in 67 games but his ERA ballooned to 4.66. The next year, after a good start, he was injured in a collision with first baseman Bob Burda and underwent facial surgery, returning before the end of the season. The Brewers acquired him for a minor leaguer in 1972, and after two moderately successful seasons in Milwaukee, he was dealt to the Phillies for his final year. /(BC)

Johnny Lipon — 1922- . SS-3B 1942, 46, 48-54 **Tigers**, Red Sox, Browns, Reds 758 g, .259, 10 hr, 266 rbi.
    Manager 1971 **Indians** 18-41, .305

As the Tigers' regular shortstop from 1948-51, Lipon was more adequate than outstanding. But after his playing career, he became a highly respected minor league manager, often rumored to be in line for a major league job. His only opportunity came when he replaced Alvin Dark at Cleveland for the last 59 games of the 1971 season. /(BC)

Nelson Liriano — 1964- . 2B 1987- **Blue Jays** 268 g, .259, 10 hr, 86 rbi. *1 LCS, 3 g, .429, 1 rbi*

Liriano was handed Toronto's second base job at the beginning of 1988 but slumped badly at first and lost playing time to Manny Lee. He won it back in 1989 after Lee temporarily replaced injured shortstop Tony Fernandez. That April 22, Liriano broke up Nolan Ryan's bid for a sixth no-hitter with a ninth-inning triple; a week later, he broke up a Kirk McCaskill no-hitter in the ninth. /(SOM)

Joe Lis — 1946- . 1B-OF 1970-77 **Phillies**, Twins, Indians, Mariners 356 g, .233, 32 hr, 92 rbi

Lis led two minor leagues in home runs, but struck out too often to stay in the major leagues. In the only season he approached regular status (253 at-bats as the Twins' first baseman in 1973), he had career highs of nine HR, 25 RBI, and 37 runs, batting just .245. /(WOR)

Hod Lisenbee [Horace Milton] — 1898-1987. RHP 1927-32, 36, 45 Senators, **Red Sox**, A's, Reds 969 ip, 37-58, 4.81

In his 1927 rookie year with Washington he was 18-9 with an AL-leading four shutouts. He beat the "Murderers' Row" Yankees five times that season (and gave up Babe Ruth's 58th HR). After that Lisenbee was a journeyman pitcher in both the majors and minors. Following his retirement in 1942, he came back in 1944 with Syracuse (International League) and pitched a no-hitter at the age of forty-five. The next year, he pitched 31 games for the Reds, mostly in relief. After the war, he continued to pitch in his native city of Clarksville, TN (Kitty League) until he was fifty. /(LRD)

Ad Liska [Adolph James] — 1906- . RHP 1929-33 **Senators**, Phillies 351 ip, 17-18, 3.87

A submarine pitcher who suffered a boyhood injury that prevented him from throwing overhand, Liska had a brief major league career. He excelled in the Pacific Coast League, where, from 1936 to 1949, he won 248 games for Portland. /(JK)

Mark Littel — 1953- . RHP 1973, 75-82 Royals, **Cardinals** 532 ip, 32-31, 3.32. *2 LCS, 7 ip, 0-1, 2.35*

Big (6'3" 210-lb) Littel was the American Association Pitcher of the Year in 1973. The strikeout pitcher used his blazing fastball to become bullpen ace for the Royals and later the Cardinals, but in the 1976 ALCS he surrendered a pennant-winning home run to the Yankees Chris Chambliss in the bottom of the ninth inning of Game Five. He saved 56 games from 1976 to 1981 until elbow spurs cut short his career. /(FJO)

Bryan Little — 1959- . 2B-SS 1982-86 **Expos**, White Sox, Yankees 327 g, .245, 3 hr, 77 rbi

Little was the Expos' starting shortstop in the first part of 1983 but was otherwise a utility man. He led the NL with 24 bunt hits in 1983 and was voted the major leagues' best bunter in two separate polls. His father and two brothers, Tom and Grady, all played minor league ball. /(JCA)

Dick Littlefield — 1926- . LHP 1950-58 Red Sox, White Sox, Tigers, Browns/Orioles, **Pirates**, Cardinals, Giants, Cubs, Braves 762 ip, 33-54, 4.71

Littlefield was dealt 10 times during his nine-year career, in trades involving 38 other players. He lasted longest with the Pirates—almost two years—winning a career-high 10 games in 1954. Pittsburgh then stole Bill Virdon from the Cardinals for Littlefield and Bobby Del Greco in a May 1956 trade. The Giants traded him to the Dodgers for

Jackie Robinson in December 1956, but the deal was voided when Robinson retired. /(ME)

John Littlefield — 1954– . RHP 1980–81 **Cardinals**, **Padres** 130 ip, 7–8, 3.39

Called up during the 1980 season, reliever Littlefield led the Cards in appearances (52), relief wins (5), and saves (9). That winter he was one of seven players dealt to the Padres in the Rollie Fingers deal. /(FJO)

Danny Litwhiler — 1916– . OF 1940–44, 46–51 **Phillies**, Cardinals, Braves, Reds 1057 g, .281, 107 hr, 451 rbi. *2 WS, 10 g, .229, 1 hr, 3 rbi*
☛ *All-Star—42.*

Litwhiler had to overcome serious knee injuries in the minor leagues. Called up by the Phillies late in the 1940 season, he batted .345, hitting in 21 straight games. The following year he had a career-high 18 home runs, collecting one in every NL park. In 1942 he became the first major league outfielder to play at least 150 games in a season without making an error. He was traded in 1943 to the Cardinals, who won pennants in 1943 and 1944. His was one of two Cardinal homers hit in their 2–0 victory over the Browns in Game Five of the '44 World Series. Because of his badly damaged knee, Litwhiler was originally classified 4F, but in 1945 the Selective Service began targeting ballplayers. After spending 1945 in the military playing baseball at Fort Lewis, Litwhiler was solely a platoon player for the rest of his ML career. /(JK)

Bud Lively [Everett Adrian] (Red) — 1925– . RHP 1947–49 **Reds** 249 ip, 8–13, 4.16

Lively spent 19 months fighting in Europe before getting a shot with the Reds in 1947. His father Jack was 7–5 for the 1911 Tigers. /(JK)

Mickey Livingston [Thompson Orville] — 1914–1983. C 1938, 41–43, 45–49, 51 Senators, **Phillies**, Cubs, Giants, Braves, Dodgers 561 g, .238, 19 hr, 153 rbi. *1 WS, 6 g, .364, 4 rbi*

A career backup, Livingston caught more than 100 games only in 1943, split between the Phillies and Cubs. Then, after military service, he was a surprise hero in the Cubs' WS loss in 1945, with three doubles and four RBI. /(ARA)

Winston Llenas — 1943– . 2B-OF-3B 1968–69, 72–75 **Angels** 300 g, .230, 3 hr, 61 rbi

Llenas interrupted his career as one of the Mexican League's greatest third basemen to spend five seasons with the Angels, primarily as a pinch hitter. In 1973, he led the AL in pinch hit at-bats (56) and hits (16), with a .269 batting average overall. A top slugger in the Mexican League before his ML stint, he returned there in 1977 for seven more seasons, including three .300 years. /(MC)

Nelson Lloyd — 1851–1925. *Executive.*

As a part owner of the Reds and Giants, Lloyd was not known to the public. He was often credited with being a behind-the-scenes peacemaker in the many bitter battles that were fought among the owners over control and direction of the game in the early years of the century. /(NLM)

Pop Lloyd [John Henry] (El Cuchara) — 1884–1964. SS-1B-2B-C Negro Leagues 1905–31 Macon Acmes, Cuban X-Giants, Brooklyn Royal Giants, Philadelphia Giants, Leland Giants, New York Lincoln Giants, Chicago American Giants, Columbus Buckeyes, Hilldale, Bacharach Giants, Atlantic City Bacharachs, New York Black Yankees .342, 26 hr (inc.)
☛ *Led League—ba 10, 15, 28. Hall of Fame—1977.*

Pop Lloyd, premier Negro League shortstop and baseball nomad, was promoted by many as the greatest player of all time. He played on at least a dozen different teams in his 26-year career. When asked why so many teams, Lloyd replied, "Where the money was, that's where I played." A tall, angular man with a Dick Tracy profile, Lloyd was a nondrinking, soft-spoken gentleman who seldom cursed. He was a complete professional, on and off the field.

Lloyd was a lefthanded line-drive hitter who used a closed stance. He held the bat in the cradle of his left elbow, and would uncoil to unleash a controlled attack on the baseball. A gifted runner with long, smooth strides, he deceived opponents into under-rating his speed. He was often compared to Honus Wagner. Connie Mack of the Philadelphia A's, who spent 50 years in the game, said, "Put Lloyd and Wagner in the same bag and whichever one you pulled out, you wouldn't go wrong."

Lloyd began as a catcher in 1905 with the Macon Acmes, who could not provide him with a mask. After one season, he moved to the Cuban X-Giants as an infielder. He helped the Philadelphia Giants to a league championship the following year and stayed

.329 batting average and twice led the league in triples. He excelled in a 1910 series played in Havana against the Detroit Tigers. The Tigers won 7 of the 12 games, with Ty Cobb hitting .369 in five contests. But Cobb's average was only good enough for fourth place; Lloyd batted .500 in 12 games and added insult to injury by tagging Cobb out on three consecutive basestealing attempts. In 29 recorded games against white major leaguers, Lloyd batted .321.

As Lloyd's legs began to go, he moved from SS to first base. Approaching age thirty-five, he signed with the Brooklyn Royal Giants as player-manager, and was active for three abbreviated seasons before going to the Columbus Buckeyes in 1921. Then thirty-eight, Lloyd led the Buckeyes in games, hits, doubles, and stolen bases while batting .337. Rejuvenated, he topped the .320 mark for Hilldale in 1923 and for the Bacharach Giants in 1924–25. He was forty-four when he hit a league-leading .564 for the New York Lincoln Giants in 1928; he also led with 11 HR and 10 SB in a 37-game schedule.

When Babe Ruth was interviewed by pioneering announcer Graham McNamee, he was asked who was the greatest player of all time. Ruth asked, "You mean major leaguers?" "No," replied McNamee, "the greatest player anywhere." "In that case," responded Ruth, "I'd pick John Henry Lloyd." Lloyd was elected to the Hall of Fame by the Committee on Negro Baseball Leagues in 1977./(LL)

Hans Lobert [John Bernard] (Honus) — 1881–1968. 3B-SS 1903, 05–17 Pirates, Cubs, **Reds**, Phillies, Giants 1317 g, .274, 32 hr, 482 rbi.
    Manager 1938, 42 **Phillies** 42–111, .275

A four-time .300 hitter, Lobert was a top NL third baseman in the days before WWI. Bearing a slight physical and facial resemblance to Honus Wagner, the speedy, bowlegged Lobert stole 30 or more bases seven times in 1907–14. His six steals of home as a Phillie tie him for second on their all-time list. He stole second, third, and home on September 27, 1908 and he once raced a horse around the bases following an exhibition game. On October 12, 1910 at Field Day in Cincinnati, he was clocked rounding the bases in 13.8 seconds. Following his playing days, Lobert coached at West Point (1918–25), spent nearly two decades as a minor league manager and ML coach, and managed the Phillies for two games in 1938 and all of 1942. He was influential in transforming Bucky Walters from a marginal ML

Pop Lloyd

two more. He spent 1910 with the Leland Giants, who posted a 123–6 record, before moving on to the New York Lincoln Giants, for whom he hit .475 in 1911 and .376 in 1912.

Rube Foster enticed Lloyd to join his Chicago American Giants, and from 1914 through 1917 Lloyd batted cleanup for the four-time Western League champions. His teammates there included such greats as Oscar Charleston, Bingo DeMoss, Louis Santop, Smokey Joe Williams, and Cannonball Dick Redding. Chicago won world championships in '14 and '17.

Lloyd played 12 seasons in Cuba, where he earned the nickname El Cuchara — The Shovel. He was known for scooping up handfuls of dirt while adeptly fielding his position. In Cuba, he compiled a

Hans Lobert

infielder into a star pitcher. His brother Frank played 11 games in the Federal League. /(ME)

Don Lock — 1936- . OF 1962-69 **Senators**, Phillies, Red Sox 921 g, .238, 122 hr, 373 rbi

The Senators traded the aging Dale Long for Lock before he had played a single ML game, and six days later Lock homered in his debut to give Washington a 1-0 win over Chicago. Always a home run threat when he made contact, Lock was plagued by strike-outs, fanning once every four plate appearances. He hit 27 and 28 HR in 1963-64 but also struck out 151 and 137 times. /(FK)

Larry Locke (Bobby) — 1934- . RHP 1959-1965, 67-68 **Indians**, Cardinals, Phillies, Reds, Angels 417 ip, 16-15, 4.02

The flaky Locke, a hairstylist, spent just one full season in the majors—with the Indians in 1961. From November 1961 through April 1962, he was alternately the property of the Indians, Cubs, Cardinals, and Phillies. /(ME)

William H. Locke — 1869-1913. *Executive.*

Locke was sports editor of the Pittsburgh *Press* for ten years until 1903, when he was named secretary of the Pirates. In January 1913 he headed a group including W.F. Baker and Governor Tener of Pennsylvania that bought the Phillies. He was named president but died suddenly on August 14 of that year. /(NLM)

Bob Locker (Foot) — 1938- . 1965-73, 75 **White Sox**, Pilots/Brewers, A's, Cubs 879 ip, 57-39, 2.76. *2 LCS, 3 ip, 0-0, 10.13. 1 WS, .1 ip, 0-0, 0.00*

In 1965 sinkerballer Bob Locker joined knuckleballers Hoyt Wilhelm and Eddie Fisher in the White Sox bullpen. Locker led the American League with 77 appearances and saved 20 games in 1967. When asked about his success, the geology major explained that he derived his powers from consuming honey—nature's essence. Locker was traded to the Pilots in 1969 and sold to Oakland a year later. He went 7-2 in 1971, and 6-1 with 10 saves for the 1972 World Champion A's. When Rollie Fingers established himself as Oakland's ace reliever, Locker was traded to the Cubs, for whom he won 10 and saved 18 in 1973. He retired with 95 career saves. /(RL)

Gene Locklear — 1949- . OF 1973-77 Reds, **Padres**, Yankees 292 g, .274, 9 hr, 66 rbi

A full-blooded Cherokee, the lefthanded batter had 150 pinch-hit at-bats in 292 ML appearances. Locklear had a .321 batting average for the Padres in 1975, his only 100-game season. After a .240 season for the Nippon Ham Fighters of Japan in 1978, he retired to pursue a career as an artist. /(MC)

Whitey Lockman [Carroll Walter] — 1926- . 1B-OF 1945, 47-60 **Giants**, Cardinals, Orioles, Reds 1666 g, .279, 114 hr, 563 rbi. *2 WS, 10 g, .186, 1 hr, 4 rbi.*
   Manager 1972-74 **Cubs** 157-162, .492
☛ *All-Star—52.*

Lockman homered in his first ML at-bat, July 5, 1945 and once led off consecutive games with home runs, but he was never a feared power hitter. He hit a career-high 18 homers in 1948, his first full season, and had his only .300 season in 1949. Still, he was a consistent contributor and one of the hardest men to double up in ML history, hitting into one double play every 87 at-bats. In the Giants-Dodgers playoff series in 1951, his ninth-inning double drove Don Newcombe from the game and set the stage for Bobby Thomson's famous home run. /(FK)

Skip Lockwood [Claude Edward, Jr.] (Jaws) — 1946- . RHP 1965, 69-80 A's, Pilots/Brewers, Angels, **Mets**, Red Sox 1236 ip, 57-97, 3.55

Lockwood received a $100,000 bonus to sign with the A's as a third baseman in 1964, but he didn't hit and converted to pitching in 1968. He failed again, as a starting pitcher, and began the switch to relieveing in 1973, his last year with Milwaukee. He finally achieved a modicum of success as the ace of the Mets' bullpen in the late 1970s; his 19 saves in 1976 tied him for second in the NL and 20 saves in 1977 (when he set a since-broken Met record with 63 appearances) was good for a tie for fifth. He got his nickname of Jaws (after the shark movie) at this time for "chewing up" batters. But in 1978 he dropped off to 15 saves and tied Rollie Fingers for the league lead with 13 relief losses, the third-worst NL mark ever. In June 1979 he went on the DL with tissue tears in his shoulder and missed the rest of the season; a comeback attempt with Boston in 1980 failed. /(SH)

Dario Lodigiani (Lodi) — 1916- . 3B-2B 1938-42, 46 **A's**, White Sox 405 g, .260, 16 hr, 156 rbi

When Lodigiani played second base at San Francisco's Lowell Junior High, his double play partner was Joe DiMaggio. He missed 1943-45 in military service, and an elbow injury in 1946 hindered his comeback. He had a long career in the Pacific Coast League and as a White Sox scout. /(NLM)

Billy Loes — 1929- . RHP 1950, 52-61 **Dodgers**, Orioles, Giants 1190 ip, 80-63, 3.89. *3 WS, 22 ip, 1-2, 4.91*
☛ *All-Star—57.*

Renowned for his wacky reasoning, Loes advised against becoming a 20-game winner, because "If you win 20 games, they expect you to do it every year." Loes never did win 20, but was 50-25 over four seasons in Brooklyn. /(FK)

Tom Loftus — 1856-1910. OF 1877, 83 St. Louis NL, **St. Louis AA** 9 g, .182, 0 hr, inc rbi.
Manager 1884, 88-91, 00-03 Milwaukee (UA), Cleveland (AA), Cleveland (NL), Reds, **Cubs**, Senators 455-583, .438

Loftus's career as a ML manager was far longer than his ML playing career. He often had a part ownership in the clubs he managed. He did not believe in changing pitchers during a game, and in 1890 he worked to change the rule prohibiting a manager from being a third base coach. For a time he was president of the Three-I League. /(NLM)

Bob Logan (Lefty) — 1910-1978. LHP 1935, 37-38, 41, 45 Dodgers, Tigers, Cubs, Reds, **Braves** 223 ip, 7-15, 3.15

Logan spent most of 1932 through 1943 with Indianapolis (American Association), starting more openers for them than any pitcher in their history. His only major league wins came at age thirty-five with the war-decimated 1945 Braves. /(NLM)

Johnny Logan (Yatcha) — 1927- . SS-3B 1951-63 **Braves**, Pirates 1503 g, .268, 93 hr, 547 rbi. *14 WS g, .154, 1 hr, 4 rbi*
☛ *All-Star—55, 57-59.*

Scrappy Johnny Logan never backed down from a fight and never lost one. His quick hands compensated for an average arm at shortstop and were an asset when, outraged by beanballs, he took on opponents as big as Don Drysdale. In Milwaukee, he was a minor league star for four years and a major league standout when he moved there with the Braves in 1953. He was the shortstop for the 1957 and 1958 NL pennant winners; in '57, he led the league with 37 doubles and reached career highs with 83 RBI and a .297 batting average. Traded to Pittsburgh for Gino Cimoli in 1961, he served the Pirates as a backup infielder and pinch hitter through 1963. /(JK)

Lucky Lohrke [Jack Wayne] — 1924- . 3B-2B-SS 1947-53 **Giants**, Phillies 354 g, .242, 22 hr, 96 rbi. *1 WS, 2 g, .000*

Lohrke gained the nickname Lucky when he was called off the Spokane (Western International League) team bus 15 minutes before its departure. Lohrke was headed for Triple-A; the bus was headed for disaster. It crashed into a ravine, killing eight players. Lohrke went on to become the Giants regular third baseman in 1947 and a utility man thereafter. /(JK)

Bill Lohrman — 1913– . RHP 1934, 37–44 Phillies, **Giants**, Cardinals, Dodgers, Reds 990 ip, 60–59, 3.69

According to some historians, Lohrman invented the slider. Others merely credit him as one of the first to use the pitch extensively. A Giants starter from 1938 to 1941, he was traded to the Cardinals in December 1941 as part of the deal that brought Johnny Mize to New York, but after pitching five games for St. Louis in 1942 he was sold back to the Giants. Lohrman went on to have his best season, 14–5 and a 2.48 ERA. /(BC)

Mickey Lolich — 1940– . LHP 1963–76, 78–79 **Tigers**, Mets, Padres 3639 ip, 217–191, 3.44. *20 wins: 71–72 1 LCS, 19 ip, 0–1, 1.42 1 WS, 18 ip, 3–0, 1.67* ☛ *Led League—w 71. Led League—k 71. All-Star—69, 71–72.*

Portly lefty Lolich stole the spotlight from teammate Denny McLain in 1968, despite McLain's 31-win season. Lolich won three games in the 1968 World Series, giving up only five runs in his three complete games, including a 4–1 victory in the seventh game

Mickey Lolich

against Bob Gibson on two days' rest. In the sixth inning of that victory, he picked off both Curt Flood and Lou Brock. A notoriously poor hitter (a career .110 average), Lolich cracked his only major league homer in Game Two of the Series off Nelson Briles.

The picture of consistency throughout his career, Lolich struck out 200-plus seven times and finished 12th all-time in strikeouts with 2,832, second only to Steve Carlton among lefties. Lolich was not a natural lefthander. A childhood run-in with a motorcycle left him with a broken left collarbone. Rehabilitating his left arm actually made it stronger than his right. Lolich came up the same year as McLain but was far more consistent, never winning fewer than 14 games in his 11 full years in a Tiger uniform. In 1968, while McLain piloted planes and played the organ, Lolich rode motorcycles and played the drums on his way to 17 wins, going 10–2 over the last two months of the season. In 1971 he had a league-leading 25 victories and 308 strikeouts. He would have won the Cy Young Award but for Vida Blue's spectacular rookie season. Lolich won 22 the following year with a career-best 2.50 ERA and again felt he deserved the Cy Young Award, but he lost a close vote to Gaylord Perry.

Lolich was traded to the Mets for Rusty Staub after the 1975 season, then "retired" after going 8–13 for New York in 1976. He sat out the entire 1977 season to get out of his contract, then signed with San Diego for two final seasons. /(SEW)

Sherm Lollar — 1924–1977. C 1946–63 Indians, Yankees, Browns, **White Sox** 1752 g, .264, 155 hr, 808 rbi. *2 WS, 8 g, .308, 1 hr, 6 rbi* ☛ *All-Star—50, 54–56, 58–60. Gold Glove—57–59.*

Lollar, a quiet workhorse who led by example, was the White Sox' catcher through the "Go-Go" years. This was ironic, since he was painfully slow. But he was a dangerous hitter with good power and was outstanding on defense. He led AL backstops four times in fielding and his .992 career average ranks in the top five all-time. In 1962 he equaled the ML record by catching six pop-ups in one game.

Lollar came up with the Indians in 1946 but was traded to the Yankees that December in the deal that sent Gene Bearden to Cleveland. After he put in two years of backup work in New York, the Browns acquired him in one of their many deals with the Yankees. In 1952 an eight-player deal brought him to Chicago, where he appeared in over 100 games for ten straight seasons.

On April 23, 1955 he became the third major leaguer in history to collect two hits in one inning

Sherm Lollar

twice in the same game. He slugged a pair of homers and had five RBI as the Sox defeated Kansas City 29–6. His best season was 1959. He hit 22 homers and had 84 RBI while handling Sox pitchers faultlessly as Chicago won its first pennant in 40 years. /(RL)

Tim Lollar — 1956– . LHP 1980–86 Yankees, **Padres,** White Sox, Red Sox 906 ip, 47–52, 4.27. *1 LCS, 4 ip, 0–0, 6.23. 1 WS, 2 ip, 0–1, 21.60*

Lollar looked like one of the NL's up-and-coming lefthanders when he went 16–9 for the 1982 Padres. He had a 90-mph fastball and was extremely tough on lefthanded hitters. Troubled by a bad elbow in 1983, he dropped to 7–12 and quickly faded. He didn't survive the second inning of his 1984 WS start, allowing the Tigers four runs on four hits and four walks in Game Two. Lollar played first base as well as pitcher in his first two minor league seasons,

and he was one of baseball's best-hitting pitchers during his ML stint (.234). He hit three homers in both 1982 and 1984 and came through with a pinch hit when given one at-bat by the 1986 Red Sox. /(JCA)

Stan Lomax — *1899–1988. Broadcaster.*

After graduating from Cornell, Lomax wrote for the Bronx *Home News* and the New York *Journal-American* and shared a 15-minute nightly sportscast with Ford Frick. When Frick became NL president in 1932, Lomax left the newspaper to do the radio show full-time and was heard on WOR from 1932 until his retirement in 1978. /(NLM)

Ernie Lombardi (Schnozz, Bocci) — 1908–1977. C 1931–47 Dodgers, **Reds**, Braves, Giants 1853 g, .306, 190 hr, 990 rbi. *2 WS, 6 g, .235, 2 rbi*
☛ *Most Valuable Player—38. Led League—ba 38, 42. All-Star—36–40, 42–43. Hall of Fame—1985.*

Famed for his long hits, lead feet, and large nose, Lombardi was one of baseball's top catchers during the 1930s and 1940s. The only catcher to win two batting titles, his consistently high batting averages were achieved despite his legendary lack of speed. Contemporary Billy Herman said later: "I don't think anybody could top him. But he was so slow afoot that those infielders could play him so deep that he just didn't have any place to hit the ball. He had to hit it over the fence or against the fence or just too hard for anybody to be able to make a play." Lombardi's powerful line smashes were legendary; he hit with his fingers interlocked so he could grip his bat, the league's heaviest, closer to the end.

Lombardi broke into baseball with Oakland of the Pacific Coast League at age eighteen. After being sent out to Ogden for seasoning, he had three outstanding seasons, catching 120, 164, and 146 games and hitting .377, .366, and .370. The Dodgers bought his contract in 1931, but though he hit a strong .297, they traded him to Cincinnati in a six-player deal in March 1932.

His greatest years were with the Reds, catching over 100 games for ten straight seasons and hitting .300 in seven. Twice he led NL catchers in fielding. In 1938, he won the NL MVP award by becoming only the second catcher to ever lead a major league in hitting (.342), while cracking 19 homers and driving in 95 runs. That season he caught Johnny Vander Meer's consecutive no-hitters. He was a mainstay for the 1939 Reds pennant winners and 1940 World Champions.

Ernie Lombardi

The 1939 WS saw an incident that haunted his career. In the 10th inning of the fourth and final game, Yankee Charlie Keller crashed into him in a close play at the plate. Lombardi was stunned and another Yankee run scored while he lay on the ground. Newspapers unfairly called it "Lombardi's Swoon."

Sold to the Braves in 1942, he won his second batting title (.330) and then spent his final five ML seasons with the Giants.

In his later years, he was bitter because he was not named to baseball's Hall of Fame. Eight years after his death, he was enshrined by the Veterans Committee./(MC)

Vic Lombardi — 1922– . LHP 1945–50 **Dodgers**, Pirates 945 ip, 50–51, 3.68. *1 WS, 7 ip, 0–1, 12.15*

Lombardi fanned 19 batters in a game twice in one week in the 1941 Penn State Association. Scouts who went to check him out were surprised to find he was just 5′7″ and 158 pounds. But by the last year of WWII, with talent scarce, Lombardi's size was overlooked. Given a chance, he won between 10 and 13 games a season as a .500 pitcher for the 1945–47 Dodgers and the 1948 Pirates./(JK)

Steve Lombardozzi — 1960– . 2B 1985– **Twins**, Astros 444 g, .233, 20 hr, 107 rbi. *1 LCS, 5 g, .267, 1 rbi. 1 WS, 7 g, .412, 1 hr, 4 rbi*

Lombardozzi was the second baseman for the 1987 World Champion Minnesota Twins, batting just .238 for the season but .412 (7 for 17) to lead all hitters in the World Series. As a rookie in 1986, he led AL second basemen with a .991 fielding percentage. But the Twins wanted more run production, and in April 1988 they traded slugger Tom Brunansky for the Cardinals' Tommy Herr. When Herr did not pan out, the Twins acquired Wally Backman for 1989 and traded Lombardozzi to the Astros./(JCA)

Jim Lonborg — 1942– . RHP 1965–79 **Red Sox**, Brewers, Phillies 2,465 ip, 157–137, 3.86. *2 LCS, 9 ip, 0–2, 5.79 1 WS, 24 ip, 2–1, 2.63*
☛ *Led League—w 67. Cy Young Award—67. All-Star—67.*

Gentleman Jim is mainly remembered for his gutsy performance in the 1967 World Series, after a Cy Young 22–9, 246-strikeout career season. The tall and articulate Lonborg had compiled just a 19–27 record in his first two seasons before leading the Red Sox to their first pennant in 31 years. He ensured the pennant by beating the Twins and Dean Chance on the last day of the season, the only time the Red Sox were in first place in a wild three-team race between the Red Sox, Tigers, and Twins. Four days later in the World Series, he beat the heavily favored Cardinals with a one-hitter 5–0 to knot the Series at one game each. He lost the perfect game when he walked Curt Flood with two out in the sixth on a 3–2 pitch, then lost the no-hitter when Julian Javier doubled with two out in the eighth. Lonborg then tossed a three-hit, 3–1 victory in Game Five to give Boston a 3–2 Series edge. A Roger Maris homer in the ninth spoiled the shutout and Lonborg's 17-

inning scoreless skein. By the seventh game and on only two days' rest, however, Lonborg finally gave out, losing a 7–2 decision to Bob Gibson, who won his third Series game. After the dream season, Lonborg was largely ineffective, winning just 27 more games for the Red Sox in the next four years. He won 14 games after being traded to Milwaukee in 1972, then spent the remaining seven years of his career in Phildelphia. In 1974 he won 17 games, but the highlight of his season was a grand slam he hit on June 29 against Montreal, only his third career homer. He won 18 games in 1976 and went 11–4 in 1977 before fading out two seasons later. /(SEW)

Bill Long — 1960– . RHP 1985, 87– **White Sox** 456 ip, 21-25, 4.33

A product of the San Diego farm system, Long was a throw-in on the 1984 deal that sent Ozzie Guillen to the White Sox for LaMarr Hoyt. He was twenty-seven when he got his first ML win, a two-hit shutout against the Yankees on May 5, 1987. He became a long reliever and an adequate starter. /(RL)

Dale Long — 1926– . 1B 1951, 55–63 Pirates, Browns, **Cubs**, Giants, Yankees, Senators 1013 g, .267, 132 hr, 467 rbi. *2 WS, 5 g, .250, 1 rbi*
☛ *All-Star—56.*

The 6'4" 205-lb Long turned down a contract from the NFL Green Bay Packers to play pro baseball. He stuck with the Pirates in 1955 after 11 minor league seasons (2 as a home run champ) and led the NL in triples. In May 1956, he hit eight homers in eight consecutive games, a record equaled by Don Mattingly in 1987. Traded to the Cubs in 1957, he found cozy Wrigley Field to his liking, hitting 55 HR over the next three seasons. In 1958 he caught two games using his first baseman's mitt, becoming the first lefthanded catcher since 1906. In 1959 he tied a then-NL record by hitting back-to-back pinch homers. He also helped the Yankees down the stretch in 1963 with timely pinch hits. After his playing career, he worked as a minor league umpire. /(DB)

Herman Long (Germany) — 1866–1909. SS 1889–1904 Kansas City (AA), **Braves**, Yankees, Tigers, Phillies 1872 g, .279, 92 hr, 1052 rbi
☛ *Led League—hr 1900.*

With a powerful arm, a quick release, and outstanding range, speed, and agility, Long played shortstop, according to the Boston *Globe*, "like a man on a flying trapeze." He joined Fred Tenney, Bobby Lowe, and Jimmy Collins in the Braves' (then called

Herman Long with the Braves

the Beaneaters) infield that was probably the best of the 19th century. His career chances-per-game (6.4) tops all shortstops.

One of three Beaneaters to play on five NL pennant winners in the 1890s, he was a strong run producer, twice knocking in over 100 and scoring over 100 seven times. His 149 runs scored led the NL in 1893 and his 12 home runs led in 1900. Noisy and uncouth on the field, he urged teammates to greater efforts, ragged opponents, and stirred up fans. He always played all out, once breaking Pittsburgh catcher Connie Mack's leg with a ferocious slide when there was no play at the plate.

After his playing days, he managed in the minors. However, he contracted tuberculosis, moved far from the scenes of his success to Colorado, and died broke and friendless. /(ADS)

Tommy Long — 1890–1972. OF 1911–12, 15–17 Senators, **Cardinals** 418 g, .269, 6 hr, 140 rbi

Long led the NL by cracking 25 triples for the Cardinals in 1915, the most by a rookie in this century and the second highest rookie total ever. After hitting .294 and .293 in his first two seasons as a Cardinal, he slumped badly in 1917 and disappeared from the majors. /(BC)

Ed Lopat [born Edmund Walter Lopatynski] (Steady Eddie, Junk Man) — 1918– . LHP 1944–55 White Sox, **Yankees**, Orioles 2439 ip, 166–112, 3.21. 20 wins: 51
5 WS, 52 ip, 4–1, 2.60.
    *Manager 1963–64 **A's** 90–124, .421*
☛ *Led League—era 53. All-Star—51.*

To frustrated hitters he was the Junk Man. Lopat turned his lack of a fastball into an advantage, keeping hitters off stride with an assortment of slow breaking pitches thrown with cunning and accuracy. Free-swinging teams like the Indians became easy victims; Lopat was 40–12 lifetime against Cleveland.

After four seasons with the White Sox, Lopat was traded to his hometown Yankees in February 1948, and manager Casey Stengel pitched him between flamethrowers Allie Reynolds and Vic Raschi, the contrast making Lopat's slow stuff all the more unhittable. He averaged 16 wins a year in the World Championship seasons of 1949–53, won a career-high 21 games in 1951, and led the AL in ERA (2.42) and winning percentage (.800, 16–4) in 1953. In the 1951 WS, he pitched a pair of complete games, beating the Giants 3–1 in Game Two and 13–1 in Game Five. When his playing days were over, Lopat remained in baseball as a coach, manager, general manager, and scout. /(MG)

Stan Lopata — 1925– . C 1948–60 **Phillies**, Braves 853 g, .254, 116 hr, 397 rbi. *1 WS, 2 g, .000*
☛ *All-Star—55–56.*

A decorated WWII veteran and the first NL catcher to wear glasses, Lopata didn't see much action behind Andy Seminick and Smokey Burgess until he assumed a deep crouch at the plate at the urging of Rogers Hornsby. He then hit .290 with 14 home runs in 1954 and belted 22, 32, and 18 HR the next three seasons before a dwindling batting average put him back on the bench. /(JK)

Davey Lopes — 1946– . 2B-OF 1972–87 **Dodgers**, A's, Cubs, Astros 1812 g, .263, 155 hr, 614 rbi. *6 LCS, 22 g, .282, 2 hr, 11 rbi. 4 WS, 23 g, .211, 4 hr, 11 rbi*
☛ *All-Star—78–81. Gold Glove—78.*

One of the most effective thieves in a basestealing era, Lopes stole five in a game on August 24, 1974 to tie a 70-year-old NL record and in 1975 he set a since-broken ML record with 38 consecutive successful steals. He was the league leader in 1975 (77) and 1976 (63), and he stole five in the 1981 LCS and added four more in the World Series. He set the NLCS career record of nine, and his ten in the WS ranks third. He stole 47 bases at age thirty-nine and 25 at forty. His career total of 557 stolen bases ranked 10th all-time as the 1980s ended.

Perhaps the best moments in Lopes's career came in the 1978 World Series against the Yankees. He hit two HR and drove in five runs in Game One, and added another HR in the sixth and final game. In a losing cause, he hit .308 with two steals for the Series.

When the Dodgers traded Lopes to the A's following the 1981 World Series, they broke up the longest-running infield ever. Lopes has played with Steve Garvey, Bill Russell, and Ron Cey for nine seasons. Lopes won the 1978 Gold Glove at second base and had excellent power for his posi-

Davey Lopes

tion. He hit a career-high 28 HR in 1979 and hit 17 twice. He coached for the Rangers following his playing career in the late 1980s. /(TG)

Al Lopez — 1908– . C 1928, 30–47 **Dodgers**, Braves, Pirates, Indians 1950 g, .261, 52 hr, 652 rbi.
  Manager 1951–65, 68–69 Indians, **White Sox** 1422–1026, .581. First place: 54, 59 *2 WS, 2–8, .200*
☛ *All-Star—33, 41. Hall of Fame—1977.*

The 5'11" 165-lb Lopez had a long and distinguished career as a catcher and manager and was enshrined in the Hall of Fame in 1977.

Not much of an offensive threat, Lopez hit higher than .275 only three times in his 19-year career. His career high in home runs was eight (1936 and 1939) and in RBI was 57 (1930). His great value was as an extremely durable receiver. For many years he held the record for most games caught in the major leagues (1,918) and the NL (1,861), and for most years in the NL catching 100 or more games (12). These endurance marks were somewhat inflated by the fact that he was largely a defensive replacement

Al Lopez

the last two and a half seasons of his career. He tied the record for most games caught in the NL without a passed ball (114 games in 1941) and led NL catchers in assists three times (1932–33, 1936) and fielding average three times (1940, 1943–44).

Lopez also left his mark as a manager. He led the Indians from 1951 to 1956 and the White Sox from 1957 to 1965 and 1968 to 1969. He was the only AL manager to finish ahead of the Yankees in the 1950s, winning pennants with the Indians in 1954 and the White Sox in 1959. He finished second every other year that decade, and nine times overall. His record as a manager was 1,422–1,026, with a .581 winning percentage that is ninth on the all-time list.

In a poll taken among retired major leaguers in the mid-1980s, Lopez was rated the seventh-best defensive catcher as well as the seventh-best manager of all time. /(JJM)

Aurelio Lopez — 1948– . RHP 1974, 78–87 Royals, Cardinals, **Tigers**, Astros 910 ip, 62–36, 3.56. *2 LCS, 6.1 ip, 1–1, 4.26. 1 WS, 3 ip, 1–0, 0.00*
☛ *All-Star—83.*

Dubbed Senor Smoke for his lively fastball, the portly veteran of 12 seasons in Mexico was one of the AL's top relievers for several years with Detroit, all after the age of thirty. Lopez had pitched professionally in his native Mexico for nine years before joining the Royals at the tail end of 1974 but returned to his longtime team, the Mexico City Reds, the following season, and in 1977 was the Mexican League MVP with a 19–8, 2.01 record. The Cardinals purchased his contract that fall and traded him to Detroit a year later, where Lopez quickly became the Tigers' bullpen stopper. He saved 21 games in 1979 and 21 more in 1980 while leading the AL with 13 relief wins. He recorded only six saves in 1981–82 but rebounded with 18 in 1983, then added 10 wins and 14 saves in 1984 working primarily as a set-up man for Cy Young Award winner and MVP Willie Hernandez. Lopez won the deciding fifth game of the WS against the Padres with two innings of relief, then suffered an off-year in 1985 and signed with the Astros as a free agent. He pitched exclusively in relief for Houston in 1986–87, saving eight games. /(SCL)

Carlos Lopez [born Carlos Antonio Morales Morales] — 1950– . OF 1976–78 Angels, Mariners, Orioles 237 g, .260, 12 hr, 54 rbi

Lopez played five years in his home country Mexican leagues before being purchased by the Angels' organization after the 1973 season. The Mariners selected him in the expansion draft, and he had his best season in 1977, batting .283 with 16 steals, eight HR, and 34 RBI in 297 at-bats (all career highs). He slumped to .238 with the Orioles in 1978, his last year in the majors. /(WOR)

Hector Lopez — 1932- . OF-3B-2B 1955-66 A's, **Yankees** 1451 g, .269, 136 hr, 591 rbi. *5 WS, 15 g, .286, 1 hr, 7 rbi*

The versatile Panamanian was traded from the A's to the Yankees during the 1959 season and was with New York for five straight pennants (1960-64). He played mostly third base for Kansas City, mostly outfield for New York, and he provided timely hitting as both a regular and pinch hitter. In the 1961 World Series against Cincinnati, he drove in seven runs—five in the final game, a 13-5 Yankee victory. /(JK)

Marcelino Lopez — 1943- . LHP 1963, 65-67, 69-71 Phillies, **Angels**, Orioles, Brewers, Indians 653 ip, 31-40, 3.62. *1 LCS, .1 ip, 0.00. 1 WS, .1 ip, 0.00*

The tall Cuban was named to the Topps All-Star Rookie team in 1965 after a 14-13, 2.93 ERA season with the Angels. Often wild, the next year he slumped to 7-14 while leading the AL in hit batsmen. Arm problems over the next few years handicapped his ML career. /(MC)

Bris Lord [Bristol Robotham] (The Human Eyeball) — 1883-1964. OF 1905-07, 09-13 **A's**, Indians, Braves 741 g, .256, 13 hr, 236 rbi. *3 WS, 16 g, .159, 4 rbi*

Signed off the sandlots by the A's 1905 pennant winners when their regular centerfielder was injured, Lord was a stocky journeyman with a fine arm. Later, the A's reacquired him in one of the all-time lopsided trades: even-up for Shoeless Joe Jackson. /(ADS)

Harry Lord — 1882-1948. 3B 1907-15 Red Sox, **White Sox**, Buffalo (FL) 972 g, .278, 14 hr, 294 rbi. *Manager* 1915 **Buffalo (FL)**, 59-48, .551

At times, Lord inspired his teammates with his hustle, earning the White Sox captaincy; at other times, it seemed he didn't want to play. The two years he batted more than .310 (1909 and 1911), he followed with marks of .267. He excelled at stretching doubles into triples. But as a fielder, he was virtually immobile. In 1913, he set single-season AL records for fewest chances accepted (364) and fewest assists (221) by a third baseman in 150 or more games. He jumped the White Sox in 1914, returned only to demand his release, and disappeared again

when Charles Comiskey turned him down. Ten days later, Buffalo (Federal League) announced they had signed Lord, who didn't show up until the next year to serve as player-manager. /(DB)

Los Angeles Dodgers — 1958- . Team. 2866-2389, .545. *NL West Champions 74, 77-78, 81, 83, 85, 88 NL Champions 59, 63, 65-66, 74, 77-78, 81, 88 World Champions 59, 63, 65, 81, 88*

When Dodger fans stopped dodging the Brooklyn trolleys that gave the team its name and started dodging traffic on the notorious Los Angeles freeways (eventually starting a local tradition of leaving the ballpark early to beat the traffic) America entered a new era.

"Dem Bums" had gone Hollywood. Leaving behind revered Ebbets Field, considered too small by owner Walter O'Malley, they wound up in the stadium considered by many the best ever built, and became the most successful sports franchise ever fielded, setting the ML single-season attendance record several times. They also became known for a succession of great pitching staffs starting with Koufax and Drysdale; bringing back the running game with Maury Wills; and the long tenures of their managers, Walter Alston and Tommy Lasorda. Los Angeles continued the Brooklyn tradition of appearing in every NL playoff, winning in 1959 and losing in 1962 and 1980. The 1959 win followed a seventh-place finish, a record comeback. /(TG)

Los Angeles Memorial Coliseum Los Angeles Dodgers 1958-61. LF-252, CF-420, RF-300

Expanded to 105,000 seats for the 1932 Olympics, the Coliseum was easily baseball's largest stadium, but was structurally incapable of containing a normal baseball field. Its oval-shaped playing area created 250' and 302' foul lines in its first season, and 120' of unused space between the centerfield fence and the seats. A 42' screen was erected in the left-field corner in an attempt to reduce the number of pop fly home runs, while the right-field fence shot sharply out to an almost unreachable 440' in 1958. That year, 193 home runs were hit in the Coliseum: 182 to left, 3 to center, and 8 to right. In only four seasons the Dodgers set several attendance records at the Coliseum, including 92,706 for Game Five of the 1959 WS against the White Sox and 93,103 for a May 7, 1959 exhibition against the Yankees on Roy Campanella Night. /(SCL)

The 1966 Los Angeles Dodgers

Baldy Louden [William] — 1885–1935. 2B-SS-3B 1907, 12–16 Yankees, Tigers, **Buffalo (FL)**, Reds 599 g, .261, 12 hr, 202 rbi

Louden was earning $2,700 a year with the Tigers when he chose to join Buffalo of the Federal League in 1914; he batted .313 as their shortstop. When the Feds folded in 1916, he hit .219 for the Reds while leading NL second basemen in fielding average. /(NLM)

Slim Love [Edward Haughton] — 1890–1942. LHP 1913, 16–20 Senators, **Yankees**, Tigers 119 g, 517 ip, 28–21, 3.04

Although he never had a losing ML season, wildness kept the 6'7" lefty from real success. In 1918, the only season he pitched regularly, Love was 13–12 for the Yankees but led the AL in walks. /(JK)

Joe Lovitto — 1951– . OF-3B 1972–75 **Rangers** 306 g, .216, 4 hr, 53 rbi

Lovitto hit .300 in the minors the season before he was called up, but his best major league mark was .224 in his rookie 1972 season. /(JFC)

Grover Lowdermilk (Slim) — 1885–1968. RHP 1909, 11–12, 15–20 Cardinals, Cubs, **Browns**, Tigers, Indians, White Sox 590 ip, 23–39, 3.58. *1 WS, 1 ip, 0–0, 9.00*

Grover and his brother Lou Lowdermilk both pitched for the 1911 Cardinals. Grover was 6'4" and lean, with long fingers, and was favorably compared to Walter Johnson—except that he couldn't control his blazing fastball. He was a member of the 1919 Black Sox but was not involved in the scandal. /(WAB)

Bobby Lowe (Link) — 1868–1951. 2B-OF-3B-SS 1890–07 **Braves**, Cubs, Pirates, Tigers 1824 g, .273, 70 hr, 984 rbi.
Manager 1904 **Tigers** 30–44, .405

A righthanded-batting leadoff man with fair power, the handsome, mustachioed Bobby Lowe (along with Kid Nichols and Herman Long) starred on all five Beaneater (later known as the Braves) pennant winners of the 1890s, playing second base in an infield that has been called the 19th century's best. On Decoration Day 1894, Lowe became the first

Bobby Lowe

major leaguer to homer four times in one game, doing it off Cincinnati's Elton "Iceberg" Chamberlain. The home runs came consecutively, in six at-bats, all over the 250-foot left-field wall of Boston's Congress Street Grounds, the Beaneaters' temporary home while their regular park was under repair. After the 20–11 Boston victory, the crowd showered Lowe with $160 in silver coins./(ADS)

John Lowenstein — 1947- . OF-DH-3B-2B 1970–85 **Indians**, Rangers, Orioles 1368 g, .253, 116 hr, 441 rbi. *2 LCS, 6 g, .167, 1 hr, 5 rbi. 2 WS, 10 g, .308, 1 hr, 4 rbi*

After spending eight of his first nine ML seasons as a utility man with the Indians (1970–77) and the Rangers (1978), Lowenstein was picked up on waivers by Baltimore. The lefty was platooned against righthanded pitchers and became a favorite of manager Earl Weaver for his intelligence and attitude. Lowenstein reached his peak in 1982 when, platooning in left field, he hit .320 with 24 HR, 66 RBI, 69 runs, and 54 walks (all career highs) in just 322 at-bats (122 games). His .602 slugging average and 7.5 HR percentage would have led the majors if he had had enough at-bats to qualify. And he led all outfielders in fielding, going the entire season (111 games) without an error.

Even when not posting such spectacular numbers, Lowenstein was consistently valuable for the Orioles. In 1979, he missed much of the stretch run with a badly sprained ankle, but in Game One of the LCS he pinch hit. In the bottom of the tenth inning with the score tied 3–3 with two out and two on, he hit an opposite field homer off the Angels' John Montague. Lowenstein followed this in the World Series with a pinch two-run double in the eighth inning of Game Four as the Orioles rallied for six runs after being down 6–3. In 1983 he hit a WS homer in Game Two to tie the game in an eventual 4–1 victory as Baltimore won the first of four straight to become World Champions./(WOR)

Turk Lown [Omar Joseph] — 1924- . RHP 1951–54, 56–62 **Cubs**, Reds, White Sox 1032 ip, 55–61, 4.12. *1 WS, 3 ip, 0–0, 0.00*

Lown was a hard-throwing but very wild starter with few successes in his first three years with the Cubs. Switched to relief, he blossomed into a star. His top season was 1959, when he helped the White Sox to their first pennant in 40 years with a 9–2 mark, an AL-leading 15 saves, and a 2.89 ERA. His nickname came from his fondness for turkey./(AA)

Peanuts Lowrey [Harry Lee] — 1918–1986. OF-3B 1942–43, 45–55 **Cubs**, Reds, Cardinals, Phillies 1401 g, .273, 37 hr, 479 rbi. *1 WS, 7 g, .310* ☛ *All-Star—46.*

Lowrey came to the Cubs during the war years. When Chicago won its last pennant in 1945, he contributed a .283 BA and 89 RBI. But after several years of steady play, he was traded with Harry Walker to the Reds in 1949 for Frank Baumholtz and Hank Sauer in one of the best deals the Cubs ever made. Lowrey slumped in Cincinnati, but upon his sale to the Cardinals in 1950, his career enjoyed a rebirth. He batted a career high .303 in 1951 and led the NL in pinch hits with 13 in 1952 and 22 in 1953.

His nickname stemmed from the fact that his grandfather described the infant Lowrey as "no bigger than a peanut." Later, when he performed in child bit parts in silent films, actress Thema Todd reportedly gained his good behavior with promises to buy him peanuts. He also had a speaking part in *The Winning Team*, which starred Ronald Reagan as Grover Cleveland Alexander./(ARA)

Mike Loynd — 1964- . RHP 1986–87 **Rangers** 111 ip, 3–7, 5.82

Loynd tied an NCAA record with 20 wins for Florida State in 1986 and defeated Cleveland in his debut with the Rangers that July 24 after just five minor league starts. He was sent to Houston after being hit hard in 1987. /(JCA)

Tony Lucadello — Unk.–1989. *Scout.*

Lucadello became a full-time scout with the Cubs in 1948 after part-time scouting during WWII. He joined the Phillies' scouting staff in 1957. He discovered Mike Schmidt, Ferguson Jenkins, Alex Johnson, and Toby Harrah, and he signed 50 major leaguers. His brother Johnny was an infielder for the Browns and the Yankees. /(FVP)

Gary Lucas — 1954- . LHP 1980–87 **Padres**, Expos, Angels 669 ip, 29–44, 3.01. *1 LCS, 2 ip, 0–0, 11.57*

Normally a good control pitcher, Lucas entered Game Five of the 1986 LCS with a 5–4 lead and no one on base, needing just one out to send the Angels to the WS. He promptly hit Rich Gedman with his first pitch (his first hit batsman since 1982), setting up Dave Henderson's home run off Donnie Moore in the next at bat. The lanky lefthander debuted with San Diego in 1980, and from 1981 to 1983 he saved 13, 16, and 17 games, leading the NL with 57 appearances in 1981 while posting a career-best 2.00 ERA. He was traded to the Expos for Scott Sanderson after the 1983 season, and then to the Angels two years later. /(SCL)

Red Lucas [Charles Fred] (The Nashville Narcissus) — 1902–1986. RHP-PH 1923–24, 26–38 Giants, Braves, **Reds**, Pirates 907 g, .281, 3 hr, 190 rbi; 396 g, 2542 ip, 157–135, 3.72

Lucas broke in as a pitcher but lacked a good fastball, so efforts were made to convert him into an infielder to take advantage of his hitting ability. His exceptional control eventually made him a top NL righthander, but his reputation as a good-hitting pitcher far overshadowed his accomplishments on the mound. He won 109 games for the perennial second-division Reds from 1926 through 1933, with highs of 18 in 1927 and 19 in 1929. In 1933 he walked only 18 in 220 innings, and his 1.61 bases on balls per nine innings places him 20th all-time.

In 1929, '31, and '32 he led the NL in complete games and in one stretch in 1931–32 completed 27 consecutive starts, a modern record. For his career he completed 68% of 301 starts. Among his best-pitched games were a 15-inning, 1–0 win over the Giants (7/16/33) and a 3–0 win over the Dodgers (7/22/27) in which he issued no walks, faced the minimum 27 batters, and gave up only one scratch hit.

His career batting average was .281 and his 114 pinch hits and 437 pinch at-bats (a .261 average) were ML records for many years. He still ranks in the top ten in both categories. /(LRD)

Frank Lucchesi — 1926- . *Manager* 1970–72, 75–77, 87 **Phillies**, Rangers, Cubs 316–399, .442

A light-hitting minor league outfielder, Lucchesi first became a manager in the low minors at age twenty-three. After 19 years, he received his first ML assignment with the Phillies in 1970. He later managed the Rangers from mid-1975 until mid-1977 and ten years later finished the 1987 season as interim manager of the Cubs. With the Rangers in spring training in 1977, he was physically attacked on the field by Texas second baseman Lenny Randle, who was outraged at being benched. Lucchesi suffered a black eye, fractured cheekbone, and other injuries. He had Randle arrested a month later after turning down a settlement (Randle was also fined by the team for Lucchesi's medical expenses). The bad publicity led to Lucchesi's June firing. Randle was later found guilty of assault, and Lucchesi sued him for $200,000, saying that the incident cost him his job. It was finally settled two years later. /(BC)

Ron Luciano — 1937- . *Umpire* AL 1968–80 *3 LCS 1 WS 1 ASU*

"I was an umpire, but beneath my chest protector beat the heart of a fan," said Luciano. He applauded great plays, shook hands with home run hitters, and congratulated players after a good game. His on-the-field histrionics delighted the fans but were often frowned upon by players and fellow umpires. In 1975 Cleveland manager Frank Robinson levied $200 fines against Indians caught talking to Luciano during a game.

The only things that bothered Luciano were long games and making decisions. Boredom and the pressures of his profession often spawned his theatrics. He would frequently render an out call by pumping his arm several times or with a mock shooting gesture with his right hand.

Luciano's clashes with Baltimore manager Earl Weaver were legendary. The first time the two met was in Rochester (International League), and Luciano ejected the feisty manager in four straight games. In the majors, Luciano ejected Weaver eight times. The feud between the two was so severe that the AL took Luciano off Baltimore games.

Upon his resignation, the comic ump worked as a color commentator for the NBC Game of the Week for two seasons. His three books (with David Fisher), *The Umpire Strikes Back*, *Strike Two*, and *The Fall of the Roman Umpire*, have all been highly successful.

A football standout at Syracuse University, the burly 6'4" 260-lb tackle played in the 1959 Pro-College All-Star Game and briefly with the Buffalo Bills in the AFL before becoming an umpire. /(RTM)

Fred Luderus — 1885–1961. 1B 1909–20 Cubs, **Phillies** 1346 g, .277, 84 hr, 647 rbi. *1 WS, 5 g, .438, 1 hr, 6 rbi*

Luderus was Grover Cleveland Alexander's first baseman in the Phillies' few strong years before 1920. By the standards of the time, he was a power hitter, batting fifth behind NL HR leader Gavvy Cravath to give the Phillies their middle-of-the-order punch. A lefthanded batter who threw right-handed, he was the first to hit two over-the-fence homers at Baker Bowl in a single game, long clouts even in that stadium's modest confines.

He came up with the Cubs, filled in for the ailing Frank Chance for a few games, and was traded for Bill Foxen, an undistinguished pitcher. He captained the pennant-winning 1915 Phillies and was their only strong hitter in the losing WS with the Red Sox, batting in six of his team's meager total of ten runs. An iron man, he played 533 consecutive games and was proud of never having been lifted for a pinch hitter. /(ADS)

Steve Luebber — 1949– . RHP 1971–72, 76, 79, 81 **Twins**, Blue Jays, Orioles 206 ip, 6–10, 4.62

Luebber never overcame control problems. In his best season, 1976, he went 4–5 with a 4.00 ERA while walking 62 in 119 innings. /(SFS)

Urbano Lugo [Rafael] — 1962– . RHP 1985- **Angels**, Expos 138 ip, 4–7, 5.01

The son of a Venezuelan pitching great of the same name, Lugo was rated the Eastern League's top pitching prospect in 1984 and was 3–4 while spending most of 1985 with the Angels. He won just one more ML game after a January 1986 elbow operation. /(JCA)

Fred Luderus

Mike Lum — 1945– . OF-1B 1967–81 **Braves**, Reds, Braves, Cubs 1517 g, .247, 90 hr, 431 rbi. *2 LCS, 3 g, .667*

The Hawaiian hit three HR against the Padres on July 3, 1970. He was most productive with the 1973 Braves, hitting .294 with 16 HR and 82 RBI as a first baseman and outfielder. But he achieved his greatest success as a lefthanded pinch hitter. His 103 career pinch hits and 418 pinch at-bats put him among the all-time leaders. In his second stint with the Braves, in 1979, he led the NL with 17 pinch hits in 52 tries, and pinch homered in consecutive games on September 4 and 5. He left in 1981 standing second to Hank Aaron in games played for the Atlanta Braves. /(PB)

Harry Lumley — 1880–1938. OF 1904–10 **Dodgers** 730 g, .274, 38 hr, 305 rbi.
   Manager 1909 **Dodgers** 55–98, .359
☛ *Led League—hr 04 .*

The Dodgers drafted Lumley after he led the Pacific Coast League in batting in 1903. As a rookie rightfielder, he led the NL in triples (18) and homers (9). Named Dodger player-manager in 1909, he guided the team to a sixth-place finish. /(AL)

Jerry Lumpe — 1933– . 2B-3B-SS 1956–67 Yankees, **A's**, Tigers 1371 g, .268, 47 hr, 454 rbi. *2 WS, 12 g, .231, 2 rbi*
☛ *All-Star—64.*

A line-drive hitter but a defensive liability at third base and shortstop for the Yankees, Lumpe was traded to the A's in 1959 and became a steady second baseman. In 1962 he reached career highs in average (.301), HR (10), and RBI (83) and put together a 20-game hitting streak. /(FK)

Don Lund — 1923– . OF 1945, 47–49, 52–54 Dodgers, Browns, **Tigers** 281 g, .240, 15 hr, 86 rbi

Five of Lund's seven seasons consisted of fewer than 55 at-bats. He hit .257 as the Tigers' right fielder in 1953, his only year as a regular. /(FK)

Carl Lundgren — 1880–1934. RHP 1902–09 **Cubs** 1322 ip, 90–55, 2.42

Lundgren was a starting pitcher on three successive Cub pennant winners (1906–08), but despite going 17–6 (2.21) in 1906 and 18–7 (1.17) in 1907, he was never used in a World Series; always, there were even better pitchers ahead of him. He later replaced Branch Rickey as baseball coach at the University of Michigan. /(JK)

Dick Lundy (The King) — 1899–1965. SS-2B-3B-MGR Negro Leagues 1916–48 Bacharach Giants, New York Lincoln Giants, Hilldale, Baltimore Black Sox, Philadelphia Stars, Newark Dodgers, New York Cubans, Newark Eagles, Jacksonville Eagles statistics not available

Lundy was one of the top shortstops in Negro League history, a great star and showman respected for his quiet professionalism, leadership qualities, and ability to perform suberbly under pressure. An exceptional fielder, he had great range and an outstanding throwing arm. He was a consistent, powerful switch-hitter who posed a threat on the basepaths.
   Lundy moved north with his hometown Jacksonville, FL team in 1915 when they became the

Atlantic City Bacharach Giants. In 1921, he led the club with a .484 batting average. His 13 home runs in 1924 led the Eastern Colored League. He became the Bacharach Giants' player-manager in 1925 and led them to pennants in 1926 and 1927. In the 1926 Black World Series against the Chicago American Giants, Lundy hit .325 with six RBI, four runs scored, and six stolen bases in a losing cause.
   Lundy joined the Baltimore Black Sox in 1929 and became part of their "million-dollar infield" with Oliver Marcelle, Frank Warfield, and Jud Wilson. The Black Sox were Negro American League champions that year. In 1933 Lundy moved to the Philadelphia Stars, and though he was no longer in his prime, he was selected to play in the first East-West all-star game.
   Lundy played eight years in the Cuban Winter League, compiling a .341 average; he led the league in stolen bases in 1924. In 33 games against white major leaguers, he hit .289. He retired as an active player in 1937, after 22 seasons in the Negro Leagues. /(ETW)

Tony Lupien [Ulysses John] — 1917– . 1B 1940, 42–45, 48 **Red Sox**, Phillies, White Sox 614 g, .268, 18 hr, 230 rbi

A Harvard graduate, Lupian succeeded Jimmie Foxx as Red Sox first baseman during WWII, but he carried a better glove than bat. After leaving the ML, he managed in the minors, coached at Dartmouth, and wrote a book about baseball's reserve clause. /(EW)

Al Luplow — 1939– . OF 1961–67 **Indians**, Mets, Pirates 481 g, .235, 33 hr, 125 rbi

Luplow's ML career as a journeyman outfielder was highlighted by his selection to the Topps Rookie All-Star team in 1962 and a brilliant catch for the Indians at Fenway Park (6/27/63). He raced head-long toward right-center, grabbed Dick Williams's drive backhand, and flipped over the fence into the bullpen. /(EW)

Dolf Luque (The Pride of Havana) — 1890–1957. RHP 1914–15, 18–35. Braves, **Reds**, Dodgers, Giants 3220 ip, 193–179, 3.24. 20 wins: 23 *2 WS, 9 ip, 1–0, 0.00*
☛ *Led League—w 23. Led League—era 23, 25.*

One of the first Cubans to succeed in the majors, Luque came to the U.S. in 1912 to pitch for Long Branch (NY-NJ League) and was 22–5 in 1913. After a couple of unsuccessful trials with the Braves, he caught on with the Reds during WWI and stayed for 12 seasons. In the 1919 WS, he relieved twice

Dolf Luque

without allowing a run, and the next year he became a regular Cincinnati starter. He led the NL in losses (23) in 1922 but had his career year the next season, leading the league in wins (27), winning percentage (.771), and ERA (1.93). Although he never again topped 20 wins, Luque led again in ERA with 2.63 in 1925. In the 1930s he turned to relief pitching for the Giants. His 4–1/3 shutout innings earned him the win in the 10-inning fifth and final game of the 1933 WS. /(EW)

Billy Lush — 1873–1951. OF 1895-97, 1901-04 Washington (NL), Braves, Tigers, **Indians** 489 g, .249, 8 hr, 152 rbi

Lush was a fast but unproductive switch-hitter. Playing for Washington in 1896, he compiled an .885 fielding percentage, the worst among National League outfielders. His brother Ernie played one game for the 1910 Cardinals. /(DAS)

Johnny Lush — 1885-1946. LHP-OF-1B 1904-10 Phillies, **Cardinals** 369 g, .254, 2 hr, 94 rbi; 1239 ip, 66–85, 2.68

As an 18-year-old first baseman/outfielder with the Phillies, Lush was the youngest regular ML player of the 20th century. He became a full-time pitcher for

Philadelphia in 1906, when he had a career-high 18 wins and a no-hitter against the Dodgers, but he had only one more winning season. /(JK)

Rube Lutzke [Walter John] — 1897–1938. 3B 1923-27 **Indians** 572 g, .249, 4 hr, 223 rbi

A gifted fielder, Lutzke was weak at the plate and was often removed for pinch hitters. He led American League third basemen in putouts, assists, and errors in 1923. /(ME)

Greg Luzinski (The Bull) — 1950- . OF-DH 1970-84 **Phillies**, White Sox 1821 g, .276, 307 hr, 1128 rbi. *5 LCS, 20 g, .274, 5 hr, 12 rbi. 1 WS, 3 g, .000*
☛ *Led League—rbi 75. All-Star—75-78.*

Luzinski earned the nickname The Bull with his bulging arms, thick neck, massive body, and vicious righthanded batting stroke. As the Phillies' left fielder in the 1970s, he teamed with third baseman Mike Schmidt to form a potent slugging combination and help the Phillies to four NL East championships in five years.

The 6'1″ 220-lb Luzinski reached the ML for good in 1972, with two minor league home run crowns, one minor league batting championship, and three minor league strikeout titles on his resume. He hit .281 with 18 HR as a rookie, and .285 with 29 HR and 97 RBI in 1973, the year Schmidt joined the lineup. From 1975 to 1980, the pair averaged nearly 66 HR a year. Luzinski was hobbled by knee surgery in 1974 but rebounded in 1975 to hit .300 with 34 HR and a NL-best 120 RBI. The Bull still routinely struck out 100 times a season, yet pushed his average up to .304 the following year as the Phillies won the first of three consecutive division titles, and in 1977 he logged career highs in all three Triple Crown catagories, batting .309 with 39 HR and 130 RBI. In LCS play, Luzinski was just as dangerous, slugging home runs in Game Two in 1976, Game One in 1977, and Games Three and Four in 1978, but the Phillies lost all three series. Luzinski's production fell off badly in 1979, and in 1980 his average dropped to .228, but the Phillies finally advanced past the LCS with a five-game victory over the Astros, as Luzinski homered to win Game One. In the WS, the Phillies used the clumsy-fielding Luzinski primarily as the designated hitter and he failed to get a single hit, but the Phillies beat the Royals in six games.

Luzinski was sold to the White Sox before the 1981 season and he immediately became Chicago's full-time DH, where he no longer had to endure criticism for his wretched defense. He played four seasons in Chicago, helping them to the AL West title in 1983 with 32 HR and 95 RBI, then retired after hitting .238 with 13 HR in 1984. The Bull is fourth on the Phillies all-time home run list, behind Schmidt, Del Ennis, and Chuck Klein. /(SCL)

Sparky Lyle [Albert Walter] — 1944- . LHP 1967–82 Red Sox, **Yankees**, Rangers, Phillies, White Sox 1391 ip, 99–76, 2.88. *3 LCS, 11.2 ip, 2–0, 2.31. 2 WS, 7.1 ip, 1–0, 1.23*
☛ *Cy Young Award—77. All-Star—73, 76, 77.*

Lyle was one of the AL's best relievers for over a decade with the Red Sox and Yankees, leading the league in saves in 1972 and 1976, and in 1977 he became the first reliever ever to win the AL Cy Young Award. A wisecracking lefthander with a sizable paunch visible beneath his uniform, Lyle relied on a crackling slider almost exclusively in his heyday but also possessed a good fastball and a capable curve. He never started a ML game.

Lyle pitched briefly for the Red Sox as a rookie in 1967, but not at all in the WS, and in 1968 he began to emerge as their bullpen ace, finishing 6–1 with 11 saves and a 2.74 ERA. He saved 17 games in 1969 (third in the AL), 20 in 1970, and 16 in 1971, but before the 1972 season he was traded to the rival Yankees even-up for first baseman Danny Cater, one of the worst trades in Red Sox history. Lyle immediately led the AL with 35 saves for the Yankees in 1972 while recording a 1.91 ERA, and he added 27 saves in 1973, a career-low 1.66 ERA in 1974, and an AL-best 23 saves in 1976 as the Yankees won the AL championship. In 1977 Lyle was even better, winning 13 games and saving 26 (second in the AL), then adding a win in the WS as the Yankees beat the Dodgers in six games and Lyle captured the AL Cy Young Award.

By the spring of 1978, however, Lyle was feuding with Yankee management, irked over owner George Steinbrenner's decision to sign relief aces Rich Gossage and Rawley Eastwick as free agents despite the presence of Lyle in the club's bullpen. Gossage became the club's closer, and after the season Lyle was traded to Texas in a 10-player-deal that brought Dave Righetti to the Bronx. By 1980, Lyle's slider had lost its snap, and he saved only 15 games in three final seasons with the Rangers, Phillies, and White Sox. He made his feelings about playing for the Yankees known in *The Bronx Zoo*, a book he wrote with Pete Golenbock in 1979. /(SCL)

Sparky Lyle

Ed Lynch — 1956- . RHP 1980–87 **Mets**, Cubs 940 ip, 47–54, 4.00

After pitching for the lowly Mets of the early 1980s, Lynch was 10–8, 3.44 as their third starter when they finished second in 1985, but he was traded to the Cubs for a pair of minor leaguers in the middle of 1986 as the Mets were storming toward a World Championship. Lynch had excellent control (2.2 walks per nine innings in the ML) and could pitch in relief as well as start, but a 2–9, 5.38 record with Chicago in 1987 ended his ML career. /(SCL)

Jerry Lynch — 1930– . OF 1954–66 Pirates, **Reds** 1184 g, .277, 115 hr, 470 rbi. *1 WS, 4 g, .000*

Lynch's outstanding pinch hitting (19-for-47, .404) was a major factor in the 1961 Reds' surprising NL pennant. Overall, he had career-high averages of .315 (batting) and .624 (slugging) for the season, with 13 HR and 50 RBI in only 181 at-bats. When he retired, the poor-fielding outfielder ranked first all-time in pinch HR (18) and second in pinch hits (116) and was tied for first in pinch at-bats (447). The lefthanded-hitting Lynch led the NL in pinch hits twice (19 in both 1960 and 1961).

Lynch joined the Reds after missing most of the 1956 season due to illness. With Pittsburgh, he had been a part-time outfielder and occasional catcher, but not a very successful pinch hitter (9-for-49, .184, over three seasons). He was a semi-regular outfielder in 1958 and '59, reaching bests of 17 HR (1959, 379 at-bats) and 68 RBI (1958, 420 at-bats). He returned to the Pirates in mid-1963./(SFS)

Mike Lynch — 1880–1927. RHP 1904–07 **Pirates**, Giants 655 ip, 43–32, 3.05

A crafty collegian from Brown University, Lynch won 32 games for Pittsburgh in his first two seasons. He led the Pirates in strikeouts in 1904 but tended to walk as many as he whiffed./(ME)

Thomas J. Lynch (King of the Umpires) — 1859–1924. *Umpire* NL 1888–99, 1902

Lynch was a National League umpire known for his honesty. He was instrumental in increasing the prestige of umpires through such actions as leaving the field rather than continue the game in face of heavy fan abuse. He became National League president in 1910 as a compromise candidate and served until 1914. Although his tenure was largely uneventful, his brusque manner and forthright opinions offended several club owners and brought about his replacement./(BC)

Fred Lynn — 1952– . OF 1974– **Red Sox**, Angels, Orioles, Tigers 1879 g, .284, 300 hr, 1088 rbi. *2 LCS, 8 g, .517, 1 hr, 8 rbi. 1 WS, 7 g, .280, 1 hr, 5 rbi* ☛ *Rookie of the Year—75. Most Valuable Player—75. Led League—ba 79. All-Star—75–83. Gold Glove—75, 78–80.*

Despite ten 20-HR seasons, one batting title, and All-Star appearances in each of his first nine seasons, Fred Lynn always fell short of expectations--betrayed by a fragile body and burdened with one of the finest rookie seasons in ML history.

In 1975, Lynn captivated Boston with his effort-

Fred Lynn

less lefthanded swing, ringing line drives, and almost daily sprawling catches in centerfield as he led a young Red Sox club to within one win of the World Championship. On June 18 he bombed the Tigers with 3 HR, 10 RBI, and 16 total bases in one game, and by season's end Lynn had hit .331, led the AL in runs and doubles, and became the only player ever to be named Rookie of the Year and MVP in the same season. In 1979, he was even better, leading the AL in batting (.333) with 39 HR and 122 RBI. Lynn, however, longed to play in his native California, and the Red Sox obliged by trading him to the Angels in January 1981. Away from Fenway Park, Lynn would never hit .300 again.

He remained one of the AL's better-fielding outfielders when healthy, and had six consecutive 20 HR seasons (1982–88). His grand slam in the 1983 All-Star Game (the only grand slam in All-Star play) was his fourth All-Star Game home run, second only to Stan Musial in ML history. But he was never the Hall of Famer he had appeared destined to be in 1975, and the main culprit was injuries. While some were the result of reckless play (he broke a rib crashing into an outfield fence and twice tore up his knee breaking up double plays), more often it was nagging strains and sprains that kept him off the field. The only year in which he played 150 games was 1978. /(SCL)

Barry Lyons — 1960– . C 1986– **Mets** 188 g, .241, 7 hr, 64 rbi

Lyons finally got a chance to play regularly when Gary Carter had knee surgery early in the 1989 season. Lyons was hot at first, hitting two HR in his first week as a regular, but soon he slumped and then went on the DL with a broken foot. He came off the DL the same time as Carter. /(WOR)

Denny Lyons — 1866–1929. 3B 1885–97 Providence (NL), **Philadelphia (AA)**, St. Louis (AA), Giants, Pirates, Cardinals 1121 g, .310, 62 hr, 569 rbi

A fine righthanded hitter and remarkable fielder for those gloveless days, Lyons ranks second among ML third basemen in putouts per game. His best seasons were 1887, when he hit a career-high .367 and set the ML record for putouts at third base (255); and 1890, when he hit .354, led the AA in slugging (.531), and led league third basemen in fielding. /(FIC)

Jimmy Lyons — Unk.–Unk. OF-MGR Negro Leagues 1911–32 New York Lincoln Giants, St. Louis Giants, Chicago Giants, Brooklyn Royal Giants, Indianapolis ABC's, **Chicago American Giants**, Detroit Stars, Cleveland Browns, Louisville Black Caps statistics not available

Jimmy Lyons was a vital cog on Rube Foster's great Negro League Chicago American Giants of the early 1920s. Winners of pennants in each of the first three years of the Negro National League (1920–22), the Chicago American Giants relied on the swift, left-handed outfielder for his defensive skill, speed on the bases, hitting, and expert drag bunting. Teammate Willie Powell noted that Lyons "didn't know what it was to get up to bat and take his full swing, 'cause Rube always had him put it here, lay it down there." According to Powell, the 5'6" Lyons was faster than Hall of Famer Cool Papa Bell—a statement naturally disputed by Bell. Lyons was a feared baserunner known to sharpen his spikes. He led the NNL with 22 steals and a .394 batting average in 1920. He finished his career as manager of the Louisville Black Caps in 1932. /(PG)

Steve Lyons (Psycho) — 1960– . OF-3B-2B 1985– Red Sox, **White Sox** 596 g, .262, 14 hr, 164 rbi

Lyons was Boston's first pick in the June 1981 draft. Though signed as an infielder, he played 88 games in centerfield as a Red Sox rookie in 1985. Known as Psycho because of his reckless hustle and flakiness, he became a Boston fan favorite and hosted a local call-in show. On June 29, 1986 the White Sox accommodated Tom Seaver's desire to play for an East Coast team by shipping him to Boston for Lyons. Relegated to a utility role, Lyons became an attitude problem and was sent down in 1987. He later returned to bat .280 and was made Chicago's third baseman two months into the 1988 season. /(RL)

Ted Lyons — 1900–1986. RHP 1923–42, 46 **White Sox** 4161 ip, 260–230, 3.67. 20 wins: 25, 27, 30
   Manager 1946–48 **White Sox** 185–245, .430
☛ *Led League—w 25, 27. Led League—era 42. All-Star—39. Hall of Fame—1955.*

Lyons never pitched in the minor leagues and never pitched in a World Series, but 21 seasons of yeoman work for the seldom-contending White Sox earned his 1955 election by the BBWAA to the Hall of

Ted Lyons

Fame. He attended Baylor University with plans for a law career, but his college pitching made him a sought-after prospect. Upon graduation in 1923, he turned down an offer from the A's to sign with Chicago for $300 a month and a $1,000 bonus. He joined the team in St. Louis on July 2 and relieved in the first ML game he ever saw, retiring the three Browns he faced.

By the next season he was a regular starter, and in 1925 he led the AL in victories (21) for a fifth-place team. He repeated as AL win leader in '27 and won 22 in 1930. In 1925–30, he averaged nearly 19 wins a season, although the White Sox never finished in the first division. Late in 1925, in a game that Chicago uncharacteristically won 17–0, he held the Senators to no hits for 8-2/3 innings. On August 21, 1926 he no-hit the Red Sox, winning 6–0.

Then, in 1931, he injured his arm and lost his fastball. His manager, Donie Bush, pronounced his arm "dead." But Lyons developed a knuckleball and was soon pitching effectively again. In 1936, he helped pitch the club to its first finish in the AL first division (third) since he had joined the team 14 years earlier.

His most important weapon was excellent control. Never a strikeout pitcher, he walked only 1,121 batters in 4,161 innings pitched over his career, and at one point in 1939 he hurled 42 consecutive innings without issuing a base on balls.

In 1939 White Sox Manager Jimmie Dykes began pitching him once a week, always on Sunday, to save his arm and to take advantage of Lyons's tremendous popularity to draw large crowds. The Sunday-only pattern continued through 1942, with Lyons's .634 winning percentage (52–30) the best for any four-year section of his career. In 1942 he led the AL in ERA (2.10) while completing all 20 of his starts and winning 14.

In the fall of '42, the 41-year-old lifelong bachelor joined the U.S. Marines, spending part of his three-year hitch in combat. In 1946 he returned to the White Sox and pitched five more complete games, winning only one, his 260th. Thirty games into the season he replaced Dykes as White Sox manager. His managerial record through 1948 was 185–245, with the main criticism being that he was too easy-going to enforce discipline. He later coached and scouted before retiring in 1966 to help his sister manage a Louisiana rice plantation. /(RL)

Rick Lysander — 1953– . RHP 1980, 83–85 A's, Twins 257 ip, 9–17, 4.31

Signed by Oakland, Lysander bounced around the minors for six seasons until a 10–3 season of relief for Ogden of the Pacific Coast League earned him a short trial in 1980. He was traded to the Astros and then to the Twins. In 1983 he pitched in 61 games with a 3.38 ERA but his performance later suffered because of overwork. /(MC)

Jim Lyttle — 1946– . OF 1969–76 Yankees, White Sox, Expos, Dodgers 391 g, .248, 9 hr, 70 rbi

Lyttle hit .310 in 126 at-bats for the 1970 Yankees in his most active season. He was a good outfielder, but had little power and lacked consistency. /(JFC)

Printed in the United States
103555LV00001B/85/A